DAUGHTERS OF DALLAS

A History of Greater Dallas Through the Voices and Deeds of its Women

VIVIAN ANDERSON CASTLEBERRY

Odenwald Press
Dallas, Texas

Daughters of Dallas

Copyright © Vivian Anderson Castleberry

All rights reserved. No part of this book may be used or reproduced in any manner whatsoever without permission in writing from the author.

Published by Odenwald Press, Dallas, Texas

Editor: Sylvia Odenwald
Layout/Design: Lynn Holt
Jacket Design: Barbara Nehman
Graphic Artist: Bob Forston
Graphics Coordinator: Louie Wilson, Lumar Graphics
Author Photograph: Barbara Jones

Library of Congress Cataloging-in-Publication Data

Castleberry, Vivian Anderson, 1922-
    Daughters of Dallas: a history of Greater Dallas
        through the voices and deeds of its women/
        Vivian Anderson Castleberry
            p.   cm.
    Includes bibliographical references
    ISBN 0-9623216-8-0 : $35.00
    1. Dallas (Tex.)—History. 2. Women—Texas—Dallas—History.
I. Title.
F394.D2157C37   1994
976.4'2812—dc20
                                                      94-14920
                                                          CIP

Printed in the United States of America

For my own five daughters

Carol, Chanda, Keeta, Kimberley, Catherine

and, especially, for

Curtis Wales Castleberry, my life partner

who made *them* and *this* possible

ACKNOWLEDGMENTS

• • • •

My mother, Jessie Lee Henderson Anderson, taught me to say thank you, and two men, my ministers, Dr. William G. Fletcher and Dr. W. B. J. Martin taught me that none of us can take credit for what we do because all of us "stand on the shoulders" of past giants. For my mother, I must say thank you to all who have made this work possible and to my mentors—Drs. Fletcher and Martin—I acknowledge my gratitude to those who paved my way.

The entire staff of the Dallas Public Library with special appreciation to Gail Bialis, Joan Dobson, Sharon Van Dorn, Jimm Foster and Carol Roark.

Barbara Jones was the official photographer for the book. Most of the other pictures were in my files at *The Dallas Times Herald*, which were given to me when I retired in 1984. I deeply appreciate the camera's eye view of photographer Andy Hanson and the photography staff there.

And to historians, writers, researchers, friends and family including Mike Hazel, Thomas Smith, Darwin Payne, A. C. Greene, Barrot Sanders, Fred Longmore, Elizabeth Enstam, William F. Jacoby, Ruth Rydell, Edith Roberts, Keeta Castleberry Rupp, Elma Knight, Margaret McDermott, Willie Lewis, Quinton Anderson, Florence Phelps, Bertha Galloway, Grace Gage, Pearl Anderson, Barbara Middleton, Mary Collett, Ruth Spence, Rowena Rutledge, Anne Cochran, Dorothy Bruton, Margaret Ackerman, Catherine Ann Castleberry Tracy, Betty May Stewart, Howard Hooper, John C. Phelps, Alvernon Tripp, Ernestine McGowan Castleberry, Adlene Harrison, Jo Ann Sweet, Deanna Anderson, Anne Rawlins, Helen Hodge, Natalie Ornish, Calvin Hodge, Idelle Rabin, Louis Didrickson, Jackie DeGaugh, Janet Romanyshyn, Patti LaSalle, Gretchen Ferris, Lucille Boynton, Maura McNiel, Juanell Kris Burton, Virginia Whitehill, Lindalyn Adams, Carol Castleberry Tate, Hortense Sanger, Juanita Hamilton, Patricia Currin, Jane Guzman, Delia Reyes, Julia Scott Reed, Chanda Castleberry Robertson, Patricia Meadows, Hibernia Evans, Belen Ortega, Julia Brown, Gertrude Shelburne, Elizabeth Robinson, Margaret Thomas, Irene Garcia, Anita Martinez, Cordye Hall, Pat Zahrt, Kathleen Zahrt, Kimberley Castleberry Saucedo, Raven Hail, Faustina Martinez, Vera Ford, Juanita Craft, Joy Mankoff, Joe and Bessie McLemore Trees, George Galerstein, Elizabeth Blessing, Ruth Altshuler, Yvonne Ewell, Elizabeth Ann McMurray Johnson, Ruth Prouse Morgan, Mary Jennings, Helen Kemp at Minute Man Press of Mesquite.

And, with gratitude beyond my words to express, some who questioned, read, edited, kept the computer working and pushed—my husband, Curtis Castleberry; Rosann Naim, publisher, Sylvia Odenwald; Lynn Holt, and Barbara Nehman.

Many of you made contributions and/or pre-ordered "Daughters of Dallas" to cushion the birth process and bring the work to life. Here's to you . . . .

Susan Abrahamson, Suzanne Ahn, Mary Louise Airhart, Betsy Alden, Trish Aldredge, Leona Allman, Ruth Altshuler, Barbara Anderson, Jean Anderson, Quinton Anderson, Roserma Arnold, Sue Autry, Sallie Bailey, Jessie Barbee, Ruth Barnhouse, Carolyn Barta, Mittie Lee Beaird, Frances Bearden, W. E. Beeman, Eunice Beene, Gerry Beer, Rebecca Bergstresser, Taunee Besson, Lucy Billingsley, Elizabeth Blessing, Susie Bowman, Lillian Moore Bradshaw, Terri Breitling, Wanda Brice, Lottye & Alan Brodsky, Mr. & Mrs. Henri L. Bromberg, Jr., Debbie Bronson, Brenda Brown, Terry Brown, Tina Bruner, Doris A. Budner, Kristeen L. Burks, Juanell Burton, Rebel Brown Calhoun, Adelfa B. Callejo, Barbara Cambridge, Dolores Carruth, Jackie Caswell, Clare Buie Chaney, Hazel Chaney, Gloria Chapman, Doris Chrones, Cynthia Watkins Clanton, Diana S. Clark, Ann Classe, Johanna Clevenger, Anne A. Cochran, Kay Cole, Billie Maxine Cook, Dorothy Porter Copeland, Janice Corley, Betty Cosgrove, Barbara Cottrell, Lerabeth Covin, Rita Cox, Vernie Crabtree, Jeannette Crawford, Charles and Garland Cullum, Eloise Cullum, Lee Cullum, Claire Cunningham, Patricia Currin, Jack Daniel, Pat Davidson, Mildred Davey, Kim Dawson, Roslyn Randolph Dawson, Mary Alice Dealey, Mrs. E. L. DeGolyer, Jr., Liz Deuillet, Anne Dickson, Rhonel Didrickson, Lucy Dulin, Alice M. Dykeman, Ann Early, Janice R. Edgin, Aileen Edgington, Leota Edwards, Marcelle Egbert, Harryette Ehrhardt, Rowena Elkins, Margaret Estes, Linda Evans, Jeanne Fagadau, Dorothy Fagg, Suzan E. Fenner, Elizabeth Francis,

Emme Sue Frank, Billie Frauman, Valerie Freeman, Bennie Houser Furlong, George Galerstein, Catalina E. Garcia, Irene Martinez Garcia, Ann Garrard, Deborah Garrett, Mary B. Garrison, Claire Gauntlett, Marjorie Ann White Giles, Kathlyn Gilliam, Regine Ginsberg, Jo Fay Godbey, Allene Goldman, Hannah Goldstein, Sue Goolsby, Betty Gordon, Sneh Goyal, Greenhill School, Joanne Greening, Pat Greenwald, S. Brooks Gremmels, Johnnie-Marie Grimes, Bill Brice & Gail Griswold, Margaret B. Guy, Jane Guzman, Nancy Halbreich, Sandy Haley, Cordye Hall, Eileen Hall, Eulaine Hall, Joyce Hall, Kathryn & Craig Hall, Ebby Halliday, Vera Hallmark, Elizabeth Ann Hamill, Juanita Hamilton, Bettye Hammond, Andy Hanson, Mamie Harris, Adlene Harrison, Helen Harwig, Cherry Haymes, Cheryl Haynes, Mary Frances Henderson, Mary Jo Henry, Nelle Henson, Lyda Hill, Helen Hilseweck, Pauline Hines, Helen Hodge, Betty Holcomb, Ann Hollingsworth, Nancy Horowitz, Phil Huey, Mr. and Mrs. R. Bruce Hughes, Waunell Hughes, Helen Hunt, Mrs. H. L. Hunt, Carla McNamara Hunter, Mrs. George E. Hurt Jr., Molly Ivins, John Jagger, Amelia Core Jenkins, Mitch Jericho, Linda Jinks, Elizabeth Johannaber, Mary John, Eddie Bernice Johnson, Scherry Johnson, Nelle Johnston, Nellie Johnston, Barbara Jones, Barney C. Jones, Mardi B. Jones, Patti Jones, Roger Kallenberg, Susan Kaminsky, Anne Kasper, Alexina Keeling, Jan M. Killen, Flo Kilmer, Gayle Reaves King, Donna Knox, Cecina Koeijmans, Peggy Ladenberger, Paula Lambert, Erie Darnall Land, Leslie Lanes, Bettina Lang, Mrs. J. L. LaPrelle, Dorothy Latham, Valerie Lawlor, Yana Lipscomb-Davis, Barbara Lischer, Deborah DeBerry Long, Harriet Lowe, Julie Lowenberg, Sally Luoma, Mary Lyman, Marty Lynch, Carol Madison, Dian Malouf, Madeline Mandell, Sandra Manfre, Joy Mankoff, Anita Martinez, Mr. and Mrs. Reuben Martinez, Barbara Materka, Linda Mayberry, Ellen McCready, Effie McCullough, Loretta McDaniel, Margaret McDermott, Jean Black McDowell, Frances McElvaney, Mary Lynn McEntire, Diane P. McGauley, Ann McGee-Cooper, Trisha McGowan, Dorothea McGrath, Sally McKenzie, Betty McKool, Maura McNiel, Mary Gail Meadows, Patricia Meadows, Carmen M. Michael, Barbara Middleton, Lester Miller, Gloria Milliken, Junanne Mitchell-Peck, Cynthia Mondell, Carolyn Moomaw, Patricia Moore, Gloria Moores, Joshua Morales, Ruth Morgan, June Mounger, Eloise Myers, Rosann Naim, John and Jan Neal, Priscilla W. Neaves, Barbara Nehman, Nicki Nicol, Carolyn Norgaard, Liz Oliphant, Noel O'Reilly, Natalie Ornish, Theresa Overall, Joanna Pace Partain, Rev. Sheron C. Patterson, Ronnie Pearce, Elsie Pearle, Pat Pearson, Catherine Perrine, Gail Peters, Barbara Peterson, Morena & Marvin Petsch, Mrs. R. J. Price, Caren Prothro, Tegwin Pulley, Marjorie Purnell, Emilie C. Quade, Mary Quesnel, Louise B. Raggio, Sue Rascoe, Meg Read, Amo Redus, Carol Reed, Trudy Thompson Rice, Virginia Riley, Ellen Rogers, Julian Rogers, Marilyn & Earl Rose, Sue Gill Rose, Mary Louise Rowand, Billy Ruth & Richard Rubottom, Therese Ruffing, Rose-Mary Rumbley, Ruth Rydell, Pat Sabin, Jan Sanders, Ruth Sanders, Hortense Sanger, Karin Sawhill, Marge Schafer, Howard Schultz, Emily Schumacher, Shirley Schwaller, Karen Seaman, Sheila Seifert, Glenna Foster Seipp, John Harvey Self, Janice Sharry, Sara & Wayne Shaw, Helen Sherman, Marilyn Sherrod, Carole Shlipak, Patsy A. Shockley, Mrs. Marvin G. Shwiff, Mary Sias, Ann Cook Slicker, Gail Smith, Jean Smith, Mary Ann Smith, Maryann Smith, Sue Smith, Kitty Alice Snead, Beth Son, Pauline Steele, Anne Stewart, Judge Annette Stewart, Betty May Stewart, Marion Strange, Annette Strauss, Susie Streng, Mrs. L. R. Strickland, Dorothy Stuck, Alice Fleming Stultz, Sue Swann, Mary Lois Sweatt, Julia Sweeney, Frances Spruce Syphers, Charlotte Taft, Ouita Theunissen, Doris Thomas, Mrs. Bascom Thomas, Ruth, Angie & Linda Thomas, Elizabeth Thompson, Martha Tiller, Martha Tiner, Beverly Tobian, Shirley Tobolowsky, Marguerite Topper, Ronda Vecchio, Carol Duncan Vesey, Nora Vincent, Liz Stewart Wally, Madeline Wardell, Linda Wassenich, Barbara Lord Watkins, Betty J. Watson, Sharon Watson, Beatrice Weisbrod, Clint West, Jane Wetzel, Bonnie Wheeler, Olivia Masih White, Virginia Whitehill, Danna Wharton, Alinda Wikert, Ruthe Winegarten, Margot Winspear, Kathleen Zahrt.

PREFACE

• • • •

Dallas has a richer heritage than it knows about. From the very first decade, Dallas was a city of diversity. It was a land of Afros, Anglos, French, Germans, Irish, Mexican, Swedish and Swiss. And, after these, other settlers from other countries added to the rich cultural mix. Sometimes Dallas was not even aware of this. Sometimes it still is not.

The first settlers of any race, color or religious persuasion are inclined to keep to themselves. Not to do so is to be lost in a strange land. The early French at La Reunion seldom met the early Germans who came halfway around the world to till the land. The early Mexicans seldom consorted with the early Irish, for in a large sense, they were competing for the few jobs in the new territory. The early Anglos, who arrived by ox-drawn covered wagons from Alabama and Illinois, Indiana and Kentucky, Missouri and Mississippi, met the few Swiss and Swedes only as shopkeepers who supplied their needs in a world alien to all of them.

And, from the second decade of Dallas, its Black citizens have contributed their rich and unique talents to the city. From their arrival, in bondage as slaves, they have been constant and consistent contributors to the city that, until the late 1950s, has done them the greatest injustice possible, ignoring them. Through it all, their gifts have continued. They have, whether they are aware of it or not, continued to help keep Dallas "safe" for a new generation to move on.

Dallas has one more thing going for it that has been almost totally ignored: its women. Brown, black, white and yellow, and all shadings of those colors, the women have been the harbingers of social change, the keepers and conveyers of the culture. From the 1840s, by surviving and thriving in an alien land, in special club meetings since the 1870s, in the training and guidance of their children and in "pillow talk" with their men at night, they have wielded an important and continuous influence that has been ignored when the histories of Dallas were written.

This is a partial story of those ignored, overlooked, forgotten people—the blend of ethnicities that would, long ago, have made Dallas truly an international city had it only taken better advantage of its priceless cultural diversity. It is especially a story of the unheralded half of the population of all colors—THE WOMEN OF DALLAS.

The above, written early in the compilation of this book, is as true today as it was when I first set it down to try to explain to people what I was doing and why I was doing it. Now, as I complete the long journey of researching and writing, I know that this is but one more piece in a continuing effort to find and document the story of Dallas. I have included here much that has been ignored by other researchers, and I have corrected a few past errors while, I am confident, making many original ones. My hope is that future historians, researchers and writers will take what appears already in all the books and continue to improve what has been done. Many of the individuals in the pages of *Daughters of Dallas* deserve a book of their own. This I leave to you . . . with my blessings.

CONTENTS

• • • •

Chapter 1: In The Beginning — 1

Charity Morris Gilbert, the first white woman to enter Dallas, "sailed in" on a river raft and Margaret Beeman Bryan, its first First Lady, begin women's remarkable contributions.

Chapter 2: The City's Premiere Entrepreneur — 11

Widowed at age 39 with four small children, Sarah Cockrell, the city's first capitalist, catapulted the family business into a fortune so vast that her will was published in pamphlet form.

Chapter 3: Petticoat Pioneers — 23

From a few hovels on the prairie at Three Forks on the Trinity River, Dallas acquires an identity—and women, often lost in the "cracks" of its past—give it substance and sustenance.

Chapter 4: The Seven Sisters from Tennessee — 31

The indomitable Hughes sisters—seven of them—imbue Dallas with a rich legacy—leaving their married names on streets, buildings, cemeteries, churches.

Chapter 5: The Multiple Millers—Millermore and More — 39

In their houses, writings and progeny, a host of women, white and black, stamp the Miller name indelibly on Dallas.

Chapter 6: From Vision to Village — 51

From camping on the banks of the Trinity and trudging from the Gulf to establish a utopia to presiding over the city's first mansion, Dallas women exhibit courage, tenacity, perseverance.

Chapter 7: The Dallas Peaks — 59

Streets are named for men in the family—Peak, Carroll, Worth, Junius. The women leave their mark as Harwood and Field. The town's first philanthropist is Juliette Peak Fowler.

Chapter 8: Dallas Becomes a City — 70

The city incorporates—and Dallas pushes its boundaries eastward when the Motleys settle Mesquite and northward when the Coits settle on the county's northern boundary.

Chapter 9: The 1860s—A Decade of Chaos — 78

The town burns, the Civil War rages dividing families, friends and countrymen; vice, gambling, prostitution and corruption take their toll—and the women of Dallas survive and prevail.

Chapter 10: Dallas's Dawning Days   96

From backgrounds of education and culture, women arrive in Dallas expecting the "good life" for themselves and their children. Where it does not exist, they establish it.

Chapter 11: Women—The City's Conscience   106

From poet laureate—the state's first—to political activist—the city's first—Dallas women assume responsibility for the social graces to civilize the growing city.

Chapter 12: The Genteel Decade   114

As Dallas gets its first "paved" streets, its first "electric" lights and its first social clubs, its women gentle its growth.

Chapter 13: The 1880s—A Decade for Education   121

From Mary Ann Ryland West, who opened its first school, to the present, women are Dallas's principal educators.

Chapter 14: Women Organize to Change Their World   133

From their first groups in their places of worship, women organize to bring about countless human and social changes.

Chapter 15: A Decade to Play—the Gay Nineties in Dallas   149

As it reaches its half century mark, a carnival atmosphere prevails in Dallas. While social protocol is clearly defined, women continue to progress toward personal autonomy.

Chapter 16: The Twentieth Century Arrives   163

The first automobile comes to town, neighborhoods expand into the suburbs, and Dallas becomes a fashion center.

Chapter 17: A Library Is Born   170

Dallas women learn that a "young upstart," Andrew Carnegie, is giving away millions to establish public libraries. Led by May Dickson Exall, they secure a grant for Dallas.

Chapter 18: Women as Cultural Arbiters   179

Dallas's cultural climate buds with women leading the way in art, beautification, concert, song and symphony.

Chapter 19: Dallas's Denizens of Darkness   192

Beneath its veneer of respectability, another Dallas exists—where segregation is entrenched, prostitution legalized, lawlessness widespread and the Ku Klux Klan proliferates.

Chapter 20: Women Embrace the Children   205

Women respond to the growing needs of children and youth—organize the Baby Camp, forerunner to Children's Medical Center; Hope Cottage, an adoption agency and the YWCA.

Chapter 21: The Mexicans Find a Home in Dallas 217

Fleeing uprisings in their homeland, Mexicans arrive in Dallas and unconsciously stigmatize their new lives by occupying houses in what was the Red Light District.

Chapter 22: Education for Women and Girls 225

Ela Hockaday founds a school of excellence for girls and a woman enrolls as the first student in a new Methodist-sponsored university out on a weed patch north of the city.

Chapter 23: Toddling Toward Equality 241

Nonie Boren Mahoney convinces a state senator that Dallas women are serious about suffrage by dumping a petition with numerous signatures on his desk during a legislative session.

Chapter 24: The Pacesetters 254

Edith Wilmans, Charles Etta Jones, Florence Martin, Genevieve Shea, Juanita Wade, Vareta Gulley, Maria Luna and others lead women into agriculture, business, dentistry, law, medicine . . . .

Chapter 25: Courage to Conquer—Women as Survivors 266

The 1930s decade begins in panic with the Great Depression, and women in the workplace are the first to lose jobs. With the Centennial, they celebrate survival.

Chapter 26: Six Daring Daughters 272

In legislation, contraception, sports, health, philanthropy Dallas's daughters leave a trail of contributions—and one's name is carved in the annals of crime.

Chapter 27: Women at War—the 1940s 287

In times of national crisis, there are no limits to what women are asked to do, nor what they accomplish. Some who find independence during war years refuse to go home again.

Chapter 28: The Power–Four 296

Ebby Halliday, real estate; Mary Kay Ash, cosmetics; Mary Crowley, home accessories, and Bette Graham, founder of Liquid Paper all personify the rags-to-riches American dream.

Chapter 29: The Message Carriers 309

The media, in its multiple forms, carries Dallas's message to the world. Hundreds of women from Pauline Periwinkle to Judy Jordan to Julia Scott Reed are among the messengers.

Chapter 30 —Unease in Utopia 327

In a decade marked by apathy, Dallas—still a man's town—continues advancing with women leaders—among them Connie Condos, Juanita Craft and Mary Louise Rowand.

Chapter 31: Tides of Change   337

The gales of change heralding a new day for women blow gently in Dallas with women embracing a more promising future while retaining a stable framework.

Chapter 32: Faces of Feminism   352

Women singly and in groups find freedom for new futures. Their illustrious names include Hermine Tobolowosky, Maura McNiel and Barbara James.

Chapter 33: Preserving the Past   365

Stigmatized by a reputation of blatant progress, Dallas is called by its women to seek broader values, preserve its past and seek connections including international diversity.

Chapter 34: Connecting the Pieces   375

From other parts of Texas, other states and other countries a new migration of women arrives to incorporate values beyond expansion and wealth as Dallas approaches the 21st Century.

Chapter 35: Expanding the Circle   390

New styles of leadership that seek connection rather than confrontation give Dallas new direction as women and other minorities become a significant and valued part of the whole.

Chapter 36: Future Unlimited   401

At 150, Dallas—having lost the brashness of youth and the uncertainty of adolescence—is led by its women and people of color toward a time of full partnership for all its people.

PART II

The body of the text, Chapters 1 through 36, written as nearly as possible by decades, has been enriched and personalized with the addition of individual chapters on women, most of whom are native Dallasites and whose experiences epitomize the growth of the city. They are:

Margaret Boone Ackerman	**411**
Ruth Elaine Collins Seaman Sharp Altshuler	**418**
Cordye McLaurin Hall	**424**
Adlene Nathanson Harrison	**433**
The Martinez Women—Faustina, Irene Garcia and Anita	**442**
Maria Belen (Correa) Ortega	**455**
Florence Harllee Phelps	**462**
Idelle Goodman Rabin	**468**
Gertrude Terrell Aldredge Shelburne	**476**
Ruth Potts Spence	**482**
Alvernon Verita King Evans Tripp	**488**
Martha Bell Leonard Zahrt and Lily Vertrees Bell Leonard	**494**

Part I

1

IN THE BEGINNING

In the beginning was the river.... The river was the Trinity[1] and from its earliest days, Dallas has had a love\hate relationship with it—expecting more than it could deliver, using its resources unmercifully, changing its course for the advancement of industry, recurrently expecting it to provide an outlet to the Gulf of Mexico—and thus to the world—or, at the very least, to be the nucleus of a major recreational center. Dallas has longed to be on the water—and the water, badly used and badly preserved, has all but dried up. The Trinity overflows its boundaries only now and then in extremely rainy seasons, proof that it still has power. Literally dozens of master plans for the city's improvement—always with the Trinity as the focus—have been advanced through the years only to be stored away and forgotten.

It is entirely fitting that the Trinity and Dallas's first female resident are inextricably intertwined, for neither its river nor its women are to be ignored.

Only the barest of facts remain to herald Dallas's first woman. Her name was Charity Morris Gilbert[2] and she arrived in Dallas by water, floating down the Trinity River on a raft from Bird's Fort 22 miles to the northwest.[3] So far as history records, she is the only Dallasite ever to "sail" into the city.

This extraordinary entry set the pattern for all women who would follow her to Dallas, for their exceptional contributions have, like the river, been treated with recurrent fascination and disdain.

Charity entered Dallas in the waning winter of 1842. She was pregnant with her ninth child. It had not been her idea to travel by raft, but Mabel Gilbert, her husband, had been adamant. A former Mississippi river boat captain, he was most at home on the water and insisted that it was the quickest and most efficient way to move to their new home. He and his friends spent days felling cottonwood trees, lashing them together and caulking them to make a raft. Then he and Charity loaded their few pieces of furniture, trunks and boxes of clothes, quilts and family memorabilia onto the crude conveyance. Charity boarded the raft with the family pet, a parrot, and they were off.

Mabel Gilbert's persistence in "sailing" down the Trinity was ill-advised, for it was no Mississippi River. Sudden bends in the stream, snags and snarls all along the way and its meager width detained them several times. Only the winter's heavy snowfalls and spring rains had swelled the river to make it possible for the barge to get through at all. The trip they had thought would take three or four days lengthened to almost two weeks.

Mabel Gilbert rode on horseback on the river's bank, using the butt of his rifle to part the dense shrubbery, alert for Indians or animals that might attack them. He had killed birds and wild game to augment their food supply, but the larder was almost bare and everybody was hungry, tired and out of sorts.

Charity recalled the promise of new opportunities that had brought them on this journey. John Neely Bryan had visited them at Bird's Fort early in February and described a new city he was founding at the Three Forks of the Trinity downriver. He said it offered unlimited possibilities.

Bryan had told them fragments of his personal story—enough to make them believe that he was no itinerant dreamer:

He had been born on a Fayetteville, Tennessee, farm on December 24, 1810. As a very young man, hardly more than a boy, he set out for Nashville where he "read" law and was admitted to the Tennessee Bar. In 1833, during an epidemic, he had cholera and was advised by doctors to seek a cure in the wilderness. He moved into the uncharted

From this serene setting on the West Fork of the Trinity River, the first woman settler, Charity Morris Gilbert, moved to Dallas in the spring of 1842.

The Texas State Historical Marker at Bird's Fort.

"wilds" of Arkansas where he lived for several years among the Cherokee Indians, regained his health and, with a friend, established and began to develop the town of Van Buren.

Lured by the promise of free land and unlimited opportunity in Texas, Bryan moved to Preston Bend on the Red River where he clerked for a time at Coffee's Trading Station, near what would later become Denison. The trading post was owned by his friend, Holland Coffee, a pioneer Indian trader. There Bryan learned about the Three Forks area and in 1839 made a trip south. He found what he considered the ideal spot for a town on a bluff of the Trinity River and marked the spot, but he seemed in no great hurry to develop it.

He returned to his Indian friends in Arkansas, bought supplies and stopped on his return trip for another visit with Coffee. By the time he arrived back at the Trinity River, it was November of 1841. He hastily erected a crude cabin, only a little more than a lean-to, using the river bluff as shelter, completing it barely in time to protect himself from a gruelling winter.

Bryan was a great story-teller and the area he described had sounded like a new Promised Land. Mabel Gilbert and his friends were enthralled. He and another Bird's Fort resident, James Beeman, returned with Bryan to his cabin on the Trinity and scouted the terrain. Lured more by what they heard than by what they saw, the two were convinced to move to Dallas.

There were other reasons the families were eager to leave Bird's Fort. It was more than adventure that compelled them. It was also fear. Bird's Fort, commanded by Jonathan Bird of Bowie Company, was one of several forts commissioned by the Republic of Texas to safeguard settlers from Indians. Located near the West Branch of the Trinity River some seven miles south of what would one day be Arlington and six miles north of the present town of Euless, Bird's Fort offered only a modicum of protection to its residents. The winter had been especially dire. In the fall of 1841 residents of the isolated fort discovered they did not have sufficient food to last through the winter and three men set out for the nearest trading post on the Red River for supplies.

By November, near the time that Bryan was building his lean-to on the banks of the Trinity, the wagons were long overdue. Three other men—Hamp Rattan, Alex W. Webb and Solomon Silkwood—went to search for the missing men and supplies. Their attempts were unsuccessful. On Christmas Day, near the present site of downtown Carrollton, while cutting an ash tree for the wild honey stored in its trunk, Rattan, Webb and Silkwood were ambushed by Indians. Rattan was killed and scalped. The other two escaped and made their way back to the Fort where Silkwood died within a few days from exposure to the cold. Webb went on a second scouting expedition, found the delayed wagons with provisions and made it safely home.

There were also rumors that the fort was about to be closed. Indian raids, the weather, lack of security in the buildings, the distance from supplies and the sparse population all made it difficult to maintain the fort.

Doubtless, Charity mulled over these things, hoping that this time her husband's constant search for new adventure, would be satisfied. She longed to rear her children in a stable community. She wanted to plant seeds and set down roots. She wanted a home, and she hoped Dallas would be it. If she had to make the trip by water, there was no better time of the year to do it. The water moccasins that infested the river bottom and the copperheads and rattle snakes that lived along its banks were still lethargic from their winter hibernation and not dangerous, and the insects that later in the year would make river travel unpleasant were not yet crawling or flying about.

The raft rounded a bend, with rare ease this time and Charity's wandering gaze focused on a figure on the riverbank up ahead. She saw him and recognized him even before he called out:

"Welcome," he shouted. "I have been waiting for you . . . ."

The greeting could not have been more cordial. Capt. Gilbert heard the shouts and galloped down. He and Bryan exchanged cordial greetings and both were on the bank to assist Charity from the raft. Bryan was everywhere at once, it seemed, overjoyed by the arrival of this first family to his new settlement. He hoisted the trunks with great efficiency and invited the Gilberts into his home for refreshments. If Charity was disappointed in

The site of Bird's Fort Texas Historical Marker: Take #157 (Collins Street) north out of Arlington for 1.8 miles past the West Fork of the Trinity River. Turn east on obscure Callaway Cemetery Road. Travel to dead end past cemetery and over railroad track. Turn south for .8 miles through gate (often locked) into Silver Lake Gun Club. Marker is .4 miles beyond gate.

Beeman Memorial Cemetery is on land homesteaded by John and Emily Hunnicut Beeman.

Emily lies beside her husband, John Beeman, at the back of the Beeman Cemetery.

the accommodations, she did not show it. The cabin was so tiny that they could not all fit into it at once, but a meal of buffalo meat and wild honey revived her spirits.

The two men piled their plates and went outside where they propped themselves against a log to relish their food and talk about the future while Charity fed and quieted the children. Their meal completed, Bryan insisted that she join him and her husband.

Then, with the grace of the old country gentleman/lawyer that he was, Bryan delivered an official welcoming speech climaxed by presenting Charity with a city lot. It did not matter that the territory had city lots only in the imagination of the genial host. It would be another two years before streets would actually be laid out and Charity would learn that her lot was on Commerce at Houston Street. It would be 14 years before the city would be incorporated and the landmarks Bryan had laid out in his mind would become realities.

After Bryan himself, Charity was the first landowner in the new town. More important, she brought the nucleus of a new population in her several children. No matter that in a few years, she would again be uprooted and moved on by a husband whose vision of the good life always lay just beyond the present.

Charity Morris Gilbert was Dallas's first remarkable woman. There would be countless more to come . . . .

A few days after Charity and Mabel Gilbert were welcomed by John Neely Bryan, two of the Beeman families traveled north of the site that its founder had chosen for his town. On April 4, 1842, the day after leaving Bird's Fort, John and Emily Hunnicutt Beeman and James and Sarah Crawford Beeman stopped for lunch on the banks of a creek. The day was unseasonably warm. The trees dressed in new green were reflected in the tranquil water. Birds called greetings to one another. A fat turtle sunned itself on a boulder lodged at the edge of the creek. The children spotted it and called out to their parents. James said that they should call the place Turtle Creek. And thus Turtle Creek got its name.

Emily Hunnicutt Beeman was a Georgia native; John was from South Carolina. They had married on June 19, 1823, in Alton, Illinois, where both families had gone to farm. The Beemans had come to Texas in 1840 to homestead, leaving behind their oldest daughter, 16-year-old Elizabeth, as the bride of Henry Harter in Illinois.

Thus, their second child, 16-year-old Margaret, was the oldest of the Beeman children arriving that spring day in 1842. No special bells rang out, no ceremony marked the appearance of the young woman who for the next 70 years would play a vital role in the development of the new city—for already its founder had singled her out as a person of unusual charm and spirit.

No diaries or journals record the auspicious meeting and it was years later, in 1892, before the *Memorial and Biographical History of Dallas County* recorded:

> (He) had for five or six months been monarch of all he surveyed . . . (but) . . . he entertained them with the best he had—chiefly bear meat and honey— perhaps without recalling the adage about entertaining angels unawares, yet it was verified in this case, for ere a great while, the lonely son of Tennessee gave his heart and hand to a comely and pure-hearted daughter of Illinois in the person of Margaret, a daughter of Mr. and Mrs. John Beeman.[4]

Charity Gilbert was doubtless disappointed when the Beemans chose to locate a distance away from their own downtown Dallas property. While the Gilberts chose a 640-acre headright on the west side of the Trinity River, the Beemans settled on another 640 acres some three miles to the east. They named their area White Rock for the white shale near the surface of the earth, a distance away from the area later known as White Rock.

Upon their arrival, Charity and Mabel found a 14 by 14 foot oak cabin on Charity's city lot ready for them, it having been completed by their older sons with Bryan's supervision and help. They moved into it but later sold it to Mabel's brother, Wilson Gilbert, and his wife, Martha, and built a larger house on their 640-acre grant on the

Charity Gilbert's bravery under stress was recorded in a letter by her daughter, Nicy Gilbert Hampton in 1893 . . .

west side of the Trinity. There, Charity and the children worked with their husband and father to cultivate the earth and plant, grow and harvest food for themselves and the animals and to share with other individuals and families who found their way to Dallas. It was a herculean task. The heavy black soil, indeed as fertile as their mentor had promised, defied their best efforts to conquer it. When it rained, the soil turned to a gummy paste. When it did not rain, the earth cracked after a few days and the crops not already ravaged by birds, insects, rabbits and squirrels, parched and dried up. Tools were meager—an ax, a crude hoe and a wooden plow—mostly sticks, stones and their own bare hands.

An added frustration was Gilbert's total lack of knowledge about farming. He was a seaman, not a man of the soil, and, like so many men of early Dallas days, he was often away from home on hunting trips or traveling to distant places to buy supplies leaving Charity and the children to cope alone. Charity's bravery under stress was recorded in a letter written by her daughter, Nicy Gilbert Hampton:

> Indians frequently came to our house and partook of the bounty of my father, who always treated them kindly . . . . My father and all of the men were away . . . . We saw about twenty Indians approaching the house, all in war paint. There being no men left . . . my mother, then nursing a babe, realized that it was impossible for her to escape . . . . She called all of us children to her and told us to flee through the forest to Fort Inglish (located near the present city of Bonham) and give the alarm . . . . She said she was tired of this kind of life and would stay and die. Of course we were all greatly alarmed, and all vanished in the woods . . . . She then advanced to meet the Indians with her babe in her arms. To her great surprise, they began to make signs of friendship and one of their number who could speak English gave her to understand that they were friendly and meant her no harm, and asked permission to camp in the grove nearby. She readily consented and gave them bountifully of what she had . . . . A runner was sent after us children and we were informed of the glad tidings.[5]

Some of the older children were not found by the runner and eventually reached Fort Inglish to give the alarm. A Captain Ballard quickly organized a group of heavily armed men and galloped off to the Gilbert home.

> He was about to attack the Indians when my mother interfered and prevented the battle . . . my mother rushed in between them (the Indians and the troops) with her babe in her arms, and after much persuasion prevailed upon Captain Ballard to not molest the Indians.[6]

The babe in Charity's arms was Morris, the first child born in Dallas. Mabel Gilbert made numerous trips to Fannin County where the Gilberts had lived before seeking sanctuary at Bird's Fort. During the winter of 1844, they left Dallas and returned to Bonham. He received a patent for land in Fannin County on February 20, 1845, having sold his Dallas property to William Coombs. Charity's new home, three miles from Bonham, became a flourishing ranch, part of which was purchased years later by Sam Rayburn while he was Speaker of the House of Representatives.

The Beemans, experienced in farming in Illinois and accustomed to the vagaries of weather, fared much better. Even though the soil all but defeated their attempts to conquer it, they persevered. They were encouraged by the arrival of the third Beeman brother, Samuel, with his family. Together they erected a 15-square-foot blockhouse with lookout holes and a projecting outer wall on the upper part of the building as protection from Indians. Though they never needed the "fortress," there was reason to believe they might. On the day after his arrival, John Beeman rode his horse into town to collect mail from a Peter's Colony agent. On his way back to his farm, several Indians rode out of a clump of trees and chased him.

In all, the three Beeman families added 25 children to the Dallas population, eleven of them the daughters and sons of John and Emily.

The courtship of Margaret Beeman and John Neely Bryan is a matter of conjecture rather than record. One visitor to early Dallas noted that Bryan was living in the "bonds" to marry his wife, a common practice in the days when it was difficult to secure a marriage license and even harder to find a licensed official to perform a wedding ceremony.

Margaret became the first First Lady of Dallas on February 26, 1843, ten and a half months after she moved to the area. Born on September 29, 1825, she was a 17-year-old bride. Her husband was 32.

The couple rode horseback to Fort Inglish, near what is now Bonham, to be married in a civil ceremony. It was the nearest place with a licensed official who could perform weddings. The bride wore a calico dress and the bridegroom a buckskin suit. Both wore moccasins Margaret had made.

The couple returned from their 120-mile horseback ride and settled into their honeymoon cottage, a single 14 by 15 foot room made of rough-hewn cedar logs. It had a door in the front, an opening for a chimney and a fireplace on its left wall, no windows and no floor. Bryan had built it for his bride to replace the even smaller lean-to that had served as his home.

Margaret found it a "lovely place to make a home." In a rare interview in the latter years of her life, she reminisced:

Margaret Beeman married Dallas founder John Neely Bryan when she was 17.

> We lived happily in a lovely log cabin. Buffalo, deer and turkey for meat and wild honey for sweets. We ground our meal on a steel mill and raised the corn on the ground where your fine courthouse now stands. We had an Indian pony and wood plow made from a fork of bois d'arc tree and harness made from buffalo skins. We crossed the river in our little canoe dug out of a cottonwood tree.[7]

Glimpses of Margaret as a young wife and mother indicate her to be shy, but she was a bride of not quite five months and not yet 18 when Englishman E. Parkinson visited the Bryans while on an excursion through the Republic of Texas with President Sam Houston. Parkinson's diary notes that he and his traveling companions first visited the Beemans at White Rock Springs "where we were regaled with an acceptable and plentiful supply of buttermilk." Then the party went "to another settler's cabin on the banks of the river. It was inhabited by a Col. Bryan . . . ." (no mention of Margaret)

> He was a hardy backwoodsman, and a sensible, industrious, ingenious and hospitable man. I remained with him the two following nights.[8]

John Neely Bryan, as a 32-year-old bridegroom, already looked gloomy.

Margaret was only 18 years old in January of 1844 when Mrs. J. P. Dumas dismissed her with only a slight reference. The Dumases and 12 male companions arrived in Dallas with 100 head of cattle and a wagon loaded with corn. Dumas was a surveyor who laid out the original town of Dallas in 200 x 200 foot blocks extending eight blocks East to West from the Trinity to Poydras and 10 blocks North and South from McKinney to Young. Mrs. Dumas was "a gay soul who traveled in an ancient hack drawn by the two old steers named Buck and Broad." She kept a diary on her journey from the Falls of the Brazos to Dallas where she and her husband made their home within a few yards of the Bryan cabin.

Her diary barely notes Margaret's existence:

> Col. Bryan met us ten miles from the village 'We are glad to have you locate with us,' he said, 'as we are about out of corn . . . .' We found living there John N. Bryan and his wife and a Mr. Lundy and his family. Mr. Lundy was a blacksmith. [His shop] was in a log hut. In a shed room Mr. Lundy opened a store. His stock consisted of a barrel of whisky and three bolts of calico. The

first dress I ever got in Texas was off those bolts. I won this dress in a horse race from Mr. Lyle. He paid 50 cents a yard for the goods.[9]

Margaret was not a total recluse. Early in the spring of 1844, she accompanied her husband to Red River for supplies. While they were away, rainstorms swelled the Trinity and it overflowed, badly damaging the cabin. They returned to find it uninhabitable. Also, they needed a larger house because Margaret was pregnant. They lived in a tent made of wagon sheets while a second log cabin, two rooms with a breezeway between, was built. It was up the bluff further from the river than the first cabin.

The fate of the first cabin is unknown.[10] One story is that it was moved to White Rock Creek northeast of Dallas where it served as shelter for several tenant families until the land was purchased by Dr. R. C. Buckner as the site for the Buckners Orphans' Home and that Dr. Buckner, knowing the cabin's history salvaged it and eventually presented it to the City of Dallas. The story further claims that the cabin, now restored, was moved in 1976 to Dallas County Historical Plaza at Main, Market and Elm Streets where it sits only a little more than 100 yards from where it sheltered Dallas's first bride. Many researchers and historians believe that the downtown John Neely Bryan cabin is an impostor and that, at best, it contains only fragments of the original cabin.

The John Neely Bryan Cabin—which may be an imposter—sits on Dallas's Commerce Street.

In any event, the cabin has become a downtown Dallas landmark, known as the John Neely Bryan cabin. It should be named the Margaret Beeman Bryan Cabin, for she did a lot more living in it and in their subsequent homes than her husband ever did.

Their second cabin, built in the spring and summer of 1844, was completed before the birth of the Bryan's first child on August 26, 1844. The baby was a boy; they named him Holland Coffee in honor of Bryan's long-time friend. This baby, like so many infants on America's frontier, died in July of 1845 when he was 11 months old. His final resting place is in the Beeman Cemetery,[11] on Osage Road off Gault just behind the present Sheareth Israel Cemetery. The baby, quite likely, is the first person buried in the plot which is located where Hatcher now merges with Dolphin Road, on land homesteaded by his grandparents and where they and other family members also rest.

Almost five months after Holland Coffee died, on January 9, 1846, Margaret gave birth to a second son, John Neely Bryan, Jr. Many Dallas historians record Bryan, Jr. as the first child born in the new town, but Dallas's first child was Morris Gilbert, the second Holland Coffee Bryan. John Neely Bryan, Jr. was its third.

Margaret and John had four more children, two of them born in the cabin and two after they had moved again. Elizabeth Frances Bryan (Dillon) joined the family on December 4, 1847; Edward Tarrant Bryan on June 2, 1849; Alexander Luther Bryan on October 3, 1854 and Thomas Pinkney Bryan on October 9, 1861.

Margaret did a lot more living in the Bryan cabin than her husband, whose wandering ways found him, more often than not, away from her and the children.

The arrival of the children chronicle the wanderings of their father. After five years of marriage, Bryan reverted to his nomadic ways. The babies appeared almost regularly nine months after he returned from one trek after another.

Edward, the Bryan's third living child could not have been more than a few months old, perhaps but a few weeks, when Bryan left his family to follow the Gold Rush to California in 1849.

Margaret stayed home with her own three babies—the infant Edward, John Neely, Jr. 3 1/2, and Elizabeth, 18 months. She also had her uncle James's children, Mary Frances, Emily Elvira, Francis Marion (Frank) and Melissa Anice Beeman, who ranged in age from 10 years to 28 months. James, who had lost his wife, Sarah Crawford Beeman, the year before, hired a Negro girl to live in and help out with the children. This meant that the cabin housed nine people, seven of them children. With the help of her parents and friends, Sarah and Alexander Cockrell, she kept the home, grew the garden, looked after her children, replenished supplies, traded with the Indians and waited for her husband to come home. A year passed before he gave up his dream to strike it rich in gold and returned to his family.

Early in the 1850s, Margaret Bryan had yet another trauma to face. Her husband began to drink heavily.[12] The man whose vision had founded a city, secured a charter for the county, and successfully battled for his town to be the seat of county government, seemed to lose sight of his vision.

He had sold 86 of his prime city lots and given away many others including the site for the first county court house on a plot next to his own home. Here, soon after learning that the Republic had granted Dallas the right of county seat, city fathers erected a 16 x 16 foot cabin on the site, moving the building to the northeast corner of the lot so as not to interfere with Bryan's corn crop. It was roofed with four flat boards and floored with puncheon logs. A large fireplace with a clay chimney provided warmth when county business was handled. There was no provision for cooling in the summer, not even windows for breeze cross currents. Furniture consisted of split logs mounted on stumps.

By 1852 the Bryans were deeply in debt and in August of that year Bryan sold Dallas and the ferry concession he had founded to Alexander Cockrell for $7,000. The sale became effective in March of 1853 and included everything which Bryan had not already sold or given away, including the cabin where the family lived.

Margaret and the children, now 4, 6 and 7, continued to live in the cabin on the Trinity and welcomed their husband and father when he was sober enough and interested enough to come home. At 43, he had let a city and, with it, a fortune slip through his fingers.

Frank Cockrell, Alexander and Sarah's son, in a history he wrote of early Dallas, described Bryan in the early 1850's as "gloomy." He added that Bryan drank heavily, lost his mental alertness and showed only sporadic interest in the town he had founded. Several times he was arrested and brought into court on minor charges.

Cockrell, the historian, adds it would be erroneous to think that Bryan did not love his family. "He was a man of honor devoted to his family all of his life," Cockrell wrote.

Surely Margaret would have preferred less expression of devotion for his family to his friends and more evidence of it at home, for again she was left alone to cope with her home and children. This time there were four little ones.

In October of 1854 Margaret gave birth to a fifth child and fourth son, Alexander Luther. The baby was not a year old when his father got into a fight with a man over what Bryan described as an affront to Margaret. In the altercation, Bryan shot the man and, thinking him dead, saddled his horse, Neshoba, and rode out of town pausing only long enough to meet Cockrell, his lawyer, on the west bank of the Trinity River Bridge and sign papers necessary to look after his business while he was absent.

There was little business left to look after.

In her wildest dreams, Margaret could not have imagined how long this episode would last. The children grew, the oldest two to become teenagers before she would see her husband again.

He wrote letters—but more often to his friend, Alexander Cockrell, than to her. His behavior indicates that the mental incapacities he was to suffer later had already

John Neely Bryan's oldest son was 10 when he rode away from Dallas and 16 when he returned.... His children didn't know him.

manifested themselves because the man he had wounded not only recovered, but made it clear that he had never intended to file charges.

Letters Bryan said he wrote and received from Margaret presumably were destroyed, for only two are preserved from Alexander Cockrell's files[13] to suggest anything of what was happening in Bryan's life during the six years of his absence. We have even less in preserved history of how Margaret, John Neely, Jr., Elizabeth, Edward and baby Alexander survived.

The first letter to Cockrell:

Creek Nation
February 25, 1856

Mr. A. Cockrell:

Sir, I have received your letter of December 4 a few days since and I was very glad to get it. I have received one from my wife only. I am now living with Jesse Chishalm in the Creek Nation about 40 miles north of Fort Arbuckle. Chishalm is a half-breed Cherokee and an old friend of mine. I have done nothing yet to make a living. I have been out on the plains 3 times to look for gold mines, but did not find them and think I shall start again soon but will return here again. I sometimes think it would be best for me to go into the western part of Texas and make me a new home for I want to see my family and shall not be satisfied until I am again with them. I wish you would write to me and advise me as regard to this course and let me know if you think it would be safe for me to do so or not. I was in a storm sometime since and a tree blowed down on my horse and broke him down in the line. Since which I have had to borrow. I am surprised at Colonel Stone and the other attorneys in Dallas for turning against me and I shall meet them when they least expect it and then I will know the reason why they do so. If I have any friends among the people of Dallas, I want you to write and let me know who they are. Give my love to my wife and children and say I will be with them as soon as I can. I shall depend upon you to act for me as well as you can and I hope to live to thank you and pay you for it. Give my respects to your lady. I remain your friend.

J. N. Bryan

The second letter was written almost two years later:

Jamestown, California
January 2, 1858

I received a letter from you which was written in June last and I answered it at the time of reception, but I have not heard from you since. I received one from my wife at the same time and have not received any since. What can be the cause is a mistery to me. But I continue to write . . . . I hope you will write to me and let me know the cause, if any. I do not write to anyone at Dallas except you, for I cannot place my confidence in any of the rest. I am not able to come home yet, but as soon as I can I shall start home on the mail route from here to El Paso. I have worked harder than I ever did in my life, but it takes all I can make to pay expenses, and everyone here that I am acquainted with is in the same situation. I sometimes get out of heart and conclude I will not be able to see my wife and children again. The gold mines are so worked out that men can make but little now and still a man's expenses are the same they were before the mines failed. I am mining now but the water freezes up and I can make nothing. You could not believe that there was in this country hundreds of them that are almost on the starve, but such is the case, and there are but a few but what eats up at night what he makes in the day. IT IS THE HARDEST COUNTRY, I think, on earth. I shall be on my way out as soon as I can make the money. I shall not remain here one day longer than I can help, for I want to see my wife and children.

When I mention that this is the cause for my coming home you know I am in earnest. I want to see my wife, tell her what I have written and say to her it is not my fault I don't come home. Give my love to my wife and children. My respect to Mrs. Cockrell and any others that you know to be my friends if I have any about. I remain your friend.

John N. Bryan

P. S. If you write, direct your letters thus Col. John Bryan, Jamestown, California.

If letters come after I leave I have friends here that will send them to me wherever I go. I do not want any more sent to Stockton for there are too many there that know me. J. B. Bryan was there not long ago.

There is mystery in the time elapse between Bryan's leaving the Indian Creek Nation and arriving in California, and in his concern that too many people know him in Stockton. Surely Margaret must have pondered that puzzle as she waited in Dallas for her errant husband.

He returned in 1861 after six years of wandering. Frank Cockrell recorded the homecoming:

It was night when he reached the Trinity River. The bridge over which he had passed years before on his flight had fallen and the ferry was re-established. The ferryman was off duty. His wife heard his loud calling and recognized his voice and awoke the ferryman. He was haggard and worn and his children did not know him.[14]

Margaret recognized his voice and sent the ferryman to fetch him home? He was so worn and haggard that his children did not know him? Of course not. He had not often communicated with them, and those were the days before photographs so they could have no idea what he looked like. Imagine what it would be like to Margaret—the mother of children 10, 8, 6 and less than a year when their father went away to have him return to sons and a daughter 16, 14, 12 and almost 7.

Margaret was barely 30 when her husband "honored" her by shooting a man and then deserting her for six years. She was 35 when he returned and within weeks she was pregnant again. Her youngest and last child, Thomas Pinkney Bryan, was born in October of 1861, ten days after her 36th birthday and almost nine months to the day from her husband's return.

Bryan did not tarry for the baby's birth. The rumblings of secession from the Union by southern states already were brewing by the time he returned home. On February 8, 1861, the Confederate States of America were formed and by the middle of April the Civil War was in full force. Bryan immediately enlisted in Darnell's Cavalry Regiment on the side of the South and became a scout for the regiment. His soldiering did not last long, for he was 51 years old and in failing health. After a year he came home to the family he had left three times before—once to seek his fortune, once to flee from justice and once to join the Confederate Army.

Shortly after arriving back in Dallas, the Bryan family moved to White Rock near Margaret's family home. It must have been a vast relief to her to be closer to her family, who had helped her so many times in so many ways while her husband meandered about the country. Her father, John Beeman, had died five years before, on March 12, 1856. He had acquired a small fortune and after the estate was probated in 1858, it was dispersed among his many heirs. Margaret inherited 40 acres at Big Spring on White Rock where they built their new home. She also inherited other lands. It was her money—money she inherited from her family—that built and furnished their home and provided the livelihood for the family.

After moving to White Rock, John sporadically showed renewed interest in Dallas. He surfaced as a leader following the 1866 floods that destroyed a large portion of the city and he headed a campaign to renew citizenship rights to Confederate veterans. He led a support group seeking speedy completion of the Houston and Texas Railroad to Dallas.

His moments of renewed interest in his town were laced with longer and longer periods of melancholy. Margaret and the children lived in fear that he would wander off again or, worse, harm himself or someone else. Frank Cockrell, who often accompanied him on their horseback rides from White Rock into Dallas wrote, "It became manifest that the once fertile mind was entering into the shadows, and impaired intellect."[15]

Bryan's family admitted him to the State Mental Hospital in Austin on February 20, 1877. Six months and 25 days later he died there.[16]

No records exist of the disposition of his body. This raises many questions. Is it possible that Margaret and the children—the oldest was 32 years old at the time of his father's death—had completely severed the relationship with their husband and father? Or, perhaps, all their money had run out and they could not afford to bring the body home? Or could they have had a private burial in or near their home and let nobody know?

Strangely, nobody ever asked Margaret these questions, or if they did she kept the answers to herself. Perhaps the shame that accompanied mental illness in those days sealed her lips. Or maybe guilt over things she perceived she might have done rendered it impossible for her to talk.

Or, it could be, as Margaret Ackerman, a third-generation descendant in the family would say wistfully: "I don't think Cousin Margaret was very happy."[17] Perhaps she simply wanted to forget.

Margaret lived for 42 years following the death of her husband. She never remarried. She died on September 6, 1919, only 23 days before her 94th birthday. First buried at Charlie, Texas, her body was later moved to the family plot in Riverside Cemetery near Wichita Falls.[18]

2

THE CITY'S PREMIERE ENTREPRENEUR

Through the years, Dallas has always honored entrepreneurship above other values. Making money has been the primary game, and the man who pulled himself up by his own bootstraps was held in great esteem. Men have been the players . . . .

And yet, it was a woman who played the game first, by all the rules set down by the males, and won in a fashion far bigger than most individuals who followed her. Her name was Sarah Horton Cockrell. She was Dallas's first entrepreneur, so overwhelmingly successful that the 1892 *Dallas City Directory* listed her occupation as "Capitalist."

Sarah's arrival in Dallas was inauspicious. She was 25 years old, an old maid by the standards of her time, when a covered wagon brought her to Dallas with her parents, Enoch and Martha Stinson Horton. They came from Russell County, Virginia, arriving on November 29, 1844. They settled at Mountain Creek in what was then called Hord's Ridge and later Oak Cliff. At that time Dallas and Hord's Ridge and several other small settlements of a few families each were all separate villages, none any more significant than the other.

The fifth of the 11 Horton children, Sarah was a quiet, somewhat somber girl who often looked after her younger siblings, cooked, helped with the housework and at times, assisted with the planting and harvesting.

Sarah's appearance was as unpretentious as her manner. Willow slender and straight, she was gifted with the flexible but tough traits of that enduring tree. Her erect carriage made her appear taller than her five feet five inches. She wore her dark hair parted in the middle, braided at the ends and caught into a bun at the nape of her neck. Heavy arched brows framed deep-set gray eyes, their green flecks vibrant and sparkling when she was animated, blazing on the rare occasions when she was angry, retiring behind darker pigment when she was reflective, and always unfathomable.

She was a quite ordinary-looking young woman and nobody could have guessed that she was a person of destiny who would form and shape her new world in such a way that it would forever be imprinted with her deeds.

The Hortons moved to Dallas with 10 of their 11 children plus several children-in-law and grandchildren, leaving only their oldest daughter Mary, who was married to Martin M. Thompson and would move to Dallas 10 years later. The new Dallasites were Jane, John, James, Sarah, Enoch, Jr., Robert, Martha, Rachel, Lucy and Emarine. In following years, Jane married William Bradshaw; John wed Elizabeth Margaret Hopkins; James married Jane Phillips and, later, Mary (Mollie) Morton King; Enoch, Jr. had two wives: Nancy C. Reed and Lucy Lanier; Robert died single. Martha married her cousin, William Horton, and Rachel wed Joseph Read. This litany of spouses is significant because it shows how families were interrelated through marriage during those early days. Young people often married cousins and even more often siblings of their own sister or brother.

Not Sarah. Even in those days when an unmarried girl was an old maid with all the stigma attached to that condition—no man of her own, no children, no support, destined to make her home as an unwelcome adult in the home of a brother or sister after the death of her parents—Sarah gave every evidence of being serenely unperturbed by her single state. Perhaps she dreamed of love, marriage and children as she went about her daily chores, but always she seemed separate and apart—living, not in loneliness, but aloof from prevailing conditions.

Alexander Cockrell was an intrusion into her world—literally as well as figuratively. At 26, he was as totally into his world as Sarah was apart from hers. Born in Kentucky into an affluent family, he moved with his parents to Missouri when he was four years

Sarah Horton Cockrell was Dallas's first entrepreneur whose wealth was so extensive that her will was published in a 24-page pamphlet.

Sarah Cockrell's gentle manner is revealed in this portrait of her by Nadine Steele Cockrell and in letters to her daughter.

old. Shortly thereafter his mother died and his father left the little boy pretty much alone. When he was 14, Alex left home. Like John Neely Bryan, the man who would become his friend in a new world called Dallas, Alexander lived for a time with the Cherokee Indians.

Those were the days when a man with more guile than education could support himself by finding and returning runaway slaves to their masters. Alexander took up the trade. In 1846, this brought him to Dallas where he stopped off for a visit with his cousin, Wesley Cockrell, a neighbor of Enoch and Martha Horton. Always on the alert for an opportunity to make money, Alex volunteered to deliver merchandise to the Horton home. Though he had a sturdy wagon and a good team of oxen, he had not reckoned with the vagaries of the Trinity River crossing from Dallas to Hord's Ridge nor the deep mud that would impede his progress. Doubtless, he had also loosened his tongue with a nip or so in town, for Alex was not known to exit quietly when the drinks went around. So it was that he reached his destination swearing and calling out for someone to come out and claim the freight.

Sarah met him with ice in her eyes. The few words they exchanged were curt. She claimed the freight and slammed the door. The tall black-haired, dark-eyed deeply tanned young man might be a relative of a neighbor, but it was clear that he was no gentleman, and Sarah dismissed him as quickly as possible.

Or, so she thought. She saw him again a few days later, before he took off for the Texas border to fight in the Mexican War, when she went with her family to visit the Wesley Cockrells. On this occasion, Alexander was as handsome and charming as he had been uncouth at their first encounter. True to her nature, Sarah shared with no one the effect of this unconventional young man on her. True to his nature, Alexander Cockrell took an indelible picture of a gray-eyed young woman with him along the trail and into battle. When he could not, with his usual ability to run away from involvement and responsibility, shake the vision, he backtracked to Cousin Wesley's house.

His arrival coincided with a party, and his appearance on the scene set many a heart aflutter. He scanned the dancers and greeted several of her brothers and sisters, but did not see the girl he had come home to find.

Alexander found Sarah in the kitchen. Taking her hand he led her out under the stars of the late summer night and there, typical of his act-first, think-later manner, told her that he had come back to marry her. Sarah said yes. She did not even seemed surprised.

On September 9, 1847, over the objections of her father who warned her of Alexander's unsavory character, and her mother, who spoke guardedly about the roving ways of many men, Sarah Horton married Alexander Cockrell. She was 28. He was 27. She wore, for her wedding, a new calico dress and the bridegroom was resplendent in his freshly laundered army uniform.

Alexander and his bride went home to the 640-acre homestead adjoining the farms of her parents and his cousin for which he had applied immediately after Sarah said yes. They built their home, one large room with a half-story loft and a shed room to store supplies. It was the talk of the entire countryside because, again, Alexander did things with a flourish. Not only was it bigger than most of the other houses nearby, but it was painted! Whitewashed! The first house in the entire area to be other than natural, rustic logs. The bride began housekeeping with one pot and a skillet. Their stove was the open hearth.

Alexander broke and planted a few acres of his farm, but his restless nature demanded a faster-paced life. He bought a few cattle and shortly was operating the first ranch in the area. He also ran a freight service from Dallas to Houston, Jefferson and Shreveport using oxen to transport supplies.

When he was away, Sarah managed the business. She could read and write; he could not. Though her formal schooling had been limited, she had educated herself and it was she who kept the company records, wrote the letters and was both cashier and banker. She read to her husband whatever she thought he ought to know. When he was away on long freighting trips, she managed alone. She traded corn for hides and honey with the Indians.

Alexander Cockrell was as flamboyant as Sarah was serene. She brought order into his life . . . he brought excitement into hers.

Sarah was as steady as her husband was flamboyant, as organized as he was mercurial, as discerning as he was dashing. He dreamed wild and wonderful visions; she put fences around them. He brought her the world, often along with it the seamier sides of life. She gave him stability, often filling the mother role he had never had.

Sarah lost her first baby. The child of their wild and wonderful first passion, Logan Morgan Cockrell[1] was born in 1848 only a few weeks after his parents' first wedding anniversary. A beautiful, happy baby, he seemed to give Alex Cockrell the roots that had always been missing in his life. Shortly afterward, Sarah was pregnant again. In February of 1850, following a brief illness, Logan Cockrell died. Alex was inconsolable. After the funeral, he mounted his horse and rode off. He was gone for a month, leaving Sarah alone with her grief, seven months pregnant and in charge of the family business.

Aurelia Effie Cockrell was born on May 25, 1850. The mother-daughter bonding was instant, intense and inclusive. Through letters that the two exchanged and through stories passed down through the family, there is clear evidence that Sarah taught her daughter to be independent, even when she longed to protect her from the harder aspects of life. As she grew up, Aurelia assumed much of the responsibility for the care of her three younger brothers, even though Sarah always had help. In many ways, Aurelia was a carbon of the younger Sarah.

One of Sarah Cockrell's several homes. She moved several times to make way for a growing city.

Though John Neely Bryan was 10 years older than Alexander Cockrell, the two men became close friends, comrades and drinking buddies. Their similar backgrounds—both adventurers and self-made men, both visionaries, both having left home as boys and both having lived with the Indians—gave them endless topics for discussion. So did their mutual dreams for the growth of the town they had chosen. While the men were companionable, Sarah and Margaret Bryan were almost like sisters. Like their husbands, Sarah and Margaret shared many similarities. Both had been reared in large families. Both had come to Texas leaving behind older sisters. Both were married to men who were temperamental, who drank—sometimes heavily—who were sometimes in trouble and who often needed looking after. In addition to being dear friends, Sarah often assumed the mother role for the younger Margaret.

While Sarah looked on her husband's peccadillos with amused tolerance, she found it difficult to forgive Bryan for his treatment of Margaret. Her keen business sense gave her a clear insight into the way Bryan was mismanaging his affairs. She kept her counsel, as usual, when Margaret complained about her husband's behavior, but Sarah did not always keep her opinions to herself when Alexander defended his friend.

Robert, the third Cockrell baby, was born in 1852. He was still nursing the day Sarah's reverie was broken by shouts from her husband as he galloped into the yard waving a piece of paper above his head and shouting. "Mrs. Cockrell, may I present you with a town?!"

And he laid at her feet the city of Dallas. For $7,000 cash he had bought outright all of the remaining city lots that Bryan had not already given away or sold. To do it he had liquidated most of the family holdings. What Sarah thought or said history does not record, but in her usual manner, she turned adversity into opportunity, determined to help make their new enterprise profitable. She also began to save some of the family assets. Since there were no banks, Sarah kept all of her accounts, including large amounts of cash, in a small black trunk.

Sarah and Alex had been married for five and a half years when they left their White House Ranch and moved into downtown Dallas into the house vacated by the Bryans. For Sarah it was not altogether a happy move, for she had enjoyed the privacy of living on the ranch and she longed to rear her children as much as possible away from public glare.

Their business mushroomed. One of Cockrell's first acts as the new owner of Dallas was to establish a ferry across the Trinity River to link Hord's Ridge with Dallas, for already there was conflict between residents of the east and west sides of the Trinity River. This animosity was rooted in the battle between the frontier towns over which would become the county seat. In 1846 when Dallas County was established, Dallas had become the temporary seat of county government principally because Bryan offered a cabin to house the offices. Hord's Ridge and Cedar Springs, which at that time were the two largest settlements in the region, protested. An election held in 1848 gave Dallas 191 votes, Hord's Ridge 178, and Cedar Springs 101. Two years later in 1850, Dallas was named permanent county seat when it won a run-off election by 28 votes—244 for Dallas and 216 for Hord's Ridge. Hord's Ridge was not a happy loser.

The residents west of the Trinity were still smarting from the defeat, which the Cockrells understood because they had lived in Hord's Ridge during the clash. Added was their difficulty in transacting business with the county. When rains swelled the river, it was often impossible for them to reach downtown Dallas to file official papers.

Cockrell took steps to mend the rift. He replaced the slow, sluggish ferry with a tall bridge across the river. To build it, he erected a steam circular saw mill, the first in the area, on the river's east bank. As soon as timbers were cut for the bridge, he moved the saw mill further east, and began cutting lumber to sell. He bought additional property along the river's edge. He began a brick yard and erected the first brick building in town, a two-story structure on the southeast corner of his downtown holdings.

By this time there were four Cockrell children. Sarah had been pregnant twice more and had given birth to two more sons, Frank Marion in 1854 and Alexander in 1856. Alex and Sarah had also built a new home, a five-room house on the east end of Commerce Street. Sarah's involvement in the business never wavered. She continued to handle all the paper work, collect money owed them, issue receipts and accept freight. Money in the bank, still the small black trunk, mounted.

When John Neely Bryan left Dallas, it was Sarah who assumed the role of day-to-day caretaker for Margaret Bryan and her children because Margaret's parents lived too far away. Sometimes Alex and the Cockrell children resented the time Sarah devoted to the Bryan family. When letters from the roving Bryan came to Alexander rather than being sent to Margaret, Sarah was provoked. Shirley Seifert describes one scene: A letter has just arrived from Bryan and Sarah is reading it to her husband. She pauses in her reading and says to her husband: "Over and over . . . he says to give his love to his family. But it wasn't only the family . . . . There was the town . . . . If it had not been for that shooting . . . ." Alex takes up for his old friend. "Look . . . What can a man do but shoot a feller that insults his woman?" Sarah levels those gray eyes on her husband. "He could have turned his back," she says, "and stood by Margaret. That would have been a better way to show what he thought."[2]

The Cockrells continued to expand their holdings. By the beginning of 1857, he had completed plans for a grand new hotel and before the year was out had begun construction, in the meantime ordering lavish furnishings and equipment to be shipped from the nation's leading manufacturers.

He did not live to see the hotel completed. On April 3, 1858, he was killed on a downtown Dallas street by City Marshall Andrew M. Moore.

Marshall Moore was new in his job, having been elected to the post only two days before, but resentment between the two men had been brewing for a long time. Details are sketchy. What is certain is that Moore owed Cockrell money, either money he had

A Fatal Recontre . . . eight shots from Moore's gun took effect on the deceased . . . .

borrowed or for merchandise he had agreed to purchase. Early in the morning Cockrell rode his horse into town intending, among other things, to collect the debt from Moore. As was his usual habit, he had a drink—or two—or more. Moore, nervous about any encounter with Alex, was doubtless feeling cocky about his new status. He was attempting to arrest Alex on an ordinance involving the new hotel, when the gun went off. Moore said Cockrell was resisting arrest. Observers said very little, because the community suddenly had become a smoldering tinderbox and the least spark could have set off a conflagration.

The *Dallas Herald* called it a "fatal 'rencontre,'" a French word meaning a hostile meeting. The newspaper story:

> On Saturday evening last, a distressing and fatal rencontre occurred in this place between A. M. Moore and Alexander Cockrell, two leading citizens of town, resulting in the death of the latter. Both parties were armed with double barrelled shotgun and revolver, and Moore at the time was attempting to arrest the deceased, under a writ for violating a corporation ordinance. Eight shots from Moore's gun took effect on the deceased, most of them in the lower portion of the abdomen. He survived about an hour and a half. As the whole affair will undergo judicial investigation we forebear making any comment or from stating the circumstances in detail as we do not wish to prejudge or prejudice the case one way or the other in advance of the trial. Moore was admitted to bail in the sum of $5,000. We will only add that this unfortunate occurrence has thrown a gloom over this community. It is a distressing affair that cannot be too much deplored.[3]

Sarah prepared her husband's body for burial, then called the photographer to take a picture. She did not have time to mourn. She had several businesses to run. The city's future rested on her shoulders.

Sarah did not seem at all surprised when the townsmen brought Alex's body home. She was, wrote Shirley Seifert, "so calm . . . so quiet . . . in perfect command of herself and everything else."[4] She directed that his friends lay the body out in the living room. She took charge of preparing it for the funeral. She sent for Maxime Gouhenant, the town's photographer, to take pictures. She made funeral plans. She sent some of the Black people who had long been with them to report Alex's death to family members and friends. Her children were spending the night with friends in Hord's Ridge and she sent for them. She received Berry Derritt and took the tin box of money he had collected during the day for bridge toll fees. She received a young lawyer who had only recently moved to town and who, for reasons he did not explain, returned the watch Alex had entrusted to him only moments before he was killed.

Then she asked that the "bank," the little black trunk, be brought to her, and she worked the rest of the night checking and rechecking family holdings. When the first hint of dawn came gently to Dallas on the morning of April 4, 1858, Sarah knew precisely what they owned, knew exactly what was owed to them, and knew, to the last penny, what she could count on collecting, what she would need to write off, how she would run the businesses and who she would trust to help her.

In the meantime, the town was in turmoil. Alexander Cockrell paid the salaries that provided the livelihood of many townspeople. Will Toomy, foreman of the mill, was concerned about his job and wondered how he would pay the mill hands. Pere Frichot, foreman at the brickyard, had similar disquieting thoughts. Rudy Horst, hauling a piano and chandelier for the new hotel from Shreveport, learned about the catastrophe from a horseman before he got to town and worried about what he would do about unloading his cargo, who would pay him for his services and what would happen to the hotel. There were not many demands for a grand piano. He could not know, nor could the rest of the people, that Sarah was making plans for the future even as they fretted.

Nobody, in their wildest dreams, imagined that Sarah would, or even could, carry on. Abraham Shirek and Hyman Hirsch, merchants who were at that moment expanding their business at the behest and encouragement of Alex, talked about moving. "While her husband lived, she was his bookkeeper, and that is all. She can't do what he did," they told each other that night.[5]

Her son, Frank, summed it up: "She had been his amanuensis (secretary), counselor, bookkeeper and was acquainted with the details of his work, his finances and contracts and very efficient. When the blow fell, her acts indicated where her thoughts were, as does the buoy where rests the anchor, to complete the works of her husband in memorial of him . . . . The great responsibilities resting upon her seemed unsurmountable."[6]

Sarah did not have time to mourn. Thirty-eight years old and the mother of four children, the oldest eight and the youngest two, and with a large portion of the economic stability of the town resting on her shoulders, she walked away from her husband's funeral to manage the family businesses. A newspaper account, some years later, describes her:

> Carefully dressed in her best black alpaca with skirts sweeping the floor, hooped bodice and tight-fitting black bonnet, she stepped out to grapple with the man-sized job that awaited her in an exclusive man's world at the time.[7]

Sarah wrote to her husband's family in Missouri, directing her letters to his brother, Francis Marion Cockrell, for whom Frank M. Cockrell, the son who would later become the family historian, was named. Francis was an attorney and Sarah requested his legal advice. The responses were less than enthusiastic. Her brother-in-law was "deeply pained to receive the bad news," sympathized with her and the children, advised her to hire "able lawyers," and regretted that he could not come to Texas.[8]

The three-day trial that followed in July was sensational. Sarah hired John C. McCoy, the town's first lawyer, to prosecute Moore. The defense team of four lawyers was headed by Col. Warren Stone. Public sentiment ran high in Moore's favor and when the verdict "innocent" was rendered, the courtroom burst into spontaneous applause.

Sarah again corresponded with the Cockrells in Missouri—this time, not to Alex's brother, but to Alex's sister, Polly Fulkerson and her husband. In December, Sarah received a letter from Francis, full of platitudes and advice, but still offering no help. The future was now up to her.

Sarah's toll bridge across the Trinity River replaced the ferry until it washed away and had to be replaced.
—Texas/Dallas History and Archives, Dallas Public Library

Sarah set about collecting debts, including the one that her hot-headed husband had lost his life arguing about, paid what they owed, and began to expand the businesses.

Four months after Cockrell's death, floods loosened the west arch of the Trinity bridge and the entire west section of the wooden structure collapsed. Only momentarily daunted, Sarah renewed the ferry license, which had lapsed when the bridge was in operation, and using a family-owned ferryboat which was already anchored in the Trinity, she reopened the ferry service.

Sarah shunned the spotlight. One of her greatest strengths was her ability to evaluate people. She chose workers carefully, gave them responsibility and rewarded them with appreciation as well as money for jobs well done.

Berry Derritt was typical of her employee success stories. She put him in charge of the ferry, and he refused to leave "Miss Sarah" when emancipation of slaves gave him his freedom in 1863. He allowed regular customers to charge their fares, but no stranger was allowed on his boat without paying full fare. He scrupulously kept account of all money and turned the day's receipts over to Sarah every evening. The fare for people travelling by foot was 5 cents; horse and buggy, 25 cents; wagon and one pair of horses or oxen, 30 cents; each additional pair of animals, 10 cents; each head of sheep or hogs, 2.5 cents; each head of loose horses or cows, 5 cents.

All of Sarah's businesses prospered. She moved the sawmill southward to a grove of hardwood trees and added circular saws to speed the process of turning logs into lumber for a building-hungry community. She improved and enlarged the brickyard and opened a flour mill. She operated the farm and continued to upgrade both the cattle and facilities on Mountain Creek ranch.

Friends and business associates tried to dissuade Sarah from building the hotel she and her husband had planned, but she refused to listen. There was only one small wooden hotel in town, and Sarah's business sense, honed through the years by keeping company ledgers, convinced her that Dallas was going to expand and required a first class hotel.

She completed the St. Nicholas, named for its manager, Nicholas H. Darnell in 1859. Made of brick and towering three stories upward on the northeast corner of its 100 square foot lot on Commerce at Broadway, it was the city's first skyscraper, the grandest building for miles around. A hallway ran the full length of the first floor separating a large office and waiting room on one side from a spacious dining room on the other. The kitchen was in another building separated from the dining room by an archway. A wide staircase opened from the hallway to the second floor and a smaller stairway from the second to the third floor.

The hotel was opened with a grand ball—Dallas's first major social event. Kerosene lamps reflected the highly polished woodwork where the dining room had been turned into a ballroom. The livery stable, an integral part of the hotel's plan, sold out. Surreys and stylish carriages drawn by horses especially groomed for the occasion drew up to the hotel's entrance to spill out men and women transformed from their usual buckskin and calico garb into persons of regal splendor. The women had sent to St. Louis or Philadelphia or Boston for ball gowns or they had resurrected satins and old lace from boxes which they had protected on their long trek to Texas, and remade them into the era's highest fashion—tightly fitting bodices with high necklines and leg-o-mutton sleeves over full skirts sweeping into trains. Some of the gowns were adorned with handmade silk flowers. Almost all the women carried bouquets. Treasured heirloom jewelry was brought out of its boxes, cleaned and polished, and made its debut on Texas soil. The men wore Prince Albert evening wear with white high-stiff collared shirts.

An orchestra led by violinist Frank Leonard sat on a raised platform and played symphony music while the ladies and gentlemen overflowed the reception hall and ballroom into the hallways and on the staircases conversing about the splendor that lay around them. At the stroke of 10, a bugle call announced the Grand March, and Col. John McCoy with a beautiful young girl led it.[9]

The St. Nicholas Hotel was opened with a grand ball—Dallas's first major social event.

It would be interesting to know the identity of "the beautiful young girl" because of the tragedy that shaped Col. McCoy's life. At the time he led the Grand March, he was one of the area's most eligible bachelors. He had arrived in Dallas in 1846 as a field representative for the Emigration Land Company, promoters of Peter's Colony in Texas. Originally from Indiana, he had practiced law in Missouri and Kentucky and somewhere had met and fallen in love with Cora M. McDermott of Pennsylvania. Once established in Dallas, he asked her father, Col. J. B. McDermott for permission to marry his daughter.

The two were married in 1851 and she died two years later in childbirth. (For details, see Chapter 6.)

So, it was widower Col. John McCoy, the same McCoy who prosecuted the man who killed Sarah's husband, who led the Grand Ball at the opening of the St. Nicholas Hotel. Logic would have it that Sarah was the beautiful young woman he escorted at the opening ball, but this is not likely. At her own party, she was her usual unobtrusive self, staying on the periphery of the festivities. The conventions of the day demanded decorum from women in public places, especially widows, but there is strong evidence that Sarah preferred it that way. She did allow her children to attend the ball and mingle with guests who had come from all over the state. Honored guests were seated on a half circle balcony with balustrade above the dining-ballroom which was decorated with boughs of cedar and other evergreen and garlands of wild flowers with the flags of the United States and Texas at either side.

Frank Cockrell, then only five, recalled attending the opening ball:

> The dances were the waltz, the schottish, the mazurka, the polka, lancers, the Virginia Reel, and the slow stately and dignified minuet. As they played the goodnight waltz, this little ditty was sung by Frank Leonard:
>
> We will hang up the fiddle
> and the bow,
> We will hang up the fiddle
> and the bow.
> You've danced all night 'till
> broad daylight,
> We will hang up the fiddle
> and the bow.[10]

The grand hotel lasted for a year exactly—from July 1859 to July 1860—when it was destroyed on Sunday, July 8, by the great fire that burned most of Dallas.

While the clouds of the Civil War moved ever closer, Sarah Cockrell was becoming the town's most outstanding business person. She continued to keep a low profile, managing her multiple businesses through her highly skilled employees, but when the occasion demanded, she spoke out. During the time she was building the St. Nicholas, she was also making plans to rebuild the Trinity River Bridge. Her lawyers drew up a charter for the Dallas Inn and Bridge Company to be presented to the State Legislature. It would be, like the collapsed causeway of the past, a toll bridge.

Merchants and other leading professional men wanted a free bridge. They had no resources to pay for it, nor any plans for raising the money to do so, but 54 of them signed a petition asking the Legislature to deny Sarah Cockrell's request and to authorize a free bridge. This was presented on December 1, 1859.

Sarah went to Austin. She appeared before the Legislature and presented her case. It was the first time a woman had done such a thing in Texas.

The Legislature, both shocked and titilated at the appearance of a woman, voted overwhelmingly in her favor. She came home and immediately started construction. The war's outbreak postponed the venture.

For Sarah, the Civil War demanded additional giving—both of her time and her money. She paid for many of the uniforms of men who enlisted for the Confederate Army. She saw that their businesses were in order and often helped to look after their families while they were away. She continued to help Margaret Bryan, moving her and her four children to White House Ranch after John Neely enlisted.

As soon as the war was over, Sarah renewed preparations to build the Trinity Bridge. She was the sole owner and financier, but the board of directors she personally selected

When Dallas business leaders asked the state legislature to deny Sarah's request to rebuild her toll bridge, she went to Austin where she was the first woman to testify before the State Legislature.

did not even include herself. The new bridge was completed in 1872, the same year that the first train puffed into Dallas. The train arrived on July 16, to shouting ovations from a crowd estimated to be between 4,000 and 5,000 people, quite a feat when you consider that the total population of the town stood at around 1,000. The Houston and Texas Pacific Railroad tracks that brought the train (including one passenger car, bearing honored guests, among its several freight cars) was completed only the day before.

Sarah's bridge built to handle intercity commerce and the railroad, shortly joined by a second, the Texas and Pacific, provided intra-city shipping and paved the way for a burgeoning city. Sarah's interests expanded with the growing city.

The "soft" side of Sarah is seldom mentioned, yet she was as devoted a wife, good friend, loving mother and dedicated community supporter as she was a successful businesswoman. She was determined that her children would not suffer any deprivations, either physically or emotionally, because of their father's death and her involvement with business affairs. Both from letters that have been preserved and from family history passed orally through the generations, it is clear that Sarah struggled to keep her family life and her personal commitments as rich as possible. It is also clear that she did not wish to marry again.

There were suitors—and at least one proposal of marriage that came from a most unlikely source, the Methodist minister. The Rev. James Anderson Smith, an early circuit rider, had come to Dallas as a part of Peter's Colony, had served as a minister as well as active community volunteer and was as stable and community-committed as Alexander Cockrell had been charismatic. He was first president of the Agricultural and Mechanical Association, the parent society of the State Fair of Texas, and had distinguished himself as a captain of the Davis Home Guards of Dallas County during the Civil War. In 1960, his wife died and some time afterward he proposed to Sarah Cockrell. The depth of their commitment is unknown, but his letter of proposal indicates that there had been some conversation between them of a deeper-than-friendship commitment. His letter of proposal is undated:

My Dear Mrs. Cockrell:

The many and pressing claims on your time and attention preclude the possibility of a personal interview. I therefore pen a few lines for your perusal with the hope of eliciting an answer that will relieve me from this painful suspense. I entreat of you by that undying love I have for you to give the subject a favorable consideration.

I have reflected on it maturely and prayerfully and the more I think of it the more thoroughly am I convinced than no evil of any kind to us or injury to anyone else can possibly grow out of our union and am the more convinced our happiness would be mutually promoted and secured. Then why my dear Sarah should there be any further hesitation why postpone those sweet enjoyments that belong alone to conjugal love and domestic affection—My very soul longs to call you mine please my sweet loved one to answer me favorably though it should be ever so briefly—If only that one sweet word yes twill be enough to complete my happiness and life's devotion to your happiness will be the least return that I can make. Select your own time and manner of answering this but my dearest one Let the answer be favorable. Yours most respectfully and affectionately.

Jas. A. Smith[11]

There is no record of Sarah's response, but she did not give him the yes he desired for she died still the widow of Alexander Cockrell. She and the Rev. Smith remained friends and she was one of the city's most lavish philanthropists. She had given the lot on the corner of Commerce and Lamar to the First Methodist Church and added money gifts for the building.

It is likely that Sarah's devotion to her children, together with her overwhelming involvement in business, gave her the knowledge and insight to know that she could not

Sarah, doubtless, had many suiters, among them the Methodist minister whose "very soul longs to call you mine." He did not get the "sweet yes," he longed to hear ... for she died still a widow.

begin a new romantic alliance. Her children were her life. The oldest of the children, Aurelia, most missed her father and most wanted to know his side of the family.

Aurelia was just 20 when Sarah put her in charge of 18-year-old Robert and sent them to Missouri to visit their father's family. They were the guests of their father's sister, Polly, and her husband, Reuben Bradley Fulkerson, in Walnut Grove, Missouri. Aurelia was charged with looking after her brother and enrolling him in a school his uncles chose. At first Aurelia, who had never been away from her mother except for overnight visits with friends, was exceedingly homesick and wrote her mother of her fears and illnesses. The letters did not reach Dallas, and on September 2, 1870, Sarah wrote to her brother-in-law:

Mr. R. B. Fulkerson

My Kind friend and Brother this morning I conclude to write you a few lines as I cant hear from Aurelia. I have never received a line from her but once since she left. I got the letter she wrote to me the morning after she got to your house. I now (sic) she had wrote to me though I feel shure that someone intercepts her letters that I may not get them. I fear she has not got our letters. We have sent the Herald every week since they left home and has written every week. If Aurelia does not hear from home I am shure she will get homesick and if I new (sic) she was homesick I would start after her this day. You dont now how dear that child is to me. Since her health is poor I can't hardly bear her out of my sight though it appeared as if nothing would satisfy her only to send her to see her Father's relations. As to you and Polly I felt shure you would be a Father and Mother to them. As to Gen. (Francis Marion) Cockrell I had nothing to expect of him for a silence of six years is enough to satisfy anyone that he was not interested much in the welfare of his Brother's children . . . .[12]

Sarah told her brother-in-law in the same letter, "I will be satisfied for you to do what you think is best in the choice of a school for Robert. I want him placed in a strict school, and I want him to be kept their (sic). I don't want him to have but very little money at his command . . . ."

From Aurelia's records, her letters home and letters written from Fulkerson to Sarah, it is clear that Robert was somewhat irresponsible. Aurelia kept careful records of the money with which her mother entrusted her. On September 15, 1870, she provided a comprehensive list of expenditures, including not only fares for transportation and expenses for her brother's school wardrobe, but the few cents she paid for postage stamp and writing paper, concluding her letter with:

Mama I paid all of this out of the money you gave me also paid for everything we used on the road out of mine, for Brother would get nothing. As to what he did with the ten dollars he left home with and the ten you sent him I cant tell . . . .[13]

All of Aurelia's letters to her mother revealed her homesickness. Her health was fragile. In October she wrote, "I have now been sick since Wednesday, confined to my bed with high fever and rising in my head . . . . How I did wish for home." Later the same month she wrote, " I . . . am very anxious to start in the first days of December for home . . . ." Another time she wrote that she would die if she could not be back in Dallas by Christmas. But Christmas came and went and she was still in Missouri. There were several mentions that a cousin might return home with her, but this did not happen. Sarah often suggested ways she might work out getting home. Her return was complicated because young ladies did not travel alone at that time. Aurelia had to wait until a relative or friend could travel with her.

In lengthy letters addressed to "my sweet child, my own dear Aurelia, my own beloved child . . . ." Sarah kept her daughter apprised of the family business, local news and gossip in her hometown. In November she complained that her taxes for 1969 were

Aurelia Effie Cockrell Gray was Sarah's only daughter. The two were unusually close. Aurelia died at age 21, only nine months after she married Mitchell Gray.

exorbitant—$150! She wrote at length about births, weddings, illnesses and death of people Aurelia knew. On November 17, 1870, she wrote about a new kitchen appliance. "I have the finest stove," she wrote. "I had rather cook for 20 on it than for 2 on the fireplace."

Sarah's longing for her daughter is especially poignant in a letter written on November 28:

> My Dearest Darling. I will wright (sic) you a few lines that you may now (sic) that you are always present with your mother. Oh, how I do hope to see you soon. I feel my Darlin' if I had to weight another month to see you I don't know if I could wait with any kind of patience.[14]

Except for the times when she was ill and longed for her mother's comforting presence, Aurelia began to enjoy the social life with her Missouri cousins. She attended parties and balls, danced and flirted and showed concern for Robert now enrolled in McGee College. Her letters to her mother, not quite so frequent, were still written to express great interest in what went on in Dallas and continuing love and affection for her relatives and friends. At one time, details of which do not exist in the preserved letter, Sarah said something that Aurelia took to be criticism of her behavior or her responsibility to Robert and the daughter wrote a heart-broken letter home. Sarah's good opinion, as well as her love, mattered deeply to the young woman.

Sometime in the late winter or early spring of 1871, Aurelia arrived back in Dallas to a joyous reunion with her mother. But her days to live at home were few. On May 11, two weeks before her 21st birthday, Aurelia married Mitchell Gray. Though details of the union are few, it was, without a doubt, a love match. His work took the young couple to Groesbeck, only a short distance today, but more than a day's journey at that time. The hotel rooms and boarding houses where the young couple lived were sweltering in the summer and freezing when winter came on early. In early June, less than a month after she was married, Aurelia wrote to Sarah:

> Mama, I must tell you of Mr. Gray and my happiness. I do know he is one of the best men, husbands, in the world, and I am one of the happiest beings that ever lived . . . . he is so kind to me. I always thought him perfect but I find him more so than I thought.[15]

Into the fall, the young couple's living accommodations and financial outlook improved and Aurelia became the proud owner of a sewing machine. On September 4, she wrote to Sarah: ". . . So, you see, the total cost was $81.00 . . . a gift from my husband. I feel that I can never fully repay him for this gift."

In the fall, Aurelia wrote her mother about the trip she and her husband made to visit his family for the first time. She seemed apprehensive about the visit, but was thrilled at the outcome, telling her mother that she had been lovingly welcomed. Even so, she missed her mother in Dallas. "I long for Christmas to come," she wrote.

The holidays came. Sarah and Aurelia had a joyous visit in Dallas. Together again, mother and daughter were never closer. When the couple returned to his work, Aurelia wrote about being chilled through on a late night trip with her husband, about the fever that came and lingered, about the "risings" that kept her in intense pain, the sore throats that were her constant nemeses. And, sometimes, Mitch wrote about the girl he had married, what he should do to insure her health, how much he loved her . . . .

On February 28, 1872, Aurelia Effie Cockrell Gray died. She was three months shy of her 22nd birthday, less than a year removed from the day she had promised Mitchell Gray "until death do us part." She is buried in the Cockrell plot in Greenwood Cemetery.

Sarah had lost the third of those who added depth, joy and meaning to her life: her firstborn son; then her husband, and the daughter who had been almost a younger replica of herself.

But there was still work to be done. Sarah Cockrell began to lay the foundation for her legacy. She carefully planned how she would give back to Dallas the important things she had acquired.

On August 14, 1882, the county assumed ownership of Sarah's bridge, with her blessing. She enlarged her flour mill located on Pacific Avenue where it runs into the Trinity River. Known as Todd Mills, it was managed by her son, Frank Cockrell, and her son-in-law, Aurelia's husband, Mitchell Gray.

As the town grew Sarah moved to make way for it. Her house on the Trinity, where the Triple Underpass is now located, became a business establishment; she built a new house at Live Oak and Pearl and moved. When the city again encroached, she again moved, this time to South Dallas, building her home on Lamar at Arnold.

In 1887 she erected the first office skyscraper, a five- story building on the eastern boundary of the growing downtown, that housed many of the city's law and business offices until it was razed in 1930. As befitted ladies of that time, she moved into the home of her son.

Sarah Cockrell died on April 26, 1892, at the age of 73. Her will was published in a 28-page pamphlet.

No one before her and no one after her has owned so much, given so much, or cared so much about the City of Dallas. Her personal holdings amounted to about one quarter of the entire downtown. Other property, in addition to the ferry, city lots and other philanthropies she had given away prior to her death, would have made her wealth equal to about one half of the entire city. Yet, she was as unobtrusive in death as she had been in life. The story of her death occupied but a four-inch space on the inside page of the paper:

A PIONEER GONE
Death of Mrs. S.H. Cockrell in
This City Yesterday

At 4:10 yesterday afternoon there died at the residence of her son, Alex Cockrell, on South Lamar street, Mrs. S. H. Cockrell, an old landmark of the early settlement of this county, she having settled near Eagle Ford in 1811. She was the third daughter of Enoch Horton, a Virginian, and the widow of Alex Cockrell, a Missourian, who settled in Dallas one year after the time that the afterward (sic) Mrs. Cockrell came to this county. She was an honored member of the Dallas County Pioneers' Association and was well know (sic) for her good old-time hospitality. Frank M. Cockrell and Alex Cockrell, both well known and prominent business men of this city, are her only surviving (sic) children, one brother and one sister having died. Mrs. Cockrell leaves a magnificent estate, embracing large farms and some of the best business property in the city.

The funeral will take place to-morrow afternoon at 2:45 from the Commerce Street Methodist Church. Rev. C. O. Jones will preach the funeral sermon.[16]

Sarah lies in Greenwood Cemetery where the giant skyscrapers of downtown Dallas cast their shadows on late summer afternoons and where the joyous music of the Meyerson Symphony Center hovers and where the progress of the Arts District encroaches, but never interferes with the sleep of those who lived to make Dallas great. Her beloved husband, his remains removed from the family plot where she first buried him, lies beside her.

3

PETTICOAT PIONEERS

The year 1846 was propitious for Dallas. It was the year that Dallas County was chartered, and thus official business could be conducted.

Anna Minerva Kimmel was the first bride to be married in Dallas County. She and Crawford Trees applied for a license to wed on July 20, 1846; vows were exchanged and the marriage recorded on July 22. They were two of only 350 people who inhabited the area when Texas, which itself had been admitted as the 28th state of the United States on December 29, 1845, recognized it as a county.

Both Anna Kimmel and Crawford Trees had come to Texas in 1845, she with her recently widowed mother, Catherine Hunsaker Kimmel, and he traveling alone. He was a 22-year-old single man and she a teenager. Both had been born and reared in Union County, Illinois, but had never met until they settled on farms adjoining each other in Dallas County. The Kimmels and Crawford Trees arrived within months of each other, and it was not long before the 22-year-old bachelor was courting his 14-year-old neighbor. Anna married him the following year when she was 15.

They built their home on the highest geographical location in North Texas on a white chalk bluff escarpment surrounded by cedar trees.[1] Since the Kimmel and Trees families were the first settlers west of the Trinity, Anna had only family for neighbors. They were some 15 miles from the John Neely Bryan cabin, a day's wagon trip. At the time of their marriage, Crawford had already been granted 640 acres of land from Peter's Colony, property to which they acquired free title after they had lived on it and cultivated it for three years. By the time they had the title, they were already accumulating additional land.

Anna gave birth to their first child on April 11, 1848, making her a 16-year-old mother. They named the premature baby Catherine and kept her alive through sheer determination and ingenuity. Helen Joy Straus Hodge, Anna's great-granddaughter, tells the family story of her grandmother's survival. "She weighed only two and a half pounds. Her cradle was a padded wooden box. Her incubator was the back of their wood-burning stove. They kept constant vigil, forcing drops of milk into her mouth."[2] All the infant wanted to do was sleep, so when she was too tiny or too disinterested to nurse, Anna expressed her milk and forced it into her baby's mouth.

Survive and thrive the infant did. She grew up to marry Jesse M. Ramsey and continue the lineage of the family through Winnie Ann Ramsey Straus to Helen Straus Hodge. Catherine was the first of Anna's 10 children, which included Beatrice, born January 31, 1852; David, born May 15, 1854; Philip Wilson, born March 28, 1857; Samuel Henry, born August 24, 1859; Crawford, Jr., born January 20, 1962; Texanna, born November 20, 1864; Mary Ellen, born June 4, 1867; Robert E. Lee, born June 12, 1870 and George Washington, born February 6, 1873. Anna had given birth to her first child when she was 16 and her last when she was 41.

In 1849 when baby Catherine was less than a year old, Crawford, along with most of the other Dallas men, went to California on the gold rush and was gone for two years. Anna was left to manage the farm and livestock. She had two St. Bernard dogs for protection.

Crawford was more successful in his search for a fortune than most of the men who made the trip to California. He returned with several thousand dollars in gold and a thin gold watch and chain, which he willed to Catherine and which was handed down in the family to the first daughter of each generation for more than a hundred years. Crawford invested in land—rich black soil ideal for growing cotton and for raising cattle. At one

Anna Minerva Kimmel, above, was only 15 when she wed her neighbor, Crawford Trees, below. They were the county's first bride and groom. She outlived him 33 years and managed the family property which at one time was the largest acreage in the county owned by one family.

time the Trees owned more acreage in Dallas County than any other family. They gave the property for the first combination church/school in the area. Known as Little Bethel, it was located in what is now Duncanville.

Slaves helped to farm the land and care for the livestock. On record, November 7, 1953, is the sale of a slave Patsy, about 35 and her two children, Clarinda, 4 or 5, and George, about 6 months, from John Neely and Margaret Bryan to Crawford and Anna Minerva Trees.[3]

The Trees gave 160-acre farms to each of their children. When Crawford died on January 31, 1899, Anna owned 3,858 acres of land plus some $40,000 in cash and stock. Family historian Bradley C. Hodge, writes that Crawford was literate but usually signed his signature with an "X." Joe Trees, a grandson, believes that "Grandpa could not read or write." In either case, it was Anna, who handled the family's written records.

Anna outlived her husband for almost a quarter of a century. She continued to live on the family property and to manage it. At her death the remaining family assets were divided among the surviving heirs. Catherine's part of the family farm came down to her daughter, Winnie and to her daughter, Helen. When Helen Hodge sold it on November 15, 1973, it had been owned and managed by succeeding members of a single family for 128 years.

Anna Minerva Kimmel Trees died on November 18, 1913. She is buried in the Trees Cemetery in Cedar Hill beside her husband in plots adjacent to that of other family members. Historian Bradley Hodge says that the cemetery was established on August 21, 1856, when Philip Trees, Anna and Crawford's fourth child died.

A woman filed Dallas County's first law suit. She was Charlotte Hewitt Dalton, who divorced her husband—and married Henderson Couch, foreman of the jury that granted her divorce, before the day was over.

It was also in that first year of Dallas as a county that another woman, Charlotte Hewitt Dalton Couch, made history. She filed the first court case in the county. On December 7, 1846, Charlotte sued for divorce from her husband, Joseph B. Dalton. She paid all of the court costs. The jury granted the divorce. That same evening Charlotte married Henderson Couch, who had served as foreman of the jury that had rendered the verdict in her favor. What is recorded clouds rather than elucidates the event:

> Henderson Couch, as foreman of the jury at the first court ever held in Dallas county, December, 1846; he and his eleven colleagues divorced Mrs. Charlotte M. Dalton from her husband, Joseph Dalton, and before the sun of that day glided to the 'heathen Chinee' side of the globe; the said Henderson Couch and Charlotte M. Dalton, legally and constitutionally, were husband and wife. It was the first civil suit—Dalton vs. Dalton—ever tried in Dallas county; yet some people of this day imagine that the 'early times' of Dallas were of the backwoods . . . . Let all such realize the eclectic dispatch business in early Dallas days . . . then tip their beavers to the memory of Henderson and Charlotte Couch.[4]

Records of the earliest Dallas settlers are sparse and the stories of women virtually non-existent. Most early records were kept by men, and men pay attention to things males value—things they can weigh, measure or count. Women are more likely to value things that cannot be quantified—things that they feel, sense and envision. So it is that early Dallas history is replete with names of settlers, their birth dates, the number of wives and children they had, acres of land they acquired, military units in which they served, titles and honors they accumulated, dates of their deaths and where they are buried. Only occasionally did a historian include the flavor, fabric, texture, color and climate of those early Dallas days. There are, in short, in early records, a great many "facts," but few feelings.

Women are also sparse in history because they get lost. They change their names when they marry and lose their own family connections so that it is increasingly difficult through the years to trace them. The fragments of their lives are handed down, if at all, in quilts and other handwork and an occasional letter. In those early days of Dallas, their names, if mentioned at all, were dropped between commas, their actions noted in parenthesis and their identities relegated to footnotes.

Bema Hearne is a typical example of this kind of record keeping. Sandwiched between commas in the listing of her father and husband in the earliest recorded history of Dallas, the *Directory of the City of Dallas 1861-1881,* Bema is remembered this way: "S. J. Adams, born in Stewart County, Ga., April 14, 1837, studied law in Arkansas, married Bema Hearne, Oct. 16, 1867, daughter of Col. H. R. Hearne . . . ." There follows a lengthy story about Col. Hearne and S. J. Adams but no further mention of Bema. She was an individual in the shadows of their male lives.

Some of the women are nameless:

> In 1854, he [Judge John B. Goode] was married to Miss . . . Floyd of the country who blessed him with six interesting children, and who still lives, sharing the happiness of her family, and enjoying the comforts of a delightful home acquired by the industry and patient perserverence of her husband.[5]

The woman who distributed the mail for the first appointed postmaster is credited in parenthesis:

> A new U. S. postmaster, Charles M. Durgan, arrived to assume Bryan's duties with the mail. (Durgan was postmaster in name; his wife, Elizabeth B. Thomas Durgan, actually fulfilled the function of organizing and sorting the mail.)[6]

Elizabeth B. Thomas Durgan organized Dallas's first post office, sorted the mail and saw that it was properly delivered, but her husband, Charles M. Durgan, had the title of postmaster . . . . Laura Lively was one of seven women whose biographies are among 742 entries in an early Dallas history. She got in because the writer wanted to include her late husband; she got three lines of the lengthy entry.

The first official city records (1846) lists 53 entries of families and/or men who moved to Dallas. Thirty of these make no note of the wife's name. They are listed "John L. Anderson and family from Tennessee; James Armstrong and family; Micajah Goodwin and family; Weston Perry and family of 13 children; Dr. Samuel B. Pryor and young wife; Elder William Rawlins and family," and on and on. There is no way of knowing how many new citizens this added to the young community, for even in instances where a wife's name is mentioned, children are often omitted.

The names of only seven women appear among the 742 biographies in *Memorial and Biographical History of Dallas County 1892.* One is a Catholic nun and the other six are widows, listed so that their late husbands can be included. Such is the fate of Laura Lively:

> Laura Lively, widow of Patrick Henry Lively . . . (followed by a long story about him. Then it picks up) She was his third wife, Laura Turpin, (followed by another long sketch about her late husband including his two prior wives and all of his children. It concludes) In matters of religion he inclined to the Campbellite faith, his widow being an Episcopalian.[7]

The scarcity of material has often led historians to conclude that there was little of interest about these early Dallas women, that they were young uneducated kids who packed up from their homes in Kentucky, Tennessee, Illinois, Missouri and other points to the east and north and docilely made the long trek to Dallas at the bidding of their husbands or fathers.

Such a picture, accurate as it is in many instances, is far from the whole truth, for among those first settlers were women who were exhilarated by the promise of a new life in a new land, who came to Dallas willingly and who filled their children's lives with fun as well as hard work. Even the photographs are misleading, for once in awhile there is the picture of rare beauty among the austerity. Many of the women were from established families in eastern and southern cities. Often Dallas's rugged frontiersmen, who are credited with carving a city out of nothing, brought with them wives who were both educated and refined and who, from the very beginning of Dallas, demanded schools for their children, churches in which to worship, cultural advantages that often taxed the limits of the frontier town, and social events to relieve the monotony. From the very first, it was the women who insisted on books, art, music and theater in their expanding village.

Though buried in the texts of their husbands', fathers' and brothers' biographies, there are fascinating glimpses of early Dallas women who worked side by side with men to settle Dallas.

Lucinda Blackburn Smith is one among them. One of Dallas's earliest settlers, she arrived with her husband John W. Smith three years after Margaret and John Neely Bryan were married and four years after the Beemans and the Gilberts came to town.

Lucinda Smith was born in 1815 into an eminent Kentucky family and was accustomed to amenities nonexistent in the village of Dallas. Her ancestors were landed gentry; one uncle was a state judge and another a candidate for governor. Her biography lists only her father as a parent; the chances are that, as the eldest daughter, she remained at home to look after her father after her mother died. She was 28 years old when she married John W. Smith in Allen County, Kentucky, on February 22, 1843. A native of Richmond County, North Carolina, John was ten years older than his bride.

As newlyweds, Lucy and John moved to an unsettled area in Cass County, Missouri, but John was still not satisfied. He had heard glowing stories of riches to be found in both California and Texas and he longed to settle in one state or the other though neither state was yet a part of the Union.

In 1845, 13 months after he and Lucy were married and a year after they stopped off in Missouri, John left his pregnant wife to go explore Texas. He was gone for seven months, returning in November to Lucinda and his baby daughter, Mary Frances, who was born shortly after her father began his trip to Texas. The family packed and almost immediately set out for Dallas. They were accompanied by a friend, James Martin Patterson, and took horses to sell along the way to fund their travels.

In Cairo, Illinois, Patterson and the Smiths temporarily parted, Patterson going to New Orleans on business and the Smiths traveling on to Texas through Mississippi.

The arduous journey in a covered wagon with an infant was relieved by the promise of riches that lay ahead. Imagine how Lucy must have felt when, on a cold February day in 1846, the wagon arrived in the tiny hamlet called Dallas, a "city" that consisted of four tiny cabins surrounded on every side by a wilderness.

Lucinda Blackburn Smith, from a prominent Kentucky family, arrived in Dallas on a cold February day in 1846 to find only tiny cabins surrounded by a wilderness.

> Indians roamed at will on all sides of them; buffalo, deer, antelope, bear and all the wild animals native to the country quenched their thirst in the Trinity river . . . and fed upon the luxuriant mesquite and buffalo grasses indigenous to the soil . . . . [8]

James Patterson was waiting for the Smiths in Dallas, having arrived 10 days ahead of them. The two men formed a partnership to establish and run a general merchandise store called Smith & Patterson. It was the first retail establishment in Dallas, preceded only by William Lundy's blacksmith shop and "store," the Lundy store which stocked only a barrel of whiskey and the three bolts of calico.

Lucy Smith had little time to worry about the life she had left behind. While her husband concentrated on the business, she ran the home, cared for it and the children. She had four more children in Dallas—Ellen, Lloyd, Elden W. and Lula C.

But what about Lucy the person? One must read between the lines of the bare facts of her life—her birth in Kentucky, the date of her marriage, her arrival in Dallas—to conjecture a little more about her. She was older than most of the wives who came to early Dallas, and at age 30 when Mary Frances was born, she was considerably older than most first-time mothers of her day. She gave birth to her last child at the age of 40. She lost her oldest son under conditions not altogether clear. The records state only that "Lloyd Blackburn was killed at the age of nineteen, November 2, 1870, by Tom Caudle of Lancaster, Texas; Tom evaded justice then and is running at large now."

Lucy saw the town grow from a dozen or so people to somewhere between 5,000 and 8,000. (There were 800 residents in 1872, 10,000 in 1882, and 50,000 in 1892.) She lived through business affluence and business failure, and watched the railroads come and the city streets laid out and churches and schools take form. She joined the Episcopal Church shortly after it was established in Dallas.

Her husband and four surviving children were at her bedside when Lucinda Blackburn Smith died on March 16, 1879.

She, who for 33 years managed a home and family, looked after the business while her husband was away from home, and gave the city substantial citizens for future generations, appears little more than a sweet old lady in her obituary:

> Mrs. Smith was one of those unostentatious Christians whose unobtrusive manners, devotion and duty to her family and friends has gained for her the love of all who knew her. She was truly a woman of pure thought, pure words and pure deeds . . . . She has left to all who knew her a rich heritage of goodly deeds and loved and glad memory.[9]

John Smith outlived his wife eleven years, dying in Dallas on July 13, 1890, at the age of 85.

Sarah Patterson and Lucinda Smith had little in common except that they were both born in Kentucky and married to partners of the first retail store in Dallas. Sarah was 18 years younger than Lucy, and James Martin Patterson was old enough to have been his bride's father. He was 36, Sarah Elizabeth Self, 15, when they married on October 5, 1848, in Farmers Branch.

While Lucy remembered a childhood of wealth, privilege and social position, Sarah's had been an entirely different life. Her father had died when she was a small child and her mother, Rebecca Self, married William Bowles, a Baptist minister. Sarah was 12 when she arrived in the Dallas area with her mother, stepfather, her sister Ann and her half siblings, Harrison H. Bowles and Hannah F. Bowles in 1845 and settled near Farmers Branch. At 15 she was a bride and within the year, a mother.

For the next 25 years Sarah was either pregnant or nursing an infant. She gave birth to 11 children. Only six—Florence Belle (who married John Spellman), Kitty (who wed Joseph Shuford), James, Edward, Rowena (who married Thomas H. Patterson), and Emma, survived to adulthood.

Sarah Patterson appears nothing more than the docile wife in her husband's biography:

> . . . cheered by the presence of the devoted wife whose willing hands and cheerful disposition have done so much to make attractive the home . . . ever ready to listen with due consideration to any suggestion, or with alacrity, to gratify any wish he may express.[10]

Sarah Elizabeth Self Patterson, at 15, married 36-year-old James Martin Patterson and gave birth to 11 children.

Sarah Shelton Huffman Perry arrived in Dallas with her husband, Alexander Wilson Perry, in 1844 from Illinois. Sarah had married 21-year-old Alexander on January 9, 1840, two days before her 16th birthday. Four years later, at age 20, Sarah Perry was already the mother of three children—the first born eight months and 16 days after she was married; the second 16 months later, and the third less than two years later. With their three babies, Sarah and Alex left Illinois for Texas, arriving in Dallas with two teams, three extra horses and $30 in cash.

The Perrys took a headright under the Peter's Colony grant. Only seven families lived within a radius of five or six miles of their first home. In 1850 the Perrys moved from Peter's Colony to an 800-acre farm which included the land on which the present city of Carrollton is located.

Alex bought and sold land, traded in cattle, and farmed—his first crop was "enough for himself and to spare, and has ever since had plenty."

Sarah had babies, 14 in all, from Margaret, who arrived September 25, 1840, to Roxanna, who was born February 15, 1867. In between Margaret and Roxanna were Rebecca A., January 7, 1842; William E., December 16, 1843, and the 11 born in Dallas: Mary L., February 23, 1846; Harriet M., August 30, 1848; Alexander, December 25, 1850; Sanford C., November 1, 1852; twins John H. and Sarah, March 5 and 6, 1855;

DeWitt C., January 10, 1858; Waid H., February 15, 1860; Carry H., May 9, 1862; Louria, November 25, 1864.

The listing of births and deaths gives scant attention to the relentless tragedy that stalked those early Dallas settlers, and many historians—all male—assume that because death was so ever-prevalent, it was an accepted condition of life. Seldom, if ever, does one get a glimpse of a mother's tears over the crude coffins of baby after baby after baby. Sarah Perry buried six of her children—Alexander when he was 2, Rebecca when she was 18, Mary when she was 14, Sanford when he was 23, Sarah when she was 8 and Carrie when she was 18. Many, many women died in childbirth. Then, as now, teenage pregnancy increased the chances of childbirth death. In a frontier town with the barest of medical facilities, only home-produced remedies, poor nutrition, no prenatal care and little knowledge of how to avoid pestilence, death was an ever-present possibility, but that does not mean that it was ever easy for a mother to lose her children.

Sarah and Alex Perry's surviving children all settled within three miles of their home on property given to them by their parents.

Polly Marsh also arrived in the very early days of Dallas with her husband, Harrison C. Marsh, and their five children from Kentucky. Born Mary Raymond on February 2, 1810, she acquired Polly as a nickname as a child and carried it all of her life. The couple was married in Paris, Kentucky, on November 11, 1828, and left two baby boys, William Raymond and Harrison Franklin, buried in their hometown. Thomas C., Sarah Ellen, John David, Mary Frances and Elizabeth Jane traveled in the covered wagon with their parents. In Dallas, Polly gave birth to two more children, Martha Ann, on February 27, 1848 and Charlotte Maria, on March 30, 1851.

Even with the responsibilities of such a large family, Polly Marsh filled her home with love and laughter. It was a popular meeting place, something akin to a community center. George Jackson in his book, *Sixty Years in Texas*, wrote: "The old home of Polly and Harrison Marsh . . . was where the young people loved to meet. We had many a party there and always had a good time." Dallas's Marsh Lane got its name from this early Dallas family, the street named specifically for Thomas C. Marsh, the oldest of Polly's Dallas-born children.

At 21 years of age in 1845 when she arrived in Dallas County from Illinois, Rachel Haught Lumney was following the pioneering spirit of her Dutch-ancestry parents, Peter and Sallie Carver Haught, born in Pennsylvania, who were among the first families to settle three states—Virginia, Ohio, and Illinois. Rachel Haught married Thomas Lumney when she was very young. Records say she was born December 18, 1824, and married on September 25, 1832, but this is not likely for it would make her an 8-year-old bride. In any event, she was already the mother of Ara and James when she arrived in Dallas. Mary Elizabeth, Sarah Jane, Turner, Thomas V., William H., Charles and Emily were all Texas-born.

Rachel Lumney had a vivid memory and was a wonderful story-teller. In later years, as an old woman, she said that few families endured more hardships and privations that hers. At times, she said, when her husband was away at work and she saw the Indians camping near, she would yoke up the oxen, put her children in the wagon and drive to the nearest neighbor—several miles away—for protection. Pregnant often and constantly caring for young children, she also helped out with the field work. For clothing she dressed and tanned the bear and deer hides of the wild game that supplied the family's larder. Hunger was seldom a problem, she said, because wild game was plentiful, but the variety of foods was limited to what was in season. The first pigs the family bought were kept penned against the house in the chimney corner to keep the wolves from catching and killing them. Widowed one month shy of her 49th birthday, Rachel had learned the coping skills that made her old age secure. After her husband's death, she purchased a 137-acre farm and continued to live there for the remainder of her life.

Polly McDonald Cole and her husband, Dr. John Cole, arrived in Dallas in December of 1843 with nine of the 11 children. The first six—Calvin, Malinda, Lucinda,

Mary (Polly) Raymond Marsh filled her north Dallas County home with love and laughter while giving birth to nine children. She is the matriarch of the family for whom Marsh Road is named.

James Madison, Eliza Jane and John Higgs—were born in Sumner County, Tennessee; and the other five—William Alfred, Louisa Elender, George Washington, Martin Van Buren and Joseph Larkin—in Crawford and Washington Counties, Arkansas.

Polly was 49 and her youngest son two when the family arrived on Cedar Springs Creek about two and a half miles north of John Neely Bryan's settlement. The oldest son, Calvin, had married Elvira Ann Reeder in Arkansas and remained there for another year before he joined his parents' family in Dallas in 1844, and Lucinda had died at the age of 9. Polly Cole managed the large family while her husband, a physician and later a judge in Dallas County's first probate court, practiced medicine, operated a pharmacy and, for a time, ran a store, and bought and sold land. Polly is the matriarch of numerous Dallas-area Coles and the mother of the family for whom Cole Street is named. Her sixth child, John Higgs Cole, married Elizabeth Preston, for whose family Preston Road had earlier been named.

Elizabeth and John Cole built a three-story red brick home on Cole Avenue at the spot just east of the present North Dallas High School. Each brick in the house was imprinted with the Cole name. Martin Van Buren Cole married Margaret Preston, younger sister of Elizabeth. Margaret and Martin owned property on Turtle Creek bounded by what is now Mockingbird Lane and Eton, Gillon and Douglas. Their home was just south of the present location of the Dallas Country Club. James and William Cole also married sisters—James wed Sarah Ann Bennett and moved to San Antonio taking with them her younger sister, Mary Jane Bennett. On November 8, 1858, William Cole and Mary Jane were married. The two couples lived in San Antonio until 1866 when Sarah Ann and James returned to Dallas and bought 80 acres along Turtle Creek.

Lucy Jane Monroe Browder was Dallas's first realtor. She sold the houses which her son built in the Cedars, Dallas's first exclusive residential area.

Lucy Jane Monroe Browder, who bought and sold property in early Dallas, is the city's first recognized realtor. The niece and ward of President James Monroe, she was accustomed to a secure and privileged life, but chose to cast her future in an unsettled part of the country. She arrived in Dallas in 1845 as a widow, traveling through from Missouri with her two sons, Edward Cabell Browder and Isham Bell Browder. Upon arrival, the trio camped out in the settlement of Cedar Springs. As soon as he had secured the title to his Peter's Colony land grant, Isham went home to Missouri and married Lucy Ann Breeze. He brought her and their infant son back to Dallas in 1847.

Two years later, on September 26, 1849, Elizabeth Coats married Edward Browder. Elizabeth, according to stories passed down through the family, was a direct descendant of Pocahontas and for decades the name "Pocahontas" had been conferred on the female children in the family. Elizabeth stopped that tradition, giving her four daughters the simple names of Annie, Emily, Fannie and Jane. Her two sons were Pleasant and Edward.

The Browders were a close family. The sisters-in-law—Elizabeth, whose home was on Commerce Street, and Lucy, who lived at Browder Springs, named for the family, on the site that is now Old City Park—often did their laundry together at the spring. Annie and Emily, the little girls, would often be placed in a tub and floated out onto the pond. The tub, tied by a long rope to a tree on the bank, provided the children a delightful time to play on the water while their mother and aunt visited and washed and rinsed the family laundry on the bank nearby.

While her daughters-in-law followed the prescribed routine for married women of the time by working exclusively in their homes, Lucy Jane went about helping newcomers to secure property and homes in the new settlement of Dallas. Together she and Edward planned The Cedars, Dallas's first exclusive residential area. Edward, a surveyor, laid out the lots. Lucy Jane sold them.

Isham died in 1862 from a Civil-War connected illness. His mother and older brother continued to contribute to the growing Dallas. Edward and Elizabeth were neighbors and close friends of Richard Cooke Buckner and encouraged and assisted him with the founding of Buckner's Orphans Home. Annie and Emily would ride side-saddle out to the orphanage in Mesquite to help care for the children and sew for them. "Father" Buckner conducted the wedding ceremonies at Buckner's Home when Emily Browder married James McCorkle and Annie Browder wed Ed Prickett. While Buckner was a confirmed Baptist, the Browders were equally devout Methodists; and the First Methodist

Church of Dallas sometimes held services in the Browder home during the time that its minister, the Rev. William C. Young, and his wife, Rebecca Young, were building their home nearby.

The Browders were influential in the bringing the first railroads to Dallas and the family name is connected with the city's early water supply when 1,500 Dallas residents had water delivered through wooden pipes from Browder Springs to their homes beginning in 1869 until White Rock Lake was completed and filled in 1911. Browders Springs was then covered over and today lies under R. L. Thornton Freeway.

Browder Street bears the family name. Edward also honored his wife's famous Indian ancestor by naming one of the streets in his subdivision "Pocahontas." The street, to the north of the present Old City Park, now is Griffin East feeding into R. L. Thornton Freeway. Lucy Jane made her home with Edward and Elizabeth for many years. All three of them and Isham Browder are buried in the Masonic Section of the old Masonic and Odd Fellows Cemetery that lies in front of the Dallas Convention Center a short distance from their former homes.

Lucy Jordan Latimer brought the first piano to Dallas in 1849—and gave an impromptu recital on the downtown street before unloading her household supplies in her new home.

As the first decade of Dallas was drawing to a close, a momentous event occurred with the arrival of Lucy Jordan and her husband, James Wellington Latimer. They came in 1849 from Red River County in an oxcart, she with her rosewood piano and he with his printing press. Latimer, the first newspaper publisher in Dallas County, is credited with establishing Dallas's cultural climate, but her contributions are barely mentioned. Young, married only two years, vivacious, educated and energetic, Lucy had her husband stop the oxcart on Dallas's public square—what little of a square existed at that time—sat down at the keyboard and gave an impromptu recital on the first piano that ever came to Dallas, all before she unloaded her household goods.

Latimer set about publishing a newspaper first called the *Cedar Snag*, but soon changed to the *Dallas Herald,* a paper that rarely mentioned the name of his wife. Had he not been so cautious about giving her credit, future generations would know more details about this remarkable lady. Elizabeth Enstam in her "When Dallas Became a City," notes:

> Lucy Jordan Latimer came in (an) ox-drawn wagon . . . with her rosewood piano and thorough education . . . . As a teacher, Lucy Latimer brought Dallas contacts with the wider culture, especially through her training and music and her personal interests, like astronomy.[11]

Lucy is mentioned briefly in this news story:

> The semi-annual examination of the pupils of the Dallas Collegiate Institute came off on Monday and Tuesday last. The courthouse was procured for the exercises and crowded to its utmost capacity by one of the most intelligent audiences we have seen assembled in Dallas . . . . The exercises were diversified by entertaining and amusing dialogues, declamations and original compositions, interspersed by instrumental and vocal music from Mrs. Latimer's music classes.[12]

Years later Bruce Roche, in writing about early Dallas, said: "Lucy Latimer was stately and commanding, beautiful and attractive, the toast and idol of the whole country, the cynosure of all eyes, the loved of all circles high and low, the equal of her newspaper husband, James Wellington Latimer."

The first decade of Dallas ended with a Christmas Eve dance at a tavern owned by William Beeman, brother of Margaret Beeman Bryan. Ten couples attended and danced on puncheon floors made of split logs whose upper surface had been smoothed with an ax. A scribe noted that Nat M. Burford and Captain W. H. Hord were among the dancers, that they treaded the minuet and the Virginia reel "to the witching music of a good fiddle."

One might think that their dancing partners were women, but there is no record that this is so.

4

THE SEVEN SISTERS FROM TENNESSEE

In the first decade of Dallas, a remarkable family of sisters made a deep, lasting and—through their descendants—continuing contribution to Dallas. They came, one by one, with their husbands between 1843 and 1854.

They were the Hughes sisters from Tennessee.

And there were seven of them!

Buildings, parks, schools, neighborhoods, churches, cemeteries and streets are named for their families, usually in the names of the men to whom they were married.

But in many cases, it is the women who made the contributions.

Nancy Jane Hughes Cochran was the first to arrive, in March 1843, with her husband, William M. Cochran, and their four small children. The children, all under six years of age, were John Hughes Cochran, born June 28, 1838; Archelaus Madison Cochran, born September 28, 1839; William Porter Cochran, born January 24, 1841, and Margaret Elizabeth Cochran, born September 27, 1842, who died January 1, 1848.

Nancy was 26 years old, her husband 36. They left Greene County, Missouri, in the dead of winter, and, traveling with their children, all under six, they arrived at Mustang Branch, the name of which was later changed to Farmers Branch, just as spring began. William was issued Land Certificate #2116 in Peter's Colony, and the Cochrans began to make their mark on the new territory. In the next nine years, Nancy would have five more children—and would be joined in Texas by six sisters and their husbands and a brother and his wife:

Nancy Jane Hughes Cochran was the first of the seven amazing sisters to arrive in Dallas. She and her husband, William M. Cochran, arrived in March of 1843.

Mary Hughes Webb and her husband, Isaac Blackmon Webb, arrived January 27, 1844.

Sarah Matilda Hughes Williams and Thomas Carroll Williams came in December of 1845.

Serena Caroline Hughes Knight and Obadiah Woodson Knight arrived November 30, 1846.

Margaret Morris Hughes Bachman and John Branahan Bachman came in 1850.

Aisley Amanda Hughes Record and her husband, George Washington Record, arrived in 1853.

Martha Letitia Hughes Dennis and her husband, the Rev. Levi R. Dennis, came in 1854.

William Holmes Hughes, the brother, and his wife, Zuleika Ruth Kittrell Hughes, arrived in 1852.

Mary, Nancy Jane, Sarah, Aisley, Serena, Margaret, Martha and William were eight of the 13 children of William and Aisley Carr Hughes of Tennessee. The parents and three of their offspring—Archelaus Madison Hughes, John Findall Hughes and Anne Maria Hughes (later, Doss)—remained in Tennessee, their home state. Two were deceased—the youngest child, David Leander Hughes, and Elizabeth Dalton Hughes Record.

Nancy and William Cochran had an excellent first year. They settled on a 320-acre Peter's Colony land grant and grew enough corn, which they ground by hand, to supply ample bread for their family and to share with other families who arrived too late to grow crops of their own. A year after their arrival, they introduced the first wheat into the county and two years later planted the first cotton.

Nancy, born in North Carolina on October 24, 1817, and reared in Tennessee, worked on the land along with her husband, ran the home and looked after the children. On July 26, 1845, she gave birth to a fifth child, Mary Mariah Cochran, who died the same year. The next year Nancy had James Monroe Cochran on June 1, 1846, to be followed with Martha Alice Cochran on Christmas Day of 1848, George Washington Cochran on January 11, 1851, and Sarah Jane Cochran on March 29, 1853.

Like other families who had been lured to Dallas by the promise of a virtual utopia in Peter's Colony, the Cochrans were soon disenchanted. Peter's Colony did not live up to its promises. It had been established by William C. Peters and Associates of Louisville, Kentucky, as the Texas Emigration and Land Company. It promised Texas, then a republic, to deliver between 250 families annually between 1843 and 1848 as settlers in an area which began at a point on the Red River and extended south 100 miles to near Waxahachie. This took in all of Dallas County except a three-mile strip on the east. The organization, quickly known as Peter's Colony, advertised throughout the country and in Europe. It promised heads of household from 320 to 640 acres of rich river bottom land that would produce corn, rye, barley, oats, peas, beans, melons, figs, sweet and Irish potatoes, hemp, fruits and grapes. And, it promised that the Trinity River, on which these lands were situated, was navigable to Galveston on the coast.

Nancy was 36 and the mother of six children, the oldest only 25, when her husband died. She managed the property and educated her children while having to get the court's permission for every penny she spent—because women could not legally manage the business of their minor children without court approval.

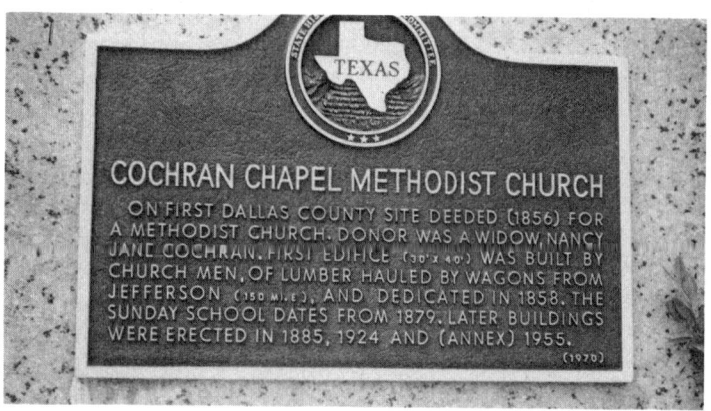

Nancy Cochran personally walked off the area and wrote the specifications for the property she gave to establish Cochran Chapel Methodist Church.

Eight years after they arrived, on April 30, 1851, the Cochrans bought 640 acres of land on Browning Creek five miles nearer to the growing city of Dallas and moved. Even though he had already moved his family away from Peter's Colony, William Cochran was one of five committee members named at a mass meeting of settlers held on May 15, 1851, to draft resolutions against the Texas Emigration and Land Company for failing to live up to its promises. The result was that agents of Peter's Colony absconded, taking some of the records with them, only a step ahead of possible punitive action.

On their new farm, the Cochrans also prospered. They built the second cotton gin in the county and added a corn mill. They had become popular and highly respected citizens of the community. William had been elected County Clerk of the new Dallas County in July of 1846 at the first election held in the county. In 1847 he was elected Dallas County's first representative to the State Legislature.

In the spring of 1853, during a typhoid epidemic, one-year-old Sarah Cochran died. Hers is the first grave in what would become Cochran Chapel Cemetery. Nancy had lost two other children in Dallas—Margaret Elizabeth at age 7 and Mary Mariah shortly after birth. Both were buried in Farmers Branch Cemetery near the Cochran's first Dallas home.

Seventeen days after baby Sarah's death, on April 24, 1853, William M. Cochran died, also with typhoid. He had lived and worked in Dallas for one decade.

Nancy Cochran managed the family property for almost 24 years after the death of her husband, but she is buried in Cochran Chapel Cemetery as "wife of" Wm. M. Cochran.

At this time, Nancy was 36 years old. She had six children. Her oldest son was not yet 15 and her youngest, 27 months.

A superlative manager, Nancy took over the business. She consolidated the family holdings, retaining what she could reasonably manage, and selling or deeding property to others. In 1856 she sold the cotton gin to John Coit. That same year she deeded a piece of the farmland to the trustees of the Methodist Episcopal Church South for Cochran Chapel Church and to establish Cochran Chapel Cemetery where her husband and baby were buried.

Her gift provided the land and her additional financial contributions helped construct the first deeded church in Dallas County. Lumber to build the church was hauled by wagon 150 miles. She named the church and cemetery for her late husband.

Nancy Jane Hughes Cochran was the first Methodist to settle in or near Dallas and the first known Methodist sermon in the county was preached in her home. Once worshipers were in the middle of a service when they noticed Indians nearby. It is said that the men interrupted the service, picked up their guns, straddled their horses and gave chase to the fleeing Indians, then returned to the church and completed the worship service.

Loving and generous in many ways, Nancy was uncompromising when it came to her children's moral principles. She took literally the Biblical admonition to rest on the Sabbath day to the point that all food to be eaten on Sundays had to be prepared ahead; nobody did any work, including cooking and cleaning, on Sundays. A family joke was that on weekends she sewed the boys' underwear onto them so that they could not go swimming on Sunday.

Nancy Cochran was, according to family members, equal to any task. She could make a speech or preach a sermon—and did. She personally surveyed the land that she gave for Cochran Chapel Church, and specified directions in her own handwriting, noting that the property would continue north to the bois d'arc tree, then west to an oak and on and on until she had outlined exactly the area on which the church and cemetery would be located, both within a short distance from her home. She could run the farm, operate the cotton gin, survey a piece of property, cook a meal, make the family clothes, draw up a deed and defend her actions in court when necessary.

But, legally, she could do none of these things without court supervision. Her husband had died very suddenly when he was 53 years old leaving no will and in those days, and for years to follow in Texas, a woman was a non-person in the eyes of the law. From the time of William's death and for the next 19 years, until her youngest child was 21, Nancy had to account for every cent the estate made and every expenditure that went out because, under Texas law, she inherited half of what her husband left and her children divided the other half. Ironically, her youngest child died only 20 days before he was 21.

Her great-great granddaughter, Anne Cochran, when opening Nancy Jane Cochran's records in the Dallas County courthouse, and seeing the meticulous handwriting of these written records over a period from 1853 to 1872, "got goose pimples. There were tiny slips in there noting that my great-great grandfather owed $2.75 for feed, $6 for lumber, things like that. There were receipts for the cotton and for the grain. There were expenses for clothing and food and schooling. There were receipts for college tuition, notations for books and supplies. As guardian of the children, she had to report to the court every year about everything that came in and everything that went out. And she had to be bonded."

The farm made money. With Nancy Jane's management, all four of the older boys—John, Archie, William and James—were college-educated at McKenzie College in Red River County, the only college in the state at that time. George, the fifth son, did not live to attend college.

John married Martha Jane Johnson, was elected to the State Legislature and became historian for the county. They had six children, two of whom died young.

Archie studied medicine and was the first physician to practice in Dallas. He married Laura Knight, his first cousin, who died four years later leaving a daughter. He was remarried to Mary Jenkins Collins in January of 1871 only 10 months before he died at the age of 32.

William settled on the family farm to help his mother; he married Amanda Maria Lawrence and they reared seven of the nine children born to them.

James was a pharmacist who later returned to farming. He was married to Margaret B. Lively who died in 1878 leaving three children. The next year he married Nannie M. Clark who lived only a year. Three years later he was married for the third time to Hattie M. Bowlin. They had three children.

Martha Alice, known as Mattie, the only surviving daughter, was 11 at the beginning of the Civil War. All four of her older brothers served in the Confederate Army and all returned safely, though James Monroe was wounded.

During the war, Nancy and other women of the community gathered at sundown daily in a grove of trees in the corner of Cochran cemetery for prayer. It was, she told family and friends, the source of her strength to carry on the business during those trying times.

Two years after the war ended, Mattie, at the age of 18, married William Harris, whom she had met in 1858 when he was teaching school at Cedar Springs. Her uncle, the Rev. William H. Hughes, performed the ceremony on April 9, 1867. Mattie had seven children, Laura J., who married H. H. Jacoby; Clara Arvilla; James H., who died at seven months; Mary Mattie, a teacher who did not marry; William Randolph, who married Minnie Beulah Bookhout; Archie Bentley, who married Shirley Adelia Terry; and John Cochran Harris, who married Nellie Hunt Wilson. Many of the offspring of Mattie Cochran Harris, grandchildren of Nancy Jane Hughes Cochran, have been prominent attorneys in Dallas and environs.

Nancy Jane Hughes Cochran died on October 15, 1877, in Dallas nine days before her 60th birthday. She is buried in Cochran Chapel Cemetery beside her husband. Though she is personally responsible for both tangible and intangible contributions to the city, the marker at her grave reads "Mother," and below it "Nancy J., wife of Wm. M. Cochran."

Nancy's sister, Mary, was her closest friend. They were only a year apart in age, and less than a year elapsed after the Cochrans moved to Dallas before Mary and her husband, Isaac Blackmon Webb, and their five children arrived on January 27, 1844. The Cochrans and Webbs had been neighbors in Greene County, Missouri, and planned together to come to Texas. Descendants of the Cochran and Webb families surmise that Mary and Isaac were delayed in traveling to Texas because Mary was pregnant and not well. The Webbs set out on the journey only weeks after Mary gave birth to Mary Jane. The baby was two months and a day old when the group arrived in Dallas. The other children were William Douglass Webb, eight; Joshua Whitfield Webb, six; Alice E. Webb, four, and Sarah Almira Webb, two. Four more children were born to Mary and Isaac in Dallas: Isaac Newton on August 21, 1846; Nancy Ann Mariah on April 8, 1849; Margaret Sophronia Frances on August 23, 1852, and Samuel H. on May 30, 1854.

When the Webbs arrived in Dallas, they moved into the Cochran home and lived with them until their own home could be completed. It was crowded quarters. There were four adults and nine children, the oldest only 8, living together in a very small space.

The Webbs took a headright near the Cochrans. The historian John Cochran, Nancy Jane's oldest son, wrote that the Cochrans and the Webbs exchanged property very early so that the Webbs could have the more desirable living accommodations because of Mary's poor health. Their farm prospered until they eventually owned most of the land now included in the present city of Farmers Branch.

Sarah Matilda Hughes Williams and her husband established a school on Cochran property soon after they arrived in 1845. She was the county's first public school teacher.

Almost a year to the day after Mary and Isaac Webb set down roots in Dallas, the third Hughes sister, Sarah Matilda, arrived with her husband Thomas C. Williams. Sarah was a beautiful woman, 26 years old, educated at Columbia Female College in Tennessee as a teacher and married on June 24, 1841, at age 22 to Williams, only a week older than she, who was also a teacher. They established their first home in Bedford County, Tennessee, but moved to Dallas in December of 1845 with their two little boys, George E. V., three, and Archelaus Madison, one. They settled at first in Peter's Colony with other family members but purchased a farm in Cedar Springs in 1855.

Sarah and Thomas Williams established the first school in the county on the Cochran property and Sarah was Dallas's first public school teacher. Her husband also taught for one year before devoting himself to farming and public service. He was comptroller of state during the Civil War. When he took office the county was deeply in debt and scrip was worth only 50 cents on the dollar. During the four years he served as collector, the county liquidated all its debts, and he left office having raised money to build a courthouse and to leave a surplus in the treasury. Williams also conducted the first school census in Dallas County.

In addition to teaching, Sarah was busy as a wife and mother. She had 10 children, adding eight Dallas-born to the family—William Hughes on September 3, 1846; Alice Ann Elizabeth, January 3, 1849; Thomas Jefferson, January 2, 1851; Sarrenar Margaret Oleria, September 17, 1853; Mary Jane, June 20, 1855; Ben Hester, May 18, 1857; Buck Holmes, August 31, 1859, and Jesse Beauregard, December 14, 1862. She lost four of them, George when he was 15; Archie and William, both in 1848 when they were 4 and 2, and Sarah when she was one.

Sarah Hughes Williams died two months before her 50th birthday. Her oldest surviving daughter was 20 and her youngest child, 6. She was buried in Cochran Chapel Cemetery where 22 years later her husband was also buried. Strangely, no schools bear the name of these first two public school educators in Dallas County.

Serena Caroline Hughes Knight was the fourth of the Hughes sisters to settle in Dallas. The eighth child of William and Ailsey Hughes, she was the second wife of Obadiah Woodson Knight, who was 14 years her senior. His first wife, Mary Ann Knight, died leaving him with five children, William A., John W., Mary, Elizabeth B., Gabrial A. The oldest was 10 and the youngest three when Serena and he were married in 1845.

Serena, according to family stories, did not want to leave her comfortable Tennessee home and move to Texas, but her persistent husband prevailed and on November 30, 1846, she settled in Dallas in the Cedar Springs area near her sisters.

Serena was 24 years old, was the mother of five stepchildren, had lost an infant, Henry, and was pregnant with Laura. She would add to the family nine more children, Monroe D., Mattie A., Kate, William Hughes, Margaret Amanda, Epps Gabriel, Robert E. Lee, Archelaus J., and Josephine, making her the mother of 16 in all. Six of her children preceded their mother in death, among them Monroe at age 12 after being kicked by a horse, and Laura, the young wife of her cousin, Dr. Arch Cochran.

Three of Serena's daughters, as married women, bear names significant in Dallas annals.

Mary married Nathaniel M. Burford in 1854 and gave birth to eight children. Her husband became a prominent attorney, was elected to the State Legislature and speaker of the 11th Texas State Legislature. He served in the Confederate Army as a colonel, authored the charter for the City of Dallas when it was incorporated in 1856, served as district attorney, and was elected a judge. As an orator and writer, he was a highly respected public speaker and recorded an early history of Dallas County. Mary, who died in 1888, is remembered as "a faithful wife, a fond and careful mother and a woman of great nobleness of character."

Laura, Serena's oldest daughter, married her first cousin, Dr. Archelaus Cochran, Dallas's first physician, on February 22, 1866, when she was 19 years old. He became a city alderman and adjutant general in the Confederate Army and served for a time as postmaster of Dallas before he entered politics and was elected to the State Legislature. Archie and Laura Cochran were a brilliant couple, destined to become leaders in the city's future, but their contributions were cut short when both died very young, Laura at 23 and Archie at 32.

Mattie, the tenth of the 16 Knight children, married William Hughes Lemmon, a teacher, agricultural implement salesman and army captain, whose name is synonymous with the early development of near North Dallas. In 1887 he and his partner, O. P. Bowser, purchased 1,500 acres on the city's north side and began to develop it. William and Mattie Lemmon, at one time, owned most of what is now the Oak Lawn area. They built their home, Elmwood, on the corner of Lemmon and Cole, which at the time was described

The Hughes sisters—in the names of their husbands—have schools, parks, streets and city areas named for them. They are the Bachmans, Cochrans, Knights, Records, Webbs and Williams.

as suburban Dallas. Lemmon Avenue is named for the family and Bowser Street for Lemmon's partner.

Serena outlived all of her sisters, dying in Dallas on April 5, 1914, at the age of 92. She is buried in Cochran Chapel Cemetery beside her husband, who died April 1, 1868. Serena had more children than any of her Hughes sisters who moved to Dallas, but, strangely, there are no known surviving Knights in the city.

Margaret Morris Hughes Bachman and her husband, John Branahan Bachman, arrived in Dallas in 1850. She was 26 and he 29. They settled on property adjacent to that owned by her sisters. The Bachmans became parents of nine children, arriving with William Fletcher, four; Almira Zuleika, two, and Samuel Hughes, an infant. In Dallas, they added Daniel, Allis Amanda Dorcas, Letitia Jane, Mary Ann Mariah, John Holmes and Charles Levi. John Holmes died when he was four and Charles when he was six. All the other children lived to adulthood and married into Dallas families.

Although he was a minister, ordained in the Methodist Church, John Bachman spent most of his time farming and developing his land which included all of the area on which Bachman Lake and its surrounding streets are located. In 1901 the Bachmans sold a part of their farm to the City of Dallas to form Bachman's Lake on Bachman Creek as a source of water for the city.

In 1917 when the United States entered World War I, the city bought 120 acres more of the original Bachman property for $1,000 an acre on the south side of the lake and 40 acres of land settled by William Cochran. The city then leased this land to the Army for a dollar a year for a flying school. When the war was over, the property reverted to the city. By that time, the flying field had its name, Love Field, chosen by the Army in honor of Lt. Moss Lee Love, who lost his life in 1913 in an accident in California. A group of Dallas business leaders held the acreage together for 10 years until, in 1928, Dallas voters set aside $400,000 in bonds to pay for a municipal airport, $325,000 of which was paid for the 167.2 acres of the original site of the field.

Margaret Bachman had been a widow for nine months when her oldest daughter, Zuleika Bachman Taylor, died in childbirth at the age of 35. Infant twins died with their mother. Two daughters and three sons survived their mother's death, and Margaret, along with the children's father, William Berry Taylor, took over the rearing of her grandchildren. Bill and Zuleika Taylor had built an imposing white colonial home on the hill overlooking Bachman's lake. When the children reached high school age, Bill Taylor bought a townhouse on Cedar Springs. "Grandmother" Bachman moved into it and took charge of the rambunctious young Taylors, all of whom attended Dallas High School. Their father, who lived to age 85 and never remarried, continued to live on the farm.

John Bachman died in 1867. Margaret outlived him 37 years, long enough to see the city acquire the property for its municipal water supply from the land on which she had settled as a young woman newly arrived in the area. She died on June 12, 1904, at 80 and is buried in Cochran Chapel Cemetery.

The Rev. William Holmes Hughes, youngest surviving brother of the Hughes sisters, and his bride, Zuleika Kittrell Hughes, also moved to Dallas. They built a large home on Oak Lawn Avenue. He was a presiding elder of the Dallas district, Methodist church, and served as a chaplain during the Civil War. The Hugheses had five children, William Reddick, Eliza Alice, Hugh Bracom, Leander Hinton and Larissa Margaret, but reared only three. For 60 years "Uncle Buck," the nickname by which the Rev. Hughes was known, kept a croquet court in his large front yard and when not at Oak Lawn Methodist Church could often be found playing croquet with one or more of the town's leading citizens. Zuleika died on December 21, 1901, and William on October 24, 1916. Both are buried at Oak Grove Cemetery in Dallas.

Ailsey Amanda Hughes Record, her husband George Washington Record, and their four children, John Sherwood Moody, eight; Joseph W., seven; George Washington, five, and Virginia Alice, one, joined the growing Hughes clan in Dallas in 1853. Earlier they

The Bachman property "houses" Love Field and Bachman Lake— among many other points of interest in the city. The property also provided Dallas's first city water supply.

had lost two other children, William H., at 18 months, and Margaret at age six, both buried in Talley Cemetery in Tennessee.

Amanda was 32 and her husband 43 when they moved to Dallas. She was the second wife of G. W. Record, who had first married her oldest sister, Elizabeth Dalton Hughes. Elizabeth died in childbirth in 1835 at the age of 22. Amanda was 15 at the time of her sister's death. Seven years later, at the age of 22, she became the wife of her sister's widower. They made their home in Marshall, Tennessee, until they moved to Dallas where they added four more children to the family, Narcissa Jane in 1854, James C. Rush in 1857, Mary Ann Paralee in 1859 and Elizabeth Zuleika in 1863. James died at the age of 15 months.

The Records amassed a fortune in Dallas including the dubious distinction of owning 100 slaves, the largest number of anyone in Dallas County. Amanda, who died November 24, 1882, at the age of 62, and George, who died nine years earlier on February 10, 1873, are both buried in Cochran Chapel Cemetery.

The seventh sister, Martha Letitia Hughes Dennis and her husband, the Rev. Levi R. Dennis, arrived in Dallas in 1854, but moved on to Tyler after three years where he became pastor of the Marvin Street Methodist Church, the oldest Methodist Church in Tyler. Martha and Levi had married in 1848 when he was 28 and she 22. Their oldest child, Mary Elizabeth Jane, was born in Stokes, North Carolina. Three more daughters were born in Texas: Alice Amanda, who lived only 11 months; Margaret Ann Mariah and Sallie Serena. Both Amanda and Levi Dennis are buried in Tyler's Oakwood Cemetery.

Though many stories abound of the seven Hughes sisters who came to Dallas in its infant days, finding them was difficult. They were all known by their husband's names, with no indication on the markers at their graves that they were sisters. Their grave markers recognize them as wives and mothers, but not daughters or sisters. They finally became realities in the biography of T. C. Williams. There, buried in the next to last paragraph was this:

> The subject of this sketch, Thomas C. Williams, is the only survivor of the seven brothers-in-law who married sisters, daughters of William and Alcy Hughes, in Tennessee, and who emigrated to Dallas county, Texas in an early day in the order in which they are named, to wit: William M. Cochran, Isaac B. Webb, Thomas C. Williams, O. W. Knight, John B. Bachman, George W. Record and Levi R. Dennis.... All of the above named were leading citizens of Dallas county in their day, none of them ever having been arraigned in the courts or charged with any dishonorable act. In fact, the characters of all seven were above reproach and worthy of emulation.[1]

Sam Acheson, an eminent Dallas journalist/historian recognized the "Six Sisters in Love Field's Past," in one of his Dallas Yesterday columns in 1968.

> Descendants of these families comprise today the large and well-known clan of Cochrans-Knights-Hughes-Harris-Records-Bachmans and related in-laws whose members since pioneer days have had a major part in the development of city and county, (and adding that) their large farms extended in an almost unbroken chain northward from Turtle Creek across Bachman's Creek to the Elm Fork of the Trinity, and eastward to present far North Dallas and Farmers Branch.[2]

Throughout Dallas there are dozens of tangible reminders that the Hugheses of Tennessee made endless contributions to the area, the most important of which were their children. There were 62 in all—Bachmans, Cochrans, Denises, Hugheses, Knights, Records, Webbs and Williamses. Their descendants continue, by countless names, to populate and contribute to the city and county.

Five of the seven Hughes sisters—Margaret Bachman, Nancy Cochran, Serena Knight, Amanda Record and Sarah Williams—are buried in Cochran Chapel Cemetery. Mary Webb is buried in Webb Chapel Cemetery in Dallas and Letitia Dennis in Tyler where her husband was the minister of Marvin Street Methodist Church when she died.

They are present in schools—the Nancy Jane Cochran School at 6000 Keeneland in Oak Cliff, dedicated on November 16, 1969, and Obadiah Knight at 2615 Anson Road.

Among the streets that bear the names of family members and their spouses are Bachman Boulevard, Cochran Street, Cochran Chapel Circle, Cochran Chapel Road, Cochran Heights Court, Cochran Heights Drive, Hughes Lane, Knight Street, Lemmon Avenue, Record Street, Record Crossing Road, and Webb Chapel Road.

The Bachman area of Dallas and Bachman Lake and recreation center are reminiscences of the early Dallas families.

Cochran Chapel Methodist Church, Cochran Chapel Cemetery and Webb Chapel Cemetery are all named for family members.

5

THE MULTIPLE MILLERS—MILLERMORE AND MORE

While the Hughes sisters and their husbands were amassing large blocks of land in fertile farms north and west of the infant city of Dallas, the Miller families were acquiring land and building showcase homes across the Trinity River to the west.

It is difficult to trace the Miller families because two Millers, not related, came to Dallas in 1845 or 1846—the years vary according to who is telling the story. They were Madison Moultrie Miller and William Brown Miller. The William Brown Miller family history[1] says that "In 1846 William Brown Miller left his wife and children in Independence, Missouri . . . and set out alone to ride to Texas." The Madison Moultrie Miller family history[2] says "In 1845 Madison Moutrie (sic) Miller arrived in this area with . . . William B. Miller, no relation, who later was known for building Millermore." The two histories agree that the men were friends. The histories are further complicated by the fact that Millers married unrelated Millers in succeeding generations—including one Miller who married the widow of another Miller. Children are named for parents or grandparents. One prominent Miller—Minerva or Miss Minnie—is named for her father's first wife. When mothers died, their children were sometimes reared by half siblings, the children of their fathers by prior wives. As if that weren't complicated enough, the men and women brought to Dallas by one of those Millers as slaves took the Miller name after the Emancipation Proclamation. Both white and black Miller families continued to live on family property for more than half a century.

William Brown Miller was born in Alabama in 1807, and Madison Moultrie, in Georgia in 1814. Though there was seven years difference in their ages, the two Millers became acquainted and forged a lifelong friendship. William was educated in the public schools in Alabama, farmed and opened a general store in New Market, Alabama, in 1834. Though he moved on to Tennessee and then to Missouri, he maintained connections with Madison, who had moved to Alabama as a child and was the overseer of three plantations near New Market.

If the two men came to Dallas together, the date of their arrival would have to have been some time in 1845 because Polly Rawlins said, in a letter written to her family back in Illinois in the early spring of 1846, that she had selected her future mate from among her many suitors. His name was Madison Miller.

In the meantime, William Miller had arranged to buy property on a hillside southeast of Dallas and left on horseback for Independence, Missouri, to move his family to their new home. On the way, he was stricken with "Asiatic cholera." He was unconscious when his horse delivered him into an Indian village. He was nursed back to health by the Indian squaws. When he finally got well enough to travel, six months had elapsed and his family had given him up for dead.

When they moved to Dallas, the William Brown Miller family included Miller, his wife, Minerva Barnes Miller, their five children, Alonzo, 8; Mattie, 6; Mary Brown, 4; Virginia, 2, Susan, only a few months old, and Charilaus (Crill) Miller, 17, his son by a prior marriage. Traveling with them were at least four family slaves, couples Charlotte and Arch and Bettye and Clayton.

Charlotte and Arch and Bettye and Clayton are the third chain of the convoluted Millers of early Dallas. They, and most of the other freed slaves, chose Miller as their own name after the Emancipation Proclamation, and several generations of the family continued to live in and near Dallas 150 years later.

Two Millers—William Brown and Madison Moultrie—came to Dallas in the mid-1840s. After scouting the area, they both returned with their families, William Brown Miller bringing slaves who would later take the Miller name. Furthur complications ensued when both William Brown and Madison Moultrie married the same woman—at different times, of course.

William Brown Miller and Madison Moultrie Miller each had three wives, for a total of five women because one of the women was married to both Madison and William.

Before becoming hopelessly entangled, let us begin to individuate these three Miller chains that have made countless contributions and enjoyed great prominence in the building of Dallas County.

William Brown Miller was a man of the land. He was the son of a farmer and had continued to help his father on the farm during his school days after the family moved to Alabama. He farmed on land he rented in Alabama, on land he bought in Tennessee, and on land he probably rented from his parents-in-law in Missouri during the brief period he lived near Independence. An adventurer, an astute business man, a devoted family man, and a community builder, William Brown Miller had married Elizabeth Waddy in 1828 when he was 21. Her ancestry was Cherokee Indian. Their only child was Charilaus—known as Crill—born October 16, 1829. Crill was six years old when his mother died in 1835.

Millermore, the house built by William Brown Miller in Oak Cliff that now is the gem of Old City Park.

Not quite two years following Elizabeth's death, Miller married Minerva Barnes in Kentucky. Minerva was only 25 when she arrived in Dallas with her five children, her stepson and the black families.

On his first trip to Texas, William paid $1,280 cash for 1,280 acres. He also claimed a headright of 640 acres on the Oak Cliff side of the Trinity River, which he eventually increased to 6,000 acres, and all of which he purchased for approximately one dollar per acre. He bought and sold land according to the vagaries of the market place and his own whims. Once he sold seventy acres for $30 an acre. Later, deciding that he needed some of it back, he paid $12,500 for two acres!

Minerva gave birth to three more children in Dallas—Bettie Hickman on October 11, 1848, and William Brown Jr. on December 13, 1853. A third baby, unnamed, died at birth in 1856.

Minerva and William Brown Miller started their showcase Dallas home in 1855. The ante-bellum home, like almost all other buildings in Dallas, bears the name of the male in the family. It was—and is—known as the William Brown Miller house, but there were far more Miller women who lived in it and for much longer periods of time than the patriarch himself.

The house was typically Southern colonial with four white pillars connecting the expansive front porch with the roof above the second story. The floor plan was pegged out at night with the North Star serving as a compass so that the house would face due south and catch every breeze. A wide entryway hall centered 20 by 20 foot rooms on either side. Center-cut oak logs were hauled from Jefferson in East Texas, sliced, trimmed and fitted together with handmade wooden pegs. Beams, floors and roofing shingles were made from cedar dragged by oxen out of the dense woods surrounding the property, then hand-cut and hauled to Jefferson for finishing, then brought back to the hillside in

Oak Cliff and meticulously fitted together. Chimneys and hearths were made of native Texas stone hauled from Mountain Creek west of Dallas. Painted white, the house stood in majestic splendor on a hilltop five miles south of downtown Dallas where, surrounded by undeveloped land, it could be seen for miles.

The new house stood only a few feet from the log cabin in which the Millers had lived for eight years following their arrival in Dallas. With the exception of the Bryan cabin—or its replica on Commerce Street in downtown Dallas—the Miller's log cabin is the oldest known structure in Dallas County. It consisted of one large room heated by a fireplace with a chimney of native stone and an attic above. It was made of hand-hewn oak and cedar logs and had a wide veranda some 20 feet in length stretching across its front.

Minerva Miller did not live to see her new home completed. She died on September 18, 1856, shortly after the birth and death of her eighth baby.

William Miller completed the house and moved his family into it. As soon as they were settled into their new home, the log house in which they had lived was converted into a school for the children. Sarah B. Gray was hired in Kentucky and brought to Dallas to teach the five Miller daughters. Later, Sarah Gray taught at a school in the Masonic Hall on Houston Street.

Seven of the Miller sisters' girlfriends were invited to move into the log house and study with them. They paid no tuition. Mrs. Gray and the 12 little girls lived in the log house. During the day they held school on the first floor and at night they climbed up the sturdy oak staircase, now missing from the cottage, where they slept.

The McGuffey reader and other McGuffey texts were used. In the evenings William Miller brought out his fiddle, played dance tunes and taught the girls to dance.

The marker designating Miller-more as a Texas historic landmark.

> William Brown Miller had definite ideas that young ladies should be taught social graces, as well as the three Rs.... He would get out his fiddle, play dance tunes and teach the girls to dance. This caused quite a scandal among some of the more conservative pioneers—there was talk of putting him out of the church....[3]

The girls also rode horses for recreation, and at least once William Miller organized a jack-rabbit hunt, a pioneer version of the fox hunt, and climaxed it with a hunt breakfast afterward.

Though the school did not last long, it was the first private school in Dallas and the place where the five Miller daughters—Martha, Mary Brown, Virginia, Susan and Bettie—and their friends Elizabeth A. Griffin, Mattie Hord, Mary Elizabeth McDoniel, Fanny Palmer, and three others began their formal education. Since no records remain, the names of the other three little girls who lived and studied in the log cabin are unknown.

The cabin in which Minerva and William Miller lived was converted into a school for their daughters and seven friends.

While William Brown Miller was settling on land five miles from the heart of the little village of Dallas, Madison Moultrie Miller was casting his fortune in southwest Dallas County some 15 miles away.

It was on his first trip to the area to scout the land that Madison met Mary Parks (Polly) Rawlins, the 19-year-old daughter of Roderick Alexander and Mildred Parks Rawlins, who had settled in the area in 1844. Madison's wife, Isabell McClusky Miller, had died in Alabama in 1844 leaving him with their two surviving children—Mary Cordelia and William D. They had lost two other infants, Josephine and an unnamed baby.

Through her several surviving letters and a book, *Polly Rawlins Miller*, by Kathryn Smith Miller, Polly emerges as a high spirited, well-educated young woman. While on the wagon trip to Texas with several families, Polly wrote to her siblings back in Illinois describing some of the group's experiences.

In one letter, dated November 12, 1844, to her brother, she wrote that the wagon train had traveled 12 to 25 miles a day, had been on the road for seven weeks and had reached the Republic of Texas. They had crossed four rivers—the Mississippi, Marimec White, and Arkansas twice, once in Missouri and again in Arkansas. The trip had been costly; they had paid from 25 cents to 75 cents per bushel for corn and about the same amount for potatoes. She said they had reached the Red River on the last day of October and had then come to "a beautiful prairie which we liked very much . . . green and rolling, the ground black and rich . . . timber much like that of Illinois . . . . We are all very much pleased with the country . . . and we hear it is better out towards the Trinity."[4]

The Rawlins family, among the first to arrive in the south/southwest part of what would be Dallas County, was widely known for its hospitality. In *History of Lancaster, Texas, 1845-1945,* published by the Lancaster Historical Society, A. B. Rawlins is quoted as saying, "At this hearth the spirit of family glee and comfort has always prevailed and the stranger never was a stranger long."

So, it was entirely likely that Madison Miller found lodging with or near the Rawlins home. In any event, Madison and Polly met, somewhere around her 18th birthday, she wrote to a friend in Illinois:

> From among my suitors I have selected a gentleman of Alabama. He is there at present, but expects to return about the first of March. If he does and proves to be what he represents himself to be, I expect we will be married sometime in the spring. He is a widower with two children and is about twenty-eight years old. I have received the approval of parents and I hope you will not be dissatisfied—[5]

Polly grew impatient while waiting for Madison Miller's return. The wedding did not take place in the spring as she had said it might. On April 9, at about the time she had hoped to be a bride, she wrote again to the friend: "I am nothing but Pop (another nickname for Mary Parks) Rawlins yet, and it is doubtful whether I will be or not. However, we have received two letters from Mr. . . . . that let us know that he could not settle his business as expected."[6]

On June 2, 1846, from the State of Texas, Polly wrote again to "Dear Brother and Sister," and after filling them in on the health of family members, the weather, the condition of the crops, the restlessness of the Indians, and other smaller details, she got around to her big news:

> Now for the charm news of this letter. I am no longer Pop Rawlins. Mr. Miller and I were married on Monday the twenty-fifth of May when everything looked pleasant and gay. Mr. Miller is not here at this time. He started to Houston a few days since but expects to return in five or six weeks. We will move to the place he is improving, about five miles from here on Bear Creek. I have not been down to see the place, but I expect that it is a good one.[7]

The 19-year-old bride and her 32-year-old husband—he was four years older than she had estimated—did move to Bear Creek, but did not live there long. Polly was happy. "I have an affectionate husband and two children, a boy 5 and a girl 7—both beautiful and interesting," she wrote to the friends back home.[8]

At the time Madison and Polly married, the main trail from the Trinity River west to Johnson's Station, (which later would be called Arlington), and on to Fort Worth ran along a high ground on Dowdy Ferry Road just north of Pleasant Run Road in Lancaster. Madison and Polly Miller and the two Miller children moved there in the late fall of 1846. Polly was pregnant.

The Millers built a two-room home, one room for a store and the other for living quarters. They prospered and the family increased. Benjamin Franklin Miller was born in 1847, Fredonia Ann Miller in 1849, Madison Moultrie Miller, Jr. in 1851 and Blanche Amalia Miller in 1854.

The store grew even faster than the family. In 1848, Miller used his two-room house as the center for a new 15-room home. It was the biggest house in Dallas County. He built a separate store and a warehouse. Lumber came from Houston by ox cart. Because

Madison Moultrie Miller, a widower, brought his two children, Mary Cordelia and William D., to southwest Dallas County where he married Mary Parks (Polly) Rawlins, the popular daughter of Roderick Alexander and Mildred Parks Rawlins.

it took about six weeks for the round-trip to Houston, building consumed more than a year. Constructed of oak, the house was put together with square nails and wooden pegs. The lumber was hand-hewn. Floors were cedar and gutters were copper. It had two brick chimneys; the bricks were made of lime mortar.

When completed, the house had seven downstairs rooms, six upstairs rooms and two large attic rooms. There were three staircases, one at the back, one at the front, and another from the second to the third level. The house had no halls, so that those who "roomed" in the two attic rooms at the top had to go through bedrooms to get to their sleeping quarters. The four large rooms, two up and two down, had white plaster walls and large fireplaces with mirrors the full length of the mantle. The forty-foot dining room had a table its entire length.

The big house served as both as a home and a hotel. It accommodated the family, the workers in the flour and grist mills, the store, the post office, boarders, and, from time to time, travelers on the stage coaches passing through.

In 1848 Madison Miller was appointed postmaster at Pleasant Run, Texas, probably named by the surveyor hired to plat the area. He was from Virginia where little creeks, such as the one running through the area, were called runs. Mail came bi-weekly. Until that time, the closest post office had been at White Rock (no connection to the present White Rock area) near Waxahachie.

A stage coach route from Galveston, another from San Antonio and others east and west ran through the little village two to four times a week, so the Miller's 40-foot table was usually filled with diners. The food was under the supervision of Polly Parks Rawlins Miller.

The general store was the center of the community and carried more ware than any other place in that part of Texas. Most of the merchandise came from New York by way of Galveston, where it was shipped overland in ox-drawn wagons. Miller's chief driver was a 220-pound black man named Sam, who, according to legend, was so good at cracking his whip that he could kill a horsefly on the third oxen, three teams away, and not disturb the other oxen.

The store's merchandise was so extensive that Miller offered a pair of shoes free to anyone who asked to buy any needed thing that he could not supply. The only person who ever collected was a man who asked for a dozen monkeys. Miller did not quibble over whether, or not, they were *needed*. The man got the shoes. Almost everything else was in stock, from liquor to saddles to drugs and medicines to food to perfume to wedding dresses.

In the early 1850s, the area was so successful that Madison laid out a town and sold lots. He hired a water witch to locate the source of the town's water supply, on Clear Creek. He advertised a stage coach stop, hotel room (doubtless his own home), a blacksmith shop, a tin shop, a woodworking shop and a steam-powered grist mill. Four blocks away the first school in the area was opened.

And then Polly Parks Miller died at age 30. She had been in Texas only 12 years; she had been married for only 10 years. She had given birth to four children and had been a stepmother to two others. She had been a "helpmeet" to one of the most successful of the early settlers of the southern part of Dallas County, which was still a part of the free Republic of Texas, not even a county when she arrived. In the late evening of November 30, 1856, Polly called her husband to her bedside and gave explicit instructions about the disposition of her most valued treasures. Madison Miller sat at her bedside and wrote down her instructions:

> For Fredonia Ann Miller—one Bible, one black silk dress, one white worked counterpane, one blue Mexican Quilt, two daguerreotypes, of her Grandmother's likeness, one her Father's likeness, one pen holder and one pen knife.

> For Amalia Blanche Miller—one Bible, one quilt (Rose in the Wilderness), one white muslin dress and skirt, one daguerreotype her Mother and her likeness on one side—her brothers and sister in the other—one gold pen and case and chain.

Madison and Polly Miller operated a general merchandise store at Pleasant Run (later Lancaster) which was the community center, stage coach station and hotel. Its merchandise was so extensive that people came from miles around to buy everything from lumber to wedding gowns.

Ben Franklin's presents by his Mother—one Bible, one Mexican quilt different colors.

Madison Moultrie Miller's presents by his mother—one Bible, one quilt (Irish Chain).[9]

Polly had the articles brought to her bedside, looked at them, identified each, designated to whom they should be left, talked about her children, and died that night.

In late 1858, when he was 44, Madison met and married an 18-year-old beauty, who he had met in New York City. She was Emma Angeline Dewey. Born in 1840, the daughter of Silas H. and Amy Spencer Dewey, the bride was 12 years *younger* than Mary Cordelia, her stepdaughter, who already was married to Quincy A. Sweatt. (Cordelia's brother, William, had died in 1849.) Madison's younger children by Polly ranged in age from three to 11.

Madison died April 1, 1860, two years after he took his young bride home to Pleasant Run. He was 46 years old. The four children were "farmed out" to relatives and friends. Benny, 16, joined the Confederate Army at the beginning of the Civil War and died while in service with typhoid fever. Fredonia Ann went to live with relatives and died in February of 1864 at the age of 16, also of typhoid. Moty (Madison, Jr.) moved into the home of Sam and Lucinda Keller who reared him as their own. He considered them family. He married Lou White and lived to be 82. Blanche was only two when her mother died and 6 when she lost her father. She was welcomed into the home of her half sister, Mary Cordelia, and Quincy Sweatt. She married J. Hall Baskin, and following his death, a man named Ezell who lived only three weeks after the marriage. After his death Blanche went to live with her brother and sister-in-law, Moty, and Lou Miller and died when she was 59.

Emma was not long a grieving widow. When William Brown Miller went to comfort her and settle the estate, he stayed to court and wed her—four months after Madison died. This photograph hangs in the master bedroom at Millermore.

And Emma? She was not long a grieving widow. William Brown Miller, administrator of Madison Miller's vast holdings, took over settling his friend's business and stayed to court the comely Emma. Four months following Madison's death, Emma and William were married. The bride was 20; her husband was 54. She brought no children of her own to the marriage, but inherited six stepchildren, most of them older than she.

Emma moved into the not-yet-completed estate of her new family on Bonnie View Road. She brought with her many fine pieces of furniture from her home in Pleasant Run. These treasures included her rosewood square piano, mahogany secretaries, marble topped tables, a mahogany sofa, a pair of heavy gilt framed mantel mirrors, and other treasures. Having been married to Madison Miller for less than two years, Emma created a schism in the Miller family that still smoldered more than a hundred years later. The ancestors of Madison Miller claim that she had no right to everything left by her late husband; the ancestors of William Brown Miller claim that she was justified, as his widow, to claim whatever she wanted.

Minerva's daughters were not exactly pleased to acquire a stepmother who could very easily have been their playmate and a schoolmate when they were children. Emma, William's bride, and Martha, his oldest daughter, were exactly the same age. In the five years that followed, Emma Dewey Miller Miller gave birth to three children: sons Charles Malcolm on July 11, 1861; John Hickman (Dick) on October 14, 1862, and Minerva Hortense on December 2, 1865. In a gesture of peacemaking with her step-daughters, Emma told them that they could name this third baby if she was a girl. The girls named her Minerva—Minerva Hortense—for their mother.

In the meantime, the "big house" was completed. Emma and William, along with his children, and their baby moved into it shortly before the birth of her second child.

Minerva Hortense Miller, who married Barry Miller (same name, no relation), named Millermore and lived in it all but 15 of her 95 years. A socialite who made her debut at Idlewild's first ball in 1884, she also was an astute business woman who ran the farm. Minnie Miller and her daughter, Evelyn Miller Crowell, deserve credit for preserving Millermore records. The house was the setting over many years for some of the most lavish social events of the entire Dallas community.

Minerva Hortense Miller, known all of her life as Minnie, was the youngest of William Brown Miller's 12 children. She was born two months after his 58th birthday. He doted on the little girl and gave her every cultural and educational privilege that his money and the times could provide.

Minnie Miller spent all but 15 of her 95 years as a resident of the house in which she was born. It was she who named it Millermore.

Because Minnie kept meticulous records of Dallas's social life during her lifetime, her more serious contributions to the growing community have been obscured—and they were many. Minnie not only inherited Millermore; she managed it. She was in the first class to enroll at Ursuline Academy. She made her debut at the first Idlewild Ball and she was the first woman to serve as a trustee of Dallas County schools.

The farm was large, the help abundant, the money plentiful, and the times easy and pleasant. As a child, Minnie was free to roam the hillsides, ride horses, and have playmates for overnights. She was seven when the first train puffed into Dallas in 1872. Her father was 65. He was one of the men who had worked hard and given money to secure a railroad into Dallas, and he was not about to miss the arrival of the first Houston and Texas Central train. When Minnie begged to go with him, he pulled her up in front of the saddle and they set out. "Father always rode spirited horses," she told Sam Acheson in an interview once, "and the one he was riding that day was scared out of its wits by the wood-burning engine and the shouts of the crowd....as that train huffed its way into town. We watched it cross the new trestle over the Trinity just east of our old Ferry . . . it was all my father could do to keep the horse reined in."

Educated at Ursuline Academy in Dallas and Hamilton College in Lexington, Kentucky, Minnie transferred to Ward-Belmont in Nashville, Tennessee, where she graduated in May of 1884. Returning to Dallas, she made her debut the same year when Idlewild presented its first debutantes. She was one of five young women making bows. Her escort was Barry Miller, another unrelated Miller. He had moved to Dallas from Washington, and was "reading law' in the offices of Henry C. Coke and Judge Sawnie Robertson. A year later, after he passed the Texas State Bar, Barry Miller and Minnie Miller were married. He was 21; she was 20. Minnie spent her early married years "in town."

In 1899 Minnie's parents died within less than three months of each other, William Brown Miller on January 4, 1899, and Emma Dewey Miller on March 17, 1899.

Minnie and Barry moved back to Millermore. There they reared their four children: Thomas Barry Miller, William Brown Miller II, Philip Richard Miller, and Evelyn Dewey Miller. An astute business woman who managed every detail of the family business, Minnie was also a devoted wife and mother. She claimed she was not the slightest interested in politics, but she followed the career of her husband and went to Austin for every session of the State Legislature at which he presided during the time he was lieutenant governor of Texas.

Evelyn Miller Crowell's playhouse, now together with the southern farmhouse and the log schoolhouse at Old City Park.

Minnie and her daughter, Evelyn, are due a great deal of the credit for saving and sharing the history of the Miller family and of early Dallas.

By the time Evelyn was grown, the city was reaching out to engulf farmlands to the south, east, north and west. Roads that had been mere wagon trails were lengthened; areas were annexed. And so it was that Millermore, once a sprawling farm, acquired a city address, 3110 Bonnie View Road.

But, before that, in 1907, a third tiny building, a miniature of the original log cabin, had been added to the property. Evelyn had begged for a playhouse just like the one her grandfather had built for his family when they first came to Texas. Born on October 31, 1899, Evelyn was not born when her grandparents died, but grew up on stories about the pioneer days of Millermore. The log cabin playhouse was completed in time to be the setting for her eighth birthday party.

Hundreds of parties and thousands of meals were served to family and guests in Millermore. In the early winter of 1884 it was the setting for an elaborate dance when Minnie entertained for her college roommate, Carrie Moore Davidson. One of its most splendid events was Evelyn's June 9, 1925, wedding. Evelyn had been educated at Holly Hall in Dallas, the elite forerunner of Hockaday, was graduated from Ursuline Academy, attended a private school in New York and then attended Columbia University. The bridegroom was a New York newspaperman. For the wedding, Millermore was turned into a fairyland with an aisle of white satin flanked by ferns and flowers stretching across the lawn ending in the altar under a giant elm tree. The 600 wedding guests included an ultra-sophisticated array of politically and socially elite friends and acquaintances to hear the vows of one of its First Daughters to a New York journalist. The wedding was reported in detail:

> The wedding was colonial in style and was solemnized on the lawn of the estate, the white pilloried facade of the old Southern manor house forming a perfect background for the moonlight garden setting.
>
> From the gallery steps, the bridal path extended the full length of the lawn to the altar lit with candles beneath a giant oak tree.
>
> The bride's gown was instep length and featured a floating veil created especially for her by Bendel. Designed on colonial lines, it was of white chiffon over a silver slip featuring a straight long bodice of white finished at the bateau neckline with a frill of tulle. The skirt was three tiers of white lace over chiffon worn over hoops. The train was the full length of the gown and sprays of orange blossoms outlined the hoops in the skirt and were scattered down the train.
>
> The bride's attendant's wore colonial styled frocks of white tulle with basque waists, bateau necklines, tiny puff sleeves and flounced skirts over white satin. Their dresses were trimmed with satin ribbons in pastel shades matching the colonial bouquets of garden flowers they carried.[10]

Evelyn Miller was married to Alfred Wright Pierce in 1925. A New York journalist, he died young and Evelyn returned to Millermore where she lived with her mother.

The bridegroom's name, somewhat incidental to other details in the story, was Alfred Wright Pierce.

Minnie Miller filled many scrapbooks with mementoes of her young girlhood and of the parties and balls that kept music and laughter plentiful in the grand old house. These are now the property of the Dallas Public Library. Most concentrate on Minnie's social life and the social life of the growing city. There is not a trace of sorrow or scandal among the yellowed clippings, dance cards, social programs, and pressed flowers.

But Minnie Miller was far from frivolous. She ran the farm "according to traditions handed down by her father," said her daughter, Evelyn, while Barry went off to his law office in town. Steeped in the social customs of her time, which allowed no hint of pain or trouble to become public, Minnie gave the impression that life at Millermore was a utopia.

Minnie always said she did not believe in women's suffrage. Taking his cue from his wife, as do most men who are forming public policy, Barry, as a state senator, insisted that Dallas women did not want to vote and that he would oppose the state's approval of the Nineteenth Amendment. Nonie Boren Mahoney and the League of Women Voters changed his mind. When the Nineteenth Amendment became law, Minnie took her responsibilities as a voter very seriously. Barry had just been elected lieutenant governor of Texas when Evelyn was married. He served until 1930. Minnie was a charter member of the Dallas Woman's Club, and a trustee of the Dallas Historical Society from 1939 until her death.

Evelyn Miller Pierce followed closely in the footsteps of both of her parents. She was a writer, newspaperwoman, political activist, and author. Following her marriage she lived in New York until her husband died. Then, she returned to Dallas. On October 24, 1935, she married Chester T. Crowell. She had begun her newspaper career as a feature writer for the *Dallas Times Herald* in 1919 and was its art and music reporter for a year in 1931. In 1932 she became a research assistant for the Democratic National Committee and a year later became the editorial director of Press Intelligence for the U.S. Government in Washington, D. C. She held this job until 1936 when she returned to Millermore where she became a contributing editor for a number of magazines including *New Republic* and *Southwest Review*. A canvasser for the Democratic Party in numerous campaigns, she was a potent campaigner for her father when he ran for the Texas Senate and for lieutenant governor of the state.

Evelyn Miller Crowell chronicled family stories in two books, *Texas Childhood*, her personal memories of growing up at Millermore, and a novel called *Hilltop*. Though fictional, the latter had its setting in Dallas and its characters were based on Dallas citizens. Shortly after it was published, Evelyn said she went to a party where she was the most popular and sought-after dance partner. All of the men were courting her in an attempt to get her to reveal the identity of the characters in her book.

At Millermore, Evelyn wrote, entertained, collected Texas history, and helped her mother begin to restore the family home and the adjacent buildings.

Evelyn's *Texas Childhood*, authenticates many of the stories of early Dallas, stories she gleaned from family scrapbooks, photo albums, and stories passed from one generation to the next. She wrote about her grandparents, Emma and William Brown Miller, who died a few months before she was born, but whom she felt she knew. Her dressing table had been her grandmother's and above it hung the portrait of Emma when she came to Millermore as a bride. As a child, Evelyn sometimes was allowed to open her grandmother's little leather trunk and finger the white satin wedding gown, the size one and a half satin slippers and the "second day" lavender silk gown. In those days, Evelyn explained, when people had to travel great distances to attend a wedding, the festivities lasted two or three days and the bride's "second day" dress was almost as important as the wedding dress.

In many ways the black Miller families invested more of themselves into Millermore than did the families whose names were on its deeds. As explained by Dorothy Spruill Edwards in her book, *Somerset Homecoming,* ". . . the lifeblood of this plantation (Somerset in South Carolina) had been the slaves, not the whites . . . . the fabric, the texture, the resonance of this lakefront land came from the hundreds of black people who lived there."[11] It was the black Miller men at Millermore who tilled the land, felled the trees, built the house and its surrounding buildings, tended the stock, and harvested the crops. It was the black Miller women who cooked and served the meals, swept, dusted and cleaned, washed and ironed, tended the chickens and gathered the eggs, polished the silver, cared for the children, and often helped in the fields during planting and harvest time.

Evelyn's *Texas Childhood* gives glimpses of the relationship of the white and black Millers from her vantage point. It was, through her eyes, a happy and loving relationship:

> I would have had the loneliness of an only child had it not been for Maybelle and the other darkies on the place who, from the oldest to the youngest, were my friends and playmates. When I was very young there were still a few of the old slaves left; their children and grandchildren continued to come back around holiday time . . . . My own, particular darkies were from South Carolina, brought to Texas by my mother when she took over the farm. One family, in its various branches, provided field as well as house servants. They ranged from my beloved Granny, whose age no one ever knew, but who was grown and had children at the time of the Civil War, through her various children and their husbands and wives, and her grandchildren, including Maybelle, who was assigned to me when I was a year old . . . .[12]

June 'Teenth was a very special day for Southern black people, the day they celebrated the proclamation that freed them from slavery. The slaves had actually been freed on January 1, 1862, but it took months for the news to travel west and it was not until June 19 that it reached Texas. At Millermore it was a day of great anticipation and even greater celebration:

> The preparations always began weeks ahead . . . . Our darkies all came to mamma to ask for contributions of chickens, hams and the various ingredients for cakes and pies . . . . These were always given gladly. They were given gladly by all of the people we knew, with perhaps some good-humored smiles over the fact that they were being asked to contribute to the celebration of a

Proclamation which, by freeing their slaves—valuable properties in themselves—and, in so doing, taking away the workers from their fields, had in many cases bankrupted their families....

> When the great day dawned... I was up almost as early as the darkies and impatient to be off on a round of their cabins.... They would be standing over their wood stoves frying great skillets of chicken. The hams were baked the day before, the pies and cakes made, but the potato salad would have to be put together and the baskets—usually wash baskets, lined with some of mamma's old table clothes—packed.[13]

Children were scrubbed with lie soap. Everybody dressed in their best. Granny always wore a blue and white calico dress with a red bandanna around her neck and another around her head. Maybelle always had a new dress made from fabric Evelyn gave her for Christmas each year. Once Maybelle covered her "lovely, shiny, black skin" with face powder Evelyn had given her. Evelyn always begged to go to the June 'Teenth celebration, but was never allowed to. Once, two of her brothers slipped away and went. A fight broke out. Granny saw the two little white faces among the brawling black ones, pushed herself through the crowd, grabbed a little boy under each arm and demanded to be given room so that she could get "Mis' Minnie's chillun" away from the fighting.

There are no early written records by the black Millers of Millermore, but the stories that have come down through time are of both hardships and of benevolence, stories both similar and different from those told by the record-keeping white Millers.

For the women, in the days before electricity at Millermore, laundry was especially gruelling. They took it in baskets half a mile to the creek where they did the washing. They gathered the wood and made fires under giant black pots and boiled the dirty clothes and the white linens. The clothes worn by the white folks got special attention. The cold water in which the clothes were rinsed was icy in the wintertime. Their hands chapped and sometimes bled from wringing the water from denim and other heavy fabrics. Clothes were hung to dry on whatever bushes were available, then gathered, folded and stored again in the baskets where they were carried up the hill to Millermore and ironed.

Some members of the black Miller families continued to live at Millermore on property deeded to them by the owners. Some continued to work for Miss Minnie until her death. Arch and Charlotte, one of the two original black couples, stayed on their acreage on the Miller farm. Clayton and Bettye moved into town and once lived on Convent street near the present location of Baylor Hospital. John and Lucy Miller, another couple who came to the Miller farm as slaves, moved to Five Mile Creek.

Once, in the 1930s, Minnie Miller wanted to tell Ernest Payton the story of how slavery had brought the two Miller families together to Texas, but at that time, Payton later recalled, he didn't want to listen to her. Ernest Payton, who was a fourth generation descendant of John and Lucy Miller, later said: "I wish I had listened. At the time it really didn't interest me. I was angry about it."

Donald Payton, Ernest's son, a fifth-generation descendant of Lucy and John, is the family historian and record keeper. "The women in my family were very strong," Donald said. "They were *Miller* women and that meant something. In our family it is understood that men don't marry bad women and the women don't marry fools."

His research has taken Donald through most Dallas records and back through history to Missouri, where he found the records of the birth of his great-great grandmother, Lucy Miller, in 1870. He also found the records of the birth of Archie in 1824 in Alabama, no mean feat when you consider that slaves usually went by first names only.

Along the way Donald has picked up some striking family memorabilia and many poignant vignettes. In 1989 he made a pilgrimage back to Tennessee, South Carolina, and Kentucky and found the house built by his great-great grandfather. It had a broken upstairs window. He asked permission from the owner, a white Miller, to repair it. Then he went to the hardware store, bought what he needed, returned to the house, found a ladder and put in a new window. While working, he gathered quite an audience. Later, at a restaurant in the town, he was recognized and someone asked why he, a visitor, would

In many ways the black Miller families contributed more to Millermore than their employers, but their contributions went unrecorded except for mentions by white historians—until Donald Payton began researching and writing about them.

go to the trouble of putting a new window in the old house. He told them: "My great grandfather built that house and he built it to stand against the ravages of time. If he could have been here, he would have put in a new window. He couldn't be here, so I did it for him."[14]

After a story on Donald's work with the Dallas Historical Society appeared in the *New York Times* in August of 1990, he got a call from a woman in Colorado. She said she was a direct descendant of Clayton and Bettye Miller. "I *thought* she was a white woman, but I couldn't be sure," Donald recalls his telephone conversation. "Finally, I asked her, 'Do you know that Clayton and Bettye Miller were black?' and she laughed and said, 'And did you know that their son married an Irish girl?' Since then, she and her husband have made a trip to Dallas and I showed them all of the spots that were special to our family when they first came to Dallas as slaves."

In 1975, after several years of searching through historical papers, letters, deeds, tax receipts, cemeteries and family Bibles, Donald sent out invitations to the first reunion of his Miller family. Every year since then, around June 19, descendants of the Miller family gather from all over the world to meet each other and to talk about the past. They celebrate in Cedardale Park in South Oak Cliff near the site where their great-great-great grandparents lived and helped to build Millermore. Every year the gathering has grown. In 1990, over 1,200 people showed up.

Minerva Hortense Miller Miller died on November 7, 1960, two months before her 95th birthday. Her daughter, Evelyn Dewey Miller Pierce Crowell, died two months before her mother.

Evelyn's years of research, preservation and writing have sometimes seemed to have fallen to uncaring individuals who were deaf to her plea that "Dallas should never get so big that the pioneers responsible for this city are forgotten" and blind to its past accomplishments.

Millermore with its two adjacent log cabins became the target of vandals. (See Chapter 33) As early as 1950, when the neighborhood was beginning to change, the two women had called police officers for assistance and protection. The log cabins were used by kids for target practice. Sometimes the cabins were rifled and the interior damaged. Sometimes the fire department was called to extinguish nearby grass fires.

Through the years the Miller property had been sold off and/or given away. Much of the property deeded to the former slaves was sold to pay debts; some sold to the City of Dallas and some was reclaimed for non-payment of taxes.

Millermore, the stately old house that was largely built by black Millers, and both of the log cabins are now at home in Old City Park on Ervay Street just south of I-30 in the shadows of downtown Dallas. Refurbished into its original grandeur, the house is a centerpiece of the Dallas County Heritage Society's efforts to preserve as much as possible of the area's early history. At one time in 1966 Millermore was only hours away from the wrecking ball. The property had been sold to Good Street Baptist Church, which had given the Heritage Society until Easter to move the house. Easter was still a few weeks away when the Society learned a public auction had been announced for March 1 to sell the three structures piece by piece if necessary. Dallas women led by Mrs. Sawnie Aldredge swung into action to save the house. When George Dawdy of the Texas Wrecking & Salvage Co. arrived to raze the structures, he was met by a few men and dozens of determined women and by Constable Robie Love with a restraining order.

Through the years the Dallas County Heritage Society, other historical groups, and individuals have contributed money and time to restore and refurbish Millermore, the log cabins, and other buildings at Old City Park. Open to the public, these homes, a church, one of the original train depots, and other buildings give present Dallasites a visual and emotional history of the city.

Requiem: Evelyn Miller Crowell lies among her ancestors in The Miller Family Cemetery, which she had once described as "my favorite spot on the whole place" where she often went as a child to be among "people who had lived before I lived and were gone . . . I was interested in them, felt close to them." Every landmark except the resting places themselves are gone now. It was "about half a mile from the old log house . . . on a little knoll, in a grove of beautiful cedars." The trees have become scraggly with limited upkeep as the years have passed. The little knoll, if it exists at all, is invisible against the backdrop of brick homes on every side. It is not easy to find, tucked away behind 2907 King Cole Drive in Oak Cliff and reached through an alleyway between 2823 and 2907 King Cole. But the granite monument still stands in the center bearing the names: Alonzo Miller, Minerva Barnes Miller, Mary B. Miller; Bettie H. Miller, William B. Miller, Jr. Flat granite slabs cover the graves of William B. Miller and Emma Dewey Miller, the same slabs with the same names and dates that Evelyn meticulously copied when she sat among her ancestors as a small girl. Beside them lie Minerva Hortense Miller, Barry Miller, and Evelyn Crowell Miller and on the other side Crill Miller. And around them lie the black Millers identified by name, but with no dates: Arch Miller, Charlotte Miller, Willis Boozer, Della Boozer, Dick Hines, Lula Hines, Charles C. Jennings, Sarah Jennings and Evelyn's childhood playmate, Maybelle Shelby Stevenson.

6

FROM VISION TO VILLAGE

The 1850s dawned. Dallas was a tiny village. In 1851 the *Texas Republican* recorded 160 people. There were 123 white inhabitants and 37 Negroes. There was an abundance of lawyers—seven. There were three doctors, an editor, three dry-goods store owners, two grocers, a cabinet maker, a stone mason, and two tailors.

For the handful of citizens already present and for those yet to come, it would be a decade of unlimited possibility. It would be a time when inhabitants of the new town and county would decide whether they would move forward toward the next century or be content with the progress they had made. There would be no standing still. The adventuresome spirit that had brought settlers halfway across a continent by ox-drawn covered wagon under conditions sufficiently adverse to dissuade any but the most hardy, demanded that they move on with determination, vision and positive expectation.

The women would continue to create homes and rear children under whatever conditions prevailed. They would survive bad weather, recalcitrant growing seasons, failed crops, poor living conditions, pregnancy, the loss of their babies, loneliness and homesickness. And, they would continue to hold fast to the vision that had brought them from Missouri and Tennessee, from Kentucky and the Carolinas, from Louisiana and Alabama, from New York and Virginia to a new world. *And,* there would continue to be a wonderful blending: women from established, affluent families and women whose families barely survived. What united them was a will to a new destiny. They made the best of what they could not change and looked forward to a better future.

Consider Eliza Ann Joyner Barker. It was a cold December day in 1852, two weeks from Christmas. She had crossed the Trinity River with her husband, Charles Barker, and their four small children. Everybody was chilled. Everybody was hungry. Night was coming. The persistent rain that would have been welcome in planting time chilled her, but there was no time to rest.

Eliza helped her husband make camp. When they had made a fire and had begun to dry out, conditions appeared a little better, even though the larder was almost bare and everybody, worn from what seemed like an endless journey, was hungry.

The Barkers had been in their wagon following the trails from Franklin County, North Carolina, to Texas for exactly three months. It had not been easy. Back in September several families in a caravan of wagons had begun the trek to Texas. Eliza, 32, and Charles, only a year older, were more experienced with the vagaries of nature than many of the co-travelers. They had been married for 10 years and were determined to provide a better life than they had known for their children.

Of all the wagons that had set out on September 13, theirs was the only one that had made it to Texas. Along the way, the deeply religious Barkers would not travel on the Sabbath day, resting both themselves and their livestock. Now that they were camped on the banks of the Trinity, so far as Eliza could see, the promised land was not very promising. She could easily have wondered if the God they worshipped had forsaken them.

In his first letter home, in the winter of 1853, Charles Barker described some of the hardships the family endured. On their journey to Texas, he said, the roads were poorly marked. Rains had turned what ruts there were into muddy holes. The wagons, loaded to capacity with precious cargo, bogged down. The men, who usually walked beside the wagons, were often joined by the women and the children who were old enough to walk.

From Missouri and Tennessee, from Kentucky and the Carolinas, from Louisiana and Alabama, from New York and Virginia, they came seeking a new life. The women were a wonderful blending, from affluent families and from backgrounds of poverty, united in a single purpose—to create a city out of a wilderness.

FROM VISION TO VILLAGE / 52

Charles Barker topped a hill and there, laid out before him, was a blanket of bluebonnets. When he told his wife, Eliza, she agreed that they had, indeed, reached the promised land. . . .

Eliza had begun to prepare their evening meal. After a night of rest they would move on, hoping to reach their destination a few miles farther west before another nightfall. A lone rider distracted Eliza's reverie. As soon as she and Charles were certain that he was not there to harm them, they made him welcome. His name, he said, was James Horton and he was an old-timer in those parts. He had come to Texas in 1844 with his parents, Enoch and Martha Horton, when he was a young man, among the very first families to settle in Dallas. Not that he lived in Dallas, he added. He really lived in Hord's Ridge across the Trinity and was on his way to his new home in Eagle Ford. He had married last year when he returned from the California gold rush, and his wife, Jane Phillips Horton, was waiting for him.

Garrulous and friendly, Horton added that his brother-in-law was Alexander Cockrell, who had just bought the whole city of Dallas from John Neely Bryan, the man who had founded it, and that its future was unlimited. His sister, Sarah, who was Alexander's wife, was one smart woman and would help her husband turn the town into a profitable adventure for everybody. Not that he wanted to discourage them from going on, but surely not now. The roads westward were just as bad, maybe worse, than what they'd seen, the Indians were likely to attack and the weather would be dreadful. They had experienced only a mere sample of how cold Texas could be in the wintertime. Besides, he added, he had an empty cabin on the place that the family would be welcome to use for the winter.

By the time Horton was ready to say good-by, Eliza was eager to accept his offer and Charles was not hard to convince. James Horton rode off into the evening with a family of new Dallasites ready to occupy his vacant cabin. Eliza and Charles settled in and made the old dirt-floored cabin as comfortable as they could. From time to time James Horton rode by and Eliza met one or two of the other women who lived not far away.

When spring came, Charles Barker joined Horton on a cattle roundup. On horseback, topping a hillside, he viewed his first blanket of bluebonnets spread across the land almost as far as his eyes could see. Explaining it to Eliza later, he said he had seen the promised land that they had envisioned when they left North Carolina. Eliza's enthusiasm almost matched her husband's. The Barkers had come to Texas to stay. Another year passed before they could make arrangements to buy a few acres from Horton in South Dallas County. On it, in 1854, they built a large one-room, two-story house, hauling the lumber for it from Groesbeck by wagon. That first winter, the cabin had no doors and Eliza covered the openings with their tents. Her cook stove was a fire in the middle of the room on the dirt floor.

The Barkers prospered. By the following year they built a fireplace and room-dividers in their frontier home. To the four children (Etna Ann, Sarah Elizabeth, Richard and Lewis), who camped with them on the Trinity their first night in Dallas, Eliza and Charles added four native Texans—Charles Thomas, John Samuel, Martha Carolina and James William.

The family continued to be deeply religious and helped to establish the first Methodist church west of the Trinity River on what is now U.S. Highway 67 and Camp Wisdom Road. They called it Wesley Chapel. Charles Barker served as secretary of his church from 1866 until 1874. Eliza Joyner Barker lived for more than half a century on the Barker land. She died October 22, 1905, at age 85, ten years after Charles' death. They are both buried at Little Bethel Cemetery in Lancaster.

Even while Eliza Barker was camping on the Trinity River, the paradoxical side of Dallas that has always been present, was being lived out in a beautiful new residence on the corner of Commerce at Lamar Street. There, in a city show place home, Cora McCoy was getting ready for Christmas. She and her husband, John C. McCoy, had been in their new home less than six months.

Considerably older than Cora, John enjoyed the attention that his distinctive personality afforded. He was a learned man from Indiana who had come to Dallas in 1844 as an agent for Peter's Colony and was greeted personally, as he would write to the folks back home, ". . . by Colonel (John Neely) Bryan who came out in buckskin leggings and moccasins and a red and black plaid blanket coat cut in high-water style. Through the solicitations of the colonel, aided by the sight of the inevitable gourd, the contents of which could readily be guessed, we were at home with him." As the town's first practicing attorney, his courtly manners, his pleasant demeanor and his affluence, John McCoy's perceived idiosyncrasies were forgiven by the townspeople, for he did not always agree with most of them. In fact, he was one of three, out of a total of 32 voters, who opposed Texas joining the Union in 1845, and he was, he said later, the only able-bodied man in town who did not go California during the 1849 gold rush.

A handsome bachelor, McCoy caught the eye of almost every young girl who came to town and was considered a prize catch by all of their mothers. He had been gracious, comforting and sometimes financially helpful during the year or so that their husbands had been off to California. They were both intrigued and a little envious when they learned that he had chosen as his bride a beauty from Pennsylvania. Cora M. McDermott arrived in Dallas in the summer of 1851 and the two were married in a log cabin that stood about a mile and a half east of the public square on the Kaufman highway. He had hoped to have their home completed before the wedding; he was building the most lavish and beautiful building to date, the first frame house in Dallas. Delays in the arrival of materials hampered the building and it was not until they had been married almost a year, in August of 1852, that they moved in.

John loved company and he enjoyed showing off his new home and his young wife. Soon, as a historian would recall:

> Theirs was a home of gayety and frequented by all who delighted to steal away from the cares of the busy life.[1]

John C. McCoy, Dallas's first lawyer, bought this lot at Oakland Cemetery for his 21-year-old bride, Cora M. McCoy, and their infant daughter, who died at birth on July 15, 1859. McCoy remained a bachelor until he was buried beside them in 1887.

Even though she loved her husband and was happy in their new home, Cora found it increasingly difficult to entertain in the manner expected of the wife of one of the town's leading citizens. She missed her family and the affluent lifestyle to which she was accustomed. She was sick and lonely. Even when spring came, she spent more and more time in bed. Every day she expected to be better, and, certainly, when the child came, she would return to her normal self.

It was not to be. On July 16, 1853, in the beautiful house that her husband had built for her, Cora McCoy died in childbirth. The baby they both had so badly wanted died with her. In the years ahead the grieving widower would bring most of his wife's relatives to Dallas from Pennsylvania to live in the house—her aging father, Col. J. B. McDermott, and some of her siblings. And, when Col. McDermott died, John McCoy continued to care for his maiden sister, two of his late wife's unmarried sisters and four little boys. He saw that the children were properly educated. In due time, he resumed his courtly ways and was much in demand as an escort for the town's socially elite, but he never remarried. He died in 1887 at the age of 67 having spent only two of those years as a married man. He rests in Oakland Cemetery in a grave next to his 21-year-old bride and their infant Cora who was buried in her mother's arms.

Far to the north of Dallas, yet another story of contrast was taking place in the vicinity of Audelia Road and Walnut Street. Diana Jane Davis Jackson and her husband, James Everts Jackson, were settling on a 320-acre farm on what is now the present site of Richland College. She had come from Harrison County, West Virginia, with her parents, Henson Cole and Sarah Parrish Davis, and her husband had come from Missouri at about the same time as a single man. He took a headright of 320 acres, the allowable for a single person, in the Peter's Colony at the southwest corner of what is now Audelia Road and Walnut Street. The Davis and Jackson families lived near each other. The two young people met and, on January 10, 1850, were married.

The Jacksons were successful farmers. They improved their property, adding both acreage and livestock. They were devout Methodists; he served on the Democratic committee for his area and was on the school board. She supported his efforts and raised children. There were seven little Jacksons: Andrew Clark, Ardelia Ellen, Henson Coleman, John Thomas, Benjamin James, Jefferson Davis and Caleb William.

When an early map maker misread the handwriting and thought an "r" was a "u," the name of a street was changed. That is how the street named for Ardelia Jackson West became Audelia Road.

James Jackson was a stern and exacting father. The six boys found ways to survive, and even thrive, under the austere conditions that existed on their farm, but Ardelia, as the only daughter, was as rebellious as she was protected. There was constant pressure to conform. Her father forbade her to have suitors. When her older brother died at fifteen, Ardelia also became the oldest child. Her father did encourage education, and Ardelia took advantage of every opportunity for learning and cultural enrichment. She read, wrote, and played musical instruments, joining with her musical family in church socials and entertainment. She was church organist and, later when there was a school, she played for all school programs.

Ardelia also noticed the boys, and on May 22, 1869, when she was one month past her 16th birthday, she eloped with John Chenault. The marriage might have worked if her father had supported, rather than opposed, the union, but such was not his nature. James disliked his daughter's young husband so intensely that he soon succeeded in running him off. Ardelia did not protest too much or she would have run away with him. Instead, she remained in her parents' house where her father redoubled his efforts to keep her away from the boys. Time passed—eight years. Ardelia helped her mother, played the organ, taught children in Sunday School—and kept an eye out for an escape.

It came in the person of John Frederick West. Not a great deal is known about West, who was 25 and single and who lived near the Jacksons. The family story is that Diana sent her daughter to the orchard to pick peaches for a cobbler, but Ardelia never came back. Instead, she stopped off to see John West. Undoubtedly the two had plotted an escape at the first opportunity and this was the chance they had been waiting for. They eloped. The cloudy thing about this story is the timing. John Frederick and Ardelia Ellen Jackson West were married on January 23, 1877, and trees do not produce fruit in January. Either the wedding date is erroneous or Ardelia was on another errand when she and her fiance eloped. Her father, discovering that his daughter was not home, set out in hot pursuit, but the couple outran him, made it to Dallas and got married.

In November of the first year of their marriage, Ardelia and John had their first child, a daughter, Mildred Elizabeth, who was known as Annie, to be followed by three more daughters, Diana Jane (Jennie) born in 1879, Mary Ellen born in 1883, and Lucy N. born in 1887 and who died in within the week of her birth. Ardelia continued to savor life. When Benjamin Prigmore, a neighbor, gave land for a school, located on the northwest quadrant of what is now Audelia and Walnut, it was named the Jackson School and Ardelia was one of the teachers.

Her father not only forgave the young man for eloping with his daughter, but went into business with him. They opened a general store on the southeast corner of Audelia and Forest Lane. Soon the neighbors referred to the road running in front of it as Ardelia Road and before long the entire area was known as Ardelia Community. When streets were laid out and named on early maps, all records were in handwriting and the "r" in Ardelia looked like a "u." That is how the present Audelia Road got its name.

Many other women in Dallas's second decade demonstrated spirit and independence—some from necessity and some by choice.

Celia Ann Lair Anderson and her husband, William, followed their third son to Texas. She was 44 when they arrived in 1852 and set up housekeeping on the summit of a rise overlooking Rowlett Creek, which today is on the west marina peninsula of Lake Ray Hubbard off Highway 67 adjacent to Faulkner Point. Celia Ann Lair, born in Lincoln County, Kentucky, was proud of her family name and took it with her through Missouri and into Texas and handed it on in the names she gave her seven children. Her four daughters got her middle name "Ann" and her three sons, her birth name, Lair. The girls were Elizabeth Ann, Frances Ann, Celia Ann and Lucy Ann Anderson and the boys William Lair, Thomas Lair and Andrew Lair Anderson. The three older children—Frances, Elizabeth and Andrew—remained in Missouri when their parents came to Dallas, but William and his wife, Eliza Morris Anderson; Elizabeth Ann and her husband, Silas Bryant; Thomas Lair and his wife, Naomi Elizabeth Jones Anderson; and Lucy Ann and her husband, Wormley Carter, all became early Dallas County settlers.

The earth was rich and the crops bountiful where the Andersons settled. They grew vegetables, corn, wheat and cotton. They planted orchards with seeds they brought from Missouri. Meat was abundant—sheep, hogs, cattle, deer, birds and fish. There was no sugar, but wild honey was an excellent substitute. Salt was abundant, provided by the "salt lick," located on their farm, and now covered by the waters of Lake Ray Hubbard.

Celia Ann Lair Anderson inherited the family property when her husband died in 1858; his is the second will probated in Dallas County. Seventeen months later she died. Both are buried in the Anderson family cemetery near Lake Ray Hubbard in Rowlett.

As the decade dawned, so began what would become University Park. Pioneered by women, children, and black slaves from Alabama, it is now one of the most affluent of the Dallas satellite cities with a population of more than 20,000. But it began with one woman, Frances Sims Daniel, and her family in 1849. Frances was 50 years old and a widow, having lost her husband, the Rev. John M. Daniel, the year before. They arrived by covered wagon—Frances with six of her eight children and her widowed sister, Nancy Sims Harlan. The children were William, who later married Mary Chandler; Jesse, who wed Ann Purvis; Francis R., who married Mary Robinson; John F., who married Mary Harvey; Eliza, who wed Levi Windham; Thomas B.; Isabella O., who married Alexander Harwood, and Margaret S., who married the Rev. Joseph L. Smith.

Frances Sims Daniel and her family camped on the spot where SMU's Dallas Hall stands when they arrived to become the first settlers of University Park.

Choosing the best spot they could find, they camped first on a rise some five miles north of Dallas on the spot where Dallas Hall of Southern Methodist University now stands, but they soon discovered that there was no water available. They then moved their campsite a short distance to the north and centered their home in 640 acres which Frances bought for 50 cents an acre. The house was located just north of the present Daniel Cemetery. Her property was roughly bounded by what today is Lovers Lane on the north, Turtle Creek on the west, Haynie on the south and Central Expressway on the east.

A century and a half later, all that was left of property in the Daniel name was the Daniel Cemetery, one and a tenth acres at the eastern end of Milton Street on Airline Road. Some of the bois d'arc trees that Frances planted around her home still spread their shade over the graves. A fence, erected by Margaret, the youngest daughter, shields the place from would-be predators:

DANIEL FAMILY CEMETERY

Frances Sims Daniel (1796-1853) moved to Dallas County with her family in 1849 and purchased land in what is now University Park. An orchard planted near the Daniel home became the site of a family cemetery in 1850 when "Old Frank," a family slave for over forty years, was buried there. The gravestone of Isabella Harwood (1836-1851), daughter of Frances Sims Daniel, is believed to be one of the oldest in Dallas County. Interred here are Daniel family members, family slaves, and Daniel descendants, including veterans of four wars.[2]

A slave, "Old Frank," was the first person buried in the cemetery. Isabella Harwood was the first family member buried there. She had married Alexander Harwood at age 13; he was 17 years her senior. She died in childbirth a year after she was married. Her daughter, Fannie Belle Harwood, survived but died as a child when she was nine. The little girl is buried beside her mother in the Daniel plot. Nancy Harlan died in 1851 and Frances on October 29, 1853. She was 57 years old and had been in Dallas only four years.

Some 90 Daniel descendants and spouses rest in the family plot. As long as she lived, Margaret Daniel Smith kept the family history current. Now, generations removed from this first daughter of University Park, many of the connections are lost.

In southeastern Dallas County, Virginia Bledsoe was taking her first job as a teacher in the first school opened in her community near the present town of Lancaster. She was not more than 21. Many of her students were bigger and almost as old as she, among them Roderick Alexander Rawlins. The eighth and youngest child of Roderick and Mildred Parks Rawlins, Roderick Alexander was 11 when he arrived at an area staked out by his family southeast of the present town of Lancaster as their home.

His sister, Nancy Rawlins Taylor, later reminisced about the family's journey from Illinois in 1844. She, 14 at the time of the migration, recalled that a wagon train of some 30 people had left Illinois for Texas in September. It took them two months to get as far as Lamar County, Texas, where they sent two of their party, her brothers-in-law, Pleasant Taylor and Samuel Keller, ahead to select their new home. The young men chose a site which was totally uninhabited and returned to Lamar County for the rest of the party. They arrived back at their new Texas home in December and camped for the winter. She recalled:

> We camped the first night at Cedar Springs. The next morning we started for our home, as we called it, on Ten Mile Creek. There were no roads in those times and we had to head the creeks, which made the distance so much farther that we could not reach home that night; in the meantime it clouded up and commenced raining, we could find no water therefore we stopped somewhere, I never did know exactly where, we had been lost, we had neither dinner, supper, nor breakfast. As soon as it was light we made another start for our destination and reached it on the second day of January 1845 at two o'clock in the afternoon. The boys that had gone on ahead of us had made a shelter for us, out of some old boards that were found by some of the party and pressed into service.[3]

By the time Virginia Bledsoe began teaching school, Roderick Alexander was a serious boy whose behavior and manners belied his age. Born January 20, 1833, he was five and a half years younger than she. There is no record of whether she taught other Rawlins children. In any event, a romance began between the young teacher and her student and on September 30, 1852, when he was 20 and she was 26 they were married. Three children—A. Bledsoe, Addie Blanche and Betty Alexander—were born to them. Virginia was killed in a freak accident in 1890 when she was thrown from a buggy. Her husband outlived her 10 years. Both are buried in the Pioneer Section of Edgewood Cemetery in Lancaster.

Mary Ann Hill Goodnight and Esther Jane Patton Bell both started out for Texas in the very early fall of 1854; Mary Ann and her husband, James Paris Goodnight, from Kentucky, and Esther Bell and her husband, Jackson Bell, from Virginia. They traveled by wagon under the usual conditions—overgrown and difficult trails, bad weather conditions, and illness.

Esther and Jackson Bell left Virginia on September 11, 1854, and arrived in Dallas in record time, 39 days later. Along the way they buried their oldest daughter at Preston on the Red River.

It took Mary Ann and James longer to make the trip. They left Allen County, Kentucky, on October 5, 1854, two weeks after they were married, and arrived in Dallas in 45 days, on November 19. They settled on acreage in the Lisbon area of Dallas County and by 1878 had completed a large home at what is now the intersection of Beckley and Overton Roads. In their chosen county on the raw frontier of Texas, Mary Ann had 13 children: Pauline Jane, Isaac Henry, Amanda Ellen, Thomas Mitchell, John B., Fanny L., Frank Hill, Allie May, James Paris Jr., William Blackburn and three other little girls who died in infancy. Mary Ann and James Goodnight, who served as an elder, started the Cumberland Presbyterian Church. James was also tax assessor-collector for five years and was secretary-treasurer of the building committee for the first church-school erected in Lisbon.

That there is no mention of Mary Ann Bell Goodnight's activities other than what surely was her preoccupation with being pregnant, birthing babies and rearing children is typical of the times, for, beginning around 1854 and lasting until the Civil War broke out, much of the press and a lot of the gossip centered on the behavior of women. Men were outraged when women expressed opinions in public and the man who "let" his

School teacher Virginia Bledsoe married her student, Roderick Alexander Rawlins, when she was 26 and he was 20. Their three children carried on a family lineage in south Dallas County that began in 1844 and continues to the present....

wife behave in such a manner was scorned. The editor of the state's leading newspaper at the time wrote this editorial:

> . . . when woman leaves her sphere, disorder in the social circle is the inevitable result. She has not the power to rule the outside world, but by the genial influence of her smiles, and the deep pathos of her calm and gentle love, she may control . . . the human heart.
>
> There are two orbs of pre-eminent importance to us in the solar system . . . . The one is brilliant, glorious, powerful. On him is our dependence—he lights the way, and governs all our movements. The other is calm, placid, and benign wooing us from the cares of the day, to the genial lanes of the home. Such should be the organization of every household. Man should be looked to as the source of light and support; while woman as the embodiment of love and happiness. The one is fitted to rule by the strong arm—the other by the persuasive eloquence of the affections only.
>
> . . . woman come down from the desk and leave forever to the colder hearts and harder hands than you have by rights, and study out the ends that are waiting for you to accomplish.[4]

A week later *The Standard* must have been pleased to report a new law that had just been enacted in by the Illinois legislature:

> Resolved that a fine of $500 be hereafter imposed on any young lady who shall lecture in any part of the State without first putting on gentleman's apparel.

In the spring of 1855 Dallas had a sudden population explosion with the arrival of 200 new residents at the same time. On April 26, 1855, men, women and children, worn and bedraggled from their long 26-day trek from Houston, arrived in town. They were a motley crowd and, to the townspeople who were already agitating for an independent city, looked strange, indeed. A few were riding horses, but most were walking beside overloaded ox-drawn carts. They wore wooden shoes or no shoes at all; their clothes were strange. They spoke a language that most people could not understand.

They were the founders of La Reunion. They were Europeans—mostly French, but with some Germans and Swiss. They came to establish a utopian community. A year earlier Victor Considerant, an idealistic Frenchman who led the socialist movement following the death of its founder Charles Fournier, had come to the Dallas area with Arthur Brisbane, an American idealist, seeking a place to establish a utopian community. Several Texas sites appealed to them, but he chose what must have been the least desirable land for the group, comprised mostly of artisans and craftspeople. He selected the limestone hills overlooking the valley of the West Fork of the Trinity three miles west of the village of Dallas. Today the site is bounded by the West Fork of the Trinity River on the north and by Westmoreland and Davis Streets.

Considerant returned to France where he founded La Compagne Franco-Texienne to finance the purchase of 2,000 acres of land and where he wrote a book, *Au Texas*, lauding the qualities of his chosen land. In his words, "the promised land is a reality." He had seen a place where the weather was mild the year around, where the soil was much like that of the grape-growing areas of France, where everything that grew was edible and tomatoes grew as large as watermelons.

Considerant had replaced John Neely Bryan as a promoter. His "perfect place" to establish a utopian socialist community would be laid out according to exact principles set down by the late Fournier. Everybody would live commune-style in a phalanstory, a U-shaped complex of housing units around a 150-foot square. Work would be shared, with each person contributing what she or he did best, and with the domestic work allotted so that all worked equally and shared equally in the rewards.

In 1855 Dallas had a population explosion with the arrival of 200 residents, a rag-tag contingent of "foreigners" who would immeasurably enhance the artistic and cultural climate of the city.

By the time the La Reunion group reached Dallas, they were already disillusioned. They had planned to sail to Galveston and there take boats that would bring them up the Trinity River to Dallas. The first part of their plan went fine, but when they disembarked in Galveston and discovered that the Trinity was not navigable, they rented horses and carts for the rest of the journey. Tradespeople along the coast took advantage of their inexperience and they paid far too much for the conveyances that brought them to Dallas. It was a footsore, weary and disenchanted bunch that began to claim its utopian dream. It was also a determined bunch.

Throughout 1855 and into the next year, the Europeans continued to arrive in Dallas to become a part of the dream. They cleared land, built a storehouse and a dining hall where they all shared their meals and built the town's first brewery. The first disappointment was that the chalk-like land, no matter that it looked like the grape-growing regions of France, was totally unsuited for agriculture. Even worse, they were not prepared to provide goods and services that were needed in a tiny frontier town. They were aristocrats, artists, musicians, botanists, milliners, couturiers, tailors, winemakers, shoemakers, weavers, jewelers, stonemasons, lithographers, chefs and poets. Only two of them were farmers. Their tools for tilling the land were crude to non-existent, and some found the swords used by their fathers in the Battle of Waterloo and brought to America as souvenirs to be useful in harvesting the meager first grain.

Material available for buildings did not lend itself to the prescribed edicts of the deceased French idealist. They had to settle for tiny limestone rock houses. And then there was the weather. Texas weather, never predictable, was especially ornery that year. There came a very late harsh blue norther, followed by a few weeks of suffocating heat and then a prolonged drought.

Even as new settlers trickled in, by the end of the first summer the utopian dream of everybody living and working together in harmony had given way to confusion and frustration. As a business, the settlement was poorly run. As an experiment in utopian living, it was even more of a disaster. Where there is no money to buy the basic necessities of life, dreams soon founder. Considerant was the first to pull out. He left for San Antonio declaring La Reunion a failure. Some families moved into Dallas. Others went home to Europe. Several Swiss families moved to Moon Lake a short distance north on the Trinity River and established farms. Others gave up on the utopian dream and began farming on their own. All that is left of the physical site of the original LaReunion Settlement is Fishtrap Cemetery where some of the original settlers are buried.

What La Reunion gave to Dallas is much more important than a failed utopian community. It brought in new ideas, a new texture, and a new flavor to the frontier town. Its residents brought music and poetry spiced with European character. It was the first international settlement in the territory and its individuals added to Dallas a dimension that made it different and lifted it above the norm for towns of its time. Further, the gifts of those who ventured to Dallas with La Reunion and stayed continue to enrich Dallas.

7

THE DALLAS PEAKS

All of near East Dallas was first settled by the Peak family of Kentucky beginning in 1855 when Jefferson and Martha Malvina Reser Peak bought a large farm in the country east of downtown. Their farm was located between the boundaries of what is now Haskell to the west and Carroll to the east and by Capitol to the north to Elm on the south. Peak Street runs northwest-southeast right through the middle of it.

Most historians credit William Henry Gaston for opening up East Dallas. Important as he was in all of the ways men measure success—founder of two banks, real estate investor, merchant, utility executive, transportation enthusiast, state fair promoter and more—he did not arrive in Dallas until 1868.

The Peaks were there 13 years ahead of Gaston and were already firmly settled in East Dallas. Both the men and the women in the Peak family contributed to the work and the rewards of the frontier territory. Though little is recorded about Martha Peak, family stories reveal her to be a woman of intelligence, charm and courage. Martha was known by her family as Malviney, "whose elegant manners presented ever a queenly appearance."[1] The grandchildren remembered her as a tiny woman always clad in silks and wearing a lace cap.

But she was not always the gentle woman the grandchildren remembered. Though slight in stature, she was a woman of great strength who gave birth to 12 children and reared 10 of them. She left family, friends, an affluent lifestyle and a two-story brick home on Main Street in Warsaw, Kentucky, on April 3, 1855, to travel halfway across a continent and establish new roots.

She was the pivot from which the many members of her family went their separate ways to contribute to their new world, and she was the lodestone that lured them back again to the large laughter-filled house at what is now Peak and Worth streets. There she set a lavish table for returning prodigals, whether they were family or friends. Grandson Howard Peak remembered climaxing a long wagon trip from Fort Worth by arriving "through a big gate into the great yard of Grandpas's to the great delight of not only ourselves, but those with whom we were to spend a fortnight" and sitting down to a supper that included "a great steak from Nussbaumers, the Butchers, fried chicken with milk gravy, fresh eggs, vegetables of all kinds, cornbread, hot biscuits, butter and sorghum molasses, milk, tea, peach cobbler, etc., etc. etc."[2]

Martha was 14 years old when she married Jefferson Peak. Among family papers is this yellowed clipping:

> The clerk of Gallatin County (Kentucky) is hereby authorized and requested to issue a license authorizing the performance of the marriage ceremony between my daughter Martha M. Reser and Jefferson Peak given under my hand and seal this 13 day of August, 1826. Wm. Reser[3]

It was three years later when Carroll Marion, the couple's first child was born on November 13, 1829. Martha bore children two and three years apart until she was 45 when her last, Matthias L. Irving, was born on February 11, 1857. Between Carroll, the oldest, and Matt, the youngest, there were William Wallace, January 29, 1831; Sarah Ann, February 10, 1833; Jefferson Jr., May 16, 1836; Juliet Abbey, May 8, 1838; Martha Hellen, February 29, 1840; Junius, September 5, 1842; Junius II, April 5, 1845; Worth, April 24, 1848; Florence Chalfant, July 25, 1850, and George Victor, August 19, 1852. Matt was the only native Dallasite, born two years after the family arrived.[4]

The Peak women contributed many firsts for Dallas. Martha Malvina Reser Peak was the first lady of East Dallas.

Sarah Ann Peak Harwood, oldest daughter of Martha and Jefferson Peak, kept vigil over her family and was half of the Alexander Harwood family for whom Harwood Street is named.

Jefferson, who had been stationed in Texas during the Mexican War (1846-1848), had written long letters to his family filled with glowing stories about what was happening in the newly settled territory. Carroll, then a teenager, was especially enamored by his father's letters and longed to see the area. But, by the time Jefferson returned from service, Carroll was ready for college and left home to study medicine.

In the fall of 1852, Jefferson, Carroll, and Wallace, the second son, set out to explore the possibility of moving the family to Texas. They were away for several months.

Sarah Ann, 19, was left at home to help her mother care for six younger children. A brilliant and talented young woman, Sarah Ann had graduated the year before, in June of 1851, in the fifth graduating class at Georgetown (Ky.) Female Seminary. A handwritten note by the seminary's headmaster dated May 28, 1851, preserved among the Peak papers, reads: "Miss Sarah Peak: Being fully entitled to the honors of your class, you are hereby appointed to give the valedictory address on the occasion of the graduation of the Senior Class." The commencement program, dated June 25, 1851, lists Sarah not only as delivering the valedictory speech but also entertaining with a piano solo.

Assuming the prerogative of an oldest daughter as the family historian, teacher, counselor, correspondent and mediator—roles she would play for the rest of her life—Sarah Ann kept her father and brothers apprised of what was happening in the family while they were away. This is a portion of a long letter:

> . . . hog killing time is most over . . . . We . . . are getting our full choice of the meats. We won't get so much lard . . . as we did last winter. We have already got about a hundred pounds of sausage meat. Ma is salting a barrel of nice bones. Mart (Martha Hellen) and I beat thirty or forty pounds of sausage meat and have put it away for you.
>
> We are getting along very happily. All this family keeps well . . . . Mart and Juliet . . . have not much time. They do almost all the washing now. They study every night and whenever they can during the day. June does very well when he does at all, but it is hard to get him to study at all. You would laugh to see Worth [4-1/2] saying his lessons . . . . The first morning I told him he must say his lesson, he hollered "I won't." Ma took down a great long whip and told him he should. He ran as fast as he could until he reached the gate and stood there I suppose for an hour ready to go through should any of us make an appearance. At last he got so cold that he came in. Ma again told him he must learn his lessons. Then, amid sobs and coughs he commenced "A.B.C. . . ." Since then the last thing at night and the first thing in the morning [he says] Sarah I want to learn my lesson.
>
> We are all in Ma's room seated around a good fire. Worth sits beside me on a high chair. I told him I was writing you and what must I tell you he said. He says must I tell Pa I can black my boots by myself? . . . . Flora [2-1/2] and Victor [4 months] are well and fat.[5]

Juliette Peak Fowler established Fowler homes and became the city's first philanthropist.

Jefferson, Carroll and Wallace spent several weeks in Dallas and went home to Kentucky convinced that the infant city held the best promise for the family's future. Unlike many others who were lured by inflated promises, they carefully planned their move.

Carroll went back to the University of Louisville medical school, completed his training. On April 26, 1853, at the age of 24, he married Florence Chalfant in Madison, Indiana. The Peak and Chalfant families had doubtless long been friends because in 1850, three years before Carroll and Florence married, Martha and Jefferson had named their 10th child Florence Chalfant Peak.

In December of 1853, Martha Hellen (Mart) Peak died at the age of 13. She was the second child Martha and Jefferson would leave buried in Kentucky. Their baby son, Junius I, had died when he was 21 months old.

Though the Peaks had planned and dreamed for most of a decade about moving to Texas, there is strong evidence that their final decision was spurred by Sarah Ann's health. She had developed a persistent cough, and doctors—including her brother Carroll, the new doctor in the family—encouraged a warmer, drier climate lest she develop tuberculosis. The decision finally made, the Peaks moved to Dallas in style.

Dr. Carroll and his bride and Wallace went ahead to find living accommodations, and Jefferson, Jr., almost 19, stayed in Kentucky and joined his family later.

Before they left, Jefferson and his older sons built and outfitted two big sturdy wagons to transport the family and all their possessions. The wagons were not only covered, but also carpeted! Into them went all the household goods plus books and lessons for the children along the way. Special care was given to Sarah's spinet piano which was lashed to the carpeted side of one of the wagons.

The family left Warsaw on the morning of April 3, 1855. After traveling through Tennessee, Arkansas, Louisiana and East Texas, they arrived in Dallas on May 11, 1855. They moved into a large two-story log house on the banks of the Trinity River. A few weeks later they bought 160 acres between Main and Haskell streets and started building their large rambling two story home at what is now Peak and Worth streets. It was the first brick house ever constructed in Dallas.

Jefferson Peak proved far more adept at buying and selling property than in farming it. He named a street in his development for each member of his family. The most prominent on the western boundary of the property was Martha Avenue. Many years later, after his death in 1885, Martha petitioned the city to change the street's name to Peak. It was done and so has remained.

Seven Dallas streets bear Peak family names—Peak, Carroll, Jefferson, Junius, Victor, Worth and Flora, the latter a family name for Florence Peak Field. Harwood and Field streets are named for Peak sons-in-law, the husbands of Sarah Ann and Florence. Already there was a Jefferson Street in downtown Dallas, one of the original 18 streets laid out and named by John Neely Bryan.

Streets named for other Peak family members have been changed. Juliet became Munger Avenue at the request of Dr. S. I. Munger, who wished the street back of his Ross Avenue home to bear his name. Already there was a Munger Boulevard. These two streets, in close proximity to each other, have continued to confuse and frustrate people searching a Munger address. Sarah Ann Street became Haskell when Captain H. N. Haskell refused right of way through his property unless the connecting street bore his name. Wallace Street was changed to Gaston Avenue for Captain W. H. Gaston when, in 1870, he bought 40 acres extending from Worth to Bryan Street and built a mansion on Swiss Avenue. Matt Street was changed to Sycamore when developers of a new addition named one of their streets Watt and decided that Matt and Watt were so similar as to be confusing. It is ironic that this should seem confusing when two Munger streets did not.

Dallas proved an exciting place for the large and exuberant Peak family. Young people flocked to their home, then two miles out in the country east of Dallas. Carroll and his bride, Florence; Wallace, an eligible young bachelor; Sarah Ann, whose musical talents earned her the title of the city's Jenny Lind; Juliet, noted for her beauty and high spirits; as well as the younger children made the Peak home a magnet for the young crowd. Too, Jefferson and Martha were genial hosts who made their guests feel welcome.

There were also times of great sadness. Sarah Ann was engaged when the family left Kentucky; her fiance planned to join the Peaks in Dallas where he and Sarah Ann would be married and make their home. He began his journey to Dallas, but he never arrived. The steamer bringing him down the Mississippi River exploded in the Gulf off the Coast of Louisiana killing all aboard. Though Sarah Ann mourned, a Dallas widower had already determined to marry her. Five months after her arrival in Dallas, on October 14, 1855, Sarah Ann married Alexander Maury Harwood, whose first wife, Isabella Daniel Harwood,[6] had died in childbirth. The child, Fannie Belle Harwood, was four years old when her father and Sarah Ann were married.

Dorothy Laura Collins Cason, a granddaughter of Sarah and Alexander Harwood, recalled her grandparents:

> Fate had already taken a hand. When Jefferson and his sons, Carroll and Wallace had come to Dallas in 1852 to look the situation over, one of the people they met was Alexander Harwood. He had moved to Texas, to Peter's Colony,

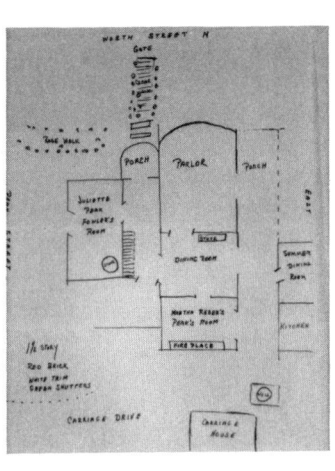

A sketch of the first floor house plans for the large, rambling two-story house, the first brick house in Dallas, built by the Peak family on Peak and Worth streets, is among remaining Peak papers.

settling first at Harwood Springs, today named Kleberg. During a conversation, Carroll Peak showed him a picture of his sister, Sarah Ann, to Alexander, who exclaimed that he was going to marry her. Within a few months after the Peak's arrival in Dallas in 1855, Alexander Harwood did that very thing.[7]

Alexander Harwood had "received as much education as the common schools of his time afforded," according to a newspaper clipping on prominent early Dallasites. He had arrived in Dallas in 1845 from Franklin, Tennessee, with his parents, Alexander Maury and Nancy G. Barksdale Harwood, and a brother, Nathaniel B. Harwood and his wife. He had spent most of his first Texas year (1845-46) exploring the branches of the Trinity River and remained as a staunch advocate of making the river navigable until his death in 1885. When he and Sarah Ann married, Alexander was county clerk of Dallas County, first elected to that post in 1850 and reelected in 1852 and 1854. Later, in 1873, he was elected for two years as clerk of both the county and district courts of Dallas County and served in that public office for a total of 12 years. A political conservative, he was one of three men who voted against annexing Texas to the United States.

Sarah Ann was 13 years younger than her husband. The difference in their ages, their dispositions and their politics must have created friction between Sarah and Alexander Harwood. Though her letters and family remembrances reveal her to be a dutiful wife, devoted daughter, caring sister and loving mother, she does not appear to be an entirely happy woman. As a young girl, she loved to travel, a luxury she curtailed after her marriage. There is evidence, too, that she gave up most of her music; she would later emerge, after her husband's death, as a powerful businesswoman administering the estate of her sister.

Dorothy Cason remembered her grandmother as a woman of leisure. "Grandma never had to do any housework of any kind," she noted in handwritten reminiscences that are among family papers. "She did not have to do any kind of work such as dusting, sweeping or cooking."

Even so, the younger Sarah surely did her share of the housework, cooking and caring for her children. She reared two, a son, Ripley Barksdale Harwood, and a daughter, Juliette Harwood (Collins), and lost two. Babies Pauline and Caroline, born after the Civil War in 1866 and 1869 respectively, died a month apart in August and September of 1869, Caroline at age 3 and Pauline at 6 months.

The Peak family had been in Dallas only a few weeks when Dr. Carroll was called to Fort Worth to minister to Capt. Julian B. Feild, one of Fort Worth's first merchants. Settled as a fort, Fort Worth had lost its only doctor when the army moved out. Its leading citizens, pointing out that Dallas already had two doctors, petitioned the young physician to establish his practice in Fort Worth. After consultation with his father, Carroll decided to take them up on their offer. He and Florence moved into a former barracks from which Dr. Peak served the community within a 30-mile radius as physician, surgeon and dentist. It is a strange quirk of fate that Dr. Carroll Peak, who had chosen Dallas as the place for the family's future, would instead be remembered by history as a "first" citizen of Fort Worth. Dr. Peak was the mentor and benefactor of John Peter Smith, who later served Fort Worth as mayor. With his move to Fort Worth, Dr. Peak established the first major link between Dallas and Fort Worth.

If "serious" was the word for Sarah, "merry" must have been the word for Juliet Peak. According to family legend and letters, Juliet walked to the beat of a different drummer. She was the family's will-o-the-wisp, who was slight of figure, pretty and possessed a bubbling personality. Her niece, Olive Peak, the daughter of Junius, remembers:

> Aunt Juliette was . . . different from Aunt Sarah and Aunt Florrie. She had fine poise, a keen sense of humor and a most pleasing address, gracious manner, strong Christian character, a tenderness of heart, a helpfulness to all and a gay spirit, despite 25 years of mourning in her widows weeds.[8]

Dallas proved an exciting place for the large and exuberant Peak family . . . . but there were also times of great sadness. Sarah Ann's fiance died in a steamer explosion on his way to marry her. She then married Alexander Harwood, a widower, 13 years her senior.

Juliette Abby Peak, crowned Dallas's first May Queen, when she was 19, succumbed to the courtship of popular Fort Worth attorney, Archie Y. Fowler, and married him in April before her 22nd May birthday. He was 26.

Juliette's fierce independence is evidenced, among many other ways, in the spelling of her name. Christened Juliet Abbey, she decided in her teenage years to change the spelling to Juliette Abby. Her parents and other relatives, including Sarah, continued to address her as Juliet. That is the spelling found in the letters Sarah wrote, in her obituary and on her tombstone, but Juliette herself always added a "te" to her name as in her will in her own handwriting dated February 26, 1889, which begins: "Know all men by these presents that I, Juliette A. Fowler . . . ."

As time passed, even Sarah acquiesced to her sister's wishes, changing the spelling of the name her own daughter, who was named for her sister, from Juliet to Juliette. More than a century later, in 1966, in correspondence with Sam Acheson, columnist for *The Dallas Morning News* who was researching a story on the Peak family, another Florence Chalfant Peak, the daughter of Junius, said it was time to forget the controversy over the name spelling and comply with Juliette's wishes. It is just as well. Four generations of Peak ancestors bear the name of their illustrious Aunt J-U-L-I-E-T-T-E.

Within two years after she arrived in Dallas, Juliette was crowned the town's first Queen of the May. The ceremonies on May 1, 1858, were held during an all-day picnic in a densely wooded area on Patterson and Sycamore next door to the home of Sarah and James Patterson.[9]

Juliette's popularity drew many suitors, but it was a young Fort Worth lawyer who claimed her heart and hand. Juliette met Archibald Young Fowler through her brother and sister-in-law, Carroll and Flora. At 26, he was the senior partner in the law firm of Fowler and (J.P.) Smith. Fowler must have appeared very debonair and sophisticated to the pretty 19-year-old May Queen.

One month shy of her 22nd birthday, in April of 1859, Juliette Peak and A. Y. Fowler exchanged wedding vows in a ceremony at the Peak home that was the highlight of the Dallas social season.

Sarah, a solemn wife of four years, the mother of a baby son and three months pregnant with what would be another Juliette, wrote to her younger sister:

> You are ill prepared for the world of care and responsibility you seem so desirous of entering."[10]

Wedding festivities over, Juliette and her new husband moved to Fort Worth. Caught up in domestic and social responsibilities, establishing her new household and enjoying the status of being the wife of the town's most promising young lawyer, Juliette was lax in communicating with her family in the manner Sarah Ann thought appropriate, and her older sister chided her:

> You have doubtless expected a letter from me long in the past, but Mary, [Sarah Ann's housekeeper] has been sick for two weeks and I could get no one to assist me . . . . I have looked with eager desire each mail to hear from you. Although I know you would apprise us of any important event, I am not satisfied that you do not make a sort of journal of small things and send us once a week.
>
> Are you keeping house yet? My dear Sister, you little know the world of care and responsibility you seem so desirous of entering. I wish it were possible for us to exchange feelings in reference to it.
>
> I am putting up pickles for you and some for Florence if she will come and get them. We have squashes, beans, sweet potatoes, potatoes, pumpkins, tomatoes, butter beans, etc. now in our garden. How I wish you and Brother Archer, Carroll and Flora could dine with us today . . . . You must try to have a good garden. It will repay all your labor and it will be good exercise for "The Master."
>
> We are counting the days 'till the hours return' that will bring us home with thee . . . only eighteen more and Juliet will be here.
>
> I suppose the Fair will take place . . . . My quilt is not finished, which you know would been have an object of much interest. (Sarah Ann's Flower Garden)[11]

The fair was the social event in which everybody participated and which drew people from Texas' hinterlands. Interesting is Sarah Ann's reference to the quilt she would have exhibited had it been finished because there is disagreement about whether, or not, she actually made the quilt. Dorothy Cason said of her grandmother: "The framed quilt square is a piece of one of her quilts, but she did not make it. This . . . was labor she did not have to do". . . . Other family members are equally certain the quilt is Sarah Ann's handwork. A framed square of the quilt hangs in the home of Edith Rydell Roberts, Sarah Ann's great-granddaughter.

Sarah refers to her husband as "Mr. Harwood;" well into the 20th century, women when speaking to others, always called their husbands "Mr." The letter makes no reference to either her own or Juliette's pregnancies. At the time it was written, Sarah Ann was only six weeks away from the birth of her daughter and Juliette was five months pregnant. Women did not go out in public after their pregnancies became apparent.

Juliette's daughter, Ada Fowler, was born in February of 1860. Doubtless "Malviney" Peak went to Fort Worth to care for her daughter and baby granddaughter as she did for most of the children, though at the time, Matt, her own baby, was only three years old. Ada lived only nine months, dying November 21 of the same year she was born. In her obituary are these words:

> . . . there is that conveyed in the folding of those little ones that passeth our understanding . . . . Thus perisheth in life's early morn the tender bud — its petals scarce unfolded . . . Gone the rosy tints that greet the sunshine, gone the sweet smile from the cherub face. the prattle from the infant tongue, the liquid light from the bright eyes, all are gone. But stricken parents, ah . . . not forever . . . though it shall not return, yet you may go to it.[12]

A block of Sarah Ann's Flower Garden quilt she wanted to show in the State Fair of Texas hangs in the home of her great-granddaughter, Edith Rydell Roberts.

Ada's death was the first of several tragedies in Juliette Fowler's life, devastating in their ferocity but honing the once, almost frivolous young girl into a woman of strength, whose largess continues to impact the lives of hundreds of people.

The second tragedy happened in July of 1861. Juliette had lost her baby daughter only nine months before and was pregnant with her second child when she and her husband journeyed from Fort Worth to Dallas for an Independence Day picnic and celebration. Festive occasions usually lasted all day and into the night. Then, everybody who had traveled more than a few miles went home with family and friends to spend the night. Children were bedded down on pallets made by spreading out quilts in any convenient corner. Juliette and Archer doubtless were treated royally. Her health was fragile.

The picnic was held at Cold Springs. The springs formed a brook that ran through the park and here the picnickers got their drinking water. Fowler, well-known and highly respected in Dallas—the *Herald* carried his professional card weekly—was appointed to guard the springs and see that no animals were allowed to drink from the area set apart to provide water for the people. The heat was excessive and tempers were almost as hot as the weather. The Civil War was raging. Six months before, on February 4, 1861, 42 delegates from South Carolina, Georgia, Alabama, Mississippi, Louisiana and Florida had met in Montgomery, Alabama, and set up a provisional government of the Confederate States of America. Jefferson Davis had been elected provisional president. By the time of Dallas's Independence Day celebration, 11 states had seceded—South Carolina, Mississippi, Florida, Alabama, Georgia, Louisiana, Texas, Virginia, Arkansas, Tennessee and North Carolina. The Texas legislature had voted on February 1, 166 to 7, in favor of secession, which was ratified by the people on February 23, (34,794 voting for and 11,325 against). Dallas men had voted 741 to 237 to secede.

It seems odd that the Dallas revelers should have been celebrating Independence Day at all, for by July 4, 1861, they—and their 10 like-minded states—were no longer a part of the Union which Texas had joined in 1846. Settled by Southerners, Dallas was very much pro-Confederacy, but the 237 who had voted against seceding included some of the town's leading citizens. Sentiments were intense, loyalties deeply divided—none more so than the Peak family. From Kentucky, a state that did not secede, they were bound by many loyalties of family and friends back home. Their two sons-in-law were passionate secessionists. Alexander Harwood, from Tennessee, had already been called to Richmond as a leader in the South's government. Archie Fowler was from South Carolina, the first state to secede from the Union.

Voices rose and liquor flowed freely. It was sometime after lunch. The little children were napping, the older children playing games and the ladies fanning themselves while they chatted under the trees. Another picnicker, John C. York, the Fort Worth sheriff, who had imbibed freely of the liquid refreshments, tried to water his horse at the area set aside for people. Archer tried to prevent him. The men, who had known each other for years, got into a fierce argument. Archer, the younger of the two, tried reasoning, but York was adamant. The picnic ended but the disagreement smoldered and the next day the two met on the street. (One family record says "York stalked Archer.") York pulled a knife on Fowler and stabbed him.

"Archer Fowler was not killed by an assassin's bullet but by a Mr. York, a well-thought-of man and sheriff of Tarrant County," wrote Olive Peak, daughter of Carroll, to her first cousin, Florence. (Her letter was among Florence's papers after she died in 1983. Florence Peak, at 89, was the last surviving granddaughter of Jefferson and Martha Peak. Until a few years before her death, she lived at 4409 Worth Street.)

Olive Peak's letter continues:

> They were both hot-headed; the atmosphere was charged with excitement. 'Men!', Ma used to say. It was during the Civil War not long before Lily's (Olive's sister) birth. They quarreled with the terrible result Mr. York stabbed Uncle A. Y and Willie Fowler, (A. Y's nephew) shot and killed Mr. York. Willie was gotten off by the men to the war and was killed in battle — poor young boy. He, as his uncle, was from South Carolina and felt, as they did then, that he must avenge his uncle's death.[13]

And so it is that A. Y. Fowler did not die at the Fourth of July picnic as many Dallas historians have written. He lived until August 26, 1861. He probably died from infections from the stab wounds. He was 28 years old.

A widow at 23, Juliette never remarried. Olive Peak, in recalling family history, wrote, "She could have married again a number of times, I'm sure. The boys—her brothers—used to tease her about several men, but she was true to her lover-husband."

When the Confederate government was moved to Richmond, Virginia, on July 20, 1961, men capable of running the government were recruited from all of the Southern states and Alexander Harwood was picked by President Jefferson Davis and the Congress to serve as assistant postmaster general.

Sarah wrote to Juliette from Richmond where the Harwoods were stationed:

> Mr. Harwood brought me your letter this morning announcing the arrival of tiny Luly. (Lula Berry Peak, daughter of Wallace and Mary Frances). I was so glad to hear it was over . . . . I like the little one's name. Luly Peak is very sweet to me.
> Well, Juliet we are keeping house. We have a nice and comfortable house . . . .
> . . . the war looks very threatening, but you must not be frightened. The people here seem to have unlimited confidence in the ability of the South to sustain itself . . . . Oh, would it were over, this terrible war—and would we were together . . . . I am so hungry to see you "and Ma and Pa all the dear little ones . . . .[14]

There is no record of how long it took for Sarah's November 10 letter to reach Juliette in Fort Worth. With the war raging in all of the southern states between Virginia and Texas and railroads being destroyed and with the normal uncertainties of mail delivery, it would have been weeks or even months.

Juliette Peak Fowler's life was fraught with tragedy. She lost her first child at nine months, her husband in the summer of 1861 when she was 23 and her baby boy in December of 1862 when he was a year old.

It seems strange, judging by today's standards, that Sarah could have written to her beloved sister with no mention of Archie Fowler's death only three months before and no mention that Juliette was about to give birth a second time.

In early 1862 Sarah again wrote to her family in Dallas. This time baby Archie is a topic:

> Confederate States of America
> Post Office Department
> Contract Bureau
> Richmond, Virginia
> January 25, 1862
>
> I was no little relieved on hearing of your condition and no little gratified that you have a fine boy and that, too, like Mr. Fowler. I had been looking for a week for letters and felt greatly disappointed when Mr. Harwood would return each day without any.... we are very well now and Juliet is just as much as I can lift—as hearty as a pig. Rip is well.... Pork is $14 per hundred in the pen, sausage 25 cents per pound. You are so much better off than so many others and I know you can't need very much dry goods for awhile. I think you are very extravagant drinking coffee unmixed and three times a day! I use one tablespoon full of coffee and better than two of rye for breakfast and have all rye for supper. Mr. H. thinks the war just commenced.
>
> I think Pa has done astonishingly well in your business matters.... When I left Dallas Mrs. Irving used a little stratagem in making me a farewell present. She wrote me a sweet note and enclosed $10 in gold. I did not suspicion what it was till long afterwards as she told me not to open it till I got here. I have purchased some excellent books with it.... Continue (to) read good books....
>
> Tell Pa I am much obliged for his letters. I shall write to him next. He writes of Ma's continued good health.... I want her and Pa to live a long time after we go back to Texas.
>
> I enclose five dollars for Ma to buy coffee or to help her toward anything which she chooses. I wish I had more to send. Don't mention it when you answer. I am so proud.... I looked for a bugle lace collar but found none. They are not worn here but crape altogether... write me as soon as you are able and let me know all you do and think about and if little Archie is anything like Ada.[15]

Juliette's joy in having a fine boy was short-lived. This baby, too, was taken from her after a year. He died in December of 1862 shortly after his first birthday.

Before the end of the war, the Harwood family was back in Dallas, where Sarah and her children, Ripley and Juliette, and Juliette Fowler shared a home while Alexander served in the war. Soon after the war ended, the Harwoods built their home at 4117 Swiss Avenue, between Peak and Haskell, in the heart of the Peak Addition. It, like most of the houses that were built along Swiss, was a work of art. For years, as the house passed from one family to another, repairmen marveled at the high grade materials and fine workmanship that had gone into the structure. Its solid walnut staircase was highlighted with a handcrafted newel post. The mantels and doors were also solid walnut. Some later owners painted over the walnut, but as people began to value past treasures, the paint was removed and the old walnut wood finished into a new sheen.

Sarah was granted her wish that her parents live "a long, long time." Both remained active through reconstruction days following the Civil War. Jefferson, a dedicated Christian of the Campbellite faith, donated the money (along with three friends—Jack Cole, Billy, Miller and Josiah Claypool who donated lumber and land) to build the first Christian church in Dallas. It was located on Carondelet Street, now lower Ross. The result was a 40 by 60 foot building where Brig. Gen. Richard M. Gano, ex-Confederate cavalry leader, physician and leading Dallas businessman turned free preacher, held forth with powerful sermons every Sunday. In 1877 the booming new church reached a crossroads in its life. Jeweler John M. Oram, whose family was musical, gave the church an organ—and all hell broke loose. In Peak's brand of the Christian church—and those of many of the other parishioners—instrumental music was forbidden in church. Sunday morning came. The anti-organ faction sat on one side of the church led by Jefferson Peak and Gen. Gano. The pro-organ group sat on the other side of the aisle led by Oram, Ed C. Smith and C. M. Wheat.

> On each side the two, tall old Kentuckians contended. Each had a roll of paper in his hands which they (sic) used in their gestures for emphasis.
> Frivolous, unsuitable, unauthorized by the Bible, irreligious, a profanation, declared Capt. Jefferson Peak.
> Countered Wheat, an organ is not a fiddle, we plan no dance in God's house. We would raise paeans with organ as well as voice to Jehovah.[16]

Sarah Ann Peak Harwood intervened. "The lovely dignified Mrs. . . . . Harwood, daughter of Captain Peak, with trembling lips begged that the two flinty old men not desecrate the house of God. "Do not have discord," she begged. "Do not break up the church."[17]

But the lines were drawn. After the third Sunday when the battle between the organ and anti-organ factions showed no signs of abating, some of the church's leading members, including the minister, withdrew. Thirty-six of the members, led by the organ faction, established worship services at Field's Opera House and later established the Commerce Street Christian Church, which eventually became Central Christian Church.

Jefferson Peak and Richard Gano had won—for the moment—and Peak intended to keep it that way. On June 18, 1879, he made out his will:

> . . . I will and bequeath to the first Christian Church of the city of Dallas one half of a block of land in my suburban addition to the City of Dallas, this half block to be selected out of said addition by the trustees of said church and my executrix. This bequest to said Church is for the building of a Church House on the lan d . . . the lot or its proceeds are to be used solely for Church purposes, this bequest is, however, upon the condition that if the said Church should hereafter at any time use instrumental music in said church services or any Sunday or Lord's day or school in said Christian Church then this bequest is to become absolutely void and the said property hereby bequeathed or any other that may have been purchased arising from sale of the land hereby bequeathed is to return and become part of my estate . . . .[18]

Jefferson Peak died on October 21, 1885. Some of his younger children joined other Christian churches where instrumental music was a part of the worship service. And, in an ironic twist, Gen. Gano also compromised. In 1890 a beautiful auburn-haired, high-spirited young woman of the church, impeccably educated, a painter and musician, planned to be married. But she announced that she would not go through with the ceremony in her parents' church unless she could have instrumental music. So it was that the young woman, engaged to one of the town's leading young doctors had her way. Katie Gano, the apple of Gen. Gano's eye, prevailed on her father to have a piano moved into the church. It arrived under the cover of darkness on April 23, 1890. Fifteen minutes later Katie Gano said, "I do," to Dr. Hugh McLaurin and 15 minutes later the piano was discreetly whisked away.

While the city went through the Civil War and Reconstruction, the third daughter in the Peak family was growing up. Florence Chalfant Peak, who was not quite five when she came to Dallas and only 12 when the Civil War started, grew up in a world entirely different from that of her two older sisters. She was 17 years younger than Sarah Ann. By the time she came of age, her family was settled into Dallas. She was known as Flora and family papers reveal her to be the social one of the sisters. She married Thomas W. Field and the couple built their rambling three-story Queen Anne-styled mansion on Peak between Gaston and Junius. One historian said that "Field flamboyantly promoted

Jefferson Peak left property in his will to build the first Christian Church in Dallas with the stipulation that the property would revert to his heirs if, at any future time, instrumental music was allowed in the church.

his extensive East Dallas holdings . . . with the construction of a palatial residence in the middle of *his* property." But the house was located on the eastern edge of the Peak Addition on land owned by the Peaks. It was the setting for many lavish social functions and masterful business deals."[19]

Flora Peak Field gave birth to two children, Herbert Field, who died as a youth, and Carrie Field, who married John Peter Smith, Jr. In her later years, Flora assumed many of the responsibilities for her family that her oldest sister had handled. "Grandma's health wasn't too robust . . . (She) was not of the same active type as Aunt Juliette or Aunt Sarah . . . (she was) adored by her grandchildren."[20]

Flora Street in Dallas is named for Florence Chalfant Peak. Its name in the area that runs through what once was the Peak Addition was changed to Roseland. Once lost into almost obscurity as it approached downtown Dallas, it regained its luster when it became a key street in the Dallas Historic District. Field Street is named for Flora's husband.

When Alexander Harwood returned home after the Civil War, Juliette Fowler went back to live with her parents and helped to nurse her father in his final illness. Her health was fragile and she sought rest and medical attention in the north and east as well as in Dallas. While resting one summer in Monteagle, Tennessee, she bought lots where she planned to build a cottage for Texas women teachers as a retreat where they could "enjoy the recuperative powers of the mountain atmosphere for their bodies and feast upon the fat things of the Southern Chatauqua for their minds." She continued medical treatment after she returned to her mother's house in Dallas. In the spring of 1888, she lost her hearing. A year went by.

Juliette Fowler left most of her fortune to establish and maintain a home for widows and orphans in East Dallas. For many years it was administered by her sister, Sarah Ann Peak Harwood, and later was administered by the Christian Church.

On May 9, 1889, Juliette went to New York City where she was the houseguest of her best friend, Mrs. M. I. Barkley, who had made arrangements for her to see specialists. In New York, very suddenly on June 4, Juliette died. She was returned to Dallas and laid to rest beside her husband in the Old Masonic Cemetery. She was 52 years old. One of her last acts, just before she left Dallas, had been to update her will in her own handwriting. She had become the guardian of an orphan boy and, in her will, provided for his education. She set up a trust fund for Matt, her youngest brother, who was living in Mexico, with the stipulation that the money be returned to her estate upon his death.

She designated 15 1/2 acres of land in East Dallas at the end of Columbia Avenue as a site for a home for needy and orphaned girls and for aged women. She also left money to begin construction on the property. In so doing, she became the city's first major philanthropist.

Without the guidance and creative genius of her sister, Sarah Ann Harwood, who was the executor of her will and director of the board of the institutions, Juliette Fowler homes would never have happened and could never have survived. Sarah Ann looked after the good name and business of her sister just as she had always cared for family members while they lived.

Juliette Fowler Homes, founded with money left by Juliette and administered by Sarah Ann, eventually were given over to the Christian Church. The first buildings on the property did not begin until after the turn of the century when Matt died and the residue of his stipend reverted back to the estate.

A year after Juliette's death and five years after she lost her husband, Martha Malvina Peak died on July 7, 1890, at the age of 78. Only six of her 12 children survived her.

Sarah Ann Peak Harwood lived in Dallas for just short of six decades. She could, according to her family members, "do anything," and was usually the person who kept peace in the family and connections between family members.

It was she who wrote the letters, she who arranged the women's meetings in the church and secured the speakers, she who gave money to build East Dallas Christian Church, she who managed her sister's affairs. She was, said the *Christian Courier* at her death, "one of the best-known women in Texas brotherhood." But she was not a "public woman. She was a modest, cultured, refined, Southern lady, refined and literary in her tastes, who used a purer speech, a limpid and rich English, who showed a clearer intelligence and acquaintance with affairs, especially in things of the church . . . and yet she could not even talk in prayer meeting if there were men present who could lead; her womanly modesty forbad it."[21]

Sarah, whose husband died in 1885, spent the last years of her life in the home of her daughter, Juliette Harwood Collins and her funeral was held in Juliette's 4207 Live Oak home. Sarah, the oldest daughter of the pioneering Peaks, outlived her parents, her husband, two children and seven of her siblings. Her survivors included her own two children, Ripley and Juliette, 10 grandchildren, three great-grandchildren and her siblings, Florence Chalfant Peak Field, Junius, Worth and Victor Peak.

8

DALLAS BECOMES A CITY

Dallas was growing in every direction.

The Peaks, joined soon by the Gastons and other prominent First Families, were laying out streets and building homes and small businesses in East Dallas. A bit farther out, the Beemans had been joined by several new families around the White Rock area. The La Reunion experiment, though an official failure, left in its wake many valuable citizens for the tiny town. The Jacksons and Davises were expanding their farms to the north and inviting new residents to join them. To the northwest, the Hughes sisters, bearing the names of the men to whom they were married, were setting down roots, rearing children and establishing religious foundations. Across the Trinity to the west, the Hords who built the first house in that area, had been joined by the Hortons, Millers, Barkers and dozens of other families. To the southern and southwestern part of the county the Trees, Rawlins and Taylors had new neighbors named Nance and Voorhies.

The area had become a county, but it had not yet become a city. It was about time. Like everything new that has the aura of success, Dallas had accumulated a large measure of riffraff. Very often the first people to attach themselves to any new experiment are those with a personal unfulfilled agenda who see any new experiment as the ideal place to impose their wishes. So it was that the new town, expanding in every direction, lured a large share of malcontents. At best there was a host of dreamers seeking an elusive utopia, and, at worst, a collection of derelicts and delinquents lured to the lawless frontier. Dallas had lawyers, but no law. The county was functioning reasonably well, but the city hardly at all. Progress had brought goods—but few services. The earliest settlers whose word was their bond were now supplemented, if not replaced, by increasing numbers of ribald opportunists.

Some historians say the official act of incorporating the town came about as a direct result of the murder of the son of one of the town's leading families over a gambling debt. This, or a number of other associated incidents, pushed the City Fathers to do what they had long talked about—to attain the credentials to make their town official. The official incorporation is dated February 1, 1856, when the State of Texas issued Dallas a charter. Some citizens opposed incorporation that made them answerable both to a municipality and a county. To some this seemed like double taxation. To many it still does.

Dallas held its first election on April 5, 1856, and named Dr. Sam Pryor its first mayor. Hardly had the polls closed and the votes been counted—white males only casting ballots—when the honeymoon was over with their new mayor. Dr. Pryor is remembered as "brusque, officious and overbearing," chiefly because he insisted on doing what he was elected to do—create a community in which order prevailed.

Women continued, mostly through pillow talk and gentle persuasion, to exert a civilizing influence on the new town. In the privacy of their homes, they had often tried to persuade their men to take action because conditions had become so bad that they were afraid to enter public places and afraid to allow their children to walk on city streets. Even so, genteel and educated women still arrived weekly to make their home in Dallas.

In 1856 Harriet Rector Cabell came to Dallas from Fort Smith, Arkansas, the bride of Gen. W. L. Cabell, who would become mayor of Dallas in 1874. History records her as "a woman of rare virtues, and greatly beloved by those who were in a position to know her many merits." Her seven Cabell children were Benjamin E., Kate Doswell,

Dallas was expanding in every direction with settlers who, at best, were dreamers determined to build a new utopia and, at worst, were a collection of lawless riffraff lured to a lawless frontier.

John Joseph, Lawrence Duval, Lewis Rector, Pocahontas Rebecca and William Lewis, the last two dying in infancy. Harriet is the first of three Cabell women who would be First Lady of Dallas following the election of their husbands as mayor. Her son, Ben Cabell served as mayor from 1900 to 1906 and Earle Cabell was elected mayor in 1961.

Eugenia Dev Les Goodere, who also would become a First Lady of Dallas, the wife of Benjamin Long, came to town in 1856 with the family of her step-father, Jean-Baptiste Goetsells. Born and reared in Louvan, Belgium, she was a young girl when she arrived in the already failing La Reunion Colony. Her family, along with several others, moved to an undeveloped street in East Dallas which they named Swiss Avenue in honor of their European heritage. In the spring of 1862, Eugenia and Benjamin Lang (who altered the spelling to Long), were married on Swiss Avenue in the home of Jacob Nussbaumer. Six years later Benjamin Long was appointed mayor during Reconstruction when Federal troops occupied the city following the Civil War.

Only 30, the new mayor had assumed a prominent role in the young city. Arriving in America at the age of 17 from Zurich, Switzerland, he was one of the La Reunion settlers who walked to Dallas from Galveston. Soon after his arrival in America, he was captured by Indians. Awakened in the middle of the night by an old Indian man who felt sorry for him, he escaped on a pony the old man provided. In 1870 Mayor Long traveled back to Switzerland to see his mother and returned with several additional families to become residents of Dallas. Many of his countrymen had a difficult time integrating the glowing tales they had heard from Long in Switzerland with the tiny, undeveloped town they found upon arrival in Dallas.

In 1872, Mayor Long was returned to office by popular vote. He continued to promote the city, not only with his services, but with his resources. He was a mayor who governed by persuasion, and much growth took place during his four years in office. Dallas got its first outdoor street lighting, its first fire department and its first public transportation—horse and mule-drawn streetcars. After he retired as mayor, Long was appointed United States Commissioner for the Northern District of Texas.

While visiting a friend, another Switzerland native who owned a saloon on Austin Street, Long was shot by a disgruntled customer. He had intervened on behalf of the proprietor when three young people tried to leave the bar without paying their bill. One of the young men returned with a gun, wounded the owner and shot Long in the chest. His death on June 23, 1877, left Eugenia Dev Les Goodere Long, as a very young widow to rear their five children alone. Their son, Ben, died with a cerebral hemorrhage. The youngest daughter, Eugenia, only a little more than a toddler when her father was killed, grew up to marry Ferdinand Riek, a musician. Annie wed Jerry Houston and, after his death, Silas Lotzenhiser. Mary married Price Bowen and Lucia married Louis F. Rick of the Rick Furniture family.

By mid-summer of 1856, *The Herald* was full of news every day about the city's progress. Streets which had originated in the mind of John Neely Bryan and been laid out by surveyor J. P. Dumas, were now, with the city's incorporation, official. The square was bounded by Main and Commerce, Jefferson and Houston. North to south beginning at the Trinity River and reaching eastward the streets, in order, were Water, Broadway, Houston, Jefferson, Market, Austin, Lamar, Poydras, and two without names. Running east and west, beginning on the western boundary, they were Columbia, Polk, Wood, Jackson, Commerce, Main, Elm, Burleson, Carondolet, Walnut, Calhoun and one without a name.

A remarkable paper for its day, *The Herald* discoursed on matters of international and national concern as well as stories of local interest. On May 10, 1856, a tornado dipped down in Cedar Hill and the paper reported: "It swept the village of Cedar Hill from the face of the earth." Eight persons were killed and 12 injured.

Supplies were still scarce and dependent on the arrival of wagon trains from the east, but on June 14, 1856, J. V. Grigsby bragged in a *Herald* ad that he had a stock of supplies "which I warrant to sell from 50 to 25 per cent lower than any other house in town." There was a "Splendid Stock of Ladies' fine dress goods, Silks, Satins, Berages (sic), Delunes, Swisses, Lawns, Poplins, Jaconnettes and Calico. Also a fine assortment

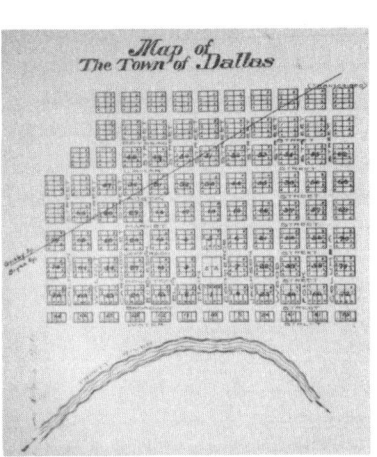

Several names of earliest streets have disappeared, but many are as familiar today as they were in 1856 when Dallas became a city.

of Shawls, Tianas,(sic) Capes, Collars, Laces and Edgings." The same wagon train brought "Sugar, Coffee, teas, and etc., and a host of other articles too numerous to mention."

While supplies were still scarce, transportation was improving, for in 1856, the first regularly scheduled stage coach from the east listed Dallas on its route.

The same lure of the wide open spaces that brought families to Dallas also induced many of them to seek land and homesites at a distance from the downtown community.

In 1856 when they arrived from Kentucky, Mary Lynn and Thomas Zachariah Motley settled on acreage he had staked out on a prior visit to Texas. Eventually they would stretch the Motley farmlands to 6,352 acres that took in what is now north Mesquite and a portion of Garland from a point connecting to Dallas on the west, including Eastfield College and stretching across to include all of what is now Town East Shopping Center and adjacent residential and commercial development.

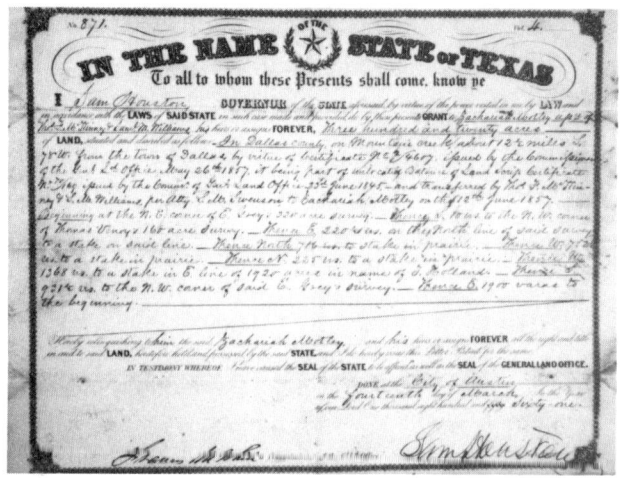

Sam Houston, governor of the State of Texas, issued this land grant to "Zachariah Motley and his heirs or assigns forever" on March 14, 1861.

At 51, older than most of the people who settled in Texas, Zach led a wagon train that included several couples, their children, slaves and household goods from Bowling Green, Kentucky, to Texas. A third-generation grist mill operator, as well as a successful farmer in Kentucky, Zach had liquidated his holdings and arrived in Texas with a small fortune in gold. Some stories tell about the chest holding the gold that Zach used as a wagon seat. Other stories are that Mary Lynn was almost weighted down with gold tucked in her underclothing. Parts of both stories are, doubtless, true, for it was the custom in pioneer days for women to "bank" their money by hiding it in their undergarments. Their modesty was such that they were confident no highwayman or marauding tribe would tear away their clothes in search of treasure.

Nine years younger than her husband, Mary Lynn was 42 when she arrived in Texas. She had left behind in Kentucky the two oldest of her 10 children, James Edward, born February 11, 1834, and Martha Elizabeth, September 14, 1836. She and Zach brought with them Jefferson Lynn, July 26, 1840; Penelope A., June 14, 1842; Francis Marion, September 22, 1844; William H., April 22, 1846; John Thomas, January 18, 1848; Robert Page, February 3, 1850; Mary Henry, April 20, 1853, and Sallie Ann, September 14, 1854. Considering that Mary Lynn traveled in a wagon with eight children, ranging in age from one to 16, for hundreds of miles, it is not surprising that she is remembered as "strong, brave, and capable of doing anything."

The Motleys built a two-story 10-room farm mansion to accommodate their family which grew to include two grandchildren and assorted in-laws, other family members, and friends who came to visit.

Zach Motley accumulated his vast holdings in only 12 years. He bought some of his land for as little as 25 cents an acre. Other land he acquired by homesteading and

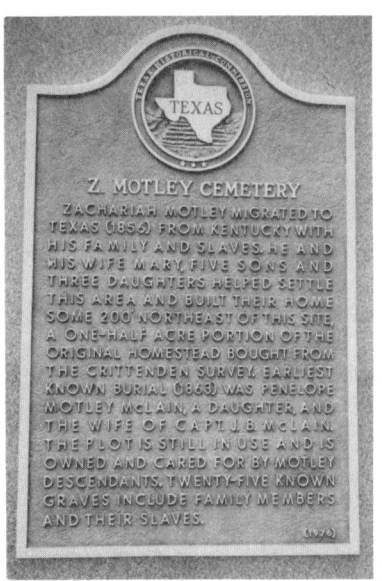

This Texas Historical Marker was erected at the Motley Cemetery on the campus of Eastfield College in 1976.

Mary Motley lies among her family members in the Motley Cemetery.

other by consignment. Among the family papers is a deed signed by Gov. Sam Houston in 1861 granting to "Zachariah Motley . . . and his heirs or assigns forever, 320 acres of land . . . on Mountain Creek, about 12 1/2 miles . . . from the town of Dallas."

The private Motley cemetery was located some 200 yards west of the house . . . .

• • • • •

The following is a time capsule, a personal requiem to and for the assorted Motleys by the author:

It is a bright, sunshiny day in late April, 1989, with the cool wind blowing gently across 35 Motleys and/or their direct descendants, by birth or by marriage, who lie beneath neatly marked stones. One additional marker, "Known Only to God," encloses the area that used to lie outside the cemetery where Motley slaves were laid to rest. Current members of the Motley family have chosen to include this area within the white picket fence that surrounds the plots. An ancient cedar, gnarled in its age as must have been some of the people buried here—several were well into their 80s—stands in the northeast corner of the cemetery. Birds nest and call out to one another in the branches of five other small trees that shade the resting place.

Some 300 feet to the west of this historical burial site, bare-chested young men in shorts lob a tennis ball back and forth. To the east, just behind where the grand old house used to stand, large serif letters adjacent to a rich brown-and-orange logo spell out "Eastfield College."

I stand on a piece of Texas history, six steps away from where the first burial took place here and, could be, in the exact spot where Mary Lynn Motley stood 125 five years ago for the burial of her second-born daughter, Penelope A. Motley McLain. Penny was 21 when she died in childbirth, on December 27, 1863, while her husband, Capt. J. B. McLain, was off fighting the Civil War. The baby may have died and been buried with her. Another child, J.B. McLain, Jr., born in 1862, died at the age of 22 months, three weeks following the death of his mother, and lies in a grave beside her.

A quarter of a century has gone by since I once drove my five little girls out Gross Road to the old Motley cemetery. They stood between its weed-covered graves marked by tilting tombstones and looked eastward to the old house which they, along with their generation of youth, called "haunted." Its ancient black caretaker would rouse himself from his nap on the wrapped-around porch to ascertain that we were there to do no harm and then he would fall asleep again. The few times I tried to engage him in conversation, he was noncommittal—either unaware of the historical significance of the edifice or protective of its lore and not willing to share family stories with an outsider.

Now it seems such a friendly place. The old house is gone, destroyed by a fire that took it away in 1966 only months before it would have been razed to make room for Eastfield College buildings. When it went, the wallpaper that "Aunt Sallie" Ann Motley had pasted on when she redecorated several years before her 1922 death still hung tenaciously and even looked almost new in some spots of the old house. Aunt Sallie was a woman of her times. She never married. Does one dare speculate why? The youngest of the Motleys, Sallie was an infant when her parents brought her to Dallas and only nine years old when her sister, Penny died. She was 14 when she lost her father. She and her mother and older brother, Will, continued to make their home in the old place after the other children married and went away. She must have had a special bond with her sister, only 17 months older than she, and she surely was devastated when this sister, Mary Henry Motley Lawrence, died in 1885, six days after the birth of a daughter. That baby, Mary Lawrence, lived only a month and lies beside her mother. Sallie took Mary's surviving children, Joe (christened Jefferson Zachariah), 5, and Nannie, 3, home with her. She, with "Uncle Will" and Grandma Motley, reared the children and their names, along with the name of all 10 of the Motley children are engraved on the marker inside the Motley cemetery.

Then, there was Mary Lynn Motley. Widowed at 52, she lived until she was 76, and those were the days when children rarely left their widowed parents to live out their lives alone. Often married children took them to their homes, or, as in the case of Sallie, a daughter remained unmarried and cared for them.

• • • • •

Still a family plot for the Motleys, the cemetery now is in the shadows of Eastfield College. A wide avenue, appropriately, Motley Drive, curves gently to its west. It is often visited by Eastfield College students and others. A granite monument reads: "A Memorial to the Motley Family." On the west side is engraved "Our Father and Mother Zachariah Motley, June 10, 1805-March 10, 1868. His wife Mary Lynn, January 18, 1814-October 31, 1890. They were a kind and affectionate husband and wife, a fond father and mother and a friend to all." On the opposite east side is a poem and on the north and south sides are the names of their 10 children and the two grandchildren who lived with them. Seven of the 10 sons and daughters—Penelope, Mary, John T., Frank, J. L., Will and Sallie—lie near their parents. Jefferson Z. (Joe) Lawrence, the grandson, also is buried in the family plot. Visitors are stopped by the bronze marker reading, "Arm of John S. Motley." The story is that when John was 17 he was working at the old Reinhardt Gin and reached in to remove rocks that had stopped the mechanism. When the saw started, it almost cut off his arm before he could remove it. Later that day the arm was amputated and buried in the family plot. The foot of Cleve Motley, Mary Lynn's grandson, also is buried there with a marble stone marking the spot. Cleve's foot was caught in a stirrup when his horse threw him. It was broken, became infected and was amputated.

Westward from the Motley Cemetery on a clear day, the skyscrapers of downtown Dallas are outlined clearly 10 miles in the distance and it is there, among those in the old Masonic Cemetery, that another woman who began a family empire in Dallas reposes. She is Rebecca Serena Allison Stemmons, the foremother of the Stemmons family dynasty in Dallas. Born in Dade County, Missouri, to Mary A. and Judge Matthias W. Allison, she married John M. Stemmons in 1857 and came to cast her lot in and make her contributions to the city of Dallas. Rebecca, as befitted the daughter of a Missouri judge, was well-educated and did her part, mostly indirectly through her husband, to see that their 10 children had every educational opportunity. Beginning the year after she was married, she had children every two to four years for two and a half decades. Walter was born in 1858, Beverly L. in 1860, Harriet Ann in 1863, Mary Belle in 1867, Lilia Belsterling in 1869, Cora Lucille in 1872, Leslie A. in 1874, John J. in 1878, Sidney A. in 1879 and Robert L. in 1881.

Col. Stemmons had a long and illustrious career in the Civil War. Taken prisoner, he escaped from a northern encampment and went to Richmond, Virginia, where his family was living at the time, rejoining them after a long absence. Some records state that he was away for five years, but this is not likely when you consider the birth of the children. Four of the children died young, but the others survived to give their time, money and name to posterity. Stemmons Freeway is named for descendants of Rebecca Serena Allison Stemmons.

The Coit School was named for John, but it was Cattie Coit who administered it and taught while her husband served in the Civil War.

Education in Dallas got a boost in the spring of 1859 when Catharine Malloy Bunting Coit arrived in town as the bride of John Taylor Coit. He had recently taken a law degree from Princeton University, and she had graduated as valedictorian of Harmony Female College in North Carolina after studying at private schools in Cheraw, South Carolina. A bride at 20, Catharine Coit had her first child on Christmas Day eleven months following her marriage and five days after her 21st birthday. When her son, John Clinton Coit, was three months old, Cattie and John with the baby, and their servants, Caesar, Daniel, George, Mary and Sam, left their South Carolina home for Dallas traveled to Montgomery and Mobile, Alabama, then to New Orleans and Shreveport, Louisiana, where they stayed long enough to purchase furnishings for the new home they were building in Dallas. They traveled by boat up the Red River to Shreveport and overland by wagon to Dallas arriving in the spring of 1859, still early enough to do some planting on the 320-acre farm John had bought the year before when he traveled to Texas to research combining a law practice with farming. He had chosen a site in north Dallas County, part of the acreage spilling over into Collin County.

Catharine set up housekeeping in her new frontier home while John got busy with planting and hunting for wild game to supply fresh meat for their larder. When baby John was 19 months old, Mary Henrietta Coit, who was to be Cattie's only daughter, was born. Her arrival on July 12, 1860, was the spark that would determine Dallas's participation with the South in the Civil War. It was a period of great stress for Catharine. She had two babies, and before the war was over, a third, Henry William, born on March 4, 1862. Her husband, busy recruiting a company for the Confederate army before the birth of Henry, left for an Arkansas training camp when the baby was less than a month old. Joining as a captain, John advanced to the rank of lieutenant colonel before the war was over. Wounded in the battle of Chicamauga, he was in an out of hospitals until his discharge from service in 1865.

Catharine, who managed the farm and took care of the children, also opened a school in order to provide early childhood education for her own children, to utilize the college training she had received and to provide schooling for neighbor children. She had help from her uncle, Duncan Malloy, her mother's brother, and from the family's seven slaves. They made a profit from the farm, if not from the school. Almost as soon as her husband was home from the war, Catharine was pregnant again. She had Charles Malloy Coit in 1866 and at his birth, had the lower portion of one of her legs amputated to relieve the pain of an old injury. Her fifth and final child, George Erasmus Coit was born in December of 1869 and lived only six months.

John Coit, frail from wartime injuries, and Catharine, slowed down by the amputation of her leg, moved into Dallas in 1870. As his health would allow, John practiced law and Cattie continued private teaching. They were charter members of the First Presbyterian Church in downtown Dallas. Their oldest child was soon to be 12 and their youngest four, and Dallas did not yet provide public schools for its children. Cattie Coit's one imperative was education and she gave her life to it, continuing to teach and pushing her children to the best possible education they could afford. With limited finances following the Civil War, there was no money to send the boys east to college as she and John had planned.

John was not quite 43 when he died on March 3, 1872, leaving Cattie, at age 34 with four children to rear and educate. She gathered up the bunch and took them back to the farm. Even as they worked to produce the family livelihood, Cattie was determined that her children would go to college. She sent John to Austin College in Sherman where he completed his degree. Charles attended Washington and Lee University and went to Capetown, Africa, as a missionary. He died there in 1895 not long after he began work. Mary Henrietta married Philip Bethea Hamer and had one son, Robert Coit Hamer. Henry William Coit was the son who loved the farm. He and his mother lived together until her death in 1883.

Coit Road is named for the early family that settled far north Dallas County. Catharine and John started it all when they arrived in 1859.

Following the death of his mother, Henry began to experiment with advanced agricultural methods and tools. He not only farmed the original 320 acres, but began to increase acreage. He acquired the interests of the other heirs in the home place. On November 16, 1889, when he was 27 years old, he brought his bride, 20-year-old Florence Graham Routh, to the farm.

In addition to the home place, which grew to 1,400 acres under his management, he leased a 2,400-acre ranch in Krum in 1901 and sowed it with wheat. Henry found the 20-horsepower steam engine he was using to thresh the crop altogether too slow so he bought a 35-horsepower tractor, an experimental model and the only one in existence in the entire Dallas area. With this engine and six triple-disc plows, he could cultivate 40 acres a day. His machine and the speed with which it worked was so unusual that it created a sensation. People came from miles around to watch.

Henry was a farmer's farmer. He experimented with new crops, organized support groups for farmers and headed organizations to promote agriculture. He served as president of Renner Farmers Gin Company, president of the Texas State Cotton Ginners Association and director of the United States Grain Growers Association. He was an organizer and a director of the National Farm Bureau.

Florence had a full and busy life. She and Henry had eight children, four boys and four girls, the last two twins, a boy and a girl. Although he did not attend college as his mother urged, Henry also valued education and served on the Renner School board, one term as its president.

The close of the second decade of Dallas was, like all years, a mixture of the frivolous and the significant, of the mundane and the unique. On April 13, 1859, every column of *The Herald* was edged in black announcing the death of its publisher, J. W. Latimer. But life went on and later the same month, on April 27 there was this:

> At the residence of the Bride's father, near Dallas, this morning, by Rev. James A. Smith, Mr. A. Y. Fowler, Esq. of Fort Worth, and Miss Juliet Peak, daughter of Capt. Jeff Peak, April 27th, 1959.
>
> Domestic happiness, then only bliss of Paradise that has survived the fall. The fairest bird of all the prairies has been ensnared in the magic net of love by this Fowler, and having secured the prize, he leaves the field, her sweet notes no longer charming our ears, her soft eyes no longer giving high happiness to sad hearts at home.
>
> Were there no bonnie dames at home,
> Or yet no lovers here,
> That in shock cross the land to win
> The fairest of the dear?
> Alas, for pleasure on the sea
> And sorrow on the shore.
> The smile that blessed one lover's heart
> Has broken many more.

A choice of delectables accompanied the notice.

It was the custom of the day to take with the nuptial notices to the newspaper some of the wedding feast including a sampling of the wedding cake for the editor, society writer and the man who set the type. It would be interesting to know who actually wrote the words, including the poem, that announced Juliette's wedding, for there is a sense that the young lawyer from Fort Worth was not a popular contender for the hand of the belle of Dallas. (See Juliette Peak—A.Y. Fowler story, Ch. 7.)

If it was not all right for a *foreigner* to ensnare Dallas belle, it was assuredly appropriate for a young man in the city to capture the affections of a beauty from another place. So, it was with approval that the *Herald* announced, on May 12, the marriage of Juliette's brother, Jefferson Peak Jr. The only time his bride's name is mentioned is in the story headlines!

JEFF PEAK & FANNIE V. MOTT, LATE OF BALTIMORE

> Our friend, Jeff and his accomplished Bride so long the bright and particular star of the circle of friends who loved her well, for her many excellent qualities of head and heart, carry with them the blessing and good wishes of their many friends. After a sumptuous feast . . . the happy couple started on a short bridal tour, with the bright morning sun shedding its golden beams upon the flowery pathway, and smiles and blessings from happy hearts showered upon them. May sorrow never come to mar their happiness so auspiciously begun, and never a cloud intervene to darken their lives.
>
> The Printer was not forgotten, and the elegant lunch sent to the Herald office was discussed in an appropriate manner.

While The *Herald* was reporting on society, it was equally adept at reporting the news of the day in everything from politics to Paris fashions. In 1859, a story on the front page said "grenadine gauze has been introduced in Paris . . . so aerial in texture it reminds one of the impalpable garments mentioned by the ancient poets." White was the only color for fashionable ladies and, of whatever fabric (grenadine gauze?) a dress

A double standard existed. Boys were expected to be the "man of the family" in crises and girls were expected to be compliant. In truth, it was often the women whose efforts kept the family together.

should have flounces . . . plaited ruches and frills at the top of the sleeves." Paris fashions took precedence in news space over the announcement that Gen. Sam Houston was a candidate for governor of Texas. Almost every issue of the paper editorialized on the town's need for a railroad and one fine summer day the editor "took a stroll through the splendid new brick hotel of Mrs. Cockrell, now nearly completed . . . . The building is of brick, 100 by 40 feet, 3 stories high!"

There was, without question, a double standard of behavior for men and women. Boys were trained, almost from babyhood, to be men. Many a youngster was called to the bed of his dying father and told that he would now be the man of the family. This popular ploy placed an impossible burden on a child and a double burden on young mothers who not only had to assume responsibility for rearing the children, but pretend that her son/child was shouldering the responsibility. Girls were trained to be belles, to be pliant, yielding and to obey their parents, then their husbands. Girls were getting a double message—the words of the society that insisted they be submissive to their men and the example of their mothers, aunts and grandmothers who were shouldering the burdens of care for their children. *The Herald* was ambivalent in its advice. Once it outlined the plight of boys in an editorial that was especially cruel to girls:

> The next great trial (that) a boy is to be obliged by a cruel master, is to sit with the girls in school . . . to be pointed out as a gal-boy . . . To be placed beside a girl who has no handkerchief and no knowledge of the use of that article, is a trial of no mean magnitude. We have been obliged to sit up close with Big Rachel laughing and blushing till we came to hate her name. We wonder where the overgrown frowzy creature is now?

Women were the guardian angels of morals and manners, certainly, but there was a question about their submissive roles. This story began as a routine report of a social event, but read on:

> A gay party of ladies and gentlemen had a delightful PicNic (sic) near town on Saturday last . . . . We left the scene of feasting with a decided opinion that the ladies of Dallas are angels, and with a vague fear that when they return to their native homes (heaven, of course), they will be assigned to the kitchen.

When the nation's newspapers were chiding women for flirting, The *Herald* treated the subject in a page one editorial, but held both women and men responsible for what it perceived as inappropriate behavior:

> One of the worst features of modern fashionable society is a disposition to flirt, existing among married people of both sexes. The wife arrays herself in silks and satins, loads her fingers and ears with jewelry and, rigged in flounces and laces, lays siege to some poor puppet arrayed in broadcloth, who has more money than brains and very little of either. On the other hand, the husband plays off his tricks in turn, and flirts with the reigning belles amid the smell of fresh paint and the exhibitions of maudlin and puerile nonsense . . . . This is a growing evil. Flirtation carried on by married people . . . destroys the sanctity of married life and is destructive of common virtue.
>
> This is no trivial matter.

On September 8, 1958, the entire front page of The *Herald* was devoted to the topic of slavery and states' rights. Throughout the remainder of the year and all of the last year of that decade, there were rumblings of war. On February 16, 1859, it reported: "Burning a Negro at the Stake."

It was not a good time for black people. Or children. Or women. Or, for that matter, men. Only, most of the men didn't know it.

9

THE 1860s—A DECADE OF CHAOS

The 1860s was, perhaps, the darkest, most divisive and most difficult decade in all of Dallas history.

It opened with the burning of the town and closed with the fledgling city struggling to overcome the Civil War. There were intense conflicts, not only between the North and South, but among members of the same family. The battle of ideas, of words and finally of warfare raged over the question of slavery. Early in the decade, on February 1, 1861, Texas, in an extralegal convention voted to cast its lot with the slave-owning South. The seventh state to do so, Texas seceded from the Union and sent its sons to take part in the struggle. Not all of its citizens were philosophical Confederates. Among its well-traveled and better-educated there was, if not overt sympathy for the Union, at least the understanding that the Southern Cause was a lost cause. Many Dallas families had come from states that remained solidly in the Union, among them Illinois and Indiana. Many others were from Kentucky and Missouri, both torn within their own boundaries between loyalty to the Union and secession.

So it was that many people in the South rallied behind the Confederacy not because they were proponents of slavery, but because they were loyal to their states. Among the opponents were two of the Dallas delegates, R. W. Lindsay and John W. Lane, who voted against secession. Many prominent national leaders also opposed slavery and the splitting of the Union, among them Robert E. Lee, a Virginian who commanded the Confederate troops. He did not own slaves and did not believe in human bondage, but he was caught up in the Southern cause. Slavery, like *causes* in all wars, was fanned to a hot flame. It was treason to oppose the prevailing point of view—and extremely dangerous. There is no count of the number of people who lost their lives—not on a battlefield, but at a community gathering—when tempers flared over whether Texas should secede from the Union.

Headlines in the newspapers of the early 1860s are full of war rumblings. The Southern Cause was taken up by the press, in legislative assemblies, in pulpits, in bars and restaurants and living rooms, and on almost every highway and byway where people came together.

When the 1860s dawned, about one-sixth, 12 per cent, of the population of Dallas consisted of black slaves. The census that year lists 1,074 slaves, no free negroes. The census was probably skewed, for had there been "free negroes" in the town, they would have evaded being counted. To be black and free in Dallas in 1860 was to court disaster. "Free negroes were frowned upon; they created trouble among the slaves. Vigilance was necessary and strict laws were passed against the runaway."[1]

The prevailing attitude was that black people enjoyed and thrived in bondage. "They were not overtasked, they had their holidays, their religious festivals, their place of worship and the usual frolic of song and dance on the plantations," wrote Frank Cockrell. "Where there were only a few, they were members of the family, and the house servants accompanied their mistress, and more especially the maid to the young mistress, in rounds of visits."[2] Cockrell is one of several early historians who glossed over that period in Dallas history and/or placed the onus of slavery somewhere else.

> Slavery was an institution fostered by the New England States. They had purchased slaves for their own profitable use from the slave traders and had encouraged the importation of the blacks from the jungles of Africa and elsewhere. When they realized that the blacks were unsuited for their tasks and

The prevailing white attitude was that black people enjoyed bondage and thrived in slavery . . . were not overtaxed, frolicked and sang and danced on the plantations.

that the climatic conditions were too rigorous and that they were better adapted to the cotton and rice fields of the South they without compunction readily sold them to the South."[3]

Historians—exclusively white males because they were the only citizens deemed worthy to write and publish records—say that slavery was never a major part of the Dallas economy. "The sale of Negroes in Dallas County was not frequent as the immigrants who brought them needed their labor to develop their lands . . . . mother and children were not sold separately, but together; human and mother instinct frowned upon separation, and never in the knowledge of the writer where the children were small and needed the care of the mother were they separated."[4]

Cockrell's observations, doubtless true in most cases, does not obscure the fact that early Dallas was a slave-holding city, nor do the stories of benevolent owners erase the fact of human bondage. In its buried past are shameful stories dealing with slavery, hundreds of them lost to posterity because Dallas's history is so one-dimensional and incomplete.

For proof of the goodness of slave-owning individuals, Cockrell cites the sale by "one of the leading physicians in Dallas" of a woman and her three children:

> Have granted, bargained, sold and conveyed, and do by these presents bargain, sell, convey and confirm unto_____following described personal property, to-wit: One negro woman, aged about 23 or 24 years and a slave for life; one negro boy, aged about 6 years and a slave for life; one negro girl, aged about 3 years and a slave for life; one negro child, aged about 1 year and a slave for life. To have and to hold unto the said____, heirs and assigns forever. And we do hereby warrant and will forever defend the title to the said above described negro property to the said ____ against all persons claiming or to claim the same by, through or under us. And we do also warrant the said negroes to the slaves for life, and to be sound and healthy in all respects.[5]

Several points need to be considered here. If the sale of human beings one to another were benevolent, why were the names of the seller and the buyer omitted? And, where was the father of these children? Had the mother been encouraged to beget offspring casually? Were the children sired by different fathers? Or, was there, perhaps an adult male—husband, father—left behind or sold off to somebody else when the young woman and her children were being so gallantly looked after?

An ugly record in Dallas history involves a black woman, Jane Elkins, the first person in the community to be legally hanged. Through "due process of the law," in 1853, she was convicted of murdering a man named Wisdom near Farmers Branch. There were no black people on the jury. And no women. Only a scant notice of the legal proceedings remain. Jane, as a slave and thus a non-person, had no legal counsel. When asked if she were guilty, she said nothing. When a former owner was asked for a comment, she said nothing. So, records of what happened are virtually non-existent. All that is known is that Jane was taken into Wisdom's home in Cedar Springs to care for his "recently orphaned" children and that after a period of time, she took an ax and murdered him in his sleep.[6] It is impossible to know what really happened, but it is unlikely that a black woman would have murdered a white man without extreme provocation.

Another tragic incident was the hanging of three black men hastily convicted of burning the city.

Dallas burned the summer of 1860. The fire started mid-day on July 8, one of the hottest days of summer, and continued until it had destroyed almost all of the downtown and parts of the adjacent buildings.

The story of the city's burning, published in the *Herald* and printed on a borrowed press in McKinney because the offices of the paper were destroyed in the fire, gave this account:

Facts of Dallas County's first legal hanging are a mystery. Jane Elkins, a slave, was hanged for murdering her white employer, but why? She had no legal counsel at her trial.

The fire that burned Dallas in 1860 may—or may not—have been started by slaves, but it is almost certain that the three singled out and hanged for the crime were not responsible.

On Sunday last, 8th inst., the town of Dallas was nearly all reduced to ashes, and almost wiped out of existence. Such a calamity has never before befallen this community—so overwhelmingly a disaster afflicted an enterprising and industrious people; nor so complete destruction of valuable property ever occurred in a small town. The fire originated in some boxes in front of W. W. Peak Brothers Drugstore, and in less than five minutes the entire building was enveloped in flames. The wind was high, blowing from the southwest, and the thermometer at the time [half past 1 o'clock] was standing at 104 Fahrenheit in the shade. The fire was then communicated to the old drugstore, and the building and warehouse of A. Surek, and the HERALD offices on the northside of Peak's and on the other to the large brick store of Messrs. Smith and Murphy, and three-story brick building of Mrs. Cockrell, known as the Dallas [St. Nicholas] Hotel. Thus at one and same time, the whole west side of the square was a blazing mass of ruins.

The Crutchfield House, Westers Barber Shop, the frame of the new building for A. Simon, the old tavern stand, the office of B. W. Stone, young Carr's saddlery shop, the large storehouse of Herman Hirsch, Darnells livery stable, A. Simon's storehouse and warehouse [Caruth's old stand] D.B. Sayres' old drugstore, W. Burtle's old shop and residence, E. M. Stackpole's store and warehouse, Lynch and Son's saddle shop, Messrs. Caruth and Simon's storehouse, R. R. Fletcher and Co's storehouse and J. C. McCoy's law offices followed. From this the fire extended to a blacksmith shop on the north side of the street, and for a time threatened a number of private residences.

There were also several small buildings near and in the rear of those on the square, consumed.... The old drugstore was vacant but had a few of Smith and Murphy's goods in it which were burnt. Over Mr. Shirek's store, and in the front room of the HERALD office, was the office of E. C. McKenzie who lost all in the room with a trifling exception. In the Crutchfield house was the post office.... a portion of the mail was gotten out, but afterwards was destroyed in another building. The entire contents of the post office were burned with the exception of postage stamps, most of which were saved. All the postage envelopes in the office were burned. Nearly everything was destroyed in the Crutchfield house, even to the wearing apparel of the occupants, furniture and everything. The stable belonging to the hotel was also destroyed together with its contents [no Horses (sic?), however]. The total loss is variously estimated—some say between $200,000 and $300,000 and others over that amount. The destruction is nearly total and complete.

It was a fire that touched the life of every citizen. Rumors quickly spread that the fire had been set by Negro slaves.

There is some evidence that an insurrection among the slaves was brewing. Fires on that sweltering summer day, when the temperature stood in excess of a hundred degrees, started in a number of other towns on the same day that Dallas burned. But no proof ever existed that slaves set the Dallas blaze. And, even if they did, the three who were hanged— Uncle Cato, Pat Jennings and Sam Smith—were scapegoats. "I think the hanging of the three negroes for burning the town is unjust, because I don't think they were guilty,"[7] W. P. Overton said in an interview later.

Fear distorts justice, and in those days preceding the Civil War, Dallas men allowed fear to control many of their actions. They restricted the civil rights of those who disagreed with them. Often they said, as men still say, that their actions were to protect their women and children. But nobody asked the women if they wished such protection. Women had no vote and no public voice.

It would be erroneous to suggest that most Dallas women were unsympathetic to the Civil War Cause. Most were as loyal as were the men in their lives. But they had not sat in the halls where decisions were made, had not heard the arguments pro and con, and had not cast one of the 741 votes in Dallas County to secede from the Union nor one of the 237 against secession. Nor had they been included in the Texas vote when 31,432 men voted yes and 14,697 voted no to joining the Confederate states.[8] Although it is doubtful that women's votes would have made a difference, in all of history in all situations, when women have had a voice, they have been far less likely than men to vote for war.

For the most part, women's role in the Civil War was like that of women in most wars. They assumed responsibility for everything at home. With a third of the men away fighting in the Confederate Army between 1862 and 1865, the women were overworked. They birthed and raised the children; handled the family business, and sowed, cultivated and harvested the crops. And they waited. With long delays in receiving accurate information from the lines of combat, they were constantly anxious. Even if their husbands, sweethearts or brothers were not in the army, all women knew personally someone who was. Many of them were torn, too, between love and loyalty to their families and neighbors and the families and friends of their childhoods, now their enemies.

Women did what women have always done: Assume whatever tasks need to be done, usually without complaint, to free their men to do the important work—killing each other on battlefields.

It is an eternal mystery why men killing each other in war is more important to history than women bearing and nurturing children, binding up human wounds and caring for the countless mundane tasks of the human family. Civil War records in Dallas list, almost endlessly, the names of fighting men, their regiments, their commanders, their escapades and episodes. Only very occasionally is there a glimpse of the women who kept Dallas moving forward while the men were away. Nancy Hughes Cochran survived those grim days by convening her "sisters" under a tree in the corner of the Cochran Cemetery to meditate and pray. The touching of lives for those in mutual distress was as essential to their survival as the "support groups" have been to their "sisters" five and six and seven generations later.

One other reality stands in the way of understanding what women really did during that war that tore a nation apart: There are few records of immediate and timely accounts because, during the crises of their lives, people do not write. At life's junctures—peaks when joys overflow and depths when emptiness pervades—individuals are too busy living life to record it. So it is that most of the records we have of events come after their actual occurrence. Time and distance always changes the event itself, for, given time to reflect and put into perspective, the meaning, texture, color and character of an event alters. While this is essential to an individual's survival, it revises truth.

Dallas was a Confederate quartermaster and commissary headquarters during the Civil War. Though actual fighting never reached the city, its people endured shortages of food and supplies. Clothing was virtually non-existent. A simple calico dress sold for $100; it had cost only a tenth that amount before the war started. Women and children wore shoes made of cloth and saddle leather. Story after story admonished the women to sacrifice for the troops on the front lines.

The best record of the Civil War conflict as it impacted the lives of individuals in Dallas is preserved in the letters of John and Susan Anna Floyd Good (the nameless Miss . . . . Floyd in the *Directory of the City of Dallas* with Good's name misspelled).[9] The letters [10] express the range of business and emotional crises representative of the many Dallas families in the war.

> John J. Good was provost marshall of Dallas County. He issued an edict that all males 16 and over were required to register for the military. Out of a population of 8,665 at the beginning of the war, 1,300 were in service—one out of every three males. "Anyone," Good said, "engaging in conduct injurious to the Confederacy will be arrested and imprisoned."

Though he was an educated man, a lawyer and a natural leader, Good was a military man and always at the center of controversy. Born in Mississippi on July 12, 1827, he moved with his family to a farm near Moscow, Alabama, as a child, was graduated from Cumberland University in Lebanon, Tennessee, and admitted to the Alabama bar in 1849. He was elected a brigadier general of the Alabama militia in 1850 and arrived in Dallas

During the Civil War, women did what women always have done. They ran the homes, reared the children, took care of all business, managed the farms, worked in the factories—and waited.

on November 25, 1851, where he immediately became involved with the Peter's Colony controversy. By taking sides with the colonists, he acquired instant popularity among his new peers and was elected to lead the group in the raid on the offices of Henry O. Hedgecoxe, Peter's Colony agent. Though Hedgecoxe was tipped off about the invading *army* and left town taking most of the records with him, the raiders ransacked his offices, took whatever remaining records they could find and returned to Dallas to be lauded as heroes.

Susan Anna Floyd was the youngest daughter of Nathaniel and Susan U. Hart Floyd. At 16, she was a stunning beauty, who soon caught the eye of the suave young bachelor, and seven months after the Floyds moved to Dallas, Susan Anna Floyd and John Jay Good were married on July 26, 1854, shortly after the bridegroom's 27th birthday on July 12. The couple moved to a cedar log cabin outside the city limits, a mile northeast of the courthouse.

Susan Anna Floyd Good, who usually signed her name Sue, but sometimes as Anna, and occasionally with both names, proved competent in every way. She not only managed her home with ease, but was knowledgeable about her husband's professional life as well. His legal work demanded long absences away from home as he followed the Ninth Judicial District court circuit from town to town in Anderson, Dallas, Ellis, Henderson, Houston, Kaufman, Navarro, Tarrant and Van Zandt counties. Theirs was a love match that grew warmer and more tender with the years as evidenced by the many letters they exchanged, and though her formal education did not equal his, her spelling and vocabulary and her ability to express herself was his equal.

John Good was southern to the core. Sue, born in Kentucky, but very much in love, was a ready convert to her husband's point of view. In the spring of 1860 he was appointed to the Board of Visitors to the United States Military Academy, an honorary but highly esteemed post, and left in May for West Point. There he was an avid observer of cadet military drills. He was often in discussion on the slavery question and disagreed, as would be expected, with the views expressed by many of the Northern representatives. Basing his arguments on states' rights rather than on the right of individuals to own each other, he wrote to Sue that he had told his Republican inquirers: ". . . so sure as there is a God in Heaven, just so certain would they (the Southern states) do it (secede), or by force of arms maintain their equal rights in the territories."[11] He added that he would be glad to leave behind the ". . . abolitionism, republicanism, fanaticism, and all the other odious isms and heresies so congenial to the North."[12]

Good did not arrive home until late July. By that time Dallas had burned and was enduring a senseless explosion of hysteria. Beatings, floggings and public hangings were the order of the day. Susan, a mile removed from the center of the storm, was kept busy with two little boys—John Jay Good, Jr., born January 26, 1856, and George Good, born December 10, 1958. Good immediately got involved in politics supporting the Southern plank of the Democratic Party, which had nominated John C. Breckinridge as its candidate for president. The Northern plank of the splintered Party had named Stephen A. Douglas as the nominee from the Northern plank. This left the cohesive Republican Party—with Abraham Lincoln as its candidate—a sure winner. Lincoln won 180 electoral votes to Breckinridge's 72 and Douglas's 12. He had been in office for less than a month when South Carolina led the procession of Southern states in seceding from the Union.

While leading the secession segment of the Dallas community, Good was also preparing the *Dallas Light Artillery* company for combat. It was a military group he had helped organize in 1859 that was as much social as military. As captain, he commanded the unit and now prepared it for battle. On April 20, 1861, Texas Gov. Edward Clark ordered Good to march his troops to Austin as soon as possible, thence to San Antonio where they were mustering 2,000 soldiers. He pulled the unit together, augmented it with additional recruits, and set out for Austin at daybreak on April 27.

Two days later from Waco he wrote the first letter home to Sue. Throughout the next year their correspondence was constant.

By mid-year of 1861, conditions for Confederate soldiers were deplorable and the war had only started. John wrote to Sue from Mount Vernon, Missouri, on August 27:

The love letters exchanged between John and Susan Anna Floyd Good during the Civil War gives a human dimension to a country divided.

Many of our troops went on the field without shoes, hats, pants and coats . . . . many soldiers pick a Union man as his target and call out . . . . "My shoes . . . my pants . . . my coat." . . . It is strange how reckless we become and how blunted are our sensibilities amid the perils of war. Those who were of the most sensitive at home are perfectly callous on occasions of this kind. Men ride over the Battlefield and laugh at what would once shock them . . . ."[13]

Though clothing was sometimes issued to Southerners fighting in the Civil War, most of the men depended on their families and friends to outfit them. John repeatedly told his wife about the lack of uniforms for the men in his company, and on September 13, Sue responded:

> You requested the ladies of Dallas to form themselves into societies and do something for the soldiers. I believe they have already been making some arrangements to that effect. Today was appointed for their meeting. I don't know what success they will have. Ma and I could not attend on account of Jay (their son, John) not being very well . . . .[14]

On September 30, she wrote that the clothing was almost ready to leave Dallas and that some of the citizens had bought caps for the boys. "I have heard of several giving as much as $25," she wrote. "Some are sending blankets. Goods are very high here now and very scarce. No new goods since you left. Shoes and boots are extremely high and very scarce . . . ."[15] George W. Laws, then County Clerk, and "Mr. Guess" did leave Dallas during the first week of October with wagons loaded with clothing and supplies for Good's men, but before they reached Arkansas, the troops had already been dispatched to Missouri.

By early December, Good knew, but admitted only in carefully veiled terms, that the South was in financial jeopardy and would likely lose the war. He sent money home to Sue, advising her to pass it along as quickly as possible. He had already confided that he would not be paid what he expected. "I regret that I have not heretofore written you to rent out our place . . . . It will yield you some revenue and ought to have been let some time ago."

On December 12, Sue's sister, Bettie Hart, wrote to John:

> . . . you have another fine *Boy*. He weighed 10 lbs & a half, has a fine forehead, black eyes & a big Floyd mouth. Johnnie & George are very fond of their little brother. George has named him, calls him Tommie Floyd. I expect he will go by that name until you return . . . . you have great reason to feel proud of your Wife & Boys. Anna has borne up under her affliction remarkably well considering your absence . . . . Do not give yourself any uneasiness about Anna & the Boys. They will have every attention that kind friends can give them.[16]

Sue scribbled a postscript: "In order to let you know that I am doing finely I scribble you a line while lying in bed . . . . Do wish you were here . . . . Our boy was born yesterday the 11th at half past 1 O'clock . . . ."[17]

Sometime in the early spring of 1862, John got home on furlough to visit Sue and the children and chose a name for his son, Ben McCullooch Jr., named for a Confederate officer he greatly admired. But the Jr.?

Shortly after he returned to his troops, John resigned his commission and returned to Dallas. In April of 1863, he and Sue moved to Mississippi where he continued to be active in politics and in military endeavors. On July 26, her tenth wedding anniversary, Sue lost her son, George, 4, to typhoid. She was alone and pregnant for the fourth time. On February 6, 1864, she gave birth to her first daughter, Betty Hart Good.

The battery Good had organized distinguished itself in three years of hard service under new leadership. Sue and John moved back to Dallas following the war. He was elected judge of the 16th District Court in 1866 but was removed as "an impediment to reconstruction" by Republicans in power following the war.

Susan Anna Floyd Good had four more children in Dallas—Nathaniel Stanley on January 4, 1867; Fannie Sue on October 12, 1871; Cerelle on September 1, 1874, and Willie Connor on December 12, 1876. The last baby, born four months before Sue's 40th birthday, lived only five months.

Sue Good became a widow in September of 1882. Her husband died in El Paso en route to California seeking a healthier, drier climate for the "consumption" that plagued him. He is buried in the downtown cemetery on the north side of the Dallas Convention Center. Sue lived another 30 years, until January 23, 1912, making her home with her daughter Fannie Sue Southworth at Naples. The Goods, who had a lifelong love affair, were separated in death. Her children buried her in Grove Hill Cemetery because, at that time, there was one of the many threats to raze the downtown cemetery as a nuisance to progress.

Though the Dallas population grew slowly during the 1860s, a few women arrived during the decade who made a lasting impact.

Elizabeth Jane Routh Thomas moved to Dallas at the outset of the Civil War with her husband, Captain James Thomas, and their four small children, Oliver, seven; Mary, six; Clara, four, and Martha, three. A veteran of the Mexican War, Thomas had enlisted with the Confederate troops, and Elizabeth felt that she would be safer in the city than on their farm in Richardson.

Elizabeth was accustomed to coping. At the age of 23, she had come to Texas from her native Tennessee on a wagon train with two brothers, Jacob and Joseph Routh, her widowed mother, and an orphaned niece, Rachel Elizabeth Mann. They spent $171.93 on the 44-day trek across country, leaving Tennessee on October 2 and arriving in Collin County 44 days later on November 15, 1851. At the time Elizabeth was a bride, having married James Thomas the year before on October 25, 1850. Business detained Thomas, she was to come to Texas with her family, and he would come for her later. When he arrived in 1852 to take her back, he liked what he found and decided to stay.

In Dallas, Elizabeth and James bought 40 acres of property lying between McKinney Street on the north and Pearl on the west and bounded by a branch, which now is roughly the location of Woodall Rodgers Freeway, on the south. They built their home on the southeast corner of McKinney and Pearl.

Subdivided, the property became known as the Thomas Addition with the principal east-west street, Thomas Avenue, given the family name, and the north-south street, Routh, Elizabeth's maiden name.

Following the war, Captain Thomas went into the mercantile business with J. M. Patterson and took an active role in the development of the young city. Elizabeth had two more children, Willie in 1865 and James Colby in 1870. She was an early active member of the First Baptist Church and reared all six of her children in the church. When James died in 1875 at the age of 53, Elizabeth had six children still at home, the oldest 20 and the youngest 5. She raised all of them in the McKinney house and continued to make her home there until her death on January 13, 1922. She had outlived her husband almost half a century.

A woman was Dallas's first restaurateur—though in the language of that day, she would likely have termed her career as running a boarding house.

Her name was Mariah L. Hickman Ervay. She got into business almost by accident. When she and Henry Sleigh Ervay were married on June 3, 1862, they moved to a large house on property near downtown Dallas. Henry was a promoter and land developer speculating in acreage to the south-southeast of Dallas. To provide the home base and stability to support them, Mariah opened a boarding house and provided breakfast and dinner for many of her roomers. She was an excellent cook and a gracious host. Those who stayed at her place and took their meals at her table spread the word. It was not long until business and professional men who lived at home but took their noonday meals

The State-Thomas division of near north Dallas originated when James and Elizabeth Jane Routh Thomas settled on 40 acres and built their home on the southeast corner of McKinney and Pearl.

Dallas's first restaurateur was a woman—Mariah Hickman Ervay, a no-nonsense woman who saw no reason to give up her lucrative business even after her husband, Henry S. Ervay, became mayor.

downtown were clamoring for the good food that visiting businessmen talked about having at Mariah's table. By popular demand, she began offering lunch as well as breakfast and dinner and thus, became the city's first restaurateur.

Mariah continued her "boarding house business" even after her husband became mayor and through the personal tragedy of losing two children. Harry Ervay was born February 17, 1864, 20 months after his parents were married and died when he was seven months old. The following year, on September 8, 1865, Jimmie Ervay was born; he died when he was four and a half. Two Ervay children, Henry S., Jr., and Maud, lived to adulthood.

Henry, whose land holdings increased in value, was appointed mayor in 1870 during the Reconstruction Period following the Civil War. He was a popular and benevolent mayor, and his popularity increased after federal officials, questioning his loyalty, tried to remove him from office. When he refused to step down, Gov. E. J. Davis ordered him ousted or jailed. He stubbornly declined to be intimidated and was locked up. A few days later after the Texas Supreme Court ruled that the governor was overstepping his authority, Henry walked out of jail a free man and a hero. During the ruckus, Mariah's table provided a popular setting for conversation and debate.

The Ervays moved away from Dallas about 1890, first to Cripple Creek, Colorado, and then on to San Diego, California, but when Henry died on August 21, 1911, his family brought him back home by train for burial. The funeral was August 31. He is one of the five former Dallas mayors buried in Oakland Cemetery. Mariah's family, doubtless buried her elsewhere because there is no record of the demise of this early Dallas businesswoman in Texas. But their name is ever-present in downtown Dallas because Ervay Street is named for them.

Mary Susan Carolyn Pipkin Young was the third woman who moved to Dallas in 1863 who would make a lasting impact on the city. The second wife of the Rev. William Ceiton Young, an early circuit riding Methodist minister who had preached in Arkansas, Illinois, Indiana, Kentucky, Louisiana and Tennessee before coming to Texas. Mary Pipkin married William Young in Arkansas on October 16, 1857. He was 30. She was considerably younger, probably no more than 20. She was about 25 when she moved to Dallas. The entire "city" had a population of not more than 700 people and the business district was confined to a single small square downtown. The Youngs settled not far from the center of the village into a home near the Trinity River on a site near what is now Union Station. He began spreading the Methodist branch of the Christian faith. While supporting him in his efforts, Mary gave birth to and reared their nine children.

On November 1, 1868, 42-year-old Rev. Young abandoned his horseback ministry to settle down with his growing family as pastor and leading founder of the Lamar Street Methodist Church, the first church of Methodist denomination in town. Its first sanctuary was a small frame building on the corner of Commerce and Lamar. The building burned in October of 1879 and was replaced with a brick church at Commerce and Prather. It is the origin of today's First United Methodist Church of Dallas. Young served as minister for two years before becoming presiding elder of the Dallas district for four years and then presiding elder of the adjoining district for six years.

Mary Pipkin Young died at the age of 93, a year before her husband. Like most ministers' wives of that era, Mary stayed in the background and the men, who were the record keepers, knew her only in relation to her role as a wife. So it was that she is remembered as "a true and faithful companion, a helpmeet . . . who shared . . . all the privations and toil of their pioneer life, bearing her part of the burden with unflinching fortitude. She is a lady of cultivated mind, refinement of manner, fine personal appearance, combined with rare graces of character, and has been a zealous and efficient laborer in church work."

The Youngs donated land for a city park, the site of the present Dallas City Hall. They also gave the property for the Scottish Rite Building on Harwood Street. Young Street is named for them; Canton Street bears the name of the Rev. Young's birthplace in Kentucky. Marilla Street is named for his mother, Marilla Ingram Young. The Youngs all rest in the shadows of their home place in Old Masonic Cemetery in front of the Dallas

The Caruth/Carruths of Dallas had their beginning with the marriage of sisters Mattie and Anna Worthington to two early successful bachelors—William Barr and Walter Caruth. The latter family added the double (rr) to Caruth following a family feud.

Convention Center. The bushels of mail delivered daily to Dallas city officials reach them on Marilla Street.

The Caruths/Carruths are widely acclaimed for their civic, religious and educational contributions to Dallas, but the Caruth women are barely acknowledged—and they were formidable.

Mattie Caruth (the first Mattie Caruth) deserves a large share of the credit for holding and enlarging the vast Caruth land estate in North Dallas. Her husband died as a relatively young man; it was Mattie who kept the estate together, managed it and passed it on to future generations.

Sisters Mattie and Anna Worthington (who would become Caruths) came to Dallas in 1865 in a 30-caravan wagon train with their parents, Thomas and Rebecca Hart Worthington, several slaves, and an almost limitless supply of household furnishings. Reared in the genteel south where the most important thing for a lady to learn was to charm the gentlemen, the young women left their Mississippi plantation as the Civil War was drawing to a close and only days ahead of advancing federal troops. In Dallas County, the Worthingtons settled at Scyene and New Hope, today's Sunnyvale. Mattie was living with her brother, Tom Worthington, Jr., in town when she received a letter from Anna telling her that she had met two interesting young bachelors. The young men, Walter and William Barr Caruth, had come to Dallas County in 1852 from Kentucky, opened a general store a block from the courthouse on Main and Record Streets and started buying property. Their first purchase was a section of land six miles north of Dallas, which they later expanded to include property extending from White Rock Creek on the east to beyond Preston Road on the west. In 1862 they bought a 420-acre tract lying between the present Armstrong Avenue and Mockingbird Lane, for which they paid $3,840, or about $9 an acre. Shortly before the Worthington women met the Caruth men, William deeded his interest in the property to his brother, Walter, and in 1889 Walter sold the tract and 72 additional acres to Fidelity Real Estate and Trust Company of Dallas for $150,000.

The Worthington sisters became the brides of the Caruth bachelors in weddings eight months apart. Mattie married first. On July 4, 1864, she and William Barr Caruth exchanged vows. The next year, on March 5, 1865, Anna and Walter Caruth were married. Prior to their marriages, William and Walter had persuaded their parents, John and Catharine Henderson Caruth, to come to Dallas. In 1858, they moved into a one-story frontier-styled farmhouse on the North Dallas property. Clapboard-sided and with native oak logs for joists, the house was roofed with hand-hewn shingles. John and Catharine Caruth became noted for hospitality they extended to travelers between Dallas and McKinney.

Mattie and William Caruth had their first child, a son, Aaron Wickliffe Caruth, in 1865. The baby died in infancy the following August 17. It would be eleven years before they would have another child. In the meantime, in 1872, eight years after she was married, Mattie designed her dream house to be constructed on the North Dallas property. She patterned it after the Mississippi plantation home of her aunt and uncle, Aaron and Polly Wycliff, where she had spent many happy hours as a child and young woman. Numerous treks to East Texas in wagons were required to haul the lumber to build the two-story Southern plantation house. The lumber was processed and finished in a sawmill on the Caruth plantation. Every inch of the house was constructed to perfection with square handmade nails holding the timbers together. Rooms were large; ceilings, high. Long, wide hallways both separated and united the rooms, each of which had its own fireplace. It took four years to complete the masterpiece. William planted bois d'arc trees in the 1870s. Mattie added a formal garden in the spring of 1877 and raised four o'clocks, marigolds and zinnias. The house sheltered several generations of Caruths.

The house was completed in time for the birth of their second child in 1876. They named him William Walter for his father and his uncle, thus beginning the repetition of names that would continue through generations of Caruths. The first Mattie, for instance, is the aunt of the second Mattie, Anna and Walter's daughter, Mattie Caruth McMillan.

Mattie Caruth designed her family's dream house which was built on their property across Northwest Highway from NorthPark. She ran the family business which amounted to a small town for 22 years after her husband died.

The third-generation Mattie is the daughter of William Walter Caruth, also named for the first Mattie, her grandmother. As if this is not sufficiently complicated, the names continue to be repeated for generations until the present.

The first Mattie Caruth outlived her husband 22 years. When he became ill, they traveled together seeking a cure, to no avail. Back in Dallas, he spent countless hours teaching Mattie the intricacies of the farm operation, drawing diagrams of where things were located, jotting down the amounts of food and supplies required for persons and livestock on the wagon trips to and from various points of the family holdings. He helped her understand the financial implications of the vast estate, which by that time resembled a small town. Two cotton gins, a sawmill and a dairy were among the thriving businesses located on the 5,000-acre Dallas farm. Mattie and William Caruth also owned 1,800 acres in Kaufman County and 7,500 acres in Johnson County.

William Barr Caruth died on October 19, 1885. Mattie was exhausted. She had spent hours learning from her husband and longer hours caring for him. Then came the emotional wrenching from one who had been partner, lover, confidant and friend. Mattie was persuaded by relatives to take a vacation. This she did, traveling with Mattie, her niece and namesake, for several months of rest and recuperation to California and Mexico. She left the farm in the care of her brother, Tom Worthington, and left her eight-year-old son with her sister Anna.

Rejuvenated, and remembering the concern of her husband that the Caruth properties needed a firm guiding hand and that she was capable of managing, Mattie came back to Dallas and took over.

> Surprisingly, it is Mattie who actually deserves the credit for having accumulated some of the Caruth's most valuable Dallas land,[18]

Not surprising at all. Dallas women have always done what was required of them. Shortly after William died, Mattie purchased a residence on Ross Avenue where she, her son, and the servants, many of whom were former slaves, spent their winters. It was an imposing house, even for its time, three stories over a basement, both spacious and gracious, located on the corner of Masten at Ross Avenue, which, at that time, was still a narrow street, that was muddy when it rained and dusty in dry weather.

Earle Clark, the stepdaughter of Robert H. Stewart, a prominent Dallas banker, joined the Caruth family on April 5, 1905, when she married William Walter Caruth, Mattie's almost-30-year-old bachelor son. Walter had inherited his father's work ethic, his mother's belief in caring for others, and both his parents' love of the land. An only child, he had sometimes been lonely and, the story goes, considered it his amazing good fortune when he won the hand of the beautiful and talented former debutante Earle Clark as his bride. The couple enjoyed wealth, social position and popularity. They spent their winters in the Ross Avenue town house and their summers in the spacious North Dallas plantation home. Two children, a son and a daughter, were born to Will and Earle—William Walter Caruth, Jr. and Mattie Caruth, who later would marry Col. D. Harold Byrd.

Will and Earle cared for the land and continued the family's philanthropic good deeds, which was passed on to their son, William Walter Caruth Jr. and his wife, Mabel Peters Caruth. The family is noted for its gifts to charity, to churches and to deserving individuals, the most lavish of which was its gift to Southern Methodist University in 1910. Founders of SMU were grappling with finding a proper location for a new university in Dallas when Will Caruth offered 520 acres, with one-half interest in all of the building lots out of a section of land bounded by Lovers Lane, Preston Road, Northwest Highway, and Airline Road plus 100 per cent interest in 200 additional acres east of the campus. The gift was mind-boggling—and immediately accepted.

Mattie Caruth lived for 22 years after her husband's death, until November 25, 1907. She and her son added land to the Caruth holdings, purchasing some of the property from her sister and brother-in-law, Anna and Walter Caruth.

Anna Worthington Caruth and her husband, Walter, in the meantime had moved, in 1881, to a 900-acre estate in East Dallas. The property, on Greenville Avenue, was bounded on the south by Belmont and extended beyond Mockingbird Lane to the north. The house, named Bosque Bonita, became a social hub of the city. Anna, by this time known everywhere as Annie, and Walter had four children—Martha or Mattie, Walter, William and Raymond (note the repetition of names!).

In 1926 a family disagreement over land erupted into the Dallas courts. Anna Worthington Caruth, then a widow, and her children, sued Will and Earle Clark Caruth claiming that his parents, William and Mattie, had acquired the Walter Caruth property with a promise of returning it for the same amount of money plus reasonable interest at a future date. The case, heard in Dallas courts in July of 1926, split the family into shreds, a split that continues, in some instances, until the present. The result was that the Walter Caruth heirs, who lost the case, added an "r" to the spelling of their name. Even now there are Caruths and Carruths in Dallas. Some, who sit together on community boards, may not even know how closely they are related. Caruth Street, spelled with the original one "r," bears the family name and NorthPark Shopping Center is located on Caruth property easily visible from Northwest Highway.

Lucinda Beckley Williams was a woman of rare accomplishments —both private and public—unusual for a woman of her time. She enjoyed success as a wife and mother, as a community religious leader, and later in her life as a professional counselor and writer of her autobiography, *The Golden Years*. With her husband and 10 others, she founded the First Baptist Church in Dallas.

Lucinda and William Williams started their move to Dallas from Belton in a wagon on November 12, 1867. Lucy carried their firstborn child, Ada, in her lap. It was during their trip that a plague of grasshoppers hit Texas. The insects were sometimes so thick that the travelers could hardly see and their wagon wheels slipped and slid on the crushed insects. A year and a half before, on her 22nd birthday, February 5, 1866, she had passed through Dallas on her way from her native Dade County, Missouri, to Waco to marry Col. Williams, 10 years her senior. When the Civil War ended, the Williamses, like most families of the time, were left penniless, and his law degree from the University of Missouri was virtually worthless. He took a job teaching school in Belton for a year before the couple moved to Dallas.

Arriving in the town, the young lawyer hung out his shingle and was joined the following year by John Stemmons, his war companion and old law partner from Missouri. Business was anything but brisk. In her book, Lucinda recalled:

> There were about four lawyers in Dallas well established.... There were some younger ones that were doing the best they could. These older lawyers were big hearted in most things, but did not mind at all letting the newcomer know that the ground was fully occupied without him. The newcomer could find work to do, but money conditions were hard still and lawyer's pay came very slowly. Everyone else was paid before the lawyer. We were not disquieted. We had each other and our precious baby. We knew nothing of long lonely evenings. I was perfectly content with the quiet, simple life, and we had food and raiment and every comfort.[19]

Young, energetic, educated and enthusiastic, Lucinda and William immediately became active in Dallas. One of their first acts was to help organize the First Baptist Church. Though Lucinda was pregnant often (giving birth to 10 children) she did not devote her full time to being a wife and mother. When William later became the organizing member of the Dallas Bar Association, she, remembering that she had sometimes felt ostracized in the early days of her husband's practice, devoted a great deal of time to counseling and mothering the wives of young attorneys.

In 1870 the Williamses bought their first home, located on several acres of land on Elm Street at what is now St. Paul. Seven of their 10 children were born in the house. It was also home to an increasing number of other children whose parents had died. This

Lucinda Beckley left her affluent family in Missouri and, on her 22nd birthday, traveled through Dallas to wed her sweetheart, Col. William Williams. She was a founder of Dallas's First Baptist Church.

led Lucinda to a lifetime commitment of mothering other people's children. It also helped to spark the founding of Buckner's Orphans Home. Robert C. Buckner was a wartime buddy and good friend of William Williams, and the two couples, William and Lucinda and Robert and Vienna Phillips Long Buckner, were neighbors. The two families, both committed to the Baptist church and both devoted to children, sought ways they could make a permanent contribution to the well-being of future generations. Buckner founded the Orphans Home; the Williams family contributed ideas, time, and money. In 1884 when the Williams family moved into a new home on Swiss Avenue, their oldest child, Amy, was 18 years old. Lucinda managed the large house, the increasing numbers of children, and volunteer activities, mostly centered around her church. She also began to write. When her husband died in May of 1910, she turned one of her numerous volunteer activities into a profession. She became a counselor at what is now Southwestern Baptist Theological Seminary in Fort Worth. In her book she explains why:

> I wanted something with a look ahead, a promise that would come. Best of all, the young people here, girls and boys, come to me and talk out their hearts, seeking motherly counsel and sympathy. I find them so ready to appreciate a little personal interest and kindly counsel. A kind, encouraging word seems to change the color of their hopes and ambitions for making the very best of every opportunity to count for good if they can. It is what we do for others that counts.[20]

Lucinda Williams survived all other founders of the First Baptist Church, being the last of the charter members to die in January of 1931.

By the time the Williams family moved to Swiss Avenue, an itinerant and criminal element had taken over downtown Dallas. Lucinda wrote that cowboys, after a night of revelry in the saloons, often rode through the streets shooting off their guns.

Margaret Davenport, who later married Clarence Shumate, recalled similar conditions. She was a little girl when she arrived in Dallas in the late 1860s with her widowed father, Dr. Silas Davenport, Dallas's first Episcopal rector. Father and daughter made their home in a downtown hotel. Margaret was forbidden to walk down Elm Street and was warned to stay on the right hand side of Main Street when coming or going from Akard to Lamar. "Gentlewomen," Margaret recalled in the latter years of her life, "were most careful as to the parts (of town) on which they let themselves be seen."[21] Unlike many of the citizens of that day who thought that closing saloons and dance halls would be bad for business, Dr. Davenport had no vested interest in the economics of the community and spoke out often and forcefully against the evils of his adopted city.

For his courage and because he treated the individual malefactors with dignity, the minister won, at first grudging respect and finally admiration from the hoodlum element. One day several of the town's leading gamblers went to the hotel where the Davenports were staying and asked to see the parson. When he appeared, he was handed a bag of money with this speech:

> Parson, we heard that you was figgerin' on puttin' up a meetin' house, and we figgered, too, that you was havin' an uphill pull and as you have treated us like we was more or less human, we thought we'd help you out a little, so we passed the bag around among the boys and packed it to you without delay and we want you to take and buy lumber and start your meetin' house.[22]

The news columns and editorials of the *Herald* were filled with tales of crime. "Crime is running away," read a *Herald* headline in February of 1886. But the reporting was cautious. Names were often omitted, even in cases of murder. "The front page was usually given over to reprinting sermons, to items about meetings—the Masons, a railroad gathering, those interested in making the Trinity navigable—to advertisements and to poetry. Even the poetry had an overriding theme of death and destruction. "Fair were our visions . . . . Our sleep grew troubled and our dreams grew wide," began a poem in

March of 1867. In the same month, the paper reported that "War and death have played sad havoc on the old families of the South...." "Johnson was shot twice in the heart," said one story, but who was Johnson?

In February of 1886, Caroline Wahrenberger drew the applause of the newspaper when she defended herself against an intruder:

> Saturday night about 12 o'clock, a man named Robert Howie, was shot by Mrs. Caroline Wahrenberger at her dwelling on Congress Avenue near the river, from the effect of which he died.... it appears the deceased... attempted to enter through a window into her sleeping apartment.... Howie came here with the federal troops some time since.... Under the circumstances Mrs. Wahrenberger did precisely what any other person would have done.... Alone and unprotected, she is threatened with violence. There have been so many assaults and robberies and burglaries in the city during the past few months that it is natural people should be suspicious of night prowlers.[23]

Saloons and gambling establishments flourished. Prostitutes, some from local families but many from other parts of the country, turned a section of near South Dallas into a red light district. Some of the houses in that area were owned by leading Dallas citizens.[24]

Belle Starr was by far the most famous of the female outlaws. Hers is a story more of legend than of fact. To some she was little more than a female Robin Hood bent on righting the wrongs of those dear to her. To others she was a cold-blooded murderer. To all Belle was flamboyant. Born in Missouri on February 3, 1848, to John and Elizabeth Hatfield Shirley, she was named Myra Maybelle. She was the middle child of seven: Preston, Charlotte Ann and John Allison, older siblings; Edward Benton, Mansfield and Cravens, younger brothers. When she was eight, the family moved from the community of Medoc, to Carthage, Missouri, where Myra attended the Carthage Female Academy.

During the unrest following the Civil War, the Shirley children took up with unsavory characters, and their parents, wanting to give them a fresh start, moved to Texas. Belle was a precocious, high-spirited, fun-loving 15-year-old who excelled in music and oratory but whose aggressive behavior made her unpopular with her peers and teachers. Preston and his wife, Mary Avilla Chelson Shirley, were the first of the family to move to Texas. The rest followed, Belle driving one of the Conestoga wagons from Missouri to Scyene where the family settled. In Scyene, she enrolled in a one-room school run by a Mrs. Poole. Older than most of the other students and academically advanced, she became bored and restless and attended class irregularly.

In July of 1866, a gang of outlaws including the Younger Brothers (Cole, Jim, John and Bob) and Jesse James arrived at the Shirley home. Friends from back in Missouri, they spent some time as guests of the family. The adult Shirleys might—or might not—have known that they were sheltering outlaws because the men were hiding out from the law after robbing a Missouri bank.

Eighteen-year-old Myra, whose social life had been severely limited in the tiny Texas village, was enamored. Some historians report a romance between her and Cole Younger, but this is speculation and Younger later denied it.

In any event, after the *desperados* rode off, Myra wasted no time grieving. She and James C. (Jim) Reed, a local suitor and petty criminal, were married on November 1, 1866, in Collin County in rites read by the Rev. S. M. Wilkins. Her parents were furious, and immediately shipped the 18-year-old bride off to live with Preston and Mary, who had moved to Palo Pinto. There followed a full year of feuding between father and husband over Myra. Jim won. Historians disagree over whether Jim lured Myra into a life of crime, or whether she encouraged him. Either way, they were not good for each other.

In September of 1869, at the farm home of the Reed family in Missouri, Myra gave birth to a daughter she named Rosie Lee and immediately, and for the rest of her life, called Pearl. Woven throughout the Belle Starr saga is the speculation that Pearl was the child of Cole Younger. This is hardly likely because the little girl was born 34 months after Belle and Jim were married; there is no record of Belle and Younger seeing each other during that time, and Younger denied fathering Belle's child.

Belle—still Myra—was a devoted mother. In 1870 she and Jim moved to California taking their baby with them. The next year, in 1871, a little boy was born. Myra named him Edward for her brother, who had been killed in a skirmish with the law. Now, with two babies, Belle longed for respectability and encouraged her husband to find a legitimate job so that the children could be reared in a loving, peaceful home. It was not to be. Jim soon ran afoul of the law and fled from California. Myra took the two children and returned to her parents' in Dallas. Jim soon joined them and for the next two years the couple lived on a farm in Scyene and managed a horse racing stable. In the summer of 1875, in what probably was a killing to claim a money award offered for his capture, Jim was shot by John Morris near McKinney.

After Jim's death, Myra—or Belle—made frequent trips from Scyene into Dallas. Once she moved with the children into Planter's Hotel downtown.

> Belle dressed and behaved in a most spectacular manner. She purchased a horse and a stud which she kept in the stables back of the hotel . . . . She dressed in black velvet, with long flowing skirts when she rode side-saddle, and wore white chiffon waists, a tight black jacket, high-topped boots and a man's Stetson hat turned up in front and decorated with an ostrich plume. The only peculiarity about this costume was that around her waist she wore a cartridge belt from which two revolvers were suspended in holsters. She attended the races, the circus and the county fair. She would enter bars and drink like a man or take her place at gaming tables for a try of her luck at dice, cards or roulette.
>
> When the mood struck her, she shocked the women and more respectable citizens of Dallas by changing into beaded and fringed buckskin costumes like those worn by Buffalo Bill, and riding at breakneck speed through the streets of the town, scattering everyone to the sidewalk. The constabulary and the whole town were afraid of her; and she gloried in being pointed out as the Bandit Queen. She had nothing to fear as long as there was no warrant for her arrest.[25]

For awhile, Myra ran a livery stable in Dallas and once was jailed, briefly, for being caught with a stolen horse. She then moved to Galena, Kansas, where she lived for a time with Bruce Younger, Cole's half brother.

The Galena sheriff, interviewed about Myra in 1938, remembered her as "a mighty good-looking woman, well educated, quietly dressed. Not tough." Myra's reputation as a beauty, like that of her wicked deeds, is grossly overrated. Doubtless she had a flair, the ability to dress and behave in manner that combined the flamboyant with the titillating and a certain aura that attracted men. But her pictures show her to be anything but a beautiful woman. Many men claimed to have been married to or had a relationship with Belle, but records show only two weddings.

After Bruce Younger, Belle soon surfaced as the friend and lover of Jim July, or "Blue Duck," the Indian outlaw. While with him, she became enamored with Sam Starr, a friend from former days. On June 5, 1880, Belle married Sam, a Cherokee Indian, in Ogallala, Nebraska. Sam was 23; Belle gave her age for the Cherokee Tribal Ceremony as 27; she was really 32. The couple moved to Oklahoma where they set up housekeeping in Porum in an isolated area Belle named Younger's Bend. (For Cole? For Bruce?)

Outlaws often found sanctuary at Younger's Bend. Sometimes Sam did not even know the identity of the men who were sheltered at the couple's two-room cabin with its little porch, small cellar and lean-to kitchen. There, the men behaved civilly with no hint of the behavior that made them *wanted* men. They even bowed their heads and listened to Belle say grace at every meal at her table. In one of the rare interviews Belle gave, datelined Fort Smith, Arkansas, *Belle* told the reporter:

Belle Starr was the most famous of early Texas female outlaws, but the tales of her escapades are more fiction than fact. There is no evidence that she ever held up a train, bank or stagecoach, or ever killed anybody.

You can just say that I am a friend to any brave and gallant outlaw, but have no use for that sneaking coward class of these who can be found in every locality, and who would betray a friend or comrade for the sake of their own gain. There are three or four jolly, good fellows on the dodge in my section, and when they come to my home they are welcome, for they are my friends . . . .[26]

In 1882 Belle and Sam were arrested for horse thievery, sentenced and sent to prison for nine months. Of all the letters, notes and texts that Belle may have written, a letter to her daughter, then 14, just before she left for prison is the only letter known to have survived. The children were then living with relatives. The letter was addressed to Miss Pearl Younger, Oswego, Kansas, and datelined Fort Smith, Arkansas:

My Dear Little One:
    It is useless to attempt to conceal my trouble from you and though you are nothing but a child I have confidence that my darling will bear with fortitude what I now write.
    I shall be away from you a few months, baby, and have only this consolation to offer you, that never again will I be placed in such humiliating circumstances and that in the future your tender little heart shall never more ache, or a blush called to your cheek on your mother's account. Sam and I were tried here, Jim West the main witness against us. We were found guilty and sentenced to nine months at the House of Correction, Detroit, Michigan, for which place we start in the morning.
    Now, Pearl, there is a vast difference in that place and a penitentiary; you must bear that in mind, and not think of mamma being shut up in a gloomy prison. It is said to be one of the finest institutions in the United States surrounded by beautiful grounds with fountains and everything nice. There I can have my education renewed, and I stand sadly in need of it. Sam will have to attend school and I think it is the best thing ever happened for him, and now you must not be unhappy and brood over our absence. It won't take the time long to glide by, and as we come home we will get you and then we will have such a nice time.
    Uncle Tom has stood by me nobly in our trouble . . . . Now baby, I will write to you often. You must write to your Grandma but don't tell her of this . . . . I do not want you to correspond with anybody in the Indian Territory. My baby, my sweetest little one, and you must mind me. Except Auntie—if you wish to hear from me Auntie will let you know.
    Destroy this letter as soon as read. As I told you before, if you wish to stay a while with your Mamma Mac, I am willing. But you must devote your time to your studies. Bye, bye, sweet baby mine.

BELLE STARR[27]

Sam Starr was killed by a fellow Oklahoma outlaw in 1886, and Belle died on her 41st birthday, February 3, 1889, at dusk. She was shot in the back with a shotgun loaded with turkey shot, about two miles from Younger's Bend as she rode horseback on her way home from visiting neighbors. Some historians believe she was accidentally killed by her son who mistook her for a marshal coming to arrest him. Edgar A. Watson, near whose home the killing took place, was arrested for the murder but was released for lack of evidence. The women of Belle's neighborhood prepared her body for burial; the men made the coffin and she was laid to rest, according to her own request, in the front yard of her home. The grave is surrounded by a stone wall some two feet high with limestone slabs tilted overtop into a V like the roof of a house. White marble at the head of the grave is inscribed with the figure of a horse with the BS brand on its shoulder topped by a large star and a bell. Below this is a hand clasped about a bouquet of flowers. The inscription reads:

BELLE STARR
Born in Carthage, Missouri
February 3, 1848
Died February 3, 1889

Shed not for her the bitter tear
Nor give the heart to vain regret,
'Tis but the casket that lies here,
The gem that filled it sparkles yet.

Belle Starr and Her Times, written by Glenn Shirley and published in 1982 by the University of Oklahoma Press, is probably the most authentic of all materials on Belle. Shirley, after careful research and meticulous documentation, concludes: "There is no evidence that she (Belle) ever held up a train, bank or stagecoach or killed anybody."[28]

The turbulent 1860s were drawing to a close. Natural disasters in the last half of the 1860s brought additional loss and suffering to the people of Dallas.

There were floods. In May of 1866, the Trinity River overflowed its banks. Water was 56 1/2 feet deep. The tiny town of Dallas became an isolated island with all communication cut off for a week. Ross Avenue was a river.

There was violent weather. On May 26, 1867, a tornado ripped through the countryside of what is now North Dallas wreaking its worst havoc around what is now Audelia and Forest Lane. Nine people were killed, among them Eliza Prigmore, 10, and three members of the Volney Coldwell family.

There were plagues. Yellow fever hit in September of 1867. While most of it was confined to South Texas, it created fear everywhere and a few cases were reported in Dallas. The malady was so devastating that it delayed most public meetings. In November of 1867, a grasshopper plague devastated the morale of Dallas citizens, the same plague that the Williams rode through on their way from Belton to Dallas. The invasion made housekeeping all but impossible. Nobody could walk outside without crushing grasshoppers, and, no matter how carefully a woman worked to keep her home free of the invaders, they flew, crawled or crept into everything. Although the plague was brief—at the most three weeks—it seemed like forever.

In addition to natural catastrophes—fire, flood, turbulent weather, epidemics and plagues—and human-made disasters—violence, gambling, prostitution, murder—the people of Dallas were still reeling from the aftermath of the Civil War. All elected Dallas County officials were tossed out and replaced with men who had been Union sympathizers:

> On Saturday evening last, all county officers were removed by order of the District Commander and replaced by newly appointed ones. Among those tossed out was John Neely Bryan. All the new ones will qualify to be sworn in except Mr. A. Buchanan as county commissioner. He died several weeks ago.[29]

Even in the darkest days, there were signs of hope. It was as if, in the most critical times, Dallas was—as it would prove to be again and again in the years ahead—setting its course toward the future.

Black people, freed from slavery, began to congregate together. Black communities were formed along Alpha and Noel Roads in far north Dallas, and Little Egypt began at what is now the vicinity of Abrams and Northwest Highway. In what is now Oak Cliff, a large community of black people camped at Ten Mile Creek and Bonnie View Road until they could build their homes. In downtown Dallas, Blacks established their Deep

Ellum Community at what is now Elm, Central and Good streets. This coming together provided the setting for the first black music, art and theater.

Still, freedom had not brought economic equity. Freed black men and women worked for $8 to $12 per month. While the price of farmland was a minuscule $2.50 to $7.50 per acre with unimproved acreage from $1.50 to $3.50, few could afford to buy. When income is but $10 per month, there is no way to save or invest.

In 1867 the first train arrived in Dallas. Two stories in *The Dallas Herald,* the one right underneath the other, record both the exultation and the frustration at the start of the railroad era:

ARRIVAL OF THE FIRST TRAIN

> Wednesday, August 28 will long be remembered as an important day in the history of our young city.
>
> At about 12 noon, the shrill whistle of the locomotive indicated the near approach of the long looked for train, and a large number of citizens congregated near the depot to witness its arrival.
>
> The cars now arrive here at 6 p.m. and leave about 5 in the morning, and should any change be made, our readers will be promptly notified.[30]

True to its promise, the *Herald* reported:

OFF THE TRACK

> The train due here on Wednesday evening did not arrive until the evening of the following day, having been off the track several times between here and Millican. On Friday morning the downtown train had proceeded but a few miles when it again took to the woods, but we believe none were injured either time. The continued heavy rains have rendered the road bed very soft and caused the track to sink under the weight of the train and we may expect the regular trains to be somewhat irregular for a few days.[31]

The first train to arrive in Dallas in 1867 created a sensation, but those first trains were as often off the tracks as on them.

The dream of a navigable Trinity resurfaced, as it would again and again. In 1866 the Texas legislature voted to incorporate the Trinity Slack Water Navigation Company. The state would furnish the money and collect the tolls to put boats on the Trinity with at least 35 boats to be floating within two years. Finally, in May of 1868, the first boat, Job Boat No. I, made it up the Trinity to Dallas. It had been slow going. The first steamboat built in Dallas was launched on December 17, 1868. Named Sallie Haynes for the daughter of Dr. and Mrs. John W. Haynes, the boat was 87 feet long and 18 feet "abeam." Sallie, the young woman, broke a bottle of sparkling wine over the bow to launch her ship. Wild celebrations ensued. News stories and editorials flooded the *Herald*. On its first trip to Galveston, the Sallie Haynes and another boat coming up the Trinity, met at Trinidad in Henderson County; the river was so narrow that the boats could not pass each other and finally had to exchange cargo and return to their points of origin. Undaunted, Dallas city fathers were certain that a new era had begun and on February 6, 1869, after the boat had reached Dallas on February 3, a long poem in the *Herald* lauded the future; its final verse:

> As for wagons and oxen we will have no use
> We will turn our mules and horses loose—
> And just so long as Old Time remains,
> We'll bless the builders of Sallie Haynes.

The Sallie Haynes was not long for this world. She made a few sluggish journeys up and down the Trinity before hitting a snag 10 miles southwest of Palestine and sinking.

The town had a couple of boosts to its economy in the late 1860s with John Tenison's saddlery shop opening in 1867 followed by G. H. Schoellkopf's in 1869. These two enterprises made Dallas the world center of leather and buffalo hide business. The first bank, established by A. C. Camp and W. H. Gaston, opened in 1868.

In 1869 Dallas got four more positive growth signs:

- Its first public water supply when pipes were laid from Browder Springs, now Old City Park, to residences. Water wells had proved insufficient to meet the growing city's demands.

- The formation of the Dallas County Medical Society.

- The opening of a free ferry to pedestrians and horseback riders. Of the 86 members of the Free Trinity Association, Sarah Cockrell was the only woman.

- Ten new streets. Dallas was growing eastward and to John Neely Bryan's original 18 streets, these were laid out and named: Sycamore (now Akard), Oleander (now Ervay), Harwood, Bryan, Live Oak, Masten, Bullington, Martin, Murphy and Stone.

Dallas was on the threshold of a new decade and the women of the city were ready for it.

10

DALLAS'S DAWNING DAYS

Dallas was ready to begin, or more appropriately, ready to burst forth into a blossoming period, but you wouldn't have known it to look at the facts at the outset of the 1870s decade.

The city was growing—in numbers of people, as a business base, in national recognition with a reputation as a good place to rear children.

Dallas County's population had increased almost 50 per cent between 1860 and 1870 growing from 8,775 to 13,329, but the town itself had almost quadrupled from 775 to 3,000 people. It had 18 stores including four groceries, a hardware store on Elm Street and two recently opened saddlery shops. It had two flour mills and three hotels: Crutchfield House, William Tell House and the Union Hotel. The Crutchfield was the most desirable. There for $2 in gold you could lodge for a week. This included room and board, but it also meant eight people to a room in four double beds with one wash bowl and one towel per person per week. Nothing was mentioned about bathing facilities.

You could worship in any one of 11 churches: Baptist, Catholic, Christian, Colored (!), Episcopal, Methodist, Presbyterian (Old School or Cumberland)—your choice of two for some of the denominations. The court house and city hall served as houses of worship on Sunday mornings for some of the sects that had not yet built places of worship.

In size, Dallas County had 576,000 acres, or 900 square miles laid out in sections of 640 acres each. The town was almost exactly in its center and was precisely 30 miles square.

On August 5, 1871, the town got its first fire department. Opened on Austin Street, and a bit later moved to Poydras, it had 14 volunteers with W. C. Conner as chief. Called the Hook & Ladder Company No. 1, it expanded to 50 volunteers within the year. Cedar cisterns at Houston and Main Street and at Market and Elm Street provided water to fight the fires. One of the department's first calls was to fight a fire at 17 Main on the north side of the street between Houston and Jefferson. Here, Professor E. B. Lawrence had established the first business college in the region, which he also used as music headquarters for bands he delighted in organizing. The facilities were large enough for band concerts and dances, and the professor often provided entertainment for Dallas citizens there. On Halloween night, the band had just struck up "The Danube Waltzes" when dancers saw flames. A lamp too close to the decorations had set them afire. The blaze was beyond the control of those who tried to smother them. Someone set off on foot to sound the alarm. Soon Dallas Hook and Ladder Company No. 1 and most of its volunteers were on the scene. They began to pump furiously; nothing happened. Alas, someone had used up the water and overlooked refilling the cistern—or the water had simply leaked out. The fire chief ran next door to the saloon and wine house of M. Caperton where he helped himself to several barrels of wine. Fire department volunteers and dancers formed a brigade and soon extinguished the fire with bucketsful of Caperton's wine. The dance then continued.[1]

Dallas also built itself a new brick courthouse in 1871 to replace the crude structure built in 1856.

Editorial commentary was glowing: "Who doubts today that Dallas will be the Empire City of the North—the depot where shall be concentrated untold wealth?"[2]

To all appearances, it seemed Dallas was ready to burst forth—and it was.... But there was another side to the story.

No streets were paved. In downtown Dallas on Elm Street the mud was from two to five feet deep when it rained. When there was no rain, the dust was so thick that

Dallas's first fire department, the Dallas Hook and Ladder Company No. 1, almost flubbed its first conflagration when it found the cisterns dry. It put out the fire with spirits from the liquor store next door.

women venturing forth covered their faces with their handkerchiefs. Housekeeping was a daily losing battle because the dirt seeped in and dust covered floors, ceilings and furniture. Cleaning equipment consisted of old rags, which were not plentiful, soap which was scarce, and water which had to be drawn from wells and heated on wood stoves.

Vice was rampant. The "Tenderloin District" on the southwest corner of downtown was open 24 hours a day. Gambling halls were solid on the north side of Main from Houston to Austin. Sixteen gambling houses, eight licensed saloons, a shooting gallery and six pool halls were attractions for "gentlemen." No women were allowed except those who served the pleasures of the men. These were the prostitutes and the handful of others, including at one time Belle Starr, who dealt cards and flirted with the men.

"The country is definitely a white man's country," exulted the *Directory of the City of Dallas,* in 1875, in what was an understatement. The best of wives were either nameless or dead and mourned.

But the women were something more than wives; they were also people, and they were about to make their presence felt in large and significant ways. The men who chose to come to Dallas were, almost without exception, adventurers. Even those with fine minds and a good education were imbued with the entrepreneurial spirit. They were determined, as the Dallas reputation so often repeats, to carve a city out of a territory that had no reason for being—no natural terrain, no inland waterways, no scenic glory.

The women were something else. Many had grown up in an atmosphere of wealth, culture, refinement and education. Some were graduates of the Seven Sister Schools. Others had gone to private academies for young women. From the first they expected the "good life" for their children. They demanded churches and schools, art, music, theater, literature. When such was not available in the frontier town, they got busy and secured it.

It is doubtful that any decade in the history of Dallas drew more women who would make a lasting impact on the city than the 10 years between 1870 and 1880. The women who came were educators and organizers, lecturers, artists, musicians, poets and businesswomen. They were crusaders and they were philanthropists. They were also—most all of them—wives and mothers.

In the early 1870s a large number of German people came to Dallas, some by way of New York and Chicago and others up from Galveston. The women among the skilled craftsmen, saddle and furniture makers were accustomed to getting together to accomplish a common goal. In 1871 these newcomers organized the Dallas German Ladies Aid Society "for the promotion of morals and benevolence." They did not call it a club and it was not chartered until February 21, 1889, thus other groups had the recognition of being "first." They were simply a group of neighbors who knew they could best accomplish a purpose in unity. They met in each other's homes and sometimes in Zion Evangelical Lutheran Church, which they soon formed. Three of the German women arriving in the early 1870s were Pauline Gunther with her husband, Herman; Sophia Gramatky, with her husband John, and Louise Dietrich with her husband Herman. The three incorporators of the club in 1889 were Fran Bayer, Mary A. Bohne and Dora Nussbaumer. From the first the society concentrated on serving others. It lent money, repaired houses and later paid light, gas and water bills for indigent people who could not afford it. Every cent was meticulously accounted for: carfare for a young boy, 25 cents; plumber for Mr. Hope, $2.50; carfare for Mrs. Wagner, 50 cents; gas (60 cents) and water (54 cents) for Mrs. Marks. As the coffers grew, so did the philanthropy. After the turn of the Century (in 1922) it gave $25 to the Dixon Colored Orphanage and $50 to the Welfare Council. By 1928 it was reaching beyond the state to give $100 to the Florida storm sufferers.

Two women, Ella M. Harris Abrams, who arrived in 1869, and Belle Fonda Schneider, who came in 1879, "framed" the decade. Working together they would impact the cultural climate of the community in ways that many women since have built upon. They founded the Dallas Symphony Club, which would one day become the Dallas Symphony Orchestra.

The city directory in 1875 bragged that Dallas was a "white man's country," and indeed it was. The best of wives were either nameless or dead and mourned.

Ella Abrams arrived in the city six months before the dawn of the decade after she married William H. Abrams on June 16, 1869. The daughter of W. A. and Fanny Murray Harris of Fauquier County, Virginia, she was educated at the Convent of Visitation in St. Louis. Her father was a United States Congressman from Virginia who later was appointed by President Franklin Pierce as ambassador to Argentina. He also edited the *Washington Union.*

Belle Schneider married Jules Edouard Schneider and moved to Dallas in 1879, where six years previously he had founded the Schneider-Davis Wholesale Grocery Company. Belle had grown up in wealth and privilege in Louisville, Kentucky, and as a 25-year-old bride, she transferred to Dallas, as fully as she could, her understanding of an appropriate lifestyle. Belle Schneider was an early prototype that women emulated for at least the next hundred years devoting both her time and her money to social, cultural and philanthropic endeavors. In the course of a few years she had four children—Florence Kate, who married Bruce F. Morgan; Elisa von Stracka who wed Leon Blum; Georgia Fonda, who married Edward H. Cary, and Jules Edouard Schneider, Jr.

Belle, Jules, Florence, Elisa, Georgia and Jules, Jr. lived in a grand house on Ross Avenue facing Akard Street. The society columns reported her parties in lavish detail and, in so doing, gave a glimpse of the opulence of the Schneider house, which held treasures, not only inherited from the childhood homes of both Belle and Jules, but with selections from their travels abroad.

Belle Fonda Schneider was a founder of the Dallas Symphony.

> ... The hostess' Steinway Grand was drawn into the spacious hall with its dome staircase, its hand-carved Moorish arch, its Arabesque frieze, its Egyptian bronzes, its lovely Byzantine chandeliers, its inlaid tables, its fleur-de-lis parquetrie, its Turkish tapestries, its tall graceful palms and its beautiful stained glass window, showing an Alhambra scene, made a fitting setting for the lyrics of the masters ....[3]

Belle Schneider's lavish parties were matched by her philanthropic contributions and she, like women who would follow her through the years, often used the house as a setting to make good things happen for the city. She was one of the founders and the first president of the Woman's Home and Day Nursery, an organizer and president for many years of the Ladies Musical Club, a charter member of the Dallas Shakespeare Club, a founder of the Dallas Art Association and of the Carnegie Public Library, a charter member of the Dallas Woman's Club and a member of Dallas Pen Women in addition to serving as a co-founder of the Symphony Club. She was "possessed of large means and the desire to use them for the benefit of mankind ... she has given generous contributions and her heart has always been open to the cries of suffering humanity."[4]

An avid churchwoman, she was an early member of St. Matthew's Cathedral, where she was assistant director of the choir and sang in a quartet. She sent two of her daughters, Kate and Elisa, to study music in Europe; they became prominent in the musical world.[5]

Amelia Huvelle was a 17-year-old school girl when Belle Schneider came to Dallas, but it was she more than any other woman of her time who followed in the footsteps of the grande dame in her concern for children and child care.

Amelia was a feisty little girl, nine years old, when she arrived in Dallas from Waco with her parents, Nicholas and Amelia Huni Antoine. Born in Alexandria, Louisiana, in 1862, she had moved to Waco when she was three years old. Six years later the family settled in the heart of downtown Dallas on Commerce Street at Akard where the Adolphus Hotel is now is located. Amelia watched the mule-drawn streetcars turn in the muddy streets at the end of the line from her living room window. Sometimes she sneaked out and persuaded a driver to allow her to drive the mules. Appalled at this unladylike behavior, Mrs. Antoine would severely reprimand her child, only to have Amelia repeat the deed at any time she thought she could get away with it.

The Antoines had family and many friends in Louisiana and went almost every year to New Orleans to celebrate Mardi Gras. It was there in 1880 that she met Camile

H. Huvelle. The two had much in common. Camile was a native of Louvignes, France, born in 1858. He had come to the United States with his widowed mother and a brother when he was 11 years old. At age 16 he had moved to Dallas and at age 22, when he met Amelia, was already on his way to being an outstanding businessman. Amelia's father was born in France and had emigrated to America as a young man.

Back home in Dallas following Mardi Gras, Camile Huvelle set out to win the vibrant and fashionable Amelia. She had said she liked music. He invited her to accompany him to the opera. He bought two boxes and included six of her relatives because a young lady could not go to the opera with a gentleman unchaperoned. The presence of a chaperon was not essential nor condoned in most of early Dallas society, but both the Huvelles and the Antoines were products of the custom.

Amelia Huvelle gave her home on South Ervay Street to the Dallas Day Nursery Association in 1929.

The year after Amelia met Camile, in 1881, they were married. Three children were born to the union—Estelle, Leon and Rene. The family moved to a large home at 577 South Ervay Street and prospered. Amelia hired the help she needed to manage her home and help with the children and turned her attention to volunteer work. Her greatest concern was the quality of health and education for children.

On January 4, 1916, Amelia was elected president of the Dallas Federation of Women's Clubs. She was elected because of her commitment to others; she, in turn, organized and directed the membership to respond to the needs of women and children. A person of great insight, Amelia understood that women could not always work profitably within their homes while they cared for their children, and she determined to establish a child care center. As early as March 7, 1916, the Federation had opened a lodge for unemployed women with a nursery attached. Here domestic sciences were taught at night, not only for the residents of the lodge, but for other women in the community. Joan Hamilton of the Department of Domestic Sciences, Southern Methodist University, donated her services as a teacher. Later taken over by the Dallas Kindergarten Association, it was named the Cora Street Nursery. In 1929 Amelia gave the Huvelle homestead on South Ervay Street to the Dallas Nursery, Kindergarten and Infant Welfare Association. At this point the Cora Street Nursery was brought in and the center rechristened the Amelia Huvelle center, the name it still bears. The nursery, starting with six babies, was soon overcrowded. One room in the house was converted into a training center for mothers. Fitted with a dozen sewing machines lent by Dallas merchants and supervised by Lena Stoneheart, the women made aprons, which Dallas merchants purchased at $1.00 per dozen. By current standards, this is a measly amount, but for many mothers at that time it meant they were able to buy milk for their babies.

Equally concerned with education, Amelia Huvelle provided food for the mind as well as food for the body. As Federation leader, she presented a series of lectures and training sessions both for the members and for the public on such topics as prenatal health, social agencies, civic federations, public health and modern fiction. Once when a county rest room became a public nuisance, she held a luncheon for the County Commissioners (all men) and persuaded them to assume expense of maintenance because "the rest room is so beneficial to country people." The Commissioners willingly agreed, but provided no money. The Federation then assumed the financial responsibility for keeping the room open and providing a caretaker.

Amelia Huvelle was the first woman to be honored with the Linz Award, established in 1924 and given annually "to the person who has rendered the greatest unselfish service to the community during the current year." It was presented to her in 1929.

In 1935 upon her retirement as chairperson of the woman's division of Community Chest, Amelia was honored at a luncheon at which time Mrs. W. P. Zumwalt read a poem. This is a portion:

The Cullum Family tree by Richard Davis Schwalm from Mary Nash's "Damn Proud People."

> There are many children being comforted and fed
> The poor and needy ones provided clothes and bed.
> And a whole community, and its social problems faced.
> There looms high for friends, Sincerity, Loyalty and Grace.
> Proof of the kind of friend that gives courage to the heart.
> Encouraging others to see their duty, and do their part
> Always bringing faith and comfort to the day,
> Smiling, boosting, scattering sunshine along the way . . . .[6]

Elizabeth Johnson Robertson Hereford, reared in New Orleans, was married to John Bronaugh Hereford on March 19, 1861, and moved to Dallas 11 years later in 1872. The great granddaughter of Gen. James Robertson of Tennessee, Elizabeth was another imported Dallasite from a family of wealth and culture. Her arrival coincided with the opening of the Cedars as an exclusive residential neighborhood and with Jane Monroe Browder's career as a realtor. Elizabeth and John owned four different homes in the Cedars, at 205, 207, and 211 Cadiz between Browder and Ervay and around the corner at 228 Browder. All were razed when R. L. Thornton Freeway skirted downtown Dallas.

Elizabeth and John had six children—Mary Chinn, John Bronaugh III, Anna Lobdell, James Stirling, Felix Senette and Catherine Stirling. The last four were born in Dallas. Elizabeth was a writer, whose book, *Rebel Rhymes*,[7] was published by G. P. Putnam's Sons in 1888.

Adding to the cultural climate of the young town, the Field Opera House opened on the South Side of Main between Austin and Lamar in 1873. On opening night, September 30, 1873, the Crisp Sisters, Jessie and Cecelia, in Bolivar Lytton's *Richelieu*, appeared to rave reviews. The theater was owned by brothers, John and J. Y. Field, the former married to Kate Knight Field, born in Dallas, the eleventh child of Obadiah and Serena Hughes Knight. She was among the first of the second generation of prominent citizens.

At about the time the *Herald* was lauding the town's new Opera House, a family that would continue to contribute to Dallas in multiple ways—religion, the arts, theater, journalism—through all its decades arrived from Tipton County, Tennessee.

Marcus and Elizabeth Cullum gave Dallas continuing generations of civic and philanthroptic leaders.

Their name was Cullum. When the Cullum stories are told and written, the emphasis is always on Marcus Hiram Cullum, patriarch of the Cullum clan, Methodist minister, church founder, pioneer. Elizabeth Jane Davis Cullum is rarely mentioned. When Eloise Cullum was asked in 1992 what her grandmother did, her answer was, "She had babies." That she did—12 of them. But there is so much more. She provided the home and the pivot that provided leadership for Dallas in every generation up to the present.

Elizabeth Cullum lost four of her children—James Lafayette at age 16; Martha Elizabeth and Margaret Alice, both at age one; and Marcus Hiram, Jr. at birth. She raised eight—four sons and four daughters—Jacob David, William Henry, Amanda Caroline (Cal), Emma Eudora, Frances Ella, Llora, Ashley Wilson and Thomas Marvin. She had 61 grandchildren. Family historian Earl C. Cullum said that 50 of the grandchildren grew to adulthood.

Sixteen Cullums comprised the original Dallas settlers—Elizabeth and her husband, the Rev. Marcus Cullum; their sons and their wives, Jacob and Lou Harper Cullum; William and Isadora (Icy) Cullum; Cal and her husband, James Isaac Jones; single daughters, Emma, Frances and Llora; little boys, Ashley and Marvin; and three grandchildren, Willie and Daisy, children of Lou and Jacob; and Viola, daughter of Icy and Will.

Traveling by stagecoach, boat and train from Tipton County, Tennessee, via Memphis, New Orleans, Galveston and Houston, the Cullums arrived in Dallas in 1873. They bought 10 acres of land in a rustic, unsettled area two miles north of Dallas bounded by what is now Cedar Springs Road and Turtle Creek.

In 1874, the Rev. Marcus Hiram Cullum founded Oak Lawn Methodist Church.

In 1873, the year before the Cullums founded Oak Lawn Methodist Church, the Dallas literary climate was enriched by the arrival of Mary Hunt McCaleb Odom, the bride of D. McCaleb, an editor of the *Herald*. A poet, she was an early Dallas feminist. Mary was a prolific writer whose articles and poems were often published in the *Herald*.

Dallas did not quite know what to do with such an outspoken woman as Mary. Many people were clearly fascinated by her but puzzled by the feminist bent in writing. Sam H. Dixon in his book, "Poets and Poetry of Texas," published in 1885, expresses a prevailing sentiment of the day: "Mrs. Odom loves her sex and has *peculiar* (underlining mine) ideas of their station." He quotes this stanza of her many poems:

Eloise Cullum, above, owns businesses in Dallas and Rockwall and Lee Cullum, below, is a triple threat journalist.

> Best and noblest part of man's life here
> Is that wherein he loves and honors woman;
> 'Tis there his soul is lifted to a higher sphere—
> In all things else his nature is but human.[8]

Mary Hunt was born around 1846 in Mead County, Kentucky, to Harper P. and Margaret Tompkins Hunt, who moved to Vicksburg, Mississippi, shortly after her birth. She was, according to Dixon, a beloved and spoiled child, whose father's wealth and mother's indulgence provided the best education of her day. She began to write poetry as a little girl and had many of her poems published in Vicksburg papers. As a teenager, she fell in love with D. McCaleb and married him around 1863 during the Civil War when she was 17 or 18 years old. Within the year she was the mother of a son; later she gave birth to two more little boys.

Mary continued to write after the family moved to Galveston where her husband joined the editorial department of the *Galveston News*.

Shortly after she was married, Mary's poems and other manuscripts were collected by her teacher-mentor, Maj. W. C. Capers, and published under the alias she used at that time, L'Eclair. Her husband found both quality and substance as well as beauty in her work and encouraged her to write under her own name. The first poem, published in the *Galveston News* under the name Mary Hunt McCaleb created a furor because it offended the sensitivity of some readers who believed that kissing was immoral. It was entitled "Just So," and ended:

> A kiss is so very entrancing,
> It bears such a marvelous charm;
> Don't tell me anything so delightful
> Could possibly be any harm.[9]

Mary McCaleb was a superwoman in writer Dixon's estimation. He said of her:

> Mrs. McCaleb was publishing a great deal . . . though no domestic duties were neglected, and her little ones lacked none of a mother's loving care . . . .
> She possesses a keen sense of the ridiculous and an almost inexhaustible fund of humor and wit, that even the longest and most severe illness has failed to subdue. Generous and devoted in all attachments . . . .[10]

Adversity deepened and strengthened Mary's writing. She was never maudlin, but often in her poetry expressed woman's ability to survive. Even as a young girl, in writings during the Civil War, her poems expressed depth not often reached in the patriotic themes of that day. Her beloved father died; she lost two children to death, an infant and a small daughter. Then, she nursed her husband through a long illness. Through all of these trials, Mary continued to write.

After her husband's death, Mary traveled and wrote, while preparing her poems for publication. A wealthy cattleman and rancher, T. L. Odom, read some of her work, was impressed and wrote to her. A correspondence ensued. The two met and soon were engaged. Mary Hunt McCaleb was married to Odom in the parlor of her girlhood Vicksburg home, where her own parents had been wed. Shortly after her marriage, G. P. Putnam & Sons, New York, published a book of her poems.

Her second husband, like her first, encouraged Mary to write. Strangely, or perhaps not so strangely, she gained the most acceptance with her gentler poems. Women responded to topics that were most familiar to them. A rare poem in this vein, called "Little Relics," is an ode to the baby she lost and begins:

> Only a baby's picture,
> With dimpled shoulders bare;
> Large blue eyes softly beaming,
> And rings of golden hair.

And ends . . .

> Why do I keep and love them,
> When so many years have fled?
> Don't you know? They were my baby's,
> And the little one is dead.[11]

It was one of Mary's earliest writings, called "Lenare," written when she was but a girl, that established her as a poet. The series were story-length and in them she viewed the Civil War, not in patriotic gushing, but as a tragedy for both the North and South.

In 1873, the same year that Mary McCaleb came to Dallas, Elizabeth D. James Mellersh also began to put her imprint on the cultural life of the city. Her contributions were equally as important as Mary's, but she did it in a different way. She turned her big, beautiful home into a haven for literary club meetings, dances, teas and other cultural and social events.

Elizabeth James was born June 26, 1837, in Memphis, Tennessee, and married George M. Mellersh there on November 24, 1858, at age 21. During the Civil War, while her husband was fighting for the Southern Cause, she lived in Memphis and later, with him, in Pennsylvania. The couple lost four babies, three in Tennessee and one in Newcastle, Pennsylvania, before they moved to Dallas in 1873. Arriving by stagecoach from Texarkana, the couple set up housekeeping on a large tract of land on what is now Dickason Street. First, they lived in a small log home, later enclosing it inside a larger frame cottage. In 1889, architect W. H. Harrell designed their home, which they named "Oak Lawn." It was a two-story showplace brick mansion located on Oak Lawn and Maple, on the spot where the Melrose Hotel is now located. Across the street from Oak Lawn Methodist Church, it was the site for many of the public meetings and social events supporting the fledgling church. The house got its name from the many oak trees around it, and is the namesake of today's Oak Lawn section of the city.

Elizabeth and George had four surviving children, all daughters. Two—Frances Maria Anne, born in 1865, and Georgie G., born in 1867—came to Dallas with their parents. The other two—Cyrene Jewel, born in 1873, and Elizabeth Sarah, born in 1867, were native Dallasites. Fannie, Georgia, Rena and Bessie, as the girls were known, brought dozens of friends of their own to the family mix so that men and women, old and young kept the house filled with excitement.

In 1874 the Sisters—six of them—came to Dallas. Related through their faith as Catholics and through the Ursuline order, they came to establish a school. Led by Sister Mary Joseph Holly, they arrived from Galveston on January 28, 1874. Their charge was to open a school for girls, as a branch of the order and educational system of Galveston. The project had been carefully planned with repeated committee meetings to determine the best way to meet educational needs of girls in the frontier town to the north of the Bay City.

The group was as diverse as it was dedicated. In addition to Sister St. Joseph Holly, born in Austria in 1842 and 12 years a nun, there was Sister St. Paul Kaufmann, Galveston-born in 1830, the first girl born in that city; Sister Mary Patrick Flaherty, born in Ireland in 1846 and three years a nun; Sister Mary Francis Xavier Vindrier, born in France and only three years a nun; Sister St. Bernard Dowd, a lay sister from Ireland, older than the others; and Sister Philomena Gerngros, born in Germany in 1869.

Dallas was not a Catholic town. There was only one known Catholic family and two Catholic bachelors in the fledgling community. Even so, the parish priest, Father Joseph Martiniere, insisted that it was imperative for his church to take the lead in educating girls and young women. The small entourage arrived by train and went immediately to the frame church, only recently erected, where they had Mass to the accompaniment of noisy pigeons in the rafters. Sister Mary Patrick, who was the resident wit, announced that the devil, "in a flutter over the sudden appearance of the army of the Lord, were plotting and planning against the sisters."[12]

Upon leaving the church, Mother St. Joseph inquired about the convent; and Bishop Dubius, who had asked the Galveston community to provide nuns for the school, pointed to a small frame cottage. The nuns were astonished when they entered the crude building. It was absolutely bare. There was no furniture of any kind, no stove, no way to heat the building, no place to sleep. Nor had their luggage arrived on the train with them. They did not know, until several people came to welcome them, that other arrangements had been made for them. The W. A. Rodgers family and a Mrs. Neville took the sisters home and invited them to stay for the night.

Mother St. Joseph Holly, above, founder, and Mother St. Paul, below, who succeeded as mother superior of Ursuline Academy.

At breakfast the next morning, Sister Bernard had them all laughing when she told that she had awakened in the middle of the night, sat up in bed and been astonished to see another old woman across the room staring back at her. It had been so long since she had seen herself in a mirror that she was not immediately aware she was viewing her own image!

On February 2, 1874, Father Dubuis blessed the little house, established the cloister and gave it canonical status. With that, Ursuline Academy, the first private school for girls in Dallas, was in session.

Ursuline opened with seven students. The long, severe winter would have defeated any but the most determined teachers. One large room served as community room, refectory, oratory, classroom and chapter room. It was heated by one stove. Adjacent sleeping quarters were cramped and cold. The roof leaked. Snow and rain splattered through, hitting the hot stove and bouncing off to blister the skin of those who hovered around it.

By the end of March, Sister St. Philomena, who was ill when she arrived and whose strength had been further sapped by the austere conditions, returned to Galveston. But the school grew and prospered. At least seven girls had crowded into the already overcrowded building as boarders. By June, four months after it opened, there were 50 girls enrolled. Even the faith of such devout Sisters as the Ursuline quintet was hard-pressed to meet the needs. They decided they must have an additional room immediately and reminded the Bishop that he had promised a two-story building when they came to

Dallas to open their school. He met their request with equal firmness. He insisted that the Ursulines go out into the community and solicit funding for their school. Never mind that this was not a Catholic community nor that its people were not accustomed to having women ask for money. Many of them, in fact, had never seen a Roman Catholic sister. Reverend Mother St. Joseph reminded him of the nun's obligations to live in confinement. He immediately lifted the cloister requirement. Astonished, the five women acquiesced, only to reverse their decision the next day. Finally, two of them—Sisters St. Joseph and St. Paul—in great trepidation, set out to follow the bidding of their bishop. They went first to the Rodgers home where they had been guests upon their arrival and whose daughter was enrolled in the school. Asking for donations was almost impossible for the two sisters, who had long lived cloistered in silence, prayer and reverence and whose talents lay in teaching children. Later one would acknowledge that the bishop's purpose, in ordering them to solicit funding for the school "was to make us practice humility and to give the inhabitants of Dallas the valued opportunity of meeting the sisters and exercising almsgiving . . . ."

The people of Dallas must have been as cautious about their new neighbors soliciting for money as the nuns were in asking for it. One man who promised them several acres of land withdrew it after his Baptist wife's minister had a talk with him. But there were also successes. Tom Crutchfield, owner of Crutchfield House, whose daughter had been to the Ursuline school in Galveston, said that he would seek subscriptions for them from his friends. Several promised a contribution as soon as their crops came in. In the meantime, Father Martiniere, with the permission of the Bishop, got the donation of eight more acres of land and a loan of $2,000 to begin the building of the new school. The land had to be turned down when a clear title could not be secured and the nuns reluctantly agreed to begin building their new facilities on the small piece of property they already owned at Masten and Ervay, facing Bryan. It took five months, from October 1874 until February of 1875, to complete the building. In the meantime, another severe winter hit. Barrels of water for mixing the mortar froze to solid ice masses. More money had to be secured and the Bishop scolded the nuns severely. In the midst of these trials, they went on retreat. The Bishop sent them into seclusion with two texts: "If you would be my disciple, take up your cross and follow me." and "It is decreed that every man must die; after death, the judgment and then heaven or hell." To these dark thoughts, he added yet another: a severe scolding for being preoccupied with a building.

The student body grew. Sister St. Claire Curtis arrived from Galveston to help out. The nuns assisted with the housekeeping as well as teaching. Sometimes their sense of humor was as essential as their dedication to their vows in keeping them at the task. In March of 1875, for instance, the Sisters came from Mass one morning to find their school yard covered in a heavy snow. Sister St. Bernard, who emerged first, pelted each of her friends with a snowball. The first full school year, 1874-75, continued to July which meant that the Sisters and their students experienced the two extremes of weather, a very severely cold winter followed by a sweltering summer. Even so, it had been a good year. Enrollment was higher than they had anticipated and the young women had studied piano, voice, French, elocution and drama as well as reading, writing and arithmetic.

Before the end of 1875 three more teachers joined the community—Mary Jane Downey, their first postulant who had been among their first seven Dallas students and who would be Sister Saint Angela; Sister Catherine O'Donnell from Ireland and Sister Augustine Hartnett. By 1878 Mother Ursula Debize from France came as a postulant. By that time the school had grown to 200 day students and 40 boarders and the nuns were sleeping in the attic. Father Martiniere was teaching upperclass math and serving as caretaker—planting and cultivating vegetable and flower gardens, caring for lawns and gardens—as well as being the spiritual leader of the community.

By 1880 when Bishop Dubuis resigned and returned to France, Ursuline again required space to expand. Father Martiniere found them 10 acres a mile and half east of where they were on Bryan Street. It had been a cotton field. They paid $2,000 and named it St. Joseph's Farm. Ground was broken for the new—and what appeared to them and all of Dallas at the time—massive four-story building in February of 1882. During the year and a half the structure was being built, Ursuline students often walked "out to the country" to check up on their new school. In March of 1883, before the building's official opening in August, two nuns took up residence at the new building at night to milk the cows and keep watch over the property. They drove to their teaching duties each day in a cumbersome buggy pulled by a yellow horse and a black mule to the vast amusement of onlookers. Festive ceremonies were held to open the new facilities. The second and third floors provided a dormitory for the boarders.

In December the school's beloved Mother St. Joseph Holly died and was buried in the cemetery on the grounds of the school. She was 42 years old. The new building had been open only a year when Mother St. Paul, who had succeeded Mother St. Joseph as superior, traveled to Galveston to ask for help with the expanding Dallas enrollment. The Dallas community was soon joined by Mother Evangelist Holly, the younger sister of Mother St. Joseph. The Holly sisters, orphaned, had grown up under the care and supervision of Ursulines and provided for the Dallas school an almost unbroken chain of dedication and educational expertise.

Ursuline Academy, through plush years and lean, with changes brought on by time's demands, continues to be a model educational institution in the Southwest. In 1950 Ursuline moved to a large campus with several buildings at 4900 Walnut Hill Lane. This location, like that on Bryan Street, was as remote and sparsely populated as the old one was when the Ursuline sisters and their students opened the school. Thirty-five years later it marks a halfway point between downtown Dallas and the burgeoning city to its north.

11

WOMEN—THE CITY'S CONSCIENCE

By the middle of the 1870s, women were taking an increasingly prominent role in Dallas. While the elite along Ross Avenue and in the newly opened residential area of the Cedars had time and money to devote themselves to philanthropy, increasing numbers of single women, heads of households, were making their way to the young city, lured to Dallas as a good place to eke out a living and rear their children.

The 1875 Dallas City Directory lists 2,489 Dallas households, 152 of them headed by women. Among these were 24 widows, 17 boarding house proprietors, 14 dressmakers, 13 laundresses, nine milliners, six cooks, three seamstresses and two housekeepers. The professionals included six teachers, one music teacher, one writer, one nurse, one telephone operator, one merchant and nine actresses. Since eight of the nine actresses listed their address at 314 Jefferson, and since there was no reason for so many actresses to have chosen Dallas as a residence, the probability is that the actresses may have had professions other than the stage. The red light district around Jefferson flourished and Dallas's actresses probably were "entertainers."

There were legitimate performers. Martha and Alice Riek, who would later become outstanding musicians, were babies when they arrived in Dallas in 1875 with their parents, Constance and Helena Theobald Riek. They grew up in a musical family. Their father was a music teacher and all family members were musical. Martha played the piano, Alice the cornet. At age seven, Martha joined her father, brother Ferdinand, and an older sister to form "Texas Parlor Quartette." In 1875 the musical family went on the road, playing throughout Texas and Louisiana. As their fame spread, they expanded their itinerary to include large and small opera houses in some of the nation's largest cities.

Dallas was always home base for the music-making Rieks. Helena sometimes traveled with her family, but often stayed in Dallas to manage their home at 115 Leonard Street. The only son, Ferdinand, formed his own orchestra and played for some of the outstanding social events, including the Idlewild ball. He married Eugenia Long, a daughter of former Mayor Benjamin Long.

Martha and Alice Riek were among the first recording artists in the United States. They recorded on the first cylinders for Thomas Edison. Though their success took them everywhere, they considered Dallas their home.

Texas' first poet laureate was a woman, Welthea Bryant Leachman, who began writing and publishing as a child. Welthea was born in Galveston on Christmas Day of 1847, the youngest of eight children, to Sarah Getchell Bryant and Maj. Gen. Charles G. Bryant, a sea captain. Hers was a family of writers including William Cullen Bryant.

Welthea grew up in Corpus Christi until she was 13 when her parents sent her to Orleans Academy in Louisiana. Stranded there during the Civil War, she resorted to writing to alleviate her homesickness. While she was still a school girl, her poetry, published in the *Galveston News*, received critical acclaim. "... her poems ... constitute a brilliant intellectual brochure," one critic enthused. At age 17, she married a man named Graham. Divorced the following year, she went to live with an aunt in Boston where she continued to write. One of her poems, "Bitter Sweet," gives insight into this period of her life. It begins:

> Under the stars that mildly shine,
> Under the dark night's cover,

A woman with sobered step then comes,
Her eye on a distant star,
She sighs in vain for a nearer gleam,
But it only shines from afar
And fades....
  Welthea Bryant
  Leachman,
  Texas poet laureate

> Down in a quiet shadowy glen,
> Where the soft breezes hover,—
> Two tarry where the shadows meet,
> Learning love's tale of Bitter-Sweet.

The last verse is:

> Ah! bitter-sweet indeed, to some
> Comes love, and love's beguiling,
> When hearts must smother fondest dreams
> And lips know naught but smiling—
> And hand that should be clasped in hand
> Meets only in the summer-land!"

In May of 1875 when Welthea was 27, she married J. S. Leachman and moved to Dallas. Described as a "prominent resident of Dallas . . . a commercial traveler for a large mercantile establishment . . . ."[1] Leachman adored his much younger bride, and encouraged her writing. Though it was a happy union, Welthea's life was still filled with pain. She lost several children. A biographer wrote that this had so preyed upon her "as to almost paralyze . . . (her talent) . . . She is a lady of indomitable courage and indisputable genius. She exhibits both fire and energy. Her poems are pervaded with . . . tenderness."[2]

Two years after she moved to Dallas, Welthea Bryant Leachman was named poet laureate of Texas. She died in 1888, having lived only 13 years in Dallas. But it was during those years that she did her finest writing.

Two events that would impact Dallas's future happened in 1875, the first that would record the daily events, and the second that would preserve the history.

The first was the merging of the *Herald* with a new paper, together called the *Daily Times Herald*. It was owned by Charles E. Gilbert, the nephew of Charity Morris Gilbert, Dallas's first female citizen. Two years after Gilbert began to operate his paper, in August of 1877, he married Gertrude Wilson, and she assumed a position among the socially elite of Dallas. Charles Gilbert, editor and manager of the *Times-Herald*, became editor of the *Evening Herald* in 1886. It became the *Evening Times* in 1888 and eventually *The Dallas Times Herald* which continued to be a major newspaper voice in Dallas until December of 1991.

The second was the Pioneer Association of Dallas County, the first organization in Dallas to admit women as full members. It was organized July 13, 1875, when 112 people met at the Dallas County courthouse. Two women, Nancy Jane Hughes Cochran and Elizabeth B. Durgan, were named vice presidents. Other officers were John C. McCoy, president, and Isaac B. Webb, W. H. Hord, Ed C. Browder, W. J. Smith and A. McCommas. The organization slated an annual reunion to be held each July 13 (unless that date came on a Sunday, in which case it would be held the prior Saturday) and scheduled a next meeting for October 30, 1875, in Hutchins.

Through the years the association has surged and ebbed in keeping with Dallasites' interest in their pasts. For many years, when the emphasis was on progress at whatever cost, the association was little more than a "sleeper," but, from time to time, it has awakened dramatically to help preserve the city's past. Many of the organization's records are lost; most of its history is from newspaper coverage of its annual picnics, the largest of which occurred in 1892 when 2,500 turned out on Friday, July 13, and 2,000 on Saturday for a two-day event.

Proud Heritage: Pioneer Families of Dallas County, published in 1986, is a rare contribution that the Dallas County Pioneer Association has made to the area. Under the guidance of its president, W. F. Jacoby, Jr., and chaired by Russell and Emily Hereford Surles, the book includes articles researched and written by those familiar with Dallas's past. Many are by direct descendants of the families included. The book more than lives up to the Association's stated purposes: (1) To perpetuate the memory and spirit of the men and women who resided in what is today Dallas County, Texas, before January 1, 1880; (2) To encourage historical research concerning Dallas County, its cities, towns, communities and early citizens so that a comprehensive knowledge of the same may be preserved for future generations; (3) To foster the preservation of historical buildings, documents and relics, and (4) to use its influence to have places of historical significance in Dallas County appropriately marked, so as to keep alive the memory of important persons, places and events.

The 1870s also brought to Dallas a child who would become its first definitive feminist. Her name was Stella White. Born February 12, 1864, in Talladega, Alabama, to Alexander and Narcissa Rodgers White, Stella and her two sisters, Linda and Abbie, were privately tutored in their father's vast library. And what a formidable library it was! Alexander White had twice served in Congress, first elected as a Henry Clay Whig in 1851, and again 21 years later, as a Republican Congressman from Alabama. Appointed by President Grant, he served briefly as Chief Justice of Utah's Supreme Court. Though he opposed Alabama's secession from the Union, he had dutifully served as an officer in the Confederate Army.

In 1876 the White family moved to Dallas. As soon as she was old enough, Stella entered Mary Baldwin College. Back in Dallas following her graduation, she was almost immediately involved in shaping her city. Far ahead of her time in some of the causes she espoused, she was called "an advance agent for the women's liberation movement."[3] In his book, *Dallas Yesterday*, Sam Acheson said she "spent her life upgrading the status of women." In the 1980s, Ruth Raymond Potts Spence,[4] herself an illustrious Dallas woman, said of her mother-in-law: "She was an activist in the most active sense of the word; very avant garde. Not afraid of anybody."

In 1887, Stella married Wendell Spence. Fortunately, for her and for the city, she had the talent, the time and the money to devote to numerous causes. A successful lawyer husband who supported her, if sometimes reluctantly, a bevy of servants, and indulgent wealthy parents formed her support system.

Stella led Dallas on two major issues: race relations and women's rights. Even as a girl, back in Alabama, she had opposed slavery, opposed the South seceding from the Union, and knew that the Southern Cause was a lost cause. Though she rarely flaunted these controversial views, she spoke out when the need arose. She looked on her "servants" as co-conspirators in good causes, Ruth Spence said, and, much to the consternation of her more traditional husband, insisted on paying them well. She believed in suffrage for women and the correspondence she left behind includes many letters from individuals supporting her work for the passage of the 19th amendment giving women the right to vote. She was equally concerned about women's health, particularly contraception and birth control. She knew and supported Margaret Sanger, the national leader of parenthood by plan, went to Washington to hear her speak, and was instrumental in bringing Ms. Sanger to Dallas where she introduced her.

There was a public Stella White Spence and a private one, but often—because of her candor—the two were the same. The public Stella Spence was an organizer of the Dallas Art Association, the Dallas Woman's Club and the Mother's Club, the forerunner of the PTA. She was an early activist for prohibition of liquor sales. She worked tirelessly for passage of the 18th amendment prohibiting the making, distribution and sale of liquor and then, when she saw that it wouldn't work, worked equally as hard to get it repealed. Her sons said: "Mother nullified her life. She spent the first half of it getting liquor outlawed and the last half getting the law repealed,"[5] One added, "Mother believes in change, even change for the worse."

She was an avid proponent of the public school system. Even though she could have easily sent her children to private schools, she kept all six in public schools and worked tirelessly to improve public education.

Humor from the public podium kept Stella from ever appearing sanctimonious, Ruth Spence said. "She cloaked her barbs, both in her speech and in her writing, so cleverly that most men felt they were being congratulated when they were, indeed, being called into question."

Stella White Spence—scholar, political activist and professional volunteer—gave women's work and worth a new dimension.

Hortense Sanger, above, and Eleanor Conrad, below, continue in the mold set by Stella Spence. Both are advocates for children.

Stella kept up a voluminous correspondence including almost weekly letters to the editor, both to Dallas papers and to national publications. When the Dallas Board of Education voted that school children could not collect and contribute money to United Charities, she fired off this missive:

> As a member of the community and a liberal patron of the public schools . . . I beg . . . to protest . . . your action rescinding the permission for the children . . . to give their annual offerings to the United Charities. Being by nature rather sociable, and believing the line between the classes to be, like the Mason and Dixon line, purely imaginary, I think I know something about the children and the schools . . . .[6]

She ended her letter with, ". . . dear boys of the School Board . . . leave it to the instinct of the women; we don't mind being without reason, for we have the assurance that blessed is he who considereth the poor . . . ."[7]

When a group of women campaigned for a candidate for Congress who opposed child labor laws and women's suffrage, Stella was indignant. She wrote: "Can you think of little children working from 6 o'clock in the morning until 6 o'clock in the evening? . . . Mr. Bailey (the candidate the group of women were supporting) says that women are too stupid to understand politics, and . . . should not speak in political meetings. The only women Mr. Bailey admires are the dummies . . . . If Mr. Bailey must be elected, let . . . men bring it to pass. Let not women . . . betray their sisters."[8]

As president of the Dallas Council of Mother's Club, Stella Spence authorized a letter to the Dallas Advertising League requesting its help in ending liquor sales at the State Fair.

> In you we recognize the power that leads the world. We know that you can make corn flakes taste like ambrosial leaves; sorghum molasses like honey. Your words are like apples of gold in frames of silver. We believe that more and more you are the universal truth . . . .

This, the praise that sets the stage for the Mother's Council request. Next, comes the non sequitur:

> The Mother's Council is composed of simple women who are trying to aid their husbands . . . to make our homes more comfortable and happier, to give your youth clean, wholesome amusement and to add to the gaiety of the little children . . . .

And then the wallop:

> The Fair Board says that the one saloon within the Fair Grounds is the life of the Fair. If this is true, why is it stuck away under the grand stand . . . ? . . . let the Advertising League advertise it as such. Let them place it in the open, the most prominent place . . . . Let them build a fine building, light it with will-o-the-wisps and let them have an avenue leading to the door, bordered with weeping willows; a terrace of widow's tears; on its right a bed of bleeding hearts; and on its left a bed of bachelor buttons. The women will furnish the flowers. Cover the home with poison ivy and erect a sign: THIS IS OUR MUNICIPAL SALOON, THE LIFE OF THE FAIR.[9]

While continuing to work for the passage of the 18th Amendment, which was ratified by Congress on January 16, 1919, and which Stella Spence would work just as diligently to have repealed in 1933, she turned her indomitable energy to securing suffrage for women. She wrote numerous letters to public officials. One response from John E. Davis on State of Texas House of Representatives stationery dated January 16, 1918, assured her:

Dallas's arts and charitable communities have been vastly enriched by the contributions of many women, among them this quartet, from the top, Betty Marcus, Lupe Murchison, Evelyn Lambert and Virginia Nick.

I am for women's suffrage, first as a matter of fair play, and then because we need the votes of the women to help bring about better economic and moral conditions. [10]

All of the letters kept by Stella Spence were mailed with two-cent postage stamps and most of them were addressed to her simply at "Dallas, Texas," with no street address.

During their campaign for the vote, Dallas women were successful in bringing national suffrage leader, Dr. Anna Howard Shaw, to Dallas. Her speech at the Adolphus Hotel, drew, according to *The Dallas Morning News* "about 140 women and a few men." Even before reporting the remarks of the nationally known speaker, it quoted Stella Spence:

No woman has a more reverent and tender love for men than I have. If necessary, I would shed my last drop of blood for them; but that has never been necessary, nor will it ever be . . . . Out of the deep love I have for them, I must confess that I think it is a man's place to stay out of politics so that he has time to run his business.

How can a man run the Government and his own business? How can he make a success of his business when he is always gallivanting around in politics?

When our Constitution is amended so that we can help them, we will let them stay at home one night at least during the week and take their place. We will bear our half of the burden of home and State. [11]

Stella Spence clipped thousands of articles during her lifetime, according to Ruth Spence. Among them is a newspaper story written by Genevieve Forbes Herrick of the *Chicago Tribune* Press Service, February 13, 1920, reporting on Margaret Sanger's appearance before the Senate Judiciary Committee in support of legalizing birth control. Stella Spence was among the "delegations from many women's organizations throughout the country and a hundred or so of Washington's most prominent wives and widows applauding this crusader whose arguments have more than once brought her to jail."

Stella White Spence, the private person, lived in a large house on Oak Lawn at Congress which her children called "The Ark" because it was always filled with a motley collection of people, animals, plants and flowers. "Mrs. Spence collected things," Ruth Spence recalled. "The house was always full of people. She took in relatives, friends and lame ducks."

There were six Spence children—two daughters, Linda and Margareta, and four sons, Alex, Wendell Jr., Joseph and Charles. Alex, Ruth's husband, was an attorney; Wendell Jr., joined the military at a very early age and died young from being gassed in World War I leaving his widow, Julia Lundsford Spence; Joseph Gilbert Spence died while a student at the University of Texas, Austin; Charles Metcalfe Spence, also an attorney, married Kathleen Talley and moved to St. Louis where he died with cancer as a young man; Linda married E. P. Brown who died with tuberculosis soon afterward leaving her with a small daughter, Nancy. Stella took her granddaughter for a number of years while Linda went to the University of Chicago to complete graduate work in nutrition. Margareta married James Haven and, after his death, Harrison Hines, and moved to Atlanta.

Even with all of her sorrow, "Mrs. Spence ran a merry household—a beautiful house," Ruth said. "She set a good table and you never knew how many people would be around it. There was always a silver service at one end. Mrs. Spence arrived at the table with an encyclopedia in one hand and dictionary in the other. She insisted that her children read the papers before they came to the table. Every evening at dinner, her table was a sparring match."

Ruth, who had been reared as the only daughter by a mother who was "gentle, calm and always very ladylike and proper," said that when she married Alex and became a member of the family, she sat at the Spence table in utter fascination. "I could never keep up with them," she said. "They would transfer from one side of an argument to the other without missing a beat. The meal lasted forever with everybody talking and laughing and arguing. And everybody drank oceans of tea and coffee."

Stella Spence was "an ample woman in the days before thin was the only thing to be," Ruth said. "Her interests were boundless. She was an omnivorous reader. Her children said, when there was a new baby, she rocked the cradle with one hand and held a book in the other." She was the consummate non-conformist—a great gardener, an avid student of the stars and planets and animal and bird life.

As a political activist, she kept her ear tuned to the people. She would often come home and announce to her family that some candidate would win an election, or another one would be defeated. When they asked how she knew, she told them she had been talking to the street car conductor. "She was almost always right," Ruth Spence said. "She took her political activism seriously and no job was beneath her. Once she took a bucket of water and a scrub brush and went about town scrubbing off signs opposing one of her projects."

Sometimes, Mrs. Spence overloaded her life with projects, became overwhelmed and got sick, her daughter-in-law said. "She would spend one to several days in bed reading, organizing her numerous projects, writing letters and resting,' said Ruth. "Linda said you could always tell the length of Mother's illness by the depth of the books stacked at her bedside."

Wendell Spence usually looked "with resigned tolerance on his wife's many activities," Ruth Spence said. She described him as "a tall, handsome, elegant man who presided over the family with great dignity. He had such conventional ideas. He kept two jersey cows on two city lots so that he would have fresh cream all of the time. He always had a little jug of clotted cream by his plate and would drown everything in it. He always went to Alexandria, Minnesota, for the summer. When he became ill, he was accompanied there by Charles and his friend, Dr. Flynn. The doctors told Mrs. Spence that he would take his own life and he did. Charles and Dr. Flynn had taken him out for a drive and stopped to service the car. Mr. Spence escaped, went into a hotel next door and slashed his throat. It was so out of character—but then he was a sick man.

"After Mr. Spence's death, Mrs. Spence had a period when she did so many things she had always wanted to do," Ruth recalled. She kept the house going. She took in a new family of boys and started a series of discussion groups for them. After she was 60 years old, she learned to drive a car. "She'd always had a chauffeur before," Ruth said. "Alex was so worried and I had to convince him that she was entitled to spend her life the way she wanted to. Her sense of humor was sharpened and she became gentler. Alex always took her out for a ride on Sundays. One sweltering summer day he had a flat while they were out and was chagrined. His mother said, "But Alex, it's such a little flat!"

She took up writing. She traveled. When she was 74 years old, Stella Spence moved to Virginia to live with her daughter, Linda, who was director of food services for Sweet Briar College. Her will, which she wrote herself, is a masterpiece of love and brevity and reads:

LAST WILL AND TESTAMENT OF STELLA WHITE SPENCE

Living on borrowed time and nearing my seventy-eighth birthday, I realize that the adventure of life is drawing to a close. I have had a life full of griefs, sorrows, happiness and joys. I have loved life. There has never been a grief so black but there was a light to lead me, never a sorrow so deep but there was a balm to aid me. Happiness has underlaid all my life and of joy I have had my share. I shall leave life with pain. I know not of the future but I feel that I shall, in any world, be homesick for the earth I have loved so long, homesick for my good fellow travelers, for the stars and the shadows on the lawn.

> "Sometimes Mrs. Spence would take to her bed to read, write and rest. Her daughter said you could tell the length of her mother's illness by the depth of the books at her bedside."

Anna Buhrer Moses ran the dairy, college-educated her six children and accumulated property in East Dallas for 45 years following the death of her husband.

> I hope that there is another world where the unfortunate will have another opportunity, where the righteous who had little here shall be rewarded; where the murderers will learn the sweet quality of mercy; the thief will feel the cleanliness of an honest life and the haughty will know the gentle dignity of meekness. I claim nothing for myself. If God in his infinite goodness grants a better life, I thank Him with all my soul. I acknowledge all the mercies of God our Heavenly Father, and am grateful for His love.
>
> To leave life now, in the most interesting time of the world, when so much will be done to help humanity and when I hope that mankind will be guided by the teaching of Jesus Christ, is doubly hard. Nevertheless, I hope to leave before my mind and body are too feeble to be of any use to mankind or be a burden to those who love me.[12]

Stella Spence died at Sweet Briar on April 5, 1943.

Two other women who arrived late in 1879, as the decade was ending, must be noted in the list of Dallas's outstanding contributors—Anna Buhrer Moser because she was another who proved that women can be capable, independent entrepreneurs and Mary Kittrell Craig because she established the first long-term study group for women that has provided intellectual stimulation to thousands of women for more than a century.

Anna Moser took over the family dairy business following the death of her husband. She arrived in Dallas in the Spring of 1879 as Anna Buhrer, a 22-year-old native of Switzerland. Born April 3, 1857, Anna migrated to the United States when she was 12 with her widowed mother, Anna Scherer Buhrer and a brother, Jacob Buhrer. The family settled first in West Virginia and remained there for a decade, moving on to Dallas in 1879.

The Buhrers had been in Dallas only a few weeks when Anna met Christian Moser, also a native of Switzerland. He had come to Dallas as a penniless youth, had worked hard, saved his money, bought a few cows, gone into the dairy business and prospered. There is no record of how Christian and Anna met, but the Swiss colony in Dallas was close-knit. Both Chris and the Buhrers belonged to the German Evangelical Lutheran Church, and it is likely that they met at church. Anna was 22 and Chris 34 on their wedding day in the fall of 1879, only six months after she arrived in Dallas.

One morning when he delivered their milk, Chris promised his customers a surprise when he came the next day. The surprise was his bride, radiant in her best dress and hat. During the 14 years that the Mosers were married, Chris and Anna had six children: August Charles in 1880, Freda in 1883, Christopher Otto in 1885, Matilda in 1887, Ernest Frank in 1890 and Huldah in 1893.

Anna and Chris prospered in their dairy; they made two trips back to Switzerland to visit family and friends. On their first trip, the couple gave a dinner party in Bern for creditors of Chris's failed cheese business, and guests found under their napkins checks in the full amount he owed each.

August was 13 and Huldah only a few months old when their father died at age 48 on September 22, 1893, leaving Anna, at 36, to rear and educate the children. She took over the family dairy, located on 37 acres at Ross Avenue and Henderson just outside the Dallas city limits. She sent all of her sons to Texas A&M and her daughters to St. Mary's College. In 1910, when the children were grown, she subdivided her property into residential lots and called it Moser's Ross Avenue Addition. By that time, the city had enveloped it. Today's Moser Avenue runs through the center of the Moser diary farm. Anna continued to live in her home in the northwest quadrant of Ross and Henderson. When she died in 1938 at age 81, having outlived her husband for 45 years, the home place was sold to make way for Merchants State Bank.

Mary Kittrell Craig and her husband, Emmett C. Craig, a cotton planter, moved to Dallas in 1879. At 37, Mary was at the peak of her energy and enthusiasm. Born November 17, 1842, in Mississippi, she was a graduate of Wilcox Female Academy and had done graduate work in Chicago and New York. She had taught at Oxford Male and Female College in Alabama. For the five years prior to her arrival in Dallas, she was president of Synodical Female Institute, a private school, in Talladega, Alabama.

In Dallas, Mary found that other women felt, as she did, that their intellectual horizons were limited. They decided to get together and talk, and from these informal conversations for intellectual stimulation came the Mary K. Craig Class.

In the beginning Craig Class participants met in each other's homes to discuss things that shaped their lives—books, current events and how they impacted Dallas. Soon they were using their forum to discover changes that needed to be made—though the Craig Class remained just that, a place for intellectual discussion. The ideas that were planted found root and flourished in the myriad other organizations to which its members belonged.

Throughout the lifetime of its founder, the Craig Class was small. Twenty-five to 30 women met on the dot of 10:30 every Wednesday morning to discuss "whatever happened to be interesting at the time." Sometimes there were outside speakers, sometimes not. The meetings were always over by noon. There was no business conducted. Dues were $10 a year. Until into her late 70s, Mary *was* the Mary K. Craig Class. She was an inspiring teacher, always open to new information. Not only did she continue to read and study, but she became chairperson of the English Department in the Mary Connor College in Sherman in 1896, continuing in that post for several years. She also gave birth to a daughter, who became a musician, and a son.

Gifted with a charm and diplomacy, Mary kept her small group together all of her life. The women considered it an honor to be included in her coterie. After she died, on August 31, 1921, many wanted to continue meeting. So it was that the Craig Class was officially organized with Mrs. Henry Spear as its director. They also decided that the intellectual wealth should be shared and voted to take in anyone who wanted to join until membership reached 300, at which time applicants would be put on a waiting list. Within months there was a waiting list of more than 200!

The decade ended just as it had begun with women carrying almost the full responsibility for expanding education, culture and social graces into the little town. One of the characteristics that makes Dallas unique among Texas towns has always been the gifts of its women. While their husbands put up buildings, the women furnished them with heart and art, mind and milk, care and kitchens, soul and sociability. The men poured the concrete. The women provided the conscience. At the beginning, there could have been no better combination.

12

THE GENTEEL DECADE

Dallas was nearing its fortieth birthday. Still a frontier town, it boasted a population of 25,000 in its city limits and 60,000 within a 12-mile radius. It had 111 miles of streets, all dirt. It had two large hotels and several smaller ones, 90 to 100 boarding houses, 20 churches—and 300 saloons! By 1884, according to records kept by M. Monduel's brewery, Dallasites and the itinerants who rode through were consuming 52,000 kegs of beer a year. Five railroads had made the town a transportation center. Those who needed work were lured by 12 manufacturing plants: three flour mills, two soap factories and one each making railroad cars, wagons, carriages, buggies, furniture, vinegar and cider and a foundry.[1]

Though it bragged about a public school system, what it offered was privately financed and subject to the economic vagaries of the times and to benefactors. There were six private schools, almost all of them for girls. Ahead of many of other frontier towns in goods and services, Dallas required the greatest ingenuity of its women to create anything resembling a comfortable lifestyle.

Sanger Bros., which had reached Dallas along with the first railroad in the early 1870s, set the fashion pace, and in the early 1880s advertised a new arrival of the latest fabrics: Organdy for 12 1/2 cents a yard; gingham for 10 cents, lawn for eight to 10 cents, and silks and satins for 50 cents to 70 cents a yard. Nun's veiling, used to make facial covers women wore in mourning, came in black only, all wool, and sold for 30 cents a yard. Dresses required from six to 10 yards, so fabric for a dress cost about a dollar, and for the most plush fabric, not more than five dollars. Numerous seamstresses advertised daily in the papers; they made garments for 30 to 50 cents each. Seamstresses often went out to work in homes of clients, sewing for a week or two for an entire family for a daily wage. Many women sewed their own and their family's clothing. There were no ready-made garments. Patterns were non-existent. Women usually ripped apart their husband's shirts and their own dresses and used them as guides to cut new garments. The children were another matter; their speedy growth elicited the best talents of mothers or seamstresses to create any semblance of fit and style.

New citizens moving to Dallas could purchase almost everything they needed for less than a thousand dollars including a large farm ($640 for a headright) a team of mules ($50 to $90 each), and an extra $25 for the harness, (up to $200 if you were a fancy dude out to impress the girls), $25 to $40 for a milch cow with calf and $30 to $50 for a horse. A barrel of coal oil cost $2.00 and supplied fuel needs for an entire family's lamps and lanterns for about six months. Those setting up housekeeping needed a washboard, 85 cents; clothes pins, 65 cents per hundred; a well bucket, 35 cents; and a dipper, 10 cents. Most women cooked family meals in two to three pots—a skillet, a large pot for soups and main dishes (potatoes, peas, beans, rice) and a smaller one for the occasional extra dish. The more luxurious kitchens also had a coffee pot. Meat was abundant—buffalo, squirrel, rabbit, fish. Many people butchered their own beef and pork. Meat was almost inevitably fried in the one skillet.

Variety in menus was severely limited, but the available basics cost very little: sugar was 11 1/2 cents a pound; salt, $2.50 per barrel; potatoes, sweet potatoes and/or onions, $1.00 a bushel; beans, 7 1/2 cents a pound, about a cent per average serving; bacon, 13 1/2 cents per pound; pickles, $11 per barrel; cabbage, 3 cents per pound; hominy and grits, $6.50 per barrel; dried peaches, 14 cents per pound. Fresh fruit, when available, was more expensive: bananas, $2.50 per bunch; apples, $7.00 per bushel; lemons, $4.00 per box; dates, 7 cents per pound, grapes, $10 per barrel, and chestnuts 18

Sanger Bros. set the fashion pace for Dallas women who had to buy yardage and have their dresses made. Seamstresses, many of them widows supporting their children, worked for 50 to 70 cents per day.

cents per pound. A pound of candy sticks was 13 cents. If the man of the house was doing the shopping—and he usually was—he might add a gallon of liquor, $2.50, to the grocery list.[2]

Everybody shared similar supplies and services. While this made life tolerable, even worthwhile, the women of Dallas knew there was a better life. The mail service, though irregular, was inexpensive, and families corresponded regularly. Letters and newspapers mailed from New York, St. Louis, Cincinnati or Richmond usually arrived in Dallas within a month. Women living near the post office collected their mail immediately and devoured it for news of family and friends, for information on the latest fashions, and for views of those closest to them about world conditions. Those who lived farther from downtown often let their mail stack up for weeks and the *Herald* regularly ran lists of people who had not claimed their mail.

Travel also brought news of the latest world events. As rail service expanded, the more affluent went to visit families in the north and east, though only the most daring women traveled unchaperoned. Some went abroad. Every day the *Herald* was filled with items about residents traveling to other cities and about family members and friends arriving in Dallas for visits.

Through memories, reading, correspondence and travel, Dallasites were keenly aware of the progress being made in other parts of the world and determined that their city, too, should benefit. And benefit, it did.

The continuing arrival of outstanding people, plus six watershed events in the 1880s irrevocably impacted the town and pushed it toward becoming a major city. The six events:

- The first hard-surfaced roads.
- The telephone.
- Electricity.
- The power-operated streetcar.
- The public school system.
- The women's club movement.

Though the first five of these are lauded in other histories of Dallas, there is little understanding of the impact and influence of women's organizations on the city, nor the influence for good that has come from the programs and projects created and administered by women. Both the educational system and the women's club movement deserve special attention.

Telephones were the first of the big six. The telephone exchange was installed by engineer D. M. Clower[3] with connections for 1,200 subscribers, but opened on June 1, 1881, with only 40. Jennie E. Thompson, the first *telephonist,* ran the board all by herself and earned only pennies per day. Jennie was one of the first of the millions of working women who would follow her into downtown Dallas to earn a living. Jennie's offices were at 224 Elm Street, and like the next several women telephone operators, she knew every subscriber personally. Judge John Bookhout, the first subscriber to this new service, and his 39 compatriots were soon joined by an avalanche of others. In 1882 the first long distance lines opened to Lancaster, Waxahachie, Ennis, Waco, Denton and Cleburne. A year later, in 1883, the telephone company knew it had a success. It enrolled its 250th subscriber and opened long distance service to five more Texas towns: Fort Worth, Terrell, Sherman, McKinney and Gainesville.

Electricity came in 1882 when the privately owned Dallas Gas and Fuel Company opened on the northwest corner of Austin and Ross, then known as Carondelet, and secured a charter from the city to begin supplying power. At that stage, it delivered both gas and electricity. The *Herald* editorially opposed electric lighting.

> Electricity does not give a regular steady light. It suddenly flares up, burns unevenly for a moment or two, and then depreciates in intensity. New York and London both have tried and abandoned it . . . .[4]

Mayer's Summer Garden, a popular amusement park on the north side of Elm Street at Stone, where large crowds of men gathered to listen to a German band and sip nickel beer, was the first place to install electricity. It was deemed "the most brilliantly illuminated place in town" by the very paper that weeks before had decreed it wouldn't work. Because saloons were the first to sign up for this new power, many people thought electricity was the work of the devil, even while they made fortuitous trips downtown at night to see "a light so bright that it's like the sunshine!" Shortly, the St. George Hotel installed one electric light, the Grand Windsor Hotel got two and Sanger's put in three!

There would follow 34 years of competition between 11 different power companies for control of electrical and gas power to the city. The resolution did not come until 1917 when Col. J. F. Strickland bought out his chief competitors, consolidated them and formed Dallas Power and Light Company. In the meantime, Jules Schneider had retained the gas service, renamed it Dallas Gas and Fuel Company and built a plant at Ross and Akard. In 1909, gas control shifted to the newly chartered Lone Star Gas Company, which had built a 16-inch pipeline to Dallas from Clay County 150 miles away to deliver gas from the Petrolia oil fields. On May 7, 1909, several thousand people gathered on a Saturday night to watch a gas torch atop the Cotton Belt Terminal Building at Commerce and Lamar shoot flames 40 feet into the air to celebrate the inauguration of natural gas service in the city.

The citizens in the 1880s could never have imagined how electricity and gas would alter their lives. By 1883, they had stopped debating the merits of the new power and were eager to install it. Most major businesses installed fixtures for both electricity and gas, a necessary precaution because one or the other, and sometimes both, often failed. All private residences were still heated by coal or wood, but efforts had begun to extend the service into residential areas.

The Dallas Herald editorialized against electricity declaring its light unsteady. Both London and New York had tried it and found that it failed, the paper said.

The city began installing street lights. The 1883 City Directory notes that electricity "beautifully illuminates the streets in the heart of the town with its pale, ghostly and weird rays." Two years later, in 1885, the highlight of the second Idlewild Ball came when guests left the music and the dancing to rush to the windows of the Merchants Exchange Building to see the first electric light on Dallas streets turned on in front of the old *Dallas Morning News* building.

It is not surprising that, with 300 saloons operating in Dallas with little or no regulation, prostitution would proliferate—and it did. The rapid growth of the town, its relative affluence and lagging regulatory laws allowed prostitution virtual free rein. Since no woman listed her occupation as "prostitute," no records exist showing how many ladies of the night plied their trade in Dallas. Prostitution was not yet legalized by the city fathers as it would soon be, nor were the prostitutes openly soliciting business. Ministers did not yet touch the subject. Husbands and fathers, some of whom were financially—if not personally—benefitting, did not take the stories home. For these reasons many, maybe most, wives and mothers were unaware of the existence of prostitution in neighborhoods near their homes.

Virginia Knight Johnson was aware. A native of Lynchburg, Virginia, where she had been educated by private tutors, Virginia married William Hudson Johnson at the age of 29 in 1872 and eight years later moved with him to Dallas. By the time women's groups were organized to attack the adverse conditions of their town, Virginia already was a one-woman welfare organization.[5] The back porch of her home was a storage center for food and clothing for the needy. She said that women did not become prostitutes by choice, but by what they perceived as necessity, and, if given an opportunity, preferred work more acceptable to society. She founded Sheltering Arms, a rescue home for prostitutes. When few of the women responded to Virginia's dream for their futures, she was philosophical. No respectable occupation afforded women the income to which the prostitutes had become accustomed, she said, and most preferred to sell sex rather than accept the measly wages offered to them in more respectable occupations.

Virginia Knight Johnson became a one-woman welfare organization who established Sheltering Arms, a home for prostitutes, but was philosophical when they failed to come to her shelter.

Though some of the town's leading male citizens viewed prostitution as detrimental to their businesses, many others profited from it, either directly or indirectly. One of the town's leading banks is a case in point.

Banker J. S. Armstrong was sitting in his office one day when a fashionably attired woman with gracious, refined manners was ushered in. She wanted to borrow $5,000. While he was conferring with her about the loan, a clerk slipped him a note. The "lady" he was so courteously entertaining, the note said, was the madame of one of the town's leading brothels. Unperturbed, the banker turned to his visitor and inquired when she thought she might be able to repay the loan. She told him that she knew she could have the money, with interest, back to him as soon as the fair was over in October. She soon left with her money. In September she was back to repay the loan and Armstrong called her into his office.

> ... I thought you said you couldn't pay back this money until after the Fair in October," he began .... "That's so, Mr. Armstrong," she replied, "But ... I forgot all about the preachers' convention coming in August.[6]

By 1884 the Dallas population had reached 30,000. Young bachelors were in abundance. Many young men had come to Dallas seeking the fortune that they were certain the new town offered. Others were the sons of the gentry, home from universities in the East. Though most of them frequented the bars and brothels, they knew that they would not find women they wanted to marry and mother their children in the prevailing limited social settings. Almost all longed for the genteel good times that they had enjoyed in more sophisticated settings. The first several social clubs organized by the young men were almost a joke. They had little purpose and no direction. Their very names repelled the young women they most wanted to attract. Among them were the B.B's (Bully Boys) and the Willing Fellows.

In the summer of 1884, a small group of men—both married and bachelors—met in the home W. C. Conner on South Ervay Street and organized a dancing club. Its purpose was "to give a ball to honor attractive young ladies recently returned from boarding school." There were eight organizers: Owen D. Burnett, Frank Cockrell (Sarah's son), Conner, Charles Dexter, George Dexter, Paul Furst, Charles Henning and Frank Meeks. They selected the membership of their new "club" as carefully as they chose the young women they would honor. They named it Idlewild.[7]

Idlewild had added 27 men for a total of 35 members when it held its first ball on October 13, 1884. Among the members were A. D. Aldredge, Ed Fonda, J. J. Eckford, Milton Hickox, George K. Meyer, Jules Schneider, H. B. Strange, and Will H. Waters. The ball was held in the Merchant's Exchange Building at Commerce and Lamar. It honored five young women, the city's first debutantes: Misses Philo Eagan, Minnie Miller, Effie Rauch, Dela Slaughter and Minnie Slaughter. Two hundred and fifty guests saw them presented. President Paul Furst opened the ball in a grand march with his date, Miss Mattie Burford, who was not a debutante.

Paul Furst's invitation to Mattie Burford and her acceptance epitomizes the protocol of the times. An informal invitation to a formal party was not appropriate and when Paul, in talking about the upcoming dance with Mattie, asked her if she would do him the honor of accompanying him to the ball she said she would give him her answer when his official invitation came. The next morning a servant delivered Paul's invitation and she responded by note that she would be glad to accept. The written word was the approved method of communication and young people used it in much the same manner that young people later used the telephone.

When they had chosen the gown they would wear to the ball, young women wrote a note to their escorts telling them its color and style. The young men then chose flowers appropriate to complement the gowns. Debutantes, their escorts and invited guests wore the most elegant clothes they owned to Idlewild. The women chose elaborate gowns in velvets and satins, but in the early days men could get by with dark dress suits if they did not own formal attire.

Minnie Miller, the only debutante in the group who married her escort, chose a gown of white brocaded velvet with a front panel of crystal beading. Her wrap was a fur-trimmed white brocade velvet cloak. Her flowers were pink silk roses.[8]

At about the time the young men were meeting to form Idlewild, Dallas's first *paved* streets were being completed. The hard surfacing had begun a couple of years earlier when merchants along Elm Street determined to improve the property in front of their stores. A mule-drawn street car delivered customers to businesses along Main Street, but few ventured over to Elm because in rainy seasons the stores were fronted with deep-rutted mud during rainy times and black clay-baked dust during dry seasons.

In 1881 Thomas Marsalis had hired city engineer, William Johnson, who had been in charge of track construction for the T&P railroad, to pave the street in front of his wholesale grocery business on Elm near Murphy with bois d'arc blocks. By 1884 most of the downtown area was surfaced with this hard wood. At first the system seemed to work, but proved to be only a slight improvement over the former mud holes and sand ruts because the wood shifted during inclement weather and when rains came, the mud washed over the wood creating a dangerous slippery surface.

In 1885 Johnson tried out a new hard-surfacing process created by J. L. McAdam in Scotland and widely used in Europe. Called macadam, it consisted of rolled crushed stone combined with gravel. Johnson tried it first on a small stretch of Ross Avenue between Ervay and the H&TC railroad tracks. It was imperfect, but a vast improvement over former hard-surfacing methods and soon was being used on all of the downtown streets. It would be a quarter of a century, 1910, before the city would assume the responsibility for laying and maintenance of streets.

The women of Dallas still seldom ventured outside their homes unescorted, but the hard-surfacing of the streets and their lighting—meager though it was—made for greater comfort when they did. The women also made much use of the telephone which was now installed in all the affluent homes along Ross Avenue and in the Cedars. A telephone was a mark of distinction much as ownership of an automobile, and in later years a television set and a computer would be. Even with such examples as Sarah Cockrell and Jennie Thompson, women rarely worked at jobs outside their homes. They were expected to aid their husbands in whatever the men chose to do.

Emma Gilliam Madsen is typical of the *average* housewife of the mid-1880 decade; her husband's biography in one of the early histories gives her more credit than most wives got for her part in making the family business a success. Most women were silent and unrecorded *helpmeets*.

Married to Hansen Madsen on December 16, 1884, Emma moved to Dallas as a bride and helped her husband open a feed business at 1617 Elm Street. Years of struggle followed. First, his partner died. He took a new partner who proved unsatisfactory; Madsen bought him out. Emma had a good education and common sense that helped to ease the family business through many difficult times. "Emma Madsen proved in every respect a helpmate to her husband and her advice, when acted upon, always proved to be sound and very advantageous.... With the assistance of his worthy wife and one (other) man, he succeeded in moving his mill to more commodious quarters, increased the capacity from 60 to 250 bushels per day. His plant is valued at $10,000."[9]

The growth and spread of transportation was the fourth component in the 1880s that created a major growth in Dallas. Rail transportation, though still in its embryonic stages, had linked the town with major cities to the north, east, west and south. What remained was safe and convenient linkage within the town so that workers could reach jobs in its flour mills, saddlery shops and other manufacturing plants.

Street car lines proliferated in the mid-1880s forming this linkage. The Dallas Bell Street Railway Company line under the direction of J. E. Henderson, Jules Schneider and Col. J. T. Trezevant ran up McKinney Avenue to Thomas Street and opened that area of near North Dallas to residential development. The next year residential construction

In 1885 Dallas got its first hard-surfaced roads, macadam, to replace the bois d'arc blocks on Elm Street. Even though women still seldom ventured on downtown streets, electric lighting made life easier for them when they did.

began from the Cedars and along Ross Avenue, and streetcar lines ran the length of Harwood Street linking McKinney on the north with the Cedars on the south.

Transportation lines utilized all kinds of power seeking the most efficient both for service and economy. Mules and horses, providing original power, gave way to steam locomotives around 1887. Cable cars were tried on Elm Street in 1890 but proved unsatisfactory. Electricity was the wave of the future. The Pearl Street line inaugurated the use of electrical power in 1889.

William L. McDonald best tells the story of the streetcar:

> The full history of Dallas's streetcar and transit system is a complex and convoluted one, including dozens of mule-drawn, electric, steam-and-cable-powered operations involved in an intricate system of expansion, bankruptcies, and take-overs; but the streetcar was unquestionably the most influential factor in the growth of the suburbs, and the traffic patterns it established help to explain why certain areas developed while neighboring ones did not.[10]

Real estate promoters then, as now, had a great influence on the city's growth. McDonald says:

> Several new lines were built by real estate promoters into essentially wild, overgrown farmland miles from the city. A distinct operating formula... became widely used by nearly every Dallas promoter. Either the land around an existing lake or park would be sub-divided for resale, or a lake and/or park would be built on salable property; a streetcar line would then be built to connect the property to the city, enticing Dallasites with the nickel fares to ride out on Sundays to take in the pure country air, have a picnic, swim or canoe about the lake and (just incidentally) to look over the beautiful, rustic lots offered for sale.[11]

Competing transportation lines in the early days, essential as they were to Dallas's growth, proliferated almost to their own extinction until in 1898 most of the lines were merged in the Dallas Consolidated Electric Street Railway Company. In 1901 Pierre du Pont, the grandson of the founder of E.I. du Pont de Nemours, arrived in Dallas seeking investments for the family business. He noted both the disarray and the potential of the transportation system:

> The whole street railway outfit here is strictly "bum"... the road is operated very badly, cars are dirty and run with very little system. The track is so rough that riding is very uncomfortable, in fact, everybody keeps a horse and buggy and the streets are crowded with vehicles in the evening. Three railway companies, owning 43.45 miles of tracks with 56 good cars, can be purchased for $1,300,000. And considering the earnings of the Electric Railway during the past year, which amounted to $114,000, and the condition of the property it (Dallas) seems to be an excellent field for investment.[12]

By mid-summer of 1901 du Pont had purchased the Dallas Consolidated Electric Street Railway Company and the North Dallas Circuit Railway Company. Though the entire town had prospered by the influx of money and talent from outside its borders, it did not take kindly to the arrival of what it considered blatant wealth from the East. Very soon an all-out battle for control of the city transportation system ensued. The electric company raised rates for power almost prohibitively. A rival line, the Metropolitan Street Railway Company was chartered; it would parallel and sometimes duplicate the du Pont line.

The conflict was solved when Eugene du Pont, Pierre's father, died and the son had to return to Delaware to run the business. He did not fair badly. He had owned the

Dallas transportation system for a little more than a year, paying $1,075,000 plus $50,000 in stock for the company and selling it for $300,000 profit.

Dallas's transportation system has continued to be controversial through the years with one "master" plan and another proposed, accepted, adapted and discarded. Profit and service have, more often than not, been out of balance with the result that those who depend on public transportation to get to their jobs and back to their homes have often been poorly served.

Improved communication and transportation that came in the decade of 1880-1890 formed the framework for the burgeoning growth of Dallas. It is relatively easy to document the progress of transportation because roads and rail lines can be measured in miles. It is also fairly simple to understand the impact of improved communication which is measured in numbers of telephones, publications and mail services.

The contribution of improved education and the impact of women's club work on the growth of the city are more tenuous and deserve more careful scrutiny.

13

THE 1880s—A DECADE FOR EDUCATION

From the first decade, education figured prominently in Dallas—and women deserve most of the credit. They instigated the founding of private schools and were, with rare exceptions, the teachers—though they usually prevailed upon men—their husbands, fathers or brothers—to be administrators. Even when they were creating the schools and teaching the children, women deemed it inappropriate to appear as managers.

Women founded the schools for their daughters. They sent their sons—if they could afford it—back East to school. If they could not afford it, they took the boys out of school after they learned the basics to help on the farms. In some circles it was considered effeminate for a boy to have an education.

Mary Ann Ryland West opened Dallas's first school in her home on the banks of the Trinity River after she arrived in 1845. She brought books and supplies from her home in Tennessee.

Only four years after John Neely Bryan set out to make Dallas a city, its first school opened a short distance from where he had spent his first lonely winter. The school was founded by Mary Ann Ryland West in her home on the banks of the Trinity River. Mary Ann was a teacher from Washington County, Tennessee, who moved to Dallas with her husband, J. R. Ryland, in 1845. She brought with her books and papers she had used back home. When she saw that there were no facilities for educating children in Dallas, she turned her living room into a school room. Though her pupils were few and the facilities meager, Mrs. West's school was a success. A year after it opened, she moved into a separate building half a mile west of her home near the present Triple Underpass. The log building had puncheon floors and wooden shutters for windows. Pupils used slates, and all examinations were given orally. Students who excelled earned hand-painted awards done by their artist-teacher.[1]

While Mrs. West was conducting her downtown Dallas school, Sarah Matilda Hughes Williams was starting her Texas teaching career in a small church at Cedar Springs and Oak Lawn. She is credited with being the first woman to teach in Dallas and may have preceded Mary Ann West by a few days or weeks. Sarah was educated in public and private schools and was a graduate of Columbia Female College in Maury County, Tennessee, where she had trained to be a teacher. She had taught in Tennessee before coming to Texas with her husband, Thomas C. Williams.[2]

Sarah was the fourth of the seven Hughes sisters (See Chapter 4) who moved to Dallas in its first decade. Though there is some question about who taught first—Mary Ann West or Sarah Williams—there is no doubt that Sarah, together with her husband, was the area's first public school teacher. She started teaching children in her home before her brother-in-law, Obadiah W. Knight, built the first public school building in the Dallas area in 1846. This combination church and school was located at what is now Oak Lawn and Cedar Springs. The building cost $300 in gold. The next year, Knight gave three acres of land to build a separate public school. He and Williams, Sarah's husband and Knight's brother-in-law; another brother-in-law, George Record, and John Howell were trustees. Sarah was the teacher.[3]

Sara B. Gray, another early teacher, came to Texas in 1855 from Kentucky to teach the Miller daughters and their friends. The year after her arrival, she and Miss M. Greenleaf opened a private school opposite the J. M. Patterson residence on the northwest corner of Sycamore (now Akard) and Patterson. Sarah Jennings was then hired by Miller to take over as teacher of the Miller daughters. Miss Jennings, from Virginia, continued to teach for three more years in the private Miller school.[4]

The John T. Coit Private School opened in far North Dallas County on the Coit property in 1859. Though it was always referred to as his school, it was Catherine Malloy Bunting Coit who was both administrator and teacher, and she who opened it with three students. By the end of the first week the enrollment had increased to eight. Cattie not only ran the school, her chief source of income, but also managed the farm while her husband served in the Civil War. Princeton educated, he was an attorney with offices in downtown Dallas. Cattie had gone to school in Salisbury, North Carolina, and had graduated from Harmony Female College in South Carolina as valedictorian in 1854.

By mid-1859, there were seven schools in Dallas. The tuition ranged from $1.60 a month for primary pupils to $2.50 a month for higher English. If a pupil wanted instruction in languages, there was an additional fifty-cent charge.[5]

In 1865 a new private school, the Coughanour School, opened for girls in downtown Dallas. It was owned by Hallie Gibson Coughanour, a teacher from Kentucky. Opened on September 4, 1865, it was very popular for several years. Known as Lou, Mrs. Coughanour was an astute businesswoman and an educator who understood that parents wanted more than reading, writing and arithmetic for their children. She hired faculty trained in art, music and elocution. Mary Owen was the popular music instructor. By the time her school was three years old, in September of 1868, Lou began holding classes in a two-story brick building at Main and Lamar and in 1876 moved into a new building on the corner of Griffin and Still. It was described by reporters of the time as "a building of architectural conceit, very chaste and charming." Its total cost was $500. To attend this "chaste and charming" school, pupils paid $30 to $50 per year. At its peak, the school enrolled 40 students a year. Using $40 as the norm, this would mean that she collected some $1,600 per year in tuition. By the time she paid utilities and upkeep, one wonders what kind of salaries were paid to teachers.

The private school system was outstanding principally because educated women did what educated women in Dallas have always done. They gave their time to serve their community. Married women who did not have to support families often taught because teaching was an accepted career option. Single women teachers, unless they lived at home, or in approved homes with friends, lived in genteel poverty. Teaching, then as now, did not pay well.

The public school system was in chaos—erratic at best and non-existent much of the time. Terms were short; school was closed when the money ran out. Children missed class as often as they attended. They were kept out to help with family chores and were absent in inclement weather. In 1880, records show a total enrollment of 1,218 students; 1,351 in 1881; 1,453 in 1882 and 1,760 in 1883.

The City Council operated the schools. It chose four trustees, one from each of the four wards. It appointed examiners for teachers, and beginning in 1877, levied a tax, one-half of one per cent, for school purposes. Indirectly the City Council also hired the teachers who were paid, pittance though it was, from city funds designated for that purpose. Teachers' salaries, according to state law, depended on the attendance of pupils. In 1883 a special tax was levied in Dallas to build a free school house in every ward. In short, the school system was in a mess and getting worse instead of better.

By 1884 there were seven public schools with a total of 15 teachers, only one teacher more than in 1877 when the city first took over the schools even though the enrollment had increased by 558 students. In numbers, this meant 15 teachers scattered among seven schools, teaching all subjects, with a teacher class load of 117 pupils. There were no high schools.

Then came Sunday, June 16, 1884. It was a sweltering day, 102 degrees outside when three men—R. D. Coughanour, L. M. Martin and E. M. Tillman—met in Coughanour's office and outlined a public education system. They made very short work

Private schools serving a few pupils each proliferated in Dallas's early days. They were founded by educated women who gave their time freely. When teachers were hired, they were paid a pittance.

The Dallas Public School system was established on June 16, 1884, in a matter of hours after the Texas Legislature had revised its educational system earlier in the year. Schools opened the third Monday of September and continued until the money ran out—which usually came very early in the spring.

of setting up a new school system—so short, in fact—that their work had to have been the culmination, rather than the start, of the project. Reorganization of the schools probably was surreptitious. In early 1884, the State Legislature, in a special session, revised laws governing Texas' public school systems; the new laws had become effective on February 6. There is no doubt that some of Dallas leading citizens, versed in law, recognized the impact of the new laws and their value to the city and acted immediately to see that Dallas had its share of state funds for public schools.

Five days after the Sunday meeting, on July 21, 1884, Mayor W. L. Cabell ordered "That all former Ordinances in relation to the city public school are hereby repealed." With the mayor's blessing and the new school board's persuasiveness (there were now added to the original three organizers John Loucks, G. M. Swink and John H. Jones as board members), the board's first important business was to divorce itself from the City Council. Whatever reservations the city may have had of letting go of the schools did not come up as a public issue. As was the custom in those days and for many years to come, controversy was avoided by a small group of men getting together, deciding what should be done, persuading any objectors, and turning their ideas into law before the public knew what was happening. When the city granted the schools autonomy, the board officially became the Board of Education with members elected by the people.

What went on behind the scenes was largely business as usual. A small handful of influential men still determined who would run for office and, thus, who would run the schools just as they decided who would run the city. It was not until 1947 when the State Legislature amended the city's charter that the school system was officially divorced from the city and became an autonomous entity, the Dallas Independent School District.

The first board of education elected L. M. Martin as its president and began the search for a superintendent. Shortly thereafter it hired W. A. Boles.

The Texas legislature decreed that public schools should begin on the third Monday of each September and continue until the money ran out. In 1884, September came in on a Monday, so the third Monday fell on September 15. In Dallas, eight schools opened for classes—four elementary white schools, two elementary black schools and one high school each for blacks and whites. A total of 703 students enrolled for the first term, 181 of them black and 522 white. The total faculty consisted of 16 white and six black teachers, an average of two teachers per school. The total operating budget was $13,153.85 for the year, or $18.71 per pupil. Money ran out in March and school was over for the year.

Two women were among the first eight principals. Blanch Adelhoff headed White School No. 3 and Leila Cowart was principal of White School No. 4. While the schools were still in their infancy, Miss Cowart moved to White School No. 1 and Miss N. P. Crane became principal of No. 4. Little is known of the Misses Adelhoff and Crane, but Miss Cowart remains a major presence in Dallas education with Leila P. Cowart School, 1515 South Ravinia, named for her.

All writers of early Dallas schools mention Leila Cowart. A heavy-set, slow-moving woman whose teaching methods were as unorthodox as they were successful, Leila (and she would have been horrified to have been addressed by her first name) lived with her sister, Lora Cowart, in the home of their brother, Robert E. Cowart in The Cedars near downtown Dallas. Lora ran the private Cowart Hall School for girls and was a thinner, more fashionable version of her older sister. Leila was principal of one or another Dallas elementary school for years, serving for many years as principal of Columbian School, but her career got off to a rocky start.

Within a couple of months after the organizational meeting for the Dallas public schools, and a month before school actually opened, Leila's teaching certificate was validated. Nineteen days later, on September 6, the action was rescinded, even while the board was hiring her as principal of School No. 4. She began her teaching career without certification and without pay. In January of 1885, almost five months into the school year, her brother, Robert Cowart, an attorney, took the issue up with the school board which promptly issued her a check for $100 (less than $20 per month!) and validated her certificate.

John William Rogers, in his delightful book, *The Lusty Texans of Dallas* tells wonderful stories about the Cowart sisters:

> ... Miss Leila and Miss Lora Cowart ... were both teachers. Miss Leila ... ruled as a kind of majestic autocrat who thoroughly impressed teachers and pupils alike. Now and then she interrupted her regular classes to discourse upon what she called "ethics."
>
> In her later years just about the time horses were being crowded off the streets by cars and traffic was becoming complicated enough to demand intersection policemen to direct it, Miss Leila acquired a buggy and old horse named Taylor. Behind Taylor she ambled comfortably along, slowing traffic, making U turns and otherwise violating ordinances in a fashion to arouse the most violent gesticulations and reproachful noises from the guardians of the law. So many hundreds of boys and girls had been in her school that whenever anyone spoke to her whom she did not recognize, she assumed it was an old pupil. To her, the policeman was simply one more ... whose violently remonstrating gestures expressed his extreme pleasure at seeing her again. She would nod graciously and slapping the reins against Taylor's fat back, continue serenely on her way, leaving the policeman with the feeling that there were some things too august even for the law.[6]

Rogers relates other stories that help to make the Cowart sisters human beings rather than pedagogues. Once, he said, a friend was commenting on the fact that neither sister ever married and Miss Leila came back with: "It's *vulgar* for all the women of a family to be married! In every common family, you'll find all the women married!" Her sister had a more philosophical view: "If you don't marry and have your own troubles," Miss Lora said, "you have other people's."[7]

The first few years of public education was a daily test of survival for teachers, administrators, children and the public. Unaccustomed to *forced* education by the state, many parents refused to enroll their children. When the kids did enroll, they often created havoc in the classrooms. For several years, sons of the *landed gentry* were still sent back to the east and north to school. Many boys who enrolled in the public school attended class sporadically and usually dropped out as soon as they were old enough to help in the family business. There are three times as many girls as boys in early classroom pictures.

In 1888 when the Dallas high schools graduated the first class, eight students received diplomas. All were girls—Nettie Bailey, Mattie Boyer, Mary Childress, Mattie Helm, Rosa Miller, Blanche Seiden-Bitel, Vesta Stokey and Minnie Terry. Until 1910 girls continued to outnumber graduating boys. The senior class picture of 1901 shows 21 girls and 10 boys and the class of 1906, 17 girls and seven boys. For a few years after boys were listed among the graduates, commencement programs noted career choices for the boys and family dreams for girls.

Through the years, many educators have looked back to *the good old days* when kids came to school eager to learn, parents were cooperative, discipline was no problem, and the community held education in esteem. Except for brief intervals, this has never been the norm in Dallas's public schools. It has probably never been the norm anywhere. The very nature of a public school system creates conditions that must be solved time after time after time. As soon as one issue is resolved, another surfaces, and resolution inevitably lags behind challenge. At its best, educated, dedicated teachers—determined to teach kids regardless of their backgrounds—are the glue that has held the public education system together.

Women have been the major part of that glue, for it is women—at least four to one—who have been the classroom teachers. For the most part, these women have been exceptional for at least two reasons: Because teaching was one of the very few avenues that society condoned for women, the most gifted and educated women of the community

Educators have looked back to the good old days when kids came to school eagerly, learned quickly and gave no trouble. Except for brief intervals, this has never been the norm. The very nature of public school education creates challenges that must be repeatedly resolved.

chose to teach. Second, the training and conditioning that girls got both in their homes and in their schools gave them the skills and patience to deal with daily minutiae that characterizes the average classroom.

Because men have headed the schools, and because in the natural order both credit and blame stops with the leader, the thousands of outstanding women teachers have been ignored. Their contributions to the city and the nation literally drop through the cracks of history into oblivion.

Though women headed almost half of the schools during the first decade of the public school system, this quickly changed. In its second decade, only three women, Emma Haley, Annie Moore and Margaret Henderson were advanced to principals. Emma was the third principal of the Oak Grove School, originally White School No. 4. A new building had been erected in 1889 at a cost of $20,000 and Miss N. P. Crane, who had been principal was replaced with W. R. Pitman at a salary of $1080. (There is no record of Miss Crane's salary, but her predecessor, Leila Cowart, earned only about $50 a month.) The new building was known as Oak Grove School. Pitman served one school year and was replaced with W. H. Kimbrough from 1890 to 1893 after which Emma Haley took over for four years. Annie Moore became principal of White School No. 3. She was recognized as a firm but gentle disciplinarian when she reported, by the end of the term, only three cases of corporal punishment while the other seven reported 147 for an average of 20 each. Margaret Henderson headed San Jacinto School from 1898 until 1926, a period of 28 years. She was revered as principal emeritus when she retired on July 13, 1926. During the next decade, 1900-1910, Mary Spears was the only woman promoted to principal of Dallas schools. She was named principal of Sam Houston School in 1907 and served 11 terms. In the next decade, 1910-1920, two women became principals. From 1920 to 1930, 14 headed schools. From 1930 to 1940, schools were headed by 11 women. In the 1940s, 13 women were principals. In the 1960s things began to change when 33 elementary schools had women principals and the change continued until by its 100th anniversary in 1984, 24 per cent (45 of the 189) of the principals of Dallas schools were women. At the 150th anniversary of Dallas, 1991-92, that percentage increased to 46 per cent (91 of 199).[8]

Even though their numbers have been small and totally out of proportion, women principals have made a lasting impact on the school system. Measured by longevity, they are more stable than their male counterparts. During the first 80 years of the public schools, men principals remained in their positions an average of 4.41 years while women stayed 6.57 years. While many factors other than longevity determine the quality of the educational system, one consistent factor is stability. While there has been criticism that some principals have been locked into jobs for which they are not qualified, there is clearly more evidence that most schools benefit when their leaders remain long enough to understand the climate of the school, the quality of the teachers and the surrounding community conditions.

Women were not deemed capable of administering junior high and high schools. The first woman to become principal of a high school was Julia C. Frazier assigned as acting principal at Dallas Colored High School in 1919 to complete the term of B. F. Darrell who died in mid-semester. In making the appointment, Justin F. Kimball, superintendent, said: "Mrs. Julia C. Frazier is scholarly, progressive, an excellent instructor, splendid in discipline, a woman of sterling character who stands for the best in her race in every phase of life. I know of no more worthy teacher than she." Even so, she was replaced at the beginning of the next year by C. F. Carr of Palestine.

Mrs. Frazier[9] studied at Howard University, Clark University and Columbia University. She specialized in foreign languages and taught Latin, English and German before becoming principal. After losing the post of principal, she returned to teaching at Booker T. Washington High School and retired in 1924. Born Julia Caldwell on October 10, 1863, in Sommerville, Alabama, she grew up in Columbus, Georgia. It took her eight years to work her way through Howard where she graduated as the only woman in a class of six in the late 1880s. She moved to Dallas in 1892, married W. W. Frazier, a

Julia Caldwell Frazier was the first woman to be principal of a Dallas school. She assumed the post following the death of Principal B. F. Darrell in mid-semester. Even though her work was exemplary, she was replaced for the next term by a male.

professor, in 1908, and died in 1929. Today, at 4600 Spring Avenue, a kindergarten-through third grade elementary school bears the name Julia C. Frazier.

Jimmie Tyler also assumed an administrative post in DISD schools in 1929. She was the first African-American woman to be named a supervisor and administrator of grades one through five. The following year she was married to high school track coach and science teacher A. W. Brashear of Lincoln High School. She was not allowed to have an office in the administration building or use any of its facilities.[10] She worked alone with an office in one of the segregated black schools. She had to get approval for what she did from one of the white supervisors whose position was equal to her own. It was not until after the Civil Rights Act of 1964 that DISD administrators met together for the first time and that offices were provided for them in the Ross Avenue building. Jimmie helped to start the Reading is FUNdamental (RIF) programs in the Dallas schools. In 1967, she retired from DISD after a career of 38 years. She then taught at Bishop College for the next four years. During her career, she studied for an advanced degree at a number of colleges and received a master's in supervision from the University of California at Berkeley. She was honored with a wing of the East Oak Cliff subdistrict complex being named the Jimmie Tyler Brashear Early Childhood Center.[11]

Jimmie Tyler Brashear became a DISD supervisor in 1929, the first African American woman to hold an administrative post.

In the past, overall, the quality of education taught by black teachers excelled that of white teachers—for two very specific reasons. First, their training was superior. Texas did not offer certification to teachers of African-American heritage and those who aspired to advancement went to other states to study, usually choosing the country's superior colleges and universities. For this reason, they brought to their classrooms a broader educational background and more specific skills than their white counterpoints. Second, African-American teachers, overall, were more dedicated to their professions. They had to be. Positions for black teachers were very limited and only top quality professionals survived. Many observers of the public school system in Dallas say that the overall quality of African-American teachers declined after Texas began to certify them. At the very least, a more provincial quality invaded the classrooms.

Edna Rowe spans a century of public school education in Dallas from early 1883 when she entered the third grade until she retired as a teacher in 1944 after 55 years, as student and teacher. She was graduated as salutatorian of her class in 1893. During her senior year she had taken teacher training and immediately, upon her graduation, was hired in the McKinney Avenue School as a *supernumerary* teacher. Her responsibilities included taking charge of the principal's fifth grade class when he was on other official school business. Edna was only a teenager herself, but she had little trouble with her charges, some five to seven years younger than herself. After a year in the McKinney School, she entered the University of Texas where she completed her bachelor of arts degree in three years and returned to Dallas to teach. She was assigned to Oak Grove school where she took her responsibilities so seriously that she failed the entire class on a history examination. The principal pointed out that something was amiss when nobody in the class could pass the course and Miss Rowe relented—somewhat. She re-tested the class and failed only half of them. Edna Rowe went back to school and was among the first of the DISD teachers to earn a master's degree. Though she taught history and English and later became a senior counselor, one of Miss Rowe's contributions to the schools was persuading Wylie Parker, principal of Forest Avenue High School, to open a home economics class for boys. She remained vitally interested and a strong advocate of the public school system until her death in 1965.

Marilyn Calhoun is one of many Dallas principals who have excelled in their roles.

Fannie Chase Harris was one of the first three teachers hired by the new school board of Dallas public schools. Born into slavery on a plantation in Georgia, she was the daughter of Jane (no last name) and the son of the plantation master. When freedom came for African-Americans, she was adopted by a friend who sent her to the Quaker public schools in South Carolina, after which she earned a teaching certificate from the Clafton Normal School in Orangeburn, South Carolina. She became a master teacher. As a young woman, she moved to Texas, settled in Corsicana and began her teaching career. Married to an attorney, she had a daughter, Frederica Chase. Later, following Chase's death, she married F. L. Harris, a prominent Dallas civic leader.

At Booker T. Washington School where she taught first grade for many years, Fannie Harris achieved phenomenal success that may be unmatched throughout more than a century. She was the school's only first grade teacher and one month, May 29, 1908, she had 145 children enrolled in her class! One school year, October 1908 through June, 1909, she averaged a monthly enrollment of 113.78 first graders and had an attendance record for that period of 94.11 per cent.[12] The same records show that enrollment for children of African-American descent diminished dramatically from one grade to the next through high school.

Birdie Alexander, who lived well into her 90s, was another teacher whose indefatigable enthusiasm for education stretched the minds and hearts of generations of Dallasites. Her greatest enthusiasm was for music, and she became the music director for the Dallas schools shortly before the turn of the century. Principals, encouraged to add music training to their curricula, were thwarted by their inability to hire trained teachers and had to accept anyone who could play a little on the piano, had a good voice, knew the rudiments of directing and was willing to be talked into taking on the extra chore. Birdie Alexander was a good persuader and a tireless cheerleader. As music supervisor, she traveled from school to school where she was able to meet every class for a thirty minute lesson once every 22 days!

It was about this time that some school leaders and board members began to clamor for physical education in the schools. Miss Alexander was not opposed to it; she just thought her music classes were providing all the physical exercise a child needed. In 1899 she wrote: "Consider its (music) benefits to the physical nature. No other exercise, no tonic can compare with singing in strengthening the lungs . . . . Circulation is quickened, the blood purified, and the nerves aroused to activity."[13] Not only was she convincing, but so persuasive that physical education was voted down at that time.

The best view of almost anything comes from those who live it, and an essay by Lillian Elliott Salisbury offers a glimpse of education through the eyes of a pupil during those early days:

MY SCHOOL DAYS

. . . I believe that I started school in the year of 1894.

There were four rooms. Our Principal Mr. Moore taught in the lower right hand room.

. . . there were three schools in Dallas, the East Dallas High, the Alamo, and the Lagow; there was one school in Oak Cliff.

There was one street car in Dallas then and it was a mule car. It was a small street car and it had to be drawn by small mules. The driver carried a whip and the wheels ran on a track from the Alamo School to the Adolphus Hotel downtown.

In the year 1900 the Mayor's daughter of Dallas drove the first electric street car . . . to the school and back to town; from then on we had no more mule cars.

We went to school by eight thirty each morning and if our grades were good enough we left at four.

. . . if we missed five words in spelling we remained after school and wrote each word five hundred times upon the black board. We had no school on Friday afternoons, nor did we take any books home on Friday.

We always went to Mr. Moore's room on Friday afternoon, and there we recited poetry and sang songs. The janitor would pin a sheet upon the wall and

Birdie Alexander thought that music and singing provided all of the physical exercise a student needed. As DISD's music supervisor, she traveled from school to school where she taught the music class for 30 minutes each every 22 days.

show what was called slide pictures. A kerosene lamp was lit and slides passed in front of the light and we enjoyed seeing the Katzenjammer Kids....

Mr. Moore came to each room before class started each morning and he would read a verse from the Scriptures and then pray a short prayer.

One time just after Thanksgiving I remember I got a surprise of my life. Our teacher sent each one of us to the board to decorate the boards for Thanksgiving. I drew a huge turkey; we went home for Thanksgiving and when we returned our teacher, Miss Cassell, passed out some photographs and among them was a picture of my drawing. I was so happy.... She gave the photograph to me and I kept it for a good many years.

The streets of Dallas had no electric lights in these days. On Main, Elm and Commerce there were lamp posts, there was a kerosene lamp in a glass box upon each post. A man would go each day from post to post and clean and light the lamps.

... The school ... had no side walks, nothing but board walks, although the front of the building resembled the Alamo.[14]

Without organized physical education, students worked off their energy in any way they could. Maggie May Fife once recalled that when she was a student at Central High School, the girls would slide down the banister railing for exercise and then sit and wave at the business men on Bryan Street as they drove to town in their buggies.[15] After her graduation from East Dallas School, Maggie May passed the state examinations in 1903 and became a supernumerary at the Alamo School assigned to teach gymnastics because, her principal told her, she was little and frisky and could do anything! She earned $15.00 a month. She reached her classes by riding the Hickory Street trolley.

It was also in 1903 that Dallas got two new public schools, Colonial Hill and Davy Crockett, the later name changed in 1955 to the more formal David W. Crockett. Mrs. C. J. Nilsson, as an adult, wrote:

MEMORIES

In the "olden days," it was fun to go to school at Davy Crockett—more fun than any other school in East Dallas—because in those days the school grounds (what is now the playground) were on a creek! You know where Victor Street runs along the playground now? Well, Victor Street used to be a CREEK, with steep banks and huge trees and all kinds of underbrush and growth, and water trickling along over the rocks and pebbles. And you know where Carroll Avenue crosses Victor Street now? Well, Carroll Avenue ran over a bridge, and that is the way we got across the creek to come to school. And in those days, some of the boys used to lean over the bridge rail and "fish" for craw-dads—and then scare all the little girls with them!

Inside, the school was ... all dark brown, and there were no light-colored walls and halls, like now. And each room was heated by its own big, round stove in one corner—and those sitting close to the stove nearly roasted, and the ones in the far corners of the room nearly froze. But there was one nice thing! Every so often during the day, the janitor would come in with a big coal scuttle of coal, open up the stove door and with an awful clatter, pour in the coal—which made such a noise, the teacher couldn't tell what anyone was doing and you could whisper or throw notes to your heart's content!

The Janitor's wife made a pot of chili on cold wet days. There was no lunch room in those days, so the children lined up at the fence next to the janitor's house and traded their nickels for a bowl of chili.[16]

In 1904 home economics, domestic science and arts—or, more precisely, cooking and sewing—was added to the curriculum. Industrial drawing for the boys had been added in 1897 and manual training introduced the next year. A few girls had been admitted

The quality of black educators was superior. Because Texas did not grant teaching certificates to blacks, they went out of state for their degrees and brought back to Dallas classrooms excellence gleaned from some of the country's best schools.

into manual training programs—designing, bench work, bent and beaten metal work, free-hand drawing, pen sketching, decorative designing, architectural drawing, sketching and painting and art, metal, leather and clay work—were still eligible to study with the boys if they chose.

Frances Sullivan was the first domestic arts and sciences teacher. The classrooms were in a building that previously had been a firehouse, with the "foods laboratory" on the first floor and sewing and drawing on the second. At age 23, Miss Sullivan felt and many times behaved as one of the girls and boys (she also taught mechanical drawing to the boys) who were her students. She roomed on Bryan across the street from her school with a family who also had a roomer named Alderson. Before the year was out Miss Sullivan became Mrs. Alderson. Judge J. E. Gilbert, the board member who oversaw home economics, had to approve all purchasing for the department and was often teased by the others on the board for the size of his grocery bill.

By 1908, most of the girls had abandoned manual training courses for domestic arts programs. They seemed content to cook and serve meals, as class projects, to their mothers, school board members and visiting dignitaries. Though they were not excluded from "shop" courses, the few girls who asked to be enrolled in manual arts courses were looked upon as strange creatures both by the boys who were their classmates and the girls in domestic science classes.

In 1904 Lida Hooe took over as supervisor of penmanship and drawing, an acceptable way to introduce art into the schools. Highly creative, Miss Hooe was also a pragmatist. She knew that the esoteric forms of art she favored would never succeed unless she introduced them in ways acceptable to the public. While teaching drawing, she introduced pottery. She was also an astute politician, who convinced the administration and the board that drawing would be greatly enhanced with the addition of a small annual fund to purchase "necessary equipment." Through the years "her vision directed and tempered the development of the art department. Fine arts continued to minister to man's emotions, but practical arts, aimed at ministering to man's physical and material needs, were never neglected."[17]

The first special school to teach English as a second language was opened in 1900 with Margaret Mosby as teacher. It was an evening school open to both adults and children who were first generation Americans. It was created at the prodding of the Daughters of the American Revolution; all expenses were paid by that organization for the first year until the school district recognized its merits and took over its operation.

In 1906 Priscilla L. Tyler returned to her native Dallas as a teacher. Born to the first freed Negro to own property in Freedman's town, Miss Tyler had completed elementary and high school in Dallas before going to Howard University and continuing her education at Colorado State Teachers College where she specialized in Spanish and excelled as a pianist and vocalist. She began her "home" teaching career at Dallas Colored School on Holland and Flora but transferred to Booker T. Washington School in 1924 where she taught Spanish for the remainder of her career. Her gift to the city was the organization of the Civic Music Guild to present Negro musical artists. She also organized the Pierian Club, the first scholastic society for children of color. In addition to her teaching career, Miss Tyler was involved in the cultural development of the community. She formed the Reading Circle and the G Clef Club and initiated efforts that opened the doors of Fair Park Auditorium to African-Americans who wanted to attend operas there.[18]

Mary C. Spears headed an unusual teacher training program that began in the fall of 1914 and continued for several years. When Justin F. Kimball became superintendent of Dallas schools (1914-1924), he determined to raise the qualification and training standards for Dallas teachers. At that time, only 13 of the 409 elementary teachers and 42 of the 97 high school teachers had college degrees. With the approval of the board, but understandable anguish among the teachers and in the community, he required all future applicants for teaching positions to have a college degree. Further, he stipulated that all teachers then in the school system should "get a degree as soon as possible." Had the decree gone into effect overnight, chaos would have resulted, for only three per cent of the elementary teachers would have been qualified to continue teaching. As a bridge, several outstanding, experienced but academically unqualified teachers were chosen to work with new teachers as counselors and coordinators. In addition, a teacher training program was organized with bright Dallas high school girls given instruction and experience as cadet teachers under older and more experienced teachers. Coordinated and supervised by Mary Spears, this program continued in effect until 1924 when a plan of cooperation between the education department of Southern Methodist University and the Dallas schools became effective. SMU trained a "pool" of young women qualified to teach and DISD having "first choice" of their services. (See Ackerman, Part II).

Sudie Williams became acting supervisor of the music department of the Dallas schools in 1913 and through 27 years until 1940 when she retired, led an increasingly outstanding program of music education and appreciation. Her Sudie Williams Choral Club was an unusual choir comprised of more than 100 elementary school teachers who met weekly to study music, sing, support each other and make frequent appearances at public gatherings. Sudie knew what she wanted to do with public school music—and she knew how to make it happen. Shortly after her appointment as supervisor, she determined to put Victrolas (record players) in every Dallas school. Instead of going directly to the superintendent with her request, she chose a committee to study the situation and, no doubt, planted in each member of that committee the idea that "awakening and developing a taste for the best in music by intelligent listening" was imperative to a well-rounded education.[19] When the first committee report came back, the school board promptly granted her request for $25.00 to buy phonograph needles. (One wonders about the record players that had not yet officially been bought?) In 1926 the board approved buying 12 phonographs and in 1931 the business manager was authorized to take bids on phonograph records. This resulted in a circulating library of phonograph records in the public schools that Miss Williams decreed second to none in the country. It had taken awhile, but Sudie Williams had accomplished her goal. Music spread until it encompassed an entire city. Orchestras and bands, along with accredited teachers, were organized in almost every school. Sometimes it was impossible to determine which came first—the music program or the instructor to manage it. As if by magic, instruments appeared for students with a desire to participate in musical programs, but whose parents could not afford to buy them.

Sudie Williams was not only an excellent musician; she was also a diplomat. When she needed money to provide record players, she appointed a committee to report the need to the school board. —Texas/Dallas History and Archives, Dallas Public Library.

In 1916 Ethelyn Mildred Chisum joined the Dallas public school system. She, too, was a Dallas native, Born on June 9, 1895, to William Henry and Virgie Collins Taylor, she was educated in the Dallas schools, graduated from Prairie View Normal College with a master of arts from Prairie View University. During her career as a teacher and, later, dean of students at Booker T. Washington High School for 32 years, she studied counseling at the University of Michigan. She was one of the petitioners of the YWCA for the establishment of the Maria Morgan Branch to serve the needs of African-American girls and women. She served on the board with Ruth Potts Spence who acted as liaison between the various community segments to create the Maria Morgan Branch. Mrs. Spence recalled in an interview shortly before her death the "amazing qualities of Ethelyn Chisum and Esther Dyson" in forming that organization in the segregated Dallas of 1940.

Ethelyn Taylor married Dr. John Oscar Chisum in September of 1923. She organized the Dallas Counselors Club and served as president for 10 years of the Dallas Teachers Council, later rerenamed Classroom Teachers of Dallas. She retired in 1965 and enjoyed 14 years of travel and community activism with her husband prior to his death in 1979. Two years after she retired from DISD, she joined the staff of SMU to work with the Upward Bound program and continued teaching, guiding, directing and inspiring young people until 1982 when at the age of 87 she retired from her second teaching career, a career that had spanned 66 years! A few months later, on January 27, 1983, Ethelyn Chisum died.

As important as it was, music was not the *only* exercise, (as Birdie Alexander had stated), required to develop healthy bodies. It was time for a physical education program in the schools and Bessie Keller was chosen to institute one. To prepare the community for this new program, Superintendent Kimball said:

> No nation is ever stronger in physical constitution or in moral fibre than the race of women who are its mothers. A danger that threatens the Americans, especially in the South, is the feeble, undeveloped physique of its women . . . . Thousands of women grow to womanhood with flabby muscles and undeveloped bodies that have never had an hour of vigorous, hearty, red-blooded, wholebodied exercise in their lives.[20]

Miss Keller reported in 1915 on the physical education program in the elementary schools: "Swedish gymnastics, rhythmic exercises consisting of marching and mimetics, indoor and outdoor folkgames are all being used to build healthy bodies." She also reported that proper seating and ventilation was required and that in 16 schools a toothbrush contest had proved to be of great interest.[21] In the meantime Margaret Holmes was placed in charge of working with girls at Oak Cliff High School.

While the administration and faculty was focusing on healthy bodies and minds of students in ever increasing numbers, students with special needs had been ignored. Unless the children could be *mainstreamed* into regular classrooms they were either kept at home or allowed to fend for themselves at school. In 1915, this changed when the school board granted Superintendent Kimball's request to "employ suitable and competent teachers specially trained and experienced in the work of elementary instruction of deaf mutes." The first school for non-hearing children was a two-story residence at Washington and San Jacinto streets where Edna Washington, the school's first teacher, stored her educational materials in the large parlor, and bedrooms were turned into classrooms. Sixteen children enrolled. Siblings of the deaf children were allowed to accompany them to school and to attend a regular school, San Jacinto, across the street. The program for deaf children was so successful that it continued through the summer with a teacher hired, for $75 a month, to continue it. During the same year, 1915, a class was begun for pupils who stammered and in 1919 a special class was set up in each school for retarded children.

The schools ventured into early education of children with the introduction of its first kindergarten program in 1922. Verina Pegues was elected the first kindergarten teacher. For a number of years, then as now, the early education program came and went at the dictates of the school board and the economic and societally conditioned whims of the community. Then, as now, many people think that the only place for young children to be educated is in their homes by their mothers.

While freedoms for girls enrolled in the Dallas schools expanded, women teachers did not enjoy equality. A double standard for male and female teachers was clearly in evidence. Married men with families were much sought after and were paid much higher salaries. Married women were discouraged from teaching and finally, in 1923, were disqualified altogether by the board of education:

> The marriage of any woman teacher after election or during the scholastic term shall be considered a resignation and cancellation of her contract without further notice.[22]

The regulation remained in effect for two decades until it was rescinded on November 17, 1943. It stripped Dallas schools of many excellent teachers, among them Waymond Blythe Hood, who moved to Athens, Texas, where as an English teacher and sponsor of the *Athenian*, the high school newspaper, she wielded a great influence on my personal life. The regulation also denied many women, because of their home responsibilities, the option of teaching elsewhere. Mrs. Hood was one of the rare teachers whose husband encouraged her to seek a teaching position elsewhere. He continued his career in Dallas. She commuted on weekends. Their son was cared for by family members.

Throughout the early days of the Dallas schools, community women were studying what was going on with their children, assisting educators with special programs, instituting projects for the improvement of education and persuading their men to improve the system. Though women were excluded for many years from direct participation in forming school policy and in school organization and curriculum, they wielded continuing pressure both as individuals and through their clubs. And, though their first clubs were not organized as adjuncts of child education, almost every woman's club had the welfare and education of the next generation as one of its consistent threads.

14

••••

WOMEN ORGANIZE TO CHANGE THEIR WORLD

By uniting their efforts, women gentled the boisterous adolescent Dallas and gave it the foundation to grow into a well-rounded healthy adult. They did it through their clubs.

Often misunderstood, scorned and taunted, clubs have provided Dallas with untold benefits and the women who participate in them avenues to alter their circumstances and control their worlds, or at the very least, survive prevailing conditions with some degree of equanimity.

May Dickson Exall, at 22, became president of the Shakespeare Club, the first club organized by women outside their worship centers. Considered the "mother" of the women's club movement in Dallas, May organized the Dallas Federation of Women's Clubs for the specific purpose of establishing a library. She not only garnered the women's support for the library, but personally wrote the letter asking Andrew Carnegie for a grant, and she headed the campaign to elicit the financial backing of the men.

Women organize into three kinds of clubs, all of which allow them to study their environment, discover their talents, support others and make changes that enhance their lives and improve the community. The three types are:

- Clubs that enrich their personal lives: literary, music and art clubs, social organizations, consciousness raising groups and women's identity groups.

- Organizations that support their families—husbands and children: Auxiliaries (medical, dental, legal, realtors, etc.), families and lineage (DAR, Daughters of the Confederacy, Children of the American Revolution, pioneer and genealogical groups), and children (PTAs, mothers' clubs of all kinds).

- Groups that meet community needs and resolve problems: All social welfare and philanthropic organizations (survival—homes for the homeless and shelters for victims of abuse, for example—and physical and emotional health—muscular dystrophy, cancer, AIDS, AA, Depressives Anonymous, for example); environment and beautification (garden clubs and improvement and enhancement groups of all kinds.)

Often what starts as an organization to fill one special need spills over into others, and equally often an organization meets many needs simultaneously.

Dallas women join clubs to bring meaning into their lives; men join to bring fun into theirs. Men usually find meaning for living in their work; their clubs are for relaxation. Women, for years forbidden and always discouraged from working outside their homes, united to improve themselves and their surroundings.

Women's clubs have proliferated in Dallas for three distinct reasons: One, young women seldom join clubs already in existence. They establish new ones. Inexperienced and believing in utopia, they have no history of what has been accomplished; they see only what is left undone and organize a group to fulfill unmet needs. Second, every group, from its beginning, develops a bureaucracy that is difficult for younger members to penetrate. They feel lost and their voices insignificant. They create their own groups which they can control and where they can see the difference they are making. The third reason for the proliferation of women's clubs is that new issues surface and an organization is formed to meet the needs of individuals afflicted by new diseases or long-smoldering, but largely ignored, problems. Good examples are centers for the treatment of AIDS patients and families, shelters for the homeless and victims of abuse, environmental organizations and anti-nuclear groups.

The growth and development of the community itself is easily traced through its women's clubs because a new group is often a direct or indirect offspring of one already in existence, some of whose members perceive that the parent organization is not fulfilling the purpose for which it was founded. The Dallas Woman's Club, for instance, is the daughter of the Shakespeare Club, and its child is the Women's Council of Dallas County. Positive Parents of Dallas is a later-day arrival of the Parent Teacher Associations, which was the offspring of the Mothers' Clubs of an earlier era. Executive Women of Dallas is the child of the Business and Professional Women's Clubs. Women's Issues Network, the Summit and Women's Political Caucus are but three of the offspring of Women's Center of Dallas.

Acceptance is another, and perhaps even more significant, reason for the hundreds of different women's organizations. Many organizations are, or appear to be, exclusive. They are limited to members of a certain social strata or a particular interest area or have age limits or territorial boundaries. In Dallas, when women feel ostracized they soon form their own group to counteract what they perceive as privileges enjoyed by others. This is the main reason for the large numbers of similar groups trying to meet the same need. Groups, sometimes consciously but more often unconsciously, define parameters for themselves and establish territorial boundaries that dare others to penetrate their turf. This overlapping diminishes both the people power and the finances for problem solving and is a sad waste of resources.

The most effective women's organizations in the city have built-in systems of renewal and for keeping alert and vigorous. They accomplish this by making new members feel wanted and needed and by immediately involving them in meaningful projects that bring them personal rewards. They also put new members through training that teaches them the history of the organization, its purpose, its goals and its current and future plans. This helps make members feel a part of community while preserving their personal identity and nurturing individual talents. The Junior League has an exemplary training program. So do others, among them the Dallas Section, National Council of Jewish Women; League of Women Voters; Women's Council of Dallas County and Explore. Organizations that continue to do the same thing year after year with little regard for changing conditions soon die.

Thousands of Dallas women have found their niche for volunteer service among them—top to bottom, Sally McKenzie, Junior League president, 1968, with Bets Whitman, Annette Strauss and Grace Stemmons.

Women and women's organizations are the first to observe human need and organize to solve problems, either through groups to which they already belong or new groups they form for those specific purposes. Usually they have credited the men in their lives for the work they do.

Dallas women's organizations were born in places of worship. Given the fact that women were largely sequestered in their homes and that churches and synagogues were the only places they could go unescorted, it is not surprising that their religious centers provided the setting, the impetus, and the inspiration for their first organized work.

The Dallas German Ladies Aid Society, organized in 1871 "to promote morals and benevolence," was the first church women's group, but it was not officially chartered until February 21, 1889, when Dora Nussbaumer, Fran Leopold Bayer and Mary A. Bohne filed papers of incorporation with the city and state. Because of this delay, other groups came first. The fact that it did not officially exist never stopped the organization from trying to meet the needs of its adopted city. It lent money, repaired houses, paid light, gas, and water bills, and made donations to orphanages and other welfare groups. Its records show paying a water bill, $3.97; a gas bill, 60 cents, and providing carfare, 25 cents for Mrs. Marks; providing a plumber, $2.50, for Mr. Hope and lending Mrs. Grossman $10.

From 1880 to 1891, 23 women's organizations within the Dallas churches were created. The Ladies' Aid Society of Central Christian Church, organized in 1881, was the first *official* women's organization in Dallas. Within the next decade, there were 22 more. The First Baptist Church had two, the Ladies Missionary Society and the Ladies Benevolent Society, both established in 1884. Two other Baptist churches had women's groups. There were five Catholic associations; four Christian groups; one Episcopalian; three Methodist; five Presbyterian and one Seventh Day Adventist. Because of their commitment to each other and the needs of the community, these women's groups exercised an impact far beyond their total membership of 767.

The women's club movement in Dallas outside religious institutions began January 26, 1886, when "more than a score" of women gathered in the Grand Windsor Hotel to form the Dallas Shakespeare Club.

From that winter day in 1886, the women's club movement mushroomed. Thousands of organizations have been formed by and for women. Many have folded, changed names, evolved into different organizations or merged with other groups, but many still exist. A woman's club, like her personality, is unique to her alone and no woman can judge for another the value of an organization.

The clubs included here are but a fraction of those thousands, chosen to show the diversity of interests and commitment to the city of women through a century and a half. They are:

The Ladies' Musicale, organized by Belle Fonda Schneider, to present and promote outstanding musical programs. Some historians say this organization preceded the Shakespeare Club.

The Standard Club, organized in 1886 by women in the Cedars, their answer to the exclusive Shakespeare Club, as a study group, but "ever ready to cooperate with any charitable or laudable enterprise," according to its charter. Mrs. Theodore Wallace was its first president.

The Chautauqua Scientific and Literary Circle, a group with 25 members organized by Mrs. C. C. Ardrey and Isabelle Gay Smith in 1888. Chautauqua was reorganized in 1894 by Katie Cabell Muse and renamed the Pierian Club.

Allegro Club, organized by Belle Fonda Schneider and "the Society Matrons of Dallas" in 1894 to "entertain three times a year with brilliant affairs—one, a formal ball; two, a large card or theater party, and three, a garden party.

WOMEN ORGANIZE TO CHANGE THEIR WORLD / 136

St. Cecelia's Club, organized by Alice Bryan Roberts in 1895 to "bring the finest choral works and outstanding professionals to Dallas." The 26 female singers met for years at 10 a.m. on Wednesdays at the YMCA Building, 293 Elm Street.

Dallas Federation of Women's Clubs, organized by May Dickson Exall and members of the Shakespeare Club on November 4, 1898, with one specific goal—to establish a public library.

Wednesday Morning Choral Club, "one of the first musical clubs open to all interested women" established by Elizabeth Frierson Crawford in October of 1903.

The Dallas Art Association, organized in 1903, by May Dickson Exall, to promote the study and acquisition of good art and to encourage and promote the Museum of Art.

The Dallas Woman's Forum, the first "department" club, each department related to public improvement," established by Adella Kelsey Turner and friends on March 20, 1906, with 200 members, The departments: Art, Bible and Sacred History, Congress of Mothers (PTA forerunner), Current Events, Household Economics. Literature, Music, Philosophy, and Civic and Philanthropy.

The Halycon Club, organized in 1907 in the home of Mrs. J. D. Padgett as the Priscilla Club to encourage philanthropic work and to promote the social welfare and development in the city.

The Suffragettes, an organization of high school girls organized in 1909, Dallas's first equal suffrage society. Members met at McKinney Avenue Baptist Church. A "partner" group of the Forean Literary Society for boys, it conducted "hot debates on voting rights for women." When Dr. Anna Howard Shaw spoke in Dallas, the Suffragettes were ushers.

Dallas Pen Women, organized in 1911, to promote excellence in writing and to be a support group for women writers.

The Stratford Club, organized in 1911 as a Shakespeare study club, to provide membership to women interested in Shakespeare and other literary figures who were not invited to membership in the Dallas Shakespeare Club.

Priscilla Arts Club, organized in 1911 by Esther Juliet Dyson shortly after she moved to Dallas as the bride of Dr. Albert Homer Dyson. The oldest club for black women in Dallas, it served for women of color in those days before integration in much the same way that the Shakespeare Club did for white women.

The Dallas Section, National Council of Jewish Women, organized March 13, 1913, with 75 members, the city's first club for Jewish women. Minnie Wertheimer Hexter was the first president. The group's purpose was "to promote faith, education and humanity." Since that day it has often been a definitive leader in service to the community, but at first it was cautious and circumspect. ". . . they undertook activities considered appropriate and socially acceptable . . . for middle-class ladies of their time."[1] Mostly, they were married to successful Dallas business and professional men and were "curiously uninvolved" in social conditions central to them as women, principally the right to vote. And, for more than half a century the majority of the members continued to think of themselves last, if at all. They founded kindergartens and day care centers, homes for abandoned children, the abused and the aged; established programs for the sick, handicapped and underprivileged, sought redress through the courts for the helpless (the foster child program, the child advocacy program), those in poverty, those in prison and their families, conducted educational programs for the alien, the illiterate and the

These women leaders include, from top, Marian Dillard (Crump), a YWCA executive, the first African-American president of Church Women United; Willie Newbury Lewis, a founder of the Women's Council of Dallas County, and Ann Richards, who honed her political skills as a member of the Dallas League of Women Voters.

WOMEN ORGANIZE TO CHANGE THEIR WORLD / 137

In numerous areas to the people of Dallas, these women made their mark. Top to bottom they are Anita Marcus, a children's advocate; Erin Bain Jones, the first professional woman to head the Dallas Woman's Club, with Margaret Jonsson, and a Woman's Club year opening with Mrs. Wesby Parker, left and Mrs. J. Curtis Sanford.

alienated. Whatever worthwhile things they did not initiate, they signed on to co-sponsor or cooperate.

The Jewish women were not always the *first* involved—remember the women going into the public schools to provide food and beautification—but they were the first to do it on a consistent, well-trained, organized basis and to go through established boards for backing. The Dallas School Board turned down their requests to be involved in projects time after time after time, but without exception they finally got what the community needed—the first trained school volunteers, the Penny Lunch program in Cumberland Hill School, the first medical facilities in Dallas Public Schools, the first services to the blind, the first services to the hearing impaired, the first free milk program to infants and children in the city, the first organized class for handicapped children, the first after-school recreation program in a public school. The list goes on. And in all of these, they did their homework meticulously to create a firm foundation of support in the community before they went public. Because of their commitment to community, it is difficult to ferret out individuals responsible for the different projects. "A 75th History of the Greater Dallas Section, National Council of Jewish Women—1913 to 1988" explains why:

> If we had given credit where it was due . . . we would have been forced to compare the relative contributions of the Section President and the line volunteer. Some very important people would have been left out. Further, it has been our intention to relate the efforts and accomplishments of an organization—the power of women joined together in the common pursuit of their shared ideals.[2]

Usually the women of the Council worked diligently to work themselves out of a job. They brought their projects along like good mothers rear their children, nurturing and caring for them with unabated dedication until they were old enough and strong enough to be let go. Because of this letting go, few remember—and, likely, none remember after a few years—the hundreds of large and small deeds initiated by NCJW for the good of the community. Through the years, some individuals stand out, not because they accomplished the projects single-handedly, but because they assumed the leadership and remained faithful, often under the most trying of conditions. Here are some:

Minnie Wertheimer Hexter, first president, 1915-1919, who guided the 75 charter members in its formative years. Born in Cincinnati in 1868, Minnie moved to Dallas when she was 20 and three years later married Victor H. Hexter, a young lawyer from Baltimore. She lived at 2534 South Boulevard, and at the time of her death on December 20, 1948, she was survived by sons George J. Hexter and Louis J. Hexter. Minnie initiated the Milk Fund in response to an appeal by the Dallas Tuberculosis Association shortly after she took office as president of NCJW. She fostered, molded, and sustained it for 30 years. In 1946 the Fund became independent of the Health Committee of NCJW and was named "The Minnie Hexter Milk Fund."

Blanche Cahn Greenburg, who founded the Dallas Infants' Welfare and Milk Association, the first organized program to provide nutritional supplements to poor children. Blanche began her work, first through the Dallas Free Kindergarten Association to meet the needs of immigrant children when she asked her personal friends to donate milk for children in the day nursery at the cotton mill and for a kindergarten in East Dallas prior to the founding of NCJW. The wife of Rabbi William Henry Greenburg, Blanche, born in New Orleans and educated in New York, was the daughter of Samuel and Bettie Amelia Levy Cahn and the mother of Edith Rachelle.

Mildred R. Sack, president, 1946-48, who established the Dallas School for Blind Children, the first day-school for these children in the South, followed by an intensive educational program for the parents of blind children. Mildred and her husband, Alfred N. Sack, personally financed all of the investigation, travel and the total budget of the Dallas School for Blind Children, Inc. until the school system took it over.

Hortense Landauer Sanger, under whose guidance the first social worker was assigned to the Dallas Police Department and whose work with children resulted in the first cooperative day care center in the housing projects of South Dallas.

Pat Peiser and Margaret Hirsch. Pat was president of NCJW in 1960-62 when it instituted Operation LIFT—Literacy Instruction for Texans—to provide a fourth grade reading and writing level through television to the approximately 7,000 illiterates in the Dallas area. With the co-sponsorship of *The Dallas Morning News* and WFAA-TV, Council members gave 9,000 hours in contacting students and teachers, supervising and promoting the project and giving financial assistance. Margaret Hirsch was the volunteer project director.

Anita Golman Marcus, president in 1962-64, whose major contributions were in the area of juvenile justice.

Jeanne Fagadau, president in 1968-1970, who initiated the school volunteer program.

Geraldine Muriel Danzer Beer, who founded the Domestic Violence Intervention Alliance and the Family Place to care for victims of violence within the family.

Sylvia Lynn Benenson, president 1978-1980, who worked in health and with the Asian population.

Joy Shechtman Mankoff, president 1984-1986, who from a 1979 program, "The Dallas Woman: Progress into the Eighties," exploring the status and roles of area women and their potential for the future, founded Women's Issues Network. It was the first time that an organization dealing directly with women's issues had come out of NCJW.

The only two women who, at Dallas's 150th anniversary, had served as mayors of the city—Adlene Nathanson Harrison and Annette Greenfield Strauss—were NCJW members. The training the organization gives its members provides them almost limitless opportunity to serve in an area of particular appeal to each. During the past several years, NCJW's major achievements have been in cooperation with other groups.

Those who wrote NCJW's 75th history best sum up the organization's intent and its value to the community:

> With each project the Section has uncovered deeper roots and causes, as its concern for delinquency led it into projects and programs dealing with child abuse, as its care for the elderly brought it into the battle with Alzheimer's disease, as—in its earliest days—its work with the blind immersed it into generations of service to the disabled. Every one of these areas has had a multitude of constituencies, and it has been the Dallas Section that has been the proficient convener and coordinator.[3]

For many years, most women made their contribution to the city through their hundreds of clubs. Top to bottom, the Dallas Bankers' Wives, Mrs. J. Darrell (Elizabeth) Francis and Mrs. Lockett Shelton, the Dallas Lawyers' Wives, founder Mrs. Kenneth Foree, seated with Jan Sanders, May Sanders, Gladys Scurlock and Jeanne Foree, and, Eleanor Sutherland and Lucy Polter, League of Women Voters.

The University Woman's Club, organized in 1915 for faculty women and wives of faculty of Southern Methodist University to meet the social needs of women and to support the university.

The Dallas County Medical Society Auxiliary, organized in the 4105 Live Oak home of Katherine Seay McReynolds (also its first president) with 17 charter members (71 before the year was out) on May 4, 1917. Established to "promote better health by teaching hygiene, nutrition, and safety measures in the home," it was the first medical auxiliary in the country and served as the model for the state auxiliary established May 15, 1918, and for the national auxiliary founded on May 24, 1922.

WOMEN ORGANIZE TO CHANGE THEIR WORLD / 139

Eunice Beene, right, and Rhobia Taylor were often speakers at small business women organization events.

Celeste Guerrero directed many successful volunteer projects for Dallas.

A trio of Women's Center of Dallas activists, left to right, Helen Schilling, Peyton Davis and Susie Streng.

The Sunshine Club of Dallas, organized on October 18, 1920, "to inspire kind and helpful deeds" for its members and as an outreach to the less fortunate in the city.

Sisterhood of Temple Emanu-El, organized "to revivify the home and inspire the best in womankind," on October 19, 1921, with Minnie Wertheimer Hexter as its first president.

Business and Professional Women's Club, (Dallas BPW), established in 1921 by Grace Whiting to support working women, to study laws and customs pertaining to women in the workplace, and to seek fair treatment for women in business and the professions.

The Dallas Southern Memorial Association, organized in 1922 by Mrs. Frank M. Field, with 72 members as "the last surviving link in the Confederacy."

The Dallas Woman's Club, founded by Katherine Seay McReynolds at the prodding of May Dickson Exall and the Shakespeare Club with its first meeting December 6, 1922, "as an intellectual center for all women of Dallas, to promote civic interests and to embrace every woman seeking enlightenment regardless of creed or economic status." It was the dream of May Exall that the Woman's Club would unite all Dallas women who were interested and able to provide social services to their city. Instead, the organization became exclusive almost from the start to the extent that years later, in 1984, Ruth Potts Spence, one of the founding members, would shake her head sadly and say, "The Dallas Woman's Club did not live up to the expectations of Mrs. Exall and Mrs. McReynolds. It very quickly became elitist, so we had to establish other groups to fill the void." In the early years the Woman's Club brought to the city many notable speakers including Carrie Chapman Catt, Fannie Hurst, Edna St. Vincent Millay, Gertrude Stein, and Margaret Bourke-White.

Junior League of Dallas, organized in 1922, with 40 members to "use their leisure time in volunteer service to the community." The Dallas League was organized 21 years after the first League was formed in New York City in 1901 and a year following the federation of leagues into the Association of Junior Leagues with 30 leagues. The Dallas Junior League was admitted to AJLA membership on May 4, 1922. Through the years, the Junior League has been *the* major contributor of service, including both hands-on volunteer work and financial backing to innumerable community efforts.

Church Women United, organized nationally in December of 1941 as the United Council of Church Women. The Dallas group, organized in 1912, preceded the national group, and helped in 1937 to establish the committee, which four years later brought the group together under the new name, Church Women United. The Dallas group remains one of the nation's strongest groups. Mary Louise Rowand headed the national organization from 1977 to 1980.

Dallas Lawyers Wives Auxiliary, organized as the Dallas Lawyers Wives Clubs by Edna Fisher Foree on March 17, 1926, with 93 charter members, to support their husbands' club and to serve as hostesses for visiting dignitaries. The organization now provides legal education for the young and serves as docents at Belo Mansion, the legal educational center. In keeping with women's inclination to credit men for their ideas and accomplishments, the organization's official history states that M.N. Chrestman, president of the Dallas Bar Association in 1926, founded the auxiliary, but charter member Christine Thompson said: "Many of the leading lawyers (there were between 100 and 150 when I came to Dallas in 1924) were of the 'old school' who thought the 'little woman's place was in the home,' but Mrs. Kenneth Foree, wife of the distinguished judge, was not easily discouraged and patiently waited for an opportune time to organize . . . . When Mr. Chrestman became president, Mrs. Foree made her move . . . ."[4]

The Dallas Women's Foundation, inspired by Helen Hunt, top, is an eminent success story. Becky Sykes, its first president, gets a hug from Pat Sabin, executive director; next, Pat with Helen Hayes, one of its annual speakers, and, bottom, Gloria Chapman, 1992-93 president, with star guest Jacqueline Joyner-Kersey.

Zonta, a "classified service club," established in 1924, "to serve the community." Its diverse membership is assured by one member from each profession. Three other "service clubs—Altrusa (1928), Quota and Soroptimist—followed Zonta to provide similar support and volunteer outlets for women.

League of Women Voters, organized in Dallas in 1938, with 16 women, the fifth League in Texas, affiliated with the national LWV organized by Carrie Chapman Catt in 1919. Nell Goodrich DeGolyer was the Dallas League's first president. It was established to recommend legal, political and social change following in-depth study of the issues and to work for improvement of conditions. The League's birthmother was the Dallas Equal Suffrage Association organized in 1920 with Nonie Boren Mahoney as its founding president. Some records credit Nonie as the first president of the Dallas League of Women Voters, but the Suffrage Association was disbanded following the passage of the 19th amendment and reorganized as LWV.

Women's Council of Dallas County, an association of individuals and organizations concerned with the quality of life in Dallas, and responding through research, service, education and action. It was organized May 4, 1954, by Mary Batts Aldredge, Katherine McLaurin Callaway, Betty Moore Chambers, Willie Newbury Lewis, and Louise Snow Phinney who felt that other clubs to which they belonged were not meeting the city's changing human needs.

Women's Center of Dallas, organized in 1972 by 13 women as **Women for Change, Inc.**, "to change society's expectations of women through research, education, counseling and communication." Maura Anderson McNiel was its first president and its Maura Awards, named for her, go annually to women helping women.

Two other organizations that support women's issues are the **Dallas Women's Coalition,** a federation of clubs devoted to women's issues, and **Women's Issues Network (WIN)**, organized in 1980 whose board *is* its membership and which, by its charter, can act quickly on issues.

The Dallas Women's Foundation, organized in 1985 by Helen Hunt, to teach women how to make money, handle money, and give money. It supports organizations that help women and girls, and has succeeded in bridging women of all ages, ethnicities, interests, political persuasions and religious heritages.

Many women's groups have struggled to be inclusive, but with limited success. Prior to the Women's Foundation, Church Women United and the Women's Council of Dallas County pioneered the bridging of ethnic, age and interests. Indeed, until the Civil Rights Act of 1964, only a few individuals and sporadic efforts were made to unite women of different ethnic backgrounds for common goals.

Some women still find value in forming their most intimate bonding with others of similar ages or heritages. Older women, for instance, do not often attend groups on the care of young children, and women of different heritages say they have unique needs that are not addressed in mixed groups.

Nellie Tafalla, past president of the **Mexican American B&PW** and an organizing member of the **Hispanic Organization for Women**, explained the need for groups exclusively for Mexican American women. "It's the only way we can develop organizational and leadership skills," she said. "It is difficult for Hispanic women to deal with highly organized Anglo groups. Young women, especially, feel uncomfortable. An Hispanic organization is something of our very own—a place where we are free to talk and know that other women understand."

Often, clusters of organizations with similar purposes form coalitions, councils or federations that include groups of clubs. Typical is the **Dallas City Council PTA** with representatives from the individual school PTAS.

Marion Price Scruggs, a leader in the early women's garden clubs in Dallas, served as president of both the Texas and National Council of Garden Clubs. She was the founder of the Federated Council of Garden Clubs in Dallas.

Mary Ray, one of many garden enthusiasts in Dallas, tends her own garden.

Garden clubs are another. In the 1920s, and extending through the 1970s, garden clubs blossomed in Dallas, resulting in the **Dallas Council of Garden Clubs**.

From the first, women had grown whatever flowers they could in their own yards, but the city fathers—intent on erecting buildings, laying transportation lines, providing utilities and running their businesses—showed little interest in beautifying their surroundings. Beginning in the 1920s, women's interest in gardening expanded to city beautification—and attention to the city's aesthetic image had its birth. The women did it against all odds. They were often ridiculed for their frequent flower shows, floral arrangement classes and gardening seminars.

Ella Harris Abrams was the first woman to push for city beautification. In the early 1920s she returned from a visit to Philadelphia and regaled her friends with stories about the beautiful gardens she had seen there. She was determined to replicate those gardens at her home, but her enthusiasm waned when the different climate and growing seasons made it impossible to create in Dallas what she had seen in Philadelphia.

But the seeds had been planted and other Dallas women joined her, determined to beautify their city. Several went to Houston for a club meeting and returned to talk about beautification projects in that city. Again, many of their efforts to transplant seeds and plants failed to work in their Dallas gardens.

John William Rogers provides insight into the interest and extent of gardening in the city:

> Miss Elizabeth Gordon, editor of *The House Beautiful*, said in the late 1940s that in Dallas and San Francisco there was more activity in gardening than in any other cities in the United States. The interest which Dallas had developed in gardens has certainly come from the fact that only recently has the community begun to discover what it can grow. It is in the intoxicated state of someone who has unexpectedly found gold in his back yard . . . water was scarce . . . the long hot summers made impossible...the sort of gardens which thrived in other parts of the world . . . there was lack of reliable information about cultivation in the Dallas climate.[5]

Prior to 1930, books and pamphlets on gardening, written in the north and northeast, did not provide information suited to the soil or climate of the Dallas area. The regions of Texas are, in fact, so diverse that information on what will grow and thrive in Houston or Tyler or Amarillo or El Paso cannot be used successfully by gardeners in Dallas.

It was not until 1932 that the first book researched and written specifically for the Dallas area was published. The book, *Gardening in the South and West*, was written and illustrated by Mrs. Gross R. Scruggs and her daughter, Margaret Scruggs Carruth. Marion Stuart Price Scruggs chaired the gardening committee for the Dallas Woman's Club which organized the city's first beautification group, the Dallas Garden Club. So many women were interested that one organization was unwieldy and a second group was organized. Its members wanted to name it for their founder, but Marion Scruggs adhered to the protocol of her time which dictated that ladies' names and photographs were never published. And, though she was the driving force behind the garden movement in Dallas, Marion Scruggs refused the use of her name. So it was that Marion became Marianne, a combination of Marion and Margaret Ann, the mother-daughter writing team and is the name of the second Woman's Garden Club.

Marion Scruggs started the Texas Federation of Garden Clubs and was a member of Dallas's first Planning and Beautification Committee. In fact, it was her behind-the-scenes prodding that created the committee. She chaired the planting committee for the 1936 Texas Centennial. From 1935 to 1937, she was president of the National Council of Garden Clubs. Her interest reached beyond the borders of the United States to Great Britain where she was a member of the Royal Horticultural Society. What she learned, she shared as a writer for numerous gardening and horticultural magazines.

At the peak of the garden movement, there were 252 clubs in Dallas.[6] Many of them were small neighborhood organizations that served members' social as well as educational needs, and many did not belong to the Council of Garden Clubs.

Minnie Marcus, right, matriarch of the Neiman-Marcus family, for many years was the executive in charge of flowers and gardens at the famed Dallas emporium. She was also a principal in the founding of the Dallas Garden Center.

Garden clubs were not the only organizations multiplying as Dallas expanded into the suburbs and beyond. Hundreds of individuals found their interests in specific topics supported and augmented by banding together. By the 1960s, women's clubs—large and small, neighborhood and community-wide—that admitted women to full membership numbered more than 1,000 in Dallas County.[7] Since then, as more and more women have gone into the paid workforce, many neighborhood clubs have disbanded. On the other hand, as the population grows and as human needs change, other groups have been established.

Throughout the years, every group of women has pushed and prodded, beginning in 1871 when the German women began their philanthropic work.

The Grand Windsor Hotel was the meeting place for the controversial first gathering of Dallas women outside their places of worship. The women met there at 10 a.m. on the morning of Tuesday, January 26, 1886, at the invitation of Mamie Trezevant, to form the Dallas Shakespeare Club.

The Shakespeare club, mother of women's groups outside their churches, germinated in the mind of Mamie Trezevant, a young bride in Dallas. Mamie was "the second Mrs. J. T. Trezevant," so described by one writer of the time. Accompanied by her friend, Miriam Morgan, she "seated herself in her dog cart for a long drive around Dallas to deliver invitations to a meeting at the Grand Windsor Hotel to a list of carefully selected guests. The purpose of the meeting was not divulged, and there was much speculation as to what this gay, energetic, and original young matron from St. Louis might have in mind."[8]

The speculation was justified. It was unprecedented for women to meet in the middle of a morning—and in a hotel at that! Every invited woman shared the titillating news with her family, neighbors and friends. There was much speculation and many questions exchanged over the women's newly installed telephones. Should they attend? What were they getting themselves into?

The day came and every invited woman showed up! Mrs. Trezevant presided. By today's standards, her suggestion that the ladies organize a club to study Shakespeare would be ho-hum. By the standards that prevailed in Dallas in 1886, it was mind-boggling. First there was profound silence as women exchanged shy glances. And then, with unanimous accord, they endorsed the idea.

The *Dallas News*, itself new in the city having only the year before been founded, reported the event:

> A number of ladies have organized a plan by which at least one afternoon each week will be devoted to exercise which promises to be at once pleasant and instructive. Shakespeare will furnish the topic for discussion on such occasions. The club is composed exclusively of ladies and it is understood it is to be their intention to exclude the sterner sex entirely . . . . This may appear cruel to the men but it will doubtless be helpful to the ladies . . . .[9]

The men were more than a little perturbed by their exclusion. They were baffled. Some felt threatened. Since there had been so much secrecy about plans for the meeting and what would happen once the women were in the hotel, an oft-repeated story—understandably omitted from official club records—has it that some of the men got together and hired one of the servants to hide in a closet off the ballroom where the meeting took place and report back to them what the women were up to. They doubtless were even more baffled when they learned that the ladies really did intend to study the Bard.

So enthusiastic were the women that they planned to hold a second meeting immediately. It took place two days later, on Thursday, January 28, in the home of Jeannette Ennis Belo on Ervay Street. They agreed on the framework of their organization and elected officers. The *News* reported:

> The ladies organized a Shakespeare Club last Thursday morning. They elected Miss May Dickson president and Miss Bessie Stephenson secretary, and are to read Shylock next Friday afternoon at Mrs. Trezevant's. I do not know who is to read the different parts. The business meeting was great fun. While each lady hesitated to speak out in a meeting somehow they were all willing to speak at once. The Club has a right to feel much encouragement for it will be the means of forming many friendships and will tend to inaugurate a diligent study of the great writer. We in New Haven think, as you are well aware, that Southern women have not kept up with us in this direction but I have not found it so. Many of the women in this little town could adorn the social circle of any community.[10]

The Dallas Shakespeare Club was the second women's club in Texas. The first was a similar club in Victoria a few weeks before the Dallas organization.

Like the Woman's Club and other organizations that followed, the Shakespeare Club was elitist. "Social lines were tightly drawn and requirements for eligibility were rigid," wrote Willie Lewis.[11] But, she added, "Texas was too new and the Civil War too recent for the development of fabulous fortunes. So there was no prestige of wealth; there were no social upstarts. The gently born were recognized by their interests, their attitudes, and their behavior." Even so, she said, ". . . membership was so eagerly sought that (it came to be understood) 'One is not elected to the Shakespeare Club but has to be born in it'."[12] The club's history also notes:

> In forming the original list, Mrs. Trezevant was wise enough in the ways of the world to know instinctively that it is neither moral nor intellectual superiority, but social prestige, that gives distinction; and that, even in a literary club, it is often not the most erudite and scholarly members but those with energy and imagination who make the greatest contribution . . . .
> One's church affiliation must also have had some influence, for almost without exception the charter members were all Episcopalians or Presbyterians.[13]

Though records say that membership was limited to 40 women, 43 are listed as charter members of the Shakespeare Club. Not a single woman invited to membership declined. Charter members are:

Ella M. Harris (Mrs. W. H.) Abrams; Sally K. Howard (Mrs. A. D.) Aldridge; Mrs. James Arbuckle; Miss Estelle Archinard; Elizabeth Mayo Harrison (Mrs. George T.) Atkins; Jeannette Ennis (Mrs. A. H.) Belo; Lulu Smith (Mrs. Robert) Berrey; Mrs. E. D. Childs; Katherine Moore (Mrs. Clifton) Church; Roberta Rosser (Mrs. Henry) Coke; Ada Ryan (Mrs. W. C.) Connor; Effie Rauch (Mrs. Milton) Dargan; Mrs. Alfred Davis; Grace Leake (Mrs. Charles) Dexter; May Dickson, soon to be Mrs. Henry Exall; Mrs. Sallie Dickson; Mrs. Frank Doremus; Miss Douglas Ewell; Laura Gaston (Mrs. W. P.) Finlay; Elizabeth Lucas (Mrs. William H.) Flippen; Zillah Lee (Mrs. Charles) Grey; Jessie Pace (Mrs. Edward) Grey; Mrs. W. C. Howard; Mary Leake (Mrs. Harold) Keating; Mrs. J. E. Lett (Archinard); Mrs. John Locke; Mrs. Marcus McClelland; Mattie Caruth (Mrs. Neil) McMillan; Miss Miriam Morgan; Mrs. Richard Morgan; Mrs. M. A. Morrill; Mrs. D. H. Morrow; Mrs. Annie Pfouts Mumford; Mrs. J. T. Murphy (Mrs. H. J. Pettingill); Miss Irene Ransome; Belle Fonda (Mrs. Jules) Schneider; Mrs. Seth Sheperd; Bessie Stephenson Thompson; Lillian Jenkins (Mrs. H. G.) Strange; Mamie Lackland (Mrs. J. T.) Trezevant; Mrs. Charles Fred Tucker; Frances Aikens (Mrs. Henry) Van Mater, Mrs. C. E. Wellesley.

Occasionally an "outsider" has gained membership in one of the elite women's organizations, but not often. Willie Lewis shook her head over a new Woman's Club member in 1953. Pointing to the portrait of May Dickson Exall, she said, "Mrs. Exall would turn over in her grave if she knew we had made *that* woman a member."

Mrs. Trezevant was the logical choice to be Shakespeare's first president, but she declined, saying that as soon as she had the idea for the organization, she knew who its president should be. Her choice was May Dickson.

And so it was that May Dickson Exall (See also Chapter 18) became the "mother" of the Dallas women's club movement.

May Dickson was 25 years old and recently returned from Vassar College. The daughter of Joseph and Sallie Epperson Dickson, May was born in 1861 in McKinney. Her father was killed in the Battle of Shiloh during the Civil War, and her mother supported her children—May and her brother, Joseph M. Dickson, Jr.—by teaching piano lessons. When they reached college age, Sallie took them East where May enrolled in Vassar and Joe in Annapolis. Getting an appointment to Annapolis was relatively easy in those days, but being able to meet the physical examination was difficult. Joe lacked half an inch being tall enough to pass Naval Academy requirements. Undaunted, Sallie devised stretching exercises and saw that her son did them. He passed the examination and created a legend. When the family gets together, someone always tells the story of the time Grandma stretched Joe.[14] He graduated from Annapolis, but resigned his commission, went to Harvard Law School and for many years, as a bachelor, practiced law in Dallas and lived with his mother and later his sister.

May Dickson, as history records, was the perfect leader for the fledgling Shakespeare Club, a woman who became a legend in her own time. She was president of the organization for 50 years, and had just been reelected for two more years at the time of her death. The office then remained vacant for a number of years because no one who knew her would dare try to fill the position. "She gave everybody the opportunity to perform and to excel," says Betty May Exall Stewart, her granddaughter and namesake, "but she expected things to be done right. If somebody failed at a paper or a task, she did it—extemporaneously and perfectly.... But you only made that mistake once!"

In the several decades following the Civil War, there was a clear demarcation between one's public and one's family/home life, and because May was a very private person, few knew her well. Mrs. Stewart, who idolized Daddeese (the name she called her beloved grandmother), is puzzled by the way others viewed her. The public adulation was coupled with awe and sometimes fear. The private woman was complex, but exceedingly loving.

A year after May became president of the Shakespeare Club, she married Henry Exall. He was 10 years her senior and as relaxed and fun-loving as his wife was organized and proper.

The Exalls moved into a home on Ross Avenue at Harwood, though he spent a lot of time at his Loma Alto farm whose northern boundary was Lovers Lane and whose southern boundary was below what is now Mockingbird. Lovers Lane was a narrow dirt road bordered on either side with overhanging bois d'arc trees, secluded in the daytime and dark at night. It was the perfect trysting place for romantic couples and May Exall named it "Lovers Lane." She also named Mockingbird for the birds that kept up consistent song and chatter among the trees.

While May, fortified by a multitude of servants, found her profession in establishing and managing women's clubs, her husband developed his farm lands. He bought 1,326 acres at the southern boundary of his property and dammed Turtle Creek between what is now Beverly and Wycliff along Lakeside Drive to form Exall Lake. His intention was to develop an exclusive residential area to be called Philadelphia Place. He selected one of the most prized lots as site for the dream house he would build for his wife and young son. He died in 1913 before fulfilling his dream.

May and her mother Sallie Dickson built the house—at 4808 Lakeside Drive. Two mothers and their two sons—Sallie and Joe Dickson and May and Henry Exall, Jr.—moved into it.

When World War I interrupted the idyllic growth of Dallas, young Henry joined the army and was sent off to Tucson, Arizona, to train troops. There, on a Sunday afternoon, he and a friend went to a reception given by ladies of a church who had planned special entertainment for the soldiers. The star of the show was a beautiful blonde dancer. Henry turned to his friend and announced that he had seen the girl of his dreams and he planned to marry her. He had and he did, but not without complications. Her name was Dorothy Brannen. She was the oldest daughter of a Canadian family who had gone to Tucson for the mother's health. The Brannens were all musical. They all danced, sang, played instruments and spoke several languages. They were Catholic. Dorothy was also engaged to be married.

Henry pursued Dorothy with undivided devotion until, one day, she made up her mind to break her engagement. She spent hours writing two letters, one to her fiance explaining that she was not sure of her feelings and, so, was compelled to call off the engagement, and the other a carefully constructed letter to the young man from Dallas. She mixed the envelopes. Henry got the letter breaking off her engagement. Her fiance got the letter of encouragement. "It was quite a mess," Betty May Stewart says of the story she heard many times from her parents.

World War I ended. Dorothy Brannen and Henry Exall, Jr. were married on July 16, 1919, in Santa Monica, California, where the Brannens had moved. Henry brought his bride back to Dallas where their four children were born, Elizabeth May, named for her two grandmothers, but always known as Betty May; Dorothy (Flippen), Phyllis (Galbraith), and Henry Exall III.

Betty May was three years old when her great-grandmother, Sallie Dickson died. "I remember her," Mrs. Stewart said. "She played baby with me. I would be the mother and she would pretend to be the baby. She was a tiny little thing. I'll never forget when she died—that frail woman in her lace cap in that *big* bed."

Dorothy and Henry and their children moved into the Lakeside house with his mother. The combination had the ingredients for a family catastrophe. May Dickson Exall was an executive—organized, aloof, wise and a social perfectionist. Dorothy Brannen Exall was an actress—impetuous, effusive, warm and flexible. May worshipped in the Presbyterian Church, Dorothy in her Catholic faith.

Dorothy and Henry were married for 17 years when his mother died. For 12 of those years they shared a home. "In that entire time, we never had a cross word," Dorothy said.

Betty May Stewart agrees. "It was my grandmother's house," she said, "and Grandmother ran it. Mother never interfered. Mother raised us, and Grandmother never interfered. There was lots of help. This left Grandmother free to do her club work and Mother free to be her own person. Mother sang on the radio and acted and did what made her happy. My father was more like his mother, but he adored my mother. When she would come into the room, he would say, 'There's Dorothy Exall!' as if each time she were a lovely surprise. When he was older he wanted Mother to stay home more and she did—only to please him."

Betty May Stewart's memories of life in the Lakeside house are vivid—reflective, often funny, sometimes poignant.

"I think it worked so well,' she muses, "because everybody had a sense of humor—even my grandmother, who came over to other people as being so serious. For instance, when we kids got the giggles at the table, she would say, 'Let them laugh! Never hold back laughter. It's good for the digestion!'"

This from a woman who ran a household bounded by protocol. Dinner was at six—sharp. Everybody was present, properly attired and pleasant. Everybody stood until all were at their places. "Woe be unto anyone late for a meal!" Everybody sat. The meal was served by the butler. The adults talked about what they had done during the day and about ideas and books and travel and news, but nothing unpleasant. The children spoke only when they were addressed. The meal was leisurely; nobody left the table until everybody was finished. "Sometimes it was maddening," Betty May said. "I would ask for another serving and my sisters and brother would glare at me because that meant we would be delayed in getting back out on the lake to play."

There were times of great joy for the kids. To some of the adult neighbors, the Exall children were strange "because we were Catholic—at a time when Dallas wasn't aware of Catholics!" But on Lakeside Drive "we kids had no problem. We formed a club we called the Infant Jesus Club. We collected money to buy baskets of food for a poor family. I suppose Grandmother's actions rubbed off on us. Once we found in Grandmother's wastebasket some old tickets to a program that had already taken place. We formed a chain across Lakeside Drive and stopped the one car that dared to come down it—there were few cars in those days—and sold a ticket for a dollar. You could buy a large basket of food for a dollar and a half."

Betty May would sit at her grandmother's feet and listen to Shakespeare by the hour. "Later when I was in Hockaday, I would read Shakespeare to her in Latin. If I mispronounced a word or quoted incorrectly, she always knew it. My sisters escaped those sessions, but I was like a blotter, absorbing everything. She knew all of Shakespeare and could quote most of it from memory.

"I was 12 years old before I knew that her dear friend Shakespeare, was dead. It made me very sad. Once she and a group of her friends went to a Shakespeare performance. She sat with her eyes closed to enjoy the program. Before long, she opened her eyes, glanced to her neighbor to the right and the left and all the other women were glancing around, too, and soon as a single person, they got up and left. The cast was misquoting! I guess they thought the ladies in Dallas wouldn't know the difference if they took some liberties with the Bard."

But she did not correct her granddaughter, when at aged three Betty May made her first stage appearance. "I said, 'Is you as wise as you is beautiful?' and Grandmother applauded the loudest." Mrs. Exall once told Ruth Potts Spence that she'd rather have a conversation with her granddaughter—Betty May—than most any other person she knew.

Betty May was a teenager when she met Peter Stewart at a Dallas Country Club dance. A native of Kansas City, he was a Culver student whose family had only recently moved to Dallas. "I was extremely near-sighted and vain—wouldn't wear glasses," Betty May said. "My mother said everything would be fine if I just smiled a lot. So that's what I was doing. Peter asked a friend who was that girl who kept giving him the come-on." He cut in. And so they were married on July 18, 1942 . . . .

But not without complications! On their second date, Betty May a very young 16, was due home by 10 p.m. She didn't make it. "We really were innocent," she insists. "There really was a mix-up," but her parents were waiting up and pacing the floor. "I opened the door and saw Grandmother down the hall with her door open beckoning to me. I shot into that room and I stayed all night! Grandmother told me everything would be fine. My parents were just concerned about me. Not to worry." Her father ordered Peter out of the house and told him never to come back. He refused to go. At the height of the two men's frustration, the younger man explained. The older one was forced to listen. "They became the greatest of friends."

This, the comforting "angel" was yet another facet of the indomitable May Dickson Exall. She was:

Tiny.

Educated.

Articulate. "Her meetings were organized to the last sentence and at the podium, she seemed six feet tall."[15]

Tireless. "When she decided to do something, there was no stopping her."[16]

Formidable. "When she told the Dallas women, who had *never* been inside a downtown office, much less asked *another man* for money, that they were going to have to go to the offices of the business leaders downtown and solicit money to build the library, they were scared to death, but they did it because they were more afraid of Mrs. Exall . . . . She answered her telephone with 'Well!' If you wanted to speak with her, you'd better know what you planned to say and get it said. She had no time for dalliance."[17]

Concise. "Mrs. Exall was the first to address the assembly, stating in that simple style of hers, the story of the Ladies' Library Auxiliary, and reading the correspondence between herself and Mrs. (sic) Carnegie . . . ."[18]

Independent. "She didn't like for people to open doors for her and she wouldn't tolerate being hurried. She did not like for anyone to take her arm as if to help her. Mrs. Burgher was the only person in the world who could get her into the car after a program or meeting. She abhorred flattery. It irritated her to be given undue praise."[19]

Proper. "Mrs. Henry Exall, president of the Shakespeare Club, gave a beautifully laid and served chrysanthemum luncheon on last Saturday with Miss Abbie Hill of Houston in the seat of honor . . . . Miss Hill is a carefully schooled woman who . . . . has pursued her studies by the piercing light of Boston culture."[20]

Fascinating. "Mrs. Exall was the most interesting woman in town. She was brilliant. She had only one child and servants and limitless energy. If she had been living today she would be president of Harvard."[21]

Disciplined. "She was quite conventional, very disciplined, could be quite formal. She ran things well, the iron hand in a velvet glove."[22]

Tender. "She was warm and friendly and full of stories. When I was a baby, she took me to performances on a pillow."[23]

Peace-loving. "Her room was the Peace Room and she didn't tolerate controversy there. We went there only by invitation and at the lightest hint of disharmony, she would say 'Out!' If we wanted to be with her, we had to behave."[24]

Family-centered. ". . . a most accomplished lady who makes their home a haven of rest from the many cares of his busy life . . . ."[25] My father was her only child and she adored him. She was proud of my mother (who followed her as president of the Shakespeare Club in 1960) and she loved all of us.

Dependable. "Grandmother was a *given*. She was never sick. Never late. She took meticulous care of her health. If she were ever in pain, nobody knew it. During the summer before she died in September, at age 75, she beat me in a foot race."[26]

Modest. "She was really very shy, extremely modest . . . the most remarkable woman I have ever known."[27]

For all of the years of her life, May Exall continued to serve Dallas. From her home at 4808 Lakeside Drive, she could look out over the beautiful Exall Lake across the street, which became the gateway to Highland Park. There she lived with her mother and, later, her son and his family, from there she organized the Dallas Federation of Women's Clubs in 1899 and the Art Association in 1903 and from that house her last rites were held following her death on September 28, 1936. A widow for 23 years, she rests beside her husband in Oakland Cemetery.

Being a visionary May Dickson Exall probably knew that she was starting something significant and enduring when she devoted her life to founding and leading women's clubs, but it is not likely that even she could imagine what a profound impact clubs would make. Even as women have gone into the workplace, have found a niche in virtually every career and profession, clubs continue to be the single most significant avenue through which they impact the community, so much so that almost all women who work outside their homes have formed women's groups within their professions. Clubs provide education, support, structure and leadership training for their members and countless benefits to the city. Through their clubs women have founded and run day care centers and nurseries, schools and hospitals and clinics, social service and welfare centers, mental health associations, halfway houses, orphanages and foster homes, environmental protection groups and hundreds of other special interest organizations.

15

••••

A DECADE TO PLAY—THE GAY NINETIES IN DALLAS

The Gay Nineties could well have had its birthname in Dallas—for the 1890-1900 decade in the town was a time of unprecedented expansion and celebration. Even as the city, at its half century mark, struggled in stormy council sessions to know who it was and where it was going, a carnival atmosphere prevailed.

The Civil War was over, reconstruction all but completed, the frontier mentality melting away as education and travel increased. Amidst the "macadamizing" of the city streets, the laying of water lines, expansion of the fire department, construction of sewer lines and the erection of electric light poles throughout the downtown and into residential areas, the city's 67,042 people were merry. They could well have had more parties per capita than any other place in the nation.

The women on Ross Avenue and in the Cedars, now near South Dallas, the two most elite residential areas, were involved in a great many things other than giving elaborate parties, but it was the parties that drew the press. And, if you did not know better you would think, from reading the newspapers of that time, that all women had to do was compete with each other over who could throw the most elaborate and well-attended party. The several papers themselves were jockeying for position and, it would seem from reading them today, seeking out the most sensational gossipy news that the hidebound conservative climate would allow.

The Dallas Herald, which had begun publishing in the first decade of Dallas, by the 1890s, had been joined by a number of other publications. In 1879 an Ohioan, James Alonzo Adams, began publishing the *Daily Times*, which he sold to Edward C. McClure and William Green Sterett in its first year. *The Dallas Morning News*, arrived on Friday, October 1, 1885, publishing this birth announcement: "*The Dallas Morning News* was born at 4:15 yesterday morning. There were 50 people present .... Every man took the infant's birth to heart. The baby was born and is doing well."[1] Before the year was out, *The Dallas Morning News* bought out the *Dallas Herald,* but not before several other publications had begun publishing. Some were short-lived; others existed for longer periods of time, among them the *Morning Call* and *Norton's Intelligencer.* In 1888, the *Daily Times* merged with a new paper, the *Herald,* combined the two and became *The Dallas Daily Times Herald*. Totally unrelated to the old *Dallas Herald,* it thrived for most of its 103 years until 1991 when it sold to the *Morning News* and ceased publication.

By the beginning of the Gay Nineties decade, both the *Herald* and the *News* were excellent publications that devoted space to social activities and to feature articles including fashions and housing with an occasional article on home decor. Privacy prevailed. Even in their coverage of Society, the intimate details of local people were never published, but the capers of the rich and famous elsewhere, particularly the royalty of Europe, were reported in great detail. In retrospect, the long stories—often several columns—devoted to the color scheme, the flowers used for decoration, the number and description of what guests wore, the gifts and their donors lavished upon honorees smacks of superficiality. Judging with the perspective of history, it was not that at all—but the very human dimension of thinking and behaving in a manner consistent with the times. Predictably, even in those days, there were Dallasites who avoided having their names in the social columns. Stella White Spence and May Dickson Exall, for instance, both of whom were social meritocracy, are mentioned rarely and only in connection with their volunteer work in the community.

Each Sunday, lengthy articles on etiquette, along with sketches showing the right and wrong, were published. One, written for women, detailed the proper way to board a street car. Others outlined proper calling cards and proper behavior for leaving them. One lengthy article showed the right and wrong way to handle the reins when driving a horse. "When you drive a horse, you mustn't sit bolt upright . . . . Cross your reins through the palm of your hand, letting the rein which comes between your first finger and thumb pass over the thumb . . . by turning your wrist, you can control your horse . . . . Some horses know more than the men who drive them."[2]

Wedding etiquette filled much space. In the Spring of 1890, "The custom begins to obtain of offering wedding gifts to the parents of the bride as well as the young couple . . . . It is," the article continued, "a pretty spring fancy to have the bridal party enter . . . to . . . the air filled with "Lohengrin" sung by the bride's girl friends." It was decreed that "the bride must be in conventional attire . . . . White faille is the current favorite for wedding gowns . . . . it is not necessary that the bridesmaids wear white gowns."[3]

In many ways, the headlines of those days could be transplanted to today's newspapers: "Dallas City Council A Long and Stormy Session,"[4] and, again, "An Adjourned Session Last Night That Lasted Until Midnight."[5] Or, "The Turbulent Trinity Flooding,"[6] adding that "Gangs of men were working all night on the Oak Cliff and Santa Fe roads" to keep the water from rising into their business establishments and homes. "Dallas Bonds (were much) in Demand,"[7] and the Board of Trade had "A Turbulent Meeting on the Railroad Question."[8]

The city budget was passed rather haphazardly in one session with no debate when "Secretary Jones . . . estimated the amount needed for the city budget for the fiscal year ending April 1, 1891, would be, among other things, $20,000 for street work, $6,000 for lights, and $30,000 for salaries.[9]

Sanger Brothers was still the harbinger of fashion in the early '90s, and was selling ladies' and children's gauze and silk underwear for 50 cents, white aprons for 19 cents, and wool serges for 37 cents a yard.

An article on fashion proclaimed that a woman could have a vacation wardrobe that would make her "look like a queen" for $1.50. The article showed sketches of dresses for traveling and "simple fete gowns" for country wear.[10]

Speculative home building began in Dallas in the 1890s, with one of the first mentions in an article by R. W. Shoppell, an architect, who wrote about a three-story, seven-bedroom home of brick and clapboard with shingle roof, circular and three stained glass windows that could be built for $3,800.[11]

Speculative building doubtless caught on fast, because by early fall, the "neat double cottage," that later was called a duplex, was being touted. Eventually, as single family housing became the vogue, the duplex fell from favor only to be revived almost a century later as condominium for the socially elite.

Simultaneously with speculative building came real estate development with Dallas expanding north and east. Newspaper ads extolled the virtues of the different developments. Fairmont Place on Lemmon and Cedar Springs would "arrange terms to suit all buyers." Monarch Place readied 114 lots, each 50 by 135 feet. Caruth Heights offered "large lots" for $75 to $100, $10 to $15 cash, the balance on easy terms, all on the "rapid transit line."

For less adventuresome folk, or for those who did not have the $10 or $15 as a down payment, there were many houses advertising for sale and for rent. One lot, 149 by 213 feet on Swiss was offered for sale at $4,000.

Furnishing the living quarters was also inexpensive. In the winter of 1894, you could furnish an entire house for less than a hundred dollars. One full-page sketch of furniture could be bought "at Christmas bargains." Shown was a roll-top desk, 48 by 33

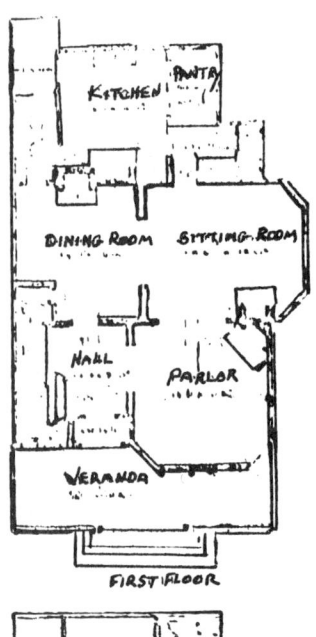
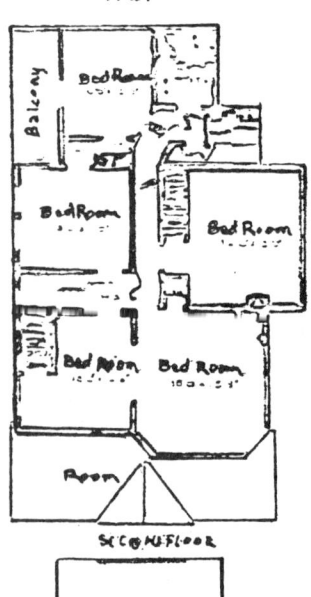
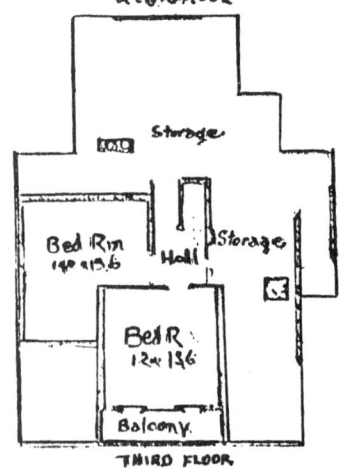

This three-story house, over a basement, could be built on Swiss Avenue in Dallas in 1890 for $3,800 when speculative building was first introduced in the city. The price did not include mantels.

inches, 45 inches high for $21.75. A combination bookcase in oak, 5 feet 6 six inches by 3 feet 4 inches with a French bevel mirror went for $16.75. An oak wardrobe with antique finish sold for $9.75, a solid oak bedroom suite consisting of bed headboard, dresser and chest was priced at $16.75, a polished oak occasional table was $1.45 and cane seated, elm chairs sold for 85 cents each. For the children's Santa Claus there was doll furniture, buggies for $1.95 to $2.95 and tricycles for $6.00.[12]

Religion, then as now, played a significant role in early Dallas. The women met in their churches, not only for mutual support in the good works they provided for the community, but also to provide religious training for their children. It was a woman, Mary E. Cogburn Oliver, who started the city's first Sunday School. She enlisted the help of her husband, F. N. Oliver, owner of the first business built in Oak Cliff, to establish a religious training program for children in the First Methodist Episcopal Church South in Oak Cliff. Mary, the daughter of Elizabeth and David Cogburn, and Oliver married December 13, 1868, and moved to Oak Cliff where their eight children were born and where he became mayor of Oak Cliff and owner/publisher of the *Sunday Weekly,* the first newspaper in Texas to print on paper manufactured in the state. Mary taught the first Sunday School class on Sunday, January 1, 1888. She did it to provide religious education for her six children—Ben F., Frank M., Claudie Lee, Mabel, Coke and Clifton. She had lost her first two children, Charlie Lee at 3 1/2 and Mabel Clair at 18 months.

The annual meetings of Baptists and Methodists in 1890 were already grappling with topics that continued to occupy them a hundred years later. At the Southern Baptist Convention in Fort Worth in May of 1890, a keynote speaker, H. R. Harris of Columbus, Georgia, expressed concern about foreigners: "We must not disregard the foreigner. We dare not treat him wrongfully. (But) can we (Baptists) be kept pure from the incoming herd? . . . Isms must be stamped out. . . . European and Asiatic heathenism might be crystallized by the gospel of the son of God." At the same conference, a speaker, identified only as Mr. Murrow, reported on the church's study of the Native American. "The saying that the only Indian you can trust is the dead Indian is a mistake. They can be converted . . . . Remove whisky from him and give him the gospel and he will rise. We must educate them. . . . We took their country . . . . now let us give them an education and the gospel." B. D. Gray of Mississippi delivered the report on the "colored population." He said ". . . colored people are powerfully inclined to the Baptist faith. Our advancement in these southern states depends much upon how we solve the problem of the negro. . . . They love us. They are eager to hear the gospel." B. R. Womack of Arkansas reported "7,000,000 colored people in the south and 1,200,000 are Baptists." After much debate, the men voted to have special meetings for the colored and have special places set aside for them in their churches.

While the Baptists were voting on their Native American and African-American members, the Methodists, meeting in St. Louis, Missouri, were arguing the "woman question." "Though there has been strong sentiment in the church against admission of women to preach, women have for a long time been engaged in missionary work. A woman is at the head of an important branch of this work . . . authorization of an order of deaconesses (should be) agreed to." The resolution passed. At the same meeting speakers made an impassioned plea for better living accommodations and better furnishings for the parsonages for its ministers. While they debated at length about how to handle this problem, a woman stood up to address the conference. She ignored the undertone grumbles of resentment from the audience as to the propriety of her speaking up and challenged the women of the church to accept the responsibility in their local churches of better housing for ministers and their families. There was not a dissenting vote from the men over such an arrangement.

Marriage license applicants and divorce petitioners were routinely published in the newspapers in the 1880s, and child custody, then as now, often made the news. In one case headlined: "Mrs. M'Daniel Gets the Child; Her Husband Gets Roasted,"[13] there is the story about a man suing for custody of his child. The judge's verdict "was that Mrs. McDaniel have custody of the child, but that its father be permitted to see it once a

Religious controversy was as prevalent in the 1890s as it has continued to be throughout the years. At that time, the Baptists were divided over racism—not only the Negro question, but the Native American as well—and the Methodists were overwhelmed with the "woman question."

week . . . as the mother designates." The judge chastised McDaniel for writing for the *Sunday Sun,* which he termed "a most disreputable publication that should not be allowed to circulate in the state." Child snatching was prevalent then as now. A Mrs. Lee, divorced in Greeley, Colorado, was awarded custody of her daughter with the father getting visitation rights. When he took his child and her pet kitten out for a buggy ride, he did not stop until he had traveled through Montana, British Columbia, Oregon, California and to Texas where he was arrested in Wharton.

Work was beginning "tomorrow macadamizing Grand Avenue from the Houston and Texas Central railroad to the fair grounds" in June of 1890, "the improvements to be completed in time for the fair," for "of all factors contributing to the advance of Dallas . . . the fair has been unquestionably the most important," said Col. J. B. Simpson,[14] Dallas loved its fair! In the same edition of the paper Mr. James Howrie, who had been hired to organize a Dallas Choral Union, to perform at the fair requested that "all ladies and gentlemen who read music please sign up." He already had signed up 100 voices and was soliciting 500 singers from throughout the state to perform.

While this was taking place, Miss May Thomas was sending out her card to a few intimate friends announcing that she would be "at home to receive them at 11 a.m. tomorrow. Imagine their surprise when, upon arrival, they learned they were invited to be present at the marriage ceremony of Miss Thomas to Mr. Frank A. Miller of Denver, Col."[15]

Mr. and Mrs. A. C. Ardrey "opened their palatial home on Swiss Avenue to introduce their daughter to society." There followed a 12-inch story listing names of all Dallas debutantes who were in the house party along with what they wore, names of house guests from McKinney, Waxahachie and Terrell, lists of numerous guests—but never the name of the honoree!

Women were beginning to experiment with politics, much to the amazement of the press. Again, the news of such shenanigans was gleaned from across the nation with no mention of anything going on in Dallas. In 1894, for instance, *The Dallas Daily Times Herald* headlined a story from Colorado: "Women in Politics—Experiment to be Tried in Colorado." Three women, it said, "will assist the men to revise the old laws and form new ones . . ." and then added, ". . . whether it is possible for a woman to deal in a practical manner . . . remains to be demonstrated."

The actions of Dallas women, both their charitable works and their social life, would not have been so carefully chronicled had it not been for two outstanding journalists of the period:

Pauline Periwinkle and Alice Parsons Fitzgerald.

Each deserves to stand alone in the annals of Dallas history, for it was they, as no other individuals, who were the bridges for Dallas women activists and who, in a large sense, paved the way to the future for women.

Pauline was the intellectual. Alice was the erstwhile debutante. Their contributions, individually and collectively, were as important as they have been unheralded.

Pauline Periwinkle was the pen name of a woman born Sara Isadore Sutherland in Battle Creek, Michigan, in 1863, the daughter of Mason Montgomery and Marie L. Tripp Sutherland. Her father died of injuries he sustained in the Civil War when she was an infant. She and her only brother, Daniel Sutherland, were reared by their mother and stepfather, Franklin Frisbie LaMoreaux, until around 1877 when she moved into the home of her "Auntie Rose" in St. Clair, Michigan, because her stepfather, she said, was "rather inconvenient . . . so much so that I never lived at home with any peace." She graduated from St. Cloud High School at the age of 18 and two years later went to work for the *Review* and publishing company owned by Dr. John Harvey Kellogg of the Kellogg cereal company. In 1884 she married James Miner, a co-worker, and began her lifelong crusade to sanction, through her writings, enhancement of living conditions for women and children. By 1890 she had risen to the position of editor. Under the by-line S.I.M. (Sara Isadore Miner), she wrote "what the wage-earning women of our land have most need of is not money aid, but sympathy and help in securing their rights."

In March of 1891 (some records say her husband died, others that they divorced), Isadore Miner moved to Toledo, Ohio, where she took a job with the *Toledo Commercial*. From there, two years later, she moved to Dallas and joined *The Dallas Morning News*. Her mother and stepfather had preceded her, moving to Dallas in 1875.

The earliest mention of this remarkable Texas journalist, other than her own columns, is in a book published in Ohio in 1896.

Sara Isadore Miner Callaway, as Pauline Periwinkle, wrote for The Dallas Morning News *from 1889 to 1916, columns and stories that helped to create a new era for women.*

> The only woman in Texas who has ever been honored by a temporary seat in the presidential chair of an assembly composed exclusively of men is Mrs. Isadore Miner. The Texas Press Association was the source of this compliment, and her reading of an appreciated paper before that body was the occasion.
>
> Mrs. Miner came to Texas two years ago; prior to that, with the exception of a two years' newspaper engagement at Toledo, Ohio, she had passed her whole life in Michigan, of which State she is a native. On arriving in Texas she immediately took service on the staff of the *Dallas Daily News* and the *Semi-Weekly Dallas and Galveston News,* editing the society columns of the first, and the Woman's and Children's Department of the other. Vastly important is this dual service on which she has entered, and rare must be the powers that can evoke the rich results that lie buried in its field of labor . . . .
>
> As an adjunct to her system of conducting the Children's Department of the *News*, Mrs. Miner employs the plan that has been elaborated from the Chautauquan idea. During the vacation months of the little ones, she teaches, through her columns, a "summer school," keeping alive the children's interest the studies they have temporarily laid aside . . . .
>
> Mrs. Miner's labors in behalf of the young have not been restricted to newspaper work . . . . she has written, with and without collaborators, seven books devoted to the instruction of children.
>
> Mrs. Miner is a member of the State Press Association of Texas; of the Texas Woman's Press Association, of which she is vice president; of the Toledo Press Club, and of the Michigan Woman's Press Association, which she helped to organize. She is also one of the organizers, and secretary of the Texas Woman's Council, by which she was lately chosen one of its delegates to the National Woman's Council, to represent the interest, the progress, and the culture of her sex in the State of her adoption.
>
> Ten years altogether is the sum of her journalistic experience . . . . The mere enumeration of her labors and her affiliations with literary bodies indicate the purpose and energy of her life; the list of her achievements the measure of its success.[16]

Isadore Miner had been in Dallas a little less than three years when the above tribute was written. She would continue to seek out and write about social issues especially critical to the needs of women and children during a Dallas newspaper career that lasted almost a quarter of a century. Among her numerous causes—mostly successful were: founding the Texas Woman's Press Association; writing and speaking on suffrage for women, being a founder of Sorosis, an organization of women writers; being the first woman to address the all-male Texas Press Association, where she made a strong case for better coverage of women's issues. When May Dickson Exall and the Federation of Women's Clubs founded the Dallas Public Library system (see Chapter 17), in addition to consistent coverage of the story on her weekly women's page, Isadore wrote more than a hundred personal letters to businessmen urging their support. Their published responses of approval helped to win favor for the library. When the library was built, Isadore was named secretary of the association.

She wrote about the value of free public kindergartens, a struggle that was accomplished only after her death. But she was more successful in her campaign to establish the juvenile court system, a singular feat because it required convincing the state legislature to enact new laws. The campaign began when she learned about two six-year-olds in a nearby city being sent to a reformatory for stealing bread. She penned the opening volley for juvenile courts with a column stating "little children do not need reformatories; what they need is a home . . . ." When the legislature failed to act, she followed with "the . . . house that killed the bill . . . passed one to protect goats and squirrels . . . . We boast of our . . . wealth . . . (but) until we direct the prosperity of the State to the upbuilding of its people, we have little of which to boast.)." The bill establishing the Juvenile Court system was passed in 1907.

Isadore and women's clubs comprised an almost undauntable team. Sometimes the club women studied conditions and presented the journalist with material for her columns. Sometimes she learned about unsavory conditions and shared these with the women who acted to correct them. She was undeterred by defeat, regrouping and finding another way to accomplish what her city needed. "The progressive woman can always console herself with the knowledge that people have opposed everything new from time immemorial," she wrote. "The inventor of the umbrella was stigmatized for interrupting the designs of Providence, for when showers fell it was evident God intended man should get wet." Together Isadore and the club women secured matrons for the jails, established parks for children, passed a pure food law in the city and worked tirelessly to see that the new ordinance was entrusted to a competent person who would enforce it.

When Isadore wrote that "people have opposed everything new . . . .," she may well have been writing about herself. She was fortunate that she had the backing of her publisher, George B. Dealey, because her popularity was not universal. Sam Acheson, in his book, *Dallas Yesterday,* was cautious in his appraisal. Pauline Periwinkle, he wrote was "a polemicist who espoused advance guard ideas ranging from votes for women to spitting on city streets." In a later book, *35,000 Days in Texas,* after history had time to evaluate her contributions, Acheson was far more generous. For many years, he wrote, she "helped shape . . . the outlook and interests of thousands of her sex in the Southwest toward public affairs . . . . Through her the *News* was the primary force in establishing the women's club movement in the Southwest." He credited her as being the first person to campaign for free playgrounds for children. The first such park was Trinity Play Park dedicated in 1909. The Trinity flooding in 1908 and its aftermath of illness and disease caused by water contamination was the catalyst for her to begin a successful campaign for pure water.

But many of her contemporaries, men as well as women, did not need to wait for history's evaluation to know that she was a remarkable person. Among her legion of followers was a 47-year-old Dallas attorney. One Sunday afternoon, he rang the doorbell at her Forest Avenue home. When she answered, he thrust two dozen red roses into her arms and introduced himself. "My name," he said, "is William Callaway. My object is matrimony." Her response: "Thank you, but I don't have a vase." That is no problem, he said, leaving her with the armful of roses and returning soon with a tall intricately decorated vase.[17] A short time later, in July of 1900 the two were married.

William Callaway, family stories go, was a bachelor who for years had courted a young woman who would not marry him. The son and grandson of leading Southern Baptist ministers, he had studied law, espoused counterculture ideas, and was an avowed atheist. Having followed Pauline Periwinkle's writings, he considered her an ideal choice to share his mature and aging years. Following their wedding, they left for a two-month honeymoon in Europe where, for the first time in her life, she had the time and the money to indulge in luxury. They bought china, crystal and silver in the capitals of European countries.

Upon their return to the states, William built a small but meticulously planned home for his bride at 3112 Peabody Street. She had complained that the clop-clop of so many horses hooves outside of her home distracted her from her writing. The house was

William Callaway, an eccentric 47-year-old bachelor, presented himself along with two dozen red roses to Sara Miner one sunny Sunday afternoon, and shortly thereafter took her on a European honeymoon. But he continued to encourage her writing.

planned around a special office for her, insulated against outside noises. There, according to family stories, she wrote, smoked cigars emulating a fashion she had picked up in Paris, and chewed gum—no doubt, according to her great-niece-in-law—to camouflage the tobacco odors.

Her husband encouraged her to continue writing—columns for the *Dallas Morning News,* stories and books for children, articles for magazines. Though they had acquired numerous treasures of household items, they rarely if ever entertained. Instead they traveled. In Dallas she was included in the inner circle of women whose activities she had long reported. In 1907 she was elected president of the Dallas Women's Federation.

Perhaps, because of their full professional lives, myriad interests and constant travels—and because they began building a house immediately after they returned from their honeymoon—two of the trunks holding treasures from their European honeymoon were stored in servant quarters behind the home of his brother, Francis Gadsden Callaway. There they remained, obscured by family accumulations for years, until Anne Tyler Rawlins, a great-niece of William Callaway, and her family cleared out her great grandfather's estate.

That is how Anne Rawlins came to inherit many of the treasures collected by her great uncle and aunt, William and Isadore Callaway. She owns the Callaway family Bible, several pieces of antique furniture, china, crystal, serving dishes, trays, silver flatware engraved "I.S.C."—and the vase that William presented to Isadore almost a hundred years ago. "I was always interested in family history and in keeping family mementoes," Anne explained. "Nobody else in the family was."

Pauline Periwinkle, also known as Isadore Sutherland, also Mrs. Isadore Miner, also Mrs. William Allen Callaway, also Isadore Sutherland Miner Callaway, died on August 9, 1916, at the age of 53. Contemporaries quoted in her obituary said she ranked with the country's outstanding suffragists, Dr. Anna Shaw, Jane Addams and Carrie Chapman Catt. She was buried in Oakland Cemetery in the lot she had bought where the graves of her mother, stepfather and two nieces are among several others. On September 30, 1927, her husband had her re-interred at Restland a little more than three years before he was buried beside her on November 15, 1930. Their marker reads: "They lived as they saw the right and were ready when called."

Isadore Callaway never had children, but reared two nieces, Alberta and Isadore Fetterly (Coleman), the children of her half-sister, Eugenia May La Moreaux Fetterly.

While Pauline Periwinkle concentrated on the activists among women in Dallas, reporting only occasionally on the more frivolous side of the city scene, Alice Parsons Fitzgerald did exactly the opposite.

Alice sprinkled her writings with nuggets of news, demands for improvements in the city and editorial opinions on the scope and shape of the environment, but her chief interest lay in writing society news. When neither the *Times Herald,* where she first worked after coming to Dallas in 1889, nor *The Dallas Morning News* where she was later employed would allow her the space she wanted for her stories, Alice established her own magazine-newspaper, *Beau Monde,* which she published for 15 years, from November 15, 1895, until her death, December 14, 1910.

A newspaper woman and writer all of her life, Alice inherited her practical streak from her paternal ancestors who came to America with the Puritans and her genteel, at-home-anywhere-in-the-world self confidence from her maternal forebears who were among the landed gentry of Virginia. She was born Alice Martha Parsons in February of 1860 in Washington County, Iowa, to Lucy Draper Parsons and Dr. R. F. Parsons, a physician, both active in Iowa during its formative years. She was educated in the Iowa schools and then went to Poughkeepsie, New York, to attend Vassar College. She traveled widely, writing wherever she happened to be and freelancing her stories. In 1883, she made up her mind to become a professional journalist and joined the Sedalia *Morning Democrat* where for three years she was literary, society and exchange editor and a regular correspondent for the St. Louis and Kansas City newspapers. At age 19, in 1879 she married Hugh Nugent Fitzgerald, a South Carolina journalist. They, with their three children, moved to Dallas in 1889.

She joined *The Dallas Times Herald* shortly after her arrival in the city and for four years was literary and society editor during which time her husband was an editor. *The History of Dallas County* says of them: "It is but right to state its (*The Times Herald*) present popularity is also due to ability and talent displayed by Mr. Gilbert's splendid corps of assistants especially to the facetious writer Mr. Hugh Fitzgerald, and his talented wife, who is society editor." But Alice Parsons Fitzgerald was never content to be anyone's "talented wife.". . . He was managing editor and staff correspondent of *The Dallas Morning News* for fourteen years and editor of the *Dallas Times Herald* for another ten. But it is through his wife that his name will be remembered."[18]

While Pauline Periwinkle hid behind a pseudonym, was self-effacing and avoided personal involvement in her stories, Alice was the opposite. She was her own best press agent, valued her opinions highly and broadcast them to the world. Writing about herself, she said:

Alice Parsons Fitzgerald wrote for both The Dallas Times Herald and The Dallas Morning News before creating her own newspaper, Beau Monde, that for 15 years heralded society.

> Mrs. Fitzgerald is a trained reporter, and ably fills assignments in any department of the daily paper, although her specialty is society reporting, in which she is especially happy, having been reared in that atmosphere, possessing a keen sense of the beautiful and artistic, and ever keeping herself *en rapport* with the forms, frills and flutters of *Le Beau Monde*." She has traveled extensively in this country, and is well known in the journalistic circles of the North and East. She is the regular society correspondent from Dallas of the Fort Worth *Gazette* and the *Globe Democrat,* and during her husband's absence last winter at Austin filled his place as special correspondent for those papers, the New York *World* and several other metropolitan dailies.[19]

Alice left *The Times Herald* in 1893 and joined *The Dallas Morning News*, where for another two years she was society editor. She resigned, she said, because of ill health, but had already decided to launch her own publication and after a summer recuperating in Colorado, she did so. During her "illness," she wrote columns for the *Fort Worth Gazette,* the St. Louis *Post-Dispatch,* the Kansas City *Journal*, and the *Denver Republican*. She also had by-lines in the Manitou *Society Journal* and covered the flower show and parade of Colorado Springs for the special carnival edition of the *Daily Telegraph*.

Only a few treasured copies of *Beau Monde*, the publication Alice launched in late 1895 and published for 15 years, remain and most of them were printed in 1898 and 1899. Published on 9 by 11-inch slick paper, it has the appearance of a newspaper but is laid out like a magazine. And it is crammed with surprises. Alice's flowery descriptions, liberally sprinkled with French words and phrases, that describe weddings, debutante parties and other social events often are relieved by blunt, no-nonsense news items and by opinions that, in later more sophisticated newspapers, would not be tolerated even on the editorial pages. John William Rogers believed that the crisp news stories were the work of her husband and the society stories her own, but the acerbic turn of a phrase in the news stories brands them all as pure Alice:

> By a vote of eleven to one the City Council declared for the adoption of asphalt as a paving material. *Beau Monde* congratulates the aldermen individually and collectively . . . .[20]

> There are queer men in the Dallas City Council . . . . The City Fathers should be elected at large and not by wards. Men break into the Council from wards, who, if forced to run the gauntlet of all the voters of the city, would be buried so deep beneath an avalanche of ballots that the tooting of the Angel Gabriel's horn would never awaken them. This is not a theory. It is a 90-ton fact.[21]

Alice routinely scolded individuals in print for breaches of protocol, often cloaking her blunt criticism in veiled innuendos. A typical oblique slap is this directed at Dallas business men after a heated meeting about whether, or not, to allow an out-of-state company to open a Dallas branch:

> It is unwise and un-American to go into spasms or convulsions at the mere mention of the word 'corporation.'[22]

The State Legislature was fair game for her barbed comments:

> With the press muzzled, insurance agents scared into convulsions, the corn crop annihilated by the drouth and the Texas legislature still in session, Texas is in a bad way and conditions are chaotic so to speak ....[23]

> ... When the women of Dallas get that library established, they can organize a kindergarten ... and show ... the Texas legislature ... the difference between a legitimate enterprise and a gold brick device ....[24]

The City Council got its full measure of criticism, too:

> Mayor Traylor and his city fathers should force the property owners to repair sidewalks. From the postoffice to the river, on Commerce Street, there are spots which are a constant menace to the life and limb of pedestrians. This is a sharp message to the statesmen ... to give the city first class sidewalks.[25]

Alice's opinions on public issues were often ahead of the times and her views on world issues often proved prophetic:

> All the parks will be permitted to keep open on Sunday and this is as it should be. Those who wish to go to the parks should be permitted to go there, while those who wish to go to church three times on Sunday will have that pleasure without hindrance .... Law-made Christians are the poorest brand of Christians.[26]

> To discuss prohibition is to discuss an impossibility, for prohibition never prohibited .... Church and Society are responsible ... for the weakness of men ... for from the beginning they have condoned the man and condemned the woman ....."Can A Woman Be a Christian If She Has to Live With a Drunken Husband?' is a question to be taken up by a prominent woman's club shortly. It is dollars to doughnuts that the bunch will decide in favor of the man and claim the woman should be a saint whatever her lot.[27]

> Emperor Wilhelm is on the war path again ....[28]

> Kaiser Wilhelm ... is approaching the danger line .... History will be made across the water before the Twentieth Century has added many years.[29]

Beau Monde (read that, Alice Fitzerald) was a staunch admirer and tireless advocate of Dallas, calling it to task often, bluntly suggesting ways for it to improve itself but always promoting it. She was equally blunt in her ridicule of Dallas's competitors. And, in the opinion of its publisher, what *Beau Monde* said was gospel, and she never missed an opportunity to self-promote:

> Greater Dallas should be the slogan from this day on. Dallas leads all in material wealth and commercial advancement ... 10,000 of her population live just beyond the present city limits .... *Beau Monde* wants to see Dallas grow to a city of 100,000 population by 1905.[30]

> The city of Dallas should pay its mayor a salary commensurate with the importance of the position ....[31]

The greatest fair in the history of the Southwest will open on September 28. This is not an idle boast. It is a fact.[32]

Sometimes the reporting changed the subject so abruptly that the reader is startled, wondering how, or even if, a second sentence connects to the one above it:

Mr. John Philip Sousa was here last week. His band was with him and so was his strut. The mercury shot down 40 degrees and never stopped until it was 10 below zero. Whisky froze in decanters and the cocks refused to crow. Sousa is incomparable . . . . He is a genius.[33]

Alice Fitzgerald often gave terse, unsolicited advice to her readers on everything from etiquette to politics:

"Greater Dallas" should be brought about by the progressive citizens who reside on either side of the river . . . .[34]

In selecting bridesmaids . . . it is not beauty that counts so much as style and carriage . . . . The wedding marches are more suited to grand opera stages than to church aisles.[35]

At the inaugural ball this winter sidearms will not be worn . . . .[36]

The Texas anti-trust law should be kicked into the everlasting subsequent.[37]

Vote early, but not often . . . .[38]

Take a bath and be a public benefactor would be a motto for some people to adopt.[39]

Alice, who knew nothing about sports, did not let that stop her from reporting on a new Dallas craze. When golf was introduced by Britisher H. L. Edwards, it became an almost overnight rage. Mrs. Fitzgerald, glowingly reporting the new craze, wrote that "the charming Helen Adams could be seen on the links almost every day gracefully swinging her caddy."

Alice never mentioned, nor alluded to, pregnancy among the socialites in Dallas, but she had no such reservation about public figures:

. . . an able-bodied stork has been seen flying in the direction of the home of Mr. Grover Cleveland . . . the stork will arrive . . . in the spring . . . .[40]

The long-legged bird is expected to alight . . . upon the residence of ex-President Harrison. The ex-President . . . is past his 65th year. He prides himself on his activity . . . . Mrs. Harrison is dark and slender of figure, not a pretty woman but high bred . . . .[41]

Alice's comments on well-known figures were often startling:

Lady Churchill is 50 and frisky . . . .[42]

Lady Randolph Churchill's engagement to young Cornwallis West is said to be really a fact. His mother is two years younger than his finance (sic) and his finance's (sic) son, young Winston Churchill, is said to be stoutly opposed to the marriage.[43]

. . . The difficulties which stood in the way of Lady Randolph Churchill's wedding now seem to have been overcome and the event is fixed . . . .[44]

Beau Monde, for all its terse advice, its gossipy tone, and its constant need to applaud itself, specialized in society coverage with stories sometimes as long as four pages covering every detail of an event. In the Gay Nineties there were countless stories to cover—teas and receptions, engagement parties and weddings, "at homes," family reunions, luncheons, banquets and nine-course dinners and numerous club socials.

The Idlewild Club, which has been the most enduring of Dallas's social clubs, got bare notice in the paper in its infancy, but by the mid-1890s, editor Fitzgerald knew it was, as she put it, the *creme de creme* and she introduced its 16th annual reception this way:

> The Idlewild whose opening reception keeps belledom in a state of ecstatic anticipation for one half of the year and in a dream of rosy remembrance for the other, rounded up the carnival gaiety last Friday night in a blaze of brilliance and beauty at the Oriental Hotel.[45]

There followed six full pages reporting the story, detailing the gowns worn by debutantes Nelle Belt, Sara Doolittle, Gertrude Flippen, Catherine Herford, Jessie Padgitt, Ethel Ryan and Bess Wathen, plus 102 of the women guests!

On November 11, 1899, the marriage of Fannie Ione Dillon and Edward Chilton Craig of Mattoon, Illinois, was reported. "Had the bridal gown been designed for a young princess, it need not have been more beautiful." It was pearl white imported satin de chine trimmed in lace and pearls, all in glowing detail. And the bride's lingerie was hand-made by the French nuns of New Orleans.

Miss Minne Mae Armstrong, described as a "thoroughly swell girl" in a special edition of the paper on December 31, 1898, got four full pages of copy complete with a photograph of the families and wedding party when she married in April of 1899. Hers was a wedding where "at high noon . . . she was led by Mr. Edward Lucus Flippin from the garden of girlhood into the kingdom of wifehood." For the event, the Armstrong home, where the wedding took place, was "transformed" by 2,000 white lilies.

In the January 14, 1898, edition of *Beau Monde* the engagement of Miss Nonie Boren to Mr. Joseph P. Mahoney was discreetly announced in a three-line item. But when the wedding took place in February, six full pages were devoted to its coverage. The Boren-Mahoney wedding (not in the detail it was first published) serves as an example of Editor/writer Fitzgerald's style—a mixture of colorful reporting, French phrases, political innuendo, fashion coverage, worldly knowledge, music and literature information all with snobbish overtones:

> Marriage bells, that began ringing with the autumn sunsets and have been chiming ever since for Cupid's victims, rang gaily out for notable and brilliant nuptials on Tuesday, when Miss Nonie McKellar Boren, daughter of Mr. Benjamin N. Boren, became the wife of Hon. Joseph P. Mahoney, state senator of Illinois. Probably no alliance in the social sphere of Dallas ever put its votaries on such *qui vive* of interest and anticipation, accentuated, no doubt, by the facts that the bride was a typical Southern girl, the heiress of one of the oldest and wealthiest Protestant families; that the groom, though of distinguished political prestige, came out of the North, and was the scion of an equally prominent Catholic family. These facts lent color to the alliance and caused the usual speculation, but they had no bearing with friends who know of the pretty love story that had been running along for years, in which neither creed, sectional lines, prestige or position played any part. In the consummation was evidenced this tender romance, as well as the elaborate preparation, which has been going on for months in the Boren home for the bridal of its only daughter. Nothing was spared . . . . The trousseau which had called forth the taste and skill of New York *couturiers*, as well as our own dressmakers, which showed laces and satins from famous looms of Europe; lingerie, as dainty as cobwebs, from the smartest and most exclusive house in New York; hats, gloves and fans from the *ateliers* of Paris' artist . . . . Equally splendid was the array of presents, representing not

only a wealth of plate, cut glass, silver *porcelaine de chine* and bric-a-brac, but the names of many first families of the state . . . and distinguished ones from the native state of the groom . . . . For her bridal she had arranged a most beautiful and fitting altar room, something unread of and unthought of before. The entire suite was resplendent with the marbles, paintings, buhls and porcelaines brought from other climes, but the *place de resistance* was the room where the vows were taken . . . ribboned off by broad white streamers of taffeta . . . . Here and there the proud, chaste bloom of a calla lilly peeped . . . . Some feet out on the velvet carpet were two stately white columns, after the Corinthian style . . . delicately entwined with cobweb fern. Connecting the two columns was a wide scarf of pearl shiffon caught in the center to the *plafond* by a silver spangled butterfly—mates of which quivered here and there on a marble Venus, on a Correggio Magdalen and other art gems in the room . . . . Carrico's orchestra . . . announced the processional by Mendelssohn's Wedding March. Down the handsome staircase came the bride's pageant of beauty, grace and gallantry . . . . Rev. B. H. Carroll of Waco officiated . . . . The bridal picture was fit for a canvas—the bride, in her superb gown trailing in lustrous folds behind her, with her four beautiful maids . . . . During the ceremony the orchestra played Mendelssohn's Spring Song. The bride wore a magnificent gown of white satin duchesse, with court train lined with white taffeta and flounced *a la* Marie Antoinette with deep rose point headed by a chiffon ruche. The French yoke corsage was overlaid in the back with solid rose point and draped very full and low in front with the point, agleam with her handsome diamonds. The yoke and sleeves were of white chiffon heavily encrusted with beaded pearl pendants; strings of Roman pearls were twined about the stock, catching a diamond sunburst, and a girdle of pearls was about the waist tied in a friar's knot and falling to the hem of the gown. She wore a wreath of the historic orange blossoms over her veil, which was caught to her hair by a superb crescent of fourteen first water diamonds, the gift of the groom, and her bouquet was composed of two dozen long-stemmed Bride rose.[46]

And on and on, all of this strung together without paragraphs. The day after the wedding, the bride's mother, Mrs. Boren, whose name was not mentioned in the write-up, entertained at a "large and handsomely appointed reception" honoring the ministers of the Baptist church who performed the ceremony. Alice Fitzgerald, in her reporting, left no doubt that though the bridegroom was Catholic and from the North, the Boren family's Southern Baptist heritage was entirely in place. In describing the bride, she had said, "she was ever a girl distinctly individual, with a rare mentality and engaging personality all her own; never copying but always doing things in her own sweet way, which, in consequence, were always interesting and never commonplace." This observation was to prove true, for Dallas would hear much in the future from Nonie Boren Mahoney.

For all of her flowery phrasing, Alice—though she would doubtless have vehemently denied it—was a dedicated feminist. In reporting a banquet given by the Dallas Commercial Club at the Oriental Hotel honoring Governor-elect Sayers, she wrote: "Petticoats were barred from this brilliant banquet," and then went on to describe in detail the event, leaving one to speculate about how she knew everything if she were barred from the party.

She supported education for women and wrote scathing editorials about a legislature that refused to provide public funding for women's education. This is the lead of a long editorial:

The Texas legislature has adjourned . . . . The representatives of the masses refused to appropriate money to educate the daughters of the masses, which is a strong reminder that many mossbacks break into the Texas House of Representatives . . . . the women of Texas should make it their business to see that men endowed with liberal hearts, expansive brains and 20th century ideas are sent to Austin to make laws.[47]

Women's campaign for equal legal rights in Texas was a long time in coming. An article published in *Beau Monde* on December 7, 1912, made this clear.

THE MARRIED WOMAN'S RIGHTS IN TEXAS

The campaign for giving married women in Texas the same property rights as are now enjoyed by married men and unmarried women got under full headway at Fort Worth at the recent convention of the State Federation of Women's Clubs when the leaders of the convention agreed to invite Judge Speer of Fort Worth, Judge Dibrell of Austin and Mr. Lewis R. Bryan of Houston to confer in the final drawing of a bill for presentation to the next legislature. The injustice done to married women by the present laws was eloquently described and denounced by Judge Speer.... A comparison between the laws of Texas and those of other States was outlined ... by Mr. William Hard of the staff of *The Delineator* which is conducting a department devoted ... to laws concerning wives and mothers .... reports calling attention to the need of immediate reform were presented by Mrs. E. P. Turner and by Mrs. J. B. Dibrell. No subject brought before the convention was given more consideration or aroused more enthusiasm.

When a woman in Texas gets married she loses her head and cannot be trusted ... to make contracts or enter into business dealings any more. So says the law .... A married woman not long ago hired a nurse to look after her invalid husband. This nurse sued for her money. The Supreme Court ... held that she couldn't collect it, and said: "The wife's separate estate is not liable for these services, even though contracted for by her." The married women of Texas are rightly dissatisfied with this low view of their capacity to give their word and stick to it ....

Not one man in ten thousand wishes to control his wife's property against her will. The law should represent the ideals of the nine thousand, nine hundred and ninety nine ....

The bill for giving married women in Texas the legal management of their own separate property and of their own personal earnings continues to receive the endorsement of many large organizations and will be one of the first measures to be presented to the Texas legislature when it meets in January ....

The voice of Alice Parsons Fitzgerald ended shortly before Christmas in 1910. She became violently ill on Sunday morning, December 11, 1900, and was rushed to St. Paul's sanitarium where she underwent surgery on Monday, rallied and was doing well when she took a sudden downturn and died at 4 a.m. on Tuesday. Her at-home funeral, 343 San Jacinto Street, as was the custom those days, was conducted by Bishop A. C. Garrett of the Episcopal Diocese. Pallbearers were among the socially elite of the city including Edward Titche, Ben E. Cabell, Edwin J. Kiest, Alex Sanger, I. Lorch and Judge U. F. Short. She was buried in Oakland Cemetery. Both the *News* and the *Herald* published a large photograph and lengthy story of her death on the papers' front pages. The *News*, as was often the custom of the day, after reporting the details of her death, reverted to lauding the contributions of her husband:

Hugh Nugent Fitzgerald is one of the most widely known newspaper men in the Southwest. He served with distinction as war correspondent during the early days of the West, when Gen. Nelson A. Miles and other famous soldiers were leading arduous campaigns against the Indians. Later he saw service throughout the country as staff man for some of the big papers. He came to Texas many years ago and won recognition both here and elsewhere for his writings on politics ....[48]

The *Herald*, on the other hand, devoted space to Alice's life that would have been right at home in *Beau Monde:*

> ... an apostle of fidelity to the ideals which enrich the early history of the Republic, an unflagging foe of Humbug and Sham and False Pretense, *Beau Monde* has made its own place not only in Texas journalism, but in the broader field of American journalism. It is known and read in many states, and it has wielded a potent influence for good in the promotion of true independence of thought, and in the stimulus of individuals and communities to greater and better achievements.
>
> Mrs. Fitzgerald united in a degree rarely witnessed an artistic and a practical mind. She wrote a dramatic criticism, analyzed a poem, and admired a beautiful picture, and with equal aptitude and vigor dealt with the sternest problems of business life. Her courage and her faith never faltered. She typified unflagging industry. Work was a passion with her, and success was the natural fruit of all she attempted because she earned it by patient, earnest, faithful work. Travel in many states and cities, and a wide range of literary work and business and social connections had broadened her education and given her a breadth and liberality of view, a range of thought, and a catholicism of opinion that marked her as one of those who deserve to be classed as the makers of states .... Her business activities never obscured the domestic life and as a wife and mother she exemplified the virtues which she taught so vigorously.[49]

Alice herself couldn't have said it better.

16

••••

THE TWENTIETH CENTURY ARRIVES

As the century turned, Dallas had become a big city—not nearly the hundred thousand that *Beau Monde* had predicted. But, by the standard of cities of its day, big. Its population stood at 68,372 representing a growth of 3,112 for the year 1889-90. And it was about to grow bigger—for in 1903 a long-smoldering debate over the annexation of Oak Cliff was resolved when the voters approved an ordinance to unite with Dallas. The winners could claim only an 18-vote victory, but it was enough to stake Oak Cliff's future with "Big D." Ever since, there have been periodic threats by Oak Cliff citizens to secede.

In 1900, Dallas was a city with 160 factories that employed 3,000 people. It had five banks with a capital of three-quarters of a million dollars. There were 95 churches and 194 saloons. The ill had their choice among 146 physicians, surgeons and faith healers of all kinds. There were 13 horseshoers, 59 dressmakers, eight milliners and 6 harness makers. The *Daily Times Herald*, with 7,000 subscribers, claimed it had the largest circulation of any paper in Texas. You could have *The Dallas Morning News* delivered daily to your home for 75 cents a month.[1]

As the downtown area grew, the people moved out, setting up new residential parameters. The State-Thomas area became a smart address just as it would again a hundred years later. Ted Dealey, seven years old as the century turned, lived with his parents at 195 Thomas Street. He recalled what life was like:

> Housewives . . . didn't have their dresses altered in specialty shops or department stores. Neither did they send their clothes across town to a resident dressmaker. Instead, the seamstresses came and lived with a family for three or four days, sleeping and eating at the respective family residences while the seasonal overhauling of the wardrobes took place . . . our seamstress was a Mrs. Harding . . . . a genius with a needle and a sewing machine . . . . She and my mother would set up headquarters in the sewing room and woe betide anyone who disturbed them . . . (Clothes) were repaired and renovated for the summer season or the wintry weather, as the case might be.
>
> Meantime, around town, things were happening of a more or less dramatic nature . . . .
>
> . . . every local grocery store had a "grab bag" on the counter. By paying a penny, you could reach through a hole in the center . . . of the grab gag, and get a small box of hard candy. If you were extremely lucky, you pulled out a sack that had a nickel in it. There was one nickel box in every grab bag.
>
> . . . all the girls rode side-saddle. And some of the side-saddles were quilted, or padded, so that the equestriennes wouldn't get too sore after a canter as to interfere with their more social duties of the evening, such as dancing the two-step and the waltz.
>
> . . . cowboys staged cattle drives right through the residential sections of the city . . . . I remember hundreds of steers being prodded down Thomas Avenue, filling the street from fence line to fence line . . . .
>
> . . . there weren't any automobiles . . . runaway horses were in vogue and it was quite a thrilling sight to see the usually docile old carriage horse come tearing down the street, red nostrils distended and flecks of foam at his mouth, pulling the remnant of a buggy behind him . . . . Heroes were made when some

courageous soul flung himself in front of the steed and halted him ... by hanging on to the trailing reins.

... people who were ill stayed home instead of hiking off to a hospital. They just sent word to the family doctor that they were about to die ... and the family doctor came .... (The doctor) didn't tell you go to go to the hospital ... or refer you to his secretary who might be able to arrange an appointment at his office for next week. ...there was no hospitalization insurance.

... young ladies of the city wore knee-length white cotton "drawers" and had webbed steel cylinders called "rats" over which they would drape their front hair to make a "pompadour." All the girls wore black cotton stockings and high-button shoes.

... male kids wore shoes with metal tips at the toes ... teen-agers went for "peg-top" trousers. To get a pair of peg-tops trousers, you selected a pair of pants about two sizes too big ... and then narrowed them at the bottom, leaving the tops just below the hip line, flaring from east to west so that the well-dressed young man ... resembled a small gas-filled balloon or the top part of an hourglass.

Most of the houses in the early 1900s were heated by Bunsen Burners, or by open fireplaces. There was no such thing as central heating. The nearest thing to central heating was furnaces in the residences of the most affluent people .... These furnaces were tremendous in size. They were located in the cellars of the houses and were powered by soft coal. Chutes leading to the basement on a downslope permitted coal dealers to unload a whole wagon of fuel to the basement floor where it was confined to a coal bin or stacked up in a corner .... Large metal pipes covered with asbestos carried heat to all parts of the house. The outlets at the end of these pipes were grilled radiators that were controlled manually in each of the separate rooms .... When someone was in the cellar stoking the fuel or stirring it up with a long-handled poker, the noise reverberated all over the house as if an earthquake was in progress.

These cellars were fascinating in that they were the storerooms of the house. There was usually a barrel of apples down there, plus crates of dried halibut, finnan haddie, codfish and buckets of salt mackerel .... In case of disaster, a whole family could have subsisted for weeks in these dark dungeons of plenty.

Upstairs in the kitchen of the more well-to-do persons were huge Majestic ranges, wood burning on one end, gas burning on the other. There were two huge ovens below, one for the wood-burning side and one for the gas-burning end. Above were two commodious warming ovens. I would guess some of these cooking ranges would be from eight to ten feet wide. In the corner of the kitchen stood a huge wood box ....[2]

True, there were no automobiles in Dallas as the century turned, but a car had been there in the early fall of 1899, and it had created a sensation. It was owned by Edward Howland Robinson Green, a wealthy Texas playboy. Known as Ned, Green had moved to Texas a few years earlier when his mother, Hettie Green, at that time the world's richest woman, bought him a toy, the rundown Texas-Midland Railroad for $500,000. Ned, 25 years old, had arrived in Terrell on January 27, 1893, with the admonition from Mama to stay out of jail and never to get married. He not only turned the money-losing Texas-Midland into a profitable enterprise, but fell in love with everything mechanical. And he didn't wed until after Mama died. He yearned to own one of the horseless carriages he had read about, and in 1899 had the St. Louis Motor Company build him one. It cost him $1,250 and was shipped to him on his railroad. It arrived in Terrell on the first Tuesday of October together with a representative from the manufacturer to teach him how to drive it. By the following Sunday, he felt sufficiently experienced to drive it to Dallas. On Monday morning, Dallasites learned:

> Hon. E. H. R. Green, chairman of the republican state executive committee, created a sensation in this city last night. At 7:30 o'clock he rode up and down Main Street in a horseless carriage at the rate of 15 miles an hour. Nothing that

has passed along the streets of Dallas since the parade of the Kaliphs has attracted greater attention.

. . . Mr. Green left Terrell in his new possession yesterday afternoon at 2 o'clock for Dallas, more than thirty miles away. Near Forney, they were crowded off the roadway into a gulley by a farm wagon and the water tank was damaged so that it began to leak, and a stop of an hour at a blacksmith shop was necessary in order to make repairs. Mr. Green arrived in Dallas at 7:30 o'clock having made the trip in five hours and ten minutes.

(Green said of the experience) . . . .When we left Terrell we struck a very sandy stretch of road, and because of the dust thrown up by the vehicle, we had to go very slowly. After this bad stretch was passed we turned on more power and fairly flew.

It was amusing to notice the sensation our appearance caused . . . . Cotton pickers dropped their sacks and ran wildly to the fences to see the strange sight. And the interest was shared by the farm animals, too. One razor-back sow that caught sight of us is running yet . . . a dozen horses executed fancy waltz steps on their hind legs as we sped silently by . . . .

I have no idea of the speed of the vehicle. We did not put on full power on the country roads because it would have been too dusty for comfort and when we struck the asphalt pavement on Main street we dared not do so because the thoroughfare was so crowded that it would have been dangerous to human life . . . ."

The vehicle . . . is propelled by a gasoline engine of 5-horse power, secured in place under the seat. It consumed two quarts of gasoline in making the run to Dallas and holds three gallons. The wheels are supported on enormous bicycle tires. The weight of the outfit is 1,600 pounds . . . .[3]

Ned Green, who had elegant bachelor quarters in a converted opera house in Terrell, later moved to Dallas where his first home was a three-story building on the northeast corner of Elm at Griffin. Then he built a three-story mansion at 2013 Commerce in Dallas described as "quarters so elegant they rival the Sultan of Siam's palace." Though he was never fully accepted into Dallas society, he was popular with the girls because he took them for automobile rides and for extensive trips on his trains, always including chaperons of impeccable esteem. His close friends, Edwin and Elizabeth Kiest, often served as escorts.

He was generous with his money in other ways, too, He provided educational scholarships and grants to several girls. Mothers responded to his attention to their daughters with both anxiety and anticipation—for Ned Green was immensely wealthy. At one time in 1907 when the Security National Bank of Dallas was on the verge of failure, Ned went down to the bank and with much fanfare announced that he was certain it was sound. To show his faith, he deposited $100,000 which stopped the run. Not only did the bank make him a director, but he became a director of 26 other Dallas business institutions.

Ned's love, in addition to mechanical contraptions, was a beautiful red-haired young woman named Mabel Harlow. She lived with him for a time in his opera house quarters. Shortly after his trek to Dallas in the horseless carriage, but before he moved to the city in 1909, he had George Pullman Co. design him a luxurious private car for his train emblazoned with the name "Mabel" on both sides. Mama was shocked and referred to Mabel as "Miss Harlot." After Hettie died, Ned married the young woman. She was snubbed by society in both Terrell and Dallas, so Ned moved to Florida with her where she became one of the reigning society queens.

Not only were several lawsuits filed against Green as a result of chasing wagons off the road and making the horses do the waltz on his way to Dallas from Terrell, but many other lawsuits were filed against those aggressive enough to try out new methods of transportation. Mrs. C. N. Arrington and her three children "suffered many inconveniences" while riding a train from Mesquite to New Orleans during the Christmas holidays of 1900 and their husband and father sued the Texas and Pacific Railroad for

$26,999 on their behalf. The suit did not say what the "inconveniences" were.[4] Four days later, February 22, 1901, Carrie Famback sued the Dallas City Electrical Street Railway Company for $5,000 for one of its cars colliding with the hack in which she was sitting on January 23, 1901.

For those who had the time and the money to travel, trains were still the quickest and most efficient transportation. They seldom ran off the tracks anymore. You could buy a round trip ticket, excursion rate, from Dallas to Washington, D. C., for $37.55 or go to San Francisco and back for $55.

But Dallas was in love with the automobile and has been ever since Ned Green brought his first car to town. In 1902 Henry Garrett opened the first automobile dealership in Texas, where he sold the National Electric car and, later, the Locomobile. The same year, R. L. Cameron opened the Steamobile auto salesroom, also the first in Texas, in Dallas. He later became an agent for Buick and put salesmen all over Texas selling cars. Dallas's first car was owned by L. S. Thorpe, (Green still lived in Terrell), general manager of the Texas and Pacific Railway, a gift of Jay Gould, who owned the railroad. As a result of so many lawsuits, the city council passed its first traffic ordinance in 1901. It prohibited speeds of more than seven miles per hour on downtown streets. In 1907 the state required that cars be licensed. J. M. Oram was the first person to license a car in Dallas. The fee was 50 cents per year.

Many other significant signs of progress were taking place in the first decade of the twentieth century.

On February 8, 1901, the Barber Asphalt Company began putting down asphalt on Elm Street. "A crowd that stretched from curb to curb and interfered with the workmen watched . . . for several hours. Elm Street (is) the mecca of thousands of Dallasites. All . . . like to watch the progress . . . . The street makes a pretty picture."[5]

In 1902 the first interurban ran from Dallas to Fort Worth.

In 1904 the first wireless message in Dallas was sent, all the way to Fort Worth.

In 1905 the first movie theater opened, the Dixie on Elm Street, and a short time later the Majestic, "the largest and finest vaudeville theater in town." Between 1905 and 1915, 20 movie houses stretched along Elm Street.

In 1906 a new residential area named Junius Heights opened, made accessible by extending the new streetcar line more than a mile. The lots were so desirable that the night before the official opening, prospective owners camped on their favorite lot and at midnight, with the sound of a pistol shot, they removed tags from stakes to secure their purchases. Within hours, 340 of the 343 lots were sold. In 1907 the city expanded north when J. S. Armstrong bought a horse farm from Henry Exall and adjoining property from Turtle Creek northward and turned it over to Hugh Prather and Edgar Flippen, his sons-in-law, to develop. They called it Highland Park.

Everybody was caught up in the frenetic pace. The Dallas woman with money devoted countless hours to running her household that usually included a staff of several people, planning her wardrobe and shopping, entertaining and doing club work, much of it welfare work, and preparing long and complicated papers for presentation. The Dallas woman without money was often the person serving the needs and wishes of the rich. Her life, for the most part unrecorded because those on the fringes of life rarely left records of their experiences, consisted of long, relentless days of labor without time-saving conveniences.

The women who had hired help were advised, in a column by Pauline Periwinkle, to treat their "serving girls" well. The "girls," they were told, should be given an appropriate room of their own, be adequately fed and clothed, should have one day a week and two evenings free, should be allowed a private life "within reason" because most young girls wanted to become wives and "you don't want your girls cavorting with men on the street." Mistresses were also advised to treat their girls fairly, but not to pay them above the "going" wage and to be certain they did not flirt with the butcher, baker or any other deliveryman.

Entertaining continued to be lavish and endless, most of it still in the homes. The genteel hostess set her table with the finest white napery, used her best china and silver and fresh flowers, "always." There was no indication of where she secured these posies in the middle of winter when, on February 23, 1901, she was advised in the columns of *The Herald* that, for a small luncheon, an appropriate bill of fare would include fruit, clear soup, deviled oysters on toast, tournedos with mushrooms, boiled fowl with celery sauce, potato rissoles, spinach with butter, chartreuse of pear, savory biscuits, ices, cake and coffee.

Choices of foods were limited, utensils for preparing the fare even more limited and recipes virtually non-existent. Women learned to cook in their mothers' kitchens. When recipes did begin to appear in the press, they were so incomplete that any novice cook could expect a disaster. A recipe for roast goose left out as much as it offered:

Recipe for Roast Goose

Get a goose. Draw the goose. Let it hang for several days. Truss it into shape. Stuff it with sages and onions. Roast before a clear fire or in a moderate oven until it is done. Make the gravy by simmering giblets in a quart of water with half a pound of gravy beef, an onion, an apple and 3 sage leaves for three hours. Thicken the sauce and serve it in a tureen.[6]

If you had guests for breakfast, you wanted to send them out into the world well nourished. An excellent menu would consist of fruit, french fried potatoes, larded steak, muffins, raspberry jelly and coffee.

With what was available, meals could still be prepared for large numbers of people for a few pennies per serving. A grocery ad for C. E. Hunt, 338 Elm Street, in February of 1901 offered: sugar-cured ham, 8 cents a pound; breakfast bacon, 12 1/2 cents; potatoes 20 cents a peck, 4 packages of oat cereal for 25 cents or a box of Quaker oats for 10 cents; 4 pounds of flour for 25 cents; butter for 25 cents a pound, 3 large cans of tomatoes for 25 cents, and a large can of California pears for 15 cents. Eggs were 18 cents per dozen.

The family in need of a new home, or who had one to sell, could advertise it in the "want" column in the newspaper, 18 words, one insertion for 10 cents. If you longed for the country life you could buy 154 acres unimproved blackland, 100 acres of it suitable for fine farming, one mile south of Cedar Hill for $15 an acre. Or, if you desired city life, you could purchase a six-room house on Junius Street in the "best neighborhood" for $1,250. You could buy a residence at 915 Ross Avenue, all seven rooms of it on an 80 by 175-foot lot for $4,000.

To furnish the house, you get everything from rugs to pictures for the wall from "the birthplace of easy payments," J. F. Zang, $100 worth for $10 down and $2.50 a week. A handsome rocking chair "with a golden finish" was $1.75, and a white enameled metal bed at A. Harris & Co. was $3.05. Hemmed sheets at A. Harris were on special for 29 cents each. Arthur A. Everts, the jeweler, charged $12.50 for 12 solid sterling silver forks.

Being properly attired for every occasion was very important. No woman was well dressed without a hat and gloves. Hats were lavish with wide brims rolled out or up or under and trimmed in lace and flowers and ribbons. For church, a lady wore two-button or four-button white or light tan kid gloves. If the gloves were tan, heavier kid was called for; if white, thin leather. Every week the papers carried stories on the latest Paris fashions—the frillier and fussier the garment, the better.

When a woman wasn't entertaining in her own home, or attending luncheons, dinners and other festive events in the homes of others, there were ample opportunities for her to get dressed up and go out for an evening. She could attend the fourth anniversary celebration of the Young Men's Christian Association, or, if she were fortunate enough to have received an invitation, the wedding uniting Gertrude Kahn and Albert Linz, decreed by *Beau Monde* as "one of the swellest of the season."

And there was always the club meeting. A club meeting was not only appropriate, but the most significant measure of a woman's acceptance into society. Few were the women who did not succumb to join one or more organizations. Programs in almost all of the clubs were by members. To be asked to read a paper was a very high honor.

The proper procedure for a woman reading a paper appeared in the *Daily Times Herald* March of 1901.

> When a clubwoman gets a commission to read a paper, the first thing she does is go to her milliner and order a new bonnet . . . . Then she attends to the second—the paper. She consults her pastor . . . . then she goes to the library for a week. Then she writes . . . . It (the paper) will not (have the proper effect) unless she has a brand new pair of gloves to hold it. White kid gloves are proper this season . . . . Stick out your little finger while reading. Pleasantness and propriety are the two effects aimed at . . . . subjects and thoughts that "shake mankind" must be ruled out. In delivery . . . never look your audience in the face . . . . Keep your eyes down and read in a level, ladylike voice.

Much attention was given to proper etiquette. It was inappropriate for women to kiss, "even your dearest friend, on the lips. That kiss is sacred to lovers and to husbands and wives. In polite society the kiss upon the cheek is the accepted form of greeting." Women were advised, in the spring of 1901, that "the afternoon tea fad has palled. The modish new thing is to serve a cup of chocolate topped by a snowy mound of whipped cream."

Advice to the lovelorn columns were making their appearance. One must surely assume that the adviser was only kidding when she advised young women: "Don't marry a man with a glass eye. Don't marry a man who objects to your playing the accordion. Don't marry a man who demands that you go against the politics of your "folks." If you are a widow, don't marry a man who will not let you sound to him the praises of your first husband."

Most women did their own housework and the press did not altogether ignore them. They were advised to start with the least used rooms, remove all the furniture, take down all pictures, and take up rugs and carpets. Every inch of the room had to be cleaned, washed and polished and every piece of furnishings cleaned before being replaced. Then, the cleaned room was sealed off before the housewife went on to the next.[7]

The same article held out great hope for the future:

> By the year 2000 women will not have to clean house. When the name of the superior sex is spelled with a capital W, each city will have its own brigades of cleaners organized for the care of houses (like) present street cleaners. (They) will arrive with mops, brooms, pails, soap, brushes . . . toil for six hours, then the legal working day, and at twilight peace will reign—the mansion spotless.[8]

Often, women not only did their own housework, but the work in the households of the more affluent. Stories of their lives are more difficult to find because they did not have time to keep records or write letters, but occasionally there is a glimpse. Sarah Ann Paralee Rupard is a typical example. Shortly after the turn of the century, her husband died leaving her with seven children. She supported them, sometimes earning only pennies per day, by taking in laundry and by sewing in the homes of other women. Sometimes her work day stretched to 20 hours.

On the other end of the scale, there were women like Electra Waggoner Wharton Bailey Gilmore who in 1902 was 20 years old. The pampered only daughter (there were four brothers) of William Thomas and Sicily Halsell Waggoner, Electra was born on a giant ranch in northwest Texas where oil was discovered, making the Waggoners, already wealthy, the richest family west of the Mississippi. On her 20th birthday, the young woman's gift from her father was having the name of the town changed to Electra. On another birthday her father gave her a ranch in Wilbarger County. She named it Zacaweista, Indian for tall grass. Electra spent a great deal of her time in Dallas where, between marriages, she owned a palatial home at 4700 Preston Road, referred to in the press of the time as "the palace." There, her shoe cabinet housed 350 pairs of shoes and she had a new pair delivered every day. She was the first person to spend $20,000 on one shopping spree at Neiman-Marcus after it opened in 1907. The day following she had another $20,000 in clothing and accessories delivered in items she had overlooked or couldn't make up her mind about during her first day of shopping.

When Electra married Albert B. Wharton of Philadelphia, every item in her trousseau bore a Paris label. There were two children by her first marriage, followed by two more husbands. For all her wealth, education and travel, Electra could not buy happiness. John William Rogers says of her, "Electra . . . was a vivid, somewhat tragic woman whose life became complicated by the oil millions that flowed in. She was, perhaps, full of the family energy that made an empire while she lacked a proper channel to express it."

Electra died on Thanksgiving Day in 1924 in New York City at the age of 42.

Electra's is an exaggerated story of what happens to a woman with boundless energy and no approved ways to channel it, but there are thousands of less dramatic incidents of women who have destroyed their lives in an attempt to live out the roles that society decreed for them.

Fortunately for Dallas, most of these women have directed their talents to improving their city. Ruth Potts Spence, recalling some of these women, said, ". . . the men looked with tolerant amusement on their wives' activities—so long as they did not have to be personally involved. The men were busy making a living and considered it effeminate to be interested in art and music. They provided servants for their wives that freed the women to do things in the community." Sooner or later most of the men of substance were "roped in," more often than not by seeing who would write the biggest check.

Mary Collett, who for many years had a ringside seat to the activities of the city as secretary to Edwin J. Kiest, editor of *The Times Herald*, said that men not only tolerated, but approved of the civic work their wives did. "It was just fine that their wives did club work," she said. "The social contacts that they made were good for business."

17

• • • •

A LIBRARY IS BORN

The Dallas Public Library system is exemplary evidence of a project dreamed, nurtured and brought to fruition by women which also won the approval, backing and financial support of the men in their lives—their husbands and brothers as well as the business community. One of the most important events of the early twentieth century and one of the most significant to the city of Dallas throughout the years, the birth of the Dallas Public Library system spanned the 19th and 20th centuries. It has been the root system, the branches or the support of all cultural, educational and business organizations that have followed, sometimes directly but more often indirectly.

Often taken for granted even by those who most use its services, the library has, for more than a century, been the one place serving everybody—citizens of all ages, both sexes, all ethnicities, every possible interest. There is no way to measure its contributions to Dallas, the scope of its gifts, the undergirding it has provided for education, its help in directing generations of young people to grow to autonomous adulthood, the preventive work it has provided to counteract crime, and the challenge it continues to give its thousands of patrons to stretch, grow, flex, focus, expand, and relax.

It is a story of romance, struggle and humor. It is a story of women's work at its very best. The fact that it has also been of prime concern to the city's most forward-thinking men is a tribute both to them and to the city.

The library story began before it ever really existed—as a brainchild of a forward-thinking individual. It began when a member of the Dallas Shakespeare Club arrived at a meeting with a clipping from an Eastern newspaper sent to her in a letter from her sister. The article said that Andrew Carnegie of Philadelphia was giving away his steel fortune to cities to establish public libraries. Shortly, the story circulated around Dallas that a "young upstart by the name of Andrew Carnegie who had made millions in steel" was now giving his money away. To many men in Dallas, this was a startling, unbelievable tale, but the women did not laugh. They went to work.

May Dickson Exall and the Dallas Shakespeare Club took the lead. Mrs. Exall knew that past efforts at building a library had failed because there was not widespread support, so she was determined to have the entire city behind the project.

As early as 1872, there had been a sporadic effort to establish a library. *The Herald*, in February of 1872, reported a musical and dramatic program sponsored by the Young Men's Literary Society to raise library funds. A few books were purchased. The next year the Dallas Library Association was formed and a rental library with 1,000 books and 75 daily and weekly newspapers opened. There were not enough subscribers to keep the project alive and it was abandoned. The association itself continued in existence and 11 years later, in 1884, Col. John C. McCoy rented a room above Charles H. Edwards' music store on the north side of Main Street between Poydras and Murphy and declared it a "free reading room." Mrs. R. D. Finn was employed the following year as Dallas's first librarian to preside over the reading room. In June of 1885, a musical at the Dallas Opera House raised funds for the reading room, and women organized one benefit after another to keep it open.

In 1889, the reading room, with its 1,647 books was moved to the new City Hall, the present site of the Adolphus Hotel. By that time the women of Dallas had heard about Mr. Carnegie and were already at work to secure a real library for the city. They knew that the generosity of the steel magnate came with strings attached and that the city itself would have to provide both money and property if it qualified for a stipend. May Exall planned carefully. She made securing a library her personal priority and talked about it to everybody she met to gather support from the cities' male leaders. Shakespeare Club members, inspired by their president's enthusiasm, trained themselves and each other to garner support from every possible quarter.

The combined efforts of women's groups was critical to the plan. In the waning days of 1898, The Dallas Shakespeare Club hosted a meeting at the First Christian Church to which it invited leaders of all women's organizations in the city. By the close of the meeting, the women agreed to form a Dallas Federation of Women's Clubs. The help of the press was solicited. Pauline Periwinkle wrote 140 personal letters to city leaders asking each to express in writing their thoughts and ideas on a public library. She received 50 responses, most of which were published in her *Dallas Morning News* column. This effort was underscored by an editorial in the paper:

> The present movement (for a library) has begun under more favorable auspices than previous attempts which, for some reason, have failed. The interest is more widespread and personnel of its promoters, which includes public-spirited women, is calculated to inspire prediction of a more satisfactory result.[1]

A formal portrait of May Dickson Exall, definitive founder of the Dallas Public Library, hangs at the Dallas Woman's Club. Standing beside her grandmother's likeness is her namesake, Betty May Exall Stewart. Mrs. Stewart followed her grandmother and her mother, Dorothy Brannen Exall, as president of the Woman's Club.

But talk alone would not suffice. Mrs. Exall sent the ladies out to raise money, an exceedingly painful chore because they had never asked for money, many of them not even from their own husbands. With fear and trembling, they accepted the challenge. May Exall led the way:

> I well remember with what a faint heart I went to ask advice from (Colonel A. H. Belo, publisher of the *News*). I can never forget . . . the ready sympathy and interest he showed and his immediate offer to start the library fund with $1,000. (with more to come if we could raise as much as $10,000).
>
> His gift was quickly followed by gifts of a similar amount from J. S. Armstrong, Colonel C. C. Slaughter, the Sanger Brothers, and . . . Colonel W. E. Hughes. There were other generous gifts—$400 from Miss Helen Gould, who later made additional gifts; $250 from J. C. O'Connor and others that swelled our fund to such proportions as to inspire us.[2]

It is entirely appropriate and true to the democratic principals that have prevailed at the library that its first gift came not from a wealthy individual, and not from someone whose name was well-known but from the Dallas Salvation Army. Its humble 50 cents started the fund for today's Dallas Public Library. Gifts came in tiny amounts and in large amounts representing the conviction of a community determined to build a library. The Dallas teachers, who then were making $1.00 a day got together and contributed $500. Shopkeepers, secretaries and school children gave their nickels and dimes. In all, the drive netted $12,000 from 1,000 contributors. The fund was turned over to trustees Joseph M. Dickson, May Exall's brother; Jules E. Schneider and Alex Sanger "to hold and disburse . . . and to buy a building for a public library."

Raising money came simultaneously with educating the community. On March 1, 1899, the Shakespeare Club was host for a meeting at the Oriental Hotel to which leading citizens of Dallas and Oak Cliff, still a separate town, and all of the women who were members of the planned Federation were sent invitations. The Rev. W. M. Anderson and Rabbi Alexander Kohut both spoke about the need for a library and its value to the city. Rabbi Kohut agreed to chair the ways and means committee. The success of this meeting called for a second which was held on March 30. Two hundred people showed up. It was from this meeting that the Dallas Federation of Women's Clubs was formed with Mrs. Exall as its president and Sally Griffis Meyer as secretary.

Having done the groundwork and secured sizable funding, May Exall then sat down to write a letter to Carnegie.

Members of her family, including granddaughter Betty May Exall Stewart, remember the stories Mrs. Exall told about writing that letter. "She said she wrote it and rewrote it and rewrote it again. It had to be perfect. She was so afraid she would not get the money after all the effort. Finally, her brother (Joseph Dickson) convinced her to stop agonizing and put the letter in the mail."[3] Mrs. Exall put it this way:

> I well remember how I labored over the wording of this letter, not stopping to think it would never come under the eyes of the Honorable Andrew at all, but would be coldly perused by his secretary, who would be empowered to give the decision . . . . An answer was eagerly awaited, but week after week passed with no results. The summer came on; club activities ceased, and I departed for a summer vacation with a heavy heart.[4]

Away on vacation, Mrs. Exall continued to wait and worry. Her recollections continue:

> In the early part of September, the long-looked-for letter, bearing the magical name, "Andrew Carnegie" on the envelope, was forwarded to me from Dallas. With trembling fingers, I opened it to find that the great philanthropist agreed to make a gift of $50,000 to Dallas for a library on certain conditions: a suitable site for a building must be provided by the City of Dallas, and a fund of $4,000 a year provided for operation and maintenance of the library.[5]

May Exall was ecstatic. She called her brother, who said that she must keep the news a secret until a mass meeting could be held to make the announcement. By that time, everybody in Dallas felt a personal stake in the library and all deserved to hear it at the same time. "I went about with this important secret concealed in my breast," Mrs. Exall remembered, "and I must confess this gave me a feeling of great importance."

It was not a secret for long. The news leaked and on September 19, 1899, *The Dallas Morning News* announced the gift in a front-page story. Two days later, on September 1, the mass meeting was held. It was, of course, Alice Parsons Fitzgerald in her *Beau Monde* on September 23 who applauded Carnegie in the most glowing terms. She relegated coverage of the meeting to secondary status while editorializing on the merits of the "great philanthropist" and approved what surely no one else took seriously, the suggestion by one speaker that the "resolutions of the ladies (be) printed on satin—good satin, not shoddy!" Alice's story in part:

> *Beau Monde* has ever been an admirer of that noted philanthropist and broad-gauged champion of republican principles, Mr. Andrew Carnegie . . . . (who) has given millions, and . . . is not ready to cease his good work. Since January, 1899, he has given away $1,250,000 . . . . he has promised Dallas $50,000 . . . .
>
> The mass meeting on Thursday night demonstrated the fever pulse of the public over the munificent offer of Mr. Carnegie. The city hall was filled with a representative and enthusiastic assemblage. The long-felt want of an intelligent, enterprising people was about to be realized and the very atmosphere was throbbing with anticipation.
>
> The meeting was presided over by Mayor Traylor and seats on the rostrum were given to the promoters of the cause, members of the clergy and prominent educators. Among them were Mrs. Henry Exall, president of the Library Association; Mrs. Sydney Smith; Mr. and Mrs. Jules E. Schneider; Mrs. Kate Cabell Currie; Mrs. George K. Meyer; Bishop A. C. Garrett; Revs. R. C. Buckner, W. M. Anderson, George C. Truett; Col. John F. Elliott; Messrs. J. M. Howell, C. L. Wakefield, Joseph M. Dickson and members of the school board. Mrs. Exall was the first to address the assemblage, stating, in that simple style of hers, the story of the Ladies' Library Association, and reading the correspondence between herself and Mrs. (sic) Carnegie, which showed that it had fallen into excellent as well as enthusiastic hands.
>
> . . . Mr. Patrick O'Keefe, the irrepressible, spoke to the point and caught the house. His motion to have the resolution of the ladies of the Library

Mrs. Exall not only wrote the letter to Andrew Carnegie to secure a grant for the library, she led Dallas women in creating a climate of acceptance for it in the community and prodded them to request money from business leaders.

Association, read by Col. Elliott, printed on satin—good satin, not shoddy—showed he was up on the elegant form of doing things.[6]

There were snags to be resolved. The City Charter provided only $2,000, not $4,000, for library support and had to be amended before Carnegie would provide the grant. This meant that the City charter must be amended at state level. Col. Henry Exall, May's husband, a friend of the governor, was sent off to Austin where he quickly took care of the matter. The city's lot, only 50 by 100 feet, on Commerce between Ervay and Akard was deemed too small to accommodate the new library, so with the permission of the city council, it was sold and the money applied to a new site, two adjoining 100 by 100 foot lots on Commerce at Harwood.

The first two sets of plans chosen for the Dallas library were by Fort Worth architects! But the grumbling about the choice of plans quieted when people saw the drawing. It looked like a library.

A building committee—May Exall, Jeannette Belo, Belle Schneider, J. S. Armstrong and Joseph Dickson—was named with Attorney Dickson chairing it. The committee agreed on tentative plans and announced that bids were open for an architect. Thirteen entries were submitted. The committee, working without knowledge of who had submitted what plans, unanimously agreed on one set of plans only to learn that it had been submitted by an architectural firm from Fort Worth. A brief flurry of consternation ensued. The committee knew that the choice of an architectural firm in Fort Worth would not be acceptable, so a second set of plans was chosen. This, too, was the offering of a Fort Worth firm. The committee then went back to the first set of plans and chose the Fort Worth firm of R. Sanguinet and Carl G. Staats. Ironically, a bit later Fort Worth chose plans of a Dallas firm for its library.

If Dallasites were dismayed by the choice, this was quickly alleviated when the plans were published. The two-story building would be both massive and classic, fronted with Roman pressed brick with terra cotta enrichments, numerous windows for proper lighting relieved by Ionic columns of gray Bedford stone. A massive celebration marked the laying of the cornerstone on January 16, 1901, and, as the building went up, the construction firm (Sonnefield and Emmins of Dallas) worked behind a host of "sidewalk engineers" gawking and offering advice. As nothing else had ever been, the library was their own. They approved. It *looked* like a library. Clifton Church volunteered to oversee construction and he, along with building committee that watched every penny, brought the project to completion for $50,097.53, only $97.53 above budget!

As soon as the building of the library was assured, the association began looking for someone to run it. There was some pressure to hire a person already in Dallas, but the committee adhered to the advice of national experts, which urged that cities hire "competent librarians" to administer Andrew Carnegie's largess. They consulted Frank M. Crunden, a nationally recognized library expert who directed the St. Louis Public Library, and he recommended Rosa Leeper, an assistant on his staff, who was a native of Sherman. In a few days a formal letter of application came from her.

Rosa's was one of many applications that the committee sifted through; they carefully studied all that were qualified. They invited a small number to Dallas for interviews. Then they offered Miss Leeper the position. She got the word that she was the committee's choice a month after she had visited Dallas while she was attending an American Library Association convention in Montreal, Canada. She accepted. Her salary was $1,200 annually. She would go to work on October 1, 1900, in Dallas, but before that she toured libraries in 20 cities so that she could bring the latest techniques to her new position.

Rosa Leeper personified the stereotype of an early twentieth century librarian. Stockily built, she pulled her dark hair that tended to be curly and unruly, into a severe bun at the back of her neck. Her round, rather flat face was set off with severe rimless glasses. She wore high collars and long skirts. A woman who could have been beautiful, she was, instead a librarian! She lived the role to perfection. Women librarians were spinsters. Rosa never married. She dedicated her entire life to the library. In Dallas almost a year before the library opened, she supervised the hiring of the staff—because of limited funding, none were qualified librarians—the purchase and cataloging of the books and, to some extent, their placement.

The Dallas Public Library system marked the first time that women who had created an organization administered it. May Exall was president of the first 12-member board; her brother, Joseph Dickson was treasurer and Rosa Leeper, the librarian, a non-voting member, was secretary. Others were a Who's Who in early Dallas and included Jeannette Belo, Isadore Callaway, Belle Schneider, J. T. Howard, E. M. Kahn, A. V. Lane, M. E. Locke, G. K. Meyer, Alex Sanger and C. L. Wakefield.

At the library opening on October 30, 1901, almost everything was in place. An ecstatic crowd of 2,000, four times the capacity of its Carnegie Auditorium, jostled one another for a glimpse. Joseph Dickson, arriving a bit late, had to use a little-known back stairway to reach the podium where he was to speak. Rosa Leeper had been allotted $7,000 to buy books, a sum that was augmented by gifts from individuals so that 10,000 volumes were purchased, at an average cost of 87 cents each. Rosa had been careful to hedge her professional expertise with the wishes of the Library Association that had hired her and paid her salary. Everybody, then as now, had definite ideas about what should be included for people to read and what should be withheld. Even May Exall was cautious. At the dedication, she said: "Some critics . . . have made the mistake of decrying the circulation of novels as an end too low to merit public attention. But good fiction (does not) require an apology." Then she hedged: ". . . obviously, no library ought to issue fiction except under the constant oversight of a librarian . . . . Some women librarians are wielding an influence for good second to that of no preacher or teacher."

Rosa Leeper, in her own estimation and that of the committee that oversaw her work, believed she was just such a librarian. She viewed her assignment as keeper of public morals, particularly as this applied to children, as well as custodian of the books. She was, in every sense, a product of her times and dutiful in carrying out her assignments. She arrived for work at precisely the appointed hour and tried to meet the expectations and demands of everybody. She had no secretary, but kept her own records in longhand carefully and precisely.

On some things she was adamant. When, prior to the library's opening, the public clamored for a listing of the titles to be available, Miss Leeper said there would be no printed catalog. "The modern way is to list the works by author, title and subject on file cards in a dictionary arrangement, using the new Dewey Decimal System," and that is precisely what she planned to do. "To print book catalogs of the issuable volumes would be as old-fashioned as using a wood-burning stove in the kitchen in this age when housewives are cooking with gas," she sniffed.

From the first, service to children was an essential component of library services. In her opening remarks, May Exall said, "we have devoted a commodious room in our building to the exclusive use of children . . . . no child in Dallas need any longer be deprived of the privilege of reading good and attractive books . . . . all the children of Dallas will be welcomed, and amid beautiful and ennobling surroundings, will receive courteous treatment and wise guidance in the choice of books." The schools began a cooperative program with the library that has continued, with few exceptions, through the years.

Miss Leeper's records reveal both the joy and some of the frustrations of the library's infancy:

Rosa Leeper, librarian chosen for the new edifice, looked after the books and the morals of Dallas readers.

Lillian Moore Bradshaw, whose tenure spanned 22 years, directed the largest expansion in the library's history, but she almost didn't get a chance to do the job because she was a woman.

> . . . (because of) lack of funds it was considered best to start with untrained assistants. One disadvantage of this plan is that it sometimes takes months to prove . . . an assistant . . . ; another is that just when a promising assistant is beginning to be of real use, she sometimes marries. Both of these unforeseen disadvantages have stricken this library and it is now being run by a force new since the opening. The present staff consists of five persons—the librarian, two regular assistants, one extra assistant, a young man for evening and Sunday work, and a janitor. The statistics during the first 10 weeks were: Registration 2,908; Issue, 15,208; not counting either reading room.[7]

Through the years, only in rare and brief times, has there been enough money to provide the services required of a metropolitan library and, without exception, a dedicated staff of professionals has provided a service to the community far beyond the financial support provided by the city. Married women were considered unqualified to be librarians as if saying "I do" meant they lost their ability to catalog, care for and distribute books. No matter how good she was and no matter how much her services were needed, when she got married, a woman lost her job. This continued until World War II when the library, desperate for qualified personnel, began taking applications of married women. Lillian Moore Bradshaw was the first married women it hired. In the minds of many, she is the greatest librarian Dallas has ever had.

Rosa's early reports show her frustration in trying to guide Dallas readers to "appropriate material." Here are excerpts from a few of her records:

> The library is classified by the Decimal System and book numbers are not used—following the plan of the St. Louis Public Library. The catalog has not progressed beyond the author and title stage, though some subjects of local interest, such as Cotton, Mexico, the Race Question, Texas History, and all Biography, have been brought out. The shelf list supplements this, and is made to take the place of a classic catalog until a dictionary catalog can be completed. The Newark Charging System is used, and free access is permitted in the reference, reading, and children's rooms. Access to the stack room may be had on application.
>
> All new fiction and a constantly varied assortment labeled "Good Fiction" is kept on the issue desk, where it may be examined and selections made.[8]

As use of the library expanded, Miss Leeper's work and frustrations increased. By the end of the first year, the library had 11,436 volumes and had circulated 83,006 books to its 5,400 card-holding readers. She was hard-pressed to meet her professional responsibilities and increasingly stymied by the demands required of a keeper of public morals. Sometimes she spent precious time trying to determine what, exactly, her readers needed or wanted and at other times she was inhibited by the demands of those for reading material she deemed inferior.

> Four out of five persons using the library for reference work either hesitate to let it be known what they want or are unable to express that want. Having learned what is wanted, it is not enough for the librarian to get the book giving the desired information. The page and paragraph must be found and pointed out . . . .[9]

Some of the Library's earliest rules bring a chuckle to today's readers; others are a shameful reminder of our past prejudices; only a very few are in effect today:

> Any white person of good deportment, character and habits may use the Reading Rooms. No person who is intoxicated or unclean in person or dress may use the facilities. No person shall be allowed to use tobacco, lounge or sleep (in the library). All white persons who reside within three and a half miles of the Dallas postoffice shall be entitled to draw books for home reading.

> Marking a book . . . will be considered an "injury." The offender is liable to prosecution under the City Ordinance . . . . In the event of contagious and infectious diseases existing in the household of a book-borrower, such borrower shall be immediately notified to turn over such library books to the Health Officer for disinfection.[10]

Miss Leeper continued as librarian until 1916 when she asked for a year's leave of absence to regain her health. It was granted, but she did not return to the post. Her contributions to the library are enormous. She was the "midwife" at the baby's birth. She purchased the first books and directed their cataloging and distribution. She presided over the expansions including the installation of the "art room" in 1902, the first public art gallery in Texas. Among its first acquisitions was an Elizabet Ney painting, an artist already well-known, who would become one of the leading artist of her time. Rosa also accepted the 167-volume Julien Reverchon collection of French literature and she saw the library's first expansion with the opening of the Oak Cliff Branch Library on November 23, 1914.

Rosa Leeper was succeeded in 1916 by Betsy Wiley, a young woman who had been her protege but who was not academically as qualified for the post. Betsy remained for six years until 1922 when she resigned to get married.

Through some of its most turbulent years, Cleora Clanton headed the library. Even her eternal optimism sometimes waned as books increased from 10,000 to 157,000 and were housed in a building where cracking plaster and crumbling ceilings sometimes damaged them.

Cleora Clanton became head librarian in 1923 and remained in the post for 22 years. She began her tenure by pointing out that the library was "overcrowded. Plaster is cracking and falling in some places." She repeatedly reminded everybody who would listen that a building that had started out gloriously with 10,000 volumes had, by 1923, grown to 66,851. One-fourth of Dallas's citizens owned library cards. Of the $7,000 appropriated annually to the library, about a third of it went to repairing books already in circulation. She was convinced that branch libraries were the only way to reach the citizens who needed library services and she worked tirelessly to secure them. She saw the opening of the Dunbar Branch (in the dedication story following her name, it was noted that she was white) in March of 1931, the South Dallas Sanger branch in 1932, the Oak Lawn Branch in a few months later and the East Dallas (Lakewood) branch in 1938. Even as Miss Clanton pointed out its problems, she was its strongest and most persistent advocate, and no matter how bad things were, she presented a positive attitude to the public. She knew that the library served as the heart of education for the city and that it must survive. "While its physical appearance and ability to function have suffered during the years, its heart is sound and its spirit unbroken," she said on its 40th anniversary in 1941, only eight days before the outbreak of World War II. She reported that the city had spent $1.3 million on the library since its beginning, an average of 27 cents per year per person. Its volumes had increased to 157,000 books, plus thousands of documents. It had circulated 15.3 million books in its first 40 years.

Through the Great Depression from 1929 until 1935, through World War II, 1942-1946, through the booming years following the end of the war when the population swelled and the library remained intact, Cleora Clanton was the librarian struggling with impossibly low budgets, dowdy surroundings and an always expanding reading public. During the Depression, the library became a haven for the poor, the idle and the cold just as it did again in the late 1980s when the street people all but took over the facilities.

Cleora managed to survive and prevail because of the dedicated women who joined her staff and remained even though their salaries were pitifully inadequate. Many deserve accolades, among them Violet Hayden, who would later be Violet Hayden Dowell, who joined the team along with Cleora and survived to become assistant librarian. In 1938 Marion Underwood became the librarian of the East Dallas branch. Marion's personal charisma charmed the old and the young, the rich and the poor, the women and the men and most of all the children. To several generations, she *was* the Lakewood library, so popular that she was known as the mayor of Lakewood. Equally significant, Siddie Joe Johnson joined the force in 1938 as director of Children's Services. She inaugurated the children's story hour, organized a creative writing club for kids and authored several children's books. When she retired in 1965, she was more important in stretching the minds of children than many of their parents and teachers. For 27 years she represented stability to kids in a world that was forever changing. Of equal significance was Alma Deere Venters, the first director of the Dunbar Branch Library. Alma, a native Texan with advanced library degrees earned in Virginia, was better qualified academically than many of the white librarians. These women stayed, not because they were financially rewarded, but because they were dedicated. In 1942 Bertha Landers established the library's visual education department, became one of the nations' leading authorities on library film departments and wrote many of the early manuals that became national "how-to" books.

The library was staggering under an impossible task—crowded facilities and pitifully few books. It was, in the words of Cleora Clanton, and of many nationally recognized authorities, a disgrace to the city. But in the darkest hours, comes often the brightest possibilities. For the Dallas Public library system it came in the formation of Friends of the Library. The brainchild of Violet Hayden, an assistant librarian, with the full approval of Miss Clanton and the backing of Erin Bain Jones, who was its first president, Friends has been a consistent force for improving library facilities. It was they who rallied the City and the citizens in 1952 to approve bonds that included a new library in the heaviest vote in the city's history.

The downtown branch of the Dallas Public Library on Young Street across from Dallas City Hall is named for J. Erik Jonsson. By all accounts, it is one of the finest library systems in the country.
—*Photo by Vivian Castleberry.*

But having a library approved and having it built proved to be two different things. Coming as it did in the midst of national controversy when Sen. Joseph McCarthy and his ilk were finding Communists under every cabbage leaf, the Dallas citizenry was divided over every public issue from where the new facility should be located to what kinds of books could be on its shelves. Many leading citizens rallied to affirm its value. Women's groups were especially persistent, among them Evelyn Lambert and Fashion Arts, Inc., a non-profit group of women working in fashion and related fields. Since fashion had become the third largest industry in the city, its support was a decided plus. On October 5, 1953, after more than a year of haggling, the City Council voted to retain the library at the Commerce and Harwood location. That meant moving books, furnishing and personnel while a new building took shape and so it was that Union Railroad Terminal became Dallas's central library for almost two years, from late in 1953 until the grand opening of the new building on September 25, 1955. The facilities were so crowded that Cleora Clanton's office was in the space formerly occupied by the men's rest room.

In the midst of the chaos, Miss Clanton retired and was succeeded by James D. Meek who took over as chief librarian on January 3, 1955. He was a different breed of librarian for Dallas. In a city where men often bragged about their lack of formal education and prized self-determination, Meek, at 34, was erudite and sophisticated. He held a graduate degree in library science from Columbia University and had gained experience in New York City, Denver and St. Joseph, Missouri. He hit the ground running. His vision was to turn the Dallas library system into one of the nation's best facilities, to blend the classiness of its neighbor, Neiman-Marcus with the folksiness of the Lakewood branch. Toward that end he hired more professionals and, at the same time, insisted on the friendliness and helpfulness that made Marion Underwood so popular in Lakewood. He ran seminars for his staff on how to dress and how to act. With the brashness that often accompanies youth and in his hurry to achieve results quickly, Meeks stepped on the sensitivities of many Dallasites, among them some of his most valuable staff as well as some of those whose votes paid his salary. He lasted less than seven years.

In 1961, followed Meeks' resignation, Lillian Bradshaw was named acting librarian. When she applied for the top job, she was informed that married women were not considered prime candidates. The search committee went looking for a good man. Seven applied. Seven were interviewed. In March of 1962, the Library Board agreed that the best "man" for the job was the woman already in the position and gave acting director Bradshaw the title "Librarian." Until 1984, for the longest tenure of anyone since the library's founding, Lillian Bradshaw headed the Dallas Public Library system.

The expansion of the system was phenomenal under Lillian's direction. Branch offices expanded to 16. A few were closed or consolidated, others expanded, many new ones established. Within the system, the numbers of books, the numbers of departments, the attention of personnel to serving an ever increasing clientele catapulted. Lillian led the campaign to name the downtown central library for J. Erik Jonsson, citizen, businessman, philanthropist, mayor. In this act, she did what most women of Dallas have always done, honor the great men who have led the city. To many people who watched it all take place, it should be called the Lillian Moore Bradshaw Library.

When Lillian retired in 1984 and was replaced by Patrick M. O'Brien, for all but six of its 83 years the Dallas Public Library had been headed by a woman.

18

••••

WOMEN AS CULTURAL ARBITERS

The advancement of culture in Dallas has always been woman's work. For every library, every symphony hall, every theater, every art museum attributed to a man, and in many instances named for him, there are women behind the scenes who have done the research, created the climate, and over a long period of time pushed, prodded and prayed to make the advancement possible. True, it is men who have, until very recent years, controlled the money and written the checks that made these advancements possible. But it is women who determined that Dallas should be a cultural center, that it should have art, music, literature and theater and the educational facilities to foster them. And it is women who have always done the support work required to make things happen.

The responsibility for developing the cultural life of Dallas has always been the work of women. They, individually and through their organizations, have been the beacon of hope for art, dance, music, theater and education.

Seldom have the contributions of women to the arts been noted, and even more seldom have they been honored. Instead, women as artists have been disparaged and the work they do dismissed as insignificant. Art that is indigenous to women—principally fabric art and china art—has only recently begun to be honored, cherished by new generations of families and, in some instances, placed in museums. How many settings of hand-painted china have been relegated to trash heaps, packed away in attics or hidden in out-of-the way china closets by daughters and granddaughters because they were embarrassed to show it? A society that does not value the gifts of its women creates a climate in which the women themselves and their lineage diminish, dismiss or deprecate their talents.

Fabric art, just as china painting, until very recent years, has been taken for granted, at best, or devalued and often destroyed. Quilts stitched by hand, crocheted bed spreads, doilies and mats of all kinds, knitted pieces, lace tatting, embroidery, cross stitch and other forms of women's fabric work were not perceived as art. It would be impossible to speculate on how many quilts have been relegated to pet quarters or used as tents by children or otherwise destroyed. One story in the Peak family illustrates the status of fabric art in early Dallas. Edith Rydell Roberts owns a beautiful quilt block which she framed and has hanging in her Arlington home. It came to her through her great-grandmother, Sarah Ann Peak Harwood. A niece said the block was not made by Sarah Ann, who had several servants. "She didn't have to do *that* kind of work," the niece said, dismissing the fact that women pieced quilts as an outlet for their artistic talents. Today, fabric creations are increasingly cherished as creative art and granddaughters

Dancer Toni Beck, with arms raised heavenward, personifies women's feeling about culture.

and great-granddaughters are rescuing them and preserving them, often in museums, or cherishing them as family heirlooms.

If their work was to be at all accepted, the women of early Dallas who were considered to be artists always emulated their male counterparts. To create in any medium that was considered "women's art" was to de-value their talent—just as women who wrote for the "women's pages" of newspapers were downgraded. Real journalists wrote "hard" news—stories about crime and violence and thievery and deception—and got their by-lines published on the front pages of the papers. Women's writing, along with women's art, was consigned to second class status regardless of the fact that both dealt with the very essence of human life from birth to death.

So, women who took their artistic talent seriously usually painted in oils on canvas or they were sculptors. They rarely married because, wedded to their art and with no support from the public, they could not continue their creative lives along with myriad details of running a household and rearing children. The women who were serious about their art, and whose families would support them, went east to study, or, better, to Europe. Only a small number of these artists returned to Dallas to make their homes, settling, instead, in eastern cities that would support their talents and where they could find like-minded individuals to nurture them.

A few early artists did return to Dallas where, for the most part, they pursued their work in a climate that was sometimes hostile, but which more often ignored them. Their talents blossomed, if at all, in a foundation and climate still directed primarily to physical survival and growth.

> As a pioneer community Dallas was filled with a populace busy making a living and accumulating property of a somewhat less abstract nature than art. Itinerant artists here as elsewhere drew crude likenesses of persons who could pose and pay for a portrait . . . .
>
> As an increasing number of Dallas families accumulated property some gesture towards art and art collecting naturally evolved . . . . The movement was without direction as there was no American art. Dallas, like all of America, gave obeisance to the established forms of European art . . . . Artists stayed away from what they regarded as the philistinism of Dallas . . . . Largely (they) ignored Texas as subject material.[1]

The first collection of art ever shown in Dallas was the brainchild of a woman, Margaret Isabel Gay Smith. Married to Sydney Smith, a longtime secretary of the State Fair of Texas, Belle was asked, according to records, or insisted, as is more likely the case, on having a "ladies department" at the State Fair. Born in 1840 on the family plantation near Starksville, Mississippi, Belle married Sydney Smith in 1865 and moved to a plantation on the Yazoo River and later to Okolona, Mississippi. She was 38 and the mother of three children when she moved to Dallas in 1878. She quickly became a social leader.

Belle helped to organize the first Ladies and Textile Departments at the State Fair in 1885. The next year she added an art show. It was the first art ever assembled as an exhibit in the city and the first time the State Fair had included art as a regular fair feature. Newspaper columns in the mid 1880s often encouraged women to assist with Belle's project and *Beau Monde* scolded them on more than one occasion for not supporting her. John William Rogers said the 1886 show was not only the first exhibition of painting ever seen in Dallas, but probably the first ever in Texas.[2] Six years later, in 1902, Belle assembled the paintings for the "picture room" of the new library.

Belle Gay Smith walked a tight rope of propriety. It was totally inappropriate for a woman of substance to have a career and her name always appeared as Mrs. Sydney Smith, as if being the wife of the secretary of the State Fair gave her permission to use her talents so long as she did it in obscurity. In 1888, with Mrs. A. C. Ardrey, she organized the Chautauqua Literary and Scientific Circle, later rechristened the Pierian Club. In 1893 she established a congress at the fair where women could exchange ideas and find mutual support. Scholarly papers were presented on topics such as "Equality, Not Supremacy." The women were interrupted by a gathering of snickering male bystanders, one of whom was heard to say that the appearance of a mouse would disrupt the whole proceeding.

Belle not only created the Women's Department of the State Fair, but enlarged and improved it every year. Though ill, she had made all of the plans for the 18th women's department in 1903 and, in an outline left with the editors of *The Dallas Morning News*, had termed it "the best ever" when she went to Marlin for her health. There, on the early morning of September 5, she died. Her funeral at St. Matthews Cathedral drew most of the city's elite including all of the staff and the board of the Dallas Public Library, of which she was a member. The library closed for the 4 p.m. funeral. She was survived by her husband, a son, Sydney Smith, Jr. and two daughters, a Mrs. W. H. Stratton, Jr. of Shreveport, Louisiana, and Tallulah Smith of Dallas. She is buried in Greenwood Cemetery.

The first art gallery in Dallas, often attributed to W. L. Crawford, was, instead, the dream and the work of his wife, Kate Lester Lamar Crawford. She had a private gallery built onto her home on Ross at Washington, later 3709 Ross Avenue, in the late 1880s and kept it open to the public for half a century. The gallery had long been a dream of Kate Crawford. Growing up in Oxford, Mississippi, the daughter of Dr. J. D. and Josephine Oliver Lester, she showed a marked artistic ability at a very young age. Her parents provided every advantage. She was educated in private schools in Mississippi, graduated from Oxford Female College and went abroad where she studied in Paris and other European art centers with the outstanding artists of the time. She traveled extensively in Europe and painted in many cities. She came home to study at the Art League of New York and was a charter member of the Carcassonne Art School in Washington, D. C.

She married L. Q. C. Lamar, Jr., the son of a Mississippi senator who was later Secretary of the Interior in President Cleveland's Cabinet and later a Supreme Court justice. Beautiful, vivacious and cultured, Kate was her widower father-in-law's official hostess. This gave her the status of a cabinet lady and afforded her the role of government representative in her extensive travels. It was a role she cherished and in which she performed magnificently.

Kate Lamar was still a young woman when her husband died. She accepted a position as art instructor at Professor Jones Female College in Dallas. She later directed the art department at North Texas Female College—later renamed Kidd-Key College—in Sherman. In 1895 Kate moved back to Dallas planning to open a school of arts. She taught for a year while finalizing her plans. In 1896, still planning to open an art school, she married Col. W. L. Crawford, a wealthy trial lawyer who was considerably older. It was a second marriage for both. As a busy wife and mother to Lester Crawford, she turned her attention to collecting rather than teaching art. Shortly after her marriage, her dream to own a gallery became a reality when her husband added a wing to their home to house her art. Upon its completion, she opened it to the public. For almost 50 years she continued to open it to visitors and personally guide them through. Much of the art was Mrs. Crawford's own work, for she continued to paint and sculpt for most of her life. In art circles, Kate's work was rarely acknowledged and, as a person, she was considered somewhat eccentric, something of a curiosity.

For whatever else she may have been—an artist whose talents were diminished by the Dallas of her day, a person of less than monumental talent, someone who turned inward and failed to develop her potential—Kate Lester Lamar Crawford was a woman ahead of her times. Her training in art and her generosity of spirit made a lasting impact on Dallas. Her greatest contribution was in following through on her vision to open an art gallery in the city; in this she was the first, thereby creating a climate for all the galleries and museums that have followed. Kate Crawford died March 4, 1947, and is buried in Oakland Cemetery alongside Col. Crawford. She outlived her husband, who died February 17, 1920, by 27 years.

Katherine Lester Lamar Crawford opened Dallas's first art gallery in her home on Ross Avenue in the late 1890s. Though a private gallery that featured her own art among the collection, she kept it open to the public for many years.

The Picture Room at the library, 1901, was the first public museum in the city. (See also Chapter 17) Belle Gay Smith assembled the art for it and patrons were charged 25 cents to view it. Those purchasing tickets had the privilege of voting on their favorite canvass. Proceeds, after expenses, were used to purchase the favored painting. There was a tie between Herbert Faulkner's "My Gondolier's Kitchen" and Childe Hassam's "September Moonrise." Both were purchased to become the first paintings for a permanent art museum.

Margaret McDermott, in white gown at left, for three decades, set the pace and supported the arts with both her service and her finances. At the left is Norma Young, founder of Theater Three. On the right is Patsy Nasher, who with her husband, Ray, was a definitive art connoisseur and collector.

The time had come to create an organization to support the many different art interests in the community and serve as a sounding board and nurturing oasis for artists. Again, it was women who led the way with May Dickson Exall the natural leader to undertake the task. Having already served for many years as president of the Dallas Shakespeare Club and been the definitive founder of the Dallas Public Library, she was willing to give the time and the accumulation of her experience and wisdom to the fledgling art groups. In January of 1903 the Dallas Art Association was chartered with Mrs. Charles Dexter as president. It began with 50 members. By 1905, it had 62 active and four honorary members whose names are a Who's Who of Dallas. Forty-eight of the 66 were women.[3]

With the Art Association in place, with the Picture Room at the library inadequate for showing art and the space needed for library expansion, it could not be long until Dallas considered a museum of fine arts. And it wasn't, though it must have seemed an eternity to the handful of art devotees. The Fine Arts Building in Fair Park was completed in 1909 and the art collection of the Dallas Art Association was placed on exhibition and formally presented to the city.

It was in that year, 1909, that Sallie Griffis Meyer became president of the Art Association. Though other art enthusiasts came and went, burned out by the herculean chore of acquiring canvasses on a financial shoestring and competing with other cities more artistically sophisticated, Sallie Meyer had come to stay. For 18 years she headed the Art Association. She almost single-handedly kept it alive during lean times when most other people were backing away and giving up. No task was too menial for her. She served in every capacity from janitor to director. "She was the *whole* thing," said Ruth Spence, who had known and worked with her during the lean years. "Nobody has ever given Mrs. Meyer the credit she deserves."[4]

During the time she was its president, Sallie concentrated on bringing outstanding Eastern artists to show in Dallas, sometimes to the consternation of local folk who were seeking an outlet for their own talents. It was difficult for them to understand that in order to be recognized on the national and international scene, they would be helped by residing and working in a city noted for its art climate. Putting Dallas on the map was

Mrs. Meyer's contribution. In order to create the quality she was determined for Dallas to enjoy, Mrs. Meyer had to develop great diplomacy, for it was as important to refuse a gift as it was to accept one. The minutes of those early Art Association meetings show discreet and tactful refusals of some offered pieces that failed to meet the committee's standards of quality and that, eventually, would have been an embarrassment to the collection. It was Sallie Meyer and her small coterie of art enthusiasts that set the standards, and piece by piece, acquired the nucleus of what is today the Dallas Museum of Fine Arts.

Exposure brings, along with it, curiosity followed by interest, education, knowledge and, finally, the desire to be included. So it was with art in Dallas. As the Art Association gradually accumulated pieces and as the State Fair exhibitions grew in numbers as well as in quality of paintings, citizens of Dallas and of Texas were exposed, many for the first time, to art—and they wanted pieces for themselves. By the early 1920s and for a number of years thereafter, art sales at the fair exhibit exceeded those at the annual National Academy Show in New York. This, more than anything else, attracted dealers and artists from throughout the country and some from Europe.

It also included a growing art colony in Dallas. When artists of that early period are mentioned, predictably it is men who are remembered: R. J. Onderdonk and his son, Julian Onderdonk; Frank Reaugh; and later Harry Carnohan, who became head of the art department of Columbia University; Everett Spruce, who became art director of the University of Texas; Otis Dozier and William Lester, who were associated with the Art Center at Colorado Springs; Alexander Hogue, who headed the art department of the University of Tulsa; Olin Travis and E. G. Eisenlohr, who founded the Dallas Art Institute—and Jerry Bywaters, who became director of the Dallas Museum of Fine Arts (1935 to 1964) and who, for years until his death in 1989 was the definitive Dallas art expert—artist, writer, teacher communicator and impresario.

In the 1930s, perhaps more a diversion from the poverty of the Great Depression as an interest in art, the Alice Street Carnival drew hundreds of celebrants. The street, a smidgen of a block in a half-circle between Maple Avenue and Cedar Spring, was unpaved and the houses on either side tiny, run-down and unpainted—the perfect spot for a carnival. Students of the thriving Dallas Art Institute loved it. For two days in June they roped off the street, decorated it with wildly colored paper streamers and sand-filled paper bags holding lighted candles, and turned it into an outdoor art center. The bohemiam atmosphere, complete with fortune tellers, soda pop and hot dog stands, kissing booths and an open air dance floor lured people from everywhere—rich and poor alike. Artists sold their works from a few cents to a few dollars. The Alice Street Carnival "was well on its way to becoming one of the town's most colorful traditions . . . . then the Art Institute was moved to the Museum of Modern Arts in Fair Park . . . . the carnival was revived . . . in the plaza. With no dust underfoot and the stately building as a background, the setting seemed far more ideal than Alice Street, but the 'grandeur' of the surroundings were formidable."[5] Well publicized, the transferred and transformed event drew 15,000 people during its several evenings in 1938, its first year. Now big business, it created disharmony among the artists and failed to attract the diversity of individuals who had been its chief attraction. By the end of its first season, it had lost its heart. The artists tried one more year and then gave up.

Women who were artists during that period are not as well known as the men. Some, like Vivian Aunspaugh continued to live in Dallas and to establish a climate of acceptance that has made it easier for other women to follow. Others, like Clyde Chandler, found the atmosphere so alien to their talents that they moved.

Vivian Louise Aunspaugh, with Clyde Chandler, in 1898 founded a school for general art work. It was not only the first complete art school in Dallas, but the first in Texas. Four years later, in 1902, the school was renamed the Aunspaugh Art School of Dallas, and a full art curriculum, including painting, drawing, modeling, outdoor sketching, illustrating, cartooning, commercial art, decoration and designing was introduced.

Sally Griffis Meyer became president of the Dallas Art Association in 1909, collected the first art for the museum, diplomatically declined art that was inferior, and piece by piece acquired the nucleus for the Dallas Museum of Fine Arts.

Vivian, born in Bedford, Virginia, in 1869, moved to Dallas as a small child with her parents, Virginia Fields Yancey Aunspaugh and John Henry Aunspaugh, a cotton man. They encouraged her art talents. At Shorter College in Georgia where she took her bachelor's degree, she won the highest art award offered by the college. She studied in New York at Art Students League and miniature painting in Chicago with Cecile Payne. She then went to Paris to the Carlarossi School and on to Italy where she studied in Rome. She gained teaching experience with brief stints at Union Springs Female College in Alabama, McKinney College, public schools in Greenville and Bonham before returning to a position at St. Mary's Episcopal College. This position brought her back to Dallas in 1898 where for the next 50 years, until her death in 1960, she was a commanding and highly respected part of the art community.

Vivian's was the first school in the Southwest to use live models, both draped and nude, which earned her, in some settings, the reputation of being a woman of loose morals. For the most part, however, she was considered an eccentric young woman and tolerated because of the sterling reputation of her parents. What, indeed, could one expect, when a young woman went off to Paris and Rome to study and work? Vivian not only weathered the small storms of protest, but went serenely on her way painting—mostly landscapes, flowers, figures, portraits and miniatures in oils, water color and pastels, teaching art and conducting summer workshops. For 12 years she headed the St. Mary's art department. Her work was exhibited at the Paris Exposition in 1900 and was shown annually at the State Fair. She directed the art department of the Dallas Women's Forum for years where she taught art history as well as painting, and probably more than any other person, helped women to appreciate their talents as artists.

Clyde Giltner Chandler was an eminent artist and sculptor who worked in Dallas, Chicago, and California in the late 19th and early 20th centuries. Born in Evansville, Indiana, Clyde was brought to Dallas by her parents, William W. and Flora Giltner Chandler when she was a baby. The drawings, clay figures and colors that enthrall most children held Clyde's interests to the exclusion of other toys. Her parents encouraged their daughter and provided educational support for her. She attended St. Mary's College and studied art with R. J. Onderdonk. Following her graduation, she studied for two years in Boston, then toured the eastern galleries. She then returned to Dallas to open the art school with Vivian Aunspaugh. The project was in its infancy when Laredo Taft, director of the Chicago Art Institute, saw her work, and invited her to study with him. In 1903 she left for Chicago. Following three years of study, she became Laredo's assistant, after which she left on a long period of study in England, Italy, France, Sicily and Greece. When she returned, she moved to Santa Monica, California, where she continued to work and study in her home studio.

Clyde Chandler's most notable work is a sculpture called "Gulf Cloud," a tribute to Sydney Smith, the first secretary of the State Fair of Texas from 1886 until 1912. Of bronze and gray granite, it stood on a plaza near the main gate of the fair and was unveiled on October 14, 1916. In 1936, just before the Texas Centennial, it was relocated in front of the Centennial Exhibit Hall. In 1972 it was moved again, some 150 feet across First Avenue so that the auditorium could be enlarged for the State Fair Music Hall. Its last move cost $40,000—exactly twice the amount Clyde Chandler received for it. Rooted in her Texas heritage, Miss Chandler sculpted the piece into four female figures symbolizing the four distinct regions of the state—the Gulf of Mexico, the Coastal Plains, the Table Lands and the Mountains. A reporter at the time it was installed explained:

> The Gulf lolls against the feet of the Coastal Plains who rests in the lap of the Table Lands, while the figure with wings, representing the Gulf Breeze, brings the rain which showers down nurturing the state. Around its base is a garland of fruits, flowers, grains and vegetables which grow in Texas."[6]

Gulf Cloud, sculpture in front of the Music Hall, State Fair Park, was created by Clyde Giltner Chandler in 1916.

Through the years Dallas has had many controversies concerning the selection and display of its art. While it does not have a monopoly on controversy, Dallas—more than most cities as they grow and mature—has harbored rugged individualists whose opinions are often as clamorous as they are uneducated. This is further complicated by the fact that persons schooled in one discipline often have a low tolerance level for those whose training is in a different genre. And if "beauty is in the eye of the beholder," many of the eyes that have viewed art in Dallas have been, at one time or another, baffled, bemused, aggravated or repulsed by what they saw. At the first art showing at the state fair, a farm boy wandered into the "gallery," viewed a few of the paintings with puzzlement and then called out to his friends: "Come on in here, boys and *look at this*. Them things are painted *by hand!*"

Artist Joan Jackson, in her studio home, painted pieces that hang in many Dallas homes.

In 1955 the Dallas Public Library had itself a humdinger of a controversy over a mural. A 10 by 24 foot metal sculpture by Harry Bertoia, it hung on the first floor of the library behind the registration and book-return desk. Three-dimensional, it was made of hammered metal bars of various shapes and sizes inside a metal frame. It was lighted from above by 14 focus lamps and also hung so that it caught the light from the outside through glass windows. Commissioned by library architect George Dahl, it cost $8,500. At the unveiling, there was a hushed silence and then Mayor R. L. Thornton expressed the sentiments of many when he said, "It looks like a pile of junk to me, but it has good advertising possibilities." Mayor Pro Tem Vernon Smith added that "people will forget what they came here (to the library) for when they see this pile of junk." The mayor was right; it became the conversation piece of the entire city and the kind of story that the national press adored telling about Dallas. Some, in the conservative climate that prevailed in the mid 1950s, saw it as a sinister plot to undermine the morals of youth. Many, including Jerry Bywaters, director of the Dallas Museum of Fine Arts, and Lon Tinkle, columnist and book critic of *The Dallas Morning News*, were its staunch defenders. Lynn Landrum, a *Dallas News* columnist, was the most outspoken opponent. He wrote that he hadn't seen the screen and didn't intend to because he wanted to remain objective. Bertoia, the artist, said, "It is a mirror of the man who looks at it. Those who find significance and meaning in it are those prepared to give it significance and meaning." Then he kept quiet. Dahl, disappointed and discouraged, offered to pay for the piece. When asked what he would do with it, the architect replied that he might "throw it in the river." At one point, the controversy was so intense that the sculpture was removed, which prompted humorist Paul Crume in his *Dallas News* column to write:

> The mural of Bertoia
> Will no longer annoia....

A second almost certain controversy was avoided when artist Marshall Fredericks observed what was happening in Dallas and sidestepped it. Fredericks was famous for his monumental sculptures, one of which graces the U. S. Department of State building in Washington, D. C. His design for the exterior of the Dallas library featured an unclothed youth standing in the open palm of a giant hand with his left arm extending away from his body and holding a book in his left hand, and his right arm reaching heavenward. The figure, the artist said, represented "the hands of God supporting youth reaching for learning through the medium of literature." Dallas nay-sayers were primed for a second bout of shrieking. And then the 880-pound aluminum and magnesium alloy figure arrived. There was a belt at the waist, cuffs at the ankles and short-sleeved shirt on the upper torso! The artist, clearly, had had the last laugh.

A 10 by 14-foot metal sculpture, on the first floor of the Dallas Public Library, created a controversy in 1955 that kept art critics, writers and politicians buzzing for months.

Allie Victoria Tennant, a sculptor, was also a noted artist in the early twentieth century. Born in St. Louis, she came with her parents Thomas R. and Allie Virginia Brown Tennant to Dallas when she was a child. Encouraged by her father, Thomas R. Tennant, who also was an artist, Allie studied first with Vivian Aunspaugh and later with Herr Kunz-Meyer of Munich, Germany, and Gatina Bianchi of Italy. She finally went to New York to study in the mid 1920s but by that time already had earned the critical approval of several visiting artists for her sculpture. She worked principally in brass and bronze.

Mary Ellen Mitchell Jericho, among her many services, became president of the American Symphony Association.

The Crystal Charity Ball annually provides funding for cultural and civic improvement. Annette Strauss, left, with sister-in-law, Helen Strauss, raised a record amount when she chaired it.

Sis Carr has long been an advocate for Dallas's cultural improvement.

Allie Tennant's was the largest art work featured at the 1936 Texas Centennial, the giant statue of a Tejas Indian brave over the entry way between two columns at the Texas Hall of State. Her work demanded a permanent place in many buildings and gardens throughout the South. She continued to live and work in Dallas at 5315 Live Oak, both her studio and her home, until her death on December 19, 1971, at the age of 79. Her private graveside rites at Oakland Cemetery was noted in a tiny four-line agate-type obituary in both of the Dallas newspapers.

Margaret Ann Scruggs Carruth earned acclaim both as an etcher and a writer. The daughter of Gross Robert and Marion Stuart Price Scruggs, Margaret was born in Dallas, was married to R. V. Carruth in 1912 and divorced from him nine years later. Her one child was Walter Carruth. She was educated in private schools, attended Bryn Mawr and was graduated from Southern Methodist University. She studied at Pennsylvania Academy of Fine Arts. She was invited to exhibit her etchings in several of the nation's outstanding galleries. She collected etching reference books and in 1928 was said to have acquired one of the largest libraries on the subject in the country. Her wood interiors were especially notable with foliage detail that caught the critical acclaim of experts in the field. Her love of nature led her, in 1932, to collaborate with her mother, an avid gardener, in writing *Gardening in the South and West*, the first book on gardening ever published specifically for the Dallas area.

In the early 1900s, Elizabeth Patterson Lyon Kiest opened a gallery exclusively for china painting where lessons were taught and art work displayed until shortly before her death in 1917.

The Parent Teachers Associations in Dallas started as a result of women's interest in art. Olivia Allen Dealey organized the Public Schools Art League at William B. Travis School in 1895 to beautify the drab surroundings, both the school rooms and the school grounds, where her children and their friends spent so much of their time. Her intention was to provide better lighting, brighten the surroundings with paint, hang some pictures on the walls and plant some flowers and shrubbery on the surrounding grounds. She and her coterie of interested mothers had no idea what they were going to discover. Sanitary conditions were deplorable. Some of the school children had little or no food. The mothers began immediately to prepare a noon meal in their homes and take it to the schools.

The second organization of mothers to respond to the needs of school children was organized at San Jacinto School and named the Colonial Hills Mothers Club. For the first few years, most of the efforts of the Mothers' Clubs were centered around the lunchroom, providing a safe water supply and other health programs and the welfare of needy children. But, simultaneously they hung pictures in the classrooms, saw that the rooms were cleaned and, as nearly as possible, aired and heated and that the school grounds were kept clear of clutter and were safe from hazards that could injure the children. They came in for their full share of criticism. Many pointed accusing figures at the "meddlesome mamas." In the early 1900s when they vigorously insisted on central heating of new buildings rather than room heaters or steam heating, one official referred to the group as the "misguided Mothers' Clubs."

But they persisted. The two organizations, The Mothers' Club and its companion, the Dallas Public School Art League were duly credited by school superintendent J. L. Long for founding, in November of 1897, the Parents' and Teachers' Roundtable, the forerunner of the Parent Teacher Associations.

> About a month ago the principal and teachers of the Oak Grove School organized a Parents' and Teachers' Roundtable for the purpose of discussing questions of mutual interest to both parents and teachers, in order to better harmonize and unite the influence of the home and the influence of the school for the mental, moral and physical improvements of the pupils .... These monthly meetings cannot fail to bring about a warmer sympathy and more hearty cooperation between the home and the school and will therefore become a greater power for the good of the children. This movement can not be too highly recommended.[7]

It was the continuing work of the mothers and their prodding of the administrators and the school board that brought about most of the advancements in the physical surroundings for the children. They tirelessly researched, carefully documented and fed information to administrators, teachers and the all-male school board.

The determination of Dallas women to improve the public schools, and their establishment of organizations for this purpose preceded by two years the founding of the National Congress of Mothers by Alice McLellan Birney and Phoebe Apperson Hearst on February 17, 1897. The first PTA Council was organized in Dallas on March 24, 1906, when the Dallas Mothers Club Congress was organized. Six clubs—San Jacinto, James W. Fannin, David Crockett, Colonial Hill, Fair Park and Stephen F. Austin—were charter members. They elected Mrs. William M. Reilly president.

Members of the Mothers' clubs often found reform difficult because they could participate in making policy only through persuasion. This often meant that the programs they started were pushed aside by the all-male boards whose value systems were different. Finally, in 1908, they were successful in having two women appointed to the board. Ella Stephenson Tucker and Adella Kelsey Turner were appointed from their clubs to observe and report back. It would be some years before a woman was *elected* to the school board. But it was a beginning.

In the meantime, women were forging ahead with the cultural development of the community.

Ella M. Harris Abrams and Belle Fonda Schneider organized the first symphony orchestra in 1890. It was the happy result for Dallas of a musician's misfortune. Hans Kreissig came to Dallas as a musician with the touring Grau Opera Company. After its Dallas appearance, it went to Little Rock, Arkansas, where it ran out of money stranding all its artists. Ella and Belle saw their opportunity, rallied everybody who had ever expressed an interest in music—and many who had not—and invited Kreissig to return to the city and form a symphony orchestra. They gave him their full support by organizing the Symphony Club. To augment his meager salary, Kreissig supported himself while assembling the orchestra by directing the Dallas Frohsinn Singing Society, a male chorus, for $25 a month! Eventually he married Louise Cretien, one of the daughters of the famous La Reunion families.

When the orchestra made its first appearance in Turner Hall on Harwood and Young on May 22, 1900, it had 21 violinists, far less than the full orchestra Dallas musicians had dreamed about and that Alice Fitzgerald considered acceptable.

> ... A symphony orchestra is the real article, or better told, the orchestra of orchestras .... the difference between it and a band is as much as a grand piano and an upright—the latter being the make-shift for the former. The highest class of music and the most ennobling musical ideas are given to the symphony orchestra ....[8]

She went on to outline in detail the instruments required for a full orchestra. Her total was 70; Dallas had 26.

The progress of the Dallas Symphony Orchestra, akin to development of the fine arts in most United States cities, was erratic. Its beginning makes it one of the oldest symphony orchestras in the country (those in Boston, Chicago, New York, Philadelphia and St. Louis came into being about the same time or a little earlier.) Only a handful of Dallasites have been willing or able to afford the tremendous amount of money required to support a superior symphony. So it is that, through the years when individuals, flush with either musical talent and/or the ability to raise money surfaced, the orchestra flourished. There has been campaign after campaign after campaign to raise money. Musicians, who should concern themselves with honing their talent, have sometimes played without contracts and without pay checks, worried that there was no money to support their families. People with money often have not supported music, or have supported it reluctantly, only as a business proposition good for the city. Mayor R. L. Thornton once verbalized what many of his cronies thought when he said he would be glad to support the symphony if he didn't have to go and listen to it. Musicians with the talent to make Dallas a first-class musical city have usually not been business-oriented, and it is not fair to expect them to be. Conductors, who should be devoting their energies to securing and honing the talents of the orchestra, often have been forced to serve as money-raising public relations people. So it has been, until recently at least, that when the economy took a downturn, the orchestra very often plunged, too.

While the top symphony positions have been held by men for the last century, it is mainly women who have worked tirelessly behind the scenes to keep it—and all other art forms—functioning. It is their telephone calls and money-raising benefits that have made survival possible. The contributions of two women to the Dallas symphony—Gertrude Aldredge Shelburne and Mary Ellen Mitchell (Mitch) Jericho—stand out.

The symphony's indebtedness to Gertrude Shelburne is included in her personal story (see Gertrude Terrell Aldredge Shelburne, Part II.)

It is the good fortune of the symphony that Mitch Jericho focused her considerable energy and experience on it—for her volunteer contributions are enormous and span the spectrum of women's activities. Born in Muskogee, Oklahoma, on September 12, 1924, to L. B. and Ruby Hall Mitchell, Mitch enrolled in SMU at age 18 and graduated four years later with high honors. She joined Neiman-Marcus where she worked in personnel, sales, and employee training until she retired shortly after her marriage to Eugene Jericho in 1952. Their three daughters are Bonnie, Jennifer and Judy. Bonnie and Jennifer are both physicians and Judy an allergy specialist.

Mitch was president of the Women's Council of Dallas County in 1968-69. Among her other contributions: organizer, Women's Division, American Cancer Society; a founder of Dallas Volunteer Center, Dallas Big Sisters and Friends of Timberlawn Psychiatric Foundation; president, Visiting Nurses Association; leadership trainer for United Way; co-chair Dallas Commission on Children and Youth. By the time she focused on the symphony, Mitch knew Dallas from the outside in and the inside out. She was president of the Dallas Symphony Orchestra League, national president of the Volunteer Council and on most local and national symphony boards. In the 1980s, she began to focus her energy on leadership training programs which she does throughout the country and on Young Audiences, which takes music into the schools. With Edith O'Donnell she founded the Dallas chapter of the organization and serves on its national board.

With the opening in 1989 of the Morton H. Meyerson Symphony Center in the Arts District of downtown Dallas, the city had reached a point of maturity to include and honor the performing arts.

One of Dallas's more successful cultural endeavors was organized by a woman, had all women in its performing coterie and was responsible for bringing outstanding talent to the city in its early days. It was the St. Cecelia Club, organized in 1895 by Alice Bryan Roberts with 26 members and a two-fold purpose: (1) to give members an outlet for performing, and (2) to bring to the city the world's most outstanding musical talent.

Alice Roberts was born on July 14, 1869, to Henry Monroe and Alice O'Neill Bryan in Talboton, Georgia. The family moved to Dallas when Alice was a little girl. Her musical talent surfaced early and after graduating from high school in Dallas, she studied at the College of Music in Cincinnati where she specialized in voice, piano and musical history. She married Jules D. Roberts in 1897 and had two children, Jules D. Jr. and Alice Bryan Roberts. She taught the history of music at St. Mary's College and then moved to Ursuline Academy where for 12 years she was professor of voice and teacher of musical history. Alice continued to study and to perform. For many years she was soloist and/or choir director, at one time or another, of First Presbyterian Church, Grace Methodist Church and St. Matthews Cathedral. Alice was an organizer of the first choral society and of the first oratorical society in Texas.

In writing about St. Cecelia Choral Society, historians have underestimated or misinterpreted its significance. The members, according to John William Rogers, "had the courage of innocence and their efforts often ended in complication if not disaster." True, the women were far better trained in the fine arts than in business, but what they accomplished for the city is a foundation for musical excellence that continues to the present.

Alice Roberts said the purpose of St. Cecelia was to "elevate music in Dallas by presenting the finest choral works and the best artists available." The club, whose members' vocal and musical talents varied widely, met at 10 a.m. every Wednesday to practice and conduct its business and it performed almost weekly from September through May.

Willie Newbury Lewis remembered some of those meetings. "Mama was a member. From the time I was a little girl (she was born in 1892) I would sometimes go with her. I loved to go with Mama, but I had to be very quiet.... There were very strict rules for children and we knew to obey them. From the age of two, I was taken to the concerts. I remember going backstage with Mama after a performance to meet Richard Mansfield."[9]

St. Cecelia brought many of the outstanding musical artists of the day to Dallas, among them Schumann-Heink, Johanna Gadski, Teresa Carreno, Edward MacDowell, Lillian Nordica, Walter Damrosch and the New York Symphony, the Pittsburgh Orchestra with Emil Pauer, Marcella Sambrich and many, many others.

If they were naive, the women were also innovative and persistent. When Fannie Bloomfield Zeisler demanded that her fee of $1,200 be in her bank in Chicago before she set out on a three-city tour—Dallas, Galveston and Austin—St. Cecelia members got busy and raised their share of it. Ticket sales usually could be counted on to raise funds for the appearances and the halls were usually filled—for two reasons. Those trained in music were starved to hear good performers and the untrained were not about to show their ignorance by staying away. There were misfortunes—which Alice Roberts met with equal amounts of ingenuity and stubborn determination.

Gadski, singing on a contract that guaranteed her a percentage of the receipts, refused to perform when she learned that her audience was tiny. Alice threatened to retaliate by seizing the star's luggage—at which stage Gadski not only honored her contract but sang so well that she was given repeated standing ovations by the sparse audience.

Marcella Sembrich had made two successful appearances in Dallas. When she agreed to make a third appearance, the fee was $2,000. On opening night, advance sales had brought in only $1,200. This was handed to the singer in her dressing room backstage at the Dallas Opera House. She counted it and refused to go on until every penny of the contracted cash was in her hands. Fortunately there was a line at the ticket counter. Every few minutes the house manager, George Anzy, would hand the star a new batch of bills. She would count it and make a notation on the pad in front of her. Finally, shortly after the 8 p.m. curtain time when the last ticket had been sold and nobody else was waiting to purchase one, Madame Sembrich had $1973.11 in her possession. She refused to sing until she had the rest of her money. Alice Roberts wrote her a personal check for $26.89—which the star insisted on having a banker certify before accepting it!

But there were other artists and other stories. When Walter Damrosch brought the New York Symphony to Dallas, his fee was $1,450. At 9 p.m. on the night of the concert, only $524 had been raised in ticket sales. He immediately discounted his fee to $950 and Alice Roberts gave him her note for $426. It took St. Cecelia two years to raise the money. When Alice sent it to him, he returned the check with a charming note:

> That little debt of yours is outlawed long ago. I cannot take your check, but
> I am delighted that you wanted to pay it. Good luck to you and best greetings.
>
> Sincerely yours,
> Walter Damrosch[10]

Opera in Dallas has enjoyed and/or been handicapped by many of the same enthusiasms as have plagued and benefitted the symphony.

The first opera, with an orchestra, was presented in Dallas in 1875 at the Field Opera House which had been built two years previously. The opera, "Martha," was conducted by Professor Otter. The theater had been built without dressing rooms and the actors had to climb out a window, cross a roof and a bridge high above the street to the Windsor Hotel for costume changes and return by the same route. That they performed at all is a testament to their dedication and to the determination of music-loving Dallasites who sat patiently when an actor was delayed in returning to the stage to go on with a scene.

By the mid 1880s opera, with varying degrees of excellence, was a regular feature of the theaters. On February 22, 1885, *The Herald* ran an ad for "The most popular grand chorus and orchestra... in America," the Emma Abbott Opera Company. Appearing at the Dallas Opera House (the second one built in 1883 with a seating capacity of 1,200 and located at Commerce and Austin Streets), the two-day event presented "Mignon" on Friday, "Martha" at the Saturday matinee and "Traviata" on Saturday night. Ticket prices were matinee, reserved seats, $1.00; general admission 75 cents and balcony 70 cents. Night prices were, lower floor, $2.00 and balcony $1.50 and $1.00.

In 1905 the Metropolitan Grand Opera arrived to present Wagner's "Parsifol." Though the performance was highly praised and the Met claimed the Dallas stop on its tour was a success, it did not return to the city for 35 years. Throughout the years that Dallas was a part of the Metropolitan tour, there were cliff-hanging moments when it looked as if there would not be the money to pay the city's portion of the fees; once the Met agreed to make the trip at a lesser stipend than the contract called for. But, almost always, at the last moment opera lovers and/or business men would provide the funding. On December 23, 1984, the Met cancelled its 1985 season.

Perhaps it was time. The fine arts—opera, symphony, musical concerts, theater, painting, writing and all the cousins of these—develop excellence only when the best models are held up to them. But there always comes a time when the baby must toddle on its own. This growing up to walk tall among the best in the fine arts has, by its very nature, come slowly to Dallas.

The Dallas Civic Opera began in 1957 and, with a name change to The Dallas Opera, has continued to excel. Its opening event starred Maria Callas in a gala concert featuring the American debut of Franco Zeffirelli. Even though the Dallas Opera has experienced many of the financial handicaps that plague the development of others in the fine arts family, there have been peak artistic moments. In 1958 Ms. Callas appeared in the new Zeffirelli production of "La Traviata," and appeared in her only staged performance in the United States of "Medea." It was that season that also introduced Jon Vickers in his American debut, and the following year, 1959, Ms. Callas appeared in Zeffirelli's "Lucia de Lammermoor." Joan Sutherland made her American debut in 1960 in Dallas. In 1962 John Houseman staged a new production of "Otello" with Mario del Monaco. Glittering personalities in opera who have made their American debuts in Dallas include Montserrat Caballe, 1965; Gwyneth Jones in 1966, and Elena Soullotis and Renata Scotto in 1968. Dallas has also been the debut site for several new or revised productions. Having successfully staged hundreds of performances and presented some of the world's outstanding talents, it continues to excel.

For many years talented artists of color were not mainstreamed into Dallas's cultural community, a much greater loss for the city than for the individuals among them who were musicians, painters and dancers.

In the 1930s and 40s a musician who went by the name of Madame Pratt lived and worked in the State-Thomas area where she operated a private music studio in her home and turned her living room into a virtual concert hall where talented musicians congregated. She mastered almost every musical instrument and taught them to her students. She owned and displayed a variety of musical instruments that captivated the girls and boys she taught. On Sunday afternoons, she held open house and citizens from all areas of the city congregated there for concerts. Dallas lost a great musical talent and the black community one of its definitive artistic resources when Madame Pratt and her husband, a Dallas educator, moved away with their two children.

What Madame Pratt did in music, Rezolia Grisson-Thrash contributed in art. She was the first black artist in the city to receive the "Still Life" art award from the Dallas Museum of Fine Arts and the only African American artist to participate in the Seventh Annual Dallas Allied Arts Exhibition in 1935. Rezolia completed her undergraduate and graduate degrees in art and began her professional career as an art teacher in the Dallas schools. She taught at Booker T. Washington and at Lincoln High School and, like Madame Pratt, lived with her husband in the State-Thomas area near downtown Dallas. She and her husband had no children of their own, but reared a niece whose name was also Rezolia.

On its 150th anniversary in 1991-1992, Dallas may, indeed, have reached the maturity to appreciate the imperative for a cultural climate aspiring to excellence and to nurture its artists of all colors and persuasions.

19

• • • •

DALLAS'S DENIZENS OF DARKNESS

By 1910, Dallas had, indeed, become a city. Its population stood at 92,104, representing a 46 per cent increase in just one decade. Worley's 1910 *Directory of Greater Dallas* records the look and the feel of a thriving metropolis. A combination street guide, cross-city and business directory and telephone book, it lists 57 dressmakers; 83 music teachers, 63 of them women, and 65 nurses, all but two of them women. Though there are pages of advertisements for automobiles and auto dealerships, the horse and buggy was not yet replaced. There are listings for 15 livery and boarding stables.

Interspersed with this phenomenal expansion, there was another side of the city—restive, sordid, illicit, and ugly:

- Segregation was entrenched.
- Prostitution was legalized.
- Gambling, drinking and carousing was prevalent.
- Lawlessness was widespread.
- Difference (language, customs, religion, skin color) was not tolerated.
- The Ku Klux Klan and other "secret" organizations proliferated.
- Crime escalated.

Until well past the dawn of the twentieth century, Dallas was able to keep its sordid side hidden. Its women, especially, were "protected" though some of them, in the "sanctity" of their own homes were the beneficiaries of their husbands' secret other lives. They became infected with the venereal diseases their mates brought home from the brothels that rimmed the north and west sides of downtown Dallas.

The Civil War had been over for half a century, but Lincoln's Emancipation Proclamation, issued on January 1, 1863, was rarely practiced in Dallas. Both blacks and whites were deprived by the prevailing separatist mentality. Impassioned speeches fed the basest of human instincts and fanned smoldering incidents into major issues. Many whites took to the streets with hoods over their heads. Blacks survived, for the most part, in silence. Reasonable and caring people of all colors and persuasions are still sickened by some things that happened. Inflammatory words, none more vehement than in a speech by Henry W. Grady of the *Atlanta Constitution*, kept dissension brewing. His speech at the State Fair of Texas began at 11:30 a.m. on October 27, 1888, and lasted for an hour and a half. The crowd, estimated at 10,000, repeatedly interrupted him with applause. He spoke on "certain problems—" namely, race and economics—upon whose resolution rests the "glory and prosperity of the south."

> This problem is to carry within her body politic, two separate races, equal in civil and political rights, and nearly equal in numbers. She must carry these races in peace, for discord means ruin. She must carry them separately, for assimilation means debasement. . . .
>
> What of the negro? This of him. I want no better friend than the black boy who was raised by my side . . . , I want no sweeter music than the crooning of my old "mammy," . . . as she held me in her loving arms, and bending her old black face above me stole the cares from my brain and led me smiling into sleep. I want no truer soul than that which moved the trusty slave, who for four years while my father fought with the armies that barred his freedom, slept every night at my mother's chamber door, holding her and her children . . . safe . . . . History has no parallel to the faith kept by the negro in the South . . . .

> . . . Into hands still trembling from the blow that broke the shackles was thrust the ballot. In less than 12 months from the time he walked down the furrow a slave, the negro dictated . . . the policy of twelve commonwealths. When his late master protested . . . from a hedge of Federal bayonets he grinned in good-natured insolence . . . .
>
> . . . The clear and unmistakable domination of the white race . . . is the hope and assurance of the South.
>
> . . . Through education the negro must be led to know, and through sympathy to confess, that his interests and the interests of the people of the South are identical . . . .
>
> The races and tribes of the earth are of divine origin . . . . What God hath separated let no man join together . . . . No race has risen or will rise above its ordained place . . . . the white race can never submit . . . must and will control the South . . . .[1]

The attitude of God-ordained white supremacy is the root of many evils in Dallas, the most horrid of which are known. Among these are the legal hanging of Jane Elkins without counsel for the murder of a white man; the selection and hanging of three black men as tokens for the perceived arson that destroyed Dallas; the seizing from the red courthouse of Allen Brooks, charged with assaulting a child, by a white vigilante mob, and flinging him with a rope around his neck from a second floor window before dragging his body through the streets. These shameful atrocities must never be overlooked, but even more devastating was the erosion of selfhood by those with white skins toward those with black skins. There is no way to measure the harm done to an individual or a group that is consistently assigned to a lower rung—the back door mentality that looks not at value of a human being but at color and automatically assigns her to an inferior position.

At death and in the final resting places, segregation continued. Even though people who were black and people who were white usually died from the same kinds of diseases, hospitals systematically separated them into separate wings. And, only in 1990 was the final resting place of many of Dallas's early black citizens rescued from oblivion. By then it was almost too late. Freedman's Cemetery, the site of some 2,000 freed slaves and their descendants, was partially buried under Central Expressway. The rest had been turned into a city-owned playground. (See Chapter 34)

Within the memory of every Dallasite born within the past 50 years is segregated transportation when a young mother holding a small child and several bundles had to push her way past empty seats to the back of the bus. "No colored allowed" was a fact of life, sometimes written but more often simply understood: No colored allowed for children on public playgrounds, at water fountains, in restaurants, in rest rooms, in schools. Even in libraries. When May Dickson Exall said, ". . . no child in Dallas shall be denied the privilege of reading good and attractive books . . . ." this did not include children who were black. All human services were segregated. Ruth Spence remembers struggling for years to convince the YWCA, "the most liberal of the organizations of that time" to allow Esther Juliet Dyson, president of the Maria Morgan Branch of the YWCA, to attend board meetings and make her report. "The first time she came, a number of women sat with their hands over their faces while she spoke."

There was also a double standard in the local press. For years the major accomplishments of black women were reported in a separate column in *The Dallas News* written by Julia Scott Reed. Without her contributions, many people and many stories would be forever lost. *The Dallas Times Herald* led the way in publishing pictures and stories about black brides—but not until the 1970s. Year after year women staffers struggled to secure equality of news space for brides, and year after year were turned down. Then, a woman, at a public meeting at Southern Methodist University, queried the women's page editor: "How do you justify publishing the photograph of a white debutante seven times during a single social season and refuse to print the picture of my daughter when she married?" This, reported to *Times Herald* management finally was the breakthrough.

In 1916, a Dallas city ordinance made it illegal for blacks and whites to live in the same neighborhood. It was a full decade before the law was declared illegal and almost half a century—after the Civil Rights Act of 1964—before neighborhood segregation began to disappear.

Juanita Craft, a lifelong law-abider and champion of youth, said with tears in her eyes as she arrived at Salado for the first session of Goals for Dallas as an invited guest, that she could not count the times she has brought her NAACP (National Association for the Advancement of Colored People) youth past those portals yearning to stop with them for a much-needed rest but knowing that they would be turned away. Florence Harllee Phelps, a soft-spoken professional teacher and social worker, said sadly that "they" finally ran her off from the home on Boll Street where she was born and where her own two daughters began life. Pearl Carina Bowden Anderson, doyenne of Dallas's black philanthropists, whose name graces a Dallas child care center and whose deeds for the American Red Cross live on as testaments to her courage, wondered why her landlady made her move when she learned that Pearl's white skin covered a black heritage. Women of color wonder, as do all decent Dallasites, why their children were required to walk past schools nearest their homes to others farther away. "They said it was a colored school," said Florence Phelps, "but it looked gray to me. The only difference was more and shinier equipment on the playground." And it still goes on. Even now, as a black, an Asian and a Caucasian child—doubtless all of mixed heritage—skip happily together on a neighborhood sidewalk headed for Charles A. Gill School, and a brilliant chocolate-skinned young woman, only two of her color in a class, raises her hand to answer a question at Skyline High School, and a small white girl finds herself the only person of her color in her third grade class in Bushman Elementary School, race is a matter of curiosity. And, for many, a matter of prejudice.

Residential segregation was legalized. In 1916, a statute was passed making it illegal for blacks and whites to live in the same neighborhood. The action came following a petition brought by the all-white Deene Park Improvement Board. The law was struck down in 1926 when the Texas Court of Civil Appeals invalidated it, but the practice of segregation continued in Dallas until after the Civil Rights Act of 1964 when neighborhoods began to mix. Even then integration came slowly and painfully.

Caught up as they were in their rounds of social activities, or among those of less affluence burdened with trying to survive, most women found it easiest to practice the prevailing adage of the day: "Hear no evil, see no evil, speak no evil."[2]

White women and black men were especially at risk. For totally different reasons, both groups dared not make too many waves. White men were the decision makers. White women were their chattels. Black men, less than half a century freed from slavery, were their serfs. Or so they thought. White women, in the words of Simone de Beauvoir were inextricably tied to the enemy—their fathers, brothers, husbands and sons.

> . . . women lack concrete means for organizing themselves into a unit. . . . They have no (shared) past, no history, no religion of their own; and they have no . . . solidarity of work and interest. . . . They are not even promiscuously herded together in the way that creates community among the American Negroes, the ghetto Jews, the workers of Saint-Denis, or the factory hands of Renault. They live dispersed among the males, attached through residence, housework, economic condition, and social standing to . . . men more firmly than . . . to other women . . . . The bond that unites (women) to (their) oppressors is not comparable to any other . . . .[3]

The invisible bonds of love and loyalty made it virtually impossible for most women to make any move that would threaten the lives or lifestyles of their beloveds. Black men were "kept in their place" by fear and intimidation. "Those were dark days. Dark. Dark. Dark," says John C. Phelps of this period in Dallas's past. "We (males) were cornered. Folks thought we wanted to be with their daughters. If we got too far up, they couldn't use us as servants." From 1920 to 1928, J. C. was janitor at the F. W. Woolworth store in downtown Dallas where he was friend and confidante to many of his co-workers. One day he overheard a white male complaining to the Woolworth manager: "Every time I come in here, I see that nigger smiling and talking to the white girls." Overhearing it, J. C. said, "it was enough to chill my blood."

His childhood gave J. C. Phelps a foot in both white and black worlds and conditioned him to understand, to withstand and react without violence to most unjust conditions. When he was a small boy in Millican, Texas, J. C.'s family moved into the home of a white family named McGregor following the death of the wife and mother who left daughters nine months, nine years and 14 years. J. C.'s mother, Pearl Phelps, also mothered the white orphan girls. Mrs. Phelps did the homemaking, prepared the food and reared the children. They sat down to meals together. Once when a jobber, invited to stay for dinner, declined because he wouldn't eat with "those niggers," Mr. McGregor asked J. C. to bring the dictionary and look up the word "nigger." The little boy learned that such a word was "offensive and disparaging" and Mr. McGregor assured him that anyone who used the term was the one who was "offensive." On another occasion J. C.'s sister and their white sister, both third graders, were studying together at the dining room table when Mr. McGregor noticed that the black child's reader was old and out of date. "The next day he hitched up the wagon and went to Bryan, 20 miles away; when he came back everybody in our school had brand new books."

The McGregors and the Phelps lived together for five years until the oldest girl married. When her fiance asked McGregor for permission to marry his daughter, the father replied, "You'll have to ask Pearl if she would like you for a son." Pearl agreed and the wedding took place. Many years later J. C. and his white sister raised other sets of eyebrows in an exclusive residential area of Houston when J.C. stopped in for a visit and she answered the doorbell and welcomed him with an effusive embrace. "He is the only brother I have ever had," she explained to an incredulous neighbor.

In 1922 most Dallas citizens paid their utility bills at City Hall, and J. C. went to pay his light bill. "I was coming out of the building when a man greeted the police officer on the corner, 'Well, I see you made it!' pointing to the new badge on his uniform. 'Yep,' the officer bragged, 'I've just been licensed to kill me a nigger.' I turned around and went back into City Hall to the office of the police chief and told him what I had heard. He sent for the officer and told him what I had reported and asked him if it was true. The officer said, 'You mean, you gonna take the word of that nigger?' The police chief said, 'Give me your gun, butt first.' Fired him on the spot . . . . If you know how to understand all this, you can make it.'

By contrast with restraints under which black males existed, black women were largely ignored by those in power, except, sometimes, when they were used as objects of lust. As maids and cooks, black women spent most of their waking hours in white homes where they were exposed to a world that included books, music and social graces. Often silent at their tasks, they nonetheless absorbed, as if by osmosis, another lifestyle. And, it is no secret that the genteel lives led by many of the white women depended on the services of their black sisters.

And, there have always been in Dallas some affluent, highly educated citizens of color who sent their children north and east to college. Their sons were encouraged to find careers away from Dallas because it offered such limited opportunity to black males. Their daughters, like the daughters of the whites, were restricted to a very few professional outlets and could come home and teach. Out of this period came a great many wonderfully gifted women educators.

John Phelps explained an important reason that the daughters of aspiring black families were often given preference over sons to advanced education. "It was for economic survival," he said. "Opportunities for males were so limited and conditions were so scary. We had to educate our daughters so they could take care of the family if anything happened to us."

Just as women were sometimes as racist as men, but more often perpetrators of racial prejudice by their silence, women were also leaders in efforts to end discrimination. In 1965 Carolyn Tobian Clark organized the Panel of American Women. It included four to five women, one Black, one Caucasian, one Hispanic, one Jewish and sometimes one of another minority race who, upon invitation, spoke to members of clubs, church groups

Dallas has always been the home of many affluent, highly educated citizens of African-American heritage. When they sent their daughters out-of-state to be educated, the young women could come home again and teach, but the young men usually did not return.

Led by Jewish and African-Americans, women began to sit down together to talk and socialize. Church Women United and the League of Women Voters were leaders for a more inclusive community.

and neighborhood organizations about personal problems each had encountered because of race, religion or heritage. Those who heard often discovered similar pockets of prejudice in their own lives.

At about the same time, informal discussion groups, first of Black women and Jewish women, but later opened to any woman who wanted to attend, began to meet in homes to talk and socialize. The women learned that they shared the same kinds of triumphs and agonies regardless of their color. Black professionals began to move into neighborhoods that had always been white. As pioneers, they were impeccably model citizens with the neatest trimmed lawns and hedges, the best behaved children, the most normal of comings and goings; they "suffered" the usual scrutiny of being first. Even though this "goldfish" existence must have been extremely frustrating, only once did someone feel safe enough of our friendship to tell me to "buzz off," though she was much more polite in the telling. Invited to my church, Barbara Lord Watkins declined, saying: "Please don't expect me to make a political statement on Sunday morning. On Sunday, let me go and worship at the church I love among my own people."

Shortly after the Civil Rights Act of 1964, an organization called Amigos was formed in Dallas to demonstrate that individuals whose colors of skin were different, who lived in different parts of the city and whose work/professional interests were varied could not only abide together harmoniously, but had a lot to share and learn from each other. There was nothing heavy about this organization. For the most part, individuals in it simply went out together to dinner usually in public places where they sat in the most visible spots in a club or restaurant and enjoyed their conversation as much as they enjoyed their food. It was a silent statement of sharing.

Many women's clubs began to integrate memberships long before all-male clubs willingly opened their doors. Church Women United was the first group to give more than lip service to integration. Open to women of all churches throughout the city, it welcomed the first black church membership shortly after it was organized and its first black leader in 1971 when Marion Dillard was installed as president. Its meetings were held in churches throughout the city with total disregard of color.

Among private organizations for women, the Dallas Women's Foundation has been eminently successful in recognizing talent—leadership skills as well as financial clout—among women. Elite and, or exclusive groups have been slower to change. But, once the novelty is past, women find their similarities far more important than their differences. They all give birth; most are the nurturers of the human race. They all want "the good life" for their children, however differently they may define this. They all want a chance at moving out and up in their careers or professions, whether this be in paid employment or in their homes. They all need to feel wanted and included by others—family, friends and lovers. Most want children. And they share common problems—domestic abuse, child care, divorce, custody battles, the glass ceiling, sexual harassment, caretakers of family members and, finally, loneliness and old age. Through shared experiences women are learning, far sooner than their male counterparts, that color makes no difference in life's crises.

Prostitution was once *quasi* legal in the city. The original red light district was centered around 400 South Houston where Union Station is now located. Ultra-fashionable houses of prostitution were run by Clara Barclay, Kitty Wilson and Fanny Harris where WFAA-TV station is now located. On Record Street from Young to the courthouse, courtesans plied their trade, often with their names painted on the doors of the "cribs."[4] In 1910, Dallas city commissioners unanimously adopted an ordinance designating boundaries in which prostitutes could live and work. The area was loosely bounded by Griffin, Carter, Laws, Broom and Summer streets, a block or two north and south of McKinney. Commissioners justified their action by saying that prostitution was a condition that would not go away, and they could better control it within established boundaries. A report held that . . . "under existing conditions . . . bawdy houses and bawds are promiscuously scattered throughout the City, greatly menacing the decent neighborhoods and offending decent and respectable communities."

Saturated as it was with saloons (there were 168, almost all of them in the downtown business district, listed in the 1913 city directory), it is not surprising that a great many "ladies of the night" found Dallas a lucrative place to do business. City leaders were inclined to look the other way. For some men, the presence of prostitutes was good for business and few took a public stand against it. Ministers did not mention it. Women of the city did not know about it or pretended they didn't. For others, it was a matter of solidarity with the "establishment." So it was that most agreed it was a good idea to designate a special place for prostitutes and require them to have an annual health examination. Within the boundaries set aside as the red light district—never called that in any official document—the women openly made their bid for customers, appearing in the doorways of their "cribs" heavily made up and scantily clad. The area was known as "the reservation." Unofficially, as early as 1900, it was called Frogtown.

From city directories of the period, it is easy to spot some of the women whose business likely was prostitution. They are listed on two blocks in the heart of the red light district by their names, and all of them, in the cross-city directory which lists occupations, are still listed by names alone. On Ardrey Street (the name changed to Brown Street the following year), in 1912 these women made their homes: Miss Alice Jones, 1003; Miss Stella White, 1007; Mamie Brown, 1007 1/2; Miss Eva Fulton, 1101; Miss May Wilson, 1101 1/2: Miss Lillie Drake, 1103 1/2; Miss Goldie Pryor, 1105; Miss Camille Davis, 1105 1/2; Miss Ella Wiggins, 1109. In 1913, along Broom Street between Carter and Laws two young women were listed; between Laws and Griffin, three; between Griffin and Summer, 11. Wesley Street two blocks east of Griffin had 13 women listed at addresses between 2106 and 2119. Twenty "Misses" lived on Griffin Street. The few who listed their occupation were "actresses" and "entertainers." In 1913, within the confines of the designated red light district, it was estimated that between 200 to more than 400 women made their homes. There could have been more. No records were kept.

Even as late as the early 1940s, remnants of the red light district still existed along McKinney. Women often sat, heavily painted and garishly dressed, in upstairs widows of seedy hotels and rooming houses and whistled, called out or made beckoning gestures to potential customers walking on the streets or riding past in the streetcars along McKinney.

That many men answered the siren call is a matter of public record. Some men openly responded to the invitation for sex. Others slipped surreptitiously into the area and hoped that they would not be seen by their neighbors who also were making the trip into Sin City.

Lily Virtrees Bell Leonard, who worked in a doctor's office in the Medical Arts Building shortly after the turn of the century, said she was appalled at the number of patients her employer was treating for venereal diseases.

What the local ministers would not do, itinerant or visiting preachers were not afraid to tackle. They had nothing to gain or lose by reporting what they learned.

In 1912, J. T. Upchurch founded a Dallas chapter of the Berachah Rescue Society, a national organization for the Redemption of Erring Girls and the Overthrow of White Slavery. In a public sermon and later in a printed brochure called "The Unchained Demon," he published pictures of the houses of prostitution and called by name the Dallas men who owned them. He also published photographs of two of the young women he identified as "White Slaves." Strikingly beautiful girls, they are photographed in stylishly simple pristine white dresses standing outside their "cribs." One of the young women pictured, Miss Viola Campbell, lived at 1205 Broom Street in 1912; that address continued to be her home in 1913. In 1914 the house was "vacant."

Upchurch delivered his sermon against the brothel to what he described as hundreds of men; many of them, he said, came forward at the conclusion to give their hands and to kneel in prayer. He took as his text, the seventh chapter of Proverbs omitting verses 19 and 20. It is the story of Solomon's exhortation to young men about the wiles of whores and the lures she casts.

> My son, keep my words, and lay up my commandments with thee . . . .
> keep thee from the strange woman, from the stranger which flattereth with her

This young woman was identified in J.T. Upchurch's book, "The Unchained Demon," as a white slave, one of the many prostitutes who legally plied their trade in Dallas between 1910 and 1913.

> words.... I discerned among the youths a young man ... and he went the way to her house ... and..there met ... a woman with the attire of an harlot.... she (is) now in the streets and lieth in wait at every corner.[5]

And so on. With a text so long (25 verses) one can but conjecture at the two verses he omitted from his text, "For the goodman is not at home; he is gone a long journey; he hath taken a bag of money with him and will come home at the day appointed."

Solomon's charges to the young men of Biblical times were no more pointed than Upchurch's in 1912. The difference is that Pastor Upchurch had a great many more words than the wise man of old. Here are but a few of them:

> ... Dallas is rapidly developing into a city beautiful.... As you stroll, behold the skyscraper(s), admire the push and thrift of its citizens there comes stealing over you an intense desire to live in such a city. (But) there are mighty problems to solve, among which is that of the Social Evil....
>
> Some of the most defiant uptown haunts of shame have been closed.... but Dallas still believes in and practices public prostitution. Her Vice District is bad to the core. Some hundreds of girls are kept in this district as White Slaves.... Thousands of men and boys visit these ... weekly and carry from (them) moral pollution and physical disease to scatter ... all over the land.... There is not a school boy or girl in the city ... but who knows where the city has its reservation or tenderloin district.[6]

In lengthy, fiery sermons, pamphlets, letters, newspaper articles and a small book, J. T. Upchurch condemned prostitution. He exhorted the men to stay clear of the vice district and declared that the prostitutes were martyrs and Dallas should erect a monument to them.

"I am informed by good authority that eighty per cent of the male population of Dallas has already contracted the black plague, the nameless, sexual disease which is God Almighty's withering curse of an unchaste life,"[7] Upchurch boomed. (This sentence is printed in capital letters in the published version). Doctors, he charged, do not dare tell their women patients the real cause of the "female trouble" that is making it necessary to remove her ovaries and destroy the possibility of her ever becoming a mother again.

The prostitutes, he said, are martyrs "giving their lives to be burned out in an early hell ..." and because they are martyrs there should be a monument directed to their memory when they die. He appeals to the prostitutes:

> Sister, suppose you have been wrecked and are now giving your life as a sacrifice upon the altars of lust ... know you not that in a few days you will be thrown aside to die a nameless death while the great army of base men will remain and have to be gratified? ... if you had a daughter would you desire her to be what you are today? ... It requires one hundred thousand recruits annually in the United States to be sacrificed.... it has not been so many days since you were dandled upon a loving mother's knee. You were pure then.... forsake the wicked life you are living and we shall ... be glad to help you back to a life of honorable womanhood.[8]

On Saturday night, August 31, 1912, Upchurch said, he held an open-air service in the red light district taking with him a band of workers. "... possibly a hundred men stood around while I told them what I thought of a city that would allow ... a vice district. (I told them) they were not as good as the poor, silly girls who lived in the dens of infamy.... My wife was with me and a man wanted to know why I dared bring my wife into such a district. I replied ... : 'What right has any city to tolerate any street in its limits where my wife cannot go ... ?'"

If the vice district is necessary to the welfare of the city, Upchurch contended, "then there can be no objections to my giving pictures of some of the houses and tell who owns them. These property owners will be proud to have their names exploited, because they are doing so much for the protection of the pure women of the land." Photographs of a two-story white house at 2227 Griffin listed B. K. Boosterchill as owner; a two-story house at 2306 Griffin was owned by R. M. Chastain. F. M. Donely was listed as owner of "a two-story house in the vice district." G. M. Ezell was the owner of the 1205 Broom Street house, and R. M. Chastain and Dr. W. W. Samuell owned large two-story co-joined houses at 2114-2116 Griffin. "It was impossible for me to give the pictures of all of the houses in the district, and I trust that those who have been overlooked will take no offence (sic) for I mean none."

Speaking to the women of Dallas, Upchurch added that "a woman has just as much right to live an immoral life as a man . . . . men have delegated to our women folks the responsibility of keeping the home pure, while we permit ourselves to indulge in almost all kinds of living . . . . but just let one of our wives step aside from the plain beaten path of virtue, and we brave men are ready to go on a six-shooter spree.

"We men have drifted into a careless way of thinking . . . (where) it is all right for us to make improper use of *those* parts of our bodies . . . . When we men get to believing it is our duty to protect the women from all dangers, including ourselves, conditions will marvelously change . . . . We must remember some women are passionate."[9]

> Of all the low-down contemptible, dirty, worthless curs on earth . . . the man or boy who ruins a young girl and then deserts her like a sneaking coyote, is the meanest, stinkingest vulture in existence; he is not fit to shoot; he ought to be eunuched and branded "C" on the forehead.
>
> My fight against the segregated vice district is a fight for the protection of unborn generations, and I contend that no man or set of men have any right to set aside the solemn laws of Jehovah God.[10]

Upchurch's was not the only voice in Dallas opposing prostitution, but his was the loudest and most persistent. By 1913 the Council of Churches denounced "commercialized vice (as) the greatest menace . . . confronting the people of this city" and on October 5, 1913, passed a formal resolution against the practice. Police commissioner Louis Blaylock opposed the resolution because ". . . it would be unwise to break up the reservation to scatter these women over our own city or else drive them to other cities . . . . (it would be like) tearing off the scab instead of curing the disease that caused it."

The Texas Supreme Court had already ruled that Dallas's red light district was illegal, but city and county law officials had simply ignored the ruling. The Council of Churches' resolution was enough to persuade County Attorney Currie McCutcheon to enforce the law. Police Commissioner Blaylock and Chief John W. Ryan agreed to cooperate. On the last day of the reservation's existence, Monday, November 3, 1913, "a veritable parade of moving vans, trucks, drays and carts loaded with furniture, trunks and boxes of personal effect moved from the reservation . . . . Last night the section was dark and deserted. The houses were unlighted and apparently unoccupied. There was no sound of music or dancing."[11]

The city did not erect a monument to the large number of women put out of work by enforcement of the law, as Upchurch had suggested. The ministers established Hope Hall as a "home for fallen women," but it was no more successful than Virginia Knight Johnson's earlier Sheltering Arms had been. Virginia had been able to attract five prostitutes; five moved into Hope Hall. Though Police Matron Mrs. J. J. Farley was "sorely disappointed at the attitude of the women regarding the homes offered them," she was not surprised. "The majority seemed to consider their own case hopeless," she said. "They told us they had to have money and couldn't make it any other way. They could not," she added, "earn enough as clerks and secretaries to support their families."[12] Many moved out of town. Others found homes within the city and continued to do business.

The Ku Klux Klan is another scar on the face of Dallas. First organized in the South to terrorize the newly enfranchised Blacks and keep them from voting, it disbanded between 1869 and 1871, but was revived in 1915, spread across the United States— and grew at such a phenomenal rate that by 1923—200,000 members attended a tri-state conclave in Kokomo, Indiana.[13]

Dallas was a fertile ground for Klan activities and its women were involved. The Klan claimed to have "upholding of the law" as its primary aim, but beyond that even its

The Texas Supreme Court had already ruled that Dallas's red light district was illegal, but officials ignored the ruling for three years until the Council of Churches brought pressure. On November 3, 1913, the music ceased and the big houses stood in darkness.

acknowledged purposes are frightening and many of its unacknowledged activities terrorizing and disgusting. Because its members worked in secret and in silence, there was no way of knowing who they were or where they were, but it is clear that many of the so-called leading citizens of Dallas were members. Grand Cyclops Z.E. Marvin, in his speech at ground-breaking ceremonies for Hope Cottage in 1922 bragged, "There are 10,000 in the Dallas Klan." At that time, the Dallas Klan, No. 66, was the largest in the nation. Marvin is one of the few mentioned by name. When phenomenally large numbers of Klansmen and women paraded the streets of downtown Dallas hooded and bearing flaming torches, the press rarely singled out an individual. It gives one pause to ask whatever happened to basic good journalism—who, what, when, where and why? It also makes one ask who, among the elected elite in the city, could be trusted? Who among the publishers and editors of the press might be Klan-involved?

Ku Klux Klan No. 66 of Dallas was the largest Klan in the nation, according to its grand cyclops, Z. E. Marvin. Usually hooded and robed so as to be anonymous, the Women KKK Drum Corps posed with their faces clearly recognizable—but they were not named.—Texas/Dallas History and Archives, Dallas Public Library.

On May 21, 1921, 789 shrouded figures emerged from the Majestic Theater on Main Street at about 9 o'clock.[14] It was a Saturday night. The parade was timed for the moment the theaters spilled their movie-going crowds onto the city streets.

> The Stars and Stripes and the flaming cross of the Ku Klux Klan were carried down Main street last night—and up Elm—while downtown Dallas stopped to watch. As if by prearranged signal, the street lights were extinguished over the route of the parade at 9 o'clock at the minute the first white-clad figure emerged from the old Majestic Theater building bearing aloft the American flag. He was followed by a second carrying the burning emblem of the Ku Klux. By single file, and with ten feet distance between marchers, the long silent procession wended its way into the hurrying Saturday night crowds, down Main Street to Murphy and across to Elm, up Elm to the theater . . . . Not a word was spoken by the 789 shrouded figures in the line . . . . Traffic was practically halted during the entire forty-five minutes occupied by the parade.[15]

Both the *Times Herald* and the *Dallas News* reported that they had received, through the mails, a statement of the purposes of the Klan. The *Herald* published the objectives:

> To the citizens of Dallas county, greetings:
> This organization has caused to be posted the following proclamation:
> Be it known and hereby proclaimed
> That this organization is composed of native born Americans, and none others.
> That it proposes to uphold the dignity and authority of the law.
> That no innocent person of any color, creed or lineage has just cause to fear or condemn this body of men.
> That our creed is opposed to violence, lynchings, etc., but that we are even more strongly opposed to the things that cause lynchings and mob rule.

That this organization stands for the enforcement of all laws without fear or favor. It recognizes, however, that situations frequently arise where no existing law offers a remedy. It hopes to see such conditions remedied by the power of public opinion and the enactment and enforcement of proper laws.

That this organization does not countenance and will not stand for the cohabitation of blacks and whites of either sex. It does not countenance and it will not stand for social parasites remaining in this city. It is equally opposed to the gambler, the trickster, the moral degenerate and the man who lives by his wits and is without visible means of support.

The eye of the unknown hath seen and doth constantly observe all, white or black, who disregard this warning. "Whatever thou sowest, that shall ye also reap." Regardless of official, social or financial position, this warning applies to all living within the jurisdiction of this Klan.

"Your sins will find you out. Be not deceived. You cannot deceive us and we will not be mocked.

This warning will not be repeated . . . .

This organization further believes that the certainty of perpetuating American liberties lies in the solid support of our public school system, adding thereto love of country and veneration for the Diety. With this in view, it wants to see an American flag raised each day with appropriate ceremonies over every public school house in the state, and each pupil in those schools instructed in the principles of morality. We believe in the enactment of a statute to that effect.

Hereafter all communications from us will bear the official seal of our Klan.

KNIGHTS OF THE KU KLUX KLAN.[16]

Two years after the Klan took to the streets in a public march, the women—in even larger numbers—joined them. The *Times Herald*, in a front page story, reported:

Robed, hooded and masked with their regalia of white trimmed with bloodred, more than 1,500 members of the Order of American Women, the Texas auxiliary to the Knights of the Ku Klux Klan, Saturday night paraded downtown Dallas while 30,000 spectators, banking the line of march, cheered or applauded.

It was the first time since the klan was organized that the auxiliary, frequently whispered of, attempted a parade and marchers were said to be from all parts of the state.[17]

By the time the women marched on the streets of Dallas, many leading citizens were openly opposing Klan activities. Dallas was the first city in the nation to originate an anti-Klan group.[18] In April of 1922 it formed the Dallas County Citizens League to oppose Ku Klux Klan activities in Dallas County. The meeting made front page headlines in *The Dallas Morning News* on four consecutive days. About 500 people signed the petition calling for a mass meeting and more than 5,000 attended at 8 p.m. on March 4, 1922, filling the City Hall auditorium to its 2,000 capacity and spilling out onto Harwood Street where 3,000 more cheered as results of the meeting reached their ears. In its call to the mass meeting the petition said, in part:

TO THE PEOPLE OF DALLAS:

Recent events constitute . . . this call. Some of our citizens have been driven from the communities in which they live by threats of personal violence. Others have been seized in the presence of their wives and daughters and dragged away to some secluded spot and there brutally beaten and otherwise maltreated. Some of those committing those crimes admit that while disguised they have punished at least sixty-three . . . . Many . . . were afraid to report . . . their punishment for fear of greater violence, or probably death. Yet, not one of these marauders has been indicted. The officers seem to be powerless .... It is therefore plain that these crimes are being committed by an organization thoroughly trained and disciplined. They must know that if they can commit crimes and escape punishment, they can commit others as well and likewise escape, and thus inaugurate an absolute reign of terror in this county.

The undersigned . . . believe that these crimes were committed by the Ku Klux Klan . . . .

. . . In view of this situation . . . we call upon all citizens of Dallas County who are not klansmen to meet with us, the undersigned, at the City Hall in the city of Dallas, on Tuesday evening, the 4th day of April, 1922 at 8 o'clock for the purpose of considering what shall be done in the emergency that now confronts us.[19]

The meeting was *endorsed* by Dallas Mayor Sawnie R. Aldredge, who declined to sign the petition because, he said, it condemned the entire police department . . ."many . . . of whom . . . are good, conscientious officers endeavoring to do their duty . . . ." Among those signing the petition were Alex Sanger, George Dealey, Ben Cabell, Wendell Spence, Bishop H. T. Moore, Rabbi David Lefkowitz, Sam Cochran, R. H. Vogel, and on and on.

Several women signed the petition, among them Alice Whitefield, Mrs. Charles Harvey, Mrs. Moroney, Mrs. J. C. Muse, Mrs. J. A. Whyhte (sic) . . . . But thousands of women who did not sign, were also actively involved. Ruth Potts Spence recalled:

"Alex (her husband) was on the school board in the hey-day of the Klan (he served from 1922-1934). Many were reluctant to oppose the Klan because it was so strong. Alex said the board must take a stand against the Klan. It put up an entire slate of candidates to oppose the board. We rallied the women and they did a brilliant campaign against the Klan. Women covered the entire city, knocking on doors and handing out campaign material. Our entire board was re-elected. It was the first major defeat of the Klan in Dallas."[20]

Human suffering has always been a condition of living. People of every generation have clucked their tongues and wagged their heads over the indiscretions of its youth. It has always been so. And, except for a changing of names and a few pertinent details, crime has always been a part of the scene—in the city of Dallas, as elsewhere. We have only to read old newspapers to find that today's lawlessness is a repetition of what has always gone on. The difference is that now we know. What once was a scandal or a disgrace or a tragedy within a neighborhood where information traveled from person to person by word of mouth, then within a town where newspapers headlined crime; then by telephone and telegraph as individuals communicated with each other across continents, now news flashes around the globe in a matter of seconds. Too, there is a vast difference in the manner in which crimes are reported. What once were items on the inside pages are now more often banner-headed on the front pages. The gorier the detail, the more likely it is that a crime will grab the top spot on television news casts and on the front pages of newspapers.

In 1913, when the Dallas population was 116,834, a total of 16,293 arrests were made, 13,802 males and 2,491 females. Six hundred and thirty-five were for "major crimes," 28 for murder. Four people were arrested for speeding during the entire year and 1,560 were jailed because they were "suspicious persons."

On Saturday, March 1, 1913, Anna Schwartz, eight years old, was killed on Elm Street in downtown Dallas by a bullet gone awry. The little girl was walking home with her mother, Mrs. Ike Schwartz, a little brother, Julius, four, and two sisters, three and six months of age. The family had been to the opening of Armour and Company's new facilities and were on their way home to 2520 Florence Street. The bullet, fired by G. W. Brite, "a former city detective," was meant for Lillian Arant, 29. She and a 25-year-old man were wounded. In the hysteria surrounding the murder, little Anna's body lay on the sidewalk for some time with curious bystanders so shocked they did not know how to act. Mrs. Schwartz and her three surviving children were shuttled off to city hall where

People often think that the world is growing more wicked by the moment, but crime and poverty have always been a part of the human condition and early newspapers are filled with reports of murder, rape, family violence and other inhumane behavior.

the mother, after crying out "We were all so happy. I and my babies. We were going home," fainted. The family later was driven home in an automobile.[21]

During the same week in March "automobile drivers" clashed at Fair Park while opera star Mary Garden was appearing as "Thais" in what was described as "to the largest audience in musical history at Fair Park . . . the social event of the season." The fracas began when white drivers attacked black chauffeurs waiting with their automobiles to drive the white owners to the Adolphus Hotel for dinner after the opera. Only blacks were arrested. The next morning the automobile owners registered a formal complaint. "The white opera goers protested that their negro chauffeurs were threatened and some were mistreated."

Wife abuse was prevalent. In September of 1913, Stella Drouilhet died in her 709 North Harwood Street home when her husband, Raymond, broke her neck. He fled the scene and was arrested the next day when he was found. He explained that it wasn't his fault. He and his wife were having an argument. She wanted him to help cook breakfast and he had told her that was her job. When she continued to "nag" him, he hit her and she fell. The fall broke her neck.

One of the great unsolved murder mysteries of Dallas is that of Florence Brown, a secretary from a prominent family who was found slain in her Field Street office on July 28, 1913. Women were honorary pallbearers before she was interred at Oakland Cemetery.

One of the most brutal crimes in the city, one never solved, occurred on the early morning of July 28, 1913, in the heart of downtown Dallas. Miss Florence T. Brown, the pretty, popular young daughter of highly respected Dallasites, was found murdered in the washroom of the offices at 110 Field Street where she worked as a stenographer for Robinson & Styron Realty Company. She was 23 days past her 32nd birthday.

Florence Brown had left her 2713 Cedar Springs home where she lived with her parents, Rebecca Robinson Brown and Patrolman J. Randolph Brown of the Dallas Police Department, at 8:05 a.m. on Monday, July 28. She was picked up by S. B. Cuthbertson in an automobile owned by her uncle, Jeff D. Robinson, the senior partner in the firm. Her father said he did not accept an invitation to ride with his daughter and Cuthbertson because the street car would take him nearer to his work. The auto trip probably took about 10 minutes. Cuthbertson said he opened the offices, turned on the fans, picked up some material from his desk and left for city hall and the court house at about 8:20. He said Miss Brown watched him crank the car and drive off. At nine o'clock Cuthbertson returned to the Field Street offices. Three minutes later, W. R. Styron (co-owner with Robinson who was at his summer home in Colorado,) and G. W. Swor, employee of the firm, arrived. Swor said he drove to work in his buggy, tied his horse on the west side of Field Street and walked over to the office where he met Mr. Styron. They walked into the office together. Swor reported:

> Mr. Styron removed his coat and walked to the southeast corner of the room to hang it up. I came through the private office of Mr. Robinson, the door of which was standing wide open. I looked into the private office, but saw no one there, and then I started into the toilet room to open the vault door. Miss Brown and myself were the only persons here who knew the combination. The door is heavy and I have been in the habit of opening it for her.[22]

The young woman's body, covered with blood, was lying on the floor just inside the washroom. Doctors said she had been beaten unconscious and then her throat cut with a single slash that almost severed her head from her body. Evidence indicated a terrible struggle. The murder weapon was never found. Her father was the first officer on the scene. He said his daughter had left with Cuthbertson at "exactly 8:05. I know no more of what happened until Cuthbertson came running up to me and notified me of my daughter's death. This was at 8:30 o'clock exactly." By the time he arrived at the Field Street offices, Patrolman Brown said, "I rushed over to the place, but as everything was in a stir, I could not make a thorough investigation."

Patrolman Brown was right. Had he been only an officer doing a routine examination and not the father of the deceased, he could not have conducted a thorough investigation because the body was removed in a wagon of the Weiland Undertaking Company before police were notified. "Chief of Police John Ryan and Chief of Detective

Henry Tanner, together with Assistant Chief Brown, did not view the body on the scene of the crime and were handicapped in their initial investigations."[23]

Cuthbertson said he had been employed the prior December as a city salesman with the real estate company of Robinson & Styron. "Mr. Robinson is out of the city and I had been driving Miss Brown to and from home and the office in one of the firm's automobiles. Mr. Robinson generally did so while was here and asked me to do so during his absence."

The three men—Styron, Swor and Cuthbertson—who discovered the body all said they were in shock. Cuthbertson ran to find a doctor and to notify her father. Styron and Swor moved her body out of the pool of blood and washed the blood from her face.

For five days, the *Herald* headlined the story on its front page. It also started a fund for the arrest and conviction of the slayer. In their frantic search to find the assassin, police arrested dozens of "suspicious" men. Countless rumors circulated. Jeff Robinson arrived in Dallas three days, almost to the moment, after his niece's murder. He was closeted with the family and then with police officers for hours. He shed no new light on the murder.

Evidence was scant. A bloody shirt button was found by Officer Will Moffett in Jeff Robinson's office six feet away from the corpse. Its owner was never found. Nothing resembling a murder weapon was located. A sinkful of bloody water and a blood-streaked towel was in the washroom across from the body. The young woman's inside right wrist had been bitten. The imprint was so deep that it brought blood. A wax imprint of the wound was made and turned over to officers. Missing was one tooth—a center right hand molar in the upper jaw. A crushed gold ring that belonged to the victim was found on the floor near her body indicating that it had been dropped during the struggle and stepped on. The safe was still locked. Nothing was missing from the offices. Officers who went through her personal files in her home found a packet of love letters from an out-of-town sweetheart. From these they learned that Florence Brown was planning to be married, "The love letters were of an entirely innocent nature," said Chief Tanner, ". . . of the nature that one would expect from a sweetheart," The writer had not been in the city for months. Chief Tanner declined to give the young man's name or location or the contents of any of the letters. Tanner and a Dallas photographer, following up on a suggestion that "a likeness of the slayer has been found reflected in the eyes of murdered people," went to the funeral home to photograph Miss Brown's eyes, but upon examination, decided that it was useless.

Florence Brown was a model citizen. Her pastor, the Rev. J. H. Moore of McKinney Avenue Baptist Church, described her as "an exemplary individual." She had attended church with friends the night before she died.

Two days after her murder, Florence Brown was laid to rest in Oakland Cemetery. Styron and Swor were among the pallbearers. Cuthbertson was not. Seventeen women, her close friends, were honorary pallbearers: Misses Elva Peacock, Edna Rogers, J. N. Parker, Mazeppa Guyer, Ella Halfer, Sadie Edwards, Nell Weir, Mary Florer, Grace Whiting, Mary Loue Roscoe, Maggie Merrill, Edith Florer and Annie Dixon and Mmes. Clarence Burton, Lucy Alexander, Johnston Franks and N. L. Long. Hundreds of grief-stricken mourners attended the funeral.

Thousands of hours went into investigating the murder. For months the stories of arrests of possible murderers played on the front pages of the papers. By November of 1913 when the case was no nearer to a solution than in the first confusing days following the murder, Meade Barr, in prison in Indiana, admitted in lucid detail that he had committed the crime. Brought back to Dallas for questioning, he retracted his admission and a lengthy investigation proved that he was not the murderer.

In the late fall, a woman, Ellie M. Lake, was arrested and held for several days. Declaring her innocence, Ellie Lake, "a tall, slender woman, a decided brunette, her black eyes snapping," declared: "I have lived in Dallas long enough for people to know me and if they don't know me, they will never get acquainted with me through the newspapers."[24] With that she refused to make any other comment to news reporters. Eventually she was released without charges.

Today, the murder of Florence Robinson Brown remains one of the city's many unsolved crimes.

20

••••

WOMEN EMBRACE THE CHILDREN

May Dickson Exall sounded both the challenges that lay ahead and a note of nostalgia for the past in opening remarks to the Shakespeare Club in 1911. "We are looking forward to another year of study and companionship," she said, in a city where "life . . . is beginning to assume the complications of a large place."[1] Indeed it was. That was the year Elm Street became "the Great White Way" when 110 street lights were turned on all at once; it was an event that made the headlines in other parts of the country. It was a time when a family, just starting out, could buy a maple rocker on cash or credit from Rick's Furniture store for $2.65, three pounds of dried blackeyed peas for 19 cents; a second-hand two-passenger Maxwell car for $15.00, a Hudson seal wrap at Neiman-Marcus for $295, and a Universal Encyclopedia. "a reference book that will tell you all you want to know," for 49 cents. A can of red salmon was 19 cents; corn, eight cents a can, and Jonathan apples a penny apiece at Star Cash Stores.

Margaret Cone, for many years director of Child Care Dallas, under several different names, at left with some of "her" family of children in 1971. She was especially pleased that hers was the first agency in Dallas to integrate —both its staff and the people it served.

Life for women was not bounded by leisurely meetings—though there were plenty of those. World conditions, both the celebrations and a brewing international conflict, encroached daily. Woodrow Wilson, the son of Presbyterian minister Joseph Ruggles Wilson and Janet Jessie Woodrow became president on March 2, 1913. A lawyer and college professor (Bryn Mawr and Wesleyan), he was well-known and admired by influential Dallas women who backed him. In 1916 he was re-elected on the platform,

Three special people who made children and their needs their first priority, top to bottom, Rhea Wolfram, advocate and mentor, Ann Hughes, counselor and friend, and Terry Ford, creator and teacher.

"He kept us out of war." Then, three months into his second term, on April 6, 1917, following the sinking of four American ships including the Lusitania by German submarines, he asked Congress for war. He led the country through World War I, led the declaration for peace on January 8, 1918, in a "Fourteen Points" state paper that won worldwide acclaim and went to Paris to help negotiate the peace treaty that called for a League of Nations. The Senate rejected the peace treaty including the League of Nations in 1920. Even so, in 1919, he was awarded the Nobel Peace Prize, an honor denied pacifist William Jennings Bryan, who resigned as Wilson's Secretary of State over what he felt was the president's war-like handling of relations with Germany.

At home, in those first years of the twentieth century, the welfare of the expanding population was a growing concern and women responded, again, by forming organizations. For the first time, these were broader based, not confined to women who were of similar religions, or from a similar social plane, or economic status or educational background. The groups came out of shared concerns for community problems. Women, then as now, who see with their own eyes children who are hungry will feed them; children who are sick will secure health care; children who are without shelter will house them; children who are not in school will insist that they have access to education. The problem lies with the *seeing*. Since those simpler days when the city was small enough that everybody could see everything, individuals have become more and more insulated and have not been able to see what goes on beyond their immediate confines. The women of the early 1900s saw: They saw when beggars came to their doors asking for a handout, when they went into the schools and saw children without food and children who were malnourished and dirty and infested with lice and other vermin. They saw similar hungry and ragged children, not in schools but on the streets; they saw when abandoned infants were left dead or dying within their own neighborhoods. "Wrapped in dirty clothes, an infant was found dead by James Kent, a negro, at Rawlins and Reagan yesterday. There were no clues. The baby was two days old and white. The infant will be buried at the city's expense."[2]

At any time when a city is growing, when it is perceived by those outside its environs as affluent, it is a magnet that draws the homeless, the jobless and the disenchanted. And Dallas was both affluent and growing.

Within a short span of time, about 10 years, Dallas had several organizations founded by women to meet the needs of the children. Among these were the Dallas Free Kindergartens that grew through name changes into Child Care Dallas; the Halcyon Club, Dallas's first welfare organization; the Young Women's Christian Association; the Dallas Infant's Welfare and Milk Association; the Dallas Baby Camp, which would eventually, along with other groups, become Children's Medical Center, and a shelter for babies that would become Hope Cottage. What started out as specific help for infants and children very soon spanned into assistance to their families, for women understand that children cannot grow up in safe environments unless their families provide it. There is no way to calculate the long, tedious hours and the use of their own resources that women devoted to building these institutions to help others.

The Dallas Free Kindergarten Association was neither free nor a kindergarten in the purest sense. "Free" meant on a sliding scale according to ability to pay, and kindergarten, a place to educate young children, meant a safe place for children to stay. And the history of child care and kindergartens in Dallas is virtually impossible to view in any sequence because sporadic efforts to look after the needs of children other than by their parents started soon after the town began and continues to the present. Throughout the years facilities have been combined, consolidated, duplicated and fragmented. There have also been numerous name changes. And imperfect records kept. All of this, coupled with changes in local and state laws governing child care and with vacillating conditions, principally tied to money, obscures what should be perfectly clear: That the care and education of young children is imperative. Women know this and women have, eternally, struggled with it. The world, until very recent times, has been content to let them. Child care has been, erroneously, termed a "women's issue." In 1990 during Operation Desert Shield thousands of women in the military went to the Middle East and left fathers to cope alone with young children, and men began to know personally that child care is a very difficult job, far more than a women's issue. Colorado Rep. Patricia Schroeder, long a child care advocate, commented that women going off to war could be a more powerful consciousness raiser than women succeeding in more workaday jobs. "The men are finding out that it is easier to be a brave soul than a tender of the hearth," Rep. Schroeder said. She added that women leaving home in response to a national crisis could help to change the devaluation of women's work "in this society . . . . Maybe child care will stop being just a women's issue."[3]

Other than individual efforts to care for other people's children—Margaret Beeman Bryan looking after nieces and nephews while their father went on the California Gold Rush, is but one of hundreds of examples—women in groups undertook to provide facilities for children in groups as early as 1897 when the Day Nursery for Children opened at 155 Belleview Avenue. Ida Gano headed a group of women who provided the center for children of widows and widowers who were Dallas residents with no place to leave their children while they worked. The center charged a dollar per week for one child, 75 cents per week for two children, and fifty cents per week for three children. This successful endeavor prompted the opening of a second facility on Alexander Street near the cotton mill. The centers were clean, safe, and convenient but offered no educational programs.

Throughout the city, as projects of their newly organized clubs and in church groups, women established child care projects. In 1901, fresh from its successful campaign to establish the Dallas Public Library, the Dallas Federation of Women's Clubs embraced the Dallas Free Kindergarten Association as one of its projects, consolidated many of the fledgling efforts and became, officially the foremother of Child Care Dallas. Through the years, Child Care Dallas has gone through a series of name changes—from the Dallas Free Kindergarten and Industrial Association, to the Dallas Day Nursery Association, then the Child Care Association of Metropolitan Dallas and, in 1982, Child Care Dallas. Simultaneously, child care centers have continued to be organized—mainly by churches and church women—and by individuals. Much later arriving on the scene are the national child care chains. All of these vary widely in quality, and finding quality care for their children at a price they can afford to pay has continued to be a grave problem for parents.

Kindergartens were started in the Dallas public schools in 1922 when Verina Pegues was hired as the first public kindergarten teacher at City Park School. By 1929 more than 1,000 children were attending the 29 DISD kindergartens. The program was discontinued that year, 1929, and did not reopen until many years later. It would be amusing if it were not so tragic that the education of young children is tied to the emotional and economic whims of society. In times of national crisis when women are needed in the work force, propaganda preaches the beneficial effects of child care outside the home. When the economy plummets, the same propaganda mills predict the downfall of civilization if parents leave the care of their children to anyone other than their mothers.

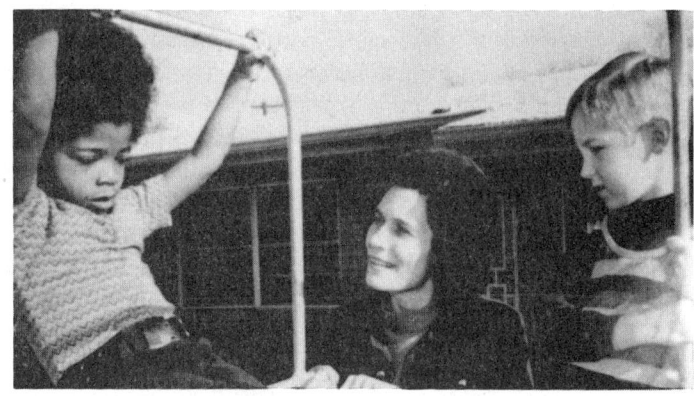

Their lives were centered in responding to the needs of children: above left, Carmen Michael, one of Dallas's firsts to believe that every child is valuable, and above right, Carol Jones, founder of the Children's Center, who understood that each child is unique.

Great-grandparents Mr. and Mrs. J. E. Mulkey of Mary Lou Mulkey Michero, above, and Alice Mulkey, below, gave the first residence for young women to the YWCA in 1911. Mary Lou later was a YW administrator and Skip (Alice) Mulkey made her contribution through the Girl Scouts.

Since the first decade of the twentieth century, the Young Women's Christian Association (YWCA) has struggled to meet the ever-changing needs of women, girls and families. It officially began on February 21, 1908, when a provisional committee was formed to give structure and national status to the Girls' Cooperative Home which had been established in the late 1800s by a group of concerned Dallas women. Mrs. John W. Everman was named president and served for five years. Grace Sheppard was the first general secretary, the name later changed to executive director. Less than a month after its founding, in March of 1908 the YW received its state charter and became an affiliate of the National Young Women Christian Association. It was located in a small rented house at 303 Commerce just east of Field Street. In June of 1912 it moved to larger quarters at 1219 1/2 Main. Soon it outgrew this and moved again to 1515 Commerce.

In 1911 Mr. and Mrs. J. E. Mulkey gave a residence at 1919 North Haskell to the YWCA that became is first residence for young women. More than half a century later, in 1965, a great-granddaughter, Mary Lou Mulkey Michero, was named associate director of the Dallas County YW, a position she held until retiring in 1976. Her sister, Alice Harriett Mulkey, served girls and women for 35 years on the staff of the Girl Scouts of America and after retiring was tapped by the Dallas Girl Scouts to head a successful campaign to build the Bette Perot Girl Scout Camp in East Texas.

In 1912, the YWCA Business Girls Clubs were formed under the direction of Grace Whiting, secretary, and in the fall of 1918 the Club Work department was organized by Louise Gies, another secretary, who remained a part of the YWCA for 46 years.

In 1919 a successful building campaign with a price tag of $800,000 was completed and two years later the second residence, Proctor Hall, opened at 1206 North Haskell, where the Hockaday School had been previously located. The gift of W. C. Proctor, a Magnolia Petroleum Company official, the new residence was named for his wife, who later became YWCA president.

In 1923 a new activities building was completed, furnished and dedicated at 1709 Jackson. Located downtown, it was YW headquarters for the next half a century.

In 1926 a gift of 10 acres at Glen Rose became the first part of YWCA's Camp Tres Rios; the acreage has increased to 76.66. In 1927 the first camp building, the main lodge, was erected and a year later an artesian well was drilled to fill its new swimming pool.

In November of 1927 the Homemaker's Industrial School deeded all of its holdings to the YWCA. This was the start of the first facility for black women. It began with a group of individuals interested in training black women and girls and included a day nursery for the young children of working mothers.

Ruth Spence remembers those days well. "My job with the YWCA was the first and only paid work I ever did," she recalled. "It didn't last long." Her salary was $25.00 a month and she was both a social worker and an instructor. "There weren't many jobs for girls back then," she said wistfully. "I was glad to work for the YW. I thought there was an opportunity to make some progress for the community." Her tenure was brief, she said. She was graduated from the University of Texas in 1917 and married in June of that year. "It was the organization in town most concerned with equality for all people. Both Alex (her husband) and I had an overriding interest in the fate of Black people."

After resigning from the YW, Ruth served on its board of directors and, for years after that, in an advisory capacity. She credited her initial involvement to Sallie Little Hanna, one of her many mentors. Mrs. Hanna was vice president of the YWCA of the United States of America from 1922-1924 and president from 1926-1930. She served on its national board of directors from 1914 until 1937. "Mrs. Hanna was a very unusual woman for her time," Ruth Spence remembered. " A native of Marquette, Michigan, Sallie Hanna, the daughter of Henry S. and Anna H. McCarer Little, was educated at Ferry Hall, Lake Forest University and Lindenwood College. She moved to Dallas after marrying John M. Hanna in 1888 and, until her death, gave her business address as the Dallas YWCA. "She was one of the most capable people I have ever known," Ruth said.

"She was very religious. I always said the Lord was with Sallie Hanna in everything she undertook."[4]

Maybe not *quite* everything. Neither Sallie Little Hanna nor Ruth Potts Spence could persuade the YWCA board of directors to respond to the needs of all of its citizens. "I was working with the black women," Ruth said, "and tried to persuade them to let our people use Glen Rose Camp. The board refused. I quit."

Whether from a guilty conscience or true altruism, the YWCA and the Council of Church Women began to raise money in 1927 to build a special facility to address the needs of its black clientele. It took a long time, but persistence paid. In 1940 the Maria Morgan Branch of the YWCA opened at 3525 State Street.

While this was going on, the depression years from 1929 to the latter part of the 1930s hit, and all human services agencies tried to meet increasing needs and to provide innovative programs toward recovery. At the YWCA, training courses were offered to girls seeking household employment. It provided training to both boys and girls under the auspices of the National Youth Administration. A neighborhood girls' program became popular, was organized into the Girl's Reserve and was the forerunner of the Y-Teens. In 1940, the YWCA became an agency of the Community Chest; it had taken more than 30 years to prove itself an indispensable part of the community.

And then World War II hit. The YWCA on Jackson Street in Dallas, like that of most YW's throughout the country turned, almost overnight, into a home away from home for those in uniform. The National YWCA assumed responsibility for United Service Organization (USO) activities and shortly Dallas's Jackson Street YW was overwhelmed with events. Dances, card parties, discussion groups, musical programs, sing-alongs and other social and educational events kept the staff and volunteers busy. Buses went to and from nearby military bases transporting young men to the YW for these occasions. Rules were strict. All social events were heavily chaperoned. Girls were encouraged to dress in feminine attire, but not provocatively. A flower tucked into a pompadour, a light fragrance, a swirly skirt and high heeled shoes were appropriate. Plunging necklines and short skirts were not. Girls were not allowed to leave a YWCA-sponsored event with one of the guests, to meet him later, or to invite him to her home. To do so was to be dismissed from future participation in the USO events. But almost everybody found ways around such restrictions and many romances began at YWCA-sponsored social events during World War II.

One romance that began at a USO-sponsored event was that of June Hanby and Kenneth Mounger, who were married in January of 1945. It has endured for almost half a century and produced three outstanding young men, Kenneth, Kevin and Mark.

The Young Women's Christian has always been a leader in helping girls and women respond to the needs of their time and to prepare for them what lies ahead. At left is a YW sewing class; at right, a typing class, circa 1912.

It was during 1944, that the community finally recognized the value of the YWCA and gave it a $49,000 grant to clear it of its indebtedness. Questions to which there are no answers arise here: Was the organization suddenly valuable because it was serving men? Did its visibility as a center to aid the war effort make it more acceptable to those who had the power to write checks? Throughout the history of Dallas, programs for boys and men have always been better financed than those for girls and women. Is this because men, who run things, know about the needs of boys firsthand, but not the needs of girls?

Or is there is a lingering feeling that girls should be home learning all they need to know at the elbows of their mothers? Whatever the reasons, the YMCA in Dallas, for instance, has always been better funded than its sister YWCA. It took 32 years after its founding for the YWCA to be provided funding by the Community Chest.

The 1950s was a decade of decentralization of facilities and programming for the YWCA. In 1960 the Garland branch opened; in 1961, the Oak Cliff Branch; in 1964, the South Dallas Branch, later combined with Maria Morgan; in 1964 the Irving Branch; in 1968, the North Dallas Branch (it closed in November of 1986); in 1968 the Richardson Branch. Even as it reached out, the YW continued to reach in, offering programs at its downtown central branch, which now was almost overwhelmed with administering its many pieces. Mistakes were made, as they always are in quickly growing organizations, in hiring and training. Women who were unparalleled in the people skills did not necessarily possess business and administrative talents. As the YW, in the goldfish existence of what was acceptable during the time for women to be and do, struggled to find its special niche, many individuals were hurt. Sometimes its physical growth took precedence over service. Between 1972 and 1989, for instance, there was overwhelming physical growth, all of which was needed.

In 1975, after a successful capital funds drive, the Downtown Branch moved to new quarters at 4621 Ross Avenue. Along with the jubilation of getting into a lovely new "home" many women shed tears for the old place on Jackson Street that had been headquarters for half a century. The war's end and changing social conditions that allowed young women more freedom in their lifestyles and better salaries forced the YWCA to evaluate its residential facilities for young women. In the late 1960s Proctor Hall was closed and the property sold to the Dallas Theological Seminary which used it as a dormitory.

The physical growth included a new building for the Garland Branch, (1977) completion of new facilities for Irving, Widner Oak Cliff and Richardson, (1986) new Metropolitan offices, (1987) additional Garland facilities, (1988) opening of Metrocrest Center in Farmers Branch/Carrollton (1989), and opening of the Mesquite Center, (1989).

Along the way another capital funds drive for $4.6 million was successfully completed. During this amazing growth, the Dallas YW often lagged in meeting the needs of women and girls in a vastly changing society. It was not, for instance, until 1980 that it opened a Women's Resource Center, even though the women's movement had been in full swing in the city for a decade. It started its first day care programming in 1976 as a reaction to, rather than being in the lead of, families needs' for child care. It held a conference on racism in 1976 six years after its national parent set "the elimination of racism wherever it exists and by any means necessary" as its "one imperative" in 1970. Three of its latest projects fill some programming gaps: the Intergenerational Center at Maria Morgan with a Positive Enrichment for Teens and School-age Fathers Program; the Vogel Alcove, a child care center for the homeless started by the Dallas Jewish Coalition, and Teen Mentor and Teen Leadership Programs as a regular YW feature.

Cautiousness in assuming leadership is to be expected. Many people accurately point out that limited resources have made it impossible for the YW to respond to many things that it would like to have done. And there is a community to bring along. To have assumed responsibility for new programs before they were socially acceptable might easily have handicapped already valuable projects. To have done so in the midst of a drive for money could have been disastrous. All this is true. Nor is the YWCA unique in its wariness. All groups accumulate bureaucracy that make it difficult for them to respond to new demands, and all organizations whose primary function is to serve the needs of women and girls are especially at risk. It is still widely believed, emotionally if not realistically, that women and girls *ought* to be at home, *ought* to behave themselves, and do not need public assistance to get on with their lives. With remnants of an antiquated mentality, it is all right for boys to sow their wild oats, but unthinkable that a girl might do so. All of this means that individuals with a vision have often found minimum response from the YWCA and have circumvented it in order to accomplish their purposes.

Its name, Young Women's *Christian* Association, has also been problematical. Though it serves individuals without regard to religious affiliation or with none at all, and though some of its strongest leaders have been women—and men—of other religious convictions, principally from the Jewish community, there are some strong feelings both within the organization and in the community that its name is restrictive. As Dallas reached its 150th anniversary, the YWCA operated out of six branches—Central, Garland, Irving, Maria Morgan, Richardson and Widner—and two centers—Women's Resource and UTA Child Development.

During World War II, the YWCA met the social needs of military men stationed nearby with events that were highly regulated. No girl could leave the YW with a man and no one was allowed to make a late date. At right, a group of women and soldiers meet the approved restrictions. Even so, many romances that culminated in lifetime partnerships had their start at the USO dances, among them that of June Hanby, left, and Kenneth Mounger, who will soon celebrate their golden wedding anniversary.

The Dallas Baby Camp was just that—an outdoor camp on the grounds of Parkland Hospital, Maple and Oak Lawn—to take care of sick babies whose parents could not afford to pay for medical care. It came about as a direct result of the vision and determination of women, is a living testament to what women can do in a very short time when they make up their minds, and flourished because of the lifelong dedication of one woman—May Forster Smith, a registered nurse.

May Smith and a group of her nurse friends were having a tea party on a rainy Saturday afternoon in March of 1913 and talking about the hot summer months that lay just ahead. Many of them, including May, were public health nurses and their work took them into the seediest parts of the city. They remembered that during the past steamy summer, and in the years before, many babies had died from dehydration brought on by viral enteritis or summer diarrhea. Air conditioning was non-existent anywhere. Sanitary conditions were negligible in the homes where their duties took them. Flies and insects were abundant. Milk spoiled and food rotted. And babies, the most vulnerable of their patients, did not survive. What to do? If they only had a place where sick babies could be brought, the nurses were willing to give their skills and volunteer their time.

A Baby Camp! That was the answer. May Smith, who was a native of South Carolina, born on May 24, 1874, and a graduate of Cooper Hospital in Philadelphia, had lived in Dallas for only five years. A public health nurse, she worked from a local sanitarium. In her rented room near City Park, she lay awake nights "thinking about the need" for a hospital in Dallas to care for sick babies whose parents were not able to pay. A tiny woman, 39 years old, who had grown up in comfort if not affluence, May was "married" to nursing. In short order, she enlisted the cooperation of the Dallas County Graduate Nurses Association, borrowed four tents from the Red Cross and got permission from Parkland to set them up under the shade trees adjacent to the hospital. The tents were furnished with donated baby beds, laundry baskets and other make-do equipment. The nurses tore old sheets to make diapers and asked for used clothing.

May's next move was to enlist the aid of physicians. Several offered assistance, chief among them Dr. Hugh Leslie Moore of Baylor Medical School and Dr. J. W. Embree of the Southern Methodist University Medical School. Dr. Moore, one of the few physicians of the day with special training in pediatric care, encouraged the nurses almost from the start.

The Baby Camp opened on April 6, 1913, only a month after May's dream was voiced. One of the four tents served as administrative headquarters, one for a kitchen, one for the nurses' dormitory and the fourth, equipped with eight spic-and-span sleeping baskets, was the nursery for the babies. In its first two days of operation, the Baby Camp had only one infant patient; a second arrived two days later. But word spread and soon the trickle became a stream of poor mothers, sick babies in their arms, arriving for care. The facilities were primitive, but sterile and the results amazing. Babies who would surely have died without attention often left the Camp on their way back to rosy health.

The nurses not only nursed babies; they nurtured mothers. They taught them hygiene and the basics of nutrition. They often saw older children in the family and referred them to the City Health Office for free smallpox inoculations and other health care. The Dallas Federation of Women's Clubs got involved and provided clothing—some for mothers and older children as well as for infants—and other supplies. The Baby Camp, which the nurses had pledged to keep open during the summer months, drew 48 babies by early fall. It was time to close the Camp, but the need for it was growing daily. The Women's Federation offered to provide financial support and the Graduate Nurses pledge to have two of their members on duty at all times if the city would provide a permanent structure. The city agreed. On April 14, 1914, just 13 months after the nurses at a tea party conceived the idea, May Smith, Mrs. J. C. Muse, Federation president, and Mrs. E. D. Sewell, chairperson of the Federation's Baby Camp committee, met with Mayor W. M. Holland and E. B. Patterson, the city architect, to view the latter's plans for a building. His design called for a small frame cottage. A 15-foot wide screened porch along the front would serve as the "hospital." Inside was a "ward" where the sick babies would be housed in inclement weather; a kitchen; the nurses' sleeping quarters and a bathroom. Using day labor, Patterson estimated that the house could be built on the grounds of Parkland for $1,500. It would be ready by May 1. And it was! On May 16, during a pouring rainstorm, formal ceremonies were held to open the new Baby Camp. Children from San Jacinto School brought wild flowers to decorate the facilities. Beaming white-capped nurses welcomed a large crowd that had turned out to see the facilities hung with fresh white muslin curtains behind a row of tiny beds ready for sick children.

May Smith was in charge all the way. When funding ran low, she "begged and borrowed" to keep the camp open. She buttonholed business executives for money to expand. A year after it opened the Baby Camp had to add a room for another nursery, glass the front porch and build a screened sun porch at the back. The Federation, itself in bad straits, suspended the Camp as a project in 1916, but May Smith had no intention of giving up. She had, in fact, a dream to expand. Officially designated as "Nurse in Charge" in 1917, May directed a hospital that now stayed open 24 hours a day all year. In June of 1922, the Baby Camp was moved across the street from Parkland and refurbished. An outpatient care facility was added. It had its own board of directors. Finally, a decade after it began, the Community Chest accepted it as a full-time project. May added a pediatric nursing school to give third year nursing students from anywhere in Texas an opportunity to train in the care of babies.

And still May dreamed. She wanted a regular hospital outfitted with all of the latest equipment. She worked quietly, behind-the-scenes in the manner that was the most comfortable for her. The aggressive, hands-on approach was never her style, even though she did it when the needs of her babies required it. In 1929 a personal friend, Tom L. Bradford Sr., gave $100,000 to build a hospital in honor of his wife and daughter. His tribute to May Smith came as the result of her having nursed his daughter, Elizabeth, when she had been stricken with polio and his wife through a serious illness. The family friendship with May had continued and Bradford had been a champion of the Baby Camp from its beginning.

Bradford Memorial Hospital opened on January 1, 1930, just at the outset of the Great Depression. Bradford, who doubtless would have funneled more money into the facility, was one of many who was deeply hurt in the 1929 stock market crash. Nobody else had spare cash. The need for medical care throughout Dallas was critical. The population was growing; the depression brought an influx of people from the countryside who hoped to find work but found, instead, a new kind of poverty. Even though Bradford had paying patients as well as caring for the indigent from its beginning, those who could not afford to pay increased speedily. Illness proliferated among babies alongside

Dallas's Children's Medical Center, one of the nation's finest health facilities, had its start when a group of nurses headed by May Smith created the Baby Camp on the grounds of Parkland Hospital. Through several name changes in more than half a century, the facility continues to be child-centered. — Texas/Dallas History and Archives, Dallas Public Library.

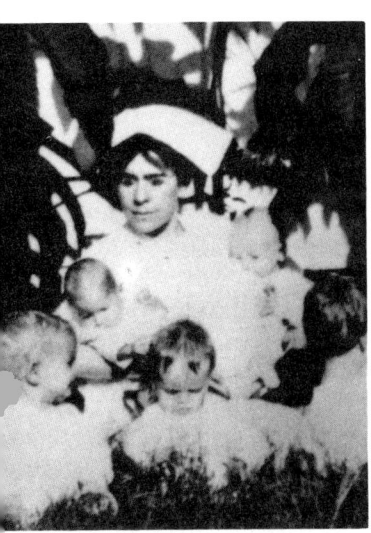

May Smith, a public health nurse, with five of her babies about 1915. Saddened by the number of babies dying for lack of health care, she created the Baby Camp from ideas suggested at a nurses' tea party.

diminishing money for medical care. May kept pushing. The Community Chest, which had accepted the facility as one of the city's most needed services, continued its support. A dedicated board, headed by Hugh Prather, kept it open. Dr. Moore, as chief of staff and a growing number of caring doctors, set bones, performed surgery. During its first year of operation, Bradford "saw" 2,104 children, admitted 503 to the hospital, and doctors performed 36 major operations and 78 minor ones.

And the facility grew. A well-baby clinic was added. The Violet Ray Clinic, open two days a week, treated children with rickets and malnutrition. Pediatric lectures were given to medical students at Baylor. Mothers were routinely offered courses in nutrition and health care. Even though the hospital had accepted all children from its beginning, black parents seemed especially reluctant to ask for its services, so in 1931 a special facility for black children was added. From the start, residents of Little Mexico, located nearby, brought their children.

Through it all May prevailed. In 1933 the staff was reorganized; salaries, from top to bottom were cut 20 per cent. May, who had been making $200 a month was cut to $160. The head nurse drew $100 and John Gardner, the janitor, electrician, engineer, painter and general handyman, who worked nine hours a day, plus being on call for night duty in an emergency, earned $54 a month.

People did all sorts of things to raise money, many of which sound insensitive or even fiendish today. For instance, during the 1936 Texas Centennial, an Incubator Baby Exhibit was set up where glass separated the infants from a visitors' gallery in a Fair Park building and viewers paid 25 cents each to see the premature babies and watch while physicians and nurses cared for them. The baby exhibit was co-sponsored by the Dallas Pediatric Society and Women's Auxiliary of Bradford, which had been organized in 1931. Parents, rather than being offended by their babies being on display, were pleased at the advanced medical care the tiny ones were receiving.

Late in January of 1938, May Smith became ill. She said it was the flu, but it turned out to be pneumonia. She died on January 31 at Bradford surrounded by her nurse friends. Though she never married and never gave birth, May was mother to the 55,000 children she cared about in the quarter of a century she nursed Dallas babies. There is no doubt that Dallas, more sophisticated and more affluent through the years, would have built a quality Children's Medical Center. There is, equally, no doubt that the one Dallas enjoys began and was nurtured by May Smith.

Hope Cottage, which started out as a shelter for babies nobody wanted and which has become a haven for infants everybody wants, can also be traced back to the vision of one woman—Emma Wylie Ballard. Hope Cottage was born in 1918. Its founder was born January 10, 1865, in Memphis, Tennessee, the daughter of an attorney, William D. and Emma Wilmans Wylie. Reared in the Presbyterian Church where she was trained in social service all of her life, Emma could trace her ancestry back through a long line of Presbyterian ministers. She was educated in private schools, Miss Kate Nelson's Young Ladies' Seminary in Shreveport, Louisiana and Mrs. C. T. Dickinson's School in Dallas. She married John M. Ballard soon after she moved to Dallas and had two children, a daughter and a son. Her husband's premature death left her a single parent. She had been quite active in the volunteer community as a charter member of the YWCA and the Women's Christian Temperance Union, an officer in the Professional Women's Club and several other organizations. Through this work she had acquired skills that fitted her for professional service to children.

Her first job was with United Charities which gave her a chance to see what was being done for the city's neediest people and to observe the gaps in service. She went from there to the Dallas County Juvenile Court where she spent five and a half years during which time she was the guiding force behind the first Dallas County Detention Home for dependent children and the Dallas County Industrial Home for delinquent girls at Elam. After supervising girls' work in the Juvenile Court, Emma became Child Welfare Director of the Dallas Humane Society where she spent another six years—more than 15 years in all—working for the well-being of children. It was during her tenure with the Humane Society, which had been established in June of 1900 with the double responsibility of preventing cruelty to children and animals, that she determined something must be done to care for throw-away babies. The children's division of the Humane Society, the Child Welfare Department, which Emma Ballard headed had, until 1918, been able to find individual women who would take care of abandoned and neglected children, but the increase of children in desperate circumstances made this no longer feasible.

In March of 1918 Emma Ballard suggested to the Dallas County Commissioners that the answer was a special home to care for these children. In presenting her case, Emma displayed 17 articles from recent newspapers, among them "Body of Baby Found at Fair Park," "Body of Infant Found in River," "Body of Baby Found 1300 Block of Browder." The Human Society gave its approval and selected a five-room cottage at 1406 Seever to house the children. Through her community connections, Emma began to assemble donated furnishings and supplies, working as May Smith had done with the Baby Camp and as other groups including the Family Place, Dallas's first home for abused wives, would do in the future. Merchants gave new supplies and women throughout the city donated used items to furnish and equip the house. The Dallas Federation of Women's Clubs paid the salary of Kate Lee, the first "mother" hired to care for the babies.

Hope Cottage, the shelter's new name, filled beyond its capacity during its first two weeks of operation and another building, the vacant Presbyterian Mission Home, was rented. For three years, from 1918 until 1921, the shelter barely managed to endure. Health care, especially, was inadequate. Because the shelter accepted sick and malnourished babies, the death rate was extremely high. In its first four years, 178 of the 542 babies died. The rest found families and homes through adoption.

Without the assistance of the Ku Klux Klan, Hope Cottage could not have survived. Today Hope Cottage ignores if it can—and minimizes when it cannot—the influence of the Klan in its early days, but its records show clearly that KKK contributions were essential. Two things must be remembered: One, in the days following World War I through the mid 1920s, the Ku Klux Klan was a highly visible, albeit secret, organization in which many of the leading citizens were involved. Two, individuals and groups that are suspect often make contributions of great value.

The story of the Klan's involvement in Hope Cottage began quite innocently. In June of 1921 Annie Jackson, who lived at 5736 Gaston Avenue, wife of Dr. Rice R. Jackson and mother of two-year-old red-haired twins, was persuaded by a friend to go with her to Hope Cottage to select a baby. In those days adoption was almost that easy. While the friend checked out the babies, Annie Jackson checked out the surroundings. She was appalled. Too many babies were stuffed into too small a space with too few attendants and sanitary conditions were deplorable. She corrected one condition the next day—buying and installing a covered container for dirty diapers so that the flies and insects could not get to them. Then she tackled the bigger problem—finding help to provide bigger, safer accommodations.

She appealed to the Presidents' Club, an organization of men who were leaders of their companies. She persuaded its president, Z. E. Marvin, to make a trip to Hope Cottage. He was head of the Grand Jury and the next day he took the entire panel to see the place and, on the spot, took up a collection to alleviate the most critical conditions.

Soon, Marvin became grand cyclops (leader) of Dallas Chapter 66 of the Knights of the Ku Klux Klan. One of his first moves was to persuade the group to support Hope Cottage. They pledged $40,000 immediately and raised it to $85,000 to buy and furnish a permanent home for the babies. From July of 1921 until July of 1922 when Emma Ballard broke ground for the building, the Klan again and again made substantial contributions. Somebody had to. Hope Cottage was $2,800 in debt. Merchants had stopped credit. Some Dallas County commissioners were indignant over the expense of running the shelter. When Mrs. Ballard reported that it cost $29 per month per baby to run the house, Commissioner C. D. Smith said, "That's too much!" He proposed that Hope Cottage be closed and the babies sent to the Dallas County Detention home.

Emma Ballard fought tirelessly for the house she had founded. In August of 1921, following relentless bickering and interference from the Commission, she resigned and became director of a new organization, the Hope Cottage Association, created to administer the home. Its continuing support brought letters of appreciation to the Klan from Emma Wylie Ballard.

The Klan continued to contribute money even when there were clear signs of disapproval over the organization's involvement. At one time in 1921, this was written into the records:

> Hope Cottage was not built from funds of the Ku Klux Klan . . . but by public and voluntary donations from its membership . . . augmented by donations from many individuals outside the Klan.
>
> The funds of furnishing Hope Cottage . . . came from many clubs and individuals—Jews, gentiles, Catholics. Hope Cottage belongs to Dallas, although it was made possible by an appeal from Z. E. Marvin to Klan members. Hope Cottage will be given debt free to the Hope Cottage Association . . . supported and run by public funds from the Community Chest.[5]

Unrest continued. In August of 1922, Marvin told the newspapers that if the Ku Klux Klan disbanded, he and others had proposed that its remaining money be turned over to Hope Cottage. At one point, Marvin resigned as a board member. His letter, though the Klan is never mentioned, indicated that he was reacting to the unease of other board members to his and the Klan's involvement. The board voted not to accept his resignation and, at a later date, he was its president.

The Klan continued to be visible for some time. When the cornerstone was laid for the new building on September 7, 1923, "robed Klansmen filed to the rostrum and a fiery cross could be seen through the green foliage of the trees with Old Glory waving in the background." And, on April 25, 1925, at vaudeville night benefit with a 165-piece band and 36 of the babies attending, J. D. Van Winkle, exalted cyclops of the Dallas Klan, was introduced as one of the guests of honor.

Even so, women and women's groups continued to be the most solid support for Hope Cottage. Groups and individuals regularly gave baby clothes and blankets, linens and kitchen supplies. The Presbyterian women gave a linen shower to supply sheets, pillow cases and clothing when the new center opened. Many times women donated food. Church groups and Sunday school classes, girls' clubs and individuals "adopted" one or more of the babies and provided special attention to them until they were adopted.

Through the years Hope Cottage has adapted its services to changing community needs. It has merged with other organizations offering services to children and families and its scope to include crisis intervention and long-range counseling. It has responded, not only to the needs of new adoptive parents and their children, but to birth parents who—for whatever personal reasons—give up their children for adoption. It has reached out to teenage mothers with support groups as well as individual counseling. It has been years since there were babies at the Cottage and even more years since citizens could walk in and adopt a child with very little screening.

Emma Ballard died on July 15, 1935, after becoming ill on June 27, the 17th anniversary from the date she founded Hope Cottage. She is buried at Restland Memorial Park.

The dream and hard work of Emma Wylie Ballard, enhanced by the vision and commitment of hundreds of others over time, has met the challenges of change with one uppermost commitment—to give every child, no matter what the circumstances of its birth—the best possible care, and the personal attention lavished on Hope Cottage by the women of Dallas has kept it safe through many bad times. The tenacity of outstanding directors from Emma Wylie Ballard to Aileen Edgington and including Selby Fly have been matched by women from the volunteer community who have headed its board.

Hortense Landauer Sanger, who was its president in 1966-67, is among its many exemplary supporters. Born in 1911 in South Dallas near where City Hall now stands, she was seven years old when Hope Cottage was created. The daughter of Horace Haas and Gertrude Pandres Landauer, she enjoyed a carefree childhood that included visiting in the homes of her numerous nearby relatives, playing in the wide streets with her

Emma Wylie Ballard's career as a social worker brought her in direct contact with the city's "throw-away" babies and led her to establish and direct Hope Cottage.

cousins and other friends, attending school and worship services in nearby Temple Emanu-El. When she spoke in June of 1982 at the dedication of South Boulevard-Park Row Historical District, Hortense reminded her audience that she was born into a Dallas with a population of 90,000 and that the changes had come "year by year, block by block, house by house, street by street." She did not say that she had been responsible for many of the most innovative, creative changes, but she has. Her total commitment to Hope Cottage and her continuing interest in it come right in the middle of the many other contributions she has made to the city.

Except for her college years—Wellesley, 1928-1932—she has lived in Dallas all of her life and in the same house in near north Dallas since 1937. Married to Morton Sanger in 1934, she is the mother of Anne Feld, John Morton Sanger and Mary Sanger. To scan her resume is to be convinced that she has nurtured the entire city, concentrating on children and health. Among her accomplishments are the development of a school lunch program in Dallas, placing social workers with the Dallas Police Department, establishing the Rhoads Terrace Preschool program, and the Dallas Commission on Children and Youth. She worked with Goals for Dallas, the Dallas County Community College Foundation, the Red Cross, East Dallas Health Coalition and chaired the Visiting Nurse Association, among many other things.

While assiduously avoiding the spotlight herself, Hortense is determined that her younger proteges are recognized. She has mentored hundreds of them, empowering them by showing them what needs to be done, including them in the planning, encouraging them in the tough times, and trusting them to do the job. In every group where expertise in planning for the future of Dallas is a topic, hers is among the first names mentioned.

She sees her city clearly. "I don't idolize the past, even when I remember much of it fondly." Her first volunteer job was with the Community Chest where she wrote stories on the human dimension of the Great Depression—homelessness, hunger, illness, hopelessness. "I saw long lines around the United Charities building, makeship tin-can and cardboard shacks under the viaducts, soup kitchens, beggars on the street, throwaway children. There was no cushion—no social security or unemployment insurance."

She sees a Dallas today that is devastated by the death of downtown, a city that is torn by racial polarity, a city where the educational system is in shambles. "I keep looking for some good news," she said, "and I remember the Spanish proverb: 'Take what you want, said God, and pay for it. There is a price to be paid for growth and it should be paid willingly . . . .'"

21

THE MEXICANS FIND A HOME IN DALLAS

Dallas's first recorded population lists only one person with a Mexican surname—Lucio Bamarus, 16, "a Mexican laborer living with John and Mary Pancoast, farmers." Other residents of Hispanic heritage came very slowly. By the mid 1890s only six others with Mexican surnames were on the census list—Jose Martinez, Michel Martinez, Vincent Rivera, Librado Torres, Joseph Villareal and Gavino Vindorez. If any of these men, who were in their 30s and 40s, had wives or families, they are invisible, which is not at all unusual.

Doubtless, not all Dallas residents from Mexico, then as now, are listed in the city directory. Many conditions create this chasm of being counted—fear of reprisal because they are not citizens, language barriers to understanding, cultural conditioning—what is important and significant to one group may be negligible to another—among them. Whatever the reason—whether they were just not in the city or in the city and uncounted—the directories of the day include very, very few citizens with Spanish surnames.

Until recently, the culture and conditioning of the Mexican-American population has kept women largely invisible—even when they have been the adhesion that held families together and, with their insistence on educating their children, are often responsible for the survival and progression of Hispanics.

How to identify them—these women, men and children with golden tan skins and beautiful brown eyes? Some insist on being Mexican-Americans and are insulted if they are otherwise identified. Some want to be Chicanos and Chicanas, meaning literally "an American born of Mexican parents," but which has come to mean "of or pertaining to Mexican-Americans." Some insist on Hispanic, which originally meant Spanish, then enlarged to be Latin American and finally has come to be an American citizen or resident of Spanish descent. Some want to be identified as Latins or Latinos, but this all-inclusive term fails to identify the unique heritage of Dallas's residents from Mexico.

They began to arrive in Dallas in large numbers in late 1914. They left their native land, many fearing for their lives, because of political upheavals and continuous revolutions in Mexico. It was impossible for many to have either security or economic survival. They came across the Rio Grande, paying a nickel each for the privilege. Most settled in South Texas, but many came on to Houston and Dallas.

Faustina Porras Martinez (See Martinez Women—Faustina, Irene and Anita, Part II) and her family were among the first to arrive in Dallas. In a 1980 interview she remembered:

"I was 14 when the Mexican bandit, Pancho Villa, took over Chihuahua where I lived. I remember him driving down the street in our neighborhood. It was the first car I had ever seen. Everybody was frightened. We did not know what was going to happen."

When Faustina and Miguel were married the Mexican population in Dallas was estimated to be 3,000. At its peak, about 1920, it was 10,000. Then it slowly dropped for two decades, as people moved and fewer arrived, to stabilize at 6,000. In 1940 it was 6,650 and since that time has steadily increased until, in 1980 it was 11,120 representing 12.3 per cent of the total Dallas population.

For many years the Mexicans who first arrived and those who came afterward continued to cluster together in "Little Mexico," the 10-block area on the northern part of the city. Their own heritage plus difficulty with understanding and being understood—most did not speak English and most Dallasites did not speak Spanish—tended to keep them isolated. And they were poor. Many, well-off in their native land, came with few possessions into a land where they were not understood and where their professions and crafts were not appreciated.

The WPA Papers, one of the most dependable resources about early Dallas, dismisses the entire Mexican population in an unflattering four-page essay. "Little Mexico," it says, ". . . is one of the few slum areas in Dallas possessing individual character." The report continues:

> Though its Mexican residents are considerably Americanized and the colony is recent in its origin compared to the Mexican quarters in San Antonio and other south Texas cities, it possesses sufficient color to attract the tourist, and its restaurants, curio shops, and motion picture theater are patronized by many non-Latin Dallas people . . . .
>
> Surrounded by the huge warehouses and towering smokestacks of Dallas's wholesale district, Little Mexico is a close-packed mass of flimsy, tumbled-down frame shanties and "shot-gun" houses threaded by narrow, twisting, unpaved streets . . . . Two or three families live in a single house with others sheltered in sheds and outhouses arranged around dirt courtyards at the rear . . . The dominant notes are poverty and squalor with a relatively high ratio of malnutrition . . . and other diseases, but the inhabitants appear to endure their lot with the patient resignation of their race, and crime, drunkenness and disorder are rare.[1]

When Anita Nanez Martinez remembers Little Mexico, she talks not about the poverty that is recorded in early records of Dallas, but of the sights, sounds, smells, tastes and feelings of family closeness that gave her the foundation to become a city leader.

The report goes on in this vein, blaming the victim for the crime, as so often happens when insensitive individuals view those they have not bothered to know. "The Dallas colony is overwhelmingly working-class . . . and normally finds employment as dishwashers, bus boys, dining room foremen, gardeners and yard men, tailors, ditch diggers and common laborers . . . ."[2]

Largely true. And what wonderful dishwashers and gardeners and laborers they became, with many becoming owners of the establishments they formerly cleaned and polished.

Anita Nanez Martinez (See Martinez Women, Part II) grew up in Little Mexico. She was born in 1925, 11 years after the great influx of 1914—long enough for the neighborhood to have stabilized—and she remembers a place far removed from that described in the WPA papers. For her as a child and for most of the other children of her time, the entire neighborhood was their playground. She remembers it through her senses—the sense of smell and taste, sight and sound, but most of all, perhaps, the sense of touch.

There was the touch of somebody who cared. Everybody in that neighborhood knew everybody else and even though they sometimes felt slighted by the rest of the community it was not, for the most part, an uncomfortable alienation. It was a close-knit, caring community where loving arms comforted children and where a child willingly "paid the price" to belong. There was the touch of a new down comforter her grandmother made from the duck feathers she plucked and cleaned, the touch of children's elbows as they assembled almost every afternoon on the bench outside her uncle's grocery store and pummeled each other playfully for the best spot. There were even the feels that *hurt*. Anita, the youngest and smallest of the crowd of children, longed to belong. "I'd put up with anything to be included! They would pick me up by my hair and say, 'Did that hurt?' and I'd say no even when my eyeballs were almost popping out! If I passed those initiations, I could belong." There was the touch of other bodies at night when children shared beds in the tiny houses.

There were the smells—the smell of roasting meat from her uncle's grocery store (Uncle Frank Mongaras)—"he put in a counter at the store and served lunches, mostly to the workers from the nearby Burrus Mills; the store's still there on Caroline Street" and the fragrance of Campbell's tomato soup that her grandmother, Thomasita Trevino Mongaras sneaked under her apron from a grocery shelf and prepared for the little girl while her son (Uncle Frank) was busy serving customers. There was the smell of talcum powder and fresh starch and Bull Durham tobacco ("she rolled her own cigarettes") in the home of the one Anglo lady who lived in the neighborhood and sometimes gave Anita a dime to help her clean house. There was the smell of permanent waving lotion from the living room of her home where her mother had a beauty shop. There was the smell of fresh coffee brewing—"My mother always had a pot of coffee for her customers."

There were the sounds—the sounds of muffled laughter and happy voices as the women worked together at one of their endless quilting parties, the sound of silence as mothers shushed their children during the afternoon siestas that were a ritual to all of the men in the family—and to all the women whose children would let them rest. There was the sound of bodily contact ("Uncle Charles had a boxing ring in his back yard and put on fights for the neighborhood. When I was a little girl I wanted to wrestle, too, and tried to convince my cousin to go in the ring with me until my father heard about it and put an end to that!")

There were the tastes—the taste of tomato soup, the taste of fried chicken after her grandmother had wrung the chicken's neck, plucked it clean and cooked it, the taste of an occasional piece of penny candy, the taste of cookies at the Wesley Rankin Community Center, the taste of wine at her first communion.

There were the sights; the view of "shotgun houses," one after the other all attached that to a little girl growing up provided a view of closeness and love. There was the sight of her Aunt Beatrice's "great big beautiful green Buick" leaving the neighborhood and coming back again, the sight of flowers in the springtime, the sight of freshly scrubbed children trekking off together to nearby Cumberland school, the sight of the nearby Ashland and Akard junk yard where Anita and other neighborhood children searched for burned-out light bulbs and tinfoil. The screw-in portion of the light bulbs were copper which could be salvaged. Gum wrappers and occasionally candy bars had tinfoil linings that could be rolled into balls. All of this could be sold for pennies. There was the sight of the window-pane taffeta dress resplendent in moss green, harvest yellow and tangerine with a huge white collar and a great bow in the back that Anita chose when a minister took six little girls to Young Ages and told them to "Pick any dress you want. I saw that dress and it was *my* dress. I didn't know it was the most expensive one in the store." And there was the sight of the great, wide Turney Street (now Harry Hines) where the automobiles rushed to and fro and, on the other side of it, St. Ann's School where "I watched the nuns walking back and forth. It was so tranquil. So serene. I watched them across the street from the Wesley Rankin Center, and I longed to go there and find out what that world was like. One day, with my heart in my throat, I raced across the busy street and went in . . . ." And then, there was the sight of all those uniforms in the attic at St. Ann's, uniforms that had been worn and donated and where Anita, with the sanction of the Sisters, chose her own uniform after the nuns had waived the tuition so that she could go to school at St. Ann's.

Anita Nanez Martinez was in the fourth grade at the time, the fifth of the six children of Jose Franco and Anita Mongaras Nanez. The years ahead would bring a wealth of deserved recognition to the child growing up to become Anita Nanez Martinez.

She would become the bride of Alfred Martinez on January 27, 1946, and the mother of Alfred Joseph, Steve Dan, Priscilla Ann, and Rene Orlando—and she would become—

- The first Hispanic elected to the Dallas City Council, for two terms, 1969-1973. Up to 1991 she would be the only Hispanic elected to a second term.
- President of the Dallas Restaurant Wives Association and the founder of Taste of Dallas to benefit the community.
- Board member of the YWCA Metropolitan Board.
- Goals for Dallas participant establishing designs of the city.
- Founder of the Anita Nanez Martinez Ballet Folklorica, a dance group, to promote a feeling of value and self-worth to Mexican-American children.

Anita Martinez, often rebuffed and rebuked by the very people she chose to serve who do not know her heritage and see her as, in her own words, "a coconut—brown on the outside, all white beneath the shell," has stayed in the fray year in and year out. She sees as her greatest contribution being a presence for the Dallas Hispanic community. Life has been both wonderful and very hard for her. Years ago when she became the first Hispanic to win a seat on the Dallas City Council, she spoke of how difficult it was to break away from a culture that tended to keep women out of sight in the home serving the male members of the family and rearing children.

"We are like crabs," she once said. "When one of us tries to crawl out of the barrel, there are hundreds of hands grabbing hold and pulling us back down." She is only one of many, many Mexican-heritage women in Dallas who have continued to experience a similar fate. Those who have "crawled out"—and they are legion—are tough, courageous, resilient and irrepressible . . . .

None more so than Maria de Jesus Carreon Moreno. She arrived in Dallas in 1927, when Anita was only a wide-eyed little two-year-old and she brought with her a background far different from those who had fled Mexico only a decade and a half before. Maria was born to Pedro and Herlinda Hortiz Correon in Mexico on January 3, 1896. Orphaned as a very young child—her mother died when she was one, her father when she was five—Maria was reared by relatives, among them an aunt who saw that the child had every possible educational exposure. Her excellent grades brought her to the attention of government authorities who provided a twenty-peso scholarship. To augment that stipend and to provide money for food and lodging, Maria scrubbed floors at night. She was graduated from State Normal School in Guanajuato, Mexico, on December 26, 1912, when she was not quite 17 years old with a teaching degree in elementary education and became a fifth grade teacher in Guanajuato's public schools. As the revolution—or revolutions, as many historians point out, there having been uprising after uprising—increased, Maria made her way to Mexico City where she worked in the primary annex to the normal school. In 1917, at the age of 21, she resigned her job, secured a passport and moved across the Rio Grande to Texas traveling with a lifelong friend, another young woman also eager to move to the United States.

In the states, she worked wherever she could find a job that would also allow her to learn and, if possible, teach. In Yukon, Oklahoma, in 1917, she worked in the Yukon Mills, a grain company; in Fort Worth in 1918, she worked for Armour and Company. In Chicago, in 1919, she was a secretary translating and answering letters in Spanish for a business while teaching Spanish classes at night at the YWCA. In El Paso, from 1920-21, she taught Spanish in the high school while cashiering at a drug store at night. In 1921 she was back working in Fort Worth as director of the Spanish Department while taking religious education and English classes at Texas Woman's College. In the summer of 1923, on her way to accept a teaching position at Roberts College in Saltillo, Mexico, she stopped off for a visit with friends in Bridgeport and met Dolores Moreno. She never made it to Saltillo, Instead, she and Dolores were married and shortly moved to Kansas City. There, while he worked in the meat packing industry, she taught Spanish, counseled women and families, conducted conferences and workshops, established and ran a nursery for children.

The Morenos moved to Dallas in 1928 bringing with them their year-old son, Samuel Alexander, born on the Fourth of July, 1927, in Kansas City. Maria, who had converted to the Protestant faith from Catholicism while living in El Paso, went to work almost immediately at Wesley Community Center and shortly became affiliated with United Charities of Dallas. She found deplorable health and sanitation conditions among "her" people in Little Mexico. She was appalled that the houses were strung together, one after the other, in what seemed to her an endless chain of poverty. Thin connecting walls sent noises from one domicile ricocheting down the line to several other families. There was no running water, no electricity. Outhouses did little to contain human waste and stench. Tuberculosis proliferated.

Maria Moreno was most appalled by the lack of education and the apparent lack of interest among the masses in education. She found girls of 12 who had never been to school. Adults could not read or write the language of their adopted country. Many of them could not even speak it.

Maria de Jesus Carreon Moreno, above, and below walking with a friend, was known as Madre de Floyd Street. She arrived in Dallas in 1927 and for the next four decades never stopped creating educational, health, financial and social outlets for Hispanic heritage children.

Maria rolled up her sleeves and went to work. She teamed with Mrs. H. A. Hudspeth to establish a Mexican Mission under the Mission Board of the Dallas Methodist District, which was eager to grant the ladies what they wanted but had little money to fund such an undertaking. When the board agreed to pay $50 a month for a center director, Maria grabbed it—though she could have been making four or five times that much teaching school.

She started a kindergarten for children, ages three to six, the first preschool program for Mexican-American children in Dallas. She canvassed the neighborhood and cajoled and charmed parents into sending their children to school. She badgered the city fathers into condemning a row of shacks as a health hazard, saw them razed and helped to find better housing for those displaced. She organized the women into a sewing and quilting club and persuaded them to give tamale suppers to buy materials for their work. While they were sewing and quilting, she taught them to speak English and many of them to read and write it. She brought city health officials to the neighborhood and conducted a campaign to get all of the children inoculated for smallpox and typhoid. When the parents rebelled, out of fear of the unknown, and children cried for fear of pain, Maria bared her arm first for the shots—though she did not need them. "It will hurt—but not for long," she told the children. "If I cry, you can cry!"[3] By this time Maria Moreno was known as Madre de Floyd Street—the mother of Floyd Street—the toughest part of Little Mexico. Everybody knew her and everybody called on her.

> ... many a night there have been running footsteps, a knock on the door, a fire, a child lost, a doctor or ambulance needed, family trouble. She had the only telephone in the area for a long time but what was more she was counselor, teacher, preacher, leader—in short Madre de Floyd Street and many another street as well.
>
> Every hospital in Dallas knows her; there are few, if any, courts in which she has not been interpreter or witness or amicus curiae, and when Tech High or Stephen F. Austin schools note Latin-American students playing hooky they call Mrs. Moreno ... Mother to them all is she.[4]

Maria Moreno scattered the seeds of love and good deeds in Little Mexico from the time she arrived in the city in 1927 until she died on October 6, 1965. Thirty years after she began her campaign to clean up the area and educate the people in it, she could count 350 children in her kindergarten, Boy Scout and Girls Scout troops, mothers clubs and church services. The seeds she planted spilled over into surrounding areas and, for the first time, gave residents of Little Mexico and other parts of Dallas a rich cultural exchange.

When the Exchange Club of Dallas penned the name of Maria Moreno as the first person in its Book of Golden Deeds in 1956, she begged for the recognition to go to her people rather than to herself. And, indeed, said her son, Dallas business leader Sam Moreno, others deserved the accolades she so willingly shared.

"She was way ahead of her time as a woman," Sam said, "especially a Mexican woman in a rigid society. But without my father's acceptance of what she did and his support of her, it might not have been possible. He thought she was wonderful; he was so proud of what she did. That was extremely rare in a Mexican man of that time. As a child, I sometimes resented what she did because it took time away from the family, but my father always made it seem right. They were a perfect match. Probably no other Mexican man in Dallas at that time would have allowed his wife to be out late at night like she was. He cushioned her and accepted the upheavals in our own family life in a way no other man would have tolerated."[5]

It is easy to stereotype Mexican-American women and men and to miss entirely the nuances that make up individual human beings. The *macho* image of the Mexican male is only one of these stereotypes. There are men of Hispanic descent who are tender, loving, caring, supportive males—excellent husbands and great fathers. The submissive image of the Senorita with perpetually downcast eyes is equally misleading. Many women of Mexican descent are brilliant, confident, bold and assertive.

This does not mean they have had an easy time. When one or a few individuals are walking against the grain of the *status quo*, acting and talking in a way not approved by the masses, she or they are often ostracized or ridiculed, and it is only in the quietness of their hearts or with a very few safe people that their real feelings are allowed expression.

Sam Moreno speaks of the "psychology of ambivalence" that pervades the Spanish/Mexican heritage, of the ingrained cultural differences between Hispanic and Northern European people. The basic difference, he said, is that for Hispanic people life is inner directed and for Anglos life is outer directed. "The concept of life in the Hispanic culture is that the individual can do a certain amount, but there comes a point when the consequences are out of your hands. You cannot control the environment, and the final outcome is in the hands of something beyond yourself. The thrust of the Hispanic culture, then, is to take care of the inside of yourself; the outside will be taken care of in one way or another. The concept of life in the Anglo culture is that man is in control of his destiny, that when the outside world is safe, then the inside of self will automatically be all right. When things go wrong, man looks for a savior. A child is born; a new weapon is perfected. The child grows up to be the leader, to take control of the weapon and to slay the dragon and everybody lives happily ever afterward."

The psychosis of ambivalence, he explained, places Hispanic people at a distinct disadvantage because these conflicting cultures are acted out daily. "In the Spanish culture, a sign of deference and respect is *not* to look someone in the eyes. The predominant view in this country is that if you don't look at me, you are not listening to me. You are not to be trusted. The Hispanic child is caught in this ambivalence when his parents demand that his eyes be cast down while they speak to him and his teacher demands that he look at her while she speaks to him. I have heard judges say before sentencing Mexicans, 'You know he is guilty. He can't look me in the eye.' I see a lot of our people, in the midst of success, still troubled by this. We live daily in world of ambivalence."

For women the ambivalence is doubly painful because, out of their homes, they must function in an environment established and managed by white males and at the same time in their more personal relationships, adhere to the cultural conditioning of their ancestors.

Adelaida R. Del Castillo studied Mexican women in the United States and published a paper that revealed, "while Mexican students fought for the democratic rights of Mexican people in general, the manner in which they implemented much of their political and organizational activities particularly limited the . . . participation of women."[6]

Leadership is a male prerogative in the Mexican culture, she found, and though women often were the leaders, organizing projects and following through with details, their male peers expected them to assume a subordinate role in public. Women often did all or most of the work, but were silent in meetings. "It was not unusual for a female, in the same class with her boyfriend, to take notes while he listened, type his term papers before typing her own, and tolerate his psychological and/or physical abuse as well as put up with his infidelity."[7]

In doing the tedious work to prepare for a meeting or conference, in writing proposals and confronting officials, women honed their political awareness and abilities, Adelaida found, but "they were central only within a personal sphere of human interaction as wives, mothers and lovers . . . . Men found it difficult to relate to women other than as sexual conquests."

When a woman did assume a leadership role, either because of her superior skills or because there were no men available, she risked alienation. "Often, assuming leadership . . . meant the risk of having one's personal integrity and emotional stability threatened. The revengeful and denigrative campaigns against women by men were . . . effective and successful. Commonly, women in leadership were labeled unfeminine or deviant." Further, they were often castigated by their own families and by other women. "The influence men had on each other and on other women in their peer group facilitated the alienation of female friendship."

As unfair as all this sounds, it is not the whole story as Senorita Castillo made clear. A system that categorically places a large percentage of its population at disadvantage—in this case Hispanics—can little tolerate a division within its own ranks. Mexican women who are often at the very bottom of the economic ladder and whose need for survival—jobs, child care and health care—is paramount have no interest and no energy to seek liberation. Further, a women's liberation movement presented by the media as white, middle class, affluent, bra-burning man-haters, as erroneous as this is in reality, holds nothing but contempt for the average Mexican wife and mother. She cannot afford, nor does she want to risk alienation from the only life she knows. "It was politically incorrect for Mexican women to blame Mexican men for their oppression when both were oppressed by socio\economic conditions—high unemployment, poor housing, lack of medical care and inferior education."[8]

Though the study was conducted in California and is outdated, as papers tend soon to be, many of the ideas expressed are echoed by Dallas Mexican-Americans, men as well as women. A professional Mexican male, the husband of a professional woman, admitted that he was struggling. "I love my wife and am very proud of what she does," he said, "but I have problems. My father and my brothers and some of my friends give me a bad time. I want to support her—but I need somewhere to find my own support."

For a master's degree thesis, "Dallas Barrio Women of Power," in 1982, Jane Bock Guzman "was surprised to discover that few . . . studies examined the roles Mexicans, and particularly Mexican women, played in the Dallas community . . . . These women . . . have contributed . . . to the development of Dallas, Their lives are American success stories . . . ."[9]

When asked, almost two decades after she had served on the Dallas City Council, to name the 10 most outstanding women in Dallas, Anita Martinez put together a list that had nine Hispanic women on it. The only exception was a black woman. She, as many other people, sees individuals of Hispanic heritage as *included*. It isn't something they have to battle to become; it is something they are.

It has been a long time since the Dallas Mexican population confined itself to Little Mexico, although many proudly still do. Some of the boys and girls who were reared there have grown up to be men and women who own estates in North Dallas and lovely homes on tree-shaded cul-de-sacs in Oak Cliff and small castles on the lakes of Ray Hubbard and Tawakoni. Now, every part of the Greater Dallas Metroplex is home to those of Hispanic lineage.

And, in Dallas, Mexican-American women are real, not token, leaders. They are physicians, lawyers and company presidents, teachers, professors and artists, computer programmers and government officials and a host of other professions. They may, and often do, feel oppressed by a system that makes little effort to understand and almost none to respond to their needs as professional women who are also wives, mothers and private citizens. These feelings they share with *all* women who have careers, even though conditions for them as a group—or any other group with language, customs or traditions that make it unique—may be more acute, more ingrained and more difficult to ferret out and correct than for women as a whole in the work force.

From almost the first, Little Mexico drew "Good Samaritans" with a will to share. These "helpers" were all Anglos, mostly from Dallas's established churches. They were principally Baptists, Methodists and Presbyterian, were inured in their own churches and faiths, were almost all women and almost exclusively English-speaking. Doubtless they were often helpful, certainly more with food, clothing and some health care than with religion. Since almost all of the inhabitants of Little Mexico in the early days were Catholic, some did not take kindly to the brand of missionary zeal of some mainline Christians.

It was from individuals of their own faith and customs that came the most help and the most healing.

Agapita Ponce lived and worked in Little Mexico from the early 1900s until her death in the 50s. As a *curadora*, she was often the only physician available to the Hispanic community. Anglos often dismissed her as a faith healer, but she was loved throughout the Spanish-speaking community and was often the first person that they thought of when there was illness in the family. For almost half a century she presided as the midwife and only medical person present at the birth of many babies who drew their first breath in Little Mexico.

Sister Phillipa Perez, a nun from Mexico, though she came much later, was dearly beloved by all of the Little Mexico residents. She was the first Hispanic female social worker, based at St. Ann's Church, who understood the plight of her charges and their most intimate needs because she connected with them culturally, verbally and empathetically.

Teodora Escobedo was another of their own that Little Mexico took to its heart. A woman of great strength and vision, she founded Iglesia Metodista Unida Emanu-El on Akard Street in 1923, the first Methodist Church in Dallas to serve the Hispanic Community.

22

EDUCATION FOR WOMEN AND GIRLS

Educated women have been the lifeblood of Dallas. Many of the women who moved to the town in the early days, married to adventurers and entrepreneurs, were graduates of the Seven Sister Schools and many others had been trained by private tutors before "finishing" at the best colleges and specialized schools of the day. For at least a century, until after World War II which ended in 1945, these women and the daughters who followed them devoted their time and talents to the community as volunteers. The city reaped gargantuan benefits from these gifts and the women who served the city created a "democracy" among themselves that has yet to be achieved by the men in the city.

> "The social and club activities of the town are carried on in a democratic fashion that makes the woman of modest competence completely at ease . . . her contact with a woman who may have millions and it should perhaps be added that the woman with millions takes it as a matter of course that she should be."[1]

Elizabeth Almquist expresses the opinion of most Dallas women— that education is the single most important factor in enriching their lives and the lives of their children.

This exchange among women—rich and poor, old and young, liberal and conservative, educated and illiterate—working together for a common purpose opened vistas for girls rarely accessed by boys. It gave women a view of life beyond the limits of their own homes. Every participating woman benefitted by association and exchange with others.

Affluent parents who sent their sons away to school were reluctant to allow their daughters to leave home, so if girls were to be trained beyond the social graces and the three "Rs," there would have to be schools for them in Dallas.

The schools were not long in coming. Ursuline, already well established, was joined by a host of other liberal arts and specialized schools for girls. Several, founded with limited resources and/or with a curricula limited in scope, did not last long. The Dallas Female College was established by the Methodist Church as a boarding school for girls in 1865. Located on Bryan Street between Pearl and Crockett, it went bankrupt in 1906 having lasted only 19 years. The building was bought by the city and became Central High School, Dallas's first public high school.

St. Mary's College (or Institute), a private preparatory school, was built between 1884 and 1886 at a cost of $100,000 including furnishings, in East Dallas on the block bounded by Ross, Henderson, Garrett and San Jacinto. Its centerpiece was a four-story building on 20 acres. Under the direction of the Protestant Episcopal Church, it was the brainchild of the Rt. Rev. Alexander Garrett who desired a school "for purposes of educating Christian women." The curricula consisted of mathematics, science, history, literature, logic and ethics, ancient languages, Spanish, French, oratory, rhetoric and composition, penmanship, vocal culture, tone reproduction and china painting. St. Mary's served as the educational base for many prominent young Dallas women in the late 1800s and early 1900s. Wedding write-ups and social tid-bits of the day often mentioned the school in their columns and several outstanding educators who made lasting imprints came to the city first as faculty members at St. Mary's. It was highly successful for a few years, but began to lose both students and faculty to other schools when the curricula failed to meet young women's changing educational needs.

The Oak Cliff College for Young Ladies opened in 1892 in a mammoth three-story Victorian building on the southwest corner of Jefferson and Crawford in Oak Cliff. It

First Lady Eleanor Roosevelt, (top) with Ela Hockaday, left, when she was a speaker at The Hockaday School. Mary Ann Allan (middle) espoused educational excellence for many years. Lenora Pipkin Hall (bottom) was the first woman elected to the Dallas School Board. Ella Stephenson Tucker and Adella Kelsey Turner were appointed prior to that. Pictures 1 and 3—Texas/Dallas History and Archives, Dallas Public Library.

was built as the Park Hotel, part of a resort spa complex planned by Thomas Marsalis, who lost his fortune in the crash of 1893. The building was cumbersome and the curricula limited. It was chartered to "teach the arts, social culture, parliamentary law, self-government, essay writing, reading, singing in public, grace and beauty of carriage and proper physical development," all of the appropriate talents in the view of its male benefactors for young ladies. Touted by its founders as "the best college in the Southwest," it lasted but 15 years.

Oak Cliff Female Institute didn't even open. Also planned by Marsalis, it was chartered in 1889. It was planned for the south side of Eighth between Marsalis and Lancaster. An architect was hired to draw the plans and a handsome rendering of a stately four-story building remain. Marsalis invested well over a million dollars in his Oak Cliff projects before his fortune collapsed.

Lora Cowart opened Cowart Hall, a private preparatory school for girls, in 1891, in her residence on Marsalis Avenue near Tenth Street where she lived with her father, Judge Robert Cowart. When he died, she and her sister, Miss Leila, both noted educators, moved in with their brother, Robert E. Cowart and his family on Grand Avenue—not the present Grand. Cowart Hall moved with them. Students ranged in age from beginners to teenagers. The faculty was limited but the curriculum stressed French, literature and art. Miss Lora attracted the daughters of leading Dallas citizens.

Frances and Josephine Holley, sisters from Alabama, moved to Dallas to teach at St. Mary's College and stayed to establish Holley Hall in 1906. During its brief existence, it made a lasting impact on Dallas. Its most enduring gift was that its Wellesley-educated founders were responsible for sending a whole generation of Dallas girls to Wellesley. Dallas is still reaping the benefits of these women, among them Gertrude Aldredge Shelburne and Hortense Landauer Sanger, many of whom then sent their own daughters to Wellesley.

In 1913 The Hockaday School opened in Dallas. Not even Ela Hockaday, a woman of total dedication to education for young women, could have envisioned the growth and popularity of her school. As the largest girls' school in the country, its reputation for academic superiority, and its popularity endures to the present.

Ela Hockaday was an unlikely person to have become an educational icon. Born on March 12, 1876, in Ladonia, Texas, to Thomas Hart Benton and Mary Elizabeth Kerr Hockaday, Ela grew up in a home of old-fashioned Presbyterian tenets. Her parents had moved to Ladonia from Georgia shortly after the Civil War where her father opened an academy for boys. His curriculum was based on the classics, principally mathematics, Greek and Latin. Ela's early education was at home where her parents' discipline and strict adherence to moral standards were alleviated by their deep love for their daughter.

A somewhat frail, shy child, Ela attended Denton Normal School and did her advanced work at the University of Chicago and Columbia University. She began her teaching career in Sherman, only a few miles from her Ladonia home, and from 1907-1910 was principal of the Sherman public schools. In 1910 she moved to Oklahoma where she was an instructor in science at Durant Oklahoma State Normal School. Disenchanted with Oklahoma politics that ran the schools, she resigned her job at the close of the 1913 school year and moved with her friend, Sarah B. Trent, back to Texas where the two women planned to farm.

Like all good teachers, Ela envisioned the ideal school—a school for girls which would be based on educational excellence. She dreamed of a place that would train girls to become ideal wives and mothers who would spend their spare time as community volunteers. Sometime during the hot summer of 1913 Ela received a telegram from a former teacher, Menter B. Terrill, who ran the Terrill School for Boys in Dallas. He was seeking a woman capable of establishing a school for girls that would be a sister to the Terrill school.

One summer of farming was all Ela needed to convince her that teaching was not so terrible. She packed her bag and left for Dallas. A meeting was held sometime during the first days of September in the home of Ripley Barksdale and Annie Lucy Keller Harwood *or* in the home of James Johnson and Juliette Harwood Collins. Ripley and

EDUCATION FOR WOMEN AND GIRLS / 227

Juliette, brother and sister, were children of Alexander M. and Sarah Ann Peak Harwood. They lived on Ross Avenue in twin houses their parents had built as wedding presents for them. Both families believe that the Hockaday School was founded in their living rooms. Both are likely candidates for they both had daughters they longed to educate.

Things moved fast. On September 21—a Sunday—Ela called Sarah and asked her to come immediately to Dallas. There followed a frantic week of papering, painting and minor remodeling of an old gray, frame house on Haskell Avenue. On September 25, Miss Hockaday's School for Girls opened with 10 students, $1,200 worth of maps and two Webster's unabridged dictionaries.

Miss Hockaday founded her school on four principals that have been re-stressed through the years: character, scholarship, courtesy and athletics.

Her own life was one of contradictions. Though she taught her students that the highest ideal for a woman was wife, mother, homemaker, church worker and welfare aide, she never married. Though she taught equality, her school from the very first catered to the economically privileged even while she bristled at the perception it was elitist. Though she taught self-awareness and self-confidence, most of her students and a lot of the faculty were in awe that bordered on fear in exchanges with her. Though she held athletics in high esteem, her own life seemed more bound by her first and third tenet—courtesy and character—than by either profound scholarship or athletic ability.

But if she, herself, appeared inconsistent, there was never any vacillation about the school she ran. From the first, she was *in charge* of her school—and nobody ever forgot it. Everybody agreed that she was an excellent administrator. Tall and distinguished-looking, almost austere, she was said to be shy and self-effacing by those closest to her. If so, these were characteristics rooted in an absolute self-confidence that she tried to instill in all her girls. To promote the equality she held in high value, Miss Hockaday required all students to wear a uniform. They were not allowed to wear make-up or jewelry.

During its second year, Hockaday became a boarding school so that girls from other cities could take advantage of the opportunities it offered to study French, Latin and German, English, mathematics and history. Miss Hockaday and Miss Trent, who remained with the school throughout her life, taught most of the courses themselves. By its third year, Hockaday had 18 boarders and Miriam Mary Meredith Morgan was hired to direct the boarding department. Strangely—or perhaps not so strangely—neither Miss Trent nor Miss Morgan appear in any of the biographical sketches of the early Hockaday period. Miss Hockaday was *it*. This is a custom that largely prevails until the present. The Hockaday faculty, consisting of many distinguished scholars—more than half with advanced degrees—rarely take leadership positions in the community. It is as if their sole identity is wrapped up in Hockaday.

Times changed, Hockaday along with them—though not nearly as speedily as many of its students would have liked. For years boarding students, if they were allowed to leave the campus at all, had to be in by 6 p.m. They were allowed a chaperoned shopping expedition on Saturdays, a movie downtown, refreshments at an approved place and church on Sunday. Boarders could have one weekend per semester off campus with parents or approved relatives. There were no casual visits to girl friends' houses; boys were off limits. Male students were allowed on campus only to approved dances—usually tea dances—and, occasionally, to an athletic event.

As late as 1941, when I was living with the Jake L. Hamon family and tutoring their Hockaday daughter, Lucretia, boarders were not allowed to leave campus with anyone except approved chaperons. I, a college sophomore, had neither the age nor the appearance for Miss Hockaday's approval, but Lucretia convinced me that it was imperative for me to chaperon a boarder friend for an off-campus movie and shopping expedition. Attired in a longish skirt and a long-sleeved white blouse with a high neckline and a tiny cameo broach on a black grosgrain ribbon at the neck, sensible low-heeled Oxfords, my hair plastered to my head and covered with a felt cloche as uncomfortable as it was unfashionable and no make-up, I arrived at Hockaday. I was to keep my mouth shut other than uttering a pleasant response in a well-modulated voice when introduced. Somehow I passed muster; I was allowed to sign out the boarding student. I was promptly

Ela Hockaday among the flowers at the school she created.

Johnnie-Marie Grimes, above, assistant to President Willis Tate, wielded great influence over SMU for many years, and Margaret Hudgins Hyer, below, burst into tears when her husband told her he planned a university on the site where they stood.

dumped and thought of no more until shortly before time to return the boarder to campus before 6 p.m. This story points up the lengths to which students went to circumvent Hockaday rules.

Emmie Baine began the Symposium on the Education of Women for Social and Political Leadership as a part of SMU's 50th anniversary. In 1994 it was the longest-running university-sponsored program of its kind in the country.

Sandy Tinkham with a group of SMU student Symposium planners. Sandy has been involved in Symposium since its beginning, first as a student leader, then as an assistant to Emmie Baine, then as a community volunteer and in 1992 was hired as director.

The school grew speedily. By its fifth year, the little old gray house on Haskell could no longer hold its burgeoning student body and Hockaday bought "Bosque Bonita," the three-story home of Walter and Anna Worthington Caruth. Located on 900 acres of farmland at the end of Greenville Avenue. Bonita Bosque was renamed the Trent House for Miss Sarah Trent and served as a residence hall for older boarders. At the time of its move to the Greenville campus in 1919, the school was incorporated. The next year an alumnae association was formed.

For many years "Hockadaisies" were required to wear "proper" dresses, hose, high heels, hats and gloves every time they left the campus. In 1928 the school introduced the tour group as a regular part of the curriculum and travelers were required to write weekly reports. They stayed three weeks at each arranged stop during their trip where they studied with local tutors.

The strict rules and the unrelenting decorum was relieved by a graciousness that permeated everything about Hockaday. Who can fault fresh flowers on white linen, antique silver and paper-thin china and cut-glass crystal, furniture of the finest woods polished to a splendid sheen? When one is surrounded by these things, they become a way of life—which is exactly what Miss Hockaday had in mind even as she espoused equality.

At home with the world's most erudite writers, artists, musicians and educators, Ela Hockaday met them on their home turfs and encouraged them to visit her school in Dallas. Some came—Eleanor and Franklin D. Roosevelt, at separate times, Gertrude Stein and Alice B. Toklas, Sir Thomas Beecham and Edward Teller. Many Hockaday alumnae recall that these great and near-great enriched their education in ways that they were not even aware when they, as students, were exposed to them.

The composition of the classes, as well as the curriculum, changed through the years. In 1931 a junior college was organized; it existed until 1951 when it was discontinued. During 1943 and 1944 the first, second and third grades were eliminated and reinstated in 1951. In 1937 Miss Hockaday's School for Girls became The Hockaday School, a private non-profit organization and five years later it became an independent entity with authority vested in a board of trustees. Miss Hockaday was named president emeritus when she retired in 1946. She had *been* the school for a period of 33 years and continued to reside on campus in The Cottage until her death on March 26, 1956. For the next 33 years Hockaday was headed by men—six of them: Hobart Mossman, Herbert W. Smith, Dr. Bernard D. Shea, Herbert W. Smith, Robert S. Lyle, and Glenn A. Ballard until Idanelle McMurry became headmistress in 1979 and served for a decade.

Today The Hockaday School is at home at 11600 Welch Road, where it moved over the Thanksgiving holidays in 1961 on a 100-acre site given by board chairman Karl Hoblitzelle. The school is a symmetry of buildings befitting the Hockaday heritage. Though it is still largely supported by gifts from men who have held the purse strings in Dallas, women's names increasingly appear among its big donors because Hockaday alumnae are, increasingly, career women who not only inherit money but make it on their own. A survey during the 1973-74 term found that 80 per cent of the students planned to become traditional homemakers and mothers. During the 1979-80 school year, a similar survey found that 80 per cent planned to be career women.

The uniform has changed. Guests invited to speak on campus have changed. This became strikingly clear in 1974 when feminist Gloria Steinem was invited to the school. Students at the all-male St. Mark's School, which by then had become the brother school of Hockaday, vehemently protested, going so far as to hang a banner at Hockaday equating Ms. Steinem with Joseph Stalin. It was the best lesson Hockaday students could have had in feminism—for even though many of the young women had not been especially eager to hear the Steinem message, they were adamantly opposed to having the boys dictate what they could do.

The stories of the beginning of Southern Methodist University are legion and the names of its founders and early leaders synonymous with the church and business men in the second decade of the twentieth century. But it is almost impossible to find and credit the women who were such an integral part SMU's founding. Without their contributions there would have been no university on the Hilltop.

One of the most colorful stories of SMU's founding is told by John William Rogers:

> As the city (Dallas) more and more took on the aspects of a city, its leaders ... began to feel the imperative need of having a great university.... Sometime about 1910 the news came that the heads of a respectably old university—Southwestern at Georgetown, Texas—were considering moving the school.... Dallas saw its opportunity and made offers to become the new home.... Georgetown got wind of what was up and for a while the fight to keep or get the church university was tinged with a violent and unholy bitterness.... Indignant Georgtownians burned in effigy President Robert Hyer who was known to favor moving, and ... Southwestern University remained where it was....
>
> Dallas ... was willing to pay the price of what it wanted. The town offered sufficient inducements including a magnificent campus site of 123 acres ... located in what was then at the northern edge of the city, and in 1911 Dallas was selected as the home of the new institution....
>
> In the fall of 1915, Southern Methodist University opened its doors.... among the graduate students was a young man named Umphrey Lee, who was destined some thirty years later to be (its) president.... there has never been a sign (since then) that either its sponsors or the town have regretted their collaboration....
>
> SMU is a Methodist school, but it is not sectarian. A recent check on its enrollment shows that beside Methodist there were twenty-eight faiths represented....
>
> Degrees are offered ... in eight schools ... (there) are twenty-six impressive permanent buildings. The overall value of the university including equipment, assets and endowment is ... a little under $20,000,000. As a privately owned institution, SMU receives no tax revenues. Operating funds come from these major sources: tuition and fees of students, income from investments, gifts for building and endowment and regular contributions from Dallas firms and

EDUCATION FOR WOMEN AND GIRLS / 230

businessmen .... In 1949 the university became the third Texas institution to be granted a chapter of Phi Beta Kappa, national honor society.[2]

Before opening its doors to the first class in 1915, SMU had been three years in the making, years in which many dedicated individuals worked diligently to bring it about.

Alice Armstrong, the widow of John S. Armstrong, father of Highland Park, donated 100 acres of land to the Methodist Episcopal Church South in 1911 to establish SMU. Additional land, adjoining, was given by William and Earle Clark Caruth. Ruth Potts Spence recalled the day Robert Stewart Hyer went to the Caruth home to get his friend to sign the papers. "Mr. Caruth was not at home. He had gone to trade a rooster and Mr. Hyer had to wait for him to return to sign the papers."[3]

Dr. Hyer was an indefatigable proponent for a major university in Dallas. When the Southwestern move failed, he resigned as its president and set up offices in the Methodist Publishing House on Commerce Street where, with a small staff—mostly volunteer—he created SMU. He made speeches, secured funding, selected the site, outlined the plans, approved the architecture, hired the faculty, bought the equipment and started the library. Every step of the way, with one exception, Margaret Lee Hudgins Hyer, his wife, was his best cheering section. The one exception was when he took her and their children to see the site he had chosen for the university.

"There we stood," said his daughter, Margaret Hyer Thomas, "on top of a little hill covered in tall grass. My father said, 'This is where Dallas Hall will be,' and my mother burst into tears. 'Oh, Mr. Hyer, what *have* you done? You've lost your mind. You can never build a university in the middle of this prairie!'"[4]

But build he did and from that day on, Margaret Hyer behaved as if the choice for the college site had been her own idea. The entire family, which had moved from Georgetown to Dallas in 1911, was caught up in the founding of the college. "My older sister (Ray Hyer Brown) was very involved. She was already a young woman (born in 1899), 13 years older than I. Most of the original decorating ideas were hers. She helped select furnishings for the dormitories and the first buildings. I was only nine when we moved to Dallas and 13 when the college opened, so I was more involved with playing and making friends and going to school. My brother was between my sister and me; all this was happening at a time when he was really disinterested ...."[5]

SMU opened for the fall semester on September 23, 1915. Its centerpiece and one of the two buildings on the "grass-covered prairie" was Dallas Hall, named for the city in which it was located and because Dallas citizens had donated every cent of the money to build it. When a visitor commented that the Methodists must be very proud of the beautiful Georgian-styled edifice topped by its dome with a skylight, President Hyer quickly set the record straight. The Methodists hadn't done it by themselves, he said, adding that individuals from every denomination in the city had made contributions. "There's as much money from our Jewish citizens in the building," he said, "as there is money from Methodists."

President Hyer wanted the university named something else, Mrs. Thomas, said. He foresaw the day when the Methodists would reunite and the name "Southern" would stigmatize the institution and offend Methodists from the north. His belief that Methodists would some day reunite was foresighted, for indeed they did in 1968 to become the United Methodist Church, but doubtless the "Southern" part of the institution's name has been no more of a handicap than the "Methodist" part of the name in some circles.

Because funding for administration and faculty was very limited, Dr. and Mrs. Hyer moved into Clements Hall, a three-story brick building that served as a women's dormitory and held some offices. Mrs. Hyer was housemother for the female students. Although the rules, by today's standards, were very strict, she was often criticized for being too lenient. Someone saw one of the women students chewing gum. Horrors! Another said the girls were dancing with each other some evenings and right in the dormitory under the eyes of Mrs. Hyer. And, worst of all, a few were caught sneaking out and going to the movies downtown.

SMU's exemplary educators includes, from the top, Ruth Morgan, an expert on politics, who twice served as provost, Bonnie Wheeler, English professor, who is a renaissance woman, and Barbara Reagan, a chair of its Economics Department, who is an advocate for equality of women in hiring and promotion.

EDUCATION FOR WOMEN AND GIRLS / 231

"Mrs. Hyer was a beautiful person and an excellent dorm mother," Ruth Spence said. "She was a gentlewoman. She cared very much about the girls and wanted to give them every opportunity to grow and take responsibility for their own lives."[6]

Margaret Hyer "walked a tight rope," her daughter recalled, "because of the severe demands of the Methodist Church. My parents were far ahead of their time. My parents had broken away from the literal interpretation of the Bible.... My father was the first person to teach Darwin.... It was not an easy life for Mother. She was expected to uphold all the restrictive rules for young women—no dates, no riding in cars—rules she didn't believe in....

"I never abided by those rules," added Margaret Thomas, who moved with her family out of the dormitory when she was 16. "I danced and had car dates when I was in high school." Margaret and her husband, Bascom Thomas, met while waiting on the same street corner for buses that would take her to high school and him to SMU. They were married in 1930 and reared two children, Robert Stewart Hyer Thomas and Gretta Thomas.

If Mrs. Hyer didn't enforce rules while she was the dorm house mother, it was because she believed them restrictive, Ruth Spence said. "She led more by example than by any other means of discipline. If the girls got the best of her, it probably was because she was looking the other way."

Looking the other way is a ploy followed by succeeding generations of house mothers, faculty members, disciplinarians and monitors of women at SMU. When I was a monitor on the third floor of Snider Hall in 1942-43, women students were still kept on a very tight leash. Not until they were seniors were they allowed to come and go from the residence halls with any degree of freedom, and even as seniors they had to adhere to strict curfews: be in by 10 p.m. on school nights and by midnight on weekends. Fifteen minutes before the witching hour a warning bell announced that it was time for final good-night kisses and at the stroke of 10 p.m. the doors were locked. Heaven help the young woman caught on the outside! She got demerits for each minute she was late. Somebody—and sometimes I was elected—had to sit up with the door key to let the laggards into the building; it was not a joyous occasion for either the culprit or the keeper.

Smoking was forbidden, to the point of expulsion. By that time many, many mothers smoked and their daughters smoked at home, often with the parents' permission. No matter. At SMU it was forbidden. Monitors were required to bed-check every room every night to be sure that all residents were accounted for. Though mine was the freshman floor to monitor, one suite—two rooms with a bath between, two girls to each room—was occupied by four seniors. They had lobbied for, and secured, a corner room. I was well aware that the corner room afforded them the opportunity to sneak out at night. I also knew they all smoked. Everybody knew it, with the possible exception of Ina Braselton, our dormitory mother, and doubtless she knew, too. I told them that I knew they smoked; I knew their parents knew they smoked, but smoking was a cause for expulsion from SMU and that I would report them if I ever caught them smoking. It became a matter of collusion. I have been in their rooms when the smoke was literally boiling out from under the bed covered to the floor with the spread. But I never caught them smoking, and they all graduated from SMU, two of them with high honors.

When SMU opened, girls were still considered delicate creatures to be protected and the rules applied seem laughable now. The dormitory curfews stayed in place until the 1960s when Radcliffe president Mary Bunting, speaking at an SMU Women's Symposium, said in her keynote speech that if women had to be locked up to keep them safe it was only fair that the boys be locked up, too. The women students, following that program, effectively worked to change the curfews.

A woman, Flora Ellis Lowrey, from Hillsboro was the first student to enroll in SMU. She transferred—she wrote from the University of Texas; SMU records say Southwestern University—as a senior so that she would be in SMU's first graduating class. Her parents, Alfred Lawson and Ella Lang Lowrey were friends of the Hyers and strong supporters of the new school. At 20, Flora—born May 29, 1893—was one of 706

The doors closed and were locked ... and woe be unto the Coed—and they were Co-eds—left outside.... When the smoke was curling in great clouds from underneath the bed covers, no one saw anyone else smoking.

EDUCATION FOR WOMEN AND GIRLS / 232

individuals to enroll, a record number for its first enrollment of any university. Five hundred and fifteen of the young women and men were entering freshmen. Flora was among the 181 advanced students. Umphrey Lee, who was the first SMU student body president, was also a transfer student. He later served as SMU president from 1939 to 1954.

Flora Lowrey became a teacher. After receiving her degree from SMU on June 25, 1916, she taught at Vernon and Cleburne. She began graduate work at the University of Chicago but returned to SMU where she completed her master's on June 25, 1945. She taught in the Dallas schools from 1922 to 1963, most of that time as an English teacher at Woodrow Wilson High School. She also taught in the Public Evening School. A writer, Flora had articles published in the *Southwest Review* and book reviews in the *Dallas Morning News*.

In the 1930s Flora lived at 2803 Oak Lawn and was a volunteer in Little Mexico. She sought out talented Mexican students, encouraged them to stay in school and go to college if at all possible. In the 1960s she was living at 6710 Dickens and complied with a request from SMU to write an essay of her memoirs of the early school. Here are excerpts:

> In the third floor rotunda of Dallas Hall is a plaque, which by now is a memorial to the Founder's Club of Southern Methodist University. The plaque is worded: "This tablet is erected in honor of the following members of the 'Knickerbocker Special Club' each of whom gave one thousand dollars or more toward the founding of this University."
>
> Two of these people whose names appear on this plaque, A. L. Lowrey and his close friend, J.K. Parr of Hillsboro, Texas, were responsible for sending me on a June day to enroll in S. M. U. Their enthusiasm and devotion to the new school led them to want me to be the first student to enroll. The *Dallas Morning News* of June 15, 1915, carried a small drawing of the steps of Dallas Hall with me perched on the steps. The caption under the drawing read, "First student to enroll at S. M. U. was Miss Flora Lowrey of Hillsboro, Texas . . . ."
>
> My registration took place in Mr. Reedy's (bursar) office with him and Dr. Hyer, the first president, and Mr. Ellis W. Shuler. My credits had been sent in from the University of Texas and the University of Chicago. I was ranked a senior, to graduate in the first class. My credits were, I feel sure, in good order, but I think I would have been accepted on any basis to insure the school of another upperclassman to help launch the 300 (later increased to 515) freshmen and to start activities for the first time.[7]

Especially amusing was the menu for the faculty, students and families served at Scottish Rite Cathedral on SMU's first day. It included Cliff Celery, Salted Munger Almonds, Brooklyn Lemonade, Fruit Salad a la First; Grace Olives, Sweet Trinity Pickles, Roast Spring Chicken Sensabaugh Style with Methodist Dressing, Potatoes au Ervay, Green Peas en Grand Prairie, Dressed Forest Tomatoes *avec* Tyler Mayonnaise, Epworth Ice Cream, Assorted Oak Lawn Cakes and Demitasse S.M.U. Anyone familiar with Methodist terminology of the early 1900s will understand the terminology and agree with Flora that "the menu was parochial, if not cosmopolitan . . . . We were METHODIST in those days!"[8]

Her reminiscences continue:

> The class of 1916 with Robert W. Goodloe as its president, chose the motto, *A posse ad esse* (from possibility to actuality). Their task was to start things . . . establish precedents . . . . The first student body was organized October 9, 1915, with Umphrey Lee as president. A constitution was adopted . . . .
>
> A popular course was public speaking taught by Miss Mary McCord . . . . We loved our social life . . . we walked and kicked bois d'arc apples . . . (along) what is now Lovers Lane . . . . Most of our opposite sex companionship was in

The University of Dallas provided opportunity for this trio of educators, from the top, Louise Cowan, who set the pace for intellectual stimulation for women, Gail Thomas, who found her educational stimulus at UD, and Joanne Stroud teacher and leader of women's groups.

> the classrooms and the halls . . . if one was popular she was invited to dinner at the boys' dormitory.
>
> . . . Mrs. Hyer and Mrs. Hyer alone gave permission to leave the campus. Couples in groups of four . . . on rare occasions got special permission. One of those glorious times Umphrey Lee, Harrison Baker, Gaynell Hawkins and I were allowed to go to the city to a show at the Majestic. We missed the last dinkey (the shuttle bus from the main line) and had to walk from Knox Street. We felt delightfully wicked . . . .
>
> . . . I remember Dr. and Mrs. Hyer best from the dining room which was in the basement. There was a family table for the Hyers and a faculty table. The rest of us sat at assigned tables. We filed down the steps and remained standing until Dr. Hyer said grace. On one occasion . . . the ritual was broken when Mrs. Harold Hart Todd . . . a piano teacher . . . who spoke with an accent . . . slipped on the top step and bumped, sitting upright with her feet forward, to the floor and exclaimed loudly, "I tink I say damn." Even the Hyers were amused . . . .[9]

Flora recalled that Dr. Minnie L. Maffett was house doctor and gave the best medical attention, "but no sympathy at all . . . in any maneuver . . . designed for a sick leave to miss classes. One went to the infirmary or to class . . . ." She recalled several faculty members who were exceptional—John H. McGinnis "who encouraged young talent—often where there was none!," Frank Seay, Ellis W. Shuler and Dorothy Amman . . . the first librarian.

> Memories surged as I roamed around and I felt the same thrill as of years ago as I stood at the front entrance and looked at the beautiful view . . . .[10]

Flora Lowrey is not the only SMU graduate whose memories surge as we stand at the entranceway and look out across the ever-changing quadrangle down Bishop Boulevard to Highland Park Methodist Church on its southwestern-most boundary. When I was a freshman there in 1940, one of my first acts, even before I enrolled in college, was to join HPMC and to help organize the youth group. There were already such leaders as Paul Deats, Ruth Harkey, Ruth and Betty Zumbrunnen, Jo Fay Harrison, John Godbey and a host of other sophomores, juniors, seniors and theology students who knew far more about it than I did. I, too, had gone to SMU because a man—in this case my mentor, the Rev. Dr. William G. Fletcher, pastor of the Methodist Church in Athens. I had a scholarship, but it would pay only tuition and I needed *everything*. My mother, Jessie Lee Henderson Anderson, was my challenger and my principal mentor who had always said "when you go away to college," even in the days when we had no money to make it possible. Dr. Fletcher, light years before his time, was the one who drove me to Dallas from East Texas, gave me street car fare on a downtown Dallas Street and sent me out to SMU with the directive that I was to get myself enrolled. I didn't have a choice. There was no way I would have failed Jessie Anderson or Dr. Fletcher, so—with fear and trembling—I found the SMU street car, made my way to campus (the street car line ended there in 1940), presented myself to Dean of Women Lide Spragins, told her I needed a job, got the position of tutor to Lucretia Hamon and then marched across from Dallas Hall to the administration building and enrolled. It was somewhat later that I learned Dr. Fletcher had prepared the way to make all this possible for me.

I knew several of the people that Flora Lowrey writes about and my stories, as stories will, confirm, embroider and sometimes differ from hers.

Mary McCord was a special favorite of mine, too. A maiden lady of indeterminate years when I met her as an SMU sophomore, having decided to minor in speech, she seemed *old*. The better I got to know her, the younger and more beautiful she became and by the time I graduated, she was not old at all, but in her prime and ready to take on new generations of students—which she continued to do until after I graduated. She taught me how to breathe, how to relax in front of an audience, how to project my voice, how to communicate on a person-to-person basis with those listening ("Select two or three people at the very beginning of your speech who seem interested in what you are

EDUCATION FOR WOMEN AND GIRLS / 234

Educational leaders, from the top, Eleanor Ott, president of Eastfield College, Terry Brown, Hockaday teacher and international advocate, and Margarita Deschner, German professor, with husband, John.

saying and speak directly to them. If you find that one or more of them are wandering, shut up and leave the podium.") Only, she never said "shut up." She had a genteel word, which I have forgotten in time. I was especially privileged because Edith Gaye Hanby (who married Noel Hunt McRoberts), who also was working her way through school, moved into the McFarlin Street apartment with Miss McCord to help look after her aging sister and I got to know Mary McCord as a friend as well as a teacher. A proper spinster lady who devoted her life to teaching, including courses for would-be ministers at Perkins School of Theology (and how many of them needed her guidance!), Mary McCord had a warm and loving side to her nature that few people ever saw. Like so many of those early dedicated teachers, she—who was among SMU's first faculty—went to work when the pay was "peanuts" and she, like the rest, was never financially rewarded for the quality of service to the university.

I knew Umphrey Lee when he served as president of SMU. He was a very special person. When I was a senior at SMU in 1943-44, I edited the *Campus*, SMU's semi-weekly newspaper, and at least once a month we published an editorial advocating a student center. At that time we had no student center. When it finally came, one of the first buildings to be erected after World War II, I claimed a portion of the victory—for the Umphrey Lee Student Center was my brainchild. Never mind that it also was the vision of hundreds of other individuals—most of whom could help pay for it! I claimed it as my very own. A personal poignant memory is that the very last major event held in the Umphrey Lee Student Center was the International Women's Peace Conference which I chaired beginning on 8-8-88. I had come full circle—from being a young woman from Athens, Texas, advocating a building where SMU students could be community together to an ending where the world was coming together in community. Shortly after the close of "From Vision to Reality: An International Women's Conference" that drew more than a thousand women delegates from 62 countries and 37 of the 50 states, the building was converted into classrooms that hold, in addition to other things, the headquarters of Journalism, my college major! I was afraid to walk into the renovated building. When I did, I was transformed—as it had been. It is a beautiful building and a major tribute to Umphrey Lee, who served as SMU's president for 15 years.

I knew Dr. Minnie Maffett. She was still SMU's women's doctor when I entered the university. She had been its women's physician for a quarter of a century and had heard "everything." I was fresh from the country where I had been surrounded with love but little money. My parents had been married for 21 years when I left home to go to college and, to all eyes, were devoted to each other and to their children. They never passed each other without touching. I left this protected environment where my relationship with my mother was especially close to go to college where I lived in a home of extreme wealth that was virtually devoid of close personal relationships. Everybody told me how fortunate I was—to have a job that required only that I use my brain; I did not have to wash dishes or wait on tables. In fact, I was *waited on*, along with other family members by a chauffeur and a butler and a maid. I told myself how lucky I was. Dr. Fletcher told me how lucky I was. Dean Spragins told me how lucky I was. Only my mother understood that my good fortune had limitations, but she said I must continue my education. One day, some three months into my first semester, in the women's lounge in Dallas Hall while studying for an algebra test, I began sobbing and could not stop. A senior, Barbara Tone, who I barely knew, became alarmed. When her ministrations did not stop my tears, she hauled me off to Dr. Minnie Maffett.

A large woman, silver-haired, with a stentorian voice, Dr. Maffett examined me, sat back and pronounced: "You are not college material. You would do yourself and the university a favor if you go home to the country and marry the farm boy next door and have babies."

That was it. To this day my anger at her lack of empathy is coupled equally with gratitude, for I got off that examining table and fled with the absolute determination that I would show her! I would show the world. She went on to become national president of the Business and Professional Women's Clubs, to serve several more years as the physician for women at SMU (I did not see her again until my senior year!), to garner the respect and admiration of women nationwide. I went on to do my own thing and to forgive her!

Years later when I sat beside her and introduced her as a speaker to a Dallas audience, I told them only a small segment of this story. She leaned over to me later and said, "I didn't do that!" and I could then feel a rush of compassion for a woman who had given up every fragment of her personal life to become a success in her professional life. She had trained for medicine at a time when it was almost impossible for women to go to medical school and, further, had practiced long before the day when emotional and/or mental stress was acknowledged to be an illness. In her estimation, if there was nothing wrong with the body, there was nothing wrong.

The two women who picnicked on that "glorious day" in 1916 followed traditional roles for women. She was the first woman to be president of the SMU Alumnae Association in 1918-19; the second woman, Linda McElroy, was not elected for another 60 years! Flora Ellis became a teacher of other people's children. Gaynell Hawkins became a social worker. Neither Flora nor Gaynell ever married. Umphrey Lee became president of SMU. The fourth member of the picnic, Harrison Baker, became an outstanding Methodist minister who served numerous Texas churches including Munger Place and Oak Cliff Methodist in Dallas before being named district superintendent for North Texas Conference of Methodist Churches, Dallas District, in 1954. Both married and had families along with careers. So much for equality of the sexes who started out intellectually equal in their halcyon college days—only to become terminally entrenched in society's permissible adult roles.

Dorothy Amann, SMU's first woman employee, longed to become a doctor. Born in Ripley, Mississippi, to Conrad and Elizabeth Hammersmith Amann, she was educated in private schools and attended Woman's College in Mississippi. When there was no money for medical school, and at a time when women were strongly discouraged from applying, Dorothy went to work for a medical firm and helped to start *Southern Medical Journal*. She attended medical lectures and reported on them. She was an editorial assistant when she quit to "read law" while assisting attorneys in Midland. Frank Reedy, SMU's first bursar, persuaded her to come to Dallas and work for SMU President Hyer. As a payoff, she was named the school's first librarian where "she had little money to work with, but she used her meager resources wisely. She was an intelligent, capable person who guided the growth of the library."[11] She organized Mortar Board, SMU's honorary group for academically achieving women.

Mary McCord taught four generations of thespians and theologs to stand up straight, look their audience in the eye and deliver what they had to say correctly, clearly and concisely.

Mary McCord, with a bachelor's from Peabody College in 1894 and a master of oratory from the National School of Oratory, 1917, was the sole speech department at SMU for years. She put together the first drama group, Arden Club, and presented Arden's first play for the first commencement in 1916. With strictly amateur actors who had no prior experience on stage, with no stage, no scenery and no equipment, she improvised. She presented Shakespeare's *As You Like It* in a grove of trees between the main campus and Highland Park Methodist Church that came, from that time until it was cut down to make way for additional classroom buildings and dormitories, Arden Forest. She directed many more plays, in the forest, from the steps of Dallas Hall and, finally, in the Mary McCord Theater, on the third floor of Dallas Hall named in her honor only after her death. She never married, giving up her personal life for a professional career that was as unheralded as it was exceptional.

My personal flood of memories are numerous. Ward, my religion professor, and Amo Atchley Redus, made their home my safe harbor many times. Her sister, Leota Atchley, who lived with them, was one of my first college-made friends, and it was she who first took me to the Reduses. Many times Amo and her professor husband gave us Sunday night supper after youth group at Highland Park Methodist Church. It did not occur to me until years later when I was rearing five daughters on a limited budget how much they sacrificed to make the world a little better for some of us who were working our way through school. I stayed as a "member" of Dr. and Mrs. Redus's household long after Leota left school to marry Frank Edwards.

Things began to change for women students at SMU when Emmie Vida Slaughter Baine joined the faculty as dean of women in 1962. A soft-spoken Alabaman, Emmie was born to Vida Foshee Slaughter and Dr. Myles Jasper Slaughter on November 17, 1916. She earned a degree in sociology at Southwestern University in Memphis, Tennessee, and her master's from Tulane University and became a social worker. She moved to Dallas in 1946 as the wife of Ogden Baine, chemistry professor and followed the traditional role of wife/mother/community volunteer while rearing a daughter, Mary Baine (Carr) and son, Robert Baine. SMU President Willis Tate enticed her to accept the dean of women post following the death of her husband. Once convinced that she could do the job, she never looked back. She became one of the definitive change agents, not only for SMU's female students but for all Dallas women. A voracious reader, she absorbed by osmosis the world outside her home, suffered vicariously the limitations of women everywhere and opened the constrained atmosphere of SMU to the windows of life for its women students. Like Ela Hockaday, she was on the alert for women role models from throughout the world who came to Dallas and persuaded many of them to visit SMU. While encouraging female students to take leadership roles for many of the advances born in her own mind, she orchestrated dozens of informal discussions in dormitory settings and in town meetings between women in the community with SMU women students.

Mary Miller, right, with daughter Jamie Miller West, the first woman to be named a dean at SMU, created courses to meet the needs of a changing community for 25 years.

In 1966, as a part of the celebration of SMU's 50th anniversary, Emmie started the Symposium on the Education of Women for Social and Political Leadership. It institutionalized what she had been doing for five years: With SMU women students in charge, it brought keynote speakers to the campus from throughout the world, mixed them with community leaders and outstanding people from other college campuses and provided formal and informal settings for them to probe the leading academic and realistic issues of the times. The Symposium was approaching its 25th anniversary when Emmie retired in 1989 and turned its reins over to Sandra CorSette Tinkham, who had been involved with it in multiple roles—in 1966 as one of the three students who "birthed" the first Symposium, then as a part of Emmie's staff, next as a volunteer, and finally as its director.

The Symposium was birth mother, either directly or indirectly, of multiple organizations seeking equality for women. Two—Explore and the Women's Center of Dallas—are its first generation children. Explore is an eight-week educational program designed to help women examine their needs, set goals and take control of their lives. It was organized in 1968 by Gail Smith, Jean Swenson and Jeanette Ivy. The Women's Center of Dallas, established first as Women for Change Inc., was organized after Ann Chud voiced the longing of many Symposium participants for an ongoing support organization. "Once a year," said Ann, "the symposium gives us an intellectual feast; the rest of the year we starve." The Women's Center was born in 1971 when 15 Symposium participants, Emmie Baine among them, met in Ann's living room to do *something* that would provide ongoing intellectual stimulation and activism. Maura McNiel was its first president.

The Symposium, indirectly, has been the impetus for Women's Issues Network, founded in 1980 by Joy Mankoff and others; The Dallas Women's Foundation, established in 1985 by Helen Hunt Hendrix and headed by Becky Sykes with Pat Sabin as executive director; the Dallas Chapter, National Organization for Women formed by Marjorie Schuchat and Jane Baker in 1972; the Women's Equity Action League, formed in Virginia Whitehill's living room in 1971; the Women's Political Caucus and the Women's Coalition, both formed in 1972. All of these groups have one thing in common: They seek equality for women in all areas of life, from Explore that focuses on individual growth to the Women's Center that concerns itself with issues indigenous to women's lives, to the Women's Foundation that helps women educate themselves about money. The proliferation of organizations is understandable. As individuals and small groups of women fail to have their personal needs met by a group, they form "splinter" groups to address specific needs. Emmie Baine has said she had no idea where her one-time Symposium in 1966 would lead.

Johnnie-Marie Brooks Grimes, who hyphenated her name only after 1980 when she grew weary of being addressed as "Mr.," an educator, volunteer, elected official, writer and world traveler has likely been the single most significant of all women contributors to SMU throughout its entire history. For 20 years, from 1954 until 1974 she was assistant to President Willis Tate at the time when SMU was expanding rapidly and determining its destiny. Always "behind the scenes" to President Tate, she was a profound mover and shaker in her volunteer life—and uniquely competent in separating her public and private life. Her dedication to families, to women and to children have been lived through her work with the Young Women's Christian Association—she was national board member for 18 years and elevated to honorary boardship in 1976—as a leader of Family Guidance Center and as a member of the Texas State Board of Education. After retiring from SMU, Johnnie-Marie wrote *Willis M. Tate: Views and Interviews*, a book delineating his leadership—a leadership for which she deserves a great deal of the credit. She and Billie Frauman, a professional consultant who has given countless volunteer hours, are two of the Symposium's birthmothers who continued to be present in its life through its turbulent adolescence to its adulthood.

Ruth Collins Altshuler, (see Ruth Collins Sharp Altshuler, Part II) for whom the first drama building at SMU was named, is the first woman to serve on the university's board of trustees, a singular honor that she both appreciates and laments. "This is still a male-dominated community," she said in 1989. "I am the only woman in the 55-year history of the Dallas Citizens Council ever to serve on its board. That tells you something." Ruth has been a contributor, a standard-bearer and a breakthrough person in so many fields—drama, mental health, volunteerism, among them—that it is not possible to categorize her, but she is especially at home at SMU, her alma mater, to which she has made a lifelong contribution. Since 1989, several women have been SMU trustees.

A consummate Mustang, Mary Elizabeth Buford Miller was the first woman to be named an SMU dean. She was a teacher and administrator in various departments of the university all of her adult life. From 1957-60 she was coordinator of informal courses; from 1960-68 director of Continuing Education and in 1975 named dean of the School of Continuing Education. A Florida native, Mary moved to Dallas with her parents, Jesse Elmer and Kathryn Spann Buford when she was in grade school. She was graduated from Woodrow Wilson High School in 1936, and in 1940 took a double degree—English and journalism—from SMU; a year later she was awarded a master's in English, also from SMU. She taught English at Dallas College from 1944-1957, took a year's leave of absence for the birth of her daughter, Linda Jamie, in 1948 and then went back to teaching. She joined the administrative staff of Dallas College in 1957 as director of informal courses.

EDUCATION FOR WOMEN AND GIRLS / 238

Barbara Anderson of SMU, top, is an educator, archaeologist and author on aging. Claire Cunningham directed special events at the Edwin L. Cox School of Business and Eleanor Tufts, third, an art professor, directed the National Women in Arts project.

She was a strong proponent of adult education. "The grown-ups keep us honest," she once said. "They are in school because they want to be. Papa's not paying for it; they are. They come into the classroom and say, 'I'm here because I want to *know*. There are hundreds of other places I *could* be . . . .' It's very flattering. But not easy. They know instantly if you're filibustering. "

Many adult courses were available, but Dallas College excelled, especially before there were community colleges in the area. Mary was the artisan and practitioner for SMU's numerous non-credit short courses, seminars and conferences. She saw change coming, welcomed it, tailored a course to help people understand it and sought the best informed people she could find to teach it. Her enthusiasm for everything from a course on firefighting to one on foreign policy, from one on practical parenting to one on philosophy was contagious. In 1964, she offered the first Career Clinic for Mature Women in the country. In 1963 she presented SMU's first Management Seminar for Women Executives. When it ended in 1980, it had continued longer than any other in the nation.

Often she was the transcendent feminist she denied being. She loved her home, her husband, Lester E. Miller, her daughter Jamie and Jamie's husband, Clinton West, and her granddaughter, Jennifer, and she had no patience with women who suggested, by word or innuendo, that women deny their femininity and/or their love for family and children.

Mary's focus on her work excluded politicking. As a result, her gifts were often underrated by the college administration, by the public and by the very people she served including women who often left her out of the planning, perhaps because she was ahead of them and perhaps because she raised issues they did not want to hear. In 1971, she said: "To those who say that women are doing no better than men in outlawing war, savagery and disease, I say, just give us time. Women have not had much practice in running things and they are still trying to do things just like men. But just be a little patient and give us a little time and things will get better."[12]

Mary Miller retired in 1985. In 1990, she lost a long battle to cancer. She lived only seven months after Jamie also died with cancer. Jamie, at 40, showed every indication of following in the footsteps of her mother. Back in 1973, Mary chided me gently—as was her nature—to write a book on the contributions of women to Dallas. She said:

> Perhaps we should coerce each other into writing the essays of our times and trials, fun and games. It is staggering to think of the magnitude of change that has occurred in *everything* in the last 25 years . . . . the subject of changing sex roles is familiar in outline to most people because of the flood of words that roll off the presses, but real understanding has not yet come . . . the subject will be paramount for the rest of this century—and into the next.
>
> "I am . . . proud of the women who are . . . going to school to formalize their learning . . . . It is wonderful when a grown woman pockets her pride to present herself at a school or college to take up where she left off, sometimes years before. Education does not perform miracles . . . but with education and faith combined, who can tell what might happen! I think we are on our way . . . ."[13]

Mary Miller was one—a very important one—who served as an impetus for this book.

In the last decade of the twentieth century, Ruth Prause Morgan surfaced as the most significant woman at SMU. She had climbed the ladder of ability, acceptance, authority, and admiration step by step since she joined the faculty as an assistant professor in 1966. She was the first person to chair SMU's University Assembly, three times voted outstanding professor, one of the few women to serve as faculty representative to the SMU board, the first woman to serve as president of the Faculty Senate and the first to serve as provost of the university—titles that affirm the esteem afforded her by administration, community, faculty and students. One of the country's foremost political analysts, she was born in California, the daughter of Ervin and Thelma Prcesang Prause.

SMU educators in three different areas of expertise are, from the top, Conchita Winn, Spanish; Virginia Currey, political science, and Jo Fay Godbey, Dedman School Lecture Series founder.

She grew up in Austin where her father, an astro-physicist, taught at the University of Texas.

Ruth Morgan's intelligent, rational, sensitive, consistent, creative behavior both in times of crisis and in routine day-to-day decisions comes out of a foundation of rearing, preparation, "normal" family responsibilities, academic experience and exposure to a world of reality. With an older sister and a younger brother, she was reared in a loved and loving family that gave her both support and models for excellence. She was educated at the University of Texas at Austin (first in her class) and at Louisiana State University, (master's 1962 and Ph.D., 1966). She taught in the public school system and in a community college before joining the SMU faculty. A prolific writer (three published books and numerous scholarly papers and manuscripts), Dr. Morgan was named provost of the university in 1986 after being assistant professor, associate professor, professor, academic director of SMU in Paris; director of the college's master of liberal arts program, assistant provost and provost.

Ruth experienced her first sexual discrimination at SMU. "The dean (who hired her) told me he would have to give me a starting salary lower than my male counterpart who joined the faculty at the same time because I had family responsibilities," adding that she was not as dependable as the man because she had a husband and children. At the end of the first year, she asked for and got a salary adjustment when she presented the dean with her solid record of achievement. The man, hired at the same time, left SMU before reaching tenure.

"If you grow up in a nurturing family—as I did—you do not experience sex discrimination. Our young people do not (know) that this is a society that does not operate gender-free. Our young women think their merit is sufficient and it isn't. It is very important for women to have role models. My own role models were my grandmother, my mother, some of my teachers, public women including Elizabet Ney, Florence Nightingale, Eve Curie—women who dared to be a little different. Many students have told me it is important for them to have female role models—principals and administrators, and I feel honored to respond to this . . . ."

Married to Vernon Morgan and the mother of two adult children—Glenn Edward and Renee—and a grandmother, Ruth also takes her role as a community participant seriously, responds to its needs with her academic and political expertise and encourages faculty members to do the same.

Dr. Morgan sees the political arena in a state of flux bordering on crisis. "We have no mechanism to give people a . . . handle on how to deal with the complexities of government. They (have) a feeling that they are powerless to effect change. We have a bombardment of information . . . where citizens get their information . . . from seconds of watching television. We have become a nation of single issue politics with special interest lobbies controlling decisions at every level of government . . . input at the local level in political parties is almost extinct.

"All thinking people agree that many court-ordered decisions . . . brought about changes that had to happen. But many (also) tamper with the very roots of democracy. When . . . the state has to guarantee an outcome by designing districts to assure that the winner be one of a particular majority or minority, then we pervert what democracy is all about—to guarantee the vote, not to guarantee the outcome. We have . . . too much court intervention."

These changes (political parties, individual responsibility, single issue interests, passive participation, court intervention) render policy-making bodies at every level from city councils to Congress virtually ineffective. "It is very difficult to build coalition to get anything done. The best way to build coalition is in the electoral process so that you don't have to fight things out at the policy-making level." When the electoral process breaks down . . . every issue becomes a single agenda item . . . (and) consensus is virtually unattainable.

In public education, "our resources are being mis-applied. The biggest problem in education began when the emphasis shifted from . . . substance to . . . technique. My teacher training courses—in what was considered one of the best colleges in the state— were absolutely worthless. What a teacher needs is inspired enthusiasm and something

Janice Bromberg, above, has served education in many capacities, among them as a member of the Dallas School Board and as a member of the SMU Board of Governors.

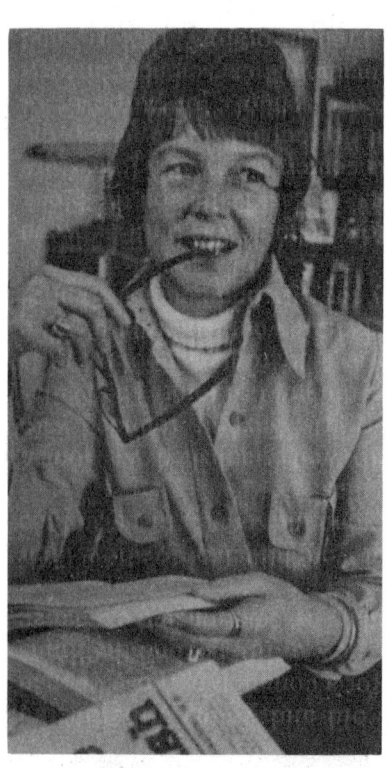

Peggy Ladenberger was a typical "child" of her generation who put her own career goals on hold to marry and get her three daughters started to school. Then she returned to the classroom, completed her doctorate and, as a psychologist, stressed education as a way out and up for hundreds of clients.

to teach. State-imposed standards take away from teaching and center on boondoggles. If the Mickey Mouse lesson plan requirements were stripped away, teachers were permitted to be professionals and paid like professionals, if they were provided with an office and a chance to be together to plan and learn from each other, if we did not require them to be policemen and bureaucrats we could turn things around overnight. I don't see us doing this. But . . . I am optimistic because where there is a will, there is virtually immediate response. Look what happened to science education after Sputnik. Look what happened to the number of quality of students under the G.I. Bill."

The quality of public education directly impacts SMU and other educational institutions because "it reduces the pool of potential applicants." This means that colleges must recruit students from across the nation and around the world, (which) is highly valuable (but) diminishes the possibility that graduates will remain in Dallas to serve the community.

The love/hate relationship of the city with SMU is a matter of concern and frustration for faculty, administration and students, Dr. Morgan said. "Dallas has never fully appreciated (SMU's) quality educational system with a faculty that willingly gives time to serve the community and students who are deeply involved in volunteer efforts. "SMU's reputation is far better outside the city than inside the city . . . . (at the heart of the problem is) the "perpetuation of the stereotype that SMU is a party school—with selective, isolated incidents rather than evaluating it from a whole range of possibilities." This stereotype prevents some quality students from even considering SMU and it limits gifts to the university.

The liabilities and assets of SMU are two sides of the same coin. "It is a private university. It is located in one of the wealthiest parts of the community. It has an attractive setting. Its Georgian architecture and architectural purity, its effort to refurbish and repair buildings and to beautify the campus all add to the stereotype that the University is elitist." Also, "our tradition of civility" is sometimes counted against SMU." It is a university that listens, usually politely, to individuals of all political and societal persuasions. It is seldom judgmental. Its students rarely rebel, though they sometimes have, its faculty mostly does what it was hired to do—teach students. The bonus is that the faculty also become involved in the community.

At this "rich party school," more than half of the students are on financial aid. The ethnic composition is "not as balanced as we would like it to be . . . but it is increasing." We emphasize recruiting African American students . . . (and) inclusivity. SMU (also) has a very important . . . role . . . in the development of Hispanic leadership of this state for the twenty-first century.

"SMU is in the fortunate position of having seen ahead volatile changes and to have positioned (itself) to meet the challenges." Because of this, SMU is in a . . . stable place to cope with the diminishing numbers of young people of college age coupled with an economic recession.

Another asset/liability is that SMU is a young university . . . . It does not have access to . . . large gifts . . . because . . . its supporters able and willing to give are limited. (But) it is not over-burdened with bureaucratic expectations and, thus, has the opportunity to carve out new directions.

"SMU is a solid institution. It has the largest private library in the state . . . . its academic program is excellent. It has the potential to become a great university. Only a few places in the southern half of the country have this possibility."

Though the numbers of women on the faculty and administration at SMU through the years has been small, their influence as teachers, mentors and role models for women on campus and off has been far in excess of their numbers. A very selective group of these women not already mentioned include Ima Herron, Barbara Anderson, Virginia Chancey, Megan and Allesandra Comini (the only mother-daughter duo), Claire Cunningham, Virginia Currey, Margarita Deschner, Ann Early, Jo Fay Godbey, Betty Maynard, Augusta Nance, Judy Mohraz, Barbara Reagan, Eleanor Tufts, Bonnie Wheeler. And so many others.

23

TODDLING TOWARD EQUALITY

Before Dallas had reached the second decade of the Twentieth Century, many of its women had joined the national trend to seek personal identities separate from that of males. True, the unchaining of the female psyche was by no means universal. The masses, many women as well as most men, still clung to the idea that women were best served who served others and that good women neither needed nor desired personal freedom. They could endlessly cite authorities to prove their contentions—pundits from all the world religions, leaders and law-makers of all governments. Never mind that all of these "authorities" in every culture were male, determined—whether they recognized it or not—to maintain existing conditions.

Throughout the country, the movement for emancipation was led by an unlikely liaison—women at the apex of the socio-economic ladder and women on its lowest rungs. The economically privileged women were educated; their reading convinced them that they were capable of making decisions for their lives and acting upon them. Women without financial clout often worked, and experienced the limitations for advancement and financial gain imposed on them. Thus, from the two poles—education and experience—women in Dallas wanted freedom to work and advance in their careers, to vote and elect those who made decisions affecting their lives, to run for public office, to control their own property.

Nor was all of Dallas averse to the liberation of women. Though many of its founders were rugged pioneers with ingrained machismo, not many were tyrants. There were dozens of men who also were caring, educated human beings often more puzzled by, than resistant to, the needs of their womenfolk for emancipation. Further, women liberation leaders were supported in Dallas both by precedent and the media—so long as they did not go "too far" and expect total equality. From its start, Dallas had more "working" women than anywhere else in the nation.

The fact that Sarah Horton Cockrell had successfully managed and increased her fortune and had been a decision-maker for Dallas in the early days established beyond any doubt that it was not impossible for a woman to manage her own affairs and those of the city. As early as 1887 *The Dallas Herald* editorially supported a woman's right to work:

> There are hundreds of ladies employed as book-keepers, copyists, typewriters and other important like positions in Dallas and it is a well known fact, be it said to the credit of the business capacity of their sex, that they not only do their work satisfactorily, but reach that degree of such perfect satisfaction as to commend the sex for this particular class of work. They are very efficient and more painstaking and careful than men, neater, nicer and altogether more desirable. The Herald hopes that Dallas business men will all give to young women such work as they are naturally suited to....[1]

Unusually advanced for newspapers of its day, the *Herald*, and later the *News* apprised its readers of what was going on in other parts of the world. "Montreal has an association for the professional education of women," The *News* reported on June 9, 1889. "The society aims to fit its members for different branches of professional life." Further down in the article, entitled "The Field of Women's Work," it was reported: "A celebrated New York physician recently ... said 'Women physicians, though they have

Nonie Boren Mahoney, a Dallas society girl, led the campaign for women's voting rights. As president of the Dallas Equal Suffrage Association, she used a unique method to convince Texas Sen. Barry Miller that women really did want to vote.

labored under very great disadvantages, are a success, and they have come to stay. A larger proportion of them than of men are a real honor to the profession . . . ."

The first organized wave of the Women's Liberation Movement in the United States came simultaneously with the outbreak of World War I. Throughout history, crises have served simultaneously as a profit and a privation for women—a benefit because it has called forth the best in them and taught them that they can do almost anything, and a disaster because it has robbed them of the men in their lives. Throughout history, too, until recently, women have fallen back into familiar, traditional roles as soon as the crisis passed.

World War I, short-lived as it was—April 6, 1917 to November 11, 1919 for the United States—goaded women into going to work filling jobs left vacant by the 4,743,826 males in service. Many of these women, who lost husbands or sweethearts among the 53,513 killed in battle did not marry again or marry at all and kept their jobs after the war ended. A very few others whose husbands and sweethearts did return continued working.

Simultaneously with the national need for women to work came their motivation for a share in decision-making.

Their first national struggle was for suffrage. It began before World War I and continued with rising voices throughout the country and with increasing numbers of supporters. Even the Shakespeare Club, whose members were "gently born (and) enjoy a pleasant, leisurely life," got into the act. In 1912 guest speaker Anna Buxton Beck spoke on "The Emancipation of Women—Is It Possible or Probable?" Her program was followed by a lively discussion on woman's suffrage. By 1914 the women were debating: "Resolved: That women should have the vote." Mrs. Greer Taylor, Mrs. W. W. Caruth and Mrs. Edwin J. Reeves presented the affirmative and Mrs. John O. McReynolds, Mrs. Lewis Dabney and Mrs. William B. Robinson the negative. The affirmative won.[2]

On Saturday, March 15, 1913, at the home of Mrs. J. B. Adoue the Dallas Equal Suffrage Association was formed. Its membership was open to both women and men. Most of its 39 charter members had already distinguished themselves in the community, among them Alice (Mrs. John S.) Armstrong, Isadore Miner (Pauline Periwinkle) Callaway, Earle Clark (Mrs. W. W.) Caruth, Minnie May Armstrong (Mrs. Edgar Lucus) Flippen and Katherine Seay McReynolds. Another charter member, a young woman who had only recently returned from Chicago, emerged as the definitive leader of the Dallas suffrage movement. She was Nonie McKellar Boren Mahoney, a fourth generation Texan, born in East Texas and reared in Dallas. She had always been a trailblazer.

When Nonie married Illinois State Senator Joseph P. Boren on February 1, 1898, her wedding write-up consumed three pages of Alice Parsons Fitzgerald's *Beau Monde*. Among the grandiose verbiage were detailed descriptions of the guests, from "many first" families; the bride's attire including "a superb crescent of fourteen first water diamonds" which attached her veil to a "wreath of historic orange blossoms." The splendid gifts including "a chest of solid silver . . . with congratulations" from the Forty-First Assembly of Illinois; decor for the at-home wedding included "two stately white Corinthian styled columns delicately twined with cobweb fern that wandered from tangles . . . at the base into great ball clusters of white Jardin roses . . . on the top." The bride had just returned from an extended trip in Europe and the Orient. She had brought with her prizes from the world's capitals to enhance the decor for her wedding. Her trousseau was designed and made by New York couturiers from laces and satins from the famous looms of Europe. Her lingerie was as dainty as cobwebs; her hats and gloves and fans from the ateliers of Paris. But with all this, Alice Fitzgerald managed to convey that the bride was something of a maverick:

> Everything from the bow of the footman to the cutting of the snowy bridal cake was stamped with that clever originality that has ever given the bride a special and unique place in the social sphere. She was ever a girl distinctly individual, with a rare mentality and engaging personality all her own; never

copying but always doing things in her own sweet way, which, in consequence were, always interesting . . . .[3]

All the splendor did not guarantee marital bliss. The couple left following the ceremony to make their home in Chicago where Nonie gave birth to one child, a son, Joseph Boren Mahoney.

By 1913, as Mrs. Nonie Boren Mahoney, she and the child were back in Dallas. A beautiful woman, born somewhere around 1880 or shortly thereafter, the great-granddaughter of Mary Moore Dickson who molded bullets to battle Indians during early Texas Indian raids, Nonie was in her early 30s when she became the Dallas leader for women's suffrage.

One of Texas's leading senators, Judge Barry Miller of Dallas, was strongly opposed to giving women the vote. Like many men of his day, he was certain that women, given the vote, would desert home and family. "The ladies in Dallas," he insisted, "do not want the vote. They are not interested in the hurly-burly world of politics." Nonie did not argue with him, but mustering all of her Southern charm, asked what it would take to convince him to change his mind. The dapper senator answered her with what he considered an impossible challenge. "Dear Lady," he said, "it will take the names of 5,000 Dallas women on a petition for me to change my opinion." Four days later Nonie walked into the State Legislature in session in Austin with a huge suitcase. Escorted to the podium, she drew out a petition with the names of 10,000 Dallas women![4] True to his word, Sen. Miller voted "yes" for Texas to ratify Amendment 19 to the United States Constitution.

Nonie and her followers had their right to vote. It had not been easy. Throughout the country, as early as the 1800s, women had insisted on the right to help shape the laws that governed them. The Territory of Wyoming, on December 10, 1869, had been the first state to give women the right to vote, not because it was particularly enlightened, but because the number of citizens it could claim would increase its chances for statehood. After March 30, 1870, when the Fifteenth Amendment gave black men the right to vote, women redoubled their efforts. Repeatedly the issue was argued in Congress with "gentlemen" from the South especially adamant in their refusal to consider a constitutional amendment. Rep. Tom Heflin, on March 2, 1913, speaking on the record in the House of Representatives, said; "Troubles (occur when) the hens quit the barnyard . . . . It frustrates the rooster who don't know what to do to get them back."

Southerners were not the only "frustrated roosters." On March 4, 1913, in a speech supporting suffrage, the speaker described how one of his constituents, a beautiful young girl, riding on a float in a parade in Washington had been insulted when a ruffian climbed onto the float and accosted her. "She ought to have been at home with her mother," snapped back Rep. Mann of Illinois, "and this wouldn't have happened."

Texas' statewide organization in support of women's suffrage came in 1916. Many women, as always happens, bought into the male notion that the home and family would be destroyed if women left it, even to cast a ballot. Even as the clamor rose, the opposition waned, until, by the time the Constitutional Amendment was introduced in Congress on June 4, 1919, its passage was assured, and "The right of citizens of the United States to vote shall not be denied or abridged by the United States or by any State on account of sex," became the law in all 48 states. (Hawaii and Alaska had not been admitted to the Union.)

Economic necessity had begun to make it essential for many women to work outside their homes, but still far into the twentieth century a double standard prevailed for and among women. By 1910, to be a lady, it was no longer essential that an unmarried woman live with her father or brother or in the homes of others as a virtual servant doing housework or caring for children. She could work for pay, but if she took a room or, heaven forbid, an apartment alone, there remained suspicion about her morals. Still, by far the most coveted role for a woman was marriage, a home and children. A man had "arrived" when he could afford to support a wife and, as his affluence increased, so did the riches he lavished on the female members of his family.

Widows were exempt from the rules of protocol; they were not only allowed but were expected to work. There were, of course, acceptable and unacceptable jobs for them. They could be cooks, seamstresses, boarding house directors, dressmakers, laundresses, milliners or housekeepers. If they were professional, they could teach school or be nurses. Women came to Dallas, as we have seen, with teaching credentials. Most of the first nurses were also trained elsewhere, but in September of 1906 St. Paul Hospital incorporated the first training school for professional nurses in Texas. Other than these two professional careers, most of the work women did—cooking, sewing, laundering—was within their own homes or the homes of more affluent women and fell within prescribed roles for women. Some, like Sarah Cockrell, who was widowed, and Mariah Ervay, who eased from running a boarding house into opening the first Dallas restaurant, were role models for ambitious women.

Sarah Ann Paralee Rupard Erickson followed the stipulated role for working women when she was forced to become the full support for her family in 1903. She was 38 years old when her husband died leaving her to support their seven children ranging in age from one to 14. She moved the family from the eastern part of Dallas County into the city and bought a home at 4011 Kentucky. As a laundress and seamstress, she managed her "cottage industry" alone, providing the economic support for her children. She saw that each was educated.

Proud, as were many women of her time, Sarah did not relate the stories of her struggle to her children and grandchildren. "Letters written to her husband, George Benjamin Erickson, in 1901-1902 indicate that a relative was running their business while Papa was away from home being treated for cancer," says Sara Jane Hibbits McGee, granddaughter of Sarah Erickson. ". . . after Papa died, she took in washing and ironing for folks. I remember helping her, though I did not know at the time they were not family clothes. She had two huge black iron cauldrons in the back yard under which she built fires. She made her own lye soap, used a scrub board and a shortened broom handle for poking the clothes into the boiling water and moving them from one pot to the other, then on to the tubs of cold water for rinsing . . . . I spent as much time as possible with her, but she didn't talk much about her life . . . ." As her children grew up and became self-sufficient, Sarah spread a special kind of loving care community-wide. "She is best remembered for her gifts of love and service to others. In time of crisis she was always there to cook, clean, tend the ill and hold the hands of the dying. She was known throughout Dallas as Aunt Sallie."[5] Sarah died on August 6, 1962, at age 97, and is buried in Grove Hill Cemetery.

Sara Hibbits McGee recalls stories of her grandmother, Sarah Ann Paralee Rupard Erickson, who earned money to support her children by sewing and taking in washing, work that was typical for widows of her time.

Sonoma Beeman Myers was one of the first women to work with heavy machinery. Sometime during the first decade of the twientieth century, she worked for a saddle and harness-making shop. But her greatest pride came from the needlework she did finishing some of the equestrian equipment. Her granddaughter, Ruth Cooper remembers:

> She was at her machine ready to start work by 7 a.m. and did not quit until 6 p.m. except for a brief lunch period, six days a week. It was dark when she left home and dark when she arrived home. She was the only woman that we ever knew to operate the heavy power machines . . . . She worked on harnesses and saddles but her pride and joy were saddles. She did the fine quilting on the fancy saddles. One year, one of her saddles won first prize at the Texas State Fair and she was so proud.[6]

A working woman from an entirely different background and with entirely different gifts emerged on the Dallas scene in 1907 when Carrie Marcus Neiman, her husband, Abraham Lincoln Neiman, and her brother, Herbert Marcus, opened a new specialty store in Dallas on September 10. The store, soon known as The Store, was Neiman-Marcus. Carrie was 24 years old and, in everybody's judgment, a raving beauty. Born in Louisville, Kentucky, she grew to maturity in Dallas tand, by the time she was 21, was top saleswoman and blouse buyer for A. Harris and Company. When her brother, Herbert, was refused the raise he wanted at Sangers where he was working, he quit and persuaded Carrie and her husband Al to move to Atlanta with him and his wife, Minnie, and their six week old son, Stanley. There they went into business holding distress sales for merchants. Carrie and Minnie both wanted to come home to Dallas, so after two years the two families moved back to Texas.

Carrie Marcus Neiman, left, set the fashion pace for Neiman-Marcus, the store she and her husband founded with her brother, Herbert, in 1907. At right, Sally Marcus gives a rousing salute to one of the store's lavish Fortnights.

On the morning of Sunday, September 8, 1907, the Dallas newspapers carried an ad centered by a line drawing of an exquisitely gowned woman in a crushed-tulle-decorated wide-brimmed hat. On either side of this eye-catching lady, the copy promised what the picture suggested, the opening of a new emporium in the city: "We have secured exclusive lines which have never been shown in Texas," the ad promised, "garments that stand in a class alone. As well as the store of Fashion, we will be known as the Store of Quality and Superior Values. Only the finest productions of the best garment workers are good enough.... Every item... will be an evidence of exclusiveness, chic, grace and splendid finish."

Carrie Neiman lived what that ad promised. Idelle Rabin, (See Idelle Goodman Rabin, Part II) founder of another exclusive specialty shop, DelAnn's, "went to finishing school" when she was employed at Neiman-Marcus. She remembers Carrie: "Carrie Neiman and Stanley Marcus were my true mentors. She was *so* elegant! I was absolutely in awe of her. I do things instinctively that she taught me. She never appeared in public without being exquisitely groomed with every item of her apparel coordinated and fitting exactly the image she wanted the store to convey. It would never have entered her head to carry a black bag and wear brown shoes. In the earlier days of my business, sometimes when I was tired or things were not going well or I was in a hurry, it was tempting to leave the house without being well put together. Then I'd remember Miss Carrie and I wouldn't dare. Now, it's as much a part of me to be matched up appropriately as it was for her. Her gift to me was being my role model. His was in giving me such a sense of self-worth. Stanley had such taste level and genius for nurturing talent. When people criticize me for being a perfectionist, I think, 'I have Stanley to thank for that!'"[7]

Mary Collett, who for many years was secretary to Edwin J. Kiest, publisher of *The Dallas Times Herald*, also remembers Carrie Neiman. As a girl growing up in a wealthy Dallas family and later as a single career woman, Mary shopped at Neiman's. "Miss Carrie's title was bridal consultant—but she did so much more. She was one of the three founders. She was on the board of directors and there's no doubt that in the beginning, she set the fashion image for the store—both in her personal appearance and behavior and in the merchandise in the store—what was bought and how it was displayed. She insisted that every person who walked in the store be treated like a person of importance. When a woman came to shop, whether she was a secretary, a bride-to-be with her mother or the wife of a millionaire, she was made to feel that she was the only person shopping at that time. I always thought that in the early days, Carrie was the one who made the store live up to its promise."[8] The success that the store enjoyed did not carry over into Carrie and Al's personal lives and in 1929 they were divorced. Herbert bought out Neiman's shares. For the next 39 years, the Store was run by Marcuses and their offspring; there is a touch of irony in the fact that it is known nationwide and, in some circles, world-wide as "Neimans."

In 1924, Anita Trevino Mongaras Nanez was the first woman in "Little Mexico" to open a business of her own. She moved the furniture out of the family's 1608 Caroline home and turned it into a beauty shop. Then she sent her two older daughters, Ninfa and Olivia to the Marinello Beauty School on Oak Lawn to learn the fine art of hair setting, permanent waving and manicuring.

Anita Nanez Martinez remembers growing up there. "Mother's business was central to our lives. She was an entrepreneur—a term I didn't even know until much later."

Anita Nanez, the mother, was already in business, when Anita, the daughter, was born in 1925. "There were six of us—I am next to the youngest. With such a large family and so little money, Mother wanted to work, but my father was very strict. He would not hear of her getting a job. So one day she moved all of the furniture out of the living room and turned it into a beauty salon. That was acceptable to my father. She didn't defy him, she got around him."

Anita Martinez remembers her mother, Anita Nanez, as "very busy always. But very joyful. She became an inspiration for lots of young women in the neighborhood. I didn't know it at the time. I just took her for granted. It was always a pleasure to be in the beauty shop. Mother kept a pot of fresh coffee brewing all of the time. The shop was filled with women. All of them were Mexican except one Anglo woman with long red hair. There was a lot of talk. A lot of laughter."

Even before she started to school, little Anita was helping out in the beauty shop handing curling papers to her mother and sisters, cleaning combs and brushes. Senora Nanez charged $1.50 for a permanent wave and later, when they came in, $3.00 for an oil permanent. A shampoo and hair set was 75 cents and a manicure 50 cents to a dollar. Sometimes, when there was a crisis in a family—a death or a wedding, for instance—the Nanez beauty operators would give their services free.

The permanent waving machine was, by today's standards, a monstrous piece of equipment that stood in the corner of the shop. Hair would be rolled on special curlers and each curl encased in a clamp protruding from the machine on wires. When all of the clamps were in place, electricity was turned on and fed through the wires, thus curling the hair. It was a tricky business. If the machine fed too much electricity, the scalp burned and sometimes blistered. And, sometimes, the hair would be too "cooked," and be brittle and break off when it was uncurled. If the heat was too cool, the hair came out limp and unmanageable. Wishes of the women varied along with the texture and quality of their hair. Some wanted a tight curl that would last a long time; others wanted a soft manageable wave. It took a lot of know-how to operate a beauty business.

Anita Nanez was on the cutting edge of the nation's burgeoning beauty business, opening her salon at the time when the industry was in its infancy. In a five-year period from 1921 when women, in large numbers, first began to cut and curl their hair, until 1926, beauty shops in the United States increased from 5,000 to 21,000.[9] The Nanez shop was one of those 21,000.

In 1930 or '31—Anita Martinez remembers "I was five or six," the Caroline Street home burned. "I can still see my mother running out of the house in her nightgown, her hair flying in the wind, with that permanent wave machine in her arms. It was the Saturday night before Easter. She had managed to buy us all new clothes and they were lying out ready for us to get dressed for mass on Easter morning. Everything went up in flames—except Mother's permanent waving machine. She managed to rescue us and her

Anita Mongaras Nanez opened the first woman-owned business in Little Mexico, a beauty shop in the living room of her home. When a fire destroyed the house, she ran out with her livelihood, the permanent wave machine.

livelihood." The family moved to 1906 Akard Street, Akard at Cedar Springs. The first thing Anita Nanez did was plug in her machine to see if still worked. It did, and she was back in business. She barely missed a day of work.

Anita Trevino Mongaras Nanez died in 1950. "She was a woman ahead of her time," her daughter said. "She was strong. She was stubborn. She was responsible. She was resilient. She gave us (her children) lots of room to develop our own identities. She brought us up to have personal integrity. She was reared in the Catholic faith, but she was not dogmatic. She left us free to explore other options. She supported us if she thought we were right and she chastised us if she thought we were wrong. Sometimes she was wrong, as when I had a good job after Daddy died and she wanted me to leave school and continue working full time. I was a stubborn as she was. I convinced her that I could be a lot more help to her after I got my diploma. And I went back to school against her will . . . . She was a trail blazer for younger women in Little Mexico. I am one of them . . . ."

Mary Collett did not prepare herself to be a working girl, was disenchanted with the world of work and, typical of so many women of her time, did not trust other women, those who worked and the wives of the men she knew. Born in Memphis, Tennessee, on March 5, 1900, she moved to Dallas with her parents in 1910. She grew up on Junius Street in East Dallas just below Carroll and some six blocks west of Collett which bears her family name. Her playground was "all of East Dallas. We ran and played in a world bounded by Haskell and Junius and Peak and Worth and Reiger and Columbia, even as far out as Fowler's Orphan's Home. We knew all of the people in all of the houses and we skipped in and out of them. I had a wonderful, carefree childhood. We were a part of the Munger family and the best families were our friends."

Mary's father was a cotton buyer and general manager of Continental Gin Company. Her mother was a homemaker "not trained for anything except being a wife and mother." Mary attended Holley Hall and had her bags packed to go Wellesley in the early fall of 1921 when her father died in his sleep. "It's a beautiful way to go—but when a cotton broker dies, the family support goes. We were penniless. I was the second child in our family of five children. My older brother had already left home and was living out of town. My sister was at SMU, so I became my mother's financial support. I was *it*. Instead of going to college, I went to work. I knew how to type. I took shorthand at night. I went to work for Southwestern Life Insurance Company filling in policies. I *hated* it. I had to make myself get up in the mornings. Then I got a job with the city attorney's office. It was a lot better."

When the *Times Herald* moved to Pacific and Griffin, Edwin J. Kiest, publisher, called Mary and asked her to come to work for him. "I really hated to leave the city, but Mr. Kiest and my father had been friends and I thought I would have a good job and a good time, so I went. Mr. Kiest thought working for a newspaper was all the honor anybody needed—and paid his employees accordingly. Not any of us made much and our lives were not our own. We worked from 8 to 5 six days a week and any other time we were needed. I was expected to be at my desk and at his every call when Mr. Kiest was in his office. I got there in the mornings before he did and saw that everything was neat and clean and in place for him. I was free to leave when he left but I was always on call. There was no overtime. We got one week of vacation in the summertime. We got Christmas, Thanksgiving and New Year's off—if there wasn't anything that had to be done. On State Fair Day and the Fourth of July when everybody else had a holiday, I went to the office and cleaned out all the boss's desks and spiffed the place up. This was expected. I got nothing extra for it, even bought my own lunch and paid my own carfare . . . . I went to work for a pittance—I don't remember how much but when I was finally raised to $125 a week, I thought I was the richest girl on earth. It didn't occur to me to expect a promotion. No woman in Dallas held an executive position. Executive secretaries were the peak; we all knew each other. We could get things done in the city because we kept the records for our bosses and we made suggestion. Really we controlled things because everybody had to go through us to get to our bosses. It never occurred to us to expect any personal credit."

When things were running smoothly at the paper, Edwin J. Kiest "sent me out to stir things up. He said newspapers should never be quiet . . . . He said women ruined newspapers, but it didn't keep him from expecting me to be on call 24 hours a day . . . ."
—Mary Collett, 1984.

In 1924 Mary moved to 2454 Haynie and lived there for more than half a century. "It was close enough that I could walk to SMU and when I had the time and money I started going to night school. I have enough credits for a Ph.D, and I don't even have a bachelor's."

Even though her social life was severely limited by the restrictions her job placed on her, Mary was having a good time. She was young and healthy and "thought I was in control of my life. Mr. Kiest would say to me. 'Mary, go out in the news room and stir something up around here. It's too quiet. A newspaper shouldn't be this quiet.' I settled two strikes before they had a chance to get going. All you have to do is know a few of the right people, listen to what they say and take care of their needs. I liked working for the *Herald*. I knew all of the prominent men in Texas.

"But, I couldn't join anything. When the Junior League was formed, I was asked to be a charter member, but couldn't because I had to work. I was invited to join the Shakespeare Club. I wanted to so badly, but I couldn't do that either. They met in the daytime and no secretary asked for time off to do anything. My aunt lived with us and she'd say, 'Mary's just a working girl; she isn't a part of the life we know.'

"I arranged for all the company parties, everything from ordering the food to arranging the flowers to inviting the guests to hiring the help. I'd stay to see that every detail was in place and then I'd go home. I loved doing it. It made me feel important. I really wouldn't have wanted to stay—fifteen to twenty men and one woman. Not me.

"Mr. Kiest didn't trust women. He'd say, 'Banks and women ruin newspapers. They move too slow.'"

Edwin Kiest lived at the Adolphus Hotel. His wife, Elizabeth Patterson Kiest, had died in 1917 leaving him one of the most eligible bachelors in the city. "His wife had died before I went to work for him. I knew her, but never well. I was always running errands for Mr. Kiest. I'd run across the street for cigars and tobacco. Sometimes I worked as much at Mr. Kiest's Adolphus suite as at the *Herald*. I did the shopping for all the men's gifts. Neiman's, A. Harris, Sangers, Linz, Everts. I had more fun shopping than anything. When he was in a lavish mood, Mr. Kiest loved to give presents.

"Mr. Kiest had an operation and was given eight months to live. He lived eight years and I was on call every minute of that eight years. No matter where I went—picture show, church, even on vacation—I left a telephone number where I could be reached in case of an emergency. One night I was at a dance in Fort Worth and I got a call at midnight that Mr. Kiest needed me. I took a taxi all the way to Dallas. When I walked in, he wanted to know if his *Western* magazine had arrived that day.

"Mr. Kiest promised I'd be well taken care of in his will and I was...I know because I kept all his records. Two weeks before he died he changed the will. I know how it happened. He gave the *Herald* to seven men—Tom Gooch, B. C. Jefferson, Skye Meade, Allen Merriam, Johnny Runyon, Clyde Taber and Albert Switzer. Two of them convinced him to change the will and leave me out. If my mother hadn't been living, I would have sued the hell out of them. I didn't because they would have said I was his mistress and it would have killed Mama.

"When Mr. Kiest died, those men cut my throat. Mr. Kiest was a just man, but I want my justice tempered with a little mercy. I made Tom Gooch fire me. I went to work every day for a year, hung up my hat and sat in my office with nothing to do. People who didn't know thought I was a little crazy, but every day, just by being there, I made them remember what they had done."

After she left the paper in 1942, Mary worked for a few months in real estate and then went to Korea as a recreation director to the troops.

"I miss the Dallas I grew up in. I miss not knowing the bus driver by name—and having him wait for me a second when he saw me coming. I miss Miss Mary at Sangers. I miss not knowing the policeman on the corner. I miss being a part of a neighborhood. Once I knew every prominent man in Texas. Now I'm living on bread and water. Do you understand why I won't let the *Times Herald* come into my house?"

Mary Collett, a typical executive secretary and working woman of the 1920s through World War II, never married, never had children, was survived by all four of her siblings when she died on January 25, 1986. She is buried at Restland.

Nelle C. Johnston, president of the Foundation for the Callier Center for a decade, 1964-1974, is typical of a generation of executive secretaries who could run their company's businesses equally as well as could their bosses.

The influence of women as executive secretaries has been vastly underrated. For about half a century—1920 when women first began to work outside their homes in large numbers until 1970—men in power required the help of at least three women. In a perfect pecking order, their wives managed their homes and their children, their mothers headed their cheering sections, and their personal secretaries managed their offices. The purpose of all three was to make the executive look good. Only his mother, of the three, dared to question his importance and she rarely did because the other two made him appear as significant as he thought he was.

As his importance mounted, the executive required an additional support system—a pool of secretaries, file clerks and typists, but the executive secretary was the most indispensable. She was the business manager, the chief public relations person, the office hostess, the troubleshooter and the diplomat. Usually, she also was the liaison between her boss's private and public lives. She knew his wedding anniversary, his family's birthdays and other important personal data. She kept addresses and telephone numbers of everybody he might need to contact and could reach them in a matter of seconds. She opened his mail, arranged it by priority of importance on his desk, sharpened his pencils, emptied his wastebasket, answered his routine correspondence, personally typed any sensitive letters and/or contracts and filed everything he considered significant under lock where she could retrieve it in moments. She made his travel arrangements and knew, often better than his wife, what he was doing and where he could be reached. She anticipated his every need, whether it was a contract for a major business deal, a cup of coffee, a clean shirt or an aspirin.

In Dallas—and doubtless in other places—executive secretaries had an clique of their own. They dressed and acted as the most important woman in the company. Executive secretaries knew each other, mostly by telephone, set time and place for their bosses to confer, scheduled luncheon dates and golf games. But they rarely confided their grievances to each other because to do so would have threatened their own ability to handle everything.

Women in the lower echelons of the organization were both jealous of and in awe of the executive secretary. If they were ambitious, they emulated her behavior. If resentful, they gossiped about her in the ladies lounge. In both cases, they were cautious of their appearance, behavior and conversation around her—because they knew it would go directly back to the Boss.

Often, when companies under pressure from laws and changing social customs found it expedient to list women on their letterheads, executive secretaries were the first to be included. They became executive assistants and office managers. Some were listed as secretary of the company. Mostly, they continued to do what they had always done.

The organization and the secretary were both fortunate when the executive deserved the adulation heaped upon him. Sometimes he did. Dallas produced many men who led companies with both ability and kindness. But the untold truth is that many of their secretaries could have handled the business just as well as they.

Many executive secretaries had very limited personal lives. Many did not marry because their time was consumed by the men for whom they worked and they were, thus, wedded to the company. But the real tragedy is that few are remembered for their enormous contributions. While the names of their bosses are recorded and regaled, they are not.

Nelle Johnston is an exception. She may be the most outstanding executive secretary that Dallas has ever known. Long after it is forgotten that she managed the office for Erik Jonsson before, during and after he was mayor of Dallas, she will be lauded for her personal contributions to the city. She is rare in another important way: She carved her own niche of service to the city separate and apart from the enormous contributions of her larger-than-life boss. She has been publicly lauded for her contributions to the Callier Center for Communications Disorders, but she is equally proud of chairing the task force on family planning for Goals for Dallas. "My contribution was being smart enough to find the right people for it," she said.

TODDLING TOWARD EQUALITY / 250

Julia Haswell Brown became the owner of Ripley Shirt Company where she began her career as a 17-year-old high school graduate.

Nelle Johnston was honored October 27, 1992, with the Nelle C. Johnston Chair in Communication Disorders established by Callier Center for Communication Disorders of the University of Texas at Dallas. She was lauded as "the person most responsible for the existence of the Callier Center . . . . an indefatigable force in the early efforts to form an institution that house . . . educational and clinical programs to help those who suffer from communication disorders, as well as research program to understand their causes and treatments." During the ceremonies a sculpture, "The Joy of Sound," by Annie Davis, was unveiled.

Nelle Johnston, like most executive secretaries, was "very uncomfortable with public recognition," she said in a 1992 interview. She, like most women who gave their lives in service to the city in the names of the men for whom they worked, are sources of untapped treasures of information.

A few women, like Julia Josephine Haswell Brown, rose to positions of personal responsibility from their beginning as secretaries. Julia went to work for Ripley Shirt Company as a 17-year-old, a month after graduating from Adamson High School. Forty-two years later she was sole owner of the company. The daughter of Joseph S. and Jettie McCombs Haswell, Julia was born in Cedar Hill on October 24, 1909, and moved to Dallas when she was an infant. The family lived at 304 West 12th Street only a short walk from the Ripley Shirt Factory at 410 South Beckley. Julia Brown talked about her life[10] as a working woman in Dallas:

"I lived at home with my parents. It was a short walk, only a few blocks to work. I went home for lunch. I worked in the office. I was George Ripley's secretary. Katie Rice Ripley—(see Chapter 26) supervised the sewing room. The business was going beautifully. She branched out. Did a lot of community work. Got into the birth control business with Margaret Sanger. As her work became more involved, I helped her. I worked about 50/50 on shirts and birth control. She was easy to work with."

Julia's starting salary was about $25 a week. "Everybody worked by the hour. Nobody had a set salary. If we worked three days, we got paid for three days. But we were making 300 shirts a day, so there were very few short weeks. I don't think I ever missed a paycheck." Employees worked an eight-hour day, longer if there was a contract to fill."

Julia met her husband at Ripley Shirt Company. George Jerald Brown was in charge of the cutting room. They were married on March 7, 1930, in the apartment over the shirt factory. "My, what a wedding! Everybody in the company came. And our families. And friends. We had about 300 guests!" The newlyweds moved in with her parents, continued to walk to work and to save their money. He was making $26 a week, a dollar more than his bride." Still working by the hour, "We brought home over $60 a week. We were rich! We could go to the grocery store and spend $3 and have several sacks. We had to haul it home in a little red wagon."

The Browns and the Ripleys shared far more than an employee-employer relationship. They were friends. "When they would go to New York on a buying trip, my husband and I would stay in their apartment and oversee everything. When they moved to Plymouth Road, we still stayed in their house when they would be out of Dallas." In 1934 the Browns bought their first car, a Plymouth. Gasoline cost 9 cent a gallon."

In the late 1930s, the Ripleys decided to sell the shirt factory to five of their stockholders. "We bought as much as we could." One by one as the other partners wanted to be free, the Browns bought more and more stock. "This hasn't been as easy as it sounds," says Julia Brown at 81. "I worked hard. I worked hardest during World War II. My husband and I made shirts. We had contracts with the Army. Employees were hard to get. We kept the place going. Lots of nights we'd finish an order at 3 o'clock in the morning. We'd go into the rest room and sleep three or four hours and go back to work . . . .

"My husband had a deferment because the government said he was doing an essential job. But I needed more insurance. If he had to go into service, I wanted to be sure he got into something he enjoyed. So right after the war started, we went out to Lou

Foote's (a flying school) and signed up for lessons. I took lessons with him. We both got our pilots' license. I had no intention of using mine, but it was sure fun doing it together. I've enjoyed my life—wouldn't exchange any part of it!"

In 1946 the Brown's only child, Joseph Jerald Brown, was born. "He grew up at this plant. I stayed home until he went to school. The next day I was came back to work." George Brown died in 1964. Very suddenly. With a heart attack. At the factory. "It nearly killed me. It was a whole year before I could walk in here without crying.— We did everything together. I am often asked how we could live so closely together 24 hours a day and still be such great friends and companions. It's just as much a puzzle to me why other people can't."

Jerry Brown was 18 when his father died. He wanted to get right into the business. "This company was all he wanted, but I wanted him to have all of the experience possible away from it so that he would know how other companies did things." He went to SMU, holds degrees in engineering and administration, worked for several companies including Texas Instruments. By 1970 only two people remained as owners of Ripley Shirt, Julia Brown and her partner, Sid Henry. "He wanted to sell out. I called my son—he was still at SMU—and asked him if he'd like to run Ripley Shirt Company and he said it was what he had hoped for all of his life. Then, I picked up my books and went to the bank. They loaned me the money. I am sole owner—except for what I've given Jerry. He's president. He runs it. He brought in some wonderful fresh new ideas. It's exciting to see the changes . . . ."

As 1991 dawned, Julia Brown still went to work every day. "I keep the books. Make all of the deposits. Pay all of the bills. It keeps me busy."

Daisy Spillman Adams owned a fish market . . . . She also owned vast farmlands, helped operate an oil company and was active in numerous women's clubs. And, she painted.

While the best stories of what life was like for working women in Dallas are told by those who live it, the conditions of the world, the country and the city formed the framework in which they performed. In 1915 the Dallas Shakespeare Club heard Stella White Spence deliver a paper on "Women in Power," in which she said, "Woman's instinct has now grown into reason. Modern woman is turning to professions in life, but in the breast-plate of her profession she still carries the distaff of the home." Another paper on the same day held that "It is woman who is the final standard of the race. One that is not engaged in productive labor is a parasite, and with parasitism comes decadence."[11]

Volume II of the *Encyclopedia of Texas*, published in 1922, gives biographical sketches of 1,782 prominent "Men of Texas." Included are 13 women, less than one per cent of the total. All but two of the 13 are artists, music teachers and expression teachers. The two are Daisy Spillman Adams, who ran a fish market on Main Street and Fannie Galloupe, proprietor of a family-styled hotel. Both women took over the businesses following the deaths of their husbands. But, in both cases, the women had worked with their husbands in running the businesses.

Daisy Adams was far more than a fish market owner. Born in Fort Worth, the daughter of William and Cora Spillman, she grew up in Kansas City and moved to Dallas with her parents in 1895. The next year she married Charles Pennel Adams. Together they studied the prevailing industrial conditions, opened the fish market at 802 Main Street, bought farm land and invested in ship building, truck farming, banking and oil. Charles Adams died in 1910, 16 years after the couple married leaving Daisy with a teenage daughter, Jacqueline, and as sole owner of the extensive businesses. By the time Jacqueline married Ed Thomas and moved to 4726 Drexel Drive, Daisy was vice president of the Tarver Oil Company, vice president of the Tarver Ship Building Company, vice president of the Liberty National Bank in Waco and owner/manager of a 2,500-acre truck farming enterprise on the West Dallas Pike. In addition, typical of most successful Dallas women, Daisy had eclectic interests and contributions beyond the business world. She was a founder of the Dallas Woman's Forum and a founder of the Dallas Art Association. She was a member of the Dallas Woman's Business Club and served on the executive board of the YWCA and was a devoted, contributing member of the First Baptist Church. She was an artist—pictures and tapestries—whose work was recognized in art circles of the Southwest.

TODDLING TOWARD EQUALITY / 252

In the early 1920s women lifted themselves out of the past—literally. They bobbed their hair, lifted their skirts, powdered and rouged their faces, wore lipstick and some—the more daring—nail polish, went to work, smoked cigarettes (it would be 50 years before they would learn this was killing them), moved out of their parents' homes when they grew up, began to work their way through college if their families could not afford to send them, often took jobs in other cities when they graduated and chose the men they married.

Women's short skirts and short hair caused all kinds of problems in the 1920s. Lowering moral standards, break-up of marriage, break-down of motherhood, rising health problems were all blamed on women—the way they looked, the way they dressed, the way they behaved. An article in the *Times Herald* on Thursday, January 27, 1921, is headlined "Short Skirts Cause Epidemic of Flu Among Women Folk" and attributes to Dr. R. S. Copeland, health commissioner the claim that "Short skirts and exposed necks and knees cause more colds and pneumonia that most people realize."

By 1926 bobbed hair, still controversial, had arrived. Most of the socially elite pictured in the papers had short hair, but shorn locks on women was still new enough to be newsworthy. On March 22, 1926, the *Times Herald* ran a story headlined, "Bobbed Hair Brings 21,000 Beauty Shops." The vast increase in beauty shops (from 5,000 in 1921 to 21,000 in 1926) was serving 25 million American women, who "now visit beauty shops regularly to have their hair trimmed, shingled, waved and treated . . . . the bob has democratized the art of beautification. Formerly only women of wealth could afford to patronize the beauty shop. Now beauty shops derive their chief support from stenographers, office workers, housewives and shop girls. Popularity of the bob has led to the almost universal adoption by American women of aids to personal adornment . . . . It has helped to build a business involving millions of dollars annually."

In 1925 house dresses cost 69¢, swim suits $3.98, window shades, 15¢ each and tomatoes, 4 2/3¢ each . . . . A tree-covered country home on seven acres near Garland sold for $3,500.

My mother was one of those women who had her hair bobbed in 1926. She had always been proud of her lustrous tresses, long enough that she could sit on her hair and she wore it in a coronet halo around her head, a style she again adopted in the later years of her life. But the day she had her hair cut "wind-blown style," layered and marcelled and came home to four-year-old me, I thought she was the most beautiful woman I had ever seen. I sat at the kitchen table and gazed at her. My less enthralled father, like many men of his time, had opposed the hair cut. He would hardly look at her.

By the middle of the 1920s decade, the cost of living had climbed a little, but prices were still unbelievably low when compared to the present time. At Sanger's one could buy lingerie imported from France—slips, teddies and gowns—for $2.98, a swim suit in the latest style for $3.98 and a gingham housedress for 69 cents. Window shades at Weir's Furniture Store were 15 cents each, a gas range could be had for $59.75 and an eight-piece genuine mahogany dining room suite—table, hutch and six chairs—for $135. Or, if you couldn't afford the $135, you could rent a furnished five-room duplex at 4506 Swiss Avenue for $67.50 month. It contained a piano, an electric vacuum, Sealy mattresses, a Herrick refrigerator and a Detroit Jewel range. Further out, a country home site of seven and a half acres on a paved road 2 1/2 miles east of Garland with numerous pecan trees, two spring-fed lakes, one stocked with white perch, partly sheep-stock fenced and with a two-room camp home could all be purchased for $3,500.

At the grocery store you could buy new potatoes for two and a half cents a pound and fresh tomatoes, 6 for 28 cents. Ked's tennis shoes were $1.23. At the drug store you could re-supply your bathroom with essentials for less than $4.00—79 cents for a box of Coty's face powder, Palmolive Shampoo, 3 for $1.00; a large Listerine for 72 cents; 3 bars of Lux soap for 29 cents and 8 rolls of Silk toilet tissue for 98 cents.

With so many women going out to work, it was only natural that conflict would develop between women who stayed at home to manage the family and those who brought home a pay check. As essential as her income may have been to support the family, women who worked were perceived as lacking *something*. And as valuable as the services of a wife and mother were, many of them resented their flapper sisters who had money, without asking any man for it, to get their hair bobbed, paint their nails and go out dancing.

In 1926, Dorothy Dix, the arbiter of homespun advice, devoted a column to the value of the housewife in which she said the housewife spends 91 hours a week working for her family and earns only $39 doing it. She computed the tasks a housewife performed at market value, adding that "she has no holidays nor time off.... Is it any wonder that ... women, knowing they have earned a good salary and that they are being cheated out of (it) ... come to hate the husbands who are so unfair?"[12]

As information of this kind began to creep into homes throughout the country, women began to ask questions. It does not take much imagination to know that many husbands had Dix's column served along with their morning coffee, and even when women could not change their husbands, it helped wives know that they were not all alone, that other women were speaking up in their behalf.

What it did, more than anything else, was make women think, prod them into asking questions before they rushed blindly into matrimony. As a result, the age at which a girl married moved up slightly. In Dallas as industry and services increased, more and more women went to work for a paycheck.

By 1927, 15,000 Dallas women were working in 125 occupations, trades and professions. There were 2,329 stenographers, 1,510 clerks, 1,193 salesladies, 380 bookkeepers, 315 cashiers, 622 nurses, 895 school teachers, 371 seamstresses, 162 dressmakers and 295 milliners. Five hundred and seventy two women were managing their own businesses. These statistics were compiled by the first Dallas chapter of the National Association of Business and Professional Women. This group, organized in 1921 by Grace M. Whiting, intended "to bring into closer relationship women of the different professions and vocations, and, by precept and example, assist the coming businesswomen to attain a credible position in the world of business." For years to come B&PW would play a significant role for women in Dallas. It produced some of the outstanding women leaders—Judge Sarah T. Hughes, Dr. Minnie Lee Maffett, Ruth Fox and Atty. Hermine Tobolowsky, among them—who would remain in the forefront in the ongoing struggle for equality for women. It is significant that 3,413 of the total of 15,000, 23 per cent of the working women in 1927, were married.

This indicates a subtle but significant change in society toward women who worked.

24

••••

THE PACESETTERS

In 1925, professional women and those holding jobs in non-traditional fields were very few—a percentage so low that it barely made a dot on the scale. Of the 15,000 working women in Dallas found by the Business and Professional Women in 1927, only a handful held non-traditional jobs.

The few women who were in non-traditional jobs and the even fewer who ran their own organizations were break-through pioneers, especially significant because they were the harbingers of the future. Among them were Charles Etta Emory Jones in insurance; Frances Hexamer in law; Florence George Martin in agriculture; Mary Winn Smoots in publishing; Genevieve Shea in medicine; Juanita Wade in dentistry; Vareta Pinkston Gulley and Maria Luna in business and Edith Therrel Wilmans in politics.

Edith Eunice Therrel Wilmans, in 1923, was the first woman to serve in the Texas Legislature. Barely a toddler when she moved with her family to Dallas around 1885 from her native Lake Providence, Louisiana, she was educated in the Dallas public schools and at age 18 married Hall Wilmans. She followed the traditional role of wife/mother until she became a founding member of the Dallas Equal Suffrage Association where she worked directly with Carrie Chapman Catt, the national president. She was also a founder of the Dallas Housewives League and of the Democratic Women of Dallas County. Elected president of the Democratic Women's Association of Texas, Edith became increasingly frustrated by Texas laws that curtailed advances for women. She studied law and was admitted to the Texas bar in 1918. She opened her offices in Dallas. Four years later, at the age of 40, she was elected to the legislature.

Edith was such a curiosity among the Good Old Boys and such a fascination with their wives and other women that it was difficult for her to concentrate on her job. When she arrived in Austin, she discovered that no rest room facilities had been provided for women.

The press was fascinated with her, but seemed far more interested in how she looked than in what she thought. Her every move was dutifully reported to the public. She arrived for work on her first day as a lawmaker wearing a brown satin dress, a gray astrakhan sport coat, a gold and gray turban, and brown shoes and hose. She did not wear "the proverbial bouquet."[1]

She was also expected to be a social creature. From women's groups, where she had garnered the support that elected her, there were constant invitations to speak. The multiple roles she was expected to perform occurred in an atmosphere where male guffaws and off-color jokes limited her ability to slip easily into the professional role she coveted.

When the Democratic Women of Travis County met in January of 1923, "There was some disappointment at the failure of Mrs. Edith Wilmans, state president of the organization and the first woman representative to the Texas legislature, to arrive in time for the meeting."[2]

The women continued to be disappointed. They felt shunned when she did not respond to them.

> "Mrs. Edith Wilmans of Dallas . . . will be a figure in the life of the Capitol city during her stay in Austin . . . . It is not to be supposed that Mrs. Wilmans will give herself much time from her duties to enter into social affairs . . . but the Travis county democratic women are planning to entertain with a dinner in her honor at some time which will suit her convenience.[3]

The story continued that there were some 300 members of the organization and they were "anxious to meet the woman who has gained recognition as a leader."

It did not take long for the new female legislator to make waves. On the second day of her tenure, following an opening address by William Lusk of Bonham, "at an informal assembly of legislators held on the mezzanine floor of the Driskill . . . some heralded as a rally for Lewis T. Carpenter for speaker . . . events began to turn the meeting into a fun-fest. Mrs. Wilmans got the floor and condemned in strong terms two speakers whom she charged with attempted tactics at ridicule. After Mrs. Wilmans left the floor, the tone of the meeting was considerably different . . . ."[4]

Edith Wilmans was the first woman to preside as Speaker of the House. She served out her one term (1923-1925), but did not run for reelection because Gov. Pat Neff, in 1924, appointed her a special judge of the Texas Supreme Court. While serving in the legislature, she organized and was the first president of "Women Legislators of the House." Twice she ran for governor and was defeated both times.

Somewhere along the way her teen-age marriage to Wilmans was dissolved and in 1929 she married Henry A. Born of Chicago and left Texas. The marriage soon ended in divorce and she returned to Dallas where she again practiced law. In 1935 she retired and bought a farm in Jack County 16 miles east of Jacksboro. She lived there alone, raised a few cattle and goats. She did most of the farm chores. She personally refinished the exterior of her ranch home with native rocks from the hills of her farm. In 1958 she fell and broke her hip. Her failing health compelled her to leave the land she loved and return to Dallas where she spent the last eight years of her life living with her daughter, Mrs. R. L. Bentley. She died March 21, 1966, at the age of 84.

Charles Etta Emory Jones was the first Dallas woman to become an executive in a Dallas insurance company. She began her career in 1916 as a clerk in the offices of the Excelsior Life Insurance Company. She had moved to Dallas at age eight from Sherman where she was born. Educated in the Dallas schools, she went to work shortly after she graduated from high school and worked her way up to become secretary-treasurer, the first woman to hold an executive position in a Dallas life insurance company. She retired in 1958 after a 42-year career in insurance.

Florence George Martin excelled in agriculture. She came by her love of the land naturally. She grew up in Mississippi to landowning and landloving parents, Zachary Taylor and Sarah Jane Snelson George. Educated in private schools in Mississippi, she absorbed agriculture and the care of farm animals and show horses by osmosis and as a very young child assisted in the care of the farmlands and animals, asking questions and honing her natural inclinations. As a young girl, she moved with her parents to Hood County, Texas, where the family settled on a ranch near Granbury. She enrolled in Methodist College at Granbury and took extension courses in agriculture at Texas A&M College before it was designated as a university and long before women were allowed to enroll as full-time students. Her "degree" from Texas A&M, with riders, is one of the first ever issued to a female.

In 1899 Florence George married William Clifton Martin and moved to Dallas. She lived in two different worlds—as a society matron in the city and as a landowner and ranch manager experimenting in all of the latest agricultural advances in Texas. Strongly encouraged by her husband, she managed a 6,000-acre ranch in Bosque County from 1913-1915. Five years later she took over the operation of an experimental community near Marshall. Located on 2,400 acres, it was known as the Darco Community. She divided the land into 100-acre tracts and established an experimental model community that drew national attention. By 1924, 28 families lived in the Darco community. They moved onto the land as tenants but worked to become owners of their 100 acres. Florence selected the tenants and served as overseer, adviser, financier and often as confidante of the families. In 1924 she termed the experiment highly successful. In Dallas, Florence was a Red Cross volunteer and a member of the Mary K. Craig Class, the Dallas Woman's Club, the League of Women Voters and the Dallas Art Association. As a writer, she concentrated on farming and ranching subjects and published

When Edith Wilmans joined the State Legislature in 1923, the first woman to be elected, she was a cause for great curiosity. The women who elected her were disappointed when she wanted to make law rather than socialize with them and the press was more concerned with what she wore than with what she said or did.

many articles. She was active in the Dallas Pen Women and the Texas Press Association. She united many of her interests in 1920 when she was named rural life chairman of the Texas Federation of Women's Clubs and spent four years outlining and instituting a program of work for rural districts which served as a model in the country.

Frances Hexamer, in 1918, was the first woman to be admitted to the Dallas Bar, but for years afterward law and other professions were considered a man's world and any woman who wanted to enter them abnormal. In an otherwise complimentary biographical sketch in "Men of Texas," an encyclopedia published in 1922, Frances is termed "a refutation of man's old contention that a woman would lose her feminine charm by mingling in the affairs of men." The daughter of Mr. and Mrs. C. F. Hexamer, Frances was a small child when her parents moved to Dallas from Canton, Ohio, in 1897. She went to work for a Dallas law firm when she was 18 years old and was successfully representing six companies when she reached the legal age of 21 and became eligible to be admitted to practice law. Those were the days when a person could "read law" as an apprentice with another attorney or attorneys and be admitted to the bar without going to law school or passing a state bar examination. Not only did this allow favored individuals without sufficient credentials to become lawyers, it also served to entrench good old boys in the profession and to exclude female intruders. That Frances was accepted is a testament, not only to her legal ability, but to her genius at having the male lawyers support her.

Though she was lauded as an example of female independence, Frances continued to live at home, 3015 South Boulevard, with her parents. She did practice alone with offices at 811 Great Southern Life Building. As secretary of the Professional Women's Club in Dallas, she encouraged other women to enter professions and as legislative chair of the State Federation of Business and Professional Women, she lobbied the legislature for the equal treatment of women in hiring and promotion. She was also active in the Dallas Bar Association and in the Young Lawyers Club. She was held up as a role model: "Miss Hexamer is one of the trail blazers . . . (who) has made her way, unassisted, in a difficult profession and her experience ought to be of value to women who follow after her."[5]

Edalah Connor Glover was the first female advertising executive in Dallas, manager of the Beau Monde Publishing Company. Edalah began her advertising career in 1918 at the *Dallas Dispatch* for $30 a month. In June of 1919 she was named advertising manager of a new publication, the *Dallas Saturday Night*. She helped to organize the new Beau Monde Publishing Company, the successor to Alice Parsons Fitzgerald's earlier newspaper. Edalah was a Dallas girl. Born on June 21, 1892, to Mr. and Mrs. Meyers Connor, she was educated in the Dallas public schools and as a young child showed an artistic talent. Her father, a physician, also excelled in art. She entered Baylor Medical University while her father was a professor there, but withdrew from both art and medicine when she married Robert C. Glover with the determination to devote her life to being a conforming housewife and society matron. It didn't take long for this existence to pall. She began to look around for work that would use her talents and provide for her an independent income. She found it in advertising. She went to work as automobile editor of the *Dispatch* and after a year was offered a position as real estate and home building editor of the *Times Herald*. She combined advertising with column writing and in one week secured $42,000 worth of advertising to launch *Saturday Night*. Six months later when she and a group of friends decided to form Beau Monde Publishing Company, she broke her own advertising sales record by securing $47,000 worth of advertising in one week. This was a spectacular record for the time and a record that would be honored in today's market. Edalah Glover founded the Woman's Advertising League of Dallas and served as its first president, a title she held until her untimely death at the age of 29.

Juanita Wade was the first practicing woman dentist in Dallas. She was born in Maryville, Tennessee, on January 11, 1896. Her parents William and Sophia Morton Wade, moved to Dallas when Juanita was six months old to escape family friction brought about by the Civil War because some family members were Confederates and others were Unionists.

Juanita, a bright and precocious child, was educated in the Dallas public schools and at Lady of Good Counsel. She graduated from high school in 1911 at the age of 15. Her brother, her only sibling, was but an infant. Her father, a Tennessee farmer, unaccustomed to the vagaries of Texas soil and climate, barely made a subsistence livelihood. He died when Juanita was preparing to enter college leaving her mother to take in sewing and washing to earn a living. There was no money for college.

For most of her life, the young girl had harbored a secret yen to become a doctor. Her mother was adamantly opposed, not only because she could not finance a medical education, but also because she felt that such a career was inappropriate for a woman. Without money and without family encouragement, Juanita enrolled at North Texas State Normal College and completed a degree in education in 1914. She was 18 years old and had a teaching certificate she did not want to use. Her mother's brother offered a lifeline. He was a physician and would help Juanita go to medical school if she would come to California and work in the small hospital he owned. She was elated. She entered the University of California at Berkeley Medical College in September of 1914.

The boys in her medical school class harassed Juanita unmercifully, doing everything they could to make her drop out.[6] Letters from her mother constantly reminded the young struggling student that medicine was not a suitable profession for a woman. Deathly afraid of earthquakes, Juanita returned to Dallas.

In the fall of 1915 Juanita Wade transferred her medical credits to Texas Dental College, later to be Baylor Dental College. She received her doctor of dental surgery in 1917 and set up practice, the first woman to do so in the city. As assistant instructor in preventive dentistry in 1921 and professor of periodontia the following year at Baylor Dental College, Juanita led the group that formed the first dental care clinics in various locations of the city for children whose families could not provide for their care.

Juanita combined a successful career with volunteer work. For many years she was a mainstay at Freeman Childrens Clinic. She spoke on dental health to organizations throughout the city including a series of radio programs. Professionally, she was assistant professor in periodontia from 1930-1943 and again from 1945 to 1949. She was a Fellow of the American Academy of Periodontology and a Fellow of the American College of Dentists. An active member of several dental organizations, she was the first—and until her death—the only woman to serve as president of the Dallas County Dental Society (1945-46). Earlier, in 1924-25, she was president of the Texas Society of Dentistry for Children and of the American Women Dentists.

Amazingly, Juanita accomplished all of this while being almost totally deaf. In 1917 while she was a senior in dental school, she had a mastoid infection and lost her hearing. The hearing aid had not been invented and she relied on lip reading and the help of friends to keep her aware.

In 1922 Juanita and James Roderick Turner were married. Her only daughter was born four years later. The little girl, named for her mother, grew up as a friend and assistant to Dr. Wade, serving as her ears, attending dental conventions, taking notes, doing research. It was an association made all the more poignant because James Turner was killed in an automobile accident in 1936 leaving Dr. Wade solely responsible for the rearing of their daughter, and thus repeating her mother's role.

"Mother's patients are a 'Who's Who' list of Dallas," Juanita Hamilton said. Dr. Wade's first ledger, which her daughter cherishes, lists the Frank Austin family, the Belo family, Mr. and Mrs. Alex Camp, the Lingos, Collett Munger, W. A. Brown, Lewis Jacoby, Eli Sanger and family, Karl Hoblitzelle, Master Henry Miller and many others among her patients. From these patients, Dr. Wade collected a $10.00 fee for routine dental care but charged only $1.00 for children. Gold inlays were $12.00.

"Her patients were also our friends and they were wonderful to my mother. I was only 10 years old when my father died, but I remember that so many people came to our house. They offered to lend Mother money—it's wonderful she never needed it. Her friends in the dental associations became our family. They included us in everything. We had many family parties. The adults would play games in the living room and the kids

Juanita Wade, the first woman to practice dentistry in Dallas, gave away almost as much time in serving children as she did in earning money for her work.

Nina Fay Waldrop Calhoun, the first woman to head women's health services for the Dallas schools, was equally as active in volunteer work as she was as a medical doctor.

would be in the back of the house playing their games. These professional associates and patients were our extended family."

Juanita Wade's dedication to dentistry and her involvement in volunteer charitable and cultural outlets continued all of her life. An opera buff, she never missed a performance in Dallas. She was active in St. Matthews Cathedral and in the Lyceum and Altrusa clubs.

In the early 1960s, Juanita, the daughter who had married William M. Hamilton, began to worry about her mother being alone. "Because she could not hear, I was concerned that she could not protect herself. My husband and I wanted to build an apartment for her at our new home on Park Lane. Finally, I wore her down. She said, 'Well, all right, but I won't be dependent on you!' And she wasn't. She left the house every morning at 7 o'clock on her way to work. I'd hear her car pull out when I was still in bed.

"I worried, too, about Mother eating properly . . . . sometimes she'd get busy and forget to eat." It was in 1967. Juanita invited her mother to dinner; Dr. Wade declined saying she preferred to eat a snack and spend the evening reading. When the meal was on the table, Mrs. Hamilton went again to her mother's apartment to invite her to dinner. She found her mother slumped over the table, her snack in front of her, the newspaper folded. Dr. Wade had suffered a stroke. She lived for two more years, never fully recovering. During the next two years her colleagues continued to admire and honor her. Before her death she was given the Dedication and Service in the field of Periodontology and a Good Fellow Award.

Nina Fay Waldrop Calhoun was the first woman to head women's health services for the Dallas Independent School District, but she began her career as a public school teacher. Born in Grayson County on November 2, 1894, the daughter of Mark L. and Lucy H. Taylor Waldrop, Nina Fay was educated in the Sherman public schools and earned her degree at Kansas State Teachers College. She taught home economics at Timpson, Sherman and Cuero before going to the University of Texas Medical School. "There were 10 girls in my medical class at the school in Galveston during my freshman year. Only two of us graduated. One of my professors made it clear that there was no room for women in medicine."

Although she was petite and pretty, Nina Fay never let the system stop her. "When you are in a minority," she once said, "you have to build a wall around yourself so that you can take the blows. You have to know what you want and go after it. I really understand the plight of minority groups because I know what is to be a minority."

Dr. Calhoun did advanced medical training at the St. Louis Skin and Cancer Hospital in New York and post graduate study at the New York Skin and Cancer Hospital. On July 4, 1921, she married Dr. Thomas J. Calhoun, who died in 1948. She interned at San Francisco Children's Hospital in 1923-24 before returning to Texas in 1925 where she was hired as the first physician for girls in the Dallas schools when that post was created. She continued in the position for five years before leaving for specialized dermatology training and then to establish a private practice in dermatology in the Medical Arts Building in 1929. She lived at 3621 Fitzhugh, and later at the Stoneleigh Hotel.

Dr. Calhoun's service to women and girls continued for eight decades. She headed the Business and Professional Women's Club in Dallas and was president of Altrusa International, from 1941-1946. During her tenure as Altrusa president she instituted an awards program for women graduate students from other countries to study in the United States. The program supplemented the finances of the awardees. Upon the completion of their graduate work, the young women were required to return to their own countries and put their education to use to improve social and economic conditions. Dr. Calhoun was instrumental in helping women from Latin America, Asia and African countries. Many of the awardees studied at Southern Methodist University where Dr. Calhoun took a personal interest in guiding and counseling them. Often she personally assisted with finances.

Her own life and work was integrated far ahead of that of the community at large. She chaired the scholarship fund for Jarvis Christian College at Hawkins and was a volunteer physician for the West Dallas Christian Center which provided day care for retarded children. As a member of the Disciples of Christ church, she was the first woman elected vice president of the Texas Association of Christian Churches. Later she was on the international board for her church and was a delegate to the World Convention of Churches in 1955 which met in Toronto, Canada; again in 1960 in Edinburgh, Scotland; again in 1965 in San Juan, Puerto Rico and again in 1970 in Adelaide, Australia.

Lala Devan Watts was the first child welfare inspector for the state of Texas. Born in Fort Worth in 1880, she moved to Dallas when she was 20 where she began her social work as a child welfare inspector. Her strong advocacy for children, women and the family brought her to the attention of government officials and paved the way for her appointment as the first child welfare inspector in the state. She campaigned tirelessly for women's suffrage and had hardly savored the victory of her first vote when, in 1921, Gov. William P. Hobby appointed her as chief of his labor department for the state. She resigned shortly to become president of the national Women's Christian Temperance Union. She died in Fort Worth in November of 1971 at age 91.

Mary Winn Smoots established the first women's newspaper in Texas, the *Texas Woman*, in 1907. When it merged with the *American Home Journal*, she became associate editor of that magazine. She also organized and served as the first president of the Dallas Writers Club and was an organizer of the Dallas Zonta Club. The daughter of Dr. and Mrs. E. W. Winn of Sherman, Mary was born in Atlanta, Georgia, and reared in Texas. A graduate of Kidd-Key College, she began her literary career in 1900 when her first story was published. She continued to write and publish throughout her life. She spent many years traveling from Texas to Washington, D.C., and back, serving as one of the first women covering the national scene for local newspapers. She had a keen eye for viewing politics and, in her mature years, became well-known throughout the state for her editorial columns.

Genevieve Shea, the first woman to be accepted into Baylor Medical School, practiced medicine in Dallas until she was 84 years old—and retired against her employer's wishes.

Genevieve Shea was the only woman in her class for the first two years she was in medical school at Baylor University in Dallas; in her junior year another woman transferred to Baylor from the University of Texas so that two women were in the graduating class. When she began her internship in July of 1924, Genevieve was the first woman Baylor had ever accepted.

Born on October 5, 1898, Clara Genevieve Shea was the only child of James Martin and Mary Ann Grady Shea. Her father, an official in the Bricklayer's Union, often spoke of a woman physician whom he greatly admired and Genevieve, whose favorite school subjects were the sciences, knew from the time she was a small child that she would study medicine. She was graduated from St. Edward's School in 1917 and attended Bryan High School for another year to study Latin and additional science courses. She then entered Southern Methodist University's pre-med program. Two years later she enrolled in medical school.

She was scared to death when she entered a medical laboratory for the first time,[7] not afraid of the subject matter or the long hours of study or the gruelling routine that lay ahead of her, but afraid that, no matter what she did, she would be rejected by her professors and classmates. By the time she entered medical school she had already weathered anti-female discrimination at SMU where some of her professors strongly discouraged her from aiming toward a medical career. One professor locked the door at 8 a.m. and would not let any latecomers, male or female, into the classroom. Since Genevieve had to depend for transportation on a cross-city street car that connected with an unreliable "dinkey" on Knox Street to get her to the campus, she often had to leave home by 5 a.m. not to miss his class.

In medical school, her professor announced that he would call the name of each student who should respond with the name of the person he would most like to have as a lab partner. The first name called was that of a recent honors graduate from SMU, Grady Redick, who immediately responded that he chose Genevieve Shea.

"All of her life, Mother remembered what a thrill it was to be *chosen*—especially after she had been so discouraged by some of the professors to study medicine,"[8] said Patricia Currin, her daughter.

During their senior year, medical students were on call to deliver babies throughout the city. As often as not, this meant driving into remote areas of town in the middle of the night. One night Genevieve delivered a baby for a poor family that had no clothing or supplies for the new addition to their family. She went home and told her mother, and the two women sat up the rest of the night making a layette which Genevieve delivered in person the next day when she went to check up on her patient. For some time afterward there were numerous telephone requests for the hospital to send the doctor who brings along the baby clothes.

Although she was elected president of her class, the senior annual showed a somber Genevieve Shea with a spit curl peeping from under her mortar board in the very middle of her forehead.

She graduated second highest in her class and applied to Baylor for an internship. She knew she would be chosen because the school always took students with the highest grades and the only classmate who ranked ahead of her accepted an internship out of state. The Baylor Hospital superintendent hedged. There were no facilities for women interns; the hours would be long and the hospital could not be responsible for her safety. Genevieve got the idea: Baylor did not want women interns. She did not argue and did not cry. She enlisted the aid of two doctors on the hospital board. After the board approved her, she learned that these two men had not agreed on anything for 20 years—except that Genevieve Shea should be admitted as an intern.

When she was accepted, Genevieve shared a room with a dietitian who was also studying at Baylor. Following her internship, Dr. Shea set up practice in obstetrics and pediatrics in the Medical Arts Building in Dallas and moved back into her family home on Tremont Street. A year later, while vacationing, she met C. Frank Brown, also a physician. She was 28 when they married. He may well have been the first male to follow a career woman to Dallas; he set up practice in internal medicine and later became top examiner for Southwestern Life Insurance Company.

Throughout her four pregnancies Genevieve Shea continued to practice medicine. Her oldest child, Mary Ann, died with scarlet fever when she was five years old. Three others—Patricia (Currin), Charles and Kathleen (Gardner) grew to adulthood in a home where both their parents were physicians. At age 50, Dr. Shea closed her office to devote more time to her family, to speaking and to public health issues. She lectured to girls in Dallas high schools encouraging them never to limit themselves professionally and teaching, by example, that it was not only possible but highly fulfilling to combine marriage and children with a satisfying career.

Early in the 1960s, Dr. Shea began to work part-time with the City of Dallas in its Department of Health and Human Services. She served clinics all over the city. Her marriage of 40 years ended with the death of her husband in 1967. A year later she married Claud Hern. She retired on December 20, 1982, at the age of 84 against the wishes of Public Health officials. Even while she was planning her retirement, she was asked to stay on full-time, which would have doubled the work load of the two Well Baby Clinics she had been managing. Though she did not accept the honor, she was greatly pleased, Pat Currin said. "'Imagine!" Pat quotes her mother, "'Being offered a full-time position at my age!" Dr. Shea would be pleased to know that her granddaughter, Mary Beth Currin . . ., is following the advice given by Dr. Shea as she works in a medical career.

Maria Luna was Dallas's first Hispanic woman entrepreneur and, in 1940, when it was organized the only woman to become a charter member of the Little Mexico Chamber of Commerce. She founded Luna's Tortilla Factory, the first tortilla factory in Dallas and, along with the Martinez family who opened the first Mexican restaurant, set in motion the taste of Dallasites for Mexican food. The date was February 24, 1924. Like most individuals—and all women—of the 1920s, Maria began her business from necessity in her own home at 2209 Caroline Street.

Maria Luna, Dallas's first Hispanic woman entrepreneur, created Luna's Tortillas, a business that has been continued by her family.

Maria came to the United States from San Luis Potosi, Mexico, arriving in El Paso on June 19, 1923, and on to Dallas where she joined her father and sister who already had made the voyage. She was 23 years old and the mother of two children, Carmen, 7, and Francisco, 3. She had worked as a meat vendor in Mexico and was soon employed by Jesus and Anita Porero in their grocery story on Griffin Street. They sold the corn grinder which they had provided for the convenience of their customers. The seller was unable to make the payments and the grinder was returned to the Poreros. Maria bought it on credit. It was the only non-cash purchase she ever made.

In her new home on Caroline, she opened for business—grinding corn and selling masa and tortillas. The business thrived. As it grew, she needed additional employees, but the men would not let their wives work outside their homes. Maria solved this problem by filling dishpans with masa, delivering them to selected women, and then in the late afternoon collecting the tortillas from the women who had made them in their own kitchens. Within a year, Mrs. Luna had gained credibility and, slowly, the women she employed were allowed to go to the factory to work. At this time, 1925, the business grew to some 25 workers who hand-produced around 6,000 tortillas daily. By contrast, when the business was first mechanized in 1940, the output was 100 dozen tortillas per hour.

Maria began her business by cooking the masa in large (No. 3) washtubs over open wood fires. Always intent on quality, she exercised a firm hand over her product, selecting the best corn, grinding it to perfection and seeing that it was mixed in exact proportions. Traditional in many ways, she was also alert to mechanical advances and when she determined that cooking the corn over gas would be just as good and much more efficient, she designed a long stove with openings for ten washtubs over gas burners. She had the apparatus made to her specifications. With the new machinery, tortillas production was speeded up. Four women could handle the cooking while one kneaded the dough and a sixth used a mold to turn out the tortillas.

Her children grew up in the Luna tortilla business. Two years after she arrived in Dallas, Maria married Rudolfo Gonzales. Though both tried to accommodate the relationship, troubles soon developed. In 1937 two auspicious events occurred. Maria divorced her husband of 12 years and, with Mike Martinez, bought the 1600 block of McKinney. She moved her business to 1615 McKinney. A two-bedroom apartment over the factory provided living quarters for the family. By 1951 the small apartment was home to 10 people, Maria, her daughter Carmen and her husband and their two children, and Francisco, his wife and their three children. When his wife was pregnant with their fourth child, Francisco determined to move to the house he had purchased in 1949 and rented out because he didn't want to upset his mother. Just as he expected, when he told Maria he was moving, she accused him of destroying the family. She continued to be angry until time proved her wrong; rather than being disruptive, the move brought greater harmony to the family and continued dedication to the business. Francisco had rarely defied his mother. When he graduated from Crozier Technical High School in 1939, he wanted to study medicine, but Maria, recently divorced from his stepfather, convinced him that he was the only man of the family and must help her in the business. After attending business college in Dallas, he did just that.

In 1936, Sammy's in Highland Park Village, owned by the Messina family, was the first customer outside the barrio to buy Luna's tortillas. In 1929 the tortillas were shipped to the first out-of-town customer, a restaurant in Wichita Falls. The business continued to spread—through East Texas, into Oklahoma and Louisiana and eventually as far away as St. Louis. Maria added other Mexican products to her factory to accommodate customers—salsa, rice and beans, chile con queso—all of which were made on the premises.

For most of her life Maria continued every night personally to sharpen the grinding stones because she did not trust anyone else to do it properly. Even so, she was no grind. She was a devout Roman Catholic who supported Our Lady of Guadalupe church with her presence and her money. She loved dancing; many times after the stones were sharpened in the evening, she found someone to take her dancing, in the latter years of her life often her grandson, Florentino Ramirez.

Pacesetters for women in medicine are, from the top, Gladys Fashena, the first woman to serve as president of the Dallas County Medical Society, Ellen Loeb, hematologist/ oncologist and cancer researcher, and Ruth Allen, pediatrician.

The factory that bears the Luna name now sends out tortillas nationwide from its McKinney location near downtown Dallas. Its founder, Maria Luna, continued to live in the apartment above the factory until her death at age 71 in 1971.

Louise Posey, in 1938, opened the first woman-owned grocery store and hamburger stand in her area of town. It was a business that began in the 12 by 17-foot living room of her home, 1823 East Eighth Street Extension with a 1 by 4 plank shelf nailed to the wall to hold a few cans of vegetables and fruit, a couple of 25-cent plank tables to serve customers her homemade hamburgers and a $4.00 candy showcase. The Louise Posey story is told by Kenneth Foree in a 1946 article in *The Dallas Morning News*. Louise began her career like many women of color of her time, by cleaning houses for white women. In 1922 she took on a housekeeping chore that was to change her life. She went to work for widowed sister schoolteachers, Mineola King and Dona L. Palmer. They hired her on the recommendation of friends, sight unseen, and she had worked for them three months before they ever met. Even without meeting, they liked each other. Louise got the key left for her from the next door neighbor, completed her work quickly and efficiently, ate the lunch left in the refrigerator for her, collected the couple of dollars from under the sugar bowl where her employers had put it, locked the door, returned the key to the neighbor and was on her way before the teachers got home from school. A deep and trusting friendship resulted.

Louise had been working for the sisters for 15 years when Mrs. King suggested that they go into business together. "You should become financially independent," Mrs. King told Mrs. Posey. "You are not always going to be able to clean other people's houses. If you will furnish the place and do the work, I will furnish the money and the support." Mineola King suggested a cold drink and hamburger stand. Louise said it was too late in the year for a cold drink stand to be successful and dismissed the idea. Early the next year Louise returned from work at the King house and told her daughter, Willie, that "Mrs. King brought up that foolishness about a business again." Her daughter responded, "Mama, you're always worrying the Lord to open the way. Maybe this is His way." Louise thought about it and prayed about it before reporting to her employer that she was ready to open her business. Mrs. King told her to clear her front room and she'd see about the money. They agreed to halve the profits.

Early in the summer of 1938 Louise Posey was in business. She had $25 of Mrs. King's money which she used to buy three cases of soda water, a cooling box, cookies, candy, hamburger meat, onions and buns. The first day she sold 15 cents worth of sugar cookies to Julia Cook. Louise kept careful records. At the end of five weeks she had profited $10. She took $5 of it to Mrs. King who insisted that she keep it for expansion. "This means I now have $30 in your business," her benefactor said. By November 1, the business had profited $20 more. She took $10 to Mrs. King who told her to keep it. "I gave you the $25 to start," she said. "I didn't tell you because I knew you wouldn't take it if I did. Now you are on your own. You must make a go of the business because you are going to need it."

Louise persevered. At times she was ready to give up. On one winter day she entered in her book that she had received $1.21 from Jim Williams, meaning he had paid a bill he owned; that she had earned $2.00 housecleaning for Mrs. King; that the cash register showed 21 cents income, meaning that the cigar box she used to keep her money had receipts of 21 cents for the day. Louise could not bear to see people in need and not respond. There was more credit on her books than there was income. One of her neighbors was a Mexican family with eight children and a husband-father who drank. Louise fed them and never entered a debt on her books. She was, she told Mrs. King, "doing the Lord's business. You don't keep books on the Lord."[9]

A while back she sold her grocery store for $5,000 cash. And she bought a brick home at Singleton and Westmoreland and four lots on which she is now building a 24 by 46-foot frame store costing $2,000. She's paid cash for everything, all of it from that original $25 and a 1 by 4 shelf she says she will keep forever.

(From top) Edna Gardner Whyte was the definitive pacesetter for area women aviators for many years. Sarah Menezes, one of the earliest women attorneys in Dallas, with Rae Ann Fichtner, who followed in her footsteps. Joan Tarpley Winn, judge of the 191st District Court, carved a new niche for women.

Now 59, Louise superintends her store. Willie and another women run it. Frequently she goes to see Mrs. King and Mrs. Palmer to show them her bank book with $75 to $225 weekly deposits.[10]

Vareta Pinkston Gulley, the daughter of popular and affluent Dr. Lee Gresham Pinkston, was one of the first women to open a business outside her home in the South Dallas African American community when she inherited the Hatcher Street Florist in 1941. Vareta, the oldest child of Viola Shaw Pinkston and Dr. Pinkston, had come to Dallas from Terrell with her family in 1922. She was seven years old. She was educated in the Dallas public schools. As a child, she played throughout the 3140 State Street neighborhood where her parents built a home. That address is now in the center of North Central Expressway. As she grew older, she worked as a receptionist and handy girl in the 17-room Pinkston clinic, hospital and offices which her father built. It was around the corner from their home. Groomed for a career in medicine, she left for Wiley College in Marshall. As soon as she graduated in 1922 at the age of 21, she married Steve Gulley. The young couple spent the next several years between Dallas and St. Louis. Two children, Lee Patrick and Stevonne, were born.

Dr. Pinkston, the first person of color to join the staff of St. Paul Hospital, in the meantime had begun to buy up property as an investment. In 1939 he bought a small flower shop and the house next door to it on Hatcher street. The area was in flux. Black citizens were buying homes and moving into the area that had been predominantly white. Dr. Pinkston suggested to Vareta that if she did not intend to go to medical school, she might want to take over—at least temporarily—running the flower shop. In 1941 when the shop and the house next door were bombed, Vareta came out of the experience fighting! She would protect her father's investment. As soon as repairs could be made, she and Steve moved into the house and in November, shortly after Pearl Harbor catapulted the nation into World War I, she opened for business. For the next 39 years Vareta Pinkston Gulley operated Hatcher Street Florist, at first and for many years seven days a week. For many years the business also included a greenhouse in the back of the shop. Her husband, a career teacher who also taught night classes, helped when he could—usually on weekends. Stevonne and her brother grew up "helping out" both in the floral business and at their grandfather's clinic. Through the years Vareta's floral business became a fixture in the community. She ran every phase of it—overseeing the buying, floral design, delivery, billing and collecting, delivery and the minutae of pieces that provided flowers for funerals, churches, social clubs—Idlewild Cotillion and Dunbar—and individuals.

She became one of the most effective community leaders of her area. Her daughter, Stevonne in a 1993 interview, remembers that "Mama was *always* working—if not in the shop, in the community." As a member of Alpha Kappa Alpha Sorority, she was one of three individuals who spearheaded the unification of Negro Women's Clubs and sororities to end discrimination against black women in downtown department stores. "She was warm and funny and a firm disciplinarian," said Stevonne. "She usually had help, but there was never any doubt about who was in charge." And she couldn't have done what she did without her husband. "He did a lot of the housework.... There were always nutritious meals and a strong emphasis on education."

Marzelle Cooper-Hill, the granddaughter of slaves, who was born at 1491 Villars Street in Dallas, grew up to become the first officially designated black probation officer for Dallas County. She began working for the county in 1938 replacing Halaria Morgan, who had died the year before. Mrs. Morgan had set the pattern that Marzelle would later follow when she took it upon herself to notify the parents of black children who were arrested. Marzelle, who as a married woman was not allowed to continue the teaching profession for which she was trained, wanted to work part-time so that she could have time at home with her daughter.

Marzelle grew up at 1521 Villars Street, less than a block from the three-room shotgun house in which she was born. Her mother, Genevieve Turley Cooper, was a teacher, and her father, Dr. Marcellus Clayton Cooper, the first black dentist in Texas. Her mother died when she was a little girl and her father remarried. Her only brother

(From top) Attorney Adelfa Callejo is a pacesetter for Hispanic women, Ann McGee-Cooper, an educational innovator, set up teacher training programs at several colleges. Margaret Brand Smith, an attorney and insurance executive, in 1969, represented Texas at the first national meeting of the Commissions on the Status of Women.

died when they were both children. Marzelle was educated in Dallas schools, attended Wiley College in Marshall and was graduated from George R. Smith College in Sedalia, Missouri. She returned to Dallas where she taught for the next four years at Booker T. Washington High School. Her teaching contract was not renewed, as she knew it would not be, when she married David B. Hill. Married women were not allowed to teach in the Dallas schools.

For the next few years Marzelle devoted her time to homemaking. She and her husband moved to Denver for two years, then returned to Dallas where Frances was born in 1931. The next year, still unable to get a teaching position, Marzelle went to work for the Community Chest Employment Office at a salary of $12.50 a week, considered excellent at the time. The offices were segregated even though Marzelle was the only black employee, and she was allowed to work only with black clients. That made her job doubly frustrating because it was the height of the Great Depression when there were few jobs of any kind and almost none for people of color.

When she went to work for the County, Marzelle was tucked away by herself in a corner on the sixth floor of the County Records Building and "nobody paid me any attention."[11] Finally, one of the white juvenile officers showed her where the registration book was kept so that she could find the names of the black boys ("they did not arrest little black girls") and notify their families. She learned most of her job by observation and osmosis, absorbing what went on around her. When she saw white employees giving small pieces of paper to their clients, she determined that these must be checks. "I finally found out what this was all about . . . . We had no agency looking out for people or furnishing money or groceries . . . Destitute clients were sometimes given money by the County for food."

When neighbors in South Dallas complained about a little boy being neglected, Marzelle was sent out to investigate. She found a retarded child, an unemployed mother, and no food in the house. She put the woman in her car, drove her to the Records Building and told her to talk to a Mrs. White about her problem. "They gave her five dollars every two weeks for about two months . . . . It was the first time a Negro had received a check from the County."

Once when one of her co-workers, (Emma Wiley Ballard) crossly responded to her request for information, Marzelle turned and left. Emma later apologized. Marzelle remembers telling her: "We are two grown women and when you raise your voice at me I am inclined to raise mine—even though that's not appropriate under the conditions in which I am working here . . . . From that day on, her attitude changed toward me . . . ." It was Mrs. Wiley who finally told the chief officer that Marzelle should have a desk on the fifth floor with the other employees, a move, though welcome at the time, that proved unwise, for soon afterward Marzelle had a call at home that her services were no longer needed. Because there were no reasons for her dismissal, Marzelle took the matter up with prominent men in the black community. The situation moved through the chain of command to the district judges who made up the board that controlled the Juvenile Department. It was here that one of the judges admitted he had insisted Marzelle be dismissed because he had too many complaints from his constituents about having a Negro woman down there with a desk.

The Rev. Maynard Jackson convinced officials that a black probation officer was essential and that the black community would provide office space if the County would pay her salary. The compromise worked. Marzelle officed in the education building of New Hope Baptist Church on the corner of San Jacinto and Central Avenue, then in the Leach building on San Jacinto and eventually in the Henry Ford Building on Allen Street. By that time her case load was overwhelming. She was the lone black juvenile officer handling delinquent children, dependent and neglected children, adoption investigations and everything else referred to the county that related to children of color. The County finally hired her a part-time secretary. When a new building for Juvenile offices to be located on Harry Hines Boulevard was in the planning stages, Marzelle asked where her office would be located. When she was shown the plan, there was indeed an office for her—the last office on the floor, down the hall and to the back of the building segregated from other offices and across the hall from two restrooms—one for Negro men and the other for Negro women.

Mercedes Pentecost, left, with Ruth Fox, was the first woman international banker in Dallas. At right, Martha Gilmore was the first woman ordained in a mainline Baptist Church in Dallas.

When Marzelle Cooper-Hill died June 4, 1993, at age 90, she had taught women many things, among them to retain their birth names, to honor the parentage from which they came, and to be faithful to the professions that called them. She was buried at Lincoln Memorial Cemetery.[12]

25

COURAGE TO CONQUER—WOMEN AS SURVIVORS

The 1930s was a decade of contrasts in Dallas that tested all the ingenuity women could rally to survive and persevere. The decade began in panic. Sixty-three days before its dawn, on Friday, October 29, 1929, the stock marked crashed. In Dallas, still primarily dependent on agriculture, cotton prices dropped to almost zero, leaving not only the farmers who had produced the cotton but the ginners, buyers, marketers, manufacturers and consumers virtually penniless. In all areas, prices plummeted, losing nationally an estimated $50 billion from the years 1929-31 and marking the beginning of what has come to be known as the Great Depression.

Though the direct effects of the market crash were immediately felt by only a handful of Dallasites, the pervasive climate of fear penetrated every facet of life. But, true to the optimism that has prevailed throughout the history of the city and has especially surfaced in times of crisis, Dallas refused to believe that the depression would impose permanent scars. Officially, it ignored the bread lines and apple sellers on the streets of eastern cities. While newspapers in large eastern cities were reporting suicide and murder by those who lost fortunes in the market crash, Dallas papers were reporting that the city led the state in construction of buildings, in paving streets, improving its viaducts and bridges. A survey showed $20,000,000 worth of construction work planned for 1930. Forty-eight major conventions during the year before had brought thousands of visitors to the city, the most lavish of them being the convention of Rotary International in May when 10,500 enthusiastic delegates and their families from throughout the world were guests in the city.

Dallas believed itself a city on the brink of international recognition and behaved accordingly. Though the U. S. census gave it an official population of 261,010, Dallas claimed it served 308,030. If all of its claimed population chose to go to a park at the same time and divided themselves equally among its 4,000 city parks, only 77.01 people would have been in each. To get there, its citizens could use any of the 680 miles of streets, but they would have had to choose carefully not to have been in dust, rain or ruts because only 272 miles of those streets were paved. Its school age children were provided instruction by 1,231 public school teachers.

Waddy Tate, an independent candidate, was mayor of Dallas. He had won election over a field of 30 candidates with a motto of "Golden Rule and faith in the Lord," with hot dog parties and soap box speeches that guaranteed representation to the common man. One of his first acts was to remove "Keep Off the Grass" signs from city property and to give vagrants the right to sleep in city parks. Though he attracted nationwide attention with his unorthodox behavior and effected some changes in city government for the good of "plain folks," he did not have the support of his council or most of the Dallas citizens, for in 1930 despite his opposition, Dallas voted overwhelmingly to adopt a new form of government with a city manager and a council of nine members.

Women suffered the most economically because one of the first things Dallas did was to encourage all businesses to discharge married women—leaving what few jobs were available to the male breadwinner of the family. There was no consideration about which of the two in the married pair held the most lucrative position nor which of the two would least impact a family; it was simply assumed that the woman's job was dispensable.

The Great Depression of the 1930s began with the crash of the stock market on Black Friday, October 29, 1929. But while millionaires on the East Coast were jumping from tall buildings and apples were peddled on the streets of New York City, Dallas acted as if nothing had happened.

President Roosevelt gave all the banks a holiday, some businesses paid their employees in cash, the Idlewild debutantes prepared to dance, and the "Breadline Follies," spoofed the recession—all of which is characteristic of the manner in which Dallas responds to a crisis.

The city made a number of other cut-backs. Retail stores were open only five days a week, the use of modern machinery (to speed up work) was banned by state and county governments and a number of other stop-gap efforts to curtail unemployment were instituted. Even so, 18,500 were jobless by 1931. The Dallas Chamber of Commerce instituted an emergency relief committee and raised $100,000 to fend off hunger and destitution.

Dallas, along with the rest of the nation, embraced Franklin Delano Roosevelt's promised New Deal and in the November election of 1932 voted him in as president. The period between his election in November and his taking office the following March (he was the last president to be inaugurated in March rather than the January 20 date that has prevailed since then) was the bleakest part of the depression for Dallas. Some 9,000 families were on relief. A city cannery was set up to feed the unemployed; 1,379 families received clothing from a relief depot; self-help garden plots sprouted up all over the city; citizens bartered and swapped goods and services, and—again true to Dallas's ability to be optimistic in a crisis—a Breadline Follies was staged. It was, and is, typical of the city to respond to disaster with a benefit party!

President Roosevelt's first act was to declare a bank holiday. This meant that all banks simply closed their doors. Again, Dallas citizens rose to the occasion with a minimum of inconvenience. *The Dallas Times Herald* was only one of many businesses that paid its employees in cash rather than check. The *Herald* paid them two days early "so that the money can be put into circulation." Stores extended credit and, on many occasions, accepted checks which they held until the banks reopened. The reopening soon came, but it seemed an eternity for those who suffered through it. On March 14, 10 days after they closed, "Dallas Banks Return to Normal Tempo," was the headline in the *Times Herald*.

While the economic crisis had a nation in its grip, daily life proceeded, as it always does. On Sunday, October 27, 1929, two days before Black Tuesday, ten young women were announced as debutantes by the Idlewild Club to be presented to Dallas society on Friday, November 1. Club president Albert Sidney Johnson, the story said, would lead the grand march with his date, Miss Gertrude Aldredge. (See Gertrude Aldredge Shelburne, Part II) Other belles were Misses Mary Cox, Mary Catherine Crozier, Edna May Gifford, Josephine Hughes, Elsie Nicholson, Betty Smith, Louise Smith, Elizabeth Stemmons and Bettie Timmins.

Radio—no television—was still new and the programming on KRLD anything but sophisticated. Around noon each day Bob and Bill shared "useful agricultural hints." There was a preponderance of musical programs with local talent presented in piano and violin concerts and an hour-long program in the afternoon on "lost and found" items. Late in the year of 1929 Gloria Swanson opened at the Melba Theater in the first talking picture.

Even though Dallas gave only a passing nod to the Great Depression, the papers, never identifying the columns as survival techniques, were filled with helpful information on how to save, preserve, cut costs, share goods and services and live well on less.

During March of 1933, President Roosevelt announced that experiments in the White House kitchen proved that a family could be fed nutritious meals for 7.7 cents per serving. This struck a responsive chord with housewives everywhere. Home economics departments at all the major universities tested menus and recipes and both the *Dallas News* and the *Times Herald* published results.

Typical for the 7.7 cents was a menu that included a breakfast of stewed prunes, rolled oats, whole milk, biscuits, butter and molasses; a lunch of tomato soup with crackers, bread, milk shake, and apple Brown Betty, and a dinner of hamburger steak, mashed potatoes, cole slaw, biscuits, coffee and one-egg cake. Or you could have a breakfast of orange juice, Post Toasties, whole milk, scrambled egg, butter, jelly and white toast, a lunch of tomato soup with cheese straws, prune and cheese salad, bread and butter sandwich, hot chocolate and canned peaches, and a dinner that included chicken fried steak, new potatoes, string beans, carrot and cabbage salad, hot rolls, coffee and a cookie.

The brunch—two meals in one—became the chic way to entertain and hostesses tried to outdo each other with creative menus. What about steak and French fried potatoes, sliced garden tomatoes and raspberries with cream for a depression repast?

Grocery prices indicated that these menus could, indeed, be prepared for a few cents per person per serving. On June 23, 1933, A&P advertised bread at 6 cents a loaf, coffee at 17 cents per pound; eggs, 12 cents per dozen; canned milk, three tall cans for 17 cents; veal cutlets, 19 cents a pound; wieners, 10 cents per pound; butter, 24 cents per pound; ripe tomatoes, 7 1/2 cents per dozen, and carrots, 2 cent per bunch. Fresh corn was four ears for a nickel. Recipes were printed with the ads showing that the meals could, indeed, be prepared at the prices advertised.

Dallas women embraced brunch as a way of honoring their social obligations while diminishing their entertaining dollars. Giving or being invited to brunch was chic. None of the columns ever mentioned that it also saved money because breakfast-lunch was eaten as one meal. Most of the brunch menus published were lavish. Here is one: Chilled orange juice, Baby T-bone steak, French fried potatoes, sliced tomatoes, hot biscuits or buttered toast, raspberries with cream and cookies and coffee.[1]

On June 10, 1933, President Roosevelt was given "The greatest peace-time powers ever to restore prosperity." Linz Jewelers advertised engagement and wedding rings, the most lavish of which was a half-carat blue-white diamond engagement ring surrounded by 12 smaller diamonds and a diamond-circle wedding band for $172.50. On the same day you could buy a Singer sewing machine at Sangers for $29.95 and an eight-inch electric fan at Glidden's for 99 cents.

Mildred Eldred was telling mothers, in her daily column, "Your Baby and Mine," that if their children were ill or misbehaved, it was probably their fault. These are typical nuggets of advice: "The tempery baby . . . is a mishandled one." And, ". . . there is something wrong with the environment when a child of that age (2 1/2) persists in thumb sucking."[2]

Only in the classified sections did Dallasites openly admit that they were in financial straits. Bankruptcies were announced daily. A 1929 Ford Sports Roadster was for sale for $115 and a furnished duplex cottage on the Belmont car line at Markel and Beeman rented for $7.50 a month. Near SMU, a two-bedroom upstairs apartment, 3312 Rosedale, was "depression rent" priced at $50. An out-of-work auto mechanic with 12 years experience, advertised that he would adjust the brakes on any make automobile for $5 and a paper hanger/painter said he would take any job for $1.50 per room.

By the spring of 1933, Dallas was declaring itself into recovery—though it wasn't quite, yet. John E. Owens, vice president of Republic Bank, in a newspaper column, headlined "Depression to Bring Good to Many," declared that "President Roosevelt's decision to close every bank in the U.S. was the most courageous . . . bit of financial finesse ever . . . ." A little later in the spring a story said "all signs point to a definite trend toward recovery of business conditions in Dallas . . . ." It pointed out that building was up, retail sales were good, employment was rising and manufacturing was almost in full force again.

Only after the worst of the depression was over did Dallas acknowledge that there had been one and that it had been extremely painful. On May 21, 1933, in a lengthy column headlined "Stress of Depression Has Added Millions to U. S. Sick List," Edward Spencer Cowles wrote that the strain of the depression "has added many millions of persons to the nation's sick list" and that "(the) tremendous increase in neurosis . . . can be cured by reversing the process which caused them."[3]

First Lady Anna Eleanor Roosevelt enjoyed almost universal popularity at the outset of her husband's tenure as president because she ran the White House family quarters frugally and reached out to the poor and sick. She was especially popular with women. She was the first First Lady to hold press conferences in the White House for women correspondents who were barred from regular coverage of her husband. She hosted a Feminine Gridiron in Washington:

> The president's wife was host to Secretary of Labor Francis Perkins, Minister to Denmark Ruth Bryan Owen, all women members of Congress, all women newspaper correspondents and other women prominent in politics who

Leonora Corona, who grew up and studied in Dallas and became an opera star in New York and Europe, returned to her native city to sing during the Texas Centennial.—Texas/Dallas History and Archives, Dallas Public Library.

because of their sex were barred from attendance at the exclusive Gridiron club dinner. The idea, which has been amusing Washingtonians ever since it was conceived by the independent-minded first lady, deftly points out the flaw in sex discriminations in society. Gridiron dinners have always been for the leaders of government and as such were naturally off limits to women. This year, with a woman member of the cabinet and a woman minister, as well as a woman director of the mint, no change from the old rules was observed. The women . . . were not invited.[4]

It is difficult for the wife of a public man to play a conspicuous part in public life without encroaching upon her husband's territory to his embarrassment. It proved not to be difficult at all for Eleanor Roosevelt to play a conspicuous part in public life. As the years of her husband's presidency increased—the longest tenure in the history of the United States, from 1932 until his death April 12, 1945—Eleanor's popularity fluctuated, but she never curtailed her actions nor altered what she thought was right and honorable to curry favor.

Mrs. Roosevelt welcomed Marian Anderson to the White House in 1936. In 1939 when the famous black contralto was denied the right to sing in Constitution Hall because of her color in a highly public disagreement with the Daughters of the American Revolution, Mrs. Roosevelt resigned from the DAR. There is no doubt that it was at her insistence that Miss Anderson was supported by FDR's Secretary of the Interior Harold L. Ickes and by NAACP leader Walter White to present her concert at Lincoln Memorial where 75,000 heard "Nobody Knows the Trouble I've Seen" and "America."

In 1933 Eleanor Roosevelt made her first visit to Dallas. Flown from Washington to Chicago by Col. Charles A. Lindbergh, she took a commercial flight to Dallas in what was supposed to be a private visit. The private visit turned into anything but that when she was met at Love Field by 500 enthusiastic Dallasites. Front page stories and photographs in Dallas papers lauded her. ". . . in an hour and 22 minutes (she) won Dallas affection, not as the First Lady, but as Eleanor Roosevelt . . . . Hundreds who thought she would come to the city for breakfast lined the route to downtown Dallas, and were disappointed when her party breakfasted in the American Airways offices at the field . . . . (her) graceful submission to an interview with newspaper folk . . . left the interviewers convinced she is the reporter's ideal subject."[5]

Dallasites who followed Eleanor Roosevelt in the newspapers felt that she was as much a citizen of their city as she was of all others in the country. Adlai Stevenson said, "Her glow . . . warmed the world." *Time* magazine, when it put her on its cover in 1939 called her "superlative in her own right (whose) power comes from the influence not on (her husband) but on public opinion . . . unique for any woman." Even with detractors, Eleanor was a model, sometimes secretly, for women during her lifetime and has become a mentor for countless women throughout the world. In 1988, almost 26 years after her death, evaluated by a new generation of American women, 28 per cent in a *Ladies Home Journal* poll termed her the "most admired First Lady" of all times.

The Great Depression was not, by far, the only national or international crisis during the 1930s Decade. In Europe, war was brewing, a war that would envelope the entire world during the next decade. In January of 1933, two months before Franklin Roosevelt was inaugurated as president, Adolf Hitler became chancellor of Germany. He assumed dictatorial powers in March at almost exactly the same time FDR became leader of the United States. He systematically destroyed all semblance of democracy in Germany, abolished freedom of speech and assembly, repudiated the Treaty of Versailles, conscripted the youth into the Rhineland army, annexed Austria and a part of Czechoslovakia, signed a non-aggression pact with the Soviet Union and then marched into Russia.

Dallasites could not have been unaware of what was happening in Europe because both the *News* and the *Herald* were headlining the stories daily. The American people, often faulted in later years for not speaking up and the American government for ignoring the plight of those abroad, were handling the crises in their own world.

Hitler had been in power for less than a month when the *Times Herald* reported in a banner headline on its front page that "Many Jewish Residents Flee Germany," disclosing that all trains leaving that country were crowded with Jews." The same story said, "A special detective squad from the office of Capt. Hermann Wilhelm Goering . . . of the Hitler Cabinet seized Prof. Albert Einstein's 5000 marks in a bank account."[6] The next day Dallas staged a mammoth protest of these atrocities in the city hall auditorium where *all* leading Dallas Jews were joined by *most* civic leaders including R.E.L. Knight, Dr. John O. McReynolds, R. L. Thornton, Alex W. Spence, Herbert Gambrell, Sam P. Cochran, G. B. Dealey and others. No women were on the guest list.

On April 7 (1933), Dallas learned that "Hitler's bite is as bad as his bark," but on May 17 Dallas read the encouraging news that "Germany Accepts U. S. Arms Proposal,' a story that it longed to believe. There was to follow a decade of Hitler reneging on almost every promise, of his renouncing almost every treaty as he continued to persecute not only the Jews, but everyone else who did not accept his policies without question.

At the height of the depression, Dallas gave itself the biggest party in its history—the Centennial, celebrating Texas's 100th birthday.

In the midst of a world in chaos, despite the rigors of the Great Depression—or, perhaps because of it—Dallas threw itself a party to end all parties.

The event was called the Texas Centennial. It opened on June 6, 1936, to celebrate the 100th anniversary of Texas winning its independence from Mexico. It cost the staggering sum of $25 million and drew, during its 6-month tenure, 6,354,585 visitors.

There was no reason for Dallas to have been the site for the Texas Centennial. The city did not even exist when Sam Houston and his rag-tag Texas army with cries of "Remember the Alamo! Remember Goliad!" defeated Santa Anna at San Jacinto in 1836 and declared Texas free from Mexican rule. Banker/civic leader R. L. Thornton and his cronies exhibited the same braggadocio that Dallas founder John Neely Bryan had shown back in 1842 when he convinced Bird's Fort residents that Dallas was the land of the future. They went to Austin and assured legislators that they could and would put on the grandest celebration possible. And they did it. With local, state and federal funding, with architect George Dahl in charge, and with what fair enthusiast/consultant Joe Rucker once called "a huge army of hungry workers, men who had been jobless and were eager and willing to work hard," the Texas Centennial was conceived, assembled and opened in record time.

Reporters covering the giant extravaganza forgot that they had been taught in journalism school to avoid superlatives. Andrew DeShong, reported:

> Imperial fanfare which circled the globe and brought salutes from the six nations which have figured in Texas' destiny officially opened the Centennial Exposition Saturday noon.
> Dallas was entirely submerged in the tumult and color of the fair's premiere. The city ceased to have separate identity, and all Dallas became a part of the exposition, for the day of days in Texas history.[7]

Andy DeShong was not quite right. Of the six flags that had flown over Texas—France, Spain, Mexico, the Republic of Texas, the Confederate States of America, and the United States of America—two of those entities, the Republic of Texas and the Confederate States, did not/could not send messages; they no longer existed. But never mind. DeShong's comments continue:

> Countless radio listeners heard President Roosevelt's personal representative, Secretary of Commerce Daniel C. Roper:
> "America! Here is Texas! . . . The state of Texas sends greetings to all the peoples of the world. In the name of the president of the United States, I declare the exposition open."
> A telegraph cable channel around the world was open and waiting for his words . . . . Clicking keys told of the words' progress. Listeners heard the

message pass from today into tomorrow and back into today. They heard "London! Raining. Listen to the sound as it hurdles across the old world." Then came Shanghai . . . Postal telegraph had sent Roper's words around the world in two minutes and five seconds.

Excited throngs, many from every part of Texas, and many parts of the country, pushed through the main gates. Others, in smaller numbers, had been clicking the turnstiles at other entrances since 9 a.m.[8]

The Cavalcade of Texas, an outdoor pageant featuring 300 actors, 100 horses and other livestock and depicting 400 years of Texas history was not ready for opening day, but nobody seemed to miss it—and those who didn't see it often came back a second and third time during the fair to view it. Both women and minorities played a "token" though important role and opened the way for greater appreciation of their talents in the years ahead. A. Maceo Smith, years later, credited the Texas Centennial for making Dallas aware that it had a talented black population. Dr. George Washington Carver came to speak at the Hall of Negro Life.

Sculptor Clyde Chandler's "Gulf Cloud" was cleaned and moved to the fountain in front of State Fair Music Hall. Ina Ray Hutton and her all-girl Melodears were among the famous bands (Horace Heidt, Ted Lewis, Fred Waring, Duke Ellington, Rudy Vallee and others) who appeared at the Centennial. Sculptor Electra Waggoner II, the niece and namesake of the socialite for whom Electra, Texas, got its name, unveiled her statue of Vice President, Texan John Nance Garner.

Among the luminaries appearing at the Centennial opening was Leonora Corona, a Dallas native and a Metropolitan opera star. She sang Mary Austin Holley's "Brazos Boat Song," believed to be the first song ever composed in Texas, as one of the featured performers on opening day. Leonora had studied music in Dallas as a piano student of Manna Louise Sauter, left to study and sing in New York and Europe, and had already captivated Dallas when she returned as the guest artist for the Dallas Woman's Club and as soloist with the Dallas Symphony orchestra in April of 1933. Shortly before the United States entered World War II, Leonora Corona left for Italy. Nothing was heard from her after that.

The immediate results of the Centennial for Dallas, other than a giant escape to fantasyland that doubtless relieved stress in many people, was that it pumped much-needed money into the economy. A month before it opened, almost 10,000 fairground workers were earning $400,000 a week and pumping it into the city's faltering economy. The city itself felt revitalized—and, indeed, it was. Hotels were booked almost solid. Agriculture got a boost with the inclusion of new farming possibilities including cattle farming. The King Ranch introduced Santa Gertrudis cattle at the Centennial. Actors and writers found new outlets for their talents. Fair-goers saw many miracles for the first time—among them refrigerated buildings. This proved to be the forerunner of building-wide air-conditioning that would become almost universal in Dallas a little more than a decade later. Doubtless it would have come sooner had not World War II intervened.

26

SIX DARING DAUGHTERS

The women who made an impact on Dallas during the decade of the 1930s came from all walks of life. Few were native. All made contributions, some heralded in headlines of the times and others, like many of their sisters, lost in the cracks of history. Many were women of good deeds. A few were not. Most died with honor, one in ignominy. They excelled in health and philanthropy, law and justice, business and sports, and one gained notoriety through career in crime. Among them were Pearl Carina Bowden Anderson, Nell Goodrich DeGolyer, Sarah Tilghman Hughes, Bonnie Elizabeth Parker Thornton, Kate Rice Ripley and Mildred "Babe" Didrickson Zaharias.

Pearl Anderson arrived in Dallas at the age of 21 from Winn Parish, Louisiana, because she had heard of "that city in Texas where folks can find work and get ahead if they try hard enough." Her mother, Nettie Stringer Bowden, was considered to be black in Louisiana, though only her mother, from Antigua, was black. Her father (Pearl's grandfather) was Italian. Pearl's mother was half black/half white, her father French, a physician named Thibodeaux who visited often enough that several of Nettie Bowden's nine children were fathered by him.

Pearl grew up "mixed up. I was ostracized by both the black world and the white world, alienated from both. But as a child I never knew this because my grandmother made me believe I was the most wonderful child in the world. We lived on a farm and I helped her grow and preserve everything we ate. Sometimes a meal would be a slice of ham between biscuits, but I was never hungry."[1]

Pearl Bowden arrived in Dallas in 1918. Both her mother and her grandmother had discouraged her going to Dallas, "but, somehow, I knew, that my future lay here." She had picked cotton to earn her train fare to Dallas, a city "that seemed to me like the Promised Land." She knew nobody. She asked an agent at the railroad station for help and he sent her to North Dallas to a family that he knew sometimes rented rooms. "They were so good to me . . . but, then, they didn't know my heritage. And I felt so out-of-place . . . ."

She left a note for the family and made her way to South Dallas where she rented a room on Dildock Street only a few blocks from the 3815 Myrtle Street address where years later she built her house and lived until her death in 1990. She found work selling ice. Then she talked a lumber company into giving her credit to build a grocery store. She married—a marriage, "that did not last long and I had just as soon forget"—and had her only child, a girl she named Ruth.

Pearl was taking care of her daughter and working "an 18-hour day trying to make a go of the grocery business" when she became ill and a neighbor sent for the doctor. The physician who arrived in his horse-drawn buggy was Dr. J. W. Anderson, the first black doctor in Dallas. Five and a half months later he hired her. Working in a doctor's office was a step up from selling ice and running a grocery store that was always on the verge of going under. "I liked taking care of the patients. Sometimes I'd help Dr. Anderson deliver a baby, following in the footsteps of my mother and grandmother. Both were midwives."

She had worked for Dr. Anderson two years before he told her that he had fallen in love with her the instant he had seen her as a patient. The deep admiration she had for him made it easy for her to return the love he professed and on July 19, 1929, they were married. She was 30. He was 58.

As a wedding present Dr. Anderson sent his bride to Europe. He said he could not leave his practice, but he wanted her to fulfill some of her dreams. She studied in France and traveled in Italy, Germany and the Scandinavian countries before returning home to become a full-time wife and mother to Ruth. Her daughter was nine and Pearl enrolled her in St. Anthony Catholic Church school in deference to her husband's faith. She then converted from the Baptist Church in which she had been reared to Catholicism.

In the decade of the 30s Pearl Anderson concentrated on being a wife, mother and daughter. She was the "helpmeet" of the leading physician in South Dallas, the caretaker of her aging and ill mother who had come from Louisiana to live with her, and a doting disciplinarian to her daughter. In a period of seven years, she lost all three of them—her husband in 1947, her mother in 1949 and her daughter in 1954.

To save her sanity, Pearl reached out to others. She began her community volunteer work in 1958 when she signed up as an American Red Cross volunteer. Then she went to Terrell where she became a volunteer in the state mental hospital. Next she went out to the Veterans Hospital where she sought out men who were the sickest and/or the loneliest. Soon she was also a volunteer at the Lighthouse for the Blind and, after that, a volunteer at Children's Day Nurseries. Everywhere she went, lives were soon brightened both with her personal caring and with gifts that the budget could not be stretched to cover. Few people knew that most of the extra financing came from the beautiful tall, serene white woman who moved so quietly among them, who seemed most at home with black patients and black children explaining only to those who pressed her that "Negroes are my people. I am Black. I may look Indian, or French or Italian. I am some of all of that, but in my heart and soul I am a black woman."

At the death of her husband, the benevolence he had lavished on Pearl became hers. Even though she had lived, since her marriage, in comfort and even luxury, had traveled widely, had studied where and when she wished, owned jewels and paintings, she had no idea of her financial worth until she inherited it, including vast real estate holdings in several states and on Jackson Street in downtown Dallas.

Once she said, "Most people think I'm rich. I guess I would be if I didn't keep giving it all away." She was cited numerous times for service to others. The Pearl C. Anderson Day Care Center in Garland, located on property she gave for it, is named for her as is the Anderson Elementary School on Garden Lane in Dallas. At Bishop College a dormitory was named for her and in Nashville, Tennessee, the Anderson Auditorium at Meharry Medical School, a gift of her husband to his alma mater, bears her name. He had already gifted the medical school with an anatomical building named for himself. Pearl Carina Bowden Anderson died on April 28, 1990, at the age of 91. She had loved, she said in a 1986 interview, living alone "in my little house where I can come and go as I please," but during the last few years of her life she became increasingly ill and often confused. She would be found wandering the streets and returned to her house by caring friends. She is buried in Lincoln Memorial Cemetery among "my people." Her gifts to the city knew no limitations of age or color or race or gender.

Pearl Carina Bowden Anderson grew up "mixd up" because her white skin covered a black heritage. She picked cotton to earn money to move to Dallas where she accumulated a fortune.

In the winter of 1930, a tall, lean, scrubbed-clean 17-year-old red-head with a sprinkling of freckles across her nose arrived in Dallas from Beaumont to join the Employers Casualty Golden Cyclones, an insurance-sponsored girls' basketball team. As a high school senior and an all-state basketball star, she had caught the attention of "Col." M. J. McCombs who was intent on producing a sports team for his insurance company that would command headlines.

Mildred Ella Didriksen—"the press later changed the spelling of our name to Didrikson," said her brother Louis Didrikson of Newton; in time most of us changed it, too"— was born on June 26, 1911, in Port Arthur, to Ole Nikloa and Hanna Marie Olsen Didriksen, both naturalized American citizens from Norway. She was the sixth of the seven Didriksen children—sisters Medora (Will), Esther Nancy (Koch) and Lillie (Grimes) and brothers Ole, Louis and Arthur Storm. "Lillie and I were twins," Louis explained. ". . . Arthur got his middle name because he was born right in the middle of the terrible storm in Port Arthur in 1915."

In 1923, a tall, lean, freckle-faced 21-year-old from Dallas entered every sport competition for women in Texas—and won first place in eight of them.

Their father was a shipbuilder who, in his younger days, had been a seaman. "We were poor," Louis said. "Our home was comfortable and we were loved . . . . A lot that has been written and said about The Babe isn't right . . . ." My father did not build a gymnasium in our back yard. Our gymnasium was some good solid trees, some ropes and some boards. We had a wonderful time playing on these things. The Babe was a natural athlete, but she got her early training in this kind of gymnasium along with the rest of us."[2]

By the time Mildred started to school, she had become Babe to her family as she would soon become The Babe to the world. That is the affectionate name Louis referred to her still in 1990 when he was 81.

The Babe was born into a world which lauded girls who were pretty, petite, dressed in frills and were quiet and submissive. Babe Didriksen was none of these. In high school, she won almost every game and contest she entered, from marbles to harmonica playing. While other girls dated, she ran, jumped, shot baskets in her back yard, trying each time to beat her own record, and worked out on a home-made exercise machine she once improvised with flatirons and broomsticks. She was neither humble nor coy, and often gained advantage over her competitors before a game by walking up to them, looking them straight in the eye and announcing: "I'm going to lick you." Conversely, she was meticulously fair, played by the rules and insisted on a rematch if there were any doubt that she had won.

When Babe arrived in Dallas from Beaumont on February 17, 1930, to go to work for the insurance company, it was, she later said, the longest trip she ever made in her life. It was 275 miles. She played her first basketball game for Employers Casualty the day after she got to Dallas. Leaving high school in her senior year, she had yet to complete the work for her diploma—which she soon did. From the first her work at the insurance firm consisted of playing basketball. At the end of the first season, as captain she led the team to its first national girls' basketball championship. The press called her the Texas Terror when it was not headlining her as the Texas Tomboy.

She was named to the all-star girls' team, which promptly elected her captain. Twice more, in 1930 and 1931, she headed the team that won the national women's basketball championship. In one game she scored 106 points.

The third win was a squeaker. The score was tied 24-24 with less than half a minute to play. "I called time out. I told the girls to rush under the basket, and I would try a long shot. If I missed, they could get the ball on the rebound and try for a basket. With 20 seconds left, I shot from the center of the court. The ball made a clean sweep through the basket. I almost fainted . . . ."[3]

In the summer Col. McCombs took his teams—track and baseball in addition to basketball—to practice camp. Babe tried out for the other two sports. She was okay in baseball, but excellent in track and field events where she was soon captain of the teams. On July 4, 1930, the national women's track competition was held in Dallas where Babe broke three world's records—in javelin, baseball throwing and broad jump. Two of these—javelin and baseball throwing—won her championship title.

In 1932 Babe entered all of the 11 events in the Texas women's sports competition held in Denton. She won first place in eight of them, tied for first in the ninth and placed second in a tenth. Then, accompanied only by her coach, Babe left for Chicago and the national competition. After her two teammates—the girls with whom she had tied for first place in relay race and the one who had come in first in the 50-yard dash—dropped out, Babe went to the national competitions as a one-woman team. There she scored 30 points to dethrone the Chicago Evening American team which scored 22. The Chicago team, which had held the title for three years, consisted of 17 athletes. These feats earned her the accolade: "the greatest achievement in a series of events in the history of athletics," but more important to Babe was that these had been qualifying events for the Olympics.

Two weeks later in Los Angeles, where she was allowed to enter only three of the 10 events for which she qualified, she won two golds and a silver medal for the United States establishing world records in two of the events and tying for a record in the third.

She was the first woman in history to win two gold medals in the Olympics, and she came home to Dallas to wildly cheering crowds at Love Field, a parade through the downtown streets and a luncheon in her honor. A *Times Herald* article announcing the event, said:

> Mildred (Babe) Didrikson, greatest of all-time feminine athletes and idol of the 1932 Olympic games, will be given an official welcome home by Dallas Thursday. Plans for a warm reception for the 19-year-old miss who has brought this city more favorable publicity than it ever received through any other individual are being (completed.)[4]

Babe Didrickson was the toast of Dallas in 1932 when she became the first woman in history to win two gold medals in the Olympics.

During the homecoming festivities, Babe's photograph accompanied an advertisement for an automobile company, and the AAU revoked her amateur status. Her meteoric fame brought world attention. Some of the results were genuine and long-lasting; others were staged as pranks. The Babe was usually a good sport in addition to being an excellent athlete and it is difficult to know which was a stunt and which was genuine. There was the time in Beaumont when she crawled into the ring with a young man and knocked him out in the fourth round, the time she put on boxing gloves and went into the ring in New York, the time she pitched a baseball game for the House of David's bearded men's team, the time she became a short-term exhibitionist for billiards —and the time she worked out with the SMU Mustang football team. A reluctant Coach Ray Morrison, so the story goes, invited her under pressure to scrimmage with the team. She put on the smallest varsity uniform available, that of sophomore Bobby Wilson, who would later become an All-American. The Babe amazed her "teammates" by throwing an accurate pass, then by kicking the football and then demanded to be tackled. Coach Morrison cautioned football captain Ray Fuqua to go easy on her, but Babe would have none of it. On the second tackle Fuqua threw her with a bump and the coach pulled her out of the game.

Eight months after she took up tennis, Babe beat champion Alice Marble. She played around with swimming, diving, bowling and soccer. But her great adult game was golf. She became a golfer one day when she went downtown to shop for a party dress, but spied a colorful golf bag with glistening steel-headed clubs in the window of a sporting goods store. Forgetting the dress, she marched in and bought the golf clubs. Sports writers liked to tell about the 95 she fired on her first 18-hole tour as an "unheard-of feat for a links newcomer." Associated Press writer Fred Dye and Pro Erwin Hardwicke were playing a round with Babe at Tenison Park in the early days of her career. Dye recalled that he advised her to "Grab a stick and knock it on the green." The Babe swished a club from her bag, socked the ball and it stopped only inches from the hole. Then she let out a roar: I used my putter!," she exclaimed.

What the writers failed to relate are the hours, days and weeks Babe spent in perfecting her game. In April of 1935 she won her first significant tournament, the Texas Women's Amateur.

In 1937, while on tour, Babe met wrestler and sports promoter George Zaharias, known in sports circles as "the Weeping Greek from Cripple Creek." George called it "love at first sight." They were married a year later and spent the last year of the 1930s decade touring Australia where Babe played exhibition golf matches and Zaharias wrestled. There were no children. When they were not traveling, the couple lived in Florida where Babe bragged she had become a pro at making Swedish meat balls.

In all, Babe Didrikson Zaharias won 90 golf tournaments, climaxed by her victory in the British Amateur at Guillane, Scotland, in 1947. After that she turned pro and made a fortune with appearances for a sporting good firm and in golf movies.

Six times The Babe was named Woman Athlete of the Year by the Associated Press and in a 1950 ballot she was named Woman Athlete of the Half Century. Her statements to the press, like her prowess in sports, sometimes were slanted to make a more colorful story and, like them, cannot always be verified. But there was no doubt that her candor and spontaneous enthusiasm was genuine.

> "My gosh," she said after learning that she was the woman athlete of the half century. "isn't it just wonderful! I don't know if I deserve it, but I guess they know what they are doing and I'm thrilled to death."[5]

Recalling some of the greatest thrills of her career, Babe said she remembered those earliest feats best of all.

> "I was too young to realize what I had done in the National Field and Track Meet in 1933. All I was thinking was get all the points possible. I got 14. It turned out to be the largest number of points ever earned by a woman in a track meet. Then I went out and danced all night. I sure loved to dance when I was a kid...."[6]

In 1948 Babe joined pro ranks and collected every major crown, taking the world title three times. By 1950 she had earned a new title: Queen of the Links. In 1953, a week before going to the hospital for the first of many bouts with cancer, Babe won the tournament named in her honor at Beaumont. Six months later, out of the hospital, she won in the Serbin Open. On December 20, 1954, at a luncheon at the Adolphus Hotel at one of the highlights of Cotton Bowl week, she was inducted into the Texas Sports Hall of Fame. Still fighting cancer, she appeared in person to collect the recognition. A *Dallas Morning News* sportswriter wrote:

> Mrs. Zaharias, the greatest woman athlete of all time, started her rise in the sports world as a basketball player in Dallas. She went on to dominate the women's section of the 1932 Olympics and then moved into the field of golf, where she was the reigning queen for years.
> Recently, Mrs. Zaharias conquered cancer and returned to competitive golf, and the story of this—her latest and greatest triumph—thrilled the entire world.[7]

But Babe did not conquer cancer. She fought a valiant fight, was in and out of the hospital many times. She and her husband established a Babe Zaharias cancer fund so that others with cancer might be helped. She died quietly in her sleep in a Galveston hospital on September 27, 1956.

While Babe Didrikson was putting the Dallas dateline on the map for her prowess in athletics, another woman was calling the world's attention to the city for entirely different reasons. Her name was Bonnie Elizabeth Parker Thornton, and she was headlined for a life of crime.

It is a peculiar commentary on the human condition that feats of honor are often lost to posterity while exploits of horror are recalled and talked about for years. Ask any group of contemporary high school students who Babe Didrikson is and few will know. Ask them about Bonnie Parker—especially if you team it with Clyde Barrow—and almost all will know. True, the much publicized movie, *Bonnie and Clyde*, starring Faye Dunaway and Warren Beatty did much to bring this pair of Texas outlaws into contemporary thinking. But the story of Babe Didrikson, also made into a movie, did not bring the sportswoman anything like equal recognition.

Bonnie Parker was born on October 1, 1910, in Rowena, Texas, and moved with her widowed mother to the suburban Dallas town of Cement City when she was four years old. The suburb's name tells much about what kind of place it was. One writer described it as a slum, full of wrecked or battered cars in front of rundown houses. Vacant lots, littered with beer cans and other debris abounded. The children's playgrounds were the junkyards. In many circles it was called "The Bog," a part of west Dallas that the city pretended was not there. Without a doubt, it was a breeding ground for crime.

Even so, there is every evidence that Bonnie Parker could have made it through without too many scars had not the twists of fate bent her in the wrong direction at the wrong time. She was cute and she was smart. She won a city-wide spelling contest while a student at Bryan High School. She read movie magazines, longed to become an actress, studied speech and drama.

There were few models for a girl like Bonnie Parker. Very early she emulated the movie stars she longed to be, smoked cigarettes, had her hair cut very short, loved to dance. As soon as they would hire her, Bonnie went to work as a waitress in Marco's cafe. With her quick smile, sparkling blue eyes, and ready wit she soon moved up to another waitress job at the American Cafe, a block from the Dallas County Courthouse. It was 1930. She was 20 years old. She held the job for two years.

Police sirens and the presence of officers in the Parker neighborhood were a way of life. As a teenager, Bonnie married Roy G. Thornton, described by reporters of the time as a "two-bit hoodlum." In trouble most of his life, he was finally arrested for killing a man, tried, convicted and sentenced to 99 years in prison. The one photograph of Bonnie and Roy shows a couple of kids, their arms entwined staring innocently into the camera.

With her husband of less than two years locked away, living mostly on tips—pennies, usually, if anything at all—in a depressed economy, Bonnie was pretty, popular and poor—and vulnerable. Clyde Barrow, two years older, tall and rakish, must have looked like salvation to the tiny blonde waitress—barely five feet tall, weighing, at most, 95 pounds.

The two became inseparable. He was a wanted man. He had been arrested for car theft in Dallas as an 18-year-old, in Fort Worth when he was 20, in Dallas again for attempted burglary a year later and four days after that, again in Dallas for safe burglary. In 1930 he was arrested for burglary and auto theft in Waco and sentenced to 14 years. Sixteen days later he was arrested in Middletown, Ohio, as a fugitive. Finally, in April of 1930, the law caught up with him, and he was sent to the Texas penitentiary. He was granted a general parole two years later. Then he began his real life of crime—robbing, burglarizing, kidnapping, murdering.

The stories differ on how Clyde and Bonnie teamed up in 1932. The possibilities are endless. Growing up in the same general neighborhood—his poor but hard-working parents ran a service station on what is now Singleton Boulevard—their paths were destined to cross. One version is that he found her in the cafe where she worked. Another is that he was a buddy of her husband and she met him during the time Roy Thornton was on trial.

Her mother blamed him for leading Bonnie astray, but there is no doubt that she was a willing conspirator. The social mores of the day condemned her, as much for loose morals as for murder. She, a married woman, was traveling about with a no-good man. She had her picture in the newspapers smoking a cigar and holding Barrow, a willing conspirator in the gag, at gunpoint. She dressed flamboyantly, painted her fingernails, and smoked "ready-made" cigarettes. It was said that her favorite foods were red beans and cabbage. There is some doubt about this—for she loved the good life. When they would sneak into their home territory, relatives sheltered and hid them. During the summer of 1933 they lived in the Stockyards Hotel in Fort Worth where a neighbor later described Bonnie as "pretty and very nice." Once Clyde, disguised as a woman, sneaked into Dallas for his mother's funeral.

Bonnie and Clyde lived on the road and on the run. Through Texas, Missouri, Arkansas, Louisiana and Oklahoma, they left a trail of bank robbery, kidnapping and murder.

With 12 murders to their credit—nine of them officers of the law—Bonnie knew that arrest would mean conviction and the death penalty. She also knew that their days were numbered. On her last visit to her mother she said they would never be taken alive and that she wished to be buried with Clyde. She confirmed this wish in some of the poetry she left. In hiding, Bonnie often wrote. The last verse of one of her poems, *The Story of Bonnie and Clyde* was often quoted in the press:

> Some day soon they will go down together,
> And they'll bury the two side by side,
> To few it'll be grief,
> To the law a relief . . .
> But it's death for Bonnie and Clyde.

The three verses that precede the well-known last verse, especially the one just preceding it, reveal a great deal about the tiny outlaw. The third verse:

Bonnie Parker gave up her dream of being an actress to team with Clyde Barrow for a life of crime.—Texas/Dallas History and Archives, Dallas Public Library.

When having a child became a threat to her life and birth control was illegal, Kate Rice Ripley risked imprisonment to ship diaphragms to Dallas—in Ripley shirt boxes.

They don't think they're too tough or desperate,
They realise the law always wins,
They've been shot at before,
But they neither ignore
That death must be the price of their sins.

Death came soon. In a stake-out, on a lonely country road near Gibsland, Louisiana, at 9:15 on the morning of May 23, 1934, a brown, four-door, V-8 Ford stopped, and a tall guy wearing a felt hat and sun glasses stopped and stepped out of the car to render aid to what appeared to be a crippled car by the side of the road. Six officers, hiding in ambush, opened fire. Clyde, Bonnie and the car were riddled with bullets.

Bonnie was wearing a red dress, red shoes, and a white hat. She held in her hand part of a sandwich. Her last wish was not granted. Her mother saw no reason for burying the daughter she loved beside the man who, in her opinion, had led her into a life of crime. Bonnie's funeral was conducted by the Rev. Clifford Andrews, Dallas's first jail chaplain, and she was buried in Fish Trap Cemetery in West Dallas and later moved to Crown Hill Cemetery at 9718 Webbs Chapel Road in Northwest Dallas.

In the middle of the 1930s, Dallas was headquarters for a movement in Texas that was central to the lives of women and the economic conditions of families. It was the founding of the first birth control clinic in the state, and it would garner headlines for years to come. Its founder was Katie Rice Ripley whose personal and public lives were bonded in the compulsion to see that she and other women had access to contraceptives. Her health, her money and her reputation were fused in the project.

Katie Ripley was a southern girl. Born in Dallas on December 10, 1892, to Marshall B. and Mary Leila Mitchell Rice, she was educated by private tutors, spent some time in the Dallas schools, and then went to Mississippi to "finish" at All Saints Episcopal College at Vicksburg. Back home, she discovered that she was not prepared to get a job at anything available to young women of her time, so she enrolled in Sherman Business College.

In 1917, on the day before her 25th birthday, Katie Rice married George A. Ripley. He was employed in a clothing manufacturing company in Sherman. Almost immediately the young couple began planning a business of their own, and three years later together they established the Ripley Shirt Company at 410 South Beckley in Dallas. Their home was an apartment above the factory. The lives of the young Ripleys is scant, but one private incident became the turning point in Katie Ripley's life and in the lives of countless—perhaps into the millions—of Dallas women. She became pregnant and miscarried. Her physician told her that it would be unlikely for her ever to give birth to a living infant and that having a child would endanger her life.

Birth control—even for married couples—was illegal. What to do?

The birth control movement in America was just getting underway. Margaret Sanger, a public health nurse in New York, struggling with patients who had too many babies too soon and/or too fast, was summoned one sweltering day in 1912 to the New York tenements where she found three crying babies, their mother on the floor unconscious from a self-induced abortion and a distraught husband/father. Ms. Sanger pulled her through, but three months later she was again summoned to the apartment. This time the woman died. Margaret Sanger became the champion for contraception. She established The Birth Control League of America, which later was renamed Planned Parenthood.

At that time every state in the Union banned abortion. Margaret Sanger went to Europe seeking answers and learned about a Dutch physician, Dr. Aletta Jacobs, who had perfected a "German pessary" which would interrupt the passage of sperm into the fallopian tubes. Not only did this device come in 14 different sizes, it was sold freely in shops across Holland. Ms. Sanger, now married to Noah Slee, persuaded an American company to manufacture the pesaries, or diaphragms. Often in and out of jail, Margaret spent the rest of her life establishing birth control clinics, 300 nationwide. When she died in 1966, the distribution of contraceptives was still illegal in three states.

Katie had read about Margaret Sanger and on a fabric-buying trip with her husband to New York, she went to see the controversial nurse. They worked out a solution to the Ripley birth control dilemma. Katie and George shipped Ripley shirt boxes to Margaret Sanger at her New York organization. She filled them with diaphragms and shipped them back to Dallas.

Julia Haswell Brown, (see Chapter 23) who in 1970 became the owner of Ripley Shirt Company, was a 17-year-old recent Adamson High School graduate in 1928 when she went to work for the company. "I was supposed to be Mr. Ripley's secretary," she said, "but Mrs. Ripley was into the birth control business with Margaret Sanger and I found myself at their home working on birth control as much as at business working on shirts.

"I typed all of her letters and kept her correspondence. The diaphragms came regularly. Mrs. Ripley sold them to women who could afford them and gave them away to others . . . . She gave most of them away. She showed no concern. If she ever had a single fear that she might be arrested for doing something illegal, I wasn't aware of it."[8]

But other people were. Gertrude Aldredge Shelburne, who with her husband Dr. Samuel A. Shelburne were also early advocates of contraception, said that Katie Ripley welcomed everybody's help in her crusade to make birth control legal, but she would not have a board of directors. "If anybody goes to jail over what we're doing," she told them. "It will be me."[9]

More and more as the business prospered, Katie Ripley devoted her time to community work. As a member of the board of the Dallas Federation of Women's Clubs, she headed its children's bureau where she was instrumental in educating club members that the health and well-being of children was greatly enhanced when their parents spaced birth so that the mother's health was not impaired. Further, families with only the number of children they could support were much better off financially, a point that often appealed to the men. Most important, "Every baby has a right to be wanted and to be born healthy," Mrs. Ripley said again and again in statewide speeches. With her guidance, both the Dallas Federation and the State Federation endorsed legislation to make the distribution of contraceptives legal. She led the birth control movement in Texas as state chairman for Margaret Sanger's organization and served on the national committee for birth control legislation. Under the auspices of the Dallas Federation, she invited Margaret Sanger to speak in Dallas, garnering a large audience to hear her.

Though it was the center of her volunteer work for years, legalized contraception was only one field of Katie's interests. As director of employees, which in today's terminology would be personnel director of Ripley Shirt Company, she encouraged the employees to expand their interests and activities beyond their work lives. From 1946-48 she was president of the Dallas Federation of Women's Clubs advancing to that post by heading many of its projects. She was also active in state Federation activities, serving on the boards of both the Dallas and the Texas associations. She was treasurer of the Democratic Women's Luncheon Club, and an active member of several other organizations including the Women's Auxiliary of the Dallas Art Museum. She was a writer who contributed a number of articles to *The Latchstring*.

In 1935 Kate Ripley founded the first Dallas Birth Control Clinic. The city's first family planning clinic opened in 1939.

Nell Virginia Goodrich DeGolyer, her husband Everette Lee DeGolyer, Gertrude Shelburne and Dr. Shelburne and Annette Strauss and her husband, Ted Strauss were among the Dallas intelligentsia and socially elite who became staunch allies and continuing supporters of the cause to legalize the sale and distribution of contraceptives in Texas.

Nell DeGolyer came into the birth control crusade in much the same way that Katie Ripley had entered it. She, too, had lost a child; her first was stillborn in Mexico. Born in Missouri on September 11, 1886, to Hugh G. and Emma Goodrich, Nell completed a music degree at the University of Oklahoma in 1907. One of six children, she helped to work her way through school by serving as pianist in the School of Fine Arts at OU and grading papers for the German Department. After graduation she worked for a time

Kate Rice Ripley founded Dallas's first birth control clinic in 1935. She wouldn't designate a board of directors because she did not want her supporters to be legally responsible for her illegal activities.

at the University as a piano instructor. While grading German papers, she met Everette Lee DeGolyer and they fell in love. DeGolyer was studying geology at OU, which was the first school in the nation to offer training in petroleum geology. He went to work for the U. S. Geological Survey and then accepted a position as field geologist for the Mexican Eagle Oil Company. After six months he returned to Norman, Oklahoma, where on June 10, 1910, he and Nell were married in the First Methodist Church. They returned to Mexico. There, in July, at a site he had marked for drilling, the couple got a wedding present beyond their wildest imagination when oil was discovered at Potrero del Llano #4.

Although her Mexico home was a primitive hotel with few amenities, Nell DeGolyer, as she would do in their numerous homes, became a committed part of the community. She taught piano on the rosewood instrument she had taken with her and played at the Methodist Mission in Tampico. She helped nurse at a tiny combination hospital-nursery-mortuary-drugstore. Following the birth and death of her first child, Nell was further weakened with malaria. Her health, plus political upheaval in Mexico took the DeGolyers back to Oklahoma in 1913. There a second child, Virginia Nell, was born.

Three years later, in 1916, E. L. DeGolyer relocated his business to New York and the DeGolyer residence to Montclair, New Jersey. Three more children joined the family, Dorothy Margaret in 1916; Cecilia Jeanne in 1919 and Everette Lee Jr. in 1923. When World War I broke out, the DeGolyers were in Europe. She came home on a Canadian ship. His frequent and sometimes prolonged absences on business made Nell often a single parent. She managed the home, did volunteer work in the community and served as a full partner in her husband's life.

In 1936 Nell and E. L. DeGolyer and their children 23, 20, 17 and 13 moved to Dallas, and Nell became active in the community. With her abiding love of music, she was a patron of the Dallas Symphony Orchestra and of the Metropolitan Opera Spring Season. She worked with the League of Women Voters and with Planned Parenthood. She was one of its early presidents. In 1939 the DeGolyers built Rancho Encinal, a Spanish hacienda styled home on 44 acres on Garland Road. Set far back from the street, the house was surrounded by gardens designed by Arthur Berger and sloped to the back almost to White Rock Lake. Gardening was one of Nell DeGolyer's many passions. Her New Jersey home gardens had been a showpiece of the community, and her Dallas gardens soon attracted sightseers.

Following DeGolyer's death in 1956, Nell served as president of the DeGolyer Foundation Board which gave grants and maintained the DeGolyer Historical Library. She died on March 3, 1972, at the age of 85. The library, the DeGolyers' private papers and the estate were left to Southern Methodist University. The house and grounds were acquired by the City of Dallas and became the nucleus for the Dallas Arboretum and Botanical Society.

Nell Goodrich DeGolyer's interests were eclectic ranging from symphony to birth control to women's rights to gardening. She planted the first gardens at her home, now the Dallas Arboretum.

Sarah Tilghman Hughes arrived in Dallas in 1922 as a recent graduate of George Washington University School of Law and the bride of nine months of fellow-law student George Hughes. If she did not make a profound impact on the city and the state prior to the '30s decade, it wasn't because she wasn't trying. Dallas was simply not ready for the five-foot-two inch dynamo from Baltimore and her rise to a federal judgeship and national prominence was the result of persistence, perseverance and—she once said—pushiness. "You never get anywhere by waiting in the wings for somebody to discover you," she said. "Whatever you want, you have to ask for—and never go away until you get it."

Born in Baltimore on August 2, 1896, to J. C. and Elizabeth Haughton Tilghman, Sarah was always in a hurry, afraid that she could never pack enough living into her allotted span. She started school at seven, and skipped grades to graduate at 16 as salutatorian. "I deserved the top honor, but a boy beat me out. I made up my mind this would never happen again." She entered Goucher College on a scholarship in the fall of 1912 and graduated Phi Beta Kappa three years later with a degree in biology. "I also minored in math and took three years of Latin and both subjects have taught me to think more logically," she once said. There followed two years of school teaching in Winston-Salem, North Carolina, which were "boring and distasteful." The summer of her 20th

Judge Sarah T. Hughes had no reservations about moving to Dallas in late 1922. Neither the diminutive lady nor the city was prepared for what lay ahead.

year, she went home and ran her mother's boarding house, "the most difficult job I ever did. Mother was sick. She had 30 boarders and three servants. I did all the managing and all the marketing."

When fall came, Sarah enrolled in George Washington University School of Law, and to support herself went to work for the Metropolitan Police Department of Washington, D. C, one of its first female police officers. She worked on cases involving children. At night she patrolled the streets and dance halls. She was once assigned to Union Terminal. If a woman on the police force was rare, any individual with a college degree was even more so. At that time most police officers did not have even a high school diploma. Sarah was licensed to practice law in 1922, both in the District of Columbia and in Texas.

When she could spare the time from her work and studies, Sarah liked to debate politics and social issues with her classmates. Most were surprised when she singled out George Hughes as someone special. "We couldn't have been more different," she said, "but we made a very good team. He was very good-looking. He was also an older man on campus. He had served in World War I and entered law school after he got out of service. And he was a football player!" From Palestine, Texas, he was slower paced than the effervescent Sarah. "He talked very southern. We both enjoyed sports, especially tennis. He courted me by taking me on long canoe trips. Sometimes all the boys would take their dates canoeing to a cabin his fraternity owned."

At 23, on March 13, 1922, Sarah and George were married. Despite amazing and ever-increasing differences in their personalities and interests, it was a marriage that would endure for 42 years until George's death in 1964. As newlyweds they moved into the fraternity's cabin. "We canoed out each morning to our classes; it was the last carefree time of my life.

"We had no money. All we owned were our clothes and that canoe. When we graduated and came to Texas, I tried to convince George that we should come down in the canoe. But George was always more conservative than I, and he wouldn't think of taking me home to meet his folks that way. We sold the canoe for $45.

"I had no reservation about moving to Dallas," Sarah said in a 1971 interview. "I was following the advice of my favorite law professor who always told us, 'Pick your town. You can make a living anywhere. Find a place where you can make a life.'

"George came to Dallas in September of 1922. He went to work for the Veterans Administration and as soon as he could save up the money, he sent for me. I got to Dallas in December. We boarded on Victor Street." The 1923 Dallas City Directory lists them as "roomers" at 5627 Victor. He was listed as an attorney with the VA. She was listed, in parenthesis, as (Sarah), no mention of her profession.

Sarah started job hunting. "I had written 20 letters to law firms in Dallas before I came. I followed up with personal interviews to every one of them. Nobody would hire me. I was naive. It still didn't occur to me that I couldn't find a job because I was a woman.

"One firm finally let me sit rent-free in the front office. They were without a secretary and that's the space I occupied. Once in awhile they would give me a law suit." After winning two of the suits, Sarah had added enough dollars to the Hugheses tight budget that they could move. They found an apartment over a garage at 3700 Dartmouth Avenue. They lived there for four years in what was originally servant quarters. By this time George Hughes had advanced to assistant attorney with the VA and his name was in large type black lettering in the City Directory. She was still listed in parenthesis, with no profession. In 1934, Sarah and George had moved into a house they bought at 3816 Normandy where Sarah continued to live until ill health forced her into Meadow Green Nursing home in 1982.

Sarah and George Hughes managed their home together, grocery shopped together, cooked together, walked, swam, and entertained. "George was a much better homemaker and a much better cook than I, but we both enjoyed being at home. For 42 years I was home to dinner every night when I wasn't out of town." The couple chose not to have children. "It didn't make any difference to George and I never wanted the care of young children. I don't think I could have given them what they deserve because I was too interested in a career." For years Sarah Hughes chided her women friends who had several children. I was one of them. When my fifth daughter was born, Sarah threw up her hands. "I didn't think you were going to do that again," she told me. "How are you ever going to find the time to be successful in your work when you keep on having babies?"

"George and I were very different," Sarah mused. "I was garrulous. He was quiet. I liked to be with people. He mostly preferred solitude. I liked to get involved in causes; he didn't. I loved politics. He couldn't bear them. I was an optimist. He was pessimistic. He never encouraged me to run for office because he never thought I could win, but he was proud of me when I did. I was always absolutely free to make whatever choices seemed right to me; George never objected."

Sarah Hughes, as few people are able to do, kept her public life and her private life separate. The biographical sketches that came from her office always included *her* credentials with no mention of family. She seemed puzzled when interviewers asked about husband and family, but she was never hesitant to be as candid in answering these questions as she was in talking about her political and legal career.

Sarah Hughes had no business serving in public office, the Dallas senator decreed. She was a woman and she ought to be at home washing dishes.

As the 1930s decade dawned, Sarah ran for state representative. "Those were the good days. I visited everybody in town—the car barns, factories, fire houses, police stations. I ran the whole first campaign for $300. And I won." She was reelected for terms beginning January 1, 1933, and January 1, 1937. In February of 1935, midway through her third term in the state legislature, Gov. James V. Allred named Sarah Hughes judge of the 14th District Court of Texas. Her appointment was sent to the Senate for confirmation. It was traditional that if the appointment were opposed by a senator from her home county, it would be denied. Sen. Claude Westerfield of Dallas was opposed. "Sarah Hughes is a woman," he said, "and women should be home washing dishes." Women were outraged. Support for her nomination poured in from all over the country and, even though Westerfield continued to oppose it, in an unprecedented move, her appointment to the bench was confirmed. She was the state's first female district judge.

The incident became a rallying point for women seeking advancement in their careers. It was also provided comic relief in numerous tense moments. When *Dallas News* City Editor Ted Barrett asked Judge Hughes if she would pose washing dishes, her answer was "Come and get it." She posed for the picture that went out over the wire to all principal cities in the United States. It was not the only time Sarah's sense of humor lightened an otherwise sober moment. In 1976, when rumors were prevalent that she was slowing down and should stop hearing cases, her staff gave her an 80th birthday party and presented her with a pair of running shoes because, she explained, "I'm always telling them that they are half my age but nobody can keep up with me." Photographer Philip Gould of the *Dallas Times Herald* snapped her picture sitting on the floor of her office, wearing a bonnet and lacing up her new shoes. It, too, went out all over the country.

In 1937 she ran for the office to which she has been appointed for an unexpired term, defeated her Democratic opponent, and was unopposed in the general election. In her first year on the bench she disposed of 1,834 cases, an average of five a day. She won no popularity with other district judges when in a discussion about the need for more courts, she told them, "We don't need more courts. What we need is for some of you to get off your chairs and work.

"I am not a brilliant person," she once said. "I am persistent. I work hard. I accept no invitations that interfere with court hours. I take work home at night and I work part of every weekend. I read all of the briefs on cases I am to hear; I hold conferences with lawyers. In these judges robes, I do not ever allow personal opinions to intrude. Being a good and fair judge is not complicated. I use common sense. Good law is no more subtle than that." When she had been on the bench 10 years in 1945, she boasted that she had not missed a single day of work because of illness.

Judge Hughes was reelected each four years until 1946 when she ran for Congress and was defeated. In 1958 she again ran for office as a candidate for the Texas Supreme Court and again was defeated. She continued as judge of the 14th District Court. In 1960 she was reelected to her seventh term. Politics, she said, was in her blood.

Sarah Hughes with Perle Mesta, known as the Hostess with the Mostes'. Sarah never accepted social engagements during court hours, but her appearance made a party sparkle.

Because she recognized, and had personally lived the limitations that the social structure imposed on women, Sarah became involved in the women's liberation movement long before it had a name. As such, she was leader and mentor to many women who longed to be free of the obstructions that society imposed upon them. She gave presence and her effort to the advancement of women in public life, but she did not get involved in anything she considered a waste of time. She was president of the National Federation of Business and Professional Women's Clubs after serving as the head of the Dallas B&PW and the state B&PW. She was first vice president of the International Federation of Business and Professional Women. She was also president of the Zonta Club. As her professional responsibilities increased, she gave less time to Dallas groups, but her name appeared on the membership roster of all of them. When we asked her, in 1970, to take the leadership role in the founding of the Women's Center of Dallas, she declined. "If you want it done, do it yourselves," she said. "I have given my life to promoting women. Now it's your turn." But at the initial meeting for the founding of the center, it was Sarah Hughes who designated Maura McNiel as first president of the organization— "You should do it," she told Maura. "You are intelligent. You have the interest and the energy and the time." Then she handed Sandy Tinkham a pencil and designated her as secretary.

Even though she was an avowed political animal, Sarah never compromised her principals for popularity. She advocated prison reform and an enlightened view toward crime and punishment at a time when these subjects were considered political suicide. "Outside the courtroom, I have to do what I can to shape a climate of community acceptance for some of the things that must change. People think of crime and punishment in the same breath. We'll never get crime lessened until we do something about the reason for it. These aren't controversial issues. As a citizen, it's my responsibility to take sides on community issues that matter."

In the conservative Dallas climate in 1953, she agreed to be the organizing president of a Dallas United Nations Association even when colleagues warned her against it. Nor was she ever afraid of being identified as a feminist, considered a pejorative term in many Dallas circles. In 1944 she headed Dallas's "Back to School" drive to establish a program for the care of children whose mothers worked at a time when there was extreme social pressure for mothers to stay at home and take care of their own children. When married women were not allowed to teach in the Dallas schools, Sarah said that was not only nonsense; it was illegal. The ruling was changed.

In 1952 at the National Democratic Convention, Sarah Hughes was the first woman nominated for vice president of the United States. According to a prior arranged bargain, she almost immediately withdrew her name. Wasn't such a deal contradictory to her avowed beliefs? "Not at all. I am not naive enough to think the time has come for a woman to hold such a high elective office, but it is important that a woman have this kind of recognition. Some day a woman will be president of this country and I am willing to help speed that day."

The maneuver also focused national attention on the petite Dallas dynamo, who often went to Washington to remind Rep. Sam Rayburn, Rep. Lyndon Johnson, and Sen. Ralph Yarborough that she wanted to be appointed a federal judge. "Ask for what you want," Sarah Hughes told women. "Nobody is going to find you hiding in a corner and put you in the spotlight. Women are often told 'Just let George do it. Well, I'm married to George and I learned a long time ago that it wouldn't get done if I waited for George to do it."

In 1961 President John F. Kennedy appointed her U. S. District Judge for the Northern District of Texas. Every woman's organization, the bar associations, and all of the elected officials—Johnson, Rayburn, Yarborough and many others—in whose campaigns she had been a tireless worker supported her appointment. When she was sworn into the judgeship on October 16, 1961, Lyndon Johnson said he "trusted that each of her gray hairs would represent wisdom for a troubled and critical period."

When she woke on November 22, 1963, Sarah Hughes followed her usual disciplined routine. Up before six, she swam a few laps in her heated at-home pool.

On November 22, 1963, Judge Hughes sensed a dark cloud over Dallas far heavier than the hovering rain clouds outside the Dallas Trade Mart where President Kennedy was due for lunch.

Even though it was a cloudy, drizzly morning, she took her bicycle out and rode around the block. She showered, cared for her dog, had a light breakfast while reading the paper, locked the door of her home, drove herself to work and arrived at her office in the federal courthouse building a little before nine. She would later say that she could not escape a sense of foreboding.

Judge Hughes was one of the last guests to arrive at the Dallas Trade Mart at noon on November 22 for the luncheon honoring President John Kennedy and Gov. John Connally. She joined the hundreds of other guests on the main floor of the Trade Mart. Above her, three balconies overlooking the central courtyard were also filled with people. The 20-foot-long head table was laid with white cloths, overdraped in avocado, garlanded with ribbons of greenery, highlighted with two dozen yellow roses at three foot intervals and centered with a display of the six flags of Texas. Places were marked for 16 guests: Mrs. Lloyd Berkner, Mr. Dawson Sterling, Mrs. John Connally, Senator Ralph Yarborough, Mrs. J. Erik Jonsson, President Kennedy, Erik Jonsson, Vice President Johnson, Mrs. Kennedy, Governor Connally, Mrs. L. B. Johnson, Earle Cabell, Mrs. Dawson Sterling, Dr. Berkner, Mrs. Cabell and the Rev. Luther Holcomb..

Judge Hughes who had been appointed to her federal judgeship by President Kennedy should have been seated at that head table, but a political brouhaha had erupted and many of the state's leading Democrats had not been on the guest list. Pat Zahrt said it took calls to Austin to the Governor's office to get some of the state's top Democrats included.

Judge Hughes joined a festive throng, the men in dark business suits and the women hatless or wearing off-the-face hats made so popular by the First Lady. She would be happy, Judge Hughes said, when the President was safely out of town.

At about the time she was saying this, shots were ringing out on the grassy knoll just before the President's car, leading a parade, reached the Triple underpass on Main Street.

At the Trade Mart, the crowd grew restive. The guest of honor was overdue. A few minutes delay was to be expected. But 20 minutes? Then, the east door flew open and the Washington press corps exploded into the room, their faces stark and drawn. Helen Holmes, who had handled public relations for the President's visit, was in the lead. Bob Hollingsworth, Washington Bureau Chief for *The Dallas Times Herald*, was right behind her. I followed him to the phones. He said, "The President has been shot." A pall fell over the crowd. The music stopped. A thousand people froze in mid-motion. There was absolute silence. Mayor Erik Jonsson came to the microphone. He said: "I am not sure I can say what I have to say . . . . our president and our governor have been shot. We do not know how seriously . . . ." Luther Holcomb, executive director of the Council of Churches, came to the microphone. His prayer included: "Oh God, none of us can find the words to express the deep feelings of our hearts . . . . We rely upon all the faith that we possess to see us through . . . ."

Would-be diners left untouched the steaks on their plates. Many milled about as if in communion with others they could ward off what they had just heard. In a room at the front of the Trade Mart a room had been prepared for Jack and Jackie Kennedy to relax. It was furnished with a rocking chair beside a table holding a red telephone. On a table were wrapped gifts marked for the Kennedy children, Caroline and John.

Bob Hollingsworth and the rest of the White House reporters left for Parkland Hospital where the President and Gov. Connally had been taken. Sarah Hughes was one of the people who made her way out of the Trade Mart. This is the story she later wrote about the next hour of her life:

> It was 2:15, Friday, November 22. I had just reached home from the Trade Mart where a large and enthusiastic crowd had gathered to see and hear President John F. Kennedy. We waited in vain, for he had been assassinated as he was leaving the downtown area of Dallas.
>
> Numbed and hardly realizing what had happened, I drove home. There was no reason to go to court. In the face of the tragedy that had befallen us, all else seemed of little consequence.

Judge William Taylor, Mayor Adlene Harrison and Judge Sarah Hughes holding informal court on the school integration issue.

I phoned the court to tell the clerk where I was. Her response was that Barefoot Sanders, U.S. attorney, wanted to speak to me. Immediately I heard his familiar voice. "The Vice-President wants you to swear him as President. Can you do it? How soon can you get to the airport?" Of course I could, and I could be there in ten minutes.

I got in my car and started to the airport. Now there was another job to be done—a new President who had to carry on, and he must qualify for the office as quickly as possible. He had much to do, and I must think of him, and do the job that had been assigned to me.

There was no time to find the oath administered to a president, but the essentials of every oath are the same. You have to swear to perform the duties of the office of President of the United States, and to preserve and defend the Constitution of the United States. I was not afraid. I could do it without a formal oath.

Police blocked the entrance to the location of the plane, but there was no difficulty. They knew me, and I told them I was there to swear in the Vice-President as President. One of the motorcycle officers went to the plane to confirm my statement and then escorted me to the plane.

It was a beautiful sight, the presidential plane, long and sleek, a blue and two white stripes running the length of the plane with the words, "The United States of America," on the blue stripe. It seemed to exemplify the strength and courage of our country.

I was escorted up the ramp by the chief of police to the front door, where one of the Vice-President's aides and the Secret Service met me. I was trying to explain that I did not have the presidential oath but could give it anyway when someone handed me a copy.

In the second compartment were several Texas congressmen, vice-presidential aides, Secret Service men, and the Vice-President and Mrs. Johnson. Mr. and Mrs. Johnson had been my friends for many years, but on such an occasion there did not seem to be anything to say. I embraced them both, for that was the best way to give expression to my feeling of grief for them, and for all of us.

By that time a Bible that was on the plane had been thrust into my hands. It was a small volume, with soft leather backs. I thought someone said it was a Catholic Bible. I do not know, but I would like to think it was, and that President Kennedy had been reading it on this, his last trip.

The Vice-President said Mrs. Kennedy wanted to be present for the ceremony, and in a very few minutes she appeared. Her face showed her grief, but she was composed and calm. She, too, exemplified the courage this country needs to carry on. The Vice-President leaned toward her and told her I was a U.S. judge appointed by her husband. My acknowledgement was, "I loved him very much."

The Vice-President asked Mrs. Johnson to stand on his right, Mrs. Kennedy on his left, and with his hand on the Bible, slowly and reverently repeated the oath after me: "I do solemnly swear that I will perform the duties of President of the United States to the best of my ability and defend, protect, and preserve the Constitution of the United States." That was all to the oath I had in my hand, but I added, "So help me God," and he said it after me. It seemed that needed to be said.

He gently kissed Mrs. Kennedy and leaned over and kissed his wife on the cheek.

Here was a man with ability and determination for the task ahead. Great as are the responsibilities of the office, I felt he could carry on. I told him so, and that we were behind him, and he would have our sympathy and our help.

As I left the plane I heard him give the order to take off. "Now let's get ready and go." I drove away with my thoughts on this man, upon whom so much now depended.[10]

Thirty minutes after Sarah Hughes administered the oath of office to the 36th President of the United States, she answered her own phone in her own home. Always a master of the understatement, she said that "Of course, it was a great honor for me. Mr. Johnson asked me to do it because I am his friend . . . . I took it as a job. I am not emotional about it." Later she would add, "I don't consider it one of my accomplishments."

When she was 73, Sarah said, "I will live to be a hundred because there are so many things I want to master." She missed it by 12 years. The stroke that robbed her of quality for living happened in 1982 and the light left her on Tuesday, April 23, 1985. In the prime of her life, when she was relishing work, contributing in the volunteer community, gardening, swimming, biking, horseback riding, traveling, writing and speaking she was asked to sum up the most important advice for others. She said: "Never get in an argument with someone whose mind is made up. You can't win. You only waste your time."

27

WOMEN AT WAR—THE 1940s

For women, the decades of 1940s and 1950s were a paradox. On the one hand, women were never more invisible, and on the other never more visible. The male power structure in Dallas became organized in ways that categorically—unconsciously, maybe, but no less emphatically—excluded female input. And, conversely, the break-down of past prototypes gave women their first major opportunity for widespread initiatives.

On the surface, no period in the history of Dallas has been more blatantly macho as that of the 1940s through the 1950s. It was a period dominated by war and the aftermath of war, followed by almost four decades of uninterrupted expansion of businesses, industries and professions with men and male values totally in control. Men made millions in oil, real estate, banking, insurance and other industries and businesses. In the past, women had contributed chiefly as silent conspirators and behind-the-scenes advisors. Beginning with World War II—and for the years following it until the eruption of the civil rights movement and, with it, the feminist movement—the old boys network in Dallas closed ranks. They, as Ruth Pines put it "spoke only to each other and God."

The organization that closed decision-making to women—and all but a handful of men—was the Dallas Citizens Council. It was officially organized in 1937, but did not surface as *the* city's primary decision-maker until the early 1940s. R. L. Thornton, chief of the Mercantile Bank, who had been successful in claiming the Texas Centennial for Dallas against all reasonable odds, had done so with a few telephone calls to men with money. His success in that endeavor convinced him that an organization of "Yes and No" men would be good for the city.

The 100 original members of the Citizens Council were men who wielded almost complete power in their companies and did not have to confer with anyone else before committing their organizations to an idea and, more important, money. The Council's stated purpose was "to study, confer and act upon any matter, civic or economic in character, which may be deemed to affect the welfare of the City of Dallas, the County of Dallas, or the State of Texas, and to support any educational or civic enterprise deemed to promote such welfare."

It was, in reality, a super chamber of commerce. It determined who would be in charge of everything of importance in the city. Dallas historian A. C. Greene explained it:

> It used to be so simple. Uncle Bob Thornton would make a few phone calls or Mayor Erik Jonsson would have half a dozen other members of the Dallas Citizens Council to lunch at the City Club, and the problem was solved....
>
> (it) was a machine that wasn't a machine, an aristocracy that volunteered its service but was absolute in its control. Might was inherited along business lines instead of bloodlines, and all of it based on a sort of gentleman's agreement that no one would grab for private power or overreach for personal gain.
>
> ... (It) was not (and is not) a myth, or some booger-bear that hides by day and prowls by night. It is merely a corporation chartered by the state of Texas "to study, confer and act upon any matter"
>
> .... No tricky subclauses, no legal gobbledygook or secret handshakes, a closed membership and no public meetings—but it's worked long and worked well ... a system unique ... among larger American cities, this voluntary political machine that governed and directed community life through its detached but firmly controlled management units.[1]

For many years, self-appointed leaders, operating as the Dallas Citizens Council, controlled the city. When it is considered that Dallas was safe and clean, there is little wonder that many citizens long to return to the "good old days."

Nancy Steorts was the first woman to be president of the Dallas Citizens Council.

Mary Crowley, at left, with Betty Richardson, broke the gender barrier which had been in place for 41 years at the Dallas Citizens Council. She was invited to join in 1978.

Membership in the Dallas Citizens Council was by invitation only, and it would never have occurred to the original 100 members that any woman might be eligible. This policy continued for 41 years until, in 1978, Mary Crowley, founder and president of Home Interiors and Gifts, Inc., was invited to join. By the strange coincidences that mark human progress, Mary had been denied credit by a number of institutions to start her business until the bank founded by Bob Thornton extended her the loan. Several of the more prominent and successful women business executives have never been extended an invitation. Fine points for membership make most ineligible. In 1987 on its 50th anniversary, the Citizens Council had 268 members. Five of them were women—Ruth Sharp Altshuler, chief executive officer of the Carr P. Collins Foundation; Nancy Harvey Steorts, president (the first woman president) of Dallas Citizens Council; Kay Bailey Hutchison, attorney; Caroline Hunt Schoellkopf, chairperson of Rosewood Corporation, and Lucy Billingsley, president of the Dallas Market Center. In 1990, when membership stood at 260, nine women were members. Kay Hutchison had resigned to run for and be elected Texas State Treasurer. Nancy had resigned her post. Ruth Altshuler, Caroline Hunt and Lucy Billingsley had been joined by Norma Lee Beasley, Mary Jordan DeLaurenti, Valerie Freeman, Margaret Jordan, Charlotte St. Martin and Liz Minyard.

The Dallas Citizens Council achieved phenomenal benefits for almost two decades. It promoted a $40-million master plan for Dallas expansion that included housing, transportation, sports facilities, health and medical facilities, business and real estate expansions. Lauded in its early years as a model for progressive cities, its power has ebbed and waned since the 1960s. Its unofficial slogans, What's Good for Business is Good for Dallas and the even more limiting Keep the Dirt Flying, overlooked almost everything except physical growth. There were no voices of dissent, no place for a democratic process, no input from anybody except the self-anointed oligarchy. Overlooked was almost everything that provided a quality of life, almost everything that the women of the city had long struggled to include. Historians note that the power of the Dallas Citizens Council, which has in recent years made progress in inclusiveness and openness, declined because Dallas changed. True enough, but another factor is equally significant. The sons of the men who were in the original 100 usually inherited a place on the Council just as they inherited their fathers' businesses. Very often the second generation had neither the ability nor the inclination to rule as quasi-monarchs of their city.

It is little wonder, then, that this was a period when few women surfaced as even token players in the power structure. They were defined, and they characterized themselves in traditional roles—as helpmates, wives and mothers. As a matter of record, in the two decades (1945-1965) that followed World War II, women reached a new peak or nadir—depending on your personal political bent—in appearance and behavior that defined the traditional American female. The chief objective of a woman in Dallas—and largely in the rest of the United States—was to be married, and only married women were whole women. The 1940s was a time when women, whether they were in college, working, or simply waiting out the end of the conflict, turned themselves into models of what men wanted them to be and what men wanted them to be was ornamental and inaudible. One of the first things that happens among men with newly acquired money is to turn their wives into show pieces. The women generally are only too happy to comply. Most of them were contented conspirators. In Dallas, women were ahead of the national average in these roles. The period produced, at least on the surface, a great many pedestaled American princesses.

But with all of this there lies the contradiction—for try as women did to meld their futures with that of men who would live with them in eternal bliss in a rose-covered cottage at the end of Harmony Lane, reality kept intruding. For one, the grim reaper snuffed out the prospects of countless young women to marry and have children. Two hundred and ninety two thousand, one hundred and thirty-one young men died in battle in World War II. This meant diminishing chances for thousands of brides who were already married to them, or of young women harboring a future of eternal bliss to marry at all. The aftermath of every war, at least until the present time, leaves unmarried women in its wake. But there is another, equally significant consideration. Women, called on to run the farms, businesses industries and homes while the men were away at war,

Women learned that the roses growing on their vine-covered cottages had thorns. Being the darling of an adoring man who provided her total support was the ideal for many a woman—so long as he continued to be adoring—and brought his pay check home.

discovered they could do it very well. Some of them, a small but significant few, found that the taste of responsibility and independence was exhilarating—and they could no longer be content with a rose-covered cottage they had not helped to purchase, furnish and manage. Third, the scourges of war left a great many homeless women. The war shook up the nation as nothing before it had ever done. Southern boys brought home brides from England and Italy and Germany and Holland. Kids from the agricultural belts of Iowa and Nebraska introduced wives to their families from New York and California and Utah. Only a perfunctory glance at the nuptial pages—and they were the nuptial pages—of the newspapers of the period is sufficient to show that the world population was topsy-turvy.

The changes in the social structures of America planted seeds of discord right along with the benefits of cross-cultural fertilization. Not all who wed in a state of rose-colored romance survived as couples in a postwar world of reality. Divorces climbed, and a great many women who had counted on the rose-covered cottages were left to provide small apartments for themselves—and often, their child or children.

If you closed your eyes—and most Dallasites did—to what was happening in Europe and the rest of the world, the early 1940s was a time of tranquility and limitless possibilities.

Salaries were low—$25 a week was a good wage for a working woman; a man could expect a little more—but the cost of living was also pared down.

In June of 1940, if you were in the luxury class, you could rent a five-bedroom, three-bath fully furnished house on Turtle Creek for $125 a month or a three-bedroom house in Preston Estates for $65. You could buy the house at 3734 Lakehurst for $5,050 at payments of $39.10 a month or a two-story house on Lupton Drive at Preston for $1,500 down and $60 per month.[2]

A full-page ad catering to newlyweds explained how you could set up housekeeping for $183.40. If you chose, you could pay $100 down and $1 a week for two years. For this money you got a General Electric refrigerator, a white porcelain gas range, a six-piece bedroom suite and a five-piece breakfast room set consisting of a drop-leaf table and four chairs. The deal came with a certificate in writing guaranteeing to suspend payments in case of illness or unemployment and to cancel all remaining payments in case of fire, natural disaster or death of the breadwinner.[3]

Neiman-Marcus advertised a double-breasted white pique skirt, "the first separated of its kind in America" for $11.95 and a linen jacket-blouse for $7.95. An alligator-grained bag sold for $5.00 and white cotton gloves, a "fashion classic essential," for $1.00 a pair. Andrew Geller's spiked heeled summer suede pumps were $12.95 at Dreyfuss. Men's white broadcloth shirts were $2.50 each at Neiman's, and men's suits with two pair of pants sold for $29.95 at Sangers. Fashion Editor Elizabeth Scott King of *The Dallas Morning News* decreed that novelty weaves—pique, gingham, cotton lace and froths of organdy were in high fashion for women. Skirts were just below the knee and full. Unpressed pleats were in. Buttons were big. So were silk flowers and shoulder pads. Colors were gold and white. Lipstick was the key to fashion color. Hair was done in a pompadour and hats, a fashion must, "lifted back off your brow."

At Everts, you could buy a four-piece place setting of King Edward sterling for $13.35, or a dozen crystal goblets, ice teas or sherbets for $15. You could have your mink cleaned and stored for $1.25, buy a new Pontiac for $783 or a gentle pony with saddle for $17.50.

In downtown Dallas on a Sunday night at the Majestic you could see *Johnny Apollo* starring Dorothy Lamour and Tyrone Power for 25 cents or stay at home and listen to Edgar Bergen and Charlie McCarthy on the radio. Or, you could go out to SMU and see Lanham Deal starring in *As You Like It* in an Arden Club performance. If you happened to be at SMU on June 5, you could see Mrs. W. W. Fondren dedicate the Fondren Library, total cost $458,000, to the memory of her late husband.

In 1940, already half of the women of Dallas in their twenties and almost half in their thirties were in the labor force, a good deal larger proportion than any other Texas city. At noon every day, Monday through Saturday they poured out of the office buildings to lunch and to shop, forming jewels of color in a setting of buildings and busy streets.

War, as imminent as it has been for years, was a jolting shock to the average Dallasite. Soon after December 7, 1941, the war touched every individual personally.

Dressed in their full-skirted novelty weaves and their high heels, they were amused, but totally non-empathetic with Naomi Still in Tulsa. Her story was so unusual that it made the front page in Dallas. She had worn a pantsuit into a federal courtroom to be with a friend and Judge A. P. Murrah had ordered the bailiff to evict her with the warning. "Women must wear dresses and not pants in my courtroom."

On December 7, 1941, a dreary Sunday in Dallas—clouds overcast, damp winds, intermittent rain—the world changed dramatically in moments when the Japanese unleashed a hail of bombs that snuffed out 2,300 lives, destroyed or badly damaged 19 ships and almost destroyed the air force of the United States at Pearl Harbor in Hawaii. The next day, an equally dreary-weather Monday, my classmates and I sat on the floor of the women's gymnasium at SMU and listened by radio as President Roosevelt declared that "a state of war exists." The Congress, with only one dissenting vote, agreed. Jeanette Rankin, a Congresswoman from Missouri, cast the only no vote. Three days later Congress also declared war against Germany and Italy.

Though the conflict had been brewing for months, war came as a jolting shock to most Dallasites. It hit everybody quickly and personally. Overnight, men disappeared from our college classrooms, to be replaced later by the Navy V-12 Unit, men in uniform who were completing their college work in accelerated programs before being assigned to active duty. Many of the young men in uniform were our familiar classmates, their numbers augmented by other boys studying courses essential to the war effort, chiefly engineering and medicine.

The world was, at one and the same time, caught in time capsules of seconds and spinning out of control. Plans made one moment were jettisoned the next as circumstances arbitrarily altered. On the very day, for instance, of Pearl Harbor, the engagement of popular SMU student Miss Calvert Keoun was announced to Carr P. Collins Jr., the wedding to take place in her hometown of Marshall on December 31. Instead, the couple was married on Christmas Day in Sacramento, California, so that they could have a few days together before he shipped out to war. This vignette is typical of what was happening all over the country.

There were also moments of shame, as when in early 1942, the federal government forcibly moved 110,000 Japanese-Americans, including 75,000 U. S. citizens from the West Coast to detention camps for three years. The round-up began even before that, on the day war was declared. In Dallas on December 8, Mr. and Mrs. H. Muta closed the only Japanese-owned retail store in the city, the Oriental Art Company, at 1312 Elm Street. The Mutas had been U. S. residents for half a century, and in business in Dallas since 1900. On the same day, Dallas jailed five Japanese aliens "as a precautionary measure." Most were United States citizens.

Almost instantly, the military put out a call for nurses. On December 12, the Dallas debutantes, albeit in a full-page of photographs, volunteered "to aid the war effort." On the same day there was "the biggest human tidal wave of volunteers for enlistment in the military... since the World War... 500 eager-eyed young men... enlisted in the Army, Navy, Marines and Coast Guard." By the middle of December "Business Girls Enroll for Defense Duty; to form Career Girls' Defense Corps," said a headline, and by December 18 more than 1,000 young women had registered. Mrs. Norman Johnson was named "brigadier general."

Two days after the bombs fell on Pearl Harbor and a day after the formal declaration of war, writers were already telling women what they could do. In an article entitled, "Feminine Leader Sees Women as Third Army," Mrs. Harold Vincent Millicent, president of the National Council of Women of the United States Inc. wrote:

> ...a third army is mobilizing for the protection of our homes and family ...the mothers, wives, daughters, sisters and sweethearts of the men who are serving... in the defense of our nation.
>
> ...every woman can contribute... whether or not she is able to leave her home, roll bandages, learn first-aid, or can drive an ambulance. The rising cost of food, clothing, and all household appliances presents a constant challenge to

the homemaker who must keep her family physically fit, adequately clothed, and, above all, cheerful, calm and confident.[4]

There it was: The role of women was to keep the world safe at home while the men fought to keep it safe on the battlefields. The lengthy article gave numbers of generalizations, but few specifics. Women could plan menus that were less costly; they could conserve clothing and household appliances, save energy, sacrifice luxuries, salvage paper and rubber. But, chiefly, they could be the ever-present calm in storms of international chaos.

The war, expected to be over in a few months, lasted three years and eight months, 1,346 days. It was six months before the United States won its first victory against the Japanese, June 4-7, at Midway.

At home most people shared similar annoying limitations. Fairly soon, rationing stamps were issued to everybody, and a stamp, along with money, was required to purchase almost everything—many foods, numerous items of clothing, gasoline and other fuel supplies. Many products that Americans had come to believe were essential could not be bought at any price. They did not exist. Meat was in very short supply and, when it was available, was expensive. Coffee was extremely scarce. Restaurants limited their hours and sometimes closed for days when they could not get meat. Bakeries did the same thing because of the scarcity of sugar. The five gallons of gasoline you could purchase with a stamp did not let you travel very far. Shoes were extremely scarce. Women watched ads for any indication that shoes might be available, but mostly the word about scarce commodities traveled by grapevine, and often when one went to purchase an item, it had already been sold out. More than one woman suffered with uncomfortable shoes because she settled for what she could find rather than for what would fit. Nylon hose, which had only recently come on the market, were no longer available. All of the nylon was restricted to the war effort—making parachutes and other essentials. Automobiles were not made at all, the car manufacturing companies turning their facilities into making vehicles for war.

But, while scarcities were a nuisance, fear and uncertainty was an even more eroding demon. News from the fighting areas came slowly, delayed and incomplete, only by radio and newspaper, and was highly restricted by the government. Mail was censored. Fighting men were not allowed to tell their families where they were. And it was strongly encouraged that all letters from home to the men, sometimes delayed for weeks and even months, be filled only with good news. This severely limited what could be written home or, for that matter, written to the men in uniform.

But mostly, World War II, like all crises, was an individual, first person singular experience for everybody who lived it, the wives and mothers and sweethearts and sisters as well as the men fighting it on two separate fronts, Europe and the South Pacific.

On July 26, 1945, as a 22-year-old Dallas career woman, only a year out of college, I wrote a letter to myself so that I would remember what the war years were like. Never published, these are excerpts:

> There will come a time, though now I am sure I cannot imagine it, when I shall ask myself or others will ask me: What were they like—those war years? I shall then have to turn back the pages of time and search my mind until I recapture:
> The feeling of complete desolation the day I sat on a gymnasium floor and listened with a heavy heart, but unfaltering eyes, one among several hundred other students, while I heard President Roosevelt ask Congress for war. That was Dec. 8, 1941 . . . .
> What was it like, those war years? . . . . It wasn't at all like I first thought it would be. The hatred of war had been carefully ingrained into me and our generation. And it wasn't all bad like they had said it would be.
> I remember . . . things soon settled back into what we considered "normal" . . . . boys left our classrooms. Gradually—gradually change came, but as change

Rationing stamps, along with cash, were a nuisance but not nearly as difficult to bear as the news coming out of Europe and the Pacific. The war was not going well and women whose men were on the front lines lived in constant fear.

Amidst the international conflict, daily life went on. There were businesses to run, homes to maintain, children to birth and rear, bills to be paid. For the most part, women were in charge of these things.

has a way of doing, it slipped up on us until we hardly noticed the differences . . . . we talked of war as seriously as we knew how, but it didn't make much of a dent . . . . We spoke of it as people speak of every-day occurrences. We counted it in terms of weeks, or months at best. We read our newspapers and shook our heads and pursed out lips at the idea that people of any nation would defy us. We spoke of the exploits of our friends. We scoffed at those who dared see the war as going on for years . . . .

We fell in love. Boys became men overnight. And girls became women. And everybody fell in love—with soldiers and sailors, with marines. Most of all, with flyers. Again and again the warning came from those older and wiser that so many war marriages could not work—that divorce would follow, that children would be brought into the world without homes, without fathers who lived to see their offspring. And it was true. Still we fell in love. Still we married.

During those war years, life was a gamble—so much so that my generation caught at any thread of happiness and tried to weave all of the future from the few threads that touched them in passing. Love was blind. It was a hit and miss proposition and nobody was immune.

What were they like? Those war years? They were hell. And they were heaven. They were made up of a few moments when a girl could bury her face in a uniform and close her eyes to all else. They were made up of hours and days and months and years of waiting . . . when a telephone call or a letter was all that was left to live for. They were made up of forevers. An hour could be a forever. A month was hundreds of them.

. . . there was romance and high adventure. And there were the real things. It came to pass that the unusual became the ordinary and the usual became the exception. There were times when . . . a bride made a home from four enclosed walls and a grocery box and was lucky to have it. Other brides made home with Mom and Dad and waited . . . . Names of far-away places— Pearl Harbor, Guam, Leyte, Boungainville, Malta, New Guinea, Saipan . . . became haunting, deadly missiles of reality.

Yet, it was not all bad. Those war years made what had once seemed necessity now a luxury . . . . There were lots of things we didn't have. We dared not drive our cars an extra few blocks; every windshield had a little sticker on it designating whether our car was "essential" or not, and those little A, B and C stickers told all our neighbors just how much gasoline we were allowed. You couldn't buy an electrical appliance any more . . . no refrigerators, no irons, no waffle irons, no toasters. No fans. No favorite candy bars. No chewing gum. No popular brands of cigarettes. No meat. No favorite restaurant that served your favorite food.

You bought food not only with money, but with little red and blue pasteboard stamps called points. It took so many points to buy a pound of steak—only you couldn't usually find the steak even if you had the points. Shoes had points; you got two pairs a year.

At college, one day our classrooms were over fifty per cent men; then we woke up one day to see that we were practically a woman's college. But at SMU, Uncle Sam fixed that. He gave us a Navy V-12 Unit. Which meant that we had a host of young men in Navy Blue descend upon us. Which meant that life went on pretty much as usual. Our dances and pep rallies and ball games continued. Different, yes. Under stricter regulations. But we had so much more than most girls had. Our dances had patriotic themes, sometimes were bond rallies. Our plays had mostly female casts.

. . . Those little things! A girl "blind dated" or she didn't date at all. She was lucky if she drew a gentleman. At all-girl parties the conversation ran to "That wonderful Marine . . . that drip from the Midwest, that cute sailor from California, that di-vine lieutenant . . . ." You may have been cheated out of long strolls home from the college dance or a drive into the country for a picnic. But you had other things . . . .

Ours was a generation that dreamed of white picket fences and big apple trees in the yard. But we made heaven of whatever came along . . . .

. . . war touched *every* home. Some tried desperately to shut it out. Others opened wide the doors and invited sadness in. But most of us went about our daily work, doing what had to be done. Some hopefully, some desperately, some passively. Uniforms were *everywhere*. You soon didn't stare, but you never got to where you didn't notice. And when the men started coming back, some without arms and some without legs and some crippled and maimed for life in other ways, something died inside you. But you didn't say anything. There was nothing to say.

This is January 1945. The tide turned some months ago in our favor, but we are not home free yet. Casualty lists are mounting and almost every day you hear of someone you know who won't be coming home—ever. You are often afraid—bitterly, horribly afraid. The waiting is hardest. Work helps. So you drive yourself. Manpower is at a premium . . . . Yes, the war has hit every person. Sometimes in nothing more than a steak they cannot buy. Sometimes in the form of "The War Department regrets to inform you . . . ." Usually in all those million and one little ways in between.

Everybody who has experienced this war has lived a forever. My forevers have been made up of familiar faces I do not see, loneliness when I go home to the small town where I was reared, a kid brother whose heart has always been in the clouds and who has realized his life's dream because of this war. And the other brother, transplanted now on foreign soil, who thought his future lay permanently in the crunch of new-turned sod underneath his feet and the smell and fragrance of the earth as he readied it for planting. My forevers are made up of the telephone calls I do not get and the letters that do not come and eternal waiting . . . waiting . . . waiting.

World War II ended in 1945—in the spring in Europe, during the summer in the Pacific—and Johnnie came marching home, often to discord instead of harmony.

The war ended in Germany on May 7, 1945, following the suicide of Hitler and in the Pacific on August 15, 1945, after the United States dropped two bombs on Japan, one on Hiroshima on August 6 and the other on Nagasaki on August 9.

At peace, Dallas had major adjustments. The population of Greater Dallas (including seven adjoining incorporated cities—Highland Park, University Park, Preston Hollow, Cement City, Cockrell Hill, Fruitdale and Honey Springs—was 360,212 in 1940 and 395,280—a year later. It continued to expand at a phenomenal rate. Marriages soared. Young couples and young families poured in. Housing was all but non-existent. The 79,384 residences in existence in 1940 had no growth at all during the war years and slow and sporadic expansion for a few years afterward. The classified ads of newspapers were full of "Apartment Wanted" ads. Most of them began . . . ."Veteran of. . . and bride desire apartment. Will consider anything." Charlatans swindled eager housing hunters in many ways. For one, Lois and Charlie Eddins put several hundred dollars of his service savings into purchasing furniture in an apartment with the stipulation that they could then rent the place—only to find that 26 other couples had done the same thing. Rarely did any of the individuals recover their losses from the schemes. On November 27, 1946, Col. Carl L. Phinney issued a plea with landlords to aid veterans in securing housing. He said there were 11,000 homeless veterans and their families in Dallas County.

College classrooms bulged as veterans took advantage of the G.I. Bill to go back to school. It paid tuition, some fees and most books and a minute living stipend.

The birth rate skyrocketed. Obstetricians worked overtime. The maternity wards of hospitals overflowed. At Florence Nightingale, Baylor's maternity department, some new mothers found hallways converted into temporary rooms.

Slowly, price controls were lifted. Women's clothes were among the first evidence that things were returning to "normal." In the fall of 1946, women in Dallas awoke to a front-page headline: "Women Given Longer Skirts"[5] with the announcement that the Civilian Production Association had dropped all limitations on women's clothing. It was the first time in four and a half years—since April 6, 1942, when skirt lengths and other restrictions had gone into effect to save cloth—that women could begin to find variety

Having rid itself of one scourge, it was as if the country had to find another common enemy to hate. Communism became that foe. By indirect innuendo and blatant accusation, many innocent people were labeled Communist losing their reputations and their livelihoods.

in fashion. Two days later Sanger's, in a full page ad, trumpeted "Real Clothes Are Back" and showed a red brocade taffeta evening gown priced at $97.50. Its "little topping" was a belted hip-length broadtail jacket with mandarin sleeves. It would be some time before the "new look" dropped hemlines to four to six inches from the floor. Perhaps it is my personal prejudice, because I was young and aware, but I am convinced that the most beautiful clothes ever available to and worn by women were those of the late 1940s.

On November 1, 1946, the Office of Price Administration that had controlled the price and distribution of almost everything during the war ordered 1,642 local price boards locked up. Soap that had been in severe short supply began to appear again on retail shelves. On November 10, President Harry S. Truman announced that price controls on everything except rent, sugar and rice were lifted. Before Christmas, controls on housing construction were lifted making it possible for the first wholesale housing to be built since before the war. Throughout Dallas, with delays caused by shortages of supplies, builders rushed to complete two-bedroom, one-bath houses. Some were shoddily constructed and turned, within a few years, to slum areas. A great many others, kept up and often remodeled, were still quality residences 50 years later. Veterans could finance their homes through the Federal Housing Administration (FHA, Title 6). Some of the houses were centrally heated, but not all and none were air-conditioned. Unit, room-by-room, air conditioners were not widely used until a decade later. By 1949 room air-conditioners were still high. A one-horsepower Frigidaire was available at Titche's for $495. It could be purchased for $49 down and paid out in monthly installments—for wartime controls on credit, charge accounts and installment buying was among the first to be lifted (on October 25, 1946).

As restrictions were removed, prices "eased" up, 19 per cent in one month from the time controls went off. Public transportation, frozen at seven cents throughout the war, went to eight cents (October 24, 1946). The Nickelodeon, which for five cents had provided music to millions, became the "Dime-olodeon" at the 1,100 juke boxes in Dallas.

Rent controls lingered . . . and lingered. It was not until June of 1949 that the state legislature passed a rent-decontrol bill. Four days later, on June 15, Dallas became the first big city in the nation to lift rent controls. These laws were still subject to federal interpretation, but by this time the federal government was preoccupied with other activities.

Hunting Communists was among its top priorities. The House Un-American Activities committee was hearing testimony in Washington about government officials, movie stars, writers, college and university leaders and other public figures accused, with little or no evidence, of being members of the Communist Party or "fellow travelers." A "secret" FBI report placed Frederic March, Edward G. Robinson, writer Dorothy Parker, actress Sylvia Sydney and many others on the Red list. Evidence of their un-American activities was so nebulous that it would have been amusing—except that hundreds of people were hurt, their names smudged and their careers obliterated by such as this: "(He) was singled out for praise in a German-language publication of the Moscow-dominated Comintern."

Just as the Ku Klux Klan, with its divisive tactics had impacted Dallas in the 1920s, the Red baiters found fertile soil for planting its seeds of fear and hate in the city in the late 1940s and early '50s. On Dec. 7, 1948—seven years to the day from Pearl Harbor that had united the country in a single mission—the Dallas Federation of Women's Clubs heard Madame Barry Orlova of New York:

> Termites are eating at the foundation of our government. This nation is the hope of mankind in the world. We must awaken to the danger, not at our doors, but within our houses. Ask your politicians what you want to know and demand an answer. Don't be shushed. If a man tries to shush you, he is a worker for the Soviet government. There is a secret organization in this nation seeking to undermine you. It is not sleeping. It works in gangs.[6]

This was one among numbers of speeches and programs sponsored by the Federation that helped to scatter the seeds of hatred. The organization that had been created by May Dickson Exall to establish the Dallas Public Library had come a long way from open debate. For months Federation members were subject to speakers who limited, rather than expanded, their horizons.

Strangely enough, Federation members on the same day they were listening to Madame Orlova describe conditions in Washington as "the most dangerous scandal in the history of this nation," voted to buy a Bookmobile for the Library. The library, like other public services, had been in a five-year slumber during and immediately following the war years at a time when demands for service were burgeoning. Librarian Cleora Clanton made countless speeches about inadequate facilities, lack of room for expansion, lack of money to buy new books and replace or restore old ones. She grasped at anything that would enhance the services to a clamoring public. The Bookmobile, a library on wheels, was one answer. Purchased and outfitted, it was in service before the end of 1949 and carried books, on a regular schedule, to several places throughout the city. A decade later three Bookmobiles were making 23 stops per week in shopping centers not served by branch libraries. Ms. Clanton had successfully convinced her board during the war years to issue books to service people without restriction. In 1945, she issued 339 cards to men and women in uniform at military bases throughout the Southwest. Follow-up studies showed that the experiment was a success. The number of overdue books were "infinitesimal."[7]

When she retired on December 31, 1954, Ms. Clanton had worked for the library 39 years. "I started for exactly nothing," she said at her retirement. "It was three months before I was paid anything . . . . My work carries with it a compensation above salary. There is pleasure in helping people."

Cleora Clanton, like so many women who have contributed to the quality of Dallas, at her retirement, overlooked the excessive hours, poor compensation and overwhelming expectations that her job had entailed. The "glass ceiling" for women—a term that would not be recognized for years to come—was already firmly in place. Women could be teachers, librarians and nurses, but they would not be paid what they were worth nor appreciated for what they did. This was spelled out as the 1940s decade came to a close at the national convention of the American Association of University Women in Seattle. Two thousand participants heard the results of a two-year study.

"There is," the report concluded, "an increasing demand for women's services in the labor force, but . . . unfortunately . . . the most cordial welcome awaits them in low-paid, unskilled jobs."

28

• • • •

THE POWER–FOUR

In less than two decades, between the years 1945 and 1963, a quartet of Dallasites cast a new mold for women entrepreneurs. The manner in which they have developed and ran their businesses and the successes they have enjoyed are unparalleled in the annals of American business. They share almost uncanny backgrounds and a basic tenet of the Golden Rule of "Do unto others as you would have them do unto you." Although men often sneered at initial contact with each of the four beautifully groomed, soft-spoken, quiet-mannered women—nobody questioned that their way of managing their businesses has been overwhelmingly rewarding—financially, personally and in service to others. Though each planned to be successful and each worked countless hours in establishing and managing her business, none ever dreamed that she would become a premier Dallas titan.

The four are Mary Kay Ash, founder of Mary Kay Cosmetics; Mary Crowley, founder of Home Interiors and Gifts Inc.; Bette Graham, founder of Liquid Paper Corporation, and Ebby Halliday, founder of Ebby Halliday Realtors.

They share financially deprived backgrounds. Had they been male, they would been call Horatio Algers. They are, instead Gaeas—earth mother goddesses of strong business associate daughters and sons. As young children, they were in dysfunctional birth families but were encircled with love in their extended family relationships. They were all products of the Great Depression; they assumed responsibility for themselves and the lives of others at very early ages. They all had early failed marriages that taught them, as one of the women put it, "I couldn't depend on a man to support me or rescue me. I had to be my own savior."

Of the quartet, Ebby Halliday was the first of the post World War II women business successes. She owns and manages one of the largest residential real estate companies in the world, covering the Greater Dallas Metroplex and through Relo (a network of companies offering relocation services which she was instrumental in establishing in the 1950s) 1,250 cities throughout the United States and 17 foreign countries. This giant business (in March of 1991) operated out of 20 offices plus the corporate office at Preston Road and Northwest Highway in Dallas. It had 830 sales associates and 102 salaried employees. For the "past 10 or 15 years" it has averaged 5,500 sales, half of all of them cooperative ventures. In 1990, which was considered a bad year for real estate, "we came close to 9,000." Ebby Halliday knows all of the people who carry business cards with her name on them and she knows to the last penny what her company is worth.

Born Vera Lucille Koch on March 11, 1911, in Leslie, Arkansas, Ebby Halliday was 18 months old when her father died. She and her two siblings, Virginia Lee (Huff) and Raymond Koch, went to live with their grandparents, The Rev. J. C. and Dulcina Linson Elizabeth Stinson Treece Mabrey. Her grandfather was a circuit-riding Baptist minister and the children's highly structured lives revolved around church, Sunday school and prayer meetings at a Presbyterian church which was near their home and to which they went on horseback. "We had a good moral grounding . . . . We ate lots of chicken wings at the second table on Sundays," Ebby said in a 1991 interview. When she was seven, her mother remarried and sent for the children. Her stepfather was a Kansas wheat farmer—austere, domineering and, at times, cruel both to his wife and the children. Two more babies, Frances Elizabeth and Paul Hanson, joined the family.

Vera Lucille attended a one-room school; she built a world of her own through reading when she could escape to do so. Her stepfather considered reading a waste of time and those who indulged in it lazy. At school she devoured the classics, the only books her "library" had. Once she was caught reading at home and the book was snatched away and tossed into the fire. Her stepfather, on the other hand, demanded perfection from the children in everything. He insisted that they lead their class scholastically and that they win all athletic awards. The children got up at 6 a.m., did their farm chores, went to school, did more chores, did their homework and helped around the house. "He wanted us to be No. 1 in everything; he was obsessed with competition." Vera Lucille and Virginia Lee were more pressured than their brother because he had had polio and was not strong.

Ebby Halliday, at left, in her classic pose before the real estate firm that bears her name, and, above, shortly after she opened her business in 1945.

When Vera was 14 she was ready for high school which her tiny wheat-farming town did not have. She found a room in the home of Margaret and Judge Crane in Abilene, Kansas, within walking distance of high school. She worked her way through high school with a part-time job as a salesgirl at J. B. Carson and taught Sunday school at a Methodist church. She was an A student in everything except math. "I could have done a lot better if I hadn't sneaked out all the time to play tennis." She graduated in 1929, five months before the stock market crashed and the banks closed. "I had saved $29.75—an enormous amount for a school girl. I lost it all when the banks closed.

"I wanted desperately to go to Kansas City, but the depression was in full sway and there were no jobs." Through a drummer she heard about an opening in the Jones Store in Kansas City. She got on the bus and went. She got the job. "It was a huge store—covered two full city blocks. The millinery department was leased to Consolidated Millinery. They put me in charge of the Hat Box in the basement." There you could buy a beret for 79 cents, the best hat they had for $2.00. Graduated upstairs to the better department, she sold hats for as much as $10.95. She also became Ebby. An older associate started calling her Ebby. "She said a Vera Lucille could never expect to become a success in millinery. And I looked like an Ebby." The Halliday part of her name is from an early marriage. She was divorced from this husband, now deceased, after she moved to Dallas.

Her sales ability came to the attention of Consolidated managers, and they asked her to transfer to Omaha, Nebraska, where she was in charge of the first floor—"not the elegant sixth floor"—hat department and lived with the Flannery family. "In Omaha I was introduced to sin—my first alcohol. Nell McDermott managed the upstairs hat department, and she took me to the Fontanelle Hotel and ordered a frozen daiquiri for me. It was delicious!" She "loved Omaha," but was there only a year before Consolidated transferred her to Dallas to sell hats for W. A. Green on Main Street.

Ebby moved into a room with the Milam ladies—"Miss Emma and Sister"—at 1819 Moser Street. It was 1938. She would be with W. A. Green for seven years. "Consolidated also leased the hat department at Sangers. Roxie Thedford headed that. She was an elegant person—knew everybody in town. She was wonderful to me."

Ebby sold hats and saved her money waiting for the day when she could open her own hat shop. She accumulated $1,000. Plagued with sore throats and laryngitis, she finally agreed with the doctor who told her that she should have her tonsils out. While waiting in the offices of Dr. John McLaurin, her surgeon, she heard his secretary confer with him about stock he owned. "As soon as I could talk, I told him I had $1,000 to invest and asked him what stock I should buy. He said 'I don't give women advice. If they lose money, they cry.' I said, 'Try me. I won't cry.' So, he told me to buy cotton futures. I parlayed that thousand dollars into $12,000." She opened her custom hat shop at 2603 Fairmont taking with her hat designer Pearl Kemendo and a host of customers including the Long sisters—Jody and Virginia. The hat shop she decorated herself served as a cozy meeting place for many women. "You just go along doing what you like to do to the best of your ability, saving money and taking risks—and *always* remembering to be nice to the people you serve—and you never know what's going to happen next. Life takes you in directions you never dreamed possible."

Life dealt Ebby a sharp turn, outward and upward, through one of her favorite customers. Virginia Long married Clint Murchison, Sr., he of the oil fortunes. Just after World War II he invested in a block of property along Marsh Lane and built houses of In-Cem, an insulated cement that was touted as a construction that would revolutionize housing in the entire world. The houses were all cement, walls and floors. "They were solid. They were—" she hesitates—"not very appealing." They were, in short, quite ugly. They did not sell. Clint Murchison said if Ebby could sell his wife all those hats, he was sure she could make the houses pretty enough that people would buy them.

Ebby went to see the houses and was captivated by the challenge. "I just picked one and started to work on it. It was the first model home in Dallas." Calling on the assistance of her designer and listening to the advice of other friends, she turned concrete living rooms into early American showcases and concrete bedrooms into French provincial dreams and concrete kitchens into picture-pretty settings that begged for culinary delights. "I sold one and moved on to the next. I didn't stop until I did them all. I loved it! I sold the shop and moved out into Walnut Hills Shopping Center." In all she decorated and sold 52 houses along Almazon, Bolivar, Cortez, Durango, Espanola, Fontana, Gaspar, Hidalgo, LaJoya, Linda, Manana—"the Murchisons were taken at that time with things Mexican." The area was then out in the country, and Ebby walked out of her office one day to see two hunters. She greeted them—and sold them each a house. "Their wives couldn't believe it!" The two-bedroom houses sold for $7,500, the three-bedroom for $9,000. Many of the houses, still standing, sold in the 1990s for well over $100,000. The city tore some down on Almazon to build the Walnut Hill library.

Ebby opened her own business, Ebby Halliday Realtors, in 1945. "In my wildest dreams, I could not imagine where the business would go. I didn't plan it; it just grew. I concentrated on doing each thing as it came along . . . . For a long time we didn't even have training sessions. If there is a secret to our success, it's people. I love people and I love houses. I know how to choose people and I know how to let them develop." She also knows, her associates tell you, how to develop potential, discipline, and let go if things do not work.

On Easter Sunday, April 18, 1965, she married her best friend and most admiring fan, attorney Maurice Acers. Theirs was a true partnership as they consistently tried to bring out the best in each other. He chaired the Ebby Halliday board. "He educated me in many ways. He was an only child with a strict upbringing. He was with the F.B.I. He helped me never to compromise with principle. We solved most of our business problems and all of our personal problems with pillow talk." She met him when they shared a taxi

Ebby Halliday began her real estate career by transforming concrete block houses into homes of beauty. She sold 52 houses along the Spanish-named streets in northwest Dallas for Clint Murchison before creating her own company.

in Beaumont in 1958. They dated for seven years. Even if they'd wanted to marry sooner, they might not have been able to mesh their schedules to set a date. She began her married life when he was Rotary governor and they attended an international Rotary convention in Lake Placid, New York, immediately after the wedding. Back home, they prepared for a honeymoon in Mexico that turned into a 12-person event with some of his and some of her business associates going along.

Bette Graham at left, in the serene pose characteristic of her, and above, in the cantilevered living room of her home where she painted.

Women comprise about 75 per cent of the personnel associated with Ebby Halliday Realtors. "Women's volunteerism has helped to build this community. Women have provided the threads, the fabric of our city. They have built the human part of our educational system, our health facilities, the parks, art, music, theater. Sometimes they are not as objective as men—but in our business that's often an asset. Women are very caring and concerned. Their sensibilities and sensitivities pick up nuances that are easily overlooked."

Since the earliest days of her business, Ebby has contributed time, talent and money to developing realtors and to her community. She has served on dozens of civic and professional boards. She was the first woman president of the venerable North Dallas Chamber of Commerce and is a past president of the Greater Dallas Planning Council. She is an avid beautification enthusiast and was president of Keep Texas Beautiful in the 1980s. Her honors are local, national and international. She feels keenly her responsibilities of founder/president/mentor/caretaker of a major Dallas organization. "You care," she says, shunning the first person pronoun, "and you become frustrated when there's nothing you can do about a bad situation—an ill child, a mother with cancer, an alcoholic husband. You watch these personal problems impede the progress of people and you want to reach out and take the burden away and you can't."

"I've been so blessed," she says. "Good health. Humility. Ability Inspiration. A strong desire to share." She takes care of herself—her health, her appearance, her inner self. "I read a lot. Have good friends. She drops a few names—Dale Pitt, Katherine Rix, Mary Lou Muether, Mildred Boyles, Audrey Price, Mary Louise and E. C. Rowand—that's just a few. And Maurice."

(Since the interview, Maurice Acers died on August 6, 1993) Yes, she says, there is a something she would like to leave as her message to posterity. This is her message:

We had a neighbor on the farm in Kansas—George Robinson—who had the finest corn in the country. He won the blue ribbon at the county fair every year. When he harvested his crop, he always gave his neighbors some of his prize-winning corn for seed. Someone asked George, "Why do you give your prize seed away? Aren't you afraid your neighbors will grow better corn and win the prize?" Uncle George replied, "My neighbors must grow good corn to insure the quality of my crop. The wind carries the pollen and if my neighbors have inferior corn, my own fields will suffer." And so it is. If we are unethical or inefficient, if we make derogatory remarks about others, we injure ourselves. If we share what we are and what we have, we build up ourselves and others and inevitably the whole human race improves.

Seeking a way to improve her typing ability, a young secretary with a child to support used her art skills and turned a product she named Mistake Out into a multi-million-dollar business.

A decade after Ebby Halliday began selling houses in Dallas, a young secretary arrived in the city from Houston. A single mother, the sole support of a preschool-aged child, she took a job as a secretary in the Mercantile Bank Building, located in downtown Dallas. To get to her job on time, she left her apartment near Love Field before daylight, with her little boy. She dropped him off at a Child Care Dallas day care center and got to her desk by 8 a.m.

Her name was Bette Clair McMurray Nesmith. She would later remarry and become Bette Graham. Her son was Robert Michael Nesmith, who later would gain worldwide fame as one of the Monkees in a singing group—but not before helping her launch a product that would become a multi-million-dollar organization.

Bette was born to Christine and Jesse McMurray on March 23, 1924, near San Antonio, Texas. She was a good student, more interested in art than in economics. She dropped out of high school in her senior year to marry Warren Nesmith on March 4, 1942, before he was shipped overseas during World War II. It was 24 days before her 18th birthday. Nine months and 26 days later she was a mother. The marriage ended in 1947 as abruptly as it had begun—and Bette was left to support her son alone. She completed a business course in Houston and found a job as a secretary. To bring in extra cash, she painted a mural at a Houston theater, wrote and illustrated children's books, did free lance commercial art and window displays. Shortly after her divorce she moved with her four-year-old son to Dallas.

Bette was young, healthy, pretty and conscientious. She continued to augment her $300 a month salary with whatever extra jobs she could find—among them modeling furs in fashion shows. Eventually she found a job as executive secretary to community leader W. W. Overton who was chairman of the board of Texas Bank & Trust Company. There she got her first electric typewriter. The touch was so much lighter than on the old manual keyboard that she started making typing errors for the first time in her life. Erasing the carbon ink was virtually impossible, especially on multiple onionskin copies. Nightly, Bette went home with a headache after retyping letters and business documents, sometimes several times, often running late in picking up her son—which did not make the caretakers happy. One night, after her son was in bed, she was painting and mulling over the erasure problem when an idea "so simple that I don't know why someone hadn't done it before," exploded in her head. She was eliminating the mistakes on her canvas by painting over them. Why couldn't she do the same thing with typing mistakes? "I put a small bottle of the white stuff I was using on my canvass in my purse. I could hardly wait to get to work the next day . . . ." She tried it on her typing errors—and it worked. Not perfectly. It needed some improving. She went home and started to improve.

Perfected to her satisfaction, she made more of the product—a simple tempera water-based paint, applied with a tiny brush. When she made a typing mistake, she whited it out on the original and all of the carbons and continued to type. She thought little of it. This went on for five years. Other secretaries noticed what she was doing. Some of them wanted to borrow her white-out material. Others asked for bottles of their own. Bette called it Mistake Out and shared it with all of her friends. Slowly, she began to charge a few cents a bottle for the product because she could no longer produce and give it away.

Her kitchen was her laboratory and manufacturing plant. Eventually, a supply dealer saw it, heard the testimony of the secretaries and suggested that she ought to market it.

Bette thought that might be a good idea, but the first big company, IBM, she contacted said she should improve it before they would be interested. With the help of a chemist teacher at St. Mark's School and a paint store employee, Bette improved the product, but she never contacted any large outlet again. She knew that Mistake Out was a good product—and that she should market it herself. In 1956 she established the Mistake Out Company to produce and market Liquid Paper Correction Fluid. Already she was producing more of the product than she could handle because she was still working as a secretary five and a half days a week. She was also serving as an artist and illustrator part-time when she could get work and continuing to model. Her son and his friends were her agents; they and she were the distributors.

In 1956 she got her first big break: General Electric ordered 300 bottles of Mistake Out in three colors. She experienced all of the uncertainty that goes with the life of an entrepreneur. "I was often discouraged. I could not afford to quit my job because I had a child to support. But I couldn't keep working the long hours I put in at the office and the long hours I worked at home. I got almost no sleep, and I was worried all the time. It wasn't until I turned my life around that I could turn my business around." Her rescue came in the form of a mistake she made. She wrote a letter on the stationery of the company for which she was employed and signed it with the name of the Mistake Out Company she had developed. She was dismissed from her secretarial position. Devastating as it momentarily was, the dismissal turned out to be the most motivating thing that ever had happened to Bette.

The year was 1958. Bette threw herself into making a success of the Mistake Out Company. She borrowed $700 to get her business started—and she did not believe in going into debt. She took a part-time job as a clerk in a church office to pay the grocery bill. She bought a bicycle for transportation. Her 16-year-old son, now exhibiting some of the reluctance of teenagers and very much into his music, still helped her bottle and distribute Liquid Paper. Two years went by, then three, then four. She was still barely staying afloat, but she increasingly believed in her product as testimonial after testimonial from secretaries throughout the country applauded Liquid Paper. Slowly, she began to advertise—in company papers, in secretarial journals. Production outgrew her kitchen. In 1960 she moved the production into her garage and the next year into a 10 by 26-foot portable building. This facility for the next four years served as office, production, packaging and shipping headquarters for Liquid Paper. In 1962 Bette married Robert M. Graham and together they toured the country promoting the product. By the time the marriage ended in 1975, the company had long since become an overwhelming American Success Story. In 1965 it was incorporated and moved into four rooms at 6959 Twin Hills, an expansion that continued to grow until it overflowed seven portable buildings.

Demand for Liquid Paper kept outstripping facilities to produce it. In 1965, the company sold 133,000 bottles for a total of $66,000. By 1977 it had a total of 331 employees worldwide and equipment that could produce 500 bottles per minute. Its output for the year was 25 million bottles and its earnings $1,500,000.

In the spring of 1966 the company hired its first manufacturers representative. In 1968 Bette changed the name of the company to Liquid Paper Corporation, and at the same time retired as president to devote her full time to being a Christian Science practitioner. She still held most of the stock in Liquid Paper and was honorary chairperson of the company. The new facilities the company built at 9130 Markville Drive, beginning in the spring of 1968, were firmly imprinted in her image. Nineteen people went to work there. There was yet another expansion in 1972, the year it spread internationally with the opening of its first subsidiary in Canada. In May of 1973 the company moved into Europe and broke ground for corporate headquarters at 9130 Markville. This again was a facility that bore all of the earmarks of Bette's artistic genius combined with her conservative financial sense. It was a building that flowed. Its several stories were reached by ascending wide carpeted ramps rather than stairways opening to the landscaped exterior rather than dark interiors. It was designed to blend outer and inner space and its work units were defined by colors and angles and lighting rather than by walls and partitions.

It was the art masterpiece that Bette had always intended to paint. She was pleased with it as she showed it off—just as she was pleased with her own home at 4604 Wautaga where her all-white glass-enclosed living room was cantilevered among the tree tops. It was in this setting that Bette's artistic achievements were most in evidence in her own paintings and sculptures.

Speaking to the Harvard Business School in 1976, Bette told the future corporate giants that a business based on spiritual values can succeed—that, indeed, the only true success is that which comes from having served others. "From the company's beginning, we've had a long-range plan . . . that sees business as something more than manufacturing and getting the product to the consumer . . . . The thinking (of employees) is our most valued asset . . . . each employee's contribution is regarded as equal in importance and value. We do not have a traditional hierarchical organization with one individual over another." She added that money had never been her motivating force.

Freed from day-to-day responsibilities in the company, Bette established two foundations: (1) The Bette Clair McMurray Foundation gave grants to help women in business and the arts. (2) The Gihon Foundation worked at making love the basis of business. Because Bette remembered those earlier days of single parenthood, she was especially empathetic to young mothers and children and because she was, first and always, an artist, she funded projects in the arts. She acquired a collection of art, Works by Women, including a Mary Cassatt and a Georgia O'Keeffe, that she opened to the public.

Attuned to the nuances that permeated big business, Bette was aware that she was often criticized and called naive. "People have dismissed me for my idealism, but all of the time I have been taking money to the bank, I have been doing the things they said I couldn't do. "I want to be a success as a human being. Everything else is secondary."

Bette had consummate faith in women. "I am very much into women's issues . . . . We must make it possible for a woman to have her opportunity . . . . Men must understand they are not doing us a favor when they protect us from reality. Women are broadening their concept of themselves—their aspirations are changing and the world is changing its thinking about women," she said in 1978. "There is discrimination; there is a power struggle . . . but the struggle is between two differing concepts of power—concepts held by both men and women: the supposed supremacy of physical force versus the genuine supremacy of grace and love . . . . One of the greatest issues we face is allowing qualities that are essentially female to blossom in the world. This has enormous potential to bring changes to the family, business and leadership . . . on a global basis."

Bette remained on the board of Liquid Paper until 1976. In 1979 when it sold to the Gillette Company for $47.5 million, Bette Graham relinquished the stock she held in the company she built and nurtured. Building on her statement, "My estate will be what I can do for others," she immediately began planning to give her money away. She purchased property on Harwood at New Jack street and hired an architect to draw up plans for a women's building that would house her foundations, include a gallery for women's art and provide offices, meeting rooms and support facilities for non-profit women's organizations. She also planned a building that would provide temporary homes to women trying to put their lives back together following catastrophes. When Bette Graham's building died with her on May 12, 1980, Dallas women lost one of their strongest advocates.

Mary Crowley was 20 years old and the Great Depression was gripping the country when she assumed sole responsibility for rearing her two children alone. Within weeks she was hired by a man who told her there was no point in interviewing her; there were no jobs.

The early life of Mary Elizabeth Weaver Carter Crowley is almost eerily like that of Ebby Halliday. And her business policies bear a striking resemblance to those of Bette Graham. In three decades Mary Crowley built Home Interiors and Gifts Inc. from nothing into a $500 million-a-year business. Forty thousand women carried business cards as her associates.

Mary Weaver was born on April 1, 1915, in Slater, Missouri. Her mother died when she was 18 months old and she went to live with her maternal grandparents, W. D. and Laura Crain, on a wheat farm near Sweetwater, Missouri. She had an older sister and a younger brother, who was only three months old when their mother died. Mary once said that her entire future life, her belief in God and the innate goodness of people was shaped in those early years when she was a much loved and cherished child in the home of her grandparents. When she was seven, her life was abruptly interrupted when "I was pulled up by the roots" and sent to live with her father and his new wife in Washington state. Her father, a Latin teacher, seemed to live in his own world totally unaware that his wife was abusing his children. The only thing he encouraged was Mary's alert mind and the time she spent reading, but he did not intervene when her stepmother perpetually interrupted Mary's studies. In an effort to keep peace in the family, Mary and her sister took over most of the household chores, and Mary did almost all of the cooking. Still the abuse continued. "I've gone to school many times wearing long stockings to hide the bruises and welts on my legs," she once said. "I spent as much time as I could out of the house. I would disappear into the woods with a book. That's where my close association with the woods, with nature, the birds, with music and with God began. There was nobody I could tell how unhappy I was, so I would go into the woods and talk to Jesus. I felt He was my only friend . . . . I really wasn't all that good. I spent a great deal of time praying that my stepmother would die."

Mary Crowley, at left, who established Home Interiors and Gifts in 1957, with Mrs. Billy Graham and Ethel Waters, and above, centering Mary Miller and Erie Darnell.

Eventually the neighbors complained that the Weaver children were being abused. The juvenile courts intervened. Mary and her siblings were removed from their father's house and returned to their grandparents, who by that time had moved to Arkansas where they were running an experimental chicken farm near Fayetteville. Mary was 13. "It was hard on my grandmother—having a teenage girl is not exactly the best time to become an instant mother. This was especially true for Grandmother who was an older woman with new career responsibilities. I was safe, but the intellectual stimulation was gone." Mary graduated from Fayetteville High School near the top of her class and took courses at the University of Arkansas in her senior year.

"More than anything in the world, I wanted a home of my own, so when Joseph Carter asked me to marry him, I thought it was the answer to my prayers." She was a bride at 17 and the mother of Donald Joseph Carter on July 5, 1933, three months after her 18th birthday. Two years later, in 1935, Ruth Carter was born. The family moved to Sherman. Mary was 20 years old, had two babies and "was married to another kid." The Great Depression was at its worst. "If anybody supported us, I knew it would have to be me."

One morning Mary pressed her best pink cotton dress, shampooed and set her hair, polished her white shoes, straightened the seams on her one pair of stockings, convinced a neighbor to keep her children, and walked two miles into Sherman. She traversed the square, selected the store that had the best-looking window display, went in and asked the first clerk she saw to direct her to the manager. She was told that if she had come to seek work, to forget it because nobody was being hired. Mary said thank you, but she *would* like to see the manager. The clerk pointed upstairs. Mary went up. The manager barely acknowledged her presence. Mary told him her name and said she had chosen his store to work for. He said that was flattering, but he wasn't hiring. She said she had to have a job. He said hadn't she heard there was a depression on. She said yes, that's why she needed a job. He said sorry, so did everybody else. She said she would come to work for him on Saturday and if she didn't sell enough to earn her keep, he didn't have to pay her. He threw up his hands and said all right, one day!

"I floated down those stairs and went through the store noting where the merchandise was and what I might do to earn my salary. I saw that the clerks there looked tired; nobody smiled. I wouldn't have bought anything from one of them...." On her way out she noticed a thread display just inside the front door. Thread was three cents a spool. Almost everything else in the store was priced at two cents less than the dollar, 98 cents, $1.98, $2.98. Sales receipts and the money were sent upstairs on a conveyer belt where change was made and sent back down. "On the way home I had a brilliant idea. When I went to the neighbor's to claim my children, I was literally walking on air."

Saturday came and Mary went to work. She was a few minutes early. She looked fresh and sparkling. Her smile was as genuine as it was attractive. When she made her first sale, she suggested that the customer include a spool of thread with her purchase—and for a penny more she wouldn't have to wait for change. It worked. "Those were the days when everybody sewed and all of the women made quilts. They had to have thread. I sold a spool of thread with almost every sale."

At the end of the day, the manager asked how she had managed to be the top salesperson in the store on her first day at work. "I just love to sell," she said. "I just love to help people find what they want. It makes them so happy." He told her to come back on Monday and see if her sales ability would continue to work. She did and it did. Her salary was $7.00 a week.

"I kept selling, but I knew that if I wanted to give my children the future they deserved, I had to make more money. I needed some solid grounding in business. Sherman did not have a business school. The Rotary Club offered scholarships to high school seniors interested in taking business courses. I wasn't a high school senior, but I needed the money, so I applied. I won." She completed the course, signed up for night courses at SMU, got a job with an insurance company and worked for Montgomery Ward on Saturdays. She rented an apartment, hired a caretaker, brought her children to Dallas and got a divorce.

One night she was invited by a friend to a Stanley party. Stanley sells home cleaning supplies and related items through the party plan. "I almost didn't go. I was tired. The children needed me at home. The weather was terrible. But the friend who had invited me needed the few "gifts" that were always given to the hostess at one of the parties. So I fixed myself up and sloshed through the rain—beginning to turn to snow—and went. My friend met me at the door with such a warm welcome. She said she really hadn't expected anybody to show up. The saleswoman, Mary Kay Eckford, went through her spiel; the guests ordered the few supplies they could afford, most of them stretching their budgets. The few guests gave the demonstrator more time to visit with each person. Mary told her that she was new in Dallas, had two small children, and needed to make more money. The demonstrator said she should become a Stanley representative. Mary said but she must do something that would earn her a hundred dollars a week. Her new friend nodded and smiled and said she sometimes earned a hundred dollars in a single day.

Mary Crowley had met Mary Kay Ash. From then on their lives would be intertwined.

Mary went to work for Stanley—part-time. She started on week-ends and occasionally she would do a night party. Within a few weeks she was making more on her part-time job than in her salaried job. She quit being a secretary and became a full-

Surely somewhere in the silent universe, bells must have rung on that cold winter night when two Marys met in Dallas, for the lives of Mary Kay Ash and Mary Crowley were transformed. This began the process that has, in turn, elevated the economic lives of millions of women.

Dallas's quartet of successful women—Ebby Halliday, Mary Kay Ash, Mary Crowley and Bette Graham—all ran their organizations by paying as much attention to the quality of life as to its quantity, approaches that sometimes caused the bottom-line-is-the-only-thing-that-matters business community to think them naive.

time Stanley saleswoman. Eventually, Mary Kay married Mary's brother and for a period of nine years they were sister-in-law before he and Mary Kay were divorced.

In 1941 Mary met a tall handsome civilian employee of the National Guard, David M. Crowley Jr. It was instant rapport, but there were obstacles. Mary's first responsibility was to her children; they were eight and six. Mary was a devout Baptist who tithed her income even when there was not enough money to cover her essential expenses. Dave was an equally dedicated Catholic. The courtship lasted seven years. For the four years he was overseas during World War II, they wrote to each other every day. They were married in 1948.

In 1954, Mary left Stanley to go to work for World Gifts, Inc., an importer who also sold through the home party plan. Again, Mary loved selling, but she did not like the company policies. A limit was placed on the amount anyone could earn—and the officers of the company included a cocktail party among the entertainment at a national convention. Mary, opposed to all liquor, wrote a letter outlining her ideas for improving company policies and her opposition to serving liquor. She asked for an interview to discuss her ideas. She expected a telephone call and negotiations. Instead, her office furniture was delivered to her front door on the following Monday morning without explanation. She was devastated. Dave left for work, comforting his wife and telling her that it wasn't the end of the world.

Mary dried her tears and recalled the axiom she had lived by: "Every ending presents a new opportunity for growth." She got out pad and pencil and started outlining what was right about the two prior companies for which she had worked and what was wrong. By the time Dave came home that evening, he was greeted by a jubilant wife who told him she was going into business for herself. "The day that had dawned with the funeral for my old career ended with the birth of my own company," Mary wrote in her autobiography, *Think Mink*.

It wasn't as easy as putting it on paper. She had several basic tenets: She would form a business that dealt in direct sales through home parties; she would utilize sales associates who were women; she would operate on a cash basis; she would establish a business that would enrich the lives of those she touched. She had made many friends among the wholesale vendors, and they were delighted, eager to help her when she decided to go into business for herself.

Home Interiors and Gifts Inc. was officially born on December 5, 1957. From the first it was a success. Mixed together on the backs of envelopes, scrap paper, note pads, blue-lined kids' school paper Mary scrawled schedules, sales meetings, speaking engagements, grocery lists, menus and company policies. Edited in her firm, sure hand, she wrote: "We believe in the dignity and importance of women. We believe that everything woman touches should be ennobled by that touch. We believe that the home should be a haven, a place of refuge, a place of peace, a place of harmony, a place of beauty." The basic tenet of Home Interiors and Gifts is "Love One Another."

Not long after she opened her business, Mary needed operating capital. Two leading banks in Dallas turned her down. One loan officer was nonplused. He could not believe that a group of under-educated, barely trained *housewives* were going to sell home accessories at *parties* in the homes of other women, call themselves businesswomen and earn a dime. Back on Main Street after two turn-downs, Mary clutched her briefcase, stopped at a red light, said a prayer and looked up to see the Mercantile Bank sign ahead of her. She marched in, went directly to the executive offices and told R. L. Thornton Jr.'s secretary that she needed 10 minutes of her boss's time to present a plan that would make both of them rich. The puzzled secretary disappeared and returned almost immediately to usher Mary into the offices of the bank president. It took only a few minutes. "He understood right off. He asked a few questions. Then he reached for a form and signed his name. I went home with the $6,000 I needed to expand."

When success came—and it soon did—Mary was asked to join the board of directors of the bank.

Mary always said she had no employees, only associates, women who worked *with* her. There were/are thousands of them scattered across the country and abroad. She spent a great deal of time motivating them. "My most important job is to make each woman feel as important as she is. I still train all new managers," she said in a 1977 interview. To do it, she took them to her Buena Vista, Colorado, mountain retreat and spent five days teaching, inspiring, and loving. She fed their egos as well as their bodies. Incentives included mink coats, vacations in exotic resorts, new cars and jewelry. Once she paid a $71,165 grocery bill after she gifted her visiting associates with a shopping spree at a Safeway store. Another time she wrote a check to cover a $50,000 medical bill after she flew 550 women to Dallas for a check-up.

Mary Kay Ash, at left, is both the reality and the symbol of the company that bears her name, and, above, as a community volunteer shortly after she created Mary Kay Cosmetics in 1963.

There were problems. In 1960 Mary's persistent tiredness finally sent her to the doctor. She had cervical cancer, radium implants and surgery. She came out from under anesthesia determined to be back at work in days. She was. When the cancer returned in another part of her body, she had chemotherapy, dressing herself up to go for her treatments in the same way she groomed herself for an important speech. When the Internal Revenue Service questioned her 1974 income tax return, she was able to prove that everything was legitimate business expense. Mary lived an integrated whole melding her business and her private lives. Her large and lavish home at 10265 Inwood Road was open house to thousands of women who sold her products. Her two Lear jets kept people in touch. Her California resort was the place she trained associates. Two things—one a place and the other a time—was sacrosanct. The place: a chapel at the back of her Inwood home which she shared with those who cared but which was her spot of solace. The time: Christmas time. All sales stopped and all women, herself included, were encouraged to be at home with those dearest to them.

Following the simple path of faith, Mary continued to teach a Sunday School at First Baptist Church, as often as possible arranging her business and personal calendar so that she would be in Dallas on Sunday. She gave away millions, $750,000 (of the $2.5 million total cost) to First Baptist Church; the complex is named for her; thousands to Colorado Women's College to keep it open. Dallas Baptist University was her special love and includes three buildings bearing her name. She provided scholarships for kids to that school and others. She helped to establish Youth for Tomorrow, an organization that operated homes for troubled youth. There was no such thing as a shy introverted person in Mary's presence. Everywhere she went she made the circuit, shaking hands, smiling, asking questions, drawing people out. Her brown eyes radiated empathy and every life she touched blossomed under her care. Strangers could read about her policies, term her naive, criticize her approach toward life and call her a Pollyanna for the way she ran her business, but all of the skeptics and critics melted under her charm and honesty. She held nothing back. She died on June 19, 1986, from cancer that finally defeated her. During her last illness, and only days before her death, she was responding to well-wishers. I was one of them. On the board of the Community Ministry Program of the Greater Dallas Community of Churches, I was raising money to provide the salary for a minister at El Centro College and I wrote to Mary. Through the years she and I had served on many projects together and I considered her a friend, but I did now know how ill she was. The check she sent came along with a note on her personal pink stationery with the red lettering: Mary C. Crowley. It was written by her daughter, Ruth Shanahan, and it was dated June 4, 1986. And it was typical of Mary:

> I am writing for my Mother who is very ill at Baylor Hospital. She wanted to encourage you with this check to serve the needs of the people at El Centro . . . God bless you all as you serve . . . .

The lives and accomplishments of Mary Crowley and Mary Kay Ash are inextricably intertwined. Since they met in 1942 where both recognized magic in the other, they served as each others models and mentors. In the beginning, it was Mary Kay who boosted Mary's career by encouraging her to get into party sales. Then, it was Mary, after she went with World Gifts, who recruited the best saleswoman she knew, Mary Kay. Both made their fortunes in party sales; both dealt with products that were indigenous to women; both concentrated on the talents of women to distribute their products. When Mary went into business for herself in 1957, could Mary Kay be far behind? Not very!

Mary Kay Ash founded her own company five years and nine months after Mary Crowley went into business for herself. Since then Mary Kay, debatably, has done more for the financial advancement and the personal esteem of more women than any other business person in the history of Dallas. She is the founder of Mary Kay Cosmetics, Inc. By its 25th anniversary in 1988, its sales totaled $406 million. Some 200,000 beauty consultants carried business cards designating them as representatives of Mary Kay. By 1992 it had 1,700 employees nationwide, a sales force of 250,000, operated in 18 countries, and posted retail sales of more than a billion dollars. Throughout the United States women driving pink Cadillacs stand out in traffic. They are women, who by superlative sales, have earned the right to drive a Mary Kay car for a year.

Mary Kay's annual sales meetings are combinations of giant football pep rallies, Billie Graham revivals, Macy Thanksgiving Day parades and Miss America beauty pageants. And Mary Kay is the queen, mentor, friend and spiritual guide of the entire extravaganza. While Mary Crowley was the consummate earth mother with a hands-on approach to the training and guidance of the women who represented her company, Mary Kay's is the regal approach—a touch mysterious and aloof. In both instances the aura is in error. Mary Crowley knew how to confine herself in the ivory tower when business demanded and pay attention to her company's bottom line, and beneath the regal splendor, Mary Kay is warm, friendly and funny. Both were/are exceptional business women and role models.

Mary Kay was born in Hot Wells, Texas, on May 12, some time before 1920, (part of her aura is that she does not reveal her age) the youngest of the four children of Edward Alexander and Lula Vember Hastings Wagner. When the little girls was two, the family left Hot Wells where they owned and managed a small hotel and moved to Houston. Her father's health was bad and her mother went to work to support the family. The job she found required up to 14 hours a day. Mary Kay grew up independent. She learned to cook and clean house and care for her father at a very early age and when she encountered an overwhelming task, Mary Kay would call her mother for direction. More often than not, Lula Wagner would respond to her daughter with a few words of advice and a determined, "You Can Do It." Those four words became the child's credo. Through financial ups and downs, marriages that did not work out, rearing three children and struggling with the quirks of building an international business including sales associates throughout the world to whom she is the model, Mary Kay has always remembered she can do it.

Mary Kay has built a financial empire on the four words, "You Can Do It," that her mother always told her when she was a little girl running the house and caring for her father while her mother worked to support them.

She started Mary Kay Cosmetics on Friday, September 13, 1963, one month—or so the story goes—after the death of her second husband. They had planned the business together, he to handle the business part of the company and she to manage the product and the people. Following his death, plans went forward with Mary's 20-year-old son assuming the business part of the organization. She opened with nine people, $5,000 and faith bringing to the endeavor a lifetime of experience in selling—most of it in party sales. With World Gifts, she had worked her way up to become an officer of the company where she remained until she was almost ready to establish her own business.

Her personal life, as the country western song goes, has had "its little ups and downs." A late-in-life child whose fate made her responsible beyond her years—her siblings were considerably older—Mary Kay attended Houston's Reagan High School. She was pretty and popular, a "redcoat" on the drill team, a debater and an extemporaneous speaker. She was 17 when she married Ben Rogers. The country, still in Depression, provided few jobs and little hope for the future. Money was scarce to non-existent. The young Rogers family moved in with his mother. Mary Kay went to work as a typist at her church to supplement the family income. The job sometimes required her to be on duty seven days a week.

Shortly after the war, Mary Kay was divorced and left with three children—Marylyn (Cates), Ben, and Richard. The Stanley job allowed her the potential of making enough money to support her children while still providing some time for her to spend at home with them, but she got off to a very shaky start. For the first three weeks she worked, she sold only $7 worth of merchandise per party—and there weren't many parties. Then she attended a sales convention, felt right at home with the people she met and loved its rah-rah atmosphere. When the company crowned as queen the woman who had sold the most products the prior year, Mary Kay determined that next year she would be wearing the robes and crown and standing in the spotlight. She was. She remained with Stanley for 13 years, then joined World Gifts. She rose to national training director.

She left World Gifts in 1963 following surgery for a rare form of paralysis on one side of her face. Recovering and bored—she had worked all of her life—she had time to think about the idea that had long been in the back of her head, a business of her own. She knew that she wanted to do something that would, as she saw it, enhance the lives of women; she wanted women on her staff; she wanted them to be independent agents and she wanted to sell through the party plan. One day, reaching for the face cream that she had used for a decade, she *knew*. The cream was mixed in small batches by a shop owner whose father had worked out the formula for tanning hides. Mary Kay got hers, as did others, in any handy container and carted out in empty shoe boxes. Her own youthful skin was testimony to the product's effectiveness. There had to be a fortune in that product if it were properly packaged and marketed. Mary Kay and her family bought the formula and were in business.

Mary Kay Ash is a living contradiction. She loves the flamboyant lifestyle—fabulous houses, furs, jewelry, cars, resorts. She is the image she projects, perfectly coifed hair, impeccable make up, flawless manicure, exquisite clothing. She is also totally guileless. She loves being with her family, likes to cook and—until she became so much in demand that there was no time for it—was an avid gardener. Her public speeches are often strung-together-maxims that rival any homily delivered from a Baptist pulpit. She makes others believe because she believes. She is a living example that her inspirational maxims work. Underneath a soft, pastel ultra-feminine exterior is a strong, enduring, astute woman who built a major financial empire. Though her title is chairman emeritus, to everybody she is the company. Her elegance derives from that fact that she attributes her success to other powers and people outside herself—her God, her family and her business associates. That's a lot of credit going to others—her husband Melville Jerome Ash, who she married in 1966 and who died in 1981; her daughter and sons, her grandchildren, great grandchildren; the company executives and employees, her Baptist Church friends; women in other businesses and thousands of Mary Kay associates.

29

THE MESSAGE CARRIERS

Without message carriers to the world, the story of Dallas would have been severely limited. Message carriers have come in many forms, among them letter writers, telephone and telegraph communicators, authors, journalists, advertisers, playwrights, producers, radio reporters, television newspeople, publishers and book distributors. For many years after Dallas was founded, women were the private message carriers and men had a monopoly on public communication. Almost all of the letters were written by women. When the telephones were installed women talked to each other over the new instruments. But when the telegraph lines were strung, it was men who used them. Men wrote and published the newspapers; men controlled the air waves both when radio was introduced and, later, when television arrived.

It was only natural, then, that the messages on public media reflected male interests and male values. The only deference to women in newspapers was in stories and columns that men believed women wanted. This proclivity is reflected in early Dallas papers. But, soon, both of the major Dallas papers and most of those that came afterward designated a *woman's page*, or eventually, a woman's section. In the beginning these were filled with personal items, social news, fashion and food. From time to time some papers added a page of interest to children. They also included picture pages, stories of intrigue—many of them highly fictionalized—and serialized romance stories.

All international, national, state and local news in the papers, all sports and financial and business news was for the male reader. Women, the consummate consumers, were lured with advertising, the financial lifeblood of papers. But for years, advertisers overlooked a basic fact: Women shopped not only for their own and their children's clothes and for almost all food, they also shopped for mens' apparel. They controlled purchases of household goods and supplies and had a voice in the choice of transportation, travel, recreation and other necessities and luxuries. In the early days, it is true that men made and controlled most of the money, even that brought to the marriage by the women. But the catering to men and male prerogatives lingered in advertising long after reality changed. It was only after 1970 that automobile manufacturers, as one major example, recognized women as major consumers. Even then, their sales pitches to women focused on cosmetics—design of the car, color, interior finish, fabric—rather than overall value—safety, dependability, economy—which women considered essential.

Newspapers, and later radio and television, positioned their messages, not only to men readers, listeners, and viewers, but to 12-year-old males. For years—and sometimes still—journalism schools teach their students to write stories as if communicating with adolescents. This continues even though more sophisticated communications capture all media awards.

Most journalists, both men and women, who have covered both *soft news* (read that women's news) and *hard news*, find a compelling ambiguity between what they are taught and their own truth. Journalism schools do an excellent job of convincing students that *hard news* is the only *news* and that writers who prefer or excel at human interest stories are working in an inferior medium. For that reason most beginning reporters aspire to front-page by-lines. It takes maturity and experience for reporters to vanquish this bias. As a rule, writers in the features sections of newspapers gain far broader experience because they meet more varieties of people, have more choice in the subjects they cover and more leniency in the way they write their stories. Beginning reporters of *hard news*, especially on metropolitan newspapers, are assigned *beats* that severely limit their exposure and expression. It is not surprising that most *hard news* reporters eventually become cynics because they have steady exposure to the violent in human nature. The feature writer, on the other hand, samples the exalted in humanity, along with the violent. Journalism schools teach students to ask who, what, where, when, why and how. The *hard nosed* reporters focus on the who and what. The feature writers ask why and how. And since *hard news*—the violent part of the human equation—never occurs in a vacuum, but always in a framework of time and conditions, a strong case can be made that the writers of *soft side* news provide a more valuable community service because they cover conditions that, unless corrected, erupt on future front pages. Feature or *soft side* news writers also chronicle indigenous lifestyle patterns. Hard news is just that—the set, slowly-if-ever changing aspects of humanity. Soft news reports changing lifestyles—the fluid nuances of society, and, arguably, advances in the human condition.

Basic tools of communication are shared by all newspapers writers—with the exception of sports which has a language all its own. Sports is the only writing done for the already initiated; unless readers know the game, its rules, and at least the major players, they cannot understand the story. Sports writers are allowed to break basic journalism rules. Verbs are bandied about with no relation to what actually happened. Those unaware of the sports lingo would never know that killing an opponent only means winning a game. Sports words are war words. Sometimes, an entire story fails to divulge the sport being played!

Radio and television are both latecomers in the history of human communication. The first radio did not occur until 1900 when American scientist R. A. Fesseden successfully transmitted the human voice by radio waves. A quarter of a century later a Scottish inventor, John Logie Baird, transmitted recognizable human features via television. There is no way to measure the impact of radio and television on human communication. Both have transformed the way we see, think, understand and respond.

Since all forms of public communication were/are male controlled, women have not been readily accepted. The first female newspaper reporters, the first women on radio and the first women in television had a hard time. If they had any chance of surviving, they had to enter by male rules because that's all there were. Some firsts among female reporters tried to emulate men in their personal as well as their public lives and were discredited by the very males who were their models. Men did not want women to be substitute men. Other women were relegated to the *sob sister* roles—that is they were assigned the human interest stories and, according to the male editors, were expected to highlight the maudlin in human nature. Sob sisters were not accepted as regular news reporters and, no matter what other reporting they did, were not respected. It took more than a hundred years for women to gain any degree of equality in American newsrooms. They came to be recognized in radio and television more quickly because human history was moving at a faster pace. But, more than thousand years after the first newspaper was published in 748 in Peking, China, almost 150 years since the first newspaper came to Dallas in 1848, almost three-quarters of a century since the first radio was broadcast from Dallas, and half a century since the city's first television, women are still extremely scarce in news decision-making roles. Who decides what is news, who writes it and who delivers it is still largely a male prerogative. The edict of the *Times Herald*'s Edwin J. Kiest that "women . . . ruin newspapers" was still being echoed in 1955 when Charlie Dameron said he couldn't find a woman qualified to be a newspaper man. It did not occur to either man that failure to find and hire appropriate women showed their own bias. The statements were as sexist as editors' *inability* to find good reporters among blacks was racist.

Throughout all of Dallas's history, some women communicators have set their own course and found their own way through the quagmires of male opposition.

For those women who broke the barriers in newsrooms, the unifying denominators appear to be that they were professional loners charting their own courses and stubbornly determined to survive. The best of them accepted the male model and male evaluation of their work, learned from this model and then circumvented it. They followed all the

Women who wanted to become news people had to conform to male views and values on what was worth reporting because all of the press was owned and controlled by men. The first women in any profession walk a tight-rope between what is expected of them and what they expect of themselves.

basic rules of professional journalism, but added an ineffable quality of humanity that has withstood the test of time.

In 1943, Dorothea Louise Lyle was the first woman hired by the Associated Press. In 1950, while reporting for the *Dallas News*, she was the first to suggest that Dallas needed a Press Club and to begin negotiations to form one. Still, in a 1991 interview, relegating her achievements more to chance than to personal excellence, Dorothea said she would never have got her foot in the door if a war had not riddled the newsrooms of male reporters. And she credits others with the founding of the Press Club. She was unaware of the barricades she had personally removed for other women journalists.

Dorothea was born in Beaumont, Texas, on October 23, 1918, the daughter of Alice and Jim Lyle. The family, including a sister and two brothers, moved to Wichita Falls when she was five. There she grew up, graduated from high school, attended junior college and completed her freshman year at Texas State College for Women in Denton. Her growing up years were "Peaceful. Wonderful. We were coming out of the depression." Her father worked for a utility company, so the family had not been deprived during the depression. She was still living in that safe, uncomplicated world in June of 1939 when she graduated from the University of Texas at Austin with a degree in journalism. Newspapers were headlining crumbling conditions in Europe, but college students—even those who would be the future newswriters—were usually insulated from that reality.

On Labor Day of 1939 while on a family vacation in Ruidosa, New Mexico, the war came home to Dorothea. She heard that Hitler was "liberating" Czechoslovakia, and soon afterward that the Athena had been torpedoed on the high seas. A friend was one of the rescued passengers on that fateful passage. "It was suddenly clear to me that there was no escaping. We would be in the war. The vacation that was to celebrate my graduation from college became the moment of my growing up."

Dorothea Lyle McGrath, with teletype operator Bernie Smith in 1944, was the first woman hired by the Associated Press and the person most responsible for founding the Dallas Press Club, but she—like most women of the early days—credited others for her achievements.

Dorothea had been working part-time for the Wichita Falls *Record-News*, living at home and earning $15 a week. Shortly after the family vacation, she was hired full-time as a reporter on the women's news desk.

On December 7, 1941, "I was sitting at the Sunday dinner table listening to radio. There was a news bulletin. Pearl Harbor had been attacked by the Japanese. Dad drove me to work. I was one of the first to walk into the newsroom; soon it was a beehive.... My claim to fame was finding a picture of Douglas MacArthur. I remembered his name was spelled "Mac..." and everybody was looking for it filed under "Mc."

Shepherd Field in Wichita Falls became a major training site for pilots, and hundreds of families moved into the West Texas town. With young male reporters going into service, women were doing more and more at the paper which often hired the wives of service men to fill vacant posts. "It was my job to train them to work on women's news. I was expected to cover the hard stuff."

In 1943 a friend got a job with United Press in Dallas. "I asked him if there were any chance of UP hiring a woman. He said to send my application. I did. And then I thought, why not write to Associated Press, too." Off went the letters. "It was a Monday night. Around 9:30. I'd been covering the city council meeting and was back at my desk writing the story when I got a call from Frank King." King was AP bureau chief in Dallas. He wanted to interview Dorothea. "We made a deal. I was going to Dallas for the Texas-OU weekend. He would interview me while I was there."

Typical of the times, and even more typical of the paternal manner in which men treated women, Frank King talked with Dorothea's boss, Henry Fulcher, in Wichita Falls. The two men put a net under the young female reporter. King would offer her a job in Dallas on six months probation. Fulcher would save her job in Wichita Falls. If she didn't work out, she could have her old job back. "I didn't know about this deal. I was so excited. I got a room at 4005 Gaston and moved to Dallas. I went to work for AP for $37.50 a week. When my six months probation was up, Mr. King gave me a permanent job and increased my salary to $65 a week. What wealth! "I must have worked out fine. After Mr. King hired me, he hired only women!"

DALLAS TIMES HERALD FORUM

For three decades, 1943 to 1984, **The Dallas Times Herald** and its Women's/Living staff opened the club year in September with a reception to which the president and publicity and program directors were invited. It was explained what and how their news could be covered. Awards were given for exceptional service and the morning was highlighted by a prominent person speaking. When Erma Bombeck, at left, spoke, she later said: "You are the only people I've ever met who invite guests to your party to tell them what you are not going to do for them."

The Dallas Times Herald went to press for the last time on December 9, 1991, after publishing for 112 years.

Garden Editor Edith Hanby McRoberts, top, and reporter Judy Beene.

Accepting awards for their clubs for serving Dallas are, top to bottom, Jeanne Fagadau and Ruthmary White, Barbara Greene and Pat Peiser, and Betty Watson and Eleanor Burns.

The Times Herald *Living Staff responsible for the annual fall forum and the summer Women's Panel included, sitting, Susan Rutherford, Mary Ann Lane, Vivian Castleberry, Dorothy Fagg, Barbara Richardson, and standing, Janet DeSanders, Graydon Heartsill, Ann Worley, Floyce Korsak, Lana Henderson and Maggie Kennedy.*

THE MESSAGE CARRIERS / 313

The 1972 Panel: Shirley Fitzjarrald, Barbara Meril, Gerrye Dunbar, Gini Seely and Frances Niles, seated; Nila Sloan, Helen Hadsell, Pat Greenwald, Kathy Ashmore, Marie Malouf, Connie Amaya and Bobbie Granberry, standing.

The 1977 Panel: Daisy Joe, Janet Keating, Joan Jackson Kent, Erika Sanchez and Judy Amps, seated; Peggy Shelmire, Judy Marshall, Julie Esely, Victoria Downing, Donna Clack and Margaret Guy, standing.

The Times Herald Women's Panel started in 1957 as the Homemaker Panel to give women a chance to examine their lives, appreciate their contributions and expand their horizons. The Panels preceded by several years consciousness raising groups in Dallas—but served the same purpose. They continued for 25 years.

The infinite variety of Panel: Upper left, Celeste Guerrero and Betty Richardson, 1976; upper right, Doris Muldoon and Sheila Seifert, 1974; across center, Ronda Vecchio, 1968, a gleeful 1967 group, and Melva Knox, 1974; at left, Juanell Burton, Bette Moncrief and Sue Goolsby, 1971; at right, Margaret Guy and Dorothy Fagg, 1977.

There was one mighty surprised hold-up man when he opened the bag he had just stolen and found it contained news stories instead of money. Small town Texas newspapers went to press the next day with trivia. Their stories had been ripped off by the gunman.

Dorothea began her Associated Press career on "The Pony." This meant she sent the news three times a day to papers all over the state and a few surrounding states. "The big cities had their own wire services. All other newspapers that belonged to AP relied on us to send their news. It was my job to determine what stories to send. Eight machines clattered constantly. Two hundred thousand words came in over those machines. I had to edit it down to 17,000 words and get it out to all the member papers. Some I had to send. Columns. Some features. The rest was up to me. There was no second guessing. I had to decide instantly whether to include it or delete it.

"I didn't dare leave my desk, barely had time to run to the restroom . . . no time for coffee breaks. And I *loved* it!"

The biggest stories clattering over the machines were *flashes,* which were accompanied by bells. Four bells indicated the biggest flash; two bells was a news bulletin. "I was on the desk when President Roosevelt died. I was on the desk when the atom bombs were dropped. The day that happened, it hit me: I was the first person in Dallas to know when a big story broke."

She worked for Associated Press throughout the war years, going to AP offices which were at the *Times Herald* during the day and at the *Dallas News* at night. It was the responsibility of whoever was in charge at the changing of shifts to put late-breaking news pages in a zipper bag and hand carry it from one location to the other. Without those stories, the papers served by AP would have no news to fill their columns. One night Jimmie Payne, an associate of Dorothea's, was carrying the bag down Poydras Street from the *Herald* to the *News* when he felt a gun in his back. "We were frantic! Jimmie finally turned up, but the news had completely disappeared. Many Texas newspapers filled their columns with trivia that day. And a hold-up man was, no doubt, severely disappointed when he opened the zipper bag and found no money."

In 1946 Dorothea went to work for *The Dallas Morning News*. She was among the first women hired on the city desk and the first person to cover the labor beat. "Labor was not a popular subject in Dallas, and reporters were not clamoring to cover it. I found it absolutely fascinating. I count it as one of my greatest achievements that I was respected by both management and labor. I'd go to a labor meeting and they'd be giving management hell and they didn't have anything good to say about the paper I worked for, but they always added, 'We're not talking about you, Miss Lyle.' When I interviewed the top men in the big companies in town, they'd apologize to me before they said nasty things about organized labor."

When she left the *News*, the labor newspaper ran an editorial commending her work and saying how much she would be missed. "It is the only clipping I've ever kept. Reporters on other beats had accolades heaped on them—justifiably so. But I worked a beat that did not pass out accolades. So, this one little editorial is my blue ribbon; it's all I need."

In 1949 Dorothea went to Houston to cover a state American Federation of Labor convention (before AFL and CIO merged) and a friend took her to lunch at the Houston Press Club. "I thought a press club was a great idea and Dallas should have one, so I came home and talked about it. Others agreed with me. Fenton Baker (general manager) gave us a room off Peacock Terrace at the Baker Hotel and we organized a small group and got the ball rolling."

To *get the ball rolling*, three reporters, Dorothea, Harry McCormick and Don McIver signed a letter they sent to Dallas newsmakers asking for donations for a Gridiron show. They forgot to mention it to their boss. When Ted Dealey began getting calls from his friends wanting to know "what the hell this is all about," he called the reporters and soundly chastised them. "We came away with our jobs. I wasn't sure we were going to! Mr. Dealey later became one of the Press Club's best supporters, but we sure had a rocky start. I learned a lot from that. He had every right to be upset.

"Clifton Blackmon and Frank King deserve the credit for starting the Press Club. Clifton worked for a company that allowed him time to do that sort of thing. We were so grateful because we (newspapers reporters) didn't have much time off for other things."

Their long and odd working hours created a special bond among journalists. Dorothea was especially popular among the single staff members. So was a blue-eyed brunette staff artist named Frank H. McGrath. They became good friends. A romance developed. Dorothea and Frank McGrath were married at the University Park Methodist Church on June 6, 1950. Both continued working for *The Dallas Morning News.*

For almost half a century Graydon Heartsill's by-line appeared in **The Dallas Times Herald.** *Beginning as a "stringer" when she was an SMU student, she covered stories throughout the country and abroad including four presidential inaugurations, two major Texas tragedies—the school explosion at New London and the Texas City Disaster—and collected almost every accolade offered to a reporter.*

"The city was blatantly sexist—but I didn't recognize it then." She does vividly remember one occasion, being escorted out of the Petroleum Club because she was not the appropriate gender. Her beat included city hall. When J. B. Adoue was mayor, he invited all of the press that covered city hall to lunch at the Petroleum Club. "I was pleased to be included. When I got off the elevator, I stood face-to-face with Jody Thompson Sr. He told me that I was in the wrong place. I assured him that I wasn't. I told him the mayor had invited me to lunch.... He said ladies were not allowed to lunch at the Petroleum Club and took me firmly by the arm and escorted me back onto the elevator. As the door closed, I was saying, 'But, Mr. Thompson, I'm not a lady!; I'm a reporter!' Even so, I found myself out on the street. Later that day the mayor called. He didn't apologize. He just laughed and said he hoped I hadn't missed lunch."

Press Club membership was also a case of sex discrimination. "I had worked really hard to get the club started. By the time it was ready to take in members, Frank and I were married. We couldn't afford two sets of dues, so his name was on the roster and mine was listed as spouse."

Dorothea continued working as a reporter until shortly before the birth of Nannette, her only child, in 1956. She had a pregnancy leave, among the first women at the paper to be allowed one. So that she could keep her benefits, the paper paid her $5 a month—and continued to do so for years. She remained "on leave" until her daughter was almost ready for college!

Native Dallasite Graydon Heartsill was one of the *Times Herald*'s early women employees. Born on July 10, 1906, the daughter of James and Eva Langston Heartsill, she was graduated from Bryan Street High School two months after her 17th birthday and entered SMU that fall. Before she was 20 years old and while she was still a college journalism student, she went to work as a "stringer" for the *Times Herald*. Her career spanned almost half a century until her retirement in 1971. People remember Graydon as the paper's "sob sister," but the euphemism derogates her solid reportorial work.

By the time Graydon graduated from college in 1927, she had accumulated a clipping file of by-lined stories that was the envy of reporters twice her age. Shortly after she went on staff full-time, she was selected to establish a women's department and for the next decade was responsible for women's news. Like most women of her time, she longed for front page by-lines and in 1937 traded her title as women's editor for that of staff writer. For the next several years her by-line appeared regularly on the front page.

Graydon approached every assignment as if her front row seat to the breaking news was a covenant with her reader. Whether standing by a grave as a widow placed a rose on the coffin of the man she had murdered, meeting Eleanor Roosevelt on her first visit to Dallas, listening to a president take the oath of office in frigid Washington, or interviewing 22-year-old Yves St. Laurent, who would become a fashion giant, as he rode a horse for the first time, Graydon took her reader along with her. She moved light years away from her beginning, when her parents registered their new arrival on that sweltering summer day in 1906 only as Baby Girl Heartsill—an anonymity that produced all kinds of repercussions when she applied for a birth certificate to attend the first Paris fashion showings. Graydon was one of those rare reporters who always remembered that she was the bridge from the breaking story to the reader—never a part of the story. Even as she covered national political conventions, major stories—the New London Tragedy, the Texas City Disaster, the Kennedy Assassination, among others—and inauguration ceremonies for four presidents, even as she garnered almost every reporting award, Graydon was the conduit.

In 1943 Graydon was named fashion editor of the *Times Herald*. She didn't want the job. "I would much rather be garden editor," she said. "I am much more at home digging in the dirt than being cramped into a smoke-filled room watching clothes parade down a runway. What does this year's skirt length have to do with shaping history?" And, yet, her writing did just that—included the length of the skirts and the shape of the silhouette into words that were history in the making. And she won every writing fashion accolade offered.

In 1948 when she went to Europe to cover the first major fashion shows following World War II, Graydon dutifully wrote about hemlines and shoulder padding, but she also sent home wonderful stories about post-war France and its people.

Graydon covered the first fashion show in New York in 1943, was one of the first writers named to its editors' committee and continued in that role until her retirement. In 1958 she won Dallas's first award for excellence in fashion reporting. In 1963 she took the first fashion award ever offered in the J.C. Penney-University of Missouri's nationwide competition, a contest that was known as the Pulitzer prize for women journalists. In 1967 she was one of seven writers awarded top accolades in New York.

Graydon most enjoyed covering politics, and in 1965 she compared the inaugurations of four presidents—Harry Truman, Dwight Eisenhower, John Fitzgerald Kennedy and Lyndon Johnson. She told her readers:

> ... every brief minute of history that ushers a man into the presidency of the United States is different.... Each time the unchanging oath might have been a script written just for the occasion and for the performer who for posterity has made it his own.
>
> The first time was in January of 1949. Harry S. Truman had been in the White House three years so there was no special novelty in hailing him as the chief.... Truman had outsmarted the pollsters. Happy days had come again.... That was the fun one.
>
> Dwight D. Eisenhower's first inauguration in 1953 saw the Republican's victorious candidate as a knight in shining armor.... That was the dedicated one.
>
> In 1961, John Fitzgerald Kennedy was sworn in on as cold a day as Washington can recall. Against its frigidity, the vigor and vision of the youthful leader seemed destined... to carry his New Frontier to global achievements.... That was the thrilling one.
>
> Last Wednesday came the fourth.... Lyndon Baines Johnson... had earned, through experience and through the calm and steady assumption of leadership the title which had come to him... in an hour of tragedy. He had been given the nations' mandate to launch his Great Society.... This was the confident one.

No matter what came before or after in history, Graydon's story, brief and poignant, made every reader a participant in the Johnson inauguration. She said: "They rejoiced in the way this husband and wife—a President and his First Lady—looked at each other when the swearing-in was done, and in the way they barely touched each other on the arms in a gesture that somehow bespoke 32 years of partnership and love more than an embrace and a kiss would have done . . . . The haze and the wisps of white that dimmed and flecked the skies left the backdrop untouched so that the majestic dome stood out against turquoise clarity."

Graydon was fashion editor when I joined the *Times Herald* in 1955. A professional without peer, she could have made my life miserable. Instead, she steadfastly supported and assisted me, an aspiring young, untested women's editor. She rarely offered advice and never criticism. She often gave approval and applause. She had never learned to drive, so as often as I could I volunteered to drive her to events, especially those in the evening. It was during these times that she told me delicious stories of the city and the *Times Herald* of the past. She often mentioned the days when automobiles were rare and never dependable. The newspaper staff worked long hours. They would come in early in the day and stay until the presses rolled, however late that might be. This often meant a six-day week, and sometimes seven. On those rare occasions when they got off on Friday night and did not have to return until Monday morning, they would all pile into someone's car and head for the beaches in South Texas. This meant driving to Galveston or Corpus Christi after a long day's work and without sleep, spending four to six hours rollicking on the beach, maybe catching a nap on the sands, and then driving back to Dallas. One weekend six young reporters made that trek. On the way home they had car trouble. It was the middle of Monday morning when they walked into the city room. Edwin J. Kiest met them and fired all of them. Graydon went home devastated. "Like a zombie. Bone tired. No sleep. And now no job. My career shattered. Pretty soon the phone rang. It was Mary Collett, Mr. Kiest's secretary." Graydon was expected back at her desk immediately. "They couldn't get a paper out with six of their key reporters missing. He had to hire us all back."

Graydon Heartsill died on March 5, 1989, at the age of 82, survived only by a nephew. It had been 11 years since her byline appeared almost daily in the newspaper and Dallas had altered dramatically in that time. A handful of us, none among the still working press of the *Times Herald*, were at Greenwood Cemetery to bid her adieu. But those who were, traded happy stories about the reporter who was a charter member of Munger United Methodist Church, an organizer of the Dallas chapter of the National Fashion Group, a charter member of the Press Club and who always relegated every plaque and statuette to the bottom drawer of her desk. Even as I write, I look at the bronze disc inscribed "J.C. Penney-University of Missouri Journalism Awards . . . presented to *The Dallas Times Herald* first place for "Best Fashion Story, National Competition, 1962." When she retired, I salvaged it from her desk. All she took home was the vintage typewriter on which she had written her first story and which, at her request, the paper gave her when she retired.

Julia Scott Reed had already been a professional newswoman for almost a quarter of a century before she went to work for The Dallas Morning News *in 1967 where for more than a decade she reported on news of black citizens.*

Without Julia Scott Reed, the acts and voices of Dallas's black population would be even more silent than they are. As a columnist for *The Dallas Morning News* from 1967 to 1978, Julia was the first person of African American descent to be hired by a Dallas newspaper and the first black reporter on a major daily in the South. She personally integrated the Dallas press. She was the first Black admitted to the Dallas Press Club, the first to cover the Dallas County Commissioners Court, the first to cover Dallas City Hall and the first to become a member of Theta Sigma Phi, the journalism honorary organization for women.

Julia was born in Dallas on July 17, 1917, the daughter of Nina Bell McGee. She recalls her father as someone who was away from home a lot and who died when she was quite small. She remembers his homecomings as a time of "feeling very special, like a princess, lots of hugs and lots of presents." There is no mention of him in any of the interviews she gave through the years and by 1991, she was physically frail and her mind unable to organize facts and present them coherently as a result of a near-fatal stroke on December 12, 1978. This condition was extremely frustrating to her, because all of the information was filed away on those mental tapes. She just could not get it out.

In a 1968 interview Julia recalled the first seven years of her life as idyllic. Her mother was a maid for a wealthy family in the Cedars and the two made their home with

THE MESSAGE CARRIERS / 318

*Natalie Ornish expected her **Pioneer Jewish Families** to be a treasured book for the people she wrote about. Its favorable review in The New York Times and its several awards were a pleasant bonus*

Sylvia Odenwald is a relative newcomer in Dallas publishing. This is her 11th book.

Evelyn Oppenheimer has been a radio personality, writer and book reviewer for many years.

the white family. Julia and the daughter of her mother's employer were exactly the same age and, until she was seven, Julia's favorite—indeed her only—playmate was the little white girl. She was never made to feel any different from the white playmate with whom she spent almost every waking moment.

Julia could not remember when she first became aware that words had the power to convey or cloud meaning, but "From the time I was a small child, I read, looked up the meaning of words and tried to use them. I never cared about big, long or flowery words. I just wanted to master simple, straightforward communication." Her columns, the "Open Line" for the *Dallas News* for 11 years prove her mastery of this simple, honest technique. About Mrs. H. C. Foster in 1968, she wrote, "It's a long distance from a little farm in Wesson, Texas, where Mrs. Foster was born to the United Nations, but she made it." And about Esther Juliet Dyson, also in 1968: ". . . Mrs. Dyson continued with her activities after the death of her husband, Dr. Albert Homer Dyson, 11 years ago . . . . the recent death of her son took its toll on her endurance. She closed her home at 2816 State St. last Saturday and has gone to live with her daughters in Detroit, Michigan." In 1969, about Sylvia Gaye Stanfield, Julia wrote, "Sylvia graduated as salutatorian of James Madison High School in 1961, holds a bachelor of arts degree in intercultural studies from Western College for Women and a master's from the University of Hawaii. She worked for the Foreign Service before being named vice consul of the United States to the Republic of China. Sylvia speaks Chinese." Julia said her role as a journalist was to tell the public about her people. "It would have been silly to embroider the facts . . . . What they accomplished was exciting enough."

When she was seven, Julia's parents moved to an all-black neighborhood and the little girl enrolled in an all-black school. "Overnight I had to get used to a new way of living. It was frightening." She enrolled in J. P. Stark School and then, by walking 10 miles daily, to Booker T. Washington where she was graduated. Her father died; her mother became ill. She nursed her mother, attended classes in the daytime and worked nights. She took business courses so that she could better support herself and her mother. On a scholarship, she enrolled in Wylie College. She wrote stories and essays and poetry to express her thoughts and feelings—and one day it came to her that she could use her interest in words and people as a journalist. Her first job was with the Kansas City *Call*. Her first assignment took her to the city jail where she was addressed as "Girl" and belittled by a white jailer who did not believe that she was a reporter. That didn't bother her nearly as much as hearing the doors of the jail clang shut behind her. "I wanted to run, but I didn't. I got my story. And that's the last time I ever considered running."

Back in Dallas she went to work as a reporter for the *Dallas Express* and advanced to city editor. She stayed for 15 years. Part of this time she was an announcer on Radio Station KNON. She went to work for the *News* in 1967. Her writing spotlighted the interesting activities and the leading personalities in the Black community, but it did more. It was the only bridge between black and white communities, and brought into focus the political, economic, educational, social and cultural contributions of individuals and groups to the whole of Dallas.

She married Scott when she was 17. On December 3, 1966, long divorced from Scott, she married Ewell D. Reed. They owned and he managed a security patrol firm. They were married only four years and three months when he died March 14, 1971. There were no surviving children by either marriage, but Julia reared Gayle V. Eubanks, a cousin and foster daughter. She once said that she considered the way black families looked after their own as one of their most positive attributes.

Julia covered the walls of her spacious den in her Oak Cliff home with her numerous awards. A place of honor on the mantel was reserved for the winged bookends, the Extra Mile award, presented to her in 1970 by the Business and Professional Women of Dallas. In 1991 the Women's Center of Dallas honored her with a special Maura Award for her lifetime of dedication to advancing the roles of women. She is a Life Member of the National Association for the Advancement of Colored People. She was B&PW's Trail Blazer in 1967. She was on the legislative committee of the Community Council of Greater Dallas and on the board of Planned Parenthood and the War on Poverty. She was

THE MESSAGE CARRIERS / 319

one of the original members of LEAD, the organization for the advancement of education in Dallas and of the Goals for Dallas planning committee.

Her speeches, many of which are lost to posterity, are filled with nuggets that, in a few words, typify her philosophy. In 1969 she responded to an award ceremony by Altrusa Club honoring her: "The doors have been closed to black people for many years.... You cannot expect overnight for people to arrive fully eligible to compete in a world they have never before been allowed to enter." In a speech at the YWCA urging peaceful, integration, she said, "There are hot heads in every group, and they are heard because their voices are loud.... emotionalism prevails over reason every time." Deploring militancy as an avenue of entry, again and again she said, "I don't want *out* of the system; I want *in*."

Julia considered the Kennedy assassination story to be the most significant she ever covered, but the one that mattered most to her came in the aftermath of the Supreme Court ruling banning segregation on public transportation. "I called the director of the Dallas Transit System and he said: 'As of this moment, the signs are coming down!' I wrote that story with tears in my eyes."

Her most important work for the city, she said, was in encouraging the people of South Dallas to vote and helping other segments of the community value the voices and votes of its black citizens. For 16 years she chaired Precinct #335. "The vote is our most precious thing. It must be used with dignity. When I first was precinct chairman, politicians could buy blocs of votes by giving people what they wanted to satisfy their weaknesses. Now we are more sophisticated and the deals offered are more sophisticated and we all have to be very careful that we're not selling out in ways that still limit us.

"I know that I am sometimes called an 'Uncle Tom' by my friends, but I and others are determined to build into our social structure a foundation that allows us to open all of the doors of life. We can't do this by tearing down what already exists. It has taken a lot time and great patience. I have seen my people come from servitude to dignity."

Radio was the first medium that carried the messages, in their own voices, from individual to individual. Dallas was the first city in Texas to have a radio station when it established WRR in 1920. Not long afterward Edwin J. Kiest bought KRLD for *The Dallas Times Herald*, and *The Dallas Morning News* established WFAA. The programming was naive. Many programs catered to agriculture of which Dallas was the hub. A farm program almost always anchored the noon hour to draw the listening ears of farmers who had come in from their fields for lunch. The stations scheduled many musical programs and included singers, small bands and piano recitals. By 1922 the music of Herman Waldman and his orchestra from 11 p.m. until midnight from the rooftop garden of the Adolphus Hotel provided at-home music for a dance-crazed city. Cooking shows and recipes, lectures from home demonstration agents on gardening, canning and household tips were interspersed with long-running radio serials, appropriately termed *soap operas* because their sad music and story lines held countless women glued to the radio while they washed dishes, did hand laundry, ironed and did other household chores.

Meg Healey was one of the early Dallas women radio personalities. She teamed with her husband for the Tim and Meg show, a light-weight chit-chat program that became very popular. Meg, like later television anchors, was much sought after to star at community benefits and as a public speaker.

Evelyn Oppenheimer had already established her reputation as a public speaker and writer before she began a career on radio as a book reviewer in 1948. Hers is the longest-running book program on the air anywhere in the United States. Her choice of the books she reviewed, her deep and resonant voice, careful preparation and articulate delivery kept her sponsored and heard by thousands of listeners after most radio book reviewers fell by the wayside.

Born to Louis and Gertrude Baum Oppenheimer on October 20, 1907, Evelyn had many opportunities for education and travel. "My mother taught me to value everything and my father made it possible for me to experience life at its fullest," Evelyn said in a

Judy Jordan, promoted by KDFW in 1973, was the first woman in the nation to be a prime news anchor.

Cynthia Mondell, with her husband, Allen, is a film maker, whose work has been extolled throughout the country.

Pat Perini was vice president of programming at KERA-TV.

1977 interview. An only child, she graduated from Forest Avenue High School "at the very experienced and sophisticated age of 16." Instead of going immediately to college as her friends did, she toured Europe for a year. Her mother sent along note paper and told her to write down her impressions of the people she met and the places she saw. It was training that she has valued for all her life. Back home, she learned that the college to which she had applied "had already filled its Jewish quota.... Anti-semitism was rampant, taught and practiced." She enrolled in the University of Chicago, earned a PhD in literature with a minor in philosophy and wrote book reviews for the *Chicago Post*. After she graduated in 1929, she became a full-time reporter for the paper, still writing about books and authors.

Invited by the Dallas Council of Jewish Women to come home and review *Mourning Becomes Electra*, Evelyn was an immediate success. "At that time, reviews were done only for clubs. "I wanted to reach a larger audience. I thought that I could do this by presenting programs in department stores." Her first venture was with Sanger's, later with Titche's department stores, which then had auditoriums where they presented fashion shows and programs of general interest to the public. Evelyn's reviews were so popular that she went from a monthly to a weekly review. Then came radio. Since then she has been a literary agent, has written or co-authored several books and taught the techniques of oral reviewing at Texas Tech, SMU, the University of Dallas, UT-Austin, the University of Texas at Austin and the University of California at Los Angeles.

Judy Jordan Greene became the first woman in the United States to anchor a news program in prime time in a major market when KDFW-TV advanced her to the co-anchor position in 1973. She began her news casting in the 5 p.m. slot and eight months later went prime time. She was, at one time, co-anchoring the news at 5, 6 and 10 p.m. She was the darling of news watchers. It was a staggering assignment for which she had little background and virtually no support.

Born in 1941 in McAllen, Texas, Judy graduated from North Texas State University in education, and taught for a year in her mother's kindergarten. When her mother died with cancer in 1970, Judy moved to Dallas to be near her siblings—Darrell, Steve, Greg and Martha Horton. Answering a newspaper ad in 1964, she was hired by KDFW as "a girl Friday. I did whatever needed to be done." Young, vivacious, energetic and bright, Judy did not miss much at the station where she continued in the role for which she was hired, for almost nine years. When Parisian designer Yves St. Laurent came to Dallas, none of the men wanted to interview him; Judy did. "I was scared to death. Women's voices and women's faces were not considered to be good on television." That interview was her break. She was given other assignments nobody else wanted or had time for. In early 1970 the station assigned her, along with Ray Walker, to co-anchor the 5 p.m. news. "I learned I could do it!" Later in the year when the station realigned its newscasters, it was rumored that they might consider a woman. Judy had lunch with me in my offices at the *Times Herald*, across the street from KDFW that day. She knew that she was being considered for the 6 p.m. news post. "When it comes to a final decision," she said, "they will not put a woman in that position." In the middle of the afternoon the decision was announced: Judy and Ray were the station's new co-anchors.

"They never did interview me," Judy said, "They did not ask me if I wanted the job. They just assumed. I was thrilled beyond words." But her lack of training to negotiate a contract, her naive approach to the position, and her absolute honesty left her vulnerable. There were no role models. She had no idea how to ask for a raise. "I learned what they paid me was ridiculous." She was expected to appear on the show daily with her hair, clothes and make-up perfect. She had no allowance for any of this. Not even her cleaning bills were reimbursed as a business expense. She knew that her co-anchor was making much more money than she, but she didn't know how much more. The rumor got around that she was going to sue the station for salary discrepancy. "I didn't start it and I wouldn't have done it . . . but it worked." Her income shot up.

Still, there was too much to do. Judy was a community star as well as a news anchor. Everybody wanted her to speak; every charity benefit wanted her to emcee. She could not shop for groceries without people stopping her to ask for an autograph. Once she was pulling weeds in her front yard and a man stopped to introduce himself. The mail was overwhelming. Judy Jordan Clubs sprang up. Men proposed to her. Women admonished her to take care of her health. Young women emulated her hair style. At work there was some envy of her spotlight role. It was a gruelling routine, and corporate America was not geared to provide a support system for its women in key positions. One's failings were noted, scrutinized, and held against them. One's strengths were taken for granted.

Gail Tomlinson Bialas, right, and Karen Page entertain Marlene Sanders, left, who was a guest speaker for Women in Communication.

Judy's personal life was virtually *on hold*, but one admirer refused to give up or be intimidated. His name was David Greene and he was a star in his own right. He had lettered in football *and* graduated as valedictorian of Hillcrest High School, was a scholar and football player at Rice University and at the top of his class in medical school when he dropped out to go into business. On January 20, 1973, Judy married him. He brought to the marriage his son, Stuart, born in 1967 by a prior marriage. Two days after the wedding, Judy went on the air in her first 5 p.m. news slot. When she was broadcasting three times daily, her husband often drove to the station and took her to dinner between the 6 and 10 p.m. news.

Women were just beginning to gain entry into national television and Judy was courted by several stations. She was flattered, but resistant. She valued home and family; she loved Dallas. For a time the lure was constant and persistent, but she did not take the bait. After making a speech in Garland, when she was rushing out to an assignment, she paused by a woman in a wheelchair, introduced herself and told her how much she had appreciated the woman's facial responses to what she had said. When she rose to accept an award and got a standing ovation, she paused at a table and told Mae Graves and Pat Zahrt, "If I stand tall, it's because I stand on your shoulders."

Her outward ebullience covered a young woman who was shy and who longed for privacy. Other women, viewing her as the star she was, were hesitant to offer the kind of support she needed. She was torn between her public life and the private life in which she felt most comfortable. She longed to have children. In 1973 she was enthusiastically pregnant and miscarried. She did not have time to mourn. By the time her daughter, Jordan Greene, arrived on August 15, 1976, Judy wanted both in and out; the corporate world was not yet prepared to grant long pregnancy leaves. Rather than promoting her talent and providing the support she needed, the station continued to treat her as a protege. Eventually Judy moved to Tyler where David had gone into business; she worked in television there, then moved to California with her family.

Lee Cullum is a three-star communicator—television, magazine and newspaper. A Dallas native, the daughter of Charles and Garland Cullum, of the famed founders-of-Dallas family, she began her career as a society columnist, but quickly learned that this was not her forte. Growing swiftly from the role of Dallas socialite, which was hers by

THE MESSAGE CARRIERS / 322

birth, rearing, education and appearance, she became interested in politics—specifically her city and how it worked. She spent six years at KERA, Dallas's public television station, where she was executive producer and moderator of *Newsroom*, a five nights per week news and public affairs program. For a part of that time she was also vice president for KERA's program development, putting together local interest pieces for the Public Broadcasting System. She followed that with a number of years editing *D*, the city's monthly news magazine. From there she went to the *Times Herald* where she became chief of its editorial department. She held that position until the demise of the paper in 1991 and moved to the *Dallas News* as a columnist.

Since the infant days of Dallas, women have been writers. Their work has been limited both by prevailing social customs—women's truths were seldom acknowledged as valid—and by their own ability.

Frances Sanger Mossiker said she frittered many years of her life away before she began writing following a bout with cancer when she lay in bed and wondered whatever happened to Marie Antoinette's necklace. As soon as she was able, she went to France to find out—and the result was The Queen's Necklace, *the first of her books published to rave reviews.*

Frances Sanger Mossiker was able to rise above both of these impediments. As a writer, she is in a class by herself. In 1961 she won the Carr P. Collins award of the Texas Institute of Letters for *The Queen's Necklace.* She was the first woman and hers the first book not set in the Southwest to earn the distinction. She authored 12 books, though she did not begin to put pen to paper until she was in her fifties. "I frittered my time away," she said in a 1969 interview, of those days before she became a serious writer.

Frances was born April 9, 1906, in Dallas to Elihu and Evelyn Beekman Sanger. Her mother was a native of Natchez, Mississippi, whose parents had emigrated from France, but her paternal roots reached back to Dallas's early days when her grandfather, Alexander Sanger and her uncle, Philip Sanger brought Sanger Brothers, to Dallas.

Known as Fanny, Frances grew up privileged and protected, both of which she resented because "they restricted me." She and her brother, Everett. often played in the attic of her grandparents' house in The Cedars, the posh residential area where Jane Monroe Browder had been Dallas's first woman realtor. She demanded to attend public school and was allowed to enroll at Forest Avenue High School—but she was driven there by the family chauffeur.

Women who excel in public relations in Dallas are noted for the savior-faire. Top, to bottom are: Helen Holmes, who handled the Kennedy visit and the Jack Ruby trial, Martha Tiller, who worked in Washington before starting her own company, and Julia Sweeney, who began her own company after working at Neiman-Marcus and The Dallas Times Herald.

She spent her summers in France with her mother's relatives who lived near Strasbourg. She was tri-lingual—English, French and German. Enrolled in Hockaday, she excelled academically while chafing at rules she considered to be too restrictive. At the age of 17 she went to Smith College in Massachusetts. During her freshman year she met Frank Beaston, an actor, when the faculty and students entertained with a tea for the cast of his Broadway play. Even years later she was not sure how this chance meeting blossomed so quickly, but blossom it did and before her 18th birthday she eloped with Beaston. She transferred to Barnard College and, in spite of domestic turmoil, graduated in 1927 Phi Beta Kappa. She did graduate work at the Sorbonne, University of Paris, and

Margaret Hartley joined the SMU Press in 1947 and became editor of Southwest Review in 1981. She died in 1983.

Patsy Swank is a reporter, publicist, art enthusiast and critic and an expert on the history of Dallas.

Kay Tiller is one of many women who successfully operates a one-woman business giving personal attention to their clients.

moved with her husband to Detroit and Hollywood before giving up on the marriage and getting a divorce.

Frances Sanger Beaston was 23 when she returned to Dallas. Skittering around the edges of propriety, she often stretched the endurance of the conservative community and her proper Jewish family. She took up Zen-Buddhism, for eight years was a vegetarian. She studied and took courses in new subjects as they surfaced, enrolling in an Esalen sensitivity training class at SMU in 1969. An insatiable reader with the voice and mannerisms of an actress, she wondered what she could find to occupy her time in Dallas. Stanley Marcus suggested radio and recommended her to WFAA. At the same time he hired her to give a series of lectures on decorative history at Neiman-Marcus. The lectures, she would say later with a smile and a shrug, were "something less than an overwhelming success. I knew very little about decorating and I told Stanley so. He said I could research and learn. I could and I did. My presentations were flawless, but I didn't handle questions well. Someone would ask about Hepplewhite when I'd barely researched past Chippendale. I didn't last long."

Radio was a different matter. She began by doing book reviews for WFAA and writing reviews for the *Dallas News*. This led to a career with Fort Worth's Station KGKO, where for several years she was host of *Woman's World*, a program that explored arts, books and current events. It was one of the first organized programs in the Southwest that recognized women as being interested in things other than homemaking and volunteer work.

In 1934 Frances married Jacob Mossiker and for a time "frittered my life away. I socialized, traveled, played bridge, took short courses and read." This "frivolous era" came to a halt in the early 1950s when she had breast cancer and a radical mastectomy. While she was recuperating, her fertile brain wandered through myriad paths—and came to focus on one of the world's great mysteries, the disappearance of Marie Antoinette's diamond and emerald necklace. As soon as she was able to travel, Frances went to France to seek the answer. The result was *The Queen's Necklace*, published to rave reviews in 1961. The *New York Times* called it "a narrative as exciting as a novel, swift moving, suspenseful, hardly to be put down; yet more important than any novel, a turning point in history explored in depth."

The writing compulsion had come to stay. Frances would never again be without something in the works. Though she traveled worldwide to research, she did most of her writing at home, first in the house she and Jake Mossiker shared on wooded acreage at 4848 Shadywood Lane, and later in their Turtle Creek apartment. The walls were lined with books, many of which found a permanent home on the shelves of the room for writers she endowed on the third floor of the downtown Dallas Public Library. For every published writing there are loose-leafed notebook pages full of hand-written notes in blue and red and green ink, almost as many of them in French as in English. "I have to know my settings and my characters intimately," Frances once said. "I have to be a part of their times—know their jokes, their restaurants, their plays, their music, the everyday life they lead, their gossip. When I am blocked, I know I'm not ready. I haven't researched thoroughly enough." She kept a note pad by her bedside to jot down ideas that came during the night and might escape before she could write them down the next day.

"I wish I'd started earlier in my life," Frances once said, but she did her best to make up for "all that lost time." Until health failed, she worked seven to eight hours a day—even on days she thought she was not doing her best. On her good days "when the story is spilling out and all I have to do is write it down," she worked as many as 16 hours. Among her 12 books, two for children and two for young adults, in addition to *The Queen's Necklace*, are *Napoleon and Josephine: The Biography of a Marriage*, a 1964 Literary Guild selection; *The Affair of the Poisons*; *More Than a Queen: The Story of Josephine Bonaparte*; *Pocahontas: The Life of a Legend*, and *Madame de Sevigne: A Life of Letters*.

Frances Sanger Mossiker died on May 12, 1985.

THE MESSAGE CARRIERS / 324

Natalie Moskowitz Ornish is a message carrier in several media. Beginning in public relations by conducting a campaign for Galveston's library, she became a newspaperwoman, then wrote radio, stage and television scripts and music productions, turned her talents to film-making and in 1989 published *Pioneer Jewish Texans*. Her book has far transcended her original purpose—to find and preserve the contributions of Jewish individuals to the state. It has won two national awards, the Benjamin Franklin Award—first place in history category at the American Booksellers convention, and the National Conference of Christians and Jews' Mass Media Award.

A precocious child, born to George and Bess Shapiro Moskowitz on Galveston Island on February 15, 1926, Natalie graduated from Ball High School at the age of 14 and entered Sam Houston State College that fall. She graduated three years later, and took her master's from Northwestern University at 18.

A national magazine featured her youthful accomplishments, and her home town asked her to return and conduct a campaign to secure public support for its privately-endowed library. Natalie took the challenge even though two prior campaigns had failed. She worked in numerous library jobs, collecting information and refreshing her knowledge of Galveston politics before she went public with the campaign. By an overwhelming majority, voters approved a public funded library.

Joining Associated Press, Natalie worked in Chicago and Omaha before returning to Dallas to join the public relations firm of Rogers and Smith. In Dallas she met Dr. Edwin P. Ornish and the two were married November 6, 1949. Their four children are Laurel Ann Ornish, a radio/TV personality; Dr. Dean Michael Ornish, whose research, care and writings have revolutionized the treatment of heart patients; Dr. Steven Andrew Ornish, a psychiatrist in San Diego, and Kathy April Ornish, a professor at Albion College.

Margo Jones, above, and Elizabeth Ann McMurray, below, were contemporaries and compatriots. Margo created an innovative theater-in-the-round and Elizabeth Ann opened a small, intimate book store where the nation's intelligentsia congregated and socialized.—The McMurray picture from the Collection of the Texas/Dallas History and Archives, Dallas Public Library.

Natalie's writing for children came out of frustration at not being able to find quality material for her own sons and daughters. In 1962 she was commissioned by Theatre Three to write a play for the juvenile audience. The result was *Just Twelve*, which eventually went on national tour. Her music was performed at Tiny Tots concerts for several seasons by the Dallas Symphony Orchestra. As the children grew, so did their mother, who turned her attention to filmmaking and produced several documentaries on a variety of subjects—the ballet, which has long been a passion; swimming, diving and Texas history. "I've done work that I could do in my home," Natalie said, and then smiled. "I write, produce, direct . . . and stand over each like a mother and watch it grow until it is just right!"

Those who write and those who publish and distribute books are soul sisters, all cut from similar fabric bent on getting the messages out in different ways. Before there was a public library, several efforts were made to form rental libraries; they had limited success, principally because they were run by individuals who loved books but had little business acumen. For several years Kate (Mrs. Wirt) Davis operated The Little Book Shop on Main Street where she catered to a limited clientele. It was a small intimate place, the kind that all but disappeared as book publishing became more sophisticated.

Elizabeth Ann McMurray was one of those rare individuals who put it all together. She was a book lover; she had solid experience and her timing was right. She opened her vest-pocket-sized book shop at 1330 Commerce in March of 1938. It was directly across the street from the Adolphus Hotel and half a block from the Baker Hotel. It was called, appropriately enough, McMurray's Bookshop, and it quickly became *the* place to be seen among the *literati* in Dallas.

Liz was born in Okarche, Oklahoma, and started out in life to be a journalist. By the age of 14, living with her parents in McAlister, Oklahoma, she was a columnist for the Tulsa *World* and Oklahoma City's *Daily Oklahoman* but she found her true calling when she went to work for the book store at the University of Oklahoma. The Texas Centennial brought her to Dallas where she managed Karl Placht's Beacon Bookshop working a 10-hour day.

Dallas was a *yeasty* place at that time for creative people. Liz was popular with them, but more important to her future, she was loved and respected by its established citizens. When the Centennial ended, many of her friends urged her to stay. Some began to talk about helping her start a business.

Elizabeth Ann was 23 years old when she opened McMurray's Bookshop. It was a tiny place, 15 by 40 feet, that quickly became a popular gathering spot for local writers, readers, publishers and bibliophiles and a magnet for national and state writers including J. Frank Dobie, folklorist; George Session Perry, novelist, and Walter Prescott Webb, historian. Its reputation grew nationwide.

In 1980 Elizabeth Ann wrote about the book store in an article published in *The Dallas Morning News*. She said it was a narrow, dark place when she first saw it, with very high ceilings and a small balcony that was perfect for an office. But she did not see the narrow cavern; she saw, instead, two sparkling front windows flanking a bright yellow door and interior lighting that would lure readers to the back of the shop where shelves on either side brimmed with books of all kinds. For a $5,000 investment, she made it happen. Her rent was $180 a month. She paid $196.39 for lumber to build the shelves and tables; $41.65 for light fixtures; $40.65 to have them installed; $37.50 for a cash register; $60 for an adding machine; $10 for a desk and chair. Two thousand dollars went into books.

"I had expected to work hard," she wrote, adding that her job at the Texas Centennial bookshop had run from 10 a.m. until 10 p.m., but she had no idea how hard. Sales averaged $8.93 per day for the first 10 days. Painful as this must have been, it set the stage for the personal service that became the hallmark of the bookstore. "Everyone received maximum service."

Liz cited four reasons that made her bookshop a success: (1) Her youth and limitless energy; (2) Interest in the people as much as the books they bought; (3) Luck—location of the shop, zest of the community; (4) caliber of her associates. "I was blessed . . . with an incredibly able and incandescent staff."

Liz kept the shop going and growing for 18 years, until 1955 when she sold it. She had moved to a new location on Commerce. She managed the business as a single mother. Her son, Richard Ellegood, was barely a year old when she opened the shop. When she sold it, she was the bride of William Weber Johnson, correspondent and domestic bureau chief for *Time-Life*. They moved to San Diego. The photograph that accompanies the article Liz wrote for the *News*, is a visual indication of Dallas's erudite thinkers who made her bookshop a household word. She is pictured with Eugene McDermott, Sari Scott, Mary Finney, E. L. DeGolyer, George Sessions Perry and Margo Jones.

Seven years after Elizabeth Ann started McMurray Bookshop another young woman hit Dallas who would make a similar striking impact on the city. Her name was Margo Jones and her talent was the theater. She was the first producer and director to establish a highly acclaimed professional theater company in Texas. Like Liz, she was young, talented, tireless and determined, and during the decade of her contributions, Margo made an indelible impact on the city leaving a legacy of excellence that is unparalleled anywhere in the country.

Margo was 33 when she reached Dallas. Born in 1912 in Livingston, Texas, the daughter of a lawyer, she began life as Margaret Virginia Jones but soon was Margo. She spent her childhood playing fantasy games, dressing up in all sorts of attire and pretending to be the various characters her costumes suggested. She turned the barn into a theater and prevailed on her brothers and sisters to present plays for the family and neighbors. She was always the director. When she wasn't playacting, she was in the courtroom listening to her father plead cases. She told everybody she wanted to be a lawyer, but by the time she enrolled in Texas State College for Women, now Texas Woman's University and the repository of Texas Women's History Project Archives, she knew the theater would be her career. She majored in drama. All of her classmates were studying to be actresses. Margo thought that was fine. She would direct them. If she felt a moment's hesitation because all directors were men, she never showed it.

As a college student, Margo attended every play she could, both on campus and in Fort Worth and Dallas. While her classmates sat back and enjoyed the performance or used it as a classroom to study the actors, Margo took notes on ways to improve the productions and on directing techniques. When she graduated, her parents gave her a trip to Russia where she went to as many performances as she could cram into a short visit. During the summers, she had studied at Pasadena Playhouse and she returned from the Soviet Union to Pasadena where she became director of the school. In 1943 she moved to Austin where she joined the drama department at the University of Texas.

During her UT years, Margo outlined her program for the ideal theater. She drew up a complete plan that included money, location, personnel, playwrights, buildings and audience. But most of all she concentrated on philosophy—which was original. She wanted a small, intimate theater in a setting sufficiently sophisticated that it had an untapped audience, somewhere midway between New York and California. She wanted to present plays both by established writers and by new talent. She wanted to work with actors intent on developing their abilities rather than in playing to talent scouts.

She chose Dallas. Having thought through every detail possible, she asked the Rockefeller Foundation for a fellowship that would let her spend a year traveling throughout the United States studying theater and interviewing theater people. She got it. Three months later she was invited by Tennessee Williams to help him direct *The Glass Menagerie*. She passed up the remainder of her Rockefeller fellowship to help launch the production in Chicago, but through it all she was determined to establish her own dream theater in Dallas.

She arrived in Dallas in February of 1945. Her job was to convince the city to catch her vision, share it and support it. The initial meeting was held in the home of Margaret and Eugene McDermott. When Margaret presented her a check for $10,000, Margo knew she was on her way. Her euphoria was short-lived. She scoured the city but could find no building sufficient to house the small, repertory theater she had in mind. It was almost three years before the theater opened, in November of 1947, in the Gulf Oil Building at the State Fair of Texas. The playing area was 20 by 24 feet. Around it were 198 seats on four sides.

Margo had $199.00 in her theater treasury when the play opened. At the close of the 16-week season she had costumed, directed and presented eight plays, five new scripts and three classics. She had paid salaries to the actors. And she had $12,000 in the coffers. Dallas embraced Margo and her new theater-in-the-round. Play-goers were thrilled that Dallas was the setting for theater innovation. The name changed annually, along with the plays—Theatre 47, Theatre 48, Theatre 49, and on. Not everything was smooth sailing, but Margo was always able to survive and rise above the obstacles. Once she said the secret of her success was no secret. "You must have a capacity for a tremendous amount of hard work, and a joy in doing so," she said. She was dreaming far, far ahead and making plans to expand the season of her theater for the entire year except for brief vacations for the actors when tragedy struck. On August 5, 1955, Margo died. She was 43 years old and was only beginning to live out her vision. The verdict was death by suffocation after she inhaled fumes from a cleaner that had been used to clean the carpets in her apartment.

Countless other message carriers, both past and present, deserve recognition—literally dozens of newspaper women; many radio and television personalities including Iola Johnson, Rosalind Soliz and Clarice Tinsley; Pulitzer-winning playwright Beth Hensley; Margaret Cousins, who for many years edited *Good Housekeeping Magazine*; native Oklahoman Ernestine Adams, a petite dynamo who in Dallas became a voice of authority in the male-dominated petroleum press; Margaret L. Hartley, who climaxed her career with *Southwest Review* by editing it for 17 years; Sallie F. Hill, who for years as "Aunt Sallie" charmed farm children with her answers to their letters in *Farm and Ranch* and advanced to vice president of the *Progressive Farmer* while garnering every honor for magazine newsprint writers. She died in 1992 at the age of 101.

The message carriers have given Dallas a panoramic view of the world—and, often, the world a glimpse of Dallas far beyond its stereotypical, superficial, glitteringly shallow image.

30

• • • •

UNEASE IN UTOPIA

When the 1950 decade arrived, Dallas showed no signs that it would never stop growing. The population stood at 522,000, a 61 per cent increase over 1940. The county population had increased by 166,436, from 398,564 in 1940 to 565,000 in 1950. The city's parameter was 117.25 square miles. It had 1,200 miles of streets, 72 parks and playgrounds and 87 totally segregated public schools. Only 15 of the schools were for Negroes.

It was a man's town. *The Dallas Morning News*, in a front page editorial on January 1, 1950, enthused: "Dallas has the high good fortune of wonderful leadership . . . men and women who step out . . . ." But, beyond that mere mention, women were invisible in the remainder of the editorial. The City Directory bragged that "industrialists, wholesalers, manufacturers, retailers, bankers, oil men, aviation men and the little business men have pooled their efforts to bring about a financial condition that . . . few cities can equal." It added that "(It's) many-sided economic structure has influenced its cosmopolitan outlook . . . . It is a city of diversity," but there is little evidence that it was really cosmopolitan or that it valued its diversity. The introduction to the directory is rife with figures of quantity. There is little evidence for the brag that "It is a city with the charm of yesterday and the spirit of tomorrow."

On the surface, Dallas was a safe, secure, sumptuous, simply superb place to live. It was clean, its burgeoning neighborhoods relatively free of crime and the cost of living nominal.

Its men were imbued with the "can do" spirit and its women were touted as models of beauty and charm. Their faces filled the rotogravure sections of the national press. They were the crown jewels of the male establishment who kept the dirt flying—both literally and figuratively. Buildings soared into the skies and on the top floors of those skyscrapers, Dallas males—perhaps unaware of what they were doing—held court and determined who was *in* and who was *out*.

While the economy was booming and the prosperity seemingly infinite, the 1950s was also a decade of social apathy. It was as if human progress were being held in suspension, and many women found conditions disquieting.

"I experienced culture shock," remembers Mary Louise Rowand, who moved from Scranton, Pennsylvania, in 1953. "Segregation was in full force . . . my children had been in schools that were totally integrated. Many women were professional; in Dallas I did not meet a single woman who worked outside her home. I was driving down the street and saw a bumper sticker, 'Get the U.S. out of the U.N.' I wondered what kind of place we had chosen to rear our children?"

Juanita Craft, who had lived for a quarter of a century in the city by the dawn of the '50s decade, was fully aware of its restrictions and limitations and was doing everything she could to remove the barriers.

Leona Allman, who had arrived in 1945 with her husband, Leo, and four-year-old Linda, found it safe but was "shocked" to see separate drinking fountains for blacks and whites. "I had never seen *that* back in Kansas," Leona said. Because of Leo's work with the U.S. Labor Department, they found people and experiences beyond the limitations of mainstream Dallas. Even though Leona, who had married at 17, followed the prescribed role of wife/mother/homemaker in Dallas, she sought courses, lectures and friends to enhance and expand her training as a home economist. She had completed her college degree after her marriage. When Lisa, her second daughter, was a high school junior,

The 1950s dawned, Dallas was experiencing a facade of boundless expansion and prosperity. Hundreds rushed in to take advantage of what seemed to be its unlimited potential. While the population soared, buildings reached skyward and highways stretched into infinity, human progress remained in a time warp.

Leona took a job two days a month at the Food and Drug Administration that eventually became full time. "My job was essentially consumer education," she said.

Consumer education was what most Dallas women needed. Almost all were full-time housewives and the goods and services they were expected to manage were growing phenomenally.

Dallas had handled its wartime and immediate postwar housing shortage. Clothing was in abundant supply. Transportation was readily available; almost everybody owned a car and those who didn't had access to convenient city transportation. On January 8, 1950, a *Dallas News* headline detailed "New Subdivision Plans for 2,000 Negro Residences" at Mountain Lake Road and Jefferson. Not a single letter to the editor followed that announcement asking why housing was segregated.

A two-story, four-bedroom home on Bordeaux was for sale at $37,500. Rent for a two-bedroom house or apartment ran from $22.50 to $70 a month, depending on its location.

Fashions at the beginning of the 1950s decade dictated that women smooth every fleshly bulge with a girdle. The silhouette featured a pencil-slim top-to-bottom look with skirts dropping to mid-calf under tightly fitted waistlines. The predominant color was navy. The favored hat—and hats were imperative—were tight-fitting cloches with veils.

By 1955 things had changed a little. Dallas Transit workers were threatening a walkout. The day before the strike deadline, Sunday, June 5, 1955, in a typical manner, the *city fathers* negotiated with labor leaders to avert the strike. Transit workers accepted a new contract that raised their pay to $1.75 per hour, a nine-cent raise.

Prices were climbing—but not much. You could buy a seven-piece chrome dinette set including table, and six chairs upholstered in "genuine duron" for $78, and for the kids, a Gym-Dandy Skooter Gym Set including two swings, two chinning bars, two rings, a trapeze bar, a sky shooter, a basketball board and a six-foot slide complete with all the tubing for assembly for $29.95. You could fly to New York on American Airlines for $63. A second hand Chevrolet sports coupe cost $995, a head of lettuce 14 cents, and a bottle of Revlon nail lacquer, 60 cents. A four-room apartment at 3622 Binkley rented for $95 a month.

Working women—and they were dramatically increasing—were paid an average of $50 a week; an executive secretary could expect to make $400 a month, no overtime and few benefits.

By 1955, women's fashions had done an about-face. Skirts were very-very full below cinched waistlines, some belted, some sashed, but women still wore them over restrictive girdles. That summer you could buy beautiful print dresses at Neiman's. The top price was $29.95. Women did not wear pants.

On December 4, 1959 Stemmons Expressway opened. An 8-mile link of I-35 cutting through the Industrial district on its way from South Dallas/Oak Cliff into Northwest Dallas and on into Denton, it was the first highway begun under the federal interstate program which would eventually link the nation in a network of coast-to-coast, border-to-border super highways. It cost $35 million and opened, appropriately enough, with a truck crashing through a barricade. Perhaps somewhere there are records showing how many deaths and injuries have occurred on that 8-mile stretch of I-35 North since it opened on the cold December morning of 1959.

Also, in December a gasoline tax war had cars lining up at the pumps before prices "got back to normal" at 26.9 cents for regular and 30.9 cents for premium.

The school board and administration's greatest worry was that too many students were getting married before they graduated from high school. To discourage this, officials took all extra-curricular privileges away from married students. Pregnant girls, married or not, were required to drop out of school. The boys who made them pregnant were allowed to continue in class.

This is but one of the many ways that girls bore the brunt of discrimination because of their gender. There was little attention paid in the echelons of power to the needs of children and youth. Facilities and funding for programs for boys, though inadequate, was many times that provided for girls. The prevailing attitude continued to be that boys must sow their wild oats and there needed to be some effort made to get them on track following this rebellious time. The prevailing notion was that girls would be protected by their families and needed no community support.

Enlightened, individual women knew better, and it was they—again through their clubs—who established the first programs to salvage and support young women.

Constance Stathakos Condos—through all of the clubs in which she held membership and most of them served as president— was the definitive leader to promote the needs of girls during the 1950s decade. She and Grace Stemmons started the Girls Foundation home. The Dallas Federation of Women's Clubs was its birthmother, but it soon became independent and operated as Girls Foundation, Inc., until it was adopted by Hope Cottage Children's Bureau. The home provided housing and care for 14 girls, not nearly sufficient to meet the need.

Connie Stathakos was born in Dallas on January 31, 1914, to Frank and Angeline Polichronopulos Stathakos and grew up with a brother and sister in East Dallas. She graduated from Woodrow Wilson High School and attended SMU. She married Anthony Condos, whose family, like hers was Greek in origin, but the marriage did not last long. Bettina Condos, who married Herman Lang, was her only child.

Connie was the first person to be awarded the three major service awards—Zonta, Arete and Linz—for outstanding contributions to the city. In April of 1972, a month before her death, the University of Dallas gave her its Athena award for public achievement. Prior to that she had been awarded Zonta's outstanding contributions award in 1962, the Arete award in 1963, and the Linz award in 1964. All cited her as the outstanding citizen of the year. The Linz award was rarely given to a woman.

At one time and another Connie served as president of most of the major women's groups, among them the Dallas Women's Forum, Junior Dallas Woman's Forum, Dallas and Trinity districts of the Texas Federation of Women's Clubs, YWCA, Dallas Sunshine Club and Women's Council of Dallas County. She was on the first committee of Goals for Dallas.

Connie established the pattern for professional volunteerism in her generation and served as the role model for many women who followed her. She wielded the president's gavel with both efficiency and compassion. When she ran a meeting, she *ran* the meeting. She was able to hear all sides of every controversy without ever losing control, and she knew how to cut off debate when arguments became trivial or vindictive. She said she learned how to manage by observing large businesses and adapting their techniques to her volunteer work. There was no secret, she said; it was a simple matter of organization. For instance? "I spend the first hour every morning, from 8 to 9 o'clock, returning telephone calls and writing notes. After that, I'm out of the house for the day. If you call me and I am not at home, I return your call within 24 hours. If I don't reach you, I will try a second time. After that, it's your turn again."

Her 7106 Lakewood Boulevard home was filled with family treasures which Connie cherished, but she was not a woman of wealth. She once said that because she had very little money she tried to make the "little things count." Among her "little things" was a personal note of appreciation to anyone who did a kindness to her—and within 24 hours after the event. She was lavish on few things. One of those was her daughter's wedding at St. Matthews Cathedral. Perfect to the last detail and very formal, it managed to convey the warmth and loving friendliness for which Connie was famous. She often gave boxes of her home-baked Greek baklava to her friends. Among those who enjoyed this largess were the printers at Dallas newspapers, who every year during the Christmas season received a box of these home-baked goodies with a note thanking them for spelling her name correctly!

When Connie died on May 15, 1972, the Dallas Community Chest Trust Fund of which she was an advisory council member, issued a tribute to her. Here are excerpts:

> . . . it seems remarkable that a woman of such natural warmth and compassion could exhibit the drive and efficiency of a board room executive.

Constance Stathakos Condos was the model for club women—intelligent, organized, articulate and directed toward serving others.

Yet it was her deeply human concern that motivated Constance Condos to a position of civic leadership in the Dallas community and contributed to her ability to organize others (to) . . . causes (including) education, cancer, mental health, muscular dystrophy, youth rehabilitation, juvenile delinquency, city planning and the legal rights of women . . . . She believed in America as the land of opportunity . . . . During her career . . . she spearheaded almost every women's campaign fund drive including the Cancer Drive, SMU Sustentation Drive, Presbyterian Hospital, United Way and University of Dallas . . . . Long before women's liberation was a mass movement, she was serving on (Texas) Commission on the Status of Women.

Connie Condos was the preeminent example of the 1950s volunteer—a person who worked full-time, accomplished countless benefits to Dallas and who was never paid for her services. Mary Louise Rowand recalls those halcyon days: "Women had all this *time!* Once they got their children in school, they devoted their lives to volunteer work. The church was at the center of most women's lives. Church Women United had schools of mission that lasted all week . . . . And people were so nice. I'd never known such friendliness. Clerks addressed me as 'Dear' and 'Hon,' and said, "Y'all come back now!' People went out of their way to be helpful. I was driving my children to the zoo and stopped to ask directions. And the man said, 'I'm going that way; I'll show you'."

On forms that asked for "occupation," almost all Dallas married women wrote, "housewife." The care and nurturing of their children was paramount—and for a very good reason. There were record numbers of children. The birth rate in Dallas, as in the rest of the country skyrocketed, producing what would come to be known as the Baby Boom. Dallas County posted a record 14,950 births in 1949. But neither the individuals nor the community valued women's at-home work. Rearing children and nurturing them to adulthood, keeping house and supporting their husbands were not acknowledged as valid contributions.

The few married women who did venture out of their homes to work were careful to keep the nurturing role at the center of their lives—or, at least, to give the impression that they did. Interviewing a working women at that time was like pushing a button and getting the *correct* line. No matter how significant was her job or how valuable her public contribution, every married woman said: "I *always* put my family first," or words that meant the same thing.

Noreen Nicol was one of those few married women with a career. She did not plan it that way when she married Bill Nicol and had two little girls, Nicki and Myra Jean, but when Bill wanted to open his own business in 1948, she encouraged him to do it and said she would help. For the first five years after they established Nicol Scales, Noreen told everybody she was just helping her husband until he got his new business going. "In one major way, I was very lucky," she once said. "Bill and I were working together and when there was a problem with someone to care for the children, we could shift our schedules and one of us—usually me—could take care of it. I realize that women who were working for other companies couldn't do that."

In 1953, Noreen gave birth to a third little girl. The baby lived three days and died with a congenital heart deformity. Her doctor advised her to keep herself busy. "Three weeks later, I was back at the company as a full partner. I told Bill if I were going to be involved, it would be more than as a helper . . . . I've been there ever since," Noreen said in a 1985 interview.

Aware that Dallas was slow to recognize the abilities of women and give them equal treatment when it came promotion time, Noreen said being a partner in the company she helped to create had some disadvantages along with the benefits. "Our company is part of the male world,"—Nicol Scales, the largest scale company in the Southwest, sells, services and engineers electronic and manual systems—"and I have to know everything about the business and still keep the soft touch!"

Noreen was on the cutting edge of another developing trend—that of a mature woman going back to college to complete a degree. A native of Corsicana, born to Mack

Women could exhaust themselves in taking care of their families and their homes, work unlimited time in serving others, utilize countless hours shopping, preen themselves endlessly and play hard at bridge or golf or planning or giving parties—but they could not work to earn money. It was an unwritten rule of the Fifties.

J. and Nora Woodward Lewis on August 22, 1911, Noreen was married to William Nicol in 1937. Because of her work at Nicol Scales and to satisfy a personal dream, she enrolled in SMU, sandwiching classes between work, home and volunteer commitments. She completed a bachelor of business administration with high honors in 1955.

Noreen Nicol, at left, was one of the few married women with a career. In the beginning, she helped her husband start a business of his own. After a family tragedy when her doctor said she ought to go to work, Noreen with Bill, at right, discovered that she wanted both of them to balance their lives while rearing their children. She became a partner in the firm she helped create.

A devoted member of Zonta International, Noreen was its special representative to the United Nations International Women's Conference in Geneva. She was a exemplary model of her message when she spoke to unbelieving high school and college women students and told them that a woman could succeed in the quadruple role of career, wife, mother and volunteer.

She advanced to become president of the company before her death on April 5, 1991. The proof that her life and her message was valid is in her two daughters. Dr. Myra Jean Nicol Williams is a molecular bio-physicist, executive vice president and CIO of Glaxo Pharmaceuticals; she is also the mother of two daughters. Nicki Nicol is president and CEO of Nicol Scales.

Dallas, through the eyes of Juanita Craft, another of its outstanding women looked quite another way. It not only failed to acknowledge the worth of all its citizens, it slammed the door in their faces when they did not fit the prescribed image. Juanita spent her life getting those doors ajar.

Juanita Jewell Shanks Craft, who denied being a feminist, was one of the strongest leaders—male or female—that Dallas has ever produced. Hers was a lifetime struggle for the rights that the United States Constitution guaranteed her, but because of her race denied her. The Civil Rights Act of 1964 had not yet been passed when she began her crusade, and there was never a day in her life that she was not doing everything in her power to make Dallas and the country live up to its promise to her.

It took her half a century—until 1975 when she was elected to the Dallas City Council—for her own personal badge of recognition. She was pleased, but not satisfied. "Dallas has accepted me—but not my people," she said. "Our minds are still enslaved . . . ."

Juanita Jewell Shanks was born on February 9, 1902, in Round Rock, Texas. Her father was a teacher for 40 years. One of the first students to be awarded a grant to attend Prairie View, he graduated as valedictorian of his class in 1895. Her mother was a homemaker. Both parents expected their only child to graduate from high school and go to college. "I was exposed to education all of my life," she said in a 1970 interview. Juanita's ancestry dated back to the earliest days of the United States.

Her paternal great-grandfather was a slave sold away from his wife and 10 children to a family in Mississippi where her grandfather was born into slavery and sold to the Harrington family in Texas. "Both of my (paternal) grandparents were born into slavery.

They were good, solid, industrious people—very intelligent. When they died, they left a 300-acre farm near Austin. Her mother was Eliza Lydia Balfour Shanks. "The Balfours, my mother's family, came to Texas from Arlington, Virginia, about 1852. One of my aunts, Aunt Caroline, is American Indian.

"I am American. There is no reason for me to be described any other way. I'm a combination of many different nationalities. So are most other Americans. Why do we talk about each other as *black* and *white* when there is no such thing? Identifying a person by the color of her skin doesn't make any sense."

Even though she grew up politically aware, Juanita began her personal crusade for equality when her mother died on November 15, 1918. "Mama was dying, but we couldn't get her into a hospital because of her race. I vowed right then I would spend my life changing that."

She was graduated from Prairie View State Normal and Industrial School in 1922. Her certificate—no diplomas were conferred—was in dressmaking and millinery. She married, taught school a year and moved to Galveston where she worked as a drug store clerk. She was widowed, she said, by the time she was 22.

Juanita arrived in Dallas on March 22, 1925. She was 24 years old. She went to work as a bellwoman (she stressed the woman, one of Juanita Craft's very few acknowledgments that there was a feminist buried deep in her psyche) at the Adolphus Hotel. She was working at the Adolphus in 1933 when Eleanor Roosevelt went to the hotel for breakfast. That visit made a profound and lasting impression on Juanita. The President's wife greeted, shook hands and spoke a word to everyone serving her. To Juanita, that handshake and few words validated what she had always known: that she was a person of worth with a mission in life. Neither Mrs. Craft nor Eleanor Roosevelt could have predicted that Juanita would receive invitations to the White House from three separate presidents.

Six years before she met Mrs. Roosevelt, in 1927, Juanita filed a lawsuit to gain voting rights for blacks in the Texas Democratic Primary. Because of legal maneuvering, it took 17 years, until 1944, for this to come about. When she became discouraged, as she often did, her response was to do something positive. This usually meant gathering a group of youth under the sponsorship of the Dallas National Association for the Advancement of Colored People (NAACP) and taking them on a trip to show them what the rest of the world was like.

In 1935, Juanita joined the NAACP. She was elected to its national board in 1941. "I've worked on everything in the NAACP," Juanita said in a 1974 interview, ticking off on her fingers the size and value of the organization—"started February 12, 1909. Purpose: To see that Negroes got full citizenship . . . ." She chaired its credentials committee, an elected position, 19 times. But most of all she liked working with youth. "I've taken them everywhere. An average of 30 kids a year to NAACP national conventions since 1960. We raise all our own money. I tried to make all the trips educational. When the convention was in Los Angeles we saw the Painted Desert and Grand Canyon on the way out. I took them to the ocean. We toured Watts. Bus loads five times to Washington, D.C. To Newark, N.J. To New Orleans. Denver. Oklahoma City. Boston. I've taken them on almost a thousand trips."

In 1955, Juanita led the NAACP youth to picket the State Fair of Texas demanding that people of color be allowed to go to the fair at any time of their choosing. Until then the fair had set aside only one special Negro Day per year. She also led their picket line at the Majestic and Palace movie theaters downtown and, with them, participated in the picket of H.L. Green when blacks were not served at public lunch counters. All of her work was peaceful. She encouraged her kids: "Never tear down where you would like to sleep tomorrow."

On October 2, 1937, Juanita had married Johnny Edward Craft. He died in 1950. There were no children by either marriage. A few years after her husband's death, Juanita said, "I have chosen never to marry again because the average man is jealous. He thinks you are putting others before him. If I were married, I'd never get my work done."

The work she did, in addition to NAACP, included chairing a Democratic precinct for 23 years, attending every Democratic state convention from 1944 until 1982, serving as a delegate to the Democratic National Convention in 1976, working with the League of Women Voters, the Community Council of Greater Dallas, the Episcopal Centers Board, Dallas's Bi-racial Committee, the Dallas County Community Action Committee, the West Dallas Service Centers, the Urban League, the Dallas United Nations and from 1975-1979 serving on the Dallas City Council.

Juanita Jewell Craft, right, moved to Dallas when she was 24 years old with a college education that got her a job as a bellwoman at the Adolphus Hotel. Through the years, while her work centered with youth through the NAACP, she helped to push ajar every door closed to citizens of her color and concluded her career by making policy for Dallas from her seat on the city council.

Honored with almost every award Dallas offered, Juanita accepted with both grace and needling. In 1968 when she was the first Negro to be given the Linz Award, the city's oldest civic award, she told the audience comprised of the Establishment of the city: "I won't stop with winning this award. I don't have sense enough to take care of just my own business. There are a lot of things I don't like about the city and I'm going to try to change them. There are too many people who do not even know someone of another race. I ask you to open your eyes and see. So, look out. You'll be hearing from me." She then added, "I'm going to have to take back what I said—that you have to be a banker to receive this award. I will continue to say you have to be rich. Because I'm one of the richest of women. I'm not a wealthy woman, but I am rich because I have the love of the people in the community and devotion from a lot of people—especially the city's youth."

Her personal needs were few. She lived in a modest white frame house in South Dallas at 2618 Warren Street, a house whose walls were "papered" with award certificates and plaques—among them a distinguished Alumni Award from Prairie View College, the Sojourner Truth Award from the Democratic National Council of Negro Women and the Zonta and Linz awards. It is a house that should/may become a shrine of education to future young people. "I live very simply. All I need is a bed to sleep in and enough to eat to keep me going . . . . I love to travel and can have a bag packed and be ready to go in 20 minutes. I make everything I wear. I have never owned a ready-made dress. This one I have on now cost $1.00. I made it in less than two hours.

"When I die, I want them to remember I raised hell with them . . . . and maybe made a few changes. I'd like to die feeling that progress has been made. Some days I do. Some days I don't. I feel like I'm going in circles. When I think of the documents of this country—that we are all free—I don't know why I have to struggle to get what belongs to us." Ill a long time before she admitted it, Juanita died on August 6, 1985. Juanita Craft, said Ted Watkins, president of the Dallas branch of the NAACP, "was a living legend."

Across Dallas in Park Cities another woman was doing everything she could to bring about changes in the way society treated its people who did not fit the *approved* image. Her name was Mary Louise Rowand and her stage of action was the world.

Mary Louise arrived in Dallas with her husband, the Rev. Edward Clem Rowand Jr. and their two children, Diane Rowand (Simons) and Edward Clem Rowand II in the fall of 1953. Side by side with her husband, whose "call" to preach at Central Christian Church brought the family to Dallas, Mary Louise worked in the church and carried the church into the world—and as far more than a "helpmeet" to her husband. She was ordained into the ministry in the Christian (Disciples of Christ) Church in 1965 with all the rights and privileges ordination entails. One of the first women in Dallas in a mainline denomination to be ordained, she modeled for women what it means to be both female and a minister of the gospel. Her presence and significance in the community opened the doors for, first a trickle, and then a flood of women whose "calling" to the ministry had been denied both by social structures and by the women themselves.

Mary Louise was born to David Harry and Dora Louise Griffith Morris on September 1, 1918, in Fairmont, West Virginia. In Fairmont College she majored in education, was the school's leading actress, won a Katharine Hepburn look-alike contest—and met E. C. Rowand. They have been a team since July 21, 1942, when they were married and Mary Louise began housekeeping in a 14-room manse with no furniture. E. C., who had just completed his bachelor of divinity degree at Yale, set up his first ministry at the First Christian Church in Scranton, Pennsylvania. Their salary was $1,800 annually plus housing and a travel stipend. "We were so eager to get started that we didn't even know we were poor," Mary Louise told reporter Maureen Garcia-Pons in 1974 when she returned to Scranton to address the 43rd annual meeting of the Congregations in Christian Mission. One of her contributions to Christian outreach, Mary Louise said, was gathering the North Scranton high school seniors together in the spring and giving them dance lessons before the senior prom. "There was this preacher's wife standing on a table top with a police whistle trying to teach those youngsters everything from the polka to the waltz," she told Ms. Garcia-Pons.

Teaching kids to dance was typical of Mary Louise's religion which she spread like a spiritual blanket over everything she touched. Hers is a faith of action, love and laughter. In the speeches, programs and sermons she gives throughout the world, she speaks in capital letters with exclamation points at the end of her sentences. Firmly centered in the Christian faith, she widened her circle of understanding to learn from people of other faiths. She once said "I am a church woman, and I emphasize both church and woman, aware that I am walking these days in a realm of controversy, a battle-ground of opposing theologies, a time in which the word heretic, liberal, modernist, conservative, fundamentalist, feminist are hurled by one set of thinkers at another! I am not come to disregard or to attack any other belief, but I must witness to my own! My relationship is with God, which is the very essence of the Christian faith, and (with) Jesus Christ but I know there are as many ways to the stars as there are persons to climb them!"

Mary Louise has shaped Dallas and it has shaped her. Twice, on June 23, 1973, and again on September 23, 1980, Dallas staged a "Mary Louise Rowand Day," proclaimed by the mayor and city council and held as an open celebration for all people of the city. The proclamation issued by Mayor Robert S. Folsom in 1980 highlighted some of Mary Louise's contributions to the city and said, in part:

> ... Mary Louise Rowand has lived in exemplary manner a life for others; for her family, her church family, her Dallas family, her worldwide family .... has inspired the hearts of many to be aware, to be concerned, to share, to have hope .... she has served in personal ways as wife, mother, grandmother, neighbor, friend, church member, teacher, preacher .... she has served in public ways as president of both the local and national Christian Women's Fellowship, as co-chairperson of the Dallas Bicentennial Celebration, as board member of the American Bible Society and Texas Christian University, and most recently

following her presidency of the Dallas Church Women United as their national president with world-wide responsibilities . . . ."

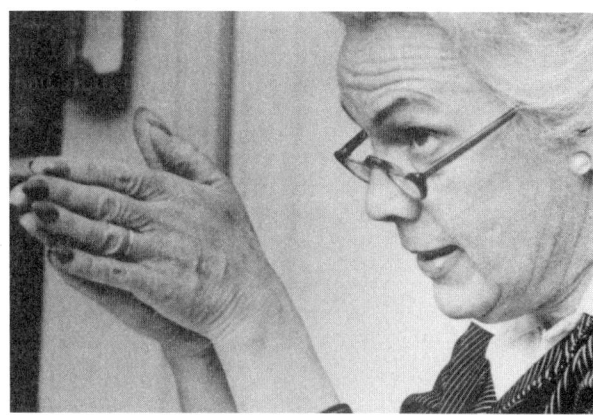

Mary Louise Roward, above, wondered what kind of place she had chosen to rear her children when she moved to Dallas in 1953. She remained to change almost every 1950s expectation of women—both for herself and for others.

Her Dallas mission? ". . . I have the ear of people with power and I try to speak for those who can't speak or cannot be heard." She counted it as a part of her spiritual outreach to know where the needs were, to help educate the women in organizations she led to know, and to hold elected officials responsible for responding to these needs.

In July of 1977 as she became president of the national body of Church Women United, she said her mission had always been "to move out from church walls into the world—to prisons, hospitals, women's centers, rehabilitation centers, counseling centers. Even as she prepared to assume the office that would take her to every continent, she learned she had breast cancer. The prognosis was not good. She was advised to cancel all travel plans. Instead, during the next year, she traveled and spoke in 55 different countries.

In May of 1980, fully recovered, she sent a letter of appreciation and gratitude to national board members who had touched her life during that critical time. In a day when so many women suffer from breast cancer, her words are a balm. She said:

> Three years ago this week, I was completing the 21st ordeal of cobalt. February 1, 1977, had dawned like any other day, but by evening I was in the hospital and on the operating table the next morning. I did not even know how to spell mastectomy! . . . Come July, only God knew . . . who would be wearing that President's Cross (the cross that designates Church Women United president). I moved in faith for 20 weeks. Not knowing, Trusting. Not anxious, nor afraid.
>
> The entire Assembly blessed me, and then that beloved Communion Service on that Purdue hillside was like a benediction laid on my anxious soul. Standing in front, I felt His arm around my shoulder, and the word to "Keep on, woman; I'll tell you when . . ."
>
> It is now 36 months later! . . . I do not remember airports and delayed flights, three keynote speeches in less than a week, back-to-back board sessions with task forces, committees. I do not remember the hot, hot tears, upset stomachs, sleepless nights . . . nor the bone-weariness of meeting deadlines . . . .
>
> I have loved being your president, and I shall miss you . . . ." I have finished the race. I have fought the good fight. I have kept the faith." All the time wanting to be more for you, but you have had all of me there is!

On June 23, 1980, less than a month after she mailed this "love letter" she presided over her last session of the World Assembly of Church Women United. Held in Los Angeles, it drew delegates from 170 countries.

Tall and regal with a crown of silver white hair, Mary Louise found it impossible to fade into the background when photographed with women of the world—women from Zambia and Kenya, Peru and Chile, Yugoslavia and Germany, Japan and Soviet Georgia, China and Australia, California and Kentucky. She represents mother/confessor/role model to thousands of young women. "When I preach downtown (during Lenten services), telephone operators, secretaries, saleswomen, file clerks come . . . . they know I am their friend." Her house was often filled with distraught kids and hurting parents that she and her husband counseled long after they retired as ministers of Central Christian. Their teamwork also included guided tours of Europe and the Holy Land almost annually beginning in 1958.

Mary Louise served on the board of trustees of Texas Christian University and on the board of its Brite Divinity School which conferred on her an honorary doctor of divinity degree giving her the title The Reverend Doctor Mary Louise Rowand.

One of the all-star women newshapers chosen by the *Times Herald* beginning in 1963, Mary Louise was a participant and speaker annually at its women's panels. She was among the first to recognize the unrest beneath the perfectly applied make-up, the teased and sprayed hair-dos and the facade of smiling serenity of the women participants. Once, after being asked to make suggestions for a women's panel program, she wrote:

> . . . It was in 1963 that women's real selves began to emerge. Until they found out how numerous they were—those unfulfilled ones—their widespread unrest had no focus. As the women around me talked, revealing more than they realized, I felt a revolution exploding. I recalled Ibsen's play: "Above all else you are wife and mother," and I heard the women saying, "I no longer believe this. Above all else, I am a human being, and . . . and I'll decide . . . . The good life has never been proven to be attainable by only one route for all. Women must choose . . . .
>
> My own speaking centered around the things that we as women in Dallas were caught up in—the civil rights movement, peace movement, the new politics and the "greening of America." And . . . all around me women in Dallas were entertaining revolutionary ideas, running risks, making bold decisions, defying entrenched power and taking lonely stands . . . .

31

TIDES OF CHANGE

Margaret McDermott and Barbara Jordan, robed to receive honorary degrees, personify here the changing roles of women.

The decade of 1960-1970 was one of heady excitement for women who stepped out, stepped up and stepped off into new dimensions of living. The storms of feminism that wreaked havoc in other parts of the country were far more gentle gales in Dallas, but the winds of change were present and what they lacked in turbulence, they made up for in tenacity.

The 1960s was the decade that women, by their own personal choices, entered politics for the first time. Elizabeth Blessing, who had served two terms on the City Council—the second woman to do so—ran for mayor, the first Dallas woman ever to do so.

It was the decade that the Dallas County Community College System was established, opening the doors to education for thousands. Margaret Milam McDermott, a cultural connoisseur, was the only woman on its first board of directors. Her gentle but firm voice helped to shape the system. It was she who deserves the credit for the aesthetics of the separate schools.

It was the decade that women discovered that their brains had not atrophied when they dropped out of college some 10 or 15 years previously and who returned to college in record-breaking numbers. Community colleges were the haven for most, but other colleges and universities also reached out to meet their needs. Carolyn Lipshy Busch Galerstein, who herself had been a graduate student while pregnant, pioneered courses for older women.

It was the decade of integration. Women's organizations had long been laying the foundation for peaceful integration, though it was the men who got the credit. The Dallas Citizens Council formed the Dallas Bi-Racial Committee that on August 15, 1961, integrated downtown business establishments. This group, "in a series of 'get tough' meetings early in the sixties," integrated the city without violence.[1] But that account and others like it including editorials in Dallas papers crediting the DCC, gave no mention of the work women had done for years to create a climate in which these orders were taken seriously. Women of all colors had been working together for several decades, exchanging stories both in their private homes and, by invitation to organizations. Women planted the seeds and nurtured the soil that made peaceful integration possible. The Dallas Citizens Council issued a decree whose time had already come.

It was the decade of the women's liberation movement, when the second wave of women's emancipation swept the country. In 1963 Betty Friedan's book, *The Feminine Mystique*, explored limitations that women placed upon themselves when they invested their entire lives in the men to whom they were related, either by birth or by marriage. In 1964, a rider on the Civil Rights Bill—women were not then and have not since gained their constitutionally guaranteed equal legal rights—gave women the legal right to freedom.

It was the decade when married women went to work outside their homes in record numbers. Dallas had a higher percentage of women working outside their homes than anywhere else in the country for three distinct reasons: (1) Dallas women had always exhibited an intelligence and independence that placed them, often, on the front lines of pioneering new ways of living; (2) Dallas was experiencing an economic boom and thousands of single mothers saw it as the promised land for a new lifestyle. In Dallas they could find work, living space and child care not available in the surrounding small towns where they lived. Or, so they thought. (3) Dallas, for this same economic reason,

Kim Dawson, Texas-born, Washington-savvy, New York-experienced and Paris-sophisticated, was the perfect choice for fashion director of Dallas's new merchandising venture.

lured hundreds of young professional women, many to seek jobs with career possibilities and many others transferred to the city by their own or their husbands' companies.

It was the decade when child care became *the* number one priority of families. With thousands of women pouring out of their homes into the workplace, the need for quality care for babies and little children and the need for concerned attention to the needs of boys and girls mushroomed. Thousands upon thousands of single parents—mostly single mothers—learned that there simply were not enough good caregivers.

In Dallas, these phenomenal social changes took place in the framework of continuing physical growth and economic prosperity. The city reached a population of 745,000 including its four "island cities"—Cockrell Hill, Fruitdale, Highland Park and University Park. Dallas County had almost a hundred thousand people. Its economic base was stable. Still dominated by agriculture, banking, insurance, manufacturing and oil, it was also becoming a city of electronics, transportation, communications and both clothing and home fashions. When the decade began, the business volume was $2,991,177,000. The land on which it rested ("The rich, loamy black soil in Dallas is duplicated in only one other place in the world, the Russian Ukraine") was valued at $120,000,000 and included 2,100 miles of roads, streets and highways, 85 per cent paved. Recreational facilities were plentiful. White Rock Lake Park, alone, attracted 1,000,000 annually. Fair Park had a $5,000,000 civic center and housed the State Fair, the largest celebration of its kind in the nation.[2]

Living costs in the city were low—building costs and housing, electricity and gas inexpensive and food costs below the national average.

The quality of life in Dallas, the directory bragged, was outstanding. "The cosmopolitan atmosphere of Dallas, more evident than in many larger cities, is due chiefly to its blending of many cultures and to its highly diversified interests. Dallas . . . attracts . . . population from all sections of the United States—the Old South, Pacific Coast, North and East. It combines the gracious hospitality of the Old South with the open-handed friendliness of the West, and these traits . . . (are) blended with the aggressiveness and business energy of the North and East."[3]

Though hyperbole exceeded reality, the Dallas economy was expanding; it was reaching in new directions. And economic frontiers always open doors of opportunity to women. Not only are new jobs created, but there is no old boys network to close ranks against intrusion. Fashion, which had been struggling in seedy lofts and showing in rented hotel rooms for years, reached a new respectability in the late 1950s and early 60s when Trammell Crow opened the Dallas Trade Mart and, the next year, the Dallas Apparel Mart. Fashion had reached the big time. Dallas officially recognized it as one of its prime industries and in its wake came all of the accessory sidelines and support businesses.

Kim Dawson was the Mart's fashion director. The embodiment of fashion/beauty in the city, she came to her new job with the appropriate personal appearance and credentials. Born in Lufkin, on July 13, 1924, to James Aubrey and Mabel Sanford Hughes, she had grown up in Center after her parents were divorced. Her birthname was Marjorie Marie Hughes, which was changed to Kim Garrett by the Harry Conover agency when she went to New York to model. Following graduation from high school, she moved to Dallas, took a business course and was just completing it when World War II began. She went to Washington to work in the office of Sen. Tom Connally. By selling a record number of war bonds, she won a trip to New York where she paused in sight-seeing long enough to interview with Harry Conover, then New York's top model agent. It was a match. Her fresh spontaneity coupled with an incredibly sophisticated presence on the runway made her an almost immediate success. She became a top couture model. When the war was over, she went to Paris where she modeled collections by famed French designers including Marcel Rochas and Jacques Fath.

After a year and a half, she was tired of the Parisian lifestyle, came back to the United States, and worked briefly in California before returning to Dallas. She married photographer George Dawson, retained the Kim for her name, added his Dawson and continued her modeling career at Neiman-Marcus. When the couple's first child, Kim Taylor Dawson, was an infant, Kim took time out from the hectic life of fitting and runway modeling to breast feed the baby, who sometimes was brought to the store by her father for that purpose! "It was," Kim said, "unbelievable—very frustrating to others. I occasionally had to hold up the whole show to feed my baby." That child grew up with a sister, Lisa Dane (Leonard) and a brother, George "Tiger" Dawson to become a physician, Dr. Kim Taylor Dawson Vernon.

Kim Dawson is an enigma. Though her entire career has been based on beauty and fashion, though she looks and lives the role of model, she is also an astute business woman. Incredibly down-to-earth and level-headed in a profession often based on artifice and sham, Kim combined mystique with acumen to be a success in her multiple roles of model, entrepreneur, wife, mother, grandmother and volunteer.

"A woman must spent long hours and do a lot of juggling to merge two jobs—that of homemaker and career woman," Kim told Jaime and Letabeth Littlejohn for *Women of '85*, "but with dedication to combine everything comes a self-fulfillment that makes it all worthwhile."

In 1962, Kim opened her own business and in 1964 when she started as fashion director of the Apparel Mart, she expanded her own Kim Dawson Agency, Inc., providing talent to the radio-TV-fashion industry. Thousands of young women and hundreds of men have sought modeling careers through her agency.

Elizabeth Blessing had earned her credentials in every way that society decreed for a woman. She had grown up in Dallas, attended Hockaday, was married, had children, but she was considered a maverick when she ran for city council in 1959.

Though the doors were open for women to run for public office—Edith Wilmans and Sarah Hughes, the two most outstanding examples—only a very few women were willing to tackle campaigns unless they were invited to do so by established political structures, always run by men. Where the established structures looked for *good* men, they sought only token *safe* women. Most of the women prominent in the early days of political involvement were not elected until the early 1970s, but the seeds of change were planted in the prior decade. Elizabeth Blessing opened the doors in 1959; Anita Martinez, elected in 1969, was the first Hispanic to serve on the Dallas City Council. Eddie Bernice Johnson, the first black woman from Dallas to serve in the state legislature, took office in 1972; Adlene Harrison, the first woman to serve as mayor, was elected to the City Council in 1973, but had been on the City Plan Commission for eight years prior to that. Nancy Judy, who began her political career on the DISD Board of Education in 1972, became the first woman on the Dallas County Commissioners Court in 1979.

Elizabeth Blessing led the way in many ways. She was the second woman to serve on the Dallas City Council and the first woman to run for mayor. She was preceded on the Council by Calvert Keoun Collins, selected and anointed by the Citizens Charter Association, in 1957.

Elizabeth campaigned for office bareheaded and without gloves! This was so startling that it made headlines in the newspapers. She was defying the beauty/fashion/happy homemaker role to which Dallas women were assigned. And that was only one of the ways she was a maverick when she ran for City Council in 1959. With a handful of other candidates, she was an independent, contesting the virtual monopoly of men chosen by the CCA. Elizabeth had all the proper credentials to fit the mold of a respectable politician—except for the fact that she was the wrong gender. She had been a Dallasite virtually all of her life. Born in Fort Worth to A. J. and Willie Johnson Cuppels, she was christened Arza Elizabeth and brought to Dallas when she was six months old. She grew up in East Dallas, the area she sought to serve on the council. She graduated from Woodrow Wilson High School and from Hockaday Junior College. She was a member of Munger Place United Methodist Church. For six years she was administrative assistant and personal secretary to Ela Hockaday. During World War II, she followed her Air Force flyer husband, William Blessing, around the country to the different places he was stationed. In 1945 the Blessings returned to Dallas and became business partners in real estate development and construction. They had four children—Brian, born in 1944, Scott in 1946, Gail in 1950, and Billy in 1956.

Elizabeth lost her first race to the CCA candidate, George F. Mixon, by 119 votes—33,861 for her, 33,980 for him. But she wasn't through with politics. In 1961 she ran again, this time being elected by 5,000 votes in a run-off. In 1963 she ran for a second term, sweeping the election with 61 per cent of the votes.

Eddie Bernice Johnson, left, with her son, Dawrence Kirk, campaigns for the state legislature. Her election began a career in public office that took her to the nation's capital in the early 1990s. Nancy Judy, above, the first woman elected to the Dallas County Commissioner's Court, kept a low profile while wielding a tremendous influence for many years.

It was apparent from the outset of her political career that Elizabeth was not a rubber stamp representative. She was constantly in the headlines because she questioned everything she did not understand. Though willing to compromise, she lived up to her campaign promise: that she would represent, to the best of her ability, the people who had elected her. In 1965 she announced for mayor. Her opponent was the CCA-sponsored, highly successful businessman, J. Erik Jonsson. The campaign was marked by several ugly incidents, many contrived or taken out of context. Some men seemed puzzled. One, shaking his head, said to Elizabeth, "I understand that you have four children. Don't you have enough to keep you busy?" Elizabeth lost. Resoundingly. She polled only about a third of the total vote.

The chief reason for her defeat? "The fact that I am a woman," she said, in an interview on the day after her defeat. Dallas was not ready for a woman mayor. It is all right for women to raise funds in campaigns and even all right for them to sit on the City Council. But it is not yet all right for them to present themselves for top public offices . . . ."

But Elizabeth left a great legacy to Dallas women: she pioneered the way for them to run for, be elected to and hold public office. Since then, many women have served on the city council, most with distinction, some with CCA approval, others as independents.

Dallas's first woman mayor, Adlene Harrison (see Adlene Nathanson Harrison, Part II) was nurtured in a Dallas family noted for its concern about human equality and its determination to effect change. From her birth on November 19, 1923, she absorbed political savvy around the dining table as she listened to her father, Hyman Nathanson, uncles and cousins—among them Julius Schepps—talk about people problems, argue about solutions and plot strategy. She served on the City Council 1973-77, was named mayor pro-tem and became interim mayor in 1976 when Wes Wise resigned to run for Congress.

From the time voters approved the building of community colleges until the first one, El Centro, opened it took only 14 months. Principals in making it happen were, left to right, Carol Zion, Bill Priest and Margaret McDermott.

When Eddie Bernice Johnson was elected to the Texas House of Representatives in 1972, she was the first black woman ever chosen for that office and the first woman from Dallas County to be a lawmaker since 1935. Born in Waco, Eddie Bernice graduated from high school there and from Holy Cross Central School of Nursing at St. Mary's College, University of Notre Dame. She took advanced training in nursing, specializing in psychology at Texas Christian University, North Texas State University and Texas Woman's University. She was chief psychiatric nurse at the Veterans Administration Hospital in Dallas when her talents became clear to women and to political leaders who urged her to seek public office. Because she could not campaign while working in her government job, she resigned to become executive assistant of the Personnel Division of Neiman-Marcus. It was position that allowed her both visibility and the time to conduct a campaign.

Nancy E. Judy was the first woman elected the Commissioners Court in Dallas County. She was elected to serve District 2, for a third term, in November of 1986 with 72 per cent of the vote. Nancy's quiet demeanor belies her ability to deliver tough decisions. A graduate of Pennsylvania State University, she moved to Dallas in 1955 and has always combined her public life with a successful private one. She is married to Robert W. Judy, an engineer. Their daughter, Robin Ann, is a high school teacher and the mother of twins. Their son, Matthew Rodman Judy, is a wildlife biologist.

Nancy began her political career on the Board of Education of the Dallas Independent School District in 1972 and served for five years. She ran, unsuccessfully, for the U. S. House of Representative from the Fifth District in 1976. Nancy is a member of many organizations and has served on countless boards from Charter 100 of Dallas to the Dallas Arboretum & Botanical Society and the Dallas Museum of Fine Arts. She served as executive director of the Dallas County Republican Party in 1977. Covering all bases, she belongs to the White Rock Republican Women's Club but is also on the board of directors of the Republican Men's Club of Dallas County. She and her husband live in Garland and she belongs to organizations in Garland, Dallas and Mesquite, the entire scope of the second district of Dallas County which she represents.

The single most outstanding and lasting event that impacted and improved the lives of women in Dallas happened in May of 1965 when the Dallas County Community colleges were founded. In that month, voters approved a $41.5 million bond issue to finance a community college district. The act would create seven colleges with El Centro downtown and the other six forming a ring around Dallas County. These schools have been a special blessing to women. For the woman who required job skills, the woman who needed alternative class hours, the woman who could not afford either the time or the money to enroll in a four-year college, community colleges were accessible and inexpensive. For the woman academician, the colleges offered opportunity for career development.

Margaret Milam McDermott was the first woman to make an impact on the new community college system. The consummate cultural connoisseur, Margaret gave to Dallas both time and money that had already made her name synonymous with art in the city. Her first gift to the colleges came out of that discipline. She insisted that each college be designed for the terrain and the setting in which it was to be located. It would have been less expensive to have commissioned one set of plans and adapted them to the different schools, Mrs. McDermott once said, "That's one thing I won . . . . I lost some arguments!"

A Dallas native, born in 1912 to attorney Lynn and Grace Hill Milam, Margaret was educated in the Dallas schools and attended Sweet Briar College and the University of Texas. In 1935 she returned to Dallas and worked briefly as a society and arts reporter for *The Dallas Times Herald*. In 1952 she married Eugene McDermott, who with Cecil Green and J. Erik Jonsson, founded what would grow into Texas Instruments.

With R. L. Thornton, Jr., Margaret co-chaired the first community college board. "They needed a woman," she said, "and I was it." That first tireless seven-member board created the foundation, established the framework and envisioned the creation of the seven colleges. "We met *every* night . . . . We had nothing—no land, no buildings, no supplies, no students. We were a close board," Margaret said. One of the board's first acts was to hire Bill Priest as its first executive, a selection that, according to Margaret, was "inspired." In 1966 only 14 months after voters approved the funding, El Centro enrolled its first students.

Mamie Abernathy McKnight, from a Dallas family of achievers, is potent on several levels. She is a college administrator, historian and bridge builder between people—women especially—in her role as community volunteer.

The first woman hired in early 1966 by the newly formed Dallas County Junior College District, as it was first known, was Dr. Carol Lee Zion, a Florida educator. Her title was associate dean of instruction. She was responsible for a minutae of details from helping to hire faculty, to determining department and classroom locations to buying auditorium curtains. Fresh from doing similar work in Dade County, Florida, she was young, vibrant and indefatigable. Carol bought a house in Dallas, loved the community and planned to put down roots, but in her haste to get things done, she made some enemies. During the last week of her short tenure with the colleges, Carol and I had dinner. She shared her vision of what the community college system should be.

She envisioned El Centro as the hub for all of the schools, serving as a resource center, administrative headquarters—a place for faculty from all schools to meet and exchange ideas, for students from all schools to unite for the same purposes and to share major programs, both academic and cultural and for Dallas citizens to tap as an educational/cultural/civic center. She saw such a center as uniting the community college system, hoping that such a place would vastly diminish turf competition. She was both tearful and philosophical about her vision as she prepared to leave Dallas. "I moved too fast," she acknowledged. "I am an innovator. The world does not long tolerate innovators. Nor does it remember them. Usually, somewhere in the future, the visions of innovators are put into practice, but by that time we should have moved civilization forward another 50 years."

The seven colleges, most of which have enjoyed phenomenal success from the time they opened their doors, were completed on a staggered basis: El Centro in 1966; Eastfield in 1970; Mountain View in 1970; Richland in 1972; Cedar Valley in 1977; North Lake in 1977 and Brookhaven in 1978. In 1972, the name was changed to Dallas County Community College District and in 1989 the Bill J. Priest Institute for Economic Development opened near downtown Dallas. It was named for the founding chancellor and serves the community through the Business and Professional Institute, the Edmund J. Kahn Job Training Center, Small Business Development Center, Center for Government Contracting, Business Incubation Center, and International Trade Resource Center. In many ways it resembles the vision that Carol Zion had in the beginning.

From the first, women have had a prominent role in the community college system, many serving as presidents of the several schools.

Mamie Abernathy McKnight joined El Centro College when it was only eight years old. A true daughter of Dallas, the third of James C. and Mamie Bell Abernathy's seven children, Mamie brought with her a host of credentials. She was born in Dallas on February 20, 1929, attended Harllee School, was graduated as valedictorian of Lincoln

High School, earned bachelor and master's degrees from Prairie View after studying at Wiley; received her doctorate in education at North Texas State where she majored in psychology and administration and minored in counseling, returned to Dallas to teach at her high school alma mater and then signed on as assistant professor at SMU. En route to her job as educational paraprofessional program director and instructor at El Centro in 1972, she also took graduate work at the University of Wisconsin, the University of Texas and Texas Woman's University and taught courses at NTSU, Bishop College, Prairie View, the University of Texas at Arlington, Wiley and Pepperdine University. Six years after joining El Centro, she was, in 1978, promoted to division chair of the communication, mathematics and development studies department and in the fall of 1985 became consultant to the chancellor for community development of the DCCCD. It was a job that is both visionary and specific—visionary in that it asks her to understand the needs of students in Dallas County and specific in that it requires her to find ways to meet the needs.

Mamie remembers—but does not dwell on—Dallas as a community closed to the talents of its citizens of African American descent. Instead, she has become one of the definitive African American historians of the area, ferreting out and preserving the accomplishments of Black Dallasites.

To read Dallas history, one would get the impression that its black people all did menial work when, in truth, many outstanding professionals including some of the best and brightest of educators were people of color. All Mamie had to do to prove this was to look at her own family. Of her six sisters and brothers, two are pharmacists, one is a lawyer, one works for the Internal Revenue Service and four are educators. Ezra McKnight, her best supporter, is the fellow teacher she married in 1952 and their daughter, Ginger Laurie McKnight, is an attorney practicing law in New York City.

Even though Dr. McKnight remembers Dallas with doors she could not enter, water fountains she could not drink from, empty bus seats she could not sit in, recreation centers where she could not play, schools where she could not enroll, she emphasizes instead the opportunities that have enriched her life. She points to parents, low on money but long on love, who *expected* each of their seven children to get a college education, her husband who has been a co-partner in their marriage, a daughter who has taken advantage of many of the doors she has helped to open, and countless friends and associates of all colors and abilities who have worked with her.

"Dallas," she said "is a city in flux. The problems we have here have been growing for years. Business moving out of downtown has left the city with a limited tax base. Middle income people have lost their jobs. But we are not hopeless. We are not like the cities where the whole inner structure is a pocket of poverty. The enrollment at El Centro (in the heart of downtown Dallas) is up. The key to progress is education, Education, EDUCATION. I can't stress that enough!"

Carole Rolnick Shlipak, also a Dallas native, brought expertise in raising money to DCCCD when she joined it in 1979. Nine years later, a study by the Council for Support and Advancement of Education, named DCCCD as the top public two-year fund-raising institution in the country for the past five years. As director of development and chief operating officer of the DCCCD Foundation, Carole was responsible for the group that raised $3.6 million. The Foundation has more than $2 million in assets and gives more than $500,000 annually in scholarships and grants.

The daughter of a Dallas businessman, George Rolnick, whose name is synonymous with hat manufacturing, and Minnie Rosen Rolnick, Carole was born on November 6, 1938, the youngest of four girls. Her mother died when she was very young and she was reared by her father and stepmother, Anne Winkler Rolnick. She was graduated from Highland Park High School and from Newcomb College of Tulane and did graduate work at the University of Pennsylvania.

When she married Dr. Louis Shlipak in 1962, Carole had no intention of becoming a career woman. With the birth of Andrea in 1966 and Michael in 1968 she further committed herself to the role of homemaker/wife/mother. But there were other factors at work in her life. Whatever volunteer work she undertook she did with such

Carole Shlipak achieved what most women discovered to be elusive: She carved a career from her volunteer work—and found that she could earn money for what she had been doing gratis. She continued to ply her expertise on both levels.

professionalism that she came to the attention of community leaders—in Irving where she lived, in Dallas where she was born and in the state. She developed her leadership skills chiefly through the League of Women Voters where she served the Irving chapter in almost every capacity from stamp-licker to president and then moved on to the board of directors of the Texas LWV. From the first, she said in a 1980 interview, she had been blessed with a husband who took seriously the volunteer work she did and who encouraged her to further stretch her wings.

By the time she went to work for DCCCD in 1979, her children were launched. Carole and the community colleges seemed a perfect fit. Because they were new and still innovative and because Bill Priest, the founding top executive, was creative and willing to try new ideas, Carole was able to present a work portfolio based almost entirely on her volunteer work. Her only jobs prior to that had been a sales job at Neiman-Marcus during the Far Eastern Fortnight and interning as a teacher of history and Western Civilization at Bishop College. Three weeks after he met her at a social event in her volunteer capacity, Dr. Priest offered Carole a part-time job. Further, he agreed that it would be fine for her to work flexible hours so that she could link home, volunteer and career responsibilities. It was a match from the first. "I got the freedom to be a professional doing a job I loved! In the beginning my contract called for half time work. From the first I worked the number of hours of a full time employee, but I was *free* to set my own schedule. I am a product of the American system of volunteerism."

Until the 1960s, mature women in college were an anomaly. An unwritten rule prescribed that people proceed along life's course in order: one grew up, went to school, went to work, got married, had children, grew old and died. There was little bending of the rules for either men or women. Then the G.I. Bill of Rights changed all that. It was passed by Congress on June 22, 1944, and set in motion a new day in higher education by providing government-paid tuition and other benefits for veterans of World War II. Thousands of men who had lost from two to five years of their normal educational lives flocked to the classrooms. These older men usually had families and often wives worked to support the family. But the women themselves, except for a few who were also veterans, had no direct benefits from the G.I. Bill and no comprehension that they, as mature adults, could return to the classrooms.

A percentage too minuscule to measure remained in college after they were married and had children. Carolyn Lipshy Busch was one of the rare married women who was a student, a wife and a mother all at the same time. This experience, teamed with her academic excellence led Carolyn to create a course called "How To Go To College When You're Over 25," which made her the perfect candidate for the University of Texas at Dallas when it established its Maturity College in 1975.

Carolyn earned a bachelor's degree and a Phi Beta Kappa key at the University of Missouri in 1951. Born to Harry and Lillie Swartz on August 14, 1931, in Amarillo, Carolyn married Dr. Sylvan Busch on April 13, 1952. She acquired four babies and two advanced degrees in the next 10 years. Susan Busch was born in 1954 between Carolyn's bachelor and master's degrees; Alan L. Busch arrived in 1956 while his mother was a graduate student at Columbia; Saralynn Busch arrived in 1959 and Lauren Busch was born in 1962 at the time Carolyn was working on her doctorate at the University of Maryland.

Carolyn began her professional career in Dallas where she was executive director of the Zale Foundation for three years. During this time her husband of 14 years died suddenly. Her children were 12, 10, 7 and 5. She took all four to Spain where she enrolled in the University of Madrid and studied Spanish literature. Back in Dallas, she took a job at the University of Texas at Arlington as an assistant professor of Spanish, a post she held until 1975 when she went to the University of Texas at Dallas where she was dean of the School of General Studies and associate professor of comparative literature with a specialty in Spanish and founding director of Maturity College.

"Older students are being courted by colleges throughout the country," she said in an interview in 1975, "but these schools are not prepared to handle older students. They (the students) are entirely different from 18-year-old kids going away to school for the first time. They are mature adults. Many of them have family responsibilities. The role is especially hard for mature women going back to school because they often have both job responsibilities and children. Many also have a low self esteem. At Maturity College, we are ready to help in many ways."

Carolyn Lipshy Busch Galerstein was one of the most effective people on the Dallas scene during her career as foundation director, professor, college administrator, leader of the Dallas Commission on the Status of Women and, not surprisingly, wife, mother and community volunteer.

On October 30, 1971, Carolyn married George Galerstein, and added his children—Nina Gagnon Fendel and Bill Galerstein—to her life. Carolyn and George were a uniquely gifted team in their multiple community responsibilities, suited in temperament, religion and politics, and dedicated parents. George supported and applauded her and was never threatened by the honors she accumulated nor by the role he played in being a full partner in their at-home life. It could not possibly have always been easy, but Carolyn always made it seem so. "Balancing career and family is women's greatest challenge," she said.

Carolyn was the first chairperson for Dallas's first Commission on the Status of Women. George was her best adviser, supporter, and confidante. Carolyn's untimely death on March 27, 1988, left a chasm in the educational and volunteer communities of Dallas. But it was women and women's groups that suffered the greatest loss. A brilliant strategist who kept a sense of balance and perspective even under the most trying conditions, Carolyn cooled the ardor of the most flaming feminists even while she ignited the passion for struggle and personal advancement in women who did not trust their own personhood.

Other Dallas-area colleges and universities also addressed the needs of older students and, especially, of older women returning to the classroom, but the fact that the University of Texas at Dallas was established in 1969, after much political haggling, exclusively for advanced students—juniors, seniors and a graduate school and remained so for years—gave it special insight and direction toward meeting the needs of adult students.

The public schools in Dallas were integrated slowly and methodically, for some time grade by grade and school by school. The children—especially the younger children—adjusted quickly with only normal bumps along the way. But there were impediments. The children came out of homes, many of which had ingrained prejudices against people of other colors and races and backgrounds. The board and administration,

Kathlyn Gilliam was uninvited to speak at a Dallas elementary school, but she was not left speechless. She became president of the DISD school board.

though well-intentioned and committed to make changes required by new laws, was also made up of individuals who came out of another time and another frame of reference. For years there were major and minor skirmishes. Court battles impeded the inevitable. Teachers also had been trained and experienced in a setting of "different but equal"—which was neither—and a few, both white and black, found it hard to let go of their past biases.

Private schools mushroomed where children of parents who found integration intolerable enrolled their kids. There were as many reasons given for the deluge of private institutions as there were children to fill them. But, whatever the reason, the results were the same: public schools suffered. In many cases, boys and girls from affluent and better educated homes, enrolled in the private schools. Increasingly, this left the public schools to serve children with greater need but less preparation. There continued to be dozens of excellent public schools in Dallas and hundreds of excellent, dedicated teachers determined to make the system work and thousands of parents and individual citizens committed to the public schools. And there are boys and girls graduating from public schools every year who make outstanding records in some of the country's leading colleges and universities.

From the first, the little children—when left alone by prejudiced adults—were soon learning and playing together without incident. All parks, swimming pools and recreational facilities were opened to all citizens. It would be years before blacks and whites would play together as well as they were learning to work together, but the day would come. On all public transportation, signs came down dividing sections between blacks and whites. Restaurants began to seat and serve everybody. Nobody who lived it will ever forget the pickets at the Picadilly restaurant on Commerce Street—a picket line that was short-lived because almost immediately the doors were opened to protesters. Nor can they forget the first sit-ins at H. L. Green on Main Street where black teenagers with their sponsors were joined by several whites who were appalled that there were public places in downtown Dallas where its black citizens could not sit and have a soft drink or eat a sandwich.

It was during these changes in enrollment and in the policies governing them that a woman was named president of the Dallas Independent School District's Board of Education for the first time. Not only was she female, but also African-American. She was Kathlyn Joy Christian Gilliam, and she—like the next woman to head the board, Mary Holland Rutledge—had worked tirelessly all of her adult life to enrich the public school system. Both had headed local PTAs. Both had moved to Dallas from small Texas communities. Both had broad community experience in the city.

Kathlyn Gilliam integrated her own life along with that of the schools. Born on October 16, 1931, in Campbell, Texas, she had moved to Dallas with her parents, Ross Christian and Lucille Donaldson Christian, when she was 13. One of seven children, she graduated from Lincoln High School in 1948 and married her high school sweetheart, William E. Gilliam, the next year on March 11, 1949. She completed a business course at Southwest School of Business Administration and did office work full and part time along with giving birth to Deborah Joyce in 1951, Constance Ann in 1955 and Edward Christian in 1964. In 1970 she was one of those older women students when she enrolled at Southern Methodist University. By that time Deborah was in college and Connie a high school senior.

During her children's early years, Kathlyn devoted a lot of time to their schools. She became president of Dallas City Council of Colored Parents and Teachers in the 1960s and was given its life membership award at the group's 28th annual Founder's Day celebration in 1969. The impact of her work and her commitment to children was already evident when, in the early 1970s, a personal affront pushed her to greater community-wide involvement. She was invited to Preston Hollow Elementary School PTA to discuss, along with a white woman, the League of Women Voters' school desegregation plan. The invitation was withdrawn after a few members of the board protested her appearance. At the time the Dallas City Council PTA was backing a proposed amendment to outlaw student busing. At the meeting itself dozens of women protested

Ethel Stewart was unprepared for discrimination when she moved to Dallas. She found racism rampant in the church she chose to attend.

the withdrawal of the invitation to Kathlyn and said they were appalled that a few board members could override the decision of the majority. Kathlyn said she was not surprised at the withdrawal of the invitation or at the confusion it created. She did not hold any animosity, she said, "toward those who left me speechless. I don't know who they are, but they seem to know me and that I don't pick my words or my people."

Kathlyn was first elected to the school board in 1974 after being defeated for the board the first time she ran in 1972. She was named vice president of the board in 1978 and president two years later and continued on the board after her tenure as president ended. Kathlyn's honors are legion and eclectic.

All teachers owe a debt of gratitude to Thelma Paige Richardson. Like Rosa Parks who refused to go to the back of the Cleveland Avenue bus in downtown Montgomery, Alabama, on December 1, 1955, touching off a new era of civil rights for black Americans, Thelma Richardson fought back at a system that was unfair. She was the Dallas school teacher who equalized the salary scale for black and white teachers when she became a plaintiff along with the Negro Teachers Alliance and the NAACP in a federal suit in 1942. Until that time there was little consistency in the way teachers were paid. Whites were paid more than blacks. Men were paid more than women. And coaches were paid more than anybody else. When promotions were passed out, it was almost always coaches who were promoted to principals.

It took years for Thelma Richardson and her co-plaintiffs to win the suit to equalize salaries, but win they did and the new ruling altered salary scales throughout much of the South. Thelma was a perfect person to put her name on the suit because she was an exemplary teacher. Born in Denver, Colorado, she earned her bachelor of arts degree in modern romance languages from the University of Northern Colorado, a master of arts from the University of Denver and a master of liberal arts from SMU. She taught at Booker T. Washington High School, Lincoln High School and North Dallas High School and then joined the staff of the East Oak Cliff Subdistrict.

Integration of neighborhoods followed the ending of segregation in public places. As long as neighborhoods remained segregated, other efforts to create harmonious diversity was, at best, artificial. Children could be bussed across town and placed in classes together; businesses could hire employees without regard to skin color; women could sit together in each other's homes and in club meetings; friends could go out to dinner together in leading restaurants and have a good time. But for a long time there was an invisible color line in the residential areas. A small neighborhood centered by Robin Road and bounded by Inwood, Mockingbird Lane, Lovers Lane and Lemmon was among the first—possibly *the* first—to achieve harmonious integration. There, in the early 1960s, led by Jodie and Victor Furnish, a white couple, and Joyce Lockley, a black mother, residents formed one of the first neighborhood associations in the city. Across town in North Dallas, professional couples who were black moved onto McShann Road. Barbara Watkins joked that she lived in the only black ghetto in North Dallas. While leading a committee for the League of Women Voters to determine segregation patterns in the city, she was frustrated to discover the dearth of records on segregated housing.

Some of the strongest resistance to integration came not in the schools and not in the neighborhoods, but in the one place that should have taken a leading position for wholeness—the churches. There is a saying, repeated so often that its origin is lost: "The color line is never so clearly drawn as at 11 o'clock on Sunday morning."

Ethel Elizabeth Johnson Stewart remembers her first experience at a church after she moved to Dallas in 1962. Although she was then 64 years old, she had never experienced discrimination and was unprepared for what happened to her. Born in Canada, the daughter of a Methodist minister, educated as a musician and home economist, she had lived in Cincinnati and Mexico City before moving to Dallas. "One of the first things I did was go and meet the priest at the nearest Episcopal church. I liked him. We got along fine and I told him I would be at worship services on Sunday morning. Sunday

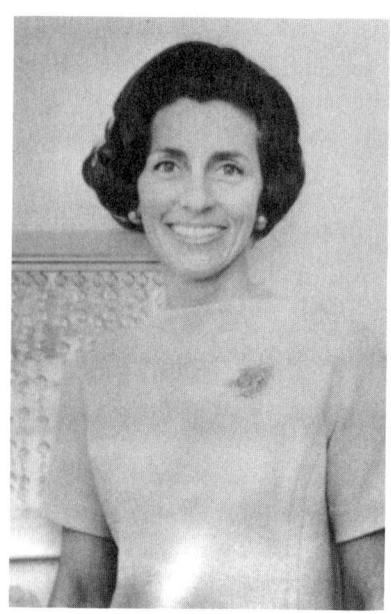

The Panel of American Women was as effective as it was low-key. Carolyn Tobian Clark founded the Panel in Dallas.

came and I went to church. When I got up to take communion, someone blocked my way to the altar. I said 'Excuse me,' and went around him. I took communion. The services ended. It was only later that I learned the church had police protection that morning. Then someone told me that there had been anonymous telephone calls. One caller had told the priest that if he gave that black bitch communion, he would be dead before sunset. Well, I went back to church and nothing ever happened . . . . People were plenty prejudiced, let me tell you!"

Three groups, two of them comprised entirely of women and the other of couples, were sparkling gems in the city's integration process. Two, the dialogue groups of Jewish and Black women and Amigos, the group that socialized in public places, have already been mentioned. The third was the Panel of American Women. Carolyn (Tobian) Clark organized the Dallas branch of this national group. It was comprised of four or five women from different neighborhoods, of different backgrounds, ethnicities, ages and skin colors. Upon invitation of organizations Panels presented programs, each woman speaking from her personal experience about how discrimination had impacted her life. Dozens of women signed up to participate in panels to assure an authenticity of voices, and new individuals were added so that stories were fresh to panelists as well as to audiences. The only criteria was that a Panel should include women with diverse histories.

In the 1960s, vast numbers of women found paying jobs outside their homes. For most, this meant that their work day increased dramatically because very few husbands added extra home chores to their responsibilities. Women's primary concern was for their children. Prior to the 1960s, most women in the labor force left their children with a relative or with a neighbor. But as the age span for employed women increased, this eliminated what was once a large pool of help with child rearing. Not only mothers of young children were working, but the mothers of those young mothers also worked.

Overnight groups rushed in to fill the void. Most aimed at providing quality care; a few gave it. Unfortunately, many were motivated by making money rather than providing a nurturing atmosphere for children. From the outside, caring for children looked easy. Instead, done right, it is the most demanding work in the world—a joy at times but also a 24-hour-a-day non-ending responsibility. A genuine love for children is a good start, but it is far from enough. There must also be tolerance for mundane chores connected with child care plus an intelligent interest and response to questions and needs of each individual child. Dallas, like the rest of the country, suffered and still suffers from a dearth of good child care providers.

Women and women's organizations have worked diligently to help fill the need. Almost every women's organization in the city has listed child care as one of its top priorities. Countless programs, workshops, seminars, symposia and projects of every sort have sought ways to increase quality care at a price that is within the reach of working parents. Salaries for child care workers are pitifully small. This brings into child care centers many who are unsuited to nurture small children.

In Dallas there are hundreds of child care, kindergarten, and early childhood learning centers. The system is confusing because there are few valuative processes and, in many people's minds, child care and early childhood education are synonymous. Some centers offer both child care and educational programs, but not nearly all of them do. Most large, and some smaller, churches offer education and/or care for young children. It does not follow that programs are excellent because they are housed in a church or even that the church is responsible for the quality of the program offered. The situation is further clouded by the fact that programs peak and wane with the economy and with individual administrators and teachers. Choices are further complicated because children have varying needs. At first when babies need to be fed, changed, loved and coddled a good, clean nurturing center may serve the needs of all of them, but as soon as their personalities and inclinations begin to develop—and this happens when they are very young—the best training derives from centers and teachers who understand that each child is unique.

Child Care Dallas, under several names, since it began serving families and children in 1901, has the most consistent record of excellence in the city, principally because it has always had quality directors and has remained child-centered. Margaret Cone became director in 1953 and steered the agency through the critical years of its most explosive change. It was the first agency in the city to be totally integrated, both in the children it served and in its staff. "We've never had a problem," Margaret said in December of 1971 as she prepared to pass the torch to Madeline Mandell. "I'm so pleased about that."

During her 19-year tenure, Margaret moved 15 times as the headquarters of the agency relocated. She was one of the first people in the nation to stress programs geared to children's individuality rather than to their chronological age, and one of the first to insist on education and training for those in charge of the eight centers she administered. She organized the Texas Association for Children Under Six in 1963. Community services director for Dallas's Housing Authority prior to becoming director of the Day Care Association of Metropolitan Dallas, as it was then known, Margaret took over a staff of 64 including one social worker caring for 365 children. On January 1, 1972, she passed along to Madeline a staff of 109 personnel, including six social workers serving 650 children.

The choice of a new administrator could not have been better—both for the children of Dallas and for the young woman who took the post. Madeline Mandell was a native of El Paso, born on October 20, 1935, to Humboldt, Casad and Evangeline Smith Mandell. She grew up with a brother, Humboldt Jr., was graduated from El Paso High School, took a bachelor's in English from the University of Texas at Austin and a master's in social work from Denver University. Several positions in Texas and California, the latter with the Girl Scouts Council of San Francisco, prepared her for the Dallas post.

Madeline's history with Dallas went back six generations to the earliest days of the city when her great-great-great grandfather, Green W. Minter, a Methodist minister, served as one of the first four commissioners of Dallas County. His daughter was Lucretia Minter who married Charles Baker. Charles helped to build the first court house in the county and to organize the first court. Lucretia and Charles' oldest child was Martha Elizabeth Baker, the first girl born in Dallas County. One of Madeline's aunts, Dorothy Ann McComas Wright, was head nurse at Scottish Rite Hospital in Dallas for many years.

Child Care Dallas, under several names since its creation, was headed by Margaret Cone, left, during its years of most explosive physical growth. She passed the torch to Madeline Mandell 1972 who guided the agency through its most turbulent human changes.

Sonya Bemporad, above, joined Child Care Dallas in 1976 and has been a definitive link between the agency, the people it serves and the Dallas community.

The child care agency Madeline administered reached into many areas as the city expanded and needs changed. As Dallas reached its 150th birthday, the agency had six divisions with a staff of 250. Madeline's title was president and chief executive officer.

She said the agency has been consistently successful because (1) it is locally based and administered—"when changes need to be made, we are free to make them," (2) it has a multi-talented staff—professional, caring and dedicated and (3) volunteers give countless hours of service that there's no money to pay for.

Sonya Bemporad, vice president of operations, is a major key to the continuing success of the agency. She joined in 1976 as executive program director bringing with her a background from Temple University, Sophie Newcomb College, the University of Cincinnati and Sarah Lawrence where she earned a master's in child development. Her giftedness lies in her ability to do long-range planning while keeping care and training of individual children firmly in mind. Her outreach into the community—she does private family counseling and therapy, designing, teaching and administering child care and family programs at area colleges and universities—brings her work full circle. It not only gives her the perceptions and experiences of a changing community but allows her to bring these talents back into her agency.

For years Child Care Dallas has monitored the achievements of children who have had their educational start in one of its centers. "We follow the children through the eighth grade. Children from no other early childhood care program in the area match our level of achievement," Madeline said. "We are very proud of that."

There are other good centers and good educational programs. Most are expensive; most top-notch ones provide financial aid to low-income parents with exceptional children.

Finally, the responsibility for selecting a good place to care for their children rests with parents—chiefly with mothers. Whether a father is present, or not—and often he is not—the mother usually assumes responsibility for child care. Fathers tend to stay out of the picture unless there is a crisis—at which time they often react with anger. Overburdened mothers, with two full time jobs, home and workplace, often ignore or overlook problems with child care facilities unless breaches of care become flagrant. And community standards of control are pitifully few.

The long view of history clearly shows that women have made progress. As Dallas celebrated its century and a half birthday, its women were beginning to be counted essential to the city's well-being and progress. This was largely due to the second wave of the women's liberation movement. Both of the thrusts by women for equality were connected with war and the aftermath of major national conflict. The first, during and following World War I, secured the vote for women and then waned. The second started during World War II when women learned they could handle almost every job and wanted the opportunity to do so.

Historically measured, women are only a step removed from having their total lives defined for them and assigned to them. In many parts of the world this is still true. Three very real contradictions face every woman who would like to feel and act upon her own autonomy: (1) *Love*. She cares about her family—husband, children, mothers, fathers, sisters, brothers, friends, *ad infinitum* and will do nothing that might hurt them. (2) *Conditioning*. Both the loud and subtle messages of her entire life assail her. It matters, or she believes it matters, what others think of her. (3). *Priority*. The doors are open and the choices infinite, but each choice has a price tag. Women see this smorgasbord of choices and often feel frustrated.

Women as groups are ambivalent, pulled by their loyalties. Cracks develop in fragile territory and chasms often follow. As divisions develop between groups, individuals tend to stand apart across the chasms and throw verbal stones at each other. And each group clamors for a spot at the head of the line. They divide by (1) *Nationality*: Cultural conditioning often keeps women apart in special ghettos even though these may be divided by only a few blocks. (2) *Ethnicity*: Blacks, Whites, Hispanics, Asians and other groups bind together apart from women of other colors. (3) *Age*: There is no comparison between

Women have many loyalties that keep them from fully cooperating with each other. They divide along lines of nationality, ethnicity, age, marital status and children, work, religion, choice, sexual orientation and economics—and this is only a beginning of the subtle nuances that keep women apart.

the world in which grandmother grew up and that of today's young women and girls. (4) *Possessions*: Those who have worldly goods tend to be insensitive to the valid needs of those in poverty, and the poor look with both envy and resentment at the wealthy. (5) *Work*: Women who work full time at home often accuse their career-minded sisters of being selfish; those who choose careers outside the home often categorize their at-home sisters of being lazy or dull. (6) *Religion*: Institutional religion has often done more to separate women than it has done to unite them. Fear and diffidence have kept women from sharing their most basic needs and desires. (7) *Choice*: Instead of uniting to control their reproductive capacities, women scream at each other over abortion which is only a minute particle of their total sexuality. (8) *Sexual bent*: Women who are heterosexual have tried to exclude lesbians and bi-sexuals and the latter, who only within the last few years have emerged from their hiding places, yell defiance at their straight sisters.

There are many other significant areas of difference, all of which create misunderstandings. And when none of these work, women are sent another message: WAIT. It's not your turn yet. For most of creation, women have internalized this message. WAIT until the wars have ended; your first loyalty is to your country and it is your duty to raise sons for the military. WAIT until the earth is safe; we are destroying it with the garbage of our lives and you, dear lady, can bring the green grass back to the parks, the birds back to the forests—if you can keep the saws out of them long enough—and plug up the hole in the ozone. WAIT until your sisters and brothers of all colors gain their place at the fountains of freedom; your work is to help bring this about, then you will have your opportunity. WAIT until your husband has safely launched his career; he is the chief breadwinner of the family and what would you do if you could not depend on him? WAIT until your children are grown; they are your first priority. When *all* of this is accomplished, then it will be your turn.

Women waited. When the women's liberation burst onto the national scene, many Dallas women were aware of it and eager to be included. But they were smart. They knew the climate of their community and moved slowly and purposefully—even when many decried that method. Through criticism—both self-imposed and other-directed—the women of Dallas created a carefully planned and solid edifice. Its painfully slow process has touched the lives of thousands of women who, in their different styles, have passed the flickering torch of freedom from one set of hands to another. Some came early to the cause, were fiery in their commitment and burned out; some were so intense that they self-destructed; some found the barbs of personal conflict or of societal conditioning too painful and dropped out; some grew weary and found other causes for their commitment.

Some stayed through all the vicissitudes.

32

FACES OF FEMINISM

Thousands of women moved individually and in concert to create changes during the 1960s decade, most of them within the confines of their societal conditioning. They had very little choice. The world—especially the world of Dallas—was not ready for a revolution as can be testified by many women who came to the city, tried to make changes quickly and left in frustration and disappointment.

Hundreds of individuals and groups worked to improve opportunities for women while continuing to value their traditional roles. Often, as they did this, outsiders saw Dallas women stagnated in their stereotypical roles. Instead, the women were moving slowly but decisively, their roots systems firmly planted while they grew new branches of expectation and opportunity. Feminist Gloria Steinem said in a Dallas interview that she was surprised at the scope and depth of the women's movement in Dallas. Expressed in a cliche of the time, Dallas women refused to throw out the baby with the bath water.

The great numbers working for creative change are Maura McNiel, Hermine Tobolowsky and Barbara James. From different backgrounds and using different methods they and others forged a women's liberation movement that was both vibrant and lasting.

Maura Anderson McNiel is considered the *mother* of the women's liberation movement in Dallas. Hermine Tobolowsky, an attorney, wanted a law or two changed so that Texas women would not be equated with idiots and infants and discovered that an entire system had to be altered. Barbara Minor James, representing both herself and her race, was a *first woman* in a series of appointive and elective offices.

Maura McNiel had been involved in almost every human rights issue as each surfaced—equal opportunities for Native Americans, Blacks and Hispanics, environmental issues, assistance to children and youth, voting rights, political campaigns, psychological break-throughs, *ad infinitum*. Through their churches and their clubs, Maura said, "women were taking care of everything in Dallas that was not profitable and was never completed. For diversion we had bridge, the Bible, and book reviews. What else was there?" She was one of those women willing to WAIT. "There was so much to do," she said. "I didn't see any problem for women . . . ." Her progression to becoming the "mother" of women's liberation in Dallas was an evolution.

Maura became a Dallasite in 1952 and became a person in her own right in the decade of the 1960s. She worked from a basic philosophy of "opening the doors and letting everyone find their own answers."

Maura—a woman "good at waking people up," but who is a "slow learner"— was born on April 11, 1921, in Minneapolis, Minnesota. She was the oldest of four children of Oliver and Hazel Anderson Anderson. Her father was an insurance man, her mother a career homemaker. The brothers were Harley, four years her junior, and John, eight years her junior and a baby sister, Gretchen, 15 years younger. Maura graduated from West High School in 1939 where, among a host of other significant events, she and Harry Reasoner had the co-leads in the senior play. Three years later she graduated from the University of Minnesota *cum laude* with a triple major—English, psychology and anthropology plus a course in logic in the law school. She studied under B. F. Skinner, Buckminster Fuller and Robert Oppenheimer. She was a supporter and friend of Hubert Humphrey before he reached national office. She joined a sorority, Kappa Alpha Theta, became its pledge captain and spent most of her time "trying to change the Greek system. I couldn't tolerate the injustices taking place in the name of sisterhood and when a student

Gerri Hair's shirt expresses the message of the Dallas Women's Center in the mid-1970s.

Wes Wise, above, with his wife, Sally, made good on a campaign promise to establish a Dallas Commission on the Status of Women if he were elected mayor.

committed suicide because she didn't make the sorority, I knew something was drastically wrong."

A host of other things were shaping Maura's life—visits in the sparsely settled Dakotas, her father's homeland; summers in her mother's northern Minnesota woods. She was taught to ride horseback and explore the Minnesota north woods by Native Americans on her grandparents' property just across the border from Canada. Everybody in her family had American Indian friends. Her mother spoke Sioux. "My earliest conscious recollection of injustice was having the Indians rounded up and herded onto reservations." It was also from the Indians that she first absorbed the knowledge that "the entire eco-system is intertwined, and disturbing one part of it wreaks havoc with other parts." These fundamental revelations fine-tuned a child growing up "determined I would do everything I possibly could to make things right for everybody."

There were detours. "The year I graduated from college was the last of the innocent times. Before World War II, kids had a chance to grow up slowly. The war ended that." She had a college degree with honors in courses that made her think, but not a single practical course that would help her earn a living in the fast-paced war economy. She enrolled in Minneapolis Institute of Art and hastily finished a course in engineering drafting. Always good in art, with "an eye for putting things together, seeing things in a sequence, knowing what's going to come out at the other end," Maura was hired by Donaldson's Department Store in Minneapolis. "I backed into that job. I was doing some art, some modeling, and it just sort of happened. The men all went to war, and they were putting women into jobs they'd never held before . . . ." She stayed at Donaldson's for three years where she handled 26 display windows, including hauling around the mannequins that were "as heavy as lead." Her job expanded to include copy for advertising and publicity. She was also responsible for a weekly fashion show at the Curtis Hotel. For this she hired and directed all of the models and coordinated all of the clothes—and commentated the show. For her regular job she was paid $30 a week. The fashion show earned her an extra $5 and she wrote and hosted a weekly 45-minute radio show for an additional $5.

"I was young and had boundless enthusiasm and energy. Nothing seemed out of my reach." And then a "gorgeous Marine lieutenant walked into my life. I fell in love. He had a college degree, was an excellent tennis player, and he danced divinely. Those were my chief requirements for a husband." They were married in 1943 and things went downhill from the start. She quit her job and moved to Erie, Pennsylvania, his hometown. When things got worse instead of better, she "just knew" that a baby would solve all their problems. Rick was born in 1945, but things did not improve. "My marriage was my reform school." When the baby was 14 months old, she took him and fled back to her mother's house in Minneapolis. When she went to buy carpeting for a house that she, her brother and his bride were remodeling, she got into a conversation with the owner, learned that the business was almost bankrupt and convinced him that he needed an interior decorator to salvage it. Somewhat skeptically, he agreed to try it. "A few months later we had the business back in the black."

She wrote a novel she called *Quicksand*. When she got a rejection slip from a publishers, she burned the manuscript. "Nothing was lost. It was good therapy."

In the meantime she and a friend were making and selling clothes. "I'd always designed and made my own clothes, so I just *did these things* and sold them and it was terrific. The war had ended. Fabric and buttons and sequins and all the little extras were back, but most of the designs were just horrible. One day I went into a fashion house to buy some zippers. They knew I'd modeled and asked me to try something on for a customer. I did. It was a terrible outfit. Didn't fit. Buttons that didn't. I said there ought to be pockets in it. That made the designer mad. She walked out and slammed the door so hard the glass broke. That left them in a real bind. There was a market coming up and no designer. So I felt responsible and said I'd do their line. I did. It just ran away with sales. This got me noticed . . . ."

She was offered a job with Wragge in New York, accepted it and quit before she went to work. "New York was no place for a mother with a young child. I couldn't find good housing for us and I was worried about child care and I didn't want to leave Rick

Maura McNiel was president of Women for Change before its name was changed to Women's Center of Dallas. She is known as the "mother" of the women's movement in Dallas.

Linda Coffee, above, and Sarah Weddington, below, filed the suit that went to the Supreme Court which made it legal for women to get abortions.

ROE V. WADE

Two lawyers, both in their 20s, in March of 1970 filed a suit in the federal district court in Dallas to make it illegal for a woman to be required to carry a pregnancy to term against her wishes. Linda Coffee, who had clerked for Judge Sarah T. Hughes, found Norma McCorvey, a 25-year-old pregnant woman, who wanted an abortion that was illegal under the laws of every state in the union. Linda called her classmate, Sarah Weddington, the only other woman who had been in her University of Texas Law School graduating class, and together they brought the suit.

The court, in June of 1970, declared the Texas law unconstitutional, but did not grant the plaintiff the right to legal abortion. After months of legal maneuvering the case reached the Supreme Court where Sarah and Linda argued the case on October 11, 1972. Three months later, on January 22, 1973, the decision was handed down. Seven of the nine Supreme Court justices affirmed the right of women to legal abortion. It was a decision that continued to plague society for years to come.

In an ironic twist, Norma McCorvey, in whose behalf the case was filed, is the anonymous Roe of what has become Roe v Wade. Henry Wade, whose name the case carries, had nothing at all to do with it. He explained: when the case was filed, it was against the state and named all district attorneys as defendants. Because it was filed in Dallas, his name came first. "I was," he said, "never involved in any way... had no time to try to help solve a social problem. I have no strong personal feelings (about abortion) either way. I think that a woman has a right to an abortion.... I do think there should be some restrictions."

with my mother." She had heard that Dallas was making a name for itself in fashion and that there were positions open for designers. She flew to Dallas. "I made an appointment with Donovan Manufacturing Company. Tom McNiel was assistant to Donovan. He interviewed me."

He also took her out to dinner, sent her notes and flowers, hired her, and explained that he never dated employees. She and Rick moved into a studio apartment on Eastern Avenue. By taking no lunch time and no coffee breaks and by taking work home, she was able to negotiate a 9 a.m. to 2 p.m. work day which meant that she could get her son to school in the morning and be at home when he got out in the afternoon.

True to his word, Tom McNiel, a graduate of West Point who also had a failed marriage, did not date his employees. He quit his job and went to work in insurance. Then, the courtship progressed like wildfire. Maura and Tom were married on February 1, 1953.

"Those were wonderful years. I was in love with everything. I did all the 50s stuff that women did. Took the kids everywhere. Opened up the city to them." Bridget was born on February 3, 1955; Andrea on November 29, 1956, and Amy on July 19, 1958. The birth of the third little girl was the beginning of years of personal anguish. Amy, a Down's syndrome child, was profoundly retarded. After consulting with spiritual, financial and legal authorities, Maura and Tom placed their daughter in custodial care. They were told that she would not live past age three, but she lived to adulthood, always in an institution. In 1959 Maura crushed a leg in a ski accident and was told she would never walk again. "I never accepted that diagnosis." She spent a year in rehabilitation. Her son graduated from Austin College and was working on his master's degree at the University of Minnesota when he developed aberrant behavior that eventually was diagnosed as schizophrenia. At 19, Andrea died following a car crash on a rain-slick Dallas street while returning home from helping to get a children's camp ready to open.

In spite of personal tragedy—or perhaps because of it—Maura was deeply involved in community activities. At first most of her work was centered in and radiated out from her church, Midway Hills Christian. She has served it as a senior high Sunday School teacher, for 11 years from 1960 to 1971; as youth education director; on its board in almost every capacity including elder, and as president of its women's organization. In the 1950s when large numbers of American Indians were relocated from reservations into cities to work and Dallas was one of the centers of relocation, Maura worked on these issues.

Charter members of the Women's Center were Maura McNiel, Flo Wiedemann, Eddie Bernice Johnson and Johnnie-Marie Grimes.

Working on issues of racism in Dallas was this trio, Anita Martinez, Yvonne Ewell and Peggy Patterson.

When the Civil Rights movement began, she devoted her time to that. "I was incensed about segregated schools and transportation." Maura moved through the 1950s and 1960s raising her children, helping her husband grow in his career and involved in almost every community effort that sought to answer limitations in the lives of others. Her work was inclusive, her interest eclectic. She was on the board of both the Dallas Council on World Affairs and Pan American Round Table in the 1950s; was a founder of Save Open Spaces and Block Partnership, served on the boards of Dallas United Nations Association, Domestic Violence Intervention Association, National Conference of Christians and Jews, Common Cause, and KERA-TV. She did taping for the blind and worked for the YWCA, serving on the board of its student chapter at SMU. During the first part of the 1960s she was deeply committed to children and youth, established a coffee house that drew as many as 200 kids for conversation, recreation and community action. She organized a job fair that, in one day, placed 3,000 teenagers in summer jobs. At another time she coordinated a conference, "Rescue the Land," with the Institute of Urban and Environmental Studies at SMU. She took leadership roles in organizations for her children—the PTA, Cub Scouts and Campfire Girls. She also wrote a book for children.

In 1968 everything came together for Maura McNiel when she signed up for a course at Northaven United Methodist Church called Explore. "It involved helping a woman look seriously at her life and take control of it. I couldn't imagine that I needed it. I was so busy, perfectly happy, but the women doing it were very serious and I thought, 'Well, maybe I will. My last child will be ready for college soon and I might could learn something'. . . ."

Explore "blew me away," as it did many women. "One of the first assignments was to introduce yourself without referring to your husband or children. I'd started every sentence with 'Tom says,' for so long that I didn't know there was any other way to think." Maura got through the first two-hour class, but she missed the second while driving around trying to decide whether, or not, to complete the course. She showed up for the third session and never missed another. The course lasted eight weeks, two hours per session. Reading and homework was voluminous. "It all seemed so casual and friendly, but it was very well organized and the four people who taught it were intentional, professional and provocative. One of the assignments was for each woman to make a chart showing exactly how she spent her time. "I discovered I was working a 33-hour day."

Economic advancement was the primary issue of Lila Williams

Scherry Johnson and Bitsy Wesner stressed equality in education.

Equal legal rights demanded the attention of Joann Peters.

As the group looked at what they did with their lives and what the men in their lives did, the discrepancies were evident. "Women did things that were not profitable—that is, that did not make money. If a job was profitable men did it. If it was tedious or if it never got finished, women did it—and, of course, men let them do it, expected them to do it. A man's idea of public service was to lend his name. Women's idea of public service was to lick the envelopes and postage stamps and make all the telephone calls and the follow-up calls—but still have dinner on the table at 6 p.m. every day. All the time we had been thinking that the men who were running things knew what they were doing—and all the time they didn't. Men didn't know beans about what was really going on in the schools or about transportation or about anything that had to do with human qualities."

It was in Explore that Maura became aware that "women have been assigned the clean-up chores of the city just as they have been cleaning up the messes at home. And, if we are serious about making our world more humane, we (women) can't afford to be marginal any longer. It is absolutely essential that we be a part of the decision-making process."

Having completed the Explore course, Maura went on its staff. The all volunteer staff was comprised of *graduates* who took seriously the evaluations of participants, searched for new material, revised the curricula, held intensive training sessions and met each class with the same dedication of the original staff. As the course spread, there were soon 500 alumna of Explore, "and they had nowhere to go. Even earlier than Explore, SMU had held its annual Symposium on the Education of Women for Social and Political Leadership. Every year we (the participants) would come away from that all revved up with no place to focus our energy. We needed a clearing house, a center . . . ."

From there to Women for Change and the Women's Center of Dallas was only a small step. It seemed like a giant leap. "Several of us were envisioning the idea of some kind of 'graduate' program to Explore and the Women's Symposium at the same time. Finally, several of us met one night at Ann Chud's house to pool our ideas. I was stubbornly opposed to an organization. When they asked for comments, I said I didn't want to sit through any more board meetings and didn't want to have to establish another set of by-laws and Judge (Sarah) Hughes said, 'Are there any more comments?' and then she or Johnnie-Marie turned to me and said since I didn't have a job or wasn't going to school, I could chair the next meeting. And then Judge Hughes handed Sandy Tinkham a pencil and said she should take notes. And that was it." The group discussed a name and came up with Women for Change. They had a late summer meeting at Maura's home which then was at 4207 Boca Bay. It was mostly a social gathering but the house overflowed with women who were exhilarated about an organization to support their needs. The first open-to-the-public meeting was held October 17, 1971. *The Dallas Times Herald* ran a coupon asking response from anyone interested in an organization "directed to the special interests of women through the creation of a Women's Center. It will support and undergird individuals and groups, initiate change and provide fresh channels for education, communication and action." The response was overwhelming. At the meeting, Maura gave the opening address; Judge Hughes gave the keynote speech; Johnnie-Marie Grimes presided. The group divided into nine task forces. "That's when I became involved almost 24 hours a day. Each of those task force chairpeople had to be carefully selected, allowed to initiate her own agenda within the framework of what was outlined by the group, sometimes convinced that she could do the job and nurtured while she was doing it. It was exciting."

Everybody agreed to get busy and meet again in six months. Carolyn Busch (who would later wed George Galerstein) negotiated office space in the Zale building. Board meetings, every Saturday morning to begin with, were endless. But the group coalesced and the organization was off and running. In February, the second meeting was held in Fincher Hall on the SMU campus. Feminist Gloria Steinem was the speaker. "It was an extraordinary meeting!" The auditorium would seat 400; it overflowed. People stood in the halls. Classes from Hockaday arrived and the kids perched on the stage surrounding the speaker. A videotape, unusual for that time, carried the speech to those outside the auditorium. Few people left. The video ran consecutively for 24 hours and was almost never without a large audience.

Women for Change grew into the Women's Center of Dallas. Maura continued to guide and direct. Every trip she made out of town, those for pleasure, for business with her husband and for her own business, included meetings with key women to learn what they were doing about women's issues. She made countless speeches in Dallas and throughout the country including the baccalaureate address to graduates of Wellesley College when Bridget graduated. She was involved in the formation of other groups to meet the needs of women—The Family Place, a shelter for battered wives and their children; the Dallas Women's Coalition; Women's Issues Network, the Dallas Women's Foundation, The Summit. She worked in some 50 political campaigns and served as the Dallas contact for the national Women's Campaign Fund. She was named by the mayor on the first Dallas Commission on the Status of Women.

The task forces of the Women's Center sometimes took on an identity of their own, with separate boards and by-laws. The Women's Political Caucus grew from the political task force. The Women's Southwest Federal Credit Union evolved from the economic task force. The Rape Crisis Center grew on the expertise of the health task force.

When the Women's Center established its annual Women Helping Women Awards in 1973, Maura was one of the first of the group to be honored. In 1988, the award that goes annually to women for service to other women, was renamed The Maura Award.

As Dallas reached its 150th birthday, Maura reflected on the progress for women during the four decades she had been pivotal to the changes. "I don't know where it will all end," she said. "There is so much yet to be done. Women are not yet in the Constitution . . . . But, it will *never* be like it once was. Everything has changed. It hasn't come as quickly as I thought it would, but then I'm still trying to learn patience. Equal pay for equal work is taken for granted. There are almost as many women as men in law schools. Medical school is fast closing the gap on admissions between men and women. Flextime is accepted by a great many organizations. A few major corporations have established child care centers. We have a woman governor of Texas and a woman mayor of Dallas. And the six largest cities in Texas are, or have recently, been headed by women. Our advances are *so* taken for granted that we don't even get credit for them!"

Hermine Tobolowsky worked for years and countered countless insults before she got equal legal rights for women in a special session of the legislature.

Hermine Dalkowitz Tobolowsky was a young attorney, living in Dallas for only six years when, in 1957 at the legislative chairperson of the Business and Professional Women's Clubs, she set out to give married women the right to control their own property. B&PW was a vibrant organization whose membership included most of the professional women of Dallas. Sarah Hughes was one of its leaders—and whatever the other women needed to spur them to action, Sarah provided with her eternal questioning and prodding. Ruth Fox, trained as a social worker, but deeply involved in community activism, provided a great deal of the nurturing and support needed by those in the forefront of a fray. They are but two of many women Hermine cites as vital to the passage of the Texas Equal Legal Rights Amendment.

Hermine was tough under her tender facade. Born in San Antonio on January 13, 1921, to Maurice and Nora Brown Dalkowitz, she grew up with a "baby brother," Marcus B. Dalkowitz, three years her junior. When she entered the University of Texas School of Law in 1941, one of 11 women in a class of 350, she was only 20 years old. She had already earned academic honors in the San Antonio Public Schools where she was graduated at age 17, from Incarnate Word College and the University of San Antonio (later it became Trinity University), earning her degree in two years.

Soft-spoken and seemingly shy, Hermine completed law school to graduate as one of only two women in her class—in spite of obstacles constantly placed in her way. One of her most vivid memories is of the professor who called each of the women into his office, lectured them on how unsuited women were to be attorneys and gave them a list of eligible bachelors so that they could pursue a more appropriate destiny. She learned in her classes how unfair Texas laws were to women. The seeds for her to tackle revising those laws were planted when, one day in class, the professor described a case. There

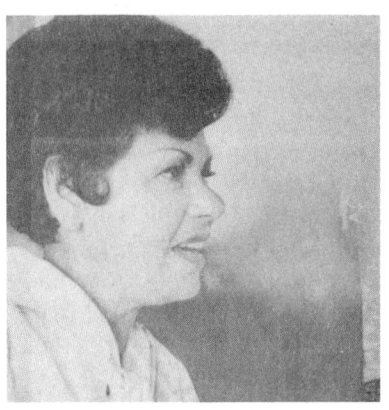

Ann Chud's living room was the birthplace of Women for Change.

Paula Latimer was a Women's Equity Action League organizer.

Margaret Estes was on the national board of the YWCA.

was a woman with five children, he said, whose husband deserted the family. She moved to another town, passed herself off as a widow, took an inheritance from her own family and opened a small business which thrived. Years later her husband showed up, took over the business and gave money and property to his mistress. Under Texas law, which gave the husband full control of the wife's property, including what she had inherited, the woman was powerless to do anything about it.

Even though she was among the 10 top students in her graduating class at law school, Hermine did not easily find a job. While being interviewed by a Houston firm, it was explained to her that no woman with their firm would be allowed to appear in court, but would do research and prepare briefs. When they later wrote asking her to return for a second interview, Hermine refused, explaining she would not work for a firm whose attitude toward women was so antiquated.

One of her professors was eager for her to clerk for the Texas Supreme Court and made an appointment for her to be interviewed. The interviewer did not even look up when she arrived. She recalls: "He didn't acknowledge my presence. He said he did not know why he was wasting his time with 'this damn fool interview,' that there's not a woman alive with sense enough to be a clerk in the Texas Supreme Court. I told him that I did not want his job. I told him that he was a servant of the people of Texas and as such he was a disgrace to be in his position. Then I walked out. Nobody, least of all a brand new lawyer, talks to a judge that way, but outside several people had overheard and the word spread. All the way out of the building, people were shaking my hand and patting me on the back."

She accepted a position with Lang, Byrd, Cross and Ladon in San Antonio after they promised her $200 and the chance to present argument in a case before the Texas Supreme Court. She accepted for two reasons: the going rate for attorneys at that time was $75 a week and it was usually years before any young lawyer got to appear before the state supreme court. She had already accepted the offer before she learned that she was allowed to prepare the brief because no other attorney in the firm would take it; it was a lost case before it ever started.

Hermine met Hyman Tobolowsky while visiting her mother, a patient, and her brother, a medical student, in Dallas. She became a Dallasite when she married Tobolowsky, vice president of a retail clothing store, in 1951. She opened her own law practice to give herself time both to be with her bridegroom and to be active in community volunteer work. Her first effort was working to gain jury service for women.

Hermine made her first trip to the Texas Legislature in 1957. The occasion was a state Senate hearing on a proposed bill for married women to control their own property. Many women from throughout the state were present to support the bill, but most showed their support by stating their names and the organizations they were representing. Hermine stood before the committee, in hat and gloves, and cited specific incidents. She told them about the woman whose husband had suffered a stroke and could no longer even hold a pen to sign his name. Medical bills were mounting, but without his signed consent, the woman could not dispose of their stocks in order to pay his bills. She told them that laws in Texas equated women with idiots, imbeciles and juveniles. She said that marrying her husband was the smartest move she ever made, but her wedding vows didn't turn her instantly into an imbecile.

"When I got down to specific cases, they got nasty. One said he had never seen any woman smart enough to sign a deed or handle property sales without the consent of her husband. Another said if I didn't like his attitude, I could just come down to his district and tell the stupid little women there what I thought. I eventually did—and we defeated him. Another passed a cigar up to me and said if I wanted to behave like a man, I might as well smoke like one."

From March 1957, until November 7, 1972, Hermine never let up in her effort to change Texas laws toward women. She came away from the Senate hearing knowing that it would take more time than she had to wipe all the discriminatory laws against women off the Texas books. She made up her mind and convinced others that it could be accomplished with the passage of a Texas Equal Legal Rights Bill. This decision did not make the effort easier, but it cemented Hermine's resolve. Through insults, innuendos and accusations to her personally as well as to the legislation she was proposing, Hermine persevered.

Those opposing rights for married women attacked Hermine because they understood that they could not insult half of the voting public and get reelected. They explained to their constituency that they were, of course, for women's rights, just opposed to the woman backing the legislation. The only time Hermine ever saw her husband angry, she said, was when they went to a political rally in El Paso. Following a speech by the legislator from that district, individuals were standing around visiting when "I saw my husband turn red and draw back his fist. The legislator had lowered his voice and confided that he was all for rights for women but he couldn't support any bill that was being promoted by that prostitute from Dallas . . . . Fortunately my husband got control. We defeated that man for reelection."

Mary Esther Gaulden helped create the National Organization for Women nationwide before moving to Dallas and becoming a leader.

Victoria Downing was one of the founders and first president of the Women's Southwest Federal Credit Union.

Edwina Cox Evans is director of Bethlehem Center which aids people when they fall through the cracks elsewhere.

A friend called her from Brownsville to say that their representative, running for reelection, had said he could not vote for the ERA because of "that woman who presented it to the legislature. I was, he told the gathering, drunk, disorderly and using foul language. I was angry, but amused, too. I never drink and I never use profanity. Never. So I told her to plan a public meeting and get him there and I would come. They did. He had to admit publicly that he was lying. He also announced that he was not going to run for reelection."

The passage of the Texas Equal Legal Rights Amendment to the Texas Constitution wiped some 40 discriminatory laws off the books at one time. After the legislature approved it in 1971, Texas voters approved the constitutional amendment by a four to one majority in 1972. The work of the Family Law Section of the State Bar of Texas already had revised family law that undergirded the new legislation.

But it wasn't all over. In the heat of defeating the Equal Rights Amendment to the U. S. Constitution, states that had enacted such legislation came under scrutiny and old sores were reopened. ERA opponents targeted Texas—because its laws had advanced women's rights from almost last in the nation to near the first with the passage of its ERA. Opponents of the law, calling themselves the Pink Ladies and dressed to prove it, swooped into Austin plying legislators with home baked bread and roses. Their spokesperson was Phyllis Schlafly, arch-rival of a constitutional amendment that would have made women equal under national law. Hermine was there, too. Columnist Molly Ivins wrote what happened next:

> A formidable speaker is Mrs. Schlafly, and she wheeled out rhetoric that had not been heard on that floor since the Senate debated the radical notion of giving the vote to women. By the time Mrs. S. was through, most of her auditors were convinced the ERA would destroy not only the family, but moral fiber

Barbara Minor James, the first woman of African American descent to head the YWCA, has built bridges across chasms of discord in her native Dallas throughout her life.

and western civilization . . . . Then Hermine Tobolowsky came to the mike in a businesslike way and we were all given an unforgettable lesson in the difference between rhetoric and substance. Mrs. Tobolowsky simply shredded the anti-ERA arguments. She would never put it this way, but she ate that lady's lunch, is what she did. Ann Richards (later to become Texas treasurer, then its governor,) said, 'She made us all so proud that night, not just because of her, but of ourselves as women and proud to have a leader with such dignity, such grace.'[1]

Grace and dignity. They continued to epitomize Hermine Tobolowsky, for she was as gracious and unassuming in victory as she had been in the throes of ridicule. "My style," she said in 1978 interview, "is working to change things that are unjust. The legislators misjudged me because they did not know how long I was prepared to do battle. I realized that some people wanted to rattle me. It can't be done. I will not adopt anybody else's belligerence."

The Women's Law Caucus at the University of Texas named its annual award for her, the Hermine Tobolowsky Award. The Women's Center of Dallas and Soroptimist International both gave her its Women Helping Women award. She has held positions and been given almost countless honors including inclusion in the Texas Women's Hall of Fame. Asked to name the things that have been most important to her personally, Hermine said:

> Passage of the Equal Legal Rights Amendment to the Texas Constitution.
> Ratification by Texas, of the ERA to the U.S. Constitution, the eighth state to do so.
> Passage of the Homestead Amendment giving single persons the same rights as married couples.
> Lobbying the repeal of approximately 30 laws that discriminate against men or women.[2]

It took Hermine 15 years and 8 months of never-ending work that justly earned her the title "Mother of Texas Equal Legal Rights."

Barbara Minor James grew up in a segregated Dallas, helped it to become an inclusive city, and in a 1991 interview said she believed "it is stuck somewhere back in the 1960s—and will be in deep trouble unless women assume leadership roles for which they are uniquely qualified."

She has never, she adds, felt apart from the women's movement. "Negro women in America have always been liberated," she said. "For the past 30 years white women have been catching up with where we have been since slavery. We've always worked, reared children by ourselves, taken the responsibility for our futures . . . ."

But she feels a part of the women's liberation movement and is grateful to it for "freeing women to become all they can be. What the women's movement did was help us all come out of the closet. It gave us the right to take charge of our own lives."

Barbara was born "at 8 a.m. on a glorious Sunday morning—or so my mother told me"—on December 28, 1930, to Irma Pierce Minor. Her father was Layton Alfred Minor and the family lived in the 3600 block of Watt Street in North Dallas. When she was a small child, hoping to improve their economic condition by better work for Alfred, the family moved to California, but the situation for a black family was very little better there. In 1934, Irma Minor brought her daughter back to her mother's house in Dallas. "My father never did come back to Dallas, so my parents were finally divorced 11 years later." Barbara's maternal ancestors, since slavery, had been educated women. Her mother was a college graduate and her mother before her. Both were teachers. Back in Dallas, jobs for professional women were scarce and for professional women of color virtually non-existent. Irma Minor found work as a first aid instructor with the NYA (National Youth Administration). It was a part of the WPA (Works Progress Administration, one of Franklin Roosevelt's programs to put the country to work during the Great Depression.) She became the city's first certified first aid teacher.

Three generations of professional volunteers, from the top, Virginia Whitehill, mentor feminist, Susan Stahl, an advocate for children, and Susybelle Gosslee, who has rescued homeless girls.

At B. F. Darrell Elementary School and at Booker T. Washington High School, Barbara was a good student and a joiner. "All of my life I have known that the way to get things done was to find a group of people who want to accomplish the same things you do and organize and make it happen." She went to Wylie College like her mother and her grandmother, Maggie Pepper Pierce, before her. She graduated *cum laude* in 1951 with a B.S. in elementary education and went to California where she earned a master's in early childhood education with a music minor at San Francisco State Teachers College.

Barbara credits her mother and two organizations—New Hope Baptist Church and the YWCA—for shaping her into a woman who knows her strengths and is determined to use them to serve her community. "The church was my first teacher. We were blessed with strong leaders who taught us, inspired us and motivated us to action, men like the Jacksons, Dr. A. S. Jackson and the Rev. Maynard Jackson . . . and from the time I was three, the YWCA was my second home." Irma Minor, her brother and sister-in-law had pooled their money and bought a house at 2511 Washington Avenue, next door to the Maria Morgan Branch of the YWCA. "Even before there was organized child care, I would stay there sometimes while my mother worked. And, oh, those women who became my role models—Marion Hill Dillard (Crump), Juanita Spencer, Gwendolyn Hill Clark, Mrs. Hudson." Barbara's first paying job was also at the YWCA. She was the receptionist at the Maria Morgan branch during the summer of 1951 before leaving for graduate school.

Back in Dallas after earning her master's degree, Barbara was hired as a music teacher by DISD. The job lasted one year "because somebody decided to look back on my application and adhere strictly to antiquated rules. Dallas had a nepotism rule—no two members of the same family could be employed in DISD at the same time (the rule, once tried in the Supreme Court, was abolished as have been many discriminatory laws) "When those in power have a need, they bend the rules. That's what happened. They needed me as a music teacher and they didn't bother to read the application." The following year Barbara taught in the Richardson Independent Schools. After she and Elbert James, a graduate of Florida State University, were married on July 20, 1957, they bought a house in Dallas. There again Barbara found herself unemployed because of a rule. Teachers had to live in Richardson to work in the Richardson schools. By that time it really didn't matter because Barbara was pregnant.

Nedra Patrice James was born on May 26, 1958. An excellent student, like her mother, grandmother and great-grandmother, she became a teacher. A graduate of Ursuline Academy, she earned a bachelor's *cum laude* from Spelman College and a master's in church music from Scarritt College and became a teacher in DISD's School of Performing and Visual Arts. Barbara was divorced when her daughter was 16.

Characteristic of her ability to see many facets of any issue and to work through difficult situations without rancor, Barbara harbors no resentment over a marriage that did not continue to work, and even though her entire life has been surrounded by, working with, and supporting women—both in her private as well as her public life—Barbara has the tenderest of feelings about men. "The plight of the young black male is intolerable," she said, citing the prison population that is overwhelmingly black male. "Black men have left their wives because they couldn't make a decent living, not because they are shiftless and lazy. Young black men resort to drugs and violence because they don't have anything meaningful to do," she added. "If America can put men on the moon, it can stop the drug trafficking. We don't stop it because some people in high places profit from it . . . ."

Barbara talks about segregated Dallas framed in words of compassion rather than bitterness. "I love Dallas," she said. "It is my home. I grew up when segregation was very much alive. I remember the water fountains with the signs "colored" and "white," and the street cars with the "colored" signs toward the back of the bus. In downtown Dallas there were few comfort facilities for Negroes. Mothers had no place to take their children to the restroom and no place where they could go into a restaurant and sit down and buy their babies a sandwich."

Even so, "In that segregated world, I did not get as many embarrassing moments as the boys did. Young black women have not been perceived as a threat like the young black men . . . . For me segregation was a way of life. I didn't think much about it either way when I was growing up, but I've always been a joiner and as I began to participate more and more in the community, I realized that the Negroes were not given the chances they deserved. Very early the YWCA chose to be inclusive in both staff and volunteers." The YW organized its first Negro branch in 1892 in Dayton, Ohio, and employed its first black staff member in 1908. In 1915 it held an interracial conference in Louisville, Kentucky, and in 1970 declared its one imperative to be "the elimination of racism wherever it exists and by any means necessary."

Her own emancipation came about slowly, oozed into every fiber of her being, felt absolutely right with each step. "I remember the Majestic theater downtown. There was a side door for Negroes and we had to buy our tickets and go upstairs through that separate door. In high school, I decided that I wouldn't go to movies any more—that they were not that important to me—until I had the same freedoms as my white sisters and brothers. Today that seems like a small step, but to a high school girl in the 1940s it was major."

During her daughter's childhood, Barbara worked as a volunteer, focusing her services through the YWCA that had nurtured her. In 1974, the YWCA asked her to become president of its board. "My first reaction was sheer disbelief. I had come up the ladder slowly. I had done almost everything. But was I ready for such a responsibility? I was the first Black—and being a first anything is not easy. I discovered anew that God has a plan for me and when I'm asked to do something, I must do it because it's God's plan unfolding. I said yes and there followed the most significant period of my life. Doors opened. Opportunities flooded in. Experiences broadened. Skills sharpened."

The YWCA in Dallas had accepted the national imperative to eliminate racism in word only. "During my administration, we got ourselves ready to begin." There was constant negotiation. "Women of color wanted to see change come overnight. Some of the white women were even worse! Others who were vital to our long-range cause didn't want to move so fast. Some didn't want to move at all! So, sometimes you have to go back to where you were in order to get to where you want to go. And if you want to make the trip permanent, you'd better take everybody along!" Almost without exception, Barbara observed women rise to positions of leadership "that were magnificent to behold! Some who seemed prejudiced and narrow-minded turned out to be our best advocates. All it took was exposure—and a little time."

The YWCA, she said, "has moved toward all inclusiveness. We are not there yet, but we're leading everybody else!" But, she added, "the city is in trouble. Like our country, we've gone backward. Unless women assume responsibilities for leadership, for putting their special skills to work, we could lose even more than we already have." And what are these special talents women have? She ticks them off:

1. Her ability to organize. A woman is a master at taking on one more thing without omitting what she's already doing. She is skilled at detail—and every detail is imperative.
2. Her ability to negotiate. The skills she has honed in her family help her to back off before she boxes herself into a corner.
3. Her ability to communicate. She knows how to say what must be said without hurting others.
4. Her ability to show love. Women can look at a volatile situation and find a way to ease it. Women care about everybody's feelings.
5. Her ability to be inclusive. We take everybody along as we move along. We look at the whole world as family.
6. Her freedom from fear. We don't have a lot invested in the status quo, so it is easier for us as women to try new ways of doing things.[3]

Once having tasted freedom, people find it impossible to go back into bondage. People of color and women of all shadings know that—and the knowing is often painful. The road to equality is booby trapped with myriad impediments. Many women long for the comfortable cocoon. But safety is a trap. It has held countless women in confinement;

FACES OF FEMINISM / 363

The Women's Center of Dallas grew out of an organization first called Women for Change which was organized in 1971. Its founders were all "graduates" of SMU's Symposium on the Education of Women for Social and Political Leadership. Because it kept a low profile until it was solidly organized and because its leaders were experienced and organized from the beginning, there were few radical edges to the Dallas movement. At the first official meeting on October 16, 1971, Judge Sarah T. Hughes said: "Women have been socialized to marry and have babies . . . fifty years ago this was a lifetime career, but times have changed. Now a woman has half of her life ahead of her after the children are grown."

Women's Center activists carried on business while having their picture made. Standing are Maura McNiel and Gay Jurgens; sitting, Sandy Tinkham, Ann Chud, Pat Greenwald and Anne Garbarino with daughter Maura.

Women were affirmed and challenged by speakers including Gloria Steinem, feminist and author; Flo Kennedy, attorney, and Maggie Kuhn, founder of the Gray Panthers of America.

Marjorie Schuchat, left, was a founder of the Dallas NOW chapter. Psychotherapist Carol Madison works with family abuse victims. Below, left, Women's Center founders Gail Smith, Maura McNiel and Pat Greenwald. Below, center, anthropologist Margaret Mead spoke many times to Dallas women.

Lily Tomlin, above, with Susan Caudill, and, below, Charlotte Stewart, left, founder of Displaced Homemakers.

once they take that first step out of the safe nest, there is no turning back. Those who try to revert to security after tasting independence find themselves fraught with frustration, often ending in depression. They are the women most critical of women achievers. Having not had the courage or opportunity to strike out for their own liberation, they heap blame and guilt on women who do make a bid for emancipation.

Even while they learn that security is bondage, they have also learned that freedom imposes responsibilities for which they are often not prepared. Striking out to claim freedom is a heady wine but the journey is perilous, the roadblocks incalculable and destination often disappointing. So, why struggle? The answer is simple. They have no choice. The world sorely needs the best talents of all of its people.

The most difficult part for women is keeping balance. Many women have lost their way and had, as Barbara James put it, "to go back to where they were in order to get where they wanted to be." In the first heady days of the women's liberation movement, beginning in the early 1960s, women were in such a rush to claim the equality to which they were entitled that a great many "threw out the baby with the bath water." They gave up trappings that had defined what it meant to be female. In the extreme, this included the way they dressed, looked and behaved. They did not, for the most part, find either satisfaction or success. The backlash, as backlashes always come after a major breakthrough, called into question separate but equal roles for women and men. This is an old trap that is no longer tolerable.

Because they had no role models, women achievers have had to learn on the job, chart their own course, make mistakes, assume responsibility for them, fail and try anew. They have had to make choices, many of them excruciating choices. They have had to decide, when their careers were rising, whether, or not to step back, and have a child before the biological clock made a choice impossible, whether to take a promotion that would send them away from a familiar setting and aging parents, whether missing camaraderie with friends or sitting down to a meal with their families took precedence over spending a gruelling weekend away at a remote area on business so they would have a better chance at partner status in the law firm; whether, after they had children, to uproot them from schools they liked and friends they loved to move across the continent or around the world to accept a new job. Men have not needed to make these choices. Cultural conditioning and societal approval for men has condoned job first, self second, family third, community fourth. For women the order is reversed: Family first, community second, job third and self fourth.

33

• • • •

PRESERVING THE PAST

The euphoria among women activists in the 1960s was followed in the 1970s with a decade of sobering reflection. The dream of complete liberation and autonomy that had seemed within easy reach of every woman who wanted it proved to be elusive. For many women, the 70s was a period of grave disappointment. Thousands of flaws, invisible to women who were setting goals and forging ahead, surfaced to make their lives miserable.

New Texas laws, liberating as they were for most women, allowed no-fault divorce and marriages crumbled in record numbers. Since those new laws did not provide alimony, many women who had paid, or at least helped to pay, their husbands' way through college, graduate school, law school or medical school were left with inadequate training and little experience to be their own sole support if they were divorced.

Mary Lynn Aldredge McEntire, standing, got involved in historical preservation first through her mother, Mary Batts Aldredge, seated, but stayed to organize the LOLITS (Little Old Ladies in Tennis Shoes) who successfully saved and restored Millermore.

Married women who had thought that a paying job would solve most, perhaps even all, of their problems learned, in countless cases, that they were free to work so long as they didn't leave anything undone at home. In most houses this meant getting up earlier than other family members and working far into the evening, for it was they who continued to do most of the shopping, cooking, child care and housecleaning.

The care of their children became a constant source of agony for many women. Whether they were single parents heading households with a limited income or married

(From top) Margaret Golden is a part president of the Dallas Federation of Women's Clubs and active in the Daughters of the American Revolution. The Women's Department of the State Fair of Texas was a major source for preserving women's talents through Leah Jarrett, past director, left, and Elizabeth Peabody. Mrs. Harry Joseph Morris is an accredited genealogist.

women working at two jobs there simply were not enough hours in the day to get everything done. Almost every working mother lived with stress—trying to find good care for her children, trying to balance family time with career time, trying to meet the countless needs of family members, coping with conflicts between themselves, their parents and society which blamed them for every real or perceived flaw in the children.

Many women were lonely—and too exhausted to do anything about it even if they were sufficiently assertive to seek social outlets. The constant demands of their work, for those who were career oriented, and the constant needs of their children if they were single mothers, left almost no time for them to make friends. The institutions that had served as social outlets for women in the past rarely provided structure or support for the emerging woman. They did not know what to do with her and, instead of creating ways to meet her changing needs, often blamed her when she did not fit outmoded molds. Working women did not have the time—and most of them not the inclination—to join garden clubs and sewing circles. Churches, which had provided the social structure for earlier families and individuals, tried—but mostly failed—to make room and welcome the single professional woman or the single mother. One single woman of that period said, in a 1969 interview, "I am never lonelier than when I'm at church on Sunday morning."

Many organizations made an attempt to meet the needs of the new woman by forming professional chapters that met at night, but these had limited success. Women who worked all day and went home in the evening to prepare dinner and do the home chores were too tired to go out to an evening meeting. Women with children could not afford baby sitters. Increasingly the workplace became the center for their lives, in most cases severely limiting their potential for growth. In too many office coffee bars, in too many teachers' and nurses' lounges, over too many hasty lunches, women limited their social lives to shallow gossip.

Adding to their misery were stories in the media of super women who were doing it all—with time left over to be president of the PTA or to run a charity league benefit. The average woman, who couldn't, or didn't want to do it all, had guilt piled atop her physical and emotional exhaustion. And Dallas had become a mecca for this very woman—the young, bright, eager professional woman recently out of college with limited experience, and the young, pretty single mother with only a high school education and one or two children to support. She came to a city bright with promise for her future.

This new woman came to a Dallas that had stopped thinking of itself as a city and started using the term Metroplex. Its metropolitan area was 4,600 square miles and included Collin, Denton, Ellis, Kaufman and Rockwall counties in addition to Dallas County. The county had a population of 1,158,400 in its 900 square miles and included 28 separate municipalities. The Metroplex had almost a million and a half people.

The physical growth of Dallas was phenomenal. In the period between January 1, 1960, and September of 1969 it had added 190,621 new residences within the city limits—a number sufficient to have founded a new city. While the power structure of the city was wheeling and dealing, its women were, many times, on a collision course. Those who worked at home viewed those who worked outside their homes with both envy and contempt. Those who had paying jobs viewed their at-home-all-day sisters as lazy and dull. The social structure of the time did nothing to alleviate the lines of conflict, and, in fact exacerbated them by playing into the stereotypes. In social gatherings, the lines of demarcation were almost visible. Carol Tate, who was reared in Dallas and graduated from its Bryan Adams High School, explained what happened at faculty parties she attended with her university professor husband. "When people ask me what I do and I tell them that I stay at home and rear our children, a curtain falls over their faces, they say, 'that's nice,' and immediately wander away to find somebody interesting to talk to."

Another area of conflict resulted from the great influx of women from other parts of the country who came to Dallas for their own or their husband's career advancement. Many of the landed gentry, while enjoying the fruits of the economic boom, would have been perfectly happy to leave the social and cultural structure untouched. Many of the new people, at least from afar, viewed the city as Neanderthal. The Dallas stereotype—

Southern, conservative, macho, intellectually, and culturally limited—prevailed even when the reality differed.

Martha Russell Tiller tells about the advice she got from her women friends when she and her husband left Washington, D. C., for Dallas in 1976. After much commiserating, one friend summed it up: "If you're moving to Dallas, remember you must not do anything, say anything or have any opinions. You must simply look pretty and keep your mouth shut." Martha—an actress (stage, television and radio) social and press secretary for President Lyndon B. Johnson and Lady Bird Johnson; with the communications department of CBS for 15 years, who had handled public relations for two presidents, two vice presidents, a senator and two governors—didn't take their advice. In Dallas, in the early 1980s she opened her own highly successful marketing-oriented public relations-advertising agency, Martha Tiller and Company, serving clients worldwide. When Martha had returned to Texas from New York, Washington and California to marry her Texas sweetheart they agreed that they would live in the city that provided the job to the one making the most money and offering the best opportunity for advancement and that the other would accommodate her or his career options to that arrangement. "There was never any contest. I *knew* I would be the one making the concessions." Martha acknowledged. "In the 70s, men *always* got the jobs making the most money."

Martha, and the thousands of bright young women like her, arrived in a city that for a long time had adhered to Mayor Bob Thornton's admonition to "keep the dirt flying." Whatever was a few years old was outmoded and useless and was destroyed. In its place rose skyscrapers that were new and shiny and were virtual clones of each other. Dallas did not know its past, or if it did, there was no appreciation for the fabric, texture, tone and quality that formed its root structure and provided its foundation. Expansion and growth were the city's gods and wrecking balls razed many architectural treasures.

It is an incongruous phenomena that the new generation of independent women which surfaced and thrived in the 1960s should have planted the seeds for preserving the past, but that is what happened. And, again, it was Dallas women who recognized the truth of the adage, "(those) who do know the past are doomed to repeat it," and put a stop to the untenable *progress.* Armed with restraining orders, they literally stood, in some instances, between the bulldozer and the buildings about to be razed.

An attitude of tolerant amusement prevailed in the community toward affluent women in their hats and white gloves who wanted to preserve old houses and barns! "We were," said Mary Lynn Aldredge McEntire, "the LOLITS—Little Old Ladies in Tennis Shoes." At first nobody paid much attention to the growing number of LOLITS, even though they were the *landed gentry* of Greater Dallas. Most of their husbands, conditioned by the growth factor that had prevailed for more than a century, considered their wives' newfangled idea to preserve old stuff a bit eccentric. At best, the general public ignored their efforts; at worst, the women were taunted and satirized. They were also determined.

The movement began with efforts to save Millermore (see Chapter 5), the dowager of Old City Park. More than any other person, Mary Batts Aldredge deserves the credit for the success of the endeavor. When Mrs. Aldredge's Founders Garden Club began the effort to preserve the visual history of Dallas County, its members discovered right away that the project was too big for one small club, and formed the Dallas Heritage Society. Mary Aldredge was its founding president.

When Millermore was built, almost nothing except flat land with a few gently rolling hillocks existed between it and downtown Dallas, but as the years went by the city underwent dramatic alterations. At first, land was sold off and developed for residential areas encroaching upon the farmhouse. Then, many of the small houses constructed as family residences between World Wars I and II became rent property or were abandoned and boarded up. People moved to the north and east. Eventually Millermore itself was left vacant. Those who had lived in it and loved it and are buried in the cemetery on its property were all gone. Eventually the property was sold to Good Street Baptist Church, a large and influential worship center for a mostly black congregation.

For a time it looked as if Millermore would be no more.

Brief stories in the 1960s newspapers reveal nothing of the drama going on behind the headlines to save the ante-bellum structure.

> Millermore, a well-known South Oak Cliff home with a pre-Civil War background is scheduled for demolition.[1]

> A temporary restraining order was issued Friday to prevent immediate demolition of Millermore.[2]

> Millermore, a stately but rumpled ante-bellum Dallas landmark, may have to weather a second Civil War over the next several weeks if it is to survive. The homestead was the scene of a wild scramble Friday as a potential house wrecker was served with restraining orders . . . . At stake is Millermore's life.[3]

> The year-old battle to save a 100-plus year-old Dallas mansion from the blade of the bulldozer appeared lost.[4]

> An out-of-court settlement Wednesday saved Millermore from possible destruction and apparently ended months of controversy surrounding the 111-year-old house.[5]

Lindalyn Adams is one of the city's most successful preservationists, was president of the Dallas County Medical Society Auxiliary when the Aldredges gave it their home.

"Mother got a lot of the credit for saving Millermore, but she had lots of help," said Mary Lynn McEntire, who has also served as president of the Heritage Society. "She just never gave up." Even in the darkest days when a permit had been issued to a wrecking company to demolish Millermore and was moving its equipment onto the site, Mary Aldredge said that the Heritage Society had not lost the war. Demolition crews were not the only hazard. Derelicts often took over the vacant house while it was at the Bonnie View address. "It was cluttered with winos, littered with garbage, more than a few times was the victim of blazes set either by careless people or arsonists. Several times J. B. (Mary Lynn's husband) would get up in the middle of the night and take Mother over to Oak Cliff when we'd get a message about a fire or vandalism."

The Heritage Society's persistence paid off. It saved Millermore, paid off the back taxes, praised Good Street Baptist Church for its patience in waiting to begin construction of its new sanctuary, paid its other bills and began a campaign to raise $10,000 to move the house. In March of 1967 Mary Aldredge, surrounded by county and city officials, broke ground for the reconstruction of Millermore at Old City Park. In July of 1968 the project was completed and the restored house opened to the public.

The women's best efforts did not save many of Dallas's other historical buildings from destruction.

Lindalyn Bennett Adams tells about one of the buildings they lost. It was at the corner of Akard and Commerce. "It was a wonderful building. We heard that it was going to be torn down, so we called the owner. He said he would delay demolition for 36 hours while we raised the money to buy it. After dinner Rube (her husband) and I drove down to look it over. A huge vehicle pulled up behind us. Printed on its side was a sign, 'We can wreck the pyramids.' Men began to pile out and put on hard hats. I found the foreman and asked what was going on. He said, 'Lady, we're tearing this building down.' I raced across the street to a telephone. For several hours there were frantic calls. Then the wrecking ball knocked a hole right through the center of the building . . . . Destruction like that can't be repaired . . . ."

Lindalyn Adams has been one of Dallas's most potent and persuasive preservationists. She was born in Wichita Falls on July 4, 1930, and brought to Dallas by her parents, Charles Carlton and LaNette Haynes Bennett when she was three months old. She grew up with one sister, Ida Beth Bennett Howes, in East Dallas, was educated in the Highland Park schools, entered SMU, married Reuben Homer Adams on September

Lindalyn Adams looks beyond a problem to its solution, listens to all voices, honors the opinions of those with whom she does not agree and patiently seeks to find a way to bring consensus to any group she chairs.

10, 1949, at East Dallas Christian Church and reared her three sons, Richard Bennett Adams, Charles Robert Adams, and William Haynes Adams, in the city. The only time she spent away from Dallas was the four years following her marriage when her husband was in medical school at Duke in North Carolina.

Lindalyn is a consummate volunteer. Back in Dallas in 1953, she joined the Junior Matrons at East Dallas Christian, where her mother was a member before her, and became its president. She centered a great deal of her work through medical wives groups, the Parkland Wives Club, the Faculty Wives of Southwestern Medical School, the Women's Auxiliary to the Dallas County Medical Society. She has served as president of all three. She points to the Junior League as her trainer for volunteer work. "It trains you thoroughly and it expects excellence. Most members respond . . . ." She had a six months hiatus between one full-time volunteer commitment and the next in 1969 when she read about the women's efforts to save Millermore. As soon as the Junior League ball, which she chaired, was completed in February, she volunteered to be a docent at Millermore. She was one of the first three, numbers she quickly augmented by getting on the telephone and calling up friends. Her father owned a candy and peanut business just across the street from Millermore. "I practically grew up in that area, so it was like going home.

"Serving as Millermore docent started my interest in the history of the city and the preservation of its past," she said. Before long she was one of Mary Aldredge's young tigers, one of Mary Lynn McEntire's "Little Old Ladies in Tennis Shoes." Many women including Ruth Ann Montgomery, Harriet Weber, Mary Frances Yancey, Mary Nelle Clampitt, Isabel Decherd, Jo Ann Wynne, Margaret Hill "and whatever expert consultant we could snag" traveled country lanes and small towns all over North Central Texas searching for houses to salvage and restore. All members of the newly formed Dallas County Heritage Society, they sat through four-hour executive committee meetings weekly defining their agenda and seeking money to finance their dreams. "It was," says Lindalyn in retrospect, "the most exciting, wonderful, special time. The feeling of friendship, comradeship, love we developed for each other—well, there is no way to describe it.

"We were," she paused, hesitated, "ahead of the men. Women have such special skills and abilities. We were like the founding fathers. We had a plan. We were never in debt. The business men were impressed. Most of all it worked because it was the right thing to do."

Most of all it worked because the timing was right and the leaders of the Heritage Society and other groups, including the Historic Preservation League, had the patience to do things right. There were no knee-jerk decisions. The women constantly called on experts, both those within the city and those of national and international repute. Lindalyn's ability to enhance projects and organizations by bringing people from all parts of the community with widely varying interests into a harmonious working relationship is legendary. She is not alone. Hers is a talent widely practiced by many other women in the community.

Lindalyn is a master at looking beyond the problem to its solution and uniting forces to bring about a creative solution. Typical is her vision that brought about the Dallas County Medical Society Auxiliary's Aldredge House. She was president of both the Dallas County Heritage Society and the auxiliary in 1972-73. "I knew that the Aldredges wanted to donate the house to an organization that would lovingly care for it and preserve it for the future," she said. "For many reasons, the Heritage Society, at least at that stage, could not undertake the responsibility. I knew that the Medical Auxiliary—it has about a thousand members—had long wanted a place of its own." It took a year of negotiations. The Aldredge family was willing to give it before the auxiliary was willing to accept it. "The house was in wonderful shape. The yard needed attention. There was strong opposition among some of the members toward our accepting such a huge responsibility." The auxiliary voted to accept the gift at the last meeting Lindalyn chaired as president. "Yes," she admitted, "I was nervous. But before the vote I had this sense of calm and peace. I knew it would work. The time was right."

There has not always been serenity, Lindalyn added. There have been long, involved negotiations with the city and with the street. "It's still a sensitive issue with some. We undertook this project before Swiss Avenue was on the National Register, when houses in the neighborhood were selling for $10,000 to $12,000. A small percentage would be happier if we weren't there. We've tried to be good neighbors. It's worked out well."

In her several roles as a preservationist, Lindalyn has worked to establish the West End. She chaired the Dallas County Historical Commission, a 35-member board, appointed by the Commissioners Court, that authenticated historical buildings and dedicated historical markers to them during the celebration of the Texas bi-centennial. She worked with the county to place historical medallions on five of its buildings—the Old Red Court House, the John Neely Bryan Cabin, the Criminal Courts Building, the Records Building, and the Dallas County Administration Building, popularly known as the School Book Depository.

When it came time for a disposition of the Texas School Book Depository, it was inevitable that Lindalyn Adams be involved. She had done her homework and paid her dues in the field of historic preservation. In 1982 she won the Ruth Lester Award, the highest citation given by the Texas Historical Commission. The city needed her expertise. Equally, she felt a commitment to give the city back some of the vibrancy it had before Kennedy was assassinated in Dallas. As president of the Medical Center Woman's Club she was holding a meeting of the organization in her home on November 22, 1963. Dr. Adams, her husband, observed the confusion from his offices at the medical school; failing to reach her by telephone, he drove home to report what little he knew. She interrupted the meeting and turned on the television in time to hear Walter Cronkite report the president's death. "It was the most traumatic experience . . . a trauma felt the world over. We had all worked so diligently to make the President's visit a warm welcome and thousands had turned out to greet him. There was such awful grief. Horror. Terrible guilt. I cried more in the next three days than I'd cried in all my prior life and I wasn't alone. It effected everybody emotionally and physically . . . and it lasted for years. The buoyancy went out of our city. There was a pall. We were almost afraid to say anything positive about Dallas. We were protective and defensive. We had a right to be. We were perceived as an evil place. Twenty years later when my husband and I were on a cruise and said we were from Dallas, a woman said, "Oh, that's where they kill presidents."

The Texas School Book Depository hovered on the brink of the Trinity River at the Triple Underpass. It had a checkered past. Built in 1899 and refurbished in 1900 after a fire as the Southern Rock Island Plow Company, it had served various purposes through the years but was notorious as the place from which Harvey Lee Oswald allegedly fired the shot from its sixth floor that killed President Kennedy. Judson Shook and Lindalyn, along with Martin Jurow of movie-making fame who was vitally interested in preservation, met to talk about the building and its future. The county desperately needed new office space. The result was that the Commissioners Court agreed to buy the building, convert it into county offices but reserve the Sixth Floor for historical purposes. Lindalyn agreed to chair its conversion and called the Texas Historical Commission for help. Conover Hunt responded. "When I saw her, a light went on. I knew we would do it. She said we should do a study to find out what to do with the Sixth Floor. She wrote the grant, worked with the Commissioners and rallied support from various historical groups."

The consensus was that the Sixth Floor should not be a museum, but a historical and educational place pertaining to the assassination, that funds to establish it should be secured from private sources and that an admission fee should be charged to help defray the cost of maintenance." The Sixth Floor had its grand opening on February 20, 1989. It has become a focal point for the thousands of visitors who once milled around across the street snapping pictures and asking questions. Done in great taste, it answers most questions that anyone could ask. The voices that opposed the project are silent now.

"It has been both my privilege and my pain to be involved with things that haven't been established yet—and in making them work. By the time a thing is established, I'm already on to something else. I've enjoyed not being stuck in one group with one kind of people doing the same thing over and over. I like variety," Lindalyn said.

In the midst of one especially difficult time when Lindalyn was trying to pull everything into a working unit, her husband took her out to dinner. Spilling her problems to him, she felt the tears begin to fall. He did not suggest that she back off from the task.

His only comment was a quiet, "I just want you to be happy." "I am happy," she responded. "I'm doing exactly what I should be doing, what I want to do. It's just *so hard* sometimes." She paused. "I have to believe in what I am doing. I know when it's right. I can feel it. It needs to happen. When that happens, I just do it."

It was in the 1970s, July 9, 1973, to be exact, that the Dallas City Council officially designated Swiss Avenue as its first historic preservation district. That, too, had taken years and had called forth the best efforts of those interested in preserving Dallas's past. In the summer of 1972 a special report prepared by city planners urged quick action by city officials to preserve Swiss. Weiming Lu, assistant director for the Urban Design Division of the city's Department of Planning and Urban Development, told a *Dallas Morning News* reporter, that beyond preserving Swiss Avenue, the ordinance was vital "because it is the only way the citizens of Dallas can be assured that visible reminders of city heritage will not be destroyed."

Builders, with permits in hand to begin apartment construction on Swiss, were understandably frustrated and angry. On the day of the City Council vote to change zoning, 27 people spoke in favor of the zoning change and nine against it. When the vote for approval was announced, onlookers jumped to their feet, smiling, whistling, cheering and applauding. Dallas had just won its first major hurdle in preserving its history.

Harryette Ehrhardt and her husband, who wanted to live in a big house in East Dallas, moved onto Swiss Avenue at the time it was zoned commercial and helped to turn it into a city showplace.

Dorothy and Wallace Savage, a former mayor of the city, had continued to maintain their home at 5703 Swiss. Most Swiss Avenue homeowners had sold their homes and moved away after 1964 when the City Council approved zoning that would allow apartment buildings between Fitzhugh and LaVista, but the Savages and a few others remained. In the atmosphere of the 1960s, it is not surprising that developers did not rush in to build, but as Dallas continued to expand in the latter part of that decade and into the early 1970s, developers decided they were sitting on a gold mine and moved to begin apartment construction. Swiss Avenue residents, including new families who had bought and remodeled the once palatial homes on faith that the city would return the area to a single family residences, rebelled.

Harryette and Jack A. Ehrhardt were among the first of the *new* families to see the potential of Swiss Avenue. They bought their 5731 Swiss home in early 1972. What they found was typical of other houses in the area—houses that were structurally sound and very large with assorted garages, apartments that had once served as servants' quarters, extra outbuildings, many gardens gone to seed and all in deplorable conditions.

Harryette Bushong Ehrhardt was born in Hattiesburg, Mississippi, on August 5, 1934, and moved to Dallas when she was four years old. Except for a time during World War II when the family followed her father across the country when he was in service, she was educated in Dallas and Highland Park schools, received her bachelor and master's degrees from SMU and her doctorate in education from the University of Houston. She became a teacher and taught in grade schools in Texas, Louisiana and California. In 1955 she married Dr. John Allen Ehrhardt and for the next several years was a lecturer and then assistant professor at SMU; a visiting professor at Texas Woman's University, Virginia Polytechnic Institute and New York State College, and a consultant in education for the Dallas Independent School District while having five children—Harryette Pickett in 1957, Helen Elizabeth in 1959, Ralphanna Lynn in 1960, John Allen, Jr. in 1962, and Kathryn Maulice in 1972.

From 1977 to 1981 Harryette served on the board of DISD. A political activist, she was a founding member of the Dallas Area Women's Political Caucus and a founder of the Historic Preservation League. She chaired political campaigns, mostly for candidates who were ethnic minorities. She was the spokesperson for individuals who needed expertise in impacting established systems. While she concentrated in enabling individuals to speak and act for themselves, she was also an articulate voice for groups—women, minorities and the poor—who had not yet learned to speak for themselves.

In 1989 Harryette and Jack allowed their home to be shown on the annual Tour of Homes, and during this event she described the neighborhood, the process of securing a historic preservation district and her own home:

> This home was built in 1918 by Theodore Marcus . . . . we bought it in 1972 . . . . It was located in . . . an inner city slum. There were cars jacked up in front yards. Many (houses) were sub-divided. Many were vacant. Ours had "squatters"—then called Hippies—who had lived here for some time. They continued to live in the back apartment—we left the heat and electricity on for them—until summer when the days and nights were warm. Then we left a note asking them to leave . . . . We never saw any of them (any more), but for several years after that once a month or so a van of "Flower Children" would come to the house and bring carnations . . . . They would admire the house and we would ask if they wanted to see it. When they had walked through the house, they would thank us and leave. We never asked . . . but they must have lived here . . . .
>
> (We found) the walls on the top floor painted black and saffron pink. The upstairs bedroom doors had locks on the outside and holes cut in the middle. (What she did not include in the presentation was that her husband, Dr. Ehrhardt, had fallen through some flooring in the basement while doing repairs and had to have assistance to get out of the tiny "prison.")
>
> We bought the house when our fifth child was on the way. We certainly were attracted by the size, with nine bedrooms and five and a half baths, but the real reason we wanted to live here was that this . . . was the only integrated neighborhood in Dallas. We wanted our children to have the advantages this neighborhood with its rich cultural diversity offered.
>
> Others also bought on Swiss Avenue at this time. We were an adventurous group ripe for the persuasion of the Savages who live on the corner to the south. They had lived here all of their lives, through Wallace's tenure as mayor, through Swiss's glorious days and through her fall from grace. They loved this street and made us feel we were smart enough to save this irreplaceable part of history. About half a dozen of us set about to do just that. We were laughed at by City Hall . . . which scoffed at the idea that we might become an historic district. We became an effective band of citizens to save our area.
>
> We formed the Historic Preservation League—incorporated in this living room.
>
> We took on the absentee landlords who had bought the houses for speculation awaiting the change in deed restrictions which would allow the homes to be torn down and high rise apartments built.
>
> We lobbied residents frightened of the implications of an historic designation.
>
> We printed and distributed pamphlets.
>
> We produced an emotional guaranteed-to-make-you-moist-of-eye slide presentation, and we spoke at every organization that would have us.
>
> We brought to Dallas the attorney who had written the New Orleans French Quarters ordinance and he generously worked with our city staff to write Dallas's Historic District ordinance.
>
> We held the first annual Swiss Avenue open house hoping for a few hundred people. Our home was on that first tour. We had 2,500 . . . .
>
> Then we returned to City Hall and were the darlings of the city. We easily got our area declared an historic district.
>
> This house has three stories and a basement served by an elevator. It has about 9,000 square feet in the main house and 730 in the apartment over the three-carriage garage. There are fireplaces in the living room and in the upstairs sitting room, three working wells and a greenhouse which we converted to a sauna.

Once when the Drs. Ehrhardt—Harryette and Jack—were remodeling their Swiss Avenue home before they moved in, she took the children back to their University Park home to put them to bed. When Jack failed to show up, she back-tracked and found him stuck in a hole in the basement where he had crashed through the floor and was wedged.

Our youngest child, Katy, is the only one now living at home in the main house. She will enroll at Texas A&M after her graduation from Woodrow Wilson High School this June. Woodrow, incidentally, is celebrating its 60th anniversary this year and honoring Wallace Savage along with my aunt who were in its first graduating class. Our daughter, Lynn, lives in the carriage house. She will finish her residency at Parkland in seven weeks and join her father full time in the ophthalmology practice he started here in East Dallas more than a quarter of a century ago. Ginger, Taffy and John, our other children who grew up in this house, are all products of the neighborhood and of the Dallas Public Schools . . . .

On and adjoining Central Expressway, arguably Dallas's busiest thoroughfare, another major restoration and preservation project got underway in 1990. And, again, it was a woman who led it. Her name was Jerry Henderson and she was an anthropologist. Assigned by the Texas State Highway and Transportation Department to study the effects on the environment and historical integrity of the area before construction could begin on the $636-million-dollar widening of North Central Expressway, Jerry was not thrilled with her assignment even though she was a Dallas native. At the time, she was the only woman archeologist on the department's staff and her passion was Native American culture and history. The assignment to Dallas looked both dull and mundane.

What she discovered boggled her imagination and indefinitely postponed the widening of the major artery.

She unearthed—quite literally—Freedman's Cemetery, a link to many of Dallas's early black citizens who were buried there in a four-acre plot following the Civil War. Part of the cemetery was already underneath North Central Expressway and more of it had been turned into an abandoned park.

Jerry Henderson did not want the Dallas assignment for widening Central Expressway believing it to be mundane and uninteresting. But she got it and what she found is an anthropological gold mine.

Jerry's life began in Dallas July 26, 1948, when she was born to Dana Dell and Ida Watson Henderson. Her father was a professional baseball player; the family lived at 1317 Cedar Haven. Jerry attended Roger Q. Mills Elementary School, Boude Storey Junior High and Adamson High School. At 17, a high school senior, she fell in love with a sailor, married him and ran off to California. Her son, Jeffrey Crouch was born in 1960. When the marriage failed, Jerry returned to Dallas and worked as a secretary at Dallas Power and Light. In 1969 she married architect Lynn McDonald "because he was such a nice man and promised me I could go back to school." She entered the University of Texas at Austin that same year and eased into anthropology. "It was a gradual thing. At first I was just taking courses—and then it grabbed me!" She earned her degree in anthropology in 1974 and her master's in 1976 at about the same time she got her second divorce. Her first professional job was with the University of Texas as a contract archeologist. The next year, 1977, she was hired by the Highway Department, later to be renamed the Texas Department of Transportation. She was its first—and for a long time—its only female employee.

When Jerry arrived in Dallas to take over the project, she walked the area—looking for any one of three criteria that the highway department uses to ascertain value: (1) anything over 50 years old; (2) one-of-a-kind items; (3) architectural treasures. She stumbled onto a sign: "Freedman's Memorial Park," and stopped in her tracks. It is illegal in Texas to cover a burial plot without first removing the graves. Jerry began calling around and asking questions. Her best resources were elderly black citizens. A key was Dr. Robert Prince, who—as it turned out—had been trying for years to get the city to do something about the cemetery where several members of his family were buried.

Jerry headed a team of 24, more than half of them women, who began the long and difficult task of locating the graves and painstakingly marking their outlines with string. Alongside the concrete artery hundreds of graves were located, but the team did not stop there. By shutting down the expressway one lane at a time, where daily an average of 75,000 cars whiz past, they used hand picks to remove the pavement and search for the long-ago interred bodies. Eventually the bodies will be exhumed for reburial.

"We have found hundreds of graves already,' Jerry said in the spring of 1993 while still in the process of exploration. "We may not find everything, but we have to try." And not only try. Every effort is made to identify the remains. "We are helped immeasurably in this effort with new demographic information." When the project is completed, Jerry aims to see that families are reburied together just as they were in the days following the Civil War when they were first interred. Reburial caskets stand waiting for the remains. "We need to know everything that is possible to know about the original cemetery," Jerry said, "and put everything back like it was. This won't correct the wrong we've done all these years but it's our job to make it as nearly right as possible."

34

CONNECTING THE PIECES

Dallas has been vastly enriched by women who moved to the city from other areas. Whether they came from other parts of Texas or other states or other countries mattered little. Their initial reaction to what they found in Dallas varied according to the time they arrived, their backgrounds, experience and education, their expectations and the framework of family and friends into which they moved. What they gave to the city is immeasurable—ideas and experiences that have expanded, enlarged and amplified the provincial confines of their new residences. They and their gifts are eclectic. Among them are Gerry Beer, Anne Dickson, Joy Mankoff, Patricia Meadows, Louise Raggio, Delia Reyes, Barbara Watkins and Virginia Whitehill.

At the opening, in 1978, of the Family Place, Dallas's first shelter for victims of family violence, Gerry Beer, right, Joan Wales, Sandy Hanson and Fran Goodwin held a press conference before welcoming their first residents. Women have seldom united across age, economic and ethnic lines to accomplish a single purpose as they did to establish the Family Place, clear evidence that family violence occurs among the rich as well as the poor, in all social brackets and to women of all ages.

Louise Hilma Ballerstedt Raggio began her commitment to, and concern for, Dallas when she arrived in January of 1946 to La Reunion's Mustang Village. She had a three-year-old son and was pregnant. She came from the South Texas home of her parents where she had lived for three years while her husband served in World War II. Even though her La Reunion apartment had no refrigerator, no washing machine, and no telephone, "it was wonderful to have plumbing!" The rain fell incessantly the first few months she was in Dallas and her converted barracks home was surrounded by mud bogs. The couple's second-hand car had 125,000 miles on it, and when Grier Raggio drove it to work at the Veterans Administration, Louise was isolated with a young child and no friends . . . .

Louise was the only child of Louis and Hilma Lindgren Ballerstedt, born June 15, 1919. She grew up on a Travis County farm that operated without electricity and was

Louise Ballerstedt Raggio, one of the country's top family lawyers, had a rocky start in Dallas in her converted army barracks home.

reached by unpaved roads. Her early education was in a tiny country school. When she was ready for high school, Louise and her mother moved to Austin where Mrs. Ballerstedt opened a boarding house to support them. Louise graduated from Austin High School at 16 as valedictorian and from the University of Texas, *magna cum laude* at 20. Because teaching was one of the few approved careers for women, Louise dutifully got a certificate and found a teaching position. But while waiting—and dreading—for school to start, she heard about Rockefeller fellowships that would give young college graduates a year of study in public administration in the nation's capital. She applied for one and was accepted. In the fall when she was due in the classroom, she was, instead, headed for Washington, D. C. Her parents, who had been so protective of their only fledgling through college, sent her off with their blessings because their friend, Lyndon Johnson was a Congressman, and her mother decreed, "Lady Bird and Lyndon will look after Louise."

The Johnsons were gracious to Louise, but it was the nation's First Lady who was her idol. Eleanor Roosevelt often invited the 48 Fellows—30 men, 10 women—to the White House for Sunday night supper. "Eleanor Roosevelt was so warm . . . . I felt if I got too homesick I could crawl up in her lap and she would make me forget my problems."

Following her year in Washington, Louise returned to Texas where she was a National Youth Administration counselor, and where she met Grier H. Raggio. They were married three months later on April 19, 1941. Grier, ruggedly handsome, a graduate of George Washington University School of Law, was a private in the Army. His heritage was Italian, his look and manner *macho*, his humor contagious, his temperament sometimes fiery, his advocacy for the rights of all people uncompromising, and his support of Louise and, later, their children, absolute.

Grier got out of the Army in the fall of 1945 and went to work in Dallas. It was three months before Louise and their son could join him because "there was *no* housing in Dallas. Young couples by the thousands were pouring in." When she did arrive, it was to a city "that was no place for a woman with a profession and even harder on a mother who wanted to continue a career. The attitude of Dallas equated a professional woman with a street walker. I was going crazy . . . .

"Grier said I needed to get out of the house. The cheapest way to do it was to go to law school. Tuition was $8 an hour." Grier, Jr. was six and Thomas Louis, one, when Grier accompanied Louise to SMU "where he literally pushed me through the door to my first law class." She began in night school, taking as many courses as she could. In the middle of her studies, Louise was pregnant again. "Dean Potts (of the SMU law school) was so puzzled by me. Some of the faculty was very upset when I was obviously pregnant and still attending class." In October of 1949, Kenneth Gaylord Raggio was born. By the time Louise enrolled as a regular daytime student, she occasionally pedaled him in a bicycle basket to SMU where he played quietly in the corner while his mother attended class. Four male Raggios were in the applauding audience when Louise graduated in 1952.

"There were no jobs for women lawyers. The employment services at SMU would not accept my application, so I worked at home taking whatever jobs I could get. I became one of Dallas's original Super Moms. I baked cookies and cakes for the PTA, went to every meeting for parents at the boys' schools. I was a Cub Scout mother and a Sunday school teacher. I gave birthday parties and chaperoned kids' overnights and camp outs."

Louise and Grier soon were among Dallas's "fringey liberals." They joined the Unitarian Church and she found intellectual sisters in its women's group. They were charter members of the Dallas United Nations. They joined the Young Democrats Club where she was introduced to Sarah Hughes . . . as Mrs. George Hughes.

In 1954, Sarah Hughes called Louise and told her to go and apply for a job in the District Attorney's office. Henry Wade was district attorney. "Henry hired me to get Sarah off his back." Her job as an assistant district attorney paid $350 a month, "half of what the men were making. Icicles hung all over the place the day I reported for work. The guys thought the office was going to the devil. I was given the Juvenile Delinquency Department . . . . Nobody else wanted it. I handled all domestic relations. I began to gain a reputation as a family lawyer. Henry was a wonderful boss. He allowed me to run my

Louise with her law and life partner, Grier Raggio, who pushed her through the door to her first class at SMU's law school.

own department, and I always had his support. Some of the guys who at first were the most obnoxious became lifelong friends."

Meager though the salary was, it provided the security the Raggios required for Grier to quit his job and, in 1956, to open his own practice. Before the year was out, Louise joined him; the fledgling firm became Raggio & Raggio. Her climb to become one of the nation's top family lawyers appears spectacular to those unaware of her long, hard, often lonely, financially bleak, societally ostracized, professionally arduous journey . . . . All three of her sons are attorneys and her granddaughters, as well as her grandsons, are growing up with free options to become professional people if they choose. "People don't realize that the only way you keep your kids is to let them go. You must let them hear their own drummer even if it's one entirely different from yours. With her own strong family ties as examples, Louise will do anything within the integrity of her profession to keep children from being harmed in divorce and custody battles. "A family lawyer," she said, "must have all of the abilities of other lawyers plus a sensitivity to the family."

Louise chaired the Family Law Section of the State Bar Association that rewrote the marital property laws for Texas and, eventually, completely revised the Family Law Code.

In the 1980s decade, having earned almost every accolade given by the bar associations, she turned her attention toward removing the subtleties of discrimination that still kept women imprisoned in the lower echelons of the socio-economic ladder. She was president of the Summit, established in 1989 "as a force in Dallas so that women become full participants in all decision-making processes to create a whole, just and abundant community." She was a charter member of The Dallas Forum, an elite group of corporate executive women. She became an overt activist for women while retaining her credentials in her profession. "I could not spend energy on women's things until I had paid my dues. I couldn't be known as a flaming feminist because I had to have the votes of men who were still in charge." While "paying her dues," she was, in 1979, elected a director of the State Bar Association and was the first woman to be a trustee of the Texas Bar Foundation, which she chaired in 1984-85. She was elected a Fellow of the Texas Bar Association and in 1982 a Fellow of the American Bar Association, which selects into membership only a fraction of one percent of all lawyers in the United States. In 1983 she was named one of the 22 best family lawyers in America and later in the 1980s was one of 29 original members—only six of them women—of the Matrimonial Network made up of the country's most prestigious attorneys working in family law.

"I reserve the right not to believe tomorrow what I espouse today; I never intend to stop growing."

What really has happened is that Louise Ballerstedt Raggio has only become more of the person she has always been, a person leading the way into a more humane future. What Louise did for women is largely unheralded because of the lawyer-client relationship that keeps personal stories sacrosanct. What Dallas has done for Louise is provide the setting, sometimes in positive supportive ways, often in negative ways, that challenged her to overcome obstacles.

Today, Louise said, Dallas is "a city divided. I arrived in a city almost 50 years ago that was run by a very few males. We all marched to their tunes. Minorities and women were invisible. *Nobody* not anointed by the rulers got in. Now discrimination is much more subtle and much more evil. Women and minorities are promised that the doors are wide open—but most of them have inside locks."

Geraldine Muriel Danzer Beer thought she was leaving civilization when she moved to Dallas in June of 1946. "I'd lived in New York, Boston and Washington, D. C. After that, Dallas? I was horrified . . . .

"And, I was wrong." Invited to a restaurant for dinner with Lawrence and Ruth Kahn, Gerry expected the stereotypical Texas woman—"big, raw-boned, blowzy, somebody who would greet me with a booming 'how y'all.'" What she got was a petite, beautifully groomed, cultured, friendly lady. "Ruth stood up and said, 'Hello, Gerry,' and I was in love with her!"

Geraldine Beer did her homework thoroughly, educated the public and garnered support from leaders in Dallas before she went public with her plan for a shelter for victims of family abuse.

The Kahns had invited the Beers to come to Dallas "to see if it were a place we might like to live. I *knew* it wasn't.... I fell in love with it the moment I arrived. The heat was unbelievable, but I never knew people could be so wonderful."

Gerry was 25 years when she and her husband, Bob Beer, decided that their future was in Dallas. Born in Brooklyn on July 8, 1920, to Dr. Charles and Elsie Rappaport Danzer, she grew up with an only brother, Herb, who arrived when she was 13 months old. Her parents were separated when Gerry was four. Her mother took the two children back to her mother's brownstone house in the heart of Brooklyn. "I really loved living there." What could have been an idyllic childhood was marred by bitter friction between her parents.

To celebrate her birthday, Gerry and her mother took a trip from New York through the Panama Canal to California. On shipboard she met Bob Beer. By the time the ship had made its round-trip voyage and returned to New York, the girl-child who celebrated her 17th birthday in the middle of that trip and the 19-year-old boy were in love. She went back to high school, he off to college. In the fall of 1938 she entered Barnard. At the end of her junior year, a month before her 21st birthday, Gerry and Bob were married. They moved to Cleveland, Ohio, where she completed another semester at Western Reserve University.

"The world had turned topsy-turvy. An evil man in Germany had gobbled up several small nations and was murdering Jews." On December 7, 1941, the Japanese had bombed Pearl Harbor all but demolishing the United States Air Force. The world was at war.

The Beers were living in Washington when Bob went into service and, after six weeks training, was shipped to New Guinea. "I wept for two days, then moved back with Mama in Manhattan." Gerry went to work for Saks Fifth Avenue, then moved to Abraham and Strauss where she was an assistant buyer in the millinery department. She was working there when Bob came home.

Like most people whose lives were disrupted by World War II, the Beer's initial jubilation was soon replaced by frustration. How would they manage? What would they do? Where would they live? The answer came in the Kahn's invitation to visit Dallas. They moved to Dallas in June of 1946. Bob went out to work. Gerry raised their children—Alfred, born on July 9, 1947, David, December 2, 1949, and Jonathan, May 23, 1953. As the children grew, Gerry grew. "Dallas was a totally different world from what I'd known. Women in volunteer work intrigued me. What they did mattered. And, it was fun!" She started her volunteer work "helping Ruth Kahn" on the Dallas Jewish Federation Women's Division's publicity committee. "There I met Hortense Sanger and my life has not been the same since." In 1961 she chaired the Women's Division of the Federation and went to Israel during the summer of 1962 where she observed personally the plight of the Holocaust victims. "On my way back, I asked the question over and over, 'What is my mission in this world?'"

Friends advised her to go back to school and complete her college degree. She worked out an arrangement between Barnard and SMU, completed her college credits and was awarded her degree in psychology in 1965. Then, seeking a spot to use her training, she heard Lucy Patterson speak on the unmet needs in South Dallas which focused on the lack of educational facilities for its young children. "Lucy blew me away! I had found my niche."

With the support of Temple Emanu-El, women developed and ran the Rhoads Terrace Institute of Early Childhood Education and Developmental Day Care. Sue Lichten was its first chairperson, Gerry its second. Located in the Rhoads Terrace Public Housing Project, it began as a half day preschool that developed into a full day care program. It was funded by a federal grant and local money; Temple Emanu-El supported it, partly through its budget, but mostly through individual subscriptions.

"We had all kinds of ideas about what should be done. We were often wrong. We learned to listen to the parents, and we learned to hear what the kids were saying. We learned that mothers needed caring for, too." Parents got very involved in Rhoads Terrace. A sense of community developed there. Adults learned responsibility for taking care of their own lives. When something needed fixing, they learned to go to the proper city officials to get it done." Deep and continuing friendships came out of the associations. The children blossomed. "Our work together provided clear evidence for projects like Head Start. I know it had a lasting effect on the children."

While working with Rhoads Terrace, Gerry experienced her first uneasiness in the city she had chosen. "I saw the first bars on the windows of their homes. I heard about repeated robberies in their neighborhoods." Gerry was with Rhoads Terrace for 10 years. "It was very gratifying, and letting go was like divorcing a member of the family, but it was time. There was some growing resentment in the community about those rich Jewish women. I was not treated like a professional, but I was expected at all times to behave like one. I was working full time and not being paid. I phased myself out." Rhoads Terrace became a part of the Dallas Day Care Association.

Gerry was one of thousands of women of the 1970s who found herself in an internal struggle. "It was no longer appropriate for me to be a full-time mother (her youngest son was almost 17 at the start of the '70s decade). Bob had begun to want to travel. My time was his; all our plans revolved around his. He earned the money and it was appropriate that he make the decisions, but this was not satisfying. I was unhappy and this put a terrible burden on Bob." After much reflection and some counseling, Gerry decided it was time to find a focus for her life.

Reading that Lord & Taylor was establishing a store in Dallas, Gerry knew that with her background in merchandising and her knowledge of the community, she had skills that would be helpful to them. She had hardly sent off her resume when she was called for an interview and was hired as an executive service manager. "I was the trouble shooter," she said, reflecting on the two and a half years she worked for money.

But she found work limiting. "I was no longer free to do community work. I didn't need the money, so I quit and became a professional volunteer," first at the Women's Center of Dallas.

"That led me to the Family Place," Dallas's first shelter for victims of family abuse. The Family Place was Gerry's brainchild. It became, for the entire country, a model program of how to shelter and heal women abused by the men in their lives.

Gerry began it reluctantly, asked questions of everybody she respected about the need for a shelter for abuse victims. It was hard for her to believe that women were hurt by those who said they loved them. Once committed, Gerry built a foundation of solid mainstream community support. By the time the shelter opened in a reconverted frame house on McKinney Avenue in December of 1978, everything needed for its success was in place. The board was comprised of community professionals. But when it came to the program, Gerry listened to the experts—women who were victims of abuse. On its opening day, the occupancy was at capacity and continued to be so. Additional shelters have helped, but the need continued to grow. Gerry devoted a decade to the Family Place before she again moved out and on.

As Dallas celebrated its 150th birthday Gerry chose to be at the Health Special School, DISD's school for pregnant girls. "The abuse of kids is awful," she said. "We don't have enough professionals. Volunteers *must* fill in when our tax dollars don't stretch. Taking chances is something volunteers can do that institutions can't—or don't. I don't have a single regret for the way I've chosen to serve my community."

Joy Shechtman Mankoff moved to Dallas in 1959, the bride of Ron Mankoff, a tax attorney. She was 25 years old and her first impression was "how warm and friendly everybody was! The city was so different then. I remember driving down Central Expressway when there was nobody on it but me!"

Joy had a full decade of experiencing the city as a woman in the traditional mold before she took her first steps to involvement in 1970. "I was an inactive housewife. My world was centered in my husband. I did the *mother* kind of things"—managing the home, playing golf and enjoying bridge every Friday. She was "surrounded by friends whose lives were similar. None of us was employed. I took on no major responsibilities until Douglas was 7." Douglas, born in 1963, is the younger of Joy and Ron Mankoff's two sons. Jeffrey, their older son, was born in 1961.

Joy Mankoff, at right, and Bette Miller, who was president of the Greater Dallas Section, National Council of Jewish Women in 1975. Joy later chaired a program that led to the formation of Women's Issues Network.

Born to George and Hannah Walker Shechtman on August 31, 1934, Joy met Ronald M. Mankoff while she was a student in Connecticut College. They had a four-year courtship before they were married on November 3, 1959. With a mother who was very active as a volunteer in her community and a college that encouraged its women to leadership, "I should have learned to be independent, but after I met Ron I spent those last two years of college writing Mrs. Ron Mankoff on all my papers and book covers."

One jarring incident marred Joy's early Dallas days. Her mother had been president of the women's opera board in her Connecticut home town and encouraged her daughter to contact the women's group of the opera in Dallas. Joy did. "They were very gracious. They said they had *never* received a call like that before and they would most assuredly be in touch with me. I never heard from anybody again. I learned later that the way it's done in Dallas is to donate at least a thousand dollars and wait to be asked to join."

When she began to hear political and racial comments at social gatherings that disturbed her, Joy kept quiet. "I was really shy in those days," she said. She joined the National Council of Jewish Women at the urging of Emme Sue Frank and became involved in Operation LIFT (Literacy Instruction for Texas), a group that taught adults to read and write, but did not discover her own voice until four years later when Kennedy was assassinated. "I wanted to move away, but Ron and I decided we must stay and stand up for what we believed. Everybody was speaking out then. Dallas wasn't a city of hate, just a city that had allowed a small vocal minority to make it seem so."

Once out of her cocoon, Joy could not be stopped. She began by writing NCJW's bulletin, then worked up its budget. "They sent me to the United Nations Institute and I came back all fired up." The SMU Symposium on the Education of Women for Social and Political Leadership "had a profound effect on me." She recalls: "My name card read Mrs. Ron Mankoff. William Sloan Coffin was a speaker and he said to me, 'I know what a Ron Mankoff is, but what is a *Mrs.* Ron Mankoff?' I was shaken! I had allowed myself to merge into my husband; it was his identity that defined me. To disappear under the name of someone else is a terrible thing.

"As we progressed into the 1970s, many things that had held such promise for women were disappearing. The Women's Law Center had fallen apart. The Women's Center had closed its doors. The City Council had dismantled the Dallas Commission on the Status of Women . . . . It was time for some others of us to speak up."

Joy was vice president of the Women's Council of Dallas County and program chair for the NCJW in 1979 when she encouraged the two groups to work together on a program called "Dallas Women Into the Eighties." Many outspoken participants, all with their own agenda, brought to the event problems that demanded attention. When the rhetoric ceased, it was clear, Joy said, that Dallas needed a small group, unfettered by bureaucracy and free of outside restraints, that could act quickly and decisively to meet the needs of women.

The result was Women's Issues Network (WIN). Joy was its first president. A 501 (C) (4) organization, not as restrictive as a 501 (C) (3), it is tax exempt but not tax deductible. It cannot be partisan, but it can take up issues. Its board is its membership. Former board members usually continue a close bond. Because it is small, WIN can and does react quickly on anything that curtails or limits women's rights.

The calendar moved on, from the 1970s decade, through the 1980s, and into the 1990s, and it was as if Joy Mankoff had been issued a mandate to be everywhere that social conditions were unfair to any member of the human family. "Fairness has motivated me," she said, "fairness to women, fairness to the aging, fairness to minorities.... If it isn't fair, then you work to make it fair.... Equality may not come in my lifetime, but I can get the world started in that direction...."

Except for her one fiat of fairness, Joy gave her time to groups that were unrelated— the League of Women Voters, Mental Health Association, Committee on Crime, Goals for Dallas, Dallas County Historical Building Advisory Committee, Dallas Women's Foundation, Boys and Girls Clubs of Dallas, and on and on. By the time she became president of Planned Parenthood in 1988, her credentials were sterling, and she was able to assemble a Planned Parenthood advisory council of city luminaries.

"We've come a long way in Dallas." Joy said. "We have had a woman mayor, a woman city manager, a woman city attorney, a black superintendent of schools, but many people are unaware of all the closed doors. The glass ceiling is still there...."

Virginia Bulkley Whitehill with her mother, Myrtle Bales Bulkley, and her daughter, Margaret. Ginny is the consummate Dallas volunteer, a role model for many younger women. Myrtle was a lifelong advocate for women's rights.

Virginia Bulkley Whitehill knew right away that she was an "outsider" when she moved to Dallas in 1960. Born in New York, she had grown up in Pelham Manor, but had lived in several states before moving to Dallas. "I transferred my Junior League membership thinking I would make friends quickly. But it didn't happen . . . the Junior League would have been much happier if I had not intruded and started asking questions."

She soon stopped telling people she was from New York "because they acted as if I had some incurable disease. I'd mumble that I was from 'back East' and then change the subject.... Jim and I were not social in the way Dallas was. We didn't enjoy huge crowds with a lot of supercilious comments that you couldn't hear because the noise was so loud. Our idea of a party was six to eight people at dinner talking about ideas. We didn't find that in Dallas."

Born on July 9, 1928, to Myrtle and Harold Bulkley, Ginny grew up with one brother and took a degree in history at Mount Holyoke College. She married young, divorced and had two little girls when she met and married Jim Whitehill. Patricia and Margaret, her daughters, were nine and six when the Whitehills moved to Dallas.

Ginny enrolled her children and herself in Sunday School at Highland Park Presbyterian Church "where I lost my religion regularly on Sunday mornings." She remembers the incident that caused her to withdraw. The class was studying the Old Testament, specifically about leprosy and the treatment of lepers. Virginia said that nobody she knew had leprosy, that she thought the purpose of the study was to find parallels in the Bible stories that applied to the present. "I added that I thought Dallas treated its Black people the way lepers were treated in Biblical times. Every eye turned to me. Nobody said anything for a few seconds and then they began the discussion again as if I hadn't spoken. After class a pretty, beautifully dressed lady, came up to me and said that I couldn't be expected to understand because 'you haven't lived heah very long.... We love our Negroes, but they aren't like us. It's their nature to be like they are. When you live heah awhile, you will understand.' She said a lot more. The longer she talked, the angrier I became. I said I didn't agree with her and left. I did not go back."

In the almost third of a century since Ginny moved to Dallas, she has watched and helped it change. "With my background in history, I tend to look at situations in long spans of time. I see progress...."

Anne Ponder Dickson moved to Dallas from her native El Paso in late 1963 as a bride. She had visited the city often and thought she knew it, but she found Dallas "very strange. As a young married couple, we were entertained lavishly, but I had a hard time ... At the country club I heard blatant racist remarks. In El Paso *we* (the Anglos) were the minority and racist statements like I heard in Dallas never happened—not even in private."

Born August 7, 1939, the daughter of Daniel Ray and Winifred Kennedy Ponder, Anne grew up on a ranch in the Davis Mountains with one sister. Her father was the youngest mayor El Paso had ever elected. In college she majored in bio-chemistry and had been accepted to a medical school in Virginia when she came home for a year to please her parents, met Robert Miller Dickson, married him on September 28, 1963, and moved to Dallas.

"I didn't fit in Dallas. Fortunately Bob sensed that I was lonely and felt unaccepted—and he began to view his city through my eyes. We both grew. We both have very good friends now, but it wasn't that way at first. I found Dallas women superficial. Brittle. Insulated. And the men in Dallas were hard on women . . . ."

The Junior League was Anne's channel for growth and change, though she had a shaky start there, too. "I worked in West Dallas—and I couldn't get *anybody* interested in working with me there." She kept at it. After 14 years as a full time homemaker, wife and mother, under League leadership, she created a Career Development course which she taught for four years. "I did my best to get this huge, profitable women's organization stirred up about issues that were affecting their lives. It was too threatening." But, slowly, there were flickerings. The three dreaded "Ds"—death, desertion and divorce—found victims among League members. The Career Development course gave several of them their first survival kit. "It helped a lot of women break out into being their own persons," she said,. "It didn't help me. I hadn't a clue of what I wanted to do with my life!"

But even while searching for her own identity, Anne was building her future on her past. When her father died in 1965, Anne and Bob began to assume responsibility for the Ponder ranch in West Texas. After the death of her mother and the illness of her sister, they assumed the full responsibility. "I have never met a person in Dallas who knows the cattle industry," Anne said. "Ranch work is so hard. So dirty. Back-breaking work. It is not Dallas. Dallas is a finance place, a sophisticated place."

For a less flexible person than Anne, there were the makings of a split personality. She lived in North Dallas, belonged to the Junior League, socialized with Dallas's economically affluent, mothered Stephanie Ponder Dickson, born in 1964, and Robert Kennedy Dickson, born in 1968. Two or three times a month she flew to El Paso, drove the 200 miles to the Ponder ranch and did the grungiest kind of work. After her mother's death, she also cared for her grandmother, who died in 1990 at age 100.

As busy as she was, Anne's Career Development program compelled her to continue reexamining her life. One night at a party she overheard a discussion about a new publishing company about to be established. She was intrigued, asked questions, and offered to invest. In 1978 she became vice president of New London Press, and in 1981 established her own company, Pressworks Publishing. Totally untutored in publishing, she took crash courses while she did on-site, hands-on training. "I loaned it a lot of money," she said. "I published high quality books—little jewels." She has not issued a title since 1986, principally because, "I cannot bend with some of the practices . . . ."

And what has changed about Dallas? "A lot," Anne said. "Economics and immigration are the chief reasons. Women of accomplishment were not valued here. Now they are."

Patricia Ann Blachly Meadows moved to Dallas in 1963 "where everything was under control. Erik Jonsson and the men ran the business community and the women handled the cultural affairs. Women ran their charity events like CEOs of major companies. I was impressed!"

More than any other woman, Patricia has provided the support for women artists to accept their talent, the setting for them to show their work, and the atmosphere for the city to approve their gifts. Though women have always been the city's art preservers and displayers, their own art has not been taken seriously. They worked in a negative climate that choked their talent, channeled it into areas deemed appropriate for women, or kept them closeted in their garrets.

"I said I thought Dallas treated its black people the way lepers were treated in Bible times. Every eye turned to me . . . . Then there was complete silence. After a long pause, the conversation started again as if I had not spoken . . . ."

Anne Ponder Dickson with Linda Gale White in Austin in 1984. Anne created a course that changed the lives of many women, but it took awhile for her to apply the training to herself.

Patricia changed all that. But first, she had to learn how. On the day she arrived in Dallas, there would have been no way to guess the impact that she would have on her adopted city. She was pretty, proper, polite and a pampered product of the 1950s. Married to Curtis W. Meadows, Jr., scion of one of Dallas's leading families, Patricia arrived into an atmosphere of acceptance. Many of the young couple's friends were classmates from the University of Texas School of Law, from which Curtis had just graduated. The friends of her husband's family and the wider social circles of Dallas reached out to include and embrace her.

Patricia was born between two brothers, Bill and Bob Blachly to William Douglas and Irene Bond Blachley on November 12, 1938, in Amarillo. Her father's government job required him to transfer from one place to another. Her mother, the daughter of a Baptist minister, took the children and went along. "She was very supportive, very protective of her children." The family had moved 11 times by the time Patricia was eight. "We were living in Austin. It was wartime. Mother requested no more moves. She needed some permanency in our lives, so we stopped our nomadic ways and settled on a working farm near Austin. I cherish those (four) years of farm life. They gave me a very practical background, a sense of birth, death, the changing of seasons."

When she was 12, the Blachlys moved into Austin and built their home. Patricia thought she would become a professional dancer and for a number of years was a serious student of dance. She graduated from Austin High School in 1956 and entered the University of Texas where she studied history and English as a major and anthropology and Spanish as a minor.

She wanted to learn how these different disciplines fitted together. "I have always been interested in relationships, and everything I studied has worked itself out as pieces in the life I eventually chose." For the first three years she was in the University, Patricia was enrolled in what was called Plan II, an advanced academic curriculum. During her junior year, she began to believe that, for her, there were connections she was missing in the smorgasbord of academic wealth, and she decided to leave Plan II. John Silber, who later became one of the most controversial educators of the twentieth century, was her adviser. "He sneered at my reasons, said they were very shallow." But leave she did. It was the first time that Patricia held to her convictions against someone of power and prestige.

By that time Curtis Meadows was in her life. They had met when she was a freshman. "I was doing a can-can dance in a very abbreviated costume in a follies program, and he was intrigued. Later I was at his fraternity house watching him jitterbug, and I was intrigued. But our romance did not progress smoothly . . . .

"Curtis Meadows is one of the world's most gentle, caring people. He soon asked me to go steady. I thought going steady was boring. I have a very low tolerance level for boredom. So we'd go steady and I'd break loose. Nobody has ever understood his tolerance for my behavior. About the time I was graduating, I realized what a very special man he was. I called him up and asked him to forgive me and take me back. I said I'd mended my ways. And I had!"

Patricia and Curtis dated for five years. She took his pin. She graduated; he was in law school. She was working for the University of Texas for $1.00 an hour. "Both sets of our parents were happy about us, but we couldn't afford to get married." Finally, Curtis told his father that he wanted to marry Patricia and his father agreed to continue his support through school."

They were married June 10, 1961. "We lived a very meager, happy life. There was a good group of young marrieds. I was welcomed into the law wives group. We played an inordinate amount of bridge." When Curtis graduated from law school, he moved to Dallas and Patricia remained in Austin for the birth of their son, Michael Lee Meadows, on February 13, 1963. She was only beginning to feel at home in Dallas when Curtis's brother, Algur, died. "It was a terrible blow to the family . . . . Our baby gave us all a reason to hang on and heal. . . . Among all the weeping, there was laughter at the antics of a tiny little boy . . . . New life grows out of the saddest times."

Curtis was hired by a Dallas law firm and the couple moved into an apartment. Patricia joined the Junior Bar Wives. "Linda Custard invited me to join the Junior

"The men ran the city and the women ran their charity events like CEOs. I was so impressed! My models were people like Sis Carr, Evelyn Lambert, Betty Marcus, Lupe Murchison, Virginia Nick, Grace Stemmons.... And then Evelyn held up her award and said it was time for the younger women to take over and she looked right at me...."

Symphony League. Then the Junior League invited me. That made me focus. I began to feel a part of the city."

John Morgan Meadows was born on December 17, 1965, and Patricia was a full-time mother and a part-time volunteer. "Then a friend convinced me I was drifting. She said I needed a five-year plan, so I made one. Painting and dance were my passions. I signed up for the Junior League Follies and joined the dance choir at our church. It was all sheer joy."

Her volunteer work introduced Patricia to the city's leaders. "People like Virginia Nick, Lupe Murchison, Betty Marcus, Evelyn Lambert, Sis Carr, Grace Stemmons.... They ran things with such efficiency. When Evelyn got the Arete award, she held it up, looked right at me and said, 'I've worked hard for this. I deserve it. Now it's time I had some fun. So I'm turning the reins over to younger women....'

"Grace Stemmons was the great encourager. She took time to show us how. The Junior Bar Wives was picked by Neiman-Marcus as the recipient of one event of its annual Fortnight. It was to be our great money-maker, but we were so naive that we didn't get a contract of what we would furnish and what Neiman's would supply. We assumed too much. None of us had any money at that time. We couldn't even afford a Fortnight ticket. And then we had to get our hair done and buy a dress and hire a baby sitter. So we were horrified when we learned that our organization was to provide the wine and other refreshments for the event that was supposed to benefit us. Grace Stemmons went with us to Neiman-Marcus. We were embarrassed to admit that we had not considered all of the expenses involved and that we did not have the money to put on the event. Grace spoke up and said, 'Stanley, you have to help these girls.' So, we worked out a compromise. That taught us to make sure of the bottom line before we committed ourselves to anything else.

"It taught me never to be cowed or awed, and to run things like a business. Working as volunteers sent us all out on the street to meet people with money. I remember I went to Uncle Al with a shaking heart to ask him to buy a table for the Fortnight event. I was *so* nervous. It cost $250. He was amused. He was used to being asked for thousands....

"...And that's the way I learned. We are all sum totals of all our prior experience—and everything comes in handy."

It was around 1975 that the many pieces of Patricia's interests focused on art. "Curtis gave me my first set of oils. At first I painted just for fun, but I felt myself moving more and more to art. It was a time when women were beginning to be encouraged to have careers. Then I became aware that all of the artists were garreted in their studios. We needed a place of our own." "We found an old warehouse on Swiss Avenue, in a terrible condition, but I could see the possibilities. I had no intention of doing anything except finding us a place. The furthest thing from my mind was to become personally involved in it. All I wanted to do was paint."

In the beginning, wearing overalls and sweat shirts, Patricia cleaned and mopped and painted, climbed ladders and cleared cobwebs, scrubbed floors and refinished them. All the while she sought women in their remote garrets, offering them a chance to show their work to the world. There were false starts, detours, disappointments. The first who attach themselves to any new project are usually opportunists, people who are perpetually disappointed and who constantly seek outlets for their personal agendas. Because women have little experience in separating the wheat from the chaff, and because they are connectors, eager to give every voice an opportunity to be heard and, in this case, every artist an opportunity to be shown, there were days that the project seemed bogged in a mire. But Patricia persevered. Two things kept her at it: one, a husband who believed in her dream, provided support for her and for it and, in many ways, filled the role that women usually fill for their artist mates, and, two, a coterie of women who were determined that the project succeed.

They called their place D'Art. "I was one of the few with experience both as an artist and as a community volunteer. I had learned how to make connections, Patricia said. "I didn't want to take a leadership role, but it was so important to so many people that I could not turn it down." The result has been that Patricia is the spokesperson for

Patricia Blachly Meadows, above, is surrounded by the works of Dallas artists in 1983, the year after D-Art opened. Below, in a testament to the fact that art is not all glamor, she and Sherry Owens wrestle Jerry Daniel's sculpture into position for the "Senses Beyond Sight" show.

other artists. Patricia is mentioned, if at all, as a member of the board and, occasionally, as the chairperson. But she does not show. It is a supreme gift.

Patricia has gifted Dallas in many other ways. When official boards meet, she is there to represent the women. In unofficial places, hers is the presence seen and the voice heard. "I was mentored by men who controlled the art world," she said, "so I have only deep appreciation for what they have added to my life and my art. And because of this, I am heard." She has lived inclusiveness, earning her credentials with membership on boards such as the Dallas Museum of Art, where she has served on its acquisitions committee. But the rebel side of her surfaces often as it did when she insisted that her family move near downtown Dallas in the renewed State-Thomas area. When she was president of the State-Thomas neighborhood association, she encouraged her Black and Hispanic neighbors to retain their residences.

Her resume reflects the new person Patricia is. She lists her profession as artist, art administrator, and art consultant. Her professional activities are art related: National Museum of Women in the Arts, Washington, D.C.; D-Art Visual Art Center, co-founder, director and board member; Dallas Arts District Management Association; juror for many art exhibitions, and on and on and on.

"Things have worked together, Patricia said. "Community colleges offered the first career opportunities for women art teachers. Because of budget crunches, support staffs of museums are almost all women. True, some of this is economic, but I don't see this as a negative. I see it as a way for women to get their foot in the door." There are many women curators and some women directors and, she added, a good 80 per cent of all gallery owners are women. Women artists are being recognized. Women are creating art that is cross-gendered. Men curators are choosing women to show. The guerrillas are out there, too. Whether you agree with their tactics, or not, they have been in the lead to make the presence of women known in the art world. Some guerrillas wear pearls!

"Women need to celebrate the contributions we have made. Because we have been accessible, work for less money and incredibly harder than the average male, we are making it to the big time. I am not at all threatened. I am encouraged."

Barbara Earline Lord Watkins and her husband, Dr. Myron Watkins, moved to Dallas in 1964, choosing it over several other cities as the place they wanted to live and rear their family. Myron, an obstetrician/gynecologist, had few obstacles placed in the way of his professional path, but Barbara felt the barbs of exclusion very soon. "Like any good wife, I wanted to help my husband in his career, and I thought it important to be a member of the medical auxiliary." She expressed her desire to join, and "they wrote me back that if I had X number of members to second me and other stipulations, I could join. In the meantime, I learned I could not have one vote against me, so I gave up. Then I learned that a fraction of my husband's medical dues went to the auxiliary and that infuriated me." Barbara began a one-woman campaign to open the auxiliary to black women. "I fought the good battle. Wrote letters. Told everybody. Got the word out. The auxiliary opened up, but I did not join until 1988 . . . . They often asked me. I simply could not . . . ."

Barbara, the daughter of Edward Adolphus and Madeline Yvonne Parsons Lord, was born October 7, 1935, in Jacksonville, Florida. Her mother, a medical assistant, and her father, a physician and minister, lived in Bainbridge, Georgia, where Barbara—along with three brothers and a sister—were reared, "but Mother went to Florida for the birth of all of us." Her father, a native of British Guyana, "did not want Georgia-born children."

Married on June 14, 1957, Barbara and Myron went to Kansas City, Missouri, where he completed his medical training and they had their first child, Cynthia Yvonne, on July 14, 1958. They next spent three years in Kansas City where he did his residency and she was director of the School of Medical Technology at Kansas City General Hospital until the birth of Elizabeth Jeanette on August 21, 1960.

Shortly after completing his residency, Dr. Watkins was ordered to report to the Army. The couple, with their two baby daughters, requested assignment "to all of the glamor spots of the world," but wound up in his hometown of Atlanta at Fort McPherson, Georgia. "There were no other African-American officers on base. It appeared we would

Barbara Lord Watkins is vice president of Parkland Memorial Hospital, a position that allows her to be out of her hospital office into the community where she builds bridges between the health needs of the people and her organization's response to those needs.

be many months getting base housing." Captain Watkins was in a catch twenty-two situation. His ob/gyn specialty demanded that he be quickly available for night calls at the hospital. Segregated housing would have put the Watkins family miles from the base. "Overnight they managed to find a place for us. Never mind that it was a converted barracks. Housing for enlisted men. Right behind the general's quarters. We moved in." Barbara did research in the laboratory. "Those two years gave us time to think about where we wanted to live. "We checked very carefully. A. Maceo Smith told us: 'If you come to Dallas and have something to give, Dallas will give you the opportunity. But remember you will have to pursue it.' That's all I ever wanted—an opportunity. We rented a small three-bedroom home on Blue Creek Drive in Oak Cliff. The van broke down in Mississippi on our way here. The temperature hit 105 degrees. We spent 10 days at Holiday Inn Central, but I never really regretted our choice."

There were moments, though, that she gasped—like when she read in the paper that the League of Women Voters was getting out a mailing supporting the repeal of the poll tax. "I thought, 'what is this? Nobody ever mentioned that I would have to pay to vote! Georgia had done away with that a long time ago. The article said that the women were meeting at Sue Lichten's house to work on the mailing, so I called Sue. She gave me her address and told me how to get to her house, and I drove down Central Expressway to North Dallas for the first time."

From the very first, "I was accepted into the League of Women Voters without reservation. The members were cordial. There was no facade. No pretense. Never once the feeling that we are doing this because we should. It was get in there and do your share and there's a place for you." There were other groups that welcomed her with open arms—but not everybody did. She made an issue only of things she felt were important. "Country clubs were not open. Still aren't, but they are insignificant." She has many times been the "token" black person in groups "if I thought it was important to be represented at the table," but she has tried never to place her children in such situations.

There are two Dallas-born children, Anne Marie, November 7, 1964, and Myron Hickman Watkins, Jr., April 20, 1966. Anne was on the way when the Watkins went house hunting. Their search took them to North Dallas where "a very gracious realtor" showed them through a house on Caladium between Preston and Nuestra. "It was just about perfect. We talked about it all the way home and were so excited. It wasn't 30 minutes before the realtor called and was very blatant, 'you know you can't live there; that street is not open to Blacks.' They heard about McShann Road, then a two-block long street less than a mile from where they had looked at the house on Caladium. The street, named for Dr. McShann, a black physician who owned a huge farm in that area, was for many years the only street in North Dallas open to Blacks. Barbara called it the "North Dallas Black ghetto." The Watkins's were among the first families to move onto McShann Road, before it had most city services. It was years later before the first white family moved onto the street integrating the neighborhood. As late as mid-summer of 1991, acts of overt racism occasionally interrupted the quiet professional neighborhood. "There are still elements that keep us from feeling safe and comfortable in our own homes."

Education has always been a top priority with Barbara. She found an excellent school for Cynthia at St. Anthony in Oak Cliff, even though she had to drive many miles after the family moved. She found an equally right school for Elizabeth at the Science Place in Fair Park. When it came time to select a pre-school for Anne, Barbara checked with Park Cities Baptist, which had been highly recommended. "They wanted me to come visit—which I was glad to do. And they wanted Anne to come visit, and then they said they had never had a black child and maybe this wasn't the right time. Maybe they needed to get to know her better. Maybe in another year. It was quite an experience. I left and went to Walnut Hill Presbyterian. Anne was readily accepted, enjoyed it, and I enjoyed the relationships. Park Cities called me back. I tried to get into dialogue with them—but there was no way I was going to put my child there."

One of the few times that Barbara and Myron Watkins made an issue of a segregated social situation was when they had invited guests and made reservations to hear an entertainer at Harper's Corner. "We arrived and were told they had no reservation for

Watkins. I looked over the list and found Watkins and was told that was another Watkins who was a guest in the hotel. It soon became obvious that we were not going to be seated. I went to the front desk and asked them to ring the Watkins who were guests in the hotel. I was told there was no one registered by that name.

"At that time LeRoy Johnson, a state senator from Georgia, was scheduled to come to Dallas to speak. He was a friend of ours so we told him that perhaps Dallas was not ready for him. It was a community still practicing segregation." Planners of the Johnson event moved fast. Barbara was told that if she would call and inform Sen. Johnson that everything was fine, there would be no incidents, that Harper's "would integrate, would let two of you, maybe as many as four, come in at a time. I said 'no! Either you are open or you are not. So they opened. I never went back."

This, and other incidents of racism, prodded the city fathers and the legal system to become more purposeful about integration of its public facilities. The Tri-Ethnic Committee was appointed and Barbara was on its first board.

Barbara Lord Watkins has been a key person in integrating the City of Dallas. She has served on numerous boards. "I choose to serve where I think I can make a contribution." When Cynthia was invited to become a member of the Junior League in 1987, one of the first three African Americans invited by the Dallas League—there had been a transfer prior to that—Barbara was asked to be a member of JL's advisory committee. "The League is to be commended," Barbara said. "No organization does a better job of training its young women to serve their community. Cynthia found it a really neat experience and I enjoyed my associations."

When Cynthia graduated from high school and went away to college, Barbara thought it was time to re-examine her own goals. "I was determined I was not going to be a parent with an empty nest syndrome. Public administration was something that I wanted to fine tune. So I applied to SMU, and after many years went back to school and got my master's in public administration, completed it in two years, finished with a 4.0 grade average. I did some work with the regional office of Health and Welfare. Also worked with the VNA as a developmental officer."

As a volunteer, Barbara "was painfully aware that I could make an impact only to a certain degree. When decisions are made in agencies, volunteers count only if they are on a board that sets policy." She wanted a professional job where she could have a voice in improving care that delivered services directly to individuals. She found it at Parkland Hospital.

"I was asked by the CEO to come to Parkland in the Department of Public Affairs. At first I was not interested." Her perception of Parkland was "something I could not be very proud of." He insisted that I check it out, said there were changes taking place that were very positive." One trip was enough to convince her that things were, indeed, heading in the right direction and she welcomed being a part of the change. "I've not had a day at Parkland that has not been challenging. I've had a part in making major changes that have made Parkland a center of excellence, one of the leading hospitals in the United States. It has a better reputation nationally than it does locally."

Barbara's title is vice president. "I've been fortunate," she said. "Along with my job, I've served in other capacities in the community. This has been *very* important to Parkland in helping us understand the external environment. Being involved in the wider community has helped us provide better services."

Barbara compares the Dallas she saw 27 years ago with today: on the surface, it is a better place for and to its citizens of African-American heritage. "Housing is our biggest breakthrough. No realtor today would dare tell us that a street was closed to us." Public education is open, but troubled. The overt signs of racism are gone, but something more imbedded and even more detrimental to healthy community life is much in evidence. We all know the right things to say and the right things to do but in many places this is a facade. It's more than a glass ceiling. Sometimes we can't even get to the table. That is *so* hard."

Delia Maria Perez Reyes was "totally surprised. Totally baffled at the Hispanic situation" when she moved to Dallas in 1976 and "totally surprised at the attitude of

Barbara was told that the Watkins name on the reservation list was that of a hotel guest. When she went to the phone and requested to speak to the Watkins registered at the hotel and learned there was no such person, she knew that discrimination was solidly in force.

women and minorities toward those conditions." For her, both the prevailing conditions in the city toward its Spanish-heritage citizens and the almost acquiescent acceptance of those conditions by its subjects were deplorable. "I had to back up and try to understand what had happened here." Her perspective was from the Dallas Hispanic Chamber of Commerce where she was the first non-Mexican American to head it.

Born in Havana, Cuba, on February 2, 1942, Delia was a child of privilege reared by "very, very strong women," her mother—Delia Perez Riaza, her grandmother and three aunts, all of whom were independent people. She was an only girl in a large, extended, happy family. "I was reared to be the star. All of my cousins were boys and they all deferred to me." While the women in her family pushed and prodded, her father, Julio Perez, supported and undergirded. "My father always said, 'You can do it,' about anything that I wanted to try."

Delia was educated in private Cuban schools and was on the threshold of going to the university when Castro came to power in Cuba in 1959. "Overnight everything fell apart." The family moved to New York in 1962. "I was 20 years old, had never worked, and had to find a job. My father was not well." What she found was a routine Girl Friday job with a Jewish insurance agency in Harlem. "It was a job. I needed a job. It never occurred to me to think that where I worked or what I did was beneath me. I just did the job. In New York I experienced no discrimination because I was Hispanic. I did because I was female. You give everything you have to a job and when you get a promotion somebody says you got it because you are a woman!"

In 1965 Delia married Adrian Reyes, Puerto Rican by birth, New York City by rearing, and "Cuban in his thinking!" Their son, Victor, was born in 1971. It was then that her mother reverted to her cultural heritage. "My mother said I must stay at home and keep my child. My father encouraged me to continue working. I did quit working. It was my tradition."

In Dallas, Adrian Reyes started the Adrian Research Group and wanted Delia to come to work with him. She did. "I was surprised when some of the women showed jealousy. My husband said he needed me in the business and wanted me there. He respects my work. We separate our turf. He *never* introduces me as his wife." Working with Adrian has given her insights into the business that she could have gotten no other way, Delia said. "Every women must know her husband's business—and so few women do!"

Business led Delia, quite logically, to the Hispanic Chamber of Commerce, "where I was soon perceived as arrogant simply because I faced issues and spoke up. Hispanic women in Dallas are extremely submissive. I didn't know how to be." She survived because she was smart and "because I was not perceived as Hispanic. My attitude was if you can do the job, do it, and don't be intimidated by anything or anybody."

"I see Hispanics in Dallas *so* behind. Afraid to speak up. Women supporting men. So much holding back. So much fear. I tell them, 'Why be afraid? You have to learn to ask. The worst that can happen to you is they'll say no.' People self-discriminate. Strong women do not fear each other. I love to mentor strong women. I'm a good listener. I learn fast. I know my strengths and weaknesses and I call on my resources."

After more than a decade of observing, Delia believes she has some insight. She thinks that the problems of Mexican-Americans in Dallas are rooted in three main obstacles:

1. The Mexicans are so close to home. They have not embraced this country. They think of Mexico as home and many of them still want to go back, even those who were born here.

2. The Mexicans who come to Dallas (at the present time) are poor. They come to get a job. To buy a TV. To buy a car. To send money home.

3. Their culture keeps them stuck. They stay together. They don't aspire to an education because they don't have a history of achieving beyond the next pay check. The women don't understand why it's important to go to college because they're just going to get married. Their parents say, 'Why do you want to study? Why do you want to go away

Delia Reyes was a child of privilege in pre-Castro Cuba, a working "girl" in New York City, and then was totally surprised and puzzled by the Hispanic situation in Dallas. But she's helping to change all that.

from us? Settle for what you have. It was good enough for your grandparents. For your parents. And it's good enough for you."

"If it were not for this country," Delia reflects, "*where* would we have gone? This is home! Our son was born here." Tiny in size, a giant in intellect and passionate in temperament, Delia is at home with herself, at home in her chosen city and doing everything she can to move it into the next century for all of its citizens.

35

EXPANDING THE CIRCLE

Dallas went through a catharsis in the 1980s. Many foundations which had been constructed and were depended upon by the City Fathers crumbled. The economic base—agriculture, then oil, banking, insurance, real estate—was convulsive. Industries toppled. Businesses, by the score, went into bankruptcy. Others combined in mergers trying to survive. Along with the economy, many other institutions that had formed the foundation for physical growth collapsed.

It was a decade of chaos. Even those most familiar with the barometers of economics could not believe the fiscal debacle. With only occasional glitches the standard of living in America had risen for almost half a century. Two generations had grown up believing that a job, a house, a car and the accouterments of "the good life" was their due. Many thought the future really was unlimited. Some believed that riches were theirs for the taking. Young couples started their marriages with what their parents had taken a lifetime to acquire, and almost all expected to improve the economic lifestyle of the older generations. Living as most did from payday to payday, and often on credit, few had any financial cushion for what most major businesses euphemistically called "downsizing."

The reaction of most—organizations as well as individuals—was to keep on doing what had worked in the past, believing that harder work, longer hours, more attention to detail would get the ship on course again.

Dallas as a city was still more concerned with physical growth than for quality of life for its people. The 1981 "Greater Dallas/Dallas County, Texas City Directory," Volume II noted that Dallas became, in 1977, one of the five leading convention cities in the nation. For the year 1977-78, it was headquarters for 1,189 conventions bringing to the city women and men from all over the world, mostly to do business. Even when the conventions were not booked as financial endeavors, but were religious, fraternal and service assemblies, they gave the city a financial shot in the arm as hundreds of delegates poured into hotels, restaurants and retail establishments. Dallas provided more first class hotel and motel accommodations than any other city in the Southwest—23,000 rooms.

The Dallas World Trade Center provided 1.4 million square feet—later doubled in size—for foreign trade transactions.

Dallas County encircled 859 square miles which included 28 separate municipalities. Its metropolitan area included Collin, Denton, Ellis, Hood, Johnson, Kaufman, Parker, Rockwall, Tarrant and Wise Counties in addition to Dallas with a total of 8,360 square miles. Just before the financial collapse of its banking and oil empires, it had 2,060 companies with assets of a million dollars or more. Its economy was diverse: 17.7 per cent in retail trade; 17.4 per cent in services—business, personnel, medical and professional; 13.3 in government; 8.9 in wholesale trade; 7.6 in banking, finance, real estate and insurance; 6.7 in transportation, communications and utilities; 4.7 in contract construction and 1.2 in mining; the remainder a host of miscellany.

As a place to live in 1980, Dallas was the least expensive of all major cities. It cost a family of four $15,313 to live in Dallas compared to $15,483 for the same family of four in Atlanta; $15,488 in Houston; $16,337 in St. Louis; $16,486 in Kansas City; $16,547 in Cincinnati; $16,516 in Pittsburgh; $17,126 in Los Angeles; $17,204 in Baltimore; $17,211 in Seattle; $17,330 in Chicago; $17,411 in Cleveland; $17,427 in Detroit; $17,792 in Philadelphia; $18,026 in Washington; $28,529 in San Francisco; $19,972 in New York; $20,609 in Boston.

By 1984, the cost of living had climbed dramatically with a U.S. average of $24,207 required to maintain a median lifestyle for a family of four. In Dallas the cost was only $22,678.

Officially, Dallas still looked on its women as ornaments, the 1981 city directory bragging, "Dallas has a world-wide reputation for well-dressed women . . . understated elegance."

But two tremendously important things had happened to Dallas women: (1) They *knew* they were vital—and for reasons far beyond what they wore and how they looked, and (2) Qualities that had always been considered female were beginning to be recognized as essential in public as well as in private life.

Women had to learn to value themselves before they could teach the world to do so. They had to define themselves *for* themselves rather than accept the assigned male opinion—and they had to do it in sufficiently large numbers to command attention. They had to stop apologizing for who they were and what they thought, to stop being substitute men in their drab dress-for-success business suits, to honor and applaud themselves and each other, to laud their unique contributions rather than edit their remarks, present their contributions and adapt their appearance, behavior and their ideas in ways they thought most pleasing to men. When they could do this, they would then be free of the onus of control by manipulation.

Individual women had long done it, managing to function and contribute in a male-defined social structure.

Women communicating with each other across cultural boundaries greatly enhance the quality of life for all participants. Jehan Sadat, left, the guest of the Dallas Women's Foundation, pauses with Kay Bailey Hutchison.

In the 1980s, many Dallas women began to make the leap. Many became entrepreneurs, establishing their own businesses, hiring and training personnel in ways different from what they had been told was the proper road to success. Tired of hitting the glass ceiling, they struck out on adventures of their own. Many emulated the male model, but many pioneered new horizons. The most successful of them—consider Mary Kay Ash and Ebby Halliday—kept a keen eye on their company's bottom line, but never forgot the well-being of their employees. They ran businesses as humane as they were financially profitable and provided new models of corporate management that nurtured the human spirit along with the bank account.

Dallas offered excellent opportunities for women to establish and profit in their own businesses. With a 23 per cent response from members of the Dallas Forum, an organization of the city's leading businesswomen, the consensus was that "a very positive attitude toward women prevails." Judy Sims, chairman and chief executive officer of Software Spectrum, said that "Dallas has an incredible energy. There's a feeling that anything is possible because so many Dallasites have done the impossible. Julia Sweeney, president of Callas, Foster & Sweeney, who created her own organization after working for Neiman-Marcus and being society editor of *The Dallas Times Herald*, found "Dallas extremely open and welcoming—once a woman takes the plunge to go out on her own." Charlotte St. Martin, president and CEO of Loews Anatole Hotel, added that "Dallas rewards results."

The women were not Pollyannas. They said that the best way for a woman to get ahead in business was to create and manage her own organization. The second best way was to work for another woman who had established her own business and proved it profitable. In addition to Mary Kay Ash and Ebby Halliday, they named Valerie Freeman and Annette Hamilton. They said that women are still handicapped in many companies by "the prevalence of old attitudes about women in business," by their inability to borrow money, and by being excluded from meetings where decisions are made. "If I have equal access, I do fine," said one, "but I'm aware that the agenda brought to the table has often already been decided on the golf course or in the executive dining room—or in the men's room!" Groups that welcomed "token" women have sometimes felt threatened at the arrival of more than a safe allotted number and have "downsized" the allotment. And, there is still the old ogre of divide and conquer: pitting women and minorities against each other when the economic pie is divided.

There is a third way for a woman to be rewarded for an excellent performance—join a company and work for a male manager who has proved openness to minorities and women. Members of the Dallas Forum said the best companies in Dallas are JC Penney, NationsBank, Southwest Airlines and TU Electric. The best male bosses are W. R. Howell, Ron Anderson, Hugh McCall, Herb Kelleher, Erte Nye, John Alston, John Scovell and Trammell Crow.

Generally, women and men manage differently. The traditional male management model is one of command and control based on the assumption that money is the most important reward required to elicit peak performance from employees. Women have traditionally managed by persuasion and mediation based on the assumption that inclusion and sharing are equally as important as salary. As time goes on, both men and women are learning from each other, in many instances taking the best of both traditional management styles and creating new ways to work together. Many men who hired minorities and women only to comply with changing laws found new wealth in the employee mix.

There are at least five areas which indicate that corporate management is becoming friendlier to women:

1. Hiring. Even though women still do more of the routine, lesser-paid jobs in most companies, almost every career and profession now has a few women among male workers.
2. Promotion. There is no doubt that the number of women in positions of responsibility in large companies is increasing, though Julia Sweeney voiced the concerns of most businesswomen when she said, "Dallas women in *almost* top positions is encouraging, but it would be much more so if we could see more presidents and CEO's rather than stopping with vice presidents. Women are receiving promotions to *almost* top levels."
3. Remuneration. Equal pay for equal work prevails, though there are still pockets of resistance. To most young women it is unbelievable that only a few years ago there were blatant—and routinely accepted—salary discrepancies between men and women doing identical jobs, with the man always paid more.
4. Training. Today, when a woman gets a promotion, she is usually eminently qualified for the position, but she also has access to company-supported training programs. This is new. Until a very few years ago, a woman promoted to a high post lived isolated in her lonely aerie.
5. Sensitivity. As men and women work together for common goals, their unique skills and talents are exchanged and blended. Males in management are increasingly allowed to encompass more than the company's profit level in dealing with personnel, and women are sometimes expected to voice opinions and perceptions in company board rooms.

Dallas women's gifts to new management styles are much in evidence whether these skills are used to create businesses of their own, change the way things are done in large corporations, shared with CEO husbands, or change the community climate by osmosis. Lyda Hill, president of Hill Development Company, pointed out the exceptional contributions to the city by the professional caliber of its volunteers "Women learn they have the skills to create and operate their own businesses and their work in the community helps them to identify needed services."

So, out of confusion, out of conflict, out of chaos, Dallas women, with their inclusive styles of getting things done, are leading the way to cohesion.

While these sparks of change were being ignited, efforts were increasing to make the city more inclusive for its residents and more realistic in its claim of being an international city.

Dallas had long called itself an international city, but its concern had been based far more in goods than in services. Its progress toward being truly international came slowly and in ways that rarely made headlines. In the world of commerce, men were the movers and shakers and from the beginning of time, the exchange of goods often was the wedge that opened the doors to international relations. But in the ongoing day-today routines, it was mostly women who quietly worked within the system to forge changes in the foundations of the Dallas/Texas social order and women moving to the city bringing their expectations and gifts from other parts of the world who led the way for Dallas to be the international city it proclaimed itself to be. It had long been an international city in commerce—countless references in its recorded history proclaim it a city of business—but a civilized city demands much more than buying and selling and trading. Again, it was its women who best understood this.

Women accepted, albeit slowly at times, the gifts and talents of their sisters from other worlds in a way that men never had. Some foreign-born men had been Dallas citizens for years and had never been accepted as equals by the Dallas male establishment. Women did not have that problem because they were united in the core of their being—giving birth, nurturing the young, supporting their fathers, husbands and sons. Underneath the jargon of different tongues, the heart language of women was identical.

The business community still expected women to help create the social climate to promote international trade and economic expansion, but women and minorities were not supposed to *meddle* in the real world. This became clear in the 1980s when the International Society/Dallas-Fort Worth was formed. Though open to the public and including women and minorities on its board, it rarely sought members or the counsel from individuals of other organizations that had long been in existence. It was an elitist organization with no residents on its board or advisory board who were foreign-born. Statements such as the one made at a board meeting that the organization could not afford to have either a woman or a black take a position of leadership stamped it as a continuation of business as usual. In many ways, there was still an atmosphere of antiquated social posturing, of college fraternity/sorority exclusivity, that the organization would somehow be less powerful if it widened the circle to include all citizens. Its women's organization fit the old model. Called the Women's Committee of the International Society/DFW, its work included raising funds and providing volunteer time to develop programs, publicizing the group and publishing a newsletter.

For years foreign-born Dallasites had united into groups, social and religious, mostly to preserve their heritage and to provide places and events where they felt at home. These groups usually were created by and for the different nationalities that moved to the city. There were, through the years, organizations of almost every nationality—English, French, Spanish, Mexican, Czech, German, Irish, Norwegian, Greek, Italian, Arab, Chinese, Japanese, Turkish, Polish—to name only a few of them. Rarely was there any effort to mingle the nationalities. Though these clubs provided many advantages for their members, they tended to perpetuate divisiveness rather than to promote community. Because they were insular, old resentments of one group against another sometimes prevailed.

Dallas began to try to become an international city following World War II. The Dallas Council on World Affairs was one of its first efforts at international connectedness. It struggled to be inclusive, but its speakers were almost always chosen from the ranks of government with a large percentage having a military background. Because of this, their political leanings were predictable, and the leaders saw little need to hear the voices of people who did not agree with them. The Dallas Council on World Affairs' Committee for Foreign Visitors, directed for years by Lorrine Emery, was one bright spot for the city. It found Dallas hosts for people from foreign countries who were visiting in the area and provided Dallas citizens who participated with a hint of the riches that were possible when diverse peoples exchange ideas with each other. Lorrine did a masterful job with the program. The women's group of the Dallas Council, Les Femmes du Monde, supported the men's projects and, later, expanded into projects of its own.

In holding onto the old, Dallas proclaimed an international mayor's ball honoring the elitists—ambassadors, leaders of cities, the affluent and the would-be affluent. The chairmanship of the ball passed from one leading business entity in the city to another and was loosely held together from the Office of International Affairs, City of Dallas, an adjunct of the mayor's office. Those who held the "power" and those with sufficient money to buy it, were included. The very wealthy often spurned organized efforts,

---

Men expected women to provide the social amenities to promote business. They were not needed in the real world where decisions were made. For the most part women willingly complied.

circumvented the connections and found their own way through the maze to new creativity. Many who were doing yeoman work of turning Dallas into a city of greater diversity worked outside the establishment, did not feel included and were, in fact, not included.

These Dallas International Cultural and Social Circle members in the early 1970s are Virginia Turner from the Philippines, Annette van Oostveen from Indonesia, Morena Petsch from Italy and Ronnie Pearce from New Zealand.

Dallas had an international ball for almost a quarter of a century before the Mayor's International Ball, whose name was later changed to the Ambassador Ball, with all its glitter, was created. In 1959, following a Christmas party in the home of Marvin and Morena Fantozzi Petsch, 30 different nationalities—both native-born and foreign-born—formed the Dallas International Cultural and Social Circle. Continuing through the years, its purpose was to "provide a social environment for those who found themselves in a strange and foreign land without friends, thus helping members of the community to grow in mutual understanding and friendship and rendering assistance to people who moved to Dallas from other countries.

The Circle in its name connoted its threefold purpose: social, educational and cultural. The social came first because, Morena Petsch said: "when people's social needs are met, they take care of the rest of their needs by themselves." The social needs were met through parties, travel, picnics, boating, sports and climaxed with an annual gala ball and international dinner, the forerunner of the mayor's international ball. Its educational contributions were in several ways. English classes were offered from the first. Other languages—Spanish, French, German, Russian, Chinese and others—were taught by educated natives from the different countries. Informal discussion groups in different languages helped to keep club members attuned to their own native tongues while providing English-speaking members an opportunity to converse in other languages. The organization also offered citizenship classes. It taught courses in American history and provided translators and interpreters. This service was of special value to the medical community as increasing numbers of foreign-born patients arrived to be treated in a country whose customs and languages were different from their own. The cultural portion of the circles helped to broaden the knowledge and wealth of people from over the world through programs featuring art, music, films, travel, food, speakers, folk dances and seminars.

Though its gifts to Dallas have been many—and largely unheralded—its greatest contribution was in helping individuals born in other lands with different customs, languages and cultures to feel like Dallas was their home. Toward that goal, its women taught new citizens how to shop in the American retail businesses, especially in grocery stores. Food that is unknown, prepared in ways that are untried, often is one of the primary causes of homesickness. Women have helped new residents find health care, have instructed them about inoculations for their children, and, in most instances, have provided transportation to physicians and support while they undergo examinations. The organization had helped people find employment and housing. Many times Morena and Marvin Petsch have hosted foreign-born guests in their home until the new arrivals complete a medical program, get enrolled in college or find suitable housing of their own.

It took her native country to recognize and honor Morena Petsch's gifts to her adopted homeland. In 1983 Italy gave her its top honor for "humanitarian effort" to America.

Women have helped their sisters from other lands to enroll their children in schools. Most of all they have been family to women whose birth families are thousands of miles away. They have been present at birth, rites of passage and death. They have planned and been present for christenings, communions, bridal showers, weddings, birthday parties, presentations, wakes and funerals.

Though she has had many helping hands during the years, Italian-born Morena Petsch and her American-born husband of German descent, Marvin, have been the adhesive that kept the organization going and the catalysts that have moved it forward. Morena is a woman whose passion for community began in the village of Pescia near Florence, Italy, on April 12, 1922. She was with the International Red Cross when she met Marvin during World War II. Following their marriage at the end of the war, Marvin brought her home to Luckenbach, Texas, and to Dallas in 1953. Brilliantly educated—pre-med at the University of Pisa, Italy; languages at Grenoble University, France, and Goethe Institute of German Language, Munich; Italian and International Red Cross Nursing in Florence; Swiss Reusch School of Nursing in Naples—she was tapped to teach Italian at Southern Methodist University shortly after her arrival in the city. The birth of two daughters curtailed her teaching career, and she and became a travel consultant and community volunteer.

With a command of eight languages, Morena communicated with most people in their native tongue. Her work as an international Red Cross nurse brought her in contact with soldiers from all over the world and made her a person of the universe. The value of the human being without regard to race, color, background, gender, political or religious bent or age was bred in her from the moment of her birth. She grew up, the fifth of seven children in a small village noted worldwide for its international flower market, "where we absorbed the worth of each human being. Our parents stressed our mutual humanity and the beauty of our individual roles in the human family. I never thought about differences in nationalities, cultures, languages, politics or religion until I was grown."

For Morena and Marvin and their two daughters, the international club brought anguish as well as benefits. Because it is an ugly story that she is not comfortable repeating, not even those who befriended her and the organization know about the innuendos and outright threats surrounding her work. "A little group of Dallasites embraced and supported us from the beginning, but to many we threatened what they called their American way of life." She referred to the period in which the organization began, the Joseph McCarthy era when many people were looking for Communists under every bush. "The Cultural part of our name was thought to refer to a cultural revolution." Threatening telephone calls kept the family on edge. "My little girl was sick one day and home from school. She answered the telephone and the caller told her to tell Mrs. Petsch they were going to kill her husband and her children. I was outside. Patti ran out of the house screaming." There were other anonymous threats. The shocking episodes continued until the Kennedy Assassination.

"Americans," Morena Petsch said, "are very generous. I can't say too much about the love and generosity I have experienced as an adopted American. But I learned through the years to be very cautious about what I said because I have been so often misunderstood or mis-interpreted. Americans know it all. They ask your opinion and then do not listen. Some of it is a carry-over from the war—an individual is blamed for the real or perceived wrongs of her country. People all the time tell me *who* I am and *what* the country of my birth is. It usually doesn't bear the slightest resemblance to the truth.

The low profile of DICSC in the Dallas area has kept its deeds largely unknown. "Good deeds are tainted when they are talked," Morena once said. So it is that the work of the organization has rarely received the credit it is due as an international catalyst. There are a few exceptions. In 1965 the James Campbell Chapter of the Daughters of the American Revolution honored Morena with its annual Americanism Medal, and in 1988 she was recognized by J.C. Penney with a community volunteer award. It was not, however, her beloved adopted country where she became a citizen in 1947, but her native land that singled her out for her most prestigious honor. In 1983 the President of Italy cited her with its Cavaliere nell'Ordino Al Merita della Republica Italiano, its top honor

Ruth Miller and her daughter, Abbie, left, and Kathie Smallwood and her mother, Sarah. At right, Nedra Patrice James, her mother, Barbara Minor James, and her mother, Irma Pierce Minor.

No better way exists to expand the circle of human understanding than for mothers to pass along their gifts to their daughters. In current American society, this has not been a popular thing to do. It is condoned and approved for fathers to support their sons, pass along their names, their influence, their wealth and often, their professions, and secure mentors for them from their own circle of associates. But mothers do not share their innermost secrets with their daughters; they do not talk about their passions, dreams, disappointments or even their reality. They communicate on a surface level and with trivia. And, so, a stereotype has been created that makes friction between mothers and daughters both natural and inevitable. This notion is aberrant. Nowhere in any society at any time, except in America, and in recent times, has it been the norm for mothers and daughters to live in discord. When mothers tell their daughters their secrets, and listen carefully for their responses, the personal relationships will be immeasurably enriched and the circle of human understanding will be expanded. On these pages are a few Dallas daughters with their mothers.

Beverly Mitchell-Brooks and her daughters, Stacy Ann and Teri Dawn Mitchell.

Olga Platko Mowchan and her daughter, Barbara Middleton.

Nellie Tafalla and her daughters, Theresa Tafalla and Roseann Tafalla Bersterman and Roseann's daughter, Stephanie, at left. Above, Sybil Hamilton and her daughters, Lea, Becky and Vicki; at right, Amy Haas Brau, her daughter, Rose-Mary Brau Rumbley, and her daughter, Jill.

EXPANDING THE CIRCLE / 397

Dr. Genevieve Shea, her daughter, Patricia Brown Currin, and her daughters, Mary Beth Currin Burns and Claire Currin Murad.

Peggy Ladenberger and her daughters, Susan Ladenberger Garza, Jan Ladenberger Person and Judy Ladenberger Burnett.

Above, left, Suzanne Ahn and her mother, Sun Tuk Ahn; center, Annette Strauss and daughter, Nancy; right, Jewel Cates and daughter, Julie. Left, Carolyn Saunders and daughter, Lisa; right, Mrs. Lindsley Waters and daughter, Virginia Waters Shuford. Bottom, left, Ruth Woodall Collins, her daughter, Ruth Collins Sharp and her daughters, Sally and Susan, and, right, Johnnie Keany and her daughters, Kim and Kelly.

to "select individuals for their humanitarian efforts." The medal of honor was presented at special ceremonies in Dallas's Lakewood Country Club.

In America, one of the rites of adulthood is the acquisition of a home and so it was especially significant to Morena Petsch and to DICSC members when the club dedicated a building of its, the International Center, at 6033 Berkshire Lane. Mayor Wes Wise, the keynote speaker for the dedication ceremonies, proclaimed it "international friendship and understanding day."

While DICSC was inclusive from its beginning, some foreign-born citizens did not find a home within its circle—and like any groups left out—formed its own.

The Dallas International Center's "angel" is Jeannette Early, left, with center supporters Carolyn Langham, Linda Evans, Rita Malik and founder/director Kwasi Ohene-Bekoe.

The Dallas International Center is one such group. Founded in the fall of 1987 to "promote international understanding and goodwill through counseling, public education, cultural interchange and through international business consulting services," it intended to reach "members from every region of the world." It has been moderately successful. Working under the motto, "Humanity is indivisible and universally interdependent," its success in the Dallas community is largely attributable to one person: Dr. Kwasi Ohene-Bekoe.

Kwasi is a native of Ghana, West Africa, who holds degrees from Osei Tutu College in Ghana and Trinity College in Ghana. He taught on a college level before arriving in Dallas in 1968 where he earned a master of theology from Perkins School of Theology at SMU and a master of arts in political science and public administration from SMU in 1973. In 1982 he received his doctorate in ministry from SMU. For a decade he was assistant director of the Martin Luther King Center where he helped to establish the Foreign Peoples Assistant Program Council. Ordained in the British Methodist Church (Ghana), he is the founding minister of the International Church of the Metroplex, whose core members are also connected with the International Center, though the two are entirely separate.

Ignored and forgotten is the fact that Dr. Ohene-Bekoe is singularly responsible for the establishment of the city's office of international affairs. The chain of events that preceded it happened in 1975. Emmanuel Olatunji, a 28-year-old Bishop College student from Nigeria was pumping gas into his car at a convenience store on Monday night, August 25, 1975, when the store was robbed by two men. Police officers arrived and Olatunji was pointed out as a possible suspect. Told to freeze, he ran instead, apparently understanding neither American customs nor the meaning of the words. Shot once in the head, he died. Subsequent investigation proved him innocent.

When Nigerian officials in Washington, D. C., began an investigation into the death of their countryman, there was nobody in Dallas available to respond. The mayor was out of the city and other elected officials had no authority to respond to calls. The

Nigerian ambassador called the ambassador from Ghana and he, in turn, got in touch with Kwasi who at that time was president of the African International Relations Association. Many telephone calls later what could have been an international tragedy of major proportions was averted. Dr. Ohene-Bekoe, in his role as a minister as well as a public servant, spoke at a memorial service for Olatunji. The lead paragraph of a news story at the time promised . . . ."he will not be a forgotten man."

Today almost nobody remembers. For Kwasi the tragedy crystallized the imperative need for a Dallas official who could respond quickly to questions of international import. He presented this message to the mayor and pressed for its resolution. Appointed by the mayor he then worked on a committee of three which recommended an international ambassador for the city to be administered from the mayor's office. Passed by the City Council, the organization was created. In 1974 George Schrader, then city manager, expressed to Dr. Ohene-Bekoe, "sincere appreciation for the many contributions you have made toward the achievement of an international understanding in Dallas."

A researcher and writer, Dr. Bekoe is the author of the *Globogram*, a series of publications on the countries of the world that includes concise but intensive information on the people, geography, and institutional and infrastructural aspects of each country. The *Globogram* is written and published under the auspices of the International Center and all profits go back to the Center. The other public service to Dallas is the Center's Humanities-International public lecture series supported by the Texas Committee for the Humanities, a state program of the National Endowment for the Humanities. This series of monthly lectures is open to the public and features eminent speakers from throughout the world followed by a question and answer period. In a 1990 interview published in *D* magazine, Kwasi said that "world-class buildings and airline schedules are mere window dressing on a truly international city. Only international people, woven into the local community at every economic, cultural and intellectual level, can give that glossy facade a global heart."

The growth of the international community in the city speaks to the global heart of the matter, for the Dallas population of foreign-born residents grew from around 5,000 in 1979 to more than 50,000 in 1989. There were, for instance, 60 residents from Poland in 1969 and 3,000 a decade later; there were only six Ethiopians in 1979 and 5,000 in 1989. The most explosive population, predictably, were the Vietnamese which expanded from 50 in 1979 to 26,000 a decade later.

Though there is scant recognition of the international lectures by the Dallas community, many who have presented programs in the series have been impressed. Professor Gordon Bennett of the University of Texas at Austin noted that: "Elitist foreign affairs organizations abound. If the International Center stands out, it for being the opposite." H. Bradford Westerfield, the Damon Wells Professor of International Studies at Yale, wrote following his lecture in 1990: "The diversity of the audience . . . was truly impressive as was their alert interest and intelligent questioning . . . .These are people who would probably not be reached by the conventional foreign affairs organizations but are attentive . . . and educated . . . (and) embody the important changes that are making Dallas an international city that connects with all of the Eastern Hemisphere not just all of the Western Hemisphere as many people have traditionally perceived Dallas . . . . you are clearly making worthy efforts to bring together people who might otherwise tend to stick in very separate narrow niches." When Dallas journalist Lee Cullum spoke in the spring of 1990, she wrote: "I was very impressed with the diversity and seriousness of the audience. Those were the most thoughtful questions and comments I have ever received after a speech." Further, Lee wrote, "I don't believe we can build one (international affairs) without the other (humanities). The only way to establish a peaceful, productive, humane world order is through the two great international languages of arts and the sciences. These are the disciplines that transcend national boundaries and speak to the hearts and minds of . . . people."

The program management council of the International Center exemplifies the diversity noted by lecturers. It is chaired by Rita Malik of Pakistan and includes 30 women and 25 men from 24 different countries. Dr. Ohene-Bekoe is married to Carol Mignon Coulter Ohene-Bekoe, who is associate director of personnel at SMU. They have three children, Ama, born December 18, 1972, who is a student at Georgetown University's School of Foreign Relations; Akua, born December 31, 1982, and Danquah, born February 27, 1984. The younger daughter and son are Lakewood school students.

Dr. Ohene-Bekoe credits women with keeping the International Center open. In addition to Rita Malik, he cites Jeannette Early, Linda Evans, Marie Wong, Anne Bavarian, Monique Norjaim, Tina Bruner and Colleen Hennicke—and four special men—Drs. Willis Tate, Russell Perry, Fred Streng and Richard Rubottom. Dr. Tate, Perry and Streng are deceased. "Mrs. Early has been the Center's angel. I would have had to padlock the door if it had not been for her."

Jeannette Brown Early, a native of Waco, was honored by the Center in 1991. She began her international citizenship at Baylor University where she made friends with a Japanese girl. In 1937 she married Allen M. Early. For the next 12 years they moved often, and lived in many states "where I made it a point to invite international students and other foreign-born people to our home on a regular basis for entertainment and informal cultural exchange." The Earlys were host family to a German boy, one of the first six students to enter the United States on the American Field Services Program. In 1949 the Earlys settled in Dallas and 20 years later established the Early Foundation, which Jeannette insists is "no big thing." Assiduously avoiding publicity because she adheres to the Biblical admonition, "let not thy left hand know what they right hand doeth," Jeannette has quietly contributed to countless causes that promote human connectedness. "It is a great feeling to contribute to something that seeks to enrich the quality of life for people regardless of race, color, creed, national origin, or ideological persuasion, she said. "I believe in the integration and interdependence of the human family."

As Dallas headed toward the 21st century, it was in many ways still an international city in name only. Its official stance was still elitist and limited though its leaders were saying the right things and its promise was unlimited.

36

FUTURE UNLIMITED

As research and interviews for this book concluded, many women spoke of Dallas as a "spiritual" place, and almost all were on a personal spiritual quest. They see Dallas facing many challenges yet to be resolved, but like their predecessors who established a city on a prairie, they expect their "can do" spirit to prevail.

Dallas, nearing the dawn of the twenty-first century, had unlimited potential. It had experienced tremendous internal agonies in the past few years, but the fiscal and political pangs of the recent past were no more critical than they had been in earlier times. The darkest days of Dallas were the 1860s when two crises almost wiped out the fledgling village. First, the town had burned leaving only a very few buildings. Then, in while trying to come to grips with that tragedy, the Civil War erupted, creating a climate of financial disaster and human distrust.

Like the mythical phoenix, Dallas rose from the ashes in greater splendor than before. It was, perhaps during this period that the "Can Do" spirit of Dallas was born.

A century later, in the 1960s it faced another kind of crisis. While the country was enjoying the most prolonged economic boom in its history, segments of its heretofore unacknowledged population—its citizens of color, its women and its youth—demanded recognition. The war in Vietnam divided Dallasites as it divided the rest of the country, though the financial heyday eclipsed both civil unrest and the women's movement in the city and hid local agitation against the Vietnam war. This failure to acknowledge and deal with problems has resulted in a much longer and more painful coming to terms with social and political issues.

Dallas will continue to encounter paroxysms in the future as some of its old guard relentlessly try to apply old methods of problem-solving to a new day and others of its emerging leadership agitate for instant innovation. It will continue to make mistakes, as it has in the past when too often its master plans for steady growth have been filed away in bottom desk drawers and forgotten.

But its future is bright. It has shown that it can survive all kinds of crises and move on to new adventures. Those who have been left out of the decision-making process are being included. Its women are gaining an equal say in what happens to it—not only in the influence they have on its men but in their own right. Its women have paid the price of participation and taken positions side by side and shoulder to shoulder with its male leaders. It has now had women in every position of responsibility in the city and will have others. It has given its daughters, as well as its sons, the unwritten and unspoken message that it is all right for them to express their opinions, vote their convictions, and manage their lives as co-partners in their city.

Women of its past wielded their power primarily through boudoir politics. Women of its present and future are expressing their opinions and voting their convictions from the seats of responsibility.

Slowly, but with absolute certainty, the day of benevolent dictatorship when the city was controlled by old white men, is passing away.

And if, as some people believe, women are being elected to city and county offices only because these positions are perceived as insignificant, so be it. If, as some people say, women are being given the chore of cleaning up the garbage of the city just as they have been responsible for clearing away the debris of the homes, they are equal to the task. Women are very good at bringing order out of the world's messes. They are, in fact, leading the way to a more inclusive future.

Redistricting so that the city can have representation from several of its ethnic groups created a city-wide brouhaha. At times, as in past crises, it seemed impossible to resolve, but it, like crises of the past, has been laid to rest to the satisfaction of many, if

Annette Strauss headed the City of Dallas during critical times—and retired at the end of her second term with conviction that she had done a good job.

not most, of the principals demanding change. In the future Dallas must be sensitive to other emerging leadership. Its Asian population has grown at a phenomenal rate, and just ahead is the time when it must have a visible position in elective and appointive offices. Whether this comes with a clamor or in the natural course of change will depend on those who hold the reins of responsibility as well as on individual leaders of the under-represented groups.

Inclusion will continue to be a problem until such a time when diversity is respected as a true wealth.

At a new crossroads, Dallas is emerging into community—again. Scott Peck, the eminent psychiatrist and writer, in his book, *The Different Drum—Community Making and Peace*, says that community-making goes through four stages: pseudo-community, chaos, emptiness and community. In Peck's analysis, pseudo-community consists of a group's attempt to "fake it," to come together in almost instant harmony. Chaos is the clamorous stage of misguided attempts to heal and convert. Emptiness is the letting go of barriers that keep individuals from hearing each other. Community is understanding of and appreciation for diversity, those who disagree as well as those who are of similar opinions. A group comes into community only when it goes through—not around or over or under—all of these stages.

In Dallas, especially among women, there is a fifth stage and none of the stages appear to be as critical for women in groups as they are for men in groups. Women, by their conditioning, see and feel the distress of others and are willing to move around, reach out and make way for new people with new ideas.

The five stages—with due credit and grateful appreciation to Scott Peck and other researchers and writers—are simulation, search, struggle, space and synergy.

At the International Women's Peace Conference, M. Scott Peck, right, delivered a keynote address at the invitation of Ruth Tiffany Barnhouse, center, who opened the conference. Barbara Middleton, who chaired the spiritual renewal center is at right.

Simulation is surface. It consists of the open smiles, hefty handshakes, casual kisses and false embraces proffered among people who are determined to be in instant rapport with each other. At its best, it is good manners, a pleasant way to greet others who will be in only limited, casual contact, but it is an entirely false premise on which to base a continuing relationship. You see simulation in every single new Dallas group. Men often circle the table or move about rows of seats shaking hands and exchanging pleasantries. Women, especially in mixed groups, are more reserved. Some hide away on the back rows. A false sense of hope often underlain with suspicion permeates the room. In all-female groups, women embrace, exchange cheek kisses, wave across space at others they recognize. For neither men nor women is there any depth of exchange.

Search is the second stage. As women begin to work together, they share confidences, becoming increasingly comfortable with each other. They are genuinely eager to understand where their experiences are similar and where they differ. They want to know what has worked best in other homes, in other organizations, in other societies. There is an atmosphere of benign gossip, the exchange of trivia, the search for commonalty. They are sometimes puzzled by the attitudes and methods of other women, but they rarely ignore or dismiss others' truths.

Struggle is the third stage, struggle because among women's groups there is rarely the total chaos of men in groups. Only occasionally does a woman find differences so painful that she leaves the group and slams the door behind her. When men and women are together in groups, the men usually dominate the conversation, ask the questions, give the answers. Women alone listen to each other much more carefully and are much more eager to reach consensus. The most dramatic example in present times is the abortion issue. When men are not present, when women are not taking their direction from male leadership, it is entirely possible for them to hear and understand each other. Though there is absolute conviction by some that women must be free to choose and absolute conviction by others that all abortion is evil, most women can move past these impediments, stop trying to convert each other and work together for common goals. The struggle toward community is not as difficult for women because they are more flexible, more willing to mediate, more determined that everybody wins.

Space is the fourth stage. Peck calls it emptiness. Space is at once the most difficult and the most essential stage on the journey to community. Space is an especially hazardous stage for women because they are accustomed to filling every niche of their time with activity. They handle the world's trivia and operate on several planes simultaneously. The minutiae and the essential get equal time. Women's actions move from the report due at the office to their children's homework, to their mother's health problems, to a budget hearing, to tonight's casserole, *ad infinitum*. Relaxation for most women means shifting gears to other responsibilities. Yet, every woman knows the compelling need to get away from it all, to clear the clutter from her brain, to become an empty vessel. In space there are no givens, no *ought* tos, few absolutes. In space, even when it sometimes feels that nothing good ever will happen again, there is healing and those who dare to go through it come out on the other side refreshed, renewed, forgiving, in peace and ready to move on to new frontiers.

Synergy is the final stage. Synergy is like a concert. In fact, one of the synonyms for synergy is concert. Like a fine orchestra, where instruments are different, each contributing its own special tone to the music, groups in synergy work in symphony to reach a common goal. Synergy is Peck's community. Synergy is sharing, joint participation, exchange. Synergy is communion.

Dallas is coming into synergy. It will not always be so. There will be differences in the days ahead among leaders and among those who are being led, a difference of opinion between ethnicities and among individuals of the same ethnic background, friction between those who have wealth and those who do not, misunderstandings between those who are divided along age lines or interest lines or religious lines or political lines—or gender lines. But it is clear again that resolutions can be reached and that many, many more of its people will have a voice in the decisions.

At its 150th birthday, Dallas was led by a woman mayor. Annette Strauss, the first woman to be elected to the position of mayor, had been preceded by Adlene Harrison, who served a few months in 1977 as interim mayor. Annette prepared for city government serving as a councilperson-at-large from 1983 until 1987, from 1984 to 1987 as mayor pro-tem. In 1987 she was elected mayor following a heated campaign during which many of the people she expected to support her did not. Nearing the end of her two terms as mayor, she speculated on the reasons for this lack of support at the outset from some of the men she had counted on.

"When I ran for mayor (the first time), the business establishment did not support me. There were many reasons for this, but I think underlying it all was fear of the unknown. A woman as elected mayor was new. These were men I knew, men I'd worked with on boards, men who said they were my friends. It was hurtful. But I have to say with few exceptions, they all called me after the election and promised their support.

"These were Good Old Boys; they *are* good old boys. And I don't use that term in a derogatory way. They are *good* for this city and I admire and respect them for what they've given and are still giving to Dallas." When she got into the political arena, her good friend, Adlene Harrison, and many men, including her brother-in-law, Robert

Strauss, who had spent a great part of his life in the public domain, told her what to expect. "I thought I was prepared," she said in retrospect, "but nobody is until they do it themselves. It's something you have to learn on the job."

Annette Louise Greenfield Strauss was heading a city that had no place for her professional talents when she arrived to make her home in it on January 1, 1947. Born in Houston to J. B. and Edith Weinberger Greenfield, on January 26, 1924, she was educated in the Houston public schools, graduated at age 16, attended Rice University for one year and transferred to the University of Texas at Austin. She completed her bachelor's degree in sociology in 1944 with honors and a Phi Beta Kappa key, having been named the outstanding woman speaker in the Southwest.

Already in love with Theodore S. Strauss, whom she had met during her junior year, she went to New York, enrolled in the graduate program at Columbia University and earned her master's in sociology and psychology in one year while working as a John Roberts Powers model. "I planned to get a degree in social work," she said, "but I really was not happy in New York. I wanted to come home and get married." She returned to Houston and worked for a year as a field case worker for the Red Cross before she and Ted were married on September 8, 1946. They spent three months in Stamford where Ted worked in his father's dry good store during the Christmas holidays. They started 1947 in Dallas in an apartment at 4124 Hyer. "That was in University Park," Annette says. "I didn't know there was a University Park. To me it was all Dallas. Still is. To be separate is dumb."

Ted Strauss went to work for the new radio station KIXL. His take-home pay was $138 a month. He earned an extra $7 a day by going to the station at 6 a.m. and conducting a call-in talk show that he called "Poor Old Ted." To supplement their income, Annette tried to find a job in her professional field. "Nobody wanted me. I tried everywhere— the Council of Social Agencies. the Jewish Welfare Federation. The Red Cross." Finally she and Adlene, as volunteers, were put in charge of a swimming class. "The only job I could get was as a model at Neiman-Marcus." She worked for special shows and as a photographer's model. "We needed the money. We were living on Ted's salary and on money we got as wedding presents." She supported Ted's work by mailing post cards from points over the city lauding his show and asking questions for him to answer on the air.

Their social life evolved around their college friends who lived in Dallas. "Bob and Helen Strauss and others, Ted's friends and mine from college days. From the second day of her residence in the city, Annette was a volunteer. "Some of my friends were working on the United Jewish Appeal Drive. They were doing a benefit. I volunteered and went to work on January 2. My first volunteer job in the city was as a fund raiser." Known as the definitive leader among women in city-wide campaigns to raise money, Annette had led campaigns that raised $10 million by 1989.

Her daughters, Nancy Strauss Halbreich (Mrs. Jeremy) and Janie Strauss McGarr (Mrs. Cappy) joined the family in 1950 and 1954 respectively. During all the years of their growing up, Annette arranged her volunteer commitments so that she could participate fully in their rearing and in activities that mattered to them.

The city of Dallas during those years was "was a *lot* smaller, really a little town. It was run by business. A lot of good came out of that. That is not true today. Today Dallas is not run by anybody. You have to hear the voices of many, many people. Sometimes there are too many voices. The clamor impedes progress, but it's the democratic way and works better for all of the people." She is reflective as she makes these comments, speaking of petty controversies that often took precedence over significant issues of city government.

As a volunteer, Annette Strauss created many organizations and headed many of the significant ones. But she began in the "vineyards" of service in what she termed her "stuffing and stamping" period, the time when she was starting at the bottom, learning her way as well as the ways of the community and advancing step by step up the ladder to leadership. When she was asked to do something, she accepted the responsibility "if I thought I could do it and people would benefit from it. I tried never to accept anything

As Annette Strauss, the first elected woman mayor in Dallas, wound down her two terms, she spoke of her vision for the city. Annette Strauss began her public service in what she called her "stuffing and stamping" stage and step by step climbed the ladder of social responsibility to the very top. Her ability to be patient and hear every voice was new at City Hall. Most former mayors had listened only to city leaders before doing what was good for Dallas.

that didn't appeal to me personally and I especially would not take something I didn't believe in wholeheartedly." Even so, that covered a multitude of tasks.

When First Lady Patricia Nixon chose volunteerism as her focus on the nation's problems during the presidency of her husband, cities throughout the country hastened to establish Volunteer Action Centers. Dallas already had one. It was called SERV (Special Effort to Recruit Volunteers). It had been organized three years before by Annette Strauss, Martha Lynch and Connie Condos in Annette's living room. She was its first president and its emphasis, like that of the new national group was to coordinate volunteer services. To take advantage of the excellent organization already in existence, Dallas answer to the new national group was called DVAC-SERV.

Annette's influence and personal service spread far beyond the local community; she sat on state and national boards, serving as president of several of them. But she always came home to Dallas with her gifts of time, money and organizational skills. In 1974 she chaired the Crystal Charity Ball, the community's *creme de creme* party that had distributed millions of dollars to local worthy causes. Predictably, she raised more money than any prior chairperson.

As a volunteer Annette Strauss had peaked. What next? In an interview following that success, as a reporter I asked that question. Her answer was, "I haven't the slightest idea." I said she should run for public office; the city needed her in a decision-making position. She said the idea was absolutely crazy; she hadn't the remotest idea of doing such a thing.

"At that time the idea was crazy," she said in a 1991 interview. But not nearly as crazy as she thought at the time. Having given all of her time as a volunteer serving always on a professional level for three decades, Annette Strauss's decision for the next period of her life was to earn a paycheck. She was persuaded to go to work as a public relations consultant for Bozell and Jacobs Inc. She did it, she said at that time, because the world evaluated a person's worth by how much money she made, "and I wanted to see if I could cut it." But she negotiated her hours so that she could retain her volunteer commitments. It was not long before she was promoted to vice president.

Five years later, in 1983, Annette ran for city council. Her victory was a landslide, 70 per cent of the total vote in a five candidate race for Place 10, an at-large position. She had hardly been seated until she was selected deputy pro-tem and, a year later, mayor pro tem. In 1987 she was elected mayor of Dallas.

History will write the chapter on Annette Strauss's major contributions. She served the city for four and a half years that turned out to be pivotal. When she was sworn into office, the economy was skidding and by the time her mayorship was half over many of the financial institutions that had supported the city were no more. The biggest banks had been consumed by outsiders. The oil industry had plummeted. Retail stores whose names were synonymous with Dallas merged or closed. Real estate had come to a standstill. Over-built in the plush times, thousands of offices in high rise-buildings were vacant. After six o'clock in the afternoon, downtown Dallas had more the look of a mausoleum than a thriving metropolis.

City government *appeared* to be virtually non-functional. Every minority group wanted representation. This would have been much easier to do if there had not been thousands of individual voices and individual needs *within* each separate group. Public meetings, including city council meetings, sometimes wound up in shouting matches. For almost two years the people of Dallas and its governmental structures haggled over re-districting. It was, as Annette Strauss would say later, "a painful time. A growing time. A hurting time. And not so much for me—though I was hurting—as for the city. We could not afford to have things blow apart."

But there was a light at the end of the tunnel, and when the history of the city during his period is written, the mayor will stand out as a beacon of light, a harbinger of hope. Her gifts were countless, but probably can be best summed up in two words: patience and perseverance. There were many who faulted her for those very traits; they remembered the "good old days" when the city fathers spoke and everybody marched in tandem behind them. They were certain that a man, someone who was tough and forceful, could have avoided most of the chaos. Some believed, as one said, "If Bob Thornton

Gail Thomas is Dallas's definitive futurist who not only envisions a new day, but works step by step to make the dreams a reality. Like the dawn of a clear day, she sees old systems breaking apart only to make way for the future.

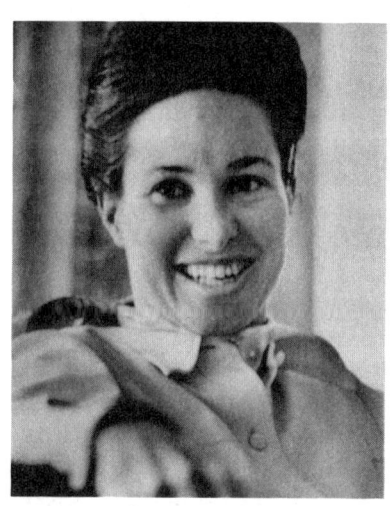

With the leadership of women like this trio, Dallas's future will be a better place to live and work. They are, from the top, Suzanne Ahn, Lyda Hill and Regina Montoya. While they center their service in their professions—medicine, business and law—each has a world view inclusive of people everywhere.

were mayor, all this nonsense would cease," and a quieter voice responded: "If a Bob Thornton were mayor today, there would be blood in the streets." The city cannot, of course, go back, do it over and know how things might have turned out differently if one of the tough guys had been in charge. But the chances are highly likely that chaos would have erupted into violence, because the world had changed, the city had changed, people's expectations of their city and for themselves had altered dramatically.

"If I had one gift," said Mayor Strauss near the end of her tumultuous tenure, "it was in my willingness to listen. I have a passionate belief that I had to make my decision, after listening to all of the voices, based on my personal confidence that I was doing the right thing. Before I took a position, I had to know how people felt about the issue. If I made a decision based on who screamed the loudest for attention, how could I be sure that somebody else wouldn't scream louder tomorrow?"

And what kind of city was she was turning over to the next mayor? "A good city. At a good time. The City Council I served as mayor *did* work together, even at times when all we saw reflected in the press were our points of disagreement. We did many good things for the city." The economy is edging upward. Many of the housing problems have been solved; most of the homeless have, at least, a place to go—whether they go there or not. Public education is headed in the right direction. Crime is down, "not as much as we had hoped it would be. But we are no longer the No. 1 crime city in the nation . . . or anywhere near it." Job opportunities are increasing as new industries choose Dallas for their home base. Real estate is moving again, sluggishly but surely.

"And the Spirit of Dallas is just fantastic. When the history of this period is written, it won't be a tale of two cities, but a story of one city struggling to give each one of its people an opportunity to take advantage of an opportunity. There's one thing that's in this city's favor: Dallas, Texas, is the best place in America to live and do business."

Gail Griffin Thomas is Dallas's definitive futurist. Standing on the cutting edge of change, she has both feet firmly planted in the traditions—the continuity—of the city and a mind that envisions the grandeur of what is possible for the future.

Gail was born with, grew up with, came of age with and matured with this double vision and, sometimes, double burden. Only as she reached the half century mark in her own life was she able to integrate and express the coming together of the things she had inherited and acquired.

Gail was born on August 24, 1937, the fourth child, third daughter of James Isaac and Electra West Griffin. Two older sisters, Gretta Griffin Coulter and Betty Griffin, and a brother, James Isaac Griffin III, were already a part of the Princeton, Texas, family. She was already married, already a professional psychologist before she understood that she had had an "idyllic childhood. I felt protected. I was loved. I grew up in a family that both shielded me and gave me the message that I must become and excel at being my own person."

The growing up, itself, might have produced ambivalence instead of the giftedness Gail inherited. From the time she was a year old the family lived for half of every year in McKinney, six miles from the place of her birth, and the other six months in Rocky Ford, Colorado. In Princeton and McKinney, a short distance north of Dallas, she was a child of the metropolis. She watched from the back seat of the family car competing with her siblings for the first sight of Pegasus, the red horse flying atop the Magnolia building that was the harbinger of a shopping expedition at Neiman-Marcus. In Rocky Ford, rural and agricultural, she lived in the fantasy land of make-believe, often lying on her back in the haystacks conversing with the birds and weaving magic stories from her own imagination. "The two sides of me were always kept alive. There was the very social side acceptable to the outside world and the very introspective side, a world of books, myths and healing. I am still living both sides," she said in a 1991 interview. I live them both every day . . . ." She paused: "Now they are more and more coming together."

Gail skipped her senior year in high school and completed the twelfth grade in a private school in Rhode Island. She enrolled in SMU when she was 16. "I felt like I had

Dallas as a spiritual center is enhanced by these three leaders, from top, Catalina Garcia, Caroline Rose Hunt and Beverly Laughlin Brooks. They are professionals in health, business and insurance, but their service to humanity is countless.

been introduced to the world. I know now it was a very narrow view bounded by the Park Cities and North Dallas, by sororities and fraternities." There she continued to lead a double life. A philosophy major, she probed ideas and issues far into the night with her professors and classmates who were interested in the world of the mind. Paradoxically, she joined a sorority and became a Mustang cheerleader. She met Robert Hyer Thomas when both were members of the Student Council. He, a veteran of the Korean conflict, was representing the School of Law. An older student, he was the grandson of Robert Stewart Hyer, founder of SMU. They married on December 14, 1957, in SMU's Perkins Chapel when she was but 20 years old. Again, she was in two worlds. As the wife of a young attorney, the heir of SMU's founder, in the North Dallas-Park Cities area she had inherited the social connections of his as well as her own forebears. As a reader and thinker she sought, but seldom found, time to be alone to develop her own path. Her mother-in-law, Margaret Hyer Thomas, became, for that period, the most important woman in her life. "Bob's mother was quite an influence on me. She was so intelligent, so interested in ideas. From the first we shared a special relationship that continues to shape and direct me."

For a period of time Gail allowed, and often reveled in, the externals of her life. She became a member of the Junior League and a docent at the Art Museum. She was active in the Art Museum League. She became president of the Dallas Society for Crippled Children. She had three children, Victoria Thomas Mannes in 1959, Stewart Hyer Thomas in 1961 and Electra Thomas Harelson in 1964. "I was doing my best to give and to serve."

But there was a missing piece. "I needed more than the social and civic world offered. By the time I was 25 I needed to demand more of myself. So I took up painting. I took my art quite seriously." With Carolyn Foxworth and others she started Art About Town. But still there was the nagging question: What next? What else? She is introspective, meditative . . . .

"The more I got in touch with the center of my soul, the more I knew there were other demands to be made of me . . . . I burn out quite easily if I try to do too much community and civic work, so I sometimes say that's all there is, I'm not going to be involved in that group anymore. And then I pull back and I see how much there is to do and how much I want to contribute and I come back and get into something else. So, I realize now there are these connections in me. I have to matter. We can't pay for all the things we require in our city and I have to be there, to do my part." And then . . . . "and then I've had to find the deeper and deeper resources in me, tap into those. Briefly, sometimes, I feel isolated, but I *never* suffer loneliness. I celebrate aloneness. I dance. I sing."

For a time the art filled the void in Gail's life, but not for long. "When I was 28 I knew I had to go back to school. I had to know! I had to have access to knowledge." She enrolled in graduate school in psychology at SMU and soon became even more frustrated. The professor was new; when he asked me to lead the class one day, I knew I was in the wrong place. I did not need to lead; I needed to learn, to be challenged totally. "I stumbled blindly into UD (University of Dallas) and was turned on intellectually." She completed her master's in 1972. It wasn't easy. Her children were 8, 11 and 17. "I did all the mommy things, too. Cafeteria duty all through middle school, Stewart's soccer games, the girls' cheerleader practice. I bought a little alarm clock and on the days I drove car pool, I'd set it. When it went off, no matter what I was doing, I left to pick up the children. I've interrupted graduate conferences, long distance telephone calls, conferences with my academic employers. The kids hated it when it was my turn to drive car pool because I would just barely make it—or be a few minutes late . . . . I was not the most popular car pool mom."

When she was 33, Gail was asked to become dean of women at UD. She called a family conference. "I told them they'd have to help me decide. We sat around the table and talked. We decided I should take the job. It was tough. I didn't know any woman at the time who worked.

"I do not have unlimited energy . . . . I had to choose, and I found it became easy to write 'regret' on social invitations. But I was suspect. I'd meet friends in the grocery store and they'd grab me and say, "Oh, Gail, *where* have you been? Are you all right?' The greatest discipline of all was not to care. It was hard on Bob. A difficult time for our marriage. Gradually I found I could find one person at a social gathering and have a meaningful conversation. I'd go. Bob would talk to everyone. I'd sit with one person all evening and learn something.

"This is a technique that women need to learn—how to meet their individual needs. None of us wants to turn our backs on the social world. Society is the realm of the goddess, the face of the goddess showing itself. The social world is the feminine world. Men serve the women. They dress up in tuxes, get the drinks. The talk is about women's realm—vacations, children. Parties are where traditions are continued, connections made, recipes for life exchanged.

"Gossip is God's messenger."

Gail has continued to live "out on the edge." Her family has "mostly become accustomed to it. They are all incredibly beautiful people. Mom has always been the weird one in this family.... None of my children rebelled... didn't run away, didn't get into drugs. My children say 'yea, Mom, go for it!'.... I do think they worry sometimes that I might go too far out.... I'm the one that comes home with the drums and the crystals.... This is the Age that's coming in and I'm trying to find out about it."

In 1982 Gail completed her doctorate, two years after she founded the Institute of Humanities and Culture, which she described in her introduction to "Imagining Dallas," as "an attempt ... to study seriously the life of the city and to provide a center of learning open to the imagination." In this work Gail has reached some of the "center" for which she has been reaching all of her life even while she continues on the "journey of the soul." The Institute is really a "think tank" with some 50 or so "fellows" from several states and six countries who think, write and usually live on the cutting edge of change. But they are, for the most part, not cloistered in convents, not hidden away in reclusive mountaintops, not continually conversant with shamans and seers. From time to time they make those journeys, but they live in the "real" world, have families, and write and speak in a communicatory language. In 1991 the Institute is a "center for learning dedicated to the re-imagination of culture in the city, housing a sizable press, Studies in Cultural Psychology, a Center for the City, and a Teachers Academy which sponsors a summer institute for teachers and an institute for principals."

Gail, herself, is a visionary for the city of Dallas. In 1982 she spoke of a city as "a construction and, with grace, a work of art ... a natural habitation of humankind: it holds us, frames our hopes and desires, and shapes our destiny. To 'imagine' the city in which we live (Dallas) is to participate actively in its making." It becomes clear as she speaks that she has a continuing love for her city and that her criticisms come from a loving mother who expects the best of and for her child. Even after years of psychology, attending countless conferences and workshops, Gail still views herself as a "child of privilege. "I was an adored fourth child, secure, protected, loved. I lived in a fantasy world."

These gifts compelled her, over and over, to rededicate herself to her city. No matter how hard she tried to withdraw—and from time to time she did to find the new centeredness of herself—she always came back to the community. In an interview in the early autumn of 1991, she was about to go off again on a pilgrimage of privacy. Reflecting on her city, Gail said:

"Dallas is in one of its most difficult times. In the 1960s and the early '70s there was a lot of cooperation. Leaders of color felt like they were a part of the city. Today ... ? In some ways, we are better off than we were a decade ago. In others, worse.

"We're going through a shedding of the old personae, a breaking down of the patriarchy of dependency. All patriarchal structures are almost fully broken down. You see a lot of flurry of activity with some people trying to keep control, but it doesn't work. It manifests itself as foolish." The institutions that governed life in the past no longer do so. Broken apart are:

- Economics. There is a demise of old Dallas money.
- Family. The family, as we knew it in the past, is gone.

- Churches. Buildings are no longer the center of spiritual life. People refuse to be controlled by dogma but find new ways to spirituality.
- Education. The educational system has broken apart.

When the structures break down, new growth inevitably begins. "At the time of breakdown a person, an entity, an institution, a city is at its most vulnerable. We are at that stage in Dallas. We can see the shoots of new growth. We see it in female leadership emerging, struggling certainly, but with a strong root system and branches taking hold. Racially, it's more difficult to see. We are in a tight place, but there are signs of new growth, and we are going to be all right.

"I see Dallas in the place of a snake shedding its skin. There is a period of several days in the shedding process when the skin completely covers the eyes and the snake is blind. That's the place Dallas is in now. But we know the movement is at work. My sense is that Dallas will be very vibrant, emerge with a lot of vitality that comes from the feminine. I see Dallas as a spiritual center." She pauses and reverts to the practical:

"People all over the world are drawn to Dallas. There is this incredible fantasy about the city. When I call people anywhere in the world and ask them to come to Dallas, they accept. I've never had anyone turn me down . . . . There's something about this place!"

"The spirit is strong and the spirit will prevail. Energy does not disappear. It transforms itself and emerges in new forms."

From the sweep of lawn in front of City Hall, Dallas appears beautiful and clean. The corner of the library at right frames tall buildings at the city's heart. It is a Dallas where the voices of its ethnic diversity and of its women offer hope for a bright and wonderful future.

Part II

Fabrics and flavors of a time and place are often best captured in stories of individuals who lived them.
Following are the stories of women who helped to shape Dallas and were, in turn, shaped by it.

Margaret Boone Ackerman is a direct descendant of Margaret Beeman Bryan.

MARGARET BOONE ACKERMAN

• • • •

December 20, 1902—November 7, 1993

Margaret Boone Ackerman moved to Dallas in 1914 as a 12-year-old school girl, but her ancestry dates to the city's earliest days.

Margaret's grandmother was Emily Elvira Beeman Baker Holmes, a first cousin of Margaret Beeman Bryan, Dallas's first First Lady. Emily was the daughter of James Jackson and Sarah Crawford Beeman, and Margaret, the daughter of John and Emily Hunnicut Beeman. Brothers, James and John Beeman, were among the city's first settlers.

Emily was 16 years younger than her cousin Margaret. When she was eight, she and older sister, Mary Jane, 10, and younger siblings, Francis, five, and Anice, three, were left by their widowed father with Margaret while he went with John Neely Bryan to California during the gold rush. Until she was 15 when she married, Emily lived off and on with Margaret where she tutored the children and helped with the house work.

When Margaret Ackerman was a little girl, her grandmother, Emily Elvira Beeman Baker Holmes, lived near them.

"My grandmother told us endless stories about the early days of Dallas," Margaret Ackerman said in a 1988 interview. My sister (Mildred Boone Haden) and my aunt (Angelina Alice Baker Nicholson) wrote her stories down and went over and over them with her to be sure they were accurate." These stories both expand and enrich the city's history:

Emily Beeman was conceived at Old Crossroads Camping Ground and born January 8, 1841, in Dalby Springs, Bowie County, near Texarkana, just across the Red River into Texas where her parents had stopped on their covered wagon trek to the Three Forks of the Trinity. She is considered to be the first girl born in the Republic of Texas.

The Beeman brothers—James, John and, later, Samuel—had come to Texas from Missouri and Illinois. Like many others, they were lured by the wondrous tales of unlimited riches spread by Peter's Colony agents. They bought script for 320 acres of land at 15 cents per acre on the Three Forks of the Trinity and had applied for a grant of 640 acres. They stopped for more than a year in Bowie County and then went to Bird's Fort for the winter of 1841-42.

Sarah and James had married in St. Charles, Missouri, on September 15, 1836. They had a son, William C., born on September 27, 1837, and a daughter Mary Jane, on March 3, 1849. The little boy died in 1840, so the Beemans reached Texas with only Mary Jane and left Bowie County for Bird's Fort with their two daughters, Mary Jane and baby Emily.

The winter of 1841 was bitterly cold (see Chapter 1), supplies extremely limited and conditions for survival at the remote Bird's Fort unsavory. When spring came, the Beeman families readily accepted John Neely Bryan's invitation to move to Dallas. They left Bird's Fort on April, 7, 1842, and arrived in the Dallas area the following day.[1]

Emily was 14 months old when her parents brought her to Dallas. The covered wagons bearing James and Sarah, along with John and Emily Beeman followed the Trinity River to Dallas. At the mouth of a wide creek, now in the vicinity of Oak Lawn and Maple, the Beemans spotted a giant turtle sunning itself on a rock. "We'll call this Turtle Creek," James Beeman told the children, and that is the way Turtle Creek got its name.

The Beeman families settled some five miles almost due east of the village of Dallas. They named their part of the county White Rock for the white shale near the surface of the earth. Here they built their blockhouse as protection against the Indians. The house was located on what is now the southeast corner of South Haskell and Dolphin Road.

Emily Elvira Beeman (Baker Holmes) lived in the cabin with Margaret Beeman Bryan while her father and Margaret's husband hunted for gold.

In October of 1843, Sarah and James had their first Dallas-born child, a baby daughter they named Gennett. She lived only two months. The next year, on November 28, 1844, a son, Francis Marion, was born, and two years later, on November 19, 1846, another daughter, Melissa Anice.

The baby was only 16 months old—Emily was seven—when their mother died on March 8, 1848. Sarah Beeman was buried in the extreme northeast corner of the Beeman land. When Scyene Road was widened from a trail to a street, the grave was protected by a small picket fence and the road laid around it. Neighbors kept the pickets in repair and painted them white. Finally, progress encroached. Sarah's grave was paved over and now lies under the intersection of Scyene Road and Buckner Boulevard.[2]

Ten months after Sarah's death, James married Catherine Napper, the daughter of a family traveling through Dallas on its way to California. When the Nappers continued on their journey, Catherine went with them. James followed on horseback for three days trying to lure his bride home, but to no avail. He was granted a divorce later that year.[3]

Sarah Beeman had taught her daughters reading, writing and arithmetic and Emily used these skills to tutor the Bryan children.

John Neely Bryan, who had lived for much of his life among the Indians, taught Margaret to trade with them. She was not afraid of them as were many early settlers, but she was terrified of wild animals, and the prairie was alive with deer, antelope, wild horses and turkeys, wolves, bears and buffalo.

Emily remembered vividly one occasion when a herd of buffalo descended on the frontier town of Dallas leveling everything except the cabin in which they lived. For three days Margaret and the children huddled in the cabin which shook so badly when the animals lunged against it that they were afraid it, too, might tumble. The buffalo milled about, eating everything—the crops, the gardens, every blade of grass—and creating such a dust storm that people could barely breathe. Sometimes there were so many buffalo crowded together in a mass kicking up so much dust that it appeared to be night in the middle of the day. The buffalo fought each other to suck the honey from the trees.[4]

Emily's father returned to Dallas some time during 1850, for on December 3 of that year, according to county records, headrights of 640 acres each were registered to John, James J. and John Smelser Beeman, the son of Samuel Beeman who had arrived with his family from Illinois in 1846 to join his brothers.

On November 29, 1851, Emily's father married Elizabeth Baker, who had been his children's teacher for several years. They added three more Beeman children: Lydia, who died as an infant in 1853, Charles A., born on January 24, 1854, and Sarah on March 9, 1857. At the time of Sarah's birth, the family lived in Weatherford where they had moved in June of 1856.

Emily Elvira Beeman Baker Holmes, sitting in the middle at right, centers her Baker's dozen, her six sons, standing, and six daughters.

It was in Weatherford on September 8, 1856, that Emily Elvira Beeman, at age 15, married William Thatcher Baker, the brother of her stepmother.

They lived for a time in Lancaster before moving to Hamilton County where, on a farm south of town, Emily gave birth to 12 children: Sarah Mehettable (Hettie), James Artemas (Jim), Francis Houston (France), William Thatcher, Jane Emily, Elizabeth Scythia (Betty), Charles Curtis, Norton Amos, John Beeman, Margaret May (Maggie), Mary Oconasta and Angelina Alice (Angie). Emily called them her Baker's Dozen. The Bakers had been married for almost 28 years when he died on August 12, 1884.

Almost a decade went by. On September 12, 1893, Emily married again. The bridegroom was David Thomas Holmes, a Methodist minister and a first cousin of Oliver Wendell Holmes. He had seven children, making Emily the mother of 19, her Baker's Dozen and the seven Holmes children. Her youngest daughter was 10.

Mary Ocanasta Baker Boone, Margaret Ackerman's mother, was the eleventh child of Emily's Baker's Dozen, all handsome, healthy, long-lived individuals. Mary earned a teaching certificate from AdRan College, taught school for a time, and married Malcolm Alvah Ackerman, M. D., on February 2, 1903. They moved to Hamilton where all five of their children—Emily, Mildred, Sybil, Malcolm and William—were born. Sybil was a baby when they moved to Dallas in 1918.

Margaret remembers a Dallas far different from the one described by her grandmother:

"We moved in two cars, both loaded down with us and our luggage. My father drove one and my brother the other. Our house was in East Dallas, 923 Grandview Avenue. Papa opened his offices at 910 Medical Arts Building. He was among the early doctors to move into Medical Arts.

"Dallas was a small town. We could walk most of the places. When we didn't walk, we rode the Dinky (an electric-powered small car). The fare was 5 cents, but we bought tokens and that way we could ride for 3 cents.

"Bread was 10 cents a loaf and eggs were 10 cents a dozen—but we almost never bought eggs. People gave us eggs to pay their doctor bill.... My father delivered lots of babies—we estimate around 5,000. He charged a $5.00 delivery fee but lots of people couldn't afford even that. Some insisted on giving him something.

"So, that's the way we got a lot of our food. People would bring us vegetables and fruits. Or they would work out the fee. My mother usually had help—someone to come on Friday and change all of the sheets, someone to come on Monday and do all of the laundry, someone to come on Tuesday and do the ironing and so on. These were almost always women who were paying their doctor fee by helping the doctor's wife with her housework. Papa would take almost anything in payment—a quilt, turkeys, chickens. Once it was hot tamales.

"The hot tamale man pushed his cart through the neighborhoods every Saturday. Usually we could hear him coming calling out, 'Hot tamales! Hot Tamales. Come and get them while they're hot,' but whether we heard him, or not, he always stopped at our house. He had six tamales all wrapped and ready, one for each of us kids. He was paying for the delivery of his twins."

Margaret and her sisters shopped at Sanger Brothers, A. Harris and Neiman-Marcus. They attended Lipscomb School and Bryan High School, located on the present site of the Plaza of the Americas Hotel. She was graduated in 1925 and, in the fall, enrolled in the freshman class at Southern Methodist University. She rode the street car to the northern boundary of Dallas at Knox Street and McKinney and from there, the Dinky to the campus.

Hillcrest was not yet paved. SMU was an infant college. There was only one building on campus, Dallas Hall, which housed all of the classrooms, the post office, the library and all of the administrative offices.

With a degree in hand, Margaret went to Whitewright to teach home economics. Years later at an autographing party following the publication of her cookbook, *Never Too Hot in the Kitchen*, more than half of the women from her first Whitewright homemaking class showed up to applaud her.

Margaret was devastated when her first teaching job did not work out, but she basked in the way her parents welcomed her home. Her mother's words at the critical time became Margaret's touchstone. "Mother said: 'Remember that when a door closes on one part of life, another opens—and behind the next door is something far more wonderful than the one that just closed.'

"My mother believed that love and discipline are one. She never belittled us, never embarrassed us and never corrected us harshly. She would say, 'Come and sit by me. We need to talk,' and she would listen to us. Sometimes she would agree that what we had done was fine. Sometimes she would say, 'You know that behavior is not what pleases you. I am certain you want to be the best person you can be for yourself.' That was just about it. I never felt I had to put on a false front or hide anything from her or deny my own best interests. I learned a lot about how to relate to my students from the care I had from my mother."

Back in Dallas, Margaret took a job teaching homemaking at Sunset High School. "Teaching was my whole life. I loved it!" Her principal was W. T. White. "He was a great principal. He expected the best from us, made us believe in ourselves and supported us absolutely. I remember one time Miss Kathleen Witherspoon, the English teacher—she was a tiny little thing, but, my, she could teach English and she could write—wrote a play about white and black relations. I don't remember what the play said, but I remember what a flap it made. People were up in arms. The school board didn't know what to do, and Mr. White said 'well, we won't do anything. She has written something she believes in and that's that . . . .'

"Sometimes I wonder why our present leaders don't just say 'that's that,' and then not talk anymore about it. The world is full of hot heads who make mountains out of molehills."

Kathleen Witherspoon continued to teach high school English, later transferring to another Dallas high school where Stanley Marcus was one of her students. "Several years later when he had completed college and joined Neiman-Marcus, Stanley was strolling the aisles one day when he ran into Miss Witherspoon. In the course of their exchange he reminded her that she had not paid her bill that month. Pulling herself to the limit of her four feet, ten inches, she fixed him with a stare. 'Young man,' she said, 'you know that as a school teacher I don't make enough to pay all my bills. At the first of the month, I put everything into a hat and the ones I draw out I pay as long as the money lasts. If you fool with me, I won't even put your bill in the hat next month.'"

William Travis White was responsible for introducing Margaret Boone to "the Colonel," who turned out to be the something wonderful her mother had promised her would be behind the next door. She had waited almost 10 years for it to happen.

"Mr. White came by my room one day and said, 'Margaret, Col. Ackerman and his adjutant are going to be here next week, and I want you and your girls to prepare lunch for them. I said we would be glad to . . . . We did that all the time. That was my job."

This was 1943, at the height of World War II, and Col. Gilbert Evans Ackerman was in charge of the ROTC units in the southern area. Some years earlier he had lost his young wife, an opera singer, to pneumonia on the day after Christmas and on the way home from her funeral was in an automobile accident that immobilized him for active duty.

Miss Boone and her homemaking students planned the menu, prepared the meal, set the tables and were about ready to serve when Mr. White appeared at her door again.

"I remember the scene vividly. He said, 'Come here, Margaret. Go brush up your hair and fix your face. The old colonel is eligible.' I laughed, and said, 'I haven't got time,' and he said, 'Oh, yes you do. You do what I tell you.' Well, he was my boss, so I did it."

The luncheon went beautifully. As the dessert was being served, her principal called for the teacher to come out and join him and his guests. She declined, but her boss insisted.

"So I pulled off my apron and smoothed my hair and went in and Mr. White pulled up a chair between him and the colonel, and I had a piece of pie and a cup of coffee and a nice visit and that was it."

Two weeks later Margaret was teaching when she looked up and Colonel Ackerman stood in the doorway. "In his uniform, of course. Spit and polished. Beautiful! I was so impressed. He said, 'May I see you please?' and I walked out into the hall and he said, 'I would like to take you out to dinner and I would like us to go to one of the operas. Which one would you like to see?' and I said, 'Let's see *Aida*' and he said 'That's one of my favorites.' He said, 'I'll be by for you; I'll call.' I went home and I said 'Well, guess what? I have a date with Col. Ackerman next Saturday night! We're going to dinner and the opera.' Now, my father never had a drink of liquor in his life, but he came home with a big bottle of Haig and Haig, and said, 'I bought the best scotch I can buy. Your mother and I are going up to your sister's and you take Col. Ackerman back to the kitchen and you get out the ice and you tell him to help himself. But you be careful. You don't know how to drink.' And that's what we did. We went to dinner and to *Aida* and during the triumphal march Gil took both my hands and every fiber in me responded."

They dated for two years, and "He courted my mother! The war was on and there were lots of things you couldn't get—sugar, coffee, toilet paper. Every time he came he brought some of those things to her. Mother thought he was wonderful . . . ."

He went to Mineral Wells to check the ROTC camp. While there, he called Margaret every night. Once it was an urgent call. "He asked if I could meet him in Fort Worth on Saturday afternoon. I knew at once something was wrong."

Col. Ackerman had received orders to go overseas. "I can't leave these men in the middle of training," he told Margaret. "I want you to go home and call Travis White and tell him to call Sam Rayburn and get these orders postponed until I can complete this job." She said she would. The colonel then pulled her close, kissed her and said, "Texas would have been pretty rough without you. Can you get ready to go to Europe with me?"

They were married on July 20, 1946. Margaret was 40; Gilbert was 52.

"Oh, what a happy time we had! I went to Cordon Bleu Cooking School. And I had a private audience with Pope Pius XII."

The colonel and Margaret were in Europe for two years while he served as president of the War Crimes Court in Dachau, Germany, and she did volunteer work. Her most gratifying job was in relocating children who had been sent away from their homeland for safety during the bombings of World War II. When the Army of Occupation determined that it was time for the children to go home, they asked Margaret to chair the relocation committee.

"Every family that had a spare room was obligated to take at least two children. Some of the children didn't know who they were, didn't even know their names. Many of their parents had been killed during the war and their families—if any were left—were scattered, so I worked very hard on their backgrounds. Of course, many things I didn't find, but I did pretty well. I also trained all of the officer's wives to take care of the children."

The friends who had arranged Margaret's audience with the pope had a very large house with five extra rooms and were obligated to take 10 of the children. Margaret and her colonel often went to the country to visit with their friends and the kids. "I knew that taking care of, clothing and feeding that many children was almost prohibitive, so one day I suggested that I could write back to the states and get whatever clothes the children needed.

"They needed everything. But we didn't know sizes. So, Gil took a roll of brown paper about three feet wide and 20 feet long. He stretched it across the floor and gave every child a number. He told them to all stand on their numbers . . . . He was fluent in

German, of course . . . and he went around and drew the outline of their feet, the length of their stockings, the length of their arms, their weight and their height."

Margaret then sent the brown paper with all of the instructions to her father in Dallas and asked him to see that the order was filled. "I knew Papa had a patient who was head of one of the departments of Sears and Roebuck who could get everything together for me." The friend meticulously filled the order, placing every child's clothing into a separate box and marking it with his number. "When the boxes came, we took them out and called the children together and gave each of them a box. You have never in your life seen children as happy. One put on his socks, another his hat, another his sweater . . . . Finally Gil said, 'Now, everybody stop! Everybody put on your socks. Put on your pants. Put on your shirts. Put on your shoes. Put on your sweaters. Put on your hats, and we'll all take pictures. And that's what we did . . . .'"

The Ackermans returned to Washington in 1949. Two years later, the colonel retired and Margaret took him home to Dallas. Dr. White, by then DISD school superintendent, asked him to remodel the warehouse system for Dallas schools. "This meant he had to fire me (Margaret was still on leave from her DISD teaching job, a concession that was made to all employees who were involved in the war work) because a man and wife couldn't both work for the school system in those days.

"I really didn't intend to go back to teaching," but the Highland Park School system prevailed on her to return to the classroom. When she declined, they persuaded her to go back from Easter until the end of the school year. The superintendent said he had two very bad classes that needed her firm discipline. In one of the classes, the kids had taken their teacher and set her out the window into the hedge.

"So, I went. Teaching English. Never taught English before in my life . . . . I should have had better sense . . . . Every day when I went into the classroom there were dirty pictures drawn on the blackboard. One day I stepped in a little early and here was this child drawing away. When he saw me, he darted to his seat. I said, 'Larry, come here, I need to talk to you.' He got a little smart but I just ignored it. I told him I wanted him to erase the board for me because I didn't like coming into the room and finding the board filled with trash. He knew I knew he had put the stuff on the board and all the kids knew I knew. But I said, 'Larry, I know how smart you are. You can be a wonderful person. You can be just great. And if you are going to be the wonderful person I know you are, you and I are going to get along just fine, but, boy, if you are not, you are not going to like the way I treat you.' He say, 'Yessum,' still sullen. But later I overheard him tell some of the kids, 'Don't fool with her!'

"That boy and I became the best of friends. His father had a florist and every day for the longest time I would find a red rose on my desk."

From Easter until school was out stretched to nine years for Margaret teaching in the Highland Park Schools. After the first few months, she took up her first love, teaching homemaking, and continued there until she retired in 1960. Her homemaking teaching career spanned 33 years.

On his 80th birthday, Col. Ackerman gave a birthday present to posterity. He demanded that Margaret collect her recipes and food tips, and together they wrote a cookbook. Into his 81st year, he typed the recipes and together they proofread them. He then, at his own expense, had the book published. When Margaret complained about the cost, he reminded her that they had often spent that amount on travel and had nothing from the travels to leave for future generations.

Gilbert Ackerman died in March of 1983 from cancer of the lungs. He had never smoked but was gassed during World War I and felt that was the cause of his illness. By this time, he and Margaret, now 22 years as Dallas residents, had sold their home and moved into a condominium because he wanted to make life as comfortable and secure for her as possible. During his illness, he often reclined or lay on the living room couch and would ask her to come sit by him. "He would hold my hand or put his arms around me and it was all the strength I needed to go on. He was 89, but he was as bright and active as a new dollar until his last month. One day he asked her to come sit by him and when she did, he said: "The closer I get to the sunset, the colors are brighter." I said,

'Oh, Gil, thank you for making that statement to me. Henceforth, I'll look forward to that last sunset so I'll know how beautiful the colors really are.'

In two hours he closed his eyes very quietly and it was all over."

Requiem: A little more than a decade later, On November 7, 1993, Margaret Boone Ackerman saw her last sunset.

Ruth Collins Sharp Altshuler, native Dallasite, who personifies optimism.

RUTH ELAINE COLLINS SEAMAN SHARP ALTSHULER

• • • •

March 10, 1924

The city of Dallas and one of its favorite Daughters, Ruth Sharp Altshuler are analogous.

Those who know and love the city speak of the Spirit of Dallas, a quality defying definition that is made up of—but not limited to—courage, creativity and confidence.

Those who know and love Ruth Elaine Collins Seaman Sharp Altshuler speak of her persistent optimism, made up of—but not limited to—resilience, radiance and reliability.

Ruth and the city both are an enigma to the uninitiated who see the surface but not the foundation underneath. To both Ruth and the city, anything unpleasant is a challenge to surmount rather than a problem that obstructs.

The two differ in one distinct way: Dallas, the city, has an overlying pseudo-sophistication, a brashness. Some casual observers and many writers call it a mean streak. Ruth, the woman, is totally guileless, gracious and genuine and so refreshingly honest that casual acquaintances think it is feigned.

Ruth Altshuler wears life well. She was to the Dallas of the 1980s-90s decade what Sarah Horton Cockrell and Juliette Peak Fowler had been in its early history—a leading philanthropist. It was a title she shunned, but one she had earned because of her generous contributions to a myriad of human services. And it was also that she supported her contributions with personal commitment.

"There's never been anyone more Dallas and Texas than I am," she said. She was born, reared, educated and—except for brief periods of schooling and a tiny stint following a young husband during World War II—has lived all of her life in the city. She loves it, understands it, supports it, chastises it, makes no excuses for its limitations and continues to believe that the repugnant can be righted and the ugly made attractive.

Ruth Altshuler was born on March 10, 1924, at Baylor Hospital to Carr P. and Ruth Woodall Collins, and welcomed into the family that included two older brothers, James M. and Carr P. Collins Jr. She grew up in Lakewood on Swiss Avenue in the last house before the street wound into LaVista.

Dallas was a simple small town and the Lakewood area one of the sparkling jewels in its setting. Her mother was a career homemaker, wife and mother "who interrupted her bridge game in the middle of it to be home when we got there from school. Mother was very practical, very calm. A tornado could come in one door and go out another and not disturb Mother." Ruth's father "very excitable, very successful," kept the house filled with a motley collection of individuals from preachers to politicians.

"I was," Ruth said, "the Golden Girl." At five, she went to Mrs. Landers Kindergarten on Bryan and continued there through the second grade. Then she went to William Lipscomb, J.L. Long Junior High and Woodrow Wilson High School. "My biggest problem was whether I was too tall to be cut in on at the dance. I was five feet, eight when I was 13 years old! I had a wonderful time at Woodrow, made good grades, was a school favorite. My biggest disappointment was that I didn't make cheerleader!" Years later, as Woodrow initiated its Hall of Fame, Ruth was called to the podium and presented a giant megaphone making her Woodrow's "permanent lifetime honorary cheerleader.

She graduated from high school in 1940 at age 16 and entered SMU that fall where she continued to live in a golden cocoon. "I pledged Pi Beta Phi sorority. My life was so uncomplicated . . . ."

In those halcyon days of Dallas, downtown was the hub of all activity. "We shopped there, went to the movies there, went to church and Sunday school there, went to the doctor there. All of the doctors were in Medical Arts. There were only two hospitals—Baylor and Parkland." At a very young age, Ruth and six of her friends were allowed to go downtown by themselves on Saturday. "Our mothers gave us a dollar. We'd take the Junius Heights street car at Harrell's Drug Store (Gaston at Abrams). The fare was seven cents. We'd eat at Hunts for 35 cents, go to the movie for another 35, and go home on the street car. We had lunch, transportation and entertainment all for less than a dollar!"

Because she assumed that life would be good to her, every good thing pleased Ruth but did not amaze her. She was a teenager when her father backed W. Lee O'Daniel for governor of Texas. The three O'Daniel children—Pat, Mike and Molly—approximated the ages of Jim, Carr and Ruth Collins and the two families were friends. When O'Daniel won by a landslide, Ruth spent several slumber party weekends in the governor's mansion. Once, she insisted on sleeping in the Sam Houston bedroom finding it "the most uncomfortable bed I've ever tried to rest in." When Molly O'Daniel married Jack Wrather, the governor invited all of Texas to the wedding "and I think most of them came. He had the ceremony piped onto the lawn." Ruth was a bridesmaid.

At the end of Ruth's freshman year at SMU, Mrs. Collins decided that her daughter was old enough to go away to school and sent her to Fairmont in Washington. "It was a girls' school. I loved it. Exciting things went on all the time."

Ruth was a 17-year-old college sophomore when the Japanese bombed Pearl Harbor. "I thought, 'What is Pearl Harbor? Who cares?' But I could see there was a panic and my first thought was to reach Jim (her older brother) at Harvard . . . and he would tell me that everything would be all right."

Everything was not all right. Ruth's safe world had just collapsed. "There's never been a war like World War II. The whole country was touched. Before it was over, every family had somebody it . . . both of my brothers were." Ruth completed her school year and came back to a changed Dallas. "Everything was rationed. You had to have stamps to buy anything. People who used to drive their cars were taking the bus. No new cars were being made. There were no tires . . . ."

In September of 1942, Ruth re-enrolled in SMU where only a few boys were left on campus, but throughout the Dallas area, the elite of the country's young men were training for military service. One group of Navy flyers secured the names of Dallas girls; the men parceled out the names and each invited a young woman to a dance. It was March of 1943 around Ruth's 19th birthday . . . .

"Your life can hang on a phone call." The man who called Ruth was Bleecker Provoost Seaman, Jr., a 1941 graduate of the U.S. Naval Academy. The courtship was wild and wonderful. In July, four months after they met, Ruth married her Navy flyer in Pensacola, Florida, where he was stationed. Her entire family went to the wedding. The honeymoon lasted for 18 months while the bride followed her young husband to Florida, Oregon and finally to San Diego. He was killed while flying off an aircraft carrier in the South Pacific leading a bombing raid on Tokyo. "I got the message he was missing in action, but I knew . . . . I was a widow a month before my 21st birthday."

Back in Dallas, Ruth got a job with Delta Air Lines at Love Field. "It saved my life." For six months she was at the ticket counter and then transferred to operations. "I was 21, out flagging planes at 3 in the morning, telling them how to park . . . going over weather reports with the pilots. One morning in August of 1945 I was in the operations room at Delta waiting for the ticker tape to give me the weather report in Shreveport when the message came over, 'Atomic bomb drops on Hiroshima this morning.' My first thought was 'Get on with it! Who cares about Hiroshima? I need the weather report.' I'd never heard of an atom bomb. Not many in the country had."

Ruth was still working for Delta when she went to a dance one night when "the best-looking man I'd ever seen walked in. We were all trying to find out who he was!"

He was Charles Stanton Sharp, recently discharged from the Navy, eight years Ruth's senior, on his way through his home town of Dallas to Harvard Business School to complete the graduate degree he'd interrupted to go into the military. "Charles had been a very poor boy." He had worked for three years day and night after graduating from Highland Park High School before he had enough money to go to college. He went to the University of Texas, took two years of pre-law, three years in law school, got his law degree, worked briefly for a law firm and then went to Harvard Business School where both of my brothers had gone."

Ruth and Charles Sharp were married in June of 1947. She returned to SMU and completed her college degree. He finished at Harvard and joined her father at Fidelity Union Life Insurance Company. "It was a decision he never regretted. He and my dad had a wonderful relationship—and as time went on it became more and more clear that his decision was the right one."

Sally Sharp was born in 1949, Charles Stanton Jr. in 1952 and Susan in 1959.

In addition to the birth of her first child, the year 1949 was auspicious for Ruth in another life-altering way. It was also the year she joined the Junior League.

"My world changed. I had lived such a sheltered life . . . . I had never seen another side of Dallas. I took the provisional course and I walked through the door of a whole new world. The door of my comfortable life slammed behind me. I've been beating on it ever since trying to get back in . . . . Once you see what needs to be done out there and how many people need you, then it's hard *ever* to be comfortable again . . . . I was at the Lighthouse for the Blind. Parkland Hospital. The Salvation Army. Goodwill . . . .

"I'm organized and I delegate, so I ended up being president of the Junior League."

Busy with two young children and the League, Ruth didn't pay much attention when her husband mentioned that there was something wrong with his leg and his arm. "He'd always been in such robust health." She ignored it until a physician friend told her at a social event that she should persuade Charles to see a doctor. He did and dropped the bomb at dinner one night. The doctor said he had Parkinson's, Charles told his wife, who was pregnant with their third child . . . ."Charles was quite matter-of fact. I knew what we were in for. I just about went to pieces . . . ." She conferred with his doctor who told her that Charles had about 10 more good years.

"We had 20 more years, 15 good ones. We didn't let it get to us. We didn't talk about it. We continued with our activities. Charles was such a gallant man, so unself-conscious. We'd sit at the head table at community events and I'd feed him."

Increasingly Ruth took on the physical care of her husband.

As the disease advanced, the Sharps faced another crisis. Their 19-year-old son showed signs of mental disturbance. It would be a long time before his illness was correctly identified as schizophrenia. "He thought all the planes were out to get him.... For eight years he lived at home running up and down the halls being psychotic."

Ruth continued her community work. On many occasions she was the first woman to serve in a leadership role. After Junior League, she became president of the Visiting Nurses Association where she worked with Bob Strauss who was its vice president, who then persuaded her to go the board of Goodwill Industries, its first woman board member. She was the first woman elected to the board of the Salvation Army, the first woman on the board of Republic Bank Corporation, the first woman to chair the executive board of Highland Park United Methodist Church. She was also president of the Dallas Woman's Club "which pleased my mother," and secretary of the board of Hockaday School. She chaired the boards of both the Collins Foundation and the Sharp Foundation. In 1986 she chaired the United Way campaign. A letter over her signature brought in a million dollars in one month after she had been advised by one of the male leaders that she could not raise money by writing a letter. She was the first woman to serve on the board of governors and the board of trustees of SMU. She has advanced to the national board of several of the organizations.

"I've been the token woman on more boards than I can count. I've enjoyed everything I've ever done, but this is still a male-dominated community. Everywhere I went, I tried to get more women on the board and it usually worked." In 1989 she said, "I am the only woman in the 50-year history of the Dallas Citizens Council ever to serve on its board. This tells you something."

Ruth and Charles Sharp, right, with SMU President Willis Tate and Mrs. Tate at the Ruth Collins Sharp Drama Building.

Ruth's eternal optimism reached a few low ebbs. Her father became "totally out of it." At one point Ruth arrived at a breakfast with the Wonderful Women of Dallas and said that her husband, her son and her mother were all in different rooms at Baylor Hospital—and she tarried to comfort another woman who had spoken about a family problem.

"I just kept marching," she said, recalling that period of her life. "I'd put on my lipstick and go out and face the world.... Women of my generation would wait to put on their lipstick if the house were burning down. There were 10 or 15 nightmarish years.... I'd complain to my friends that I was nervous, that I didn't have any energy. Bless them, they'd listen. They couldn't do anything, but they listened....

"When I was at my absolute worst, I went to the Royal Wedding (Charles and Diana).... I just kept going...."

Her parents died. Both of her brothers died, first Carr Jr. and later Jim Collins, both with the same rare lung disease. Charles died in February of 1984. Her son was in and out of hospitals and finally settled on a ranch near South Texas. "He is severely mentally ill, but he has some quality of life there. I talk to him on the phone often and see him.... If he had been at home, we both would have been dead by now."

Her son's illness was the door through which Ruth met Dr. Kenneth Altshuler, who had joined Southwestern Medical School after teaching at Columbia University for 22 years. "He was building the psychiatry department at Southwestern and trying to acquaint the Dallas community with various forms of mental illness."

Dr. Altshuler was impressed with Ruth's acceptance of her son's illness and her practical approach to handling it. He also knew about her community work.

"He called me several times. I did not respond. I was so tired of mental illness.... That was the time they were still blaming mothers." She finally went to the hospital. "I looked at those slides and could *see* the difference in a normal brain cell and one from a schizophrenic patient...."

Ruth was hooked. Once again the comfortable life she had rebuilt through refusal to wallow in sorrow and the determination to revitalize a positive outlook had been enhanced by the opening of a new door. She was able to help in three positive ways: one, establish funding for and serve on the board (and as vice president) of Southwestern Medical Foundation, (2) educate the community about mental illness, helping families and patients overcome the stigma associated with it and (3) personally encourage Ken Altshuler and the work he was doing.

The two dated for three and a half years and were married on December 5, 1987, creating a family constellation that consists of Ruth and her two daughters and her son and Ken and his son and two daughters and their three children.

Ruth's refreshing candor stuns many of her associates. She hides from nothing. Her humor is contagious and her sense of the absurd disarming. She always speaks the truth as she sees it, so there is never an occasion for subterfuge.

After her brother, Jim Collins, completed a tenure in Congress, he ran for mayor of Dallas. While campaigning for him, Ruth told a group of women friends, "Everybody knows that Annette Strauss should be elected mayor of Dallas, but my brother thinks he wants the job, so I'm going to do everything I can to see that he gets it." When he lost in the primaries, Ruth was at the Strauss headquarters the next day helping to see that Annette got elected. When Ross Perot announced that he might be a possible candidate for President, Ruth immediately got involved. Margo Perot was one of her dearest friends.

Once when Charles and she were at the head table at a VIP dinner, she absentmindedly started cutting the meat for her dinner partner—only to realize that it wasn't Charles she was assisting. "We had a wonderful chuckle over that."

When she was honored by the Texas Legislature, she told the lawmakers that she deeply honored. "You come to this building every day to work, but I may have had one experience here that some of you haven't. How many of you have slept in Sam Houston's bed?"

Seated at a dinner party with a Nobel geneticist and the top lung man from Harvard Medical School, Ruth said her two brothers had both died with the same rare lung disease and she estimated that she had a 50 per cent chance of developing the same thing. "They put their heads together and said I had only a 25 per cent chance of getting the illness. I told them I was glad I'd run into them—they'd just doubled my lifespan."

Ruth's reflections on the city and women's role in it emanate from the same hopeful attitude that pervades the other areas of her life. "It saddens me that downtown is gone. I wish we could still leave home without having to lock our doors and drive down our streets without fear and let our children play all over the neighborhood without watching their every move. I wish we did not have to be concerned about drugs or our kids drinking .... I don't know how we get that kind of security back—or even if we can.

"I think race relations are very serious. Annette was a strong mayor, kind and considerate, listened to everybody. She kept the lid on. Some criticized her for not being tough enough, but if we'd had some tough macho guy in her place during her tenure, we might have had blood in the streets ....

"Women can make a difference. In corporate board rooms, women are still tokens—invisible almost. There are not many more women there than there were 10 years ago. Progress is being made, but its very slow.

Not long after Ruth and Ken were married, Dr. Altshuler marveled at her cheerfulness. "He said 'You go to bed humming and you get up humming. How do you do that?'. . . . I was born with a good disposition. I had good parents, a loving home, financial security . . . . I do not take my good fortune for granted. My work is half out of compassion and half out of guilt.

"I don't worry and I don't live with fear. Who would have ever thought I'd be on my honeymoon at my age? . . . . Ken and I were in Leone and on the last day we were there, I was standing by the window when Ken woke up and he asked what I was thinking. I said, 'I was thinking these last two weeks might be the happiest time of my life,' and he said, 'I have been thinking the same thing.' How many people our age can say that?"

Cordye McLaurin Hall, Dallas's Peace Mother and political activitist.

CORDYE MCLAURIN HALL

• • • •

May 31, 1899

Cordye McLaurin Hall is the conscience of Dallas. She started holding up a mirror so that it could view its true image almost as soon as she arrived in the city as a student at Ursuline Academy in 1913. And she never stopped. On her black-lacquered kitchen table in East Dallas she framed political strategy, wrote letters to world leaders, statespersons, politicians, lawmakers, media moguls and financial wizards. In that kitchen she entertained senators and strategists, pacifists and politicians, journalists and family members.

Nobody escaped Cordye's demand that they get involved. Her special concern was women. "Women don't know what they can accomplish! Mothers, in their own homes, can make *the* difference between a world exploding into chaos and one in which they can rear their children with the promise of a life ahead! They must get involved at the *precinct* party level—makes no difference which party!"

Born May 31, 1899, Cordye views the world through clear, unblinking eyes and a mind that has absorbed countless information and filed it away for total recall at any moment. Personal questions bore her. She considers it nonsense to dwell on dates and names of past events; she is not interested in rehashing the past.

"There are ugly chapters in our past," she said, "but we don't have to repeat them. What's essential is that each person improve the now!"

Cordye McLaurin was 13 years old when she came to Dallas. Born to Albert Laurence and Myrtie McCamant McLaurin on a remote farm at Fort Phantom Hill near Abilene, the youngest surviving child and only daughter of a Scottish father and a Scotch-Irish mother, she had three older brothers. When she was two, her father sold the farm, loaded his family in a wagon and headed west. He planned to homestead a section (640 acres) in the Texas Panhandle. He envisioned a ranch of legendary fable, with vast acreage and wealth. The family was barely on its way when he became violently ill and they had to turn back. The stomach ache turned out to be a ruptured appendix. He died leaving Myrtie a widow with four children.

Following the funeral, the new owners of the farm offered to tear up the contract so that Myrtie McLaurin, her three sons, Mickey, Mack and Jim, and Cordye would have a home. Myrtie would not have it; she insisted that they follow her husband's dream. In the wagon, they headed west across the Texas line into New Mexico where relatives lived. They were not welcome. To make a home for her children, Myrtie pitched a tent in the remote reaches along the Texas-New Mexico border in a canyon between two mountains. The two older boys enrolled in school in Corona, New Mexico, and "boarded" in town for four months until school was out. Food was scarce—weeks with nothing but bread and beans flavored with a bit of salt pork and an occasional rabbit that the dog brought home. Cordye's earliest memory is cuddling at the foot of a feather bed she shared with her mother and little brother and feeling safe from the panthers that stalked the countryside and the boulders that rocked the earth as they came tumbling down from the mountains above.

Myrtie McLaurin, planning to stake a claim, moved her family to Dickens. She reckoned without the legal approval of her state. Women were nonpersons. They could not homestead property. She was not to be defeated. She had Mickey, the oldest son, then 13, declared "of age." As head of the household he applied for a homestead in the Panhandle of Texas. The venture failed. Mrs. McLaurin was not strong enough to cope with the vagaries of the weather. The boys were too young to cope. The family left its land, moved to several different locations, always struggling for survival and settled in Merkel, 14 miles from Abilene.

Cordye loved school and was double promoted very soon after she started, but she hated the restrictive church to which her mother took the children and was frightened by the preacher whose subjects for sermons always included loathing for the Chinese and the Catholics. "He always warned us of the 'yellow hordes' that were going to sweep down on us,' Cordye wrote in her book, *What Can One Person Do?* ". . . he preached about the terrible Catholic people. Such talk scared the life out of me . . . but eventually my common sense took over."

When Cordye was in the fifth grade, Mack moved to Oklahoma and Mickey to Corpus Christi. Mrs. McLaurin and the two younger children followed Mickey, whose employer was Catholic and encouraged Myrtie to enroll Cordye in Incarnate Word Academy.

"My mother became very ill. She asked Mack to take charge of me. I was in the seventh grade. I was very close to my mother. I was 13 when she died. It nearly killed me."

Cordye and Mack, in his early 20s, moved to Dallas where they lived with family friends, later renting a room. Mack paid for Cordye's tuition, sometimes as little as $2.00 a month, to Ursuline Academy. When he became too ill to work, the nuns took over the care and nurturing of the young girl and kept her in school. "Finding Ursuline was my lucky day." Not only did she get a good education, but through her association with the nuns, some from Europe, Cordye learned that "except for their clothing, women in all parts of the world are pretty much alike." It was her first lesson in becoming a world citizen.

World War I, the war to end all wars," imprinted Cordye permanently. She was an orphan, still in high school when all three of her brothers were called into service. Mickey, gassed in France, came home to struggle for breath the rest of his life. Mack was the last to be called up. "When he left, I felt orphaned." Two of her favorite nuns also went home to France to help out in their country's time of crisis.

Cordye graduated from high school at the time when the men were arriving home from World War I. Jobs were scarce and the few that were available went to returning servicemen. "I worked at whatever jobs I could find." She was hired by Franklin Motor Company to answer the telephone, and fired following a successful selling campaign "because they didn't like the way I answered the phone." On her next job, also dealing with customers by telephone, she was praised for her ability. "I began to understand that it isn't what you do or how you do it that's important, but how you fit into the needs of the organization. Company loyalty is a one-way street. They expect total commitment from, but have no commitment to, employees."

She rented a room for $50 a month, ate a banana for breakfast, sometimes her only meal for the day, spent six cents to ride the street car to work. If she was lucky, she brought home $20 a week. When friends asked her to go to Eastland and take a job with Homer's Buick Agency, she went.

In Eastland she met a young man and got married. She slides over this part of her life as if it doesn't exist. She does not say, "I fell in love and got married." She does not give the first name of young man she married. The marriage lasted five tumultuous years and produced two little boys.

In 1922 Cordye moved back to Dallas, into the garage house at the back of her brother's home at 5946 Belmont, and again began temporary work. If being a single working girl in Dallas had been a bad dream, being a single mother was a nightmare. "I was so grateful to my brother for a place to live," she said, "but I had no idea how I would work and take care of my children . . . . If you were smart and wanted a job, you did not tell your employer that you had children."

One temporary job was with Feedol Oil Company. "My employer traveled five states selling oil by carload lots. Once he was gone for five months. He was the smartest person I ever worked for. He would come in and grade everything I did. When he gave me the job permanently, he delegated all of the detail to me. He taught me one thing that has been my motto all of my life. He said, 'Don't ever kick a mad dog,' and I never have." Cordye worked for the company for three years until it consolidated and moved its headquarters to Kansas City.

"Then I went to work for McLarin Rubber Company for John Anderson. He was the kindest, sweetest man I ever worked for. The company was owned by a Mr. Ware. He was a 32nd degree Mason. When he discovered that Mr. Anderson had hired what he thought was a Catholic—I wasn't, but he assumed I was because I'd gone to Ursuline—he made Mr. Anderson fire me."

When Oil Well Supply Company moved to Dallas, Cordye was one of hundreds of applicants. She called Mr. Anderson and asked if he would recommend her. He did, and she was hired to do the payroll. "It was very, very difficult, exacting, confining work." she said. "I worked five and a half days a week and overtime at no extra pay. I was the whole department and the work load grew and grew. There was no modern equipment.

"They finally got me an addressograph machine." This consisted of small metal plates on which the names and addresses were imprinted. Stacked into a trough, they dropped, one by one, into a form where Cordye hand-pressed them onto mailing envelopes, checks or other paper. The addressograph machine improved, but when Cordye used it at Oil Well Supply, it was cumbersome and contrary. It saved time when it worked and added to her stress when it didn't. She had to make a name plate for each new employee, every change of address, and delete the names of those who were terminated. There was no margin for error. "The quickest way to create company upheaval is omit paying someone or to send anyone a check for the incorrect amount." Also, she was doing the payroll for employees in Mexico, England and Canada. This required keeping current with changing money rates in each of the countries and adapting the salary checks accordingly.

The million-dollar payroll—phenomenal for that time—was printed out, five checks to a sheet and came to about three inches thick. For this work Cordye earned $100 a week. There was no overtime, no Social Security, no hospitalization, no benefits of any kind. There was a job to be done and no matter how many hours it took, she did it. When the recession hit, Oil Well employees found on their desks notices that they would be cut back to a four-and-a-half-day week with a 16 1/2 per cent cut in salary. They were to sign the agreements and return them to management. Instead of signing hers, Cordye went to see her boss. "I told him I couldn't support my children on $75 a month. He said the company was not responsible for my children.

"I walked out. When I got to my apartment the phone was ringing. He wanted to know if I had come to my senses. I assured him that I was quite rational. He said he could easily replace me. I said I could not possibly work for less than $100 a month. He said he had to cut everybody alike. We compromised. He raised my salary to $125 and cut it back to $100." She later learned that a trainer the company had brought down from Pittsburgh refused to train anyone else for her job.

"I don't know how we made it," Cordye said. "I don't know how I dressed myself and the boys. Friends gave me clothes. I sewed. The boys became responsible very young. They went to Fannin (School). They walked. Before they were old enough to stay by themselves, a lady on Fitzhugh kept them. "Once I had my phone taken out when I couldn't pay the bills. We didn't own a car. But we were not hungry. We ate pretty well. As soon as the boys were old enough they got paper routes and helped out."

Illness? "Well, I just wasn't sick. Couldn't afford to be. But once when Dick was tiny, he got really, really sick and I told my boss I needed to leave to take him to a doctor. I said, 'If he isn't better by tomorrow, he won't be here.' That's when I was working for Mr. Anderson. He called the man who was driving the company truck and told him to come around immediately, that Mrs. Hall had to go home. "Dick was so fragile that I carried him on a pillow. We went to Baylor Hospital. When I tried to sign him in, they wanted to know who was the man of the house. I explained that there was no 'man of the house,' that I was the responsible person, that I had a good job and would pay them. They didn't like that, so I had to pay them $25 cash to get my child X-rayed. I waited with the baby for two hours in a drafty room before they came back and told me that Dick would need surgery on both ears.

"There was no way I could pay for the surgery in advance, so I walked out. I called St. Paul. I didn't know a soul there, but I knew the nuns would listen to me. Sister Catherine said, 'Bring your child here. We will see that he gets attention.'

"The problem was that my surgeon was a Baylor man and the two hospitals were having some kind of feud. Doctors had to choose which faction they were with. I explained my financial problems to my doctor. He said he would do the operation at St. Paul if I could get them to approve him. I did. That broke the ice between these two hospitals. It was my first experience at resolving conflict through peaceable measures."

There were many hurdles to overcome. For one, when Wally was not quite seven, the legal age for children to enter school, Cordye knew he was ready for first grade. She gave a birthday party for him, declared him seven and enrolled him in first grade. Once she applied for a job where the cut-off age for hiring was 30. She moved her birthdate back a year. "When the system is stupid, you have to do things to beat it—and it's all right as long as you don't hurt anybody else."

There was also the matter of divorce, which was considered shameful. If a woman could not 'hold her husband,' there must be something wrong with her. Cordye was supporting herself and her sons, but one's reputation was evaluated along superfluous lines. Cordye got a quiet divorce and told everybody she was a widow. It was years before many of her friends knew otherwise.

Inequality in the work force between men and women was blatant, consistent, open and totally approved—not only by society at large but by both the women and the men caught up in it. "Jobs for women were secretarial or clerical. There were no women executives. My job as a payroll clerk was exceptional, and as high as I could go. I was doing the work of several people—five were hired to replace me when I left—but I got neither a salary nor the title. She tells one story in her book:

> Frequently I was called on to handle confidential letters, and one day I was called into the office of one of the top executives for this purpose.... I stood by awaiting my orders while the men discussed the financial condition of the company and the country.... "It may take a war," I heard one of the men say. That brought me to life. I replied....'If it takes a war to make the capitalistic system survive, let it sink!"
>
> The men were taken aback... but... it was easier for them to laugh and call me their conscientious objector than it was for them to... replace me. I learned in that way that women could be more outspoken than men. Women didn't amount to anything in a man's world....

"There was a devastating salary difference (between what men were paid and what women earned). Men were being paid $250 a month for the kind of job I was doing—and they had two or three assistants. When I left in 1942, I was making $165 a month. Oil Well established a Payroll Department. They hired a man to head it. I trained him. He became my boss. When I left, he hired four more people. They got everything in such a mess that they had to hire outside experts to come in and straighten it out."

Troubles were brewing in Europe. Hitler had come into power in Germany. His inhuman atrocities still lay ahead but people who read and thought had a pretty good idea of what was about to happen. Cordye was one of those people. "I knew Hitler had to be stopped, but I also knew that we were bungling our chances to take care of the situation before we came to blows." With two young sons, she could see a repeat of what had happened to her brothers. Wally, the oldest, had graduated from high school. Dick was ready for high school and Cordye was busy buying a house.

"I had wanted a home of my own all of my life. I began to save a little every time I got a check, sometimes not more than a nickel or dime, but always something." It took her eight years to accumulate $1,000. In 1940, after President Franklin Roosevelt got a new home ownership bill approved through Congress, Cordye borrowed $3,000 against her life insurance policy and had her home built for $4,000. On a quiet street in East Dallas that has become a haven for young people of substance, the house is in the heart of a renewal area. Some of its surrounding neighbors bear price tags of upwards of $100,000.

Cordye had been with Oil Well Supply for 15 years when Wally insisted that she take some time off. The company said it couldn't spare her, so Cordye quit.

After visiting her sons—Wally in the Air Force, Dick at the University of Texas at Austin—she returned to Dallas where she worked at several jobs while finding her real vocation in volunteer work—holding individuals in responsible positions accountable for their actions, political activism and promoting world peace. None of her jobs made her any money, "but I'd never made money, so that didn't bother me. What did bother me was that people were unconcerned about what was happening in the world."

World War II ended. Wally had flown 182 missions over the Himalaya Mountains, familiarly known as The Hump. He was awarded two distinguished flying crosses, two air medals and a Presidential Unit Citation. Dick, who graduated from the University of Texas at 19, had joined the Navy V-2 program while still in college and was on active duty when the war ended.

For many, like Cordye Hall whose two sons had come home safely, it was a time for rejoicing. But there was also an uneasiness astir, as if the world, rid of one enemy, could not survive unless it found another to hate.

Communism became that enemy. The nation seemed to lose all sanity as individual after individual, many in positions of great responsibility reacted against the "threat" of communism. The Russians, who had been an ally, one of the Big Three, along with England, in World War II and who had lost 20 million people in the war, were the principal target of the hate mongers. But fear and retribution didn't stop there. Signs, "better dead than red," cropped up all across the country. Mass hysteria erupted. Thousands of people, most of whom were guilty of nothing more than being at a party or listening to a speech by a 'Red' were accused of being "fellow travelers." Some lost their jobs and their livelihood. Many lost friends. The mindset of national leaders was that Communism would take over the United States. The theory was that the "domino effect" would get one country after another until all were gobbled up by the dreaded Red disease. The national madness reached to Congress where Sen. Joseph McCarthy was able to command nationally televised hearings in which he accused citizens of being communists.

All organizations and groups that were openly working for peace became targets of the anti-Communist crusade, especially the fledgling United Nations. The UN, an organization of nations for maintenance of world peace, was structured at a conference on international organization in San Francisco in 1945 (April 25-June 26). The new charter was signed by 50 nations and, shortly thereafter, by Poland and went into effect on October 24, 1945. The General Assembly was made up of representatives of all member nations, among them—what else?—nations that were socialist and communist as well as democracies. This was so threatening to individuals looking for Communist plots everywhere that they were instrumental in getting an amendment through Congress (the Connally Amendment) that freed the United States from complying with the international laws they had just helped to create.

Cordye Hall became a fearless, feisty one-woman crusader for sanity. "I had to find out if one person could make any difference," she said.

One, she made it her business to read and study the propaganda, never to accept gossip or hearsay as truth. "It makes no sense to read or listen only to those things you agree with. How are you going to know what your enemies are up to if you don't read what they are saying?"

Two, she helped to organize the Dallas United Nations Association and served on the nominating committee to select its officers. She helped to persuade Sarah Hughes to become its first president.

Three, she helped to organize an informal committee that read, clipped articles and challenged false accusations against the UN through "Letters to the Editors" columns in newspapers. She was the designated letter writer. Louise and Grier Raggio, both attorneys, were key public speakers. All, including Sarah Hughes, later to become a federal judge, were attacked.

She started a personal correspondence with women behind the Iron Curtain, a woman in Yugoslavia and another in Poland and sent a letter to another in Russia. The first two were answered, the third not. For these efforts, she was visited by two FBI agents who insinuated that her correspondence, including mailing packages to her Yugoslav friend, with people in Communist-controlled countries was anti-American.

She personally befriended foreign exchange students, especially a young woman from Pakistan and a medical student at Johns Hopkins University from Malaysia when some of Dallas's most prominent citizens were trying to get them expelled from the United States. When it appeared that Nadira Aziz from Pakistan would have her SMU scholarship revoked for truthful responses on a radio program, Cordye started a telephone campaign to support her. She later learned that Stanley Marcus has quietly paid the girls' tuition so that she could remain in school and graduate.

She personally challenged the tax-exempt "nonpolitical" Facts Forum organization founded in 1951 by H. L. Hunt, one of the world's richest men. Invited to join the group, she visited his "nonpolitical" library where she found multiple copies of only six books, all of them attacks on Cordye's favorite organizations, the World Federalists and the United Nations. She "reviewed" the library in the United World Federalists bulletin and sent Hunt a special delivery copy. He called and asked her to please meet him for a personal interview. She welcomed the opportunity, but when she arrived Hunt was not there. He sent, instead, Dan Smoot, president of Facts Forum and radio-television commentator for the organization. "I was impressed with the big guns he'd sent to talk with me, but not won over," she said. She asked for permission to select three books to add to the Facts Forum library and was told she could submit her choices but that a reading committee would have to approve them. She chose *The Anatomy of Peace* by Emery Reves, *Introduction to World Peace Through World Law* by Grenville Clark and *Let's Join the Human Race* by Stringfellow Barr. A committee never read the books; eventually she was told to come get them. She noted guests who were invited to participate on Facts Forum programs, wrote to them and enclosed material on the organization. Eleanor Roosevelt cancelled her scheduled appearance on one of the programs in response to Cordye's letter.

She took issue with the First National Bank in Dallas when she discovered Facts Forum materials, free for the taking, on a table in the center of the main lobby. Not only did she close her account with the bank, but asked for a meeting with Dr. Arthur A. Smith, vice president and economist for the bank. He told her that if the bank did not cooperate in providing space for the materials, Hunt would take his billions elsewhere. "So, Hunt won that skirmish. His material continued to be dispersed in the bank lobby." But Cordye found a way to protest. On her lunch hour, she picked up Facts Forum material and dumped it in the trash can outside the bank. On her return, she again passed through the lobby, collected material and put it in her office wastebasket. "This gave me great personal satisfaction," she said.

She challenged *The Dallas Morning News* when, on May 11, 1953, she read the first of three columns by H. L. Hunt entitled, "Presenting Facts on Facts Forum." With a telephone call she learned that the decision to run the articles had been made by an assistant editor in the editorial department while his boss, who had declined to run the series, was on vacation. The final article revealed that the U. S. Treasury had ruled it a tax deductible group.

She began a one-woman letter-writing campaign about Facts Forum, her first letter directed to the Treasury Department. Her campaign got a boost when she sent a packet of information, at his request, to journalist Ben Bagdikian of *The Providence Journal*, who read the material, conducted his own research and wrote a series of 11 articles that appeared in a number of newspapers nationwide. The series was then bound into a booklet. Cordye ordered 1,000 booklets "which I sold at cost. This was a gamble because it put a real crimp in my small income." Sale of the booklets was greatly enhanced with the appearance of 3x4 ads on every page of *The Dallas Morning News* touting the series. "To this day I don't know who inserted those ads." Not long after the publication of Bagdikian's series, Hunt announced that Facts Forum was being discontinued because it was no longer profitable. "I learned that the IRS had canceled its tax-exempt status."

Cordye Hall, at right, with Eula McNabb in the living room of her home from which, for many years, she organized events, wrote letters and directed peace and political projects.

One thing led to the next in Cordye's life, as if for her it was a natural progression from founding organizations (United World Federalists, the UN and its UNESCO—United National Educational, Scientific and Cultural Organization) to unraveling fear-and-hate groups (Facts Forum) to upholding individual rights (befriending women by corresponding with them and sending them food and clothing), to caring for international students and to being a peace advocate).

Being an advocate of equal rights put Cordye in the forefront for integration. "The conditions under which Dallas's black citizens lived were deplorable." The Texas poll tax, one of the ways it had kept blacks from voting, had been declared unconstitutional, but there were other more subtle and insidious ways that kept the races segregated. In 1955 the American Friends Service Committee sent Almeta Robinson to Dallas to help break the employment color line. Cordye immediately befriended her. "It took us a year but we finally placed a Negro secretary with the American Jewish Committee." It was such a minute beginning, but it was a start—and we've never gone backward on that."

Cordye was one of the few people who picketed in front of the Picadilly Cafeteria on Commerce Street until it agreed to serve Blacks.

It was in politics that Cordye made what she considers to be the most important contribution to progress for black citizens. She did it without ever holding office, as a by-product to accomplish another goal and without any fanfare. The year was 1955. A small group of "loyal" Democrats, of which Cordye was a key person, decided to pool their resources and run some candidates for public office. "There were really two parties in Dallas County, Democrats and Conservative Democrats, who were really Republicans.

Our aim was to establish a real two-party system in Dallas County. We were so successful that Gov. Allan Shivers and John Connally both switched to the Republican Party."

When Cordye went to see the headquarters for the new Democratic organization, she found a table serving as a desk, a typewriter, two chairs, and an office manager who went out to lunch soon as Cordye and Sarah Hughes arrived. "I knew the operation was doomed unless we could get somebody in charge who cared, knew what was going on, and would work long hours for little pay. I decided I was that person. Sarah discouraged me. She said the job was temporary, paid very little, and I'd have to do everything from managing to being janitor. I told her my house was paid for, my car paid for, my boys grown. I resigned my job and went to work. And was it work!

"There were only three black precinct chairpersons. My first job was to increase that number and to find loyal, competent persons for all the posts. At the end of my four years in the office there were 11 Negro chairpersons, none of the original three, all substantial people." Among them was Juanita Craft and Julia Scott Reed.

"When the Young Democrats declared themselves in favor of integration, all hell broke loose. I got to my office at 8 a.m. the day the story broke. The phone rang incessantly all day. I was called 'Nigger lover' and a lot of other things, but that was mild compared to what happened to Paulia Weaver. She was president of the Young Democrats. Her life was threatened; her apartment was threatened. One of our men sat for two days and nights at her house with a shotgun in his lap."

When Cordye read an editorial in *The Dallas Times Herald* in November of 1987 commending the Dallas Citizens Charter Association for bringing about peaceful integration in the city, she was one of many people—an overwhelming percentage of them women—who knew differently. "Anybody can do a good job when their work has already been done. I know many who were already doing this work before there was a Citizens Charter Association."

Cordye Hall knew that the United States' intervention in Vietnam was a disaster, and very early joined a group that protested at Dealey Plaza near what would become the Kennedy assassination site. There, week after week from 11 a.m. until noon each Saturday, Cordye stood with a few others in heat and cold, rain and shine, sun and cloud, snow and ice in a silent, prayerful, meditative protest holding one small sign reading "Peace." Mostly it was time-consuming, repetitious and boring. But they kept at it until after President Lyndon Johnson, who had inherited Vietnam and had refused to seek a second term because of it, went out of office. And until the senseless, undeclared war ended much as it had begun—with no winners, only thousands dead.

The Vietnam Conflict was never a declared war, but at its peak in the spring of 1969, it involved 543,400 U.S. military personnel. It is doubtful that one person in 10,000 in the United States knew the history of Vietnam, but Cordye knew: settled by Viets from Central China before the Christian era; controlled by China from 111 BC until 939 AD; independent after defeating the armies of Kublai Khan in 1288; ruled by France from 1858 to 1884, occupied by Japan in 1940; retaken from France by Vietnamese in 1945. The history is, of course, far more complicated, including the division of the country into North Vietnam and South Vietnam. The United States got involved by encroachment, at first sending only a handful of advisers who then had to be protected by other advisers who then had to be protected by military force.

The United Nations had been established to resolve such international conflicts, but the United States, it will be recalled, absolved itself from relying upon international law. One horror led to a new one. The protests against being in Vietnam intensified. A record number of young men became conscientious objectors. When they refused to join the military, they were left with three choice: Become conscientious objectors (not easy), be jailed in this country or escape to another. Thousands went to Canada. The divisions within the United States were catastrophic.

Cordye's most active and far-reaching protest against the Vietnam war was in forming a Dallas group of Another Mother for Peace, the principal protest group that women—mothers and their cohorts—waged against the Vietnam War. Another Mother for Peace was a nonprofit, nonpartisan association whose goal was to eliminate war as a means of settling disputes between nations, people and ideologies. Its literature and its medallion was one simple slogan: "War is not healthy for children and other living things." Millions wore it.

Through another half century when military explosion after explosion kept the world on the brink of oblivion, Cordye never stopped. From that small black lacquered table in her kitchen, she wrote letter after letter. She responded to thousands of telephone calls. Time after time, anonymous callers called her Commie, Pinko, Fellow Traveler, Communist Sympathizer. Her eyes twinkled. "I've been called worse!"

Her own words are more potent than any other and ring out in her Open Letter to Women of the World:

> Our first objective toward ending world conflict is to find a solution OTHER THAN WAR for settling the conflicts between nations.
>
> If some wars seem justified, let's not forget there is still a better way to solve the problems that created those wars . . . . women have a unique perspective. Heretofore ignored, more or less, in matters of war and peace, women can now play a compelling role in this great undertaking for global peace. Women are a mighty force . . . (who) require security more than power; human rights rather than human sacrifice.
>
> . . . men can be quite two-faced about war. On the one hand they want the profits, the "business," and they will compete mightily to win government contracts to make weapons for war. On the other hand they give their lives, literally and bravely, on the battlefields . . . in wars both declared and undeclared.
>
> I believe the world has a way to settle disputes: The International Court of Justice, a court of law and a function of the United Nations.
>
> To a very great extent, men control most of the world's governments, and most of those governments have resisted the forum of the United Nations for settling their disputes. Even more rarely they have sought an opinion from the International Court of Justice; and when they have, and the opinion does not favor them, the entire procedure is ignored.
>
> We, women of the world, could change that . . . .
>
> . . . the steps of change are small—infinitesimal on a world scale. But, silence is the real enemy. Where injustice; slavery . . . . discrimination based on color, creed, culture, language, lifestyle, dress, or physical appearance; where deprivation, deceit, dishonor or perfidy are practiced, each . . . of us should step forward to name the foul deed . . . and try to stop it.
>
> World peace will emanate from our homes with each of us teaching, living and respecting *life*.

The Peacemakers Steering Committee that planned and presided over the 1988 International Women's Peace Conference included Margaret Estes who was not present for the picture and, sitting on the floor, Leslie Lanes and Barbara Middleton; on the couch, Ruth Barnhouse, Carole Trout, Rachel Ford, Rosann Naim, Vivian Castleberry and Donna Shellhorn; and standing, Barbara Jones, Margarette Ehrsam, Emily Scobee Schumacher, Liz Deuillet, Karin Sawhill and Rhonda Palmer.

*Adlene Nathanson Harrison flashes the "V"
for victory after winning her first election in 1973.*

ADLENE NATHANSON HARRISON

• • • •

November 19, 1923

Adlene Harrison's love affair with the city of Dallas and her determination that all of its citizens have equal access to its good and equal protection from its bad things was planted in her at birth. Her parents provided unconditional love; her mother imbued her with the conviction that family came first, her father with the feeling that family includes everybody; her husband and daughters have provided the support and the safety net that has allowed her to be a public figure. It was the love of family that brought her back to Dallas from the University of Missouri at the end of her junior year in college to be with parents who were grieving when their only son went away to war. It was love of the extended family—the community—that kept her from what she most wanted to do in life—run for mayor in 1976.

Adlene Nathanson was born in Dallas on November 19, 1923, to Russian-born parents, Hyman and Bertha Golman Nathanson who migrated to the United States in their teens and met and married in Dallas. A sister, Miriam Nathanson Feinberg and a brother, David Nathanson, were already members of the family when Adlene was born. The Nathanson children grew up at 2834 South Boulevard on the corner of South Boulevard and Jeffries in the safest of all possible worlds. The streets were their playground, all of the neighborhood children their playmates. Every woman had household help and the help was always black and all of the black children were included in the friendship ring. "Nobody in my house ever thought there was any difference in people because of their color," Adlene said. When she learned that there were places in Dallas she could not go with her friends who were black. "It made me feel bad. I grew up feeling terrible about this division in my town."

"With my mother the family always came first. She was very shy, never ran around with friends. Once a week she played bridge and that was it. She was a great cook and a great seamstress."

Hyman Nathanson was 13 years older than Adlene's mother. "They had the most adoring, sensitive marriage I have ever known," Adlene said. "I think that's one reason I did not get married until later in life. I wanted what my parents had in a marriage, and it took a long time to find someone . . . ."

While her mother's role was making the children feel secure, her father's was in opening their world. He was president of Golman Baking Company, one of the definitive employers of the time. "When I was still a little girl, I went to the bakery with him every night around 9 o'clock. The bakery was on Corinth Street. He had a ritual. He would walk through the entire bakery greeting everybody, checking to see that all was going well, and introduce me to anyone new to me. I'd grab a bun off the conveyer belt and eat it piping hot. Then we'd go home."

Her father was Adlene's model for her public life. "My father didn't preach. He explained. I absorbed how he treated people, how he related to them, how he worried about them. When I became aware of trade unions, I was baffled that anybody would strike against their employer, and my father explained that many employers ran sweat shops. He said trade unions were absolutely necessary." But his own bakery, with some 700 employees, did not unionize for many years.

"We learned about human rights around the dining room table. My father talked to us about civil rights before the movement had a name. He said it would take hundreds of years of struggle before equality was assured."

The dining room table was also Adlene's first classroom. Doubly related to the Schepps family—her dearest friend and confidante was her cousin, Olga Mae Schepps. Adlene grew up sensitive to the city—its transportation, housing, the environment, parks, recreation, the library, police protection, business and she thought everybody knew these things. Her first organized schooling was an extension of the family structure. At age three she began kindergarten at Temple Emanu El when it was still located in South Dallas. "I have a picture of myself that was in the newspaper saying that I was neither tardy nor absent for the three years I went to kindergarten . . . . I was a healthy kid. I adored school—every school I ever attended." From kindergarten, she went to John Henry Brown Elementary School where one of her favorite teachers was Virginia Treadwell, who later would be Scooter Miller of Washington, D. C. "She was gorgeous, a flaming redhead and a great teacher."

Forest Avenue High School was "wonderful. Today it's James Madison and I never walk in there that I don't have a flood of very special memories. It hasn't changed all that much. It still smells like my high school." Adlene excelled academically, but her favorite subjects were people, tennis and public speaking. "I was a people person. I would study, make high grades and walk out and not remember any of the details." She was into almost every extracurricular activity. She graduated in June of 1940, third in her class of 310. She was 16 years old.

She was still 16 in September when she went away to the University of Missouri. "I planned to major in journalism and cover all the exciting stories all over the world." She and Olga Mae went together, but having her best friend and cousin with her did not assuage the homesickness. The two girls were homesick together. "We were miserable. We cried every day." At Christmas when they went home to Dallas, Olga Mae swore she would not go back. "She did. Only long enough to pack her clothes and go home for good. I felt deserted. But I made up my mind I was going to get over being homesick and I was going to have a good time. So I started meeting people and getting involved."

In her sophomore year Adlene was elected dean of her Alpha Epsilon Phi sorority house. The requirement for dean was that a young woman had to be at least 18 and at least a junior. Most were seniors. Adlene was 17 and a sophomore. Together with the housemother, her responsibilities were to manage the house, run chapter meetings, represent the sorority at Panhellenic, counsel girls with problems and serve for the group to the university. The job had never been much of a burden—until shortly after Adlene took it.

On December 7, 1941, only two months after Adlene was named dean, the world changed instantly and dramatically. She had gone to Kansas City to spend the weekend with a friend. The radio was on and the program interrupted to flash the news that the Japanese had bombed Pearl Harbor. "A friend was picking me up to drive me back to school. He was a senior law student. As we got in the car, he said, 'I'll never finish law school now.' We drove that 127 miles back to Columbia in dead silence listening to the radio. The carefree days were over."

Adlene's duties as dean of the house expanded to include the care of the sorority house property as well as its residents. When the grounds keepers as well as the male students went into military service, the girls were their own lawn mowers and hedge clippers. "The war changed everything."

The war wore on. Adlene completed her sophomore and junior years. She had changed her major to political science and history when she realized that her real interest was not in reporting the news but in making it. When her brother went overseas as an ordinance officer with the Eighth Air Force, their mother was distraught. "I had to do something to alleviate the sadness in that house. I decided I must stay at home with my parents until the war was over."

She got a job at Neiman-Marcus. "I was out of place. I hated watching women trying on all those clothes with a war going on. It all seemed so insignificant. And I despised the cut-throat competition that went on among some of the personnel." Adlene's attitude showed; the personnel director sent her to work in the stock room on the second floor, "to see if I could survive, she said. Survive I did! It was hot there. The work was heavy and tedious. I had two co-workers. One of them read her Bible at every break and on her lunch hour. The other one couldn't read. I had no intellectual stimulation.

"The way the stock room was arranged, all of the heavy stuff—coats and suits and stuff like that—was at the back. All the light weight stuff was at the front. I got tired of lugging all the heavy things from the sales floor to the back of the stockroom. One day I rearranged everything. I put the heaviest stuff at the front so we wouldn't have so far to carry it. One of the buyers came in. She said, 'Who did this?' Trembling, I said, 'I did.' She said, 'Who told you to do it,' I said, 'Nobody,' She said, 'Why?' So I told her. She said, 'Makes perfectly good sense to me. I'd like for you to come work for me half a day every day.' I said, 'The personnel director won't let me. She wants to see if I can last in the stock room.' She said, 'Don't worry about the personnel director.' So I went to work for her and learned a lot there." Adlene became a Neiman's buyer.

Adlene's next job was with Iris Mendel at Volk's where she was an assistant to the buyer. "She is one of the most courageous women I have every known. A professional in every sense of the word. Her husband became an invalid six months after they married and she took care of him for years. Iris taught me so much."

Adlene left Volk's to volunteer in the Red Cross Motor Corps. "I thrived there. I liked feeling a part of the war effort. I liked wearing the uniform. I liked driving. I liked getting to know people. I liked the sense of adventure—not knowing what would happen next."

Adlene planned to go back to school when the war ended, but by that time she was already deeply involved in the city of Dallas. She had tried to transfer her University of Missouri credits to Southern Methodist University and complete her degree there, but "transfers were not so easy in that time. I would have had to repeat almost a year of work to get a degree, so I said forget it."

In 1953, Adlene met the man she felt could help her create the kind of marriage her parents modeled. She was working at the polls "when this nice man came in to vote shortly before it was time for the polls to close. I'd seen him around, but didn't know him. He tried to strike up a conversation with me about whatever it was we were voting on—the D/FW Airport, I think. I said 'No politicking at the polls. I was quite emphatic . . . .

"I don't know where I got this veneer of being so outspoken. I didn't get it at home. My mother didn't raise her voice at all and my father spoke very quietly. Their whole manner was gentle. All three of us kids were combative. I thought people took advantage of my father and I made up my mind that I wasn't going to be like that. I've been termed a maverick when I'd be more of an insider than anyone else in the group. But I just won't let those who are powerful take advantage of those without power.

"So, I was very brusque with this nice man. . . . I don't know why he hung around. But he did and he asked me out to dinner so that we could discuss the issues later." They talked for hours. Adlene had met someone who was as interested in current issues as she was. Separated but not divorced, Maurice Harrison had not been dating. Single but wary of entanglements, Adlene had broken two engagements shy of the altar. She and Maury Harrison did not rush a relationship. There were, to consider, his two children, Scott and Amy, who were living in California with their mother.

They married on June 14, 1953, a quiet wedding at home, and Adlene tried for a time to be the kind of homemaker her mother had been. "I worked at it, but not very hard. The prevailing attitude was that married women did not work. "So it never occurred to me to get a paying job, and we sure could have used the money. Maury's contribution to Dallas was my time. I could see so much out there to do. He encouraged me to get involved. I was still so much a part of my family. I overheard the phone calls that came to Julius Schepps from people like Tatum, Florence, Cullum, Thornton. Sometimes I didn't agree with the decisions I heard them making. I'd hear about the school board candidates, hand picked, ready for the voters to approve. I'd hear about the city council candidates; all the voters had to do was vote 'yes.' Sometimes I didn't agree. I told Julius what I thought. . . . I don't think it made any difference. Well, maybe once. I prevailed on them to quit endorsing school boards. . . ."

Two years after the Harrisons were married, their only child, Janie N. Harrison was born on June 6, 1957. Adlene has had many accolades, but nothing that has ever happened to her has come anywhere near equaling the experience of becoming a mother. It was, Adlene said in a 1976 interview, "like it wasn't real. When you have your own child, it's like everything is happening for the first time in all the world." Adlene and Amy have become close friends. Amy lives in California and "calls me from her car phone while she drives from one appointment to another. She'd talk all the way, I think, if I had the time to listen. She says it keeps her company."

Back in 1957 the city was teetering on the brink of great change—politically, economically and ethnically. Adlene became more and more involved in volunteer work in the community. "My mother kept Janie. She fed Maury and me. Everybody was supporting me. I wasn't supporting them. I think about that and I feel bad."

In 1963, Adlene was named to the City Plan Commission, a post she held for eight years. Having done all her homework very carefully, she arrived at her first meeting to be greeted warmly and told that the last woman who served on the commission always brought home-baked cookies. "She said, 'Gentlemen,' you have the wrong woman. I do not bake cookies. I'm here to help you take care of our city.'" For some time she was the only woman on the commission, a situation that was never comfortable for her in any of the jobs she has held. "I was so glad when Mo Sloan and then Kay Gallagher came on the commission. They both turned out to be strong, tough, excellent commissioners. It was the first time I'd had a chance to nurture women in any major way. . . .

"Women usually bring a different dimension, an additional consideration to the table. They are more sensitive to the needs of children and women. They care about family neighborhoods. . . . This doesn't mean that some men don't care and it doesn't mean that men are the enemy. What it means is that it takes all of us working together and taking into account everybody's best interests before we make decisions that affect everybody. . . . For a long time the attitude in Dallas was 'if it's right for business, it's right for Dallas.' I got the reputation of being opposed to business. I'm not opposed to business. It is good for Dallas. I'm for business in a way that everybody can win."

Adlene thinks that her greatest contribution to the City Plan Commission was in creating a climate conducive for neighborhood groups to organize. "It took years to get neighborhoods working together. And they still have to learn how to cooperate with each other to effect major change. Everybody is eager to speak out when something needs correcting in their own back yard, but they are not willing to work for the same protection for others."

At a family reunion Adlene greeted Joe Golman and told him she was pleased that he had announced he would be running for city council. Later at the dinner, he responded to the toast for his candidacy by announcing that Adlene would be his campaign manager. "I was astonished. I told him I didn't know anything about running a campaign and he said I would do fine. I told other family members I wasn't qualified to run a political campaign and all of them said I was. On the way home I told Maury I didn't know how to do this and he said go for it. I was a bright person; I would learn.

"So, I didn't have any choice but to do a good job. Joe was elected to office by the largest margin of any of the candidates." It was at a Christmas party in 1972 that Louis Nichols told Adlene she ought to run for the city council. Bob Hollin told her the same thing. "I had opposed their requests several times at the city plan commission and I reminded both of them. 'If I'm on the city council, my vote will count,' I told them. They said they knew it, but I'd always been prepared and I'd always been fair. I wanted to run for the council, but I didn't want to do that to my family. On the way home I told Maury this and he said, 'If you are going to work all this hard, your vote ought to count.' I thought it over a few days and then one morning we were all in the kitchen—Maury and Janie and me—and I said to them, 'Listen, you both say you want me to run for the council. I'd like to do it, but if I do, this family will be totally disrupted. Because if I do it, I'm going to do a good job. I'll be on call 24 hours a day. There'll be times when we'll all wish we were somebody else, somewhere else. If you can't live with that, tell me now and I won't run. Because I don't want any guilt trips later.' They both hugged me and said go for it! It was rough on the family. But not once did either of them say they were sorry we'd made the choice." Her mother, her sister and other members of the family were equally supportive. "My sister was the most giving person I've ever known. While I was out 'saving' the city, she was the glue that held the family together." Her mother, a woman who lived a totally different lifestyle to Adlene, "was totally supportive. She swelled with pride. Even after she was very old and living at Golden Acres and sometimes not aware of a lot of things, she would grab my hand and introduce me and talk about all the things I had done."

Adlene ran for city council with the sanction of the Citizens Charter Association, the venerable "Old Boys' Network" to which she had often voiced opposition. She was chosen for a place on the ticket after John Schoellkopf became president of CCA and vowed to bring in some new people. Many old-timers opposed her candidacy. Among the opposition was John Stemmons, who had salvaged the Trinity River bottoms. After it was confirmed that she would run for office, some of those who supported her asked if she would go to see John Stemmons. She agreed to do so.

"I walked in his office—a great, monstrous, sumptuous office. He greets me and sits down behind his desk. Before I can say a word, he says, 'I will fight with every last breath I have to keep Dallas from going single district.' That's just the beginning. He lays out the old-line business community's agenda. He says, 'We always have team work in Dallas and I know you're going to do a fine job.'" When I can finally get a word in, I say, 'Mr. Stemmons, thank you very much for seeing me. I appreciate your time,' and I get up to leave. He says, 'Just a minute, Little Lady. I want to show you something.' He walks over to the curtains of his office and pushes a button and the draperies open to the most breathtaking view of Dallas I've ever seen. He says, 'See that skyline? See that city. That's my city . . . .' I say, 'It's my city, too, Mr. Stemmons,' and I leave.

"There's so much about John Stemmons that's admirable. So much about him and all those leaders like him that we have to be grateful for . . . . When I ran for a second term, Mr. Stemmons still opposed me and once said he would run for the job himself if they couldn't find somebody to oppose me. But he didn't run and no one opposed me. I was elected for a second term."

Adlene was a Dallas City Councilwoman from 1973-1977. For the council she chaired the Community Development Committee, the Transportation Committee and the Child Advisory Committee and was a member of the Public Safety Committee, the Arts Committee and the Public Utility Committee. Often she was told by men that they enjoyed working with her because she thought just like a man and she would say, no, she thought just like an enlightened woman.

Once, she said, City Manager Alex Bickley told her that women are just like unions. He told me, 'Women never give up on anything. They keep right on coming back until they get what they want.'"

In a 1973 interview, as a new councilwoman, Adlene said that women "as individuals and as groups should . . . express their views. They are so aware of the problems of child care, school drop-outs and the aged because they are the care-takers. Our Council would be more responsive to the crises of children, youth and the aged if women would . . . talk about what they know best . . . . The responsibility of women is not only to look after their own homes but to make their voices heard for those who do not have a voice of their own . . . . We produce the kind of citizens our children will become. When we do not care enough to provide a safe and rewarding atmosphere for our children, we breed a youth who turns to juvenile delinquency, dope addiction and robbery. We would save our city a great deal of money if we put our time and our money into prevention."

As a city councilwoman Adlene said she averaged three nights a week in public work. Often she had a commitment every night. But, she "loved it! There are duties you buy when you run for public office and win."

Adlene Harrison views Dallas from atop the Times Herald building shortly after she became the first woman to be its mayor. She told civic leader John Stemmons, "This is my city, too."

In her final year of serving on the city council, Adlene was elected mayor pro-tem, second in command who chaired the council when the mayor was not present. Before her term ended, Mayor Wes Wise resigned to run for Congress and Adlene became mayor of Dallas, the first woman to hold that position. She handled the gavel with fairness, professionalism and humor. As a councilwoman, in the briefings prior to city council meetings, several of the men smoked cigars. Adlene and Lucy Patterson, who also was on the council, choked and gasped through those meetings. Finally, the two women solved the problem. Adlene bought cigars for her and Lucy. When the men lighted up, so did they, blowing cigar smoke into the faces of their male cohorts. "That solved the smoking problem," Adlene said.

During one of the council meetings which she chaired, there was a hearing on tenants' rights and the manner in which the city did not monitor properties. When Charlie Young got up to testify "he was so angry with the Council for not passing a strong tenants' ordinance, that he opened up a shoe box and let out hundreds of cockroaches. The press made quite a thing of that, but I didn't. He had made his point. It was one of those funny things that you always tell your grandchildren—and I think it made a difference in the way the Council related to tenants."

Adlene's most difficult decision was whether, or not, to run for mayor in 1977. She had everything going for her. She enjoyed the reputation of being a councilperson who was fair to all her constituents and in being a mayor who led from an even, controlled and honest basis. Everywhere she went people were urging her to announce her candidacy. "And I wanted to. Oh, how I wanted to. But there was something else to consider. I knew Judge (W. M.) Taylor's decision on school integration would come down at any time and

I wanted the community to give its children an even chance at education even more than I wanted to be mayor.

"If I had run, I would have had to resign as mayor. I felt that if I stayed in office for the judge's decision, I could help to make a smooth transition to a new way of education. If I left the position, I did not know what would happen. So, I would make up my mind to resign and run—and then I would rethink and decide I must stay. I bugged the life out of Maury. Every time we were together for any time at all I would ask him what he thought I ought to do and he would say he wasn't going to be responsible for my decisions. I would have to make them myself. So, I would decide I absolutely would not be a candidate and then I would be out in the community and people would not let up urging me to run and I would come home again and say I couldn't pass up this chance. It would be the last one I had to make a real difference in the city I loved."

She decided not to run. Thousands of people were disappointed. "I felt terrible. I didn't want to let the women down. I didn't want to let the minorities down. I didn't want to let anybody down. I didn't want to let me down. But I had to do it."

In March of 1976 Judge Taylor's decision was announced. In retrospect, she knows that her decision to remain in office and help her city peacefully to accept the ruling is the right thing to have done. On March 10, 1976, she issued a statement from the mayor's office. It urged the citizens to comply fully and peacefully with the judge's ruling. She said, in part:

> For many years, Dallas has tried to provide a high standard of public education in the best interest of all members of our community. Court decisions about how to achieve full opportunity . . . have attracted the interest and concern of many citizen groups. In this process, the fears of parents have often obscured the real issue—the needs of their children. Now is the time . . . that Dallas gather all the energy and resources available to assure a strong and viable school system for the future.
>
> Judge W. M. Taylor has rendered his long-awaited decision . . . . It is for the sake of the children . . . that I am committed to accept and help implement the findings and directions of the District Court. It is the responsibility of adults to build constructive support and orderly implementation of the court's decision for these reasons:
>
> First, because I believe the success in education can be found in mutual understanding, positive effort, cooperation—not in controversy, dissension and divisiveness;
>
> Second, because I believe that Judge Taylor has given all interested parties a full hearing and has permitted all reasonable alternatives to be studied, argued and compared . . . .
>
> Third, because I believe that the time has come to adopt strategies of positive action to overcome the frustrations caused by doubt, uncertainty and confusion.
>
> I know that the citizens of Dallas, with me, will never have another peaceful night's rest if any Dallas child is harmed—physically or emotionally—by any irresponsible act by a lawless person . . . . Even though we may not all concur with the court's ruling, we do agree on peaceful means and reasonable discussion. I am . . . confident that the majority of our citizens will work hard with the City Council all day, every day, if necessary, to achieve educational excellence . . . . For those who may doubt the will of the majority, I assure you that any act of civil disobedience will be dealt with promptly and firmly . . . .
>
> Personally, I am committed to action which will heal . . . Dallas and renew the tradition which has held for twenty-five years—peaceful integration of public facilities, open accommodations, and open housing—all in the spirit of the greatest good . . . .
>
> . . . I am asking that you join with me and other members of the community in assuring a shield of safety and the promise of educational opportunity for every child in Dallas . . . .

Helping to implement the court ruling on schools was Adlene's most personally rewarding experience as councilperson and mayor. She also sponsored the first historic ordinance in Dallas for Swiss Avenue. (See Chapter 35) and she led the rezoning ordinance for Bryan Place that brought the first major living accommodations back to near the downtown. Town houses in Bryan Place were the first residences that lured people back toward downtown Dallas to live. Adlene worked with Bryghte Godbold to create the West End, which was a maze of empty warehouses to the West of downtown Dallas. The West End very quickly became a mecca for upscale restaurants and the favorite meeting place for young professionals who poured out of the downtown skyscrapers daily for lunch or came back to meet their friends in these familiar haunts for dinner.

Adlene's most enduring struggle was for day care. "Unless a city takes care of its children, it will eventually lose the struggle to upgrade all of its other resources. "I have worked on day care all of my public life," she said. She pointed to *some* progress: the city now has ordinances that control licensing for child care. Several centers in or near downtown Dallas, nonexistent a few years ago, are there because Adlene and people like her were unrelenting in their efforts to get them. Usually this required rezoning, which she addressed with caution because she was a strong zoning proponent.

She's lost some things that mattered to her, among them the Comanche Peak Plant. "I fought Comanche Peak because it was too expensive and nothing ever convinced me that it could be made safe. It is the biggest crisis our city has faced and to most people it was a non-crisis. I still think it's treacherous; I hope I'm wrong . . . . The Council voted 10-1 to okay it."

Having closed the door on running for mayor, Adlene had no idea that she would use her talents in public life by becoming regional administrator of the Environment Protection Agency. She resigned from the city council in 1977 when Jimmy Carter appointed her regional administrator of the U. S. Environmental Protection Agency. While holding that position for four years, she was able to find and promote many outstanding women to key positions and in 1981, shortly before her term expired, she was awarded the National Federal Employment Woman Distinguished Service Award for Efforts on Behalf of Women. She had barely completed this assignment when she was appointed chairperson of the Dallas Area Rapid Transit Board, a position she held from 1982 through 1986.

Adlene became a key adviser to many people holding public office, among them Annette Strauss who sought her counsel before she ran for a Dallas City Council seat. During the two terms Annette served as mayor, she and Adlene spoke by telephone frequently. "Annette did a fantastic job," Adlene said of Mayor Strauss as she was winding down her second term and being criticized for speaking with Judge Buchmeyer about redistricting the city. "It's a tempest in a teapot," Adlene said of the fracas. "I spoke to Judge Taylor all the time when I was mayor and he was about to hand down his decision of the schools. How can we work together if we don't talk to each other?"

The wall of a long hallway in Adlene's home is a museum of her life, typically arranged and hung by Maury. On one side of the wall are family memorabilia—photographs of grandparents, parents, children, aunts, uncles, cousins. On the other wall are the tokens of her public life including the Zonta Award, the national Brotherhood and Humanitarian Award from the National Conference of Christians and Jews, the Dallas Historical Society award for excellence in public service, the Women's Center Women Helping Women award, the Headliner of the Year Award (1976) from the Dallas Press Club, the Outstanding Citizen Award from the Black Chamber of Commerce; the Community Relations Award from the American Jewish Committee and many others.

When Adlene is working on an issue, it is all consuming; she never lets up. She stops people who can be helpful to her cause anywhere and everywhere, even if there is but a moment, to explain, illustrate, argue. There is never any doubt where she stands for she is openly honest and candid. Listening to her, one might think that every civic decision is a crisis. But, once the situation is resolved, she usually views it not as a crisis but as an open door to new progress. She rarely chews over old bones. And she holds no grudges.

She is incredibly gifted to see the good in people and while she may disagree absolutely with what they do, she can give a long outline of their values. She did not accept gifts that came with strings attached. When she was running for office, this occasionally meant returning a check. "Pauline Kress was my campaign manager and she'd say, what do you mean, you want me to send this back? We have to pay our bills, and I'd say if I get a check for the wrong reasons, we send it back. I know what he wants and I can't do it and I can't accept his money."

What were the crises? "There haven't been many really volatile things. School desegregation had the *potential* of being volatile, but we had people like Jack Lowe, Sr. saying we have to make this work. We created the Magnet School System. I happened to be along and gave my best efforts to making it happen.

"It was a different climate (in the 1970s). Black people were not fighters. Big leadership threw them a bone now and then and kept control. I was never afraid of what our Black citizens would do. I was scared to death that some bigoted red-neck Anglo would blow it apart. The climate has changed now. Young Blacks do not accept the bones. And leaders have to worry about the possibility of volatility."

Adlene is a strong and consistent supporter of women in public office. "I have been in the catbird seat to watch women, and in a few instances to help women, get appointments to commissions and boards. I have been in a place where I could nurture them and sometimes give them some assistance. I have also been in a place where I could talk my male counterparts into choosing women for positions. I have been proud of these women and proud to be counted among them."

But she never filled a position with a woman just because she was female. "When I went on the Council, many women saw me as the way to gain advantages for women at all levels of government. I always said 'If you have political aspirations, put yourself through a training period.... Work in some organizational capacity for the city or for a bond issue or for a candidate. The system eats alive neophytes'." Women often said to her that her responsibility was to fill every appointment with a woman, Adlene countered that her responsibility was to fill every vacancy with the best qualified individual. "I told them that I was looking for a woman who would make all women look good.

"My life has been tied up with women's things. I've always worked with them and I've had the pleasure of finding a woman, maybe buried somewhere in obscurity, and opening the doors for her. It doesn't matter whether she's Democrat or Republican and what color she is or what age, if she had talents, I wanted her working for Dallas. I'm proud of every woman I've ever appointed.

"And there's something else. I have never disparaged or sloughed off a woman in the presence of men. I will tell *her* what I think. I may tell a few other women what I think. I may not be able to support her as a candidate but I won't put her down. And if she does win, I will do everything I can to help her."

Many people thought redistricting the city to give fairer representation to all citizens of Dallas was a potentially volatile issue. Adlene never did. Just as she predicted, with the usual amount of grumbling, single districts were approved and are working. "We've had a lot of issues that seemed a crisis at the time that turned out to be opportunities for growth and enrichment."

As long as she lives, Adlene Harrison will care about her city, will raise her voice to discipline it when she disapproves of the direction it is taking, will vocally support laws and causes she thinks are just, with equal vehemence will oppose those she feels are wrong. And, like a good mother, will love it anyway.

Faustina Porras Martinez, matriarch of the Martinez family, above, and right, with her son, Alfred, proving that she came by the title Mama Cha-Cha honestly.

THE MARTINEZES—FAUSTINA, IRENE (GARCIA), ANITA

• • • •

Faustina, 1900—1990; Irene, 1916; Anita, 1925

In 1914, a black-eyed beauty, mature beyond her 14 years, arrived to make her home at 2010 Griffin Street in Dallas. Her name was Faustina Gamboa Porras and her advanced maturity came, in part, from conditions that brought her to the city. Born on February 22, 1900, in Chihuahua, Mexico, she was one of the seven children of Epigmenio and Dominga Gamboa Porras and lived carefree in an upper middle class neighborhood. Her father was a *curadora*, a self-trained-and-experienced healer esteemed in his neighborhood. She was sent to school at an early age and encouraged to read and study. In 1913 her life and that of the family's neighbors and friends suddenly and, in some cases violently, came to an end. Since 1910 a revolution had been raging in Mexico and in 1913 it reached her village. Pancho Villa, termed by some as the "Robin Hood" of his time and by others as a bloody bandit, took over Chihuahua.

Years later, in a 1980 interview, there would still be gaps in Faustina's memory, as if some things were too painful to remember about the family's escape to the United States and the first years of its resettlement in Dallas. She wanted to remember the good times. She had written out a prayer and the interview proceeded only after she had shared it.

> Thank you, God, for letting me reach my 80th birthday and be together with my whole family. Thank You for the wonderful memories. As I look back through the years, many emotions fill my heart. I have had many satisfactions and many hardships and disappointments.
>
> Life as I know and enjoy it today is made up of all of the hard work we have put into it, day by day, throughout the years.
>
> Through my family, I have been very fortunate. Our close-knit family life has brought about the success we enjoy today. At no place on the face of this earth could all of this have been possible except in the United States and no place has given us more opportunity than Dallas. God bless America always!

Faustina paused. Looked at her daughter, Irene Garcia, and added: "In all of my life, every time I wanted to do something, I would say a prayer. Oh, God, open the door for me. Here I come!"

Faustina and her family arrived in Dallas among the first Hispanics. They came with almost nothing in worldly goods, with a language alien to that spoken in their chosen city and they settled in the area that only recently had been vacated by the prostitutes. Entirely innocent of the stigma attached to this part of town, they were glad to find houses big enough to accommodate their large families. This meant there were three strikes against them: They did not know the language, had little money and settled in an area that had only recently been a Red Light District.

Faustina, haltingly, sketched her family's escape across the Rio Grande into the United States. "I remember Pancho Villa coming to our village. He was in the first motor car I had ever seen. He looked so grand sitting in that great car. Like all of the heroes I had read about. Only he was not a hero.... We were not told a lot. We were just kids. But we knew. Things were very bad. My father was a respected citizen. The most prominent people were rounded up first. Sometimes they were never heard from again. We were in very great danger. My father said we must leave...."

They left with the clothes they could wear and what few possessions they could carry. Dr. Porras could afford the nickel per person fee to get all the members of his family across the Rio Grande. Not everybody was so fortunate and the penniless ones were often turned back. Her father also had train fare for the family to Dallas. Most escaping Mexicans settled into South Texas, which was the extent of their dreams from prosecution.

Faustina remembered her early Dallas days as fraught with frustration. She wanted to go to school, but there was no school near enough for her to attend and she had advanced beyond the Catholic schooling established for children with Mexican heritage. "I cried and cried," she said, and shrugged, "But it was not to be."

Uprooted from a privileged class, without money, set down among people whose language she did not understand and people whose attitudes made her and her family feel unwelcome, Faustina was both puzzled and determined—puzzled that the good life she had enjoyed had no value in her new home and determined that she would hurdle whatever barriers were placed in her way.

There was such hard work. "We took jobs in the field. Whatever we could find. The pay was pennies. It took all of the money we could get to eat. My father worked from early in the morning until dark. When he could find work. We worked with him. My brothers and sisters."

There was a big fenced back yard where the family lived and a swing her father attached to the limbs of a giant tree. She and her sister, Delila, a year older, were too big to play on the swing, but they were attracted by the voices and laughter of men coming from the other side of the fence, so they would swing very high and peer over to see what was going on. The hilarity came from a pool hall. Inevitably, the pretty girls were spotted by customers of the tavern. One young man, who delivered milk for a dairy, spotted the girls. The next time he delivered the one quart of milk the Porrases could afford, a note was with it. He wanted to meet the girl he had glimpsed in the swing over the backyard fence, that he would like her to be his girl friend. Delila found the note when she brought in the milk. She met the young man. There followed an appropriate courtship and eventually the two married. Half a century later, after the death of his wife, the man confessed the note had been meant for Faustina.

Faustina said she did not remember meeting Miguel Martinez. In 1914 Mike Martinez lived at 513 Griffin Street, several blocks from where the Porras family made its home. But the neighborhood was close-knit, united by a common place of worship and shared recreational outlets. In any other setting a 25-year-old bachelor might not have glanced a second time at the just-budding Faustina. He was ten years her senior, born on May 8, 1890, and had come alone to Dallas ahead of the Porras family. It is something of a mystery how he found the time to woo and win a bride because Mike Martinez, his family says, always was a workaholic. In 1914-15 he held three jobs. He was a dishwasher at the Oriental Hotel, went from there to an ice cream cone making factory where he did the clean-up work and then to a pool hall where he closed up at 2 a.m. Faustina did not remember whether it was the same pool hall of her swinging observations, but it likely was because the city directory lists only one pool hall in the neighborhood at that time.

Faustina and Mike were married on Thanksgiving Day, November 25, 1915. "It was the only time my father could get off from work long enough to get married," Irene Garcia would say later. They set up housekeeping in a three-room house on McKinney and shared it with Elvira Leal, matriarch of the Leal tortilla factory which was located on Harwood. Mike was still a pot washer at the Oriental Hotel, but an astute observer who watched and absorbed the chef at work. One night when the chef did not come to work, Mike filled in and did such a good job that the chef felt threatened and fired him. It was an auspicious day for Mike, whose 18-year-old wife was expecting their second child. He decided to go into the restaurant business himself.

The first El Fenix restaurant was opened on McKinney at Griffin early in 1918. Named the Martinez Cafe, it was a one-man, virtually around-the-clock operation. Mike served food as long as there were any customers to eat it and did all of the clean-up, managing, buying and bookkeeping after hours. At first, he served only American food, but soon, to satisfy his own palate, he introduced a few dishes from his native land. Curious customers asked for samples, liked the taste and insisted on servings. On September 15, 1918, Mexican food became the restaurant's staple.

Mike introduced the Mexican plate in the Martinez restaurant. It was the first time in Dallas, and possibly the first time in the United States, that one plate held a combination of foods, and it happened because Mike got tired of washing so many dishes. Each food, as was the custom in his country, was served in a separate dish. As the customers increased, the number of dishes increased. It was getting to be prohibitively expensive to supply the restaurant with so many dishes and an overwhelming burden to wash so many. Mike decided to use one plate and arrange the food as attractively as possible on it. At first he was very careful that no one food touched another, but as time went by the tamales and enchiladas, beans and rice topped with cheese were combined in one artistic steaming whole.

Customers began to arrive from downtown and then from across town. Soon larger quarters were needed. In 1922 Mike bought a vacant building at 1608 McKinney and converted it into a restaurant. Now that the cuisine of his native country was food that most customers came to eat, the new logo read "The Finest Mexican Food is Served," and above the new logo was the new name "El Fenix," the Spanish spelling for phoenix, the mythical bird of great beauty that lived eternally, burning itself to death at the end of each long life and then rising from the fiery ashes to renewed youth and yet another life cycle.

The new restaurant was across the street from where the family lived. Faustina, like all good Mexican wives, was not allowed to work in the restaurant. But her homemade tamales became famous there. Mike took bowls of masa home to her, she made the tamales and he took them back to the restaurant as a part of the regular fare. Her flour tortillas, becoming famous among the kids in their neighborhood, found equal favor among El Fenix customers.

Even though her husband was across the street, Faustina rarely saw him. "He worked 24 hours a day," Irene said later. "He was always going the extra mile. When the business expanded, he hired help, but he always kept an eye on the food preparation and the way it looked on the plate. He demanded that the customers be served promptly and courteously." Mike did not like the public relations part of the business. Once he hired a cook who greatly resembled him and when a customer asked to see the manager, Mike would send the cook. Whether the customer heaped praises or had a complaint, it was the "substitute" Mike who took the bow or heard the rebuke.

As the restaurant prospered and the family increased, the Martinez family required more space. They moved, first to McKinnon Street and later to Cole Avenue. They were not welcomed into either neighborhood. Faustina declined to recall specifics of those moves. Irene, reluctantly, recalled that the "edging up" and "getting out" of the entrenched

Mexican neighborhoods had their painful moments. The children were sometimes stoned by the neighborhood children on their way to school and in Pike's Park. "It was just kid stuff," Irene said. "I don't even really remember." She does remember that when the family moved to 2701 Cole Ave. near what is now the Quadrangle, into a house for which the family paid cash, the neighbors signed a petition trying to keep them out. They were somewhat appeased when Mike bought the vacant lot next door to the Martinez home thus putting some distance between the established neighbors and his family. Typically, Irene Garcia does not remember the names of the people who signed the petition to keep Mexicans from moving into the Cole Avenue neighborhood. She does remember that Emma Dove Gay Sousa refused to sign that petition, "and I'll have a warm place in my heart for her forever."

The Martinezes were good neighbors. "I don't know whether it was that the vacant lot became the neighborhood playground or whether it was our telephone that people borrowed that began to win everybody over, but mostly it was Mama's tortillas. Before we went to school in the morning, she always gave us a tortilla, an egg and a glass of milk. When we got home in the afternoon, she'd give us a tortilla, beans and a glass of milk. She was almost running a short order restaurant from our back door. The kids *loved* her tortillas and she'd pass them out to everybody.'

Faustina was kept busy with the Martinez children. She gave birth to twelve—Irene, Mike, Jr., twins Hortencia (Tencia Stickle) and Elvira, Henry, Alfred, Gilbert, Faustina (Tina) and Reuben and three other infants that did not survive. Elvira, one of the twins, also died in infancy, leaving eight children that Faustina reared to adulthood.

"Mother was a saint," Irene said. "She was very religious. She started her day every day with prayer. I don't know how she managed when we were small, but as she grew older, her prayer time increased to an hour every morning. I lived with her all of my life, married and unmarried . . . . I don't understand when I hear women complain that they can't get along with their mothers.

"My parents were a team. Papa would get home about three in the morning and Mama would be waiting up for him. She had the only key to our house so she would have to let him in. All transactions between Mama and Papa took place at that time. We kids never knew when there were problems."

Mike Martinez took his sons into the business when they were children and taught them all to cook. "Papa and all the boys cooked. The girls never did," Irene said. "He wouldn't allow us in the kitchen; he was afraid we would hear foul language. He trained us to be hostesses, bookkeepers and cashiers in the restaurant.' He did not allow them to work anywhere else.

As the business prospered and the children grew, Faustina occupied herself with church and other volunteer work, with sewing and handwork. "If I had gone to college, I would have been a clothing designer," she said. Instead, she used her creative abilities in making clothes for herself, her daughters and her grandchildren. "She could copy anything," said Irene. "All she had to do was look at a dress, no matter how complicated it was, and she could make one better!" Faustina liked brilliant colors, exotic fabrics, sequins, beads and feathers. She took a course in dying and fabric-covering shoes and had a pair of shoes to match every outfit she owned. At one time her wardrobe included 200 pairs of shoes. As the years increased, so did her pleasure in wearing beautiful clothes, especially evening wear.

All five of the Martinez sons served in the military, four of them in World War II and one in the Korean conflict. In 1943, with four of their sons in service, Faustina and Mike Martinez became citizens of the United States. She went to night classes, polished her English, learned history and government and passed the citizenship test. She found she still loved to study.

During World War II when employees were hard to get and harder to keep, Faustina began to help out in the restaurant. She learned she liked that, too. She took up several hobbies—acting, photography and ceramics. Once she won a first prize at the State Fair for a piece of her ceramic art. She signed up for a Dale Carnegie course and excelled. She loved mastering English words and phrases, and the actress in her loved to test them on others. As the years went by, she became a doting grandmother, caring for their mothers as much as for the children. "She was a supportive, loving mother-in-law," said Anita Martinez. "When Priscilla came, she made her the most beautiful clothes. She brought clothes for the boys, too. Once she arrived at our house with a whole wardrobe of baby clothes from Neiman's!" But her new independence and community involvement precluded her being the ever-present babysitting grandma. She would be glad to help them pay for a baby sitter, she told her children, but they couldn't count on her to do the sitting herself.

As long as her husband lived, Faustina planned her schedule around his, which continued to include long hours at the restaurant. She would keep the house quiet during the day so that he could rest. In February 22, 1946, her 46th birthday, Mike gave Faustina the best of all birthday presents: He promised her some of his time. Grateful for the safe return of their sons from the war, celebrating their still-new American citizenship and wanting time to do things together, the Martinezes paid the gift tax and turned the business over to their children.

He also had time for the dream he had long shared with his wife, that he would do something for his native village in Mexico. He had never forgotten his own deprived childhood when, at age seven he had begun to drive a string of burros to and from coal mines for pennies a week. When he was 15 he had gone to work in the coal mines full time to support himself, his widowed mother and a sister. He had made his way to America in 1911 and been successful beyond his wildest expectations.

For the next decade after he retired, Mike Martinez traveled to and from his village, Hacienda del Potrero, which is between Monterrey and Savinas, Mexico. He taught the villagers the latest methods of agriculture—how to sow, cultivate and harvest food. He helped to introduce sugar cane and other crops that would bring quick cash. He dug their first water well and took the first electrical equipment to them. He planned roads and put the natives to work building them. Many times he paid their wages from his own private funds. He built a huge plaza which the natives named the Miguel Martinez Plaza. He installed concrete seating under the shade around it. The names of all of his children are inscribed on one special bench. Every Saturday night, he gave a dance open to the public. When his sons and his daughters and their families came for these parties, he was especially pleased. "But one of his absolute rules was that if we came, we had to dance with everybody. No exceptions," said Irene. "I didn't always like to dance with all of the men. Some smelled bad. Some wore their hats. One, I remember, was real short and he wore his hat and it hit me in the face all time we were dancing. Sometimes they couldn't dance. I would say, 'But, Papa . . .' and he'd say, No buts. Everybody deserves to have a good time. You go. You dance."

Faustina often accompanied Mike on the trips to Mexico, and always she went for special occasions. He was there and she was preparing on fly down to celebrate her birthday on February 22, 1956, when he had a heart attack and died.

The entire family rallied, pulling together as they had always done in a crisis, but Faustina would not be comforted. "I thought my mother was going under," Irene says. For two years she lived enveloped in her own sorrow. She did not sleep well. She almost gave up eating. She spent long hours in her room with the door closed. Her few outings with her children and grandchildren were perfunctory. There was no joy to anything."

Her son and daughter-in-law, Alfred and Anita Nanez Martinez, had taken up ballroom dancing. "I knew she was a wonderful dancer and I suspected that might bring her out, but how to get her started?" Anita said. They gave her dance lessons as a present and everybody—children and grandchildren—pressured her to use them. "We made her think our feelings would be hurt if she didn't. We took her to the first class. In no time at all she outclassed us! Dancing gave her self-confidence."

Faustina, who had been listening while her daughter and daughter-in-law told the story, chuckled: "They got me started and now they can't get me stopped," she said.

She began to travel. She joined the Dallas International Cultural and Social Circle to help welcome Dallas residents of foreign birth to the city—so that she would have another wonderful place to dance. She lent her special expertise and support to newcomers in the women's auxiliary of the Dallas Restaurant Association. She found new pleasure in worship at Christ the King Catholic Church where she was a "life member" of the altar society. She was especially proud of her "volunteer for life" award from St. Paul Hospital auxiliary and of the honorary membership awarded her by the Daughters of the American Revolution. She encouraged the family to hold its El Fenix board meetings at home so that she could cook for them.

Dancing was the impetus of Faustina's life for three more decades. She danced her way into the hearts of Dallas. She took class after class. She "graduated" from four dance instructors, finding a new one when she thought she had learned everything that each could teach her. She mastered the rhumba, the mambo, the samba and the tango along with the waltz and the foxtrot. Dallas called her Mama Cha-Cha. Her favorite, she said in 1980, was the samba. "I like fast music. I don't get tired. Slow music is for old folks. It's boring." She would be on the dance floor almost every night, she said, if she could find partners with as much energy as she had. She gave up ceramics because she said it kept her home too much. "Dancing," she said, "is exercise with pleasure. I used to go to the old folks home and dance for them," she said. "I quit when I found out I was the oldest one there." She collected so many trophies that her children bought a special case for them.

She was in her 80th year when the telephone rang at 2 a.m. at Irene Garcia's bedside. "What are you doing?," asked a chipper Faustina. "Sleeping . . . like all sane people," said Irene. There was a pause. "Oh," said Faustina. "I didn't realize it was so late. I just got home. I've been out dancing with *your* grandson." Her escort had, indeed, been her great-grandson, John Michael McBride, Jr. who at that time was a sophomore at SMU.

On her 80th birthday, her six surviving children, their spouses, her 22 grandchildren and their spouses and her six great grandchildren honored Faustina with a dinner dance at Dallas's Chaparral Club. "I'm dancing a special arrangement of 'The Last Waltz'," quipped Faustina on the day before the party, "because, who knows, tomorrow may never come!" Tomorrow did come—3,394 more tomorrows. Faustina danced many of those days away. She died on June 8, 1990, at 90 and rests beside her husband in Calvary Hill Cemetery. Six children, 21 grandchildren, 21 great grandchildren and 2 great-great grandchildren survived her.

Irene Martinez Garcia, at left, and, at right, standing next to her mother Faustina, with her sisters, Tina McDaniel and Tencha Stickle.

IRENE MARTINEZ GARCIA

The first of the Martinez children, Irene Martinez McBride Garcia, was born on September 19, 1916, 10 months after her parents married when her mother was only 16 years old. She grew up, along with her siblings in the family restaurant business. She was a toddler when her father opened the first restaurant. She is now president emeritus of the El Fenix board of directors, and like her mother, Irene has gained verve and confidence with each passing year.

There were times when Irene, like others in the four generations of the family-owned business, tried to escape. Some have done it but Irene found, for her, that "the benefits and blessings outweighed the frustrations." As long as her father lived she did not dare try to break away, and following his death, she discovered she did not want to leave.

"Running a restaurant is like having a party every day," she said. "My mother thought we were all crazy, but that's the way we are." Her parents served separate but equally important roles in the rearing of their sons and daughters, she said. "My father treated all three of his girls like babies. He was the old-fashioned patriarchal father. But, by his example and because we grew up being hostesses in the restaurant, he imbued in us a hardcore work ethic. My mother treated us like the individuals we were—and are. She provided a very safe, warm and loving home."

Irene started to school at Cumberland Hill where her natural curiosity and bright mind was handicapped by her lack of proficiency in English. "It was terrible! I thought in Spanish and then would have to translate—and that took time." She had reached the seventh grade when teachers told her that she would not be promoted. In those days when many students—and most Mexican students—did not finish high school, graduation from grade school (there was no junior high) was a significant milestone. And Irene did plan to go on to high school. To be told that she would be held back was devastating. She dissolved into tears. W. J. Morris, the assistant principal, intervened. He said that if she and the four boys in her class who also were failing, would come to school an hour early each morning, he would tutor them. Irene was ecstatic. She told her mother who told her father who said absolutely no. No girl of his could attend a class with four boys and a male teacher. Absolutely not. Irene turned on the tears again. "I cried a lot in those days," she says. "It was the *only* way I could get anybody's attention." After several days of tears, Faustina reported to Mike that Irene had stopped eating and cried all the time and was surely going to get sick. He finally agreed that Irene could attend the class if her sister would go with her. "Tencia must have hated that," Irene says, "but she went. I graduated with my class. Mr. Morris was the first teacher who believed in me."

In September of 1930, Irene was the first Mexican student ever to enroll in North Dallas High School. Getting in was not easy. Until then, the few Mexican children who reached high school went to Bryan High near downtown Dallas. Irene was exactly the age her mother had been when she first arrived in Dallas and though the community had changed, there were still invisible boundaries for its Hispanic population. "I wanted desperately to go to North Dallas because Mr. Morris said it was the place for me, but my parents discouraged me. They did not want me to feel the kind of discrimination that they had. I cried again . . . ."

In high school Irene blossomed. Her grades soared. She signed up for every English and literature course offered, but she also took science and math courses. She was elected president of the Spanish Club, then president of the Pan-American Club and then president of the Chess Club. She was popular with her classmates. "I think I was such a good student because my father would not allow me to date—or to do anything else without a chaperon. So, I just read and read. When her trigonometry teacher sent home a note that he would be taking his class on a field trip to measure a bridge at White Rock Lake, Mike Martinez said again that Irene could not go. He had heard what went on at White Rock Lake. He had heard it was a "lover's paradise" and no daughter of his could go there. Irene cried. Faustina told Mike that Irene had stopped eating and was crying all the time and was going to get sick. Mike said all right, she could go, if her mother and the other kids went too. "So there we were, Mama sitting on a park bench and all seven of my little brothers and sisters playing on the swings while I did my trig assignment."

When Irene graduated from North Dallas, Faustina told Mike he had to go. "Papa never went anywhere; he just worked all the time. But Mama persuaded him to go. There he was sitting near the front. Mama told me he was so proud . . . ."

He should have been. Irene was the first Mexican student to graduate from a Dallas high school with honors, a four-year average of 93.6, third in her class. She was given a

Linz award for extracurricular achievement. She won a citation for never being absent or tardy during high school. She planned to go to college and become a doctor, but a counselor told her that she was too compassionate and should take a business course. Her father did not object to business training, but first wanted her to become proficient in Spanish, so he sent her to live in Mexico with friends for a year.

Back home, in September of 1936 a few days before her 20th birthday, she enrolled in Metropolitan Business College. By the time she earned her diploma she was taking dictation at the rate of 125 words per minute and typing 77 words a minute. In business school, she met John Hampton McBride. He asked her to tutor him in Spanish. Papa said yes *if* he would come to their home for lessons and if her brothers and sisters stayed in the room as chaperons. "John was the first boy ever allowed to come to our house," she said. Their budding romance had its handicaps. Irene couldn't date without a chaperon. If she and John left the house, her uncle had to accompany them. "So I got my uncle dates with my beautiful girl friends. It worked out."

Irene got her business school diploma and a job with attorneys in downtown Dallas, but she did not tell her father. She simply got dressed each morning and went off to what her father thought was her class. Her destination was her new job. "I loved it," she said. "And then my father found out. He stormed. No daughter of his would work in a downtown office with men! He threatened to divorce my mother. He threatened me. I had to quit my job. But I cried and I cried and Mama told him that Irene had stopped eating and cried all the time and was going to get sick." He compromised. If Irene had to work, he told Faustina, she would work for him.

"The next day he took me to the restaurant. He put me on the cash register." She learned quickly and retained everything. More and more, Mike trusted her, taught her, trained her and depended on her.

In 1938 Irene married John McBride and moved into an apartment away from her family. "I didn't like it," she said. She continued to work long hours at the restaurant until her only son, John Michael McBride, was born in 1942. She went back to work when the baby was six months old and never left. She and McBride were divorced in 1948 and she moved back home. Mike had already given the business to his children, but he still kept a close eye on his daughters. He did not approve of divorce, but he welcomed his daughter and grandson home. When Irene dated, she did not let her father know about it.

Irene was single for 10 years. She met Santiago (Jimmy) Garcia at El Fenix where he had taken a temporary job after he was laid off by a major Dallas manufacturing company during a business slump. "I saw this man and I knew right away he was the one for me," Irene said. "My pulse beat faster." From Mission, Jimmy Garcia could not afford to be serious about a successful businesswoman, an heir to the founder of a restaurant chain, who now chaired its board and who wore diamonds and drove a Cadillac. But serious they became. They were married on the day before her birthday, September 18, 1957. His temporary job with El Fenix has lasted almost 40 years. When Irene and Jimmy bought their home in North Dallas, they encountered almost a repeat of what had happened to Mike and Faustina in the early 1930s. They had to buy two vacant lots adjoining their property. "Nobody spelled it out," Irene says. "Nobody would dare to have said they didn't want Mexicans moving into the neighborhood."

In 1990 there were 15 restaurants in Texas and Oklahoma. The business is family-owned and managed and four generations of Martinezes run things. Irene is chairperson emeritus of the board. The vote of the majority is the decision. "Everybody is equal and nobody can persuade or coerce anyone else," Irene said.

Irene thinks she has contributed to the independence of women in Dallas, particularly young Mexican women, by her example. "When I went to work with my father, few Mexican girls were allowed to work anywhere. When other girls saw me do it, they felt they could, too, and because I'd done it without compromising myself or my heritage, other strict fathers thought it might be all right for their daughters.

"Working gave me more freedom, and freedom gave me more responsibilities. El Fenix is an integral part of Dallas," she says. "It has served as the launching pad for many Mexican restaurants, and it has been a training place for both women and men who want to go into food service. "I like to train bright young people. I tell them that nobody yet has been a success with 40 hours of work a week. Maybe they work on the job only 40 hours, but there's always homework. I tell them always to save the first and last tips they get on each shift. Restaurant work is very tiring and it's natural to let down a little when you are tired. But when you know you are going to put that last tip into a savings account for something you want very much, you're going to give quality service right to the end of your shift."

It's been years since Irene had to cry and cry and stop eating and almost get sick to prove her point. If she has opened doors for other women to walk through, she is grateful. "I wouldn't take anything for the training and discipline I got," she said, "but I don't want any other woman to have to do it." At home anywhere in the world, with anybody, she recalls her past with candor, her present with pleasure and her future with optimism. "Life is good," she said. "I know *who* I am."

Anita Nanez Martinez spreads a feast on a West Dallas street to initiate the Dallas Restaurant Auxiliary's Taste of Dallas in 1969. Anita, above, shortly after she became the first Hispanic elected to the Dallas City Council.

ANITA NANEZ MARTINEZ

It would be difficult to find anyone who belongs more to all parts of Dallas than Anita Nanez Martinez. She was born in Little Mexico, reared on Akard and Pearl streets, attended schools on the boundaries of downtown, earned her "keep" with part time jobs at H. L. Green, Sangers, and the Adolphus Hotel, began her married life in an apartment in Oak Lawn, lives in North Dallas, served two terms on the Dallas City Council and centers her heart and her volunteer work in West Dallas.

Anita joined the Martinez family on January 27, 1946, when she married Alfred. The daughter of Jose Franco and Anita Trevinio-Mongaras Nanez, she was born on December 8, 1925, at 2608 Caroline Street in the heart of Little Mexico. She grew up largely fending for herself—searching for treasures in junk heaps that might be salvaged for pennies, hanging onto the sides of her father's wagon as he conducted a pick-up and delivery service, creating plays and dance recitals clad in self-made crepe paper dresses in the dirt streets of her neighborhood, learning arts and crafts in the nearby Methodist-sponsored Wesley Community Center. Though her family's religious heritage was Catholic, "my mother allowed us great lenience in the churches we attended. She thought that religious and moral training was imperative, but it didn't matter much to her whose brand we practiced. I think this is a marvelous gift . . . ."

Anita started to Cumberland public school when she was six years old, but wanted desperately to go to St. Ann's Catholic school. Her mother discouraged it because tuition and uniforms were beyond the Nanez's ability to pay. Determined that there was a way if she only wanted it and was willing to work for it, Anita made her way across the busy street from her neighborhood to St. Ann's, met the nuns and bartered her tuition and uniforms. She entered St. Ann's in the fourth grade. "I absolutely adored it," she said. "I liked the structure, the discipline, the excellent training, but most of all their demand that I give my best. I thrived in that setting." The nuns also gave Anita a sense of her own worth. "They mirrored their belief that I was unique and special."

Anita completed the seventh grade at St. Ann's and entered Crozier Technical High School. When she was not in class, she was working—for the National Youth Administration, wrapping gifts in a downtown store, serving as BBJ (bread, butter, jelly) waitress in the coffee shop at the Adolphus Hotel. When her father died in 1939, her mother wanted Anita to quit school and go to work. "She was scared," Anita says. "I was making more money than anybody else in the family at my summer job. I always gave my pay check to Mother. I was able to persuade her that I could continue to give her money while I was in school and that I would be in a better position to help her after I got my high school diploma."

Anita's first civic involvement began when she was 14 years old. Pearl Street in front of their home was unpaved. Soot from nearby mills and dirt from traffic blew a constant dust storm that settled in their lungs, left a film on every surface and permeated their clothes. In her school civics class, Anita learned that citizens who want to change conditions should join together and present a request to elected city officials. She carried a petition door-to-door requesting that the street be paved and delivered it to city hall. It was her first lesson in effective community involvement. When it worked, it became a model that she would practice for the rest of her life.

Anita had just celebrated her 16th birthday on New Year's Eve of 1943 and had persuaded her mother to allow her to attend an adult party to celebrate. Her older sister, Tommie, would spend her New Year's eve checking coats and hats at El Fenix restaurant where she worked. The employee who helped Tommie called in sick. "My mother said I would have to help my sister. I was furious. I argued and cried, but she would not change her mind. She drove me to the restaurant. I didn't say a word all the way."

Anita was further chagrined when she learned that she was also expected to wait on tables. She had just come through the door with a tray full of enchiladas when she spotted a tall, handsome boy. "Who is that boy?," she asked her sister at the first opportunity. "Oh," said Tommie, "that's Tencha's (Hortencia) little brother. His name is Alfred Martinez." Hortencia, Alfred's sister, and Olivia, Anita's sister, were good friends, but their younger siblings had never met. When introduced, Alfred's first words to Anita were, "Do you like balloons?" Her answer, "Oh, yes, though to be honest I'd never thought about it before. Then he just disappeared. A few minutes later he came back with a balloon sculpture and gave it to me."

The budding romance was totally in keeping with the couple's Hispanic culture. Eddie Mongaras, Anita's cousin and Alfred's friend, arranged for them to go to a movie together. World War II was raging and Alfred joined the Army Air Force (there was no separate Air Force at the time). Anita continued in high school, graduated in 1943, took a Civil Service examination and went to work for the Eighth Service Command. They wrote to each other every day and saw each other on his occasional leaves home. He was preparing to go overseas when the war ended in 1945.

On January 27, 1946, seven weeks after her 20th birthday, Anita Nanez and Alfred Martinez were married. "I wanted so badly to keep my job," she said, "but good Mexican wives *did not work*." So, even though she was making more money than her young husband and had only furnished rooms in which to ply her housekeeping responsibilities, Anita quit her job. She was soon pregnant.

Alfred Joseph was born in 1946, Steve Don in 1948, Priscilla Ann in 1949 and Rene Orlando in 1950. Anita was 25 years old, the mother of four children under five years of age, and married to a man whose career kept him on the job long after she had the babies to bed at night. If she ever felt depressed or deprived, she has never talked about it. Instead, she has many times called herself one of the luckiest of women.

Part of the reason is that she *is* Mexican to the core, proud of her roots and eager to share the gifts of that culture with everybody. Part of it is that she had a large, loving, extended family—both her own and her husband's—who gave her support when she needed it. Many women complain bitterly when their husbands seem to put their jobs ahead of the family; Anita said that Alfred's hours on the job he loves have given her the chance to develop her own special interests. Part of it is that the family became increasingly affluent and though she has had to wait for some of the things that mattered to her, she long since moved away from a day-to-day struggle for life's necessities. But most of it is her own buoyant enthusiasm. When she commits to a responsibility, she believes that it is going to succeed. She has lived through many disappointments but she does not give up. "I've made some mistakes," she said, "but I learn from them and use the experience to win next time." Many people mistake her cheerful optimism for naivete, but a careful look at what she has accomplished disproves this.

Eager to get out of her house and into the community, Anita took her four children and began her lifelong involvement with Dallas. When her oldest son was four, she read about a swimming class for children at the YMCA and went to enroll him. She learned that she would have to go into the pool with him. She signed up, took the three older children into the water with her and left the baby in his infant seat at poolside where she kept an eye on him. Seventy-two hours of swimming later she had earned her Red Cross lifesaving certificate and had three children who swam as if the water were their natural habitat.

Greedy for learning, she read—especially newspapers—and wrote letters to the editor, and signed up for courses wherever she could find supplemental child care. The YWCA was a fertile spot. There she learned modeling, took guitar lessons, a course in public speaking, another in community life and her first lessons in dance. She helped to bring the Ballet Folklorico of Guadalajara to the city. This would serve, down the road after a time, as a major turning point in her life.

She and Alfred bought their home in 1959 in North Dallas. They borrowed $3,000 to make the down payment. "We were scared to death. The living room and dining room were empty for a long time and the rest of the house had very sparse furnishings. We bought only what we could afford to pay for. I was willing to wait."

Part of the reason she was willing to wait was that the entire community was becoming her home, and she was more eager to live in it than the four walls in which she ate and slept. As the children entered school, she joined the PTA and the YWCA and was soon on their boards. She raised money for Children's Medical Center and became involved in Goals for Dallas. She also signed up for courses at SMU's night school.

Active in the Dallas Restaurant Association Women's Auxiliary, and on its board in 1969, she was determined that it do something significant for the community as well as support what then was an almost all male organization. She persuaded the Auxiliary to sponsor the first Taste of Dallas, a benefit to which all restaurant association members contributed the specialty of their house at a central location on one gala evening. Dallas went in increasingly large numbers for several years and proceeds from the benefit provided school lunches for hungry children. While serving on the Goals for Dallas Design of the City committee, she came to the attention of city decision-makers and in 1969 was asked by the Citizens Charter Association to run for at-large place on the Dallas City Council. When she told her husband that she was thinking about running, he said, "You . . . are . . . what? Are you crazy? Are you nuts?" She did not announce until she had his complete support as well as that of her children. "They," she says, sparkling, "did not know what they were getting into . . . . Neither did I."

She recognized that the CCA had asked her to run because they considered her "safe" and because she would represent two minorities clamoring for attention—Hispanics and women. They did not know she would be vulnerable on both counts. Some Hispanic voters saw her as "a coconut—brown on the outside, all white beneath the shell," she explained. Women saw her as distant from feminist issues. But it was clear from the start of the campaign that she was out to win. She showed up everywhere—morning, noon and night, making as many as half a dozen speeches daily. On the day before election, almost exhausted, she went home, shampooed her hair and was about to crawl into bed when she heard over the radio that a line of people more than a block long was wrapped around the Records building to renew their car licenses. She grabbed a wig, pulled it over her damp hair headed downtown where she shook hands and passed out campaign literature until the building closed and the crowd was gone.

She won, defeating her three opponents without a run-off in the primary, with 52 per cent of the vote. Two years later she was reelected without opposition. She was the first Hispanic to sit on the Dallas City Council, the fourth woman to serve on the Council and the first Hispanic woman to serve on a city governing board of any major city in the United States. Until 1991, she was the only Hispanic to be reelected to the city council for a second term.

Almost everybody underestimated Anita—those who wanted her on the Council, those who did not and those who were waiting to see what happened. Her very presence called into question all the stereotypes of what a good Dallas leader looked like and acted like. She was neither the proper color, the proper age nor the proper gender of the model city "father." Always impeccably groomed and wearing the brilliant colors she favored—no drab mannish suits for her!—she turned up everywhere driving her Cadillac and wearing her diamonds.

"I know I came on like gang busters," she says in retrospect. "I felt like there was no tomorrow. There was so much to be done and so little time!" At Council meetings she did not behave in the approved manner, sometimes asking questions that seemed naive to more seasoned politicians. But she did her homework. She was no rubber stamp for the status quo. Though she ran into noisy and sometimes nasty opposition from more militant Hispanics, she continued to be fully committed, by word and in deed, to those whose heritage she shared. Usually this has meant working behind-the-scenes within the system, but not always. She set up community meetings in West Dallas, the area most densely populated by Mexican-Americans and asked them what they wanted. They told her—reluctantly at first, timidly for many who had lost hope in the American dream, clamorously for those who were tired of waiting, belligerently for those who were compelled—for whatever reasons—to force progress—they told her. "Sometimes I felt like I had the burden of the whole world on my shoulders." Persistently she pushed their agenda: Improvement of streets and transportation, additional police protection and better street lighting, sewage and garbage disposal, health clinics, libraries and recreation facilities. In 1972, principally at her urging, $8 million was allocated for improvements in West Dallas; this was a jump from $2 million in the prior budget. Reminded repeatedly that she was an at-large council representative whose concern should be all segments of the city, she responded that in a good family its most vulnerable member was the one who most needed attention—and West Dallas was a member of the family that had been made to feel like a stepchild. She convinced West Dallas citizens that they were an important link in the chain of the city; she made it clear to city leaders that "no chain is stronger than its weakest link."

When persuasion did not work, she showed another side of her disposition, totally surprising to some. The Council was in its 1972 budget hearings. She had repeatedly asked for a recreation center in West Dallas; she had just as repeatedly been told that there was no money. Viewing a city map during the briefing, she noted that major improvements were planned for existing recreational centers in other parts of the city. West Dallas was blank. "I was furious," she says. She marched to the podium, grabbed the stick, pointed to West Dallas and demanded, "Why is this area blank? . . . . I cannot support this budget." The next Monday the Council voted to include a recreation center for West Dallas. They named it the Anita Nanez Martinez Center.

When she completed her second term, Anita told friends that she would now get some much-deserved rest and have time to enjoy her grandchildren. However President Nixon appointed her to the National Voluntary Service Advisory Council and named her one of six individuals to evaluate the Peace Corps in the 68 countries where it operated. For two years she traveled incessantly, once around-the-world in 17 days, took the responsibility for having one director replaced when she found him inadequate to do his job, helped to write the report, was present when it was hand-delivered to President Ford—and then came home and collapsed. She was hospitalized with fatigue.

Even as she lay in bed, she was already planning her next projects: get her body back in shape—walk, run, play; stimulate her brain—exercise and meditation; eat a more healthy diet—hard for someone who enjoys all rich Mexican foods; visit her children and grandchildren and be as committed to getting in touch with them as with the Peace Corps volunteers; be a good neighbor—she served as president of the Walnut Hills Home Owners Association.

Along with creating the Anita Nanez Martinez Recreation Center and its expansion in 1991, Anita breathed life into its programs with her special presence and fund raising. Dear to her from the outset were the dance and drama programs. She joined Pan American Ballet Folklorico, one of 12 women, who performed dance with a special Mexican/Spanish flavor throughout the city. She encouraged children to participate in dance programs immanent to their Hispanic roots and helped to finance teachers to guide them. "Every Spanish-speaking child is born with star quality," she once said. "All they need is for someone to recognize it and give them a chance to develop it." In 1981 she was the founding president of Friends of Anita Nanez Martinez Recreation Center to raise and disperse funds for projects with a special focus on the Anita N. Martinez Recreation Center Folklorico Dancers. This group of children and young adults appeared in programs in Dallas, the state, the nation and Mexico. Anita was tireless in efforts to raise money for instructors, costumes and travel. In 1988 the core group became Anita N. Martinez Ballet Folklorico, Inc., a subtle but significant growth because it now was a professional dance company of the city of Dallas.

Anita is puzzled over those who question a dance group—especially one that *appears* elitist—as a major advancement of the Hispanic population as an integral part of the city. "This," she said, "is the drawing out of natural talent. This raises the self-confidence of every child who participates. This gives parents and grandparents and aunts and uncles and brothers and sisters—we Mexicans are *very* family oriented—a reason for pride. When the performer hears the applause, he or she is lifted up and out of any ghetto into the limelight. When the community hears the applause, it means affirmation and hope. And everybody has something to aspire to! We have had students go on to study with the best teachers in the country. There will be others.

"You don't build self-esteem in a day or a week or a month and you never build it by pointing out weaknesses. You build it child by child by child, one at a time, by making that individual child feel wonderful about herself or himself, by stressing what can be done instead of what cannot be done. We talk preventive, but we fund emergency. I'm trying to turn that around."

Maria Belen Ortega's soprano voice thrilled audiences in leading capitals of the world.

MARIA BELEN ORTEGA (CORREA) DIAZ-MORA DAVEY

• • • •

December 22, 1914

The view that Belen Ortega has of Dallas and the conditions under which she grew up are far different from those of others who arrived in the city escaping the revolutions in Mexico. There are several reasons for this different view, among them money, mission and music. The money, though it was sparse, allowed the Ortegas to settle in a Dallas area with an ethnic mixture and to secure and furnish a single-family house. Their mission was two-fold: to build a future founded on, but not limited to their Mexico roots, and to find property that had been in their family when Texas belonged to Mexico. And music speaks a universal language. Among the furnishings of the first Dallas house, Belen's mother provided a rosewood concert piano with the determination to see that her daughter was musically trained.

But there was no way they could know the heights to which the infant would rise, for Belen Ortega is a multi-gifted musician. She began her training in Dallas, perfected it in Europe and has been applauded in the entertainment capitals of the world including New York, Hollywood, Mexico City, Rio de Janeiro, Canada, Cuba, Madrid, Barcelona, Montreal and San Juan.

A soprano, she is recognized as a leading exponent of Latin repertoire. She has sung on radio, television, in supper clubs and on the concert stage and under the batons of leading maestros. Also a classical guitarist, she has responded to the applause of countless audiences with guitar encores.

She has appeared on programs featuring luminaries including Bing Crosby, Dorothy Kirsten and Marian Anderson. She has had her own radio shows on both KRLD and WFAA in Dallas and has sung for celebrities including Eleanor Roosevelt, Secretary of

State Cordell Hull and President Miguel Aleman of Mexico. She is an educator who has taught in her own studio and at a number of Dallas's public and private schools including Thomas Jefferson and St. Mark's of Texas. She taught for four years at the American School Foundation in Mexico City and in Mexico City College. She has appeared in numerous musical festivals in Europe, Mexico and the United States. Her research among teachers, scholars, composers and musicologists has led to a vast collection of Mexican art and folk songs. She has also modeled—representing the spirit of both the United States and Mexico for Pan American Airways in its inaugural flight.

On October 31, 1937, Texas Governor James V. Allred named her "Nightingale of the Americas."

Belen was a Christmas child, born December 22, 1914, in San Luis Potosi, Mexico. She came to the United States in the arms of her mother early in 1915. Her parents, Mercedes Rocha Villanueva and Epitacio Ortega y Ortega, with their two older sons, Victor and Javier, and Belen were among the thousands of Mexican families crossing the border into Texas to escape persecution. Her father's records detail the acts of defense and loyalty, of injustice and imposition and the killing of victims—leaders, soldiers, women, children—during that awful time. "My father's writing reveals how, more than once, he was compromised by a government official or militant in authority," Belen said.

The family came to Dallas on the train and found a house on Latimer Street just south of downtown bordering on what was then the most exclusive neighborhood in the city. Most other Mexicans moved north of Dallas in the area that would come to be known as Little Mexico. Belen said she never talked to her parents about their escape from their native country. Her mother's family insisted that they try to find land that had belonged to them when Texas was still owned by Mexico. It was never recovered.

What Belen most remembers is a childhood of pure joy. Their home was a place of culture, elegantly furnished with fine oak and mahogany tables and bureaus and hand-upholstered chairs and sofas. The neighborhood was one of ethnic and ecumenical variety. An Italian family lived on one corner of their city block and a German family on the other with a variety of Anglos and the Ortegas in between. "We took it all for granted. We didn't know how rich we were."

As a child, Belen played house and dolls endlessly with two little girls her own age, blonde, blue-eyed Marian Bigby and Thelma Dixie with the lavish black curls. Sometimes Nina, the Italian child, joined their play and sometimes they all went to Nina's house where they played hide-and-seek in her family's grape arbor.

Belen and Marian began their acting careers together. "We made Hawaiian skirts out of canna lily leaves and crowns of four o'clocks and put on shows. We'd charge a penny for admission. We would stage elaborate productions with our dolls as characters or as the audience. We were always the stars . . . ."

In grade school—second or third grade—the two little girls tasted their first audience adulation—and Belen was addicted! Dressed in rompers, one in pink and the other in blue, with their cheeks and knees rouged, they went on-stage and performed in stiff, automatic doll-like gestures to recorded Victrola music. As the record wound down, so did the antics of the dancing dolls until, at last, when the music stopped two little girls collapsed on-stage. "The applause was thunderous. It was my first show stopper."

It was also Belen Ortega's spark for many show stoppers to come. When she was eight, her mother insisted that Belen stop so much playing and devote more time to music. Her mother believed that anyone with a musical talent should be trained in as many ways as possible, so it was not enough that Belen sang. She also took music lessons, going weekly on the street car to the home of Frieda B. Saunders on Marlborough Street in Oak Cliff where she took piano lessons. These music lessons were a gift of the Wednesday Morning Choral Club and were the first of several scholarships that allowed Belen to continue her training in music. "Frieda Saunders gave me an excellent foundation—one I've built on the rest of my life."

As the little girl began her lifelong career in music and performing, dramatic changes were taking place in her family. Her father, financially independent with an inheritance from his father, took one of his sons, Javier, and returned to Mexico where the political upheaval was somewhat subdued. "He intended to return to Dallas, but got caught up in the politics of his country and time went by and he never made it back."

"My father was an extraordinary man—a civil engineer. He had a fine education, had studied law. He was distinguished. Handsome. A scholar, a dreamer, a writer, a poet, a philosopher. He was not a soldier," and the Mexico of that day required that all its men be fighters. When she was older, Belen visited her father in Mexico. "I got beautiful letters and poetry from him.

"Mother was a beauty. Dynamic and outgoing. Independent. Authoritative. Quite willful. She expected my father to work harder and provide beautiful things for the family."

Not long after her parents were divorced, Mercedes married Nicanor Correa and had two more children. "Mother insisted that we all use the Correa name. That's how I came to be known as Belen Correa and how people remember me when I first began to sing. My stepfather provided the luxuries that my mother required. There was no animosity or unhappiness with my stepfather, but I felt like I had lost my identity and as soon as I reestablished contact with my father, I took my own name back."

In school musicals, Belen was often asked to take the solo parts. "The first time this happened I was in the third grade. The song was the "The Spanish Cavalier. I'll never forget it," and she sings it, her voice clear, and rising perfectly on the high notes just as it must have done that day back in early 1920s at Cumberland Hills School.

"I don't remember ever being singled out as a different because of my nationality. Instead, I was made to feel special because I was born in another country. I give my mother credit for this." While many families who had escaped the Mexican Revolution and settled in Dallas tried to bury their painful memories, Mercedes Rochea Villanueva Ortega Correa insisted that her children learn and value their past. "My mother gave me a deep understanding and a great love for our Mexican heritage. She encouraged love for the country in which I was born as well as the country to which we came. At home we spoke both Spanish and English—and it had to be good Spanish and good English. Mother did not tolerate sloppy language!"

The family home on Latimer street burned taking with it all of the family possessions included Belen's beloved piano. For a short time, the family moved into Little Mexico, and it was there that Belen began her civic work. She organized a singing group of talented young boys and girls called Mexico Musicals which performed throughout the area.

Mercedes Correa was always ambivalent about Belen's career. She was a taskmaster in making the little girl study; she wanted her daughter to sing; she wanted her to be a star. But she did not want her long out of her sight and sometimes became ill and lured her daughter home. Once Belen was in Vienna on the verge of a major breakthrough in her career and was called to come home to Dallas because her mother was very ill.

Belen's mentors and models are carefully preserved in a scrapbook she made from the time she was in grade school through her senior year in high school. While other children cut paper dolls, Belen snipped photographs and stories from newspapers and magazines about leading singers—Lauritz Melchoir, Serge Koussevitzky, Dorothy Kirsten, Marian Anderson, Jan Peerce, Ezio Pinza, Maria Kurkendo, Enrico Caruso and others. Belen never met most of them, but among her treasured memories is a conversation with Artur Rubinstein on train from Chicago to New York.

From the time she was 12, Belen appeared as a guest artist at Dallas clubs and churches. "Before I was out of high school, I'd sung in all of the biggest churches in town. I was the singer on all of the high school programs." She made her first money singing at Dunton's Cafeteria near the Palace Theater on Elm Street. For performing five nights a week, she got $10.

Her talent got her invited into the adult social world while she was in her teens. Even though her mother was very strict about her daughter's social life, she allowed Belen to attend parties in homes of which she approved. "I remember the Joseph Tallals. They just about set the music trends in Dallas at the time (late 1920s, early 30s). There were three very talented young Tallals—Sherry, Vivian and Joseph, all musical. They gave a lot of parties and I was always invited. There I met many professional musicians—

guests who were in town, members of the Dallas Symphony Orchestra. I remember especially Zelman Bruno, violinist, and Lev Aaronson, cellist, both with the Dallas Symphony. They became good friends. They would applaud and shout "bravo!" when I sang.

In 1932 Belen graduated with high honors from Dallas Technical High School and was awarded a scholarship to SMU. It was her third scholarship. She had earned her second at age 15 when she became the protege of Feodore Gontzoff, a distinguished White Russian, who had escaped the Russian Revolution to settle in Dallas. She studied voice with him for six years. Her college scholarship, $350, paid her tuition for a year, but there was a problem. It supported a liberal arts education. Both pleased at the possibility of continuing her education and disappointed that the scholarship would not cover music, Belen spent a summer being "a pretty impossible child for my mother to live with.' The issue was resolved when Mrs. Correa came up with the money to pay for one music theory course. At the end of her first year at SMU, Belen's scholarship was renewed for another year because no other qualified student applied for it.

Belen was a serious student, but singing was her first love. At the end of her second year at SMU, she passed all requirements for a teaching certificate—and left school to continue her music education and career. Her aim was to go to New York to study and sing, but her mother said she was not old enough. She got a government job working as a bilingual secretary. It allowed her to support herself while continuing her musical studies.

By word of mouth, with an occasional story in the newspapers, with appearances in the city wherever she could sing and earn a few extra dollars, Belen's reputation grew. "One day I looked out the widow and saw this limousine pulling up in front of our house—the biggest, longest car I'd ever seen. Three people got out and knocked on the door. My mother answered and they asked if this were the house where the little Mexican girl who sang so beautifully lived. My mother said she had a daughter who sang. They wanted to know if I would go to the Texaco Building at State Fair Park with them to audition. Mother said no."

"I was by her side listening. I begged my mother to accept. She finally agreed. We dressed hurriedly and the two of us went with them."

The audition led to Belen's first major professional engagement, starring on the outdoor Texaco stage at the Texas Centennial. The Centennial, the year-long celebration of the state's 100th birthday, in 1936 and the Pan American Exposition that followed it in 1937 opened up a whole new world to Belen Ortega and many musical artists in the city. "During those two years most of the world's most famous orchestras played in Dallas—and I got to sing with most of them."

The Centennial appearances led to radio shows of her own, first at KRLD and later at WFAA.

On October 31, 1937, Governor Allred designated Belen Ortega "Nightingale of the Americas," and the Rotary Club sponsored her on a goodwill tour to Mexico.

In the early 1940s Belen finally made it to New York where for four years she continued to study voice. A long-running singing engagement at El Chico in Greenwich Village provided the bread and butter support she required while her fame spread. She appeared on her own show at CBS, sang at Madison Square Garden and the Rainbow Room atop Rockefeller Center, sang in Radio City, went to Mexico City to sing on the Coca-Cola Show of XEW, had her own show on the Blue Network NBC, Chicago.

In 1946, shortly after the close of World War II, she went to Mexico City to sing at the introduction of a new radio station, XEQ—and met Dr. Alberto Diaz-Mora Beristain, author, philosopher and professor at Universidad Nacional de Mexico. For the first time she had met a man whose ambition and luminous qualities matched her own and who reveled in her fame.

"There are few men like him," Belen said. "The term 'Renaissance man' is overused, but it describes him exactly. He had an out-of-this-world quality. The way he looked, the way he dressed, the way he spoke all had a magic quality."

Love enhanced the quality of Belen's voice and manner. Her career soared. She sang on the National Hour sponsored by the Mexican government, accompanied by the famed Tatannacho Orchestra, and performed on many other occasions in Mexico, Central and South America.

On October 25, 1947, Belen and Alberto were married. "We were very much in love," and she was torn between career and marriage. "My mother had raised me to believe that it was immoral for a married women to travel without her husband. And, I had always felt a void in not having completed my college degree, so it seemed the right time to continue my studies."

Belen devoted a year to studies in Mexican history and to research in folkloric material under Manuel M. Ponce, the father of nationalistic music in Mexico. She studied musicology with Dr. Jesus Romero and Professor Vicente T. Mendoza. She studied classical guitar with J. Silva and Daniel Garate. She met with contemporary composers and collected Mexican art songs, both published and in manuscript.

"I took this year out of my life to study and research because I knew I would specialize in this very beautiful and little known repertoire. I wanted to proclaim the soul of the land of my birth."

Proclaimed Nightingale of the Americas by Gov. James V. Allred, Belen Ortega taped in Madrid a 20-selection serenade featuring the leading artists of Mexico. The response was electrifying.

At the end of the year, still reluctant to leave her husband for concert appearances, she accepted a position teaching music at the American School Foundation in Mexico City where she directed the elementary department and chaired all the bi-lingual music programs. She introduced an annual music festival and organized and directed a choral group of 70 voices. She held this position for five years during which time she was invited to teach adult courses at Mexico City College and to conduct a teacher's music summer course and workshop.

The magic of the marriage was mixed with a yearning to continue with her singing career. "Professors in Mexico did not make much money. My income as a teacher helped to support us. I did not mind that. What I did miss was the pursuit of my own career. And I wanted a baby. I couldn't convince Alberto to have a child. He said that our union was complete and that the addition of a child could not enhance it and might even destroy it. He said later we could adopt a child. This hurt. The child issue was a divisive one—and yet we loved each other so deeply. We had a marriage that existed on another plane—I can't describe it. When he received a commission from the philosophy department to write a book on aesthetics, we resolved that I should go home to Dallas to visit Mother and give him time to write and me time to sort out my feelings."

Belen was in Dallas in December of 1954 when she got word that her husband had died "in a tragic accident . . . . I still can't talk about it," she said more than a third of a century later. She went to Mexico to be with his family for the memorial services and stayed to complete his business. Then she returned to Dallas and gradually returned to singing.

Although her bookings were full and she was working throughout the United States, there was something missing. "My agent suggested I go to Spain. He said he could book me for concerts if I were only there. So I went."

At first Belen was disappointed. Her bookings consisted almost entirely of supper club engagements and she longed for the concert stage. Following an appearance at Madrid's Institute of Culture, she got the break she had been longing for. She was immediately booked into Spain's leading concert halls. There were three concerts in Madrid, two in Seville, two in Barcelona, one in Oviedo, one in Salamanca, one in Valencia and on and on.

Then came a festival featuring musicians from 22 countries. Belen won the top vocal soloist award. "It was a marvelous experience . . . . I wish I'd stayed in Spain."

The Barcelona concert brought numerous curtain calls. Among those applauding was Gabriel Sonia, president of RCA in Spain who asked to meet with her. "I had no idea he was in the audience. I was thrilled! I was even more thrilled when he asked if I would like to record. I hit the ceiling. Bounced. Came back down and said, SI!"

It was the break she had long dreamed about, but it almost didn't happen. "I rushed back to Madrid, got my other commitments in order—and came down with a terrible case of laryngitis, saw every specialist in the city. Nothing worked. It got to be the middle of December. Winter is terrible in Madrid. Weeks went by—five or six. They were ready to cancel my contract when I finally got well enough to sing. The hall where we recorded was enormous and frigid. Musicians played wearing overcoats. I shivered. Between numbers I took sips of cognac. But I recorded . . . ."

The concert on tape is "A Serenade by Belen Ortega, Nightingale of the Americas" under the baton of Garcia Morcillo. It consists of 20 selections featuring artists from many countries that highlight Belen's Mexican repertoire.

The response was electrifying. In major cities in Spain, Canada, Mexico, Puerto Rico and the United States, reviewers lauded the work . . . . "Senorita Ortega in her debut fully lived up to her advance notices . . . (we) accord her the highest possible praise," said the Montreal *Daily* . . . . "She captured the varied moods of Spanish folk songs set down by Manuel de Fallas, her eager voice spilling vivid embroideries," wrote Claudia Cassidy for *The Chicago Tribune*. Mexico's President Aleman wrote that it was "a special pleasure to congratulate you . . . for your merits as a distinguished artist of song."

But the most electrifying moment for Belen came when she was walking down the street in New York and saw a music store window featuring her photograph and overflowing with her tapes . . . . For she was back in the United States. Her mother was sick again. "I kept getting letters and wires from my sister that I would never see Mother alive again if I did not come home soon."

Her homecoming was triumphant. But her mother's illness sobered her and again she was pulled between continuing with her career that would require constant travel or staying in Dallas to care for her mother. There was also her interrupted education, the college degree she had never completed. She chose the caring role and college.

"Going back to school was difficult," she said. "Experience had taught me so much. After performing on some of the world's finest concert stages, studying theory did not excite me." Often the textbook version did not resemble Belen's truth, but she persevered. She completed her work and received her bachelor of music arts degree from SMU in 1960, interspersing her studies with professional appearances.

Following her mother's death, she opened a studio in her home where she taught private students. She continued to be a student herself, seeking opportunities to study and learn.

Ten years later she married Thomas Edward Davey, who she had met in San Miguel de Allende, Guanajuto, where she had gone to study painting. He was a "very unusual, very determined British American," who persisted in wooing her until she finally married him. The marriage lasted for six tumultuous years. "It was a mistake from the beginning; I don't know why I did it . . . . I believe in marriage. I wanted it to work. It never did. He claimed he was proud of me, liked my singing and wanted me to be successful. But he wanted to possess me, to keep me in an ivory tower. When I was out of his sight, he was miserable, so I gave up singing and I was miserable." They divorced. He died nine years later.

True to the programming of her life, Belen went back to school. While continuing to do programs by invitation and with a full schedule of private pupils, she enrolled in Texas Woman's University, and in 1977 received her master's degree in music education. In 1988 she became a columnist for *El Sol of Texas* reporting on the art and cultural events of the Greater Dallas Community for the Spanish language newspaper. She was also writing a music textbook for teachers of elementary school children.

On October 5, 1989, the Meadows School of the Arts at Southern Methodist University announced a $50,000 endowed scholarship, the Belen Ortega Scholarship which was matched by funds from the Meadows Foundation. "It had always been my dream," Belen said, "to establish a musical scholarship so that talented students could have the help they needed and possibly have a wonderful life of singing for audiences in many countries as I had. So, I thought, 'why not now?' I wanted to meet and enjoy some of the students chosen to receive the scholarship. I got in touch with my financial adviser and my attorney."

Robin Ramirez received the first scholarship grant in 1990. It was hard to tell which was more thrilled—Robin or her benefactor, Maria Belen Ortega (Correa) Diaz-Mora Beristain Davey.

"New horizons are opening daily for talented young Hispanics," Belen said. "It makes me immensely happy."

*Florence Louise Harllee Phelps, educator,
was born in the shadows of downtown Dallas.*

FLORENCE LOUISE HARLLEE PHELPS

• • • •

April 18, 1905

Florence Louise Harllee Phelps was born on April 18, 1905, at 1813 Boll Street, where the Morton H. Meyerson Symphony Center now casts its the shadows over its neighbors immediately to the north in the Arts District of downtown Dallas. The youngest of four children and only daughter of Norman Washington and Florence Coleman Harllee, she grew up both cherished and privileged.

"I didn't know black or white," she said in a 1984 interview. "I grew up with no fear. My father was one of the most respected men in town. His friends came in our home all the time, not as black men or white men but as people of value regardless of their color. My father went everywhere in Dallas. He never entered any establishment, business or home, by the back door. When he went anywhere, he went as a man, not as a black person. From the time I was a small youngster, I trailed him. I never knew we were black."

Norman W. Harllee was a teacher and principal. He came to Dallas in 1879 from Lumberton, North Carolina, with a new college degree from Biddle University to take a teaching job paying $62 a month. When he wasn't teaching, he was often in the business offices of downtown department stores. "At the first of every month one of the businessmen sent for him. He balanced their books. He was an excellent mathematician. Mostly, he worked for Mr. Sanger, but other merchants also called him." Professor Harllee also tutored the sons and daughters of his white friends. He died in 1928, having lived for the rest of his life in the Boll Street home he bought shortly after he arrived in Dallas. He is the first black person for whom a Dallas school is named. In 1927, the N. W. Harllee Elementary School at 1216 East 8th Street was dedicated.

Florence grew up surrounded by professional people—doctors, lawyers and educators. "My godfather, Doc Rowan, lived next door to us. He was a multi-millionaire who made his money in real estate. From Ross Avenue to where I lived, our neighbors were all white. My music teacher was white. I was so much younger than my brothers that I never had anyone to play with at home, so when I was a small child my playmates were all white."

The little girl got mixed messages about her city. "Both of my parents talked to me about what was going on. They explained to me that there were white people and black people in Dallas and that the colors did not mix socially, in business or in school. But they lived as if there were no color lines, so I did have something of a culture shock when I started to school."

Florence Louise Harllee was already reading and writing when she entered school at age four. She also spoke French, having grown up with a father who was bilingual and a mother who encouraged that languages other than English be spoken in their home. Even before she began school, Louise—that's what her mother called her when she was a child—was a scholar.

"Segregation became real to me when I started school. My parents tried to cushion me, but I began to recognize that I couldn't do some things I'd always done. I attended Colored School No. 2 on Flora Street. I thought it very strange that all of my classmates were black. That wasn't what the world was like. I soon learned that our school did not have the same facilities that other schools had. When I thought about it, I knew it was unjust but I was so busy learning that I let it slide by. She had not been in school many weeks before she was advanced to the second grade. "From there I just went up, up, up."

She completed requirements for her high school diploma and graduated from Booker T. Washington when she was 11 years old.

Norman and Florence Harllee would not let their child go away to school, so they had to find something for her to do.

"I started following my father around again. It was the best education I could have had." She helped him teach classes, giving individual attention to slow learners. When night classes were arranged, she taught them. "I have taught more people to read and write than I can even imagine—way up in the hundreds. I never kept score. If there was a job to do, I just did it." Most of her work was as an unpaid volunteer.

After two years, Florence persuaded her parents that she was old enough to go to college and in the fall of 1918 she enrolled at Howard University in Washington, D. C. "I was too young to date," she said, "so I concentrated on my studies."

In the summer of 1921, home from college for the summer, Florence accepted the invitation of a family friend to go swimming....

John C. Phelps picked up the story.

"It was the summer of 1924. June 24, 1924, to be exact. Sweltering. Fourteen of us had rented the only swimming pool with dressing room facilities in Dallas that was open to its black people. It was at Gregg Park on the corner of Hall where Central now is." The young bachelors did this every summer Sunday, he explained, and invited young women to come and swim. John Phelps was one of the bachelors, 21 years old. He had moved to Dallas from Millican, Texas, and was employed as a porter at the F. W. Woolworth five and ten cent store, Elm and Stone.

"My buddy and I were sitting beside the pool talking about life. I'd just bragged that I planned to stay a bachelor all my life," he recalled. "The woman I marry hasn't been born yet!"

Sixty-six years later, John Phelps remembered that day with absolute clarity.

"About that time the door opens and in walks the most beautiful girl I have ever seen in my life. Tiny. Her hair down to her waist. Almost a halo over her head. An unearthly, ethereal quality about her. Like an angel. Who's that?' I asked my friend, not able to take my eyes off her. 'That's Professor Harllee's daughter,' he said. 'Don't you mess with her! She don't run with our gang. There's no way you can get a date with her.' I was still watching her. 'That's the girl I'm going to marry,' I told him. He snorted. 'I thought you said the woman hadn't been born yet that you would marry.' 'That door just gave birth to her,' I said. 'I'll bet you $25 I marry her.' That was a fortune in those days!"

Two days later John Phelps called on Florence Louise Harllee for the first time. Never, for a single day after that did he let her forget that he was the man for her. He sent notes and tokens of his affection. He saved his money and worked for advancement at his job. When she returned to Howard in the fall for her senior year, she found waiting in her dormitory room a box of stationery with her return address printed on it and all the envelopes stamped and addressed to him. Along with it was a telegram expressing his affection. He wrote to her every day. When she came home for a visit, he monopolized her time.

"It's not surprising," said Alvernon Tripp, who remembered Florence as a beauty and John as the most handsome man in town. "She was tiny. He was tall and elegant. They always made a striking couple."

John courted Florence for five years. She graduated from Howard in the spring of 1925 and came home to Dallas. Proficient in French and also qualified to teach Latin and Spanish, she applied to teach languages. "They wouldn't let me," Florence said. "Blacks weren't allowed French." She started teaching at H. S. Thompson Elementary School in September following her 18th birthday in April. "I have taught every grade all the way from first through high school." she said.

"I saw her every day," John said. "I was trying to be worthy of her, trying to get a raise. Trying to get a promotion." It was she who proposed. He continued the story. "She said, 'Let's get married and see what happens,' and her mother said, 'If you two want to get married, go ahead. You can move in here with me.' So, we went to the preacher's house and got married." It was November 17, 1929. At the reception following their wedding, John's buddy handed him the $25 he had won in that long-ago swimming pool-side bet.

The stock market had just crashed. "It wasn't any time to consider changing jobs," John said, "But Florence thought I should, so I quit my job and went into insurance. The Atlanta Life Insurance Company, Atlanta, Georgia. The first three weeks I worked, I made 49 cents. Florence said, 'You can do it!'. . . . I thank the Lord every night for her sticking with me.

"I worked nights and holidays as a bell boy. I was Bell Boy No. 28, at the Adolphus Hotel."

To help with expenses, Florence took on a summer job in 1931 with the county as a social worker. Unemployment was rampant and many people were moving to Dallas from other cities and states and from the surrounding countryside because the future looked less perilous there than in their own parts of the world. As they came, displaced from familiar support systems, they brought along their miseries, thus creating additional stress both for themselves and for Dallas. During the summer months when she was not teaching, Florence worked to help reduce the county's case load. She was the first degreed social worker the county hired.

Florence Phelps with daughter Lucy Patterson, the first black woman to serve on the Dallas City Council.

Florence and John C. Phelps with daughter Lucy and her husband, Albert S. Patterson, and their son, Albert Harllee.

The Phelpses lived in the house where she had been born and had grown up on Boll Street. Their first daughter, Norma Belle, was born March 22, 1930, and their second daughter, Lucy Pearl on June 21, 1931. John and Florence, Norma and Lucy and Mrs. Phelps' mother, Florence Harllee, continued to live on Boll Street. Norma and Lucy graduated from high school and enrolled in their mother's alma mater. Both graduated from Howard University when they were 18 years old. Both became educators. Dr. Norma Phelps Barratt was the first woman to teach in the medical school at the University of Michigan. For several years she taught at the medical school in Saudi Arabia, the first woman to teach men in that country. Lucy Phelps Patterson, the first black woman to be elected to the Dallas City Council which she served for seven years, was professor-in-residence and director of the social works program at Bishop College.

Always aware of racial discrimination, Florence and John Phelps usually were able to circumvent it, to ignore it or to rise above it. Both were intent upon lessening tensions between the races. Neither was comfortable with confrontation. When they moved in circles where they were known, they were treated with respect. But their widening circles of involvement, both professional and personal, left them vulnerable to the rebuffs and insults cast upon other people of color.

Silence, John said, has often been the best way to react when people behave badly, as it was in the late summer of 1946 when he drove his daughters to Dallas's Union Station for them to return to college. He found an excellent parking spot. The family was about the get out of the car when another car behind them honked. John kept the door shut and sat there. The honking continued. Soon, there was a man leaning on his window. "Move, Boy," he said. "Back up. I want this parking place. I just continued to sit there, not saying a word. He flounced off. I watched as he approached a police officer on the corner. He started talking to the man with the gun, pointing at me and gesturing. The officer walked over and said, 'I understand you are having some troubles,' and I said, 'No, Sir. I'm not having any troubles. I think he might be.' Then I explained what happened and the officer turned to him and told him he would have to move. All the time Norma and Lucy were saying to me, 'Daddy, you've got to learn how to curse!' I thought that was pretty wonderful. Here I had two daughters in college and they'd never heard their father utter a curse word . . . . Turned out both the other man and I were trying to get our daughters on the train to send them off to college. The girls had a lot in common."

But neither silence nor passive resistance is always possible. There are times when action is imperative, and, usually, Mr. Phelps said, this happens when the limitations impose upon one's children. The day he took action also involved a daughter and a college experience. She had won an honor and needed an evening gown. Her parents wanted her to have the most beautiful white dress that Dallas had to offer. No store in town would allow them to try on clothes. John Phelps went to the most exclusive ladies' ready-to-wear department at Sangers and asked to see a white evening gown. He gave the clerk the exact size he wanted. The sales clerk said, 'We don't have any white evening dresses," and I said, 'Now be careful what you say,' but she insisted, so I asked to see her boss. Another lady came up and repeated what the first had told me. 'We don't have any evening dresses to fit you.' So I asked to see the manager. This young man came up and I repeated what I wanted. He said, 'I'm sorry, she is right. We don't have any dresses for you.' I said, again, 'Now be careful what you say,' and he said, 'Boy, what do you think you are doing? Trying to come down here and change our store?' and I said, 'No, sir, I'm just trying to buy an evening dress for my daughter.' He said 'Well, we don't have anything. You'd better leave.'

"I walked over to the elevators and pushed the Up button. He said, 'I told you to leave. You're supposed to be going down,' and I said, 'I'll go down when I damn well please.' I got off on the sixth floor and walked into Mr. Brown's office. He said, 'Hello, there, J.C. What's the matter? You got another committee you want me to work with you on?' I said, 'Yes, sir, and this committee is meeting downstairs in your Ladies' Ready to Wear Department.' He said, 'What's going on?' I said, 'Just come on,' and I turned and went out and he followed. We went on down there and stepped off the elevator. I pointed to the first woman and said, 'This young lady told me you didn't have any evening dresses to fit *me*. Then I pointed to the second woman, "and this lady told me I wasn't going to get an evening dress here,' and I pointed to the man, 'And this boy called me Boy and told me I had to get out of here.' I told them all, 'Now, be careful. I want to buy an evening dress for my daughter.'

"Mr. Brown looked them all over. Then he pointed to each one. 'Now *you* and *you* and *you*. Take Mr. Phelps with you and be damn sure you find an evening dress to fit his daughter. Then he turned and punched the elevator button and went on upstairs.'

"You face all these things. You go through all these things and finally you get to a stopping point."

The stopping point came for Dallas women citizens of color "about 1960" when Florence Phelps, with Maurine Bailey, chaired the integration of stores. It was, as revolutions go, amazingly quiet. Three hundred black women from all walks of life organized into a coalition and announced that they would no longer shop in Dallas until the stores allowed them equal shopping privileges. "We marched a little," said Florence, "but that's about all."

"Everybody told her she would get fired from her teaching job for doing that," added John, "but she didn't."

"Well, mostly we just had meetings with the owners and managers," she explained. For her efforts, Florence received the second annual Citizenship Award from Alpha Kappa Alpha Sorority and the lasting admiration of responsible citizens everywhere.

There have been hundreds of other rebuffs. Neither Florence nor J. C. Phelps dwells on them, and it was difficult to get them to dredge painful incidents from the recesses of their memories. "There were the 'Whites Only' water fountains in all of the stores. When Sears first opened charge accounts, we were among the very first to get one," said John. "Then, one day we were shopping in Sears on Ross Avenue. I had just had a prescription filled and needed to take my medicine. I looked around for a water fountain and couldn't find anything except a 'Whites Only,' so I took my pill. There were some stares but nobody said anything. We came home and Florence wrote a letter to the manager explaining what had happened. She wrote that the day for 'Whites Only' signs was gone. He wrote back that he agreed, was then reevaluating store policy and the next time she came in, she would see that the signs had gone. And that's what happened."

When a handbook for visiting teachers in the Dallas Independent School District was needed, Florence Phelps spent an entire year going to meetings all over the state, collecting information, doing research and writing material. Then, when the book was published, they left her out completely. The State of Texas insisted they republish the book crediting her along with the other visiting teacher experts.

Florence had given up her full-time social work career in 1941 to become a visiting teacher in the Dallas Independent School District. As a social worker, her case load was only in the black communities, and she longed to make a difference with children in the formative stages of their lives, in finding and alleviating the source of so many problems she found, especially among children who had internalized low self-esteem because of their color.

Florence earned a master's of social work from Atlanta University in 1949, a master's in education from North Texas State University in 1958; did postgraduate work at the University of Texas in 1954, at the University of Illinois in 1959, at Southern Methodist University in 1963 and at Texas State University in 1964. She became a social worker for the City/County Department of Public Welfare in 1936 and continued for five years. She was the DISD social worker from 1941-1971 and assistant professor in the Graduate School of Social Work at the University of Texas at Arlington in 1971-72.

During all the time she was employed career-wise and otherwise, Florence Phelps continued her volunteer work for Dallas. She could not remember which work she did for pay and which she did as an unpaid volunteer. She was, at one time or another, acting director of the Wiley College Extension School in Dallas; director of the C.E.M.A. Financial Corporation; consultant for special case and adoptions for Hope Cottage Children's Bureau; chairperson of the Community Round Table on Social Health and Welfare Problems; on the board of Opportunity Industrial Center; with the Visiting Nurses Association of Dallas; president of the Visiting Teachers Association of Dallas; board member of the Dallas Memorial National Association; Texas United Community Services (director from 1970-73); a member of the League of Women Voters, United Methodist Women, Iota Phi Lambda and Alpha Kappa Alpha. She was honored as social worker of the year in Dallas in 1973, as a woman of the year by Iota Phi Lambda in 1973, with the National Sojourner Truth Meritorious Service Award in 1964. She is listed in Who's Who in the South and Southwest and in Who's Who in American Women.

"We think alike and we enjoy the same things," Florence said in 1954, of herself and the man to whom she had been married for 55 years. "We both enjoy music. We like people and good conversation. We have traveled extensively—been in 48 of the 50 states. We have spent many a night on the road in our car because we were not allowed to register in a hotel.

"Our country has suffered because of segregation. Everybody here (in Dallas) has suffered from it, the white folks as well as the black. We know it. They don't because they've never looked at the situation honestly. What is needed in the world is brains—not pigmentation."

For the 1990 national census, when John filled in the blank asking about nationality with the word American, a census official called him from Washington. To every query—What nationality are you? What race are you? What color are you? John answered American. "I finally told him that I knew he was searching for a word that went before American, such as Italian-American, Hispanic-American, Afro-American, but that I was born in this country, had no connections to any other and declined to be labeled with any other. He finally gave up."

The closest Florence ever came to being bitter was when she gave up her Boll Street home. "We had lived there all my life," she said. "They forced us out. We *had* to sell. They were building all around us." It was 1962. "Did we get out of it what it was worth?" She considered the question. "No." She said it very low and with finality. Her husband added, "Is there any way to measure the value of a *home*? The place where you've lived all of your life? Where you were born? Where your children were born?" They bought property in the beautiful, rolling hillsides of Oak Cliff not far from where Sarah Horton Cockrell and her family first located, not far from where the first black Dallasites arrived with William B. Miller. There they built a lovely home on a secluded street that ends at a city park named for John C. Phelps. It is filled with mementoes of a lifetime, a life of service well-lived.

"Florence is . . . ." For a few minutes John C. Phelps, in a 1990 interview, is without words. Back while she was teaching in the UTA Graduate School, she lost her way home from Arlington one afternoon and searched for three hours before she arrived home. Very slowly, her ability to communicate in words deteriorated. John was her primary care-taker. On this day he has groomed her immaculately. She sat through the interview serene, seldom trying to speak, but the beam in her eyes, her occasional seconds of clarity when a single word come out, let it be known that she heard, understood and was greatly frustrated when she could not communicate.

"On our wedding anniversary recently, I took her out to dinner. It seems that everybody we know turned up at that restaurant that night. Everybody was stopping and hugging her and telling each other stories about their connection with her. One man came over finally and asked who she was and I said she was the first social worker in the state of Texas and he said, 'No! Don't tell me this is Florence Phelps!' Turned out he was a coach in DISD. And he turned around and started telling everybody that he'd heard of Mrs. Phelps ever since he'd been with the Dallas schools."

How have they been married so well for so long? John answered: "In the beginning, her family was one of the most respected families in Dallas. I was the one from out of town. I wouldn't have done anything to embarrass her or her parents if my life had depended on it. When we decided to get married, we made up our minds never to quarrel—and we never have. When the girls were growing up and there were things we needed to discuss, we would get in the car and drive and talk and when we came home we were in complete agreement about what we ought to do. Every night, *every night* I thank God that she has been in my life. That she has been with me. If I have to go somewhere, I take her with me. There is no way. No way at all I could ever show her how much she means to me."

Idelle Mildred Goodman Rabin, entrepreneur and consummate Dallas volunteer.

IDELLE MILDRED GOODMAN RABIN

• • • •

November 23, 1921

Idelle Rabin grew up *with* Dallas. But at her birth on November 23, 1921, there was little hope that she would live to be a part of her city's growth and change. She was born with twisted intestines, and no infant with that condition had ever lived more than three weeks. Surgery, never done on newborns, was the only way to correct the problem.

Charles and Anne Garonzik Goodman named their baby Idelle Mildred and they insisted on the surgery. At St. Paul Hospital where she was born, medical history was made in Dallas when doctors successfully performed the operation that saved the infant's life.

Idelle Mildred Goodman Rabin has beat the odds in countless ways ever since.

Dallas was a small city, when Idelle was born. Every day of her life, with the exception of three years when she was a student at the University of Texas in Austin, it has been her home. "I wasn't aware of its size," Idelle said. "I remember when I was about five or six visiting Philadelphia and hearing that Dallas had 150,000 people and I thought 'My goodness! What a lot of people! I wonder how many of them I know?' I wanted to make a list, but my mother discouraged me . . . ."

As far as Idelle knew, the entire city of Dallas belonged to her. Growing up on the corner of Pennsylvania and Peabody in near South Dallas, Idelle lived in a neighborhood that was open, friendly, accepting, caring. Her father was head of the diamond department and on the board of directors of Linz Brothers, jewelers. By example, he set the first example of professional taste for his daughter. When he went to work he was always impeccably groomed with a white carnation in his buttonhole. Her mother was a community volunteer, a founding member of Dallas Hadassah and an exemplary housewife and mother.

"South Dallas was a world unto itself. We knew everybody and everybody knew us. Nobody locked a door. In the summertime we all left our doors open. There was no air conditioning, You invited the paper boy in for lemonade. The ice man delivered large blocks of ice and left it on the back porch. Many people wrapped their ice in old quilts or tow-sacks. We had an ice box. That made us one step up to being privileged, but I never thought about it.

"It was a very good life. I was an only child, but I grew up in a close, extended family with lots of cousins, aunts and uncles. I never lacked for playmates."

If her world of Dallas was one small neighborhood when Idelle was a little girl, the stories she heard from her father were of even a smaller Dallas. He, too, was a native, born in 1890 to Briene and Max Goodman, who had migrated to Dallas from Latvia in 1875 and gone into the mercantile business. Charles told his daughter stories about growing up with his seven brothers and sisters at 500 South Ervay Street, playing in the woods surrounding their home and going rabbit hunting in the vicinity of what is now Main and Elm at the Triple Underpass. Anne Garonzik Goodman was from Philadelphia.

In the summertime her mother took Idelle to Philadelphia to visit her relatives. It was there she first began to understand that cities are different and to feel that Dallas was the best place in the world to live. "In the world where I lived there was absolutely no discrimination. In Philadelphia I heard the adults talking about red lining. I remember thinking that there was something wrong with the rest of the country.

"My very first memory was Miss Walker's Kindergarten. Emily Schepps and Ed Tobolowsky were two of my classmates. My best friend was Jean Moore. She was a part of the Metzger family. We did everything together. Girl Scouts was a big thing. Miss Gertrude Newman—she was the playground teacher at Colonial Hills School—was our leader. On Saturdays Jean and I would go to town on the Ervay Streetcar. We'd get a hot dog at Woolworth for 15 cents and a lemonade for 5 cents. Then we'd go to a movie at the Melba where we bought popcorn for another nickel. Then we'd walk over to the Palace and go to another movie. It was a great thrill to watch the organ come up out of the floor. The music was marvelous! The Majestic had a downstairs nursery and when you were a little kid and went to the movies with your parents, you stayed there while they saw the movie. When you got older, if the movie bored you, you could go there and play . . . .

"Sundays were for visiting with relatives. Everything centered around family. The maid was a part of the family. You were as responsible for her well-being as she was for yours."

Idelle can't remember a time when she didn't want to be an actress. "I took elocution and dancing lessons from Miss Triller. I loved music. When I was seven, my parents gave me a season pass to the Dallas Symphony Orchestra. They gave me a grand piano when I was 13. Getting a grand piano was *the thing*. I just knew I would be a concert pianist."

Idelle was eight when the stock market crashed. It hit her personally the year she was nine. For the first time in her life, there were no company dividends. "We'd always counted on these yearly bonanzas for the extra things in our lives. That year there was nothing extra. It made quite an impression on me!"

Growing up in Dallas was ideal, "but I didn't know it. It was just the natural thing. It was a big event to drive out into the country along Preston Road to Armstrong Parkway. The State Fair of Texas was the highlight of our lives. Weber's Root Beer stand on Forest Avenue was our hang-out. Sunday school was our socializing center.

"I have always enjoyed being a part of the Christian community. I've been a spectator, knowing I would never be a participant. This has never bothered me, never made me feel like an outsider. When I was growing up I never experienced a single case of anti-Semitism. Not one. Friends have pointed out slights and slurs, but I've have never been conscious of discrimination. Maybe it's because I've never wanted to do anything that I wasn't allowed to do. Country club life would bore me to distraction. They give great parties? Not nearly as good as I can do in my own home at a lot less expense . . . ."

Idelle Goodman graduated from Forest Avenue High School in 1938 at the age of 16 and went off to the University of Texas where, logically enough, she got involved in everything that had to do with theater. As a member of the Curtain Club, she worked with Ida Nell Brill. Years later at a social event she addressed Nellie (Mrs. John) Connally as Ida Nell Brill, "and Mrs. Connally said, even before she remembered who I was, 'I know where we knew each other!'

"I wanted desperately to go to the American Academy of Dramatic Arts. But nice Jewish girls didn't leave home and go to New York to become actresses. My father absolutely put his foot down. He was afraid I would turn out like his "flaky" sisters. How wonderful they were! One was a ballerina, another a writer for Warner Brothers and another the executive secretary for RKO Pictures."

In 1940 Idelle went to work for Neiman-Marcus. "Neiman's was my university. I spent my entire Neiman's career, five years, in one department, the junior department on the mezzanine. It was the perfect place for me. There I could act out my fantasies. Acting and selling are natural allies. Selling is not only a craft, but a fine art. At its finest, it is the height of creativity. You don't deceive. You don't manipulate. You make every person feel better by what you do for them. Stanley (Marcus) and Carrie Neiman were my mentors. She was the epitome of style and class, a fine art in the way she dressed, looked and acted. I was so in awe of her. Stanley was the professor and teacher. He had such taste! He recognized quality in his personnel and nurtured the talented. He gave me my sense of self-worth.

"Today I do things instinctively because of the way they taught me. Just by being herself, Carrie Neiman taught me to take the extra seconds to put myself together before I face the world. Stanley taught me to be discriminating, to have an eye for detail. He would walk through the store checking and snap his fingers and get the tiniest flaw corrected. Today when people accuse me of being a perfectionist—and I am,"—she laughed, "I smile and say you can blame Stanley Marcus for that."

Idelle worked for Neimans during almost the entirety of World War II. She was there when the Japanese bombed Pearl Harbor on December 7, 1941. She was still there when the Germans admitted defeat on May 7, 1945, and there when the atomic bomb was dropped on Hiroshima August 6, 1955, and on Nagasaki on August 9 and there when the Japanese surrendered on August 15. From her vantage point on the corner of Commerce and Ervay she heard the newsboys shouting "extra! extra!" time after time during those sweltering days before television.

But her thoughts were often elsewhere. Earlier in the year she had met the first man who seemed worth her time. She met him because her mother insisted that she do something she didn't want to do, "but knew I must keep peace in the family. My mother was directing a program on the weekends for servicemen at the Jewish Community Center. It was where Old City Park is now—not far from where we lived. On weekends the service men from surrounding camps poured into Dallas. There wasn't a lot for them to do. Mother's group provided some music programs, a few classes of one kind and another, but mostly fed them! Mother was tired of what she said was my youthful self-centeredness—and insisted that I do *something* for her project. She said it was my patriotic duty."

Directing the program that Anne Goodman was chairing was a young man from Philadelphia whose name was Leon Rabin. He had come to Dallas earlier that year as the community organizer for the United Service Organization (USO). With a degree in psychology from the University of Pennsylvania, he thought it prudent not to get romantically involved with anyone. He knew, he said in a 1985 interview, that Jewish mothers were eager to marry off their daughters to eligible, acceptable young men. So, to fend off any entanglements, he passed himself off as married with a wife and children back in Philadelphia.

That is, until he met Idelle Goodman.

It was hardly your typical romantic encounter. Having decided she would "keep peace in the family" by doing what her mother wished, Idelle capitulated totally and organized 23 of her friends to serve breakfast on Sunday mornings to 400 servicemen. Throughout her life Idelle spoke often and vehemently for her beliefs, but when she had done good battle and lost, she was totally gracious and cooperative. So, there she was on

Sunday morning, totally in charge. "Idelle ran the operation like a top sergeant," said Leon admiringly.

The Rabins grinned like conspirators when they are asked what happened to his tale that he had a wife and children back home. But they didn't tell. Nor did they divulge how long Idelle continued to serve breakfast to the visiting servicemen.

Idelle Mildred Goodman and Leon Rabin were married on November 4, 1945, in the Grand Ballroom of the Melrose Hotel, a portion of which became an exclusive restaurant.

Idelle bought into the societal conditioning for women of that time. She resigned her job at Neiman's. "I was," she said, "the nice Jewish housewife." What she means is that she bought into the propaganda that was prevalent at the time. Servicemen, just as they had two decades before, were returning in huge numbers. Women, who had kept the home safe, reared the children and held the jobs that kept the military supplied during four years of combat, were encouraged by every persuasion of the mass media to go home again. Movies ("The Best Years of Our Lives"), articles, the radio, public speeches—everything contrived in one simple message: If you insist on working outside your home, Honey, you not only are taking the bread from the mouths of other families, but you are denying your God-given destiny as a woman.

Idelle put up with being a typical housewife for exactly a year. She played mah-jongg with her friends. She chatted about housing. She talked baby formula and diaper-changing with "the girls." She even played bridge . . . . "Did I really do that?" she groaned. "I don't know how to play bridge. I *hate* bridge."

To save her sanity, she and her bridegroom became involved in the minuscule art and theater community in Dallas. They went to the movies, to every showing that presented itself as theater. "Not much and not often." Two energetic, enthusiastic, educated young people in love, they sought out every opportunity to view theater, music, the arts of any and all kinds. In 1946, Leon finished his master's degree in psychology at Southern Methodist University and wrote his thesis on the problems the Dallas Police Department had in trying to hire minority officers, the first study done in the Southwest on black-white relations. Idelle applauded him mightily—and was miserable.

To assuage her need to be involved in art, Idelle started to bead the blouses and sweaters her mother turned out. Beautiful works of art, they were admired and sought after by her circle of friends. People kept saying, "Why don't you go into business?" It sounded tempting. The practical Leon said yes, indeed, the blouses were beautiful, but it didn't make sense to open a business unless there was a demand for—not only the works of art his wife and her mother could turn out, (which limited the supply dramatically)—but for exclusive garments of all kinds. Was Dallas ready for such a business? Would women purchase garments bought for them personally in the marketplaces of the world? Was such a business, in short, practical and would it be profitable? Simple questions demand simple answers. Leon stood downtown on the corner of Main at Harwood and counted the number of women passing by who wore skirts and blouses.

He told Idelle that opening an exclusive shop, catering to the individual needs of discerning women, stocking merchandise that was excellent quality, not too high priced and offering personal service looked like a good bet. On November 23, 1946, at first in partnership with friends, they opened Berwald-Rabin at Lovers Lane and Inwood.

"That was the 1940s," Idelle stressed. "No *married* woman in my circle of friends worked. I didn't know any woman who worked—except for the nurses and the teachers . . . . And here I was every day going out to work. My friends couldn't understand it. I didn't fit in anymore. They thought I had deserted them and I felt left out. I wanted and needed their support. Leon—he was always the consummate philosopher—kept telling me, 'One of these days it will be chic to be a business woman'."

Hurt as she was, Idelle made up her mind that "I'm not going to live behind the store. My first outreach was in the arts. It was natural. I had freedom in the evening. And I yearned to be on stage in one way or another." Hardly had the store opened when the Dallas Community Center Players moved in with them. It was the only live theater group in the city. The store became its rehearsal stage and its prop-and-costume storage center. "Our first production was pretty awful," Idelle said. "Some of our friends had come to support us and some left before it was over—to keep from telling us what they thought of the play."

Characteristic of Idelle and Leon Rabin, they knew it was awful and they wasted no time in excuses. They got involved in other art projects. Leon made a number of radio appearances. They supported and he acted in early productions of Margo Jones's Theatre '47. (The name changed annually). He played Brenda Vaccaro's grandfather in *Twilight Park* when she was five.

Idelle and Leon Rabin with her mother and business partner, Anne Garonzik Goodman, at DelAnns in 1951.

In 1951, the partnership with friends having not worked, Anne Goodman bought into the business. Leon, who had been doing consulting work for businesses, came in as a partner and the business manager.

The store moved to 6207 Hillcrest across the street from Southern Methodist University and became DelAnns, a combination of mother and daughter names. "We planned for it to be a college shop," Idelle said, "but after a bit we looked at what we were doing. We had 600 girls and 200 women customers and the 200 accounted for three-fourths of our business . . . ."

The store was a success, but there was something missing. In 1953 the Rabins added that missing link. They adopted a daughter. On July 6, 1953, when she was 30 hours old, Charlsie Goodman Rabin came home with Idelle and Leon. "I had always known I wanted a child," Idelle said. "I wanted to be a mother. My life would have been incomplete without a child. Sure, it was hard. That was 1953 . . . . " Again, as in 1946 when she went into business, she was defying what public opinion decreed that a woman *ought* to do. Good mothers made home, husbands and children their full career. They did not need anything else to fulfill them. "I wanted to be with my baby as much as possible. I stayed home in the mornings until about 10. I bathed her and fed her and then I went to the store." Idelle, unable to be the 1950s image of the ideal woman, shared the guilt trip with other working woman of that time and, like most of them, tried to be a super woman.

Idelle has dressed countless Dallas women appropriately for the biggest moments of their lives. When she goes to market, she has each in mind and, home again, is personally on the phone, saying, "When I was in New York, I saw this outfit and it had your name on it." Almost always she is right, though if the woman tries it on and it isn't right, Idelle says, even before she can, "Take it off. It's not you, after all." There is never any hard sell. If the customer shows the slightest doubt, Idelle says, "Let's find something else." She would consider it an insult to an individual to lower a price, but as soon as she puts things on sale, she's on the phone reporting it.

Only those of us who have benefitted from her expertise in having exactly the right thing for big occasions know how to appreciate her largesse. And a personal story:

I had *never* been in DelAnns. I knew both of the Rabins, him better than her because of our involvement in the volunteer community, but I had always assumed that the clothes were too expensive for my budget. When you are working as a journalist and rearing *five* daughters, you are very cautious about the money you spend on your own wardrobe. It was early in the 1970s and the Dallas Commission on the Status of Women was new.

Both Idelle and I were on it. We worked extremely well together, my paper having said that I could serve on the Commission provided I did not become a "front" person or a spokesperson for it. Idelle and I were on the Women and Work task force and we decided to put on a work fair for Dallas women. She chaired it; I was her back-up person. Never have I been associated with anyone who was more organized, dedicated and efficient. The project was an overwhelming success. Either during, or soon after it was over, I was invited as a journalist by Braniff Airways to "One Glorious Weekend in Acapulco." This VIP event included such people as Henry and Nancy Kissinger and Lady Bird Johnson. I knew I must go; I had nothing to wear. I called Idelle. "I have a problem," I said, "and I am going to make it your problem. I have to have a wardrobe that will be acceptable for a very special four days in Acapulco. I have very little time and even less money and, in addition, I *hate* to shop. What are you going to do about it?" She said, "Come out here," and let's see what we can do." I have no idea how she assembled the wardrobe that made me feel like I belonged in that circle of individuals, but she did—and I did.

And one more personal story: When I retired from *The Dallas Times Herald* in 1984, I had been invited by the Dallas Women's Center to present its annual Women Helping Women awards. That was nothing new; I had been honored to do this on several prior occasions, so I was totally unprepared for what happened. After I had presented all of the winners, my friends turned the tables on me and presented me with one of the highest honors I have ever had—a check in the amount of $5,750, making it possible for me to go to the Soviet Union on the first of my Citizen Diplomat trips with a nest-egg left over to take a trip to Europe when this book is completed. The day following this astonishing event, Idelle called me. She said I would not find hers and Leon's name on the six-foot-long scroll of contributors to my future because they intended to present me with a "going away" wardrobe so that I could be well-dressed when I traveled. She said, as is her way of operating, "Come out here and let me outfit you!" I went and she did. I have no way of knowing how often this generosity has been repeated, but I am certain of this: Those of us who have been the beneficiaries could accept only because we knew there were no strings attached and the Rabins could do it only because they did not expect anything in return. Everything of this kind they have ever done has been anonymously. Another legacy, perhaps, from Stanley Marcus.

The Rabins had an uncanny sense of recognizing talent and supporting it early when it mattered most. They "adopted several promising young Dallasites. One day in 1949 they cashed a check for advertising executive Allen Pottasch when he was a new kid in town and nobody else would do it. They were mutually impressed. The Rabins invited him to breakfast; they helped him become oriented to his new city. He never forgot. They befriended Aaron Spelling of television production fame, when he was starting his career and directed a play at the Jewish Community Center.

Their ability to invest in people who make a difference was repeated in their ability to choose art causes that are destined for success. In 1965 when Polly Lou Moore wanted to do something special for the arts in Dallas, she said one day while in DelAnns that she would like to send out a mailing to young professionals asking for their support. The Rabins provided money for the mailing. The result was The 500, Inc. In 1977 The 500 honored the Rabins as founding sponsors with a Richard Serra sculpture in their name at the Dallas Museum of Fine Arts.

Through the years Idelle honed her interest in the arts in multiple ways. She and her husband were "first night" sponsors of countless art benefits. She is one of the first, if not *the* first person people call when they need help in raising money for art, theater and music. Along the way, she took up painting and, busy as she continued to be, escaped whenever she can grab a moment—sometimes no longer than 10 minutes at a time—to paint in her at-home studio. "A city cannot grow and thrive unless it develops the arts along with its business," her husband said repeatedly. She always nodded.

The tragedy of being recognized in one field—whether it be typecast as an actor or recognized as *the* definitive supporter of the arts is that, too often, one's options are perceived as limited in other fields. As much as it pleased her to be recognized as an arts supporter, Idelle felt rebuffed as a business person, and until recently DelAnn's was the second most successful small business in Dallas.

"I'm middle," Idelle said, "and those in the middle get overlooked. I've neither been Big Business that is automatically looked up to or Small Business that gets attention and support. We've always made our own way. We've almost always been profitable, but we haven't made a huge splash. "I am always asked to sponsor the project, get the speaker, pay for the extras, but I have been passed over again and again for the honors that usually go with this kind of dedication."

Probably the principal reason that Idelle has not had the public recognition she deserves is that she has lived and worked principally in a man's world by male standards. The three individuals she has idolized and emulated are men—Charles Goodman, her father, a man of superior intellect and style, her boss, Stanley Marcus, a man of matchless quality in merchandising, and her husband, Leon Rabin, a man of consummate wit and integrity. While this choice of mentors is clearly understandable, it has left all but the strongest of women baffled in the same way that her friends were puzzled when she "deserted" bridge and mah-jongg. Women are usually the ones who give the love and attention that every human being requires; they have been willing to lavish it on men who, after all, are *supposed* to be forceful and aggressive, but they have withheld it from their sisters who exhibit similar characteristics. Men, on the other hand, who pass out accolades—if they honor women at all, and they rarely do—choose the mother-madonna type.

Additionally, Idelle has been "left out" because she chose both to eliminate from her own value system the traditional ways women live their lives *and* the new way they are functioning. "I am not a feminist," she declared, while exhibiting all of the finest characteristics of the true meaning of feminism, *the doctrine advocating social and political rights for women* equal to those of men. Her first venture into working for the advancement of women came during her tenure with the Dallas Women's Commission, but her real conversion came in 1985 when she went to Nairobi to the United Nations' World Conference of Women. There she met women from other parts of the world who were overcoming obstacles far greater than she had ever experienced. "It hit me that I should be helping other women in business." Already a member of the National Association of Business Women Owners, she became visibly active in its projects. She became a key figure in the success of the Dallas Women's Foundation that annually gives away thousands of dollars to help women take their first steps toward personal independence. She belongs to the Dallas Forum composed of women who own or manage businesses with an international bent.

"It's awfully hard for a woman to survive in her own business," Idelle said. "Some of the reason lies in the public domain but a lot of it is their own responsibility." The social order is at fault when it excludes all except the male model to measure business success. "I made a *choice* never to let the store dominate my life. Men never understand why I didn't move to a mall or open up a chain. Their reasoning is that to be successful one must constantly try to be bigger. My reasoning is that to be successful one must constantly try to be best."

Women need practical sense as well as creative ability when they open businesses of their own and this reality, in Idelle's opinion, often is lacking. "Women see themselves as 'finished' in the male role. They think they have to have the whole thing when they start out. They want the fine office, furnished with the latest gimmicks, the designer clothes, the most expensive leather briefcase. The 'image' is important, but it doesn't have to cost the fortune they don't have. I've been in business for 45 years and it's only the last 15 or so that I can afford me!"

Because she sees things so clearly so quickly without having to wait to dissect an idea and put it back together, because she has always been so energetic—awake and every mental antenna alert at a 7 a.m. breakfast while others are getting their first sip of coffee, because she arrives at every meeting prepared having done her homework, people tend to miscalculate Idelle Rabin. They do not see her total dedication to her city . . . .

"I love being a part of Dallas. I wouldn't live any other place in the world.

"What do I see of the past in Dallas? And what do I see for the future?" She did not hesitate. It's something she'd thought about many times, something she had worked out over a long period of driving to meetings at 6 a.m. and getting home from another at 10 p.m., in the meantime having put in a full eight hours at the store with an hour's break for a business luncheon.

"Dallas has some unique problems. Having two entities—Highland Park and University Park—within its boundaries tends toward fragmentation. We are not centralized. We do not have one single purpose. Every element of this city has pockets of energy. Many of them we have not been tapped. Women are coming up. This is going to make a huge difference. The saddest thing of all is that it no longer has a downtown. We are no longer the oligarchy we once were. The price you pay for democratization is that you do not get things done as quickly. It's a price I'm willing to pay. I want Dallas to be prideful again. I want my grandson"—that's Brandon Charles Burden—"to enjoy what I have enjoyed."

Gertrude Terrell Aldredge Shelburne, a fifth generation Dallasite, whose great-great grandfather, George Whitfield Terrell, explored the area that would become Dallas.

GERTRUDE TERRELL ALDREDGE SHELBURNE

• • • •

October 19, 1907—June 16, 1993

Before there was a city, before there was a state of Texas, Gertrude Shelburne's roots were planted in Dallas.

Her great-great grandfather was George Whitfield Terrell, who was chosen by his friend, Sam Houston, to explore the area that is now centered by Dallas. Texas was then an independent country having declared its freedom from Mexico on March 2, 1836, and secured it when General Houston led his army against Santa Anna and the Mexican forces at San Jacinto on April 21, 1836. Eager to settle the new nation, the newly elected President Houston of the Republic of Texas chose George Terrell to be the emissary to the Indians. It was Terrell who negotiated the first peace treaty with them and recommended sites for peacekeeping forts so that settlers traveling from the south of Texas and from eastern and northern states would have some protection.

George Terrell had already helped to establish those forts, including Bird's Fort, before John Neely Bryan pitched his tent on the banks of the Trinity and called the place Dallas.

Though her genes are firmly planted in Dallas on both the maternal and paternal sides of her family, Gertrude also inherited their predilection to the cosmos. Her great grandmother, Rebecca Ann Terrell set the pattern. Rebecca Ann was married to James Epamananous Terrell, the son of the George Whitfield Terrell. James, imbued with the pioneering spirit, moved away from Dallas in the 1850s. He declared that the city was getting too big and too civilized and took his bride to California to live. And so it was that Gertrude's grandmother, Gertrude Terrell (who would later marry S. I. Munger), for whom she was named, is a native Californian. Born in 1859, Gertrude Terrell was a small child when the Civil War erupted. James joined the Confederate forces. Rebecca Ann came home to Texas. Because there was no dependable overland transportation Rebecca Ann took her three small children and boarded a ship that took them down the coast of California to Panama. She traveled by mule across Panama—this was some 40 years before the Panama Canal was dug—and boarded another ship which brought her to Texas.

Almost half a century later, on October 19, 1907, Gertrude Aldredge was born in Dallas. She was the oldest of George N. and Rena Munger Aldredge's four children. Her two sisters—Betty Aldredge Slater and Rowena Aldredge Edwards—and her brother, George N. Aldredge Jr.—were all born and reared in Dallas.

When Gertrude was 13 her parents bought the house at 5500 Swiss Avenue that Will Lewis built for his bride, Willie Newbury Lewis, after she declared it too big for her. Willie had sold it to an oil man whose diminishing fortune made it impossible for him to keep. The Aldredges bought it in 1921 and it was in that house that Gertrude and her siblings grew up. It was from that house she went away to college, from that house she made her debut in 1929 and in that house that she was married.

Gertrude remembered Dallas as a small town where everybody knew everybody else and where everybody was responsible for everybody else. When their good friends, the Burghers built their home on the site where the Melrose Hotel now stands, they urged the Aldredges to purchase the lot next door, but George and Rena declined because, they said, Oak Lawn was too far from Dallas.

Gertrude was a shy and very protected child, she said. "My mother was strict—very strict. She made all the decisions for me and it never occurred to me until much later that I had any choice at all about what I would do, what I would wear, where I would go to school or who would be my playmates." Her best friend, Lela Vardell, lived across the street but the two girls never spent the night at each other's home because my mother would not have allowed it.

"Reading was my greatest joy and since there was no restriction on the books I read, I spent endless hours alone in my room absorbing just about everything I could get my hands on." That turned her into an excellent student who not only read and absorbed information years in advance of other children, but taught her to edit her thoughts and write down her ideas in a clear, organized manner. For the first five grades of her schooling, she, along with the children of her parents' friends, attended Mrs. Taylor's School. When she reached the sixth grade, she enrolled in Holley Hall.

Holley Hall was the brainchild of Josephine Holley, who had come to Dallas following her graduation from Wellesley College in 1890, to teach at St. Mary's College. Soon recognizing the need for a quality education for girls that would prepare them to do college work, Miss Josie asked her younger sister, Frances Holley to move to Dallas and help her establish and operate a school. It was a school that lasted about a quarter of a century, from shortly after 1900 until 1926 or 1927. Very few records remain on the school, but its impact on Dallas continues to the present through the contributions to Dallas of its graduates.

"Miss Josie had taught my mother at St. Mary's, so there was never any doubt that I would go to their school as soon as I was old enough," Gertrude said in a 1991 interview. "Miss Josie taught Latin and English and Miss Frankie taught math. Sometimes it seemed to us that Miss Josie's sole purpose in life was to get us into Wellesley." Several other prominent Dallas women concur, because most of the girls who graduated from Holley Hall went on to graduate from Wellesley. Most excelled at Wellesley, proof that Josephine Holley knew what she was doing.

Gertrude was one of five young women who graduated from Holley Hall in 1924. She was 16 years old. Josephine Holley enrolled all five of the graduates in Wellesley. Four went. The fifth, Gertrude's friend Lela Vardell, did not go away to school. "So far as we were concerned, Wellesley was the only school in the country. I don't think I'd ever heard of Vassar or Smith or Mount Holyoke and if I had, I would never have thought of defying Miss Josie to go there."

Wellesley proved to be an educational goldmine for the shy 16-year-old from Dallas, "but I've appreciated it far more since I've been out than I ever did when I was there. I was turned loose there, on my own, for the first time in my life. You might think that a girl who had led such a restricted life would try all sorts of new and different things, but I didn't. Wellesley is a girls' school, so there wasn't much opportunity for dating and I wasn't eager to date, anyway. My passion was still books—and movies! I loved the movies. I went all the time."

Gertrude spent three years at Wellesley in pretty much the same kind of cocoon she'd lived in Dallas. She was getting ready to enroll for her junior year when her mother decided it was time to take the entire family on a trip around the world. So, instead of going back to college, Gertrude joined the rest of the family for a leisurely trip abroad. "It was the most significant experience of my life. I recognized later how college changed me—and it did change me—but I knew at the time how much traveling was broadening and deepening my experiences." The family returned to Dallas in the middle of May, 1928, in time for Gertrude to have a summer to prepare to re-enroll in college for her senior year. She graduated from Wellesley in May of 1929.

An economic disaster was just over the horizon when Gertrude came home with her diploma, "but those of us in Dallas were hardly aware of it." Gertrude was preparing for her Idlewild debut. The Great Depression hardly reached them at all. "Our plans were all made when the stock market crashed and we went on with our plans," she said.

Idlewild announced its 10 debutantes of the season on Sunday, October 27, 1929. The headline in *The Dallas Times Herald* read, "Ten Debutantes will Make Bows at Idlewild," and the underline read "Club President Albert Sidney Johnson and Miss Gertrude Aldredge Will Lead Grand March." Two days later the stock market crashed and three days after that, on Friday, November 1, Gertrude was officially introduced to Dallas society. The nine other debutantes of the season were Mary Cox, Mary Catherine Crozier, Edna May Gifford, Josephine Hughes, Elsie Nicholson, Billie Smith, Louise Smith, Elizabeth Stemmons and Bettie Timmins.

Rena Aldredge chose the dress for her daughter's debut. "I hated that dress," Gertrude said, 62 years later. It was blue moire taffeta with a tiered skirt. "I made a bargain with my mother. I told her I would wear it if she would let me choose my own dress for the Terps (Terpsichorean) dance. In those days Terps came one week after Idlewild. Mother agreed, so I wore the blue to the presentation and to my own party. But I wore a wonderful slinky black velvet dress to Terps and carried an armful of long-stemmed American beauty roses. I'm probably the only Dallas debutante who turned up at an official party in black. Mother was wonderful. She didn't say a word. She didn't even raise her eyebrows. She'd made an agreement. She even seemed to enjoy it!

"I loved it!" Gertrude said of her debut year. It served as her passage to adulthood. "From that time on, I was free to make my own plans."

Not long after the Idlewild dance, Mary Neal called to tell Gertrude that she had been chosen for the Junior League. "She asked if I would like to join and I said I supposed so and she said for me to be at the Tea Room the next day to serve lunch. Things were so simple back then. Now, Junior League provisionals go through such a long period of training and volunteer work. All we had to do was show up and do what we were told to do."

Gertrude "showed up" the next day at the Tea Room on Main Street. "The idea for having us work there was so that all of our beaus would come there to eat lunch."

Serving lunch at the tea room was the beginning of Gertrude's volunteer work. Soon she was teaching at Scottish Rite Hospital. "I was not trained to be a teacher, but the children in the hospital needed to keep up with their work and I discovered I was quite good at teaching."

In the fall of 1933 in the living room of Aldredge House, Gertrude was married to Samuel Ainslie Shelburne. A native of Virginia, six years older than his bride, Sam Shelburne was a graduate of Rice and of the University of Pennsylvania School of Medicine. He had come to Dallas in 1931. "Sam wanted to do research," Gertrude said, "but it was in the midst of the depression and there was no money anywhere for research." Dr. Shelburne began his practice in internal medicine and became an instructor at Baylor

University Medical Center. In 1934, shortly after the couple was married, he became the physician in charge of the Cardiac Clinic at Baylor University Hospital.

As a young wife, Gertrude never slowed down. "My first big job was president of the Junior League." Characteristically, she disclaimed the idea that she was chosen to head the League because of her exceptional ability. "The president was getting married and leaving Dallas," she said, "so they asked me take the job and I did." She is one of the few League members to have served for more than one year as president. "The president of the Junior League was expected to be on almost every community board, so I found my days pretty full. I've forgotten all of the things I did. When I was going through some personal papers, I found a list I'd made. I was on nine different boards at one time .... That's not possible."

But it was possible. One thing led to the next. "How could I do it? I had excellent help at home. I've never had a paying job, but I've worked longer hours than most women who get a paycheck. I learned how to work with volunteers to get things done." Along the way there were three Shelburne children—Samuel Ainslie, Jr., George Aldredge and Alice (Mrs. Edward F. Neild III). "My daughter has better sense than I did. She wouldn't think of getting herself so involved." But the granddaughters are following Gertrude's example—and it was with obvious pride that she a showed a family photograph taken on her 80th birthday that included all members of the family except one grandson who could not get away from college to attend the festivities at Aldredge House. Identifying the members of the family, Gertrude pointed with pride to a granddaughter who had studied Chinese at Stanford and then graduated from law school with a speciality in international law focusing on China.

Before the children grew up, before there was any thought of grandchildren, Gertrude was busy making a home for a very involved physician and making waves in the Dallas volunteer community. She began her married life in an upstairs apartment on University Boulevard, but soon found a house on Golf Drive and bought it. Then World War II interrupted everybody's lives and the Shelburnes moved to California where he spent two years as a physician. When he was shipped overseas, Gertrude—following in the footsteps of her great-grandmother—came home to Dallas. She took an apartment on McFarlin until her husband was discharged from service and set up his practice again in Dallas.

Gertrude's volunteer work cut across all areas of Dallas life. Her social heritage was the start, but only a start. She worked "in the trenches" in all segments of the community, and in 1991 cited five different areas that had been the most personally satisfying: Visiting Nurses Association, the Symphony, Planned Parenthood, Women's Council of Dallas County and the Council of Social Agencies, later renamed Community Council of Greater Dallas. These five represent a cross-section of Dallas.

Reflecting on the different areas in which she had served, Gertrude said: "The Junior League was trying to start the Council of Social Agencies. It was in the 1940s and I was in charge of getting it organized. Three men—Fred Florence, A. C. Bigger and Karl Hoblitzelle—told us how it should be done. We didn't agree. We knew it wouldn't work. At that time there was a man heading the Community Chest and they wanted to make him head of the Council. He was a nice man but he didn't have the education or the training to head a social agency. We wanted to bring in somebody who would do the job that needed to be done. I was appointed the spokesperson to tell those three Dallas giants that the Junior League wouldn't provide the money unless we did the job right. Everybody felt so sorry for me, but it wasn't hard. I just told them we weren't going to do it their way and they said okay, then, do it your way. We got the agency started and hired a man from out of town to head it .... He just stayed one year. He said it was too hot in Dallas for him. Most people thought he meant the weather. But he also meant the political climate."

Then, Lawrence Pollock, who was president of the Dallas Symphony, asked Gertrude to head ticket sales. "I told him I would if he would let me do it the way it ought to be done. He said all right, but he didn't understand what I had in mind. I went out to the Colonial Golf tournament and picked up one of their programs. It was filled with advertising of organizations that supported the golf tournament. I showed it to Mr.

Pollock and told him that's the way we had to go about selling tickets to the symphony because we were competing for the entertainment dollar. He asked out much it would cost and I said I didn't know, but I'd find out and get back with him tomorrow. I got on the phone and got most of the work donated. The next day I called him back and told him it would cost $2,100. He said fine; he would underwrite it. He also said, 'Why don't you be president? I don't have time to do the job.'

"I spent three weeks arguing with my husband about taking on the job as president of the Symphony. He said I couldn't do it. No woman ever had. He said why couldn't I just settle for executive vice president. I told him, 'No. If I'm going to do the work, I'm going to be the president. If I'm going to take the criticism, I'm also going to have the credit.' He finally gave in and said it would be okay if Lawrence Pollock would stay as board chairman. So that's what we did. We rewrote the by-laws so that he would be chairman of the board and I would be president." In that role, Gertrude visited almost every Dallas executive.

When birth control was mentioned in the United States only in hushed whispers, and the sale or possession of contraceptives was illegal, even for married couples, Gertrude helped Katie Rice Ripley smuggle diaphragms to Dallas across state lines from New York. Had the two been caught, it would have been a federal offense. Gertrude went on to be a founder of the first Planned Parenthood affiliate in Dallas and "I came out of retirement to help establish a new affiliate of the organization in 1982." Planned Parenthood named its original clinic on Greenville Avenue for the Shelburnes and later established the Gertrude Shelburne Volunteer of the Year Award and the Gertrude Shelburne Humanitarian of the Year Award.

For many of her most active years, Gertrude Shelburne worked from her 5358 Meaders Lane home. After she was widowed in 1979—and Dr. Shelburne had spent the final five years of his life in a nursing home suffering with Alzheimer's—she moved to a condominium on Christopher Place and from there to 3525 Turtle Creek. On her 83rd birthday, she had a stroke that affected her speech and, for a time, left her partially paralyzed. With characteristic good humor she worked at getting well. "Isn't it wonderful," she asked, "that I helped to get Visiting Nurses started in Dallas and now they are giving me therapy? Just think, we started out with two visiting nurses; now there are dozens and they are doing such a wonderful job in this community!"

There was a watercolor of Aldredge House on her dining room wall and a photograph of her mother on a living room table that made Gertrude smile every time she glanced at them.

"My mother was one of the most fun people I've ever known," she said. "She was a marvelous traveling companion. We went many places together. Mother never stopped learning, never stopped being challenged. She wrote the most marvelous doggerel. She made it up about any and all kinds of things. I remember some of the things she said. This one still makes me laugh:

> I wake in the morning
> Collect my wits
> Open the paper
> And read the obits.
>
> If my name is not there
> I know I'm not dead
> So I eat a good breakfast
> And go back to bed.

The Aldredge family gave Aldredge House to the Dallas County Medical Auxiliary in April of 1974 and on April 2, 1975, a dedication ceremony made the transfer official. "It was a good thing," said Gertrude Aldredge. "The house is serving the community well and linking the past with the present. And, they are taking good care of it." By a quirk of timing, the Medical Auxiliary is one of the few organizations in the city that Gertrude Shelburne did not serve as president.

Gertrude glanced over autobiographical material she provided to *The Dallas Times Herald* in 1969 and laughed. At that time she had summarized her career as "Housewife and Mother. Volunteer. Past president of: (1) the Dallas Junior League; (2) Community Council; (3) Dallas Garden Club; (4) Dallas Symphony Orchestra; (5) Women's Symphony League; incoming president of Women's Council of Dallas County; board of Texas Social Welfare Association and Visiting Nurses Association; past chairman of the Department of Christian Social Relations for the Episcopal Diocese of Dallas, on the National Committee on Crime and Delinquency and on the board of LEAD. She had already been given the Zonta and Arete Awards for community service and been named Dallas Chapter of Texas Welfare Association's most outstanding contributor. "I have," she wrote at that time, "been vitally interested in many aspects of health, education and welfare . . . in Dallas and have served on too many boards to list them all."

In 1991 when Planned Parenthood of Dallas and Northeast Texas, Inc. presented its first awards to people for outstanding contributions in advancing the mission of Planned Parenthood, the Gertrude Aldredge Shelburne Award was presented to Mrs. Shelburne for "her lifetime commitment to family planning; for being the first woman and one of the only two to date, to be president of the Dallas Symphony Association; to be the first woman to serve on a Dallas County Grand Jury; to be the first woman to serve as president of the Community Council, and for her continuing service to the Dallas community and to its women."

"We turned the symphony around," she said. "We saved it. We also created the Community Council . . . . Women have done everything of any significance ever accomplished in this city in the social and human relationships areas."

Gertrude Shelburne's personal service to Dallas ended on June 16, 1993, when she died, but her legacy will continue to live in the hands and hearts of all Dallas volunteers.

Ruth Potts Spence had an intimate knowledge of Dallas from the days its streets were paved with bois d' arc to the space age.

RUTH POTTS SPENCE

• • • •

September 6, 1894—April 10, 1989

From the day when the streets were paved with bois d'arc blocks to the space age, Ruth Potts Spence lived, helped to shape and was shaped by the city of Dallas. Hers was an unusual, if not unique perspective, for she was born and reared into Society. But like no other person of her time, she empathized with people whose color and financial fortunes were different from hers, and spent her entire life bridging—or trying to bridge—the chasms among and between individuals and groups of people.

In February of 1984, Ruth said she was not interested in talking about herself or relating the stories of Dallas's growth. "Oh, Honey, I've done that over and over," she said in answer to a telephone inquiry for an interview. "Everybody's heard what I have to say." It took a bit of gentle persuasion but she finally agreed to the interview in her Overbrook home "for an hour."

The minute Ruth opened the door, I knew I had found a rare gem. Tiny—not more than five feet two inches—and slender, she carried herself with the regal splendor of royalty. Her silver hair was perfectly coiffed. Her ivory colored dress, with a pinstripe in red, was buttoned down the front. Shirt-waist styled over a slightly flared skirt, it was belted at the waistline. The sleeves were turned up into deep cuffs. She wore red sandals—and her toenails were crimson!

The warmth of her reception was eclipsed only by the depth of her knowledge and, it turned out, her willingness to share what she knew. At that time Ruth Spence was a few months short of 90 years old. She had made copious notes, so as "not to waste your time, Dear," and she talked about the Dallas of yesterday as if it had been only yesterday. In the end it was I who had to break up the interview. As I left she said, "You will come back." Her eyes shot sparks. "I'll pay you if you will!"

It was the first of several interviews with a remarkable woman. She always managed to steer the interview away from herself and her own contributions to Dallas, sharing, instead, vignettes, anecdotes and endowments of other Dallas women. She knew everybody from almost the earliest days of the city; some were her friends and contemporaries, but most were the age of her indefatigable mother-in-law, Stella White Spence. Always calling them Mrs. Husband's Name, Married Name—as in Mrs. Wendell Spence—Ruth talked about May Dickson Exall, Margaret Hudgins Hyer, Sallie Little Hannah, Sallie Griffis Meyer, Leila Cowart, Lora Cowart, Margaret Carlson Munger, Janet Belo Peabody, Leonora Pipkin Hall, Adella Kelsey Turner, Pearl Bowden Anderson, Esther Juliet Dyson and others. Her personal stories of these remarkable women are laced through this work.

Ruth Spence was living totally in the present. Not once during eight hours of taped interviews did she express a longing for the days of yore. Every morning, she said, life gave her a new present to open and explore. At 90, she was still a voracious reader—everything from books to magazines to newspapers, and especially the innovative publications. Occasionally there would be glimpses of Ruth Spence, the activist, who had long since retired from the everyday fray, but who kept up with everything in the community, had incisive insights into many of the present and emerging problems and repeatedly honored a reporter by asking, "What do you think? What is your feeling?"

Ruth Potts was born on September 6, 1894. She grew up in South Dallas with two brothers. Their father, William Henry Potts, was in the leather business and their mother, Jaley Cox Potts, a native of Tennessee, was "a gentle, quiet, calm person. She felt that life for a woman was in the home. Mother spent most of her time trying to make a lady out of this savage."

Dallas was *so* different, Ruth reflected, describing the small town in which she was born to the metropolis it had become. "The street car ran right in front of our house on South Ervay Street. My earliest recollection is of the street cars drawn by mules. And downtown streets were still paved with bois d'arc blocks." Ruth attended Dallas public schools, then went to Miss Holley's School for Girls and, in 1913 to the University of Texas.

Entertainment for the young people was centered in their homes. "We did very simple things. We had lots of picnics, took long walks in the woods. In the spring we searched for wild violets and in the fall we went pecan hunting. We rode bicycles a lot and I used to ride horses.

"Athletic prowess for girls was not encouraged. My mother felt athletics was for boys, not for well brought-up young ladies.... Later on, when the man I married and I were playing tennis, he said that when I played tennis with him and he asked me for a second date, it was bound to be love".... The only place we had to swim was at Leachman's Natatorium. The Leachman laundry had a swimming pool. It was the only one around.

"The most exciting thing we did was go for trolley rides. There were open trolley cars that ran on two loops, a north loop and a south loop. We'd have pop corn and soda pop and we'd sing! The whole trolley would join in and form a chorus. The trolley rides were very gay affairs."

Ruth was barely 18 when she left for Austin and the university. The university served as an extended home and the dean of women as a surrogate mother. "Mrs. Kirby was dean of women. She didn't think well of young ladies stepping beyond their established roles. Her cardinal rule was that we must not sit on the campus with a boy. We did, of course! We would see her come out on the campus dressed in a little black taffeta dress with a bonnet tied under her chin and the girls would rise like blackbirds all over the campus where they'd been sitting with the boys."

Boys and girls did not fraternize in any of the extra-curricular activities. The all-male Curtain Club, renowned for its theatrical productions, went on tour and the officers of the all-female Asheville Literary Society took advantage of the opportunity to put on a production of their own. Ruth was cast as an idiot boy.

"I played the role brilliantly. Everybody said I was a natural!" A major crisis transpired, not over girls being cast into the parts of men, but in how they would dress while playing the male roles. "Mrs. Kirby called a meeting. She said, 'I understand—though I find it hard to believe—that some of you young ladies plan to wear trousers on stage . . . . Of course, that will *not* be permitted.' The cast then called a meeting. Katherine Wheatley was the lead and she said she simply could not do her part unless she could wear trousers. We came up with a brilliant plan. We would erect a waist-high stone wall all across the stage and all the action would take place behind that wall. That way nobody could see that we had on trousers. When we told Mrs. Kirby about it, she said 'very well. I accept that, but of course you will have to wear gym bloomers over your trousers because we will have to have a gentleman raise and lower the curtain and we can't allow any chance of his seeing you in public in trousers.' So, we wore bloomers over our trousers! We were all in hysterics."

Ruth completed her bachelor of art's degree at UT in the spring of 1917 and came home to Dallas. Her first and only paying job was with the YWCA. Her salary was $25 a month. "There weren't many jobs available for girls. Social work and teaching was about it and I had not prepared to do either. There was a world of opportunity for volunteers and the YWCA treated its volunteers like professionals. I felt that I could be far more influential as a volunteer than I ever could be as a paid worker. There was so *much* that needed to be done in Dallas and the YWCA was a good place to get things started."

Getting started was not as easy as it appeared to the tiny, feisty young woman just out of college. Ruth wanted to bring the organization into the Twentieth Century overnight and discovered that, even in the most progressive groups, wheels of change turn slowly. "I wanted the YW to really serve the black people. I was working with black girls and I was determined to open up Glen Rose Camp to them. When the board refused, I quit."

During the years 1917-1918, while World War I was coming closer and closer to the United States, Ruth was in graduate school at Columbia University, and, more important for her at the time, planning to be married. Her fiance was Alex White Spence, a law student at Columbia. The oldest son of Wendell and Stella White Spence, he had enlisted in the Army and was stationed at Leon Springs. The young couple had known each other for years, grown up with the same people and moved in the same social circles. They were married on Monday, June 17, 1918, while he was on leave. Typical of Ruth's reluctance to be in the spotlight is the story of her wedding. Buried in *The Dallas Morning News*, in a column, "Dallas Social Affairs," fourth paragraph on page 4, the story is exactly 10 lines long and reads:

> Miss Ruth Potts, the daughter of Mr. and Mrs. William Henry Potts, and Lieutenant Alexander White Spence, the son of Mr. and Mrs. Wendel (sic) Spence, were quietly married at 8 o'clock last night at the Ervay Street Methodist Church. Dr. Ivan Lee Holt performed the ceremony. Lieut. and Mrs. Spence will be at home for the present in Fort Worth.

Though their rearing was different, Ruth and Alex Spence shared the same interests. Marrying into the Spence family, Ruth said, "was like coming home. It was often said I was more like my mother-in-law than my own mother. Mother was reserved. Mrs. Spence was out front in everything. Once Mrs. Spence lured Mother into scrubbing liquor signs off sidewalks—which my mother did not find at all congenial.

"I thrived on being in a family in the center of almost every activity in Dallas. Mrs. Spence and I were the greatest of friends. We were both book people. I never once felt intimidated in her company and I took great pleasure in being with her. Next to my husband, she was the most scintillating conversationalist I've ever known."

Meals at the Spence table were "sparring matches. The table was set with a silver tea service and Mrs. Spence would take her place, an encyclopedia on one side and a dictionary on the other. They could sit for hours arguing and debating. The arguments were so lively. It was not unusual for one of them to start off arguing a point, transfer to the other side in the middle of it and never be aware of it. There were always extra people at their house—strays come to stay for awhile, visitors from out of town. She took in anybody who needed a home. Everybody was included in these lively sessions—and they'd go on for hours until one or another of the boys would have to break it up."

Ruth found an intellectual feast at her mother-in-law's table, but she was even more pleased that her young attorney husband was as interested in community activism as was his mother and as she was. "Both Alex and I had an overriding interest in the fate of Black people. In our early married life, race relations were the greatest issue of the time."

Ruth very quickly found a way to go around obstacles placed in the way of things she wanted to accomplish rather to hit them head-on. Because their first priority was the full participation of black people and because, at the time of their marriage, the Ku Klux Klan with all its propaganda about racial purity was holding full sway in Dallas, Ruth put her energy, money and time to correcting inequities at the state level.

"The League of Women Voters wasn't yet organized in Dallas, but it was a potent factor in the state. Jessie Daniel Ames (from Georgetown) was its president. She was the widow of an Army doctor who left her with three children to rear. She could see with absolute clarity what needed to be done and had the ability to pull together women to make change. Her great talent was in getting things through the Legislature. She would go to the Legislature and threaten them with the power of the League. This meant she threatened them with power she didn't have—but they thought she did!

"Mrs. Ames had all kinds of committees throughout the state working on social issues. I chaired her minimum wage and working hours committee and worked with her on prison reform. I met the most capable women in the state."

Ruth Spence was a potent force on the committee of Southern Women for the Prevention of Lynching and a member of the Inter-Racial Committee of Texas. She helped organize a committee on Negro Participation in the Texas Centennial Exposition in 1936. Though she did not get everything she wanted—there was still segregation at the hundredth birthday celebration of Texas' independence—there would have been far less inclusion had there been no Ruth Spence working for equality.

Following the Centennial, Ruth turned her talents to housing and served on the Federal Housing Committee of Dallas. Her aim was to see that "every child, every family in this community has a home of its own." She worked tirelessly to end the poll tax in Texas, a small tax levied on all for the privilege of voting and rejoiced when it was declared unconstitutional.

Again, when she could not persuade established organizations to adopt reforms that would help to embrace all citizens, she went around them. She was one of the primary organizers—perhaps *the* most important cog—in the formation of the Dallas Civic Federation. This organization brought to Dallas many of the nations' most important thinkers and writers. A lot of the guests were so controversial that no established Dallas institution, not even Southern Methodist University, would sponsor them.

In the early 1920s, when she was still a young woman, Ruth helped to defuse the impact of the Ku Klux Klan in Dallas at a time when many leading citizens were joining it or remaining quiet. Both Ruth and her husband were passionate advocates of the public schools. In 1922 Alex was elected to the school board and served continuously for 12 years including six years as vice president and two as president. It was during this time that the Klan all but took over Dallas. It ran candidates for all elective offices, including the school board. Alex was running for reelection against the Klan candidate.

The women determined to defeat the Klan candidate. "Women did it! We rallied hundreds who combed this city. It was the first significant setback to the Klan in Dallas. I have never been more proud to be a woman." Ruth said she received hate mail daily during this period and several threats on her life. "I didn't have time to worry much about it," she said.

The Alex W. Spence Middle School and Academy at 4001 Capitol Avenue is named for Ruth's husband, the longtime advocate of public education. In 1984 she was concerned that no history of the school had ever been written and wanted to do it herself, a project she did not complete.

Even when she could not tolerate some of the limitations of many of the ladies' clubs, Ruth remained a member of the most socially elite. "I was their in-house rebel," she said. "Without me and a few others like me, many would never have glanced out the windows of their refuges to see the world out there." She was a member of the Dallas Shakespeare Club, the Dallas Woman's Club and Kappa Kappa Gamma sorority. Among others, she served on the boards of the Dallas Museum of Fine Arts and the Hockaday School and was on the board of governors for the Dallas YWCA.

Only occasionally did a hint of reservation surface as she talked about the groups to which she belonged. Of the Dallas Woman's Club, she said, "it accomplished a lot with its varied programs and its lecture series, but it never became what Mrs. Exall had in mind. She wanted it to be far more than a social club, and she wanted it open to any women who wanted to join. That didn't happen. But women ran it *very* well. It has always been financially secure. They didn't build on Park Lane until they saw their way clear to pay for the building.... Women are so fiscally responsible.

Of the Dallas Art Association, she said, "It started as an organization of teachers, the teachers who were the *creme de la creme*. In the beginning, the members were all women. The men were encouraged by their wives to give money, but the sums were pitifully small. Then, a few men who were artists became involved. It took a long time for it to be an okay thing for men to be interested in the art associations. It was considered effeminate for a man to be interested in art and music." For many, many years Mrs. George K. Meyer (Sallie Griffis Meyer) kept the art association alive. She did it by sheer determination. She has never been given the credit she deserves for the work she did. Not even that wonderful Jerry Bywaters (an artist and writer on art) gave her the credit she deserves because he was younger and he just didn't know what she did."

Of the Junior League of Dallas, she said: "The League has had a *big* influence on this city. At first it was extremely elitist and *very* exclusive. One of the great joys of my life has been to watch the democratization of the Junior League."

Of the Women's Council of Dallas County, she said, "That's one I was wrong about. When Willie (Lewis) came and talked to me about another women's organization, I didn't think it would materialize. I'd seen so many things started with the idea of being inclusive and watched them fail. Maybe I was tired, or maybe I was entertaining a bit of cynicism; I'll admit I didn't think it could work.... I am glad that it has accomplished the inclusiveness that the Woman's Club never did."

Of the SMU Women's Symposium, on which she served as an advisor until her death: "It is one of the finest things that has ever happened in our community. From the very first, Emmie Baine insisted that it include a great variety of participants. Even though it started primarily for college women, it had community participants of all ages."

Emmie Baine said that Ruth Spence was "invaluable to the Symposium. She had a way of putting her finger on issues that were important. She was able to pose questions that made us all think. It would be difficult for me to overestimate the value of her contribution to the quality of the program. Ruth Spence was one of the first people in Dallas who saw clearly the injustices to black people and she never stopped doing everything she could to see that they were included."

Ruth Spence worked for pay, for the YWCA "because it was on the leading edge of change," for only a brief time in her life, but she gave herself tirelessly to Dallas for more than 50 years and led women in their successful campaign to defeat Ku Klux Klan candidates for the Dallas School Board in 1920s.

Mrs. Spence and Mrs. Baine met soon after Emmie moved to Dallas and worked together first in the League of Women Voters. "When I became Dean of Women at SMU, I had several visits with her because she had such a broad span of interests and such keen insight," Emmie said of Ruth. "She must have been lonely at times, for hers was the lone voice in some circles for social justice."

As she worked on different projects through the years, Ruth Spence made friends in all parts of the community. "I stayed with the YWCA because it was a vital, yeasty organization interested in public affairs and the development of women, and its interracial policies were liberal." But not as liberal as Ruth would have liked nor as she worked for them to become. When the Maria Morgan branch of the YW was built in 1940, Ruth was determined that it be an integral part of the YW program. "Mrs. (Esther Juliet) Dyson was their representative to the board. I tried for a long time to get them to let her come to board meetings before they finally agreed. The first time she came, some women sat with their hands hiding their faces while she spoke. I was embarrassed, hurt and angry . . . .

"Mrs. Dyson tried to comfort me. Black people had been so used to being rebuffed that she accepted it as natural. Many years later we went together to a public luncheon at a hotel in downtown Dallas. She reminded me of the time when women hid their faces to keep from looking at her while she spoke and said, 'Did you or I think we would ever live to see the day when we could sit down to lunch together in a public place?'"

"I am often comforted by something Mrs. (Sallie Little) Hannah said to me once. She was national president of the YWCA, very capable, very interesting, most religious. When she traveled, which she did a lot, Mrs. Hannah would travel up to Sunday and get off the train and lay over until Monday before traveling again. The Lord was by her side all the time. Once when she and I were rocking on my porch one evening, Mrs. Hannah had just made a speech that day. Suddenly she said, 'You know, I didn't make a very good speech today. I really made a very poor speech, but it's all right. I said to the Lord, you gave me only a certain number of talents and that's all I can use. Speech making is not one of them, so if I didn't do very well today, I can't use the talents I wasn't given.' That has comforted me many times. I've used the talents God gave me to the best of my ability. I can't use those I don't have."

"You hope you are taking a long look at things," Ruth Spence added, immediately moving from the personal back into the universal. "You hope you are doing the best you can with all the talents you are given." She paused, then added: "My personal frailty is that I've held on to my idealism too tenaciously. But, without it, I would have withered."

Ruth Potts Spence died April 10, 1989. Leon Harris, author and associate with her in several Dallas organizations, wrote in a letter published in *The Dallas Morning News:*

> "All her life, she characterized herself politically as a liberal, including those ugly periods in the history of Dallas when for many of its most important citizens, "liberal' was synonymous with "communist." And she did all these things quietly, without any stridency, without any self-righteousness and, above all, without any personal publicity . . . . To find anyone who holds this belief and practices it seems impossible. As money became the exclusive measure of men and women in Dallas, Ruth Spence stubbornly continued to apply instead the inch-rule of character and talent and service.

Alvernon Verita King Evans Tripp won almost every award given to women in Sacramento before returning to serve her native Dallas.

ALVERNON VERITA KING EVANS TRIPP

• • • •

January 3, 1898—April 21, 1993

Alvernon Tripp watched Dallas both up close and from a distance. She viewed it and participated in it as child and adult from the perspective of being black, watched it grow and change, was aware of the limitations and opportunities present in it for her participation and growth, and knew its areas of resistance.

Born in Dallas on January 3, 1898, when its population was around 80,000, Alvernon was the first child and only daughter of Benjamin and Mary Walker King. In September of 1915, as a 17-year-old, she left it to go to Prairie View A&M; she returned to teach in the city in 1921, after receiving her B. S. degree from Cheyney Teachers College, which later became a part of the University of Pennsylvania. She lived and taught in Dallas for a decade, lived and worked in Salt Lake City, Utah; Spokane, Washington, and Sacramento, California, with brief stints in Wyoming before retiring from her government position and returning to Dallas to make her home in 1970.

Alvernon lived with the pulsating, transforming city in a love/hate relationship reserved only to those who know their territory intimately. She was both a part of and apart from the throbbing metropolis. She watched changes take place in Dallas and knew the pockets of prejudice that continued to exist and she could, until her final illness, name and date them.

"My parents did not emphasize what we could not do. They stressed what we *could* do. It's a policy I've tried to follow all of my life."

Alvernon's oldest brother was only a few weeks old—she only two—when non-relenting rains turned the temperamental Trinity River into one of its periodic oceans.

Her first memory is having her father haul her in a wagon to safety on high ground, admonish her to stay put and return to the flooding house for her mother and baby brother.

As a little girl, she picnicked on the verdant greens along Forest Avenue which then was one vast pastureland. Her parents owned dairy cattle—at that time only five or six cows. "My father would put a rope around their necks and tie it to a stake along the road. Mother would give us little baskets filled with food and we would play and eat—she called it picnicking, and we considered it a rare treat—under the shade of trees while we kept an eye on the cattle while they grazed."

Education was always emphasized in the Tripp family. On her first day of school "My father took me in the wagon. The school was Frederick Douglass. It was on Preston and Gano. Oh, yes, it was all black. We called it colored then. The Colored School." She completed the advanced seventh grade at Douglass, then entered the Colored High School on Hall and Cochran. Some five miles from their home 3520 Spence, it was a long way for Alvernon and the four brothers who followed her to get to school. "We rode the street car to the end of the line and then walked. We almost never missed school. If the weather was terrible—really cold or raining or snowing—my father took us in the wagon."

"Geography was my favorite subject. I read about all those faraway places and dreamed of getting away from Dallas and going there. And I loved English. Words were wonderful! I always thought it was wonderful to know the meaning of words and be able to use them correctly. And I loved music. I played the piano from the time I was a very little girl. I liked school. I was a good student."

Every adult, both in the schools and in the neighborhood, was responsible for other people's children, she said. "Our parents expected the teachers and other adults to correct us. If they didn't, our parents wanted to know why not. We were good kids because everybody we knew kept an eye on us. We wouldn't dare let anybody down.

"Mother was well educated for a woman of her day and she always emphasized that education was imperative. Mother was—well, they didn't call it model or mentor in those days—the one we most wanted to be like, the one we most wanted to please."

Mary Walker King had, herself, been reared by a mother who valued education. Born near Guthrie, Oklahoma, Alvernon's mother was reared in a family that pioneered Oklahoma.

When Alvernon was four, she made the first trip that she remembered to visit her Oklahoma grandparents. There was a death in the family and "the house was filled with folks. When everybody left, there was this one white woman who didn't leave. It puzzled me. I asked my mother why that white woman didn't go home and Mother said she didn't leave because it was her home. 'That is your grandmother,' she said. 'She is my mother just like I am your mother.' My grandmother was so beautiful. I remember going home and telling everybody 'My grandmother is white and she has red hair.' Why did I think having a white grandmother was so grand? Because the white folks we knew were good folks. We were taught to respect them because they had more advantages than we did—and we should try to be like them."

Alvernon graduated from Darrell High School in 1915 in a class of 30, the largest that the black schools had ever produced.

College offered Alvernon her first away-from-Dallas opportunities. "I went to Prairie View because it was the outstanding school in the South for blacks. It was so exciting! But it wasn't all wonderful. The most depressing was the food. I had never had corn bread for breakfast. At Prairie View, we had fried bacon and cream gravy with corn bread. Twice a week, on Tuesdays and Fridays, we had biscuits. Those mornings we could hardly wait to get to breakfast. We had lots of beans—beans of all kinds. The food was not like my mother made at home."

At Prairie View Alvernon was introduced to sports. Tall and coordinated, she loved basketball and tennis, but she liked most of all "being one of the rah! rah!—what do you call it? The Pep Squad! I was fortunate enough to be selected for the first pep squad that Prairie View ever had. A professor from Yale came to our school to teach and he thought a pep squad was a good idea and he picked me to be on it. I did like that! I joined the music club and played piano in the college orchestra. I wanted to be on the marching band, so I took up the saxophone . . . . I was never very good on the sax, but I couldn't march around carrying a piano, so I had to do something where I could march on the football field."

Prairie View did not offer a degree, only a Life Certificate to teach. Alvernon got hers in 1917. Nor was there a teacher training program offered. "But to get our certificate to teach, we had to do cadet teaching. I spent two summers teaching in Dickson Orphanage in Gilmer."

Then she headed for Pennsylvania and Cheyney Teachers College.

"All of my life I had heard stories about the north and the west where there was no segregation. I always said one day I would go there. Well, I did, but I learned right off that things were not all that wonderful up North, either . . . .

"In Dallas I became aware when I was, probably, no more than three years old, that we were not included everywhere. We lived on Spence Street, one long block from Colonial where we would go to ride the street car. We kids always sat on the seat right behind the driver. It was the grandest thing! One Sunday we were going to church and all of us (the family) got on and we took our usual seats and the conductor said we would have to go to the back. 'See those signs,' he said, pointing to the signs that said 'Colored.' 'You'll have to go sit back there.

"Oh, indeed, I was aware there were places in Dallas we could not go. We couldn't play in city parks. All the drinking fountains had 'Whites' or 'Colored' on them. We couldn't go to the State Fair any day except the time set aside as Negro Day. We couldn't swim in most of the pools. We couldn't try on clothes to see if they fit and we couldn't take them back if they didn't. We couldn't stay in hotels when we traveled. We couldn't order food in any restaurant. In some of them we could go in the back door and get something and take it out. When we went to white folks' houses, we had to go in the back door. We knew where the boundaries were. We couldn't go to the school closest to us if it wasn't a colored school. Did we miss it?" She pondered how to answer this question she must have been asked hundreds of times. "You can't miss what you've never had . . . . Oh, there were times. When I was a little girl and it would be cold and I'd have to pass a white school to get to mine and I'd say to my brothers, 'Now, if we were white, we could stop and get out of the cold'!"

"When I left for Pennsylvania, I rode as far as St. Louis in a Jim Crow (segregated) car. From St. Louis to Cheyney, I could go Pullman. When I went to get my ticket, the agent asked me, 'Are you sure you are going to Pennsylvania?,' and I said, 'Yes! I'm going to Cheyney to college!' He acted like he didn't believe me. My brother had told me to ask for a lower booth. I did, but the agent said I would have to take an upper. 'We don't have any lower booths for you people.'

"But, I was far more aware of segregation away from the South than I was in Dallas. When I lived in Salt Lake the prejudice showed everywhere. Once a friend and I went into a dime store and asked the girl behind the counter for a Coke. She kept ignoring us and waiting on other people. I wanted to leave the store but my friend wouldn't. She said 'We're not in the South now; we have just as much right to have a soft drink at a public place as anybody. When the girl just kept ignoring us, my friend asked to see the manager. He asked where we were from and we told him. He said if we were from Dallas we ought to know better, that the only place in town we could get anything was at the station two blocks away."

Alvernon completed her bachelor's degree at Cheyney in 1921 and moved back to Dallas. She began her teaching career at Booker T. Washington, which then was an elementary school but moved two years later to Darrell High School. She was in her early 20s—and in love.

She vacillated between career and marriage. "I wanted to be married before I was 25. At 25 a girl was considered an old maid and that was a horrible fate! But then, if I got married I would lose out on my career and I loved teaching. At that time a married women couldn't teach in the Dallas schools. If she got married, she automatically lost her job."

Her solution was a secret marriage. The bridegroom was Charles Victor Evans. "I had known him all my life. Our families were friends. We all attended New Hope Baptist Church." Charles Evans was a railroad man, among the most highly respected and lucrative careers for a black man in those days. "I had such wonderful plans.... Not all of them worked out. I'll always—*always*—be grateful to my husband. He took me away from Dallas."

Native Dallasite Alvernon Tripp, as a child, tended her father's dairy cattle along Forest Avenue, grew up to teach school in her native city, then to live in several states and have several careers before returning home to become a class act volunteer. At right, she has a word with another wise woman, Johnnie-Marie Grimes.

The couple had been married for three years when the Texas and Pacific Railroad transferred Charles to Salt Lake City. He wanted to make the move and he wanted his wife to go with him. "I was thrilled! I announced my marriage and off we went!"

Salt Lake set Alvernon off on another adventure. "Married women couldn't teach there, either, so I turned to music." She was playing for a church program one night when a musician from Tuskegee Institute heard her and called her. He had been thinking, he said, of forming a jazz band and he wanted to know if she might be interested.

"I said absolutely. I'd never played jazz in my life, but I knew I could. I'd played music all my life and played with the orchestra at Prairie View. So, five of us got together and formed a band. We called it Vern's Dixieland Players. But they called it Alvernon's Band. I kept at this off and on for seven years.

"Then a drummer I'd met called from Spokane, Washington, and said he had a booking there and wanted me to come play with them. I'd always wanted to go to Washington so I was thrilled. I talked it over with my husband and he thought it was a good idea. We both loved the state, so we decided to take the band and move there."

Alvernon lived in Spokane for 14 years. She paused in her story, was very still and then added, very quietly: "My husband passed while we lived there.... I never had any children. Wanted four. Planned to have four. Didn't have any."

Alvernon continued with her music." She had spent some vacation time and holidays in Wyoming, so when she got a call from a small town to come play there, she took the band and went. "It was a winter resort where people went for steam baths for arthritis and other health problems. I'd never heard of the place until they called and asked me about booking the band, and I can't think of it now, but it was fun and added another dimension to my life.

"But I knew it was time to get into a career that was more stable, so I wrote to Austin (Texas) and asked about my teaching certificate. I was very happy to learn that it was still good." The teaching job she found was with the government—organizing and directing an educational program for the WPA.

She lived for one more year in Spokane, "where I was sick all the time. I had developed bronchitis. My doctor said my health would improve if I would get away from that cold, damp climate. So, I took a furlough and came home to Dallas for a visit.

"Then I went to Sacramento. Had no trouble finding a job with the government and getting a transfer. My health improved immensely right off. When I wasn't working, I got very involved in the volunteer community. Politics. League of Women Voters. Church work. During the war, being a volunteer at the USO . . . ."

It was at the USO in 1942 that she met Richard Tripp.

"He was the first person I'd met since Charles Evans that I felt good to be with. He was an officer, a lieutenant. From New York. Wore the uniform well. That name . . . Richard Tripp . . . thrilled me." In 1944 they were married." He reminded me so much of my first husband. I was working at McClelland Field. He was stationed at McClelland. Then he was sent to Louisiana. From there his unit was sent to Florida, then back to New York. That's where he got out.'

The marriage lasted four years. The breakup came over his drinking. "He loved his liquor and I figured I don't have to be bothered with this. My first husband drank. I was determined not to get caught in that kind of thing again. I never knew Richard drank until after we married. I asked him one time why he never drank in front of me before we got married and he said I was the only woman he had ever met that he wanted to marry and so he just didn't drink around me until afterward. He thought once we were married, I would be caught. Little did he know!"

She chuckled. Grew quiet. "I was in love. Really in love again, but I found out in time. He loved his liquor, too. So I ran. I was better off when my life wasn't complicated by men."

On vacation and sometimes for the holidays, Alvernon returned to Dallas. Her family still lived in the city. "I could see that some changes were happening in Dallas, but I wanted to find out for myself if anything was really better. It was the early '70s. I read about a meeting of the Democratic Party in downtown Dallas. It was at one of the hotels. So I went. I sat down. Right in the middle of the auditorium. Somebody I knew came along and spoke to me and said I'd better move. I said, 'No. I know where I can sit in California. I'm going to find out how the Democrats are behaving in Dallas. You know, not another soul even acted like they thought I ought to move. Nothing happened. Absolutely nothing. That's when I knew that Dallas had changed.

"Then when my brother died and I came home for the funeral, I told a friend that I needed to buy a hat and she said she would go shopping with me. She said, 'Let's go to Volk's. They have very nice hats," and I told her I wanted to *try on* hats before I bought one and she said, 'Honey, this isn't the Dallas you left. We can try on hats at Volk's. So we went shopping and we tried on hats and dresses and both of us bought things."

By this time the King family had dwindled. Alvernon's only surviving brother wanted her to move back to Dallas. "He told me that it was nonsense for us to be living 2,000 miles apart. He said he was not going to move to California and it was time I moved back to Dallas. It was our home. He said 'I need you. I will take care of you.'

"I made six trips to Dallas to check things out. I thought I would move back when I retired, but then I started working as director of a community center just to help them get started. That lasted for six years. My brother kept pestering me, so one day I said 'this is it! I'm going.'"

This was in August of 1970.

The interview was taking place in her neat home on the outskirts of Fair Park on December 13, 1990. Alvernon lived alone, but "was not lonely." Her home was a happy clutter—neat stacks everywhere, notes from friends, newspaper clippings she would send to interested people, photographs, A Bible, a couple of books. She knew just where to reach to retrieve what she wanted. The telephone rang constantly. The walls were lined with pictures and mementoes and honor certificates and citations lauding Alvernon for service. There was the resolution from the Sacramento City Council with multiple whereases citing her for volunteer services; a lengthy clipping from *The Sacramento Bee* when she was named Sacramento Woman of the Year, A certificate from Prairie View naming her a distinguished alumnae, one from the Sacramento Chamber of Commerce lauding her for outstanding professional services to the community and several others. There were also citations she had collected from the city of her birth: a plaque of appreciation from the Family Guidance Center in 1977; a plaque naming her to the Senior Hall of Fame in 1978; a certificate from the National Council of Negro Women in 1984 saluting her for outstanding service, a citation from the City of Dallas . . . .

In 1988, at a birthday celebration at Thanks-Giving Square when she was 90, Alvernon was honored by Dallas with special recognition. Mayor Annette Strauss personally read and delivered into Alvernon's hands a resolution that cited her for "talents and energies to cultivate knowledge and wisdom in herself and others," for a lifetime of "creating justice, building bridges of understanding between peoples of diverse races and beliefs," and for "leadership in organizations whose good works touch countless lives."

The program also included special recognition from Deputy Mayor Pro Tem Diane Ragsdale, from Dr. H. Rhett James and from Elizabeth Espersen of Thanks-Giving Square.

Alvernon Tripp was reflective as she voiced the progress she had observed in Dallas, carefully evaluating where the city was and where she thought it might be in the next decade. "Some people have a hard time still accepting us (the blacks) as equals. I tell my young friends that is their loss. We have so much to learn, all of us as individuals and as groups from each other. Some women, especially, still treat me like an outsider. I see them trying, but they just haven't made it yet. And some of them are such good Christian ladies! When they see me, they stand back and wait until someone else greets me. The more significant the person is in the community, the more it serves as an ice breaker. As soon as someone important, in their eyes, comes up to me, then they do, too. 'Oh, Alvernon, how are you,' they say. And all the time they've been eyeing me out of the corner of their eyes and waiting to see when it will be all right for them to acknowledge that I'm there!

"When I moved back to Dallas, I planned to get involved in only one or two things, but you know how it is. There just seemed to be so many places I was needed and so many things I could do. I've spent most of my volunteer time with the League of Women Voters and Church Women United. They are both working at bringing about good changes and they are farther along in providing the community equal opportunity for all people than any other women's organizations in the city.

"I have slowed down some now. But I haven't stopped . . . ." When she moved back to Dallas, Alvernon and her brother bought a duplex. She moved into one side and her brother and sister-in-law into the other. Her brother lived only 20 months after she returned to Dallas. She and her sister-in-law continued to enjoy a close and loving relationship until 1988 when her sister-in-law left for the Thanksgiving holidays to visit her own family. On Thanksgiving night she died while chatting with her sister. "I never have come to terms with that," Alvernon said. "She was the one who kept the yard so beautifully. The one who put up all the Christmas decorations. I haven't had the heart to do it since she passed. She was so dear to me. She waved good-by and said, 'I'll see you next week,' and then never come back."

In the early Spring of 1993, a stroke finally slowed Alvernon. She passed on April 21, 1993. She died with absolute confidence that Dallas is better today than it was yesterday, that progress will continue, and in abiding faith that, for the good of all people of all ages and all colors, "we shall overcome."

Martha Bell Leonard Zahrt "married Braniff" in 1945 and edited its company newspaper, the B-Liner.

Lily Virtrees Bell Leonard with Congressman Sam Rayburn and a portrait of his protege, Lyndon Baines Johnson.

MARTHA BELL (PAT) LEONARD ZAHRT
November 14, 1909—January 31, 1991

LILY VIRTREES BELL LEONARD
August 14, 1884—January 30, 1966

• • • •

Martha Bell Leonard drew her first breath on Ewing Street on November 14, 1909. It took three days for the birth, and her 12-pound birth weight almost ended her life along with that of her mother, Lily Virtrees Bell Leonard. Their survival gifted Dallas with two strong women whose life struggles parallel that of the growing city.

Pat—for soon, and forever afterward that's who Martha Bell would be—grew from a precocious little girl into a woman who observed with her camera and her typewriter the burgeoning aviation industry. For 30 years she was the eyes, ears and voice of Braniff Airways.

Getting born was possibly the only event that Pat Zahrt was ever slow about. As a child, she was in a hurry to explore life. One of her earliest memories was running from her Ewing Street home to the fire station a block away. The firemen would take her home and, at the first opportunity, Pat would escape again, her red curls bouncing as her long legs began yet another adventure.

It was a good life for a little girl. Pat had loving grandparents, Tyree and Martha Hardy Bell, who lived on Hibernia Street in East Dallas where she often visited. They helped to keep her well-clothed and well-fed and allowed her to grow in a world where it was safe for children to play up and down streets. Pat's father, Ernest E. Leonard, was "a brilliant, charming, congenial man," Pat said, "who could talk his way into any job, but had a hard time keeping one." At the time of her birth he was general manager for Briggs-Weaver Machinery Company and at another was head of Murray Gin Company. He eventually sought work in distant cities. When he came home "he and Mama would make another baby . . . . Mother was pregnant most of the time."

There were five pregnancies, each producing a boy. Pat's brothers were Ernest, who became a Dallas police officer and was killed in a motorcycle accident at the age of 23; Tyree Bell; John Billy; Douglass Wilbur and Turney White. Turney was the top cadet in the Texas A&M Class of 1942 and was "missing in action" in Germany in November of 1944. It was five years before his body was identified and he was brought home to Grove Hill Cemetery where he was buried with full military honors and a posthumous Congressional Medal of Honor.

Pat was graduated from North Dallas High School in 1925 in its first four-year class. She was 15 years old. Tall for her age and "neither pretty nor popular," she excelled academically. "I was a quick take. I won all the speaking contests and most of the writing contests." Her four-year 95-plus grade earned her a scholarship to the University of Chicago. Her mother gave Pat her blessing. It was all she had to give.

By that time Ernest Leonard had taken permanent leave of the family. Lily worked at whatever job she could find.

"She walked all over East Dallas selling encyclopedias. Even in the sweltering summer—once 105 degrees—my mother never stopped. She also sold Spencer corsets—every woman wore a corset. Later she worked for doctors at the Medical Arts Building. Another time she worked for Tenison Florist." Eventually Lily Virtrees Bell Leonard bought a house at 8903 Groveland near the present Dallas Arboretum, one of the first to buy there, and opened her own flower shop. "Mother reared five little boys and me on an income that averaged around $18 a week. My grandparents helped with the little boys, but I was her real helper.

"Mother had absolutely no false modesty and a delicious sense of humor. She was a flower enthusiast and often traded lilies with her friends. Once she asked me to drop some bulbs off to a wealthy friend in North Dallas. She put them in a paper bag. She also gave me the table scraps for my dog in another bag. When I got to Mrs. Penn's house, she was not at home. I left the bag at her front door with a signed note that 'Mother sent these.' Mother later got a puzzled telephone call from her friend inquiring why she had sent her table scraps.

"During prohibition when liquor was illegal, Mother decided to make some home brew. She borrowed a crock, corks and a capper. My brothers were outside and I was in the kitchen watching as she bottled the brew. The doorbell rang. I went to the door and there stood the biggest cop I've ever seen. By the time I got back to the kitchen, Mother had poured most of the brew down the sink. The officer reported that my brothers were tossing rocks at passing cars . . . . Mother never tried her hand at home brew again.

"Mother taught me to respect all people, to honor hard work and to credit everybody equally for their contributions. She was born in Kentucky but came to Dallas when she was 16. She was a leader for women's suffrage and fought the Ku Klux Klan in the 1920s. When the city street cars and busses segregated Blacks, Mother would often walk to the back of the bus to sit. When Marian Anderson was not allowed to sing in Constitution Hall, Mother resigned from the DAR, took the dues she had been paying them and joined the NAACP.

This gave Pat Leonard a model for behavior years later when she insisted on membership to the Dallas Press Club for Julia Scott Reed, the first black admitted. "Professionalism knows no color lines," she said.

Lily Leonard was Pat's model in many other ways. "Mother worked for what she believed in. She was a charter member of the Democratic Women of Dallas County and of the Texas Democratic Women's State Committee. She was a delegate to two Democratic Women's conventions. She was a delegate to the National Democratic Convention in Chicago in 1982. She was a friend of Sam Rayburn. She traveled on the Adlai Stevenson campaign bus when he ran for president. She worked for Lyndon when he ran for president and for Hubert Humphrey when he ran. Mother was fun to be with. She never gave up keeping up—and she taught me to be independent."

Pat's first real assertion of independence came when she left Dallas for Chicago and college. She was two months shy of her 16th birthday. Her grandmother had sewed her college wardrobe, suited for the Dallas climate. One pair of black bloomers had $50 sewed into them. "I got on that damn train at Union Station, took off those bloomers and put that $50 in my purse. It was the richest I've ever been."

Pat Zahrt reported almost every major Dallas aviation event for 30 years.

What lay ahead was anything but rich. She was met in Chicago by paternal relatives, who made it clear that she was not wanted. Much later, she and her aunt Lillian became good friends, but the beginning was not easy. "My aunt wrote Mother that I had all the worst traits of the Leonard family. She said I sprawled on the furniture. The truth is she didn't want to be responsible for me."

Pat found a room in a "dirt cheap" but university-approved rooming house and a roommate to share expenses. She enrolled in school and got a job in a real estate office typing listings. It paid $25 a month. Winter came. "I walked to class. Sometimes the temperature was 20 degrees below. I'd have frozen if I hadn't made friends with a classmate who gave me her brother's discarded black bear coat. It literally saved my life.

"I kept up my grades and I made friends. I wrote for the college newspaper. Many times I was hungry. I'd stand in front of a campus coffee shop and when someone came along I knew, I'd glance at my watch like I was waiting for someone. Usually the friend would invite me to go inside and have a cup of coffee. I'd eat a roll and drink a cup of coffee—and sometimes that was all I'd have to eat in the entire day."

Once at Christmas when there was no money to go home to Dallas, Pat was sitting huddled alone in her room, both homesick and heartsick, when a special delivery package arrived from her mother. It contained a roasted chicken and all the "fixings" of an at-home Christmas dinner including Mama's special fruitcake. "It was the best food I have ever tasted in my entire life—before or since. I sat in the middle of my bed all alone and had a party."

After three years of living hand-to-mouth, Pat's endurance wore thin and she dropped out of school and went to work.

"I wanted a job in advertising, but there were none. But, my height was turning into an advantage. I was tall and slender and my red hair got me lots of attention. I had learned to use make up and wear clothes well." She wound up with a modeling job in a Michigan Avenue couture working for two women who were partners. She earned $25 a week—"absolutely fabulous for those days." She made an appointment to have a portrait made and got permission from one of the partners to borrow a sequined jacket for it. When the picture arrived addressed to Pat, the other partner opened it, saw the jacket, accused her of stealing it, and fired her.

Pat next went to work for Carson-Pirie Scott and Company, using her office skills. Between typing letters, she modeled, both for individual customers and on the runway. "It ruined me for clothes," she said. "My body feels good only in beautiful clothes of the best fabrics by leading designers. I have rarely been able to afford me!" Even though the modeling was agreed upon when she took the job, her boss did not like having Pat interrupt her secretarial chores and reacted by piling more work on her desk. "The nearer quitting time, the higher the stack grew, so when I heard about a job at another company, I changed jobs."

The job was at the Chicago branch of N. W. Ayer and Son, the leading advertising agency in the United States. "I was in heaven!" The job was taking shorthand and typing letters, but with an organization that offered an unlimited future. Her boss traveled and was gone most of the time. "I handled everything!" At this job she started at $25 a week and was raised to $30.

She lived in one room which she made into a studio apartment by sawing off an iron bed, slip covering it and turning it into a couch. She stored food and supplies in boxes and stashed them in the unused fireplace. In the wintertime, a tiny balcony was her refrigerator and in the summer she bought nothing perishable that she couldn't consume immediately. The steam-heated radiator provided little heat, so during the cold months, she hovered over an electric stove on top of the radiator. She walked from Illinois Central railroad on the lake to LaSalle Street where she worked, more than a mile, in rain and snow and over ice and, in the summertime, in sweltering heat. "It wasn't gruesome," she said, "It was glorious. I was having the time of my life! There were lots of friends, lots of dates . . . ."

Then one cold New Year's Eve, a night so cold that nobody dared get out to the festivities they'd planned. The landlady gave a party in the rooming house for the residents. And Pat Leonard met Walter Zahrt. "We left the party and braved the ice and walked to a coffee shop and talked until dawn." He was from Fort Wayne, Indiana, had been to college—Purdue—had a job at a time when few men did, kept the store for a tailor shop down the street and planned to become a public relations man.

They were married on September 10, 1935, in Gary, Indiana. "He needed me and I needed someone to need me . . . . It was a good marriage for 10 years. His family situation was unusual. There was a girl and three boys. "They had money, but nobody ever had any money. It was doled out to the penny. His mother took turns being mad at the daughters-in-law and trying to pit one of us against the other."

Walter had a relative in Dallas who told him that he could find work at the Texas Centennial, and "Walter convinced me that we needed to move to Dallas." Pat resigned her job and they used her vacation pay to make the move. They found a garage apartment on Fitzhugh for $25 a month. He got a job in charge of the Frigidaire exhibit at the State Fair Music Hall, one of the Centennial exhibits. Pat spent most of her time building him up, applauding his success and waiting until it was her turn again.

Before the Centennial job ended, Walter got a job as sales manager of the top radio station in San Antonio, and the Zahrts moved to Alamo City—10 miles out in the country where they found a tiny house heated with a fireplace and one gas stove. "My career was on hold. My wardrobe was shot. I owned one pair of good shoes. Walter had an almost unlimited expense account. He dined in the top restaurants with leading citizens." Pat wrote his letters and did his brochures at home—and raised Scottie dogs for her spending money. "Christmas was coming. I wasn't feeling very well, but I had no money. So I loaded a litter of Scottie puppies in our Buick coupe and went into Dallas to try to sell them at Mother's flower shop. Nothing happened. On my way home with the puppies in the back seat, I was ill, depressed and despondent. I was pregnant and didn't know it . . . ."

Kathleen was born on August 10, 1940. Her father was ecstatic. Her mother even more so. "We had a wonderful baby and I was sure our most rugged days were behind us." Pat looked after Kathleen, kept house, cooked gourmet meals, wrote letters for Walter, compiled his sales brochures, soothed his frustrations, made suggestions. And always, *always* applauded him when the fruits of her labors paid off. "I did what all good wives do—made him look good!"

Then came December 7, 1941, and the beginning of World War II. Kathleen was 16 months old. San Antonio was a critical city to the war effort, Walter along with it. "He absolutely blossomed. He was working with all the top brass. Wives had a good time, too. I started being invited to all the parties. Everything was so intense."

Walter Zahrt had a wife and a baby and a job that required every creative effort that both he and his wife could deliver, with only one paycheck between them, but he thought he was not doing his share. In August of 1944 he joined the Navy and was sent to Camp Elliott in San Diego for training.

"I came back to Dallas," Pat said. "to Grandmother's house."

Kathleen was almost four when Pat took her daughter and went to San Diego to visit her Navy husband. They stayed for two weeks in a Quonset hut provided by the armed services. "We had a wonderful time. At least Kathleen and I did. Walter seemed to enjoy having us. I had hardly reached home when I got a letter from him saying that I, of all people, would understand that he had fallen in love with someone else. It was your typical 'Dear John' letter. He asked for a divorce.

"I wouldn't give him one for a full year. Those were extremely unsettling times, not a time for anyone to make permanent decisions. I waited for him to come to his senses, but he filed for divorce. He paid no child support until Texas approved the reciprocal child support law. Even then the money came so seldom and so erratically that I gave up. I reared Kathleen all by myself." Her father did not ask for visitation and never paid any attention to his child. It was not until she was grown and needed some closure to the relationship that she looked him up and became acquainted. By that time he had a third wife—and was a stranger.

"I was divorced in 1945 and on July 7, 1945, I married Braniff."

It was a love/hate relationship for 30 years. "The job was absolutely wonderful," she said. "I'm an optimist by nature and I'm a workaholic. No matter how bad things were I could find something good about what I was doing." When Pat went with Braniff there were two people in the public relations department—her boss and a young journalism graduate. "Everybody outside the company knew me—all of the press and a lot of other people. My boss couldn't stand the attention I got . . . . I feel so sorry for people who never learn that their employees will make them look good if they'll give them half a chance.

"I kept taking on more responsibility because I thrived on work and there was so much to be done. Everybody in the company except my boss was supportive. I inherited the job of handling the maintenance crew and checked every pilot's flight manual. At one time I was handling five jobs: I was the official Braniff photographer until 1965. I put out the company tabloid newspaper. It was a 20-page paper once a month called the *B-Liner*. I was my own typist and copy reader. I was the publicity lady, called the press on anything that had the makings of a story. I arranged all the press conferences, called the press, made all the arrangements for refreshments and stayed at the press room to see that everything went well. I wrote letters, ran the copy machine and answered the phones."

Her designated secretary really worked for Pat's boss and Pat, like most women executives at that time, found it easier "to do it myself than expect anything from anybody else. I have put the paper out many, many times on weekends in my house."

She sought out the hard-working, but usually unrecognized, employees in her company and gave them recognition through stories in the *B-Liner*. She then copied the stories and sent them, along with a photograph, to the employee's parents' hometown newspaper "where they would be published with a 2-column picture on the front page. Grandma would see it and Mama and Papa would see it, and all the cousins—and it made everybody happy.

"When Braniff executives entertained, I made all of the arrangements from issuing invitations, to planning the menu to seeing that every detail was carried out. I would arrive early at the event, see that the guests were properly treated and say to my boss, "Of course, you remember Mr. So and So" and then when they were ready to sit down to eat, I would leave. It was extremely rare for me to stay for the festivities."

Working 60 and 70-hour weeks took its toll. Even Pat's natural good humor and eternal optimism palled under the strain. She spent weeks deciding how to ask for help. She revised and rehearsed what she would say, made an appointment with her boss and requested an assistant. She said she could be much more efficient and do a better job for the company if she had someone to do the detail work. She said she could save the company both time and money. While she talked, her boss had his feet on the desk in front of her face and looked out the window. When she had finished, he told her that his understanding was that she was dissatisfied with her job and felt that it was too much for her. He said that was fine with him; she could easily be replaced. That was the end of the conversation.

"We were his 'gofers'—his serfs." Her boss often counted on her to run personal errands. "His wife was ill. I never minded doing her shopping when they were entertaining for Braniff—but it would have been nice if someone had said thank you. Once I was told to go buy food for a dinner party they were having. When I took the things to her, I was told 'I never use green asparagus. I always get the white.' I had taken two hours of my company's time to do the shopping, the time I later had to make up by proofreading the newspaper at home.

"I drove my own car on all the errands—for 26 years, but finally I got smart and I typed out on my expense account, not only the mileage, but exactly where I went and for what purpose. It was a nuisance—but it put a stop to running personal errands."

There was also sexual harassment, which in those days did not even have a name. "I was constantly fending off sexual innuendos—and sometimes downright harassment. Some men seemed to think that because I was divorced, I was fair game. When a meeting was over, somebody always would linger and suggest that now that the work was done, we could go up to his room and have a drink.

Lily Leonard celebrated her 80th birthday with friends including Judge Sarah Hughes.

"Once a Braniff vice president asked me out to dinner. I was pleased. We went to a nearby restaurant. We were hardly seated when he asked about my husband and I told him I had been divorced for many years. He said, 'What you need is a good screwing.' By that time I was inured to shock and I didn't even respond. I just lifted the menu between him and me and looked for the highest priced things on it—whether I liked them or not! I had a shrimp salad to start and filet mignon and a Caesar salad—everything to make the bill amount up. When dinner was over, I said 'thank you very much; it was a good dinner,' and I got up and walked out and got in my car and went home. I always drove my own car. It was the best protection possible. From that day on the man has always treated me like the lady I am!"

In 1956 when Pat was honored at Southern Methodist University with a Southwestern Journalism Forum award, the first it ever gave to a woman, she told her boss about it as soon as she knew. He barely responded. The day came for the luncheon honoring her and she told him, "I'm leaving now for the luncheon," and he asked "What luncheon?" Another Braniff officer overheard and said that he would be honored to escort Pat to the luncheon. On the way, they stopped at a florist and he bought her a corsage.

When her boss retired, Pat was not even considered for a promotion. A young man, almost young enough to be her son, got the position. She continued to do the work. "He was scared of his shadow. I lived in a strait jacket under him."

She was named to the national Savings Bond Committee by the U. S. Treasurer, a job that took her to Washington annually for a meeting and was cited several times for contributions to that program. She starred year after year in the Dallas Press Club's annual Headliner Award programs. In 1970 she won a "Katy" award for publishing the best company newspaper. She traveled extensively, "but almost always on my vacations or spur-of-the-moment assignments. It was uncanny how my boss could always think of reasons I should remain in the office when Braniff planned its VIP excursions. I would plan all of the details for one of these events, issue the invitations, check the guests in and wave them good-by. I was never allowed to go along as a part of the fun."

Pat retired in 1975. She was one of the first women directors of the company. Her salary was $1,200 a month.

Braniff fell on bad times and, after many ups and downs, closed. Pat saw the end coming. "It started the day they moved Mr. Beard out. The company would be flying today if its management had remained solid. There were so many mistakes . . . .

"Ah, but it was fun! There were some great moments. I dedicated the longest runway that has ever been opened at Love Field. I got Mayor (R.L.) Thornton to come out and turn the first spade of dirt when we started building the Braniff Love Field Base. I planned every detail when we opened it. It was always second nature to me to plan an event that would capture the imagination of the community and of the press. When we opened the longest runway, for instance, I bought 20 yards of 20-inch white satin ribbon and roped off the runway . . . . I never got reimbursed for that ribbon. I put it on my expense account and was told that it was 'irregular' —and they couldn't reimburse me for it!"

In her personal life, "I did two things right—bought a house and reared a great daughter."

In 1964 she paid $15,000 for a house and financed it at 6 per cent interest. From it she could drive to work at Love Field in less than 10 minutes. Her daughter called the living room "Mom's Museum," because it housed collections Pat had accumulated from all over the world—awards and plaques and framed certificates; an the oil portrait of her mother painted by Dallas artist Victor Lallier, a photograph of her brother who was lost in World War II, and hundreds of other highlights. "I was scared witless when I signed the papers to buy the house," she said, "but it was the smartest thing I ever did."

Kathleen Zahrt holds bachelor and masters degrees from Texas Woman's University in stage lighting and production. She worked to help finance her education, graduating in 1968 and earned her master's two years later. She did graduate work at Connecticut

University working with equity actors who came there for two-week runs. She worked for five years at the Los Angeles Music Center and then became a general electrician in Los Angeles. In the early winter of 1991 Kathleen moved back to Dallas. Pat had looked forward to it for months.

For 30 years, Pat was on the cutting edge of change for working women in Dallas. From the inside, as a participant, she shaped many of those changes and as a retiree she prodded companies to fairer treatment of its women employees.

At night, Pat liked nothing better than to curl up in her bed with a good book. That is where Kathleen found her on the morning of January 31, 1991. At some time during the night, Pat had stopped breathing.

NOTES

• • • •

Chapter 1: In The Beginning

Dallas's earliest settlers were so busy building a city that they apparently had little time to keep records. This chapter utilized, as a foundation, identical sources cited by other writers and includes *A History of Greater Dallas and Vicinity, Vols. I and II*, by Philip Lindsley; the works of Frank M. Cockrell and Monroe F. Cockrell, *A History of Early Dallas* and *Sarah Horton Cockrell in Early Dallas*, and John Henry Brown's *History of Dallas County, Texas from 1837-1887*. The work is greatly enhanced by "Footprints" written by James J. Beeman and found and preserved by his great-granddaughter, Mildred Boone Haden, and by interviews with Margaret Boone Ackerman, descendant and namesake of Margaret Beeman Bryan. I am indebted to historian Janet Romanyshin for the location of Bird's Fort.

1. La Santisima Trinidad, the Most Holy Trinity, was named by Alonso de Leon, a Mexican-born officer of the Spanish Crown, in 1690. Trinity means Three in One, so named for the three forks—West, Elm and East—of the river. Previously, American Indians had called the river Daycona and Arikosa.
2. United States Census, 1820, for Dixon County, TN. Both Philip Lindsley and John Henry Brown list Dallas's first woman as Martha Gilbert. Martha was, instead, the wife of Wilson Gilbert, Mabel Gilbert's brother.
3. Location source: Official Military Map of the Civil War, *Atlas to accompany the official records of the Union and Confederate Armies,* 1861-1865 Plate CLVIII.
4. Emily Elvira Beeman Baker Holmes, reminiscences recorded by her daughter, Angelina Alice Baker Nicholson, and her great-granddaughter, Mildred Boone Haden.
5. *Memorial and Biographical History of Dallas County*, 1892.
6. *The Dallas Morning News*, Nov. 18, 1993.
7. Ibid.
8. John William Rogers, *The Lusty Texans of Dallas,* 32.
9. E. Parkinson, Journal on trip to Bird's Fort with Sam Houston.
10. John William Rogers, *The Lusty Texans of Dallas,* 37.
11. Numerous, and often contradictory, stories of the first John Neely and Margaret Beeman Bryan Cabin are recorded by Dallas historians. Barrot Steven Sanders has done one of the more comprehensive researches. See his book, *Dallas, Her Golden Years.*
12. Texas Historical State Marker, Beeman Cemetery, Dallas, TX.
13. Frank M. Cockrell, *History of Early Dallas.*
14. Monroe F. Cockrell, *Sarah Horton Cockrell in Early Dallas*, 10-14.
15. Ibid.
16. Frank M. Cockrell, *History of Early Dallas.*
17. Texas State Asylum records, September 14, 1877.
18. Margaret Boone Ackerman, interview April, 1989.
19. Beeman Family Records.

Chapter 2: The City's Premier Entrepreneur

The most significant material for this chapter are Frank M. Cockrell's *History of Early Dallas* and Monroe F. Cockrell's *Sarah Horton Cockrell in Early Dallas*. Frank was the son and Monroe the grandson of Sarah and Alexander Cockrell. Monroe Cockrell's book is a compilation of family letters, pictures and clippings, most of which had been previously published in *The Dallas Morning News*. Another vital source was Shirley Seifert's *Destiny in Dallas*. Though fiction, it was termed by Sarah Cockrell's grandson and the family historian, Monroe Cockrell, as showing "remarkable fidelity to historical accuracy." The book, published in 1958, is dedicated to "my friends, the Cockrells of Texas, and to Monroe Cockrell in particular, chief polisher of the family escutcheon and keeper of the records." I am further indebted to Barney C. Jones and Mary Alice Dealey, both descendants of Sarah and Alexander Cockrell, for the stories they shared and to family member, Noel Sever O'Reilly, for his letters and the photograph of an oil painting by Nadine Steele Cockrell.

1. *Memorial and Biographical History of Dallas County, 1892,* 772.
2. Shirley Seifert, *Destiny in Dallas*, 113.

3. *The Dallas Herald*, Apr. 10, 1858.
4. Shirley Seifert, *Destiny in Dallas*, 223.
5. Ibid., 240.
6. Frank M. Cockrell, *History of Early Dallas*, 52.
7. Florrie Wade Collection, #87.26, Box 23, Folder 11, Archives, Dallas Public Library, "Dallas's First Businesswoman." #7.
8. Monroe F. Cockrell, *Sarah Horton Cockrell in Early Dallas*, 115-117.
9. Frank M. Cockrell, 57.
10. Ibid., 57.
11. Monroe F. Cockrell, 96-97.
12. Ibid., 104-105.
13. Ibid., 27.
14. Ibid.
15. *The Dallas Herald*, Apr. 27, 1892.

Chapter 3: Petticoat Pioneers

I am deeply indebted to the several family historians whose work *Proud Heritage: Pioneer Families of Dallas County*, published by the Dallas County Pioneer Association in 1986 and, especially, to William F. Jacoby Jr. whose idea it was to create such a book. It served as a rich resource for this chapter and others.

1. Bradley C. Hodge, *Proud Heritage: Pioneer Families of Dallas County*, 237.
2. Helen Joy Straus Hodge, interview, Apr. 25, 1993.
3. Original bill of sale owned by Joe Trees, interview Joe and Bessie McLemore Trees, May 25, 1993.
4. *Memorial and Biographical History of Dallas County, 1892*, 155.
5. F. E. Butterfield and C. M. Rundlett, *Directory of the City of Dallas for the Year 1875*.
6. Darwin Payne, *Dallas: An Illustrated History*, 28.
7. *Memorial and Biographical History of Dallas County, 1892*, 493-494.
8. Ibid., 815-816.
9. Ibid., 817.
10. Ibid., 879.
11. Elizabeth Enstam, *When Dallas Became a City*, 161.
12. *The Dallas Herald*, July 3, 1858.

Chapter 4: The Seven Sisters from Tennessee

1. *Memorial and Biographical History of Dallas County, 1892*, 461-462.
2. Sam Acheson, "Dallas Yesterday," *The Dallas Morning News*, Dec. 16, 1968.

Chapter 5: The Multiple Millers—Millermore and More

Five principal sources served as the foundation for material in this chapter: scrapbooks and notes kept by Minerva Hortense Miller; books and documents written by Evelyn Miller Crowell; the essay, "Before There Was Lancaster," by Kathryn T. Smith and Judge Newton Fitzhugh published in *History of Lancaster 1845-1945;* Kathryn Smith Miller's *Polly Rawlins Miller*, and writings and interviews with Donald Payton.

1. Evelyn Miller Crowell, a paper prepared at Millermore, August, 1955. Compliments Dallas County Heritage Society.
2. Newton Fitzhugh, "Pleasant Run," History of Lancaster, Texas.
3. Evelyn Miller Crowell, 5.
4. Kathryn Smith Miller and Judge Newton Fitzhugh, *Polly Rawlins Miller* and "Pleasant Run," *History of Lancaster, Texas*, 7.
5. Ibid., 45-46.
6. *History of Lancaster,* "Before There Was a Lancaster," 4.
7. Ibid.
8. Kathryn Smith Miller, 18.
9. Ibid., 54.
10. *The Dallas Times Herald,* June 10, 1925.
11. Dorothy Spruill Edwards, *Somerset Homecoming*, 178.
12. Evelyn Miller Crowell, *Texas Childhood*, 24.

13. Ibid., 45-46.
14. Donald Payton, interview, Oct. 4, 1991.

Chapter 6: From Vision to Village

Writers of family histories published in *Proud Heritage* provided the basis for several of the stories published in this chapter and include Zelda Vineyard Johnston on Eliza Joyner Barker; Mary Jackson Sutherland and Everts E. Jackson on Diana Jane Davis Jackson and Ardelia Jackson West; William Clytes Anderson Culler on Celia Ann Lair Anderson, and James M. Guinn on Mary Ann Hill Goodnight. *The Park Cities—A Walker's Guide & Brief History* by Diane Galloway and Kathy Matthews added to the story on Frances Sims Daniel.

1. *Memorial and Biographical History of Dallas County, 1892,* 560.
2. Texas Historical Marker, Daniel Family Cemetery, Dallas, TX.
3. Nancy Rawlins Taylor, interview, *The Lancaster Herald,* 1891, republished in *Proud Heritage,* family essay by Robert Westbrook Sears, 1986, 200.
4. Charles D. Morse, editor and publisher, *The Standard,* Clarksville, Red River County, TX, Apr. 28, 1855.

Chapter 7: The Dallas Peaks

While living on Gaston Avenue shortly after graduating from SMU in the 1940s, I became aware of the significance of the Peak family to East Dallas and had always heard how many of the major streets were named for family members, but the family itself was elusive—until, one day, in the Dallas Public Library, I read the obituary of Miss Florence Chalfant Peak—and learned that she was survived by a niece, Miss Ruth Rydell. At that very moment, Ruth Rydell and I were serving together on the general board of First Community Church. When I called Ruth and asked if she were a member of the Peak family, she said, modestly, that she was. She introduced me to her sister, the family historian, Edith Rydell Roberts. Almost all of the material for this chapter is the result of those happy mergings and I thank them!

1. Howard W. Peak, "Visiting Our Grandparents," an essay, Peak Papers, Dallas Public Library, Texas/Dallas History, Archives MA85.7, Box 1.
2. Ibid.
3. Peak Family Papers, Peak Family Bible.
4. Peak Family Bible.
5. Sarah Ann Peak, letter, Dec. 10, 1852, among Peak Papers in possession of her great-granddaughter, Edith Rydell Roberts.
6. See Chapter 6 on Isabella Daniel Harwood.
7. Dorothy Laura Collins, handwritten information, Aug. 4, 1891, Peak Family Papers.
8. Olive Peak, handwritten note dated Jan. 17, (no year), Peak Family Papers, undated.
9. *Christian Courier,* June 27, 1889.
10. Sarah Ann Harwood, letter to Juliette Peak, Family Papers, undated.
11. Sarah Ann Harwood, letter to Juliette Peak Fowler, Oct. 2, 1859, Peak Papers. A block of the quilt, Sarah Ann's Flower Garden, she hoped to enter in the State Fair of Texas, is framed and hanging on the wall at the home of her great-granddaughter, Edith Rydell Roberts in Arlington, TX. The pattern for it was worked out by Curtis Castleberry and made by the author.
12. Clipping, no source, Nov. 22, 1860, Peak Family Papers.
13. Olive Peak, letter to her first cousin, Florence Peak, undated, Peak Papers.
14. Sarah Ann Peak Harwood, letter to Juliette Peak Fowler, Richmond, VA, Nov. 10, 1861, Peak Papers.
15. Sarah Ann Peak Harwood, letter to Juliette Peak Fowler, Jan. 25, 1862, Peak Papers.
16. Kenneth Foree, *The Dallas Morning News,* Jan 25, 1948.
17. Ibid., July 25, 1948.
18. Jefferson Peak, Last Will and Testament, June 18, 1877, filed for probate March 29, 1890, State of Texas, County of Dallas.
19. William L. McDonald, *Dallas Rediscovered,* 137.
20. Peter Smith, grandson of Florence Peak Field, letter to author, Aug. 7, 1985.
21. *The Christian Courier,* July 30, 1914.

Chapter 8: Dallas Becomes A City

Most of the credits for material used in this chapter are cited in the text. Microfilms of *The Dallas Herald* at the Dallas Public Library were indispensable. I am especially grateful for copies of the research done by Joe B. Motley, great grandson of Zachariah and Mary Lynn Motley, which secured the Texas Historical Marker at the Motley Cemetery. Rich material was also provided in a story by Paul Rosenfield, *The Dallas Times Herald Magazine*, June 4, 1961, and by interviews through the years with Motley family members.

Mary Marcelle Hamer Hull in her essay on John Taylor and Catherine Bunting Coit, published in *Proud Heritage*, provided the background for the section on the Coits. Mae E. Riek helped enormously with her story on Benjamin and Eugenia Dev Les Goodere Long, also in *Proud Heritage*. The *Directory of the City of Dallas for the Year 1875* provided the background for stories on Harriet Rector Cabell and Rebecca Serena Allison Stemmons.

Chapter 9: The 1860s—A Decade of Chaos

1. Frank M. Cockrell, *Early Dallas History*, 62.
2. Ibid., 62.
3. Ibid., 61-62.
4. Ibid., 62-63.
5. Ibid., 63.
6. *Memorial and Biographical History of Dallas County*, from reminiscences of W. P. Overton, 177.
7. Ibid.
8. Lester Newton Fitzhugh, Prologue to *Cannon Smoke*, viii.
9. *Directory of the City of Dallas, 1861-81*, 3: 2.
10. Lester Newton Fitzhugh, *Cannon Smoke*, the letters of Captain John J. Good, with a definitive prologue and epilogue by Fitzhugh.
11. Ibid., vii.
12. Ibid.
13. Ibid., 58.
14. Ibid., 70.
15. Ibid., 87.
16. Ibid., 143.
17. Ibid., 144.
18. Barrot Sanders, *The Caruths—Dallas's Landed Gentry*, 50.
19. Lucinda Beckley Williams, *The Golden Years*, 93.
20. Ibid., 150.
21. John William Rogers, *The Lusty Texans of Dallas*, 145.
22. Ibid.
23. *The Dallas Herald,* Feb. 3, 1886.
24. See Chapter 20 for more on crime, prostitution and gambling.
25. Burton Rascoe, *Belle Starr*, 117-118.
26. Ibid.
27. Ibid., 219.
28. Glenn Shirley, *Belle Starr and Her Times,* 20.
29. *The Dallas Herald,* Nov. 13, 1867.
30. Ibid., Sept. 21, 1867.
31. Ibid.

Chapter 10: Dallas's Dawning Days

Many sources—*The Dallas Herald* on microfilm at the Dallas Public Library, out-of-print books of poetry; Mary Cullum Nash's "Damn Proud People," the story of the Cullum family; Rogers's *Lusty Texans of Dallas*; *Prominent Women of Texas—1896*, and Sister Ignatius Miller's *Ursulines of the Central Province*—formed the foundation of resource materials for this chapter.

1. John William Rogers, *The Lusty Texans of Dallas*, 229-230.
2. *The Dallas Herald*, Feb. 18, 1873.
3. Alice Parsons Fitzgerald, *Beau Monde*, quoted in Rogers, 336.
4. *Prominent Women of Texas*, 1896, 140.
5. *Who's Who of the Womanhood of Texas*, 140 and 201.
6. Dallas Federation of Women's Clubs, history, 76-85.6. Dallas Federation of Women's Clubs, history, 76-85.
7. *Rebel Rhymes*, often mentioned in biographies of Elizabeth Hereford, is out of print, and no copy could be located.
8. Sam H. Dixon, *Poets and Poetry of Texas*, 1885.

9. Ibid., 205-206.
10. Ibid., 206.
11. Ibid., 208-209.
12. Sister Ignatius Miller, *Ursulines of the Province*, 210.

Chapter 11: Women—The City's Conscience

Interviews with Ruth Potts Spence (see Ruth Potts Spence) and her generous sharing of clippings, letters and photographs that had been saved by her mother-in-law, Stella White Spence, provided much of the background for this chapter. Mary Kittrell Craig was woven together from many different sources. Welthea Bryant Leachman was discovered in the pages of *History of Dallas County 1892* and *Poets and Poetry of Texas*. From *Proud Heritage* came the history of the Dallas County Pioneer Association and from the same source, in essays by A.C. Moser and Bertha Fritz, background for the story on Anna Buhrer Moser.

1. *History of Dallas County 1892*, 852.
2. Sam H. Dixon, *Poets and Poetry of Texas*, 184.
3. Sam Acheson, *The Dallas Morning News*, Oct. 12, 1970.
4. See Ruth Potts Spence.
5. Ruth Potts Spence, in interview on her mother-in-law.
6. Mrs. Wendell Spence, undated letter to *The Times Herald*, among Spence papers.
7. Ibid., newspaper clipping, undated, in Spence files retained by Ruth Potts Spence, in possession of author.
8. Ibid.
9. Ibid.
10. John E. Davis, State of Texas House of Representatives, Jan. 16, 1918, from personal correspondence of Mrs. Wendell Spence, in author's possession.
11. *The Dallas Morning News*, Apr. 2, 1915.
12. Stella White Spence Last Will and Testament, Spence personal files, copy in possession of author.

Chapter 12: The Genteel Decade

1. *The WPA Guide and History*.
2. *The Dallas Morning News*, various issues, advertising sections, early 1890s.
3. *WPA Papers*, 70.
4. Ibid.
5. *Who's Who of the Womanhood of Texas*, 93, 194.
6. John William Rogers, *The Lusty Texans of Dallas*, 146.
7. Minnie Miller Papers, Dallas Public Library.
8. Ibid.
9. *Memorial and Biographical History of Dallas County*.
10. William L. McDonald, *Dallas Rediscovered*, 87.
11. Ibid.
12. Ibid., 86.

Chapter 13: The 1880s—A Decade for Education

I am indebted to Walter J. E. Schiebel and his *Education in Dallas*, published by the Dallas Independent School District in 1966 and to numerous sources which more definitively outlined the contributions of Dallas teachers of African-American descent—among them Sadye Gee's *Black Presence in Dallas*, Yvonne Ewell and Kathlyn Gilliam's *Black Women: Achievement Against the Odds*, and to journalists Julia Scott Reed and Norma Wade. In addition, there are those wonderful sources already acknowledged, the WPA papers, both in their original form, and in the book *WPA Guide and History* published by the Dallas Public Library and the University of North Texas Press, and to the rollickingly amusing *Lusty Texans of Dallas* by John William Rogers, one of the first copies that came into my life through Graydon Heartsill.

1. *The WPA Dallas Guide and History*, 180.
2. Ibid. Also, Cochran Family History.
3. WPA Papers, 316.
4. Ibid.
5. *The Dallas Herald*, June 8, 1859.

6. John William Rogers, *The Lusty Texans of Dallas*, 156-157.
7. Ibid., 157.
8. Dallas Independent School District, Larry Ascough, public information director.
9. Sadye Gee, *Black Presence in Dallas*, 49.
10. Norma A. Wade, *The Dallas Morning News*, Feb. 15, 1985.
11. Yvonne Ewell and Kathlyn Gilliam, *Black Women: Achievement Against the Odds*.
12. Dallas Public School Superintendent's Monthly Reports, 1896-1909, hand-written records, The Dallas Public Library.
13. Walter J. E. Schiebel, *Education in Dallas*, 22.
14. Ibid., 36.
15. Ibid., 22.
16. Ibid., 42.
17. Ibid., 61.
18. Sadye Gee, *Black Presence in Dallas*, 109.
19. Ibid., 72-73.
20. Ibid., 77.
21. Ibid.
22. Walter J. E. Schiebel, *Education in Dallas*, 156.

Chapter 14: Women Organize to Change Their World

1. National Council of Jewish Women Greater Dallas Section, 1913-1988, a history, 4.
2. Ibid.,
3. Ibid., 64.
4. Christine (Mrs. J. Cleo) Thompson, "History of the Dallas Lawyers Wives Club," delivered to opening session of organization, September 1989.
5. John William Rogers, The *Lusty Texans of Dallas*, 358.
6. *The Dallas Times Herald*, club files, 1973.
7. Ibid.
8. Dallas Shakespeare Club history, 4.
9. Ibid.
10. Ibid.
11. Ibid., 3.
12. Ibid., 13.
13. Ibid., 5.
14. Betty May Exall Stewart, interview.
15. Willie Newbury Lewis, interview, 1984.
16. Ibid.
17. Betty May Exall Stewart, interview.
18. *Beau Monde*, Sept. 23, 1899.
19. Betty May Exall Stewart, interview.
20. *Beau Monde*, Nov. 26, 1898.
21. Ruth Potts Spence, interview, 1987.
22. Ibid.
23. Betty May Exall Stewart, interview.
24. Ibid.
25. *A Memorial and Biographical History of Dallas County, Texas, 1892*, 570.
26. Ibid.
27. Dorothy Brannen Exall, interview.

Chapter 15: A Decade to Play—The Gay Nineties in Dallas

All of the newspapers published in Dallas of the 1890-1900 decade were indispensable to the material for this chapter. I am one of the last researchers who used the crumbly issues of *Beau Monde* before they were put on microfilm, and I treasure being able to read them just as they came off the press more than a hundred years ago. I am overwhelmingly indebted to Anne Tyler Rawlins, great-niece of Sara Isadore Sutherland Miner Callaway—Pauline Periwinkle—who let me hold in my own hands treasures from Dallas's first woman journalist of distinction including the Callaway family Bible and the vase that William Callaway gave his wife-to-be in 1890.

1. *The Dallas Morning News*, Oct. 8, 1885, 8.
2. Ibid., May 18, 1890.
3. Ibid., 3.
4. Ibid., May 4, 1890.
5. Ibid., May 8, 1890.
6. Ibid., May 2, 1890.
7. Ibid., May 3, 1890.
8. Ibid., May 21, 1890.
9. Ibid., May 4, 1890.
10. Ibid., May 11, 1890.
11. *The Dallas Morning News*, May 11, 1890.
12. *The Dallas Daily Times Herald*, Dec. 18, 1894.
13. Ibid., Nov. 24, 1894.
14. *The Dallas Morning News*, June 15, 1890.
15. Ibid., June 29, 1890.
16. *Prominent Women of Texas*, 1896.
17. Anne Tyler Rawlins, interview, 1992.
18. John William Rogers, *The Lusty Texans of Dallas*, 179.
19. *Prominent Women of Texas*, 130.
20. *Beau Monde*, Nov. 26, 1898.
21. Ibid., Feb. 11, 1898.
22. Ibid., Apr. 29, 1899.
23. Ibid., Apr. 22, 1899.
24. Ibid., Apr. 29, 1899.
25. Ibid., Dec. 12, 1898.
26. Ibid., June 13, 1908.
27. Ibid.
28. Ibid., July 7, 1900.
29. Ibid., Jan. 12, 1907.
30. Ibid, Jan. 7, 1898.
31. Ibid., Dec. 3, 1898.
32. Ibid., Aug. 19, 1899.
33. Ibid., Feb. 11, 1898.
34. Ibid., Dec. 10, 1898.
35. Ibid., Mar. 3, 1898.
36. Ibid., Dec. 10, 1898.
37. Ibid., Dec. 21, 1901.
38. Ibid., Mar. 28, 1902.
39. Ibid., Apr., 22, 1899.
40. Ibid., Jan. 28, 1898.
41. Ibid., Oct. 13, 1900.
42. Ibid., July 7, 1900.
43. Ibid., Sept. 18, 1899.
44. Ibid., July 28, 1900.
45. Ibid., Oct. 28, 1899.
46. Ibid., Feb. 4, 1898.
47. Ibid., June 3, 1899.
48. *The Dallas Morning News*, Dec. 14, 1910.
49. *The Daily Times Herald*, Dec. 13, 1914.

Chapter 16: The Twentieth Century Arrives

The Dallas newspapers, published during the first decade of the twentieth century provided the basis for this chapter, enriched by stories of descendants from those earlier days of Dallas.

1. *Dallas City Directory*, 1900.
2. *The Dallas Morning News*, Moments of the Past, Feb. 8, 1966.

3. Historians Tom Smith and Mike Hazel recently discovered an earlier "horseless carriage in Dallas in Apr., 1897.
4. *The Dallas Morning News,* Oct. 9, 1899.
5. *The Dallas Herald*, Feb. 28, 1901.
6. Ibid., Feb. 28, 1901.
7. Ibid.
8. *The Daily Times Herald,* Apr. 23, 1901.

Chapter 17: A Library Is Born

For this chapter, I am indebted to Lillian Bradshaw and the numerous interviews she afforded me as a journalist during our Dallas journey together when she was librarian. I thank her for writing "The First Forty Years," published by Friends of the Dallas Public Library in 1991. Larry Grove's "Dallas Public Library—the First 75 Years," published in 1977 was a wonderful source. The history was enriched by the work of Vale Frasch for *Texas Woman's News*, and Cele Berkman, by numerous newspaper articles and by the personal stories of Betty May Exall Stewart.

1. *The Dallas Morning News*, Mar. 12, 1899.
2. Larry Grove, "Dallas Public Library, the First 75 Years," 21.
3. Betty May Exall Stewart, interview.
4. Larry Grove, 21.
5. Ibid.
6. *Beau Monde*, Sept. 23, 1899.
7. *Library Journal*, Feb. 1902.
8. Ibid.
9. Larry Grove, 40.
10. Ibid., 36.

Chapter 18: Women as Cultural Arbiters

1. *The WPA Dallas Guide and History*, 229.
2. John William Rogers, *The Lusty Texans of Dallas,* 244.
3. *Dallas Social Directory*, 1904-05.
4. Ruth Potts Spence, interview, Feb. 28, 1984.
5. Rogers, 246-248.
6. Francis Battaile Fisk, *A History of Texas Artists and Sculptors*, 219.
7. *The Dallas Morning News*, Dec. 13, 1897.
8. *Beau Monde*, July 1899.
9. Willie Newbury Lewis, interview, 1984.
10. John William Rogers, 233.

Chapter 19: Dallas's Denizens of Darkness

1. John Henry Brown, *History of Dallas County, Texas from 1837-1887*, 255-271.
2. 17th Century legend of "Three Wise Monkeys," Nikko, Japan.
3. Simone de Beauvoir, *The Second Sex*, translator's (H. M. Parshley) preface, xix.
4. Pam Lange and Mindie Lazarus-Black, *Family Business in Dallas*, 213.
5. *The Holy Bible*, King James Version, Ch. 7, excerpts.
6. J. T. Upchurch, "The Unchained Demon," Berachah Rescue Society, 37.
7. Ibid., 38.
8. Ibid., 41.
9. Ibid.
10. Ibid.
11. *The Dallas Morning News*, Nov. 4, 1913, Sec. 1, 16.
12. Ibid.
13. Bernard Grun, *The Timetables of History*, 484.
14. *The Dallas Morning News*, May 21, 1921.
15. Ibid., May 22, 1921.
16. *The Dallas Times Herald*, May 22, 1921.

17. Ibid., Apr. 8, 1923.
18. Wyn Craig Wade, *The Fiery Cross*, 201.
19. *The Dallas Morning News*, Apr. 2, 1922.
20. Ruth Potts Spence, interview, Feb. 28, 1984.
21. *The Dallas Times Herald*, Mar. 2, 1913.
22. *The Dallas Morning News*, July 29, 1913.
23. *The Dallas Times Herald*, July 28, 1913.
24. *The Dallas Morning News*, Nov. 3, 1913.

Chapter 20: Women Embrace the Children

I am indebted to the YWCA and the generous sharing of its archives provided by director, Dr. Mary Sias; to The *Dallas Evening Journal* May 13, 1915, page 2, col. 5, for its excellent coverage of May Smith and the nurses she led to establish the Baby Camp that, through time and growth became the Children's Medical Center; to Aileen Edgington, who as director of Hope Cottage, allowed me to look at all of its records and to read its board minutes, and to the coverage that newspapers provided of the events during this period of time.

1. *Dallas Shakespeare Club, 1886-1954*, 25.
2. *The Herald*, Mar. 3, 1913.
3. *New York Times*, Sept. 18, 1990, A-10.
4. Ruth Potts Spence, interview, Feb. 28, 1984.
5. Hope Cottage Records, 1921.

Chapter 21: The Mexicans Find a Home in Dallas

I am indebted to Elizabeth Enstam, notable Dallas historian, who shared with me her notes and tape on Maria de Jesus Carreon Moreno when she discovered that the boundaries of dates for her own book did not include the period of time that Mrs. Moreno contributed to Dallas. I also thank Jane Bock Guzman for sharing the results of her master's degree studies and the thesis, "Dallas Barrio Women of Power." But, most of all, I am grateful for doing volunteer work in "Little Mexico" when I was a student at Southern Methodist University, 1940-1944, where I personally experienced the magnificence of Mexican American women, and for the deep friendships I share with many women of Hispanic heritage. My life has been vastly enriched by all of them.

1. *The WPA Dallas Guide and History*, 306.
2. Ibid.
3. *The Dallas Morning News*," Madre de Floyd Street," by Kenneth Foree.
4. Ibid.
5. Elizabeth Enstam, interview with Sam A. Moreno, son of Maria Moreno.
6. Adelaida R. Del Castillo, "Mexican Women in the United States—Struggles Past and Present." Los Angeles: Occasional paper No. 2, Chicano Studies Research Center publications, University of California, 1980.
7. Ibid.
8. Ibid.
9. Jane Bock Guzman, "Dallas Barrio Women of Power," a thesis for the degree of master of arts, University of North Texas.

Chapter 22: Education for Woman and Girls

It would be impossible to list the hundreds of people who have taught me and shaped my thinking about education for girls and women in Dallas. In the first writing, the chapter had 100 pages. One day I closed my eyes and cut ruthlessly. I hope you stayed!

1. John William Rogers, *The Lusty Texans of Dallas*, 335.
2. Ibid., 199-201.
3. Ruth Potts Spence, interview Feb. 28, 1984.
4. Margaret Hearne Hyer Thomas, interview, 1991.
5. Ibid.
6. Ruth Potts Spence, interview, 1984.
7. Southern Methodist University Archives, compliments Patricia LaSalle.
8. Ibid.
9. Ibid.

10. Ibid.
11. *The Formative Years, 1915-1920*, SMU archives.
12. Mary Buford Miller, interview, 1972.
13. Ibid., letter to author, Dec. 22, 1971.

Chapter 23: Toddling Toward Equality

The information for this chapter came from literally hundreds of sources, most of which are cited below. I am especially grateful to Stanley Marcus for his book, *Minding the Store*, to Natalie Ornish for *Pioneer Jewish Texans*, and to Mrs. James G. McCollum for her thesis on the struggle of Texas women to get the vote. Personal interviews enriched and humanized much of the research. I am especially indebted to Sara McGee, Ruth Cooper, Idelle Rabin, Mary Collett, Anita Martinez, Julia Brown and Pat Zahrt.

1. *The Dallas Herald*, Jan. 26, 1887.
2. *Dallas Shakespeare Club, 1886-1954*, 28
3. *Beau Monde*, Feb. 4, 1898.
4. Mrs. James G. McCollum, Thesis, June 28, 1949.
5. Sara Jane Hibbits McGee, *Proud Heritage*, 215, and interview.
6. Pam Lange and Mindie Lazarus-Black, *Family Business in Dallas: A Matter of Values*, 215.
7. Idelle Goodman Rabin, interview, Oct. 23, 1990.
8. Mary Collett, interview, Feb. 20, 1984.
9. *The Dallas Times Herald*, Mar. 22, 1926.
10. Julia Josephine Haswell Brown, interview, Jan. 23, 1991.
11. *Dallas Shakespeare Club, 1886-1954*, 28.
12. *The Dallas Times Herald*, Mar. 22, 1926.

Chapter 24: The Pacesetters

To so many I owe gratitude for the foundation and the human interest components of this chapter: To Dr. Mamie McKnight and her continuing research on the citizens of African American descent; to Sarah Weddington and her associates who wrote about Texas women in politics; to *Who's Who of the Womanhood of Texas* for the forgotten stories of Florence George Martin; to Juanita Hamilton for help with the stories of her mother, Dr. Juanita Wade; to Patricia Currin, daughter of Dr. Genevieve Shea; to the Dallas newspapers of the period; to Vareta Pinkston's daughter, Stevonne, and to Jane Bock Guzman for sharing her research on Maria Luna, and to so many more, gracias and thank you, thank you, thank you.

1. *Austin American*, Jan. 10, 1923.
2. Ibid., Jan. 6, 1923.
3. Ibid., Jan. 7, 1923.
4. Sarah Weddington, Jane Hickie and Deanna Fitzgerald, *Texas Women in Politics*, 6-7.
5. *The Encyclopedia of Texas*, 659.
6. Juanita T. Hamilton, interview on her mother, Dr. Juanita Wade, 1992.
7. Jannah Louise Abdallah, T. C. Wilemon Junior High, Waxahachie, *Texas Historian*, January 1984, 11-13.
8. Patricia Currin, interview on her mother, Dr. Genevieve Shea, Mar. 22. 1992.
9. T*he Dallas Morning News*, Dec. 8, 1946.
10. Ibid.
11. Deborah Fridia Bedford, 1988 interview for *African American Settlements of Dallas*.
12. *The Dallas Morning News*, Marzelle Cooper-Hill obituary, June 6, 1993.

Chapter 25: Courage to Conquer: Women as Survivors

Personal memories of the Great Depression and of the Texas Centennial formed the basis for this chapter which was greatly enhanced by the stories, both written and verbal, of others who experienced those days in Dallas.

1. *The Dallas Times Herald*, Allena Duff James, food columnist, June 30, 1933.
2. Ibid.
3. Ibid., May 21, 1933.
4. International News Service, Apr. 28, 1933.

5. *The Dallas Times Herald*, June 5, 1933.
6. Ibid., Apr. 1, 1933.
7. Ibid, June 6, 1936.
8. Ibid.

Chapter 26: Six Daring Daughters

Among my most enriching blessings are the people I interviewed, many of them repeatedly, during my 28 years as a journalist. My reporter's notes are filled with gems from Pearl Anderson and Judge Sarah Hughes, both of whom granted taped interviews. I am grateful to Virginia Whitehill and to Dawn Letson, curator of manuscripts, DeGolyer Library, for help with the Nell Goodrich story; to Julia Brown and the archives of the Dallas Women's Federation of Clubs for assistance on Kate Rice Ripley and to Louis Didrickson, brother of Babe Zaharias, for correcting and enriching the newspaper accounts of his sister's unparalleled contributions to athletics. The Bonnie Parker story is the first I followed day-by-day in the newspapers when I was a child. These memories, of course, were researched again through books and newspaper accounts of the Barrow-Parker escapades.

1. Pearl Anderson, interview Feb. 16, 1984.
2. Louis Didrickson, interview, Dec. 22, 1990.
3. *The Dallas Morning News*, Feb. 16, 1950.
4. *The Dallas Times Herald*, Aug. 11, 1932.
5. *The Dallas Morning News*, Feb. 16, 1950.
6. Ibid.
7. *The Dallas Times Herald*, Nov. 21, 1954.
8. Julia Brown, interview Jan. 23, 1991.
9. Gertrude Aldredge Shelburne, interview Mar. 7, 1991.
10. Sarah Tilghman Hughes, published in numerous publications, copy in possession of author.

Chapter 27: Women at War—the 1940s

1. *The Book of Dallas*, "Power and Politics," 233-250.
2. *The Dallas Times Herald*, classified advertising pages, June 1940.
3. Ibid.
4. *The Dallas Times Herald*, Dec. 9, 1941.
5. *The Dallas Morning News*, Oct. 20, 1946.
6. *The Dallas Morning News*, Ruby Clayton McKee, reporter, Dec. 8, 1948.
7. *The Dallas Times Herald*, James V. Lovell, reporter, Feb. 4, 1946.

Chapter 28: The Power–Four

Though countless newspaper stories, company reports and the writings of this quartet of women provided enrichment for this chapter, almost all of the material comes from personal interviews and from interviews with others who knew these four exceptional women.

Chapter 29: The Message Carriers

I am deeply indebted to the women of this chapter who supplied me, through personal interviews during the years, and through letters afterward, with the material that appears here.

Chapter 30: Unease in Utopia

Research through the pages of newspapers on microfilm at the Dallas Public Library served as the basis for capturing the mood and the realities of Dallas as a city for women in the 1950s. Personal interviews with Leona Allman, Connie Condos, Grace Stemmons, Juanita Craft and Mary Louise Rowand through the years served as the parameters.

Chapter 31: Tides of Change

This chapter has been a personal journey. For 28 years, for *The Dallas Times Herald*, I reported on the subjects and all of the women whose stories are told. During the writing, I reinterviewed most of them—Kim Dawson, Elizabeth Blessing, Adlene

Harrison, Eddie Bernice Johnson, Nancy Judy, Margaret McDermott, Mamie McKnight, Carole Shlipak, Kathlyn Gilliam, Ethel Stewart and Madeline Mandell. And, I am grateful to George Galerstein, who corrected my memory of details about Carolyn Galerstein.

1. A. C. Greene, "Power and Politics," *The Book of Dallas*, 248.
2. R. L. Polk, *Polk's Greater Dallas, City/County Directory*, introduction.
3. Ibid.

Chapter 32: Faces of Feminism

The three women cited here, Maura Anderson McNiel, Hermine Dalkowitz Tobolowsky and Barbara Minor James, have equally significant sisters throughout the community whose stories could have been told. These three were chosen because they have lived the women's liberation movement in their personal lives and, in many ways, are typical of the way other women have lived. In all three cases, the stories were told after extensive interviews with the subjects over many years.

1. *The Dallas Times Herald,* Nov. 18, 1982.
2. Hermine Tobolowsky, interview, 19, 1978.
3. Barbara James, interview, July 15, 1991.

Chapter 33: Preserving the Past

1. *The Dallas Times Herald*, Apr. 16, 1965.
2. Ibid. Feb. 18, 1965.
3. *The Dallas Morning News*, Feb. 19, 1965.
4. *The Dallas Times Herald*, Feb. 16, 1966.
5. *The Dallas Morning News*, May 19, 1966.

Chapter 34: Connecting the Pieces

Each of the mini-profiles included in this chapter are the result of personal interviews with the subjects. All of them are written from taped sessions with the eight women, who were reinterviewed shortly before the book was completed.

Chapter 35: Expanding the Circle

The overwhelming response of women (38 per cent) in the Dallas Forum to inquiries about changing opportunities for women in business and organizations and individuals sensitive to new developments provided the basis for evaluations in this chapter. I am deeply grateful to Louise Raggio for contacting Forum members and to the individuals in Forum for providing the answers. For assistance with the development of Dallas toward becoming truly an international city, I am especially indebted to Dr. Kwasi Ohene-Bekoe and Morena Fantozzi Petsch—and to the newest star in the constellation, Sandy Cohen, whose Holidays of People Everywhere (HOPE), the December celebration at Dallas City Hall in December of 1993 marked new official recognition and inclusion by Dallas of its citizens from throughout the world.

Chapter 36: Future Unlimited

I am deeply grateful to the books and lectures by M. Scott Peck and to the works of women researchers—notably Carol Gilligan—for establishing parameters and giving insight into ways people learn and grow. Annette Strauss and Gail Thomas afforded me unlimited time over many years and countless interviews for their part of the story. I am so grateful to them—for their generosity to me, but more important, for their service to Dallas. On a personal level, I cite four of many experiences that shaped my thinking for this chapter: (1) the Character Research Project that my husband, Curtis, and I experienced with our five daughters at First Community Church in Dallas for 15 years; (2) my work as a reporter with *The Dallas Times Herald* that took me daily into every type of situation with people of both sexes of every age, color and creed for 28 years; (3) work with Sharon Tennison, founder and CEO of Center for Citizens Initiatives, over a period of 32 years that sent me to the Soviet Union in 1984, again in 1986, and again in 1987 to learn for myself that "the bad guys" are only human like the rest of us, and (4) "Global Peace: From Vision to Reality: An International Women's Peace Conference, presented by Peacemakers, Inc. in 1988, that brought to Dallas more than 2,000 delegates—women from 63 countries and 37 states—who showed me that the human family can resolve conflicts peacefully and live together in creative diversity. I am grateful to countless individuals for the success of that conference. The group that steered it through included Dolores Pevehouse, Les Pugh, Ruth Barnhouse, Rosann Naim, Leslie Lanes, Barbara Middleton, Carole Trout, Rachel

Ford, Donna Shellhorn, Barbara Jones, Margaret Estes, Emily Scobee Schumacher, Liz Deuillet, Karin Sawhill, Rhonda Palmer, 229 volunteers, 113 host families and 560 contributors!

PART II

Margaret Boone Ackerman

Margaret Boone Ackerman talked about her grandmother, Emily Elvira Beeman Baker Holmes, and her own life in Dallas in a taped interview in April of 1988, and provided additional information, both in writing and verbally. It was edited and corrected by her sister, Mildred Boone Haden, the family historian, on November 9, 1993. The few references are for clarification.

1. "Footprints of James J. Beeman," recovered by Mildred Boone Haden, his great granddaughter, among private Beeman Papers.
2. From stories of Emily Elvira Beeman Baker Holmes recorded by her daughter, Angelina Alice Baker Nicholson, and great granddaughter, Mildred Boone Haden.
3. District Court, Dallas County records, Vol. A. Page 258.
4. Stories told by Emily Elvira Beeman Baker Holmes to her family.

Ruth Elaine Collins Seaman Sharp Altshuler

I deeply appreciate the caring/sharing interviews that Ruth Elaine Collins Seaman Sharp Altshuler has granted me through the years, her contributions both to the city we love and to me personally.

Cordye McLaurin Hall

As a journalist, I often had heard about Cordye Hall and been intrigued with her spunk and determination, but I had never done an in-depth story on her. I was an admirer in absentia. Once, in June of 1970, I sent a reporter to interview her as an organizer of Another Mother for Peace. Susan wrote, "Never before in history, have mothers organized to make war on war." The story was brief and nonthreatening, but it compelled me to join the organization and proudly wear its medallion. Later, when I was braver and about to retire from *The Dallas Times Herald* in the spring of 1984, I interviewed and did a more in-depth story on her.

But I did not know her. And the story did not do her justice. None could. Led by Cordye Hall and others of her persuasion, I was free, upon retirement, to be active in seeking peaceful resolution to human conflict. My first act was to make a trip to the Soviet Union as a Citizen Diplomat, and meet women of all ages, professions, interests, sizes and backgrounds who knew, as I did—as women do—that there are always better ways to solve problems than killing each other. With increasing conviction, I went twice more to the Soviet Union.

Then, I became the catalyst and the chairperson of Peacemakers, Inc., which sponsored on August 8, 1988 (8-8-88) "Global Peace: From Vision to Reality—An International Women's Conference." The week-long event at Southern Methodist University in Dallas drew more than a thousand participants from 63 countries, every continent, and 37 states of the United States. Thousands of personal, poignant events took place as woman after woman—regardless of age, color, family background, political persuasion, personal conviction, religious view, economic condition, educational ability—declared her commonality. It was a mind-boggling, overwhelming, positive experience.

Cordye Hall was a significant part of it. Disappointed time after time with failures of promised breakthrough to world peace, she determined to complete the book she had been persuaded to write as a money-making project for the conference. *What Can One Person Do? A Texas Woman Answers*, with the help of her friend Ken Gjemre, her daughter-in-law, Eulaine Hall; her granddaughter, Sandy Hall-Chiles; her biographer, Ruthe Winegarten, and with the push of an 8-8-88 deadline, Cordye delivered her book. I continue to stand in humble gratitude for such a giant as she—needler, nudger, monitor, mentor, instigator and inspiration.

Adlene Nathanson Harrison

Countless interviews with Adlene Harrison, both as a public official and as a private citizen, plus help from Maurice Harrison and others in her family and among her associates formed the basis for this chapter. I also had access to some of her writings including the text of her message to the citizens of Dallas following Judge W. M. Taylor's ruling on school integration. I am deeply grateful.

The Martinez Women—Faustina, Irene Garcia and Anita

Many interviews through many years with several members of the Martinez family furnished the material for this chapter. I especially cherish the time with Faustina Porras Martinez.

Maria Belen (Correa) Ortega

The concert of 20 recordings, a Serenade by Maria Belen Ortega, the "Nightingale of the Americas," illuminated the published stories and personal interviews that made this chapter possible.

Florence Harllee Phelps

Numerous interviews with Florence Phelps through the years of her career in Dallas, interviews with her daughter, Lucy Patterson, and published news stories formed the background for this chapter. I am most indebted to her husband, John C. Phelps, whose generosity of spirit pervades everything he touches and who helped me with details.

Idelle Goodman Rabin

Many associations—both in formal interviews and informally in working together—with Idelle and Leon Rabin made this chapter possible. I am grateful, not only for their time, but for their enrichment of my personal life. Along with the rest of Dallas who knew him, I mourned the death of Leon Rabin in 1992. It is entirely possible that I was one of the working girls Leon counted to determine the practicality of opening a business. At that time I was employed by the Petroleum Engineer Publishing Company diagonally across the street from where Idelle Rabin had worked at Neiman's. I spent that first year of my honeymoon life almost exclusively in skirts and blouses and sweaters, some of which I had, no doubt, purchased at Idelle's bidding.

Gertrude Terrell Aldredge Shelburne

As a reporter, I was always in awe of Gertrude Shelburne because of her professionalism. She always seemed to stand a little above the work she was doing so as to view everything with clarity. My several interviews with her after I retired revealed her to be as caring and emphathetic as she was organized and effective, and I am grateful for knowing her in both roles.

Ruth Potts Spence

For almost a century, Ruth Potts Spence lived in Dallas where she was a keen observer of its physical growth and change and, for more than half a century, helped to shape that growth into a city more inclusive of all its resources—both its people and all the institutions that impacted their lives. She was, for the critical first five years of research for this book, from February of 1984 until shortly before her death, the definitive person with whom I checked information. Many times she clarified, corrected, and in her gentle way, directed the work. I am eternally grateful.

Alvernon Verita King Evans Tripp

Alvernon was a towering presence in any gathering. Elegantly tall, she matched her height with a keen intellect and a perspective on her native city gleaned from having lived, studied and worked in six states. With this multiple experience, she observed and contributed to Dallas for many years. Our last interview occurred only weeks before her final illness and I consider my life enriched by her presence in it.

Martha Bell Leonard Zahrt and Lily Vertrees Bell Leonard

I had known from the time I began this book that I wanted to include the story of Pat Zahrt for several reasons: She was an exceptional woman, a Dallas native with a unique perspective—both as a working woman and as a single mother rearing a child alone. She dedicated her career to an organization that was uniquely Dallas and experienced both the best and the worst that the city had to offer. I had postponed interviews that would enhance the work I had done with her through the years until one day in the fall of 1990, I felt a compelling urge to get on with the story. I called Pat and she invited me to her home where we sat for almost a full day talking, visiting, interviewing each other and looking at pictures. I left and wrote the story and called her back the next week to check on details. In less than two months after that Pat died. I am so grateful we had time together.

BIBLIOGRAPHY

••••

Thousands of books, newspaper and magazine articles, photographs, oral histories, family papers, court proceedings, legal documents, cemetery records, souvenirs and personal interviews served as references during the many years of research and writing of *Daughters of Dallas*. The following is a selection of some that were most helpful.

Abernethy, Francis Edward. *Legendary Ladies of Texas.* Texas Folklore Society, XLIII, in cooperation with the Foundation for Women's Resources. Dallas: E-Heart Press, 1981.

Acheson, Sam. *Dallas Yesterday.* Dallas: SMU Press, 1977.

———. *35,000 Days in Texas.* A History of *The Dallas Morning News.* New York: MacMillan, 1938.

Achor, Shirley. *Mexican Americans in a Dallas Barrio.* Tucson: University of Arizona Press, 1978.

African American Families and Settlements of Dallas: On the Inside Looking Out. ALP Printing Co., 1990.

Anderson, Pearl C. Sunday Magazine, *The Dallas Times Herald.* October 31, 1976.

Barnes, Beatrice G. *Golden Profiles.* Chicago: Adams Press, 1981.

Beckett, Hazael Williams. *Growing Up In Dallas.* Dallas: New Hope Press, 1985.

Belenky, Mary Field, Blythe McVicker Clinchy, Nancy Rule Goldberger, and Jill Mattuck Tarule. *Women's Ways of Knowing.* New York: Basic Books, Inc., 1986.

Bella Starr or the Bandit Queen. Journal published by Richard K. Fox, New York, 1889.

Bradshaw, Lillian Moore. T*he First Forty Years*, a History of the Dallas Public Library. Dallas: Friends of the Dallas Public Library, Inc., 1991.

Brooks, Elizabeth. P*rominent Women of Texas.* Akron: Werner Company, 1986.

Brown, John Henry. *History of Dallas County, Texas from 1837-1887.* Dallas: Milligan, Cornett & Farnham, 1887.

Butterfield, F. E., and C. M. Rundlett. *Directory of the City of Dallas for the Year 1875.*

Bywaters, Jerry. *Seventy-Five Years of Art in Dallas.* Dallas Museum of Fine Arts, 1975.

Carlisle, Mrs. John C. Papers, Dallas Historical Society.

Chisum, John H., and Ethelyn Chisum. A Family Collection, Dallas Public Library, 1989.

Cochran, John H. *Dallas County: A Record of Its Pioneers and Progress.* Dallas: Arthur S. Mathis-Van Nort Publishing Company, 1928.

Cockrell, Frank M. *Early Dallas History. The Dallas Morning News.* Originally published in weekly installments in "Dallas Sunday News," May 15, 1932 to Aug. 28, 1932. Privately published, 20 papers, by Monroe F. Cockrell, Illinois, 1944.

Cockrell, Monroe F. Papers and collections, Dallas Historical Society.

———. *Sarah Cockrell in Early Dallas.* Privately published, 1961.

Conner, Seymour V. "The Peters Colony of Texas." Austin: Texas State Historical Association, 1959.

Considerant, Victor. Au *Texas*. Paris, France: Librairie Phalansteriere, 1854.

Craft, Juanita Jewell. Unpublished oral history, papers and memoribilia.

Crawford, Ann Fears, and Crystal Sasse Ragsdale. *Women in Texas*. Austin: Eakin Press, 1982.

Cristol, Geraldine Propper. "A History of the Dallas Museum of Fine Arts." Thesis, Southern Methodist University, 1970.

Crowell, Evelyn Miller. *Texas Childhood, 1846-1941*. Kaleidograph Press, 1941.

———. "William Brown Miller." A paper prepared at Millermore, August 1955, Dallas County Historical Society.

Cullum, Earl Owen. Dallas Historical Notes on Early Dallas, the Oak Lawn Community and Oak Lawn United Methodist Church, 1978.

Dallas City Directories, 1875-1992.

Dallas County Court Records, Civil and Criminal.

Dallas Federation of Women's Clubs, a history of, 1936-1946 and 1946-1956.

Dallas German Ladies Aid Society, 1907 to May 1974. Papers and memoribilia, Dallas Public Library.

"Dallas Guide and History, Writers' Program, Parts 1, 2, & 3, popularly called the WPA Papers," 1935.

Dallas PTA, 1909-1969, a history of, "Now We Are Sixty." Published by the Dallas City Council of Parent Teacher Associations.

Davis, Ellis A., and Edwin H. Grobe, comp. The *Encyclopedia of Texas*. Vols. 1 & 2. Austin: Texas Development Bureau, 1922.

Dealey, Ted. *Diaper Days of Dallas*. Dallas: Abingdon Press, 1966.

de Beauvoir, Simone. *The Second Sex*. New York: Alfred A. Knopf, Inc., 1952.

Directory of the City of Dallas 1861-1881.

Dixon, Sam H. *Poets and Poetry of Texas*. Privately published, 1885.

Earliest History of Dallas, 1861. A microfilm, Dallas Public Library.

Ewell, Yvonne, and Kathlyn Gilliam. *Black Women: Achievement Against the Odds*, 1981.

Federation of Women's Clubs, 40th Anniversary. Special section, *The Dallas Morning News*, Oct. 30, 1938.

Ferguson, Charles W. *The Male Attitude*, a historical study. Boston: Little, Brown and Company, 1966.

Fisk, Frances Battaile. *A History of Texas Artists and Sculptors*. Abilene, TX, 1928.

Fitzhugh, Newton. *Hardscrabble—Pleasant Run and the Origins of Lancaster*. Lancaster Historical Society, Lancaster, TX, text of an address, Oct. 12, 1969.

Fitzhugh, Lester Newton. *Cannon Smoke*. The letters of Captain John J. Good. Hillsboro, TX: Hill Junior College Press, 1971.

Forrester-O'Brien, Esse. *Art and Artists in Texas*. Dallas: Tardy Publishing Company, 1935.

Galloway, Diane, and Kathy Matthew. *Park Cities, a Walker's Guide and Brief History*. Dallas: SMU Press, 1988.

Gambrell, Dr. Herbert C. Papers and collections: Dallas Historical Society.

———. "Dallas, Texas," *The Handbook of Texas*. Edited by Walter Prescott Webb, Texas Historical Association, 1952.

Garrett, Howard, and Trent Humphries. *Plants of the Metroplex*. Lantana Press, 1975.

Gee, Sadye, comp. *Black Presence in Dallas*. The Museum of African American Life and Culture, 1988.

Goals for Dallas, published by Goals for Dallas, 1966.

Greene, A. C. *Dallas: The Deciding Years—A Historical Portrait*. Published by Sanger-Harris in commemoration of its 100th year in Dallas. Austin: Encino Press, 1973.

———. *Dallas USA*. Austin: Texas Monthly Press, Inc., 1984.

Grimes, Johnnie-Marie. *Willis M. Tate, Views and Interviews* Dallas: SMU Press, 1978.

Grove, Larry. *Dallas Public Library: The First 75 Years*. A History of the Dallas Public Library: Published by the Dallas Public Library, 1975.

Grun, Bernard. *The Timetables of History*. F. A. Herbig Verlagsbuchhandlung, 1946. English Language Edition, Simon & Schuster, 1975.

Guzman, Jane. "Women of the Barrios." Master's thesis for the University of North Texas, 1992.

Hall, Cordye. *What Can One Person Do?*. A Texas Woman Activist Answers. Privately published, 1988.

Hammond, W. J. "La Reunion, A French Colony in Texas." Norman, OK: *The Southwestern Social Service Quarterly*, September, 1936.

Handbook of Texas: Vols. 1 & 2. Texas State Historical Association, 1952, supplement 1976.

Hatcher, Mattie Austin. *Letters of an Early American Traveler.* Mary Austin Holley, "Her Life and Her Works." Southwest Press, 1933.

Head, Louis P. "The Kessler City Plan for Dallas, Genesis and Development of the Plan of 1910: the Supplement Plan of 1920; Progress in Fifteen Years." Dallas: A. H. Belo Corporation, 1925.

Hico, Louise Estelle. "Considerant and His Texas Utopia." Masters thesis, Southern Methodist University, 1924.

Hicks, Edwin P. *Belle Starr and Her Pearl*. Little Rock: Pioneer Press, 1963.

Hirsch, Alice, and Wilma Hirsch. Dallas County Census 1850, 1860, 1870. Hand-copied from original records, Dallas Public Library.

Holley, Mary Austin. Letters of an Early American Traveler. Dallas: Southwest Press, 1933.

Hope Cottage, Dallas. Files and minutes, 1918-1982.

Howard, James. "Big D Is for Dallas." Distributed by University Co-operative Society. Austin, 1957.

Hutto, Nelson A. "The Dallas Story from Buckskins to Top Hats." Privately published, 1959 as a souvenir.

Jackson, George. *Sixty Years in Texas*. Dallas: Wilkinson Printing Company, 1908.

Johnson, Frank W. "History of Texas and Texans." The American Historical Society, 1914.

Kimball, Justin F. "Our City—Dallas." Kessler Plan Association, Dallas, 1927.

Lancaster, A History, 1845-1945. Compiled by the Lancaster Historical Society, published 1978.

Lange, Pam, and Mindie Lazarus-Black. *Family Business in Dallas: A Matter of Values*. Dallas Public Library, 1982.

Lasher, Patricia, and Beverly Bentley. *Texas Women*. Austin: Shoal Creek Publishers, 1980.

Leslie, Warren. *Dallas Public and Private: Aspects of an American City*. New York: Grossman Publishers, 1964.

Lewis, Willie Newbury, Elizabeth Waggoner Burgher, Mary C. Swain, Bess Walcott Jones, and Elizabeth Taylor Robinson. *Dallas Shakespeare Club, A History 1886-1954*. Privately published, 1954.

Lindsley, Philip. *Greater Dallas and Vicinity, Vols. 1 and 2,* Dallas Historical Society, Chicago: Lewis Publishing Co., 1909.

Littlejohn, Jayme, and Letabeth Byrd-Littlejohn. *The Women of '85—a Who's Who and What's What About Women of the Metroplex*. Dallas: Two Byrds Publishing, 1985.

Marcus, Stanley. *Minding the Store*. Boston: Little, Brown and Company, 1974.

McDonald, William L. *Dallas Rediscovered: A Photographic Chronicle of Urban Expansion 1870-1925*. Dallas: Dallas Historical Society, 1978.

McElhaney, Jackie. "Pauline Periwinkle: Crusading Columnist. *Heritage News*, Dallas County Heritage Society, Summer 1985.

Melville, Mary Louise Hallam. "Dallas Woman's Club, the First Sixty Years, 1922-1982," published by the Dallas Woman's Club, printed by Taylor Publishing, 1982.

Memorial and Biographical History of Dallas County: The Lone Star State. Chicago: Lewis Publishing Company, 1892.

Miller, Kathryn Smith. *Polly Rollins Miller* Dallas: Eades and Associates, 1973.

Miller, Sister Ignatius. "Ursulines of the Central Province." Crystal City, MO: Ursuline Communications, 1983.

Millett, Kate. *Sexual Politics*. Garden City, NY: Doubleday & Company, Inc., 1970.

Mitchell, Donald F. *Profile of Dallas—Love Affair With A City*. Turtle Creek Gallery, 1981.

Moore, Gary. "When the Klan Resigned," *Westward Magazine, The Dallas Times Herald*, March 31, 1985.

Mora, Magdelena, and Adelaide R. Del Castillo. "Occasional Paper No. 2," Los Angeles: Chicano Studies Research Center Publications, University of California, 1980.

Moreland, Sinclair. *Texas Women's Hall of Fame*. Austin: Biographical Press, 1917.

Morgan, Robin. *Sisterhood Is Global*. Garden City, NY: Anchor Press/Doubleday, 1984.

Nash, Mary Cullum. "Damn Proud People." The story of the Cullum Family in Dallas. Schwalm Publishing Company, 1978.

National Association of Negro Women's Council, Dallas Branch. Feature article and history. *Dallas Express*, 1943.

Naturalization Records in Dallas County, Texas, an Index to. 1872-1914.

Notable Women of the Southwest. Dallas: William T. Tardy, publisher, 1938.

Oak Cliff Tribune. Special Quarterly Historic Issue, December 6, 1990.

Of Hearts and Minds, the Hockaday Experience, 1913-1988. Hockaday Alumnae Association, Ellen Higginbotham Rogers, Chairman, History Book Committee. Privately published, 1988.

Oppenheimer, Evelyn, and Bill Porterfield. *The Book of Dallas*. Garden City, NY: Doubleday & Company, Inc., 1976.

Ornish, Natalie. *Pioneer Jewish Texans*. Dallas: Texas Heritage Press, 1989.

Parker, Emma, and Nell Barrow Cowan. *Bonnie and Clyde: Fugitives*. Edited and comp. by Jan Isbelle Fortune. Dallas: The Range Press, Inc., 1934.

Patrick, Mary. "The Bureau of Indian Affairs Relocation Program," Master's Thesis, Baylor University.

Payne, Darwin. *Dallas An Illustrated History*. Woodland Hills, CA: Windsor Publications, Inc., 1982.

Planned Parenthood. Selected files and minutes.

Proud Heritage: Pioneer Families of Dallas County. By descendants of early Dallas County settlers, the Dallas County Pioneer Association, 1986.

Rascoe, Burton. *Belle Starr*. New York: Random House, 1941.

"Reminiscences: A Glimpse of Old East Dallas." Edited by Gerald D. Saxon, Dallas Public Library, 1983-1941.

Report of the Dallas Free Kindergarten and Industrial Association, 1903-1904.

Rogers, Mary Beth, Janelle D. Scott, and Sherry A. Smith. *We Can Fly*—Stories of Katherine Stinson and Other Gutsy Texas Women. Austin: The Texas Foundation for Women's Resources, 1983.

Rogers, John William. *The Lusty Texans of Dallas*. New York: E. P. Dutton and Company, Inc., 1960.

Roosevelt, Eleanor. *My Day*. Compilation of newspaper columns with an introduction by Martha Gellhorn. New York: Pharos Books, 1989.

Rumbley, Rose-Mary. *A Century of Class*. Austin: Eakin Press, 1984.

——— . *The Unauthorized History of Dallas, Texas*. Austin: Eakin Press, 1991.

Sanders, Barrot Steven. *Dallas, Her Golden Years*. Sanders Press, 1989.

——— . *The Caruths—Dallas's Landed Gentry*. Sanders Press, 1988.

——— . *The Forgotten History of the Four Cabins, by John Neely Bryan and the True Story of the Little Cabin on Our Courthouse Square*. Sanders Press, 1992.

Santerre, George H. *White Cliffs of Dallas: The Story of La Reunion*. Book Craft, 1955.

——— . Historical Series and Archives. Dallas Public Library.

Schiebel, Walter J. E. *Education in Dallas, Ninety-two Years of History 1874-1966*. Dallas Independent School District. Dallas: Taylor Publishing Company, 1966.

Scruggs, Margaret Ann. "Thumbnail Sketches: A Panorama of Dallas Social Life." Typescripts, Dallas Historical Society.

Seifert, Shirley. *Destiny in Dallas*. Philadelphia and New York: J. B. Lippincott, 1958.

Shackelford, William Yancey. *Belle Starr, the Bandit Queen*. Haldeman, Julius Publications, 1943.

Shannon, Margaret. *Just Because—the Story of the National Movement of Church Women United in the U.S.A, 1941-1975*. Corte Madera, CA: Omega Books, 1977.

Shirley, Glenn. *Belle Starr and Her Times.* Norman: University of Oklahoma Press, 1982.

Sims, Patsy. *The Klan.* Stein and Day, 1978.

Smith, Goldie Capers. "The Creative Arts in Texas." A handbook and biography, Cokesbury Press, 1926.

"Stirrings of Culture." Essays from the Dallas Institute. Edited by Robert Sardello and Gail Thomas, Dallas Institute Publications, 1986.

SMU Oral History Project, 15 women. Southern Methodist University, DeGolyer Institute.

Southwestern Historical Quarterly. Numerous copies.

Texas Almanacs published by *The Dallas Morning News.*

Texian Who's Who. Vol. 1. Edited by Sam H. Acheson, Herbert P. Gambrell, Mary Carter Toomey, and Alex M. Acheson, Jr. The Texian Company, 1937.

The Official Military Atlas of the Civil War. Arno Press, Crown Publisher, Inc, 1878.

The WPA Dallas Guide and History. Published by the Dallas Public Library and the University of North Texas Press, 1992.

The World Almanac and Book of Facts, New York: Pharos Books, a Scripps Howard Company, New York, numerous years.

Thometz, Carol Estes. *The Decision Makers.* Dallas: SMU Press, 1963.

Tinkle, Lon. *The Key to Dallas.* Philadelphia: J. B. Lippincott Company, 1966.

Trent, Lucy C. *John Neely Bryan.* Dallas: Tardy Publishing Company, 1936.

Upchurch, J. T. "The Unchained Demon—the Tribute Dallas Pays to Vice." Arlington, TX: Berachah Rescue Society, 1912.

Wade, Florrie. Research Collection Register, MA 87.26. Processed by Cindy Smolovik, archivist, Texas/Dallas History and Archives, Dallas Public Library, 1990.

Wade, Wyn Craig. *The Fiery Cross—the Ku Klux Klan in America.* New York: Simon and Schuster, 1987.

Weddington, Sarah, Jane Hickie, and Deanna Fitzgerald. *Texas Women in Politics.* Austin TX: Foundation for Women's Resources, Inc., 1977.

"When Dallas Became a City." Letters of John Milton McCoy 1870-1881." Edited by Elizabeth Enstam, Dallas Historical Society, 1982.

Who's Who of the Womanhood of Texas, 1923-1924. Published by the Dallas Federation of Women's Clubs.

Wiley, Nancy. *The Great State Fair of Texas.* Dallas: Taylor Publishing Co., 1989.

Williams, Lucinda Beckley. *The Golden Years.* Baptist Standard Publishing Co., 1921.

Winegarten, Ruthe. *Texas Women, A Pictorial History.* Austin: Eakin Press, 1986.

Witty, Kathryne Baker, and Alma Baker Ray. *The William Thatcher Baker Family 1830-1971.* Privately published, 1971.

Women's Book of World Records and Achievements. Edited by Lois Decker O'Neill, A Da Capo Paperback, Information House Books, Inc., 1979.

Zonta Club of Dallas I. A history, compiled by Ruth Guy, M.D. Dallas Public Library.

INDEX

A

Abrams, Ella M. Harris, 97, 141, 187
Ackerman, Gilbert Evans, 414
Ackerman, Margaret Boone, 10, 411-417
Adams, Daisy Spillman, 251
Adams, Ernestine, 326
Adams, Lindalyn Bennett, 368-371
Adelhoff, Blanch, 123
Ahn, Sun Tuk, 397
Ahn, Suzanne, 397, 406
Aldredge House, 369, 480
Aldredge, Mary Batts, 140, 365
Aldredge, Mary Lynn McEntire, 365, 367-368
Aldredge, Rena Munger, 477, 478, 480
Aldredge, Sawnie R., 202
Alexander, Birdie, 127
Alexander, Virginia Bledsoe, 55-56
Alice Street Carnival, 183
Allan, Mary Ann, 226
Allegro Club, 135
Allen, Ruth, 262
Allman, Leona, 327
Allred, James V. 459
Almquist, Elizabeth, 225
Alston, John, 392
Altshuler, Kenneth, 422
Altshuler, Ruth Collins Sharp, 237, 288, 418-423
Amann, Dorothy, 235
Amaya, Connie, 313
Amigos, 348
Amps, Judy, 313
Anderson, Barbara, 238
Anderson, Celia Ann Lair, 54
Anderson, Marian, 269
Anderson, Pearl Carina Bowden, 194, 272-273, 483
Anderson, Ron, 392
Anderson, William, 54
Another Mother for Peace, 431
Ardrey, Mrs. A. C., 152, 180
Armstrong, Alice, 230, 242
Armstrong, J. S., 117, 173
Armstrong, Minnie May, 242
Arrington, Mrs. C. N., 165
Ash, Mary Kay, 296, 306, 307-308, 391
Ashmore, Kathy, 313
Aunspaugh, Vivian Louise, 183-184
Automobile, Dallas' first, 164, End Note 3, Ch. 16
Aziz, Nadira, 429

B

Babies, First Born in Dallas, 6
Bachman, Margaret Morris Hughes, 31, 36
Baine, Emmie, 228, 235-236
Baker, Jane, 237
Ballard, Emma Wylie, 213, 214, 215
Barker, Charles, 51, 52
Barker, Eliza Ann Joyner, 51, 52
Barnhouse, Ruth Tiffany, 402, 432
Bayer, Fran, 97

Beasley, Norma Lee, 288
Beck, Toni, 180
Beeman, Emily Hunicutt, 3
Beeman, James, 2-3
Beeman, John, 3
Beeman, Margaret, 5
Beeman, Sarah Crawford, 3, 412
Beene, Eunice, 139
Beene, Judy, 312
Beer, A. Robert, 378
Beer, Gerry Danzer, 138, 375, 377-379
Bell, Esther Jane Patton, 56
Belo, Jeannette, 173
Bemporad, Sonya, 349, 350
Benenson, Sylvia, 138
Benjamin Long, 71
Bersterman, Roseann Tafalla, 396
Bersterman, Stephanie, 396
Bertoia, Harry, Sculpture, 185
Bialis, Gail Tomlinson, 321
Billingsley, Lucy, 288
Bird, Jonathan, 2
Bird's Fort, 1, 2
Bledsoe, Virginia, 55, 56
Blessing, Elizabeth, 339-340
Bohne, Mary A., 97
Boles, W. A., 123
Bombeck, Erma, 312
Bradshaw, Lillian Moore, 175, 178
Brau, Amy Haas, 396
Bromberg, Janice, 240
Brooks, Beverly Laughlin, 407
Browder, Lucy Jane Monroe, 29
Brown, Florence T., 203
Brown, J. Randolph, 203
Brown, Julia Josephine Haswell, 250-251
Brown, Rebecca, 203
Brown, Terry, 234
Bryan, John Neely, 1, 5, 52, 57, 93, 412
Bryan, Margaret Beeman, 5, 6, 7, 11, 16, 21, 29, 36
Buckner, Dr. R. C., 6
Buckner's Orphans Home, 6
Buhrer, Anna Moser, 112
Bulkley, Myrtle Bales, 381
Burford, Nathaniel M., 30, 35
Burnett, Judy Ladenberger, 397
Burns, Eleanor, 312
Burns, Mary Beth Currin, 397
Burton, Juanell, 313
Business and Professional Women's Club, 134, 139
Byrd, D. Harold, 87
Byrd, Mattie Caruth, 87
Bywaters, Jerry, 183, 185

C

Cabell Children (Harriet and W. L.), 70
Cabell, Harriet Rector, 70
Calhoun, Marilyn, 126
Calhoun, Nina Fay Waldrop, 258-259
Callaway, Katherine McLaurin, 140

Callaway, Sara Isadore Sutherland Miner, 152-155, 242
Callaway, William Allen, 154
Callejo, Adelfa, 264
Carnegie, Andrew, 172
Carr, Sis, 186, 384
Carruth, Margaret Scruggs, 141, 186
Caruth, Anna Worthington, 86
Caruth, Earle Clark, 87, 242
Caruth, Mabel Peters, 87
Caruth, Mattie Worthington, 86
Caruth, Walter, 86
Caruth William Barr, 86-87, 230
Caruth, William Walter Jr., 87
Cason, Dorothy Laura Collins, 61, 62
Cates, Jewel, 397
Cates, Julie, 397
Caudill, Susan, 363
Chambers, Betty Moore, 140
Chandler, Clyde Giltner, 183, 184
Chapman, Gloria, 140
Chautauqua . . . Circle, 135
Child Care Association, 207
Child Care Dallas, 207, 348-350
Chisum, Ethelyn Mildred, 130
Chisum, John Oscar, 130
Chud, Ann, 236, 358, 363
Church Women United, 136, 139
Citizens Charter Association, 437
Civil Rights Act, 194, 196
Civil War, 56, 80
Clack, Donna, 313
Clampitt, Mary Nelle, 369
Clanton, Cleora, 176, 295
Clark, Carolyn Tobian, 195, 348
Cochran, Anne, 33
Cochran Chapel Methodist Church, 32
Cochran, Nancy Jane Hughes, Ch. 4, 31
Cochran, William M., 31
Cockrell, Alexander, 7, 11, 12
Cockrell, Aurelia Effie, 13
Cockrell, Francis Marion, 16
Cockrell, Frank, 7
Cockrell, Nadine Steele, 11
Cockrell, Sarah Horton, 7, 11, 18, Ch. 2
Coffee, Holland, 6
Coffee, Linda, 354
Coit, Catharine Malloy Bunting, 74
Coit Family, 74-75
Coit, John Taylor, 74
Coit School, 74
Cole, Elizabeth Preston, 29
Cole, Polly McDonald, 28
Collett, Mary, 169, 245, 247-248
Collins, Juliette Harwood, 62, 69, 226
Collins, Ruth Woodall, 397, 419
Common Cause, 355
Communism, 294, 428
Condos, Constance Stathakos, 329-330
Cone, Margaret, 205, 349
Conrad, Eleanor, 109
Considerant, Victor, 57

Cooper-Hill, Marzelle, 263-265
Corona, Leonora, 269
Couch, Charlotte Hewitt Dalton, 24
Couch, Henderson, 24
Coughanour, Hallie Gibson, 122
Coughanour School, 122
Council of Churches, 199
Cousins, Margaret, 326
Cowan, Louise, 232
Cowart Hall School, 123, 226
Cowart, Leila, 123-124, 226, 483
Cowart, Lora, 123-124, 226, 483
Craft, Juanita, 194, 327, 331-333
Craig Class, 113
Craig, Mary Kittrell, 112, 113
Crane, Miss N. P., 123
Crawford, Katherine Lester Lamar, 181
Crow, Trammell, 392
Crowell, Evelyn Miller, 42, 44, 45, 47
Crowley, Mary, 288, 296, 302-307
Crume, Paul, 185
Crutchfield, Tom, 104
Cullum, Elizabeth Jane Davis, 100
Cullum, Eloise, 101
Cullum Family, 100-101
Cullum, Lee, 101
Cullum, Marcus Hiram, 100
Cunningham, Claire, 238, 240
Currey, Virginia, 239, 240
Currin, Patricia Drown, 397
Cuthbertson, S. B., 203, 204

D
Dahl, George, 185
Dallas Art Association, The, 136
Dallas Baby Camp, 206, 211-213
Dallas Bankers' Wives, 138
Dallas Citizens Council, 287-288
Dallas City Council PTA, 140
Dallas Council of Garden Clubs, 141
Dallas Council on World Affairs, 393
Dallas County Community Colleges, 342
Dallas County Medical Society Auxiliary, The, 138
Dallas Day Nursery Association, 207
Dallas Equal Suffrage Association, 242
Dallas Federation of Women's Clubs, 136
Dallas Female College, 225
Dallas Forum, 392
Dallas Free Kindergartens, 206
Dallas German Ladies Aid Society, 97, 135
Dallas Lawyers Wives, 138, 139
Dallas Pen Women, 136
Dallas Southern Memorial Association, 139
Dallas Symphony Orchestra, 187
Dallas Woman's Forum, The, 136
Dallas Woman's Club, 134, 137, 139
Dallas Women's Foundation, 140
Dallas Women's Coalition, 140
Daniel Family Cemetery, 55
Daniel, Frances Sims, 55
Darnell, Erie, 303

Davenport, Margaret, 89
Davis, Peyton, 139
Dawson, Kim, 338-339
Dealey, Olivia Allen, 186
Dealey, Ted, 163
Debutantes, original five, 117
Decherd, Isabel, 369
DeGolyer, Nell Goodrich, 140, 272, 279-280
Del Castillo, Adelaida R., 222
DeLaurenti, Mary Jordan, 288
Dennis, Martha Letitia Hughes, 31
Derritt, Berry, 16
DeSanders, Janet, 312
Deschner, Margarita, 234, 240
Deuillet, Liz, 432
Dickson, Anne, 375, 381-382
Dickson, Joseph, 173
Dickson, Robert Miller, 382
Dietrich, Louise, 97
Dillard, Marian, 136, 196
Domestic Violence Intervention Association, 355
Downing, Victoria, 313, 359
Dumas, Mrs. J. P., 5
Dunbar, Gerrye, 313
Durgan, Charles M., 25
Durgan, Elizabeth B. Thomas, 25
Dyson, Esther Juliet, 193, 483, 487

E
Early, Jeannette, 398
Eastfield College, 73
Edgington, Aileen, 215
Edwards, Dorothy Spruill, 47
Edwards, Leota Atchley, 235
Ehrhardt, Harryette, 371-373
Ehrhardt, John, 371
Ehrsam, Margarette, 432
Electricity, arrival of, 115
Elkins, Jane, 79
Emancipation Proclamation, 192
Emery, Lorrine, 393
Erickson, Sarah Ann Paralee Rupard, 244
Ervay, Henry Sleigh, 84-85
Ervay, Mariah Hickman, 84-85
Escobedo, Teodora, 224
Esely, Julie, 313
Estes, Margaret, 358, 432
Evans, Charles, 490
Evans, Edwina Cox, 359
Evans, Linda, 398
Ewell, Yvonne, 355
Exall, Dorothy Brannen, 145, 171
Exall, May Dickson, Ch. 14, 139, 171, 205, 483
Executive Women of Dallas, 134
Explore, 134, 236
Facts Forum, 429-430

F
Fagadau, Jeanne, 138, 312
Fagg, Dorothy, 312, 313

Fashena, Gladys, 262
Fichtner, Rae Ann, 263
Field, Florence Chalfant Peak, 59, 67
Field Opera House, 100
Field, Thomas W., 67
Fife, Maggie May, 128
Finn, Mrs. R. D., 170
Fire, first department, (Hook and Ladder Co.), 96
Fire—that burned Dallas, 79-81
First Women's Clubs, 135
Fitzgerald, Alice Parsons, 155-162
Fitzgerald, Hugh Nugent, 155, 161
Fitzjarrald, Shirley, 313
Florence, Fred, 479
Fly, Selby, 215
Ford, Rachel, 432
Ford, Terry, 206
Foree, Edna Fisher, (Mrs. Kenneth), 138, 139
Foree, Jeanne, 138
Fowler, Archibald Young, 63, 65
Fowler, Juliette Peak, 59-69
Fox, Ruth, 265
Francis, Mrs. J. Darrell, 138
Frazier, Julia Caldwell, 125-126
Freedman's Cemetery, 193, 373-374
Freeman, Valerie, 288, 391
Fulkerson, Polly, 16
Fulkerson, R. B. 20

G
Galerstein, Carolyn Lipshy Busch, 344-345
Gano, Katie, 67
Gano, Richard M., 66
Garbarino, Anne, 363
Garbarino, Maura, 363
Garcia, Catalina, 407
Garcia, Irene Martinez, 442-454
Garcia, Santiago (Jimmy), 449
Garrett, Alexander, 225
Garza, Susan Ladenberger, 397
Gaulden, Mary Esther, 359
Gies, Louise, 208
Gilbert, Charity Morris, 1
Gilbert, Charles E., 107
Gilbert, Mabel, 1
Gilbert, Martha, 3
Gilbert, Wilson, 3
Gilliam, Kathlyn Joy Christian, 346-347
Gilmore, Electra Waggoner Wharton Baily, 169
Gilmore, Martha, 265
Glover, Edalah Connor, 256
Godbey, Jo Fay, 239, 240
Golden, Margaret, 366
Good, John J. 81-84
Good, Susan Anna Floyd, 81-84
Goodere, Eugenia Dev Les, 71
Goodman, Anne, 470, 472
Goodnight, Mary Ann Hill, 56
Goodwin, Fran, 375
Goolsby, Sue, 313
Gosslee, Susybelle, 361

Graduates, first high school, 124
Grady, Henry W., 192
Graham, Bette, 296, 300-302
Graham, Mrs. Billy, 303
Gramatky, Sophia, 97
Granberry, Bobbie, 313
Grand Windsor Hotel, 142
Gray, Aurelia Effie Cockrell, 20, 21
Gray, Mitchell, 21
Gray, Sara B., 121
Green, Edward Howland Robinson, 164
Green, Hettie, 164
Greenburg, Blanche Cahn, 137
Greene, Barbara, 312
Greenwald, Patricia, 313, 363
Greenwood Cemetery, 21
Grisson-Thrash, Rezolia, 191
Guerrero, Celeste, 139, 313
Gulley, Stevonne, 263
Gulley, Vareta Pinkston, 255, 263
Gunther, Pauline, 97
Guy, Margaret, 313
Guzman, Jane Bock, 223

H
Hadsell, Helen, 313
Hair, Gerri, 352
Halbreich, Nancy Strauss, 405
Halcyon Club, 206
Hall, Cordye McLaurin, 424-432
Hall, Leonora Pipkin, 226, 483
Halliday, Ebby, 296-300, 391
Halycon Club, The, 136
Hamilton, Annette, 391
Hamilton, Becky, 396
Hamilton, Lea, 396
Hamilton, Sybil, 396
Hamilton, Vicki, 396
Hamon, Lucretia, 227
Hampton, Nicy Gilbert, 4
Hanna, Sallie Little, 208, 483
Hanson, Sandy, 375
Harlan, Nancy Sims, 55
Harlow, Mabel, 165
Harrell, W. H., 102
Harris, Fannie Chase, 126
Harrison, Adlene, 285, 340, 403, 433-441
Harrison, Maurice, 436
Hartley, Margaret, 323
Harwood, Alexander Maury, 61, 62
Harwood, Isabella Daniel, 55, 61
Harwood, Ripley Barksdale, 62, 226
Harwood, Sarah Ann Peak, 59-60, 69
Hawkins, Gaynell, 235
Hayes, Helen, 140
Healey, Meg, 319
Heartsill, Graydon, 315-317
Henderson, Jerry, 373-374
Henderson, Lana, 312
Henderson, Margaret, 125
Hensley, Beth, 326
Hereford, Elizabeth Johnson Robertson, 100

Hexamer, Frances, 255, 256
Hexter, Minnie Wertheimer, 137
Hill, Lyda, 406
Hill, Margaret, 369
Hill, Sallie, F., 326
Hirsch, Margaret, 138
Hispanic Organization for Women, 140
Hoblitzelle, Karl, 479
Hockaday, Ela, 226, 227
Hodge, Helen Straus, 23
Holley, Frances, 226
Holley Hall, 226, 477
Holley, Josephine, 226
Holly, Sister Mary Joseph, 103
Holmes, Emily Elvira Beeman Baker, 411-13
Holmes, Helen, 322
Hood, Waymond Blythe, 131
Hooe, Lida, 129
Hope Cottage, 206, 213-215
Hope Hall, 199
Horton Children, (Martha and Enoch), 11
Horton, Enoch, 11
Horton, James, 52
Horton, Martha Stinson, 11
House, first speculative, 150
Housing, segregated, 194
Houston, Sam, 72
Howell, W. R., 392
Hughes Aisley Carr, 31
Hughes, Ann, 206
Hughes, Sarah Tilghman, 272, 280-286, 363
Hughes, William Holmes, 31, 36
Hughes, Zuleika Ruth Kittrell, 31, 36
Hunt, Caroline, 288, 407
Hunt, Conover, 370
Hunt, Helen, 140, 237
Hutchison, Kay Bailey, 288, 391
Huvelle, Amelia Antoine, 98-100
Hyer, Margaret Hudgins, 227, 230-231, 483
Hyer, Robert Stewart, 230

I
Idlewild, 117
Ivins, Molly, 359
Ivy, Jeanette, 236

J
Jackson, Annie, 214
Jackson, Ardelia Ellen, 54
Jackson, Diana Jane Davis, 53
Jackson, James Everts, 53, 54
Jackson, Joan, 185
Jacoby, W. F. Jr., 107
James, Barbara Minor, 352, 360-362, 396
James, Jesse, 90
James, Nedra Patrice, 361, 396
Jarrett, Leah, 365
Jennings, Pat, 80
Jericho, Mary Ellen Mitchell, 186, 188
Joe, Daisy, 313
Johnson, Eddie Bernice, 340, 341, 355
Johnson, Iola, 326

Johnson, Scherry, 356
Johnson, Siddie Joe, 176
Johnson, Virginia Knight, 116, 117
Johnston, Nelle C., 249
Jones, Barbara, 432
Jones, Carol, 207
Jones, Charles Etta Emory, 255, 256
Jones, Erin Bain, 137
Jones, Margo, 324, 325-326
Jonsson, J. Erik, 340
Jonsson, Margaret, 137
Jordan, Barbara, 337
Jordan, Judy, 319, 320-321
Jordan, Margaret, 288
Joyner-Kersey, Jacqueline, 140
Judy, Nancy E., 341
Juliette Fowler Homes, 60, 69
July, Jim, 91
Junior League of Dallas, 134, 139, 478
Jurgens, Gay, 363

K
Kahn, Lawrence, 377
Kahn, Ruth, 377
Keaney, Johnnie, 397
Keaney, Kelly, 397
Keaney, Kim, 397
Keating, Janet, 313
Kelleher, Herb, 392
Keller, Bessie, 131
Kennedy, Flo, 363
Kennedy, John F., 283
Kennedy, Maggie, 312
Kennedy Memorial Museum, 370
Kent, Joan Jackson, 313
KERA-TV, 355
Kiest, Edwin J., 165, 247, 319
Kiest, Elizabeth, 165
Kimmel, Anna Minerva, 23
King, Mineola, 262
Knight, Serena Caroline Hughes, 31
Knox, Melva, 313
Korsak, Floyce, 312
Kreissig, Hans, 187
Kreissig, Louise Cretien, 187
Ku Klux Klan, 192, 199-202, 485
Kuhn, Maggie, 363

L
La Reunion, 57-58
Ladenberger, Peggy, 240, 397
Ladies Aid Society of Central Christian Church, 135
Ladies Musicale, The, 135
Lambert, Evelyn, 110, 177, 384
Landers, Bertha, 177
Lane, John J., 78
Lane, Mary Ann, 312
Lanes, Leslie, 432
Langham, Carolyn, 398
Latimer, James Wellington, 30
Latimer, Lucy Jordan, 30

Latimer, Paula, 358
Leachman, Welthea Bryant, 106-107
League of Women Voters, 134, 140, 196
Lee, Robert E., 78
Lee, Umphrey, 231
Leeper, Rosa, 173, 174
Leonard, Lily Virtrees Bell, 197, 494-500
Lewis, Willie Newbury, 136, 140, 189
Lincoln Memorial Cemetery, 265
Lindsay, R. W., 78
Lively, Laura, 25
Loeb, Ellen, 262
Lowrey, Flora Ellis, 231-233
Lumney, Rachel Haught, 28
Luna, Maria, 255, 260-262

M
Madison, Carol, 363
Madsen, Emma Gilliam, 118
Maffett, Minnie L., 233
Mahoney, Nonie Boren, 242-243
Malik, Rita, 398
Malouf, Marie, 313
Mandell, Madeline, 349
Mankoff, Joy Schechtman, 138, 237, 375, 370-381
Mankoff, Ronald M., 379
Marcus, Anita, 137, 138
Marcus, Betty, 110, 384
Marcus, Herbert, 244
Marcus, Minnie, 142, 245
Marcus, Sally, 245
Marcus, Stanley, 414, 429, 470
Marsh, Mary Raymond (Polly), 28
Marshall, Judy, 313
Martin, Florence George, 255, 256-257
Martin, L. M., 123
Martinez, Alfred, 442, 451
Martinez, Anita Nanez, 218-220, 246, 355, 442-454
Martinez, Faustina Porras, 217, 442-454
Martinez, Miguel, 443
Marvin, C. E., 214
McCaleb, Mary Hunt, 101
McCall, Hugh, 392
McCord, Mary, 233
McCorvey, Norma, 354
McCoy, Cora, 53
McCoy, John C., 17, 53, 170
McDaniel, Tina, 447
McDermott, Cora M., 18
McDermott, J. B., 53
McDermott, Margaret, 182, 337, 341-342
McElroy, Linda, 235
McEntire, Mary Lynn Aldredge, 365, 367
McGarr, Janie Strauss, 405
McGee, Sara Hibbits, 244
McGee-Cooper, Ann, 264
McGrath, Dorothea Lyle, 311-315
McKenzie, Sally, 134
McKnight, Mamie Abernathy, 342-343
McLaurin, Dr. Hugh, 67

McLaurin, Myrtie, 425
McMurray, Bette Clair, 296, 300-302
McMurray, Elizabeth Ann, 324-325
McNabb, Eula, 430
McNiel, Maura Anderson, 352-356, 363
McReynolds, Katherine Seay, 138, 139, 242
McRoberts, Edith Hanby, 312
Mead, Margaret, 363
Meadows, Curtis, 383
Meadows, Patricia Blachly, 375, 382-385
Meek, James D., 178
Mellersh, Elizabeth D. James, 102
Mendel, Iris, 435
Menezes, Sarah, 263
Meril, Barbara, 313
Mesta, Perle, 283
Mexican American B&PW, 140
Meyer, Sallie Griffis, 182, 183, 483
Meyerson, Morton H. Symphony Center, 188
Michero, Mary Lou Mulkey, 208
Middleton, Barbara, 396, 402, 432
Miller, Abbie, 396
Miller, Arch, 39, 48, 50
Miller, Barry, 45, 242
Miller, Bette, 380
Miller, Bettye, 39, 48
Miller Cabin-School, 41
Miller, Charlotte, 39, 48, 50
Miller, Clayton, 39, 48
Miller, Crill, 39, 40
Miller, Elizabeth Waddy, 40
Miller, Emma Angeline Dewey, 44
Miller Families, Ch. 5
Miller Family Cemetery, 49
Miller, John, 48
Miller, Lucy, 48
Miller, Madison Moultrie, 39, 40
Miller, Mary Elizabeth Buford, 236, 237-238, 303
Miller, Mary Parks (Polly) Rawlins, 41
Miller, Minerva Barnes, 39, 40
Miller, Minerva Hortense Miller, 44, 117
Miller, Ruth, 396
Miller, William Brown, 40
Millermore, 40, 367
Minor, Irma Pierce, 396
Minyard, Liz, 288
Mitchell, Stacy Ann, 396
Mitchell, Teri Dawn, 396
Mitchell-Brooks, Beverly, 396
Moncrief, Bette, 313
Mondell, Cynthia, 319
Montgomery, Ruth Ann, 369
Montoya, Regina, 406
Moore, Andrew M., 14
Moreno, Maria de Jesus Carreon, 220-222
Moreno, Sam, 221
Morgan, Ruth Prause, 230, 238-240
Morris, Mrs. Harry Joseph, 365
Mosby, Margaret, 129
Moser, Anna Buhrer, 112
Mossiker, Frances Sanger, 322-323

Mother St. Paul, 103, 105
Mothers' Clubs, 134
Motley Children (Mary Lynn and Thomas), 72
Motley Family, 71-74
Motley Family Cemetery, 73
Motley, Mary Lynn, 72
Motley, Sallie Ann, 73
Motley, Thomas Zachariah, 72
Mounger, June Hanby, 209, 211
Mounger, Kenneth, 209
Mowchan, Olga Platko, 396
Muldoon, Doris, 313
Mulkey, Alice Harriett (Skip), 208
Mulkey, Mr. & Mrs. J. E., 208
Munger, Margaret Carlson, 483
Murad, Claire Currin, 397
Murchison, Lupe, 110, 384
Myers, Sonoma, Beeman, 244

N
Naim, Rosann, 432
Nanez, Anita Trevino, 246
Nash, Mary Cullum, 100
Nasher, Patsy, 182
Nasher, Ray, 182
National Association for the Advancement of Colored People, 194
National Conference of Christians and Jews, 355
National Council of Jewish Women, 134, 136, 236
Neiman, Carrie Marcus, 244, 245, 435, 470
Neiman-Marcus, 245, 435
Nesmith, Robert Michael, 300
Nick, Virginia, 110, 384
Nicol, Myra Jean, 330
Nicol, Nicki, 331
Nicol, Noreen, 330-331
Niles, Frances, 313
Nilsson, Mrs. C. J., 128
Nussbaumer, Dora, 97
Nye, Erte, 392

O
O'Brien, Patrick M., 178
O'Daniel, W. Lee and family, 419
Oak Cliff Female Institute, 226
Oak Lawn Methodist Church, 101
Oakland Cemetery, 53, 203
Odenwald, Sylvia, 318
Odom, Mary Hunt McCaleb, 101
Office of International Affairs, 393
Ohene-Bekoe, Kwasi, 398
Oliver, Mary E. Cogburn, 151
Oppenheimer, Evelyn, 318, 319-320
Oram, J. M., 66, 166
Ornish, Natalie, 318, 324
Ortega, Maria Belen, 455-461
Ott, Eleanor, 234
Owens, Sherry, 385

P

Padgett, Mrs. J. D., 136
Page, Karen, 321
Palmer, Dona, 262
Palmer, Rhonda, 432
Panel of American Women, 348
Parent Teacher Associations, 134
Parker, Bonnie Elizabeth Thornton, 272, 276-278
Parker, Mrs. Wesby, 137
Parks, Rosa, 347
Patterson, Albert S., 464
Patterson, Albert Harllee, 464
Patterson, James Martin, 27
Patterson, Lucy, 464
Patterson, Peggy, 355
Patterson, Sarah Elizabeth Self, 27
Payton, Donald, 48
Payton, Ernest, 48-49
Peabody, Elizabeth, 365
Peabody, Janet Belo, 483
Peacemakers, 432
Peak, Carroll Marion, 59, 62
Peak Children, (Martha and Jefferson), 59
Peak Family, Ch. 7
Peak, Fannie V. Mott, 76
Peak, Florence Chalfant, 60, 62
Peak, George Victor, 59
Peak, Jefferson, 59, 67, 74
Peak, Jefferson Jr., 59
Peak Junius, 59
Peak, Martha Malvina Reser, 59
Peak, Matthias L. Irving, 59
Peak, Olive, 62, 65
Peak, William Wallace, 59
Peak, Worth, 59
Pearce, Ronnie, 394
Peck, M. Scott, 402-403
Pegues, Verina, 207
Pegues, Virginia, 131
Peiser, Pat, 138, 312
Pentecost, Mercedes, 265
Perez, Sister Phillipa, 224
Perini, Pat, 319
Periwinkle, Pauline, 152-155
Perkins, Francis, 268
Perry, Sarah Shelton Huffman, 27
Person, Jan Ladenberger, 397
Peter's Colony, 4, 18, 19, 32, 52
Peters, Joann, 356
Petsch, Marvin A., 394
Petsch, Morena Fantozzi, 394
Phelps, Florence Louise Harllee, 194, 462-467
Phelps, John C., 194, 195, 463-464
Phinney, Louise Snow, 140
Pioneer Association of Dallas County, 107
Pollock, Lawrence, 479
Polter, Lucy, 138
Ponce, Agapita, 223
Posey, Louise, 262-263
Positive Parents of Dallas, 134

Pratt, Madame, 190
Priest, Bill, 341
Priscilla Arts Club, 136
Proctor, W. C., 208
Prostitutes, 90, 116
Prostitution, 196, 197
Pryor, Sam, 70
Public Schools, creation of, 122

Q

Quilt—Sarah Ann's Flower Garden, 63, 64

R

Rabin, Idelle Mildred Goodman, 468-475
Rabin, Leon, 470-472
Raggio, Grier, 376
Raggio, Louise Ballerstedt, 375-377
Ramirez, Robin, 461
Rattan, Hamp, 2
Rawlins, Anne Tyler, 155
Rawlins, Mildred Parks, 42
Rawlins, Roderick Alexander, 41
Ray, Mary, 141
Rayburn, Sam, 4
Reagan, Barbara, 230, 240
Record, Aisley Amanda Hughes, 31, 36, 37
Redus, Amo Atchley, 235
Reed, James C. (Jim), 90
Reed, Julia Scott, 193, 317-319
Reed, Rosie Lee (Pearl), 90-91
Reyes, Adrian, 388
Reyes, Delia Maria Perez, 375, 387-389
Richards, Ann, 136
Richardson, Barbara, 312
Richardson, Betty, 288, 313
Richardson, Thelma Paige, 347
Riek, Alice, 106
Riek, Martha, 106
Ripley, Kate Rice, 250, 272, 278-279
Roberts, Alice Bryan, 136, 188
Roberts, Edith Rydell, 64, 179
Robinson, Jeff D., 203
Roe V. Wade, 354
Roosevelt, Eleanor, 226, 268, 429
Rowand, Mary Louise, 327, 334-336
Rowe, Edna, 126
Rumbley, Jill, 396
Rumbley, Rose-Mary Brau, 396
Rutherford, Susan, 312
Rutledge, Mary Holland, 346

S

Sabin, Pat, 140, 237
Sack, Mildred R., 137
Sadat, Jehan, 391
Salisbury, Lillian Elliott, 127
Sallie Haynes, 94
Saloons, 116
Sanchez, Erika, 313
Sanders, Jan, 138
Sanders, Marlene, 321
Sanders, May, 138

Sanford, Betty (Mrs. Curtis), 137
Sanger Bros., 114, 150
Sanger, Hortense Landauer, 109, 138, 215, 216
Sanger, Margaret, 110
Saunders, Carolyn, 397
Saunders, Lisa, 397
Savage, Dorothy, 371
Savage, Wallace, 371
Sawhill, Karin, 432
Schilling, Helen, 139
Schlafly, Phyllis, 359
Schneider, Belle Fonda, 97-98, 173, 187
Schoellkopf, John, 437
Schroeder, Patricia, 207
Schuchat, Marjorie, 237, 363
Schumacher, Emily, 432
Schwartz, Anna, 202
Scovell, John, 392
Scruggs, Marion Stuart Price, 141
Scurlock, Gladys, 138
Seely, Gini, 313
Seifert, Sheila, 313
Shakespeare Club Charter Members, 144
Shakespeare Club, 134
Sharp, Ruth Collins, 397
Sharp, Sally, 397
Sharp, Susan, 397
Shea, Genevieve, 255, 259-260, 397
Shelburne, Gertrude Aldredge, 267, 476-481
Shelburne, Samuel Ainslie, 478
Shellhorn, Donna, 432
Shelmire, Peggy, 313
Sheltering Arms, 116
Shelton, Mrs. Lockett, 138
Shirley, Glenn, 93
Shirley, Myra Maybelle (Belle Starr), 90
Shlipak, Carole Rolnick, 343-344
Shuford, Virginia Waters, 397
Shumate, Clarence, 89
Silkwood, Solomon, 2
Sisterhood of Temple Emanu-El, 139
Sixth Floor, 370
Slavery, 79
Sloan, Nila, 313
Smallwood, Kathie, 396
Smallwood, Sarah, 396
Smith, Arthur A., 429
Smith, Ed C., 67
Smith, Gail, 236, 363
Smith, Lucinda Blackburn, 26
Smith, Margaret Isabel Gay (Belle), 180
Smith, Margaret Daniel, 55
Smith, Margaret Brand, 264
Smith, May Forster, 211, 212, 213
Smith, Rev. James Anderson, 19
Smith, Sam, 80
Smoots, Mary Winn, 255, 259
Soliz, Rosalind, 326
Southern Methodist University, 229-242
Spears, Mary C., 129
Spence, Alexander White, 484

Spence, Ruth Potts, 108, 169, 208, 230, 482-487
Spence, Stella White, 108-112, 483
Spence, Wendell, 108
Spragins, Lide, 233
St. Cecelia Choral Society, 136, 188
St. Martin, Charolette, 288
St. Mary's College, 112, 225
St. Nicholas Hotel, 17
Stahl, Susan, 361
Standard Club, The, 135
Starr, Belle, 90-93
Starr, Sam, 91, 92
State Fair of Texas, 247, 365
Steinem, Gloria, 229, 363
Stemmons, Grace, 134, 384
Stemmons, John, M., 74, 437
Stemmons, Rebecca Serena Allison, 74
Steorts, Nancy, 288
Stevenson, Maybelle Shelby, 46, 50
Stewart, Betty May Exall, 145-146, 171
Stewart, Charlotte, 363
Stewart, Ethel Elizabeth Johnson, 347-348
Stewart, Peter, 146
Stickle, Tencha, 447
Stratford Club, The, 136
Straus, Winnie Ann Ramsey, 23
Strauss, Annette, 134, 186, 397, 403, 404-406
Strauss, Helen, 186, 404
Strauss, Nancy, 397
Strauss, Robert, 403-405
Strauss, Theodore S., 404
Streets, hard-surfaced, 118
Streng, Susie, 139
Stroud, Joanne, 232
Styron, W. R., 203, 204
Suffragettes, The, 136
Sullivan, Frances, 129
Sunshine Club, The, 139
Sutherland, Eleanor, 138
Swank, Patsy, 323
Sweatt, Mary Cordelia, 42, 44
Sweeney, Julia, 322, 392
Swenson, Jean, 236
Swiss Avenue Historical District, 371, 371-373
Swor, G. W., 203, 204
Sykes, Becky, 140, 237

T
Tafalla, Nellie, 140, 396
Tafalla, Theresa, 396
Tate, Waddy, 266
Tate, Willis, 421
Taylor, Nancy Rawlins, 56
Taylor, Rhobia, 139
Taylor, William, 285
Telephone, first, 115
Tenant, Allie Victoria, 185-186
Terrell, George Whitfield, 477
Texas A&M University, 112

Texas Centennial, 270-271
Texas Equal Rights Amendment, 359
Texas Federation of Garden Clubs, 141
Texas School Book Depository, 370
Thomas, Elizabeth Jane Routh, 84
Thomas, Gail Griffin, 232, 405-409
Thomas, James, 84
Thomas, Margaret Hyer, 230
Thomas, Robert Hyer, 407
Thornton, R. L., 185, 406
Tiller, Kay, 323
Tiller, Martha Russell, 322, 367
Tinkham, Sandra, 228, 236, 363
Tinsley, Clarice, 326
Tobolowsky, Hermine, 352, 357-360
Tomlin, Lily, 363
Train, first to arrive, 94
Transportation, 118-120
Trees, Anna Minerva Kimmel, 23
Trees, Crawford, 23
Trees, Joe, 24
Trent, Sarah B., 226
Tres Rios, 208
Trezevant, Mamie, 142
Trinity River, 1, 9
Tripp, Alvernon Verita King Evans, 488-493
Trout, Carole, 432
Tucker, Ella Stephenson, 226
Tufts, Eleanor, 238, 240
Turner, Adella Kelsey, 136, 226, 483
Turner, Virginia, 394
Turtle Creek, 3
Tyler, Jimmie Brashear, 126
Tyler, Priscilla L., 129

U
Uncle Cato, 80
Underwood, Marion, 176
United Nations, 355, 429, 431
University Woman's Club, The, 138
Upchurch, J. T., 197-199
Ursuline Academy, 45, 103-105

V
Van Oostveen, Annette, 394
Vecchio, Ronda, 313
Venters, Alma Deere, 177

W
Wade, Henry, 354
Wade, Juanita, 255, 256-258
Wahrenberger, Caroline, 90
Wales, Joan, 375
Waters, Ethel, 303
Waters, Mrs. Lindsley, 397
Watkins, Barbara Lord, 375, 385-387
Watkins, Myron, 385
Watson, Betty, 312
Watts, Lala Devan, 259
Webb, Alex W., 2
Webb, Mary Hughes, 31, 34
Weber, Harriet, 369

Weddington, Sarah, 354
Wednesday Morning Choral Club, 136
Wesner, Bitsy, 356
West, Ardelia Ellen Jackson, 54
West, Jamie Miller, 236, 237
West, John Frederick, 54
West, Mary Ann Ryland, 121
Wheat, C. M., 67
Wheeler, Bonnie, 230, 240
White, Linda Gale, 383
White, Ruthmary, 312
White, William Travis, 414
Whitehill, Margaret, 381
Whitehill, Virginia Bulkley, 237, 361, 375, 381
Whiting, Grace, 139, 208
Whyte, Edna Gardner, 263
Wiedemann, Flo, 355
Williams, Lila, 356
Williams, Lucinda Beckley, 88-89
Williams, Myra Jean Nicol, 331
Williams, Sarah Matilda Hughes, 31, 34
Williams, Sudie, 130
Williams, William, 88
Wilmans, Edith Therrel, 255-256
Winn, Conchita, 239
Winn, Joan Tarpley, 263
Wise, Sally, 352
Wise, Wes, 352
Witherspoon, Kathleen, 414
Wolfram, Rhea, 206
Women for Change, Inc., 353, 358
Women's Center of Dallas, 134, 140
Women's Council of Dallas County, 134, 140
Women's Equity Action League, 358
Women's Issues Network, 140
Women's Rights, 161
Worley, Ann, 312
Wynne, Jo Ann, 369

X
Yancey, Mary Frances, 369
Young, Mary Susan Carolyn Pipkin, 85
Young, Norma, 182
Young, Rebecca, 30
Young, William C., 30
Young Women's Christian Association, 206, 208-211
Younger, Cole, 90

Y

Z
Zaharias, Mildred, (Babe) Didrikson, 272, 273-276
Zahrt, Kathleen, 494-500
Zahrt, Walter, 497
Zion, Carol, 341, 342
Zonta International, 140

For
Natalie Ornish
Who knows what
this day means because
she's done such a wonderful
book that helped me along the
way.

Love,
Vivian Anderson Castleberry